Standardized Test Preparation Workbook

English/Language Arts Skills

Second Course

HOLT, RINEHART AND WINSTON

A Harcourt Education Company

Orlando • Austin • New York • San Diego • London

ISBN 13: 978-0-55-400811-0

ISBN 10: 0-55-400811-4

1 2 3 4 5 179 09 08 07

Table of Contents

Name _____ Class _____ Date _____

To the Student

This booklet provides you with reading and writing test practice as well as one English/Language Arts Second Course Practice Test. We have included a Mastery Grid which will help you chart your progress as you work.

This test preparation booklet also includes tips on answering the types of questions that appear in the English/Language Arts Second Course Practice Test. There are suggestions for answering multiple-choice and open-ended questions and for responding to writing prompts.

Reading Practice and English/Language Arts Second Course Practice Test

Objective	Test Item	Page Number	Mastery Yes	Mastery No	Date	Comments/ Questions
LITERATURE						
Understand and analyze prose forms and genres.	4	13				
Understand and analyze plot.	5	13				
	11	14				
	12	14				
	6	13				
	7	13				
	1	30				
	2	30				
	12	31				
	3	38				
	10	49				
	11	49				
	12	49				
Understand and analyze characteriza-tion.	1	13				
	10	14				
	9	14				
	2	21				
	11	22				
	3	30				
	10	31				
	1	38				
	2	38				
	10	39				
	1	48				
	1	146				
	7	147				
	10	147				
	2	165				
	6	165				
Understand and analyze setting.	4	38				
	4	48				
	5	48				
	1	144				

Objective	Test Item	Page Number	Mastery Yes	Mastery No	Date	Comments/ Questions
Understand and analyze theme.	8	13				
	5	30				
	7	31				
	5	146				
	5	151				
Understand and analyze point of view.	12	22				
	3	157				
Understand and analyze types and forms of poetry and elements of poetry.	4	21				
Understand and analyze elements of poetry.	2	13				
	1	21				
	3	21				
	5	21				
	9	22				
	3	151				
	4	151				
	6	151				
	7	151				
Understand and analyze style.	1	144				
	1	151				
Understand and analyze literary devices.	9	39				
	11	147				
	7	151				
	8	151				
Understand and analyze elements of drama.	6	48				
	7	48				
	8	48				
	10	49				
	3	165				
	4	165				

Objective	Test Item	Page Number	Mastery Yes	Mastery No	Date	Comments/ Questions
Analyze historical context.	8	157				
Analyze biographical information.	3	17				
READING						
Use reading strategies to clarify meaning.	1	17				
	2	17				
	6	21				
	11	31				
	10	34				
	7	38				
	2	48				
	9	48				
	10	49				
	7	52				
	6	144				
	6	146				
	4	154				
	7	157				
	5	165				
Analyze an author's perspective, argument, and point of view.	12	22				
	7	33				
	3	157				
Analyze public documents/ informational materials	6	33				
	8	42				

Objective	Test Item	Page Number	Mastery Yes	Mastery No	Date	Comments/ Questions
Use strategies to enhance understanding.	4	13				
	10	22				
	11	26				
	3	30				
	8	31				
	2	33				
	8	33				
	9	34				
	13	39				
	11	39				
	12	39				
	2	42				
	3	42				
	6	42				
	7	149				
	2	151				
	6	157				
	8	160				
	1	165				
	4	165				
	7	165				
	8	165				

Objective	Test Item	Page Number	Mastery Yes	Mastery No	Date	Comments/ Questions
Analyze and evaluate a text.	4	17				
	5	17				
	11	18				
	1	25				
	3	25				
	1	33				
	3	33				
	5	33				
	12	34				
	10	39				
	10	43				
	1	48				
	3	48				
	3	144				
	8	144				
	5	144				
	5	146				
	7	147				
	8	147				
	9	147				
	1	149				
	4	149				
	5	151				
	11	155				
	2	154				
	3	154				
	6	154				
	7	154				
	2	157				
	5	157				
	5	159				
	6	159				

Objective	Test Item	Page Number	Mastery Yes	Mastery No	Date	Comments/ Questions
Identify elements of a text.	2	17				
	12	18				
	10	18				
	5	25				
	1	42				
	9	43				
	4	51				
	6	52				
	3	146				
	2	149				
	3	149				
	8	149				
	1	154				
	10	155				
Make connections from a text.	6	17				
	7	21				
	11	34				
	5	38				
	3	51				
	12	53				
	2	144				
	2	146				
	4	146				
	4	147				
Make generalizations from a text.	6	25				
	9	26				
	2	51				
	7	144				
Make inferences from a text.	1	51				
	9	52				
Read to inquire and conduct research using a variety of sources.	10	53				
	11	53				
	1	159				
	2	159				
	4	159				

Objective	Test Item	Page Number	Mastery Yes	Mastery No	Date	Comments/ Questions
Read to increase knowledge of the student's culture, the culture of others, and the common elements of culture.	7	31				
	8	31				
	9	31				
	12	53				
Analyze and understand elements and features of nonfiction and informational texts.	8	18				
	1	25				
	4	25				
Identify and understand departures from objectivity and/or logic.	7	17				
	4	25				
	5	42				
	8	52				
	6	149				
	5	154				
	9	155				
Recognize a variety of text patterns that organize information in nonfiction.	11	43				
	8	155				
	1	159				
	8	160				
	7	160				
	9	160				
Identify structural features and the purpose of each in nonfiction.	2	25				
	10	26				
VOCABULARY						
Understand word analogies.	5	52				

Objective	Test Item	Page Number	Mastery Yes	Mastery No	Date	Comments/ Questions
Identify synonyms.	8	21				
	5	168				
Use context clues in words, sentences, and paragraphs to decode new vocabulary.	2	17				
	7	26				
	6	30				
	7	42				
	4	144				
	5	149				
	1	157				
	3	159				
Identify and understand connotative and figurative use of language.	3	13				
	7	151				
	4	30				
Identify and use correctly multiple-meaning words.	3	135				
	7	168				
		169				
	8					
Use specialized vocabulary appropriately.	9	18				
Identify and use suffixes and prefixes to understand and create words.	8	26				
	4	33				
	6	38				

Writing Practice and English/Language Arts Second Course Practice Test

Objective	Test Item	Page Number	Mastery Yes	Mastery No	Date	Comments/ Questions
LANGUAGE CONVENTIONS						
Demonstrate control of grammar and sentence structure.	1	168				
	3	168				
		169				
	10					
Use phrases correctly.	13	137				
Identify and use verbals and verbal phrases correctly.	5	141				
	7	141				
Use clauses correctly.	9	136				
	11	137				
	12	169				
Demonstrate understanding of standard English usage.	5	140				
	7	140				
	2	170				
	3	170				
Understand agreement.	11	169				
	3	171				
Demonstrate understanding of correct subject-verb agreement.	6	136				
Demonstrate understanding of correct pronoun and antecedent agreement.	15	138				

Objective	Test Item	Page Number	Mastery Yes	Mastery No	Date	Comments/ Questions
Use verbs correctly.	1	135				
	6	136				
	6	141				
	2	168				
	1	171				
	2	171				
	5	171				
	6	171				
Use pronouns correctly.	2	141				
	8	141				
Use case forms of personal pronouns correctly.	16	138				
Avoid common usage problems.	1	141				
Demonstrate control of standard English conventions and mechanics.	4	135				
	6	140				
Use capitalization correctly.	1	139				
	6	168				
	4	170				
Use punctuation correctly.	12	137				
	4	140				
	9	169				
	1	170				
Use commas correctly.	4	168				
Use apostrophes correctly.	5	135				

Objective	Test Item	Page Number	Mastery Yes	Mastery No	Date	Comments/ Questions
Use correct spelling.	7	136				
	8	136				
	10	136				
	14	138				
	2	139				
	3	140				
	8	140				
	3	141				
	4	141				
	5	170				
	6	170				
	4	171				

Objective	Test Item	Page Number	Mastery Yes	Mastery No	Date	Comments/ Questions
WRITING						
Use the fundamentals of the writing process to improve writing; Write clearly and effectively; Write persuasive essays or articles; Write to achieve a purpose	WP1	63				
Use the fundamentals of the writing process to improve writing; Write clearly and effectively; Write persuasive essays or articles; Write to achieve a purpose; Write business documents	WP2	75				

Objective	Test Item	Page Number	Mastery Yes	Mastery No	Date	Comments/ Questions
Use the fundamentals of the writing process to improve writing; Write clearly and effectively; Write to achieve a purpose; Write descriptive essays	WP3	84				
Use the fundamentals of the writing process to improve writing; Write clearly and effectively; Write to achieve a purpose; Write short stories or poems; Write narratives	WP4	96				

Objective	Test Item	Page Number	Mastery Yes	Mastery No	Date	Comments/ Questions
Use the fundamentals of the writing process to improve writing; Write clearly and effectively; Write to achieve a purpose; Use reference materials when writing	WP5	108				
Use the fundamentals of the writing process to improve writing; Write clearly and effectively; Write to achieve a purpose; Perform literary analysis	WP6	121				

Objective	Test Item	Page Number	Mastery Yes	Mastery No	Date	Comments/ Questions
Use the fundamentals of the writing process to improve writing; Write clearly and effectively; Write persuasive essays or articles; Write to achieve a purpose	Test WP1	166				
Use the fundamentals of the writing process to improve writing; Write clearly and effectively; Write to achieve a purpose; Write descriptive essays	Test WP2	167				

Reading Practice

Standardized Tests for Reading

In the Reading Practice section, you will practice for Standardized Reading Tests. You will read some general strategies for answering multiple-choice questions and open-ended questions. Then, you will be asked to read a number of selections. Each selection will be followed by a series of questions covering comprehension and reading skills and interpretation and analysis of text (fiction and nonfiction).

Scoring the English/Language Arts Second Course Practice Test

In the **English/Language Arts Second Course Practice Test** provided at the end of this workbook, you will answer sixty-four selection questions. Forty-eight selection questions will be in a multiple-choice format. Sixteen selection questions will be in an open-ended format. Each of these open-ended questions will require a short written response and should take about ten minutes to answer completely. Some of the open-ended questions require a more in-depth response. You will receive one point for each multiple-choice question you answer correctly, for a possible 48 points. The open-ended questions will be scored on a 0–3 point scale, for a possible 48 points.

Scoring Open-Ended Reading Questions:

Score of 3: This response has a correct answer as well as text-based support. It also has specific, appropriate, and accurate details or examples.

Score of 2: This response has only a partial answer. It shows awareness of what is to be answered, and has at least one text-based detail. Although this response attempts to provide sufficient details or examples, it may contain minor inaccuracies.

Score of 1: This response is incomplete, indicating that either the question was misunderstood or that no text-based details were included in the response. The details or examples are insufficient or inappropriate, and there may be major inaccuracies.

Score of 0: This response has too little information to be scored or is inaccurate in many ways. The following conditions will also cause a response to receive a score of 0.

- The response is blank or too short to be scored.
- The response is off-topic.
- The response is written in a language other than English.
- The handwriting in the response is unable to be read.

The primary goal of the Reading Practice section is to help you prepare for taking Standardized Tests for reading. These strategies and tips can help you succeed on this type of test.

Strategies for Reading Comprehension

Understanding Main Ideas and Supporting Details

The most important point expressed in a reading passage is the main idea. The main idea must relate to the entire passage, not just to a portion of it. Follow these steps in order to identify a selection's main idea.

Step 1: Read the selection and determine the topic.

Step 2: Look at what all the details have in common. The details should point to the main idea. **Hint:** Pay attention to the first and last sentences. You may find a sentence that states the main idea.

Step 3: State the main idea in your own words. Then, look for an answer that closely matches your own. Be careful not to select a detail that merely *supports* the main idea as your answer.

Step 4: Check to make sure that the details in the selection support your answer.

Identifying Author's Purpose

There are four general purposes authors have for writing. Use the steps below for help in answering questions about purpose:

Step 1: Look in the text for clues such as the ones below.

- illustrations, diagrams, maps, charts, headings, and bulleted or numbered items (**to inform**)
- words like *should* and *must*, and words that assign value such as *worst* and *best* (**to influence, to persuade, or to convince**)
- frequent use of the word *I* and emotional words (**to express**)
- use of vivid descriptions, dialogue, rhymes, drama, or humor (**to entertain**)

Step 2: Look for the response that most closely matches the general purpose you have identified.

Using Context Clues

As you read a selection in a reading test, you may discover that the author uses unfamiliar words. One way to determine the meaning of an unfamiliar word is to use context clues. A word's context is made up of the words and sentences around it. Use the following steps to answer questions about context clues in a selection:

Step 1: Look at the context of the unfamiliar word. See if the words and sentences around it provide clues to the word's meaning.

Step 2: Use the context clues to make a guess at the unfamiliar word's meaning.

Step 3: Check your definition by inserting it in the passage in place of the unfamiliar word.

Identifying Point of View or Bias

Follow these steps to answer questions about the author's point of view or biases:

Step 1: Determine whether the writer uses more positive words or more negative words.

Step 2: Try to answer the question in your own words.

Step 3: Look for the choice that best matches your own answer.

Summarizing a Text

Follow these steps to choose the best answer to a summary question:

Step 1: Look for the main idea and the most important supporting details as you read the passage slowly and carefully.

Step 2: Consider every answer choice, eliminating those that restate a single detail from the passage, make a general statement about the passage but include no important details, or have little or nothing to do with the passage.

Step 3: Be sure that the answer you choose covers the *entire* passage by including the main idea and major supporting details.

Making Inferences

Reading tests often include questions that check your ability to make inferences from a reading passage. Often there is an idea within a passage that the author is trying to convey but does not state directly. Sometimes, you must consider various parts of the passage together in order to determine what the author is implying. Use the following steps to answer inference questions:

Step 1: Skim the passage once for a general understanding; then, reread it carefully. Keep in mind that most test questions are designed to measure your reading comprehension, not your reading speed.

Step 2: Locate key words and phrases in the answer choices that match similar words and phrases in the reading passage. You may be able to eliminate some answers right away.

Step 3: Confirm your answer by considering your prior knowledge about the subject of the passage.

Predicting Outcomes

Sometimes a reading test will ask you the outcome of events in a narrative passage. Use the following process to determine the *most likely* outcome:

Step 1: Read the passage carefully. Everything you need to know is there. The correct answer must follow easily from the information in the passage—it should never depend on a change in a person or an unlikely turn of events.

Step 2: Using the information in the passage, make a prediction about what will most likely happen next. Ask yourself what will result from the events in the passage.

Step 3: For this kind of question, you will need to read all of the answers before you choose one. Eliminate answers by matching them against what you know from the passage and what you have predicted.

Drawing Conclusions

On a reading test, you may be asked questions that begin like this, "Why do you think . . ."or "Based on the information in the passage . . ." Questions like these require you to draw a conclusion. Use the steps below to respond to these types of questions:

Step 1: Read the question or stem to identify the topic of the question.

Step 2: Study the answer choices, ruling out those choices that are clearly wrong.

Step 3: Reread the passage and look for evidence that supports which of the remaining answer choices is correct.

Strategies for Analyzing an Author's Style and Technique

Analyzing Elements of Character, Theme, or Setting

Reading tests that include literary passages often ask about literary elements such as character, theme, or setting.

Step 1: Be sure you understand the three basic literary elements listed above.

Step 2: Look for information in the passage that relates to the literary element you are asked to find.

Step 3: Choose the answer that most correctly relates to the details in the passage.

Analyzing Tone

An author's tone is his or her attitude, conveyed largely through word choice. Use the following steps to respond to reading test questions about a writer's tone.

Step 1: Look at the writer's diction (word choice). In particular, identify any connotative words the writer uses. Determine what the connotations suggest about the writer's attitude toward the subject.

Step 2: Read all the answer choices, and eliminate those that are clearly inconsistent with what the diction suggests about the writer's tone.

Step 3: Examine the remaining answer choices, and choose the one that best describes the tone of the passage. (Beware of answer choices that exaggerate the writer's attitude.)

Analyzing Style

Some test questions will ask you to analyze the author's style. Style refers to the author's unique manner of expression. In addition to tone (see above), mood is a critical element of style. Mood is the feeling that the literature creates. As in tone, the author's diction (word choice) is a major component of mood. Another way to analyze style is to classify it as formal or informal. To answer questions about style, follow the steps below:

Step 1: Look at the answer choices.

- Words like *admiring, bitter*, and *comic* suggest that the question is focusing on tone or mood.

- Words like *slangy, lofty*, or *elevated* suggest that the question is more focused on formality or informality.

Step 2: Eliminate answer choices that are clearly inconsistent with the diction, tone, or mood of the selection.

Step 3: Select the remaining choice that seems most consistent with the diction, tone, or mood of the selection.

Evaluating Rhetorical Strategies

Some tests will ask you to evaluate rhetorical strategies, including strategies that are not based on solid evidence. One flawed strategy is the use of overgeneralization. Use the following steps to evaluate generalizations you find in your reading:

Step 1: Look for general statements. Words like *no one, never, every*, and *always* may signal a general statement. An example of a general statement that sounds like an overgeneralization is "All dogs love to play in the water."

Step 2: Identify the details that support the statement. If there is no support the statement is probably an overgeneralization.

Step 3: Evaluate the support. Does it really support the broad generalization or only a qualified version of the generalization? An example of an overgeneralization that has been qualified is "Some dogs love to play in the water."

Analyzing Literary Devices

Many reading tests that include literary passages will ask you to identify literary devices. Here are some of the major literary devices.

<u>Allusion</u> – a reference to a person, place, or event from history, literature, religion, mythology, politics, sport, science, or pop culture

Example: *The George M. Cohan song "The Yankee Doodle Boy" alludes to the eighteenth century tune "Yankee Doodle."*

<u>Figurative language</u> – describes one thing in terms of another and is not meant to be taken literally

A **metaphor** compares one thing to something quite unlike it.

Example: *The wind is a rake.*

A **simile** compares two things using *like* or *as*.

Example: *The thick woods were like prison walls.*

Personification describes an inanimate object giving it human characteristics.

Example: *The flower turned its gaze toward the sun.*

<u>Imagery</u> – language that appeals to any of the five senses: sight, touch, smell, hearing, and taste

Example: *At the pond, a rustling of dry reeds revealed the brown head of a grackle, who watched the cool, gleaming water with a beady eye.*

<u>Irony</u> – the contrast between expectation and reality

Verbal irony contrasts what is said and what is meant.

Example: *"Oh, I absolutely love that hat. Are those real grapes?"*

Situational irony contrasts what is expected to happen and what really happens.

Example: *A solider survives many grueling battles abroad only to be run over by an ice cream truck back home.*

Dramatic irony presents a contrast between what a character thinks is true and what the audience knows to be true.

Example: *A play's hero thinks his son is dead, but the audience knows that his son is alive.*

<u>Symbol</u> – an object, event, person, or animal to which extraordinary meaning is attached

Example: *A skull and crossbones symbolizes danger; red roses symbolize love. These are symbols that everyone uses. Writers try to create fresh symbols.*

Strategies for Answering Multiple-Choice Questions

Here are some suggestions for taking any standardized reading test:

- First, **read the passage as if you were not even taking a test**. Do this to get a general overview of both the topic and the tone of a passage. Also, keep reading even if you do not understand the passage at first.

- **Look at the big picture**. In other words, examine the most obvious features of the passage. To do this, ask yourself the following questions as you read:

  - What is the title?

  - What do you believe is the main idea of a piece of nonfiction or the theme of a piece of fiction?

  - What do you think is the author's purpose? to inform? to entertain? to show how to do something?

- Next, **read the questions**. This will help you to know what information to look for when you reread.

- Reread the passage. **Underline information** that relates to the questions. This will help you when filling in the answers.

- **Go back to the questions**. Try to answer each one in your mind before looking at the answer choices.

- Finally, **read *all* the answer choices and eliminate those that are obviously incorrect**. After this process, mark the best answer. Also, keep in mind that the people who write standardized tests often create incorrect answer choices that are designed to distract you from the right answer. Such "distractors" include answer choices that are true but not relevant to the question, answer choices that relate to the wrong part of the passage, and answer choices that are too broad or too narrow.

Strategies for Answering Open-Ended Questions

Standardized reading tests often include open-ended questions, such as short-answer questions and extended-response questions. These questions differ from multiple-choice in that they often ask you to look much more broadly at the reading passage. Open-ended questions test your ability to synthesize what you have learned from reading a passage. Here are some suggestions for answering open-ended questions:

- Read the passage in its entirety. Pay close attention to the major events and characters. Jot down information you believe is central to the passage.

- Read each question carefully. If you cannot answer the question at first, simply skip it and return to it later.

- There are some words that appear frequently in open-ended questions, such as *compare, contrast, interpret, discuss,* and *summarize.* Be sure you have a complete understanding of these words within the context of the question.

- Return to the passage and skim it. Do this to find the details or examples you need to support your answer.

- When writing the rest of your answer, be precise but brief. Refer to details from the passage. Be sure to proofread for spelling, grammar, and punctuation errors.

Reading Practice

Read the selection below. Then read each question and choose the best answer. Use the provided answer sheet at the end of the workbook to record your answers, and use a separate sheet of paper to record your response to open-ended questions.

from The Call of the Wild
by Jack London

That winter, at Dawson, Buck performed another exploit, not so heroic, perhaps, but one that made his name even more famous. In a saloon, men were talking about dogs. Buck, because of his record, was the target for several men. Thornton firmly defended him. At the end of half an hour one man stated that his dog could start a sled with five hundred pounds and walk off with it; a second bragged six hundred for his dog; and a third, seven hundred.

"Pooh! pooh!" said John Thornton; "Buck can start a thousand pounds."

"And break it out? and walk off with it for a hundred yards?" demanded Matthewson, a man who had a seven hundred- pound claim.

"And break it out, and walk off with it for a hundred yards," John Thornton said coolly.

"Well," Matthewson said, slowly and deliberately, so that all could hear, "I've got a thousand dollars that says he can't. And there it is." So saying, he slammed a sack of gold dust of the size of a bologna sausage down upon the bar.

(6) Nobody spoke. Thornton's bluff, if bluff it was, had been called. He could feel a flush of warm blood creeping up his face. His tongue had tricked him. He did not know whether Buck could start a thousand pounds. Half a ton! The enormousness of it scared him. Further, he had no thousand dollars.

"I've got a sled standing outside now, with twenty fifty-pound sacks of flour on it," Matthewson went on with brutal directness; "so don't let that hinder you."

Thornton did not reply. He did not know what to say. The face of Jim O'Brien, an oldtime comrade, caught his eyes. It was as a cue to him, seeming to rouse him to do what he would never have dreamed of doing.

"Can you lend me a thousand?" he asked, almost in a whisper.

"Sure," answered O'Brien. "Though it's little faith I'm having, John, that the beast can do the trick."

The Eldorado emptied its occupants into the street to see the test. The tables were deserted, and the dealers and gamekeepers came forth to see the outcome of the wager and to lay odds. Several hundred men, furred and mittened, banked around the sled within easy distance.

| Reading Practice, *continued*

Matthewson's sled, loaded with a thousand pounds of flour, had been standing for a couple of hours, and in the intense cold (it was sixty below zero) the runners had frozen fast to the hard-packed snow. Men offered odds of two to one that Buck could not budge the sled. A disagreement arose concerning the phrase "break out." O'Brien contended it was Thornton's privilege to knock the runners loose, leaving Buck to "break it out" from a dead standstill. Matthewson insisted that the phrase included breaking the runners from the frozen grip of the snow. A majority of the men who had witnessed the making of the bet decided in his favor, and the odds went up to three to one against Buck.

There were no takers. Not a man believed him capable of the feat. "Three to one!" he proclaimed. "I'll lay you another thousand at that figure, Thornton. What d'ye say?"

Thornton's doubt was strong in his face, but his fighting spirit was aroused – the fighting spirit that soars above odds, fails to recognize the impossible. He called Hans and Pete to him. Their sacks were slim, and with his own the three partners could rake together only two hundred dollars, all the money they had; yet they laid it unhesitatingly against Matthewson's six hundred.

The team of ten dogs was unhitched, and Buck, with his own harness, was put into the sled. He was in perfect condition, without an ounce of excess flesh, and the one hundred and fifty pounds that he weighed were all pounds of grit and forcefulness. His furry coat shone like silk. His great breast and heavy fore legs were no more than in proportion with the rest of the body, where the muscles showed in tight rolls underneath the skin. Men felt these muscles and proclaimed them hard as iron, and the odds went down to two to one.

"Gad, sir! Gad, sir!" stuttered one rich man. "I offer you eight hundred for him, sir, before the test, sir; eight hundred just as he stands."

Thornton knelt down by Buck's side. He took his head in his two hands and rested cheek on cheek. He did not playfully shake him, as usual; but he whispered in his ear. "Do it because you love me, Buck. Because you love me." Buck whined with suppressed eagerness.

The crowd was watching curiously. The affair was growing mysterious. It seemed like magic. As he got to his feet, Buck seized Thornton's mittened hand between his jaws, pressing in with his teeth and releasing slowly. It was the answer of love. Thornton stepped well back.

"Now, Buck," he said.

Buck tightened the traces, then let go for a matter of several inches. It was the way he had learned.

"Gee!" Thornton's voice rang out, sharp in the tense silence, meaning turn to the right.

| Reading Practice, *continued*

Buck swung to the right, ending the movement in a plunge that took up the slack and with a sudden jerk arrested his one hundred and fifty pounds. The load quivered, and from under the runners arose a crisp crackling.

"Haw!" Thornton commanded.

Buck duplicated the maneuver, this time to the left. The crackling turned into a snapping, the sled pivoting and the sled was broken out. Men were holding their breaths without even realizing it.

"Now, MUSH!"

(26) Thornton's command cracked out like a pistol-shot. Buck threw himself forward, tightening the traces with a jarring lunge. His whole body was gathered compactly together in the tremendous effort, the muscles writhing and knotting like live things under the silky fur. His great chest was low to the ground, his head forward and down, while his feet were flying like mad, the claws scarring the hard-packed snow in parallel grooves. The sled swayed and trembled, half-started forward. One of his feet slipped, and one man groaned aloud. But Buck continued to pull and the sled lurched ahead in jerks until it was moving steadily along.

Men gasped and began to breathe again, unaware that for a moment they had ceased to breathe. Thornton was running behind, encouraging Buck with short, cheery words. The distance had been measured off, and he neared the pile of firewood which marked the end of the hundred yards. Then a cheer began to grow and grow, which burst into a roar as he passed the firewood and halted at command. Hats and mittens were flying in the air. Men were shaking hands, it did not matter with whom, and bubbling over in loud voices.

Thornton fell on his knees beside Buck. Head was against head, and he was shaking him back and forth. Those who hurried up heard him talk to Buck with soft, soothing phrases.

1. According to the selection, why does Thornton accept Matthewson's challenge?

   A He needed the money.

   B His fighting spirit was aroused.

   C He knew that Buck could meet the challenge.

   D His friends told him to accept it.

2. In paragraph 6, Thornton's "tongue had tricked him." What does that phrase mean?

   A He had no control over his tongue.

   B He did some tricks with his tongue.

   C He said something he didn't mean to say.

   D His tongue was moving a lot.

3. Read this sentence from paragraph 26.
   Thornton's command <u>cracked</u> out like a pistol-shot.
   The connotation of <u>cracked</u> is

   A broke up.

   B exploded dangerously.

   C frightened.

   D voiced loudly and clearly.

4. What part of this story is **most** similar to a legend?

   A Thornton refuses to sell his dog.

   B Buck does an amazing thing by pulling a sled that weighs 1,000 pounds.

   C Men bet on whether the dog can pull the sled.

   D People are living in a very cold place.

5. Read the first line of the selection.
   That winter, at Dawson, Buck performed another exploit, not so heroic perhaps, but one that made his name even more famous.
   What part of this sentence foreshadows what happens in the story?

   A That winter, at Dawson

   B Buck performed another exploit

   C not so heroic, perhaps

   D but one that made his name even more famous

6. Why does everyone leave the Eldorado and stand outside in sixty below zero weather?

   A They want to see if Buck can pull the sled.

   B They want to see Matthewson and Thornton fight.

   C The Eldorado is closing for the night.

   D They want to make more bets on the dog and sled.

7. Matthewson wages his bet with

   A one thousand dollars cash

   B money he borrows from a friend

   C his word; he has no cash with him

   D a sack of gold dust

8. Which statement **best** summarizes the theme of this selection?

   A Big bets result in big efforts.

   B Kindness is often rewarded with effort.

   C The masses are usually right.

   D Betting rarely pays off.

| Reading Practice, *continued*

9. Based on his actions during Buck's demonstration, which statement is **most likely** true of Thornton?

    A He is a kind master.

    B He angers Buck often.

    C He often bets on Buck.

    D He is a reckless man.

10. Which word **best** describes the mood of the crowd at the end of the selection?

    A remote

    B horrified

    C thrilled

    D disappointed

11. How do the odds change after the men feel Buck's muscles?

12. Based on the information given in this selection, what makes the sled especially difficult for Buck to move? Use at least two details from the text to support your answer.

| Reading Practice, *continued*

Read the selection below. Then read each question and choose the best answer. Use the provided answer sheet at the end of the workbook to record your answers, and use a separate sheet of paper to record your response to open-ended questions.

Cos Gives it up

What does Bill Cosby have in common with Robin Williams and Jim Carrey—besides being funny? Cosby's 1996 and 1997 combined income was thirty-six million dollars, an amount of money which placed him on *Forbes* magazine's 1997 Top 40 list of the wealthiest entertainers. He's there alongside other famous comics like Robin Williams and Jim Carrey. Although Cos doesn't shoot hoops, model clothes, or direct blockbuster movies for a living, he's definitely making big bucks from joking on the screen and stage. However, Bill Cosby doesn't let the buck stop at the punch line.

Jokes aside, Cos is serious when it comes to money. Cosby has played many roles in television shows, movies, and his stand-up comedy routines, but he equally enjoys the role of giver and helper. As a benefactor, Cosby gives out of his own pocket to those who need it. Like other celebrities who make charitable donations, such as Oprah Winfrey, Steven Spielberg, and Michael Jordan, he can put his money where his mouth is when it comes to sharing his success with others. Frequently, Cosby does his stand-up routines or gives speeches for benefit performances that raise funds for deserving causes. He has donated twenty million dollars to Spelman College to build a variety of new facilities and pay for teaching positions. Before this, no individual had ever donated such a large

amount to an African American college; only three other individual donations to any cause had been larger than his. Cosby and his wife, Camille, have also set up a foundation to provide assistance for people with dyslexia, a type of learning disability. The Future Filmmakers Program at New York University was established by Cosby to help encourage and provide opportunities for students in the film industry.

Although his benevolence is greatly appreciated, Bill Cosby doesn't donate for recognition or fame; his acts of charity come from his heart and from his belief that the road to success starts with one important word—*Education,* This belief could seem kind of funny coming from somebody who was better at cracking up his friends in class than cracking open a book. Cosby was determined to achieve his goals, despite his resistance to schoolwork. Because he was a natural comedian but not a natural student, his road to success was not straight and immediate. At one point, he even dropped out of high school. Nicknamed Shorty because he was tall as a kid, Shorty did not come up short; he realized that he would never really succeed in a personal way if he didn't have some solid ground under him, and that ground was education. While working in the entertainment industry, he worked on his degrees. He became so focused on his goal that he eventually earned a Ph.D. in education—no joke. Although it may seem that

Reading Practice, *continued*

Cosby's dream was to be in the spotlight, his personal dream was to finish college. You could say that education is no laughing matter to Bill Cosby, and donating his income to educational causes shows how serious he is.

If you ask anybody who Bill Cosby is, chances are good you'll get answers like "comedian," "that actor who has his own sitcom," or even "that guy who does those funny pudding and gelatin commercials." I would say, "the funniest man in the business of comedy." Now you can add the role of benefactor to that list.

Reading Practice, *continued*

1. Which of the following **best** describes the basis for the donation choices Bill Cosby makes?

   A He wants people to know that he is more than just a comic.

   B He believes that education is important.

   C He is trying to be a good role model.

   D He thinks that he has too much money.

2. Which of these statements **best** supports the author's claim that Bill Cosby is a benefactor?

   A Cosby dropped out of high school.

   B Cosby has given millions of dollars to Spelman College.

   C Cosby is a famous comedian and television actor.

   D Cosby believes that education is important.

3. Bill Cosby donated money to colleges because he

   A is more than just a comic.

   B believes that education is important.

   C is trying to be a good role model.

   D has too much money.

4. Based on the selection, which statement about Bill Cosby is **most likely** true?

   A People rarely recognize Bill Cosby on the street.

   B Bill Cosby will retire from comedy soon.

   C People will realize that Cosby is more than just a comic.

   D Bill Cosby will stop giving money to charities.

5. What is the effect in paragraph 3 of the words "no joke"?

   A to suggest that everything else in the paragraph is a joke

   B to remind readers that the information is true

   C to set up the beginning of a joke

   D to emphasize that Cosby is a comedian

6. People who give money to charities and schools are **most likely** to have which of the following characteristics?

   A a willingness to look foolish

   B a desire to help others

   C a sense of humor

   D a love of literature

7. Which of these statements is an **opinion** about Bill Cosby?

   A Cosby's 1996 and 1997 income was thirty-six million dollars.

   B Bill Cosby's acts of charity come from his heart.

   C Cosby gives out of his own pocket to those who need it.

   D Cosby eventually earned a Ph.D. in education.

Reading Practice, *continued*

8. What is the effect of the use of quotations in the last paragraph?

    A to serve as a summary of Bill Cosby's accomplishments

    B to make the selection sound made up

    C to create a funny ending for a story about a funny man

    D to make sure readers know that Bill Cosby is an important man

9. Which phrase is an example of a **cliché?**

    A shoot hoops

    B model clothes

    C a natural comedian

    D the buck stop

10. Which of these statements supports the idea that "Bill Cosby doesn't let the buck stop at the punch line"?

    A He was on *Forbes* magazine's Top 10 list of wealthiest entertainers.

    B He frequently does his standup routines or gives speeches for benefit performances.

    C Bill Cosby was better at cracking up his friends in class than cracking open a book.

    D Cosby has played many roles in television shows and movies.

11. What is the **main** purpose of this selection?

12. Describe **one** cause and its effect from this passage.

| Reading Practice, *continued*

In the first part of the poem, the highwayman promised Bess, the innkeeper's daughter, that he would return to her before midnight. He went off on a dangerous mission to steal gold from the British army. Here is Part Two. Read the poem. Then read each question and choose the best answer. Use the provided answer sheet at the end of the workbook to record your answers, and use a separate sheet of paper to record your response to open-ended questions.

from The Highwayman, Part Two
by Alfred Noyes

He did not come in the dawning; he did not come at noon;

And out o' the tawny[1] sunset, before the rise o' the moon,

When the road was a gypsy's ribbon, looping the purple moor,

A red-coat troop came marching—

    Marching—marching—

King George's men came marching, up to the old inn-door.

They said no word to the landlord, they drank his ale instead,

But they gagged his daughter and bound her to the foot of her narrow bed;

Two of them knelt at her casement, with muskets at their side!

There was death at every window;

    And hell at one dark window;

For Bess could see, through her casement, the road that he would ride.

They had tied her up to attention, with many a sniggering[2] jest;

They had bound a musket beside her, with the barrel beneath her breast!

"Now, keep good watch!" and they kissed her.

    She heard the dead man say—

Look for me by moonlight;

    Watch for me by moonlight;

I'll come to thee by moonlight, though hell should bar the way!

She twisted her hands behind her; but all the knots held good!

She writhed her hands till her fingers were wet with sweat or blood!

They stretched and strained in the darkness, and the hours crawled by like years,

1 tawny: sandy colored

2 sniggering: laughing

Till, now, on the stroke of midnight,
    Cold, on the stroke of midnight,
The tip of one finger touched it! The trigger at least was hers!
The tip of one finger touched it; she strove[3] no more for the rest!
Up, she stood up to attention, with the barrel beneath her breast,
She would not risk their hearing; she would not strive again;
For the road lay bare in the moonlight;
    Blank and bare in the moonlight;
And the blood of her veins in the moonlight throbbed to her love's refrain.
Tlot-tlot; tlot-tlot! Had they heard it? The horse-hoofs ringing clear;
Tlot-tlot, tlot-tlot, in the distance? Were they deaf that they did not hear?
Down the ribbon of moonlight, over the brow of the hill,
The highwayman came riding,
    Riding, riding!
The red-coats looked to their priming[4]! She stood up, straight and still!
Tlot-tlot, in the frosty silence! *Tlot-tlot,* in the echoing night!
Nearer he came and nearer! Her face was like a light!
Her eyes grew wide for a moment; she drew one last deep breath,
Then her finger moved in the moonlight,
    Her musket shattered the moonlight,
Shattered her breast in the moonlight and warned him—with her death.

3 strove: strived, tried, attempted
4 priming: preparing their guns for firing

| Reading Practice, *continued*

1. The phrase *Tlot-tlot*
   A makes the action more dramatic.
   B builds suspense.
   C creates the sound of horse's hooves.
   D adds humor to the poem.

2. What is **most likely** the reason Bess wants to escape from the soldiers?
   A She is uncomfortable being tied up.
   B She wants to warn the highwayman.
   C She is afraid the British soldiers will kill her.
   D She wants to make sure that her family is safe.

3. To which sense do the lines in stanza 4 appeal?
   A sight
   B smell
   C hearing
   D touch

4. What is the **most likely** the meaning of this line from stanza 2?
   There was death at every window.
   A There was something deadly lurking outside the house.
   B Soldiers were waiting at the windows to kill the highwayman.
   C A deadly storm was hammering at the windows.
   D People who wanted to kill Bess stood at the windows.

5. What is the **main** effect of the simile in stanza 4?
   A to suggest that time seemed to pass slowly
   B to show how long the soldiers stood ready
   C to emphasize Bess' age
   D to focus on Bess' discomfort

6. Based on the last stanza, what is **most likely** to happen next?
   A The sound of the gun will warn the highwayman to turn back.
   B Bess's screams will warn the highwayman to draw his guns.
   C Bess's death will make the highwayman sad.
   D The sound of the gun will surprise and distract the soldiers.

7. Which type of person is **most like** Bess?
   A someone who is easily frightened
   B someone who prefers a quiet life
   C someone who enjoys a challenge
   D someone who sacrifices herself for others

8. Based on the context of the poem, the **best** synonym for casement is
   A doorway.
   B cedar chest.
   C window.
   D gun case.

9. What is the rhyme scheme of this poem?

    A AABCCB

    B ABACCA

    C AABCCD

    D no rhyme scheme

10. What is **most likely** the meaning of this line from stanza 3?
She heard the dead man say—

    A The soldiers will die.

    B Bess will die.

    C The highway man will die.

    D The highwayman spoke to Bess while he was dying.

11. Why did the soldiers put Bess near the casement?

12. Does the poet take the side of the highway man or the British soldiers? Explain.

Read the selection. Then read each question and choose the best answer. Use the provided answer sheet at the end of the workbook to record your answers, and use a separate sheet of paper to record your response to open-ended questions.

World of Dyslexia

Albert Einstein, whom *Time* magazine named its person of the twentieth century, was a genius. Surprisingly, he was a late talker and a poor student. During his early schooling, teachers thought he was not very smart. Einstein had dyslexia. Although dyslexia afflicts between 10 and 15 percent of the American population, most people know very little about it.

What Is Dyslexia?

Dyslexia is a language disorder. The word dyslexia comes from two Greek words: *dys-,* meaning "difficult," and *lexis,* meaning "word." Literally translated, *dyslexia* means "difficulty with words." Dyslexia may be a neurological condition, which means that it is caused by the way the brain functions. Dyslexia often runs in families, leading researchers to believe it may be an inherited condition. Researchers once thought that boys were four times as likely to have dyslexia as girls. The latest studies, however, show that girls are just as likely to have dyslexia as boys.

Symptoms of Dyslexia

Dyslexia can range from mild to severe, and the condition is as unique as the people who have it. Signs of dyslexia include difficulty in learning how to read and spell. In cases of mild dyslexia, this symptom might not become obvious until later elementary school or even high school, when language and texts become more complex. Confusing directions, such as right and left, is another symptom of dyslexia. Many people with dyslexia have trouble spelling words. Many cannot create rhymes. Reversing letters, such as writing a *b* for *d* or reading *saw* for *was,* may also be a symptom.

How Dyslexia Affects Learning

People with dyslexia have trouble understanding the relationship between letters and sounds. The English language has forty-four sounds, called **phonemes.** The word *cot,* for example, is made up of three phonemes: *kuh, aa,* and *tuh.* Learning to read involves identifying these phonemes, matching them to letters, and blending the sounds together to make words. Most people sound out words so quickly that the process is automatic. This decoding process, however, is rarely automatic for those with dyslexia. Thus, they often read at a slower rate than others.

Reading Practice, *continued*

Misconceptions About Dyslexia

Because children with dyslexia have difficulty learning to read, some people jump to the wrong conclusion that these children are not bright. As the example of Einstein shows, dyslexia is not a sign of low intelligence. Many people with dyslexia are highly creative and talented. Walt Disney, Muhammad Ali, Whoopi Goldberg, Winston Churchill, and Tom Cruise are people who overcame dyslexia to succeed.

Some people mistakenly believe that those with dyslexia are lazy and just need to work harder. Most students with dyslexia, however, work incredibly hard but require a different kind of instruction. They learn better by using visual aids, touch, and movement. These students may also need instruction in phonics to help them match phonemes to letters more readily.

Dyslexia can be a challenge, but it does not mean failure. Just ask any of the accomplished and successful people who have learned how to live with dyslexia.

Reading Practice, *continued*

1. Why does the author begin the selection by talking about Albert Einstein?

   A to show how a genius is different from a person with dyslexia

   B to show that a genius can be a person with dyslexia

   C to show that time magazine favors people with dyslexia

   D to show that all people with dyslexia are late talkers and poor students

2. The writer uses subheadings to

   A help the reader define dyslexia.

   B show that the essay has three main points.

   C help the reader know what to expect in each section.

   D persuade the reader to donate money to help people with dyslexia.

3. Which statement about school is **most likely** true for students with dyslexia?

   A Classes with lots of reading pose a challenge to students.

   B All classes pose a challenge for students.

   C School is a challenge few people with dyslexia can overcome.

   D School poses no challenges to really smart students with dyslexia.

4. Why does the author place quotation marks around some words or phrases?

   A to show that the words exactly as they were spoken by a source

   B to show that they are the meanings or definitions of a word

   C to show that the author did research before writing

   D to show that the words are important

5. Which statement **best** supports the idea that people with dyslexia can be successful?

   A Some people mistakenly believe that people with dyslexia are lazy and just need to work harder.

   B Many people with dyslexia learn better by using visual aids, touch, and movement.

   C Dyslexia can be a challenge, but it does not mean failure.

   D Walt Disney, Muhammad Ali, Whoopi Goldberg, Winston Churchill, and Tom Cruise are people who overcame dyslexia to succeed.

6. Based on the selection, people who have dyslexia are **most likely** to

   A become actors or public figures.

   B love word games.

   C have difficulty with reading.

   D enjoy solving tough math problems.

Reading Practice, *continued*

7. Based on the context of the section headed "How Dyslexia Affects Learning," what is a phoneme?

   A the way "sound" looks to people with dyslexia

   B smallest of speech sounds

   C letters of the alphabet

   D blended sounds

8. Dyslexia means "difficulty with words." Monograph means "a written piece on one topic." Based on these definitions, what word would mean "difficulty with writing"?

   A dysgraphia

   B monolexia

   C dysmono

   D lexigraph

9. According to the selection, why do many people with dyslexia read at a slower rate than others?

   A They are not very smart.

   B They have poor eyesight.

   C The decoding process used in reading is not automatic for them.

   D They cannot create rhymes.

10. In which section of the passage would a reader expect to learn about the school experiences of people with dyslexia?

11. Use your own words to summarize what the passage says about dyslexia.

Reading Practice, *continued*

Read the selection. Then read each question and choose the best answer. Use the provided answer sheet at the end of the workbook to record your answers, and use a separate sheet of paper to record your response to open-ended questions.

Anne's Confession: *from* Anne of Green Gables
Lucy Maud Montgomery

On the Monday evening before the picnic Marilla came down from her room with a troubled face.

"Anne," she said . . . "did you see anything of my amethyst brooch? . . . I can't find it anywhere."

"I—I saw it this afternoon when you were away at the Aid Society," said Anne, a little slowly. "I was passing your door when I saw it on the cushion, so I went in to look at it."

"Did you touch it?" said Marilla sternly.

"Y-e-e-s," admitted Anne, "I took it up and I pinned it on . . . just to see how it would look."

"You had no business to do anything of the sort. It's very wrong in a little girl to meddle. . . . Where did you put it?"

"Oh, I put it back on the bureau. I hadn't it on a minute. Truly, I didn't mean to meddle, Marilla. I didn't think about its being wrong to go in and try on the brooch; but I see now that it was and I'll never do it again. That's one good thing about me. I never do the same naughty thing twice."

"You didn't put it back," said Marilla. "That brooch isn't anywhere on the bureau. You've taken it out or something, Anne."

"I did put it back," said Anne quickly—pertly, Marilla thought. "I don't just remember whether I stuck it on the pincushion or laid it in the china tray. But I'm perfectly certain I put it back."

"I'll go and have another look," said Marilla, determining to be just. "If you put that brooch back it's there still. If it isn't I'll know you didn't, that's all!"

Marilla went to her room and made a thorough search, not only over the bureau but in every other place she thought the brooch might possibly be. It was not to be found and she returned to the kitchen.

"Anne, the brooch is gone. By your own admission you were the last person to handle it. Now, what have you done with it? Tell me the truth at once. Did you take it out and lose it?"

"No, I didn't," said Anne solemnly, meeting Marilla's angry gaze squarely. "I never took the brooch out of your room and that is the truth, if I was to be led to the block for it—although I'm not very certain what a block is. So there, Marilla."

Anne's "so there" was only intended to emphasize her assertion, but Marilla took it as a display of defiance.

"I believe you are telling me a falsehood, Anne," she said sharply. "I know you are. There now, don't say anything more unless you are prepared to tell the whole truth. Go to your room and stay there until you are ready to confess."

. . . Marilla went to her room at intervals all through the evening and searched for the brooch, without finding it. A bedtime visit . . . produced no result. Anne persisted in denying that she knew anything about the brooch but Marilla was only the more firmly convinced that she did.

Reading Practice, *continued*

She told Matthew the story the next morning. Matthew was confounded and puzzled; he could not so quickly lose faith in Anne but he had to admit that circumstances were against her.

"You're sure it hasn't fell down behind the bureau?" was the only suggestion he could offer.

. . . "The brooch is gone and that child has taken it and lied about it. That's the plain, ugly truth, Matthew Cuthbert, and we might as well look it in the face. . . . She'll stay in her room until she confesses," said Marilla grimly.

. . . Anne steadfastly refused to confess. She persisted in asserting that she had not taken the brooch. The child had evidently been crying and Marilla felt a pang of pity which she sternly repressed. By night she was, as she expressed it, "beat out."

"You'll stay in this room until you confess, Anne. You can make up your mind to that," she said firmly.

"But the picnic is tomorrow, Marilla," cried Anne.

"You'll not go to picnics nor anywhere else until you've confessed, Anne."

"Oh, Marilla," gasped Anne.

But Marilla had gone out and shut the door.

Wednesday morning dawned as bright and fair as if made to order for the picnic. . . .When Marilla took her breakfast up to her she found the child sitting primly on her bed, pale and resolute, with tight-shut lips and gleaming eyes.

"Marilla, I'm ready to confess."

"Ah!" Marilla laid down her tray. Once again her method had succeeded; but her success was very bitter to her. "Let me hear what you have to say then, Anne."

"I took the amethyst brooch," said Anne, as if repeating a lesson she had learned. "I took it just as you said. I didn't mean to take it when I went in. But it did look so beautiful, Marilla, when I pinned it on my breast that I was overcome by an irresistible temptation. . . . And that's the best I can do at confessing, Marilla."

Marilla felt hot anger surge up into her heart again. This child had taken and lost her treasured amethyst brooch and now sat there calmly reciting the details thereof without the least apparent . . . repentance.

"Anne, this is terrible," she said, trying to speak calmly. "You are the very wickedest girl I ever heard of . . .You'll go to no picnic today, Anne Shirley. That shall be your punishment. And it isn't half severe enough either for what you've done!" . . . .

Anne realized that Marilla was not to be moved. She clasped her hands together, gave a piercing shriek, and then flung herself face downward on the bed. . . .

When her dishes were washed and her hens fed, Marilla remembered that she had noticed a small tear in her best black lace shawl when she had taken it off on Monday afternoon on returning from the Ladies' Aid.

She would go and mend it. The shawl was in a box in her trunk. As Marilla lifted it out, the sunlight . . . struck upon something caught in the shawl—something that glittered and sparkled in facets of violet light. Marilla snatched at it with a gasp. It was the amethyst brooch, hanging to a thread of the lace by its catch!

Reading Practice, *continued*

"Dear life and heart," said Marilla blankly, "what does this mean? Here's my brooch safe and sound. . . . Whatever did that girl mean by saying she took it and lost it?" . . .

Marilla, . . .brooch in hand, went to Anne's room. Anne had cried herself out and was sitting dejectedly by the window.

"Anne Shirley," said Marilla solemnly, "I've just found my brooch hanging to my black lace shawl. Now I want to know what that story you told me this morning meant."

"Why, you said you'd keep me here until I confessed," returned Anne wearily, "and so I decided to confess because I was bound to get to the picnic. I thought out a confession last night after I went to bed and made it as interesting as I could. And I said it over and over so that I wouldn't forget it. But you wouldn't let me go to the picnic after all, so all my trouble was wasted."

"Anne, you do beat all! But I was wrong—I see that now. I shouldn't have doubted your word when I'd never known you to tell a story. Of course, it wasn't right for you to confess to a thing you hadn't done. . . But I drove you to it. So if you'll forgive me, Anne, I'll forgive you and we'll start square again. And now get yourself ready for the picnic."

Reading Practice, *continued*

1. At the beginning of the story, Marilla thinks Anne

   A tore Marilla's shawl.

   B took Marilla's brooch.

   C went to the picnic without permission.

   D broke her favorite set of dishes.

2. What is the significance of Anne's confession?

   A It shows how much she hates Marilla.

   B It shows how sorry she is.

   C It shows how much she respects Marilla.

   D It shows how much she wants to go to the picnic.

3. How is Marilla different from her brother Matthew?

   A Marilla has strong ideas about raising children and Matthew does not.

   B Matthew wants to take an active role in raising Anne, but Marilla does not.

   C Marilla thinks that Anne is right, but Matthew thinks Anne is a liar.

   D Matthew is kind to Anne, but Marilla is always cold and unforgiving.

4. Right before Anne confesses, the author writes that Marilla's success in getting Anne to confess was <u>bitter</u> to Marilla. How does the word <u>bitter</u> describe Marilla's feelings about the confession?

   A It shows resurrected anger.

   B It insinuates a sense of permanent loss.

   C It gives a sense of combined happiness and sadness.

   D It suggests distrust.

5. Which statement **best** summarizes the theme of this selection?

   A Trust is more important than any possession.

   B Sometimes it is acceptable to tell a lie.

   C Older people are always right and young people are always wrong.

   D Apologizing will solve any problem.

6. When Marilla tells Matthew what happened, he is "<u>confounded</u> and puzzled." What does <u>confounded</u> mean?

   A certain

   B surprised

   C confused

   D impressed

7. *The Boy Who Cried Wolf* is a story about a boy who lies so often that no one believes him when he tells the truth. How would you compare the theme of *The Boy Who Cried Wolf* to the theme of *Anne's Confession?*

   A *The Boy Who Cried Wolf* is about honesty, and *Anne's Confession* is about family.

   B The themes of these stories seem to be at odds with each other.

   C The themes of these stories are about the same—sometimes it is acceptable to tell a lie.

   D The themes of these stories are about the same—lying always gets you into trouble.

8. Which of these situations is **most like** the one described in the passage?

   A Jan steals her grandmother's necklace but returns it before her grandmother notices it is missing.

   B Leah says that she threw the eraser, even though she didn't, so the class will be able to go on its field trip.

   C Henry is caught lying about where he was after school.

   D James admits that he cheated on his test, even though he knows he will get into trouble.

9. Which of these words from the story helps show that it is set in the past?

   A brooch

   B picnic

   C confess

   D denying

10. Based on her reaction to the discovery of the brooch, which word **best** describes Marilla?

    A arrogant

    B humble

    C cruel

    D light-hearted

11. Based on the selection, what will happen next?

12. Early in the story, Anne freely admits that she tried on the brooch. What does this tell you about Anne? Is she more or less likely to tell the truth, even if it means she will get into trouble?

| Reading Practice, *continued*

Read the selection. Then read each question and choose the best answer. Use the provided answer sheet at the end of the workbook to record your answers, and use a separate sheet of paper to record your response to open-ended questions.

Making a Magic Trick

Would you like to amaze your friends with mystery and magic? Some magic tricks take lots of material, skill, and practice. Others you can learn in just a few minutes, like the Magic Ripping Trick. Amaze your friends with a magic trick they will never forget—or figure out.

Materials

The only materials you will need are

- glue
- scissors
- two strips of the same color construction paper (6 inches long by 2 inches wide)

Making the Trick

First, fold up one of the strips like an accordion or fan, folding from one end to the other. Make sure the little package you fold measures 2 inches by 1.5 inches when you are through.

Then glue this little folded package onto the very end of the back of the other strip of paper. You should now be able to hold each end of the strip between your hands and keep the little package hidden under your left thumb. Place the prepared strip in your pocket until you are ready to present the trick. *Hint:* Practice makes perfect. You might want to run through the trick once and then make another strip for the real performance for friends.

Performing the Trick

When it is time for your magic show, hold one end of the strip in your right hand and hold the end with the package in your left hand. Show it to the audience, keeping the little package on the back hidden under your left thumb.

Now tell your audience you are showing them an ordinary strip of paper. Do not let them see the back of the strip.

Say that you will now do the amazing Magic Ripping Trick. You will rip up the strip of paper and then make the pieces come magically back together like new.

Next, rip the strip in half width-wise, down the middle. Put the right half behind the left half. The right half will now be under your thumb behind the folded package.

Then rip the strip in half again. Again, put the right half behind the left half.

Now all the pieces should be about the same size as the folded package. The ripped pieces should all be behind the folded package, which still have the very end of the ripped strip glued to the front. You should be holding the ripped pieces together in a stack under your left thumb.

Finally, all you have to do is say some mysterious magic words and then pull open the folded strip. Make sure to keep the ripped pieces hidden behind the opened strip. Your audience will see a strip exactly like the one you just tore up!

While your friends sit there with puzzled expressions, be sure to put all the torn up pieces of paper into your pocket. Good magicians never give away their secrets!

1. What is the **main** purpose of this selection?

    A to warn readers of the dangers of practicing magic tricks

    B to tell about the author's experiences as a magician

    C to inform readers about the history of a magic trick

    D to teach readers how to make and perform a trick

2. In the second paragraph under "Making the Trick," why does the author put the word <u>hint</u> in italics (slanted type)?

    A because hint is an important word

    B to get readers' attention

    C because hint is a foreign word

    D to remind readers to keep a secret

3. In the first two sentences under "Making the Trick" how does the "make sure" step logically follow the "fold" step?

    A It explains how to fold the second strip.

    B It clarifies that you will have both a fan and a package.

    C It shows how easy it is to fold.

    D It provides a check on the first step.

4. In the word <u>magician,</u> the suffix <u>-ian</u> means

    A resembling.

    B belonging to.

    C one who.

    D not.

5. The last paragraph seem to suggest that magicians

    A can keep secrets.

    B love magic.

    C are show-offs.

    D hate audiences.

6. Based on the selection, why should you put the pieces of torn paper in your pocket after you perform the magic trick?

    A because there is no nearby trash can in which to throw them

    B because magicians always make a point of being neat

    C so the audience does not figure out how the trick is done

    D so you can use the pieces in another trick

7. According to the selection, what does the author think about the Magic Ripping Trick?

    A It is the most fun trick for magicians everywhere.

    B It is quite simple to learn.

    C It never surprises the audience.

    D It takes a lot of skill and practice to get it right.

8. What should you do **before** the magic show begins?

    A Tear up strips of paper.

    B Hide strips of ripped paper under your thumb.

    C Say some magic words.

    D Glue an accordion-folded paper to a strip of paper.

Reading Practice, *continued*

9. Suppose you wanted to change the heading for the section titled <u>Making the Trick</u>. What would be the **best** heading?

   A Creating an Audience

   B Preparing for the Performance

   C Finding an Audience

   D Making an Introduction

10. Under which heading would you add information about the type of glue to use in this trick?

   A Materials

   B Making the Trick

   C Performing the Trick

   D no heading, in the introductory section

11. What does the writer mean by <u>mysterious magic words</u>? Give an example.

12. Why does the passage tell you to say some *mysterious magic words?*

| Reading Practice, *continued*

Read the selection. Then read each question and choose the best answer. Use the provided answer sheet at the end of the workbook to record your answers, and use a separate sheet of paper to record your response to open-ended questions.

The Boy Who Drew Cats
by Lafcadio Hearn

A long, long time ago, in a small country village in Japan, there lived a poor farmer and his wife, who were very good people. They had a number of children, and found it very hard to feed them all. The elder son was strong enough when only fourteen years old to help his father; and the little girls learned to help their mother almost as soon as they could walk.

But the youngest, a little boy, did not seem to be fit for hard work. He was very clever—cleverer than all his brothers and sisters; but he was quite weak and small, and people said he could never grow very big. So his parents thought it would be better for him to become a priest than to become a farmer. They took him with them to the village-temple one day, and asked the good old priest who lived there if he would have their little boy for his acolyte[1], and teach him all that a priest ought to know.

The old man spoke kindly to the lad, and asked him some hard questions. So clever were the answers that the priest agreed to take the little fellow into the temple as an acolyte, and to educate him for the priesthood.

The boy learned quickly what the old priest taught him, and was very obedient in most things. But he had one fault. He liked to draw cats during study-hours, and to draw cats even where cats ought not to have been drawn at all.

Whenever he found himself alone, he drew cats. He drew them on the margins of the priest's books, and on all the screens of the temple, and on the walls, and on the pillars. Several times the priest told him this was not right; but he did not stop drawing cats. He drew them because he could not really help it. He had what is called "the genius of an artist," and just for that reason he was not quite fit to be an acolyte;—a good acolyte should study books.

One day after he had drawn some very clever pictures of cats upon a paper screen, the old priest said to him severely: "My boy, you must go away from this temple at once. You will never make a good priest, but perhaps you will become a great artist. Now let me give you a last piece of advice, and be sure you never forget it. *Avoid large places at night—keep to small!*"

The boy did not know what the priest meant by saying, *"Avoid large places—keep to small."* He thought and thought, while he was tying up his little bundle of clothes to go away; but he could not understand those words, and he was afraid to speak to the priest any more, except to say goodbye.

1. acolyte [definition]

| Reading Practice, *continued*

He left the temple very sorrowfully, and began to wonder what he should do. If he went straight home he felt sure his father would punish him for having been disobedient to the priest; so he was afraid to go home. All at once he remembered that at the next village, twelve miles away, there was a very big temple. He had heard there were several priests at that temple; and he made up his mind to go to them and ask them to take him for their acolyte. Now that big temple was closed up but the boy did not know this fact. The reason it had been closed up was that a goblin had frightened the priests away, and had taken possession of the place. Some brave warriors had afterward gone to the temple at night to kill the goblin; but they had never been seen alive again. Nobody had ever told these things to the boy—so he walked all the way to the village, hoping to be kindly treated by the priests.

When he got to the village, it was already dark, and all the people were in bed; but he saw the big temple on a hill at the other end of the principal street, and he saw there was a light in the temple. People who tell the story say the goblin used to make that light, in order to tempt lonely travelers to ask for shelter. The boy went at once to the temple, and knocked. There was no sound inside. He knocked and knocked again; but still nobody came. At last he pushed gently at the door, and was quite glad to find that it had not been fastened. So he went in, and saw a lamp burning—but no priest.

He thought some priest would be sure to come very soon, and he sat down and waited. Then he noticed that everything in the temple was gray with dust, and thickly spun over with cobwebs. So he thought to himself that the priests would certainly like to have an acolyte, to keep the place clean. He wondered why they had allowed everything to get so dusty. What most pleased him, however, were -some big white screens, good to paint cats upon. Though he was tired, he looked at once for a writing pad, and found one and ground some ink, and began to paint cats.

He painted a great many cats upon the screens; and then he began to feel very, very sleepy. He was just on the point of lying down to sleep beside one of the screens, when he suddenly remembered the words, *"Avoid large places—keep to small!"*

The temple was very large; he was all alone; and as he thought of these words—though he could not quite understand them—he began to feel for the first time a little afraid; and he resolved to look for a *small place* in which to sleep. He found a little cabinet, with a sliding door, and went into it, and shut himself up. Then he lay down and fell fast asleep.

Very late in the night he was awakened by a most terrible noise—a noise of fighting and screaming. It was so dreadful that he was afraid even to look through a chink in the little cabinet; he lay very still, holding his breath for fright.

| Reading Practice, *continued*

The light that had been in the temple went out; but the awful sounds continued, and became more awful, and all the temple shook. After a long time silence came; but the boy was still afraid to move. He did not move until the light of the morning sun shone into the cabinet through the chinks of the little door.

Then he got out of his hiding place very cautiously, and looked about. The first thing he saw was that all the floor of the temple was covered with blood. And then he saw, lying dead in the middle of it, an enormous, monstrous rat—a goblinrat—bigger than a cow!

But who or what could have killed it? There was no man or other creature to be seen. Suddenly the boy observed that the mouths of all the cats he had drawn the night before were red and wet with blood. Then he knew that the goblin had been killed by the cats which he had drawn. And then, also, for the first time, he understood why the wise old priest had said to him, *"Avoid large places at night—keep to small."*

Afterward, that boy became a very famous artist. Some of the cats which he drew are still shown to travelers in Japan.

| Reading Practice, *continued*

1. Which characteristics **best** describe the boy in the selection?

    A   clever and artistic

    B   strong and able

    C   meek and shy

    D   dull and mean

2. Which of the following **best** explains why the boy hides in the cabinet?

    A   He knows that the goblin will soon return.

    B   He feels afraid in the temple alone.

    C   He respects the priest's advice.

    D   He is sleepy.

3. What is **most** significant about the boy's decision to hide in a cabinet in the temple?

    A   He learns the reason for his desire to draw cats.

    B   He finally listens to the priest's advice.

    C   He is hidden from the deadly goblin.

    D   He becomes famous afterward.

4. Why does **most** of the action take place in a temple?

    A   There were very few other buildings at that time.

    B   The temples are metaphoric for the changes that the boy needs to make in his life.

    C   The boy was not welcome in any of the other local buildings.

    D   The boy knew he had to rid a temple of a giant goblin that was killing people.

5. Based on this story, great artists are **most likely** to have

    A   an uncontrollable desire to draw.

    B   a good teacher.

    C   a parent who is a farmer.

    D   an obedient nature.

6. Possession means "control or occupancy." Based on this definition, which word means "took back control"?

    A   repossessed

    B   possess

    C   possessive

    D   possessed

7. Which of these questions is a reader **most likely** to ask after reading this story?

    A   Why does the boy paint cats?

    B   What country does the boy come from?

    C   Why didn't the boy just go back to his parents' house?

    D   Is this a legend about a real artist, or a story about a fictional painter?

8. How would the story **most likely** be different if it were written from the **first-person** point of view of the boy?

    A   It would make the events easier to follow.

    B   It would give more explanation of the artist's thoughts.

    C   It would tell more about everyday life in a temple.

    D   It would describe the fight between the cats and the goblin in more detail.

9. What is **most** ironic about the ending of the story?

  A The boy is forced to leave the first temple because of his art, but his art ends up saving another temple.

  B The boy ends up becoming an artist after all.

  C The boy needs farmers to feed him.

  D The priest's advice ends up saving the boy's life.

10. How does the boy change over the course of the story?

  A He decides to become a farmer like his parents.

  B He learns to hide his gift for drawing in a small place.

  C He becomes an obedient student.

  D He learns that his gift for drawing has a purpose.

11. Which of these stories would **most likely** have a theme that is similar to the theme of this story?

  A a story about a girl who makes a new friend

  B a story about an art collector

  C a story about the building of the temple

  D a story about a man who discovers his talents

12. Why does the boy's family take him to the village temple?

13. Using the information presented in this story, what do you think happens during the night in the temple when the boy hears the screaming and fighting?

Reading Practice, *continued*

Read the selection. Then read each question and choose the best answer. Use the provided answer sheet at the end of the workbook to record your answers, and use a separate sheet of paper to record your response to open-ended questions.

Organizing a Benefit Car Wash

Perhaps your organization or school group would like to earn some extra funds. Maybe you need to buy new team uniforms or band instruments, host a special program, or travel to a competition in another city. If your group lacks the funds it needs, you might want to consider a fund-raiser.

One successful and enjoyable way for a school or civic group to earn money is to hold a car wash. If the adult advisors or sponsors of your group agree, the first steps are to get your school's sanction, select a date, and find a location. Usually a local-area business near your school will cooperate if the school parking lot is unavailable or inconvenient. Ask the business owners if they would like to help your school by sponsoring your car wash. Try to find a business with a location near a busy intersection so that more drivers will see you. To avoid any problems, make sure you follow all of the steps below.

Permission:

The most important first step is to get permission from your school. If this is a school-sponsored event, school officials must be informed so they can ensure that you will be covered by insurance. They will also make sure there are no conflicts with any school policies or functions.

Adults:

You will need to have adult sponsors to chaperon the benefit. It is better to have more than one sponsor. You may need a backup in case the sponsor needs a break, is unable to attend, or can be present for only part of the day. The sponsor may be the best person to handle the money. It is also a good idea to have extra parents around to help. They can run errands or make phone calls if a volunteer forgets to show up or needs a ride. Parents can also wash and dry used towels at their homes.

Equipment:

Make sure that you have all the equipment you will need. This includes hoses, buckets, soap, sponges, a large supply of towels, and perhaps even a heavy-duty vacuum cleaner for doing car interiors. Be sure the site has a water outlet for your hose(s). If only one hose is available, have one person in charge of spraying the cars while other people do the vacuuming, sponging, wiping, and buffing. Also, make sure in advance that the school or business will donate the water so you aren't surprised with a bill afterward!

Organization and Staffing:

Organize your group. Get enough members to staff the car wash for the entire time. It is best to overestimate. For example, plan on using four people per car and servicing two or three cars at a time. You will need someone to make the schedule and to assign the hours each volunteer will work. Make sure each person is allowed time for breaks.

Reading Practice, *continued*

Some volunteers may not work as hard as others. Therefore, some people might have to fill in more than their scheduled time. Try to find three or four other people who will make sure that all goes well. Usually you know who the hard workers are. They are the ones who stay after a party to help the host clean up.

Pricing:

One other suggestion is to avoid setting a fixed price. Instead, ask for donations. Often motorists will offer more than you would have charged because they know the money is going to a worthwhile cause. Always thank the customers, no matter how much or how little they pay. You are representing your school.

Wrap-up:

Set a reasonable time limit. Make sure you begin and end the benefit at the time agreed upon. Make sure a few volunteers stay to clean up. Put all posters and other papers and disposable rags in trash containers. Spray down the lot. Roll up the hose. Thank the sponsors for their help. Send thank-you letters on the school's stationery to everyone who participated.

Finally, have fun and be safe! Expect to get wet at some time during the day, but to avoid accidents, discourage unnecessary or excessive horseplay. Remember that there will be lots of moving vehicles around.

Reading Practice, *continued*

1. What is the topic of the first paragraph?

   A why a car wash is a good fund-raiser

   B how to organize a car wash

   C what equipment you will need

   D why school groups need money

2. Based on the selection, which of the following should be done **first?**

   A Get adult sponsors.

   B Get permission from the school.

   C Collect all the equipment.

   D Make a schedule.

3. Based on the selection, the **best** person to collect the money is

   A the club chairperson.

   B the school principal.

   C an adult sponsor.

   D the top math student.

4. Which statement about benefit car washes is a **fact**?

   A Parents can wash and dry used towels at their homes.

   B It is best to overestimate.

   C The hard workers are the ones who stay after a party to help the host clean up.

   D The most important first step is to get permission from your school.

5. Which statement about benefit car washes is an **opinion**?

   A Remember that there will be lots of moving vehicles around.

   B Ask a business owner to help your school by sponsoring your car wash.

   C Does your organization or school group want to earn some extra funds?

   D Some volunteers may not work as hard as others.

6. Under which heading is the importance of thanking each customer stressed?

   A Permission

   B Adults

   C Pricing

   D Wrap-up

7. Based on the context of the second paragraph, what is an <u>intersection</u>?

   A where two streets cross

   B shopping mall

   C restaurant

   D highway with four or more lanes

8. Which sentence **best** describes the writer's approach to conducting this fund-raiser?

   A Expect huge profits.

   B Make careful preparations.

   C Work your hardest.

   D Enjoy yourself.

Reading Practice, *continued*

9. What sentence gives the **main** idea of the section titled "Pricing"?

   A One other suggestion is to avoid setting a fixed price.

   B Often motorists will offer more than you would have charged because they know the money is going to a worthwhile cause.

   C Always thank the customers, no matter how much or how little they pay.

   D You are representing your school.

10. According to the selection, why is it a good idea to have more than one chaperone?

11. Why does the author use subheadings in the selection?

Reading Practice, *continued*

Read the selection. Then read each question and choose the best answer. Use the provided answer sheet at the end of the workbook to record your answers, and use a separate sheet of paper to record your response to open-ended questions.

from The Monkey's Paw
adapted from a story by W. W. Jacobs

Characters

Mr. White

Mrs. White

Herbert, their son, about nineteen years old.

Sergeant Major Morris, a tall, heavy man with a ruddy complexion who served with the British Army in India for 21 years.

Setting: The White family's home in a newly developed English suburb, around 1920.

Scene 1

A dark and stormy winter night.

[The sound of heavy rain can be heard and an occasional thunderclap. The Whites' living room is cozy and bright. MR. WHITE and HERBERT play chess, while MRS. WHITE knits by the fire. HERBERT is winning.]

HERBERT:	Not looking too good for you, is it, Dad?
MR. WHITE:	Could you please be quiet? I'm trying to concentrate. *(He pauses another moment, then makes a move.)* Listen to that wind howling out there.
HERBERT:	*(keeping his attention on the chessboard).* I hear it.
MR. WHITE:	He won't show up in a storm like this, I bet.
HERBERT:	Maybe, maybe not. *(He moves.)* Check . . .
	[MR. WHITE reaches for a chess piece.]
HERBERT:	*(triumphantly)* . . . Mate![1]
	[MR. WHITE pulls his hand back.]
MR. WHITE:	*(angrily)* That's what I can't stand about living out in the middle of nowhere like this! Every time it rains, the road gets flooded and no one can get out here. And what do those politicians in town do about it? Nothing! I suppose our three votes just don't count.

---

1 checkmate: the final move in the game of chess

MRS. WHITE: *(soothingly)* Never mind, dear. Maybe you'll win the next game.

[MR. WHITE looks up sharply and sees MRS. WHITE and HERBERT smiling at him in amusement. His annoyance fades, and he smiles guiltily. A gate bangs, and heavy footsteps are heard approaching the door.]

HERBERT: Sounds like he made it after all!

[MR. WHITE goes to the door and greets SERGEANT MAJOR MORRIS, who comes in and begins wiping his feet, shaking out his umbrella, etc.]

MR. WHITE: *(introducing them)* Sergeant Major Morris, my wife, and this is our son, Herbert.

[They shake hands, and the three older people sit down while Herbert goes to fix tea.]

MR. WHITE: Glad you made it. We didn't know if you'd come out in this storm.

MORRIS: Storm? This little shower? *(Chuckles)* You wouldn't think much of this if you'd ever been holed up in Bombay during the monsoon season. Now there are some storms, let me tell you.

MRS. WHITE: Did you live in India a long time, Sergeant Major?

MR. WHITE: Twenty-one years he's been gone. When he joined up with the army, he wasn't a day older than Herbert there—and neither was I, for that matter. We started out in the warehouse together.

MORRIS: Well, time flies, time flies.

HERBERT: *(bringing the tea).* I'd like to go to India. See the old temples, maybe catch one of those holy men performing miracles.

MORRIS: *(shaking his head and sighing).* You're better off here.

HERBERT: But you must have all kinds of great stories to tell—the place you saw, the people you met. . . .

MR. WHITE: Does he ever! What was the story you started telling me the other day, Morris? About a monkey's paw or something?

MORRIS: *(quickly)* Nothing, really. Nothing worth hearing.

MRS. WHITE: A monkey's paw?

MORRIS: Well, it's just a bit of what you might call magic, I guess.

HERBERT: Magic!

[The Whites look at Morris with interest.]

| Reading Practice, *continued* |

MORRIS:	*(fumbling in his pocket)* It looks like just an ordinary little paw all dried up.
	[He pulls a mummified monkey's paw out of his pocket and holds it out. MRS. WHITE *draws back in horror, but* HERBERT *takes the paw and looks at it curiously.*]
MR. WHITE:	So what's so special about it? *(He takes the paw from* HERBERT *and examines it, then puts it down on the table.)*
MORRIS:	*(solemnly)* It had a spell put on it by an old holy man. He wanted to show that fate ruled people's lives, and that anyone who tried to interfere with fate would be sorry. He put a magic spell on the paw so that three people could each have three wishes from it.
	[MR. WHITE *laughs uneasily.*]
HERBERT:	Well, why don't you wish on it, then?
MORRIS:	*(sadly)* I have.
MRS. WHITE:	And did you really have your three wishes granted?
MORRIS:	I did.
MRS. WHITE:	And has anyone else wished on it?
MORRIS:	*(seriously)* The first owner had three wishes, yes. I don't know what the first two were for, but the third was for death. That's how I got the paw.
MR. WHITE:	*(after a pause)* If you've had your three wishes, that thing's no good to you now then, Morris. What do you keep it for?
MORRIS:	*(shaking his head and shrugging).* No good reason, I guess. I did have some idea of selling it, but I don't think I will. It's caused enough trouble already. Besides, no one will buy it. Some people think it's just a fairy tale, and the ones who do think anything of it want to try it first and pay me afterward.
HERBERT:	If you could have another three wishes, would you use them?
MORRIS:	I don't know. *(Pauses)* I don't know. *(He takes the paw, dangles it between his finger and thumb, then suddenly throws it into the fire.)*
MR. WHITE:	Hey! *(He jumps up and grabs the paw out of the fire before it starts to burn.)*
MORRIS:	*(solemnly).* Better let it burn.
MR. WHITE:	If you don't want it, Morris, give it to me.
MORRIS:	*(stubbornly).* I won't. I threw it on the fire. If you keep it, don't blame me for what happens. If you're smart, you'll throw it back in the fire.

MR. WHITE: *(shaking his head and looking closely at the paw).* How do you do it?

MORRIS: Hold it in your right hand and wish out loud. But I'm warning you, you won't like the consequences.

MRS. WHITE: Sounds like the Arabian Nights.[2] Why don't you wish for a few extra pairs of hands for me?

[She gets up to set the table for supper. MR. WHITE *starts to raise his arm, and* MORRIS, *alarmed, jumps forward to stop him. The three* WHITES *laugh.]*

MORRIS: If you must wish, for heaven's sake, wish for something sensible. But I don't want to be here to see it.

---

[2] **Arabian Nights:** a series of tales set long ago in the Middle East

Reading Practice, *continued*

1. Why does Morris keep the monkey's paw?

   A   He has one wish left.

   B   He thinks that it will bring trouble to someone else.

   C   He has not found a buyer for it.

   D   He is looking for someone who won't waste the wishes.

2. What will **most likely** happen next?

   A   Morris will admit that the monkey paw is a joke.

   B   Herbert will throw the monkey's paw back on the fire.

   C   Morris will leave immediately.

   D   Herbert will make a wish on the monkey's paw.

3. You could **best** describe Morris as

   A   young and reckless.

   B   worldly and wise.

   C   slow and thoughtful.

   D   fussy and uptight.

4. What is the **main** effect of setting the scene during a dark and stormy winter night?

   A   to explain why the characters are unhappy

   B   to create a mysterious mood or atmosphere.

   C   to add to the cozy feeling in the White's living room

   D   to give important clues about the characters

5. What is the mood at the end of this selection?

   A   mysterious

   B   gloomy

   C   romantic

   D   lighthearted

6. What is **most likely** the reason that Morris thinks the storm is "just a minor shower"?

   A   He has a great umbrella.

   B   He can't feel the rain.

   C   He is used to the rainy season in India.

   D   He was born in India during a monsoon.

7. Where did Mr. White **most likely** first meet Morris?

   A   at the warehouse

   B   in India

   C   during grade school

   D   in the army

8. Mr. White complains about "living out in the middle of nowhere." Why does Mrs. White think that her husband is really upset?

   A   because he lost the game

   B   because she picked out the house

   C   because he is worried about his friend

   D   because he does not like the rain

9. Herbert wants to go to India because

   A   he is young and immature.

   B   he wants to join the army.

   C   he longs for adventure.

   D   they have miracles in India.

10. What is **most likely** the reason that Herbert shouts this line?
Sounds like he made it after all!

   A He is upset that Morris will interrupt his time with his dad.

   B He was right—Morris would not let rain stop him.

   C He cannot believe that Morris made it in the rain.

   D He is excited because he has been waiting all evening to meet Morris.

11. What does Morris tell the Whites to wish for?

12. Why do you think Morris does not want too watch the Whites make a wish?

Read the selection. Then read each question and choose the best answer. Use the provided answer sheet at the end of the workbook to record your answers, and use a separate sheet of paper to record your response to open-ended questions.

Ways of Fighting Germs

Until the twentieth century, surgery patients often died of a bacterial infection. As doctors learned more about disease, it became clear that simple cleanliness could help prevent the spread of some diseases. Today, hospitals and clinics use a variety of technologies to prevent the spread of some diseases. For example, ultraviolet radiation, boiling water, and chemicals are used in health facilities to kill pathogens or germs.

During the mid-1800s, Louis Pasteur, a French scientist, discovered that tiny germs or microorganisms cause wine to spoil. The uninvited microorganisms were bacteria. Pasteur devised a method of using heat to kill most of the bacteria in the wine. This method is called pasteurization, and it is still used today.

In the late 1700s, no one knew what a pathogen was. It was during this time that Edward Jenner, a physician, studied a disease called smallpox. He observed that people who had been infected with cowpox seemed to have protection against smallpox. This protection, or resistance to a disease, is called immunity. Jenner's work led to the first modern vaccine. A vaccine is a substance that helps your body develop immunity to a disease.

Today vaccines are used all over the world to prevent many serious diseases. Modern vaccines contain pathogens that are killed or specially treated so that they can't make you very sick. The vaccine is enough like the pathogen to allow your body to develop a defense against the disease.

Bacterial infections can be a serious threat to your health. Fortunately, doctors can usually treat these kinds of infections with antibiotics. An antibiotic is a substance that can kill bacteria or slow the growth of bacteria. Antibiotics may also be used to treat infections caused by other microorganisms, like fungi. If you take an antibiotic when you are sick, it is important that you take it according to your doctor's instructions, to ensure that all the pathogens are killed.

Reading Practice, *continued*

1. According to the selection, which statement is **most likely** true?

   A Smallpox and cowpox are caused by related pathogens.

   B Vaccines can cure bacterial infections.

   C No one dies of bacterial infections anymore.

   D It is possible to eliminate all bacteria in hospitals and doctors' offices.

2. Based on the selection, what was **most** significant about Edward Jenner's discovery of vaccines?

   A Edward Jenner became known as the father of vaccination.

   B Vaccines now prevent wine from spoiling all around the world.

   C Today vaccines are used all over the world to prevent serious diseases.

   D Bacterial infections are no longer a threat to people.

3. According to the selection, how is pasteurization **different** from a vaccine in preventing disease?

   A Pasteurization is a substance that slows the growth of germs, and a vaccine uses heat to kill them.

   B Pasteurization uses heat to kill germs, and a vaccine increases immunity against them.

   C A vaccine uses chemicals to kill germs, and pasteurization increases one's immunity against them.

   D A vaccine is a substance that slows the growth of germs, and pasteurization uses chemicals to kill them.

4. Which statement supports the idea that simple cleanliness can help prevent the spread of some diseases?

   A A vaccine is a substance that helps your body develop immunity to a disease.

   B Pasteur devised a method of using heat to kill most of the bacteria in the wine.

   C Doctors can usually treat bacterial infections with antibiotics.

   D Boiling water, and chemicals are used in health facilities to kill pathogens or germs.

Reading Practice, *continued*

5. Based on the information in the selection, which of the following relationships is **most similar** to the relationship below?

   microorganism : pathogen

   A mammal : reptile

   B wheel : car

   C bucket : pail

   D muscle : nerve

6. Which statement **best** summarizes the **main** idea of the selection?

   A Pasteurization, vaccines, and antibiotics fight disease and infection.

   B Bacterial infections can pose a serious health risk.

   C Modern vaccines contain tiny, dead pathogens.

   D Hospitals and clinics use radiation, heat, and chemicals to kill pathogens.

7. Which of these events happened **first** in the history of fighting germs?

   A Louis Pasteur discovered germs that cause wine to spoil.

   B Edward Jenner studied small pox.

   C Health facilities began using ultraviolet radiation to kill pathogens.

   D Louis Pasteur created a method of pasteurization.

8. Which of the following is an **opinion** about fighting germs?

   A Until the twentieth century, surgery patients often died of a bacterial infection.

   B Pasteur devised a method of using heat to kill most of the bacteria in wine.

   C A vaccine is a substance that helps your body develop immunity to a disease.

   D Edward Jenner and Louis Pasteur were very important people.

9. According to the selection, what can happen if you do not take an antibiotic according to your doctor's instructions?

   A You may not get better because some of the pathogens will not be killed.

   B You will get better anyway.

   C All of the pathogens will be killed and you will get better.

   D Your doctor will be upset with you.

Reading Practice, *continued*

10. Which of these headings would you use for the chart below?

ultraviolet radiation
boiling water
chemicals

A   Vaccines

B   The Work of Louis Pasteur

C   Technologies Used to Prevent Disease

D   Bacterial Infections

11. Where would you look if you wanted to learn more about Louis Pasteur and his work?

12. Compare the practice of medicine today to the practice of medicine in the past. Only use information from the selection.

Writing Practice

Standardized Tests for Writing

In the Writing Practice section, you will practice for Standardized Writing Tests. You will read some general strategies for responding to writing prompts and review graphic organizers that are helpful for planning your writing. Then you will have the opportunity to respond to writing prompts in commonly tested modes—persuasive, descriptive, narrative, expository, and response to literature. The writing prompts will test your ability in five domains of writing: focus, content, organization, style, and conventions. You will also be asked to answer multiple-choice questions that are designed to test your mastery of writing conventions. These multiple choice questions and will involve editing and revising items.

Scoring the English/Language Arts Second Course Practice Test

In the **English/Language Arts Second Course Practice Test** provided at the end of this workbook, you will answer twenty-four multiple-choice questions about writing conventions. In addition you will respond to two writing prompts. You will receive one point for each multiple-choice question you answer correctly, for a possible 24 points. The two writing prompts will be scored on a *4-point* scale or a *6-point* scale depending on your teacher's preference. The writing prompts will be scored for both composition (focus, content, organization, and style) and convention. If a response cannot be read, makes no sense, has too little information to be scored, or is blank, it will not receive a composition score. A response that is off-topic also will not receive a composition score. However, an off-topic response will receive a conventions score.

SCORING ON A 4-POINT SCALE:

A *4-point* response demonstrates **advanced** success with the writing task. The essay:

- focuses consistently on a clear and reasonable thesis or position

- shows effective organization throughout, with smooth transitions

- offers thoughtful, creative ideas and reasons

- develops ideas or supports a position thoroughly, using examples, details, convincing, fully elaborated explanations, or reasons and evidence

- exhibits mature control of written language

A *3-point* response demonstrates **competent** success with the writing task. In general, the essay:

- focuses on a clear thesis or reasonable position, with minor distractions
- shows effective organization, with minor lapses
- offers mostly thoughtful ideas and reasons
- develops ideas adequately and elaborates reasons and evidence with a mixture of the general and the specific
- exhibits general control of written language

A *2-point* response demonstrates **limited** success with the writing task. The essay may:

- include some loosely related ideas that distract from the writer's focus or position
- show some organization, with noticeable gaps in the logical flow of ideas
- offer routine, predictable ideas and reasons
- develop or support ideas with uneven elaboration and reasoning
- exhibit limited control of written language

A *1-point* response demonstrates **emerging** effort with the writing task. In general, the essay:

- shows little awareness of the topic and purpose for writing
- lacks organization
- offers unclear and confusing ideas
- develops ideas in a minimal way, if at all, or shows minimal reasoning or elaboration
- exhibits major problems with control of written language

SCORING ON A 6-POINT SCALE:

A *6-point* response demonstrates **advanced** success with the writing task. The essay:

- focuses consistently on a clear and reasonable thesis or position
- shows effective organization throughout, with smooth transitions
- offers thoughtful, creative ideas and reasons
- supports a position thoroughly, using convincing, fully elaborated reasons and evidence
- exhibits mature control of written language

A *5-point* response demonstrates **proficient** success with the writing task. In general, the essay:

- focuses on a clear and reasonable thesis or position
- shows effective organization, with transitions
- offers thoughtful ideas and reasons
- supports a position competently, using convincing, well-elaborated reasons and evidence
- exhibits sufficient control of written language

A *4-point* response demonstrates **competent** success with the writing task. In general, the essay:

- focuses on a reasonable thesis or position, with minor distractions
- shows effective organization, with minor lapses
- offers mostly thoughtful ideas and reasons
- elaborates reasons and evidence with a mixture of the general and the specific
- exhibits general control of written language

A *3-point* response demonstrates **limited** success with the writing task. The essay may:

- include some loosely related ideas that distract from the writer's thesis or position
- show some organization, with noticeable gaps in the logical flow of ideas
- offer routine, predictable ideas and reasons
- support ideas with uneven reasoning and elaboration
- exhibit limited control of written language

A *2-point* response demonstrates **basic** success with the writing task. In general, the essay:

- includes loosely related ideas that seriously distract from the writer's purpose
- shows minimal organization, with major gaps in the logical flow of ideas
- offers ideas and reasons that merely skim the surface
- supports ideas with inadequate reasoning and elaboration
- exhibits significant problems with control of written language

A *1-point* response demonstrates **emerging** effort with the writing task. In general, the essay:

- shows little awareness of the topic and purpose for writing
- lacks organization
- offers unclear and confusing ideas
- demonstrates minimal reasoning or elaboration
- exhibits major problems with control of written language

The primary goal of the practice in this Writing section is to help you prepare for Standardized Tests for Writing. In order to write a concise response, you must learn to organize your thoughts before you begin writing the actual response. This keeps you from straying too far from the prompt's topic.

Strategies for Responding to a Prompt

- First, **read the question carefully.** Be sure that you understand exactly what the question is asking.

- **Decide what kind of composition you are being asked to write. You should ask yourself, "What is the purpose of this composition?"** For example, are you trying to persuade your audience to take an action or to support a position? When you understand the type of composition you are being asked to write, you will have a sense of the purpose of your composition.

- Next, **organize your thoughts.** It is best to write down notes on a separate piece of paper before actually writing the composition. First, determine the main point of your composition. Your topic sentence should include the general topic as well as the main idea. It should set the tone and catch the reader's attention. Most importantly, make sure it is answering the question. This will be the anchor to your composition. Then, come up with ideas to support your topic sentence. Your ideas should include the major points that you want to cover in your composition.

- **Write in complete sentences,** and be aware of unity within the composition. In other words, make sure your sentences and paragraphs "flow" smoothly. Sentences should come together smoothly to support the main idea and should be arranged in an order that makes sense to the reader. Be as specific as possible when stating your ideas. Make use of transitional words or phrases if necessary. Also, remember to write neatly.

- **Many writing tests are timed. Plan your time carefully**. Many writing tests are timed. For a timed test, spend about one-third of the time planning your essay. This includes brainstorming, note-taking, and gathering all your ideas. Spend about one-third of the time writing a first draft of your essay. Spend about one-third of the time writing a final draft.

- Finally, **proofread your composition.** Check for spelling and punctuation errors. Look for run-on sentences and sentence fragments. Look over verb tenses to see if you have used them correctly. Make the necessary edits as neat as possible.

- If you follow the above guidelines, you should succeed on the writing section of standardized tests. Remember that practice makes perfect. Read and write as often as possible on whatever subjects you prefer, and you will see that writing compositions will eventually come quite naturally.

Graphic Organizers for Writing

Brainstorming Significant Details

You might like to start by noting significant details in a word web. Write your topic in the middle circle. Then write words or phrases that come to mind in the outer circles.

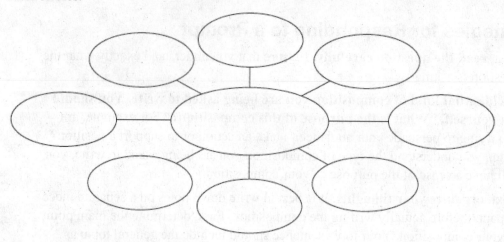

Cause-and-Effect Chart

If you are asked to write a cause-and-effect response, you might start by listing the causes and/or effects in a chart like the one below

CAUSES	EFFECTS

Compare and Contrast

To compare and contrast information, use a Venn diagram like the one below. Note differences in the outer circles (sections A and B) and similarities where the circles overlap (section C).

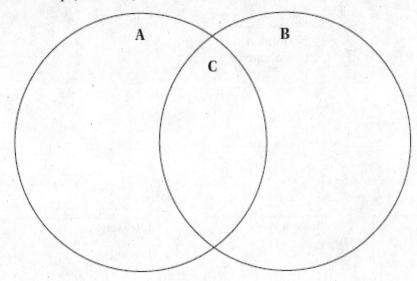

Pros & Cons

You might want to begin planning your persuasive essay by listing the pros and cons of an issue in a table like the one below.

PROS	CONS

Persuasion

If you need to persuade your reader, you might want to use this organizer. Write your opinion in the arrow at the top. Then list convincing reasons and supporting details.

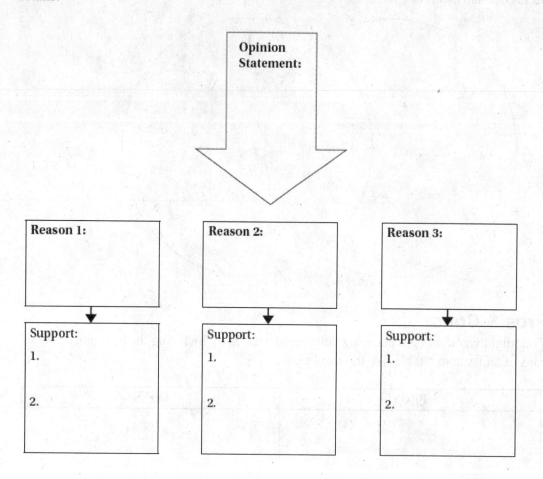

Response to Literature

To record your opinions regarding a piece of literature, you first need to organize your thoughts so that you can clearly explain your point of view. In the graphic organizer below, write your thesis statement explaining your view of the passage. Choose several examples that support your thesis. Write them in the blanks below. If you have more than four examples, just add rows to the organizer. Be sure that at least some of your examples come from the passage itself. Carefully think about how you want to organize your list of examples.

Thesis Statement:
Example 1:
Example 2:
Example 3:
Example 4:

Writing Prompt 1

Plan, write, and proofread a persuasive article in response to the writing prompt below.

> Your school newspaper has been featuring stories about schools with letter grade systems and schools with pass-fail systems. Some people in your school district want to do away with grades in favor of a pass-fail system. Others disagree. You are going choose one side of the argument and write an article for your school newspaper expressing your view on the issue.

As you write your article, be sure to

- Focus on the grades vs. pass-fail system.
- Clearly identify which side of the argument you chose.
- Use details to describe the benefits of the side of the issue that you chose to support.
- Try to convince your reader to agree with your viewpoint.
- Think about your audience and purpose.
- Organize your essay so your ideas progress logically.
- Edit your essay to correct errors in grammar, spelling, and punctuation.

Strategy for Responding to the Prompt

Prewriting

1. **Analyze the Prompt.** Read the prompt carefully to identify the purpose of and the audience for the prompt.

Purpose. In the prompt, you are asked to choose one side of the grades versus pass-fail issue. You will then write a persuasive article for the school newspaper. You are to give details that will convince your audience to agree with your opinion.

Complete the following sentence.

My purpose is to persuade _____ to _____.

Audience. According to the prompt, who is your audience? Use the following step-by-step method to analyze the audience identified in the prompt:

Steps	Explanation	Your Response
Step 1 Ask yourself, "Who is the audience for this response?"	Think about who would read a school newspaper. This is your audience.	
Step 2 Ask, "What does my audience already know about pass-fail? What do they need to know?"	Your audience will probably have a clearer understanding of letter grade systems than they will of pass-fail systems. Your challenge will be to give a detailed description of both methods and then provide supporting reasons for your choice.	
Step 3 Ask, "Does my reader already have an opinion in mind?"	When you write a persuasive essay you always have to think about how you can convince someone to change their viewpoint. At the same time, you'll need to give enough background information for a reader who has not formed an opinion before reading your article.	

2. **Develop Your Details.** Your article should tell about both grading systems and then argue for one system over the other. Use the Venn Diagram to compare the two grading systems. Write the traits of letter-grade systems in Circle A. Then write the traits of pass-fail systems in Circle B. Put any traits the two may have in common in the overlap area, marked C.

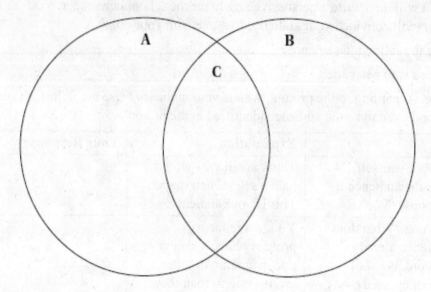

You also need to brainstorm the pros and cons of your grading system. Write the grading system you chose on the top line of the chart below. Then write the pros and cons of this grading system. You may be thinking that you will only need the pros, or arguments for your viewpoint. However, a good persuasive essay responds to the cons, or arguments against a viewpoint, too.

Grading System: _____	
Pros	**Cons**

3. **Develop Your Argument.** Now you are ready to develop your persuasive argument. First, write your opinion statement in the arrow below. This will tell the reader your exact viewpoint. It is what you want to convince your reader to think or believe.

  Next, give specific reasons for your opinion. Ask yourself, "Why do I believe that this grading system is best?" The reasons you write in the boxes should answer that question.

  Finally, for each reason, you will need to give supporting details. You may use details from the graphic organizers on the previous page. Or you may write different supporting details.

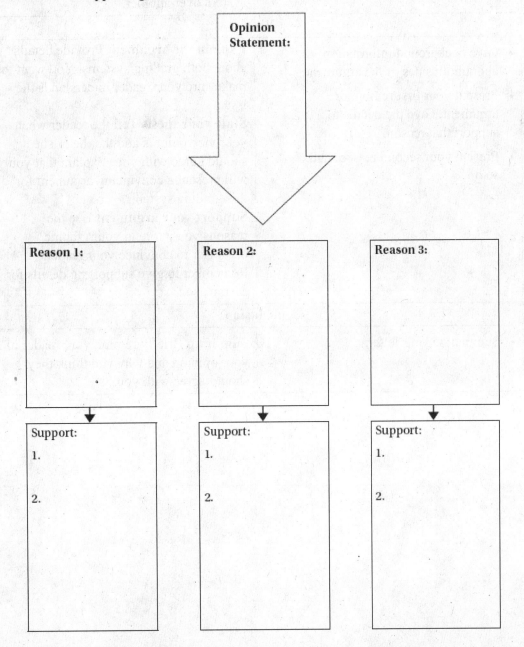

Drafting Your Response

Use the following framework to draft your response to the writing prompt. Write your draft on the lined page that follows.

Framework	Directions and Explanations
Introduction	
• Name the two grading systems and tell which one you prefer.	**Introduce your topic** Tell your reader what the subject of the article is going to be. In this case, you are going to ask your reader to choose one grading system over another.
Body	
• Give background information about both sides of the argument. • Present your first reason, or argument. Give the details to support that reason. • Present your second reason, and so on.	**Explain the argument** Provide details about both grading systems. You want to make sure your reader understands the issue. **State your thesis** Tell the reader what your viewpoint is and that he or she should agree with you. Explain that you will present a convincing argument for this grading system. **Support your argument** Use the reasons you wrote in your graphic organizer to convince your reader. Remember to give supporting details for each reason.
Conclusion	
• Summarize your letter.	**Sum it up** Briefly remind your reader of your opinion and why you think they should agree with you. ·

Drafting Your Response, *continued*

Draft your response in the space below.

_____

_____

_____

_____

_____

_____

_____

_____

_____

_____

_____

_____

_____

_____

_____

_____

_____

_____

_____

_____

_____

Name _____ Class _____ Date _____

Evaluating, Revising, and Editing Your Response

Use the following strategies to evaluate and revise your response. You may make your revisions directly on your first draft, or, if necessary, write your revised draft on the lined pages that follow.

Evaluation Guidelines for Persuasive Writing Response		
Evaluation Question	**Tips**	**Revision Techniques**
1. Does the response have a clear thesis? Does the thesis address the prompt?	Ask yourself, "Does my thesis clearly state my opinion? Does it tell the reader which grading system I prefer?"	If necessary, **revise** your thesis to address the prompt accurately.
2. Does the response use specific details to support the reasons?	Place a dot next to each example, illustration, or anecdote.	**Elaborate** on the thesis by adding more supporting details.
3. Do the supporting details clearly relate to the reasons they are meant to support?	Lightly circle each dot that represents a relevant detail.	**Cut** supporting details that do not relate to specific reasons.
4. Are ideas logically related to one another? Are there gaps in logic or information?	Study the flow from one sentence to the next. Does each idea follow logically from the one before it?	**Add** details to fill in gaps in logic. Use **transition words** or phrases to improve the flow of ideas.
5. Does the response use appropriate, precise vocabulary?	Identify words that are tired or overused by circling them. (Examples: *thing, very, great, bad*)	**Replace** the circled words with more precise, vivid language.
6. Does the response use a variety of sentence structures?	Look for sentences that start with different types of phrases. Underline sentences that seem to repeat the same structure.	**Rewrite** some of the sentences so that some of them begin with phrases, subordinate clauses, or transitional expressions.

Evaluating, Revising, and Editing Your Response, *continued*

Draft your revised essay in the space below.

_____

_____

_____

_____

_____

_____

_____

_____

_____

_____

_____

_____

_____

_____

_____

_____

_____

_____

_____

_____

_____

_____

_____

_____

_____

_____

_____

Proofing Your Response

Final Editing Guidelines
Proofread your essay to ensure that it

- contains only complete sentences, no fragments,
- shows proper subject-verb agreement, consistent verb tense, and correct use of nominative and subjective case.
- uses correct capitalization, punctuation, and spelling.

Draft your final essay in the space below.

_____

_____

_____

_____

_____

_____

_____

_____

_____

_____

_____

_____

_____

_____

_____

_____

_____

_____

_____

Scoring Persuasive Writing Prompts

Responses to persuasive writing prompts will be scored according to a *4-point* or a *6-point* rubric. The writing prompts will be scored for both composition (focus, content, organization, and style) and convention.

Using the 4-point or the 6-point rubric, a response will be deemed **unscorable** if certain conditions apply. A response will be determined to be **unscorable** for one or more of the following reasons. The paper may be:

- off-topic
- a paraphrase of the prompt
- written in a foreign language
- incomprehensible
- too brief to determine whether you have responded to the task
- a written refusal to write

Scorable responses are awarded points as detailed in the following rubrics.

4-Point Rubric

A *4-point* response demonstrates **advanced** success with the persuasive writing task. The essay:

- focuses consistently on a clear and reasonable position
- shows effective organization throughout, with smooth transitions
- offers thoughtful, creative ideas and reasons
- supports a position thoroughly, using convincing, fully elaborated reasons and evidence
- exhibits mature control of written language

A *3-point* response demonstrates **competent** success with the persuasive writing task. For the most part, the essay:

- focuses on a reasonable position, with minor distractions
- shows effective organization, with minor lapses
- offers mostly thoughtful ideas and reasons
- elaborates reasons and evidence with a mixture of the general and the specific
- exhibits general control of written language

Scoring Persuasive Writing Prompts, *continued*

A *2-point* response demonstrates **limited** success with the persuasive writing task. The essay may:

- include some loosely related ideas that distract from the writer's position
- show some organization, with noticeable gaps in the logical flow of ideas
- offer routine, predictable ideas and reasons
- support ideas with uneven reasoning and elaboration
- exhibit limited control of written language

A *1-point* response demonstrates **emerging** effort with persuasive writing. For the most part, the essay:

- shows little awareness of the topic and purpose for writing
- lacks organization
- offers unclear and confusing ideas
- shows minimal persuasive reasoning or elaboration
- exhibits major problems with control of written language

6-Point Rubric

A *6-point* response demonstrates **advanced** success with the persuasive writing task. The essay:

- focuses consistently on a clear and reasonable position
- shows effective organization throughout, with smooth transitions
- offers thoughtful, creative ideas and reasons
- supports a position thoroughly, using convincing, fully elaborated reasons and evidence
- exhibits mature control of written language

A *5-point* response demonstrates **proficient** success with the persuasive writing task. For the most part, the essay:

- focuses on a clear and reasonable position
- shows effective organization, with transitions
- offers thoughtful ideas and reasons
- supports a position competently, using convincing, well-elaborated reasons and evidence
- exhibits sufficient control of written language

| Scoring Persuasive Writing Prompts, *continued* |

A *4-point* response demonstrates **competent** success with the persuasive writing task. For the most part, the essay:

- focuses on a reasonable position, with minor distractions
- shows effective organization, with minor lapses
- offers mostly thoughtful ideas and reasons
- elaborates reasons and evidence with a mixture of the general and the specific
- exhibits general control of written language

A *3-point* response demonstrates **limited** success with the persuasive writing task. The essay may:

- include some loosely related ideas that distract from the writer's position
- show some organization, with noticeable gaps in the logical flow of ideas
- offer routine, predictable ideas and reasons
- support ideas with uneven reasoning and elaboration
- exhibit limited control of written language

A *2-point* response demonstrates **basic** success with persuasive writing. For the most part, the essay:

- includes loosely related ideas that seriously distract from the writer's persuasive purpose
- shows minimal organization, with major gaps in the logical flow of ideas
- offers ideas and reasons that merely skim the surface
- supports ideas with inadequate reasoning and elaboration
- exhibits significant problems with control of written language

A *1-point* response demonstrates **emerging** effort with persuasive writing. For the most part, the essay:

- shows little awareness of the topic and purpose for writing
- lacks organization
- offers unclear and confusing ideas
- demonstrates minimal persuasive reasoning or elaboration
- exhibits major problems with control of written language

Writing Prompt 2

Plan, write, and proofread a persuasive letter in response to the writing prompt below.

> Imagine that your school band wants to enter a contest. Everyone has been working hard, and you think your band has a good chance to win. There's only one problem—your band doesn't have any uniforms! Write a persuasive letter to a local businessperson asking him or her to contribute money toward buying uniforms. Include that, in return, all band programs for the next five years will advertise the businesses that help to purchase the uniforms.

As you write your letter, be sure to

- Focus on persuading the local businessperson.
- Describe the situation.
- Explain why your band needs and deserves the uniforms.
- Organize your letter so your ideas progress logically.
- Edit your letter for standard grammar and usage.

Strategy for Responding to the Prompt

Prewriting

1. **Analyze the Prompt.** Read the prompt carefully to identify the purpose of and the audience for the prompt.

Purpose. In the prompt, you are asked to choose a local businessperson from whom you can request a donation. You will need to present an argument to convince the businessperson to donate money for band uniforms. The prompt tells you your audience and the format for your description.

Complete the following sentence:

My purpose is to persuade _____ to _____.

Audience. According to the prompt, who is your audience? Use the following step-by-step method to analyze the audience identified in the prompt:

Steps	Explanation	Your Response
Step 1 Ask yourself, "Who is the audience for this response?"	Look to the prompt for clues about your audience.	
Step 2 Ask, "What does my audience already know about this situation? What do they need to know?"	Your audience might not know much about the band. Your challenge will be to give a detailed description about your band and their need for uniforms. Think about how you can describe the details to make your non-uniformed band seem familiar to a stranger.	
Step 3 Ask, "Does my audience already have an opinion in mind?"	Your audience may already have feelings about whether or not to donate to a school, or to this type of cause. Your challenge is to convince the reader to give money to your band.	

Name _____ Class _____ Date _____

2. **Develop Your Details.** Your letter should tell about the contest you want to enter and the difference the uniforms will make in the contest. Use the graphic organizers shown below to help you brainstorm details for your letter. Write "contest" in the center circle of one web diagram. In the outer circles list details about the contest. Write "band uniforms" in the center circle of the other web diagram. Think of different benefits of these uniforms, such as being taken more seriously. Write different benefits in the outer circles.

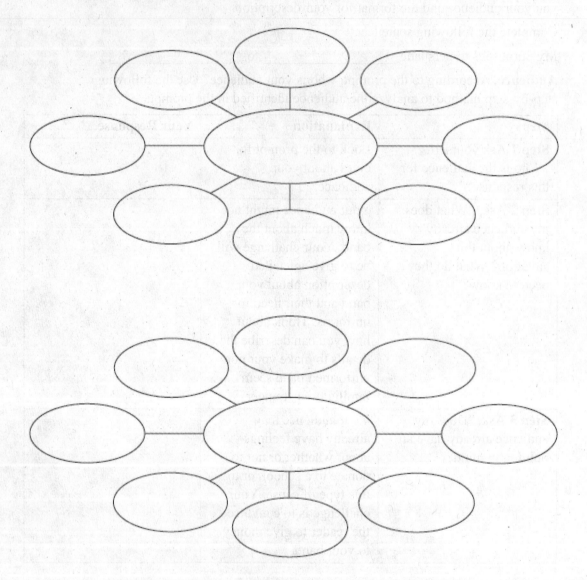

Name _____ Class _____ Date _____

3. **Organize Your Plan.** Now that you have brainstormed the details to include in your letter, you will want to organize your thoughts so that you can present them logically to persuade your audience. Fill in "uniforms" in the first-column header below. Then, using the details that you brainstormed on the previous page, add your most persuasive points as supporting reasons. For each benefit, write a sentence you could use to convince the businessperson to donate the money. As you write your sentences, add details you might use. When you are done with your sentences, write a number next to each sentence, indicating a logical order.

Benefits of _____	Persuasive Sentence	Order

Drafting Your Response

Use the following framework to draft your response to the writing prompt. Write your draft on the lined page that follows.

Framework	Directions and Explanations
Introduction	
• Use a proper greeting. • State why you are writing the letter. • State the name of your high school and the need for band uniforms.	**Get your reader's respect** Address your reader with respect. **State your purpose** Let your reader know right away why you are writing this letter. If the reader knows your purpose, it will be easier for him or her to follow along. **Introduce your topic** Tell your reader what the subject of this letter is going to be. In this case, you will be telling your reader about the upcoming band contest and the need for uniforms.
Body	
• Give background information about your band and the competition. • Present your first reason, or argument. Give the details to support that reason. • Present your second reason, and so on.	**Explain the problem** Provide details about the band and the upcoming competition. Help your reader identify with your band and its need for uniforms. **State your purpose** Tell the reader how he or she can help you. **Support your argument** Use the sentences you wrote to convince your reader to donate money for band uniforms. Arrange your details in an order that makes sense, such as type of detail or order of importance.
Conclusion	
• Summarize your letter. • Thank your reader and close with a respectful ending.	**Sum it up** Briefly remind your reader of what you need and why he or she should support your cause. **Acknowledge your reader** Thank your reader for taking the time to read the letter. Close with a respectful ending.

Drafting Your Response, *continued*

Draft your letter in the space below.

_____

_____

_____

_____

_____

_____

_____

_____

_____

_____

_____

_____

_____

_____

_____

_____

_____

_____

_____

_____

_____

Evaluating, Revising, and Editing Your Response

Use the following strategies to evaluate and revise your response. You may make your revisions directly on your first draft, or, if necessary, write your revised draft on the lined pages that follow.

Evaluation Guidelines for Persuasive Response		
Evaluation Question	**Tips**	**Revision Techniques**
1. Does the response have a clear purpose? Does the purpose address the prompt?	Ask yourself, "Does my response tell that the band needs uniforms? Does it tell why uniforms are important? Does it persuade the businessperson to donate the needed funds?"	If necessary, **rewrite** the sentence that states the purpose of your letter.
2. Is the response organized appropriately for this prompt and purpose?	This prompt clearly asks for a letter to a businessperson. Make sure that you wrote a formal business letter and not an essay.	**Rearrange** the response if needed. Include these parts of a business letter: Address and Date, Greeting, Body, and Signature. The Body of the text should include an introduction and conclusion.
3. Does the response present a logical argument with supporting details?	Look for details that support your main argument, or tell the reader why you need uniforms and why he or she should help you. Place a dot next to each supporting detail.	**Elaborate** on the letter by adding more supporting details.
4. Do the supporting details clearly relate to the reasons they are meant to support?	Lightly circle each dot that represents a relevant detail.	**Cut** supporting details that do not relate to specific reasons.
5. Are ideas logically related to one another? Are there gaps in logic or information?	Study the flow from one sentence to the next. Does each idea follow logically from the one before it?	**Add** details to fill in gaps in logic. Use **transition words** or phrases to improve the flow of ideas.
6. Does the response use appropriate, precise vocabulary?	Identify words that are tired or overused by circling them. (Examples: *thing, very, great, bad*)	**Replace** the circled words with more precise, vivid language.
7. Does the response use a variety of sentence structures?	Look for sentences that start with different types of phrases. Underline sentences that seem to repeat the same structure.	**Rewrite** some of the sentences so that some of them begin with phrases, subordinate clauses, or transitional expressions.

Evaluating, Revising, and Editing Your Response, *continued*

Draft your revised letter in the space below.

_____

_____

_____

_____

_____

_____

_____

_____

_____

_____

_____

_____

_____

_____

_____

_____

_____

_____

_____

_____

_____

_____

_____

_____

Name _____ Class _____ Date _____

Proofing Your Response

Final Editing Guidelines
Proofread your letter to ensure that it

- contains only complete sentences, no fragments.

- shows proper subject-verb agreement, consistent verb tense, and correct use of nominative and subjective case.

- uses correct capitalization, punctuation, and spelling.

Draft your final letter in the space below.

_____

_____

_____

_____

_____

_____

_____

_____

_____

_____

_____

_____

_____

_____

_____

_____

_____

_____

_____

_____

_____

_____

Writing Prompt 3

Plan, write and proofread a descriptive essay in response to the writing prompt below.

> Write a descriptive essay about the person you most admire. This essay will be posted on your history room bulletin board. Choose the person and consider the reasons why he or she is the person you most admire. Then write your description. Be sure to give details about what the person has done to gain your admiration.

As you write your essay, remember to

- Focus on the person's actions and character traits.
- Include plenty of details about the things they have done to gain your admiration.
- Describe things you like about the person.
- Use descriptions that appeal to the five senses.
- Organize your description so that your readers will admire this person, too.
- Edit your descriptive essay for standard grammar and usage.

Strategy for Responding to the Prompt

Prewriting

1. **Analyze the Prompt.** Read the prompt carefully to identify the purpose of, and the audience for your response.

Purpose. In the prompt, you are asked to describe the person you most admire. You will need to include details that show why you selected this person. The prompt tells you your audience and the format for your description.

Complete the following sentence.

My purpose is to describe _____ to _____.

Audience. This prompt offers clues about the audience. Use the following step-by-step method to analyze the audience identified in the prompt:

Steps	Explanation	Your Response
Step 1 Ask yourself, "Who is the audience for this essay?"	Look to the prompt for clues about your audience.	
Step 2 Ask, "What does my audience already know about the person? What do they need to know, or what would they like to know?"	Your audience may or may not be familiar with the person you have chosen. Your challenge will be to give a detailed description of the person so that your audience will understand your admiration.	
Step 3 Ask, "How can I help my audience see this person the way that I do?"	Remember that your audience may not be familiar with some of the traits you find admirable. Be sure to give details and background information to support your choice.	

Strategy for Responding to the Prompt, *continued*

2. **Develop Your Details.** In order to write this essay, you will need to decide what you admire about this person. Think about his or her character traits, actions, and words. Write the person's name at the top of the graphic organizer. Then add details to complete the chart.

Person I Admire _____
What this person has accomplished
What this person has said
How this person has affected me
Details of the person's character
Other important details

Strategy for Responding to the Prompt *continued*

3. **Organize Your Details.** Now that you have brainstormed details about this person, you can list several specific reasons that you admire this person. In the chart below, write different reasons you admire this person. For each reason, write at least two details that support this statement. Use the details you brainstormed on the previous page to help you. You can then use the sentences in the left column as main idea sentences of the paragraphs in your essay.

Why do I admire this person?	Detail about the person

Drafting Your Response

Use the following framework to draft your response to the writing prompt. Write your draft on the lined page that follows.

Framework	Directions and Explanations
Introduction	
• Use an attention grabber. • Introduce the person.	**Get your reader's attention** Use a statement about the person that will interest, impress, or amaze your reader. **Identify the person** Tell the person's name.
Body	
• Describe the person in an organized way. • Use sensory images.	**Begin your descriptive essay** Give one reason you admire the person. Describe how the person acts or what the person says that supports this reason. **Give a second reason,** and so on After you explain your first reason, move on to the next one. **Use descriptive language** Be sure your reader can see, hear, smell, taste, and touch what you describe. **Give plenty of details** Make sure that you describe the person in full detail. The reader should fully understand how you feel about this person. Make your reader feel like he or she has actually met the person.
Conclusion	
• Remind your audience of your choice.	**Sum it up** Restate your opening—who you chose and why he or she is to be admired. Ask your audience to think about the qualities they find admirable in a person.

Drafting Your Response, *continued*

Draft your response in the space below.

_____
_____
_____
_____
_____
_____
_____
_____
_____
_____
_____
_____
_____
_____
_____
_____
_____
_____
_____
_____
_____
_____
_____
_____
_____

Evaluating, Revising, and Editing Your Response

Use the following strategies to evaluate and revise your response. You may make your revisions directly on your first draft, or, if necessary, write your revised draft on the lined pages that follow.

Evaluation Guidelines for Persuasive Response		
Evaluation Question	**Tips**	**Revision Techniques**
1. Is the response written in the correct format to address the prompt?	Ask yourself, "Is this clearly a descriptive essay?"	If necessary, **revise** your essay so that it is in the correct format. A descriptive essay should include sensory images and other descriptive details.
2. Does the response give plenty of descriptive details?	Place a check mark next to each description. Also, make a chart listing the five senses: taste, smell, touch, sight, sound. If you wrote a sensory image for a sense, place a dot next to the sense on your chart.	**Elaborate** on the essay by adding more descriptive details. Change or add sensory images for senses you did not appeal to
3. Does the response have a clear thesis?	Ask yourself, "Does my response clearly tell who I admire and why?"	If necessary, **add** a thesis statement to your essay. Or rewrite your thesis statement so that it clearly responds to the prompt.
4. Are ideas logically related to one another? Are there gaps in logic or information?	Study the flow from one sentence to the next. Does each idea follow logically from the one before it?	**Add** details to fill in gaps in logic. Use **transition words** or phrases to improve the flow of ideas.
5. Does the response appeal to all five senses?	Read your narrative to look for descriptions that appeal to each of the senses. You may find it helpful to list the senses and put a check mark for each description that appeals to it.	Add descriptions if needed
6. Does the response use appropriate, precise vocabulary?	Identify wordy phrases, such as *at the present time, the reason that, with regard to, with the result that.*	Replace wordy phrases like those to the left with single, direct words: *now, because, about, so that.*
7. Does the response use a variety of sentence structures?	Look for sentences that start with different types of phrases. Underline sentences that seem to repeat the same structure.	Rewrite some of the sentences so that some of them begin with dependent clauses.

Evaluating, Revising, and Editing Your Response, *continued*

Draft your revised response in the space below.

_____

_____

_____

_____

_____

_____

_____

_____

_____

_____

_____

_____

_____

_____

_____

_____

_____

_____

_____

_____

_____

_____

_____

_____

Proofing Your Response

Final Editing Guidelines

Proofread your response to ensure that it

- contains only complete sentences, no fragments.

- shows proper subject-verb agreement, consistent verb tense, and correct use of nominative and subjective case.

- uses correct capitalization, punctuation, and spelling.

Draft your final essay in the space below.

_____

_____

_____

_____

_____

_____

_____

_____

_____

_____

_____

_____

_____

_____

_____

_____

_____

_____

Name _____ Class _____ Date _____

Scoring Descriptive Writing Prompts

Responses to descriptive writing prompts will be scored according to a *4-point* or a *6-point* rubric. The writing prompts will be scored for both composition (focus, content, organization, and style) and convention.

Using the 4-point or the 6-point rubric, a response will be deemed **unscorable** if certain conditions apply. A response will be determined to be **unscorable** for one or more of the following reasons. The paper may be:

- off-topic
- a paraphrase of the prompt
- written in a foreign language
- incomprehensible
- too brief to determine whether you have responded to the task
- a written refusal to write

Scorable responses are awarded points as detailed in the following rubrics.

4-Point Rubric

A *4-point* response demonstrates **advanced** success with the descriptive writing task. The essay:

- focuses consistently on describing a single place
- shows effective spatial organization throughout, with smooth transitions
- offers thoughtful, creative description
- develops the description thoroughly, using precise and vivid sensory details and images
- exhibits mature control of written language

A *3-point* response demonstrates **competent** success with the persuasive writing task. For the most part, the essay:

- focuses on describing a single place, with minor digressions
- shows effective spatial organization, with minor lapses
- offers mostly thoughtful description
- develops the description adequately, with some sensory details and images
- exhibits general control of written language

| Scoring Descriptive Writing Prompts, *continued* |

A *2-point* response demonstrates **limited** success with the persuasive writing task. The essay may:

- include some loosely related ideas that distract from the writer's descriptive focus
- show some spatial organization, with noticeable flaws in the descriptive arrangement
- offer routine, predictable description
- develop the description with uneven use of sensory detail
- exhibit limited control of written language

A *1-point* response demonstrates **emerging** effort with descriptive writing. For the most part, the essay:

- shows little awareness of the topic and the descriptive purpose
- lacks organization
- offers unclear and confusing description
- uses sensory details in only a minimal way, if at all
- exhibits major problems with control of written language

6-Point Rubric

A *6-point* response demonstrates **advanced** success with the descriptive writing task. The essay:

- focuses consistently on describing a single place
- shows effective spatial organization throughout, with smooth transitions
- offers thoughtful, creative description
- develops the description thoroughly, using precise and vivid sensory details and images
- exhibits mature control of written language

A *5-point* response demonstrates **proficient** success with the descriptive writing task. For the most part, the essay:

- shows effective spatial organization, with transitions
- offers thoughtful description
- develops the description competently, with some sensory details and images
- exhibits sufficient control of written language

Scoring Descriptive Writing Prompts, *continued*

A *4-point* response demonstrates **competent** success with the descriptive writing task. For the most part, the essay:

- focuses on describing a single place, with minor digressions
- shows effective spatial organization, with minor lapses
- offers mostly thoughtful description
- develops the description adequately, with some sensory details and images
- exhibits general control of written language

A *3-point* response demonstrates **limited** success with the descriptive writing task. The essay may:

- include some loosely related ideas that distract from the writer's descriptive focus
- show some spatial organization, with noticeable flaws in the descriptive arrangement
- offer routine, predictable description
- develop the description with uneven use of sensory detail
- exhibit limited control of written language

A *2-point* response demonstrates **basic** success with descriptive writing. For the most part, the essay:

- includes loosely related material that seriously distracts from the writer's descriptive focus
- shows minimal spatial organization, with major flaws in the descriptive arrangement
- offers description that merely skims the surface
- develops the description with inadequate sensory detail
- exhibits significant problems with control of written language

A *1-point* response demonstrates **emerging** effort with descriptive writing. For the most part, the essay:

- shows little awareness of the topic and the descriptive purpose
- lacks organization
- offers unclear and confusing description
- uses sensory details in only a minimal way, if at all
- exhibits major problems with control of written language

Name _____ Class _____ Date _____

Writing Prompt 4

Plan, write, and proofread a narrative in response to the writing prompt below.

> A teen magazine is looking for new writers. They published an illustration with a picture of machines coming to life. They want different people to write a story to go with that picture. You decide to send in a story. As you write the story, remember that the picture is only one illustration. You can make that scene a small part of your story (the beginning, middle, or end) or you can make that scene the focus of your story.

As you write your narrative story, be sure to

- Use your imagination.
- Include a scene with machines that come to life.
- Present the story logically, so that each scene makes sense.
- Use dialogue for the conversations of people in the story.
- Describe the scenes and actions with figurative language and sensory images.
- Edit your narrative for standard grammar and usage.

Strategy for Responding to the Prompt

Prewriting

1. **Analyze the Prompt.** Read the prompt carefully to identify the purpose of, and the audience for your response.

Purpose. In the prompt, you are asked to write a narrative. Your story can be about almost anything, except that it must include a scene with machines coming to life. You are to use dialogue and descriptive language in your narrative. The prompt tells you your audience and the format for your writing.

Complete the following sentence.

My purpose is to write a _____ that includes _____.

Audience. According to the prompt, who is your audience? Use the following step-by-step method to analyze the audience identified in the prompt.

Steps	Explanation	Your Response
Step 1 Ask yourself, "Who is the audience for this essay?"	Look to the prompt for clues about your audience.	
Step 2 Ask, "What is unique about my audience?"	Remember that your readers, or audience, are both the magazine editors and the people who read the magazine. Think about what teens like to read. Ask yourself what interests you and your friends.	
Step 3 Ask, "How can I make this story more interesting for my reader?"	Try to think of some ways to tease the reader and get him or her interested. For example, you might want to start with a mystery. Another way to begin is to start by telling what happens at the end, and then use a flashback.	

Strategy for Responding to the Prompt, *continued*

2. **Develop Your Plan.** In order to write your narrative, you will first have to decide what the plot will be about. You already know one scene—the machines come to life. Now you must decide what will happen throughout the story. Use the graphic organizer below to **brainstorm** the different scenes of your story. In the center oval, write a title for your story. In the ovals around it, write brief descriptions of scenes or events you would like to use in your story.

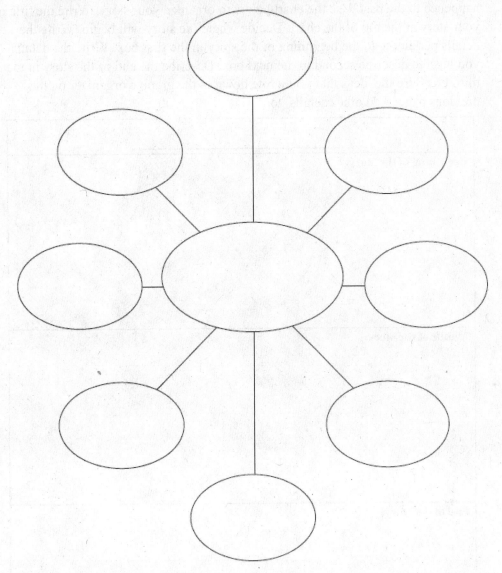

Strategy for Responding to the Prompt, *continued*

3. **Organize Your Story**. Now that you have brainstormed different scenes or events of the story, you can decide how you will present them. Sometimes it is easiest to write a story in chronological order, telling what happened first, second, and last. Other times, it can be more fun to start at the end, or in the middle. If you do this, you will need to be careful to help the reader know exactly what is happening. You can use a flashback, or you can have a character remember something that happened in the past. Use the chart below to organize your story. Write the title of your story at the top of the chart. Decide where the story will begin. Write the details pertaining to the beginning of the story in the first box. Write the details you wish to describe second in the next box. Describe the end of the story in the third box. Use the ideas that you wrote down in the graphic organizer on the previous page. Add other details, too.

_____
Beginning of the story:
Middle of the story:
End of the story:

Drafting Your Response

Use the following framework to draft your response to the narrative writing prompt. Write your draft on the lined page that follows. Remember that your narrative must have a beginning, middle, and ending.

Framework	Directions and Explanations
Introduction	
• Introduce the characters. • Make your audience want to read on.	**Describe the characters** You can help the reader picture what the characters look like. Remember to also help your reader understand each character's personality. **Get the reader hooked** Help the reader get interested in learning more about the characters by giving a funny story or presenting an interesting situation.
Body	
• Describe the location. • Discuss the actions and dialogue. • Develop your story. • Make the story real for the reader.	**Set the stage** Present a problem your characters are facing. Or tell why they are doing what they are doing. **Describe what happens** Provide details about what the characters are doing and where they are located. Use dialogue when the characters are speaking. **Give lots of descriptions** Use literal and figurative language in your descriptions. Help your reader experience the events for himself or herself. **Build the body** Use your scenes and events to build the plot of your story. Make sure that the scenes and events are in an order that makes sense.
Conclusion	
• Bring the story to a close. • Tie up any loose ends.	**Resolve the conflict** Tell how the problem is solved. If there was not an actual problem, bring the story to an end. **End the story neatly** Make sure the reader is not left with any unresolved items from the story.

Name ______________________ Class ______________ Date ______________

Drafting Your Response, *continued*

Draft your narrative in the space below.

Evaluating, Revising, and Editing Your Response

Use the following strategies to evaluate and revise your response. You may make your revisions directly on your first draft, or, if necessary, write your revised draft on the lined pages that follow.

Evaluation Guidelines for Persuasive Response		
Evaluation Question	**Tips**	**Revision Techniques**
1. Is the response written in the appropriate format for the prompt and audience?	Make sure that this prompt truly is a narrative.	**Delete** any sentences that address the audience, or seem to belong in an essay, not a story.
2. Does the story contain the required information?	Look back at the story and make sure it has a scene about machines coming to life.	If necessary, **add** the scene with the machines coming to life. Also, make sure that the scene makes sense in the story. If not, add details to make the scene fit into the story.
3. Does the narrative clearly describe the setting?	Will the reader know where and when the story takes place?	If necessary, **elaborate** your descriptions of the setting.
4. Does the narrative fully develop the characters?	Look for details about a character's actions, words, and motives.	**Add** details or descriptions as needed.
5. Does the response appeal to all five senses?	List the five senses. Write a check next to each sense that you appeal to in the story.	If most of the check marks are next to only one or two senses, **revise** some of the descriptions so they appeal to the other senses.
6. Does the narrative use dialogue? Is the dialogue effective and natural?	Read the dialogue. Circle any words, phrases, or sentences that do not sound like your character	Replace the circled words, phrases, and sentences with language that sounds natural when you read it aloud.
7. Does the story follow a logical sequence?	Ask yourself, "Does my story make sense to a reader who does not know the ending?"	Use **transition words** to help the reader, such as *before that, then, next, last.*
8. Does the story use a consistent verb tense?	Review the story. Circle any verbs that are not in the same tense.	**Change** verbs that you circled so they are in the correct tense.

Evaluating, Revising, and Editing Your Response, *continued*

Draft your revised narrative in the space below.

_____

_____

_____

_____

_____

_____

_____

_____

_____

_____

_____

_____

_____

_____

_____

_____

_____

_____

_____

_____

_____

Proofing Your Response

Final Editing Guidelines

Proofread your response to ensure that it

- contains only complete sentences, no fragments,

- shows proper subject-verb agreement, consistent verb tense, and correct use of nominative and subjective case.

- uses correct capitalization, punctuation, and spelling.

Draft your final narrative in the space below.

_____

_____

_____

_____

_____

_____

_____

_____

_____

_____

_____

_____

_____

_____

_____

_____

_____

_____

Scoring Narrative Writing Prompts

Responses to narrative writing prompts will be scored according to a *4-point* or a *6-point* rubric. The writing prompts will be scored for both composition (focus, content, organization, and style) and convention.

   Using the 4-point or the 6-point rubric, a response will be deemed **unscorable** if certain conditions apply. A response will be determined to be **unscorable** for one or more of the following reasons. The paper may be:

- off-topic
- a paraphrase of the prompt
- written in a foreign language
- incomprehensible
- too brief to determine whether you have responded to the task
- a written refusal to write

Scorable responses are awarded points as detailed in the following rubrics.

4-Point Rubric

A *4-point* response demonstrates **advanced** success with the narrative writing task. The essay:

- focuses consistently on narrating a single incident or a unified sequence of incidents
- shows effective narrative sequence throughout, with smooth transitions
- offers a thoughtful, creative approach to the narration
- develops the story thoroughly, using precise and vivid descriptive and narrative details
- exhibits mature control of written language

A *3-point* response demonstrates **competent** success with the narrative writing task. For the most part, the essay:

- focuses on narrating a single incident or a unified sequence of incidents, with minor distractions
- shows effective narrative sequence, with minor lapses
- offers a mostly thoughtful approach to the narration
- develops the story adequately, with some descriptive and narrative details
- exhibits general control of written language

Scoring Narrative Writing Prompts, *continued*

A *2-point* response demonstrates **limited** success with the narrative writing task. The essay may:

- include some loosely related material that distracts from the writer's narrative focus
- show some organization, with noticeable gaps in the narrative flow
- offer a routine, predictable approach to the narration
- develop the story with uneven use of descriptive and narrative detail
- exhibit limited control of written language

A *1-point* response demonstrates **emerging** effort with narrative writing. For the most part, the essay:

- shows little awareness of the topic and the narrative purpose
- lacks organization
- offers an unclear and confusing narrative
- develops the story with little or no detail
- exhibits major problems with control of written language

6-Point Rubric

A *6-point* response demonstrates **advanced** success with the narrative writing task. The essay:

- focuses consistently on narrating a single incident or a unified sequence of incidents
- shows effective narrative sequence throughout, with smooth transitions
- offers a thoughtful, creative approach to the narration
- develops the story thoroughly, using precise and vivid descriptive and narrative details
- exhibits mature control of written language

A *5-point* response demonstrates **proficient** success with the narrative writing task. For the most part, the essay:

- focuses on narrating a single incident or a unified sequence of incidents
- shows effective narrative sequence, with transitions
- offers a thoughtful approach to the narration
- develops the story competently, using descriptive and narrative details
- exhibits sufficient control of written language

Scoring Narrative Writing Prompts, *continued*

A *4-point* response demonstrates **competent** success with the narrative writing task. For the most part, the essay:

- focuses on narrating a single incident or a unified sequence of incidents, with minor distractions
- shows effective narrative sequence, with minor lapses
- offers a mostly thoughtful approach to the narration
- develops the story adequately, with some descriptive and narrative details
- exhibits general control of written language

A *3-point* response demonstrates **limited** success with the narrative writing task. The essay may:

- include some loosely related material that distracts from the writer's narrative focus
- show some organization, with noticeable gaps in the narrative flow
- offer a routine, predictable approach to the narration
- develop the story with uneven use of descriptive and narrative detail
- exhibit limited control of written language

A *2-point* response demonstrates **basic** success with narrative writing. For the most part, the essay:

- includes loosely related material that seriously distracts from the writer's narrative focus
- shows minimal organization, with major gaps in the narrative flow
- offers a narrative that merely skims the surface
- develops the story with inadequate descriptive and narrative detail
- exhibits significant problems with control of written language

A *1-point* response demonstrates **emerging** effort with narrative writing. For the most part, the essay:

- shows little awareness of the topic and the narrative purpose
- lacks organization
- offers an unclear and confusing narrative
- develops the story with little or no detail
- exhibits major problems with control of written language

Writing Prompt 5

Plan, write, and proofread an expository essay in response to the writing prompt below.

> The concept of honor has been an important one in all the cultures of the world. As a result, many people have thought and written about honor, both the idea of honor and the act of honoring. Read the following quotations about honor. Then write an expository essay for your local newspaper on the meaning of honor, to be published on Memorial Day or Veteran's Day.
>
> **honor,** *n.* great respect, good name or reputation, glory or recognition of one's greatness
>
> **honor,** *v.* to hold in respect or show respect for, to esteem
>
> "Fame is something which must be won; honor, only something which must not be lost."   *Arthur Schopenhauer*
>
> "Mine honor is my life, both grow in one,
> Take honor from me, and my life is done."   *William Shakespeare*
>
> "We honor the rich because they have externally the freedom, power, and grace which we feel to be proper to man, proper to us."   *Ralph Waldo Emerson*
>
> "Any person of honor chooses rather to lose his honor than to lose his conscience."   *Michel de Montaigne*
>
> "We must bear in mind the distinction between fame and honor. A virtuous person is an honorable person, a person who ought to be honored by the community in which he or she lives."   *Mortimer J. Adler*
>
> "Life and Death are fated; riches and honor lie with Heaven."   *Chinese Proverb*
>
> "Honor to the Soldier, and Sailor everywhere, who bravely bears his country's cause. Honor also to the citizen who cares for his brother in the field, and serves, as he best can, the same cause . . ."   *Abraham Lincoln*

As you write your essay, be sure to

- Focus on the meaning of honor, either as a noun or a verb.

- Consider the audience, purpose, and occasion for your response.

- Organize your response so that your ideas progress logically.

- Include relevant ideas, anecdotes, and quotations to support your definition. You may refer to, and elaborate on, one or more of the quotations above.

- Proofread your essay to correct grammar, spelling, and punctuation.

Strategy for Responding to the Prompt

Prewriting

1. **Analyze the Prompt.** Read the prompt carefully to identify the purpose of and the audience for the prompt.

Purpose. In the prompt, you are asked to read some quotations about honor. Then you are to write an essay on the meaning of honor. The prompt tells you your audience and the format for your essay.

Complete the following sentence:

My purpose is to write a(n) _____ about _____.

Audience. According to the prompt, who is your audience? Use the following step-by-step method to analyze the audience identified in the prompt

Steps	Explanation	Your Response
Step 1 Ask yourself, "Who is the audience for this response?"	Look to the prompt for clues about your audience.	
Step 2 Ask, "What does my audience already know about honor? What will be meaningful to them?"	Your audience will probably be familiar with honor, but vary a great deal as to how much they know about the people who are quoted. Your challenge will be to provide background information of the people who are quoted in order to verify their creditability. You should also think about how you can use details to make the idea of "honor" easily understood.	
Step 3 Ask, "Does my audience already have a concept of what honor is?"	You will want to give ideas that your reader can relate to, even if he or she has a personal view of what honor is. Your challenge is to present your ideas in a new or unique way without being too unusual.	

| Strategy for Responding to the Prompt, *continued* |

2. **Develop Your Plan.** Your essay should first briefly describe a general meaning of honor. Then you will want to give details and examples that support your definition. Use the graphic organizer below to **brainstorm** the details you will use to define "honor." Write the title of your composition in the center oval. Then write supporting examples and details around that center oval.

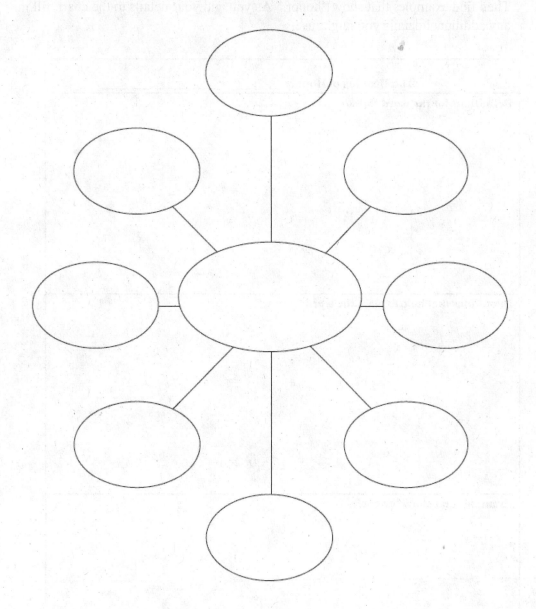

Name _____ Class _____ Date _____

3.   **Organize Your Details.** Now that you have brainstormed your details, you will
     want to organize them so that you can present them logically. Write the title of
     your essay. Then add the details that you brainstormed using the graphic organizer
     on the previous page. Separate your details in three groups. First find definitions
     for the word "honor." Next add quotations that help to explain the word "honor."
     Then find examples that show "honor." As you add your details to the chart, fill in
     any additional details you might use.

The Meaning of Honor: _____
Definitions for the word "honor."
Quotations that help explain the word "honor."
Examples that show "honor."

Strategy for Responding to the Prompt, *continued*

Draft your essay in the space below.

_____

_____

_____

_____

_____

_____

_____

_____

_____

_____

_____

_____

_____

_____

_____

_____

_____

_____

_____

_____

_____

_____

_____

_____

_____

_____

_____

_____

Drafting Your Response

Use the following framework to draft your response to the writing prompt. Write your draft on the lined pages that follow.

Framework	Directions and Explanations
Introduction	
• Use an attention grabber. • Define the word "honor." • Make the essay personal and meaningful.	**Get your reader's attention** Use an arresting statement or emotional question to introduce the word "honor." **Introduce your topic** Tell your readers what the subject of the essay is going to be. **Connect to the reader** Help your readers begin to remember the things they already know about honor.
Body	
• Share quotations about honor. • Share examples, ideas, and anecdotes. • Discuss the importance of honor. • Give proper credit to any sources you quote.	**Provide support from experts** Use quotations from experts to give your information a sense of both importance and accuracy. Arrange your quotations in an order that makes sense, such as type of detail or order of importance. **Give real-life examples** Provide honor scenarios with which your readers can identify. Arrange your details in an order that makes sense, such as type of detail or order of importance. **Give credit** Whenever you quote someone or something you read, you need to give credit to the original source. Let the reader know where you got your information. This helps show that you are not making up the facts. It also helps show that you are not stealing someone else's work.
Conclusion	
• Summarize your ideas about "honor." • Acknowledge your • reader.	**Sum it up Briefly** remind your reader what honor is and why it matters. **Acknowledge your reader** Point out that honor affects everyone; both those who have honor and those who do not. Address honor through the readers' eyes, perhaps by asking some open-ended questions.

Drafting Your Response, *continued*

Draft your response in the space below.

_____
_____
_____
_____
_____
_____
_____
_____
_____
_____
_____
_____
_____
_____
_____
_____
_____
_____
_____
_____
_____
_____

Name _____ Class _____ Date _____

Evaluating, Revising, and Editing Your Response

Use the following strategies to draft your response. You may make your revisions directly on your first draft, or, if necessary, write your revised draft on the lined pages that follow.

Evaluation Guidelines for Persuasive Response		
Evaluation Question	**Tips**	**Revision Techniques**
1. Does the response have a clear thesis? Does the thesis address the prompt?	Ask yourself, "Does my response clearly state my thesis?"	If necessary, **add** a thesis statement.
2. Does the response use specific details to support the thesis?	Place a dot next to each example, illustration, or anecdote.	**Elaborate** on the thesis by adding details.
3. Does the response contain only information that clearly supports the topic?	Lightly circle each dot that represents a relevant detail.	**Cut** supporting details that do not relate to specific reasons.
4. Are ideas logically related to one another? Are there gaps in logic or information?	Study the flow from one sentence to the next. Does each idea follow logically from the one before it?	**Add** details to fill in gaps in logic. Add transitions to improve the flow of ideas
5. Does my response sound natural?	Lightly underline any phrases or sentences that sound awkward to you.	**Rewrite** these sentences so they are more natural. Be sure the new sentences have the right tone.
6. Does the response use a variety of sentence structures?	Identify at least 1 compound sentence (2 main clauses) and 1 complex (1 independent + 1 dependent clause) per paragraph.	**Combine** ideas to create compound or complex sentences.
7. Is each paragraph centered on an organizing principle?	Read each paragraph, looking for its main idea. Put a dotted line under any sentence that does not relate to that main idea.	Decide if any of the sentences you underlined help the transition between paragraphs. Leave these sentences alone. Cut the other sentences, or change them so that they relate to the central idea.

Name _____ Class _____ Date _____

Draft your revised response in the space below.

_____

_____

_____

_____

_____

_____

_____

_____

_____

_____

_____

_____

_____

_____

_____

_____

_____

_____

_____

_____

_____

Proofing Your Response

Final Editing Guidelines
Proofread your response to ensure that it

- is written legibly.
- uses quotation marks for any quotes you used.
- uses correct capitalization, punctuation, and spelling.

Draft your final response in the space below

_____
_____
_____
_____
_____
_____
_____
_____
_____
_____
_____
_____
_____
_____
_____
_____
_____
_____
_____

Scoring Expository Writing Prompts

Responses to expository writing prompts will be scored according to a *4-point* or a *6-point* rubric. The writing prompts will be scored for both composition (focus, content, organization, and style) and convention.

　　Using the 4-point or the 6-point rubric, a response will be deemed **unscorable** if certain conditions apply. A response will be determined to be **unscorable** for one or more of the following reasons. The paper may be:

off-topic

- a paraphrase of the prompt
- written in a foreign language
- incomprehensible
- too brief to determine whether you have responded to the task
- a written refusal to write

Scorable responses are awarded points as detailed in the following rubrics.

4-Point Rubric:

A *4-point* response demonstrates **advanced** success with the expository writing task. The essay:

- focuses consistently on a clear thesis
- shows effective organization throughout, with smooth transitions
- offers thoughtful, creative ideas
- develops ideas thoroughly, using examples, details, and fully elaborated explanations
- exhibits mature control of written language

A *3-point* response demonstrates **competent** success with the expository writing task. For the most part, the essay:

- focuses on a reasonable position, with minor distractions
- shows effective organization, with minor lapses
- offers mostly thoughtful ideas
- develops ideas adequately, with a mixture of general and specific elaboration
- exhibits general control of written language

Scoring Expository Writing Prompts, *continued*

A *2-point* response demonstrates **limited** success with the expository writing task. The essay may:

- include some loosely related ideas that distract from the writer's expository focus
- show some organization, with noticeable gaps in the logical flow of ideas
- offer routine, predictable ideas
- develop ideas with uneven elaboration
- exhibit limited control of written language

A *1-point* response demonstrates **emerging** effort with expository writing. For the most part, the essay:

- shows little awareness of the topic and purpose for writing
- lacks organization
- offers unclear and confusing ideas
- develops ideas in only a minimal way, if at all
- exhibits major problems with control of written language

6-Point Rubric:

A *6-point* response demonstrates **advanced** success with the expository writing task. The essay:

- focuses consistently on a clear thesis
- shows effective organization throughout, with smooth transitions
- offers thoughtful, creative ideas
- develops ideas thoroughly, using examples, details, and fully elaborated explanation
- exhibits mature control of written language

A *5-point* response demonstrates **proficient** success with the expository writing task. For the most part, the essay:

- focuses on a clear thesis
- shows effective organization, with transitions
- offers thoughtful ideas and reasons
- develops ideas competently, using examples, details, and well-elaborated explanation
- exhibits sufficient control of written language

Scoring Expository Writing Prompts, *continued*

A *4-point* response demonstrates **competent** success with the expository writing task. For the most part, the essay:

- focuses on a reasonable position, with minor distractions
- shows effective organization, with minor lapses
- offers mostly thoughtful ideas
- develops ideas adequately with a mixture of general and specific elaboration
- exhibits general control of written language

A *3-point* response demonstrates **limited** success with the expository writing task. The essay may:

- include some loosely related ideas that distract from the writer's expository focus
- show some organization, with noticeable gaps in the logical flow of ideas
- offer routine, predictable ideas
- develop ideas with uneven elaboration
- exhibit limited control of written language

A *2-point* response demonstrates **basic** success with expository writing. For the most part, the essay:

- includes loosely related ideas that seriously distract from the writer's expository focus
- shows minimal organization, with major gaps in the logical flow of ideas
- offers ideas that merely skim the surface
- develops ideas with inadequate elaboration
- exhibits significant problems with control of written language

A *1-point* response demonstrates **emerging** effort with expository writing. For the most part, the essay:

- shows little awareness of the topic and purpose for writing
- lacks organization
- offers unclear and confusing ideas
- develops ideas in only a minimal way, if at all
- exhibits major problems with control of written language

Writing Prompt 6

Plan, write, and proofread an essay in response to the writing prompt below.

> Read the poem, "A Cowboy's Lament." As you read, you may mark
> the selection and write notes in the margins that help you think about
> what you are reading. You can use your notes to help you write your
> essay.
>
> How does the speaker of this poem feel about cowboys and the law? Write an
> essay describing the speaker's viewpoint, using examples from the poem
> itself.

As you write your essay, be sure to

- Present a clear explanation of the speaker's viewpoint.
- Give several clear ideas to support your opinion.
- Use examples from the passage.
- Use examples from your own experience or other poems, if they help you make
  your argument.
- Present your ideas in a clear and logical manner.
- Edit your essay for standard grammar and usage.

A Cowboy's Lament

As I walked out in the streets of Laredo,

As I walked out in Laredo one day,

I spied a poor cowboy wrapped up in white linen

Wrapped up in white linen as cold as the clay.

"Oh beat the drum slowly and play the fife lowly,

Play the dead march as you carry me along;

Take me to the green valley, there lay the sod o'er me,

For I'm a young cowboy and I know I've done wrong.

"I see by your outfit that you are a cowboy"—

These words he did say as I boldly stepped by,

"Come sit down beside me and hear my sad story;

I am shot in the breast and I know I must die.

"Let sixteen gamblers come handle my coffin,

Let sixteen cowboys come sing me a song.

Take me to the graveyard and lay the sod o'er me,

For I'm a poor cowboy and I know I've done wrong.

"My friends and relations they live in the Nation[1],

They know not where their boy has gone.

He first came to Texas and hired to a ranchman

Oh, I'm a young cowboy and I know I've done wrong.

"It was once in the saddle I used to go dashing,

It was once in the saddle I used to go gay;

First to the dramhouse[2] and then to the cardhouse;

Got shot in the breast and I am dying today.

"Get six jolly cowboys to carry my coffin;

Get six pretty maidens to bear up my pall.

Put bunches of roses all over my coffin,

Put roses to deaden the sods as they fall.

---

[1] **Nation:** United States of America.

[2] **dramhouse:** saloon or bar.

Writing Prompt 6, *continued*

"Then swing your rope slowly and rattle your spurs lowly,

And give a wild whoop as you carry me along;

And in the grave throw me and roll the sod o'er me

For I'm a young cowboy and I know I've done wrong.

"Oh, bury beside me my knife and six-shooter,

My spurs on my heel, my rifle by my side,

And over my coffin put a bottle of brandy,

That the cowboys may drink as they carry me along.

"Go bring me a cup, a cup of cold water,

To cool my parched lips," the cowboy then said;

Before I returned his soul had departed,

And gone to the roundup—the cowboy was dead.

We beat the drum slowly and played the fife lowly,

And bitterly wept as we bore him along;

Fro we all loved our comrade, so brave, young, and handsome,

We all loved our comrade although he'd done wrong.

Strategy for Responding to the Prompt

Prewriting

1. **Analyze the Prompt.** Read the prompt carefully to identify the purpose of your response.

Purpose. In the prompt, you are asked to analyze a poem, and answer a specific question about it.

Complete the following sentence:

My purpose is to write a _____ about _____.

Audience. In this writing prompt, the audience is not named specifically. You will need to think about what audience would read a literary response. Use the following step-by-step method to analyze how to address your audience.

Steps	Explanation	Your Response
Step 1 Ask yourself, "How do I write a story to an unnamed audience?"	Since you do not know the audience, you want to think about who would be likely to read a literary analysis. You can choose to write your analysis so it appeals to people who are a lot like you. Or you can write it to a more general audience. Either way, be sure your analysis gives details and information that a general audience can understand and relate to.	
Step 2 Ask, "What does my audience already know about the speaker of the poem?"	Your audience will likely have read the poem, so he or she will know the basic details. However, you will need to point out specific details to help make your point.	
Step 3 Ask, "Does my audience already have an opinion of the poem or speaker in mind?"	Your audience may already have a view about the speaker of the poem. You will need to give examples to help support your opinion.	

| Strategy for Responding to the Prompt, *continued* |

2. **Develop Your ideas.** Your essay should specifically respond to the question asked in the prompt. In order to do this, you will need to begin by answering the question in a few sentences. Then look through the poem to find examples that support this answer.

    As you examine the poem, you may find that you want to change your original response. That's okay. Right a new answer after the question. Then list the examples that support it in the chart.

Question from the prompt: **How does the speaker of this poem feel about cowboys and the law?**
My response:

Example from the poem	line(s)
1.	
2.	
3.	

Examples from Other Poems or Experiences	Source of the Example
1.	
2.	
3.	

Strategy for Responding to the Prompt, *continued*

3. **Write a Thesis Statement.** Look over the graphic organizer that you created on the previous page. What is your answer to the questions given in the writing prompt? Write your answer below. Then write a thesis statement, explaining your view of the passage.

My answer:_____

Thesis Statement: _____

4. **Organize Your Essay.** Now it is time to organize your thoughts so that you can clearly explain your point of view. Write your thesis statement in the graphic organizer below. Then look back at the examples you listed in the chart on the previous page. Choose several examples that support your thesis. Write them in the blanks below. If you have more than four examples, just add rows to the organizer. Be sure that at least some of your examples come from the passage itself. Carefully think about how you want to organize your list of examples. You can reorder them now, before you begin writing.

Thesis Statement:
Example 1:
Example 2:
Example 3:
Example 4:

Drafting Your Response

Use the following framework to draft your response to the writing prompt. Write your draft on the lined paper that follows.

Framework	Directions and Explanations
Introduction	
• Give the reader enough information to fully understand the poem. • Present the thesis.	**Provide needed background information** Identify the poem and briefly explain what it is about. **State your thesis** Give your opinion of the speaker's viewpoint in the poem.
Body	
• Give examples and show how they support your thesis.	**Use examples from the poem** Let the reader know when you are describing something the writer said. Use quotation marks if you are quoting the poem directly. Also tell what line(s) the quote is from. **Use personal experiences and your own background knowledge** Tell the reader how you know something or describe your personal experience.
Conclusion	
• Restate your thesis in a new way. • Tie the ideas together with a summary.	**Finish strongly** Restate your thesis and briefly review your analysis of the poem.

Name ______________________ Class ______________ Date ______________

Drafting Your Response, *continued*

Draft your literary response in the space below.

Evaluating, Revising, and Editing Your Response

Use the following strategies to evaluate and revise your response. You may make your revisions directly on your first draft, or, if necessary, write your revised draft on the lined pages that follow.

Evaluation Guidelines for Literary Response		
Evaluation Question	**Tips**	**Revision Techniques**
1. Does the essay have a clear thesis statement? Does the thesis address the prompt?	Ask yourself, "Does my thesis clearly state my opinion about the views of the poem's speaker?"	If necessary, **revise** your thesis statement to clearly address the prompt.
2. Do the supporting details clearly relate to the thesis statement?	Place a check mark next to each detail that supports the thesis statement. Draw a light line through those details that do not relate to the thesis statement.	**Cut** supporting details that do not relate to the thesis. **Elaborate** on the essay by adding details, if necessary.
3. Does the essay clearly identify statements that come from the poem itself?	Lightly underline all examples from the poem.	If necessary, **add** quotation marks around any direct quotes. **Add** statements that tell where the quote comes from in the poem.
4. Is the essay organized in a logical way? Are there gaps in logic or information?	Study the flow from one sentence to the next. Does each idea follow logically from the one before it? Or does the essay seem to jump around from idea to idea?	**Reorganize** the sentences or paragraphs to give the essay a more logical flow. **Add** details to fill in gaps in logic. Use **transition words** or phrases to improve the flow of ideas.
5. Does the response use vocabulary that is original, varied, and natural?	Lightly circle any words that are repeated several times. Also lightly circle any words that sound unnatural or out of place within the style of your piece. These are words that do not sound like something you would say.	**Replace** the repeated words with different synonyms. **Replace** any unnatural words with words that sound and feel more like words you would use.
6. Does the response use a variety of sentence structures?	Look for sentences that start with different types of phrases. Underline sentences that seem to repeat the same structure.	**Rewrite** some of the sentences so that some of them begin with phrases, subordinate clauses, or transitional expressions.

Evaluating, Revising, and Editing Your Response, *continued*

Draft your revised response in the space below.

_____

_____

_____

_____

_____

_____

_____

_____

_____

_____

_____

_____

_____

_____

_____

_____

_____

_____

_____

_____

_____

_____

_____

Proofing Your Response

> **Final Editing Guidelines**
> Proofread your response to ensure that it
> - contains only complete sentences, no fragments,
> - shows proper subject-verb agreement, consistent verb tense, and correct use of nominative and subjective case.
> - uses correct capitalization, punctuation, and spelling.

Draft your final response in the space below.

_____

_____

_____

_____

_____

_____

_____

_____

_____

_____

_____

_____

_____

_____

_____

_____

_____

_____

_____

_____

Scoring Text-based Writing Prompts

Responses to literature (text-based) writing prompts will be scored according to a 4-point or a 6-point rubric. The writing prompts will be scored for both composition (focus, content, organization, and style) and convention.

Using the *4-point* or the *6-point* rubric, a response will be deemed **unscorable** if certain conditions apply. A response will be determined to be **unscorable** for one or more of the following reasons. The paper may be off-topic:

- a paraphrase of the prompt
- written in a foreign language
- incomprehensible
- too brief to determine whether you have responded to the task
- a written refusal to write

Scorable responses are awarded points as detailed in the following rubrics.

4-Point Rubric

A *4-point* response demonstrates **advanced** success with the text-based writing task. The essay:

- offers a clear thesis, with consistent focus on the assigned task
- shows effective organization throughout, with smooth transitions
- offers thoughtful, creative ideas and an insightful, comprehensive grasp of the assigned text
- develops ideas thoroughly, using relevant, well-elaborated information, examples, and details from the assigned text
- exhibits mature control of written language

A *3-point* response demonstrates **competent** success with the text-based writing task. For the most part, the essay:

- offers a clear thesis and focuses on the assigned task, with minor distractions
- shows effective organization, with minor lapses
- offers mostly thoughtful ideas and a general grasp of the assigned text
- develops ideas adequately, with mostly relevant information, examples, and details from the assigned text
- exhibits general control of written language

| Scoring Text-based Writing Prompts, *continued* |

A **2-point** response demonstrates **limited** success with the text-based writing task. The essay may:

- include some loosely related ideas that distract from the writer's text-based focus

- show some organization, with noticeable gaps in the logical flow of ideas

- offer routine, predictable ideas and a limited grasp of the assigned text

- develop ideas with uneven use of information, examples, and details from the assigned text

- exhibit limited control of written language

A **1-point** response demonstrates **emerging** effort with text-based writing. For the most part, the essay:

- shows little awareness of the topic and purpose for writing

- lacks organization

- offers unclear, confusing ideas and little or no grasp of the assigned text

- develops ideas in only a minimal way, if at all—with little or no material from the assigned text

- exhibits major problems with control of written language

6-point rubric

A **6-point** response demonstrates **advanced** success with the text-based writing task. The essay:

- offers a clear thesis, with consistent focus on the assigned task

- shows effective organization throughout, with smooth transitions

- offers thoughtful, creative ideas and an insightful, comprehensive grasp of the assigned text

- develops ideas thoroughly, using relevant, well-elaborated information, examples, and details from the assigned text

- exhibits mature control of written language

A **5-point** response demonstrates **proficient** success with the text-based writing task. For the most part, the essay:

- offers a clear thesis, with focus on the assigned task

- shows effective organization, with transitions

- offers thoughtful ideas and a sound grasp of the assigned task

- develops ideas well, using relevant information, examples and details from the assigned text

Scoring Text-based Writing Prompts, *continued*

A *4-point* response demonstrates **competent** success with the text-based writing task. For the most part, the essay:

- offers a clear thesis and focuses on the assigned task, with minor distractions
- shows effective organization, with minor lapses
- offers mostly thoughtful ideas and a general grasp of the assigned text
- develops ideas adequately, with mostly relevant information, examples, and details from the assigned text
- exhibits general control of written language

A *3-point* response demonstrates **limited** success with the text-based writing task. The essay may:

- include some loosely related ideas that distract from the writer's text-based focus
- show some organization, with noticeable gaps in the logical flow of ideas
- develop ideas with uneven use of information, examples, and details from the assigned text
- exhibit limited control of written language

A *2-point* response demonstrates **basic** success with the text based writing task. For the most part, the essay:

- includes loosely related ideas that seriously distract from the writer's text-based focus
- shows minimal organization, with major gaps in the logical flow of ideas
- offers ideas that merely skim the surface, with a weak grasp of the assigned text
- develops ideas with inadequate elaboration, using insufficient material from the assigned text
- exhibits significant problems with control of written language

A *1-point* response demonstrates **emerging** effort with text-based writing. For the most part, the essay:

- shows little awareness of the topic and purpose for writing
- lacks organization
- offers unclear, confusing ideas and little or no grasp of the assigned text
- develops ideas in only a minimal way, if at all–with little or no material from the assigned text
- exhibits major problems with control of written language

Name _____ Class _____ Date _____

Writing Conventions Practice

Read each question and choose the best answer. Use the provided answer sheet at the end of the workbook to record your answers.

1. Choose the word that **best** completes the sentence.
   Robin _____ in her diary every night last week.

   A write

   B written

   C writes

   D wrote

2. Find the sentence that is complete and is written correctly.

   A Giraffes: up to 75 pounds of food each day; thick, sticky saliva coats sharp items they might swallow, such as thorns.

   B Giraffes eat up to 75 pounds of food each day; their thick, sticky saliva coats sharp items they might swallow, such as thorns.

   C Since giraffe's are eating up to 75 pounds of food each day and have thick, sticky saliva that coats sharp items they might swallow, such as thorns.

   D Eating up to 75 pounds of food each day, with a giraffe's thick, sticky saliva coating sharp items they might swallow, such as thorns.

3. Read these sentences. Choose the words that **best** complete **each** sentence.
   Bobbi will try out for the band in _____ weeks.
   Calvin and Missy went _____ see the play.

   A two/to

   B to/two

   C two/too

   D too/two

4. Choose the sentence that is written with the **correct** capitalization and punctuation.

   A The dodder parasite plants attach to their hosts suck off food and water and often spread diseases.

   B The Dodder parasite plants attach to their hosts suck off food and water and often spread diseases.

   C The Dodder parasite plants attach to their hosts, suck off food and water, and often spread Diseases.

   D The dodder parasite plants attach to their hosts, suck off food and water, and often spread diseases.

5. Choose the sentence that uses the possessive form of Bob **correctly.**

   A I am borrowing Bob's book.

   B I am borrowing Bobs book.

   C I am borrowing Bobs' book.

   D I am borrowing Bobs's book.

6. Choose the word that **best** completes the sentence.
   Our team _____ going to take a break from practicing.

   A be

   B are

   C will

   D is

7. Choose the sentence that is written **correctly.**

   A Were not happy about that.

   B Where not happy about that.

   C We're not happy about that.

   D Wer'e not happy about that.

8. Choose the word that **best** completes the sentence.
   _____ book is this?

   A Who's

   B Who'se

   C Whose

   D Whom's

9. Choose the **best** way to combine these two sentences.
   Let's meet after our 5th class before we go to our last class. The library will be a good place to meet.

   A Let's meet after our 5th class before we go to our next class; and the library will be a good place to meet.

   B Before we go to our last classes: let's meet in the library after our 5th class.

   C Let's meet in the library.

   D Let's meet in the library after our 5th classes, but before our last class.

10. Choose the sentence that is written **correctly.**

   A It seems mirraculous that little Benjamin is already 14 years old!

   B It seems miraculous that little Benjamin is already 14 years old!

   C It seems miraculous that little Benjamin is allready 14 years old!

   D It seams miraculous that little Benjamin is already 14 years old!

11. What is the **best** way to write the last sentence in this paragraph?
The high school chess club welcomes players of all ability levels. Weekly chess matches are held every Friday before school, beginning at 6:30 a.m. Every two weeks, the top 10 players can represent the school in a local tournament. The top four players at the end of the season have a chance to compete in the state championship tournament, which is held every year and is a great opportunity for the top four players a the end of the season.

A The top four players at the end of the season have a chance to compete in the state championship tournament, which is held every year at the end of the season and is a great opportunity.

B At the end of the season, the top four players have the opportunity to compete in the end-of-season state championship tournament, which is held every year.

C The top four players will have a great opportunity to compete in the state championship tournament at the end of the season.

D leave as is

12. Choose the sentence that is written with the **correct** punctuation.

A Maria said "she likes swimming better than running."

B Maria said, "I like swimming better than running."

C Maria said I like swimming better than running.

D Maria said she likes swimming better than running."

13. Choose the **best** way to combine these two sentences.
Theresa's long dark hair was blowing in the wind and getting in her mouth.
Theresa decided to put her long dark hair in a ponytail so it wouldn't blow into her mouth.

A Theresa's long dark hair was blowing in the wind, so she put it in a ponytail to keep it out of her mouth.

B Theresa's long dark hair was blowing in the wind and getting in her mouth, and Theresa decided to put her long dark hair in a ponytail so it wouldn't blow into her mouth.

C Theresa's long dark hair was blowing in the wind and getting in her mouth, so Theresa decided to put her long dark hair in a ponytail.

D Theresa's long dark hair was blowing in the wind and getting in her mouth, so she put it in a ponytail.

| **Writing Conventions Practice,** *continued* |

14. Choose the sentence that is written **correctly.**

   A   Do you know how to seperate spaghetti so it doesn't stick together?

   B   Do you know how to separate spaghetti so it doesn't stick together?

   C   Do you know how to separate spagetti so it doesn't stick together?

   D   Do you know how to seperrate spaghetti so it doesn't stick together?

15. Read this sentence that has a missing pronoun. Identify both the missing pronoun and its antecedent.
   Butch offered to cut the onion, but cutting ____ left a smell on his hands that he couldn't get rid of.

   A   them, onion

   B   they, hands

   C   it, onion

   D   him, Butch

16. Choose the word that **best** completes the sentence.
   Do you want to go with Tara and ____ to the store?

   A   they

   B   we

   C   I

   D   me

| Writing Conventions Practice, *continued*

A Local Play

Identify the type of error, if any, in each underlined passage. Use the provided answer sheet to record your answers to the multiple choice questions, and use a separate sheet of paper to record your response to open-ended questions.

> The new locally-written play, A day on Main Street, had just
>   1
>
> completed its premere showing. As the curtain came down,
>   2
>
> the actors looked hessitantly at each other. They walked offstage.
>   3
>
> Then smiles burst over their faces as they heard the audience applauding:
>   4
>
> enthusiastically. The cast of the play hurried back onto the Stage.
>   5
>
> They bowed with confidently. The audience threw bouquets of flowers.
>   6   7
>
> The play had been a sucess!
>   8

1.

   A Spelling

   B Capitalization

   C Punctuation

   D No error

2.

   A Spelling

   B Capitalization

   C Punctuation

   D No error

Writing Conventions Practice, *continued*

3.

    A Spelling

    B Capitalization

    C Punctuation

    D No error

4.

    A Spelling

    B Capitalization

    C Punctuation

    D No error

5.

    A Spelling

    B Capitalization

    C Punctuation

    D No error

6. Use correct grammar to rewrite the following sentence.

They bowled with confidently.

7.

    A Spelling

    B Capitalization

    C Punctuation

    D No error

8.

    A Spelling

    B Capitalization

    C Punctuation

    D No error

Summertime

Read the passage below. Choose the word or phrase that best completes each sentence. Use the provided answer sheet to record your answers to the multiple choice questions, and use a separate sheet of paper to record your response to open-ended questions.

> What do you like doing __(1)__ a summer day? Are you a person __(2)__ appreciates being outdoors? Many people enjoy the warm summer __(3)__. They participate in outdoor __(4)__, best enjoyed during warm, sunny weather. ___(5)___ basketball, swimming, golfing, or skating is a great way to spend a summer day. Gardening and cooking outdoors __(6)__ also be enjoyable summer pastimes. Just __(7)__ outside with a glass of cold lemonade suits some people just fine. No matter what __(8)__ enjoy, summer can be fun for all!

1.

   A for

   B on

   C onto

   D to

2.

   A who

   B whose

   C that

   D which

3.

   A months'

   B month

   C months

   D munths

4.

   A active

   B activity

   C activity's

   D activities

5. Use the correct form of the verb *to play* to rewrite sentence 5.

6.

   A are

   B can

   C has

   D was

7.

   A sit

   B sits

   C sat

   D sitting

8.

   A he

   B she

   C it

   D you

English/Language Arts Second Course Practice Test:
Reading and Writing

Reading Practice Test

Read the selection below. Then read each question and choose the best answer.
Use the provided answer sheet at the end of the workbook to record your
answers, and use a separate sheet of paper to record your response to open-ended
questions.

Slugging it Out
by Joan Burditt

A four-year-old gazes at the television screen and laughs as a pig hits a duck over the head with an ironing board. The duck springs back to life, running around in circles with stars spinning around his head. Does this scene sound familiar? The hard truth is, though, this is not what happens when humans get hit on the head.

Many doctors believe that as a society we close our eyes to the terrible injuries caused by a tremendous blow to the head. Doctors have expressed deep concern about boxing injuries such as those received by the former heavyweight champion Muhammad Ali. Ali suffers from Parkinson's disease, an illness probably caused by the hits he took in the ring. He was diagnosed with the disease in 1985, four years after he retired from boxing. Other famous sufferers include Jack Dempsey, Joe Louis, Beau Jack and Wilfredo Benitez.

(3) The symptoms of Parkinson's disease range from slurred speech to difficulty walking. It can also cause declining mental ability and tremors. According to doctors and researchers, a blow severe enough to render a person unconscious may result in tearing of nerve fibers and hemorrhaging, or uncontrolled bleeding inside the brain. This neurological disorder affects career boxers and others who receive multiple dazing blows to the head. It develops over a period of years. The average time of onset is about 16 years after the start of a career in boxing.

In 1984, the American Medical Association came out in support of a complete ban on boxing. The sport of boxing remains popular, however. Supporters believe that training young people to box properly instills self-control. They also point out the benefits of fighting according to a set of rules. They believe that boxing provides opportunities for individuals who might otherwise have no chance to achieve financial security. Some doctors disagree with the American Medical Association's position and believe boxing produces a few injuries because all major muscle groups are used.

The debate continues. Both sides of the issue will verbally slug it out until they can come to a resolution.

1. Which word **best** characterizes the tone of this selection?

   A   whimsical

   B   serious

   C   somber

   D   unpleasant

2. According to the selection, Muhammad Ali, Joe Louis, and Beau Jack all

   A   became doctors.

   B   became television announcers.

   C   suffer from Parkinson's disease.

   D   believe that boxing is a dangerous sport.

3. Which of the following is an argument in **support** of boxing?

   A   Symptoms of Parkinson's disease range from slurred speech to difficulty walking.

   B   Blows to the head can cause bleeding inside the brain.

   C   The average time of onset is about 16 years after the start of a career in boxing.

   D   Training young people to box properly instills self-control.

4. Based on the content of paragraph 3, what does neurological mean?

   A   related to the nerves and brain

   B   nervous

   C   related to boxing injuries

   D   serious

5. What is **most likely** the reason the author wrote this selection?

   A   to persuade the AMA to change its view of boxing

   B   to convince people of the dangers of boxing

   C   to inform readers about TV violence

   D   to entertain readers with stories about famous boxers

6. The selection suggests that in the near future

   A   boxing matches will be outlawed.

   B   doctors will stop complaining about boxing.

   C   boxing will become less popular.

   D   people will continue the argument about boxing.

7. Why does the American Medical Association believe that boxing should be banned?

8. Why do you think the author begins the selection with a description of cartoon violence?

Reading Practice Test, *continued*

Read the selection below. Then read each question and choose the best answer. Use the provided answer sheet at the end of the workbook to record your answers, and use a separate sheet of paper to record your response to open-ended questions.

from The Wife of His Youth
by Charles W. Chesnutt

[Mr. Ryder] then related, simply but effectively, the story told by his visitor [the wife]. There were some present who had seen, and others who had heard their fathers and grandfathers tell the wrongs and sufferings of this past generation, and all of them still felt. . . the shadow [of slavery] hanging over them. Mr. Ryder went on: —

"Such devotion and confidence are rare even among women. There are many who would have searched a year, some who would have waited five years, a few who might have hoped ten years; but for twenty-five years this woman has retained her affection for and her faith in a man she has not seen or heard of in all that time.

"She came to me to-day in the hope that I might be able to help her find this long-lost husband. And when she was gone I . . . imagined a case I will put to you.

"Suppose that this husband, soon after his escape, had learned that his wife had been sold away, and that such investigations as he could make brought no information of her whereabouts. . . . Suppose, too, that he made his way to the North as some of us have done, and there, where he had larger opportunities, had improved [himself] . . . . And then suppose that accident should bring to his knowledge the fact that the wife of his youth . . . was alive and seeking him, but that he was absolutely safe from recognition or discovery, unless he chose to reveal himself. My friends, what would

the man do? . . . And suppose that perhaps he had set his heart upon another, whom he had hoped to call his own. What would he do, or rather what ought he to do, in such a crisis of a lifetime?

"And now, ladies and gentlemen, friends and companions, I ask you, what should he have done?"

There was something in Mr. Ryder's voice that stirred the hearts of those who sat around him. . . . It was observed, too, that his look rested more especially upon Mrs. Dixon . . . She had listened, with parted lips and streaming eyes. She was the first to speak: "He should have acknowledged [his wife]."

"Yes," they all echoed, "he should have acknowledged her."

"My friends and companions," responded Mr. Ryder, "I thank you, one and all. It is the answer I expected, for I knew your hearts."

He turned and walked toward the closed door of an adjoining room, while every eye followed him in wondering curiosity. He came back in a moment, leading by the hand his visitor of the afternoon, who stood startled and trembling at the sudden plunge into this scene of brilliant gayety. She was neatly dressed in gray, and wore the white cap of an elderly woman.

"Ladies and gentlemen," he said, "this is the woman, and I am the man, whose story I have told you. Permit me to introduce to you the wife of my youth."

| Reading Practice Test, *continued* |

1. Which word **best** describes Mr. Ryder's attitude at the beginning of the selection?

    A cheerful

    B confident

    C bitter

    D apprehensive

2. Which type of person is **most** like Mr. Ryder?

    A someone who can't make a decision

    B someone who tries to do the right thing

    C someone who takes pride in his accomplishments

    D someone who is unwilling to work hard

3. Which statement supports the idea that "the wife" did not know she had found her husband until the end of the selection?

    A He was absolutely safe from recognition or discovery, unless he chose to reveal himself.

    B Perhaps he had set his heart upon another, whom he had hoped to call his own.

    C She was neatly dressed in gray, and wore the white cap of an elderly woman.

    D Mr. Ryder then related, simply but effectively, the story told by his visitor

4. Based on the information in the selection which of the following relationships is **most** similar to the relationship below?

    Mrs. Dixon : Mrs. Ryder

    A tenderhearted : devoted

    B proud : needy

    C wealthy : poor

    D nosy : generous

5. One theme of this selection is

    A "past events are best forgotten."

    B "out with the old and in with the new."

    C "patience and devotion are often rewarded."

    D "always listen to advice from your friends."

6. Which of the following is the **most** reasonable prediction based on the end of the selection?

    A Mr. Ryder will ask Mrs. Dixon to marry him.

    B Mr. Ryder will be happy with his wife.

    C Mr. Ryder will continue to tell the story to anyone who will listen.

    D Mr. Ryder will escape from his wife again.

7. According to the selection, how does the wife show her confidence and devotion?

   A by escaping slavery and moving North

   B by asking her friends for advice

   C by talking sweetly about her husband

   D by waiting for her husband for 25 years

8. What is the **most likely** reason that the listeners wait until Mrs. Dixon speaks before responding?

   A They are crying so hard they cannot speak.

   B They think Mrs. Dixon will interrupt them if they speak first.

   C They want to see what Mrs. Dixon wants Mr. Ryder to do.

   D They are all soft-spoken people.

9. Which of these statements **best** show that Mr. Ryder admires his wife?

   A For twenty-five years this woman has retained her affection for and her faith in a man she has not seen or heard of in all that time.

   B She came to me today in the hope that I might be able to help her find this long-lost husband.

   C Suppose this husband had learned that his wife had been sold away.

   D Suppose that he had set his heart upon another, whom he had hoped to call his own.

10. How does Mr. Ryder's story affect his listeners?

11. What is ironic about the fact that Mrs. Dixon says that the man should reveal himself to his wife?

Reading Practice Test, *continued*

Read the selection below. Then read each question and choose the best answer. Use the provided answer sheet at the end of the workbook to record your answers, and use a separate sheet of paper to record your response to open-ended questions.

Forest Fires Make Their Own Weather

As a wildfire burned near Santa Barbara, California, in 1993, huge storm clouds formed overhead. Fiery whirlwinds danced over the ground. The fire was not only destroying everything in its path—it was also creating its own weather!

Hot air rising from a forest fire can create tremendous updrafts. Surrounding hot air rushes in underneath the rising air, stirring up columns of ash, smoke, hot air, and noxious gases. Cool, dry air normally sinks down and stops these columns from developing any further. But if the conditions are just right, a surprising thing happens.

If the upper atmosphere contains warm, moist air, the moisture begins to condense on the ash and smoke. These droplets can develop into clouds. As the clouds grow, the droplets begin to collide and combine until they are heavy enough to fall as rain. The result is an isolated rainstorm, complete with thunder and lightning.

Forest fires can also create whirlwinds. These small tornado-like funnels can be extremely dangerous. Whirlwinds are similar to dust devils that dance across desert sands. Their circular motion is created by an updraft that is forced to turn after striking an obstacle, such as a cliff or hill. Whirlwinds move across the ground at 5–7 miles/h (8–11 km/h), sometimes growing up to 394 feet (120 m) high and 50 feet (15 m) wide.

Most whirlwinds last less than a minute, but they can cause some big problems. Firefighters caught in the path of whirlwinds have been severely injured and even killed. Also, if a whirlwind is hot enough, it can suck up tremendous amounts of air. The resulting updraft can pull burning debris up through the whirlwind. In some cases, burning trees have been uprooted and shot into the air. When the debris lands, it often starts new fires hundreds of meters away.

Fires are a natural part of growth of a forest. For example, some tree seeds are released only under the extreme temperatures of a fire. Some scientists believe that forest fires should be allowed to run their natural course. Others argue that forest fires cause too much damage and should be extinguished as soon as possible.

1. What is the **main** purpose of the selection?

   A to convince readers to be careful when they set fires

   B to explain weather conditions created by forest fires

   C to describe the author's experiences as a fire fighter

   D to entertain readers with scary stories about fires

2. Which statement **best** summarizes the main idea of the selection?

   A Hot updrafts caused by wildfires can result in whirlwinds and rainstorms.

   B Whirlwinds are similar to dust devils in the desert.

   C Certain weather conditions allow rain to form over a wildfire.

   D Some scientists think that wildfires are a natural part of a forest's growth.

3. Which statement **best** supports the author's claim that whirlwinds can cause big problems?

   A Most whirlwinds last less than a minute.

   B Whirlwinds start when wind hits an obstacle such as rock.

   C Most whirlwinds move quickly.

   D Whirlwinds can spread fires over distances.

4. Whirlwinds created in a fire are dangerous because they

   A move slowly and menacingly.

   B bring torrential rainstorms.

   C pick up burning debris and start new fires.

   D suck up sand into columns called dust devils

5. Based on the context in paragraph 4, an <u>obstacle</u> is

   A warm, moist air.

   B something that starts fires.

   C something that is in the way .

   D a hill or cliff.

6. Which of these statements is a **fact** about forest fires?

   A Hot air rushing from a forest fire can create tremendous updrafts.

   B Forest fires should not be allowed to run their natural course.

   C Forest fires cause too much damage.

   D Forest fires should be extinguished as soon as possible.

7. Based on the selection, how is a whirlwind similar to a tornado?

8. How does this statement expresses cause and effect?
   Some tree seeds are released only under the extreme temperatures of a fire.

Read the poem below. Then read each question and choose the best answer. Use the provided answer sheet at the end of the workbook to record your answers, and use a separate sheet of paper to record your response to open-ended questions

When You Are Old
by William Butler Yeats

1   When you are old and gray and full of sleep
     And nodding by the fire, take down this book,
     And slowly read, and dream of the soft look
     Your eyes had once, and of their shadows deep;

5   How many loved your moments of glad grace,
     And loved your beauty with love false or true,
     But one man loved the pilgrim soul in you,
     And loved the sorrows of your changing face.

9   And bending down beside the glowing bars,
     Murmur, a little sadly, how Love fled
     And paced upon the mountains overhead,
     And hid his face amid a crowd of stars.

1. Which word **best** describes the mood of the poem?

   A cheerfulness

   B forgiveness

   C regret

   D annoyance

2. What is the **best** paraphrase of line 5?

   How many loved your moments of glad grace

   A You were once admired by many people.

   B You used to be so happy.

   C You can't even remember all of your admirers.

   D You were once graceful and young.

3. Reread these last few lines from the poem.

   . . . Love fled
   And paced upon the mountains overhead
   And hid his face amid a crowd of stars.

   This is an example of

   A metaphor.

   B simile

   C personification.

   D onomatopoeia

4. In line 7, a "pilgrim soul" is **most likely**

   A someone who is religious.

   B someone who likes adventure and travel.

   C a soldier.

   D a young person in love.

5. Which statement **best** summarizes one theme of this poem?

   A Life is short and difficult.

   B Beautiful people are often surrounded by admirers.

   C People who are old are often sleepy.

   D People do not appreciate true love until it is too late.

6. What are the "glowing bars" in line 9?

   A the lover's heart

   B stories of past greatness

   C stories of past dreams

   D burning logs in the fire

7. What are the literal and figurative meanings of being "full of sleep" in line 1?

8. How does the title of the poem help you understand its meaning?

Read the selection below. Then read each question and choose the best answer. Use the provided answer sheet at the end of the workbook to record your answers, and use a separate sheet of paper to record your response to open-ended questions.

Wildlife Under Siege

The stunning lands of the national parks in the United States are being invaded. The roar of snowmobiles often rips through the quiet countryside. People who enjoy riding snowmobiles claim the machines pose no threat to the parks' animals and land. Others are not so sure. Biologists and environmental researchers have conducted studies showing that snowmobiles have terrible effects on natural resources. Whether snowmobilers mean to or not, they are harming the sensitive ecosystem that allows wildlife to survive during the winter. Snowmobiles must be banned from our national parks in order to save these animals from destruction.

Survival depends on a careful balance in nature. A few of these loud machines can disrupt the animals' habitat. Snow mobiles in large numbers are a serious problem and should be kept off public parkland. Unfortunately, there has been an increase in the number of snowmobiles zooming through these winter wonderlands. Snowmobile sales in the United States nearly doubled from 82,000 to 163,000 between 1992 and 1998. There were 2.3 million snowmobiles registered in North America in 1998. In Yellowstone National Park, only a few thousand snowmobiles were being operated in the 1970s, but the number increased to nearly 100,000 snow mobiles by 1998. The presence of all these machines means more noise and more stress for more animals.

(3) In a 1997 review that summarized more than five hundred studies, biologist James Caslick concluded that snowmobiles literally can harass wildlife to death both directly and indirectly. Although most snowmobilers do not intentionally seek to harm animals, some of them do. One writer suggests that these raiders should be banned for life from national parks. Ken Schleuter, a conservation officer in Minnesota, reports that he was called to help rescue a badly injured wolf in 1998. The snowmobile tracks around it showed that two snowmobilers had intentionally chased it and hit it. While most snowmobilers would never do such a thing, Schleuter says, "those two drivers created an awful lot of work for us, and that animal suffered. Nobody has a right to do that."

The indirect effects of snowmobiles on wildlife can be as harmful as direct attacks. Snowmobile noise alone causes trouble. Large animals like moose and elk must conserve most of their energy to survive deep snow and low temperatures. They must limit their movement to finding food. Snowmobile noise startles these animals, and they waste vital energy fleeing it. Continual stress like this contributes to the death of wildlife.

Small animals suffer, too. The packed snow on the trails is less inviting to animals that live beneath the snow's surface. Small burrowing animals must use more energy to get through packed snow, and, of course, snowmobiles easily crush these smaller animals.

Snowmobiles, while not necessarily bad, must be used responsibly. Humans should respect the very resources they want to explore with the machines.

Closing national parkland to snowmobiles will lessen the harm humans do to the winter landscape and its inhabitants.

Reading Practice Test, *continued*

1. What is the **main** idea of the selection?

   A Conservation officers are responsible for helping injured animals.

   B Snowmobiles are generally bad for wildlife.

   C Animals will learn to protect themselves against machines.

   D The noise from snowmobiles startles animals.

2. In the second paragraph, what reason does the author give for wanting to ban snowmobiles?

   A Snowmobiles damage plants and trees.

   B Too many people refuse to register them.

   C There have been too many people killed in snowmobile accidents.

   D The increased number of snowmobiles poses a greater threat to wildlife.

3. Why does the author include the third paragraph?

   A to honor the work of the park rangers

   B to give a reason for banning snowmobiles in public parks

   C to teach readers about the habits of wolves in winter

   D to show that many people do research on wildlife

4. Based on the selection, what is **most likely** to happen in the near future?

   A Snowmobiles will be outlawed.

   B The public parks will close to all people.

   C Wildlife will adapt to the snowmobiles.

   D More snowmobiles will come and more wildlife will die.

5. What **fact** does the author give about snowmobile sales in the U.S. from 1992 to 1998?

   A Not all snowmobiles are loud.

   B Sales of snowmobiles nearly doubled.

   C Snowmobiles used to be more of a problem than they are now.

   D Snowmobile sales ended in 1998.

6. You can conclude that in the winter, large animals

   A are not harmed when snowmobilers only view them.

   B should be protected at all costs.

   C should move mainly to look for food.

   D suffer from snowmobiles more than small animals.

7. Why is the statistic about the number of snowmobiles in Yellowstone National Park included?

   A to provide evidence

   B to contradict information

   C to state a reason

   D to draw a conclusion

8. According to the selection, what is the correct order of these events?
   1. Elk hear the loud noise of a snowmobile.
   2. Elk die younger because they waste energy running from the noise.
   3. Elk get scared and flee from the noise.

   A 2, 3, 1
   B 1, 3, 2
   C 3, 2, 1
   D 1, 2, 3

9. Which of these statements from the passage is an example of bias?

   A The stunning lands of the national parks in the United States are being invaded.

   B Survival depends on a careful balance in nature.

   C Large animals like moose and elk must conserve most of their energy to survive deep snow and low temperatures.

   D Ken Schleuter reports that he was called to help rescue a badly injured wolf in 1998.

10. How do snowmobiles have a negative impact on small animals?

11. Why does the selection mention that moose and elk run away from noise?

Reading Practice Test, *continued*

Booker T. Washington was born into slavery in 1856. After the end of slavery in 1865, he worked with his father packing salt. He taught himself to read, and as an adult he became an influential teacher and public speaker. Read the selection below. Then read each question and choose the best answer. Use the provided answer sheet at the end of the workbook to record your answers, and use a separate sheet of paper to record your response to open-ended questions.

from Up From Slavery
by Booker T. Washington

The first thing I ever learned in the way of book knowledge was while working in this salt-furnace. Each salt-packer had his barrels marked with a certain number. The number allotted to my stepfather was "18." At the close of the day's work the boss of the packers would come around and put "18" on each of our barrels, and I soon learned to recognize that figure wherever I saw it, and after a while got to the point where I could make that figure, though I knew nothing about any other figures or letters.

(2) From the time that I can remember having any thoughts about anything, I recall that I had an intense longing to learn to read. I determined, when quite a small child, that, if I accomplished nothing else in life, I would in some way get enough education to enable me to read common books and newspapers. Soon after we got settled in some manner in our new cabin in West Virginia, I induced my mother to get hold of a book for me. How or where she got it I do not know, but in some way she <u>procured</u> an old copy of Webster's "blue-back" spelling-book, which contained the alphabet, followed by such meaningless words as "ab," "ba," "ca," "da." I began at once to devour this book, and I think that it was the first one I ever had in my hands.

I had learned from somebody that the way to begin to read was to learn the alphabet, so I tried in all the ways I could think of to learn it,--all of course without a teacher, for I could find no one to teach me. At that time there was not a single member of my race anywhere near us who could read, and I was too timid to approach any of the white people. In some way, within a few weeks, I mastered the greater portion of the alphabet. In all my efforts to learn to read my mother shared fully my ambition, and sympathized with me and aided me in every way that she could. Though she was totally ignorant, she had high ambitions for her children, and a large fund of good, hard, common sense, which seemed to enable her to meet and master every situation. If I have done anything in life worth attention, I feel sure that I inherited the disposition from my mother.

Reading Practice Test, *continued*

1. Based on the context in paragraph 2, what does <u>procured</u> mean?

    A studied

    B obtained

    C lost

    D created

2. Which conclusion is **best** supported by the ending of the selection?

    A Washington's stepfather is angry that his son has learned to read.

    B Washington feels uneasy about learning to read.

    C Washington's mother is ashamed of her son.

    D Washington deeply admires his mother.

3. What is the effect of using the first person in this selection?

    A It allows the author to share his feelings and thoughts.

    B It emphasizes that Washington's story is a historical one.

    C It helps readers understand Washington's mother better.

    D It shows that Washington has an excellent memory for detail.

4. Which type of person is **most** like Booker T. Washington as a boy?

    A someone who stands up to a bully

    B someone who works hard to better himself

    C someone who is popular and well liked

    C someone who is shy and afraid to upset others

5. Why does Washington begin with the story of the salt-furnace?

    A to show that he always knew how to read

    B to help the reader understand why it was so hard for him to learn to read

    C to show when he first became aware of reading and its importance

    D to explain why he wanted to learn to read

6. According to this selection, what is the **main** reason Washington wanted to learn to read?

    A so he could read books and newspapers

    B so he could show his former owners that black people were smart, too

    C so he would not have to work in a salt-furnace

    D so he could become a teacher

7. Reread the last sentence in the selection.
    If I have done anything in life worth attention, I feel sure that I inherited the disposition from my mother.
    Restate this idea in your own words.

8. Explain how the historical context of this story helps you understand why Washington did not feel comfortable asking a white person to teach him to read.

Read the selection below. Then read each question and choose the best answer. Use the provided answer sheet at the end of the workbook to record your answers, and use a separate sheet of paper to record your response to open-ended questions.

Mongoose on the Loose
by Larry Luxner

In 1872, a Jamaican sugar planter imported nine furry little mongooses from India to eat the rats that were devouring his crops. They did such a good job, the planter started breeding his exotic animals and selling them to eager farmers on neighboring islands.

With no natural predators—like wolves, coyotes, or poisonous snakes—the mongoose population exploded, and within a few years, they were killing not just rats but pigs, lambs, chickens, puppies, and kittens. Dr. G. Roy Horst, a U. S. expert on mongooses, says today mongooses live on seventeen Caribbean islands as well as Hawaii and Fiji, where they have attacked small animals, threatened endangered species, and have even spread minor rabies epidemics.

In Puerto Rico there are from 800,000 to one million of them. That is about one mongoose for every four humans. In St. Croix, there are 100,000 mongooses, about twice as many as the human

population. "It's impossible to eliminate the mongoose population, short of nuclear war," says Horst. "You can't poison them because cats, dogs, and chickens get poisoned, too. I'm not a prophet crying in the wilderness, but the potential for real trouble is there," says Horst.

According to Horst, great efforts have been made to rid the islands of mongooses, which have killed off a number of species, including the Amevia lizard on St. Croix, presumed extinct for several decades. On Hawaii, the combination of mongooses and sports hunting has reduced the Hawaiian goose, or nene, to less than two dozen individuals . . .

Horst says his research will provide local and federal health officials with extremely valuable information if they ever decide to launch a campaign against rabies in Puerto Rico or the U. S. Virgin Islands.

Reading Practice Test, *continued*

1. The following diagram displays information about events in this article. Which event belongs in the third box?

```
┌─────────────────────────┐
│ Rats destroy sugar      │
│ planters crops.         │
└─────────────────────────┘
            │
            ▼
┌─────────────────────────┐
│ Effect: Planter imports │
│ nine mongooses.         │
└─────────────────────────┘
            │
            ▼
┌─────────────────────────┐
│ Effect:                 │
└─────────────────────────┘
            │
            ▼
┌─────────────────────────┐
│ Effect: Planter breeds  │
│ and sells mongooses.    │
└─────────────────────────┘
            │
            ▼
┌─────────────────────────┐
│ Effect: Mongoose        │
│ population explodes.     │
└─────────────────────────┘
```

A Mongooses do a good job of getting rid of rats.

B Mongooses threaten the Hawaiian goose.

C Mongooses destroy other species.

D Mongooses are difficult to study.

2. Where else would you **most likely** find this type of information about mongooses?

A in a chemistry book

B in a collection of stories

C in a travel guide

D in a magazine on nature

3. Based on the context of the first paragraph, the word <u>devouring</u> means

A knocking down.

B ruining.

C eating greedily.

D tearing up.

4. Which of the following is an example of a secondary source about mongoose in the Caribbean Islands?

A a journal entry from Dr. G. Roy Horst

B a Jamaican news article from 1872

C a map of Jamaica

D a college essay about the problem of mongooses

5. Based on the last paragraph, you can conclude that

A there are no mongooses in the U.S. Virgin Islands.

B health officials have not led a campaign to fight rabies.

C rabies is not a problem in Puerto Rico.

D farmers wish they had rats instead of mongooses.

6. What is the **main** effect of quoting Dr. G. Roy Horst?

A It makes the selection more interesting.

B It makes the selection more like science fiction.

C It shows that the author is a talented writer.

D It shows that the information is supported by an expert.

| Reading Practice Test, *continued* |

7. Which statement expresses an effect caused by the mongoose population explosion?

    A Some species have become endangered.

    B The Amevia lizard population has increased.

    C Sugar planters are happy with the mongooses.

    D The wolf and the coyote populations increased.

8. Why did a Jamaican sugar planter import nine mongooses in 1872?

9. Why did the mongoose population explode in the Caribbean?

Read the selection below. Then read each question and choose the best answer. Use the provided answer sheet at the end of the workbook to record your answers, and use a separate sheet of paper to record your response to open-ended questions.

from The Mazarin Stone *adapted from a story by Sir Arthur Conan Doyle*
by Michael and Molly Hardwick

Characters

Sherlock Holmes

Dr. Watson, Holmes's friend and associate

Billy, Holmes's servant

HOLMES:	But it's good to see you in your old quarters once again, my dear Watson.
WATSON:	*(concerned)* Holmes—this talk of sudden death. What are you expecting?
HOLMES:	*(simply)* To be murdered.
WATSON:	Oh, come now! You're joking!
HOLMES:	Even my limited sense of humor could evolve a better joke than that, Watson. *(Brightening)* But we may be comfortable in the meantime, mayn't we? Let me see you once more in the customary chair.
WATSON:	Pleasure, Holmes! But why not eat?
HOLMES:	Because the faculties[1] become refined when you starve them. Surely, as a doctor, you must admit that what your digestion gains in the way of blood supply is so much lost to the brain? *I* am a brain, Watson. The rest of me is mere appendix. Therefore, it's the brain I must consider.
WATSON:	But—this danger . . . ?
HOLMES:	Ah, yes. Just in case it should come off, it would be as well for you to know the name of the murderer. You can give it to Scotland Yard, with my love and a parting blessing.
WATSON:	Holmes!
HOLMES:	His name is Sylvius—Count Negretto Sylvius. No. 136 Moorside Gardens, London NW. Got it?
WATSON:	Yes. *(Hesitantly)* Er—Holmes . . . I've got nothing to do for a day or two. Count me in.

---

[1] **faculties:** natural abilities

| Reading Practice Test, *continued*

HOLMES: *(sadly shaking his head)* Your morals don't improve, Watson.

WATSON: My *morals?*

HOLMES: You've added fibbing to your other vices. You bear every sign of the busy medical man, with calls on him every hour.

WATSON: Not such important ones. But—can't you have this fellow arrested?

HOLMES: Yes, Watson, I could. That's what worries him so.

WATSON: Then why don't you?

HOLMES: Because I don't know where the diamond is.

WATSON: Ah! Billy was telling me—the missing Crown jewel!

HOLMES: The great yellow Mazarin Stone. I've cast my net and I have my fish. But I have *not* got the stone. Yes, I could make the world a better place by laying *them* by the heels; but it's the stone I want.

WATSON: And is Count Sylvius one of your fish?

HOLMES: Yes—and he's a *shark.* He bites. The other is Sam Merton, the boxer. Not a bad fellow, Sam, but the Count has used him. Sam's just a great, big, silly, bull-headed gudgeon;[2] but he's flopping about in my net, all the same.

WATSON: Where is Count Sylvius now?

HOLMES: I've been at his elbow all morning. *(He gets up.)* You've seen me as an old lady, Watson?

WATSON: *(chuckling)* Oh, yes indeed!

[HOLMES *assumes the posture and walk of an old lady.]*

HOLMES: *(in a cracked old voice)* I was never more convincing, Doctor. Never! (Watson *laughs as* Holmes *straightens up. Normal voice)* He actually picked up my parasol[3] for me once. *(Holmes picks up the parasol and gesticulates with it.)*

WATSON: He didn't!

[HOLMES *makes an elaborate bow, holding out the parasol in both hands.]*

HOLMES: *(mimicking* SYLVIUS*)* By your leave, madam. *(Holmes resumes his normal voice and manner and lays the parasol aside.)* He's half Italian, you know. Full of the Southern[4] graces when he's in the mood. But he's a devil incarnate[5] in the other mood. Life is full of whimsical happenings.

---

[2] **gudgeon:** a small fish that is easily caught and used for bait; here, a person who is easily tricked or used

[3] **parasol:** a lightweight umbrella or sunshade

[4] **Southern:** the reference is to southern Europe; the count is from Italy

[5] **devil incarnate:** the devil in human form

| Reading Practice Test, *continued* |

WATSON:	*(with a snort)* Whimsical. It might have been tragedy.
HOLMES:	Well, perhaps it might. . . .
	[Knock at parlor door, which opens. BILLY *enters, carrying a salver[6]]*
BILLY:	Mr. Holmes, sir . . .
HOLMES:	What is it, Billy?
BILLY:	There's a gentleman to see you, sir.
	*[*HOLMES *takes the visiting card from the salver and looks at it.]*
HOLMES:	Thank you. *(He replaces the card.)* The man himself, Watson!
WATSON:	Sylvius!
HOLMES:	*(nods)* I'd hardly expected this. Grasp the nettle[7], eh! A man of nerve, Watson. But possibly you've heard of his reputation as a big-game shooter? It'd be a triumphant ending to his excellent sporting record if he added me to his bag.
WATSON:	Send for the police, Holmes!
HOLMES:	I probably shall—but not just yet. Would you just glance carefully out of the window and see if anyone is hanging about in the street?
WATSON:	Certainly. *(He goes to the window and peeps cautiously round the corner of the blind.)* Yes—there's a rough-looking fellow near the door.
HOLMES:	That will be Sam Merton—the faithful but rather fatuous[8] Sam. Billy, where is Count Sylvius?
BILLY:	In the waiting room, sir.
HOLMES:	Show him up when I ring.
BILLY:	Yes, sir.
HOLMES:	If I'm not in the room, show him in all the same.
BILLY:	Very good, Mr. Holmes. *(He leaves by the parlor door.)*
WATSON:	Look here, Holmes, this is simply ridiculous. This is a desperate man who sticks at nothing, you'd have me believe. He may have come to murder you.
HOLMES:	I shouldn't be surprised.

[6] **salver:** a small tray
[7] **Grasp the nettle:** an expression that means to act boldly; nettles are plants with sharp thorns that feel soft if one grabs them firmly
[8] **fatuous:** foolish

Reading Practice Test, *continued*

WATSON:	Then I insist on staying with you!
HOLMES:	You'd be horribly in the way.
WATSON:	In his way!
HOLMES:	No, my dear fellow—in mine.

1. How has Sherlock Holmes spent his morning?

    A talking to Dr. Watson

    B following a suspect

    C posing as a woman

    D eating breakfast

2. Which characteristic **best** describes Sherlock Holmes?

    A resourceful

    B indifferent

    C obnoxious

    D polite

3. Why does Sherlock Holmes call Count Sylvius "a shark"?

    A to suggest that Slvius is a curious creature

    B to imply that Sylvius is very clever

    C to describe Sylvius's physical appearance

    D to emphasize that Sylvius is a dangerous character

4. Why does Holmes not want to arrest Count Sylvius?

    A Holmes cannot prove that Sylvius is guilty.

    B Holmes wants to find the stone first.

    C Holmes does not trust the police.

    D Holmes does not want Watson to get credit for helping him.

5. Based on the passage, you can predict that

    A Holmes will take Watson with him to meet Sylvius.

    B Holmes will wait for the police to arrive before meeting Sylvius.

    C Watson will meet Sylvius alone.

    D Holmes will meet Sylvius by himself.

6. Which line **best** shows that Sylvius did not recognize Holmes's disguise?

    A I've cast my net and I have my fish.

    B I've been at his elbow all morning.

    C He actually picked up my parasol for me.

    D He's half Italian you know.

7. What is the Mazarin Stone?

8. Why does Sylvius want to kill Holmes?

Writing Practice Test

Writing Prompt 1

Plan, write, and proofread a persuasive letter in response to the writing prompt below. Write your letter on your own paper.

> It is about the time of year when students have to take standardized state tests. The upcoming tests have caused a lot of debate about the value of state testing. Some people feel that standardized state tests are a good measure of students' academic progress and should remain. Others feel that standardized state tests should be discontinued and other factors be used to determine students' academic progress. You decide to write a persuasive letter to your school newspaper about standardized state testing.
>
> Take a stand on the issue: Either standardized state testing has value or standardized state testing should be discontinued. Give a variety of reasons and examples to support your opinion. Be sure to include plenty of convincing details.

As you write your letter, be sure to

- Consider the purpose, audience, and occasion for your response.
- Include plenty of details to support your position.
- Use transitional words and phrases to connect ideas.
- Organize your letter so your ideas progress logically.
- Edit your letter for standard grammar, usage, spelling, and punctuation.

Use the space below to plan your writing.

Writing Practice Test

Writing Prompt 2

Plan, write, and proofread a descriptive essay in response to the writing prompt below. Write your essay on your own paper.

> Picture your favorite place to eat. This can be your kitchen or dining room. It can be a fancy restaurant or a fast-food place. It can even be at someone else's house, such as a close friend or relative.
>
> Write a descriptive essay about this place for the eighth grade class journal. Describe everything about this place. Tell where it is located, what it looks like when you are sitting there, and—of course—why this is your favorite place to eat. Be sure to use specific nouns and colorful adjectives to describe everything around you, including the furnishings, wall décor, type of food, the smells, and tastes. Don't forget to describe the people around you, too.

As you write your descriptive essay, be sure to

- Clearly identify the place you are going to describe.
- Include plenty of details.
- Use sensory images so that your writing appeals to all of the five senses.
- Use transitional words and phrases to connect ideas.
- Organize your essay so your ideas progress logically.
- Edit your essay for standard grammar, usage, spelling, and punctuation.

Use the space below to plan your writing.

_____

_____

_____

_____

_____

_____

_____

_____

_____

_____

_____

Writing Practice Test
Writing Conventions

Read each question and choose the best answer. Use the provided answer sheet at the end of the workbook to record your answers.

1. Choose the word that **best** completes the sentence.
   Move _____ if you hear a clattering behind you.

   A quicker

   B quick

   C quickly

   D quickness

2. Choose the word that **best** completes the sentence.
   Kenny _____ on the ice and caught his skate on his pants.

   A slipped

   B slip

   C slips

   D slipping

3. Find the sentence that is **complete** and is written **correctly.**

   A All the pictures fit nicely in a large, divided picture frame.

   B All the pictures in a large, divided picture frame.

   C In a large, divided picture frame, all the pictures.

   D Nicely fit in a large, divided frame, all the pictures.

4. Choose the answer that shows the **correct** punctuation.

   A If you hand me the book I'll show you the page I mean.

   B If you hand me the book, I'll show you the page I mean.

   C If, you hand me the book, I'll show you the page I mean.

   D If you hand me the book, I'll show you the page, I mean.

5. Read this sentence.
   In his anger, Shawn <u>shut</u> the door.
   Choose the word that would **most** dramatically replace the underlined word.

   A closed

   B opened

   C hated

   D slammed

6. Choose the answer that shows the **correct** capitalization.

   A I live south of Granite Park

   B I live South of Granite Park

   C I live south of Granite park

   D I live South of Granite park

7. Choose the words that best complete **each** sentence.
   Guy and Hank talked about _____ hobbies.
   Did you see the dog over _____?

   A there/their

   B there/they're

   C their/they're

   D their/there

8. Choose the words that **best** complete **each** sentence.

   Be sure to bring _____ notebook.
   _____ the best person for the job.

   A your/You're

   B you're/Your

   C your/Your

   D you're/You're

9. Choose the sentence that is written with the **correct** capitalization and punctuation.

   A "Sure," Mae said, "we'll be happy to help you".

   B "Sure," Mae said, "We'll be happy to help you."

   C "Sure" Mae said, we'll be happy to help you."

   D "Sure" Mae said, "We'll be happy to help you."

10. Choose the sentence that is written **correctly.**

    A Before e-mailing become common, people communicated by writing letters.

    B Before e-mailing became common, people communicate by writing letters.

    C Before e-mailing became common, people communicated by writing letters.

    D Before e-mailing became common, people will be communicating by writing letters.

11. Choose the pronoun that **best** completes the sentence.

    The zebras took off running, and then _____ stopped and looked at the two girls.

    A he

    B it

    C they

    D we

12. Which word is a verb in this sentence?

    Neil cut the baseball in half and found string, cork, and rubber.

    A half

    B found

    C string

    D rubber

Flowers

Identify the type of error, if any, in each underlined passage. Use the provided answer sheet to record your answers to the multiple choice questions, and use a separate sheet of paper to record your response to open-ended questions.

Flowers are enjoyed <u>by many people both as landscaping, and as</u>
                                                    1
<u>indoor decoration.</u> <u>Today growing flower's is not just for amateurs.</u>
                                                    2
Horticulturists are constantly searching for a better flower. For
example, <u>Bluebonnets are wildflowers</u> that have never been grown
                        3
commercially—until recently, that is. <u>Thanks to the pioneering efforts</u>
                                                                        4
<u>of horticulturists at Texas A&M university,</u> it may soon be possible to
walk into a flower shop and purchase a bouquet of bluebonnets. What's
more, bluebonnets of the future may not be bluebonnets.
<u>The researchers are experimenting with color variations as well.</u>
                        5
They hope to develop a blossom that smells nice and <u>will last in a vase</u>
                                                                        6
<u>for several days after it has been sniped.</u>

1.

A Spelling

B Capitalization

C Punctuation

D No error

2. Using the correct punctuation, rewrite the second sentence (sentence with underlined passage 2).

3.

A Spelling

B Capitalization

C Punctuation

D No error

4.

A Spelling

B Capitalization

C Punctuation

D No error

5.

A Spelling

B Capitalization

C Punctuation

D No error

6.

A Spelling

B Capitalization

C Punctuation

D No error

Name _____ Class _____ Date _____

The Rodeo

Choose the word or phrase that best completes each sentence. Use the provided answer sheet to record your answers to the multiple choice questions, and use a separate sheet of paper to record your response to open-ended questions.

There __(1)__ nothing quite like a rodeo. Small fenced areas magically __(2)__ into arenas where cowboys, bulls, horses, clowns, dust, and sweat meld into one great event of heart-pounding excitement. What event is __(3)__ favorite? People associate riding broncos or bulls with rodeos, but __(4)__ are other exciting events. For example, barrel-racing, steer wrestling (bulldogging), and calf roping are __(5)__ by many people. There are always many things to watch at a rodeo. By evening, the memories of those who have attended __(6)__ with sounds and smells of the day.

1.
  A are
  B is
  C isn't
  D wasn't

2.
  A was changing
  B change
  C changes
  D has changed

3.
  A you're
  B our
  C your
  D this

4.
  A they
  B here
  C where
  D there

5. Using the correct form of the verb *to enjoy*, rewrite the fifth sentence (sentence with blank 5.)

6.
  A is filled
  B have been filled
  C had filled
  D were being filled

Answer Sheets

Answer Sheet

Reading Practice
Circle the correct answer.

from **The Call of the Wild**

1. A   B   C   D
2. A   B   C   D
3. A   B   C   D
4. A   B   C   D
5. A   B   C   D
6. A   B   C   D
7. A   B   C   D
8. A   B   C   D
9. A   B   C   D
10. A   B   C   D

11–12. Use a separate sheet of paper to record your response.

Cos Gives It Up

1. A   B   C   D
2. A   B   C   D
3. A   B   C   D
4. A   B   C   D
5. A   B   C   D
6. A   B   C   D
7. A   B   C   D
8. A   B   C   D
9. A   B   C   D
10. A   B   C   D

11–12. Use a separate sheet of paper to record your response.

from **The Highwayman, Part Two**

1. A   B   C   D
2. A   B   C   D
3. A   B   C   D
4. A   B   C   D
5. A   B   C   D
6. A   B   C   D
7. A   B   C   D
8. A   B   C   D
9. A   B   C   D
10. A   B   C   D

11–12. Use a separate sheet of paper to record your response.

World of Dyslexia

1. A   B   C   D
2. A   B   C   D
3. A   B   C   D
4. A   B   C   D
5. A   B   C   D
6. A   B   C   D
7. A   B   C   D
8. A   B   C   D
9. A   B   C   D

10–11. Use a separate sheet of paper to record your response.

Anne's Confession: *from* **Anne of Green Gables**

1. A   B   C   D
2. A   B   C   D
3. A   B   C   D
4. A   B   C   D
5. A   B   C   D
6. A   B   C   D
7. A   B   C   D
8. A   B   C   D
9. A   B   C   D
10. A   B   C   D

11–12. Use a separate sheet of paper to record your response.

Making a Magic Trick

1. A   B   C   D
2. A   B   C   D
3. A   B   C   D
4. A   B   C   D
5. A   B   C   D
6. A   B   C   D
7. A   B   C   D
8. A   B   C   D
9. A   B   C   D
10. A   B   C   D

11–12. Use a separate sheet of paper to record your response.

Name _____ Class _____ Date _____

Answer Sheet, Reading Practice, *continued*

The Boy Who Drew Cats
1. A B C D
2. A B C D
3. A B C D
4. A B C D
5. A B C D
6. A B C D
7. A B C D
8. A B C D
9. A B C D
10. A B C D
11. A B C D

12–13. Use a separate sheet of paper to record your response.

Organizing a Benefit Car Wash
1. A B C D
2. A B C D
3. A B C D
4. A B C D
5. A B C D
6. A B C D
7. A B C D
8. A B C D
9. A B C D

10–11. Use a separate sheet of paper to record your response.

from The Monkey's Paw
1. A B C D
2. A B C D
3. A B C D
4. A B C D
5. A B C D
6. A B C D
7. A B C D
8. A B C D
9. A B C D
10. A B C D

11–12. Use a separate sheet of paper to record your response.

Ways of Fighting Germs
1. A B C D
2. A B C D
3. A B C D
4. A B C D
5. A B C D
6. A B C D
7. A B C D
8. A B C D
9. A B C D
10. A B C D

11–12. Use a separate sheet of paper to record your response.

Answer Sheet

SCORE _____

Writing Practice

Writing Prompt 1

Your school newspaper has been featuring stories about schools with letter grade systems and schools with pass-fail systems. Some people in your school district want to do away with grades in favor of a pass-fail system. Others disagree. You are going choose one side of the argument and write an article for your school newspaper expressing your view on the issue.

Writing Prompt 2

Imagine that your school band wants to enter a contest. Everyone has been working hard, and you think your band has a good chance to win. There's only one problem—your band doesn't have any uniforms! Write a persuasive letter to a local businessperson asking him or her to contribute money toward buying uniforms. Include that, in return, all band programs for the next five years will advertise the businesses that help to purchase the uniforms.

Writing Prompt 3

Write a descriptive essay about the person you most admire. This essay will be posted on your history room bulletin board. Choose the person and consider the reasons why he or she is the person you most admire. Then write your description. Be sure to give details about what the person has done to gain your admiration.

Writing Prompt 4

A teen magazine is looking for new writers. They published an illustration with a picture of machines coming to life. They want different people to write a story to go with that picture. You decide to send in a story. As you write the story, remember that the picture is only one illustration. You can make that scene a small part of your story (the beginning, middle, or end) or you can make that scene the focus of your story.

Writing Prompt 5

The concept of honor has been an important one in all the cultures of the world. As a result, many people have thought and written about honor, both the idea of honor and the act of honoring. Read the following quotations about honor. Then write an expository essay for your local newspaper on the meaning of honor, to be published on Memorial Day or Veteran's Day.

Writing Prompt 6

Read the poem, "A Cowboy's Lament." As you read, you may mark the selection and write notes in the margins that help you think about what you are reading. You can use your notes to help you write your essay. How does the speaker of this poem feel about cowboys and the law? Write an essay describing the speaker's viewpoint, using examples from the poem itself.

Writing Conventions Practice
Circle the correct answer.

Writing Conventions	A Local Play	Summertime
1. A B C D	1. A B C D	1. A B C D
2. A B C D	2. A B C D	2. A B C D
3. A B C D	3. A B C D	3. A B C D
4. A B C D	4. A B C D	4. A B C D
5. A B C D	5. A B C D	5. Use a separate sheet of paper to record your response.
6. A B C D	6. Use a separate sheet of paper to record your response.	6. A B C D
7. A B C D	7. A B C D	7. A B C D
8. A B C D	8. A B C D	8. A B C D
9. A B C D		
10. A B C D		
11. A B C D		
12. A B C D		
13. A B C D		
14. A B C D		
15. A B C D		
16. A B C D		

Answer Sheet

SCORE _____

English/Language Arts Second Course Practice Test: Reading

Circle the correct answer.

Slugging it Out

1. A   B   C   D
2. A   B   C   D
3. A   B   C   D
4. A   B   C   D
5. A   B   C   D
6. A   B   C   D

7–8. Use a separate sheet of paper to record your response.

from The Wife of His Youth

1. A   B   C   D
2. A   B   C   D
3. A   B   C   D
4. A   B   C   D
5. A   B   C   D
6. A   B   C   D
7. A   B   C   D
8. A   B   C   D
9. A   B   C   D

10–11. Use a separate sheet of paper to record your response.

Forest Fires Make Their Own Weather

1. A   B   C   D
2. A   B   C   D
3. A   B   C   D
4. A   B   C   D
5. A   B   C   D
6. A   B   C   D

7–8. Use a separate sheet of paper to record your response.

When You Are Old

1. A   B   C   D
2. A   B   C   D
3. A   B   C   D
4. A   B   C   D
5. A   B   C   D
6. A   B   C   D

7–8. Use a separate sheet of paper to record your response.

Wildlife Under Siege

1. A   B   C   D
2. A   B   C   D
3. A   B   C   D
4. A   B   C   D
5. A   B   C   D
6. A   B   C   D
7. A   B   C   D
8. A   B   C   D
9. A   B   C   D

10–11. Use a separate sheet of paper to record your response.

from Up From Slavery

1. A   B   C   D
2. A   B   C   D
3. A   B   C   D
4. A   B   C   D
5. A   B   C   D
6. A   B   C   D

7–8. Use a separate sheet of paper to record your response.

Answer Sheet, Reading Practice Test, continued

Mongoose on the Loose

1. A   B   C   D
2. A   B   C   D
3. A   B   C   D
4. A   B   C   D
5. A   B   C   D
6. A   B   C   D
7. A   B   C   D

8–9. Use a separate sheet of paper to record your response.

from **The Mazarin Stone**

1. A   B   C   D
2. A   B   C   D
3. A   B   C   D
4. A   B   C   D
5. A   B   C   D
6. A   B   C   D

7–8. Use a separate sheet of paper to record your response.

Answer Sheet

SCORE _____

English/Language Arts Second Course
Practice Test: Writing

Writing Prompt 1

It is about the time of year when students have to take standardized state tests. The upcoming tests have caused a lot of debate about the value of state testing. Some people feel that standardized state tests are a good measure of students' academic progress and should remain. Others feel that standardized state tests should be discontinued and other factors be used to determine students' academic progress. You decide to write a persuasive letter to your school newspaper about standardized state testing.

Take a stand on the issue: Either standardized state testing has value or standardized state testing should be discontinued. Give a variety of reasons and examples to support your opinion. Be sure to include plenty of convincing details.

Write your letter on a separate sheet of paper.

Writing Prompt 2

Picture your favorite place to eat. This can be your kitchen or dining room. It can be a fancy restaurant or a fast-food place. It can even be at someone else's house, such as a close friend or relative.

Write a descriptive essay about this place for the eighth grade class journal. Describe everything about this place. Tell where it is located, what it looks like when you are sitting there, and—of course— why this is your favorite place to eat. Be sure to use specific nouns and colorful adjectives to describe everything around you, including the furnishings, wall décor, type of food, the smells, and tastes. Don't forget to describe the people around you, too.

Write your essay on a separate sheet of paper.

Writing Conventions

1. A   B   C   D
2. A   B   C   D
3. A   B   C   D
4. A   B   C   D
5. A   B   C   D
6. A   B   C   D
7. A   B   C   D
8. A   B   C   D
9. A   B   C   D
10. A   B   C   D
11. A   B   C   D
12. A   B   C   D

Flowers

1. A   B   C   D
2. Use a separate sheet of paper to record your response.
3. A   B   C   D
4. A   B   C   D
5. A   B   C   D
6. A   B   C   D

The Rodeo

1. A   B   C   D
2. A   B   C   D
3. A   B   C   D
4. A   B   C   D
5. Use a separate sheet of paper to record your response.
6. A   B   C   D

Brief Contents

Contents

3   *D*evelopment during Childhood and Adolescence   64

4 | Student Diversity 96

5 | Behavioral Theories of Learning 132

6 Information Processing and Cognitive Theories of Learning   *164*

7 The Effective Lesson   *206*

8 Student-Centered and Constructivist Approaches to Instruction   240

9 Accommodating Instruction to Meet Individual Needs   274

10 $\mathcal{M}$otivating Students to Learn   314

11 $\mathcal{E}$ffective Learning Environments   348

12 Learners with Exceptionalities

13 Assessing Student Learning

14 Standardized Tests   *492*

Features

PERSONAL REFLECTION

THEORY INTO PRACTICE

TEACHING DILEMMAS: CASES TO CONSIDER

THE INTENTIONAL TEACHER

Preface

When I first set out to write *Educational Psychology: Theory and Practice,* I had a very clear purpose in mind. I wanted to give tomorrow's teachers the intellectual grounding and practical strategies they will need to be effective instructors. Most of the textbooks published then, I felt, fell into one of two categories: stuffy or lightweight. The stuffy books were full of research but were ponderously written, losing the flavor of the classroom and containing few guides to practice. The lightweight texts were breezy and easy to read but lacked the dilemmas and intellectual issues brought out by research. They contained suggestions of the "Try this!" variety, without considering evidence about the effectiveness of those strategies.

My objective was to write a text that

- presents information that is as complete and up to date as the most research-focused texts but is also readable, practical, and filled with examples and illustrations of key ideas.
- includes suggestions for practice based directly on classroom research (tempered by common sense) so that I can have confidence that when you try what I suggest, it will be likely to work.
- helps you transfer what you learn in educational psychology to your own teaching by making explicit the connection between theory and practice through numerous realistic examples. Even though I have been doing educational research since the mid-1970s, I find that I never really understand theories or concepts in education until someone gives me a compelling classroom example; and I believe that most of my colleagues (and certainly teacher education students) feel the same way. As a result, the words *for example* or similar ones appear hundreds of times in this text.
- appeals to readers; therefore, I have tried to write in such a way that you will almost hear students' voices and smell the lunch cooking in the school cafeteria as you read.

These have been my objectives for the book from the first edition to this, the eighth edition. With every edition, I have made changes throughout the text, adding new examples, refining language, and deleting dated or unessential material. I am meticulous about keeping the text up to date, so this edition has more than 2,000 reference citations, more than one-third of which are from 2000 or later. Although some readers may not care much about citations, I want you and your professors to know what research supports the statements I've made and where to find additional information.

The field of educational psychology and the practice of education have changed a great deal in recent years, and I have tried to reflect these changes in this edition. Only a few years ago, direct instruction and related teacher effectiveness research were dominant in educational psychology. Then constructivist methods, portfolio and performance assessments, and other humanistic strategies returned. Now, emphasis on "back to the basics" is returning, which requires teachers more than ever to plan outcomes and teach purposefully, qualities that I emphasize in this edition as *intentional teaching.* In the first and second editions of this text, I said that we shouldn't entirely discard discovery learning and humanistic methods despite the popularity, then, of direct instruction. In the next editions, I made just the opposite plea: that we shouldn't completely discard direct instruction despite the popularity of active, student-centered teaching and constructivist methods of instruction. I continue to advocate a balanced approach to instruction. No matter what their philosophical orientations, experienced teachers know that they must be proficient in a wide range of methods and must use them thoughtfully.

The eighth edition presents new research and practical applications of many topics. Throughout, this edition reflects the "cognitive revolution" that has transformed educational psychology and teaching. The accompanying figure presents a concept map of the book's organization.

Concept Map: Text Organization in Relation to the Concept of Educational Psychology

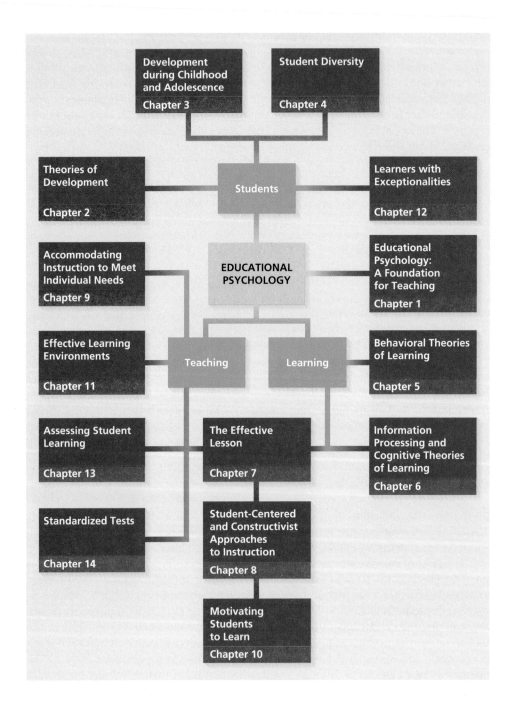

Given the developments in education in recent years, particularly with the introduction of the No Child Left Behind legislation in 2001 and the focus on standards, no one can deny that teachers matter or that teachers' behaviors have a profound impact on student achievement. To make that impact positive, teachers must have both a deep understanding of the powerful principles of psychology as they apply to education and a clear sense of how these principles can be applied. The intentional teacher is one who constantly reflects on his or her practices and makes instructional decisions based on a clear conception of how these practices affect students. Effective teaching is neither a bag of tricks nor a set of abstract principles; rather, it is intelligent application of well-understood principles to address practical needs. I hope this edition will help you develop the intellectual and practical skills you need to do the most important job in the world—teaching.

How THIS BOOK IS ORGANIZED

The chapters in this book address three principal themes: students, teaching, and learning (see the Concept Map). Each chapter discusses important theories and includes many examples of how these theories apply to classroom teaching.

This book emphasizes the intelligent use of theory and research to improve instruction. The chapters on teaching occupy about one-third of the total pages in the book, and the other chapters all relate to the meaning of theories and research practice. Whenever possible, the guides in this book present specific programs and strategies that have been evaluated and found to be effective, not just suggestions of things to try.

New AND EXPANDED COVERAGE

Among the many topics that receive new or greater coverage in this edition are the impact of educational standards on teacher certification or licensure (Chapter 1); family involvement (Chapter 4); English Language Learners and bilingual education (Chapter 4); research on the brain (Chapter 6); No Child Left Behind (Chapter 9); technology applications (Chapter 9); preventing serious behavior problems (Chapter 11); the most recent changes in IDEA (Chapter 12); and accountability aspects of No Child Left Behind (Chapter 14).

Features

Each chapter of the text opens with a vignette depicting a real-life situation that educators encounter. Throughout the chapter narrative, I refer to the issues raised in the vignette. In addition, you have the opportunity to respond to the vignette in several related features, such as the **Using Your Experience** sections that follow each vignette. Each of these sections provides critical and creative thinking questions and cooperative learning activities that allow you to work with the issues brought up in the vignette, activate your prior knowledge, and begin thinking about the ideas the chapter will explore.

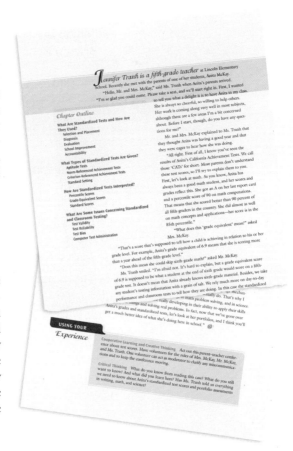

The Intentional and Reflective Teacher

One attribute seems to be a characteristic of all outstanding teachers: intentionality, or the ability to do things for a reason, purposefully. Intentional teachers constantly think about the outcomes they want for their students and how each decision they make moves students toward those outcomes. A key feature in each chapter, **The Intentional Teacher** is designed to help you develop and apply a set of strategies to carry out your intentionality. It will help you internalize a set of questions that can aid you in planning, teaching, and revising your practice in intentional ways. In each chapter, you will consider answers to the following questions from a new vantage point grounded in chapter content, and you will find new examples at all grade levels and in all subject areas to illustrate those answers. The Intentional Teacher focuses your attention on these questions:

1. What do I expect my students to know and be able to do at the end of this lesson? How does this contribute to course objectives and to students' needs to become capable individuals?
2. What knowledge, skills, needs, and interests do my students have that must be taken into account in my lesson?
3. What do I know about the content, child development, learning, motivation, and effective teaching strategies that I can use to accomplish my objectives?
4. What instructional materials, technology, assistance, and other resources are available to help me accomplish my objectives?
5. How will I plan to assess students' progress toward my objectives?
6. How will I respond if individual children or the class as a whole are not on track toward success? What is my backup plan?

The Intentional Teacher will help you combine your increasing knowledge of principles of educational psychology, your growing experience with learners, and your creativity to make intentional instructional decisions that will help students become enthusiastic, effective learners.

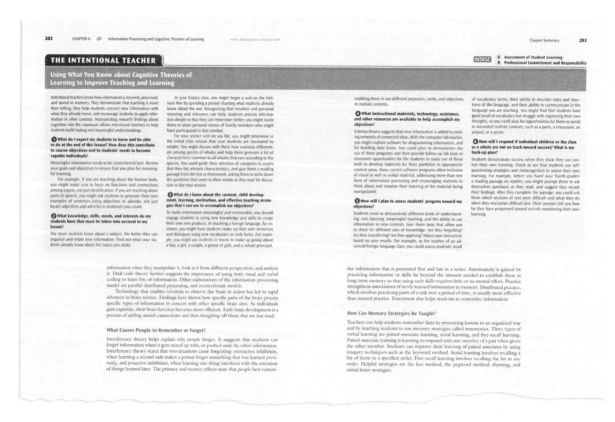

Teaching Dilemmas To support the focus on intentionality and reflection, this edition introduces new **Teaching Dilemmas: Cases to Consider** throughout the chapters. Each case offers a dialogue or vignette intended to evoke thoughtful discussion and debate on issues educators constantly face: balancing structure and freedom, colorblindness and respect for diversity, high expectations and attainable goals, focusing on tests versus focusing on children, and many more. Each of the Teaching Dilemmas ends with Questions for Reflection that prompt thoughtful consideration about the dilemma, asking students to place themselves in the dilemma and offer possible solutions. No easy answers are readily available, as there are so few in teaching, but there is plenty of room for discussion.

Personal Reflections Also in line with the emphasis on reflective, intentional practice, I've added a feature that is intended to bring a bit of myself from behind the curtain that usually divides author and readers. In sections called **Personal Reflections,** I reflect on my own experiences as a teacher, researcher, and parent to illuminate various aspects of the text. As a reader, it is important for you to know that behind each textbook is an author whose experiences, values, and perspectives shape the text.

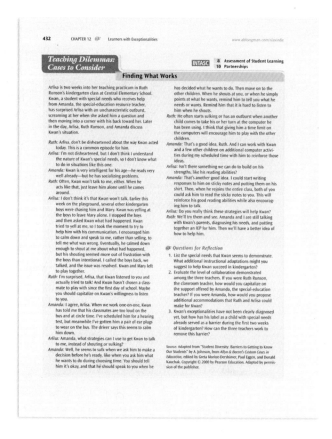

Cartoons Also new to this edition, a series of cartoons created just for this book by my colleague James Bravo illustrate key concepts in educational psychology. These are intended to be humorous but also to make you reflect. I hope you like them!

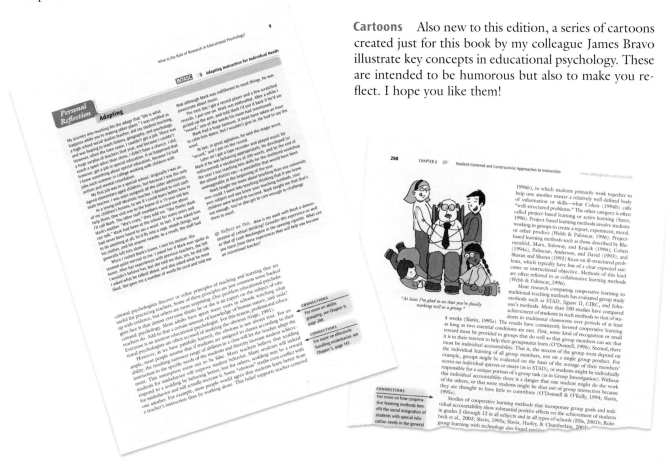

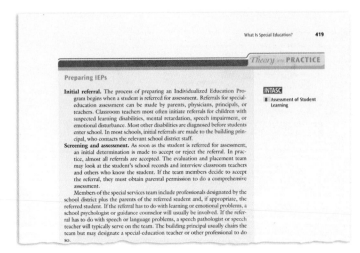

Theory into Practice   The **Theory into Practice** sections in each chapter help you acquire and develop the tools you need to be an effective teacher. These sections present specific strategies for applying information to the classroom.

Guided Study   Each chapter offers features to help you regulate your own learning: a **Chapter Outline** to guide your study objectives; glossary and cross-reference **Connections** annotations in the margins; a **Chapter Summary** to help you review your reading; and a list of **Key Terms** with page references at the end of each chapter.

Licensure   This edition has multiple tools to help you apply your learning to licensure and certification. In each chapter you can both identify and practice the appropriate knowledge and skills you have attained.

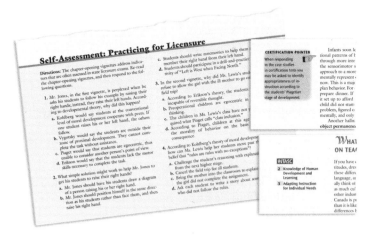

- To help you assess your own learning and prepare for licensure exams, **Certification Pointers** identify content likely to be on certification tests.

- A special marginal icon identifies content that correlates to **INTASC standards.** These correspond closely to Praxis and many state assessments patterned on Praxis.

- In addition, special **Self-Assessment: Practicing for Licensure** features at the end of each chapter are also designed to resemble the types of questions and content typically encountered on state certification tests.

Internet Connections   *Educational Psychology: Theory and Practice* also includes three special Internet connections that encourage you to go beyond the text to learn all that you can about educational psychology.

- The first is a new feature called **On the Web** that appears within the text and lists useful websites providing further information on topics discussed in each chapter.

ON THE WEB

For more on peer tutoring see the Northwest Regional Educational Laboratory at **www.nwrel.org.**

- The second is a **Themes of the Times** connection located on the Companion Website (www.ablongman.com/slavin8e) and directly linked to specially selected *New York Times* articles that present differing perspectives on contemporary topics pertinent to educational psychology.

- Finally, in the **Key Terms** sections at the end of each chapter, an icon prompts you to use **Research Navigator**™. This powerful research tool allows you to investigate key concepts and terms from the book using a collection of resources available to you online, including EBSCO's ContentSelect Academic Journal Database and *The New York Times*. Purchase of this book allows you free access to this exclusive pool of information and data. Your personal access code and instructions are included on the inside cover of this book.

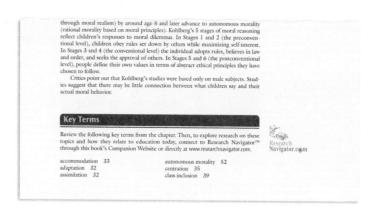

Using Research Navigator

Educational Psychology: Theory and Practice is designed to integrate the content of the book with the valuable research tool, Research Navigator™, a collection of research databases, instruction, and contemporary publications available to you online through **www.mylabschool.com.**

In the Key Terms section at the end of every chapter you'll see special Research prompts cueing you to visit the Research Navigator™ website, using the key terms in each chapter to expand the concepts of the text and to further explore the work being done in the field of educational psychology. To gain access to Research Navigator™, go to **www.mylabschool.com** and log in using the access code you'll find on the inside front cover of your text. Research Navigator™ learning aids include the following:

EBSCO's ContentSelect Academic Journal Database   EBSCO's ContentSelect Academic Journal Database contains scholarly, peer-reviewed journals. These published articles provide you with specialized knowledge and information about your research topic. Academic journal articles adhere to strict scientific guidelines for methodology and theoretical grounding. The information obtained in these individual articles is more scientific than information you would find in a popular magazine, in a newspaper article, or on a Web page.

***The New York Times* Search by Subject Archive**   Because newspapers are issued in regular installments (for example, daily, weekly, or monthly), they provide contemporary information. Information in newspapers may be useful, or even critical, for finding up-to-date material or information to support specific aspects of your topic. Research Navigator™ gives you access to a one-year, "search by subject" archive of articles from one of the world's leading newspapers—*The New York Times*.

"Best of the Web" Link Library   Link Library, the third database included on Research Navigator™, is a collection of Web links, organized by academic subject and key terms. Searching on your key terms will provide you a list of five to seven editorially reviewed websites that offer educationally relevant and reliable content. The Web links in Link Library are monitored and updated each week, reducing your incidence of finding "dead" links.

In addition, Research Navigator™ includes extensive online content detailing the steps in the research process, including:

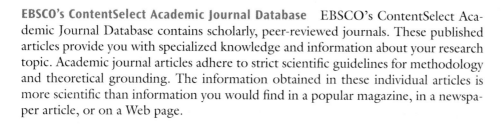

- Starting the Research Process
- Finding and Evaluating Sources
- Citing Sources
- Internet Research
- Using Your Library
- Starting to Write

Go to **www.ablongman.com/aboutrn.com** for more information on how to use Research Navigator™.

STUDENT SUPPLEMENTS

- In **MyLabSchool**, discover where the classroom comes to life! MyLabSchool is a suite of online tools, available at **www.mylabschool.com,** designed to help your students make a smooth transition from student to teacher. MyLabSchool allows students to observe real classrooms in action and helps students prepare for getting a job. With portfolio development assistance, career advice, and Praxis preparation, your students will leave your course ready for the next step. MyLabSchool includes a direct connection to Research Navigator™. Access to this valuable supplement is free with the purchase of a new text. See inside the front cover for your access code!
- A new **Teaching Dilemma Casebook,** packaged free upon instructor request, provides elementary and secondary case studies that demonstrate common dilemmas that arise in today's classrooms. The Casebook includes four detailed cases per chapter that are closely integrated with the content and augmented by guiding questions and sample responses on the text website. Students will read about the ethical, moral, and political conflicts teachers face on a daily basis and reflect upon the possible solutions, better preparing them for the split-second decision making required of them as teachers. This supplement can be packaged with the text at no additional charge. Contact your representative for details.
- **Preparing for Licensure Guides** help students prepare for special state licensure tests, such as Praxis, with exercises closely tied into specific content from the text. Special guides have been prepared for General Certification and Praxis and four state-specific certification tests: Texas, Florida, New York, and California. This supplement can be packaged with the text at no additional charge. Contact your representative for details.
- The robust **Companion Website (www.ablongman.com/slavin8e)** is organized by chapter and provides a full complement of Study Guide resources including pre-reading and post-reading study materials; self-check quizzes and practice tests; special *New York Times* articles; a complete guide to conducting research on the Internet; answers to Self-Assessment features; ongoing discussions about possible solutions to case studies in the book and in the new Teaching Dilemma Casebook; teaching strategies; lecture notes; Web links; and a correlation chart outlining the INTASC Principles and NCATE Standards addressed in the text.

INSTRUCTOR SUPPLEMENTS

- The **Instructor's Resource Manual with Test Items** contains chapter overviews, annotated lecture outlines, suggested readings and media, answers to the textbook Self-Assessment features, handout masters, and a complete offering of assessment items leveled for difficulty.
- The **Computerized Test Bank** contains a variety of testing items. The printed Test Bank is also available electronically through our computerized testing system:

TestGen EQ. Instructors can use TestGen EQ to create exams in just minutes by selecting from the existing database of questions, editing questions, or writing original questions. Testing items in the test bank include multiple-choice, true–false, short-answer, conceptual essay, reflective essay, and concept integration questions. Concept integration items ask students to apply a combination of concepts and principles to a written teaching scenario.

- The **Intentional Teacher Video** offers vignettes tied to chapter content that showcase intentional teachers and situations that educators encounter.
- The **PowerPoint™ Presentation** consists of outline slides for use in the classroom and lecture outlines for faculty. (Available for download from Supplement Central at **http://suppscentral.ablongman.com.**) New enrichment lectures in current areas of interest, such as IDEA 2004 and research on the brain, are also available.
- **Allyn and Bacon Transparencies for Educational Psychology IV** is an updated package that includes over 150 full-color acetates.
- **"What Every Teacher Should Know About" series** contains short booklets that cover the basic concepts of key topics in Education from Assessment to IDEA and NCLB. (Speak with your Allyn and Bacon/Longman representative.)
- In **MyLabSchool**, discover where the classroom comes to life! MyLabSchool is a suite of online tools, available at **www.mylabschool.com,** designed to help your students make a smooth transition from student to teacher. MyLabSchool allows students to observe real classrooms in action and helps students prepare for getting a job. With portfolio development assistance, career advice, and Praxis preparation, your students will leave your course ready for the next step. MyLabSchool includes a direct connection to Research Navigator™. Access to this valuable supplement is free with the purchase of a new text. See inside the front cover for your access code!

- **VideoWorkshop for Educational Psychology** is a new way to bring video into your course for maximized learning! This total teaching and learning system includes quality video footage on an easy-to-use CD-ROM plus a Student Learning Guide and an Instructor's Teaching Guide. The result? A program that brings textbook concepts to life with ease and that helps your students understand, analyze, and apply the objectives of the course. VideoWorkshop is available for your students as a value-pack option with this textbook. (Special package ISBN required from your representative.)

*A*CKNOWLEDGMENTS

In this edition, I benefited from the skillful assistance of my colleague Bette Chambers, who wrote the Certification Pointers and contributed content throughout the text; as well as from the feedback of special content reviewers Jean Ulman, Ball State University, and Jim Persinger, Emporia State University, on Chapters 12 (Learners with Exceptionalities), 13 (Assessing Student Learning), and 14 (Standardized Tests). I also thank the writers of the supplements: Emilie Johnson (Instructor's Resource Manual), Janet Medina and Christiane DeBauge (Certification Guides), Catherine McCartney and Therese Olejniczak (Assessment Package), Richard Giaquinto (PowerPoint™ Presentation), Carol A. Scatena (Teaching Dilemma Casebook and Companion Website).

I also wish to thank my many colleagues who served as reviewers and contributors for this edition, as well as those who participated in a special survey. Reviewers' comments provided invaluable information that helped me revise and augment the text. Contributors' work has made the features and supplements to this text first-rate.

Wallace Alexander, Thomas College
Patrick Allen, Graduate College of
 Union University
Ted Batson, Indiana Wesleyan
 University
Richard Battaglia, California Lutheran
 University
Elizabeth Anne Belford Horan,
 Methodist College
Sandra Billings, Fairfield University
Silas Born, Bethany Lutheran College
Curtis Brant, Baldwin-Wallace College
Camille Branton, Delta State University
Joy Brown, University of North Alabama
Doris Burgert, Wichita State University
Renee Cambiano, Northeastern State
 University
William Camp, Luzerne County
 Community College
Ann Caton, Rockford College
Kay Chick, Pennsylvania State
 University–Altoona
Martha Cook, Malone College
Faye Day, Bethel College
Christiane DeBauge, Indiana University
Donna Duellberg, Wayland Baptist
 University
Nick Elksnin, The Citadel
Joan Evensen, Towson University
E. Gail Everett, Bob Jones University
R. Joel Farrell, Faulkner University
Susan Frusher, Northeastern State
 University
Donna Gardner, William Jewell College
Michele Gill, University of Central
 Florida
Jennifer Gross Lara, Anne Arundel
 Community College
Raphael Guillory, Eastern Washington
 University
Jan Hayes, Middle Tennessee State
 University
James Hedgebeth, Elizabeth City State
 University
Mark Hopkin, Wiley College
John Hummel, Valdosta State University
Margaret Hurd, Anne Arundel
 Community College
Daniel Hursh, West Virginia University
Kathryn Hutchinson, St. Thomas
 Aquinas College
Karen Huxtable-Jester, University of
 Texas at Dallas
Gretchen Jefferson, Eastern Washington
 University
Carolyn Jeffries, CSU Northridge
W. Y. Johnson, Wright State University

Jeffrey Kaplan, University of Central
 Florida
Jack Kaufman, Bluefield State College
Robert Landry, Winston-Salem State
 University
Dorothea Lerman, Louisiana State
 University
Jupian J. Leung, University of
 Wisconsin–Oshkosh
Judith Levine, Farmingdale State
 University
Judith Luckett, University of Central
 Florida
Betty Magjuka, Gloucester County
 College
Laurell Malone, North Carolina Central
 University
Lloyd McCraney, Towson University
Lienne Medford, Clemson University
Janet Medina, McDaniel College
DeAnn Miller-Boschert, North Dakota
 State University
Greg Morris, Grand Rapids Community
 College
Pamela Nesselrodt, Dickinson College
Joe Nichols, Indiana University-Purdue
 University Fort Wayne
Kathryn Parr, University of Florida
Jonathan Plucker, Indiana University
Linda Robertello, Iona College
Paul Rufino, Gloucester County College
Lisa Ruiz-Lee, University of Nevada,
 Las Vegas
Carol Scatena, Lewis University
Tom Scheft, North Carolina Central
 University
Diane Serafin, Luzerne County
 Community College–Shamokin
Joshua S. Smith, University of Albany
Donald Snead, Middle Tennessee State
 University
Louise Soares, University of New Haven
Larry Templeton, Ferris State University
Leo Theriot, Central Bible College
Melaine Timko, National University
Diana Treahy, Point Loma Nazarene
 University
Kathleen Waldron-Soler, Eastern
 Washington University
Betty Wood, University of Arkansas at
 Little Rock
Priscilla Wright, Colorado Christian
 University
Ronald Zigler, Pennsylvania State
 University–Abington
Wilkins-O'Riley Zinn, Southern Oregon
 University

I am also grateful to contributors to previous editions, such as Thomas Andre, Curtis Bonk, Mary Jane Caffey, Sandra Damico, Melissa Dark, Stacie Goffin, Gordon Greenwood, Chuck Greiner, Carole Grove, Andrea Guillaume, Millie Harris, Johanna Keirns, Judy Lewandowski, Elizabeth Sterling, Kathryn Wentzel, and William Zangwill.

I'd also like to thank my Allyn and Bacon Senior Editor, Arnis Burvikovs; Development Editor, Mary Kriener; and Associate Editor, Adam Whitehurst, who oversaw the development of all the supplements; as well as Nancy Forsyth, President, and Paul A. Smith, Vice President and Editor in Chief for Education. I am also grateful to the editorial-production team at Omegatype Typography and to the education team at Allyn and Bacon who helped bring this edition to fruition: Annette Joseph, Editorial-Production Administrator; Tara Kelly, Marketing Manager; Linda Knowles, Cover Administrator; Laurie Frankenthaler, Photo Researcher; Kate Cook, Photo Editor; and Kelly Hopkins, Editorial Assistant. I am grateful to Susan Davis of the Success for All Foundation for work on all aspects of the book—including typing, doing references, proofreading, and lending general good sense—and to James Bravo, the talented artist behind the cartoons.

Finally, it is customary to acknowledge the long-suffering patience of one's spouse and children. In my case, this acknowledgment is especially appropriate. My wife, Nancy Madden, has helped on every edition as well as keeping our research going while I wrote. Our children contributed to this work by providing me with a sense of purpose for writing. I had to keep thinking about the kind of school experience I want for them as a way of making concrete my concern for the school experiences of all children.

This book was written while I was supported in part by grants from the Institute of Education Sciences, U.S. Department of Education (No. OERI-R-117-D40005). However, any opinions I have are mine alone and do not represent IES positions or policy.

R. E. S.

About the Author

Robert Slavin is director of the Center for Data-Driven Reform in Education, Johns Hopkins University, and chairman of the Success for All Foundation. He received his Ph.D. in Social Relations from Johns Hopkins in 1975, and since that time he has authored more than 200 articles and book chapters on such topics as cooperative learning, ability grouping, school and classroom organization, desegregation, mainstreaming, and research review. Dr. Slavin is the author or coauthor of 20 books, including *Cooperative Learning, School and Classroom Organization, Effective Programs for Students at Risk, Preventing Early School Failure, Show Me the Evidence: Proven and Promising Programs for America's Schools, One Million Children: Success for All,* and *Effective Programs for Latino Students.* In 1985 Dr. Slavin received the Raymond Cattell Early Career Award for Programmatic Research from the American Educational Research Association. In 1988 he received the Palmer O. Johnson Award for the best article in an AERA journal. In 1994 he received the Charles A. Dana Award, and in 1998 he received the James Bryant Conant Award from the Education Commission of the States. Dr. Slavin is pictured here with his daughter Becca.

Coverage of Interstate New Teacher Assessment and Support Consortium (INTASC) Standards for Beginning Teacher Licensing and Development

Below is a listing of the INTASC standards on education and a correlation of where those standards are addressed within *Educational Psychology: Theory and Practice, 8e.*

INTASC STANDARD		CHAPTER COVERAGE
Standard 1	*Knowledge of Subject Matter:* The teacher understands the central concepts, tools of inquiry, and structures of the subject being taught and can create learning experiences that make these aspects of subject matter meaningful for students.	Chapter 1
Standard 2	*Knowledge of Human Development and Learning:* The teacher understands how children learn and develop, and can provide learning opportunities that support their intellectual, social and personal development.	Chapters 2, 3, 4, 5, 6, 7, 10, 12
Standard 3	*Adapting Instruction for Individual Needs:* The teacher understands how students differ in their approaches to learning and creates instructional opportunities that are adapted to diverse learners.	Chapters 1, 2, 3, 4, 5, 6, 8, 9, 10, 12
Standard 4	*Multiple Instructional Strategies:* The teacher uses various instructional strategies to encourage students' development of critical thinking, problem solving, and performance skills.	Chapters 2, 4, 5, 6, 7, 8, 10, 11, 12
Standard 5	*Classroom Motivation and Management:* The teacher uses an understanding of individual and group motivation and behavior to create a learning environment that encourages positive social interaction, active engagement in learning, and self-motivation.	Chapters 1, 4, 7, 8, 9, 10, 11, 12, 13
Standard 6	*Communication Skills:* The teacher uses knowledge of effective verbal, nonverbal, and media communication techniques to foster active inquiry, collaboration, and supportive interaction in the classroom.	Chapters 4, 6, 7, 9, 11, 12, 13
Standard 7	*Instructional Planning Skills:* The teacher plans instruction based upon knowledge of subject matter, students, the community, and curriculum goals.	Chapters 1, 3, 4, 7, 8, 9, 10, 11, 12, 13, 14
Standard 8	*Assessment of Student Learning:* The teacher understands and uses formal and informal assessment strategies to evaluate and ensure the continuous intellectual, social, and physical development of the learner.	Every chapter
Standard 9	*Professional Commitment and Responsibility:* The teacher is a reflective practitioner who continually evaluates the effects of his/her choices and actions on others (students, parents, and other professionals in the learning community) and who actively seeks out opportunities to grow professionally.	Every chapter
Standard 10	*Partnerships:* The teacher fosters relationships with school colleagues, parents, and agencies in the larger community to support students' learning and well-being.	Chapters 3, 4, 9, 11, 12

EDUCATIONAL PSYCHOLOGY

Educational Psychology: A Foundation for Teaching

Ellen Mathis was baffled. She was a new teacher who had been trying to teach creative writing to her third-grade class, but things were just not going the way she'd hoped. Her students were not producing much, and what they did write was not very imaginative and was full of errors. For example, she had recently assigned a composition on "My Summer Vacation," and all that one of her students wrote was "On my summer vacation I got a dog and we went swimming and I got stinged by a bee."

Ellen wondered whether her kids were just not ready for writing and needed several months of work on such skills as capitalization, punctuation, and usage before she tried another writing assignment. One day, however, Ellen noticed some compositions in the hall outside of Leah Washington's class. Leah's third-graders were just like Ellen's, but their compositions were fabulous. The students wrote pages of interesting material on an astonishing array of topics. At the end of the day, Ellen caught Leah in the hall. "How do you get your kids to write such great compositions?" she asked.

Leah explained how she first got her children writing on topics they cared about and then gradually introduced "mini-lessons" to help them become better authors. She had the students work in small groups and help one another plan compositions. Then the students critiqued one another's drafts, helped one another with editing, and finally "published" final versions.

"I'll tell you what," Leah offered. "I'll schedule my next writing class during your planning period. Come see what we're doing."

Ellen agreed. When the time came, she walked into Leah's class and was overwhelmed by what she saw. Children were writing everywhere: on the floor, in groups, at tables. Many were talking with partners. Leah was conferencing with individual children. Ellen looked over the children's shoulders and saw one student writing about her pets, another writing a gory story about Ninjas, and another writing about a dream. Marta Delgrado, a Mexican American child, was writing a funny story about her second-grade teacher's attempts to speak Spanish. One student, Melinda Navens, was even writing a very good story about her summer vacation!

After school, Ellen met with Leah. She was full of questions. "How did you get students to do all that writing? How can you manage all that noise and activity? How did you learn to do this?"

"I did go to a series of workshops on teaching writing," Leah said. "But if you think about it, everything I'm doing is basic educational psychology."

Ellen was amazed. "Educational psychology? I got an A in that course in college, but I don't see what it has to do with your writing program."

"Well, let's see," said Leah. "To begin with, I'm using a lot of motivational strategies I learned in ed psych. For instance, when I started my writing instruction this year, I read students some funny and intriguing stories written by other classes, to arouse their curiosity. I got them motivated by letting them write about whatever they wanted, and also by having 'writing celebrations' in which students read their finished compositions to the class for applause and comments. My educational psychology professor was always talking about adapting to students' needs. I do this by conferencing with students and helping them with the specific problems they're having. I first learned about cooperative learning in ed psych, and later on I took some workshops on it. I use cooperative learning groups to let students give each other immediate feedback on their writing, to let them model effective writing for each other, and to get them to encourage each other to write. The groups also solve a lot of my management problems by keeping each other on task and dealing with many classroom routines. I remember that we learned about evaluation in ed psych. I use a flexible form of evaluation. Everybody eventually gets an A on his or her composition, but only when it meets a high standard, which may take many drafts. I apply what we learned about child development just about every day. For example, I adapt to students' developmental levels and cultural styles by encouraging them to write about things that matter to them: If dinosaurs or video games are important right now, or if children are uncomfortable about being Muslim or Jewish at Christmas time, that's what they should write about!"

Ellen was impressed. She and Leah arranged to visit each other's classes a few more times to exchange ideas and observations, and in time, Ellen's writers began to be almost as good as Leah's. But what was particularly important to her was the idea that educational psychology could really be useful in her day-to-day teaching. She dragged out her old textbook and found that concepts that had seemed theoretical and abstract in her ed psych class actually helped her think about teaching problems.

USING YOUR

Experience

Creative Thinking   Based on Leah's explanation of her writing instruction, work with one or more partners to brainstorm about what educational psychology is and what you will learn this semester. Guidelines: (1) the more ideas you generate, the better; (2) hitchhike on others' ideas as well as combining them; and (3) make no evaluation of those ideas at this time. Take this list out a few times during the semester and add to it as well as evaluate it.

What is **educational psychology?** An academic definition would perhaps say that educational psychology is the study of learners, learning, and teaching (Reynolds & Miller, 2003). However, for students who are or expect to be teachers, educational psychology is something more. It is the accumulated knowledge, wisdom, and seat-of-the-pants theory that every teacher should possess to intelligently solve the daily problems of teaching. Educational psychology cannot tell teachers what to do, but it can give them the principles to use in making a good decision and a language to discuss their experiences and thinking. Consider the case of Ellen Mathis and Leah Washington. Nothing in this or any other educational psychology text will tell teachers exactly how to teach creative writing to a particular group of third-graders. However, Leah uses concepts of educational psychology to consider how she will teach writing, to interpret and solve problems she runs into, and to explain to Ellen what she is doing. Educational psychologists carry out research on the nature of students, principles of learning, and methods of teaching to give educators the information they need to think critically about their craft and to make teaching decisions that will work for their students.

WHAT MAKES A GOOD TEACHER?

What makes a good teacher? Is it warmth, humor, and the ability to care about people? Is it planning, hard work, and self-discipline? What about leadership, enthusiasm, a contagious love of learning, and speaking ability? Most people would agree that all of these qualities are needed to make someone a good teacher, and they would certainly be correct (see Wayne & Youngs, 2003). But these qualities are not enough.

Knowing the Subject Matters (but So Does Teaching Skill)

There is an old joke that goes like this:

Question: What do you need to know to be able to teach a horse?
Answer: More than the horse!

This joke makes the obvious point that the first thing a teacher must have is some knowledge or skills that the learner does not have; teachers must know the subject matter they expect to teach. But if you think about teaching horses (or children), you will soon realize that although subject matter knowledge is necessary, it is not enough. A rancher may have a good idea of how a horse is supposed to act and what a horse is supposed to be able to do, but if he doesn't have the skills to make an untrained, scared, and unfriendly animal into a good saddle horse, he's going to end up with nothing but broken ribs and teeth marks for his troubles. Children are a lot smarter and a little more forgiving than horses, but teaching them has this in common with teaching horses: Knowledge of how to transmit information and skills is at least as important as knowledge of the information and skills themselves. We have all had teachers (most often college professors, unfortunately) who were brilliant and thoroughly knowledgeable in their fields but who could not teach. Ellen Mathis may know as much as Leah Washington about what good writing should be, but she has a lot to learn about how to get third-graders to write well.

For effective teaching, subject matter knowledge is not a question of being a walking encyclopedia. Effective teachers not only know their subjects, but they can also communicate their knowledge to students. The celebrated high school math teacher Jaime Escalante taught the concept of positive and negative numbers to students in a Los Angeles barrio by explaining that when you dig a hole, you might call the pile of dirt +1, the hole −1. What do you get when you put the dirt back in the hole? Zero.

educational psychology
The study of learning and teaching.

What characteristics of good teaching might this expert teacher possess? What behaviors does she demonstrate that might make her an effective teacher?

INTASC

1 Knowledge of Subject Matter

pedagogy
The study of teaching and learning with applications to the instructional process.

intentionality
Doing things for a purpose; teachers who use intentionality plan their actions based on the outcomes they want to achieve.

Escalante's ability to relate the abstract concept of positive and negative numbers to his students' experiences is one example of how the ability to communicate knowledge goes far beyond simply knowing the facts.

Mastering the Teaching Skills

The link between what the teacher wants students to learn and students' actual learning is called instruction, or **pedagogy.** Effective instruction is not a simple matter of one person with more knowledge transmitting that knowledge to another. If telling were teaching, this book would be unnecessary. Rather, effective instruction demands the use of many strategies.

For example, suppose Paula Ray wants to teach a lesson on statistics to a diverse class of fourth-graders. To do this, Paula must accomplish many things. She must make sure that the class is orderly and that students know what behavior is expected of them. She must find out whether students have the prerequisite skills; for example, students need to be able to add and divide to find averages. If any do not, Paula must find a way to teach students those skills. She must engage students in activities that lead them toward an understanding of statistics, such as having students roll dice, play cards, or collect data from experiments; and she must use teaching strategies that help students remember what they have been taught. The lessons should also take into account the intellectual and social characteristics of students in the fourth grade and the intellectual, social, and cultural characteristics of these particular students. Paula must make sure that students are interested in the lesson and are motivated to learn statistics. To see whether students are learning what is being taught, she may ask questions or use quizzes or have students demonstrate their understanding by setting up and interpreting experiments, and she must respond appropriately if these assessments show that students are having problems. After the series of lessons on statistics ends, Paula should review this topic from time to time to ensure that it is remembered.

These tasks—motivating students, managing the classroom, assessing prior knowledge, communicating ideas effectively, taking into account the characteristics of the learners, assessing learning outcomes, and reviewing information—must be attended to at all levels of education, in or out of schools. They apply as much to the training of astronauts as to the teaching of reading. How these tasks are accomplished, however, differs widely according to the ages of the students, the objectives of instruction, and other factors.

What makes a good teacher is the ability to carry out all the tasks involved in effective instruction (Burden & Byrd, 2003). Warmth, enthusiasm, and caring are essential, as is subject matter knowledge. But it is the successful accomplishment of all the tasks of teaching that makes for instructional effectiveness (Shulman, 2000).

Can Good Teaching Be Taught?

Some people think that good teachers are born that way. Outstanding teachers sometimes seem to have a magic, a charisma, that mere mortals could never hope to achieve. Yet research has begun to identify the specific behaviors and skills that make up the "magic" teacher (Mayer, 1992). An outstanding teacher does nothing that any other teacher cannot also do—it is just a question of knowing the principles of effective teaching and how to apply them. Take one small example: In a high school history class, two students in the back of the class are whispering to each other, and they are not discussing the Treaty of Paris! The teacher slowly walks toward them without looking, continuing his lesson as he walks. The students stop whispering and pay attention. If you didn't know what to look for, you might miss this brief but critical interchange and believe that the teacher just has a way with students, a knack for keeping their attention. But the teacher is simply applying principles of classroom management that anyone could learn: Maintain momentum in the lesson, deal with behavior problems by using the mildest intervention that will work, and resolve minor problems before they become major ones. When Jaime Escalante gave the example of digging a hole to illustrate the concept of positive and negative numbers, he was also applying several important principles of educational psychology: Make abstract ideas concrete by using many examples, relate the content of instruction to the students' background, state rules, give examples, and then restate rules.

Can good teaching be taught? The answer is definitely yes. Good teaching has to be observed and practiced, but there are principles of good teaching that teachers need to know, which can then be applied in the classroom. The major components of effective instruction are summarized in Figure 1.1.

The Intentional Teacher

There is no formula for good teaching, no seven steps to Teacher of the Year. Teaching involves planning and preparation, and then dozens of decisions every hour. Yet one attribute seems to be characteristic of outstanding teachers: **intentionality.** Intentionality means doing things for a reason, on purpose. Intentional teachers are those who are constantly thinking about the outcomes they want for their students and about how each decision they make moves children toward those outcomes. Intentional teachers know that maximum learning does not happen by chance. Yes, children do learn in unplanned ways all the time, and many will learn from even the most chaotic lesson. But to really challenge students, to get their best efforts, to help them make conceptual leaps and organize and retain new knowledge, teachers need to be purposeful, thoughtful, and flexible, without ever losing sight of their goals for every child. In a word, they need to be *intentional.*

The idea that teachers should always do things for a reason seems obvious, and in principle it is. Yet in practice, it is difficult to constantly make certain that all students are engaged in activities that lead to

CONNECTIONS

For more on effective instruction, see Chapter 7. Pedagogical strategies are also presented in Chapters 8 (p. 263) and 9 (p. 276), as well as throughout the text in features titled The Intentional Teacher.

INTASC

5 Classroom Motivation and Management

"If only I could get to my ed psych text . . ."

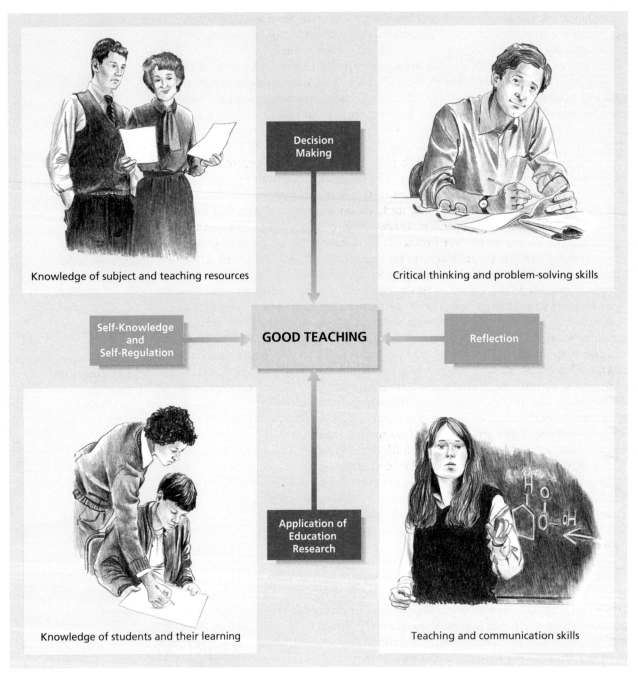

Knowledge of subject and teaching resources

Decision Making

Critical thinking and problem-solving skills

Self-Knowledge and Self-Regulation

GOOD TEACHING

Reflection

Application of Education Research

Knowledge of students and their learning

Teaching and communication skills

FIGURE 1.1
Components of Good Teaching

important learning outcomes. Teachers very frequently fall into strategies that they themselves would recognize, on reflection, as being time fillers rather than instructionally essential activities. For example, an otherwise outstanding third-grade teacher once assigned seatwork to one of her reading groups. The children were given two sheets of paper with words in squares. Their task was to cut out the squares on one sheet and then paste them onto synonyms on the other. When all the words were pasted correctly, lines on the pasted squares would form an outline of a cat, which the children were then to color. Once the children pasted a few squares, the puzzle became clear, so they could paste the remainder without paying any attention to the words themselves. For almost an hour of precious class time, these children happily cut, pasted, and colored—not high-priority skills for third-graders. The teacher would have said that the objective was for children to learn or practice synonyms, of course; but in fact the activity could not possibly have moved the children forward on that skill. Similarly, many teachers have one child laboriously work a problem on the chalkboard while the rest of the class has nothing important to do. Many secondary teachers spend most of the class period going over homework and classwork and end up doing very little teaching of new content. Again, these may be excellent teachers in other ways, but they sometimes lose sight of what they are trying to achieve and how they are going to achieve it.

Intentional teachers are constantly asking themselves what goals they and their students are trying to accomplish. Is each portion of their lesson appropriate to students' background knowledge, skills, and needs? Is each activity or assignment clearly related to a valued outcome? Is each instructional minute used wisely and well? An intentional teacher trying to build students' synonym skills during follow-up time might have them work in pairs to master a set of synonyms in preparation for individual quizzes. An intentional teacher might have all children work a given problem while one works at the board, so that all can compare answers and strategies together. An intentional teacher might quickly give homework answers for students to check themselves, ask for a show of hands for correct answers, and then review and reteach only those exercises missed by many students. An intentional teacher uses a wide variety of instructional methods, experiences, assignments, and materials to be sure that children are achieving all sorts of cognitive objectives, from knowledge to application to creativity, and that at the same time children are learning important affective objectives, such as love of learning, respect for others, and personal responsibility. An intentional teacher constantly reflects on his or her practices and outcomes.

Research finds that one of the most powerful predictors of a teacher's impact on students is the belief that what he or she does makes a difference. This belief, called **teacher efficacy** (Henson, 2002; Tschannen-Moran & Woolfolk Hoy, 2001), is at the heart of what it means to be an intentional teacher. Teachers who believe that success in school is almost entirely due to children's inborn intelligence, home environment, or other factors that teachers cannot influence, are unlikely to teach in the same way as those who believe that their own efforts are the key to children's learning. An intentional teacher, one who has a strong belief in her or his efficacy, is more likely to put forth consistent effort, to persist in the face of obstacles, and to keep trying relentlessly until every student succeeds (Bandura, 1997). Intentional teachers achieve a sense of efficacy by constantly assessing the results of their instruction (Schmoker, 1999), constantly trying new strategies if their initial instruction didn't work, and constantly seeking ideas from colleagues, books, magazines, workshops, and other sources to enrich and solidify their teaching skills. Groups of teachers, such as all teachers in an elementary school or all teachers in a given academic department, can attain collective efficacy by working together to examine their practices and outcomes, seek professional development, and help each other succeed (see Lieberman & Miller, 1999; Sachs, 2000). Collective efficacy can have a particularly strong impact on student achievement (Goddard, Hoy, & Hoy, 2000). The most important purpose of this book is to give tomorrow's teachers the intellectual grounding in research, theory, and practical wisdom they will need in order to become intentional, effective teachers. To plan and carry out effective lessons, discussions, projects, and other learning experiences, teachers need to know a great deal. Besides knowing their subjects, they need to understand the developmental levels and needs of their children. They need to understand how learning, memory, problem-solving skill, and creativity are acquired and how to promote their acquisition. They need to know how to set objectives, organize activities designed to help students attain those objectives, and assess students' progress toward them. They need to know how to motivate children, how to use class time effectively, and how to respond to individual differences among students. Like

teacher efficacy
The degree to which teachers feel that their own efforts determine the success of their students.

What do you need to know about your students in order to be an intentional teacher? How can you help your students achieve success?

Leah Washington, the teacher in the vignette that opened this chapter, intentional teachers are constantly combining their knowledge of principles of educational psychology, their experience, and their creativity to make instructional decisions and help children become enthusiastic and effective learners. They are continually experimenting with strategies to solve problems of instruction and then observing the results of their actions to see if they were effective (Duck, 2000).

This text highlights the ideas that are central to educational psychology and the related research. It also presents many examples of how these ideas apply in practice, emphasizing teaching practices, not just theory or suggestions, that have been evaluated and found to be effective. The text is designed to help you develop **critical-thinking** skills for teaching: a logical and systematic approach to the many dilemmas that are found in practice and research. No text can provide all the right answers for teaching, but this one tries to pose the right questions and to engage you by presenting realistic alternatives and the concepts and research behind them.

Many studies have looked at the differences between expert and novice teachers and between more and less effective teachers. One theme comes through these studies: Expert teachers are critical thinkers (Anderson et al., 1995; Hogan, Rabinowitz, & Craven, 2003; Shulman, 2000). Intentional teachers are constantly upgrading and examining their own teaching practices, reading and attending conferences to learn new ideas, and using their own students' responses to guide their instructional decisions. There's an old saying to the effect that there are teachers with 20 years of experience and there are teachers with 1 year of experience 20 times. Teachers who get better each year are the ones who are open to new ideas and who look at their own teaching critically. Perhaps the most important goal of this book is to get you in the habit of using informed reflection to become one of tomorrow's expert teachers.

critical thinking
Evaluation of conclusions through logical and systematic examination of the problem, the evidence, and the solution.

WHAT IS THE ROLE OF RESEARCH IN EDUCATIONAL PSYCHOLOGY?

Teachers who are intentional, critical thinkers are likely to enter their classrooms equipped with knowledge about research in educational psychology. Every year, edu-

Personal Reflection

Adapting

My journey into teaching fits the adage that "life is what happens while you're making other plans." I was certified as a high school social studies teacher, did my student teaching, and was hoping to teach history, geography, and psychology. However, when the time came, I couldn't get a job. There was a huge surplus of teachers that year, and because I couldn't coach a sport other than chess, I didn't have a chance. I did, however, get a job in special education. It so happened that I knew something about special education, because I'd had jobs each summer in college working with children with autism and mental retardation.

My first job was in a special school. Originally I was assigned elementary-aged children, but because I was the only male teacher, I was soon assigned all the older adolescents.

As a young and idealistic teacher, I decided to visit each of my children's homes, to see if I could learn better how to help them. One visit was to the home of a 15-year-old boy I'll call Mark. The other staff members warned me about Mark's mother. "She's crazy," they told me. "She thinks Mark can talk." Mark had been at the school for many years and had never been heard to say a word. In fact, if you asked him to do anything at all, he'd fly into a rage, smash things, tear his clothes, and hit anyone nearby. As a result, the staff had generally left him alone.

When I visited Mark's home, I met his mother. She seemed quite normal to me. I asked her if Mark ever spoke at home. After her experiences with previous teachers, she felt I wouldn't believe her, but she told me that, yes, he did talk. I asked what he talked about, and also asked what he most liked. She gave me a number of words he used and told me

that although Mark was indifferent to most things, he was passionate about music.

The next day I got a record player and a few scratched records. I put one on. Mark was enthralled. After a while I picked up the arm, and told Mark I'd put it back if he'd say "record," one of the words his mom had mentioned.

Mark had a huge tantrum. It must have taken an hour to calm him down, but I wouldn't give in. He had to say the word.

At last, in great agitation, he said the magic word, "record," and I put on the record.

Later on I got a tape recorder and played music for Mark if he was behaving appropriately. He developed (or rediscovered) a vocabulary of 200 words, and by the end of the year I was teaching him skills for the sheltered workshop the school district ran—a possibility that would have been unimaginable at the beginning of the year.

Mark taught me more about teaching than any university ever could. I went into teaching thinking that if you knew your subject and you knew your teaching methods, your children were bound to succeed. Mark taught me that that's not enough. You've also got to care enough to challenge them to excel.

@ Reflect on This. How is my work with Mark a demonstration of critical thinking? Consider this experience as well as that of Leah Washington in the opening vignette. What can you learn from these experiences that will help you become an intentional teacher?

cational psychologists discover or refine principles of teaching and learning that are useful for practicing teachers. Some of these principles are just common sense backed up with evidence, but others are more surprising. One problem educational psychologists face is that almost everyone thinks he or she is an expert on the subject of educational psychology. Most adults have spent many years in schools watching what teachers do. Add to that a certain amount of knowledge of human nature, and *voila!* Everyone is an amateur educational psychologist. For this reason, professional educational psychologists are often accused of studying the obvious (Gage, 1991).

However, as we have painfully learned, the obvious is not always true. For example, most people assume that if students are assigned to classes according to their ability, the resulting narrower range of abilities in a class will let the teacher adapt the instruction to the specific needs of the students and thereby increase student achievement. This assumption turns out to be false. Many teachers believe that scolding students for misbehavior will improve student behavior. Many students will indeed respond to a scolding by behaving better, but for others, scolding may be a reward for misbehavior and will actually increase it. Some "obvious" truths even conflict with one another. For example, most people would agree that students learn better from a teacher's instruction than by working alone. This belief supports teacher-centered

CONNECTIONS

For more on ability grouping, see Chapter 9, page 280.

CONNECTIONS

For more on effectively handling misbehavior, see Chapter 5, page 141.

direct instructional strategies, in which a teacher actively works with the class as a whole. On the other hand, most people would also agree that students often need instruction tailored to their individual needs. This belief, also correct, would demand that teachers divide their time among individuals, or at least among groups of students with differing needs, which would result in some students working independently while others received the teacher's attention. If schools could provide tutors for every student, there would be no conflict; direct instruction and individualization could co-exist. In practice, however, classrooms typically have 20 or more students; as a result, more direct instruction (the first goal) almost always means less individualization (the second goal). The intentional teacher's task is to balance these competing goals according to the needs of particular students and situations.

The Goal of Research in Educational Psychology

The goal of research in educational psychology is to carefully examine obvious as well as less than obvious questions, using objective methods to test ideas about the factors that contribute to learning (Levin, O'Donnell, & Kratochwill, 2003; McCombs, 2003). The products of this research are principles, laws, and theories. A **principle** explains the relationship between factors, such as the effects of alternative grading systems on student motivation. Laws are simply principles that have been thoroughly tested and found to apply in a wide variety of situations. A **theory** is a set of related principles and laws that explains a broad aspect of learning, behavior, or another area of interest. Without theories the facts and principles that are discovered would be like disorganized specks on a canvas. Theories tie together these facts and principles to give us the big picture. However, the same facts and principles may be interpreted in different ways by different theorists. As in any science, progress in educational psychology is slow and uneven. A single study is rarely a breakthrough, but over time evidence accumulates on a subject and allows theorists to refine and extend their theories.

The Value of Research in Educational Psychology to the Teacher

It is probably true that the most important things teachers learn, they learn on the job—in internships, while student teaching, or during their first years in the classroom (Darling-Hammond, Gendler, & Wise, 1990). However, teachers make hundreds of decisions every day, and each decision has a theory behind it, whether or not the teacher is aware of it. The quality, accuracy, and usefulness of those theories are what ultimately determine the teacher's success. For example, one teacher may offer a prize to the student with the best attendance, on the theory that rewarding attendance will increase it. Another may reward the student whose attendance is most improved, on the theory that it is poor attenders who most need incentives to come to class. A third may not reward anyone for attendance but may try to increase attendance by teaching more interesting lessons. Which teacher's plan is most likely to succeed? This depends in large part on the ability of each teacher to understand the unique combination of factors that shape the character of her or his classroom and therefore to apply the most appropriate theory.

Teaching as Decision Making

The aim of research in educational psychology is to test the various theories that guide the actions of teachers and others involved in education. Here is another example of how a teacher might use educational psychology.

principle
Explanation of the relationship between factors, such as the effects of alternative grading systems on student motivation.

theory
A set of principles that explains and relates certain phenomena.

Mr. Harris teaches an eighth-grade social studies class. He has a problem with Tom, who frequently misbehaves. Today, Tom makes a paper airplane and flies it across the room when Mr. Harris turns his back, to the delight of the entire class.

What should Mr. Harris do?

As an intentional teacher, Mr. Harris considers a range of options for solving this problem, each of which comes from a theory about why Tom is misbehaving and what will motivate him to behave more appropriately.

Some actions Mr. Harris might take, and the theories on which they are based, are as follows:

Action	Theory
1. Reprimand Tom.	1. A reprimand is a form of punishment. Tom will behave to avoid punishment.
2. Ignore Tom.	2. Attention may be rewarding to Tom. Ignoring him would deprive him of this reward.
3. Send Tom to the office.	3. Being sent to the office is punishing. It also deprives Tom of the (apparent) support of his classmates.
4. Tell the class that it is everyone's responsibility to maintain a good learning environment and that if any student misbehaves, 5 minutes will be subtracted from recess.	4. Tom is misbehaving to get his classmates' attention. If the whole class loses out when he misbehaves, the class will keep him in line.
5. Explain to the class that Tom's behavior is interfering with lessons that all students need to know and that his behavior goes against the rules the class set for itself at the beginning of the year.	5. The class holds standards of behavior that conflict with both Tom's behavior in class and the class's reaction to it. By reminding the class of its own needs (to learn the lesson) and its own rules set at the beginning of the year, the teacher might make Tom see that the class does not really support his behavior.

Each of these actions is a common response to misbehavior. But which theory (and therefore which action) is correct?

The key might be in the fact that his classmates laugh when Tom misbehaves. This response is a clue that Tom is seeking their attention. If Mr. Harris scolds Tom, this might increase Tom's status in the eyes of his peers and may reward his behavior. Ignoring misbehavior might be a good idea if a student were acting up to get the teacher's attention, but in this case it is apparently the class's attention that Tom is seeking. Sending Tom to the office does deprive him of his classmates' attention and therefore may be effective. But what if Tom is looking for a way to get out of class to avoid work? What if he struts out to confront the powers that be, to the obvious approval of his classmates? Making the entire class responsible for each student's behavior is likely to deprive Tom of his classmates' support and to improve his behavior; but some students may think that it is unfair to punish them for another student's misbehavior. Finally, reminding the class (and Tom) of its own interest in learning and its usual standards of behavior might work if the class does, in fact, value academic achievement and good behavior.

Research in education and psychology bears directly on the decision Mr. Harris must make. Developmental research indicates that as students enter adolescence, the peer group becomes all-important to them, and they try to establish their independence

Teachers face a number of difficult, and sometimes unexpected, decisions every day and have to be able to respond quickly and appropriately. How can you become an intentional teacher?

INTASC

9 Professional Commitment and Responsibility

from adult control, often by flouting or ignoring rules. Basic research on behavioral learning theories shows that when a behavior is repeated many times, some reward must be encouraging the behavior, and that if the behavior is to be eliminated, the reward must first be identified and removed. This research would also suggest that Mr. Harris consider problems with the use of punishment (such as scolding) to stop undesirable behavior. Research on specific classroom management strategies has identified effective methods to use both to prevent a student like Tom from misbehaving in the first place and to deal with his misbehavior when it does occur. Finally, research on rule setting and classroom standards indicates that student participation in setting rules can help convince each student that the class as a whole values academic achievement and appropriate behavior, and that this belief can help keep individual students in line.

Armed with this information, Mr. Harris can choose a response to Tom's behavior that is based on an understanding of why Tom is doing what he is doing and what strategies are available to deal with the situation. He may or may not make the right choice; but because he knows several theories that could explain Tom's behavior, he will be able to observe the outcomes of his strategy and, if it is ineffective, to learn from that and try something else that will work. Research does not give Mr. Harris a specific solution; that requires his own experience and judgment. But research does give Mr. Harris basic concepts of human behavior to help him understand Tom's motivations and an array of proven methods that might solve the problem. And using research to help him make teaching decisions is one way Mr. Harris can achieve a sense of his own efficacy as a teacher.

Theory into PRACTICE

Teaching as Decision Making

If there were no educational problems to solve, there would be no need for teachers to function as professionals. Professionals distinguish themselves from nonprofessionals in part by the fact that they must make decisions that influence the course of their work.

Educators must decide (1) how to recognize problems and issues, (2) how to consider situations from multiple perspectives, (3) how to call up relevant professional knowledge to formulate actions, (4) how to take the most appropriate action, and (5) how to judge the consequences.

Ms. O'Hara has a student named Shanika in her social studies class. Most of the time, Shanika is rather quiet and withdrawn. Her permanent record indicates considerable academic ability, but a casual observer would never know it. Ms. O'Hara asks herself the following questions:

1. What problems do I perceive in this situation? Is Shanika bored, tired, uninterested, or shy, or might her participation be inhibited by something I or others are doing or not doing? What theories of educational psychology might I consider?
2. I wonder what Shanika thinks about being in this class? Does she feel excluded? Does she care about the subject matter? Is she concerned about what I or others think about her lack of participation? Why or why not? What theories of motivation will help me make a decision?
3. What do I know from theory, research, and/or practice that might guide my actions to involve Shanika more directly in class activities?
4. What might I actually do in this situation to enhance Shanika's involvement?
5. How would I know if I were successful with Shanika?

If Ms. O'Hara asked and tried to answer these questions—not just in the case of Shanika, of course, but at other times as well—she would improve her chances to learn about her work from doing her work. Philosopher John Dewey taught that the problems teachers face are the natural stimuli for reflective inquiry. Intentional teachers accept the problems and think productively about them.

CONNECTIONS

For more on multiculturalism, see Chapter 4.

Research + Common Sense = Effective Teaching

As the case of Mr. Harris illustrates, no theory, no research, no book can tell teachers what to do in a given situation. Making the right decisions depends on the context within which the problem arises, the objectives the teacher has in mind, and many other factors, all of which must be assessed in the light of educated common sense. For example, research in mathematics instruction usually finds that a rapid pace of instruction increases achievement (Good, Grouws, & Ebmeier, 1983). Yet a teacher may quite legitimately slow down and spend a lot of time on a concept that is particularly critical or may let students take time to discover a mathematical principle on their own. It is usually much more efficient (that is, it takes less time) to teach students skills or information directly than it is to let them make discoveries for themselves; but if the teacher wants students to gain a deeper understanding of a topic or to know how to find information or figure things out for themselves, then the research findings about pace can be temporarily shelved.

The point is that while research in educational psychology can sometimes be translated directly to the classroom, it is best to apply the principles with a hefty dose of common sense and a clear view of what is being taught to whom and for what purpose.

Research on Effective Programs

Research in educational psychology not only provides evidence for principles of effective practice, but it also provides evidence about the effectiveness of particular programs or practices (Rhine, 1998). For example, in the vignette at the beginning of this

"In light of research on class size, we're not cutting class, we're helping our classmates get a better education!"

chapter, Leah Washington was using a specific approach to creative writing instruction that has been extensively evaluated as a whole (Hillocks, 1984). In other words, there is evidence that, on average, children whose teachers are using such methods learn to write better than those whose teachers use more traditional approaches. There is evidence on the effectiveness of dozens of widely used programs, from methods in particular subjects to strategies for reforming entire schools (see, for example, Ellis, 2001; Gunter, Estes, & Schwab, 2003; Slavin & Fashola, 1998). An intentional teacher should be aware of research on programs for his or her subject and grade level, and should seek out professional development opportunities to learn methods known to make a difference for children.

Impact of Research on Educational Practice

Many researchers and educators have bemoaned the limited impact of research in educational psychology on teachers' practices (see, for example, Hargreaves, 1996; Kennedy, 1997). Indeed, research in education has nowhere near as great an impact on practice as research in medicine or agriculture or engineering (Gage, 1994). Yet research in education does have a profound indirect impact on educational practice (Hattie & Marsh, 1996), even if teachers are not aware of it. It affects educational policies, professional development programs, and teaching materials. For example, the Tennessee class size study (Achilles, Finn, & Bain, 1997/98; Finn & Achilles, 1999; Finn, Pannazzo, & Achilles, 2003), which found important effects of class size in the early grades on student achievement, had a direct impact on state and federal proposals for class size reduction (Finn, 2002; Wasley, 2002). Recent research on beginning reading (National Academy of Sciences, 1998) has begun to dramatically transform curriculum, instruction, and professional development for this subject. Research on the effects of career academies in high schools (Kemple, 1997) has led to a substantial increase in such programs.

It is important for educators to become intelligent consumers of research, not to take every finding or every expert's pronouncement as truth from Mount Olympus. The following section briefly describes the methods of research that most often produce findings of use to educators.

Theory into PRACTICE

How to Be an Intelligent Consumer of Educational Psychology Research

INTASC

9 Professional Commitment and Responsibility

Let's say you're in the market for a new car. Before laying out your hard-earned money, you'll probably review the findings from various consumer research reports. You may want to know something about how various cars have performed in crash tests, which cars have the best gas mileage, or what trade-in value a particular model has. Before embarking on this major investment, you want to feel as confident as you can about your decision. If you've been in this situation before, you probably remember that all of your research helped you make an informed decision.

Now that you are about to enter the profession of teaching, you will need to apply a similar consumer orientation in your decision making. As a teacher, you will be called upon to make hundreds of decisions each day. Your car-buying decision was influenced by a combination of sound research findings and common sense, and your decisions about teaching and learning should follow this same pattern. Teaching and learning are complex concepts subject to a wide variety of influences, so your knowledge of relevant research will serve to guide you into making informed choices.

How can knowing the simple formula *research + common sense = effective teaching* help you to be a more intelligent consumer of educational psychology research? The following recommendations show how you can put this formula into practice:

Be a consumer of relevant research. It's obvious you can't apply what you don't know. As a professional, you have a responsibility to maintain a working knowledge of relevant research. In addition to your course textbooks, which will be excellent resources for you in the future, you should become familiar with the professional journals in your field. You may want to review the following journals, which typically present research that has direct application for classroom practices: *Educational Psychologist, Journal of Educational Psychology,* and *American Educational Research Journal.* In addition, check out *Annual Editions: Educational Psychology,* a yearly publication that reprints articles from various professional journals. Also, don't overlook the value of networking with other teachers, face to face or via the Internet. The example of Ellen Mathis and Leah Washington is an excellent illustration of how collaboration can expand your research base.

Be an intentional teacher. While there is no recipe for the ingredients that make up a commonsense approach to teaching, the behaviors consistent with being an intentional teacher are about as close as we can get. Intentional teachers are thoughtful. Like Mr. Harris, they consider multiple perspectives on classroom situations. When they take action, they are purposeful and think about why they do what they do. Intentional teachers follow their actions with careful reflection, evaluating their actions to determine whether they have resulted in the desired outcomes. You probably learned about the "scientific method" sometime during high school. Intentional teachers employ such a method in their teaching. That is, they formulate a working hypothesis based on their observations and background knowledge, collect data to test their hypothesis, effectively organize and analyze the data, draw sound conclusions based on the data, and take a course of action based on their conclusions. For many experienced teachers, this cycle becomes automatic and internalized. When applied systematically, these practices can serve to validate research and theory and, as a result, increase a teacher's growing professional knowledge base.

Share your experiences. When you combine your knowledge of research with your professional common sense, you will find yourself engaged in more effective practices. As you and your students experience success, share your findings. Avenues for dissemination are endless. In addition to publishing articles in traditional sources such as professional journals and organizational newsletters, don't overlook the importance of preparing schoolwide in-service presentations, papers for state and national professional conferences, and presentations to school boards. In addition, the Internet offers various newsgroups where teachers engage in ongoing discussions about their

CERTIFICATION POINTER

For teacher certifica-
tion tests, you may
need to show that you
know how to access the
professional literature, professional associations, and
professional development
activities to improve your
teaching.

work. One such group is the Appalachia Educational Laboratory listserv (aelaction). This listserv is a free, facilitated forum on the Internet. To sub-scribe, send an e-mail message to majordomo@ael.org. Leave the subject line blank and in the body of the message type "subscribe aelaction" and include your e-mail address. One day you may find yourself becoming a valued con-tributor to the field of educational psychology research, and future students and colleagues will be reading about you and your work!

WHAT RESEARCH METHODS ARE USED IN EDUCATIONAL PSYCHOLOGY?

How do we know what we know in educational psychology? As in any scientific field, knowledge comes from many sources. Sometimes researchers study schools, teachers, or students as they are, and sometimes they create special programs, or **treatments,** and study their effects on one or more **variables** (anything that can have more than one value, such as age, sex, achievement level, or attitudes). There is no one best or most useful approach to research; any method can be useful when applied to the right set of questions. The principal methods educational researchers use to learn about schools, teachers, students, and instruction are experiments, correlational studies, and descriptive research. The following sections discuss these methods (see Leary, 2004; Mertler & Charles, 2005).

Experiments

In an **experiment,** researchers can create special treatments and analyze their effects. In one classic study, Lepper, Greene, and Nisbett (1973) set up an experimental situ-ation in which children used felt-tipped markers to draw pictures. Children in the experimental group (the group that received a treatment) were given a prize (a "good player award") for drawing pictures. Children in a control group received no prizes. At the end of the experiment, all students were allowed to choose among various activities, including drawing with felt-tipped markers. The children who had received the prizes chose to continue drawing with felt-tipped markers about half as frequently as did those who had not received prizes. This result was interpreted as showing that rewarding individuals for doing a task they already liked could reduce their interest in doing the task when they were no longer rewarded.

The Lepper study illustrates several important aspects of experiments. First, the children were randomly assigned to receive prizes or not. For example, the children's names might have been put on slips of paper that were dropped into a hat and then drawn at random for assignment to a "prize" or "no-prize" group. **Random assign-ment** ensured that the two groups were essentially equivalent before the experiment began. This equivalence is critical, because if we were not sure that the two groups were equal before the experiment, we would not be able to tell whether it was the prizes that made the difference in their subsequent behavior.

A second feature of this study that is characteristic of experiments is that every-thing other than the treatment itself (the prizes) was kept the same for the prize and no-prize groups. The children played in the same rooms with the same materials and with the same adults present. The researcher who gave the prize spent the same amount of time watching the no-prize children draw. Only the prize itself was differ-ent for the two groups. The goal was to be sure that it was the treatment, not some other factor, that explained the difference between the two groups.

treatment

A special program that is the subject of an experi-ment.

variable

Something that can have more than one value.

experiment

Procedure used to test the effect of a treatment.

random assignment

Selection by chance into different treatment groups; intended to ensure equivalence of the groups.

Laboratory Experiments   The Lepper et al. (1973) study is an example of a **laboratory experiment.** Even though the experiment took place in a school building, the researchers created a highly artificial, structured setting that existed for a very brief period of time. The advantage of laboratory experiments is that they permit researchers to exert a very high degree of control over all the factors involved in the study. Such studies are high in **internal validity,** which is to say that we can confidently attribute any differences they find to the treatments themselves (rather than to other factors). The primary limitation of laboratory experiments is that they are typically so artificial and so brief that their results may have little relevance to real-life situations. For example, the Lepper et al. study, which was later repeated several times, was used to support a theory that rewards can diminish individuals' interest in an activity when the rewards are withdrawn. This theory served as the basis for attacks on the use of classroom rewards, such as grades and stars. However, later research in real classrooms using real rewards has generally failed to find such effects (see Cameron & Pierce, 1994). This finding does not discredit the Lepper and colleagues study; it does show that theories based on artificial laboratory experiments cannot be assumed to apply to all situations in real life but must be tested in the real settings.

Randomized Field Experiments   Another kind of experiment that is often used in educational research is the **randomized field experiment,** in which instructional programs or other practical treatments are evaluated over relatively long periods in real classes under realistic conditions (Levin, O'Donnell, & Kratochwill, 2003; Mosteller & Boruch, 2002). For example, Pinnell, Lyons, DeFord, Bryk, and Seltzer (1994) compared four approaches to reading instruction for first-graders who were at risk for reading failure. One of these was Reading Recovery, a one-to-one tutoring model for at-risk first-graders that requires extensive training. In each of 10 schools, the 10 lowest-performing students were identified. Four were assigned at random to the **experimental group** using Reading Recovery, and 6 were assigned to a control group. **Control group** students continued to receive the reading program and remedial services they would have received anyway.

After four months (in February), all children were tested. Reading Recovery children scored significantly higher than control students on each of four measures. The following October, students were tested again, and Reading Recovery students still performed significantly higher than control students.

Note the similarities and differences between the Pinnell and colleagues (1994) randomized field experiment and the Lepper and colleagues (1973) laboratory experiment. Both used random assignment to make sure that the experimental and control groups were essentially equal at the start of the study. Both tried to make all factors except the treatment equal for the experimental and control groups, but the Pinnell and colleagues study was (by its very nature as a field experiment) less able to do this. For example, experimental and control students were taught by different teachers. Because many teachers were involved, this factor probably balanced out; but the fact remains that in a field setting, control is never as great as in a laboratory situation (see Pressley & Harris, 1994). On the other hand, the fact that the Pinnell and colleagues study took place over a long period of time in real classrooms means that its **external validity** (real-life validity) is far greater than that of the Lepper et al. study. That is, the results of the Pinnell et al. study have direct relevance to reading instruction for at-risk first-graders.

Both laboratory experiments and randomized field experiments make important contributions to the science of educational psychology. Laboratory experiments are primarily important in researchers' efforts to build and test theories, whereas randomized field experiments are the acid test for evaluating practical programs or improvements in instruction. For example, the writing process method that Leah Washington

laboratory experiment
Experiment in which conditions are highly controlled.

internal validity
The degree to which an experiment's results can be attributed to the treatment in question, not to other factors.

randomized field experiment
Experiment conducted under realistic conditions in which individuals are assigned by chance to receive different practical treatments or programs.

experimental group
Group that receives treatment during an experiment.

control group
Group that receives no special treatment during an experiment.

external validity
Degree to which results of an experiment can be applied to real-life situations.

was using has been evaluated many times in comparison to traditional methods and found to be highly effective (Hillocks, 1984). This finding is not a guarantee that this method will work in every situation, but it does give educators a good direction to follow to improve writing.

Recently, the U.S. Department of Education has begun to strongly emphasize research as a basis for practice in education. For example, in the No Child Left Behind Act of 2001, the phrase "based on scientifically-based research" appears 110 times in reference to programs expected to be used under federal funding. What is meant by "scientifically-based research" is primarily studies in which experimental and control groups were assigned at random (see U.S. Department of Education, 2003), although well-designed studies in which matched groups were compared are also valued. These policies, and new funding to support randomized experiments, have greatly increased interest in this type of research. You can expect to see many more randomized studies in the coming years, and these studies will matter a great deal for policy and practice (see Mosteller & Boruch, 2002; Slavin, 2003).

Randomized field experiments are very difficult to do in education, as it is rare that teachers are willing to be assigned by chance to one group or another. For this reason, field experiments more often use matching, in which teachers or schools using one method would be matched with those using a different method, or a control group. For example, Calderón, Hertz-Lazarowitz, and Slavin (1998) evaluated a program called Bilingual Cooperative Integrated Reading and Composition (BCIRC) in El Paso, Texas, elementary schools. English language learners in three schools using BCIRC were matched with those in control groups, based on prior achievement levels, socioeconomic status, and other factors. After pretesting, both sets of schools were followed for two years. Students in the BCIRC schools scored higher on reading measures than those in the control schools.

Matching is much more practical than random assignment, but its results must be carefully interpreted, since there may be reasons that one group of educators took on one method while another group did not. Were the teachers in the treatment group more motivated? Did they have greater resources? On the other hand, were they more desperate to try something new? In a matched study, these possibilities need to be considered and ruled out as much as possible (Mertler & Charles, 2005).

Single-Case Experiments   One type of experiment that is occasionally used in educational research is the **single-case experiment** (see Franklin, Allison, & Gorman, 1997; Neuman & McCormick, 1995). In one typical form of this type of experiment, a single student's behavior may be observed for several days. Then a special program is begun, and the student's behavior under the new program is observed. Finally, the new program is withdrawn. If the student's behavior improves under the special program but the improvement disappears when the program is withdrawn, the implication is that the program has affected the student's behavior. Sometimes the "single case" can be several students, an entire class, or a school that is given the same treatment.

An example of a single-case experiment is a classic study by Barrish, Saunders, and Wolf (1969). In this study, a fourth-grade class was the single case. Observers recorded the percentage of time that at least one student in the class was talking out (talking without permission) during reading and math periods. After 10 days, a special program was introduced. The class was divided into 2 large teams, and whenever any student on a team misbehaved, the team was given a check mark. At the end of each day, the team with fewer check marks (or both teams if both received fewer than 5 check marks) could take part in a 30-minute free period.

The results of this study are illustrated in Figure 1.2. Before the Good Behavior Game began (baseline), at least one student in the math class was talking out 96 percent of the time, and at least one student was out-of-seat without permission 82 percent of the time. When the game was begun in math, the class's behavior improved

single-case experiment
Experiment that studies a treatment's effect on one person or one group by contrasting behavior before, during, and after application of the treatment.

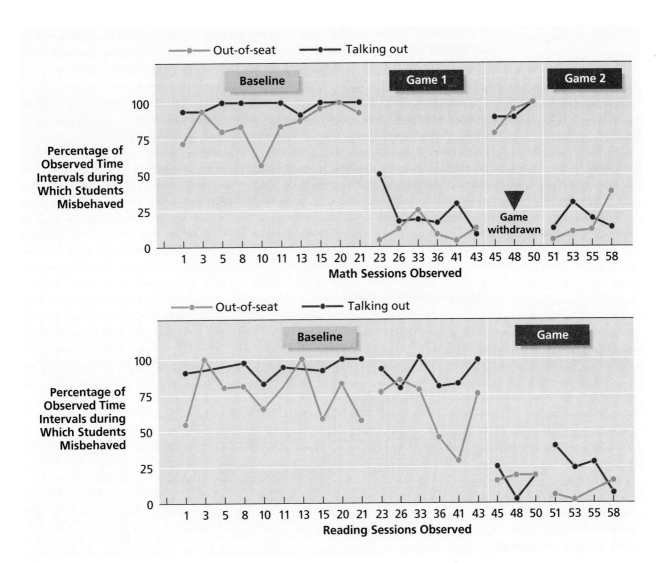

FIGURE 1.2

Results of Successful Single-Case Experiments

The effect of rewarding good behavior in fourth-grade math and reading classes is clear from these graphs. They show that misbehavior was high during the baseline period (before the Good Behavior Game was introduced) but fell during the game. For instance, in reading session 13, before the game was introduced, students were out of their seats during nearly 100 percent of the observed time intervals. In reading session 53, however, when the game was in use, the percentage of time intervals in which students were out-of-seat approached zero. In single-case experiments on treatments affecting behaviors that can be frequently measured, graphs like these can prove a treatment's effectiveness.

Adapted from H. H. Barrish, M. Saunders, and M. M. Wolf, "Good Behavior Game: Effects of Individual Contingencies for Group Consequences on Disruptive Behavior in a Classroom," *Journal of Applied Behavior Analysis, 2,* 1969, pp. 119–124. Reprinted by permission.

dramatically. When the game was withdrawn, the class's behavior got worse again but improved once more when the game was reintroduced. Note that when the game was introduced in reading class, the students' behaviors also improved. The fact that the program made a difference in both math and reading gives us even greater confidence that the Good Behavior Game is effective.

One important limitation of the single-case experiment is that it can be used only to study outcomes that can be measured frequently. For this reason, most single-case studies involve observable behaviors, such as talking out and being out-of-seat, which can be measured every day or many times per day.

Correlational Studies

Perhaps the most frequently used research method in educational psychology is the **correlational study.** In contrast to an experiment, in which the researcher deliberately changes one variable to see how this change will affect other variables, in correlational research the researcher studies variables as they are to see whether they are related. Variables can be positively correlated, negatively correlated, or uncorrelated. An example of a **positive correlation** is the relationship between reading achievement and mathematics achievement. In general, someone who is better than average in reading will also be better than average in math. Of course, some students who are good readers are not good in math, and vice versa; but on the average, skills in one academic area are positively correlated with skills in other academic areas: When one variable is high, the other tends also to be high. An example of a **negative correlation** is days absent and grades. The more days a student is absent, the lower his or her grades are likely to be; when one variable is high, the other tends to be low. With **uncorrelated variables,** in contrast, there is no correspondence between them. For example, student achievement in Poughkeepsie, New York, is probably completely unrelated to the level of student motivation in Portland, Oregon.

One classic example of correlational research is a study by Lahaderne (1968), who investigated the relationship between students' attentiveness in class and their achievements and IQs. She observed 125 students in 4 sixth-grade classes to see how much of the time students were paying attention (e.g., listening to the teacher and doing assigned work). She then correlated attentiveness with achievement in reading, arithmetic, and language and with students' IQs and attitudes toward school. The advantage of correlational studies is that they allow the researcher to study variables as they are, without creating artificial situations. Many important research questions can be studied only in correlational studies. For example, if we wanted to study the relationship between gender and math achievement, we could hardly randomly assign students to be boys or girls! Also, correlational studies let researchers study the interrelationships of many variables at the same time.

The principal disadvantage of correlational methods is that while they may tell us that two variables are related, they do not tell us what causes what. The Lahaderne study of attentiveness, achievement, and IQ raised the question: Does student attentiveness cause high achievement, or are high-ability, high-achieving students simply more attentive than other students? A correlational study cannot answer this question completely. However, correlational researchers do typically use statistical methods to try to determine what causes what. In Lahaderne's study, it would have been possible to find out whether among students with the same IQ, attentiveness was related to achievement. For example, given two students of average intelligence, will the one who is more attentive tend to achieve more? If not, then we may conclude that the relationship between attentiveness and achievement is simply the result of high-IQ students being more attentive and higher achieving than other students, not the result of any effect of attention on achievement.

Figure 1.3 illustrates two possible explanations for the correlation between attentiveness, achievement, and IQ. In Explanation A, attentiveness causes achievement. In Explanation B, both attentiveness and achievement are assumed to be caused by a third variable, IQ. Which is correct? Evidence from other research on this relationship suggests that both explanations are partially correct—that even when the effect of IQ is removed, student attentiveness is related to achievement.

correlational study
Research into the relationships between variables as they naturally occur.

positive correlation
Relationship in which high levels of one variable correspond to high levels of another.

negative correlation
Relationship in which high levels of one variable correspond to low levels of another.

uncorrelated variables
Variables for which there is no relationship between high/low levels of one and high/low levels of the other.

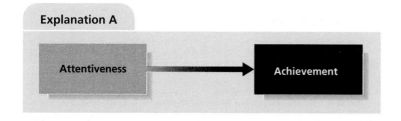

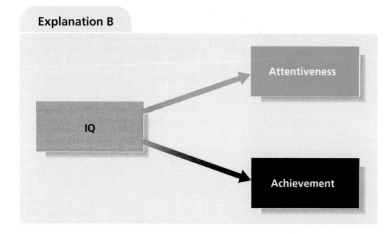

FIGURE 1.3
Possible Explanations for Correlations among Attentiveness, Achievement, and IQ

Correlational studies can show that variables are related, but such studies cannot prove what causes what. In Lahaderne's (1968) study, for example, did the attentiveness of the students cause higher achievement scores (Explanation A), or did a third factor—intelligence—determine both attentiveness and performance on achievement tests (as diagrammed in Explanation B)? Both explanations are partially correct.

Descriptive Research

Experimental and correlational research looks for relationships between variables. However, some research in educational psychology simply seeks to describe something of interest. One type of **descriptive research** is a survey or interview. Another, called ethnography, involves observation of a social setting (such as a classroom or school) over an extended period. For example, Jonathan Kozol (1991) wrote a descriptive study of life in well-funded and poorly funded schools that paints a devastating portrait of inequality in the U.S. educational system. Jeannie Oakes (1985) described teachers' practices in tracked and untracked middle schools. These and many other descriptive studies provide a much more complete story of what happens in schools and classrooms than could a study that boiled down the findings into cold, hard numbers. Descriptive research usually does not have the scientific objectivity of correlational or experimental research, but it makes up for this lack in richness of detail and interpretation (Creswell, 2002; Norcutt & McCoy, 2004; Rossman & Rallis, 2003).

Developmental psychologists use descriptive research extensively to identify characteristics of children at different ages. The most important research in developmental psychology was done by the Swiss psychologist Jean Piaget (1952b), who began by carefully observing his own children. As a result of his observations, he developed a theory that describes the cognitive development of children from infancy through adolescence.

Action Research

Action research is a particular form of descriptive research that is carried out by educators in their own classrooms or schools (Mills, 2000; Reason & Bradbury, 2001). In action research, a teacher or principal might try out a new teaching method or school organization strategy, collect information about how it worked, and communicate this information to others. Because the people involved in the experiment are the educators themselves, action research lacks the objectivity sought in other forms of research,

CONNECTIONS

For more on the use of descriptive research in developmental psychology, see Chapters 2 and 3.

descriptive research
Research study aimed at identifying and gathering detailed information about something of interest.

action research
Research carried out by educators in their own classrooms or schools.

INTASC

8 Assessment of Student Learning

> *Personal Reflection*
>
> ## Using Research to Inform Teaching
>
> As a graduate student, I conducted a study in a residential school for students with emotional and behavioral disorders. The study involved observing the behavior of a group of children who were 9 to 11 years old. The school had a program in which children earned points based on their behavior and could exchange points for various privileges or materials.
>
> Despite my attempts to be as unobtrusive as possible, I was writing notes on a clipboard, and the children were curious about what I was writing. One day, a girl in the class used her points to obtain a clipboard. She put a sheaf of paper on her clipboard and then spent all day walking around writing down all the bad things her classmates were doing. For example, she'd say, "James, I'm giving you another bad mark for not helping clean up."
>
> Of course, the other kids couldn't tolerate this for long, and soon they too used their points to get clipboards. They all then spent every free moment writing each other up for bad behavior, real or imagined. Worst of all, they started writing down bad things about me!
>
> My study was ruined, but I learned firsthand about what is sometimes called Heisenberg's Uncertainty Principle: Studying something may change what you're studying. Research in education always involves people, and people act differently when they're being studied. For this and many other reasons, even research findings with a ton of data should be taken with a grain of salt.
>
> *@ Reflect on This. Why was Slavin's study ruined? What lesson can you learn from this example about using research to be an effective teacher?*

but it can provide deeper insight from front-line teachers or administrators than would be possible in research done by outsiders.

HOW CAN I BECOME AN INTENTIONAL TEACHER?

INTASC

9 Professional Commitment and Responsibility

Think about the best, most intentional teachers you ever had—the ones who seemed so confident, so caring, so skilled, so enthusiastic about their subject. Chances are, when they took educational psychology they were as scared, uncertain, and overwhelmed about becoming a teacher as you might be today. Yet they kept at it and made themselves the great teachers you remember. You can do the same.

Teacher Certification

Before you can become an *intentional* teacher, you have to become a *certified* teacher. Each state, province, and country has its own requirements, but in most places you at least have to graduate from a four-year college with a specified distribution of courses. Various alternative certification programs exist as well. You also will need to have a satisfactory student teaching experience. In most states, however, graduation is not enough. You also have to pass a *teacher certification test*, or *licensure test*. Many states base their requirements on the 10 principles of effective teaching developed by the Interstate New Teacher Assessment and Support Consortium (INTASC) shown in Figure 1.4. They form the basis for most teacher certification tests, whether they are tests developed by INTASC, by the Education Testing Service, or by individual state departments of education.

INTASC has developed its own *Test for Teaching Knowledge (TTK)*. This is a new test that assesses new teachers' knowledge of child development; theories of teaching

1. *Knowledge of Subject Matter:* The teacher understands the central concepts, tools of inquiry, and structures of the subject being taught and can create learning experiences that make these aspects of subject matter meaningful for students.
2. *Knowledge of Human Development and Learning:* The teacher understands how children learn and develop, and can provide learning opportunities that support their intellectual, social, and personal development.
3. *Adapting Instruction for Individual Needs:* The teacher understands how students differ in their approaches to learning and creates instructional opportunities that are adapted to diverse learners.
4. *Multiple Instructional Strategies:* The teacher uses various instructional strategies to encourage students' development of critical thinking, problem solving, and performance skills.
5. *Classroom Motivation and Management:* The teacher uses an understanding of individual and group motivation and behavior to create a learning environment that encourages positive social interaction, active engagement in learning, and self-motivation.
6. *Communication Skills:* The teacher uses knowledge of effective verbal, nonverbal, and media communication techniques to foster active inquiry, collaboration, and supportive interaction in the classroom.
7. *Instructional Planning Skills:* The teacher plans instruction based upon knowledge of subject matter, students, the community, and curriculum goals.
8. *Assessment of Student Learning:* The teacher understands and uses formal and informal assessment strategies to evaluate and ensure the continuous intellectual, social and physical development of the learner.
9. *Professional Commitment and Responsibility:* The teacher is a reflective practitioner who continually evaluates the effects of his or her choices and actions on others (students, parents, and other professionals in the learning community) and who actively seeks out opportunities to grow professionally.
10. *Partnerships:* The teacher fosters relationships with school colleagues, parents, and agencies in the larger community to support students' learning and well-being.

FIGURE 1.4
Interstate New Teacher Assessment and Support Consortium (INTASC) Standards for Beginning Teacher Licensing and Development

and learning, assessment, and language acquisition; the role of student background in the learning process; and other basic knowledge and skills important for teaching. Some states are beginning to use this test. To read more about the TTK, visit the Council of Chief State School Officers (CCSSO) website at www.ccsso.org/intasc.

The Praxis Series: Professional Assessments for Beginning Teachers, developed by Educational Testing Service, is the most common test used by states to certify teachers. The Praxis Series includes three categories of assessment that correlate to significant stages in teacher development: Praxis I: Academic Skills Assessment for entering a teacher training program, Praxis II: Subject Assessments for licensure for entering the profession, and Praxis III: Classroom Performance Assessments after the first year of teaching. Praxis II would be the test you would take on completing your teacher preparation program. It offers three principles of learning and teaching (PLT) tests that relate to the content in educational psychology—one for grades K to 6, one for 5 to 9, and one for 7 to 12. These tests cover content in four areas: students as learners, instruction and assessment, communication techniques, and teacher professionalism.

Each PLT test has four scenarios followed by three short-answer questions related to the scenario. There are also 24 multiple-choice questions, for a total of 36 questions. Detailed information about the Praxis series of tests can be found at www.ets.org/praxis. From this website you can access the tests-at-a-glance page, which includes test outlines, sample questions with explanations for the best answers, and test-taking strategies. There is also a list of state-by-state requirements to determine which Praxis tests each state uses, if any. Note that individual universities may also use Praxis, even if their state does not require it.

Each state, province, or institution that uses the Praxis tests sets its own passing requirements. The passing score for each test for each state is listed on the website and in a booklet you receive with your score report.

Many states, including California, Texas, Florida, and New York, have developed or are developing their own teacher certification tests. These usually include sections much like the Praxis Principles of Learning and Teaching.

Throughout this book you will find tips on topics likely to appear on teacher certification tests. These marginal notes, called *Certification Pointers,* highlight knowledge that is frequently required on state teacher licensure exams, including Praxis Principles of Learning and Teaching.

Beyond Certification

Getting a teaching certificate is necessary but not sufficient to become an intentional teacher. Starting with your student teaching experience and continuing into your first job, you can create or take advantage of opportunities to develop your skills as an intentional teacher in a number of ways.

Seek Mentors   Experienced teachers who are themselves intentional teachers are your best resource. They are not only highly effective, but they understand and can describe what they're doing (and, hopefully, can help you learn to do those things). Talk with experienced teachers in your school, ask to observe them teaching, and ask them to observe you and share ideas, as Ellen Mathis did in the vignette at the beginning of this chapter. Many school systems provide induction programs for new teachers to help them develop in those crucial first years, but even if yours does not provide such a program, you can create one for yourself by seeking out experienced and helpful mentors.

CERTIFICATION POINTER

Teacher certification tests include a section on teacher professionalism. One aspect that is emphasized is being able to read and understand research on current ideas and debates about teaching practices.

Seek Professional Development   Districts, universities, state departments of education, and other institutions provide all sorts of professional development workshops for teachers on a wide range of topics. Take advantage of every opportunity to participate. The best professional development includes some sort of coaching or follow-up, in which someone who knows a given technique or program comes to your class to observe you trying to use the program and gives you feedback (see Joyce, Calhoun, & Hopkins, 1999; Neufield & Roper, 2003). Workshops in which many teachers from your school participate together, and then have opportunities to discuss successes and challenges, can also be very effective (see Calderón, 1999).

Talk Teaching   Talk to your colleagues, your former classmates, your friends who teach, even your friends who don't teach. Share your successes, your failures, your questions. Teaching can be an isolating experience if it's just you and the kids. Take every opportunity to share ideas and commiserate with sympathetic colleagues.

ON THE WEB

When your friends and colleagues are worn out from your passion for teaching, try virtual colleagues on the Web. Teacher-oriented websites offer opportunities to share advice, opinions, and observations. A few examples include:

Education World: **www.education-world.com**
Growing in my Job: **www.nea.org/helpfrom/growing/index.html**
The Knowledge Loom: **www.knowledgeloom.org**
K–12 Professional Circle: **www.nces.ed.gov/practitioners/teachers.asp**
Survival Guide for New Teachers: **www.ed.gov/pubs/survivalguide**
The Vent: **www.proteacher.com**

Keep Up with Professional Publications and Associations   Intentional teachers do a lot of reading. Your school may subscribe to teacher-oriented journals, or you might choose to do so. For example, look for *Teacher Magazine, Theory into Practice, Learning, Young Children, Phi Delta Kappan, Educational Leadership,* or subject-specific journals such as the *Reading Teacher* and *Mathematics Teacher.*

In addition, check out professional associations in your subject area or area of interest. The national teachers' unions—the American Federation of Teachers (AFT) and National Education Association (NEA)—have publications, workshops, and other resources from which you can benefit greatly. Your state department of education, regional educational laboratory, or school district office may also have useful resources. A few useful websites include the following:

American Educational Research Association: www.aera.net
American Federation of Teachers: www.aft.org
Canadian Educational Research Association: www.cea-ace.ca
Council for Exceptional Children: www.cec.sped.org
International Reading Association: www.reading.org
National Association for Bilingual Education: www.nabe.org
National Association for the Education of Young Children: www.naeyc.org
National Association of Black School Educators: www.nabse.org
National Council for the Social Studies: www.ncss.org
National Council of Teachers of English: www.ncte.org
National Council of Teachers of Mathematics: www.nctm.org
National Education Association: www.nea.org
National Institute for Literacy: www.nifl.gov
National Middle School Association: www.nmsa.org
National Science Teachers Association: www.nsta.org

CERTIFICATION POINTER

The teacher professionalism section of Praxis II and other certification tests may ask you to know the titles of several professional journals in your particular field of teaching (e.g., *Journal of Educational Psychology, Educational Leadership, Phi Delta Kappan*).

CERTIFICATION POINTER

Teaching certification tests might expect you to know what professional associations offer meetings, publications, and dialogue with other teachers (e.g., American Educational Research Association, International Reading Association, American Federation of Teachers, National Education Association).

Teaching Dilemmas: Cases to Consider

INTASC **7** **Instructional Planning Skills**

Choosing a New Curriculum

Jane Spivak and Maurice Brown are both teachers at the elementary level. Susana Rubio teaches in the district's high school. John Hammond coordinates the K–12 math curriculum and teaches at the middle school. Together they serve on a districtwide committee whose job is to evaluate the current math program and choose a new one.

Jane: I like some of the new programs we've looked at. They incorporate problem-solving strategies even in first grade, and they encourage cooperative learning.

John: But do they teach the basic skills? I mean, we're still getting kids in the sixth grade who don't know their basic math facts.

Susana: I agree, but they definitely need more critical thinking about math at earlier ages if they are going to handle some of the expectations at the high school level.

Maurice: I think these would work out great if you started the kids with it in kindergarten, but how about the upper grades? Are you just going to switch them from the relatively traditional program we have now into one that is much more problem-solving oriented and less teacher directed?

John: OK, OK. Another consideration is the expense of these programs, both in time and money to us and the district. I think we all agree that the easiest thing would be to keep what we've got but that the students need more.

Susana: How about a pilot study? You know, purchase materials for one or two classes at selected grade levels and do a careful comparison. We can find out both the difficulties and the benefits, then make our decision. We've certainly done some research already—the workshops we've gone to, visits to other schools using the program. But why don't we do some research of our own?

Jane: Okay, but it will have to be well done with a matched control group class using the old program for each one piloting the new. We should compare how each class does at reaching the same set of objectives we've decided on for those grade levels.

Susana: I want some qualitative feedback from teachers too. Maybe some rating scales. We could send a questionnaire home to parents.

@ Questions for Reflection

1. What are the benefits of this type of curriculum evaluation? What might be the drawbacks and limitations?
2. Devise an outline of the proposed research to compare the two curricular approaches.
3. Extend the discussion with the system superintendent. He doesn't want to spend the time or money on research before choosing a curriculum. How will the teachers defend their need for personal research?

Chapter Summary

What Makes a Good Teacher?

Good teachers know their subject matter and have mastered pedagogical skills. They accomplish all the tasks involved in effective instruction with warmth, enthusiasm, and caring. They are intentional teachers, and they use principles of educational psychology in their decision making and teaching. They combine research and common sense.

What Is the Role of Research in Educational Psychology?

Educational psychology is the systematic study of learners, learning, and teaching. Research in educational psychology focuses on the processes by which information, skills, values, and attitudes are communicated between teachers and students in the classroom and on applications of the principles of psychology to instructional practices. Such research shapes educational policies, professional development programs, and teaching materials.

What Research Methods Are Used in Educational Psychology?

Experimental research involves testing particular educational programs or treatments. Random assignment of experimental subjects into groups before the testing helps to ensure that groups are equivalent and findings will be valid. An experimental group receiving the treatment is matched with a control group whose members do not receive treatment. Laboratory experiments are highly structured and short term. All the variables involved are strictly controlled. Randomized field experiments are less structured and take place over a long period of time under realistic conditions in which not all variables can be controlled. A single-case experiment involves observation of one student or group of students over a specified period before and after treatment. Correlational studies examine variables to see whether they are related. Variables can be positively correlated, negatively correlated, or uncorrelated. Correlational studies provide information about variables without manipulating them or creating artificial situations. However, they do not indicate the causes of relationships between variables. Descriptive research uses surveys, interviews, and/or observations to describe behavior in social settings.

Key Terms

Research
Navigator.com

Review the following key terms from the chapter. Then, to explore research on these topics and how they relate to education today, connect to Research Navigator™ through this book's Companion Website or directly at www.researchnavigator.com.

action research   21
control group   17
correlational study   20
critical thinking   8
descriptive research   21
educational psychology   3
experiment   16
experimental group   17
external validity   17
intentionality   4
internal validity   17
laboratory experiment   17

negative correlation   20
pedagogy   4
positive correlation   20
principle   10
random assignment   16
randomized field experiment   17
single-case experiment   18
teacher efficacy   7
theory   10
treatment   16
uncorrelated variables   20
variable   16

Self-Assessment: Practicing for Licensure

Directions: The chapter-opening vignette addresses indicators that are often assessed in state licensure exams. Re-read the chapter-opening vignette, and then respond to the following questions.

1. In the first paragraph, Ellen Mathis does not understand why her students are nonproductive and unimaginative. According to educational psychology research, which of the following teacher characteristics is Ellen most likely lacking?

   a. classroom management skills
   b. content knowledge
   c. intentionality
   d. common sense

2. Leah Washington talks with Ellen Mathis about getting students to write interesting compositions. Which of the following statements summarizes Leah's approach to teaching writing?

   a. Select teaching methods, learning activities, and instructional materials that are appropriate and motivating for students.
   b. Have students of similar abilities work together so the teacher can adapt instruction to meet the needs of each group.
   c. When working on writing activities, consider the teacher to be the instruction center.
   d. Individualization is the first goal of instruction; direct instruction is the second goal.

3. According to research on expertise development, what characteristic separates novice teachers from expert teachers?

   a. Novice teachers tend to rely on their pedagogical skills since their content knowledge is less complex than an expert's.
   b. Expert teachers do more short-term memory processing than novices because their thinking is more complex.
   c. Novice teachers have to constantly upgrade and examine their own teaching practices while experts use a "best practices" approach.
   d. One theme that comes through educational psychology research is that expert teachers are critical thinkers.

4. Educational psychologists are often accused of studying the obvious. However, they have learned that the obvious is not always true. All of the following statements demonstrate this idea except one. Which one is obvious *and* supported by research?

   a. Student achievement is increased when students are assigned to classes according to their ability.
   b. Scolding students for misbehavior improves student behavior.
   c. Whole-class instruction is more effective than individualized instruction.
   d. Intentional teachers balance competing goals according to the needs of particular students and situations.

5. Leah Washington discusses many of her teaching strategies with Ellen Mathis. One can easily see that Leah views teaching as a decision-making process. She recognizes problems and issues, considers situations from multiple perspectives, calls upon her professional knowledge to formulate action, and

   a. selects the most appropriate action and judges the consequence.
   b. chooses a strategy that agrees with her individual beliefs about teaching.
   c. consults with expert teachers and administrators to assist with her plan of action.
   d. allows students to make instructional decisions based on their interests and needs.

6. The products of research are principles, laws, and theories. Leah Washington describes many principles and theories of educational psychology as she speaks with Ellen Mathis about teaching students to write compositions. First, describe an instruction action with which Ellen Mathis is having difficulties (e.g., Ellen assigns all students the same topic), and then describe principles and theories she can use to engage her students in exciting and meaningful lessons.

7. The goal of research in educational psychology is to examine questions of teaching and learning using objective methods. These research methods include experiments, correlational studies, descriptive research, and action research. Think of a research question, and then describe how you would go about answering your question using the above methods.

8. Intentional teachers are aware of resources available for professional learning. They continually refine their practices to address the needs of all students. List four actions you could take to find information to help you teach your students with limited English proficiency.

Theories of Development

*O*ver the course of their first 18 years of life, children go through astounding changes. Most of these changes are obvious—children get bigger, smarter, more socially adept, and so on. However, many aspects of development are not so obvious. Individual children develop in different ways and at different rates, and development is influenced by culture, parenting, education, and other factors. Every teacher needs to understand how children grow and develop to be able to understand how children learn and how best to teach them, as is illustrated in the following vignettes.

- In the first week of school, Mr. Jones tried to teach his first-graders how to behave in class. He said, "When I ask a question, I want you to raise your right hand, and I'll call on you. Can you all raise your right hands, as I am doing?" Twenty hands went up. All were left hands.

- Because her students were getting careless about handing in their homework, Ms. Lewis decided to lay down the law to her fourth-grade class. "Anyone who does not hand in all his or her homework this week will not be allowed to go on the field trip." It happened that one girl's mother became ill and was taken to the hospital that week. As a result of her family's confusion and concern, the girl failed to hand in one of her homework assignments. Ms. Lewis explained to the class that she would make an exception in this case because of the girl's mother's illness, but the class wouldn't hear of it. "Rules are rules," they said. "She didn't hand in her homework, so she can't go!"

- Ms. Quintera started her eighth-grade English class one day with an excited announcement: "Class, I wanted to tell you all that we have a poet in our midst. Frank wrote such a wonderful poem that I thought I'd read it to you all." Ms. Quintera read Frank's poem, which was indeed very good. However, she noticed that Frank was turning bright red and looking distinctly uncomfortable. A few of the other students in the class snickered. Later, Ms. Quintera asked Frank whether he would like to write another poem for a citywide poetry contest. He said he'd rather not, because he really didn't think he was that good; and besides, he didn't have the time. ◎

Critical Thinking   Why do you think Frank reacted the way he did? How could Ms. Quintera alter her approach so as to motivate Frank?

Critical Thinking   Compare and contrast these three scenarios. Explain which case(s) involved a behavioral, cognitive, social, moral, or physical development dilemma. Specify the dilemma.

INTASC

2 Knowledge of Human Development and Learning

WHAT ARE SOME VIEWS OF HUMAN DEVELOPMENT?

The term **development** refers to how people grow, adapt, and change over the course of their lifetimes, through physical development, personality development, socioemotional development, cognitive development (thinking), and language development. This chapter presents five major theories of human development that are widely accepted: Jean Piaget's theories of cognitive and moral development, Lev Vygotsky's theory of cognitive development, Erik Erikson's theory of personal and social development, and Lawrence Kohlberg's theory of moral development.

Aspects of Development

Children are not miniature adults. They think differently, they see the world differently, and they live by different moral and ethical principles than adults do. The three scenarios just presented illustrate a few of the many aspects of children's thinking that differ from those of adults. When Mr. Jones raised his right hand, his first-graders imitated his action without taking his perspective; they didn't realize that since he was facing them, his right hand would be to their left. The situation in Ms. Lewis' class illustrates a stage in children's moral development at which rules are rules and extenuating circumstances do not count. Ms. Quintera's praise of Frank's poem had an effect opposite to what she intended, but had she paused to consider the situation, she might have realized that highlighting Frank's achievement could cast him in the role of teacher's pet, a role that many students in early adolescence strongly resist.

One of the first requirements of effective teaching is that the teacher understand how students think and how they view the world. Effective teaching strategies must take into account students' ages and stages of development. A bright fourth-grader might appear to be able to learn any kind of mathematics but in fact might not have the cognitive maturity to do the abstract thinking required for algebra. Similarly, Ms. Quintera's public recognition of Frank's poetry might have been quite appropriate if Frank had been three years younger or three years older.

Issues of Development

Two central issues have been debated for decades among developmental psychologists. One relates to the degree to which development is affected by experience, and the other to the question of whether development proceeds in stages.

Nature-Nurture Controversy   Is development predetermined at birth, by heredity and biological factors, or is it affected by experience and other environmental factors? Today, most developmental psychologists (e.g., Berk, 2003; Berk, Bee, & Boyd,

development
Orderly and lasting growth, adaptation, and change over the course of a lifetime.

2003; Cook & Cook, 2005; Fabes & Martin, 2000) believe that nature and nurture combine to influence development, with biological factors playing a stronger role in some aspects, such as physical development, and environmental factors playing a stronger role in others, such as moral development.

Continuous and Discontinuous Theories   A second issue revolves around the notion of how change occurs. **Continuous theories of development** assume that development occurs in a smooth progression as skills develop and experiences are provided by parents and the environment. Continuous theories emphasize the importance of environment rather than heredity in determining development.

A second perspective assumes that children progress through a set of predictable and invariant stages of development. In this case, change can be fairly abrupt as children advance to a new stage of development. All children are believed to acquire skills in the same sequence, although rates of progress differ from child to child. The abilities that children gain in each subsequent stage are not simply "more of the same"; at each stage, children develop qualitatively different understandings, abilities, and beliefs. Skipping stages is impossible, although at any given point the same child may exhibit behaviors characteristic of more than one stage (Zigler & Gilman, 1998). In contrast to continuous theories, these **discontinuous theories of development** focus on inborn factors rather than environmental influences to explain change over time. Environmental conditions may have some influence on the pace of development, but the sequence of developmental steps is essentially fixed.

Piaget, Vygotsky, Erikson, and Kohlberg focus on different aspects of development. Nevertheless, all are stage theorists, because they share the belief that distinct stages of development can be identified and described. This agreement does not, however, extend to the particulars of their theories, which differ significantly in the numbers of stages and in their details. Also, each theorist focuses on different aspects of development (e.g., cognitive, socioemotional, personality, moral).

Today, most developmentalists acknowledge the role of both inborn factors and experience when explaining children's behavior (see Bronfenbrenner & Morris, 1998; Cook & Cook, 2005). Vygotsky's theories in particular rely on social interactions as well as predictable stages of growth to explain development.

How DID PIAGET VIEW COGNITIVE DEVELOPMENT?

Jean Piaget, born in Switzerland in 1896, is the most influential developmental psychologist in the history of psychology (see Flavell, 1996). After receiving his doctorate in biology, he became more interested in psychology, basing his earliest theories on careful observation of his own three children. Piaget thought of himself as applying biological principles and methods to the study of human development, and many of the terms he introduced to psychology were drawn directly from biology.

Piaget explored both why and how mental abilities change over time. For Piaget, development depends in large part on the child's manipulation of and active interaction with the environment. In Piaget's view, knowledge comes from action (see Langer & Killen, 1998; Wadsworth, 1996). Piaget's theory of **cognitive development** proposes that a child's intellect, or cognitive abilities, progresses through four distinct stages. Each stage is characterized by the emergence of new abilities and ways of processing information. Many of the specifics of Piaget's theories have been challenged in later research. In particular, many of the changes in cognitive functioning he described are now known to take place earlier, under certain circumstances. Nevertheless, Piaget's work forms an essential basis for understanding child development.

continuous theory of development
Theory based on the belief that human development progresses smoothly and gradually from infancy to adulthood.

discontinuous theories of development
Theories describing human development as occurring through a fixed sequence of distinct, predictable stages governed by inborn factors.

cognitive development
Gradual, orderly changes by which mental processes become more complex and sophisticated.

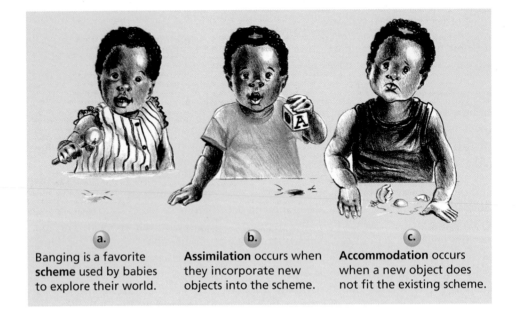

FIGURE 2.1
Schemes
Babies use patterns of behavior called *schemes* to learn about their world.

a. Banging is a favorite **scheme** used by babies to explore their world.

b. **Assimilation** occurs when they incorporate new objects into the scheme.

c. **Accommodation** occurs when a new object does not fit the existing scheme.

How Development Occurs

Schemes   Piaget believed that all children are born with an innate tendency to interact with and make sense of their environments. He referred to the basic ways of organizing and processing information as cognitive structures. Young children demonstrate patterns of behavior or thinking, called **schemes,** that older children and adults also use in dealing with objects in the world. We use schemes to find out about and act in the world; each scheme treats all objects and events in the same way. For example, most young infants will discover that one thing you can do with objects is bang them. When they do this, the object makes a noise, and they see the object hitting a surface. Their observations tell them something about the object. Babies also learn about objects by biting them, sucking on them, and throwing them. Each of these approaches to interacting with objects is a scheme. When babies encounter a new object, how are they to know what this object is all about? According to Piaget, they will use the schemes they have developed and will find out whether the object makes a loud or soft sound when banged, what it tastes like, whether it gives milk, and maybe whether it rolls or just goes thud when dropped (see Figure 2.1a).

Assimilation and Accommodation   According to Piaget, **adaptation** is the process of adjusting schemes in response to the environment by means of assimilation and accommodation. **Assimilation** is the process of understanding a new object or event in terms of an existing scheme. If you give young infants small objects that they have never seen before but that resemble familiar objects, they are likely to grasp them, bite them, and bang them. In other words, they will try to use existing schemes to learn about these unknown things (see Figure 2.1b). Similarly, a high school student may have a studying scheme that involves putting information on cards and memorizing the cards' contents. She may then try to apply this scheme to learn difficult concepts such as economics, for which this approach may not be effective.

> **CONNECTIONS**
> For information on schema theory (a topic related to schemes) in connection with information processing and memory, see Chapter 6, pages 173 and 191.

schemes
Mental patterns that guide behavior.

adaptation
The process of adjusting schemes in response to the environment by means of assimilation and accommodation.

assimilation
Understanding new experiences in terms of existing schemes.

ON THE WEB
For more on Piaget's life and work go to **www.oikos.org/Piagethom.htm.**

Sometimes, when old ways of dealing with the world simply don't work, a child might modify an existing scheme in light of new information or a new experience, a process called **accommodation.** For example, if you give an egg to a baby who has a banging scheme for small objects, what will happen to the egg is obvious (Figure 2.1c). Less obvious, however, is what will happen to the baby's banging scheme. Because of the unexpected consequences of banging the egg, the baby might change the scheme. In the future the baby might bang some objects hard and others softly. The high school student who studies only by means of memorization might learn to use a different strategy to study economics, such as discussing difficult concepts with a friend.

The baby who banged the egg and the student who tried to memorize rather than comprehend had to deal with situations that could not be fully handled by existing schemes. This, in Piaget's theory, creates a state of disequilibrium, or an imbalance between what is understood and what is encountered. People naturally try to reduce such imbalances by focusing on the stimuli that cause the disequilibrium and developing new schemes or adapting old ones until equilibrium is restored. This process of restoring balance is called **equilibration.** According to Piaget, learning depends on this process. When equilibrium is upset, children have the opportunity to grow and develop. Eventually, qualitatively new ways of thinking about the world emerge, and children advance to a new stage of development. Piaget believed that physical experiences and manipulation of the environment are critical for developmental change to occur. However, he also believed that social interaction with peers, especially arguments and discussions, helps to clarify thinking and, eventually, to make it more logical. Research has stressed the importance of confronting students with experiences or data that do not fit into their current theories of how the world works as a means of advancing their cognitive development (Chinn & Brewer, 1993).

Piaget's theory of development represents **constructivism,** a view of cognitive development as a process in which children actively build systems of meaning and understandings of reality through their experiences and interactions (Berk, 2003; Cook & Cook, 2005). In this view, children actively construct knowledge by continually assimilating and accommodating new information. Applications of constructivist theories to education are discussed in Chapter 8.

Piaget's Stages of Development

Piaget divided the cognitive development of children and adolescents into four stages: sensorimotor, preoperational, concrete operational, and formal operational. He believed that all children pass through these stages in this order and that no child can skip a stage, although different children pass through the stages at somewhat different rates (see de Ribaupierre & Rieben, 1995). The same individuals may perform tasks associated with different stages at the same time, particularly at points of transition into a new stage. Table 2.1 summarizes the approximate ages at which children and adolescents pass through Piaget's four stages. It also shows the major accomplishments of each stage.

Sensorimotor Stage (Birth to Age 2)   The earliest stage is called **sensorimotor,** because during this stage babies and young children explore their world by using their senses and their motor skills.

Piaget believed that all children are born with an innate tendency to interact with and make sense of their environments. Dramatic changes occur as infants progress through the sensorimotor period. Initially, all infants have inborn behaviors called **reflexes.** Touch a newborn's lips, and the baby will begin to suck; place your finger in the palm of an infant's hand, and the infant will grasp it. These and other behaviors are innate and are the building blocks from which the infant's first schemes form.

accommodation
Modifying existing schemes to fit new situations.

equilibration
The process of restoring balance between present understanding and new experiences.

CERTIFICATION POINTER
Most teacher certification tests will require you to know that a constructivist approach to learning emphasizes the active role that learners play in building their own understandings.

constructivism
View of cognitive development that emphasizes the active role of learners in building their own understanding of reality.

sensorimotor stage
Stage during which infants learn about their surroundings by using their senses and motor skills.

reflexes
Inborn, automatic responses to stimuli (e.g., eye blinking in response to bright light).

Table 2.1

Piaget's Stages of Cognitive Development

People progress through four stages of cognitive development between birth and adulthood, according to Jean Piaget. Each stage is marked by the emergence of new intellectual abilities that allow people to understand the world in increasingly complex ways.

Stage	Approximate Ages	Major Accomplishments
Sensorimotor	Birth to 2 years	Formation of concept of "object permanence" and gradual progression from reflexive behavior to goal-directed behavior.
Preoperational	2 to 7 years	Development of the ability to use symbols to represent objects in the world. Thinking remains egocentric and centered.
Concrete operational	7 to 11 years	Improvement in ability to think logically. New abilities include the use of operations that are reversible. Thinking is decentered, and problem solving is less restricted by egocentrism. Abstract thinking is not possible.
Formal operational	11 years to adulthood	Abstract and purely symbolic thinking possible. Problems can be solved through the use of systematic experimentation.

CERTIFICATION POINTER

When responding to the case studies in certification tests you may be asked to identify appropriateness of instruction according to the students' Piagetian stage of development.

object permanence
The fact that an object exists even if it is out of sight.

preoperational stage
Stage at which children learn to represent things in the mind.

conservation
The concept that certain properties of an object (such as weight) remain the same regardless of changes in other properties (such as length).

Infants soon learn to use these reflexes to produce more interesting and intentional patterns of behavior. This learning occurs initially through accident and then through more intentional trial-and-error efforts. According to Piaget, by the end of the sensorimotor stage, children have progressed from their earlier trial-and-error approach to a more planned approach to problem solving. For the first time they can mentally represent objects and events. What most of us would call "thinking" appears now. This is a major advance, because it means that the child can think through and plan behavior. For example, suppose a 2-year-old is in the kitchen watching his mother prepare dinner. If the child knows where the step stool is kept, he may ask to have it set up to afford a better view of the counter and a better chance for a nibble. The child did not stumble on to this solution accidentally. Instead, he thought about the problem, figured out a possible solution that used the step stool, tried out the solution mentally, and only then tried the solution in practice.

Another hallmark of the sensorimotor period is the development of a grasp of **object permanence.** Piaget argued that children must learn that objects are physically stable and exist even when the objects are not in the child's physical presence. For example, if you cover an infant's bottle with a towel, the child may not remove it, believing that the bottle is gone. By 2 years of age, children understand that objects exist even if they cannot be seen. When children develop this notion of object permanence, they have taken a step toward more advanced thinking. Once they realize that things exist out of sight, they can start using symbols to represent these things in their minds so that they can think about them (Cohen & Cashon, 2003).

Preoperational Stage (Ages 2 to 7)   Whereas infants can learn about and understand the world only by physically manipulating objects, preschoolers have greater ability to think about things and can use symbols to mentally represent objects. During the **preoperational stage,** children's language and concepts develop at an incredible rate. Yet much of their thinking remains surprisingly primitive. One of Piaget's earliest and most important discoveries was that young children lacked an understanding of the principle of **conservation.** For example, if you pour milk from a tall, narrow container into a shallow, wide one in the presence of a preoperational child, the child will firmly

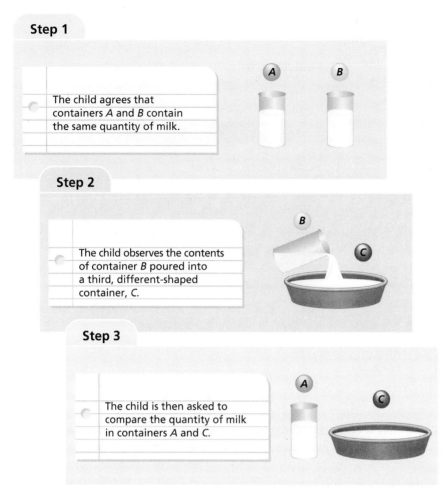

Step 1

The child agrees that containers A and B contain the same quantity of milk.

Step 2

The child observes the contents of container B poured into a third, different-shaped container, C.

Step 3

The child is then asked to compare the quantity of milk in containers A and C.

FIGURE 2.2
The Task of Conservation

A typical procedure for studying conservation of liquid quantity.

From Robert V. Kail and Rita Wicks-Nelson, *Developmental Psychology* (5th ed.), p. 190. Copyright © 1993. Reprinted by permission of Prentice Hall, Upper Saddle River, New Jersey.

believe that the tall glass has more milk (see Figure 2.2). The child focuses on only one aspect (the height of the milk), ignoring all others, and cannot be convinced that the amount of milk is the same. Similarly, a preoperational child is likely to believe that a sandwich cut in four pieces is more sandwich or that a line of blocks that is spread out contains more blocks than a line that is compressed, even after being shown that the number of blocks is identical.

Several aspects of preoperational thinking help to explain the error on conservation tasks. One characteristic is **centration:** paying attention to only one aspect of a situation. In the example illustrated in Figure 2.2, children might have claimed that there was less milk after pouring because they centered on the height of the milk, ignoring its width. In Figure 2.3, children focus on the length of the line of blocks but ignore its density (or the actual number of blocks).

Preschoolers' thinking can also be characterized as being irreversible. **Reversibility** is a very important aspect of thinking, according to Piaget; it simply means the ability to change direction in one's thinking so that one can return to a starting point. As adults, for example, we know that if $7 + 5 = 12$, then $12 - 5 = 7$. If we add 5 things to 7 things and then take the 5 things away (reverse what we've done), we are left with 7 things. If preoperational children could think this way, then they could mentally reverse the process of pouring the milk and realize that if the milk were poured back into the tall beaker, its quantity would not change.

Another characteristic of the preoperational child's thinking is its focus on states. In the milk problem the milk was poured from one container to another. Preschoolers

centration
Paying attention to only one aspect of an object or situation.

reversibility
The ability to perform a mental operation and then reverse one's thinking to return to the starting point.

Which row has more blocks?

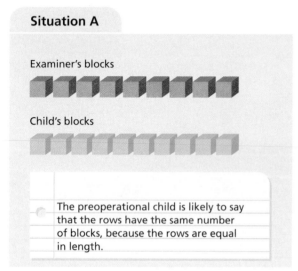

Situation A

Examiner's blocks

Child's blocks

The preoperational child is likely to say that the rows have the same number of blocks, because the rows are equal in length.

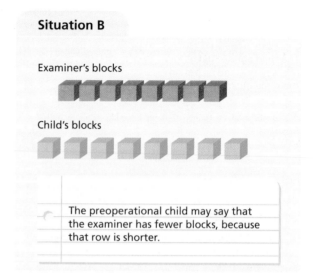

Situation B

Examiner's blocks

Child's blocks

The preoperational child may say that the examiner has fewer blocks, because that row is shorter.

FIGURE 2.3
Centration

Centration, or focusing on only one aspect of a situation, helps to explain some errors in perception that young children make.

From Barry Wadsworth, *Piaget for the Classroom Teacher,* 1978, p. 225, published by Longman Publishing Group. Adapted by permission of the author.

ignore this pouring process and focus only on the beginning state (milk in a tall glass) and end state (milk in a shallow dish). "It is as though [the child] were viewing a series of still pictures instead of the movie that the adult sees" (Phillips, 1975). You can understand how a preoccupation with states can interfere with a child's thinking if you imagine yourself presented with the milk problem and being asked to close your eyes while the milk is poured. Lacking the knowledge of what took place, you would be left with only your perception of the milk in the wide, shallow container and your memory of the milk in the tall, narrow glass. Unlike adults, the young preschooler forms concepts that vary in definition from situation to situation and are not always logical. How else can we explain the 2-year-old's ability to treat a stuffed animal as an inanimate object one minute and an animate object the next? Eventually, though,

How will this child likely respond to the Piagetian conservation task that she is attempting? What stage of development does she demonstrate? As a teacher, how might you help a young child discover errors caused by centration and irreversibility?

the child's concepts become more consistent and less private. Children become increasingly concerned that their definitions of things match other people's. But they still lack the ability to coordinate one concept with another. Consider the following conversation:

Adult: Sally, how many boys are in your play group?
Sally: Eight.
Adult: How many girls are in your play group?
Sally: Five.
Adult: Are there more boys or girls in your play group?
Sally: More boys.
Adult: Are there more boys or children in your play group?
Sally: More boys.
Adult: How do you know?
Sally: I just do!

Sally clearly understands the concepts of *boy, girl, children,* and *more.* However, she lacks the ability to put these separate pieces of knowledge together to correctly answer the question comparing boys and children. She also cannot explain her answer, which is why Piaget used the term *intuitive* to describe her thinking.

Finally, preoperational children are **egocentric** in their thinking. Children at this stage believe that everyone sees the world exactly as they do. For example, Piaget and Inhelder (1956) seated children on one side of a display of three mountains and asked them to describe how the scene looked to a doll seated on the other side. Children below the age of 6 or 7 described the doll's view as being identical to their own, even though it was apparent to adults that this could not be so. Because preoperational children are unable to take the perspective of others, they often interpret events entirely in reference to themselves. A passage from A. A. Milne's *Winnie-the-Pooh* illustrates the young child's egocentrism. Winnie-the-Pooh is sitting in the forest and hears a buzzing sound.

> That buzzing-noise means something. You don't get a buzzing-noise like that just buzzing and buzzing, without its meaning something. If there is a buzzing-noise, somebody's making a buzzing-noise, and the only reason for making a buzzing-noise that I know of is because you're a bee . . . Then he thought for another long time, and said: And the only reason for being a bee that I know of is for making honey . . . And then he got up, and said: And the only reason for making honey is so as I can eat it.

CONNECTIONS

For more on how to accommodate instruction to the developmental characteristics of children and adolescents, see Chapter 3, page 77.

Personal Reflection

Egocentrism in Action

Many years ago I was driving with my two sons, ages 4 and 2, through dairy country in Vermont. The boys were admiring the cows. "Why do farmers keep cows?" I asked them. Ben, the 2-year-old, said "So my [I] can look at them!" Jake, his older and wiser brother disagreed. "The farmer likes to play with them."

These different ideas show how egocentrism develops over time. Ben, at two, thought that everything that happens in the world relates to him. Four-year-old Jake, however, realized that the farmer had his own needs, but assumed that those needs were the same as his.

Reflect on This. How will your understanding of egocentrism help you as a teacher?

egocentric
Believing that everyone views the world as you do.

Concrete Operational Stage (Ages 7 to 11)   Although the differences between the mental abilities of preoperational preschoolers and concrete operational elementary school students are dramatic, concrete operational children still do not think like adults. They are very much rooted in the world as it is and have difficulty with abstract thought. Flavell describes the concrete operational child as taking "an earthbound, concrete, practical-minded sort of problem-solving approach, one that persistently fixates on the perceptible and inferable reality right there in front of him. A theorist the elementary-school child is not" (1985, p. 103). The term **concrete operational stage** reflects this earthbound approach. Children at this stage can form concepts, see relationships, and solve problems, but only as long as they involve objects and situations that are familiar.

During the elementary school years, children's cognitive abilities undergo dramatic changes. Elementary school children no longer have difficulties with conservation problems, because they have acquired the concept of reversibility. For example, they can now see that the amount of milk in the short, wide container must be the same as that in the tall, narrow container, because if the milk were poured back in the tall container, it would be at the same level as before. The child is able to imagine the milk being poured back and can recognize the consequences—abilities that are not evident in the preoperational child.

Another fundamental difference between preoperational and concrete operational children is that the younger child, who is in the preoperational stage, responds to perceived appearances, whereas the older, concrete operational child responds to inferred reality. Flavell (1986) demonstrated this concept by showing children a red car and then, while they were still watching, covering it with a filter that made it appear black. When asked what color the car was, 3-year-olds responded "black," and 6-year-olds responded "red." The older, concrete operational child is able to respond to **inferred reality,** seeing things in the context of other meanings; preschoolers see what they see, with little ability to infer the meaning behind what they see.

One important task that children learn during the concrete operational stage is **seriation,** or arranging things in a logical progression; for example, lining up sticks from smallest to largest. To do this, they must be able to order or classify objects according to some criterion or dimension, in this case length. Once this ability is acquired, children can master a related skill known as **transitivity,** the ability to infer a relationship between two objects on the basis of knowledge of their respective relationships with a third object. For example, if you tell preoperational preschoolers that Tom is taller than Becky and that Becky is taller than Fred, they will not see that Tom is taller than Fred. Logical inferences such as this are not possible until the stage of concrete operations, during which school-age children develop the ability to make two mental transformations that require reversible thinking. The first of these is inversion (+A is reversed by –A), and the second is reciprocity (A < B is reciprocated by B > A). By the end of the concrete operational stage, children have the mental abilities to learn how to add, subtract, multiply, and divide; to place numbers in order by size; and to classify objects by any number of criteria. Children can think about what would happen if . . . , as long as the objects are in view (e.g., "What would happen if I pulled this spring and then let it go?"). Children can understand time and space well enough to draw a map from their home to school and are building an understanding of events in the past.

concrete operational stage
Stage at which children develop the capacity for logical reasoning and understanding of conservation but can use these skills only in dealing with familiar situations.

inferred reality
The meaning of stimuli in the context of relevant information.

seriation
Arranging objects in sequential order according to one aspect, such as size, weight, or volume.

transitivity
A skill learned during the concrete operational stage of cognitive development in which individuals can mentally arrange and compare objects.

Children in the elementary grades also are moving from egocentric thought to decentered or objective thought. Decentered thought allows children to see that others can have different perceptions than they do. For example, children with decentered thought will be able to understand that different children may see different patterns in clouds. Children whose thought processes are decentered are able to learn that events may be governed by physical laws, such as the laws of gravity. A final ability that children acquire during the concrete operational stage is **class inclusion.** Recall the example of Sally, who was in the preoperational stage and believed that there were more boys than children in her play group. What Sally lacked was the ability to think simultaneously about the whole class (children) and the subordinate class (boys, girls). She could make comparisons within a class, as shown by her ability to compare one part (the boys) with another part (the girls). She also knew that boys and girls are both members of the larger class called children. What she could not do was make comparisons between classes. Concrete operational children, by contrast, have no trouble with this type of problem, because they have additional tools of thinking. First, they no longer exhibit irreversibility of thinking and can now re-create a relationship between a part and the whole. Second, concrete operational thought is decentered, so the child can now focus on two classes simultaneously. Third, the concrete operational child's thinking is no longer limited to reasoning about part-to-part relationships. Now part-to-whole relationships can be dealt with too. These changes do not all happen at the same time. Rather, they occur gradually during the concrete operational stage.

Formal Operational Stage (Age 11 to Adulthood) Sometime around the onset of puberty, children's thinking begins to develop into the form that is characteristic of adults. The preadolescent begins to be able to think abstractly and to see possibilities beyond the here and now. These abilities continue to develop into adulthood. With the **formal operational stage** comes the ability to deal with potential or hypothetical situations; the form is now separate from the content.

Inhelder and Piaget (1958) described one task that will be approached differently by elementary school students in the concrete operational stage and by adolescents in the formal operational stage. The children and adolescents were given a pendulum consisting of a string with a weight at the end. They could change the length of the string, the amount of weight, the height from which the pendulum was released, and the force with which the pendulum was pushed. They were asked which of these factors influenced the speed at which the pendulum swings back and forth. Essentially, the task was to discover a principle of physics, which is that only the length of the string makes any difference in the speed of the pendulum (the shorter the string, the faster it swings). This experiment is illustrated in Figure 2.4. The adolescent who has reached the stage of formal operations is likely to proceed quite systematically, varying one factor at a time (e.g., leaving the string the same length and trying different weights). For example, in Inhelder and Piaget's (1958) experiment, one 15-year-old selected 100 grams with a long string and a medium-length string, then 20 grams with a long and a short string, and finally 200 grams with a long and a short string and concluded, "It's the length of the string that makes it go faster and slower; the weight doesn't play any role" (p. 75). In contrast, 10-year-olds (who can be assumed to be in the concrete operational stage) proceeded in a chaotic fashion, varying many factors at the same time and hanging on to preconceptions. One boy varied simultaneously the weight and the impetus (push); then the weight, the impetus, and the length; then the impetus, the weight, and the elevation; and so on. He first concluded, "It's by changing the weight and the push, certainly not the string."

"How do you know that the string has nothing to do with it?"

"Because it's the same string."

INTASC

2 Knowledge of Human Development and Learning

class inclusion
A skill learned during the concrete operational stage of cognitive development in which individuals can think simultaneously about a whole class of objects and about relationships among its subordinate classes.

formal operational stage
Stage at which one can deal abstractly with hypothetical situations and can reason logically.

FIGURE 2.4
A Test of Problem-Solving Abilities
The pendulum problem uses a string, which can be shortened or lengthened, and a set of weights. When children in the concrete operational stage are asked what determines the speed of the pendulum's swing, they will tackle the problem less systematically than will adolescents who have entered the stage for formal operations. (The answer is that only the string's length affects the speed of the pendulum's swing.)

He had not varied its length in the last several trials; previously, he had varied it simultaneously with the impetus, thus complicating the account of the experiment (adapted from Inhelder and Piaget, 1958, p. 71).

The transitivity problem also illustrates the advances brought about by formal thought. Recall the concrete operational child who, when told that Tom was taller than Becky and Becky was taller than Fred, understood that Tom was taller than Fred. However, if the problem had been phrased in the following way, only an older child who had entered the formal operational stage would have solved it: "Becky is shorter than Tom, and Becky is taller than Fred. Who is the tallest of the three?" Here the younger concrete operational child, lost in the combinations of greater-than and less-than relationships, might reason that Becky and Tom are "short," Becky and Fred are "tall," and therefore Fred is the tallest, followed by Becky, and then Tom, who is the shortest. Adolescents in the formal operational stage may also get confused by the differing relationships in this problem, but they can imagine several different relationships among the heights of Becky, Tom, and Fred and can figure out the accuracy of each until they hit on the correct one. This example shows another ability of preadolescents and adolescents who have reached the formal operational stage: They can monitor, or think about, their own thinking.

Generating abstract relationships from available information and then comparing those abstract relationships to each other is a general skill underlying many tasks in which adolescents' competence leaps forward. Piaget (1952a) described a task in which students in the concrete operational stage were given a set of 10 proverbs and a set of statements that meant the same thing as the proverbs. They were asked to match each proverb to the equivalent statement. Again, concrete operational children can understand the task and choose answers. However, their answers are often incorrect because they often do not understand that a proverb describes a general principle. For example, asked to explain the proverb "Don't cry over spilled milk," a child might explain that once milk is spilled, there's nothing to cry about but might not see that the proverb has a broader meaning. Adolescents and adults have little difficulty with this type of task.

CONNECTIONS

For more on thinking about one's own thinking, or metacognition, see Chapter 6, page 192.

Hypothetical Conditions   Another ability that Piaget and others recognized in the young adolescent is the ability to reason about situations and conditions that have not been experienced. The adolescent can accept, for the sake of argument or discussion, conditions that are arbitrary, that are not known to exist, or even that are known to be contrary to fact. Adolescents are not bound to their own experiences of reality, so they can apply logic to any given set of conditions. One illustration of the ability to reason about hypothetical situations is found in formal debate, in which participants must be prepared to defend either side of an issue, regardless of their personal feelings or experience, and their defense is judged on its documentation and logical consistency. For a dramatic illustration of the difference between children and adolescents in the ability to suspend their own opinions, compare the reactions of fourth- and ninth-graders when you ask them to present an argument in favor of the proposition that schools should be in session 6 days a week, 48 weeks a year. The abilities that make up formal operational thought—thinking abstractly, testing hypotheses, and forming concepts that are independent of physical reality—are critical in the learning of higher-order skills. For example, learning algebra or abstract geometry requires the use of formal operational thought, as does understanding difficult concepts in science, social studies, and other subjects.

The thinking characteristic of the formal operations stage usually appears between ages 11 and 15, but there are many individuals who never reach this stage (Niaz, 1997). Individuals tend to use formal operational thinking in some situations and not others, and this remains true into adulthood.

According to Piaget, the formal operational stage brings cognitive development to a close. However, intellectual growth may continue to take place beyond adolescence. According to Piaget, the foundation has been laid, and no new structures need to develop; all that is needed is the addition of knowledge and the development of more complex schemes.

How Is Piaget's Work Viewed Today?

Piaget's theory revolutionized, and in many ways still dominates, the study of human development. However, some of his central principles have been questioned in more recent research, and modern descriptions of development have revised many of his views (see Feldman, 2003).

Criticisms and Revisions of Piaget's Theory

One important Piagetian principle is that development precedes learning. Piaget held that developmental stages were largely fixed and that such concepts as conservation could not be taught. However, research has established some cases in which Piagetian tasks can be taught to children at earlier developmental stages. For example, several researchers have found that young children can succeed on simpler forms of Piaget's tasks that require the same skills (Gelman, 2000; Larivée, Normandeau, & Parent, 2000; Siegler, 1998). Gelman (1979) found that young children could solve the conservation problem involving the number of blocks in a row when the task was presented in a simpler way with simpler language. Boden (1980) found that the same formal operational task produced passing rates from 19 to 98 percent, depending on the complexities of the instructions (see also Nagy & Griffiths, 1982).

Similar kinds of research have also led to a reassessment of children's egocentricity. In simple, practical contexts, children demonstrated their ability to consider the point of view of others (Siegler, 1998). In addition, infants have been shown to demonstrate aspects of object permanence much earlier than Piaget predicted (Baillargeon, Graber, DeVos, & Black, 1990).

The result of this research has been a recognition that children are more competent than Piaget originally thought, especially when their practical knowledge is being assessed. Gelman (1979) suggested that the cognitive abilities of preschoolers are more fragile than those of older children and therefore are evident only under certain conditions. Piaget (1964) responded to such demonstrations by arguing that the children must have been on the verge of the next developmental stage already—but the fact remains that some of the Piagetian tasks can be taught to children well below the age at which they usually appear without instruction.

Another area in which Piaget's work has been criticized goes to the heart of his "stage" theory. Many researchers now doubt that there are broad stages of development affecting all types of cognitive tasks; instead, they argue that children's skills develop in different ways on different tasks and that their experience (including direct teaching in school or elsewhere) can have a strong influence on the pace of development (see Gelman, 2000; Overton, 1998). The evidence is particularly strong that children can be taught to perform well on the Piagetian tasks assessing formal operations, such as the pendulum problems illustrated in Figure 2.4 (Greenbowe, Herron, Nurrenbern, Staver, & Ward, 1981). Clearly, experience matters. De Lisi and Staudt (1980), for example, found that college students were likely to show formal operational reasoning on tasks related to their majors but not on other tasks. Watch an intelligent adult learning to sail. Initially, he or she is likely to engage in a lot of concrete operational behavior, trying everything in a chaotic order, before systematically beginning to learn how to adjust the tiller and the sail to wind and direction (as in formal operational thought).

developmentally appropriate education
Instruction felt to be adapted to the current developmental status of children (rather than to their age alone).

Theory into PRACTICE

Educational Implications of Piaget's Theory

CONNECTIONS
For more on developmentally appropriate practice, see Chapter 3.

INTASC
2 Knowledge of Human Development and Learning
3 Adapting Instruction for Individual Needs

Piaget's theories have had a major impact on the theory and practice of education (Case, 1998). First, the theories focused attention on the idea of **developmentally appropriate education**—an education with environments, curriculum, materials, and instruction that are suitable for students in terms of their physical and cognitive abilities and their social and emotional needs. Piagetian theory has been influential in constructivist models of learning, which will be described in Chapter 8. Berk (2001) summarizes the main teaching implications drawn from Piaget as follows:

1. A focus on the process of children's thinking, not just its products. In addition to checking the correctness of children's answers, teachers must understand the processes children use to get to the answer. Appropriate learning experiences build on children's current level of cognitive functioning, and only when teachers appreciate children's methods of arriving at particular conclusions are they in a position to provide such experiences.

2. Recognition of the crucial role of children's self-initiated, active involvement in learning activities. In a Piagetian classroom the presentation of ready-made knowledge is deemphasized, and children are encouraged to discover for themselves through spontaneous interaction with the environment. Therefore, instead of teaching didactically, teachers provide a rich variety of activities that permit children to act directly on the physical world.

3. A deemphasis on practices aimed at making children adultlike in their thinking. Piaget referred to the question "How can we speed up development?" as "the American question." Among the many countries he visited, psychologists and educators in the United States seemed most interested in what techniques could be used to accelerate children's progress through the stages.

Piagetian-based educational programs accept his firm belief that premature teaching could be worse than no teaching at all, because it leads to superficial acceptance of adult formulas rather than true cognitive understanding (May & Kundert, 1997).

4. Acceptance of individual differences in developmental progress. Piaget's theory assumes that all children go through the same developmental sequence but that they do so at different rates. Therefore, teachers must make a special effort to arrange classroom activities for individuals and small groups of children rather than for the total class group. In addition, because individual differences are expected, assessment of children's educational progress should be made in terms of each child's own previous course of development, not in terms of normative standards provided by the performances of same-age peers.

Neo-Piagetian and Information-Processing Views of Development

CONNECTIONS

For more on information processing, see Chapter 6, page 166.

Neo-Piagetian theories are modifications of Piaget's theory that attempt to overcome the theory's limitations and address problems its critics have identified. In particular, neo-Piagetians have demonstrated that children's abilities to operate at a particular stage depend a great deal on the specific tasks involved (Gelman & Brenneman, 1994); that training and experience, including social interactions, can accelerate children's development (DeVries, 1997; Flavell, Miller, & Miller, 1993); and that culture has an important impact on development (Gelman & Brenneman, 1994; Rogoff & Chavajay, 1995). One example of neo-Piagetian work on cognitive development is proposed by Case (1998), who believes, as did Piaget, that children progress through developmental stages. These stages reflect the kinds of mental representations children can form and how information is processed. The stages proposed by Case are different from those described by Piaget in that ways of processing information become more complex but not necessarily different. Unlike Piaget, Case believes developmental change is based on a child's capacity to process and remember information. According to Case, short-term memory capacity not only increases with physical maturity of the brain but also becomes more efficient with practice and instruction. Research in this direction could lead to a new conceptualization of developmental stages that accounts for the fact that cognitive development proceeds at different rates on different tasks (see Flavell et al., 1993; Gelman & Brenneman, 1994; Siegler, 1998).

Alternatives to Piagetian views of stages of cognitive development include information-processing approaches (Siegler, 1991), based on the idea that people process information in a way similar to computers. Information-processing theorists tend to agree with Piaget's description of cognition but, unlike Piaget, believe that thinking skills can be directly taught. Siegler (1998) observes, for example, that children acquire increasingly powerful rules or procedures for solving problems and can be stimulated to discover deficiencies in their own logic and to apply new logical principles. In other words, they can discern rules and assess their application. In this way, children develop greater capacity for abstract thought. The implications of the rule-assessment approach for education is that stimulating new methods of instruction might actually enhance children's thinking abilities (Sternberg, 1995).

$\mathcal{H}$OW DID VYGOTSKY VIEW COGNITIVE DEVELOPMENT?

INTASC

4 Multiple Instructional Strategies

Lev Semionovich Vygotsky was a Russian psychologist who, though a contemporary of Piaget, died in 1934. His work was not widely read in English until the 1970s,

"I'm sorry, Miss Scott, but this is outside of my zone of proximal development."

CONNECTIONS

For more on self-regulated learning, see Chapter 8, page 248.

sign systems
Symbols that cultures create to help people think, communicate, and solve problems.

self-regulation
The ability to think and solve problems without the help of others.

private speech
Children's self-talk, which guides their thinking and action; eventually internalized as silent inner speech.

zone of proximal development
Level of development immediately above a person's present level.

however, and only since then have his theories become influential in North America. Vygotskian theory is now a powerful force in developmental psychology, and many of the critiques he made of the Piagetian perspective more than 60 years ago have come to the fore today (see Glassman, 2001; John-Steiner & Mahn, 2003).

Vygotsky's work is based on two key ideas. First, he proposed that intellectual development can be understood only in terms of the historical and cultural contexts children experience. Second, he believed that development depends on the **sign systems** that individuals grow up with: the symbols that cultures create to help people think, communicate, and solve problems—for example, a culture's language, writing system, or counting system.

In contrast to Piaget, Vygotsky proposed that cognitive development is strongly linked to input from others. Like Piaget, however, Vygotsky believed that the acquisition of sign systems occurs in an invariant sequence of steps that is the same for all children.

How Development Occurs

Recall that Piaget's theory suggests that development precedes learning. In other words, specific cognitive structures need to develop before certain types of learning can take place. Vygotsky's theory suggests that learning precedes development. For Vygotsky, learning involves the acquisition of signs by means of instruction and information from others. Development involves the child's internalizing these signs so as to be able to think and solve problems without the help of others. This ability is called **self-regulation.**

The first step in the development of self-regulation and independent thinking is learning that actions and sounds have a meaning. For example, a baby learns that the process of reaching toward an object is interpreted by others as a signal that the infant wants the object. In the case of language acquisition, children learn to associate certain sounds with meaning. The second step in developing internal structures and self-regulation involves practice. The infant practices gestures that will get attention. The preschooler will enter into conversations with others to master language. The final step involves using signs to think and solve problems without the help of others. At this point, children become self-regulating, and the sign system has become internalized.

Private Speech   **Private speech** is a mechanism that Vygotsky emphasized for turning shared knowledge into personal knowledge. Vygotsky proposed that children incorporate the speech of others and then use that speech to help themselves solve problems. Private speech is easy to see in young children, who frequently talk to themselves, especially when faced with difficult tasks (Flavell et al., 1997). Later, private speech becomes silent but is still very important. Studies have found that children who make extensive use of private speech learn complex tasks more effectively than do other children (Emerson & Miyake, 2003; Schneider, 2002).

The Zone of Proximal Development   Vygotsky's theory implies that cognitive development and the ability to use thought to control our own actions require first mastering cultural communication systems and then learning to use these systems to regulate our own thought processes. The most important contribution of Vygotsky's theory is an emphasis on the sociocultural nature of learning (Vygotsky, 1978; Karpov & Haywood, 1998). He believed that learning takes place when children are working

How is this parent playing an integral role in his child's learning development? How are scaffolding and cognitive apprenticeship similar?

within their **zone of proximal development.** Tasks within the zone of proximal development are ones that a child cannot yet do alone but could do with the assistance of more competent peers or adults. That is, the zone of proximal development describes tasks that a child has not yet learned but is capable of learning at a given time. Some educators refer to a "teachable moment" when a child or group of children is exactly at the point of readiness for a given concept. Vygotsky further believed that higher mental functioning usually exists in conversation and collaboration among individuals before it exists within the individual.

Scaffolding   A key idea derived from Vygotsky's notion of social learning is that of **scaffolding** (Wood, Bruner, & Ross, 1976): the assistance provided by more competent peers or adults. Typically, scaffolding means providing a child with a great deal of support during the early stages of learning and then diminishing support and having the child take on increasing responsibility as soon as she or he is able (Rosenshine & Meister, 1992). Parents use scaffolding when they teach their children to play a new game or to tie their shoes (Rogoff, 2003). A related concept is cognitive apprenticeship, which describes the entire process of modeling, coaching, scaffolding, and evaluation that is typically seen whenever one-to-one instruction takes place (John-Steiner & Mahn, 2003; Rogoff, 2003). For example, in *Life on the Mississippi*, Mark Twain describes how he was taught to be a steamboat pilot. At first the experienced pilot talked him through every bend in the river, but gradually he was left to figure things out for himself, with the pilot there to intervene only if the boat was about to run aground.

Cooperative Learning   Vygotsky's theories support the use of cooperative learning strategies in which children work together to help one another learn (Slavin, Hurley, & Chamberlain, 2003). Because peers are usually operating within each others' zones of proximal development, they provide models for each other of slightly more advanced thinking. In addition, cooperative learning makes children's inner speech available to others, so they can gain insight into one another's reasoning process. Vygotsky (1978) himself recognized the value of peer interaction in moving children forward in their thinking.

CONNECTIONS
For more on scaffolding, see Chapter 8, page 000.

scaffolding
Support for learning and problem solving; might include clues, reminders, encouragement, breaking the problem down into steps, providing an example, or anything else that allows the student to grow in independence as a learner.

CONNECTIONS
For more on cooperative learning, see Chapter 8, pages 245 and 255.

FIGURE 2.5
Teaching Model Based on Vygotsky's Theory
In (a) the child performs a learned task; in (b) the child is assisted by a teacher or peer who interacts with the child to help him move into a new zone of proximal development (unlearned tasks at limits of learner's abilities) with a new learned task.

a.
Learned task

b.
Assisted learning at zone of proximal development

Applications of Vygotskian Theory in Teaching

Vygotsky's theories of education have two major implications. One is the desirability of setting up cooperative learning arrangements among groups of students with differing levels of ability. Tutoring by more competent peers can be effective in promoting growth within the zone of proximal development (Das, 1995). Second, a Vygotskian approach to instruction emphasizes scaffolding, with students taking more and more responsibility for their own learning. (See Figure 2.5.) For example, in reciprocal teaching, teachers lead small groups of students in asking questions about material they have read and gradually turn over responsibility for leading the discussion to the students (Palincsar, Brown, & Martin, 1987). Tharp and Gallimore (1988) emphasized scaffolding in an approach they called "assisted discovery," which calls for explicitly teaching students to use private speech to talk themselves through problem solving.

ON THE WEB

To learn more about applications of Vygotsky's theories to education practice visit **mathforum.org/mathed/vygotsky.html.**

Theory into **PRACTICE**

Classroom Applications of Vygotsky's Theory

Vygotsky's concept of the zone of proximal development is based on the idea that development is defined both by what a child can do independently and by what the child can do when assisted by an adult or more competent peer (John-

Steiner & Mahn, 2003). Knowing both levels of Vygotsky's zone is useful for teachers, for these levels indicate where the child is at a given moment as well as where the child is going. The zone of proximal development has several implications for teaching in the classroom.

According to Vygotsky, for the curriculum to be developmentally appropriate, the teacher must plan activities that encompass not only what children are capable of doing on their own but what they can learn with the help of others (Karpov & Haywood, 1998).

Vygotsky's theory does not mean that anything can be taught to any child. Only instruction and activities that fall within the zone promote development. For example, if a child cannot identify the sounds in a word even after many prompts, the child may not benefit immediately from instruction in this skill. Practice of previously known skills and introduction of concepts that are too difficult and complex have little positive impact. Teachers can use information about both levels of Vygotsky's zone of proximal development in organizing classroom activities in the following ways:

- Instruction can be planned to provide practice in the zone of proximal development for individual children or for groups of children. For example, hints and prompts that helped children during the assessment could form the basis of instructional activities.
- Cooperative learning activities can be planned with groups of children at different levels who can help each other learn (Slavin et al., 2003).
- Scaffolding (John-Steiner & Mahn, 2003) provides hints and prompts at different levels. In scaffolding, the adult does not simplify the task, but the role of the learner is simplified "through the graduated intervention of the teacher."

For example, a child might be shown pennies to represent each sound in a word (e.g., three pennies for the three sounds in "man"). To master this word, the child might be asked to place a penny on the table to show each sound in a word, and finally the child might identify the sounds without the pennies. When the adult provides the child with pennies, the adult provides a scaffold to help the child move from assisted to unassisted success at the task (Spector, 1992). In a high school laboratory science class, a teacher might provide scaffolding by first giving students detailed guides to carrying out experiments, then giving them brief outlines that they might use to structure experiments, and finally asking them to set up experiments entirely on their own.

CONNECTIONS

For more on reciprocal teaching, see Chapter 8, page 251.

CERTIFICATION POINTER

Lev Vygotsky's work will probably be on your teacher certification test. You may be required to know that the zone of proximal development is the level of development just above where a student is presently functioning and why this is important for both teachers and students.

How DID ERIKSON VIEW PERSONAL AND SOCIAL DEVELOPMENT?

As children improve their cognitive skills, they are also developing self-concepts, ways of interacting with others, and attitudes toward the world. Understanding of these personal and social developments is critical to the teacher's ability to motivate, teach, and successfully interact with students at various ages. Like cognitive development, personal and social development is often described in terms of stages. We speak of the "terrible twos," not the "terrible ones" or "terrible threes"; and when someone is reacting in an unreasonable, selfish way, we accuse that person of "behaving like a 2-year-old." The words *adolescent* and *teenager* are associated in Western culture with rebelliousness, identity crises, hero worship, and sexual awakening. These associations reflect stages of development that we believe everyone goes through. This section focuses on a theory of personal and social development proposed by Erik Erikson, which is an adaptation of the developmental theories of the great psychiatrist Sigmund Freud. Erikson's work is often called a **psychosocial theory,** because it relates principles of psychological and social development.

Stages of Psychosocial Development

psychosocial theory
A set of principles that relates social environment to psychological development.

psychosocial crisis
According to Erikson, the set of critical issues that individuals must address as they pass through each of the eight life stages.

Like Piaget, Erikson had no formal training in psychology, but as a young man he was trained by Freud as a psychoanalyst. Erikson hypothesized that people pass through eight psychosocial stages in their lifetimes. At each stage, there are crises or critical issues to be resolved. Most people resolve each **psychosocial crisis** satisfactorily and put it behind them to take on new challenges, but some people do not completely resolve these crises and must continue to deal with them later in life (Miller, 1993). For example, many adults have yet to resolve the "identity crisis" of adolescence. Table 2.2 summarizes the eight stages of life according to Erikson's theory. Each is identified by the central crisis that must be resolved.

Stage I: Trust versus Mistrust (Birth to 18 Months)   The goal of infancy is to develop a basic trust in the world. Erikson (1968, p. 96) defined basic trust as "an essential

Table 2.2				
Erikson's Stages of Personal and Social Development				

As people grow, they face a series of psychosocial crises that shape personality, according to Erik Erikson. Each crisis focuses on a particular aspect of personality and involves the person's relationship with other people.

Stage	*Approximate Ages*	*Psychosocial Crises*	*Significant Relationships*	*Psychosocial Emphasis*
I	Birth to 18 months	Trust vs. mistrust	Maternal person	To get To give in return
II	18 months to 3 years	Autonomy vs. doubt	Parental persons	To hold on To let go
III	3 to 6 years	Initiative vs. guilt	Basic family	To make (= going after) To "make like" (= playing)
IV	6 to 12 years	Industry vs. inferiority	Neighborhood, school	To make things To make things together
V	12 to 18 years	Identity vs. role confusion	Peer groups and models of leadership	To be oneself (or not to be) To share being oneself
VI	Young adulthood	Intimacy vs. isolation	Partners in friendship, sex, competition, cooperation	To lose and find oneself in another
VII	Middle adulthood	Generativity vs. self-absorption	Divided labor and shared household	To take care of
VIII	Late adulthood	Integrity vs. despair	"Mankind," "My kind"	To be, through having been To face not being

Source: From "Figure of Erikson's Stages of Personality Development," *Childhood and Society* by Erik H. Erikson. Copyright 1950, © 1963 by W. W. Norton & Company, Inc. renewed © 1978, 1991 by Erik H. Erikson. Reprinted by permission of W. W. Norton & Company, Inc.

trustfulness of others as well as a fundamental sense of one's own trustworthiness." This crisis has a dual nature: Infants not only have their needs met, but they also help in meeting the mother's needs. The mother, or maternal figure, is usually the first important person in the child's world. She is the one who must satisfy the infant's need for food and affection. If the mother is inconsistent or rejecting, she becomes a source of frustration for the infant rather than a source of pleasure (Cummings, Braungart-Rieker, & Du Rocher-Schudlich, 2003; Thompson, Easterbrooks, & Padilla-Walker, 2003). The mother's behavior creates in the infant a sense of mistrust for his or her world that may persist throughout childhood and into adulthood.

Stage II: Autonomy versus Doubt (18 Months to 3 Years)   By the age of 2, most babies can walk and have learned enough about language to communicate with other people. Children in the "terrible twos" no longer want to depend totally on others. Instead, they strive toward autonomy, the ability to do things for themselves. The child's desires for power and independence often clash with the desires of the parent. Erikson believes that children at this stage have the dual desire to hold on and to let go. Parents who are flexible enough to permit their children to explore freely and do things for themselves, while at the same time providing an ever-present guiding hand, encourage the establishment of a sense of autonomy. Parents who are overly restrictive and harsh give their children a sense of powerlessness and incompetence, which can lead to shame and doubt in one's abilities.

Stage III: Initiative versus Guilt (3 to 6 Years)   During this period, children's continually maturing motor and language skills permit them to be increasingly aggressive and vigorous in the exploration of both their social and their physical environment. Three-year-olds have a growing sense of initiative, which can be encouraged by parents, other family members, and other caregivers who permit children to run, jump, play, slide, and throw. "Being firmly convinced that he is a person on his own, the child must now find out what kind of person he may become" (Erikson, 1968, p. 115). Parents who severely punish children's attempts at initiative will make the children feel guilty about their natural urges both during this stage and later in life.

Stage IV: Industry versus Inferiority (6 to 12 Years)   Entry into school brings with it a huge expansion in the child's social world. Teachers and peers take on increasing importance for the child, while the influence of parents decreases. Children now want to make things. Success brings with it a sense of industry, a good feeling about oneself and one's abilities. Failure creates a negative self-image, a sense of inadequacy that may hinder future learning. And "failure" need not be real; it may be merely an inability to measure up to one's own standards or those of parents, teachers, or brothers and sisters.

Stage V: Identity versus Role Confusion (12 to 18 Years)   The question "Who am I?" becomes important during adolescence. To answer it, adolescents increasingly turn away from parents and toward peer groups. Erikson believed that during adolescence the individual's rapidly changing physiology, coupled with pressures to make decisions about future education and career, creates the need to question and redefine the psychosocial identity established during the earlier stages. Adolescence is a time of change. Teenagers experiment with various sexual, occupational, and educational roles as they try to find out who they are and who they can be. This new sense of self, or "ego identity," is not simply the sum of the prior identifications. Rather, it is a reassembly or "an alignment of the individual's basic drives (ego) with his or her endowment (resolutions of the previous crises) and his or her opportunities (needs, skills, goals, and demands of adolescence and approaching adulthood)" (Erikson, 1980, p. 94).

CERTIFICATION POINTER
For teacher certification tests you will probably be asked about Erik Erikson's stages of personal and social development. You should know that vigorous exploration of their physical and social behavior is a behavior typical of children in Stage III, Initiative versus Guilt.

According to Erikson, what is the most important question these young people are trying to answer about themselves at this stage in their development? How might it manifest itself in their behavior? What challenges can this pose for you as a teacher?

Stage VI: Intimacy versus Isolation (Young Adulthood)   Once young people know who they are and where they are going, the stage is set for the sharing of their life with another. The young adult is now ready to form a new relationship of trust and intimacy with another individual, a "partner in friendship, sex, competition, and co-operation." This relationship should enhance the identity of both partners without stifling the growth of either. The young adult who does not seek out such intimacy or whose repeated tries fail may retreat into isolation.

Stage VII: Generativity versus Self-Absorption (Middle Adulthood)   Generativity is "the interest in establishing and guiding the next generation" (Erikson, 1980, p. 103). Typically, people attain generativity through raising their own children. However, the crisis of this stage can also be successfully resolved through other forms of productivity and creativity, such as teaching. During this stage, people should continue to grow; if they don't, a sense of "stagnation and interpersonal impoverishment" develops, leading to self-absorption or self-indulgence (Erikson, 1980, p. 103).

Stage VIII: Integrity versus Despair (Late Adulthood)   In the final stage of psychosocial development, people look back over their lifetime and resolve their final identity crisis. Acceptance of accomplishments, failures, and ultimate limitations brings with it a sense of integrity, or wholeness; a realization that one's life has been one's own responsibility. The finality of death must also be faced and accepted. Despair can occur in those who regret the way they have led their lives or how their lives have turned out.

Implications and Criticisms of Erikson's Theory

As with Piaget's stages, not all people experience Erikson's crises to the same degree or at the same time. The age ranges stated here may represent the best times for a crisis to be resolved, but they are not the only possible times. For example, children who were born into chaotic homes that failed to give them adequate security may develop trust after being adopted or otherwise brought into a more stable environment. People whose negative school experiences gave them a sense of inferiority may find as they enter the work world that they can learn and that they do have valuable skills, a realization that may help them finally to resolve the industry versus inferiority crisis that others resolved in their elementary school years. Erikson's theory emphasizes the role of the environment, both in causing the crises and in determining how they will be resolved. The stages of personal and social development are played out in constant interactions with others and with society as a whole. During the first three stages the interactions are primarily with parents and other family members, but the school plays a central role for most children in Stage IV (industry versus inferiority) and Stage V (identity versus role confusion).

Erikson's theory describes the basic issues that people confront as they go through life. However, his theory has been criticized because it does not explain how or why individuals progress from one stage to another, and because it is difficult to confirm through research (Green, 1989; Miller, 1993).

WHAT ARE SOME THEORIES OF MORAL DEVELOPMENT?

INTASC

2 Knowledge of Human Development and Learning

4 Multiple Instructional Strategies

Society could not function without rules that tell people how to communicate with one another, how to avoid hurting others, and how to get along in life generally. If you are around children much, you may have noticed that they are often rigid about rules. Things are either right or wrong; there is no in-between. If you think back to your own years in middle school or high school, you may recall being shocked to find that people sometimes break rules on purpose and that the rules that apply to some people may not apply to others. These experiences probably changed your concept of rules. Your idea of laws may also have changed when you learned how they are made. People meet and debate and vote; the laws that are made one year can be changed the next. The more complexity you can see, the more you find exists. Just as children differ from adults in cognitive and personal development, they also differ in their moral reasoning. First we will look at the two stages of moral reasoning described by Piaget; then we will discuss related theories developed by Lawrence Kohlberg. Piaget proposed that there is a relationship between the cognitive stages of development and the ability to reason about moral issues. Kohlberg believed that the development of the logical structures proposed by Piaget is necessary to, although not sufficient for, advances in the area of moral judgment and reasoning.

Piaget's Theory of Moral Development

Piaget's theory of cognitive development also included a theory about the development of moral reasoning. Piaget believed that cognitive structures and abilities develop first. Cognitive abilities then determine children's abilities to reason about social situations. As with cognitive abilities, Piaget proposed that moral development progresses in predictable stages, in this case from a very egocentric type of moral reasoning to one based on a system of justice based on cooperation and reciprocity. Table 2.3 summarizes Piaget's stages of moral development.

To understand children's moral reasoning, Piaget spent a great deal of time watching children play marbles and asking them about the rules of the game. The first thing he discovered was that before about the age of 6, children play by their own idiosyncratic rules. Piaget believed that very young children were incapable of interacting in cooperative ways and therefore unable to engage in moral reasoning.

Piaget found that by the age of 6, children acknowledged the existence of rules, though they were inconsistent in following them. Frequently, several children who were supposedly playing the same game were observed to be playing by different sets

Table 2.3	
Piaget's Stages of Moral Development	
As people develop their cognitive abilities, their understanding of moral problems also becomes more sophisticated. Young children are more rigid in their view of right and wrong than older children and adults tend to be.	

Heteronomous Morality (Younger)	*Autonomous Morality (Older)*
Based on relations of constraint; for example, the complete acceptance by the child of adult prescriptions.	Based on relations of cooperation and mutual recognition of equality among autonomous individuals, as in relations between people who are equals.
Reflected in attitudes of *moral realism*: Rules are seen as inflexible requirements, external in origin and authority, not open to negotiation; and right is a matter of literal obedience to adults and rules.	Reflected in *rational* moral attitudes: Rules are viewed as products of mutual agreement, open to renegotiation, made legitimate by personal acceptance and common consent, and right is a matter of acting in accordance with the requirements of cooperation and mutual respect.
Badness is judged in terms of the objective form and consequences of actions; fairness is equated with the content of adult decisions; arbitrary and severe punishments are seen as fair.	Badness is viewed as relative to the actor's intentions; fairness is defined as equal treatment or taking account of individual needs; fairness of punishment is defined by appropriateness to the offense.
Punishment is seen as an automatic consequence of the offense, and justice is seen as inherent.	Punishment is seen as affected by human intention.

Source: From *Social and Personality Development*, 1st edition by Michael E. Lamb, p. 213, © 1978. Reprinted with permission of Wadsworth, a division of Thomson Learning: www.thomsonrights.com. Fax 800-730-2215.

heteronomous morality
In Piaget's theory of moral development, the stage at which children think that rules are unchangeable and that breaking them leads automatically to punishment.

autonomous morality
In Piaget's theory of moral development, the stage at which a person understands that people make rules and that punishments are not automatic.

of rules. Children at this age also had no understanding that game rules are arbitrary and something that a group can decide by itself. Instead, they saw rules as being imposed by some higher authority and unchangeable.

Piaget (1964) labeled the first stage of moral development **heteronomous morality;** it has also been called the stage of "moral realism" or "morality of constraint." *Heteronomous* means being subject to rules imposed by others. During this period, young children are consistently faced with parents and other adults telling them what to do and what not to do. Violations of rules are believed to bring automatic punishment. Justice is seen as automatic, and people who are bad will eventually be punished. Piaget also described children at this stage as judging the morality of behavior on the basis of its consequences. They judge behavior as bad if it results in negative consequences even if the actor's original intentions were good.

Piaget found that children did not conscientiously use and follow rules until the age of 10 or 12 years, when children are capable of formal operations. At this age, every child playing the game followed the same set of rules. Children understood that the rules existed to give the game direction and to minimize disputes between players. They understood that rules were something that everyone agreed on and that therefore, if everyone agreed to change them, they could be changed.

Piaget also observed that children at this age tend to base moral judgments on the intentions of the actor rather than the consequences of the actions. Children often engage in discussions of hypothetical circumstances that might affect rules. This second stage is labeled **autonomous morality** or "morality of cooperation." It arises as the child's social world expands to include more and more peers. By continually interacting and cooperating with other children, the child's ideas about rules and therefore morality begin to change. Rules are now what we make them to be. Punishment for transgressions is no longer automatic but must be administered with a consideration of the transgressor's intentions and extenuating circumstances.

According to Piaget, children progress from the stage of heteronomous morality to that of autonomous morality with the development of cognitive structures but also because of interactions with equal-status peers. He believed that resolving conflicts with peers weakened children's reliance on adult authority and heightened their awareness that rules are changeable and should exist only as the result of mutual consent.

Research on elements of Piaget's theories generally supports his ideas, with one key exception. Piaget is felt to have underestimated the degree to which even very young children consider intentions in judging behavior (see Bussey, 1992). However, the progression from a focus on outcomes to a focus on intentions over the course of development has been documented many times.

Kohlberg's Stages of Moral Reasoning

Kohlberg's (1963, 1969) stage theory of moral reasoning is an elaboration and refinement of Piaget's. Like Piaget, Kohlberg studied how children (and adults) reason about rules that govern their behavior in certain situations. Kohlberg did not study children's game playing, but rather probed for their responses to a series of structured situations or **moral dilemmas.** His most famous one is the following:

> In Europe a woman was near death from cancer. One drug might save her, a form of radium that a druggist in the same town had recently discovered. The druggist was charging $2,000, ten times what the drug cost him to make. The sick woman's husband, Heinz, went to everyone he knew to borrow the money, but he could only get together about half of what it cost. He told the druggist that his wife was dying and asked him to sell it cheaper or let him pay later. But the druggist said "No." The husband got desperate and broke into the man's store to steal the drug for his wife. Should the husband have done that? Why? (1969, p. 379)

On the basis of the answers he received, Kohlberg proposed that people pass through a series of six stages of moral judgment or reasoning. Kohlberg's levels and stages are summarized in Table 2.4. He grouped these six stages into three levels: preconventional, conventional, and postconventional. These three levels are distinguished by how the child or adult defines what he or she perceives as correct or moral behavior. As with other stage theories, each stage is more sophisticated and more complex than the preceding one, and most individuals proceed through them in the same order (Colby & Kohlberg, 1984). Like Piaget, Kohlberg was concerned not so much with the direction of the child's answer as with the reasoning behind it. The ages at which children and adolescents go through the stages in Table 2.4 may vary considerably; in fact, the same individual may behave according to one stage at some times and according to another at other times. However, most children pass from the preconventional to the conventional level by the age of 9 (Kohlberg, 1969).

ON THE WEB

The Association for Moral Education (AME) provides an interdisciplinary forum for individuals interested in the moral dimensions of educational theory and practice at **www.amenetwork.org.**

CERTIFICATION POINTER

Teacher certification tests are likely to require you to know the theoretical contributions of Lawrence Kohlberg to the understanding of children's development of moral reasoning.

moral dilemmas
In Kohlberg's theory of moral reasoning, hypothetical situations that require a person to consider values of right and wrong.

Table 2.4

Kohlberg's Stages of Moral Reasoning

When people consider moral dilemmas, it is their reasoning that is important, not their final decision, according to Lawrence Kohlberg. He theorized that people progress through three levels as they develop abilities of moral reasoning.

I. Preconventional Level	*II. Conventional Level*	*III. Postconventional Level*
Rules are set down by others. **Stage 1: Punishment and Obedience Orientation.** Physical consequences of action determine its goodness or badness. **Stage 2: Instrumental Relativist Orientation.** What is right is whatever satisfies one's own needs and occasionally the needs of others. Elements of fairness and reciprocity are present, but they are mostly interpreted in a "you scratch my back, I'll scratch yours" fashion.	Individual adopts rules and will sometimes subordinate own needs to those of the group. Expectations of family, group, or nation seen as valuable in own right, regardless of immediate and obvious consequences. **Stage 3: "Good Boy–Good Girl" Orientation.** Good behavior is whatever pleases or helps others and is approved of by them. One earns approval by being "nice." **Stage 4: "Law and Order" Orientation.** Right is doing one's duty, showing respect for authority, and maintaining the given social order for its own sake.	People define own values in terms of ethical principles they have chosen to follow. **Stage 5: Social Contract Orientation.** What is right is defined in terms of general individual rights and in terms of standards that have been agreed on by the whole society. In contrast to Stage 4, laws are not "frozen"—they can be changed for the good of society. **Stage 6: Universal Ethical Principle Orientation.** What is right is defined by decision of conscience according to self-chosen ethical principles. These principles are abstract and ethical (such as the Golden Rule), not specific moral prescriptions (such as the Ten Commandments).

Source: From L. Kohlberg, "Stage and Sequence: The Cognitive–Developmental Approach to Socialization." In David A. Goslin (Ed.), *Handbook of Socialization Theory and Research,* pp. 347–380, 1969, published by Rand McNally, Chicago. Adapted by permission of David A. Goslin.

preconventional level of morality

Stages 1 and 2 in Kohlberg's model of moral reasoning, in which individuals make moral judgments in their own interests.

conventional level of morality

Stages 3 and 4 in Kohlberg's model of moral reasoning, in which individuals make moral judgments in consideration of others.

postconventional level of morality

Stages 5 and 6 in Kohlberg's model of moral reasoning, in which individuals make moral judgments in relation to abstract principles.

Stage 1, which is on the **preconventional level of morality,** is very similar in form and content to Piaget's stage of heteronomous morality. Children simply obey authority figures to avoid being punished. In Stage 2, children's own needs and desires become important, yet they are aware of the interests of other people. In a concrete sense they weigh the interests of all parties when making moral judgments, but they are still "looking out for number one." The **conventional level of morality** begins at Stage 3. Here morality is defined in terms of cooperation with peers, just as it was in Piaget's stage of autonomous morality. This is the stage at which children have an unquestioning belief that one should "do unto others as you would have them do unto you." Because of the decrease in egocentrism that accompanies concrete operations, children are cognitively capable of putting themselves in someone else's shoes. They can consider the feelings of others when making moral decisions. No longer do they simply do what will not get them punished (Stage 1) or what makes them feel good (Stage 2). At Stage 4, society's rules and laws replace those of the peer group. A desire for social approval no longer determines moral judgments. Laws are followed without question, and breaking the law can never be justified. Most adults are probably at this stage. Stage 5 signals entrance into the **postconventional level of morality.** This level of moral reasoning is attained by fewer than 25 percent of adults, according to

Kohlberg. Here there is a realization that the laws and values of a society are somewhat arbitrary and particular to that society. Laws are seen as necessary to preserve the social order and to ensure the basic right of life and liberty. In Stage 6, one's ethical principles are self-chosen and based on abstract concepts such as justice and the equality and value of human rights. Laws that violate these principles can and should be disobeyed because "justice is above the law." Late in life, Kohlberg (1978, 1984) speculated that Stage 6 is not really separate from Stage 5 and suggested that the two be combined.

Kohlberg (1969) believed that moral dilemmas can be used to advance a child's level of moral reasoning, but only one stage at a time. He theorized that the way in which children progress from one stage to the next is by interacting with others whose reasoning is one or, at most, two stages above their own. Teachers can help students progress in moral reasoning by weaving discussions of justice and moral issues into their lessons, particularly in response to events that occur in the classroom or in the broader society (see Nucci, 1987).

Kohlberg found that his stages of moral reasoning ability occurred in the same order and at about the same ages in the United States, Mexico, Taiwan, and Turkey. Other research throughout the world has generally found the same sequence of stages (Eckensberger, 1994), although there are clearly strong influences of culture on moral reasoning as well as moral behavior (Navaez, Getz, Rest, & Thoma, 1999).

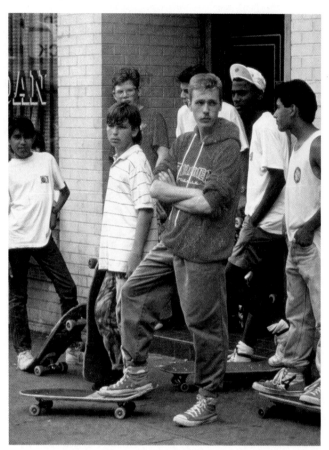

What influence can older children have on the development of moral reasoning in younger children? How can an understanding of moral reasoning help you as a teacher?

Theory into **PRACTICE**

Fostering Moral Development in the Classroom

The study of moral development is one of the oldest topics of interest to those curious about human nature, but the implementation of moral education curricula has not taken place without controversy. Educators and families active in these endeavors have grappled with the important distinction that theories deal with moral reasoning rather than with actual moral behavior. Successful programs have incorporated values education at the global, local, and individual levels.

Global Level—Districtwide Approach. Many schools have chosen to institutionalize a global, inclusive approach to character building with input from teachers, administrators, parents, and, at the higher grade levels, even students (see Kohlberg, 1980; Lickona, 1992). Here, values education is found across the curriculum, implemented throughout the school building, and connected to the home. Such programs emphasize the individual citizen as a member of the social institution and advocate particular levels of moral behavior. They provide students with a framework of expected behavior;

violations of these standards can then be addressed. At the elementary level, students receive guidelines and are invited to discuss violations and their consequences. In middle school and throughout the high school years, students are more involved in the creation and maintenance of guidelines and even play a significant role in the decision making surrounding violations of the guidelines.

Local Level—Classroom Instruction. At the more local level, the teacher might choose to capitalize on students' natural curiosity and might teach values and decision making through "What if . . . ?" discussions. The classroom is an ideal laboratory in which students can test hypothetical situations and potential consequences. Teachers must recognize the cognitive abilities of those in their class and maximize these abilities through problem-solving activities. Being an effective moral educator is no easy task. Teachers must reexamine their teaching role; they must be willing to create cognitive conflict in their classrooms and to stimulate social perspective taking in students (see Reimer, Paolitto, & Hersh, 1990).

Individual Level—Conflict Management. The shootings in Jonesboro, Arkansas; Columbine, Colorado; and elsewhere in recent years clearly showed the most horrific face of school violence and drew attention to the overall problem of violence in schools. Families want schools to provide students with the necessary tools to mediate serious conflicts without violence, and teachers and administrators are evaluating or initiating conflict resolution programs in many schools (see Bodine, Crawford, & Schrumpf, 1994).

Children's conflicts and their understanding of conflict-related events are a critical context for the development of both their moral understanding and their behavior (see Killen, 1996). Although a great deal of attention is given to aggressive conflicts because of the nature of the consequences, nonaggressive conflicts are more pervasive across all age and grade levels. Many children's conflicts require them to coordinate both moral and personal elements. In peer-peer conflicts children explore the boundaries between their own legitimate personal needs and goals and the legitimate needs and goals of others.

Teachers are in a position to foster the necessary social skills to allow students to become autonomous and socially competent individuals. Through the use of cooperative learning, a teacher builds a collaborative atmosphere in the classroom. This collaboration is an opportunity for each student to demonstrate the social competence that helps the group reach equitable solutions while fostering personal success. Noddings (1995) suggested organizing curriculum around "themes of care," to build social competence, tolerance, and altruism throughout children's development.

Through efforts like these to foster sound moral development, teachers play a tremendous role in preparing students to be good citizens in a world in which the potential for conflicts continues to increase.

Criticisms of Kohlberg's Theory

CONNECTIONS

For more on gender issues in education, see Chapter 4, page 118.

One limitation of Kohlberg's work is that it mostly involved boys. Research on girls' moral reasoning finds patterns that are somewhat different from those proposed by Kohlberg. Whereas boys' moral reasoning revolves primarily around issues of justice, girls are more concerned about issues of caring and responsibility for others (Gilligan, 1982, 1985; Gilligan & Attanucci, 1988; Haspe & Baddeley, 1991). Carol Gilligan has argued, for example, that males and females use different moral criteria: that male moral reasoning is focused on people's individual rights, whereas female moral reasoning is focused more on individuals' responsibilities for other people. This is why, she argues, females tend to suggest altruism and self-sacrifice rather than rights and rules as solutions to moral dilemmas (Gilligan, 1982). Kohlberg (Levine, Kohlberg, & Hewer, 1985) later revised his theory on the basis of these criticisms. However, most research has failed to find any male–female differences in moral maturity (Bee & Boyd, 2003; Jaffee & Hyde, 2000; Thoma & Rest, 1998); nor is there convincing evidence that women are more caring, cooperative, or helpful than men (Turiel, 1998; Walker, 1991).

Another criticism of both Piaget's and Kohlberg's work is that young children can often reason about moral situations in more sophisticated ways than a stage theory would suggest (Rest, Edwards, & Thoma, 1997). For example, although young children often consider consequences to be more important than intentions when evaluating conduct, under certain circumstances, children as young as 3 and 4 years of age use intentions to judge the behavior of others (Bussey, 1992). Six- to 10-year-olds at the stage of heteronomous morality have also been shown to make distinctions between rules that parents are justified in making and enforcing and rules that are under personal or peer jurisdiction (Laupa, 1991; Tisak & Tisak, 1990). Finally, Turiel (1998) has suggested that young children make a distinction between moral rules, such as

---

Personal Reflection

INTASC **2 Knowledge of Human Development and Learning**

Developing Character

For a number of years now a "character education" movement has sought solutions to what many in the public perceive as a decline in the moral character of the nation, in general, and of young people specifically. In an article entitled "Moral Teachers, Moral Students" in the March 2003 issue of *Educational Leadership,* author and educator Rick Weissbourd of Harvard argued that "schools can best support students' moral development by helping teachers manage the stresses of their profession and by increasing teachers' capacity for reflection and empathy." The following is an excerpt from his article:

Once again, the public frets about whether children are becoming good people. Both conservative commentators and researchers decry a steady rise in greed, delinquency, and disrespect. And once again, the public holds schools largely responsible for remedying these troubles.

"Solutions" abound. Many character education efforts in schools now focus on everything from community service to teaching students virtues, building good habits, rewarding positive behavior, and developing students' capacity for moral reasoning (Schaps, Schaeffer, & McDonnell, 2001).

There is value in these solutions. Students surely benefit from performing community service, being reminded of important virtues, and practicing good habits.

But we have been wringing our hands and trying these solutions for decades, in some cases for two centuries, without fundamentally changing students' moral prospects. The moral development of students does not depend primarily on explicit character education efforts but on the maturity and ethical capacities of the adults with whom they interact—especially parents, but also teachers, coaches, and other community adults.

Educators influence students' moral development not simply by being good role models—important as that is—but also by what they bring to their relationships with students day to day: their ability to appreciate students' perspectives and to disentangle them from their own, their ability to admit and learn from moral error, their moral energy and idealism, their generosity, and their ability to help students develop moral thinking without shying away from their own moral authority. That level of influence makes being an adult in a school a profound moral challenge. And it means that we will never greatly improve students' moral development in schools without taking on the complex task of developing adults' maturity and ethical capacities. We need to rethink the nature of moral development itself.

Reflect on This. Do you agree or disagree with Weissbourd's perspective on moral development? As a student or a teacher, have you had occasion to admit or learn from moral errors? How could your actions influence your students' moral development? Why are teachers important role models in their students development?

Teaching Dilemmas: Cases to Consider

Using Moral Reasoning

Ms. Jackson administered a unit test to students in her eighth-grade pre-algebra class. As the class began to take the test, however, she was summoned to the office for an urgent call. Rather than interrupt the activity flow, she quickly appointed Nichole, a high-achieving student who always finished tests early, to serve as classroom monitor during her absence. Ms. Jackson expected to be back in class in only a few minutes. She thought the students might not even notice she was gone. Unfortunately, Ms. Jackson was detained. As Nichole watched with growing alarm, Rafael and Martin began to discuss test items and compare answers. Gradually, other students became aware of their behavior.

Rafael: What did you get for number two? Mine doesn't look right.

Nichole: Shhhhh.

Martin: I got $x = 4$. But I can't do the first one.

Nichole and Sandy: Shhhhh.

Rafael: I think you have to divide everything by two.

Sandy: They're cheating! That's not fair!

Nichole: If you don't stop right now, I'll have to tell Ms. Jackson you were talking.

Martin: You better not. I'm not the only one. Look around. Marta even has her book open.

Marta: I'm not going to get a bad mark because you guys are cheating.

Rafael: So, if everyone does it then it's fair, right? We could all get good grades.

Dan: That's dumb. If everyone cheated, school would be a total joke. Teachers wouldn't know if we were learning anything. Grades would be worthless.

Carmen: Everybody, shhhh. We shouldn't go against the rules. You're not supposed to cheat. Everybody's going to get into trouble!

Martin: Don't be so self-righteous. The main thing is not getting caught. It's getting caught that's dumb. If nobody's

the wiser it doesn't matter, and if you're dumb enough to get caught, then you deserve whatever you get.

Sandy: Cheater!

Marta: Okay, I closed my book. My mother would die if she thought I cheated. You're not going to tell, are you, Nichole?

Nichole: I want to do whatever is best for everyone.

Rafael: Well, I'm not doing detention over this.

Dan: We could all get detention over this, because it's wrong to cheat. Meanwhile, we've lost ten minutes, so if everyone would just shut up, maybe we'll be able to finish. This is a test!

When Ms. Jackson returned to class, she knew instantly that something had gone wrong. Nichole wore an embarrassed expression and quickly returned to her seat. Martin looked angry and had a paper balled up on his desk. Rafael looked shifty and scared. Marta was gazing sadly out the window, and Sandy seemed to have some secret she desperately wanted to share. Only Dan was able to finish the test by the bell.

◎ *Questions for Reflection*

1. Analyze the differences in moral reasoning evident in the dialogue. How might Piaget have interpreted each speech in relation to stages of moral development? How might Kohlberg classify each speech in relation to stages of moral reasoning? How might Gilligan interpret the dialogue to support her view that males and females reason differently?

2. What should Ms. Jackson do to follow up on her suspicions? Assuming that she learned that cheating had taken place, how should she address cheating as a moral issue in a way that would help her students?

---

not lying and stealing, that are based on principles of justice, and social-conventional rules, such as not wearing pajamas to school, that are based on social consensus and etiquette. Research has supported this view, demonstrating that children as young as 2½ to 3 years old make distinctions between moral and social-conventional rules.

The most important limitation of Kohlberg's theory is that it deals with moral reasoning rather than with actual behavior (Arnold, 2000). Many individuals at different stages behave in the same way, and individuals at the same stage often behave in different ways (Walker & Henning, 1997). In addition, the context of moral dilemmas matters. For example, a study by Einerson (1998) found that adolescents used much lower levels of moral reasoning when moral dilemmas involved celebrities than when they involved made-up characters such as Heinz. Similarly, the link

THE INTENTIONAL TEACHER

Using What You Know about Human Development to Improve Teaching and Learning

Intentional teachers use what they know about predictable patterns of moral, psychosocial, and cognitive development to make instructional decisions. They assess their students' functioning, and they provide instruction that addresses the broad range of stages of development they find in their students. They modify their instruction when they find that particular students need additional challenges or different opportunities. Thinking about student development and watching for it in the classroom helps intentional teachers foster growth for each student.

1 What do I expect my students to know and be able to do at the end of this lesson? How does this contribute to course objectives and to students' needs to become capable individuals?

Teachers need to assess their own students' developmental functioning in light of their understanding of stages of human development. For example, if you were planning a first-grade science program, you might refer to Piaget's theory and recall that 6- and 7-year-olds have to struggle when asked to think about more than one variable at a time (centration). For that reason your science program goals might focus heavily upon students' active, open-ended exploration of their world and far less on formal experimentation requiring the control of variables. As a middle school English teacher, you might review your list of semester goals and verify that it includes not just an emphasis on a set of writing conventions but also a focus on students' moral development. You might plan to include activities that challenge students to experience characters' emotional distress or to view good and bad from different characters' perspectives.

2 What knowledge, skills, needs, and interests do my students have that must be taken into account in my lesson?

Every class group has some common, age-appropriate interests, but there is always a range of personal knowledge and interests that you can find out about to address individual needs. You might have discussions about interests, role models, favorite general icons, sports, and so on, and then use the information you gain to weave into your sessions, heightening motivation and relevance.

3 What do I know about the content, child development, learning, motivation, and effective teaching strategies that I can use to accomplish my objectives?

A broad range of individual differences can be found in each classroom, and individual students exhibit inconsistencies between their thinking and their behavior. Teachers can assess their students' developmental functioning in light of their understanding of general expectations for student development.

For example, you might discuss with students problems like those used by Piaget to assess formal operational thinking, or moral dilemmas like those used by Kohlberg to assess moral development. These will give you insight into the thinking processes of your students.

4 What instructional materials, technology, assistance, and other resources are available to help me accomplish my objectives?

How can you create a rich environment that includes a range of materials and experiences to meet a variety of needs and challenge students at all developmental levels? One solution is to introduce a range of materials likely to appeal to and inform students at a broad range of developmental levels, including magazines, newspapers, children's literature, and almanacs, maps, physical models, and real objects. You might invite students to suggest or bring materials. You might search out CD-ROMs and Internet resources relevant to the subject you teach. These resources can then be incorporated in projects and investigations that enable students of different developmental levels to find and use materials that make sense to them.

5 How will I plan to assess students' progress toward my objectives?

Effective, intentional teachers use a variety of measures to assess student growth. Students will benefit from measures that can assess psychological as well as cognitive growth. For example, you might ask secondary students to write brief analyses of current social issues, and then collect their paragraphs in folders. In spring, for each student, you might pull a sampling of essays from several points in the year to allow students to examine their evolving moral and social perspectives. In an art or shop class, you might collect an early sample of each student's work and ask the students to evaluate their work by writing a paragraph on an index card. Near the end of the term, you might collect another set of samples. Students will be pleased to assess their progress over time and their growing ability to form smooth, sophisticated pieces.

6 How will I respond if individual children or the class as a whole are not on track toward success? What is my back-up plan?

Observe your students carefully to determine whether they are working within their zone of proximal development. Are they experiencing success with the current level of support? More support can be provided for students who are working above their zone of proximal development, and additional challenges might be provided for those working below.

between children's moral reasoning and moral behavior may be quite weak (Thoma & Rest, 1999), although certain aspects of moral reasoning are related to social competence more strongly than others (Bear & Rys, 1995; Hoffman, 1993). Thoma and Rest (1999) and Rest et al. (1999) argued that explanations of moral behavior must take into account moral reasoning but also the ability to interpret correctly what is happening in a social situation, the motivation to behave in a moral fashion, and the social skills necessary to actually carry out a moral plan of action. A study by Murdock, Hale, and Weber (2001) found that cheating among middle school students was affected by many factors, including motivation in school, success, and relationships with teachers, which have little to do with stages of moral development.

Chapter Summary

What Are Some Views of Human Development?

Human development includes physical, cognitive, personal, social, and moral development. Most developmental psychologists believe nature and nurture combine to influence development. Continuous theories of development focus on social experiences that a child goes through, whereas discontinuous theories emphasize inborn factors rather than environmental influence. Development can be significantly affected by heredity, ability, exceptionality, personality, child rearing, culture, and the total environment. Jean Piaget and Lev Vygotsky proposed theories of cognitive development. Erik Erikson's theory of psychosocial development and Piaget's and Lawrence Kohlberg's theories of moral development also describe important aspects of development.

How Did Piaget View Cognitive Development?

Piaget postulated four stages of cognitive development through which people progress between birth and young adulthood. People adjust their schemes for dealing with the world through assimilation and accommodation. Piaget's developmental stages include the sensorimotor stage (birth to 2 years of age), the preoperational stage (2 to 7 years of age), and the concrete operational stage (ages 7 to 11). During the formal operational stage (age 11 to adulthood), young people develop the ability to deal with hypothetical situations and to monitor their own thinking.

How Is Piaget's Work Viewed Today?

Piaget's theory has been criticized for relying exclusively on broad, fixed, sequential stages through which all children progress and for underestimating children's abilities. In contrast, neo-Piagetian theories place greater emphasis on social and environmental influences on cognitive development. Nevertheless, Piaget's theory has important implications for education. Piagetian principles are embedded in the curriculum and in effective teaching practices, and Piaget-influenced concepts such as cognitive constructivism and developmentally appropriate instruction have been important in education reform.

How Did Vygotsky View Cognitive Development?

Vygotsky viewed cognitive development as an outgrowth of social development through interaction with others and the environment. Assisted learning takes place in children's zones of proximal development, where they can do new tasks that are within their capabilities only with a teacher's or peer's assistance. Children internalize learning, develop self-regulation, and solve problems through vocal or silent private speech. Teachers provide interactional contexts, such as cooperative learning groups, and scaffolding.

How Did Erikson View Personal and Social Development?

Erikson proposed eight stages of psychosocial development, each dominated by a particular psychosocial crisis precipitated through interaction with the social environment. In Stage I, trust versus mistrust, the goal is to develop a sense of trust through interaction with caretakers. In Stage II, autonomy versus doubt (18 months to age 3), children have a dual desire to hold on and to let go. In Stage III, initiative versus guilt (3 to 6 years of age), children elaborate their sense of self through exploration of the environment. Children enter school during Stage IV, industry versus inferiority (6 to 12 years of age), when academic success or failure is central. In Stage V, identity versus role confusion (12 to 18 years), adolescents turn from family to peer group and begin their searches for partners and careers. Adulthood brings Stage VI (intimacy versus isolation), Stage VII (generativity versus self-absorption), and Stage VIII (integrity versus despair).

What Are Some Theories of Moral Development?

According to Piaget, children develop heteronomous morality (obedience to authority through moral realism) by around age 6 and later advance to autonomous morality (rational morality based on moral principles). Kohlberg's 5 stages of moral reasoning reflect children's responses to moral dilemmas. In Stages 1 and 2 (the preconventional level), children obey rules set down by others while maximizing self-interest. In Stages 3 and 4 (the conventional level) the individual adopts rules, believes in law and order, and seeks the approval of others. In Stages 5 and 6 (the postconventional level), people define their own values in terms of abstract ethical principles they have chosen to follow.

Critics point out that Kohlberg's studies were based only on male subjects. Studies suggest that there may be little connection between what children say and their actual moral behavior.

Key Terms

Review the following key terms from the chapter. Then, to explore research on these topics and how they relate to education today, connect to Research Navigator™ through this book's Companion Website or directly at www.researchnavigator.com.

accommodation 33	autonomous morality 52
adaptation 32	centration 35
assimilation 32	class inclusion 39

Self-Assessment: Practicing for Licensure

Directions: The chapter-opening vignettes address indicators that are often assessed in state licensure exams. Re-read the chapter-opening vignettes, and then respond to the following questions.

1. Mr. Jones, in the first vignette, is perplexed when he asks his students to follow his example by raising their right hands; instead, they raise their left hands. According to developmental theory, why did this happen?

   a. Kohlberg would say students at the conventional level of moral development cooperate with peers. If one student raises his or her left hand, the others follow.

   b. Vygotsky would say the students are outside their zone of proximal development. They cannot complete the task without assistance.

   c. Piaget would say that students are egocentric, thus unable to consider another person's point of view.

   d. Erikson would say that the students lack the motor skills necessary to complete the task.

2. What simple solution might work to help Mr. Jones to get his students to raise their right hands?

   a. Mr. Jones should have his students draw a diagram of a person raising his or her right hand.

   b. Mr. Jones should position himself in the same direction as his students rather than face them, and then raise his right hand.

   c. Students should write mnemonics to help them remember their right hand from their left hand.

   d. Students should participate in a drill-and-practice activity of "Left is West when Facing North."

3. In the second vignette, why did Ms. Lewis's students refuse to allow the girl with the ill mother to go on the field trip?

   a. According to Erikson's theory, the students were incapable of reversible thought.

   b. Preoperational children are egocentric in their thinking.

   c. The children in Ms. Lewis's class have not yet acquired what Piaget calls "class inclusion."

   d. According to Piaget, children at this age judge the morality of behavior on the basis of its consequence.

4. According to Kohlberg's theory of moral development, how can Ms. Lewis help her students move past their belief that "rules are rules with no exceptions"?

   a. Challenge the student's reasoning with explanations from the next higher stage.

   b. Cancel the field trip for all students.

   c. Bring the mother into the classroom to explain why the girl did not complete the assignment.

   d. Ask each student to write a story about someone who did not follow the rules.

5. According to Erikson's theory of personal development, why did Frank react the way he did to Ms. Quintera's praise of his poetry?

   a. Highlighting Frank's achievement could cast him in the role of teacher's pet, a role that many students in early adolescence strongly resist.

   b. Students in early adolescence prefer to receive praise from teachers of the same gender.

   c. Writing poetry is developmentally inappropriate for students in early adolescence.

   d. Frank didn't think his poetry was good enough to receive praise from his teacher.

6. Write a brief description of a typical (i.e., fits the theories) student at one of the following grade levels: K–6, 5–9, or 7–12. Use the ideas of each theorist from this chapter to guide your description.

7. Make a list of developmentally appropriate teaching strategies for one of the following grade levels: K–5, 5–9, 7–12.

Development during Childhood and Adolescence

At Parren Elementary/Middle School, eighth-graders are encouraged to become tutors for first-graders. They help them with reading, math, and other subjects. As part of this program, Sam Stevens has been working for about a month with Billy Ames.

"Hey, shorty!" said Sam one day when he met Billy for a tutoring session.

"Hey, Sam!" As always, Billy was delighted to see his big buddy. But today his friendly greeting turned into a look of astonishment. "What have you got in your ear?"

"Haven't you ever seen an earring?"

"I thought those were just for girls."

Sam laughed. "Not like this one! Can you see it?"

Billy squinted at the earring and saw that it was in the shape of a small sword. "Awesome!"

"A lot of guys are wearing them."

"Didn't it hurt to get a hole in your ear?"

"A little, but I'm tough! Boy, was my mom mad though. I have to take my earring off before I go home, but I put it back on while I'm walking to school."

"But didn't your mom . . . "

"Enough of that, squirt! You've got some heavy math to do. Let's get to it!"

The interaction between Sam and Billy illustrates the enormous differences between the world of the adolescent and that of the child. Sam, at 13, is a classic young teen. His idealism and down-deep commitment to the positive are shown in his volunteering to serve as a tutor and in the caring, responsible relationship he has established with Billy. At the same time, Sam is asserting his independence by having his ear pierced and wearing an earring, against his mother's wishes. This independence is strongly supported by his peer group, however, so it is really only a shift of dependence from parents and teachers toward peers. His main purpose in wearing an earring is to demonstrate conformity to the styles and norms of his peers rather than to those of adults. Yet Sam does still depend on his parents and other adults for advice and support when making decisions that he knows have serious consequences for his future, and he does take off his earring at home to avoid a really serious battle with his parents.

Billy lives in a different world. He can admire Sam's audacity, but he would never go so far. Billy's world has simpler rules. For one thing, boys are boys and girls are girls, so he is shocked by Sam's flouting of convention to wear something usually associated with females. He is equally shocked by Sam's willingness to directly disobey his mother. Billy may misbehave, but within much narrower limits. He knows that rules are rules, and he fully expects to be punished if he breaks them.   *(Ø)*

USING YOUR
Experience

Creative Thinking   Think back to your adolescence. What was popular with your peer group that your parents disapproved of? How did you resolve this conflict between peers and parents? How do these conflicts differ from ones you have with your parents now? Do you resolve them in the same way?

Educators must know the principal theories of cognitive, social, and moral development presented in Chapter 2 so that they will understand how young people grow over time in each of these domains. However, teachers usually deal with children in a particular age range. A preschool teacher needs to know what preschool children are like. Elementary teachers are concerned with middle childhood. Middle, junior high, and senior high school teachers are concerned with adolescence. This chapter presents the physical, social, and cognitive characteristics of students at each phase of development (see Berk, 2001; Fabes & Martin, 2000). It discusses how the principles of development presented in Chapter 2 apply to children of various ages, and adds information on physical development, language development, and self-concept. Figure 3.1 identifies central themes or emphases in development during early childhood, middle childhood, and adolescence.

INTASC

2 Knowledge of Human Development and Learning

ℋOW DO CHILDREN DEVELOP DURING THE PRESCHOOL YEARS?

Children can be termed *preschoolers* when they are between 3 and 5 years of age. This is a time of rapid change in all areas of development. Children master most motor skills by the end of this period and can use their physical skills to achieve a wide range of goals. Cognitively, they start to develop an understanding of classes and relationships and absorb an enormous amount of information about their social and physical worlds. By the age of 6, children use almost completely mature speech, not only to express their wants and needs, but also to share their ideas and experiences. Socially, children learn appropriate behaviors and rules and become increasingly adept at interacting with other children.

As each of these aspects of development is discussed, keep in mind the complexity of development and how all facets of a child's growth are interrelated. Although physical, cognitive, and social development can be put in separate sections in a book, in real life they not only are intertwined but also are affected by the environment within which children grow up.

Early Childhood

Cognitive development
Language acquisition

Physical development
Large and small muscle skills

Socioemotional development
Prosocial behavior

Middle Childhood

Cognitive development
Memory and metacognitive skills

Physical development
Physical growth

Socioemotional development
Self-concept, self-esteem, and peer relations

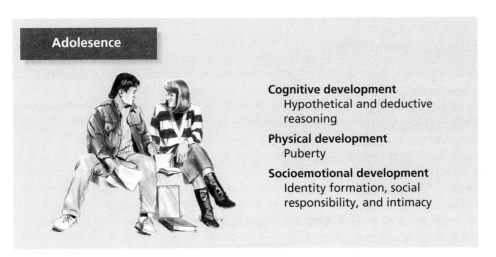

Adolesence

Cognitive development
Hypothetical and deductive reasoning

Physical development
Puberty

Socioemotional development
Identity formation, social responsibility, and intimacy

FIGURE 3.1
Central Issues in Development during Early Childhood, Middle Childhood, and Adolescence

These are some developmental concerns that are characteristically (but not exclusively) important during each of the three broad age levels discussed in this chapter.

small muscle development
Development of dexterity of the fine muscles of the hand.

large muscle development
Development of motor skills such as running or throwing, which involve the limbs and large muscles.

Physical Development in Early Childhood

Physical development describes the changes in the physical appearance of children as well as in their motor skills. During the preschool years the sequence in which all children develop motor skills is generally the same, though some children gain skills faster than others.

The major physical accomplishment for preschoolers is increased control over the large and small muscles. **Small muscle development,** or fine motor activity, relates to movements requiring precision and dexterity, such as buttoning a shirt or zipping a coat. **Large muscle development,** or gross motor activities, involves such movements

Table 3.1	
Motor Development of Preschool Children	
Age	*Skills*
2-year-olds	Walk with wide stance and body sway. Can climb, push, pull, run, hang by both hands. Have little endurance. Reach for objects with two hands.
3-year-olds	Keep legs closer together when walking and running. Can run and move more smoothly. Reach for objects with one hand. Smear and daub paint; stack blocks.
4-year-olds	Can vary rhythm of running. Skip awkwardly; jump. Have greater strength, endurance, and coordination. Draw shapes and simple figures; make paintings; use blocks for buildings.
5-year-olds	Can walk a balance beam. Skip smoothly; stand on one foot. Can manage buttons and zippers; may tie shoelaces. Use utensils and tools correctly.

as walking and running. Table 3.1 shows the ages at which most children acquire various motor skills.

By the end of the preschool period, most children can easily perform self-help tasks such as buckling, buttoning, snapping, and zipping. They can go up and down steps with alternating feet. They can perform fine motor activities such as cutting with scissors and using crayons to color a predefined area. They also begin learning to write letters and words. After 6 or 7 years of age, children gain few completely new basic skills; rather, the quality and complexity of their movements improve (Berk, 2001).

Language Acquisition

From birth to about 2 years of age, infants understand their world through their senses. Their knowledge is based on physical actions, and their understanding is restricted to events in the present or the immediate past. Only when children make the transition from the sensorimotor stage to the preoperational stage (at about age 2)

Personal Reflection

Understanding Development

For a reading program we were developing, my colleagues and I developed a set of animations to illustrate letter sounds. As part of the animation process, I supplied the voices for some of the characters. We showed our cartoons to my 4-year-old nephew, Jack, and told him to listen for my voice. He listened intently, but he looked terribly puzzled. He saw a cartoon dinosaur, for example, with my voice! Finally, he asked, "Did you have to wear a dinosaur suit?"

Jack's inability to imagine how my voice could be coming from a cartoon dinosaur is classic preoperational behavior.

◎ *Reflection on This. Why was Jack unable to disconnect his uncle's voice from the image of the dinosaur? Why would an understanding of child development be helpful to an early elementary or early childhood teacher?*

What language acquisition knowledge and skills will these children likely have by the time they enter kindergarten? As a teacher, what general approaches to formal instruction in reading and writing might you use to build on their knowledge and skills?

and begin to talk and to use mental symbols can they use thoughts or concepts to understand their world. During the preoperational stage, however, their thoughts are still prelogical, tied to physical actions and the way things appear to them. Most children remain in the preoperational stage of cognitive development until they are 7 or 8 years old.

Children normally develop basic language skills before entering school. Language development involves both oral and written communication. Verbal abilities develop very early, and by age 3, children are already skillful talkers. By the end of the preschool years, children can use and understand an almost infinite number of sentences, can hold conversations, and know about written language.

Although there are individual differences in the rates at which children acquire language abilities, the sequence of accomplishments is similar for all children. Around age 1, children produce one-word utterances such as "bye-bye" and "Mommy." These words typically represent objects and events that are important to the child. Over the course of the second year of life, children begin to combine words into two-word sentences (e.g., "More milk"). During the preschool years, children's vocabulary increases, along with their knowledge of the rules of spoken language. By the time they start school, children have mastered most of the grammatical rules of language, and their vocabulary consists of thousands of words.

Oral Language   Development of oral language, or spoken language, requires not only learning words but also learning the rules of word and sentence construction (Hoff, 2003). For example, children learn the rules for how to form plurals before they enter kindergarten. Berko (1985) showed preschoolers a picture of a made-up bird, called a "Wug." She then showed them two such pictures and said, "Now there is another one. There are two of them. There are two _____." The children readily answered "Wugs," showing that they could apply general rules for forming plurals to a new situation. In a similar fashion, children learn to add "-ed" and "-ing" to verbs. As they learn these rules, they initially overgeneralize them, saying "goed" instead of "went," for example, and "mouses" instead of "mice."

Interestingly, children often learn the correct forms of irregular verbs (such as "He broke the chair") and then replace them with incorrect but more rule-based constructions ("He breaked [or broked] the chair"). One 4-year-old said, "I flew my kite." He then thought for a moment and emphatically corrected himself, saying, "I flewed my kite!" These errors are a normal part of language development and should not be corrected (Fenson et al., 1994).

Just as they learn rules for forming words, children learn rules for sentences. Their first sentences usually contain just two words ("Want milk," "See birdie," "Jessie outside"), but they soon learn to form more complex sentences and to vary their tone of voice to indicate questions ("Where doggie go?") or to indicate emphasis ("Want cookie!"). Three-year-olds can usually express rather complex thoughts, even though their sentences may still lack such words as "a," "the," and "did." Later, children continually expand their ability to express and understand complex sentences. However, they still have difficulty with certain aspects of language throughout the preschool and early elementary school years. For example, Carol Chomsky (1969) showed children a doll that was blindfolded and asked, "Is the doll easy to see or hard to see?" Only 22 percent of 5-year-olds could respond correctly; not until age 9 could all her subjects respond appropriately to the question. Many students confuse such words as "ask" and "tell" and "teach" and "learn" well into the elementary grades.

Preschoolers often play with language or experiment with its patterns and rules (Garvey, 1990). This experimentation frequently involves changing sounds, patterns, and meanings. One 3-year-old was told by his exasperated parent, "You're impossible!" He replied, "No, I'm impopsicle!" The same child said that his baby brother, Benjamin, was a man because he was a "Benja-man." Children often rearrange word sounds to create new words, rhymes, and funny sentences. The popularity of finger plays, nonsense rhymes, and Dr. Seuss storybooks shows how young children enjoy playing with language.

Oral language development is heavily influenced by the amount and quality of talking parents do with their children. A study by Hart and Risley (1995) found that middle-class parents talked far more to their children than did working-class parents, and that their children had substantially different numbers of words in their vocabularies. The amount of parent speech was as important as socioeconomic status; children of low-income parents who spoke to their children a great deal also had large vocabularies.

> **ON THE WEB**
>
> Educators and parents can find links to other websites and resources on communication disorders at **www.familyvillage.wisc.edu/lib_comd.htm.**

Reading   Learning to read in the early elementary grades is one of the most important of all developmental tasks, both because other subjects depend on reading and because in our society school success is so often equated with reading success. The process of learning to read can begin quite early if children are read to. Research on **emergent literacy,** or preschoolers' knowledge and skills related to reading (Glazer & Burke, 1994; Pressley, 2003), has shown that children may enter school with a great deal of knowledge about reading and that this knowledge contributes to success in formal reading instruction. For example, young children have often learned concepts of print such as that print is arranged from left to right, that spaces between words have meaning, and that books are read from front to back. Many preschoolers can "read" books from beginning to end by interpreting the pictures on each page. They understand about story plots and can often predict what will happen next in a simple story. They can recognize logos on familiar stores and products; for example, very young children often know that *M* is for *McDonald's*. Further, even if they have not been read to, children have developed complex language skills that are critical in reading. Children from families in which there are few literacy-related activities can

CERTIFICATION POINTER

For teacher certification tests you may be expected to know that children's overgeneralizations of the rules of grammar are normal for young children and should not be corrected.

INTASC

3 Adapting Instruction for Individual Needs

emergent literacy

Knowledge and skills relating to reading that children usually develop from experience with books and other print media before the beginning of formal reading instruction in school.

learn concepts of print, plot, and other prereading concepts if they attend preschools or kindergartens that emphasize reading and discussing books in class (Purcell-Gates, McIntyre, & Freppon, 1995; Whitehurst et al., 1994, 1999). Similarly, young children can be taught to hear specific sounds within words (a skill called phonemic awareness), and this contributes to later success in reading (Anthony & Lonigan, 2004; Bus & van Ijzendoorn, 1999; Byrne, Fielding-Barnsley, & Ashley, 2000; Cavanaugh, Kim, Wanzek, & Vaughn, 2004).

There is a long-standing debate about methods of teaching reading, which generally pits proponents emphasizing systematic teaching of phonics against those who emphasize meaning rather than phonics. Nearly every researcher recognizes that a balance is necessary, and that both phonics and meaning are important in beginning reading (see, for example, Learning First Alliance, 1998;

Teaching Dilemmas: Cases to Consider

INTASC **10 Partnerships**

Adapting Instruction

Brenda, a first-grade teacher at Clark Elementary School, had just finished her presentation on what the class was learning this year to her students' parents on Family Night. She asked if there were any questions. Jayann's mother, Joan, raised her hand, as did Stefan's father, Ramon.

Joan: You mentioned invented spelling. There seems to be some question among many of us about whether it works. I don't know if I understand why you're using it.

Ramon: I don't either. That's not the way I was taught. I learned with phonics, and I spell fine. I can't read the writing journal my son brings home. My neighbor's child is in Mrs. Alvarez's room. I saw her journal and I could read every word she wrote. They have a list of five words each week and Mrs. Williams makes sure every one of them is spelled correctly.

Brenda: Well, actually, invented spelling is a pretty natural way for children to learn how to spell the words they use every day. I call it approximate spelling you know, close but not exact. When I read through the children's journals, I look for words I think they're ready to learn to spell. These are the words they'll want to learn because they're using them a lot.

Ramon: Yeah, but close isn't really right. It seems to me that kids either learn to spell right or not.

Brenda: Let me give you an example of how the students in our class are learning to spell. Every day, I ask the class to help me write a morning message on the chalkboard. Last week, the class was excited about a dog that had gotten into the building, so they chose, "A dog ran through our school this morning" as the message.

Several parents smile and nod, remembering how their children had still been talking about the dog in school at the end of the day.

Brenda: I write the sentence on the board as the students dictate it to me. As I call on the students, we review letter sounds, punctuation rules, and capitalization skills. Why don't you be my class and dictate the message of the day to me, and I'll demonstrate how I teach it?

Most of the parents got into the role-playing and a lively interchange ensued. But Ramon, Stefan's father, didn't join in, so Brenda decided to "call" on him.

Brenda: Mr. Martinez, this is how I try to get all the students involved at their own levels: What letter do you hear at the beginning of dog?

Ramon (getting frustrated): But that's my son Stefan's problem. He doesn't seem to hear the letter sounds the way the other kids do. How is he going to learn to spell correctly unless he is taught phonics?

Brenda took a deep breath. She understood that first-grade parents were usually anxious. Ramon's statement would only heighten their anxiety. Some children, Stefan among them, were indeed struggling. She wondered whether this approach was really working for them. She looked at Stefan's parents and the parents of the other children who were having difficulty. They were all waiting to hear her answer.

@ *Questions for Reflection*

1. Using what you know about language acquisition in children between the ages of 3 and 6, would you explain the differences in spelling ability in Brenda's first-grade class?

2. Should Brenda be a firm believer in invented spelling? What other teaching strategies might she use to help students like Stefan?

3. How should Brenda answer Ramon's question about the way in which spelling is taught?

Pressley, 1998; Wasik, Bond, & Hindman, 2002). But there remain wide differences in emphasis.

In the 1980s, the dominant approach to literacy was **"whole language"** (Goodman & Goodman, 1989), which strongly emphasizes meaning and deemphasizes phonics. Despite its nearly universal adoption, there was little research demonstrating the achievement benefits of this approach in first grade and beyond (Jeynes & Littell, 2000; Stahl & Miller, 1989). In 1990, the publication of Marilyn Adams's book *Beginning to Read,* a comprehensive review of research on early reading, was one among many factors in turning the tide, and by the late 1990s, most researchers were recommending a balance emphasizing systematic phonics. Two congressionally commissioned research reviews (Ehri et al., 2001; National Reading Panel, 1999; Snow, Burns, & Griffin, 1998) came to a similar conclusion. Children need both to be directly taught how to make letters and sounds into words, especially in first grade, and to use their new skills in meaningful text and in their own creative writing (Pressley, 2003). Teaching reading to children who are not native English speakers has particular challenges, including raising the question of whether to teach only in English or to teach English in the native language as well as in English (Slavin & Cheung, 2003). This issue is further discussed in Chapter 4.

Writing   Children's writing follows a developmental sequence. It emerges out of early scribbles and at first is spread randomly across a page. This characteristic reflects an incomplete understanding of word boundaries as well as an inability to mentally create a line for placing letters. Children invent spellings by making judgments about sounds and by relating the sounds they hear to the letters they know. In trying to represent what they hear, they typically use letter names rather than letter sounds; short vowels are frequently left out because they are not directly associated with letter names (Snow et al., 1998). For example, one kindergartner labeled a picture of a dinosaur "DNSR." Many teachers encourage kindergartners and first-graders to write stories using invented spellings to help them learn reading as well as writing (Morrow, 1993).

Theory into PRACTICE

Promoting Literacy Development in Young Children

Many of the educational implications derived from research on children's literacy development transfer findings from two sources: parental and teacher behaviors that encourage oral language development and studies of young children who learn to read without formal classroom instruction. The most frequent recommendations include reading to children; surrounding them with books and other printed materials; making various writing materials available; encouraging reading and writing; and being responsive to children's questions about letters, words, and spellings.

Teachers can use numerous props in the classroom, such as telephone books and office space in a dramatic play area (Neuman & Roskos, 1993). Classrooms can have writing centers with materials such as computers with writing programs, magnetic letters, chalkboards, pencils, crayons, markers, and paper (Wasik, 2001). Art activities also contribute to children's understanding of print. Children's recognition that their images can stand for something else helps them develop an understanding of abstractions, an understanding that is essential to comprehension of symbolic language (Eisner, 1982).

Teachers can encourage children's involvement with print by reading in small groups, having tutors read to children individually, and allowing children to choose books to read. Intimate reading experiences allow children to turn pages, pause to look at pictures or ask questions, and read along with an adult.

Predictable books such as *The Three Little Pigs* and *There Was an Old Lady Who Swallowed a Fly* allow beginning readers to rely on what they already know about literacy while learning sound–letter relationships. Stories are predictable if a child can remember what the author is going to say and how it will be stated. Repetitive structures, rhyme and rhythm, and a match between pictures and text increase predictability.

Children's understanding of literacy is enhanced when adults point out the important features of print (Morrow, 1993). Statements such as "We must start at the front, not at the back of the book"; "Move your finger; you're covering the words and I can't see to read them"; and "You have to point to each word as you say it, not to each letter, like this" help to clarify the reading process. Teachers can indicate features in print that are significant and can draw attention to patterns of letters, sounds, or phrases.

Socioemotional Development

A young child's social life evolves in relatively predictable ways (see Cummings et al., 2003; McHale et al., 2003). The social network grows from an intimate relationship with parents or other guardians to include other family members, nonrelated adults, and peers. Social interactions extend from home to neighborhood and from preschool or other child-care arrangements to formal school. Erik Erikson's theory of personal and social development suggests that during the preschool years, children must resolve the personality crisis of initiative versus guilt. The child's successful resolution of this stage results in a sense of initiative and ambition tempered by a reasonable understanding of the permissible. Early educators can encourage this resolution by giving children opportunities to take initiative, to be challenged, and to succeed.

Peer Relationships   During the preschool years, **peers** (other children who are a child's equal in age) begin to play an increasingly important role in children's social and cognitive development (Newcomb & Bagwell, 1998). Children's relations with their peers differ in several ways from their interactions with adults. Peer play allows children to interact with other individuals whose level of development is similar to their own. When peers have disputes among themselves, they must make concessions and must cooperate in resolving them if the play is to continue; unlike in adult–child disputes, in a peer dispute no one can claim to have ultimate authority. Peer conflicts also let children see that others have thoughts, feelings, and viewpoints that are different from their own. Conflicts also heighten children's sensitivity to the effects of their behavior on others. In this way, peer relationships help young children to overcome the egocentrism that Piaget described as being characteristic of preoperational thinking, and help them see that others have perspectives that are different from their own.

Prosocial Behavior   **Prosocial behaviors** are voluntary actions toward others such as caring, sharing, comforting, and cooperation. Research on the roots of prosocial behavior has contributed to our knowledge of children's moral as well as social development. Several factors seem to be associated with the development of prosocial behaviors (Eisenberg & Mussen, 1989). These include the following:

- Parental disciplinary techniques that stress the consequences of the child's behavior for others and that are applied within a warm, responsive parent–child relationship (Hoffman, 1993).

whole language
Educational philosophy that emphasizes the integration of reading, writing, and language and communication skills across the curriculum in the context of authentic or real-life materials, problems, and tasks.

peers
People who are equal in age or status.

prosocial behaviors
Actions that show respect and caring for others.

- Contact with adults who indicate they expect concern for others, who let children know that aggressive solutions to problems are unacceptable, and who provide acceptable alternatives (Konig, 1995).
- Contact with adults who attribute positive characteristics to children when they do well ("What a helpful boy you are!") (Grusec & Goodnow, 1994).

CONNECTIONS

For suggested coopera-tive learning activities, see Chapter 8, page 255.

solitary play
Play that occurs alone.

parallel play
Play in which children engage in the same activity side by side but with very little interaction or mutual influence.

associative play
Play that is much like paral-lel play but with increased levels of interaction in the form of sharing, turn-taking, and general interest in what others are doing.

cooperative play
Play in which children join together to achieve a common goal.

Play   Most of a preschooler's interactions with peers occur during play (Hughes, 1995). However, the degree to which play involves other children increases over the preschool years (Howes & Matheson, 1992). In a classic study of preschoolers, Mildred Parten (1932) identified four categories of play that reflect increasing levels of social interaction and sophistication. **Solitary play** is play that occurs alone, often with toys, and is independent of what other children are doing. **Parallel play** involves children engaged in the same activity side by side but with very little interaction or mutual influence. **Associative play** is much like parallel play but with increased levels of interaction in the form of sharing, turn-taking, and general interest in what others are doing. **Cooperative play** occurs when children join together to achieve a common goal, such as building a large castle with each child building a part of the structure. For example, Howes and Matheson (1992) followed a group of children for 3 years, observing their play when they were 1 to 2 years old and continuing until they were 3 to 4 years old. They found that children engage in more complex types of play as they grow older, advancing from simple forms of parallel play to complex pretend play in which children cooperate in planning and carrying out activities (Roopnarine et al., 1992; Verba, 1993).

Play is important for children because it exercises their linguistic, cognitive, and social skills and contributes to their general personality development. Children use their minds when playing, because they are thinking and acting as if they were another person. When they make such a transformation, they are taking a step toward abstract thinking in that they are freeing their thoughts from a focus on concrete objects. Play is also associated with creativity, especially the ability to be less literal and more flexible in one's thinking. Play has an important role in Vygotsky's theories of development, because it allows children to freely explore ways of thinking and acting that are above their current level of functioning. Vygotsky (1978) wrote, "In play a child is always

Are these children engag-ing in parallel, associative, or cooperative play? How might such play sessions benefit their development of prosocial behaviors and peer relations?

above his average age, above his daily behavior; in play it is as though he were a head taller than himself" (p. 102).

Preschoolers' play appears to be influenced by a variety of factors. For instance, preschoolers' interactions with peers are related to how they interact with their parents (Ladd & Hart, 1992). Three-year-olds who have warm and nurturing relationships with parents are more likely to engage in social pretend play and resolve conflicts with peers than are children with less secure relationships with their parents (Howes & Rodning, 1992). Children also play better with familiar peers and same-sex peers (Poulin et al., 1997). Providing age-appropriate toys and play activities can also support the development of play and peer interaction skills.

CONNECTIONS

For more on Vygotsky, see Chapter 2, page 43.

WHAT KINDS OF EARLY CHILDHOOD EDUCATION PROGRAMS EXIST?

In almost all the countries of the world, children begin their formal schooling at about 6 years of age, a time when they have typically attained the cognitive and social skills they need for organized learning activities. However, there is much less agreement on what kind of schooling, if any, children younger than the age of 5 need, and there is enormous diversity in the kinds of experiences young children have before entering school (Fitzgerald, Mann, Cabrera, & Wong, 2003; Goelman et al., 2003). The kindergarten originated in Germany in the 1800s but did not gain widespread acceptance until the turn of the last century. Since World War II, preschools and day-care programs have mushroomed as increasing numbers of women with children have entered the workforce (Scarr, 1998). In the United States, half of all mothers of infants (less than a year old) and three-quarters of mothers of school-age children worked outside the home in 1996 (Behrman, 1997). By contrast, only 32 percent of mothers with young children were working in the 1960s (West, Hausken, & Collins, 1993). Group day-care programs exist for children from infancy on, and organized preschool programs sometimes take children as young as 2. More than a million children are now in school before kindergarten, and school systems are rapidly expanding prekindergarten programs (Clifford, Early, & Hills, 1999). As programs for very young children have expanded, the quality of many children's experiences has become higher. Early childhood education has become a major focus of national policy (Carnegie Corporation of New York, 1994, 1996; Kagan & Neuman, 1998; National Education Goals Panel, 1997; Shore, 1998; Weikart, 1995).

Day-Care Programs

Day-care programs exist primarily to provide child-care services for working parents. They range from a baby-sitting arrangement in which one adult takes care of several children to organized preschool programs. Research shows that the quality of early child care can have a lasting effect (Carnegie Corporation of New York, 1994; NICHD Early Child Care Research Network, 2002; Peisner-Feinberg et al., 1998), especially for children from disadvantaged homes (Scarr, 1998). Unfortunately, research finds that the quality of day-care services provided to disadvantaged children is typically much lower than that provided to middle-class children (Sachs, 2000).

Preschools

The primary difference between day-care and preschool programs is that preschools are more likely to provide a planned program designed to foster the social and cognitive

development of young children. Most preschools are half-day programs, with two or three adults supervising a class of 15 to 20 children. Unlike day-care centers and Head Start programs (which are discussed in the following section), preschools (other than Head Start) most often serve middle-class families (General Accounting Office, 1995; West et al., 1993). A key concept in preschool education is **readiness training:** Students learn skills that are supposed to prepare them for formal instruction later, such as how to follow directions, stick to a task, cooperate with others, and display good manners. Children are also encouraged to grow emotionally and develop a positive self-concept and to improve their large and small muscle skills. The preschool day usually consists of a variety of more and less structured activities, ranging from art projects to group discussion to unstructured indoor and outdoor play. These activities are often organized around themes. For example, a unit on animals might involve making drawings of animals, acting out animal behavior, hearing stories about animals, and taking a trip to the zoo.

Compensatory Preschool Programs

Compensatory preschool programs for children from disadvantaged backgrounds were introduced on a large scale as part of the overall federal Head Start program, begun in 1965. Head Start was part of President Lyndon Johnson's war on poverty, an attempt to break the cycle of poverty. The idea was to give disadvantaged children, who are (as a group) at risk for school failure (McLoyd, 1998; Stipek & Ryan, 1997), a chance to start their formal schooling with the same preacademic and social skills that middle-class children possess. Typically, Head Start includes early childhood education programs that are designed to increase school readiness. However, the program also often includes medical and dental services for children, at least one hot meal per day, and social services for the parents.

Research on Head Start has generally found positive effects on children's readiness skills and on many other outcomes (Bracey & Stellar, 2003; Ramey & Ramey, 1998). The effects on academic readiness skills have been greatest for those Head Start programs that stress academic achievement (Abbott-Shim, Lambert, & McCarty, 2003), those that provide a strong family link (Mantzicopoulos, 2003), and those that

CONNECTIONS

For more on compensatory programs for students placed at risk, see Chapter 9, page 303.

readiness training
Instruction in the background skills and knowledge that prepare children for formal teaching later.

compensatory preschool programs
Programs that are designed to prepare disadvantaged children for entry into kindergarten and first grade.

How do compensatory programs, such as JumpStart, help level the playing field for children from disadvantaged backgrounds?

are higher in quality (Clifford et al., 1999). Research that followed disadvantaged children who participated in several such programs found that these students did better throughout their school years than did similar students who did not participate in the programs (Berrueta-Clement, Schweinhart, Barnett, Epstein, & Weikart, 1984). For example, 67 percent of the students in one program, the Perry Preschool, ultimately graduated from high school, compared with 49 percent of students in a control group who did not attend preschool (Schweinhart, Barnes, & Weikart, 1993). Effects of early childhood participation could still be detected at age 27 (Schweinhart & Weikart, 1998). However, preschool programs by themselves are much less effective than are preschool programs followed up by high-quality programs in the early elementary grades (Conyers, Reynolds, & Ou, 2003; Ramey & Ramey, 1998; Reynolds, Temple, Robertson, & Mann, 2002). The research on compensatory early childhood education might seem to indicate that preschool programs are crucial for all students. However, many researchers (e.g., Sachs, 2000) hypothesize that preschool programs are more critical for lower-class children than for middle-class children, because many of the experiences that preschools provide are typically present in middle-class homes but may be lacking in homes of lower socioeconomic status.

Despite research supporting the overall effectiveness of Head Start, questions have been raised about the current quality of Head Start programs. Because research finds lasting effects only for high-quality intensive programs (Ramey & Ramey, 1998), improving the quality of Head Start programs is beginning to take precedence over increasing the numbers of children served in Head Start (Neuman, 2003).

Early Intervention

Most compensatory preschool programs, including Head Start, have begun working with children and their parents when the children are 3 or 4 years of age. However, many researchers believe that earlier intervention is needed for children who are at the greatest risk for school failure (Carnegie Corporation of New York, 1994; Powell, 1995). Numerous **early intervention programs** have been developed to start with children as young as 6 months old. One was a program in an inner-city Milwaukee neighborhood for the children of mothers who had mental retardation. An intensive program of infant stimulation, high-quality preschool, and family services made it possible for the children to perform adequately through elementary school; nearly all of the children in a comparison group were assigned to special education programs (Garber, 1988). Several other early intervention programs have also had strong effects on students that have lasted beyond elementary school (Campbell & Ramey, 1995; Ramey & Ramey, 1998; Reynolds, 1998). A major national study of a program called Early Head Start, which provides center-based and family services to infants and toddlers, is showing positive effects of high-quality programs (Fitzgerald et al., 2003; Robinson & Fitzgerald, 2002).

Kindergarten Programs

Most students attend kindergarten the year before they enter first grade. However, some states still do not require kindergarten attendance (NCES, 2001). The original purpose of kindergarten was to prepare students for formal instruction by encouraging development of their social skills, but in recent years this function has increasingly been taken on by preschool programs. The kindergarten has focused more and more on academics, emphasizing emergent reading and mathematical skills as well as behaviors that are appropriate in school (such as raising hands, lining up, and taking turns). In some school districts kindergarten programs are becoming similar to what first grades once were, a trend that most child development experts oppose (e.g., Bryant, Clifford, & Peisner, 1991). Fifty-six percent of kindergarteners attend full-day

CERTIFICATION POINTER

On your teacher certification test, you may be required to know that compensatory education programs are designed to increase the academic success of children who are at high risk of school failure due to poverty.

CONNECTIONS

For more on early intervention programs for students placed at risk, see Chapter 9, page 307.

early intervention programs
Compensatory preschool programs that target very young children at the greatest risk of school failure.

programs and the rest attend half-day programs (Watson & West, 2004). Research on kindergarten indicates that students of a lower socioeconomic status gain more from well-structured full-day kindergarten programs than from half-day programs (Karweit, 1994b; Watson & West, 2004). Reading interventions in kindergarten, especially phonemic awareness training designed to help children learn how sounds combine into words, generally have been found to have long-term positive effects (Cavanaugh et al., 2004).

Developmentally Appropriate Practice

INTASC

3 Adapting Instruction
for Individual Needs

A concept that has become increasingly important in early childhood education is *developmentally appropriate practice.* This is instruction based on students' individual characteristics and needs, not their ages (Bowman, 1993; Elkind, 1989). The National Association for the Education of Young Children (NAEYC) (1997) has described developmentally appropriate practice for students ages 5 through 8 as follows.

Each child is viewed as a unique person with an individual pattern and timing of growth. Curriculum and instruction are responsive to individual differences in ability and interests. Different levels of ability, development, and learning styles are expected, accepted, and used to design curriculum. Children are allowed to move at their own pace in acquiring important skills, including those of writing, reading, spelling, math, social studies, science, art, music, health, and physical activity. For example, it is accepted that not every child will learn how to read at age 6. Most will learn by age 7, but some will need intensive exposure to appropriate literacy experiences to learn to read by age 8 or 9.

The NAEYC and other advocates of developmentally appropriate practice recommend extensive use of projects, play, exploration, group work, learning centers, and the like, and a deemphasis on teacher-directed instruction, basal readers, and workbooks (Kostelnik, 1992). However, a longitudinal study of children who had been in developmentally appropriate or other preschool programs found few differences lasting into the early elementary grades (Horn & Ramey, 2003).

$\mathcal{H}$ow do children develop during the elementary years?

Children entering the first grade are in a transitional period from the rapid growth of early childhood to a phase of more gradual development. Shifts in both mental and social development characterize the early school years. Several years later, when children reach the upper elementary grades, they are nearing the end of childhood and entering preadolescence. Children's success in school is particularly important during the early school years, for it is in the elementary grades that they largely define themselves as students (Carnegie Corporation of New York, 1996).

Physical Development during Middle Childhood

As children progress through the primary grades, their physical development slows in comparison with earlier childhood. Children change relatively little in size during the primary years. To picture the typical child in the primary grades, we must picture a child in good physical condition. Girls are slightly shorter and lighter than boys until around the age of 9, when height and weight are approximately equal for boys and girls. Muscular development is outdistanced by bone and skeletal development. This may cause the aches that are commonly known as growing pains. Also, the growing muscles need much exercise, and this need may contribute to the primary-grade child's inability to stay still for long. By the time children enter the primary grades, they have developed many of the basic motor skills they need for balance, running, jumping, and throwing. During the latter part of the fourth grade, many girls begin a major growth spurt that will not be completed until puberty. This spurt begins with the rapid growth of the arms and legs. At this point there is not an accompanying change in trunk size. The result is a gangly or all-arms-and-legs appearance. Because this bone growth occurs before the development of associated muscles and cartilage, children at this growth stage temporarily lose some coordination and strength.

By the start of the fifth grade, almost all girls have begun their growth spurt. In addition, muscle and cartilage growth of the limbs resumes in the earlier maturing females, and they regain their strength and coordination. By the end of the fifth grade, girls are typically taller, heavier, and stronger than boys. Males are 12 to 18 months behind girls in development, so even early maturing boys do not start their growth spurt until age 11. By the start of the sixth grade, therefore, most girls will be near the peak of their growth spurt, and all but the early maturing boys will be continuing the slow, steady growth of late childhood. Girls will usually have started their menstrual period by age 13. For boys the end of preadolescence and the onset of early adolescence is measured by the first ejaculation, which occurs between the ages of 13 and 16.

Cognitive Abilities

Between the ages of 5 and 7, children's thought processes undergo significant changes (Siegler, 1998). This is a period of transition from the stage of preoperational thought to the stage of concrete operations. This change allows children to do mentally what was previously done physically and to mentally reverse the actions involved. Not all children make this transition at the same age, and no individual child changes from one stage to the next quickly. Children often use cognitive behaviors that are characteristic of two stages of development at the same time. As individuals advance from one stage to the next, the characteristics of the previous stage are maintained as the cognitive behaviors of the higher stage develop.

In addition to entering the concrete operational stage, elementary school-age children are rapidly developing memory and cognitive skills, including metacognitive skills, the ability to think about their own thinking and to learn how to learn.

Socioemotional Development in Middle Childhood

By the time children enter elementary school, they have developed skills for more complex thought, action, and social influence. Up to this point, children have been basically egocentric, and their world has been that of home, family, and possibly a preschool or day-care center. The early primary grades will normally be spent working through Erikson's (1963) fourth stage, industry versus inferiority. Assuming that a child has developed trust during infancy, autonomy during the early years, and initiative during the preschool years, that child's experiences in the primary grades can contribute to his or her sense of industry and accomplishment. During this stage, children start trying to prove that they are "grown up"; in fact, this is often described as the I-can-do-it-myself stage. Work becomes possible. As children's powers of concentration grow, they can spend more time on chosen tasks, and they often take pleasure in completing projects. This stage also includes the growth of independent action, cooperation with groups, and performing in socially acceptable ways with a concern for fair play (McHale, Dariotis, & Kauh, 2003).

Self-Concept and Self-Esteem   Important areas of personal and social development for elementary school children are **self-concept** and **self-esteem.** These aspects of children's development will be strongly influenced by experiences at home, at school, and with peers. Self-concept includes the way in which we perceive our strengths, weaknesses, abilities, attitudes, and values. Its development begins at birth and is continually shaped by experience. Self-esteem refers to how we evaluate our skills and abilities.

> **ON THE WEB**
>
> For an article on how to strengthen children's self-esteem go to **www.kidsource.com/ kidsource/content2/strengthen_children_self.html.**

As children progress through middle childhood, their ways of thinking become less concrete and more abstract. This trend is also evident in the development of their self-concepts. Preschoolers think about themselves in terms of their physical and material characteristics, including size, gender, and possessions. In contrast, by the early elementary school years, children begin to focus on more abstract, internal qualities such as intelligence and kindness when describing themselves. They can also make a distinction between their private or inner selves and their external, public selves. This becomes especially evident as they depend more on intentions and motives and less on objective behavior in their explanations of their own and others' actions.

During middle childhood, children also begin to evaluate themselves in comparison to others. A preschooler might describe herself by saying, "I like baseball," whereas several years later this same girl is likely to say, "I like baseball more than Sally does." Ruble, Eisenberg, and Higgins (1994) have suggested that younger children use social comparison primarily to learn about social norms and the appropriateness of certain types of conduct. As children get older, they also tend to use **social comparison** to evaluate and judge their own abilities (Borg, 1998).

The trend to use social comparison information to evaluate the self appears to correspond with developmental changes in academic self-esteem. Preschoolers and young children tend to evaluate themselves very positively, in ways that bear no relationship to their school performance or other objective factors (Cole, 1991). By second or third grade, however, children who are having difficulty in school tend to have poorer self-concepts (Chapman, Tunmer, & Prochnow, 2000). This begins a declining spiral. Students who perform poorly in elementary school are at risk for developing poor academic self-concepts and subsequent poor performance in upper elementary and secondary school (Guay, Marsh, & Boivin, 2003; Ma & Kishor, 1997; Marsh & Yeung, 1997).

The primary grades give many children their first chance to compare themselves with others and to work and play under the guidance of adults outside their family. These adults must provide experiences that let children succeed, feel good about themselves, and maintain their enthusiasm and creativity (Canfield & Siccone, 1995; Perry & Weinstein, 1998).

The key word regarding personal and social development is acceptance. The fact is, children do differ in their abilities; and no matter what teachers do, students will have figured out by the end of the elementary years (usually earlier) who is more able and who is less able. However, teachers can have a substantial impact on how students feel about these differences and on the value that low-achieving students place on learning even when they know they will never be class stars.

self-concept

A person's perception of his or her own strengths, weaknesses, abilities, attitudes, and values.

self-esteem

The value each of us places on our own characteristics, abilities, and behaviors.

social comparison

The process of comparing oneself to others to gather information and to evaluate and judge one's abilities, attitudes, and conduct.

Theory into **PRACTICE**

Promoting the Development of Self-Esteem

Our society promotes the idea that people, including students, are of equal worth. That is also the premise in a classroom. But believing students are of equal worth doesn't necessarily mean that they are equally competent. Some students are good in reading, others in math, others in sports, others in art.

Some classroom activities can give certain students the impression that they as individuals are of less value or worth than other students. Research findings indicate that inappropriate competition (Cohen, 1986) or inflexible ability groups within the classroom (MacIver, Reuman, & Main, 1995; Slavin, 1987c) may teach the wrong thing to students.

This kind of research can help teachers avoid practices that may discourage children. However, it is not clear that improving self-esteem results in greater school achievement. In fact, research more strongly suggests that as a student grows more competent in school tasks, his or her self-esteem also improves, rather than the other way around (e.g., Chapman et al., 2000; Ellis, 2001).

Showing students their success can be an important part of maintaining a positive self-image. Rosenholtz and Simpson (1984) described the multidimensional classroom, in which teachers make it clear that there are many ways to succeed. Such teachers emphasize how much students are learning. For example, many teachers give students pre-tests before they begin an instructional unit and then show the class how much everyone gained on a post-test. Multidimensional teachers may stress the idea that different students have different skills. By valuing all these skills, the teacher can communicate the idea that there are many routes to success, rather than a single path (Cohen, 1984).

It is not necessary to lie and say that all students are equally good in reading or math. Teachers can, however, recognize progress rather than level of ability, focusing their praise on the student's effort and growing competence. As the student sees his or her success in school, a feeling of earned self-esteem will also result.

Growing Importance of Peers   The influence of the child's family, which was the major force during the early childhood years, continues in importance as parents provide role models in terms of attitudes and behaviors. In addition, relationships with brothers and sisters affect relationships with peers, and routines from home either are reinforced or must be overcome in school. However, the peer group takes on added importance. Speaking of the child's entrance into the world outside the family, Ira Gordon noted the importance of peers:

> If all the world's the stage that Shakespeare claimed, children and adolescents are playing primarily to an audience of their peers. Their peers sit in the front rows and the box seats; parents and teachers are now relegated to the back rows and the balcony. (Gordon, 1975, p. 166)

In the lower elementary grades, peer groups usually consist of same-sex children who are around the same age. This preference may be due to the variety of abilities and interests among young children. By the sixth grade, however, students often form groups that include both boys and girls. Whatever the composition of peer groups, they let children compare their abilities and skills to those of others. Members of peer groups also teach one another about their different worlds. Children learn through this sharing of attitudes and values how to sort out and form their own attitudes and values.

Friendships in Middle Childhood   During middle childhood, children's conceptions of friendship also mature. Friendship is the central social relationship between peers during childhood, and it undergoes a series of changes before adulthood (Hartup, 1996). Using as a basis Piaget's developmental stages and children's changing abilities to consider the perspective of others, Selman (1981) described how children's understanding of friendship changes over the years. Between the ages of 3 and 7, children usually view friends as momentary playmates. Children of this age might come home from school exclaiming, "I made a new friend today! Jamie shared her doll with me," or "Bill's not my friend anymore 'cause he wouldn't play blocks with me." These comments reveal the child's view of friendship as a temporary relationship based on a certain situation rather than on shared interests or beliefs. As children enter middle childhood, friendships become more stable and reciprocal. At this age, friends are often described in terms of personal traits ("My friend Mary is nice"), and friendships are based on mutual support, caring, loyalty, and mutual give-and-take.

Friendships are important to children for several reasons. During the elementary school years, friends are companions to have fun and do things with. They also serve as important emotional resources by providing children with a sense of security in new situations and when family or other problems arise. Friends are also cognitive resources when they teach or model specific intellectual skills. Social norms for conduct, social interaction skills, and how to resolve conflicts successfully are also learned within the context of friendships (McHale et al., 2003).

Peer Acceptance   One of the important aspects of peer relations in middle childhood is peer acceptance, or status within the peer group (McCallum & Bracken, 1993). Popular children are those who are named most often by their peers as being someone they like and least often as someone they dislike. In contrast, rejected children are those who are named most often by their peers as being someone they dislike and least often as someone they like. Children are also classified as being neglected; these children are neither frequently named as someone who is liked nor frequently named as someone who is disliked. Controversial children are frequently named as someone who is liked but also frequently named as someone who is disliked. Average children are those who are named as being liked and disliked with moderate frequency.

Children who are not well accepted or are rejected by their peers in elementary school are at high risk (Hatzichriston & Hopf, 1996; Wentzel, Barry, & Caldwell, 2004). These children are more likely to drop out of school, engage in delinquent behavior, and have emotional and psychological problems in adolescence and adulthood than are their peers who are more accepted (see also Kupersmidt & Coie, 1990; Morrison & Masten, 1991). Some rejected children tend to be highly aggressive; others tend to be very passive and withdrawn, and these children may be victims of bullying (Pellegrini & Bartini, 2000). Children who are rejected, aggressive, and withdrawn seem to be at highest risk for difficulties (Hymel, Bowker, & Woody, 1993).

Many characteristics seem to be related to peer acceptance, including physical attractiveness (Kennedy, 1990) and cognitive abilities (Wentzel et al., 2004). Studies have also linked behavioral styles to peer acceptance (see Coie, Dodge, & Kupersmidt, 1990). Well-accepted and popular children tend to be cooperative, helpful, and caring and are rarely disruptive or aggressive. Children who are disliked by their peers tend to be highly aggressive and to lack prosocial and conflict resolution skills. Neglected and controversial children display less distinct behavioral styles and often change status over short periods of time (Newcomb & Bagwell, 1998).

Theory into **PRACTICE**

Helping Children Develop Social Skills

Because peer acceptance is such a strong predictor of current and long-term adjustment, many intervention techniques have been designed to improve the social skills and levels of acceptance of unpopular and rejected children. Common approaches involve the following:

Reinforcing appropriate social behavior. Adults can systematically reinforce prosocial skills such as helping and sharing and can ignore antisocial behavior such as fighting and verbal aggression. Reinforcement techniques will be most successful if a teacher or other adult uses them with an entire group of children. This allows the child who lacks skills to observe others being reinforced for positive behavior, and it draws the attention of the peer group to the target child's positive rather than negative actions.

Modeling. Children who observe models learning positive social interaction skills show significant improvement in their own skills.

Coaching. This strategy involves a sequence of steps that include demonstrating positive social skills, explaining why these skills are important, providing opportunities for practice, and giving follow-up feedback.

The effectiveness of any intervention is likely to depend largely on the involvement of the rejected child's peers and classroom teachers. If peers and teachers notice positive changes in behavior, they are more likely to change their opinions of and accept the child than if interventions are conducted in isolation (Olweus, 1994; White & Kistner, 1992).

CONNECTIONS

For more on systematically reinforcing prosocial skills, see Chapter 5, page 140.

How do Children Develop during the Middle School and High School Years?

The adolescent period of development begins with puberty. The pubertal period, or early adolescence, is a time of rapid physical and intellectual development. Middle adolescence is a more stable period of adjustment to and integration of the changes of early adolescence. Later adolescence is marked by the transition into the responsibilities, choices, and opportunities of adulthood. In this section we will review the major changes that occur as the child becomes an adolescent, and we will examine how adolescent development affects teaching, curriculum, and school structure.

Physical Development during Adolescence

Puberty is a series of physiological changes that render the immature organism capable of reproduction. Nearly every organ and system of the body is affected by these changes. The prepubertal child and the postpubertal adolescent are different in outward appearance because of changes in stature and proportion and the development of primary and secondary sex features (Susman, Dorn, & Schiefelbein, 2003).

Although the sequence of events at puberty is generally the same for each person, the timing and the rate at which they occur vary widely. The average female typically begins pubertal changes 1 to 2 years earlier than the average male. In each sex, however, the range of normal onset ages is approximately 6 years. Like the onset, the rate of changes also varies widely. Some people take only 18 to 24 months to go through the pubertal changes to reproductive maturity; others may require 6 years

puberty
Developmental stage at which a person becomes capable of reproduction.

"No thanks, but I'll call you when I reach puberty!"

CONNECTIONS

For more on Piaget's theories on cognitive development in adolescence, see Chapter 2, page 39.

CERTIFICATION POINTER

When responding to case studies in certification tests, you may be asked to design a lesson that would be considered developmentally appropriate for a group of adolescents.

to pass through the same stage. These differences mean that some individuals may be completely mature before others the same age have even begun puberty. The age of maximum diversity is 13 for males and about 11 for females. The comparisons that children make among themselves, as well as the tendency to hold maturity in high regard, can be a problem for the less mature (Ge, Longer, & Elder, 2001). On the other hand, the first to mature are also likely to experience temporary discomfort because they stand out from the less mature majority. Early-maturing girls, for example, are more likely to engage in delinquency and have school problems than other girls (Stice, Presnell, & Bearman, 2001), and early-maturing boys also are more likely to engage in delinquent behavior (Ge et al., 2001).

Cognitive Development

As the rest of the body changes at puberty, the brain and its functions also change, and the timing of intellectual changes varies widely across individuals. One indication of this is that scores on intelligence tests obtained over several years from the same individual fluctuate most during the period from 12 to 15 years of age. Some researchers refer to an "intellectual growth spurt" at this age (Andrich & Styles, 1994). In Piaget's theory of cognitive development, adolescence is the stage of transition from the use of concrete operations to the application of formal operations in reasoning. Adolescents begin to be aware of the limitations of their thinking. They wrestle with concepts that are removed from their own experience. Inhelder and Piaget (1958) acknowledge that brain changes at puberty may be necessary for the cognitive advances of adolescence. However, they assert that experience with complex problems, the demands of formal instruction, and exchange and contradiction of ideas with peers are also necessary for formal operational reasoning to develop. Adolescents who reach this stage (not all do) have attained an adult level of reasoning. Adolescent cognitive development is characterized more by steady growth in understanding and capabilities (Eccles, Wigfield, & Byrnes, 2003).

Characteristics of Hypothetical-Deductive Reasoning

Hypothetical-deductive reasoning is one of the characteristics that marks the development of formal operational thinking, which emerges by the time children are about 12 years old (Atwater, 1996; Flavell et al., 1993). Before formal operations, thought is concrete operational in nature. Piaget found that the use of formal operations depended on the learner's familiarity with a given subject area. When students were familiar with a subject, they were more likely to use formal operations. When they were unfamiliar with a subject, students proceeded more slowly, tended to use concrete reasoning patterns, and used self-regulation sparingly. Later research has confirmed Piaget's observation that use of formal operational thought differs according to tasks, background knowledge, and individual differences (Cobb, 1995). Not all adolescents develop formal operational thinking, but there is evidence that adolescents who have not reached this level can be taught to solve problems requiring this level of thinking (Vasta & Liben, 1996).

Theory into **PRACTICE**

Promoting Formal Operational Thought

Teachers can help adolecents develop and use formal operational thought. Consider the following:

1. When introducing new information, particularly information involving abstract concepts and theories, allow students enough time to absorb the ideas and to use formal thought patterns. Begin with more familiar examples, and encourage students to apply hypothetical-deductive reasoning.
2. Students who have not yet attained formal operational thought may need more support for planning complex tasks. Pairing children who can plan with those who need support is one way of handling the situation.
3. Encourage students to state principles and ideas in their own words and to search for the meaning behind abstract ideas and theories.
4. Incorporate a variety of activities that promote the use of hypothetical deductive thinking. The following are some examples:

    - Have students write a paper that requires a debate between arguments pro and con and a discussion of the evidence that supports the two perspectives. For younger students you might want to pair children or groups and have one child or group write from one perspective and the other from another perspective.
    - Have students discuss each other's ideas, purposefully picking specific opposing positions. Debates and mock trials are two ways in which this can be done.
    - Develop cooperative activities that require substantial planning and organization. Have students work in groups composed of children with different levels of planning and organizing skills. For children who are still at the concrete operational level, provide an outline of what to think about as the planning process proceeds.
    - Develop activities in which facts come from different testimonials that may be contradictory, such as television commercials. For example, use commercials in which Brand X claims to be the best-selling domestic car and to have more features than other cars and Brand Y claims that its cars are the highest rated and have higher levels of owner satisfaction. Have the students discuss and weigh the evidence from these different sources.
    - Have students critique their own work. Ask students to generate a list of ways in which one could look for flaws in thinking or other sources that might be used to verify results.

Socioemotional Development in Adolescence

In adolescence, children undergo significant changes in their social and emotional lives as well. Partly as a result of their changing physical and cognitive structures, children in the upper elementary grades seek to be more grown up. They want their parents to treat them differently, even though many parents are unwilling to see them differently. They also report that though they believe that their parents love them, they do not think their parents understand them. For both boys and girls in the upper elementary grades, membership in groups tends to promote feelings of self-worth. Not being accepted can bring serious emotional problems. Herein lies the major cause of the preadolescent's changing relationship with parents. It is not that preadolescents care

"School uniforms! That'll take away our individuality!"

less about their parents. It is just that their friends are more important than ever. This need for acceptance by peers helps to explain why pre-adolescents often dress alike (Baumeister & Leary, 1995). The story of Sam Stevens's earring at the beginning of this chapter illustrates how young adolescents express their belongingness with other peer group members through distinctive dress or behavior.

The middle school years often also bring changes in the relationship between children and their teachers. In primary school, children easily accept and depend on teachers. During the upper elementary years, this relationship becomes more complex (see Roeser, Eccles, & Sameroff, 2000). Sometimes students will tell teachers personal information they would not tell their parents. Some preadolescents even choose teachers as role models. At the same time, however, some preteens talk back to teachers in ways they would never have considered several years earlier, and some openly challenge teachers. Others become deeply alienated from school, starting a pattern that may lead to delinquency and dropout (Murdock, 1999).

Identity Development

One of the first signs of early adolescence is the appearance of **reflectivity,** the tendency to think about what is going on in one's own mind and to study oneself. Adolescents begin to look more closely at themselves and to define themselves differently. They start to realize that there are differences between what they think and feel and how they behave. Using the developing intellectual skills that permit them to consider possibilities, adolescents are prone to be dissatisfied with themselves. They critique their personal characteristics, compare themselves to others, and try to change the way they are.

Adolescents may also ponder whether other people see and think about the world in the same way they do (Phelan, Yu, & Davidson, 1994). They become more aware

Personal Reflection

Coping with Change

My oldest son, Jacob, went through a typically stormy adolescence. At one point, when he was about 15, he had little to say to my wife and me that wasn't hostile or dismissive. However, on occasion his old loving self would still shine through. One day he spent all afternoon working with my wife to bake a couple of pies. He didn't say much, but it was heartening just to see him willing to spend time with his mom on such a prosocial activity. He put particular care into making a design on the top crust of each pie, after which he proudly put them in the oven. When the pies were done, we were astonished to see that he'd written a very bad word on each pie!

Jacob's afternoon is a wonderful example of adolescents' conflicted relationships with their parents. He was willing to bake pies with his mom, but he had to do it his way, to show that he was not dependent on his parents, and had to express his independence at every turn. Still, the pies (and the experience, in retrospect) were delicious!

@ *Reflect on This. Do you remember being conflicted emotionally in middle school or high school as you adjusted to adolescence? How might the internal conflicts have differed for adolescents of different social or ethnic groups? What kind of learning challenges does this time period pose for teachers and students?*

of their separateness from other people and of their uniqueness. They learn that other people cannot fully know what they think and feel. The issue of who and what one "really" is dominates personality development in adolescence. According to Erikson, the stage is set during adolescence for a major concern with one's identity.

James Marcia's Four Identity Statuses

On the basis of Erikson's work, James Marcia (1991) identified four identity statuses from in-depth interviews with adolescents. The statuses reflect the degree to which adolescents have made firm commitments to religious and political values as well as to a future occupation. These are as follows:

1. **Foreclosure:** Individuals in a state of **foreclosure** have never experienced an identity crisis. Rather, they have prematurely established an identity on the basis of their parents' choices rather than their own. They have made occupational and ideological commitments, but these commitments reflect more an assessment of what their parents or authority figures could do than an autonomous process of self-assessment. Foreclosure indicates a kind of "pseudo-identity" that generally is too fixed and rigid to serve as a foundation for meeting life's future crises.

2. **Identity diffusion:** Adolescents experiencing **identity diffusion** have found neither an occupational direction nor an ideological commitment of any kind, and they have made little progress toward these ends. They may have experienced an identity crisis, but if so, they were unable to resolve it.

3. **Moratorium:** Adolescents in a state of **moratorium** are those who have begun to experiment with occupational and ideological choices but have not yet made definitive commitments to either. These individuals are directly in the midst of an identity crisis and are currently examining alternate life choices.

4. **Identity achievement: Identity achievement** signifies a state of identity consolidation in which adolescents have made their own conscious, clear-cut decisions about occupation and ideology. The individual is convinced that these decisions were autonomously and freely made, and that they reflect his or her true nature and deep inner commitments.

reflectivity
The tendency to analyze oneself and one's own thoughts.

foreclosure
An adolescent's premature establishment of an identity based on parental choices, not on his or her own.

identity diffusion
Inability to develop a clear direction or sense of self.

moratorium
Experimentation with occupational and ideological choices without definite commitment.

identity achievement
A state of consolidation reflecting conscious, clear-cut decisions concerning occupation and ideology.

How do peer relationships affect one's self-concept and self-esteem? What can you as a teacher do to aid your students' emotional development?

By late adolescence (18 to 22 years of age), most individuals have developed a status of identity achievement. However, adolescents' emotional development seems to be linked to their identity status. For instance, levels of anxiety tend to be highest for adolescents in moratorium and lowest for those in foreclosure (Marcia, 1991). Self-esteem also varies, with adolescents in identity achievement and moratorium reporting the highest levels and those in foreclosure and identity diffusion reporting the lowest levels (Marcia, 1991; Wallace-Broscious, Serafica, & Osipow, 1994).

In general, adolescents need to experiment and remain flexible if they are successfully to find their own identity. By trying out ways to be, then testing and modifying them, the adolescent can pick the characteristics that are most comfortable and drop the others. To do this, the adolescent must have the self-confidence to experiment and to declare an experiment over; to vary behavior; and to drop characteristics that don't fit, even if the characteristics are supported by others. It helps to have a stable and accepting set of parents, teachers, and peers who will respond positively to one's experimentation.

ON THE WEB

For explorations of many aspects of adolescent development, including identity development and self-esteem, go to the website of Nancy Darling and her students at the University of Pennsylvania—**http://inside.bard.edu/academic/specialproj/ darling/adolesce.htm.**

Self-Concept and Self-Esteem

Self-concept and self-esteem also change as children enter and go through adolescence. The shift toward more abstract portrayals that began in middle childhood continues, and adolescents' self-descriptions often include personal traits (friendly, obnoxious), emotions (depressed, psyched), and personal beliefs (liberal, conservative) (Harter, 1998). In addition, the self-concept becomes more differentiated. Susan Harter's work has identified eight distinct aspects of adolescent concept: scholastic competence, job competence, athletic competence, physical appearance, social acceptance, close friendships, romantic appeal, and conduct (Harter, 1998). Marsh (1993) identified five distinct self-concepts: academic verbal, academic mathematical, parent relations, same-sex, and opposite sex.

Self-esteem also undergoes fluctuations and changes during adolescence. Self-esteem is lowest as children enter middle school or junior high school and with the onset of puberty (Simmons & Blyth, 1987). Early maturing girls tend to suffer the most dramatic and long-lasting decreases in self-esteem. In general, adolescent girls have lower self-esteem than do boys (Marsh, 1993; Simmons & Blyth, 1987). Global self-esteem or feelings of self-worth appear to be influenced most strongly by physical appearance and then by social acceptance from peers.

Social Relationships

Friendships   As children enter adolescence, changes in the nature of friendships also take place. In general, the amount of time spent with friends increases dramatically; adolescents spend more time with their peers than they do with family members or by themselves (Ambert, 1997). Adolescents who have satisfying and harmonious friendships also report higher levels of self-esteem, are less lonely, have more mature social skills, and do better in school than do adolescents who lack supportive friendships (Kerr, Stattin, Biesecker, & Ferrer-Wreder, 2003).

During adolescence the capacity for mutual understanding and the knowledge that others are unique individuals with feelings of their own also contribute to a dramatic increase in self-disclosure, intimacy, and loyalty among friends. As early adolescents strive to establish personal identities that are independent of those of their parents, they also look increasingly to their peers for security and social support. Whereas elementary school–aged children look to parents for such support, by seventh grade same-sex friends are perceived to be as supportive as parents, and by tenth grade they are perceived to be the primary source of social support (Furman & Buhrmester, 1992).

Relationships with Peers   In addition to their close friends, most adolescents also place high value on the larger peer group as a source of ideas and values as well as companionship and entertainment.

The nature of peer relationships in adolescence has been characterized in terms of social status and peer crowds. Social status, or levels of acceptance by peers, is studied with respect to the same status groups that are identified in middle childhood. As with elementary school–aged children, popular and well-accepted adolescents tend to display positive conflict resolution and academic skills, prosocial behavior, and leadership qualities, whereas rejected and low-accepted children tend to display aggressive and antisocial behavior and low levels of academic performance (Parkhurst & Asher, 1992; Wentzel & Erdley, 1993; Zettergren, 2003). These socially rejected children appear to be at great risk for later academic and social problems (Pope & Bierman, 1999). Wentzel and Asher (1995) found, however, that rejected middle school children who were socially submissive did not display the same school-related problems as their rejected aggressive counterparts. These findings suggest that peer rejection and negative behavior together place these children at risk.

Peer relationships in adolescence have also been studied in terms of cliques and crowds with whom adolescents associate (Brown, 1990). A clique is a fairly small, intimate group that is defined by the common interests, activities, and friends of its members. In contrast, a crowd is a larger group defined by its reputation. Allegiance to a clique or crowd is common during adolescence but not necessarily long-term or stable. Although the pressure to conform can be very powerful within these groups, only adolescents who are highly motivated to belong appear to be influenced by these norms in significant ways (Rice, 1996).

Emotional Development

Most adolescents experience emotional conflicts at some point. This is hardly surprising, since they are going through rapid and dramatic changes in body image, expected roles, and peer relationships. The transitions from elementary to middle school or junior high and then on to high school can also be quite stressful (Harter, Whitesell, & Kowalski, 1992; Midgley, 1993). For most adolescents, emotional distress is temporary and is successfully handled, but for some the stresses lead to delinquency, drug abuse, or suicide attempts (Matheny, Aycock, & McCarthy, 1993; O'Neil, 1991; Range, 1993).

Emotional problems related to the physical, cognitive, and social development of upper elementary school–aged children are common. Though preadolescents are generally happy and optimistic, they also have many fears, such as fear of not being accepted into a peer group, not having a best friend, being punished by their parents, having their parents get a divorce, or not doing well in school.

Other emotions of this age group include anger (and fear of being unable to control it), guilt, frustration, and jealousy. Preadolescents need help in realizing that these emotions and fears are a natural part of growing up. Adults must let them talk about these emotions and fears, even if they seem unrealistic to an adult. Feelings of guilt often arise when there is a conflict between children's actions (based on values

CERTIFICATION POINTER
Most teacher certification tests will require you to know how development in one domain, such as physical, may affect a student's performance in another domain, such as social.

of the peer group) and their parents' values. Anger is a common emotion at this age and is displayed with more intensity than many of the other emotions. Just as they often tell their preadolescents that they should not be afraid, parents often tell them that they should not get angry. Unfortunately, this is an unrealistic expectation, even for adults.

Problems of Adolescence

Adolescence can be a time of great risk for many, as teenagers are now able, for the first time, to engage in behaviors or make decisions that can have long-term negative consequences (Dryfoos, 1998; National Research Council, 1995).

CONNECTIONS

For more on emotional disorders, see Chapter 12, page 405.

Emotional Disorders   Secondary school teachers should be sensitive to the stresses that adolescents face and should realize that emotional disturbances are common (Galambus & Costigan, 2003). They should understand that depressed, hopeless, or unaccountably angry behavior can be a clue that the adolescent needs help, and they should try to put such students in touch with school counselors or other psychologically trained adults.

Bullying   Taunting, harassment, and aggression toward weaker or friendless peers occurs at all age levels, but can become particularly serious as children enter early adolescence (Juvonen, Nishina, & Graham, 2000; Pellegrini & Bartini, 2000).

Dropping Out   Dropping out of secondary school can put adolescents at considerable risk, as dropouts condemn themselves to low-level occupations, unemployment, and poverty. Of course, the factors that lead to dropping out begin early in students' school careers; school failure, retention (staying back), assignment to special education, and poor attendance all predict dropout (Battin-Pearson et al., 2000; Goldschmidt & Wang, 1999; Pallas, 2002). Dropout rates have generally been declining, especially among African American students, although African Americans are still disproportionately at risk (Balfanz & Legters, 2004). For Latino students, however, dropout rates remain very high (Secada et al., 1998). Dropout rates among at-risk students can be greatly reduced by programs that give these students individual attention, high-status roles, and assistance with academic deficits (Burt, Resnick, & Novick, 1998; Fashola & Slavin, 1998). Students in smaller and more academically focused high schools tend to drop out less frequently than other students (Lee & Burkam, 2003).

Drug and Alcohol Abuse   Substance use continues to be widespread among adolescents (Perkins & Borden, 2003). Eighty percent of high school seniors drink alcohol, and 31 percent have tried marijuana (Johnson et al., 2001). Drug and alcohol abuse are strongly connected to school failure (Bryant & Zimmerman, 2002).

CONNECTIONS

To learn about prevention of delinquency, see Chapter 11, page 379.

Delinquency   One of the most dangerous problems of adolescence is the beginning of serious delinquency. The problem is far more common among males than among females (U.S. Department of Justice, 1998). Delinquents are usually low achievers who have been given little reason to believe that they can succeed by following the path laid out for them by the school (Hawkins et al., 2000). Delinquency in adolescence is overwhelmingly a group phenomenon; most delinquent acts are done in groups or with the active support of a delinquent subgroup (Branch, 1998; Farmer et al., 2002; Perkins & Borden, 2003).

Risk of Pregnancy   Pregnancy and childbirth are serious problems among all groups of female adolescents but particularly among those from lower-income homes (Coley

& Chase-Lansdale, 1998; Susman, Dorn, & Schiefelbein, 2003). Just as adolescent males often engage in delinquent behavior to try to establish their independence from adult control, adolescent females often engage in sex, and in many cases have children, to force the world to see them as adults. Because early childbearing makes it difficult for adolescent females to continue their schooling or get jobs, it is a primary cause of the continuation of the cycle of poverty into which many adolescent mothers were themselves born (Hoffman, Foster, & Furstenberg, 1993). Of course, the other side of teen pregnancy is teen fatherhood. Teen fathers also suffer behavioral and academic problems in school (Hanson, Morrison, & Ginsburg, 1989). Many programs intended to delay intercourse and reduce pregnancy exist. Research on these programs finds that sex education programs that emphasize both abstinence and use of condoms and other birth control methods are more effective than those that emphasize just abstinence (Kirby, 2000).

Risk of Sexually Transmitted Diseases   Compounding the traditional risks of early sexual activity is the rise in AIDS and other sexually transmitted diseases (Kalichman, 1996). AIDS is still very rare during the adolescent years, and rates of infection have been declining (CDC, 1998). However, because full-blown AIDS can take 10 years to appear, unprotected sex, needle sharing, and other high-risk behavior among teens are what often causes the high rates of AIDS among young adults (Hein, 1993). The appearance of AIDS has made the need for early, explicit sex education critical, potentially a life-or-death matter. However, knowledge alone is not enough (Woodring, 1995); sexually active adolescents must have access to condoms and realistic, psychologically sophisticated inducements to use them (Aronson, 1995).

Sexual Identity   It is during adolescence that people begin to explore their sexual identity, including young people who begin to identify with a gay or lesbian orientation. This new awareness can cause great distress for the adolescent and for his or her parents. It also can lead to tension with peer groups, which may have strong norms against homosexuality and may engage in taunting, rejection, or even violent behavior toward gay or lesbian peers. Teachers need to model acceptance of gay and lesbian

How can Gay-Straight Alliance groups in a school help to promote tolerance among young people and ease the pressure on gay and lesbian youth? What roles do teachers play in creating a safe environment for young people conflicted over sexual identity?

students and strictly enforce school rules forbidding disrespect toward anyone, gay or straight (Koppelman & Goodhart, 2005).

Theory into **PRACTICE**

INTASC

3 Adapting Instruction
for Individual Needs

Providing Developmental Assets for Adolescents

G. Stanley Hall, an early American psychologist who studied child development, called adolescence a time of storm and stress. Whether or not that is an accurate description of all teenagers, many contemporary writers (e.g., Dryfoos, 1990) believe young people in the United States are at risk because of the choices they make. Such a view of at-risk behaviors can result in a "deficit-thinking" approach to helping teenagers. That is, our society declares "war" on teenage pregnancy, school dropout rates, drug and alcohol abuse, gangs, and violence. As Goleman (1995) noted, however, such programs often come too late and do too little. In a deficit approach we try

THE INTENTIONAL TEACHER

Using What You Know about Early Childhood, Middle Childhood, and Adolescent Students to Improve Teaching and Learning

Intentional teachers realize that students in their early years, in middle childhood, and in adolescence face different challenges as they develop physically, cognitively, and socially. They will relate student goals to the different levels of development and modify their instruction when they find that particular students need additional—or different—support in their growth toward independence.

❶ What do I expect my students to know and be able to do at the end of this lesson? How does this contribute to course objectives and to students' needs to become capable individuals?

Teachers need to build understanding of the issues that typically arise at their students' age levels, and they need to develop understanding of the stress that can be involved as students move from one level to the next. For example, you might build into your long-term plans activities that capitalize on the important influence of the peer culture. Examples include allowing students to study content through connections to topical interests such as fashion, music, and sports.

❷ What knowledge, skills, needs, and interests do my students have that must be taken into account in my lesson?

Instruction is most appropriate when it addresses students' current functioning. Both formal and informal measures can provide information about your students' linguistic, physical, and

cognitive development. For example, if you were a teacher of young children, you might check for students' concepts about print: Can they identify the front of a book? Do they track from left to right? If you were a middle school teacher, you might use informal conversation and academic materials to assess new students' English language skills. As students work, you might listen for hints that they are becoming increasingly reflective about their inner lives, a sign that marks the adolescent thought process.

As a high school teacher, you might recognize that maturing adolescents are beginning to take a more active role in the learning process, accept responsibility for their own learning, seek for real-life applications of what is being learned, and bring their own experiences into consideration. They are more autonomous, less dependent on others than younger children. You might adapt your instruction to afford more individual choice of research projects and reporting format, encouraging collaborative investigations by groups of students.

❸ What do I know about the content, child development, learning, motivation, and effective teaching strategies that I can use to accomplish my objectives?

Students' relationships with peers change over time. Observe students' peer interaction so that you can encourage prosocial behavior. For example, you might observe kindergartners during their free time, taking notes about the different forms of play you observe, or you might listen to older students' lunch

to stop adolescents from doing risky things, but adolescents don't always listen.

Instead of trying to deal with problems after they are already serious, many programs have demonstrated success with a wide range of problem behaviors by embedding preventive strategies into the regular curriculum. For example, a number of programs have succeeded in reducing high-risk behaviors by introducing "life skills training," focusing on skills such as making good decisions and resisting peer pressure (Stipek, de la Sota, & Weishaupt, 1999). Another approach is a program of prevention that focuses on building norms of cooperation, altruism, and social responsibility (Battistich et al., 1999). Involving community agencies to engage children in prosocial behaviors is another frequently recommended practice (Benson, 1997). Comprehensive, whole-school reform models can have an impact on high-risk behaviors, especially truancy and dropping out, in middle school (Balfanz & MacIver, 2000) and high school (Hammond, Ancess, & Ort, 2002; Jordan et al., 2000; McPartland et al., 2002).

CERTIFICATION POINTER

On your teacher certification test, you may be asked what is the impact on learning of students' physical, social, emotional, moral, and cognitive development.

INTASC	**7** Instructional Planning Skills	**9** Professional Commitment and Responsibility
	8 Assessment of Student Learning	

table conversations, asking yourself: "Do my students compare themselves to their peers in order to evaluate themselves?" You might make a mental note to help them make appropriate comparisons.

❹ What instructional materials, technology, assistance, and other resources are available to help accomplish my objectives?

Classroom environments may be most likely to allow for development if they include a rich variety of materials that can foster social, linguistic, physical, and academic development. For example, if you teach young children you might include a puppet center and a storytelling area to encourage oral language development. With all students, you might use classroom meetings, in which students are encouraged to share openly, to help build a sense of community and acceptance that welcomes all students, no matter what their differences.

It is important to check not just your plans and materials, but students' reaction to those plans and materials as well. Do they seem to perceive their activities as moving them forward?

You might review students' portfolios to trace their growth in self-concept, as well as academic mastery. You might watch for patterns that emerge throughout the class and use that information to adjust learning opportunities. If you teach secondary grades, you might review your lesson plans to ensure that they provide opportunities for social interaction and formal problem solving, activities that help adolescents move into Piaget's stage of formal operations, and note student comments about the assignments.

❺ How will I plan to assess students' progress toward my objectives?

Assess the information you have gathered from different sources over time. Does it suggest that students are growing in each important area of human development? For example, you might ask elementary students to write in their journals about their friends, and use their entries to help you determine whether students are developing friendships that can provide social and cognitive resources for them.

❻ How will I respond if individual children or the class as a whole are not on track toward success? What is my back-up plan?

Proponents of developmentally appropriate practice urge teachers to treat each student as an individual with a unique pattern of growth. For example, you might hold a class discussion, addressing such questions as "What can you do better now than at the beginning of the year?" "What would you still like to improve?" "How can we help each other?" By listening carefully to your students' comments you might identify any areas named as trouble spots by more than one student, determining to address such topics with further instructional activities in future lessons.

Chapter Summary

How Do Children Develop during the Preschool Years?

Physically, young children develop strength and coordination of the large muscles first and then of the small muscles (as in cutting with scissors or writing). Cognitive abilities corresponding to Piaget's sensorimotor and preoperational stages also include the acquisition of language. Oral language is usually acquired by age 3 and includes the development of vocabulary, grammatical rules, and conventions of discourse. The foundations of reading and writing are usually acquired before formal schooling begins.

Socioemotional development in early childhood can be partly described in terms of Erikson's initiative versus guilt stage. Peer relationships help children overcome the egocentrism that Piaget described as characteristic of preoperational thinking. Prosocial behavior includes caring, sharing, comforting, and cooperating. Parten identified four categories of play—solitary, parallel, associative, and cooperative—that reflect increasing levels of social interaction and sophistication. Play exercises children's linguistic, cognitive, social, and creative skills.

What Kinds of Early Childhood Education Programs Exist?

Economic and social factors have led to an increasing demand for early childhood education programs, including day-care centers, preschools, compensatory preschool programs, and kindergartens. Research findings have tended to support trends toward early intervention, school-readiness training, continuation of compensatory programs in the early elementary grades, targeting of students who are at risk, and avoidance of the potential drawbacks of kindergarten retention. Developmentally appropriate practice, instruction based on individuals' characteristics and needs rather than on age, has become increasingly important.

How Do Children Develop during the Elementary Years?

Between the ages of 5 and 7, children have slower growth but greater health and skill. They think in ways described in Piaget's theory as the concrete operational stage. Children in the upper elementary grades move from egocentric thought to more decentered thought. At 9 to 12 years of age, children can use logical, reversible thought, can reason abstractly, and can have insight into causal and interpersonal relationships.

In middle childhood, children may be seen as resolving Erikson's industry versus inferiority psychosocial crisis. School becomes a major influence on development, a place where the child develops a public self, builds social skills, and establishes self-esteem on the basis of academic and nonacademic competencies. In preadolescence, between ages 9 and 12, conformity in peer relations, mixed-sex peer groupings, and challenges to adult authority become more important.

How Do Children Develop during the Middle School and High School Years?

Puberty is a series of major physiological changes leading to the ability to reproduce. Significant differences exist in the age of onset of puberty, and both early maturers and late maturers may experience difficulties. Adolescents develop reflectivity and greater metacognitive skills, such as those described in Piaget's formal operations: combinatorial problem solving and hypothetical reasoning.

Adolescents may be seen as resolving Erikson's identity versus role confusion psychosocial crisis. They pay attention to how other people view them, search the past, experiment with roles, act on feelings and beliefs, and gradually seek greater autonomy and intimacy in peer relations. Identity foreclosure occurs when the individual chooses a role prematurely, but by late adolescence, most individuals have developed a state of identity achievement. Many factors, such as dropping out, substance abuse, and AIDS, place adolescents at risk.

Key Terms

Review the following key terms from the chapter. Then, to explore research on these topics and how they relate to education today, connect to Research Navigator™ through this book's Companion Website or directly at www.researchnavigator.com.

associative play   74
compensatory preschool programs   76
cooperative play   74
early intervention programs   77
emergent literacy   70
foreclosure   87
identity achievement   87
identity diffusion   87
large muscle development   67
moratorium   87
parallel play   74

peers   73
prosocial behaviors   73
puberty   83
readiness training   76
reflectivity   87
self-concept   80
self-esteem   80
small muscle development   67
social comparison   80
solitary play   74
whole language   73

Self-Assessment: Practicing for Licensure

Directions: The chapter-opening vignette addresses indicators that are often assessed in state licensure exams. Re-read the chapter-opening vignette, and then respond to the following questions.

1. As noted in the interaction between Sam and Billy, there are enormous differences between students of varying ages. According to the information presented in the chapter, which of the following behaviors is more likely to be exhibited by Billy than by Sam?

   a. obey parents
   b. conform to peer demands
   c. assert independence
   d. be idealistic

2. According to the information presented in the chapter, which of the following behaviors is more likely to be exhibited by Sam than by Billy?

   a. follow simple rules
   b. defy convention
   c. expect punishment for disobedience
   d. be dependent on parents

3. Typically, a young child's social life evolves in relatively predictable ways. The social network grows from an intimate relationship with parents or other guardians to

   a. nonrelated adults, peers, and then other family members.
   b. peers, nonrelated adults, and then other family members.
   c. other family members, peers, and then nonrelated adults.
   d. other family members, nonrelated adults, and then peers.

4. For students like Sam Stevens, who is entering what Piaget terms "formal operations," which of the following instructional strategies would be considered developmentally appropriate?

   a. teach Sam to hear specific sounds as he reads (phonemic awareness)
   b. allow Sam to invent spellings by making judgments about sounds and by relating the sounds to the letters he knows
   c. help Sam to resolve the personality crisis of initiative versus guilt
   d. require Sam to write assignments that require debate (argue pro or con on an issue)

5. One of the first signs of early adolescence is the appearance of reflectivity. What is this?

   a. a return to egocentric thought
   b. the development of initiative
   c. the ability to think about one's own mind
   d. joining others in working toward a common goal

6. Design a lesson that would be considered developmentally appropriate for someone Billy's age. Include an explanation as to why you believe it is appropriate.

7. Design a lesson that would be considered developmentally appropriate for someone Sam's age. Include an explanation as to why you believe it is appropriate.

8. One of the most serious problems of adolescence is delinquency. Delinquents are usually

   a. high achievers who turn to delinquency out of boredom.
   b. socially adept at leading others into crime.
   c. low achievers who feel they can't succeed in school.
   d. late-maturing adolescents.

Student Diversity

*M*arva Vance and John Rossi are first-year teachers

at Emma Lazarus Elementary School. It's November, and Marva and John are meeting over coffee to discuss the event dreaded by many a first-year teacher: the upcoming Thanksgiving pageant.

"This is driving me crazy!" Marva starts. "Our classes are like the United Nations. How are we supposed to cast a Thanksgiving pageant? I have three Navajo children. Should I cast them as Indians, or would they be offended? My Vietnamese kids have probably never seen a turkey, and the idea of eating a big bird like that must be revolting to them. I wonder how meaningful this will be to my African Americans. I remember when I was in a Thanksgiving pageant and our teacher had us black students be stagehands because she said there weren't any black Pilgrims! Besides, what am I going to do about a narrator? José says he wants to be narrator, but his English isn't too good. Lakesha would be good, but she's often out for debate tournaments and would miss some rehearsals. I've also been worrying about the hunters. Should they all be boys? Wouldn't it be gender stereotyping if the boys were hunters and the girls were cooks? What about Mark? He uses a wheelchair. Should I make him a hunter?"

John sighs and looks into his coffee. "I know what you're talking about. I just let my kids sign up for each part in the pageant. The boys signed up as hunters, the girls as cooks, the Indians as Indians. Maybe it's too late for us to do anything about stereotyping when the kids have already bought into their roles. Where I went to school, everyone was white, and no one questioned the idea that hunters were boys and cooks were girls. How did everything get so complicated?" ⓖ

USING YOUR

Experience

Critical Thinking   Spend 4 or 5 minutes writing a plausible ending to the vignette. What did Marva Vance end up doing, and what were the results?

Cooperative Learning   In small groups of four students, role-play Marva and John's situation. Then discuss the issues they are raising. After 6 minutes, report your group's conclusions to the class.

Students differ. They differ in performance level, learning rate, and learning style. They differ in ethnicity, culture, social class, and home language. They differ in gender. Some have disabilities, and some are gifted or talented in one or more areas. These and other differences can have important implications for instruction, curriculum, and school policies and practices. Marva and John are concerned with student diversity as it relates to the Thanksgiving pageants they are planning, but diversity and its meaning for education are important issues every day, not just on Thanksgiving. This chapter discusses some of the most important ways in which students differ and some of the ways in which teachers can accept, accommodate, and celebrate student diversity in their daily teaching. However, diversity is such an important theme that almost every chapter in this book touches on this issue. Teachers are more than instructors of students. Together with their students they are builders of tomorrow's society. A critical part of every teacher's role is to ensure that the equal opportunity that we hold to be central to our nationhood is translated into equal opportunity in day-to-day life in the classroom. This chapter was written with this goal in mind.

𝒲HAT IS THE IMPACT OF CULTURE ON TEACHING AND LEARNING?

INTASC

2 Knowledge of Human Development and Learning

3 Adapting Instruction for Individual Needs

If you have ever traveled to a foreign country, you noticed differences in behaviors, attitudes, dress, language, and food. In fact, part of the fun of traveling is in discovering these differences in **culture,** which refers to the shared norms, traditions, behaviors, language, and perceptions of a group (Erickson, 1997; King, 2002). Though we usually think of cultural differences as being mostly national differences, there is probably as much cultural diversity within the United States as between the United States and other industrialized nations. The life of a middle-class family in the United States or Canada is probably more like that of a middle-class family in Italy, Ireland, or Israel than it is like that of a low-income family living a mile away. Yet while we value cultural differences between nations, differences within our own society are often less valued. The tendency is to value the characteristics of mainstream, high-status groups and devalue those of other groups.

By the time children enter school, they have absorbed many aspects of the culture in which they were raised, such as language, beliefs, attitudes, ways of behaving, and food preferences. More accurately, most children are affected by several cultures, in that most are members of many overlapping groups. The cultural background of an individual child is affected by his or her ethnicity, socioeconomic status, religion, home language, gender, and other group identities and experiences (see Figure 4.1). Many of the behaviors that are associated with being brought up in a particular culture have important consequences for classroom instruction. For

culture

The language, attitudes, ways of behaving, and other aspects of life that characterize a group of people.

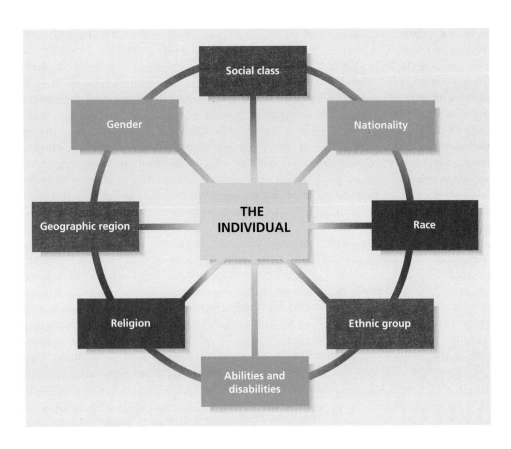

FIGURE 4.1
Cultural Diversity and Individual Identity
Reprinted with permission of the author and publisher from James A. Banks, *Multiethnic Education: Theory and Practice* (3rd ed.), 1993, p. 89. Boston: Allyn & Bacon.

example, schools expect children to speak standard English. This is easy for students from homes in which standard English is spoken but difficult for those whose families speak other languages or significantly divergent dialects of English. Schools also expect students to be highly verbal, to spend most of their time working independently, and to compete with other students for grades and recognition. However, many cultures place a higher value on cooperation and peer orientation than on independence and competitiveness (Boykin, 1994a, 1994b). Because the culture of the school reflects mainstream middle-class values (Grossman, 1995), and because most teachers are from middle-class backgrounds, the child from a different culture is often at a disadvantage. Understanding students' backgrounds is critical for effectively teaching both academic material and the behaviors and expectations of the school.

ℋOW DOES SOCIOECONOMIC STATUS AFFECT STUDENT ACHIEVEMENT?

One important way in which students differ from one another is in social class. Even in small rural towns in which almost everyone is the same in ethnicity and religion, the children of the town's bankers, doctors, and teachers probably have a different upbringing from that experienced by the children of most farmhands or domestic workers.

Sociologists define social class, or **socioeconomic status (SES),** in terms of an individual's income, occupation, education, and prestige in society. These factors tend

socioeconomic status (SES)
A measure of prestige within a social group that is most often based on income and education.

to go together, so SES is most often measured as a combination of the individual's income and years of education, because these are most easily quantified.

Levine and Levine (1996) divide the American socioeconomic class structure into five groups: upper (3 percent), upper middle (22 percent), lower middle (34 percent), upper working (28 percent), and lower working (13 percent). Within the lower working class they distinguish a very impoverished subgroup, the urban underclass, that has particularly severe difficulties in terms of unemployment, crime, and social disorganization (Danziger, Sandefur, & Weinberg, 1994; Miller & Ferroggiaro, 1995). In this book the term *middle-class* is used to refer to families whose wage earners are in occupations requiring significant education; working-class to those who have relatively stable occupations not requiring higher education; and lower-class to those in the urban or rural underclass who are often unemployed and might be living on government assistance.

However, social class indicates more than level of income and education. Along with social class goes a pervasive set of behaviors, expectations, and attitudes, which intersect with and are affected by other cultural factors. Students' social-class origins are likely to have a profound effect on attitudes and behaviors in school. Students from working-class or lower-class backgrounds are less likely than middle-class students to enter school knowing how to count, to name letters, to cut with scissors, or to name colors. They are less likely to perform well in school than are children from middle-class homes (McLoyd, 1998; Natriello, 2002; Sirin, 2003). Of course, these differences are true only on the average; many working-class and lower-class parents do an outstanding job of supporting their children's success in school, and many working-class and lower-class children achieve at a very high level. Social class cuts across categories of race and ethnicity. Although it is true that Latino and African American families are, on average, lower in social class than are white families, there is substantial overlap; the majority of all low-income families in the United States are white, and there are many middle-class nonwhite families (U.S. Census Bureau, 2001). Definitions of social class are based on such factors as income, occupation, and education, never on race or ethnicity.

Table 4.1 shows the reading performance of eighth-graders on the 2003 National Assessment of Educational Progress (NCES, 2003). Note that children of more educated parents (a key component of social class) consistently scored higher than children of less educated parents. Similarly, among fourth-graders who qualified for free or reduced-price lunches, only 15 percent scored at or above "proficient" on the reading portion of the NAEP, in comparison to 42 percent of fourth graders who did not qualify (NCES, 2003). The NAEP used qualification for free lunch as an indicator of a child's family income.

Table 4.1

NAEP Reading Score (2003) by Parents' Education: Grade 8	
Parents' Education	*% Scoring at or above Proficient*
Graduated college	43
Some education after high school	33
Graduated high school	20
Did not finish high school	13

Source: National Center for Education Statistics, 2003.

The Role of Child-Rearing Practices

Much research has focused on the differences in child-rearing practices between the average middle-class family and the average working-class or lower-class family. Many children from low-income families receive an upbringing that is less consistent with what they will be expected to do in school than that of middle-class children. By the time they enter school, middle-class children are likely to be good at following directions, explaining and understanding reasons, and comprehending and using complex language, while working-class or lower-class children may have less experience in all these areas (Slaughter & Epps, 1994). Children from disadvantaged homes are more likely to have poor access to health care, and to suffer from diseases such as lead poisoning. Their mothers are less likely to have received good prenatal care (McLoyd, 1998). These factors can delay cognitive development, which also affects school readiness. Of course low-income families lack resources of all kinds to help their children succeed. For example, children from disadvantaged families are far more likely to have uncorrected vision, hearing problems, or other health problems that may inhibit their success in school (Natriello, 2002).

Another important difference between middle-class and lower-class families is in the kinds of activities parents tend to do with their children. Middle-class parents are likely to express high expectations for their children and to reward them for intellectual development. They are likely to provide good models for language use, to talk and read to their children frequently, and to encourage reading and other learning activities. They are particularly apt to provide all sorts of learning materials for children at home, such as books, encyclopedias, records, puzzles, and, increasingly, computers (Yeung, Linver, & Brooks-Gunn, 2002). These parents are also likely to expose their children to learning experiences outside the home, such as museums, concerts, and zoos (Duke, 2000). They are more likely to be able to help their children succeed in school and to be involved in their education (Heymann & Earle, 2000). Middle-class parents are likely to expect and demand high achievement from their children; working-class and lower-class parents are more likely to demand good behavior and obedience (Knapp & Woolverton, 1995; Trawick-Smith, 1997). Helping poor parents engage in more enriching interactions with their children can have a substantial impact on their children's cognitive performance. For example, the Parent–Child Home Program (PCHP) initiative provides disadvantaged mothers of toddlers with toys and demonstrations of ways to play with and talk with children to enhance their intellectual development. Studies have found strong and lasting effects of this simple intervention on children's cognitive skills and school success, in comparison to children whose parents did not receive PCHP services (Allen & Seth, 2004; Levenston, Levenston, & Oliver, 2002).

ON THE WEB

You can learn more about PCHP programs by visiting their website at **www.parent-child.org/home**.

The Link between Income and Summer Learning

Several studies have found that while low-SES and high-SES children make similar progress in academic achievement during the school year, the high-SES children continue to make progress over the summer while low-SES children fall behind (Cooper, Lindsay, Nye, & Greathouse, 1998; Entwisle, Alexander, & Olson, 2001; Heyns, 2002). These findings suggest that home environment influences not only academic readiness for school, but also the level of achievement throughout students' careers in school. Middle-class children are more likely to be engaged in school-like activities during the summer and to have available more school-like materials. Working-class and lower-class children may be receiving less academically relevant stimulation at home and are more likely to be forgetting what they learned in school (Hill, 2001; Thompson, Entwisle, Alexander, & Sundius, 1992). The "summer slide" phenomenon has led many schools to offer summer school to at-risk students, and research is finding that this can be an effective strategy (Borman & Boulay, 2004).

The Role of Schools as Middle-Class Institutions

Students from backgrounds other than the mainstream middle class have difficulties in school in part because their upbringing emphasizes different behaviors from those valued in school. The problem is that the school overwhelmingly represents the values and expectations of the middle class. Two of these values are individuality and future time orientation (see Boykin, 1994a; Jagers & Carroll, 2003). Most U.S. classrooms operate on the assumption that children should do their own work. Helping others is often defined as cheating. Students are expected to compete for grades, for the teacher's attention and praise, and for other rewards. Competition and individual work are values that are instilled early on in most middle-class homes. However, students from lower-class white families (Pepitone, 1985) and from many other ethnic backgrounds (Boykin, 1994a) are less willing to compete and are more interested in cooperating with their peers than are middle-class European Americans. These students have often learned from an early age to rely on their communities, friends, and family and have always also helped and been helped by others. Not surprisingly, students who are most oriented toward cooperation with others learn best in cooperation with others, whereas those who prefer to compete learn best in competition with others (Kagan, Zahn, Widaman, Schwartzwald, & Tyrrell, 1985). Because of the mismatch between the cooperative orientation of many lower-class and minority-group children and the competitive orientation of the school, many researchers (e.g., Boykin, 1994a; Greenfield & Cocking, 1994; Triandis, 1995) have argued that there is a structural bias in traditional classrooms that works against these children. They recommend that teach-

CONNECTIONS

For more on cooperative learning strategies, see Chapter 8, page 255.

What additional challenges do schools and parents in poor communities face with regard to educating the children of the community? What factors make their success more difficult?

ers use cooperative learning strategies at least part of the time with these students so that they receive instruction that is consistent with their cultural orientations (see Slavin, Hurley, & Chamberlain, 2003).

School and Community Factors

Often, children from low-income families are placed at risk for school failure by the characteristics of the communities they live in and the schools they attend. For example, school funding in most areas of the United States is correlated with social class; middle-class children are likely to attend schools with greater resources, better-paid (and therefore better-qualified) teachers, and other advantages (Darling-Hammond, 1995). On top of these differences, schools serving low-income neighborhoods may have to spend much more on security, on services for children having difficulties, and on many other needs, leaving even less for regular education (Persell, 1997). This lack of resources can significantly affect student achievement (Land & Legters, 2002; Rothstein, 2001). In very impoverished neighborhoods, crime, a lack of positive role models, inadequate social and health services, and other factors can create an environment that undermines children's motivation, achievement, and mental health (Behrman, 1997; Black & Krishnakumar, 1998; Vernez, 1998). In addition, teachers often hold low expectations for disadvantaged children, and this can affect their motivation and achievement (Becker & Luthar, 2002; Hauser-Cram, Sirin, & Stipek, 2003). These factors, however, do not automatically doom children to failure. Many at-risk children develop what is called *resilience*, the ability to succeed despite many risk factors (Borman & Overman, 2004; Glantz, Johnson, & Huffman, 2002; Waxman, Gray, & Padron, 2002). But such factors do make success in school much more difficult.

School, Family, and Community Partnerships

If family background is a key factor in explaining differences in student achievement, then it follows that involving families in support of children's school success can be part of the solution. Professional educators can reach out to families and other community members in a variety of ways to improve communication and respect between home and school and to give parents strategies to help their own children succeed. Epstein and Sanders (2002) describe six types of involvement schools might emphasize in a comprehensive partnership with parents:

1. *Parenting.* Assist families with parenting and child-rearing skills, family support, understanding child and adolescent development, and setting home conditions to support learning at each age and grade level. Obtain information from families to help schools understand families' backgrounds, cultures, and goals for children.
2. *Communicating.* Communicate with families about school programs and student progress with school-to-home and home-to-school communications. Create two-way communication channels so that families can easily communicate with teachers and administrators.

CERTIFICATION POINTER

Teacher certification tests may require that you identify the factors outside of school that can affect student learning. These include culture, family circumstances, community environments, health, and economic conditions.

INTASC

10 Partnerships

"Mrs. Rogers, I think this is taking the idea of parent involvement a little too far!"

3. *Volunteering.* Improve recruitment, training, activities, and schedules to involve families as volunteers and audiences at the school or in other locations to support students and school programs.
4. *Learning at home.* Involve families with their children in academic learning activities at home, including homework, goal setting, and other curricular-linked activities and decisions.
5. *Decision making.* Include families as participants in school decisions, governance, and advocacy activities through PTA, committees, councils, and other parent organizations. Assist family representatives to obtain information from and give information to those they represent.
6. *Collaborating with the community.* Coordinate with community businesses, agencies, cultural and civic organizations, colleges or universities, and other groups. Enable students to contribute service to the community (adapted from Epstein & Sanders, 2002, p. 527).

CERTIFICATION POINTER

Teacher certification tests may require you to outline specific actions that you might take as a teacher to connect the school and students' home environment to benefit your students' learning.

Correlational research on parent involvement has clearly shown that parents who involve themselves in their children's educations have higher achieving children than other parents (Flouri & Buchanan, 2004). However, there has been more debate about the impacts of school programs to increase parent involvement. Many studies have shown positive effects of parent involvement programs, especially those that emphasize parents' roles as educators for their own children (see Epstein & Sanders, 2002; Sanders, Allen-Jones, & Abel, 2002), although there are also many studies that have failed to find such benefits (Mattingly et al., 2002). What the research suggests is that building positive relations with parents and giving parents practical means of helping their children succeed in school are important parts of any intentional educator's plan to improve the achievement and adjustment of all children, but other elements, such as improving instruction and curriculum, are also necessary.

Theory into PRACTICE

Parent Involvement

Parents and other family members have considerable influence over their children's success in school. If you establish positive relationships with parents, you can help them see the importance of supporting the school's educational objectives by doing such things as providing an uncluttered, quiet place for their children to do homework. The more clearly you communicate your expectations for their role in their children's learning in your class, the more likely they will be to play that role. For example, if you expect children to practice reading every evening for homework, having a form for parents to sign each night communicates the importance of the activity. Other strategies for involving parents in their children's learning include:

1. **Home visits.** At the beginning of the school year, it is useful to arrange for a visit to your students' homes. Seeing where a student is coming from gives you additional understanding for the supports and constraints available to the students for their cognitive and emotional development.
2. **Frequent newsletters for families.** Informing families about what their children will be learning and what they can do at home to support that learning can increase student success. If you have English language learners in your class, having the newsletter available in their first language is important both in improving communication and in showing respect.

according to ethnicity. Note that the proportion of non-Latino whites is expected to continue to decline; as recently as 1970, 83.3 percent of all Americans were in this category. In contrast, the proportion of Latinos and Asians has grown dramatically since 1990 and is expected to continue to grow at an even more rapid rate from 2000–2010. In 2001, the U.S. Census Bureau announced that Latinos had overtaken African Americans as the largest **minority group.** These trends, which are due to immigration patterns and differences in birth rates, have profound implications for U.S. education. Our nation is becoming far more ethnically diverse (Hodgkinson, 2001).

Academic Achievement of Students from Under-Represented Groups

If students from under-represented groups achieved at the same level as European and Asian Americans, there would probably be little concern about ethnic-group differences in U.S. schools. Unfortunately, they don't. On virtually every test of academic achievement, African American, Latino, and Native American students score significantly lower than their European and Asian American classmates.

Table 4.3 shows reading scores on the 2003 National Assessment of Educational Progress (NAEP) according to students' race or ethnicity. African American, Latino, and American Indian children scored significantly lower than non-Latino white or Asian American children at all grade levels. These differences correspond closely with differences among the groups in average socioeconomic status, which themselves translate into achievement differences (recall Table 4.1).

The achievement gap between African American, Latino, and white children may be narrowing, but not nearly rapidly enough. During the 1970s there was a substantial reduction, but since the early 1980s the gap has stayed more or less constant in both reading and math on the National Assessment of Educational Progress (NCES, 2003).

Why Have Students from Under-Represented Groups Lagged in Achievement?

Why do many students from under-represented groups score so far below European and many Asian Americans on achievement tests? The reasons involve economics,

INTASC

8 Assessment of Student Learning

Table 4.2

Race/Ethnicity	\multicolumn{3}{c}{Percentages of U.S. Population by Race/Ethnicity in 1990, 2000, and 2010 (Projected)}		
	1990	2000	2010
European American	75.7	71.3	67.4
Hispanic	9.0	11.9	14.6
African American	11.8	12.2	12.5
Asian/Pacific Islander	2.8	3.8	4.8
American Indian	0.7	0.7	0.8

Source: U.S. Census Bureau website, 2001 www.census.gov.

Table 4.3

NAEP Reading Scores (2003) by Race/Ethnicity: Grade 4

Race/Ethnicity	% Scoring at or above Proficient
White	41
African American	13
Latino	15
Asian/Pacific Islander	38
American Indian/Alaska Native	16

Source: National Center for Education Statistics, 2003.

society, families, and culture, as well as inadequate responses by schools (Gallimore & Goldenberg, 2001; Okagaki, 2001). The most important reason is that in our society, African Americans, Latinos (particularly Mexican Americans and Puerto Ricans), and Native Americans tend to occupy the lower rungs of the socioeconomic ladder. Consequently, many families in these groups are unable to provide their children with the stimulation and academic preparation that are typical of a middle-class upbringing (Halle, Kurtz-Coster, & Mahoney, 1997). Again, there are many exceptions; nevertheless, these broad patterns largely explain the average differences. Chronic unemployment, underemployment, and employment in very low-wage jobs, which are endemic in many communities of people from under-represented groups, have a negative effect on family life, including contributing to high numbers of single-parent families in these communities (U.S. Census Bureau, 2001).

Another important disadvantage that many students from under-represented groups face is academically inferior, overcrowded urban schools (Barton, 2003). Middle-class and many working-class families of all ethnicities throughout the United States buy their way out of center-city schools by moving to the suburbs or sending their children to private or parochial schools, leaving the public schools to serve people who lack the resources to afford alternatives. The remaining children, who are disproportionately members of ethnic minorities, are likely to attend the lowest-quality, worst-funded schools in the country (Biddle & Berliner, 2002; Ferguson & Mehta, 2004; Lee, 2004), where they often have the least qualified and least experienced teachers (Connor, Son, Hindman, & Morrison, 2004; Haycock, 2001; Viadero, 2000).

Often, minority-group students perform poorly because the instruction they receive is inconsistent with their cultural background (Boykin, 1994b; Henry & Pepper, 1990; Jagers & Carroll, 2002; Latham, 1997a; Ogbu, 1999; Vasquez, 1993). Academic excellence itself may be seen as inconsistent with acceptance in a student's own community; for example, Ogbu (1999), Spencer et al. (2001), Cross (1995), and others have noted the tendency of many African American students to accuse their peers of "acting white" if they strive to achieve. In contrast, many Asian American parents strongly stress academic excellence as an expectation, and as a result many (though not all) Asian subgroups do very well in school (Okagaki & Frensch, 1998; Portes, 1999). African Americans (Boykin, 1994a; Jagers & Carroll, 2002; Lee, 2000), Native Americans (Henry & Pepper, 1990; Lomawaima & McCarty, 2002), and Mexican Americans (Losey, 1995; Padrón, Waxman, & Rivera, 2002) generally prefer to work in collaboration with others and perform better in cooperative settings than in traditional competitive ones. Lack of respect for students' home languages and dialects can also lead to a diminishing of commitment to school (Delpit, 1995). Low expectations for minority-group students can contribute to their low achievement (Delpit, 1995; Nieto, 1997; Ogbu, 1999; Van Laar, 2001). This is especially true if, as often happens, low expectations lead well-meaning teachers or administrators to disproportionately place students from under-represented groups in low-ability groups or tracks (see Braddock, Dawkins, & Wilson, 1995) or in special education (Heward & Cavanaugh, 1997). Interestingly, though African American students often suffer from the low expectations of teachers and others, their expectations for themselves and their academic self-concepts tend to be at least as high as those of their white classmates (Eccles, Wigfield, & Byrnes, 2003; Van Laar, 2000).

The low achievement of African American, Latino, and Native American children may well be a temporary problem. Within a few decades, as under-represented groups increasingly achieve economic security and enter the middle class, their children's achievement will probably come to resemble that of other groups. In the 1920s it was widely believed that immigrants from southern and eastern Europe (such as Italians,

CONNECTIONS

To learn about motivational factors that affect some minority-group students and low achievers, including the role of teacher expectations and the phenomenon of learned helplessness, see Chapter 10, pages 330 and 331.

Teaching Dilemmas: Cases to Consider

INTASC **3** Adapting Instruction for Individual Needs **10** Partnerships
6 Communication Skills

Meeting Resistance

Fluent in both Spanish and English, Elizabeth Montgomery had changed careers in her mid-thirties to become a bilingual elementary teacher. After earning a Master of Education degree with honors and successfully completing her student-teaching, Elizabeth was hired to teach a fourth-grade Spanish bilingual class at a large elementary school in a working- and lower-class urban community. Of the thirty students in her class, twenty-six are Latino, two are African American, and two are European American.

LaShonda Brown is one of the African American students in Ms. Montgomery's class. After school she is startlingly sweet and often confides pleasant facts about her home life, but she is amazingly recalcitrant during class time. She often comes to school late and usually responds with "I ain't doin' that" to even the smallest request. In class she sits limply during assignments, makes rude noises during reading (which delights her classmates to no end), and refuses to participate in her math group. She seems both angry and dependent. By the fifth week of class, Ms. Montgomery has decided to call LaShonda's mother but plans to describe LaShonda's behavior as depression rather than anger.

Ms. Montgomery: Mrs. Brown, I'm concerned about LaShonda. She doesn't participate in class and seems especially dependent. Could she be depressed about something?

Mrs. Brown: Ms. Montgomery, that girl certainly isn't depressed because even though I'm raising her alone, I work very hard to buy her everything she wants and to make her happy. I'll admit that she's way too dependent, you might even say spoiled, but she isn't depressed.

Ms. Montgomery: Well, perhaps when you come to our class open house next week, we can talk some more about how to help LaShonda participate more in class.

During the open house Ms. Montgomery shows Mrs. Brown and the other parents around the classroom and discusses the bilingual approach she is using. The meeting is pleasant, but there is no opportunity to talk with Mrs. Brown alone about LaShonda, whose behavior is now prompting Ms. Montgomery to send her out of the classroom for small periods so her acting out does not get reinforced by her classmates.

Later that week, Ms. Montgomery receives a letter from Mrs. Brown that says, "It's too bad you can't be bothered to really teach my girl. It seems you prefer the Mexican American children in your class over the black children."

Stunned, Ms. Montgomery shows the letter to the vice principal, an African American woman with whom LaShonda has rapport. Vice Principal Johnson suggests inviting Mrs. Brown to a meeting with her and Ms. Montgomery in her office.

Vice Principal Johnson: Mrs. Brown, I'm so glad you could come in to talk with us about your concerns about LaShonda's class.

Mrs. Brown: Well, I don't mean any disrespect, but I think a white woman from the ritzy suburbs, who calls me up telling me my LaShonda is "depressed" may not be the best teacher for my daughter.

Ms. Montgomery: What would you do, Mrs. Brown, if LaShonda came into the room in the morning and refused to participate or do her work, and then refused to join the group for extra math help?

Mrs. Brown: She does that?

Ms. Montgomery: Every day.

Mrs. Brown: You've never told me this. I can't deal with her if you don't tell me what's going on. I wish you would have told me earlier.

@ *Questions for Reflection*

1. Discuss how social class, child-rearing practices, and the middle-class values of school may each be a factor in LaShonda's behavior in class.
2. If you were Ms. Montgomery, what would you have done differently with LaShonda and her mother?
3. Role-play the continuing discussion among Vice Principal Johnson, Ms. Montgomery, and Mrs. Brown. What would you say, as one of these three participants, to bring a more positive and cooperative conclusion to the meeting?

Source: Adapted from "What Would You Do, Mrs. Brown?" by June Isaacs Elia, from Allyn & Bacon's Custom Cases In Education, edited by Greta Morine-Dershimer, Paul Eggen, and Donald Kauchak. Copyright © 2000 by Pearson Education. Adapted by permission of the publisher.

Greeks, Poles, and Jews) were hopelessly backward and perhaps retarded (Oakes & Lipton, 1994), yet the children and grandchildren of these immigrants now achieve as well as the descendants of the Pilgrims. However, we cannot afford to wait a few decades. The school is one institution that can break the cycle of poverty, by giving children from impoverished backgrounds the opportunity to succeed. Most immediately, schools serving many African American, Latino, and Native American children can accelerate the achievement of these children by using comprehensive reform models and other proven practices (Borman et al., 2003; Herman, 1999; Lee, 2000; Slavin & Madden, 2001).

Effects of School Desegregation

Before 1954, African American, white, and often Latino and Native American students were legally required to attend separate schools in 20 states and the District of Columbia, and segregated schools were common in the remaining states. Students from under-represented groups were often bused miles away from their nearest public school to separate schools. The doctrine of separate but equal education was upheld in several U.S. Supreme Court decisions. In 1954, however, the Supreme Court struck down this practice in the landmark *Brown v. Board of Education of Topeka* case on the grounds that separate education was inherently unequal (Cose, 2004; Smith, 2002). *Brown v. Board of Education* did away with legal segregation, but it was many years before large numbers of racially different students were attending school together. In the 1970s a series of Supreme Court decisions found that the continued segregation of many schools throughout the United States was due to past discriminatory practices, such as deliberately drawing neighborhood boundary lines to separate schools along racial lines. These decisions forced local school districts to desegregate their schools by any means necessary (Kantor & Lowe, 1995).

Many districts were given specific standards for the proportions of students from under-represented groups who could be assigned to any particular school. For example, a district in which 45 percent of the students were African American might be required to have an enrollment of 35 to 55 percent African Americans in each of its schools. To achieve desegregation, some school districts simply changed school attendance areas; others created special magnet schools (such as schools for the performing arts, for talented and gifted students, or for special vocational preparation) to induce students to attend schools outside their own neighborhoods. However, in many large, urban districts, segregation of neighborhoods is so extensive that districts must bus students to other neighborhoods to achieve racially balanced schools. School desegregation was supposed to increase the academic achievement of low-income students from under-represented groups by giving them opportunities to interact with more middle-class, achievement-oriented peers (Lomotey & Teddlie, 1997). All too often, however, the schools to which students are bused are no better than the segregated schools they left behind, and the outflow of middle-class families from urban areas (which was well under way before busing began) often means that lower-class African American or Latino students are integrated with similarly lower-class whites (Kahlenberg, 2000; Trent, 1997). Also, it is important to note that because of residential segregation and opposition to busing, most students from under-represented groups still attend schools in which there are few, if any, whites, and in many areas segregation is once again on the increase (Orfield, Frankenberg, & Lee, 2002/03; Smith, 2002). Support for busing to achieve integration has greatly diminished among African American and Latino parents (Morris, 1999; Wells & Crain, 1997), and in fact there is a small movement toward the deliberate creation of Afrocentric academies in some urban areas.

The overall effect of desegregation on the academic achievement of students from under-represented groups has been small, though positive. However, when desegregation begins in elementary school, particularly when it involves busing children from under-represented groups to high-quality schools with substantially middle-class student bodies, desegregation can have a significant positive effect on the achievement of the students from under-represented groups (Schofield, 1995b; Trent, 1997; Wells, 1995). This effect is thought to result not from sitting next to whites but rather from attending a better school. One important outcome of desegregation is that African

Personal Reflection

Being Sensitive to Race

Long ago I carried out a pilot project in a science class that a friend was teaching in an integrated high school in Portland, Oregon. On the first day, I came to the class and explained to the students that they would be working in groups. I then asked them to select themselves into groups of four.

The students were delighted and immediately chose their groups: one composed entirely of African American boys, one of African American girls, and one of white boys, one of white girls. I was glad to see that there was one integrated group, but it turned out to be composed of students who rarely came to class!

Another time in the same school I went to visit the classroom of a friend who was teaching English. When I came into his class, the students all came rushing up. "Do you know Mr. ___?" they asked. I said I did. "Is he black or white?" It turned out that my friend, who has a dark complexion, recognized that in this school it might be good not to tell the kids his race to avoid being stereotyped as being on one side or the other.

I've now had three of my own children go through integrated high schools in Baltimore. In most ways their experiences with integration have been wonderful, and they all have friends of all races and backgrounds. Yet more than 50 years after *Brown v. Board of Education,* race is still the critical dividing line in our nation, not only in the obvious boundaries that still exist in economics, housing, and society at large, but most disturbingly in the hearts and minds of young people.

@ *Reflect on This. What was the racial or ethnic mix of your K–12 experience? What did your school do to ensure full integration among students? Did this reflect the community efforts as a whole? What discussions about diversity have you had in your education classes? How have those discussions influenced your perspectives on classrooms and learning?*

INTASC

3 Adapting Instruction for Individual Needs

American and Latino students who attend desegregated schools are more likely to attend desegregated colleges, to work in integrated settings, and to attain higher incomes than their peers who attend segregated schools (Schofield, 1995b; Wells & Crain, 1994).

Theory into PRACTICE

Teaching in a Culturally Diverse School

Following are some recommendations for promoting social harmony and equal opportunity among students in racially and ethnically diverse classrooms and schools (see also Banks, 1997b; Gay, 2004; Henze, 2001; Nieto, 2002/03).

- Use fairness and balance in dealing with students. Students should never have any justification for believing that "people like me [whites, African Americans, Latinos, Vietnamese] don't get a fair chance" (McIntyre, 1992).
- Choose texts and instructional materials that show all ethnic groups in equally positive and nonstereotypical roles (Garcia, 1993). Make sure underrepresented groups are not misrepresented. Themes should be nonbiased, and individuals from under-represented groups should appear in nonstereotypical high-status roles (Banks, 1995c, 1997b; Bigler, 1999).

- Supplement textbooks with authentic material from different cultures taken from newspapers, magazines, and other media of the culture.
- Reach out to children's parents and families with information and activities appropriate to their language and culture (Lindeman, 2001). Avoid communicating bias, but discuss racial or ethnic relations with empathy (Stephan & Finlay, 1999) and openly, rather than trying to pretend there are no differences (Polite & Saenger, 2003).
- Avoid stereotyping and emphasize the diversity of individuals, not groups (Aboud & Fenwick, 1999; Levy, 1999).
- Let students know that racial or ethnic bias, including slurs, taunts, and jokes, will not be tolerated in the classroom or in the school. Institute consequences to enforce this standard (Wessler, 2001).
- Help all students to value their own and others' cultural heritages and contributions to history and civilization. At the same time, avoid trivializing or stereotyping cultures merely in terms of ethnic foods and holidays. Because the United States is becoming a mosaic rather than a melting pot, students need more than ever to value diversity and to acquire a more substantive knowledge and appreciation of other ways of life.
- Decorate classrooms, hallways, and the library/media center with murals, bulletin boards, posters, artifacts, and other materials that are representative of the students in the class or school or of the other cultures being studied.
- Avoid resegregation. Tracking, or between-class ability grouping, tends to segregate high and low achievers, and because of historical and economic factors, students from under-represented groups tend to be over-represented in the ranks of low achievers. For this and other reasons, tracking should be avoided (Ferguson & Mehta, 2004; Khmelkov & Hallinan, 1999; Slavin, 1995b).
- Be sure that assignments are not offensive or frustrating to students of diverse cultural groups. For example, asking students to write about their Christmas experiences is inappropriate for non-Christian students.
- Provide structure for intergroup interaction. Proximity alone does not lead to social harmony among racially and ethnically different groups (Schofield, 1997). Students need opportunities to know one another as individuals and to work together toward common goals (Cooper & Slavin, 2004; Kagan, 2001). For example, students who participate in integrated sports and extracurricular activities are more likely than other students to have friends who are ethnically or racially different from themselves (Braddock, Dawkins, & Wilson, 1995; Slavin, 1995b).
- Use cooperative learning, which has been shown to improve relations across racial and ethnic lines (Cooper & Slavin, 2004; National Research Council, 2000). The positive effects of cooperative learning experiences often outlast the teams or groups themselves and may extend to relationships outside of school. Cooperative learning contributes to both achievement and social harmony (Johnson & Johnson, 1998; Slavin, Hurley, & Chamberlain, 2003) and can increase the participation of children from under-represented groups (Cohen, 2004).

*H*OW DO LANGUAGE DIFFERENCES AND BILINGUAL PROGRAMS AFFECT STUDENT ACHIEVEMENT?

As recently as 1979, only 9 percent of Americans ages 5 to 24 were from families in which the primary language spoken was not English. In 1999, this proportion had increased to 17 percent (NCES, 2004), and projections forecast that by 2026, 25 percent of all students will come from homes in which the primary language is not English. Sixty-five percent of these students' families speak Spanish (NCES, 2004). However, many students speak any of dozens of Asian, African, or European languages. The term **language minority** is used for all such students, and **limited English proficient (LEP)** and English language learners (ELL) are terms used for the much smaller number who have not yet attained an adequate level of English to succeed in an English-only program. These students are learning **English as a second language (ESL)** and may attend classes for English language learners in their schools.

Students with limited English proficiency present a dilemma to the educational system (August & Hakuta, 1997). Clearly, those who have limited proficiency in English need to learn English to function effectively in U.S. society. However, until they are proficient in English, should they be taught math or social studies in their first language or in English? Should they be taught to read in their first language? These questions are not just pedagogical—they have political and cultural significance that has provoked emotional debate. One such issue is that many Latino parents want their children to be instructed in the Spanish language and culture to maintain their group identity and pride (Cline, 1998; Macedo, 2000). Other parents whose language is neither English nor Spanish often feel the same way.

Bilingual Education

The term **bilingual education** refers to programs for students who are acquiring English that teach the students in their first language part of the time while English is being learned. English language learners are typically taught in one of four types of programs. They are as follows.

1. *English immersion.* The most common instructional placement for English language learners is some form of English immersion, in which ELL students are taught primarily or entirely in English. Typically, children with the lowest levels of English proficiency are placed in ESL programs to build their oral English to help them succeed in their English-only curriculum. English immersion programs may use carefully designed strategies to build students' vocabularies, simplify instructions, and help ELL students succeed in the content (see, for example, Echevarria, Vogt, & Short, 2004). Such models are often referred to as structured English immersion. Alternatively, ELL students may simply be included in regular English instruction and expected to do the best they can. This "sink or swim" approach is most common when the number of ELL students is small and when ELL students speak languages other than Spanish.

2. *Transitional bilingual education.* A common but declining alternative for ELL students is transitional bilingual education, programs in which children are taught reading or other subjects in their native language (most often, Spanish) for a few years and then transitioned to English, usually in second, third, or fourth grade.

3. *Paired bilingual education.* In paired bilingual models, children are taught reading or other subjects in both their native language and in English, usually at different times of the day.

4. *Two-way bilingual education.* Two-way, or dual language, models teach all students both in English and in another language, usually Spanish. That is, English proficient students are expected to learn Spanish as Spanish proficient students learn English (Calderón & Minaya-Rowe, 2003; Lessow-Hurley, 2005). From the perspective of English language learners, a two-way bilingual program is essentially a paired bilingual program, in that they are taught both in their native language and in English at different times.

language minority
In the United States, native speakers of any language other than English.

limited English proficient (LEP)
Possessing limited mastery of English.

English as a second language (ESL)
Subject taught in English classes and programs for students who are not native speakers of English.

bilingual education
Instructional program for students who speak little or no English in which some instruction is provided in the native language.

"Children, this is not *what we mean by dual language!"*

CERTIFICATION POINTER

In responding to a case study on a teacher certification test, you may be expected to know that conducting an assessment of students' oral language abilities in both their first language and in English would be a first step in helping English language learners achieve.

Research on bilingual strategies for teaching reading generally supports bilingual approaches, especially paired bilingual methods (Greene, 1997; Slavin & Cheung, 2004). The evidence supporting paired bilingual strategies suggests that English language learners need not spend many years building their oral English, but can learn English reading with a limited level of English speaking skills, and can then build their reading and speaking capabilities together (Slavin & Cheung, 2004). However, language of instruction is only one factor in effective education for ELL students, and the quality of instruction (whether in English only or in English and another language) is at least as important (August & Hakuta, 1997).

ON THE WEB

The National Association for Bilingual Education provides support for the education of English language learners at **www.nabe.org**.

Theory into **PRACTICE**

INTASC

4 Multiple Instructional Strategies

6 Communication Skills

7 Instructional Planning Skills

Teaching English Language Learners

Teachers in all parts of the United States and Canada are increasingly likely to have ELLs in their classes. The following are some general principles for helping these students succeed in the English curriculum (see Diaz-Rico, 2004; Echevarria, Vogt, & Short, 2004; Fitzgerald, 1995; Klingner & Vaughn, 2004; Slavin & Calderón, 2001).

1. Don't just say it—show it. All students benefit from pictures, videos, concrete objects, gestures, and actions to illustrate difficult concepts, but ELLs particularly benefit from teaching that includes visual as well as auditory cues (Calderón, 2001).

2. Encourage safe opportunities to use academic English. Many ELLs are shy in class, not wanting to use their English for fear of being laughed at. Yet the best way to learn a language is to use it. Structure opportunities for students to use English in academic contexts. For example, when asking questions, first give students an opportunity to discuss answers with a partner, and then call on partner pairs. This and other forms of cooperative learning can be particularly beneficial for ELLs (Calderón et al., 2004; Calderón, Hertz-Lazarowitz, & Slavin, 1998).

3. Develop vocabulary. All children, but especially ELLs, benefit from explicit teaching of new vocabulary. Give students many opportunities to hear new words in context and to use them themselves in sentences they make up themselves. Learning dictionary definitions is not as useful as having opportunities to ask and answer questions, write new sentences, and discuss new words with partners (Carlo et al., 2004; Fitzgerald, 1995).

4. Keep instructions clear. English language learners (and other students) often know the answers but get confused about what they are supposed to do. Take extra care to see that students understand assignments and instructions, for example, by asking students to restate instructions.

5. Point out cognates. If you speak the language of your ELLs, point out cases in which a word they know is similar to an English word. For example, in a class with many ELLs, you might help students learn the word *amorous* by noting the similarity to the Spanish and Portuguese word *amor*, the French word *amour*, or the Italian word *amore*, depending on the students' languages (Carlo et al., 2004).

6. Never publicly embarrass children by correcting their English. Instead, praise their correct answer and restate it correctly. For example, Russian students often omit *a* and *the*. If a student says, "Mark Twain was famous author," you might respond, "Right! Mark Twain was a very famous author," without calling attention to your addition of the word *a*. To encourage students to use their English, establish a classwide norm of never teasing or laughing at English errors.

Increasingly, research on bilingual education is focusing on the identification of effective forms of instruction for language-minority students rather than on the question of which is the best language of instruction (Christian & Genessee, 2001; Secada et al., 1998; Slavin & Calderón, 2001; U.S. Department of Education, 2000). Cooperative learning programs have been particularly effective both in improving the outcomes of Spanish reading instruction and in helping bilingual students make a successful transition to English-only instruction in the upper elementary grades (Calderón, 1994; Calderón, Hertz-Lazarowitz, & Slavin, 1998; Durán, 1994). A program called Success for All, which combines cooperative learning with one-to-one tutoring for primary-grade students, family support services, and other elements, has had positive effects on the Spanish and English reading of children in bilingual programs (Dianda & Flaherty, 1995; Slavin & Madden, 1999). Case studies of exceptionally successful schools serving Latino students (e.g., Reyes, Scribner, & Paredes, 1999) also provide practical visions for effective practice.

Bilingualism itself has not been found to interfere with performance in either language (Yeung, Marsh, & Suliman, 2000). In fact, Canadian studies have found bilingualism to increase achievement in areas other than the language studied (Cummins, 1998; Slavin & Cheung, 2003). This evidence has been cited as a reason to promote bilingual education for all students. The United States is one of the few countries in the world in which most students graduate from high school knowing only one language (Hakuta & McLaughlin, 1996).

According to research, students in a bilingual program will ultimately achieve in English as well as or better than their peers who are taught only in English. Why do you think this is true?

Bilingual education has many problems, however. One is the lack of teachers who are themselves completely bilingual. This is a particular problem for bilingual education in the languages of the most recent immigrants, such as those from Southeast Asia. A second problem is the difficulty of the transition from the bilingual program to the English-only mainstream program. Third, the goals of bilingual education sometimes conflict with those of desegregation by removing language-minority students from classes containing European American or African American students. Despite all these problems, the alternative to bilingual education—leaving students in the regular class with no support or with part-time instruction in English as a second language (sometimes known as the sink-or-swim approach)—has not been found to be beneficial for students' English language development and risks allowing the language-minority child to fail in school. For example, language-minority children are sometimes assigned to special education because of academic difficulties that are in fact due to lack of proficiency in English (Council of Chief State School Officers, 1990).

Recently, there has been a movement to abandon bilingual education in favor of English-only instruction. In California, which has the largest number of language-minority students in the United States, a referendum called Proposition 227 was passed in 1998 (Merickel et al., 2003). It mandates a maximum of one year for students with limited English proficiency to receive intensive assistance in learning English. After that, children are expected to be in mainstream English-only classes. This legislation has reduced but not eliminated bilingual education in California, as parents may still apply for waivers to have their children taught in their first language. Massachusetts, Arizona, and other states have also passed legislation limiting bilingual education (Hakuta, Butler, & Witt, 2000).

WHAT IS MULTICULTURAL EDUCATION?

In recent years, multicultural education has become a much-discussed topic in U.S. education. Definitions of **multicultural education** vary broadly. The simplest definitions emphasize including non-European perspectives in the curriculum, for example, the works of African, Latino, Asian, and Native American authors in English curricula, teaching about Columbus from the point of view of Native Americans, and teaching more about the cultures and contributions of non-Western societies (Davidman & Davidman, 2001; Diaz, 2001; Manning & Baruth, 2004). Banks (1993) defines multicultural education as encompassing all policies and practices schools might use to improve educational outcomes not only for students of different ethnic, social class, and religious backgrounds, but also for students of different genders and exceptionalities (e.g., children who have mental retardation, hearing loss, or vision loss or who are gifted). Banks (1993) summarizes this definition as follows:

> Multicultural education is an idea stating that all students, regardless of the groups to which they belong, such as those related to gender, ethnicity, race, culture, social class, religion, or exceptionality, should experience educational equality in the schools. (p. 25)

ON THE WEB

For resources and discussions of multicultural education, visit the Multicultural Pavilion at **www.edchange.org/multicultural/mission.html** and the North Central Regional Educational Laboratory at **www.ncrel.org/sdrs/areas/issues/educatrs/presrvce/pe3lk1.htm**.

multicultural education
Education that teaches the value of cultural diversity.

Dimensions of Multicultural Education

Banks (1999) discusses five key dimensions of multicultural education (see Figure 4.2).

Content integration is teachers' use of examples, data, and information from a variety of cultures. This is what most people think of as multicultural education: teaching about different cultures and about contributions made by individuals from diverse cultures, inclusion in the curriculum of works by members of under-represented groups, including women, and the like (Bettmann & Friedman, 2004; Hicks-Bartlett, 2004).

Knowledge construction refers to teachers helping children "understand how knowledge is created and how it is influenced by the racial, ethnic, and social-class positions of individuals and groups" (Banks, 1995b, p. 4). For example, students might be asked to write a history of the early colonization of America from the perspectives of Native Americans or African Americans to learn how the knowledge we take as given is in fact influenced by our own origins and points of view (see Cortés, 1995; Koppelman & Goodheart, 2005).

Prejudice reduction is a critical goal of multicultural education. Prejudice reduction involves both development of positive relationships among students of different ethnic backgrounds (Cooper & Slavin, 2004; Stephan & Vogt, 2004) and development of more democratic and tolerant attitudes toward others (Banks, 1995c).

The term **equity pedagogy** refers to the use of teaching techniques that facilitate the academic success of students from different ethnic and social class groups. For example, there is evidence that members of some ethnic and racial groups, especially Mexican Americans and African Americans, learn best with active and cooperative methods (Boykin, 1994a, 1994b; Losey, 1995; Triandis, 1995).

An **empowering school culture** is one in which school organization and practices are conducive to the academic and emotional growth of all students. A school with such a culture might, for example, eliminate tracking or ability grouping, increase

content integration
Teachers' use of examples, data, and other information from a variety of cultures.

knowledge construction
Helping students understand how the knowledge we take in is influenced by our origins and points of view.

prejudice reduction
A critical goal of multicultural education; involves development of positive relationships and tolerant attitudes among students of different backgrounds.

equity pedagogy
Teaching techniques that facilitate the academic success of students from different ethnic and social class groups.

empowering school culture
A school culture in which the institution's organization and practices are conducive to the academic and emotional growth of all students.

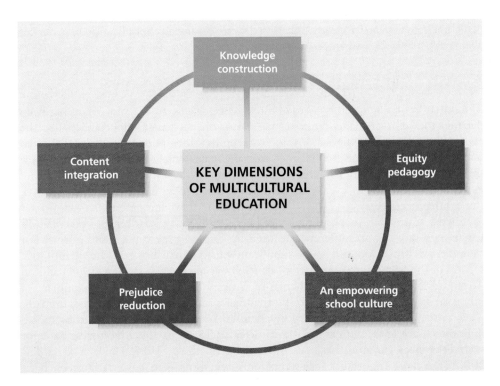

FIGURE 4.2
Five Key Dimensions of Multicultural Education
Adapted from James A. Banks, "Historical Development, Dimensions, and Practice," in James A. Banks and Cherry A. Banks (eds.), *Handbook of Research on Multicultural Education*, 1999, New York: Simon & Schuster Macmillan.

inclusion (and reduce labeling) of students with special needs, try to keep all students on a path leading to higher education, and consistently show high expectations. An excellent example of an empowering school culture is the AVID project (Swanson, Mehan, & Hubbard, 1995; Watt, Powell, & Mendiola, 2004), which places at-risk students from under-represented groups in college preparatory classes and provides them with tutors and other assistance to help them succeed in a demanding curriculum.

The first step in multicultural education is for teachers, administrators, and other school staff to learn about the cultures from which their children come and to carefully examine all the policies, practices, and curricula used in the school to identify any areas of possible bias (e.g., teaching only about European and European American culture or history). Books by Banks (2001), Davidman and Davidman (2001), Diaz (2001), Koppelman & Goodheart (2005), and Manning and Baruth (2004) are good places to start. These and other books identify some of the characteristics of various cultures and teaching strategies and materials that are appropriate to each.

CERTIFICATION POINTER

For your teacher certification test you should recognize the importance of connecting your instruction to your students' cultural experiences.

How DO GENDER AND GENDER BIAS AFFECT STUDENTS' SCHOOL EXPERIENCES?

A child's sex is a visible, permanent attribute. Cross-cultural research indicates that gender roles are among the first that individuals learn and that all societies treat males differently from females. Therefore, gender-role or sex-role behavior is learned behavior. However, the range of roles occupied by males and females across cultures is broad. What is considered natural behavior for each gender is based more on cultural belief than on biological necessity. Nevertheless, the extent to which biological differences and gender socialization affect behavioral patterns and achievement is still a much-debated topic. The consensus of a large body of research is that no matter what the inherent biological differences, many of the observed differences between males and females can be clearly linked to differences in early socialization experiences (Feingold, 1992; Grossman & Grossman, 1994).

Do Males and Females Think and Learn Differently?

INTASC

2 Knowledge of Human Development and Learning

The question of gender differences in intelligence or academic achievement has been debated for centuries, and the issue has taken on particular importance since the early 1970s. The most important thing to keep in mind about this debate is that no responsible researcher has ever claimed that any male–female differences on any measure of intellectual ability are large in comparison to the amount of variability within each sex. In other words, even in areas in which true gender differences are suspected, these differences are so small and so variable that they have few practical consequences (Fennema, Carpenter, Jacobs, Franke, & Levi, 1998; Sadker, Sadker, & Long, 1997). Far more important are differences caused by cultural expectations and norms. For example, twelfth-grade girls score significantly lower than boys on the quantitative section of the Scholastic Assessment Test (SAT) (Gallagher & De Lisi, 1994) and on Advanced Placement tests in mathematics (Stumpf & Stanley, 1996). A summary of 20 major studies by Kim (2001) found that males scored better than females in math, whereas the opposite was true on English tests. Surprisingly, males scored better on multiple choice tests, but not on other formats. There may be a biological basis for such differences, but none has been proven (see Friedman, 1995; Halpern & LaMay, 2000). The most important cause is that females in our society have traditionally been discouraged from studying mathematics and therefore take many fewer math courses than males do. In fact, as females have begun to take more math courses over the past two decades, the gender gap on the SAT and on other measures has been steadily diminishing (National Center for Education Statistics, 1997).

Bearing these cautions in mind, note that studies generally find that males score higher than females on tests of general knowledge, mechanical reasoning, and mental rotations; females score higher on language measures, including reading and writing assessments (ETS, 2001), and on attention and planning tasks (Warrick & Naglieri, 1993). There are no male–female differences in general verbal ability, arithmetic skills, abstract reasoning, spatial visualization, or memory span (Fennema et al., 1998; Friedman, 1995; Halpern & LaMay, 2000). There is an interesting argument about variability of performance in certain areas. For example, Feingold (1992) has argued that males are more variable than females in quantitative reasoning—that is, that there are more very high-achieving males and more very low-achieving males than there are females in either category. Studies of students who are extremely gifted in mathematics consistently find a substantially higher number of males than females in this category (e.g., Mills, Ablard, & Stumpf, 1993). However, there is still a lively debate about the idea that males are more variable than females in intellectual abilities (Bielinski & Davison, 1998).

In school grades, females start out with an advantage over males and maintain this advantage into high school. Even in math and science, in which females score somewhat lower on tests, females still get better grades in class (Maher & Ward, 2002). Despite this, high school males tend to overestimate their skills in language and math (as measured by standardized tests), while females underestimate their skills (Pomerantz, Altermatt, & Saxon, 2002). In elementary school, males are much more likely than females to have reading problems (Taylor & Lorimer, 2002/03) and are much more likely to have learning disabilities or emotional disorders (Smith, 2001).

Sex-Role Stereotyping and Gender Bias

If there are so few genetically based differences between males and females, why do so many behavioral differences exist? These behavioral differences originate from different experiences, including reinforcement by adults for different types of behavior.

Male and female babies have traditionally been treated differently from the time they are born. The wrapping of the infant in either a pink or a blue blanket symbolizes the variations in experience that typically greet the child from birth onward. In early studies, adults described boy or girl babies wrapped in blue blankets as being more active than the same babies wrapped in pink. Other masculine traits were also ascribed to those wrapped in blue (Baxter, 1994). Although gender bias awareness has begun to have some impact on child-rearing practices, children do begin to make gender distinctions and have gender preferences by around the age of 3 or 4. Thus, children enter school having been socialized into appropriate gender-role behavior for their age in relation to community expectations (Delamont, 2001). Differences in approved gender roles between boys and girls tend to be much stronger in low-SES families than in high-SES families (Flanagan, 1993).

Socialization into this kind of approved **sex-role behavior** continues throughout life, and schools contribute to it. Though interactions between socialization experiences and achievement are complex and it is difficult to make generalizations, schools differentiate between the sexes in a number of ways. In general, males receive more attention from their teachers than females do (Koch, 2003). Males receive more disapproval and blame from their teachers than females do, but they also engage in more interactions with their teachers in such areas as approval, instruction giving, and being listened to (Koch, 2003; Maher & Ward, 2002; Sadker & Sadker, 1994). Teachers

sex-role behavior
Socially approved behavior associated with one gender as opposed to the other.

What are various examples of how U.S. culture has changed with regard to gender roles? What perceptions have yet to change? What impact might gender bias have on you as a teacher, both personally and professionally?

tend to punish females more promptly and explicitly for aggressive behavior than they do males. Torrance (1986) found that the creative behavior of males was rewarded by teachers three times as often as that of females. Other differentiations are subtle, as when girls are directed to play in the house corner while boys are provided with blocks or when boys are given the drums to play in music class and girls are given the triangles.

Theory into **PRACTICE**

INTASC

6 Communication Skills

Avoiding Gender Bias in Teaching

"In my science class the teacher never calls on me, and I feel like I don't exist. The other night I had a dream that I vanished" (Sadker & Sadker, 1994). Unfortunately, the girl who complained of being ignored by her teacher is not alone. According to a national study undertaken by the American Association of University Women (1992), schools shortchange female students in a variety of ways, from ignoring instances of sexual harassment to interacting less frequently with females than with males and less frequently with African American females than with white females. Teachers tend to choose boys, boost the self-esteem of their male students, and select literature with male protagonists. The contributions and experiences of girls and women are still often ignored in textbooks, curricula, and standardized tests (Zittleman & Sadker, 2002/03).

gender bias
Stereotypical views and differential treatment of males and females, often favoring one gender over the other.

Teachers, usually without being aware of it, exhibit **gender bias** in classroom teaching in three principal ways: reinforcing gender stereotypes, maintaining sex separation, and treating males and females differently as students (see Grossman & Grossman, 1994; Horgan, 1995; Koch, 2003; Maher & Ward, 2002; Sadker,

Sadker, Fox, & Salata, 1994). These inequities can have negative consequences for boys as well as girls (Canada, 2000; Weaver-Hightower, 2003).

Avoiding stereotypes. Teachers should avoid promoting sexual stereotypes. For example, they can assign jobs in the classroom without regard to gender, avoiding automatically appointing males as group leader and females as secretary, and can ask both males and females to help in physical activities. Teachers should also refrain from stating stereotypes, such as "Boys don't cry" and "Girls don't fight," and should avoid labeling students with such terms as *tomboy*. Teachers should encourage students who show an interest in activities and careers that do not correspond to cultural stereotypes, such as a female who likes math and science (Sadker, Sadker, & Long, 1997).

Promoting integration. One factor that leads to gender stereotyping is the tendency for boys and girls (particularly in elementary school) to have few friends of the opposite sex and to engage mostly in activities with members of their own sex. Teachers sometimes encourage this by having boys and girls line up separately, assigning them to sex-segregated tables, and organizing separate sports activities for males and females. As a result, interaction between boys and girls in schools is less frequent than between students of the same sex. However, in classes in which cross-sex collaboration is encouraged, children have less stereotyped views of the abilities of males and females (Klein, 1994).

Treating females and males equally. Too often, teachers do not treat males and females equally. Observational studies of classroom interactions have found that teachers interact more with boys than with girls and ask boys more questions, especially more abstract questions (Sadker et al., 1997). In one study, researchers showed teachers videotapes of classroom scenes and asked them whether boys or girls participated more. Most teachers responded that the girls talked more, even though in fact the boys participated more than the girls by a ratio of 3 to 1 (Sadker et al., 1997). The researchers interpreted this finding as indicating that teachers expect females to participate less and thus see low rates of participation as normal. Teachers must be careful to allow all students equal opportunities to participate in class, to take leadership roles, and to engage in all kinds of activities (Bernard-Powers, 2001; Stein, 2000).

*H*OW DO STUDENTS DIFFER IN INTELLIGENCE AND LEARNING STYLES?

Intelligence is one of those words that everyone believes they understand until you ask them to define it. At one level, **intelligence** can be defined as a general aptitude for learning or an ability to acquire and use knowledge or skills. However, even experts on this topic do not agree in their definitions; in a survey of 24 experts by Sternberg and Detterman (1986), definitions varied widely. A consensus definition expressed by Snyderman and Rothman (1987) is that intelligence is the ability to deal with abstractions, to solve problems, and to learn.

The biggest problem comes when we ask whether there is such a thing as general aptitude (Sternberg, 2003). Many people are terrific at calculus but couldn't write a good essay or paint a good picture if their lives depended on it. Some people can walk

INTASC

4 Multiple Instructional Strategies

intelligence
General aptitude for learning, often measured by the ability to deal with abstractions and to solve problems.

into a room full of strangers and immediately figure out the relationships and feelings among them; others may never learn this skill. Clearly, individuals vary in their aptitude for learning any specific type of knowledge or skill taught in a specific way. A hundred students attending a lecture on a topic they knew nothing about beforehand will all walk away with different amounts and kinds of learning, and aptitude for that particular content and that particular teaching method is one important factor in explaining these differences. The student who learned the most from the lecture would be likely also to learn very well from other lectures on similar topics. But would this student also learn the most if the lecture were on a different topic or if the same material were presented through hands-on experiences or in small groups?

CONNECTIONS

For more on the measurement of IQ, see Chapter 14, page 504.

The concept of intelligence has been discussed since before the time of the ancient Greeks, but the scientific study of this topic really began with the work of Alfred Binet, who devised the first measure of intelligence in 1904. The French government asked Binet to find a way to identify children who were likely to need special help in their schooling. His measure assessed a broad range of skills and performances but produced a single score, called **intelligence quotient (IQ),** which was set up so that the average French child would have an IQ of 100 (Hurn, 2002).

Definitions of Intelligence

Binet's work greatly advanced the science of intelligence assessment, but it also began to establish the idea that intelligence was a single thing—that there were "smart" people who could be expected to do well in a broad range of learning situations. Ever since Binet, debate has raged about this issue. In 1927 Charles Spearman claimed that while there were, of course, variations in a person's abilities from task to task, there was a general intelligence factor, or "g," that existed across all learning situations. Is there really one intelligence, as Spearman suggested, or are there many distinct intelligences?

The evidence in favor of "g" is that abilities are correlated with each other. Individuals who are good at learning one thing are likely, on the average, to be good at learning other things. The correlations are consistent enough for us to say that there

According to Gardner's theory of multiple intelligences, which of the eight intelligences might these students use to learn? As a teacher, how would you vary your lessons to address student differences in learning style?

Table 4.4		
The Eight Intelligences		
Intelligence	*End States*	*Core Components*
Logical/mathematical	Scientist, mathematician	Sensitivity to, and capacity to discern, logical or numerical patterns; ability to handle long chains of reasoning.
Linguistic	Poet, journalist	Sensitivity to the sounds, rhythms, and meanings of words; sensitivity to the different functions of language.
Musical	Composer, violinist	Abilities to produce and appreciate rhythm, pitch, and timbre; appreciation of the forms of musical expressiveness.
Naturalist	Naturalist, botanist, hunter	Sensitivity to natural objects, like plants and animals; making fine sensory discriminations.
Spatial	Navigator, sculptor	Capacities to perceive the visual–spatial world accurately and to perform transformations on one's initial perceptions.
Bodily/kinesthetic	Dancer, athlete	Ability to control one's body movements and to handle objects skillfully.
Interpersonal	Therapist, salesperson	Capacities to discern and respond appropriately to the moods, temperaments, motivations, and desires of other people.
Intrapersonal	Person with detailed, accurate self-knowledge	Access to one's own feelings and the ability to discriminate among them and draw on them to guide behavior; knowledge of one's own strengths, weaknesses, desires, and intelligences.

Source: From H. Gardner and T. Hatch, "Multiple Intelligences Go to School," *Educational Researcher, 18*(8), p. 6. Copyright © 1989 by the American Educational Research Association. Adapted by permission of the publisher and the authors.

are not a thousand completely separate intelligences, but they are not nearly consistent enough to allow us to say that there is only one general intelligence (Gustafsson, 1994; Sternberg, 2003). In recent years, much of the debate about intelligence has focused on deciding how many distinct types of intelligence there are and describing each. For example, Sternberg (2002, 2003) describes 3 types of intellectual abilities: analytical, practical, and creative. Guilford (1988) proposes 180 types of intelligence: 6 types of mental operations (e.g., thinking, memory, and creativity) times 5 types of content (e.g., visual, auditory, and verbal content) times 6 types of products (e.g., relations and implications). Gardner and Hatch (1989) describe 8 **multiple intelligences** (see Gardner, 2003). These are listed and defined in Table 4.4.

ON THE WEB

For a summary of Sternberg's work on intelligence go to **www.indiana.edu/%7Eintell/ sternberg.shtml**.

The precise number of intelligences is not important for educators. What is important is the idea that good or poor performance in one area in no way guarantees similar performance in another. Teachers must avoid thinking about children as smart or not smart, since there are many ways to be smart. Unfortunately, schools have traditionally recognized only a narrow set of performances, creating a neat hierarchy of students primarily in terms of what Gardner calls linguistic and logical/mathematical

intelligence quotient (IQ) An intelligence test score that for people of average intelligence should be near 100.

multiple intelligences In Gardner's theory of intelligence, a person's eight separate abilities: logical/mathematical, linguistic, musical, naturalist, spatial, bodily/ kinesthetic, interpersonal, and intrapersonal.

skills (only two of his eight intelligences). If schools want all children to be smart, they must use a broader range of activities and reward a broader range of performances than they have in the past.

Theory into **PRACTICE**

Multiple Intelligences

Gardner's theory of multiple intelligences implies that concepts should be taught in a variety of ways that call on many types of intelligence (Kornhaber, Fierros, & Veenema, 2004; Krechevsky, Hoer, & Gardner, 1995). To illustrate this, Armstrong (1994) gives the following examples of different ways to teach Boyle's Law to secondary students.

- Students are provided with a verbal definition of Boyle's Law: "For a fixed mass and temperature of gas, the pressure is inversely proportional to the volume." They discuss the definition. [Linguistic]
- Students are given a formula that describes Boyle's Law: $P \times V = K$. They solve specific problems connected to it. [Logical/mathematical]
- Students are given a metaphor or visual image for Boyle's Law: "Imagine that you have a boil on your hand that you start to squeeze. As you squeeze it, the pressure builds. The more you squeeze, the higher the pressure, until the boil finally bursts and pus spurts out all over your hand!" [Spatial]
- Students do the following experiment: They breathe air into their mouths so that their cheeks puff up slightly. Then they put all the air into one side of their mouth (less volume) and indicate whether pressure goes up or down (it goes up); then they're asked to release the air in both sides of their mouth (more volume) and asked to indicate whether pressure has gone up or down (it goes down). [Bodily/kinesthetic]
- Students become "molecules" of air in a "container" (a clearly defined corner of the classroom). They move at a constant rate (temperature) and cannot leave the container (constant mass). Gradually, the size of the container is reduced as two volunteers holding a piece of yarn representing one side of the container start moving it in on the "molecules." The smaller the space, the more pressure (i.e., bumping into each other) is observed; the greater the space, the less pressure is observed. [Interpersonal, bodily/kinesthetic]
- Students do lab experiments that measure air pressure in sealed containers and chart pressure against volume. [Logical/mathematical, bodily/kinesthetic]
- Students are asked about times in their lives when they were "under pressure": "Did you feel like you had a lot of space?" (Typical answer: lots of pressure/not much space.) Then students are asked about times when they felt little pressure (little pressure/lots of space). Students' experiences are related to Boyle's Law. [Intrapersonal]

Few lessons will contain parts that correspond to all types of intelligence, but a key recommendation of multiple-intelligence theory for the classroom is that teachers seek to include a variety of presentation modes in each lesson to expand the number of students who are likely to succeed (Campbell, Campbell, & Dickinson, 1996; Gardner, 1995; Kline, 2001).

Origins of Intelligence

The origins of intelligence have been debated for decades. Some psychologists (such as Herrnstein & Murray, 1994; Jensen, 1980) hold that intelligence is overwhelmingly a product of heredity—that children's intelligence is largely determined by that of their parents and is set the day they are conceived. Others (such as Gordon & Bhattacharyya, 1994; Plomin, 1989; Rifkin, 1998) just as vehemently hold that intelligence is shaped mostly by factors in a person's social environment, such as the amount a child is read to and talked to. Most investigators agree that both heredity and environment play an important part in intelligence (Petrill & Wilkerson, 2000). It is clear that children of high-achieving parents are, on the average, more likely to be high achievers themselves, but this is due as much to the home environment created by high-achieving parents as to genetics (Turkheimer, 1994). French studies of children of low-SES parents adopted into high-SES families find strong positive effects on the children's IQs compared to nonadopted children raised in low-SES families (Capron & Duyme, 1991; Schiff & Lewontin, 1986). One important piece of evidence in favor of the environmental view is that schooling itself clearly affects IQ scores. A review by Ceci (1991) found that the experience of being in school has a strong and systematic impact on IQ. For example, classic studies of Dutch children who entered school late because of World War II showed significant declines in IQ as a result, although their IQs increased when they finally entered school. A study of the children of mothers with mental retardation in inner-city Milwaukee (Garber, 1988) found that a program of infant stimulation and high-quality preschool could raise children's IQs substantially, and these gains were maintained at least through the end of elementary school. Studies of the Abecedarian program, which combined infant stimulation, child enrichment, and parent assistance, also found lasting effects of early instruction on IQ (Ramey & Ramey, 1998). This and other evidence supports the idea that IQ is not a fixed, unchangeable attribute of individuals but can change as individuals respond to changes in their environment (Cardellichio & Field, 1997). Further, some evidence indicates that IQ can be directly changed by programs designed for this purpose (Ellis, 2001; Feuerstein & Kozulin, 1995).

CONNECTIONS

For a description of studies indicating that IQ can be directly changed by certain programs, see Chapter 8, page 266.

Intelligence, whether general or specific, is only one of many factors that influence the amount children are likely to learn in a given lesson or course. It is probably much less important than prior knowledge (the amount the student knew about the course beforehand), motivation, and the quality and nature of instruction. Intelligence does become important at the extremes, as it is a critical issue in identifying students who have mental retardation or those who are gifted, but in the middle range, where most students fall, other factors are more important. IQ testing has very frequently been misused in education, especially when it has been used to assign students inappropriately to special education or to tracks or ability groups (Hilliard, 1994). Actual performance is far more important than IQ and is more directly susceptible to being influenced by teachers and schools (Sternberg, 2003). Boykin (2000) has argued that schools would do better to focus on developing talents, rather than seeing them as fixed attributes of students.

Theories of Learning Styles

CERTIFICATION POINTER
Teacher certification tests may ask you to design a lesson that would accommodate students' various learning styles, in addition to their developmental needs.

Just as students have different personalities, they also have different ways of learning. For example, think about how you learn the names of people you meet. Do you learn a name better if you see it written down? If so, you may be a visual learner, one who learns best by seeing or reading. If you learn a name better by hearing it, you may be an auditory learner. Of course, we all learn in many ways, but some of us learn better in some ways than in others (McCarthy, 1997; Swisher & Schoorman, 2001).

There are several other differences in **learning styles** that educational psychologists have studied. One has to do with **field dependence** versus **field independence** (Kogan, 1994). Field-dependent individuals tend to see patterns as a whole and have difficulty separating out specific aspects of a situation or pattern; field-independent people are more able to see the parts that make up a large pattern. Field-dependent people tend to be more oriented toward people and social relationships than are field-independent people; for example, they tend to be better at recalling such social information as conversations and relationships, to work best in groups, and to prefer such subjects as history and literature. Field-independent people are more likely to do well with numbers, science, and problem-solving tasks (Wapner & Demick, 1991).

Students may also vary in preferences for different learning environments or conditions. For example, Dunn and Dunn (1993) found that students differ in preferences about such things as the amount of lighting, hard or soft seating, quiet or noisy surroundings, and working alone or with peers. These differences can predict to some extent which learning environments will be most effective for each child.

Aptitude–Treatment Interactions

Given the well-documented differences in learning styles and preferences, it would seem logical that different styles of teaching would have different impacts on different learners; yet this commonsense proposition has been difficult to demonstrate conclusively. Studies that have attempted to match teaching styles to learning styles have only inconsistently found any benefits for learning (Knight, Halpin, & Halpin, 1992;

learning styles
Orientations for approaching learning tasks and processing information in certain ways.

field dependence
Cognitive style in which patterns are perceived as a whole.

field independence
Cognitive style in which separate parts of a pattern are perceived and analyzed.

aptitude–treatment interaction
Interaction of individual differences in learning with particular teaching methods.

Personal Reflection

INTASC **3** Adapting Instruction for Individual Needs
4 Multiple Instructional Strategies

Understanding Diverse Thinkers

In his article "Celebrating Diverse Minds," author, physician, and educator Mel Levine of the University of North Carolina explores the importance of celebrating "all kinds of minds" as a way of making sure no child is left behind. He asks, "What becomes of students . . . who give up on themselves because they lack the kinds of minds needed to satisfy existing criteria for school success?"

Levine points out that learning differences can

constitute daunting barriers, especially when they are not recognized and managed. Most important, these breakdowns can mislead us into undervaluing, unfairly accusing, and even undereducating students, thereby stifling their chances for success in school and life.

Many faltering students have specialized minds—brains exquisitely wired to perform certain kinds of tasks masterfully, but decidedly miswired when it comes to meeting other expectations. A student may be brilliant at visualizing, but embarrassingly inept at verbalizing. [A] classmate may reveal a remarkable understanding of people, but exhibit no insight about sentence structure.

. . . Within every student contending with learning differences, an area invariably exists in which her or his mind has been amply equipped to thrive. (Levine, 2003, p. 12)

Levine proposes addressing this problem in three ways:

• **Broaden student assessment.** Our understanding of learning differences often focuses on fixing deficits, rather than identifying latent or blatant talents in struggling learners.
• **Reexamine the curriculum.** Explore new instructional practices and curricular choices in order to provide educational opportunities for diverse learners and to prepare them for a successful life.
• **Provide professional development for educators.** Provide teachers with training on the insights from brain research that will help them understand and support their students' diverse minds.

(@) Reflect on This. Did you or someone you know ever experience frustration over learning a concept or skill more slowly than peers? How would you define your learning style? What steps can you take as a teacher to become aware of your students' different learning styles and adapt your lessons accordingly?

Snow, 1992). However, the search for such **aptitude–treatment interaction** goes on, and a few studies have found positive effects for programs that adapt instruction to an individual's learning style (Dunn, Beaudrey, & Klavas, 1989). The common-sense conclusion from research in this area is that teachers should be alert to detecting and responding to the differences in the ways that children learn (see Ebeling, 2000).

Chapter Summary

What Is the Impact of Culture on Teaching and Learning?

Culture profoundly affects teaching and learning. Many aspects of culture contribute to the learner's identity and self-concept and affect the learner's beliefs and values, attitudes and expectations, social relations, language use, and other behaviors.

How Does Socioeconomic Status Affect Student Achievement?

Socioeconomic status—based on income, occupation, education, and social prestige—can profoundly influence the learner's attitudes toward school, background knowledge, school readiness, and academic achievement. Working-class and low-income families experience stress that contributes to child-rearing practices, communication patterns, and lowered expectations that may handicap children when they enter school. Low-SES students often learn a normative culture that is different from the middle-class culture of the school, which demands independence, competitiveness, and goal-setting. However, low achievement is not the inevitable result of low socioeconomic status. Teachers can invite parents to participate in their children's education, and this can improve students' achievement.

How Do Ethnicity and Race Affect Students' School Experiences?

Populations of under-represented groups are growing dramatically as diversity in the United States increases. Students who are members of certain under-represented groups—self-defined by race, religion, ethnicity, origins, history, language, and culture, such as African Americans, Native Americans, and Latinos—tend to have lower scores than those of European and Asian Americans on standardized tests of academic achievement. The lower scores correlate with lower socioeconomic status and reflect in part a legacy of discrimination against under-represented groups and consequent poverty. School desegregation, long intended as a solution to educational inequities due to race and social class, has had mixed benefits. Continuing issues include delivering fairness and equal opportunity, fostering racial harmony, and preventing segregation.

How Do Language Differences and Bilingual Programs Affect Student Achievement?

English language learners are typically taught in one of four types of programs: English immersion, transitional bilingual, paired bilingual, and two-way bilingual. Bilingual programs teach students in their native language as well as English. Research suggests that bilingual education, especially paired bilingual education, can have benefits for students. Recent legislation in states throughout the country has had a chilling effect on bilingual education.

THE INTENTIONAL TEACHER

Using What You Know about Student Diversity to Improve Teaching and Learning

Intentional teachers view student diversity as a rich resource. They learn about their students' home lives, cultures, languages, and strengths, and they value each student as an individual. Intentional teachers examine data from their classrooms and question their own practices, guarding against the possibility that their perspectives may inadvertently limit students' success. Intentional teachers use what they know about their own practices and their particular students to improve the quality of education for all.

❶ What do I expect my students to know and be able to do at the end of this lesson? How does this contribute to course objectives and to students' needs to become capable individuals?

Teachers need to examine the influence of their own cultural perspectives on the expectations they hold for students. Ask yourself, "Do my goals reflect only the values of a dominant group?" For example, you might curb your impulse to give stickers to the first five of your third-graders who earn 100 percent on their multiplication facts, deciding that your appreciation of individual competition may not be shared by all. You might decide to give students choices about how they do book reports, so that children with different learning strengths can express themselves in different ways.

Many educators feel that educational goals should reflect, at least to some extent, the community within which children are educated. Ask yourself, "How can we revise our classroom goals to better reflect the needs, values, and interests of all our students and families?" For example, you might begin a class with an informal discussion about what students would like to learn and about students' definitions of success. Students' interests and cultural backgrounds should not entirely determine your goals for a given lesson or course, but they should

be taken into account. Algebra is algebra, but there are many paths to proficiency in algebra. Find out the paths your students are most willing and able to travel.

❷ What knowledge, skills, needs, and interests do my students have that must be taken into account in my lesson?

Intentional teachers learn about their students and draw on information about their students' home lives and community resources to plan their instruction. What is your understanding of students' cultures and community? Ask yourself, "What experiences and strengths have my students gathered outside of school that can foster their learning?" For example, although you provide instruction in English, you might look for ways to value students' home language, reinforcing the idea that knowing two languages is an asset. You might design a "multilingual dictionary" activity, developing a list of classroom and family words in English, and asking students with different home languages to translate the list into their language. You could print and distribute this short dictionary at a PTA meeting as well as to the class members, who might wish to discuss similarities and differences between the languages represented and the English equivalents. In any class, you could collect colorful expressions, sayings, or slang reflecting the cultural heritages of your students. These "dictionaries" might be exchanged on the Internet or by mail with similar efforts from classes in different regions or parts of town.

❸ What do I know about the content, child development, learning, motivation, and effective teaching strategies that I can use to accomplish my objectives?

Intentional teachers may provide opportunities for students to choose ways of interacting with subject-matter content that re-

What Is Multicultural Education?

Multicultural education is calling for the celebration of cultural diversity and the promotion of educational equity and social harmony in the schools. Multicultural education includes content integration, knowledge construction, prejudice reduction, equity pedagogy, and an empowering school culture.

How Do Gender and Gender Bias Affect Students' School Experiences?

Many observed differences between males and females are clearly linked to differences in early socialization, when children learn sex-role behaviors regarded as appropriate. Ongoing research shows very few genetically based gender differences in thinking and abilities. However, gender bias in the classroom, including subtle teacher behav-

flect their learning-style preferences. You might vary grouping structures so that students work in whole-class, individual, and flexible small groups. You might employ principles of sheltered instruction, which makes grade-level content accessible to all, for your English language learners. For example, you could provide graphic organizers of the literature and bring in real examples of the items described in your readings.

❹ What instructional materials, technology, assistance, and other resources are available to help accomplish my objectives?

Effective teachers work as part of an educational team. Draw on the strengths that can come from teachers and parents working together. For example, you might survey parents about relevant summer programs. To help students maintain academic gains, you might help them acquire library cards and suggest books for them to read over vacation. You might give them each a journal and invite them—and their parents!—to write to you.

If your class includes a number of bilingual students, you might ask for volunteers to invite an older family member to talk to your art class about the particular art forms of their place of origin, and you might explain that the student would be asked to serve as translator and interpreter.

Use children's cultural backgrounds as a springboard to mainstream content and expectations. A Navajo child, for example, has as much need to learn about ancient Greece as any other child, but he or she comes with a rich background that an intentional teacher should evoke to help interpret Greek culture.

❺ How will I plan to assess students' progress toward my objectives?

Collect information on your teaching to ensure that your practices are equitable. An observer might gather information, or you might tape your teaching for later analysis. Key questions include:

Do I give equal time to interacting with males and females?

Do I praise and admonish students for the same types of behaviors, no matter what their group?

Are my expectations uniformly high for all students? Do I express this clearly?

To the extent appropriate, do I use the classroom as a forum for students to question mainstream perspectives and existing conditions? To encourage social improvement?

❻ How will I respond if individual children or the class as a whole is not on track toward success? What is my back-up plan?

You might ask yourself: "How can I confirm my current understanding of my diverse students and how can I learn more about particular groups? Have I made an effort to meet some of the adults that my students speak of as influential in their community or highly regarded by their family? Are the literature selections for class readings representative of a range of authors—by gender, nationality, ethnicity? Is my own personal reading contributing to a better understanding of diversity and individual differences?"

iors toward male and female students and curriculum materials that contain sex-role stereotypes, has clearly affected student choices and achievement. One outcome is a gender gap in mathematics and science, though this gap has decreased steadily.

How Do Students Differ in Intelligence and Learning Styles?

Students differ in their ability to deal with abstractions, to solve problems, and to learn. They also differ in any number of specific intelligences, so accurate estimations of intelligence should probably rely on broader performances than traditional IQ tests allow. Therefore teachers should not base their expectations of students on IQ test scores. Binet, Spearman, Sternberg, Guilford, and Gardner have contributed to theories and measures of intelligence. Both heredity and environment determine intelligence. Research shows that home environments, schooling, and life experiences can profoundly influence IQ.

Students differ in their prior learning and in their cognitive learning styles. Field-dependent people tend to see patterns as a whole and do better with people and social relationships. Field-independent people are more likely to see parts that make up a large pattern and do better with subjects such as science. Individual preferences in learning environments and conditions also affect student achievement.

Key Terms

Review the following key terms from the chapter. Then, to explore research on these topics and how they relate to education today, connect to Research Navigator™ through this book's Companion Website or directly at www.researchnavigator.com.

aptitude–treatment interaction 126	intelligence 121
bilingual education 113	intelligence quotient (IQ) 123
content integration 117	knowledge construction 117
culture 98	language minority 113
empowering school culture 117	learning styles 126
English as a second language (ESL) 113	limited English proficient (LEP) 113
equity pedagogy 117	minority group 106
ethnicity 106	multicultural education 116
ethnic group 106	multiple intelligences 123
field dependence 126	prejudice reduction 117
field independence 126	race 106
gender bias 120	sex-role behavior 119
	socioeconomic status (SES) 99

Self-Assessment: Practicing for Licensure

Directions: The chapter-opening vignette addresses indicators that are often assessed in state licensure exams. Re-read the chapter-opening vignette, and then respond to the following questions.

1. Marva Vance and John Rossi discuss their students' diverse norms, traditions, behaviors, languages, and perceptions. Which of the following terms best describes the essence of their conversation?

   a. race
   b. socioeconomic status
   c. intelligence
   d. culture

2. In regard to the students of Marva Vance and John Rossi, which of the following statements on socioeconomic status is most likely true?

   a. Students from working-class or lower-class backgrounds perform academically as well as or better than students from middle-class homes.
   b. Students from disadvantaged homes are more likely to have inadequate access to health care.
   c. Students from middle-class and lower-class homes are equally likely to make academic progress over the summer.
   d. Schools overwhelmingly represent the values and expectations of the working class.

3. Marva Vance and John Rossi discuss their students' tendencies to accept the stereotypical roles assigned to them by society. According to research, what should the teachers do about this stereotyping?

  a. Allow students to select their own roles, even if they make stereotypical decisions.

  b. Tell the story of Thanksgiving as realistically as possible: Indian students play Indians, girls play cooks, and boys play hunters.

  c. Themes should be nonbiased, and individuals from under-represented groups should appear in non-stereotypical high-status roles.

  d. Write a Thanksgiving play that includes the contributions of all under-represented groups.

4. José, a student in Marva Vance's class, wants to be the narrator of the Thanksgiving pageant, even though he is not proficient in English. According to research on the effectiveness of bilingual programs, which strategy might Ms. Vance use to improve all her students' English speaking and writing skills?

  a. Ms. Vance should avoid bilingual programs because they have been found to be harmful to students in their English development.

  b. Ms. Vance should learn the languages of the students in her class.

  c. Ms. Vance should support bilingual education since studies have found that students in bilingual programs ultimately achieve in English as well as or better than students taught only in English.

  d. Ms. Vance should speak out about the detrimental effects of bilingual education on a student's self-esteem.

5. Marva Vance and John Rossi discuss stereotypical gender roles in the Thanksgiving pageant. From the research reported in this section, how should the teachers assign male and female students to the roles in the pageant?

  a. The teachers should encourage students to select roles in which they are interested, not roles that society expects them to play.

  b. The teachers should reduce the interactions of males and females in the pageant.

  c. The teachers should assign males and females to authentic roles: males are hunters, females are cooks.

  d. The teachers should assign all students to nontypical racial and gender roles.

6. What is multicultural education? What steps can teachers, administrators, and other school personnel take to reach their students from under-represented groups?

7. Students differ in their prior learning and in their cognitive learning styles. What strategies can teachers use to reach all of their students?

8. List six strategies that a teacher could implement to involve parents or caregivers in helping students meet their potential.

Behavioral Theories of Learning

Julia Esteban, first-grade teacher at Tanner Elementary School, was trying to teach her students appropriate classroom behavior.

"Children," she said one day, "we are having a problem in this class that I'd like to discuss with you. Whenever I ask a question, many of you shout out your answers instead of raising your hand and waiting to be called on. Can anyone tell me what you should do when I ask the class a question?" Rebecca's hand shot into the air. "I know, I know!" she said. "Raise your hand and wait quietly!"

Ms. Esteban sighed to herself. She tried to ignore Rebecca, who was doing exactly what she had just been told not to do, but Rebecca was the only student with her hand up, and the longer she delayed, the more frantically Rebecca waved her hand and shouted her answer.

"All right, Rebecca. What are you supposed to do?"

"We're supposed to raise our hands and wait quietly for you to call on us."

"If you know the rule, why were you shouting out your answer before I called on you?"

"I guess I forgot."

"All right. Can anyone remind the class of our rule about talking out of turn?"

Four children raised their hands and shouted together.

"One at a time!"

"Take turns!"

"Don't talk when someone else is talking!"

Ms. Esteban called for order. "You kids are going to drive me crazy!" she said. "Didn't we just talk about how to raise your hands and wait for me to call on you?"

"But Ms. Esteban," said Stephen without even raising his hand. "You called on Rebecca and she wasn't quiet!" @

See Chapter 6, Information Processing and Cognitive Theories of Learning.

USING YOUR
Experience

Critical and Creative Thinking   Reflect on what Ms. Esteban might do differently in this situation to accomplish her goal.

Cooperative Learning   Discuss with another student what went wrong here. Also discuss similar ways in which you have seen inappropriate behavior reinforced in the past. Share some of these anecdotes with the class.

Children are excellent learners. What they learn, however, may not always be what we intend to teach. Ms. Esteban is trying to teach students how to behave in class, but by paying attention to Rebecca's outburst, she is actually teaching them the opposite of what she intends. Rebecca craves her teacher's attention, so being called on (even in an exasperated tone of voice) rewards her for calling out her answer. Not only does Ms. Esteban's response increase the chances that Rebecca will call out answers again, but Rebecca now serves as a model for her classmates' own calling out. What Ms. Esteban says is less important than her actual response to her students' behaviors.

The purpose of this chapter is to define learning and then to present behavioral and social learning theories, explanations for learning that emphasize observable behaviors. **Behavioral learning theories** focus on the ways in which pleasurable or unpleasant consequences of behavior change individuals' behavior over time and ways in which individuals model their behavior on that of others. Social learning theories focus on the effects of thought on action and action on thought. Later chapters present **cognitive learning theories,** which emphasize unobservable mental processes that people use to learn and remember new information or skills. Behavioral learning theorists try to discover principles of behavior that apply to all living beings. Cognitive and social learning theorists are concerned exclusively with human learning. Actually, however, the boundaries between behavioral and cognitive learning theories have become increasingly indistinct in recent years as each school of thought has incorporated the findings of the other.

CONNECTIONS

𝒲HAT IS LEARNING?

What is learning? This seems like a simple question until you begin to think about it. Consider the following four examples. Are they instances of learning?

1. A young child takes her first steps.
2. An adolescent male feels a strong attraction to certain females.
3. A child feels anxious when he sees the doctor coming with a needle.
4. Long after learning how to multiply, a girl realizes on her own that another way to multiply by 5 is to divide by 2 and multiply by 10 (e.g., 428×5 can be figured as follows: $428/2 = 214 \times 10 = 2,140$).

Learning is usually defined as a change in an individual caused by experience (Driscoll, 2000). Changes caused by development (such as growing taller) are not instances of learning. Neither are characteristics of individuals that are present at birth (such as reflexes and responses to hunger or pain). However, humans do so much learning from the day of their birth (and some say earlier) that learning and development are inseparably linked. Learning to walk (example 1) is mostly a developmen-

behavioral learning theories

Explanations of learning that emphasize observable changes in behavior.

cognitive learning theories

Explanations of learning that focus on mental processes.

learning

A change in an individual that results from experience.

INTASC

2 Knowledge of Human Development and Learning

tal progression but also depends on experience with crawling and other activities. The adolescent sex drive (example 2) is not learned, but learning shapes individuals' choices of desirable partners.

A child's anxiety on seeing a doctor with a needle (example 3) is definitely learned behavior. The child has learned to associate the needle with pain, and his body reacts emotionally when he sees the needle. This reaction may be unconscious or involuntary, but it is learned nonetheless.

The fourth example, the girl's insight into the multiplication shortcut, is an instance of internally generated learning, better known as thinking. Some theorists would not call this learning, because it was not caused by the environment. But it might be considered a case of delayed learning, in which deliberate instruction in multiplication plus years of experience with numbers plus mental effort on the part of the girl produced an insight.

Learning takes place in many ways. Sometimes it is intentional, as when students acquire information presented in a classroom or when they look something up on the Internet. Sometimes it is unintentional, as in the case of the child's reaction to the needle. All sorts of learning are going on all the time. As you are reading this chapter, you are learning something about learning. However, you are also learning that educational psychology is interesting or dull, useful or useless. Without knowing it, you are probably learning about where on the page certain pieces of information are to be found. You might be learning to associate the content of this chapter with unimportant aspects of your surroundings as you read it, such as the smell of books in a library or the temperature of the room in which you are reading. The content of this chapter, the placement of words on the page, and the smells, sounds, and temperature of your surroundings are all **stimuli.** Your senses are usually wide open to all sorts of stimuli, or environmental events or conditions, but you are consciously aware of only a fraction of them at any one time.

The problem educators face is not how to get students to learn; students are already engaged in learning every waking moment. Rather, it is how to help students learn particular information, skills, and concepts that will be useful in adult life. How do we present students with the right stimuli on which to focus their attention and mental effort so that they will acquire important skills? That is the central problem of instruction.

$\mathcal{W}$HAT BEHAVIORAL LEARNING THEORIES HAVE EVOLVED?

The systematic study of learning is relatively new. Not until the late nineteenth century was learning studied in a scientific manner. Using techniques borrowed from the physical sciences, researchers began conducting experiments to understand how people and animals learn. Two of the most important early researchers were Ivan Pavlov and Edward Thorndike. Among later researchers, B. F. Skinner was important for his studies of the relationship between behavior and consequences.

Pavlov: Classical Conditioning

In the late 1800s and early 1900s, Russian scientist Ivan Pavlov and his colleagues studied the digestive process in dogs. During the research, the scientists noticed changes in the timing and rate of salivation of these animals. Pavlov observed that if meat powder was placed in or near the mouth of a hungry dog, the dog would salivate. Because the meat powder provoked this response automatically, without any prior

stimuli
Environmental conditions that activate the senses; the singular is *stimulus.*

unconditioned stimulus
A stimulus that naturally evokes a particular response.

unconditioned response
A behavior that is prompted automatically by a stimulus.

neutral stimuli
Stimuli that have no effect on a particular response.

conditioned stimulus
A previously neutral stimulus that evokes a particular response after having been paired with an unconditioned stimulus.

classical conditioning
The process of repeatedly associating a previously neutral stimulus with an unconditioned stimulus in order to evoke a conditioned response.

Law of Effect
Thorndike's law stating that an act that is followed by a favorable effect is more likely to be repeated in similar situations; an act that is followed by an unfavorable effect is less likely to be repeated.

operant conditioning
The use of pleasant or unpleasant consequences to control the occurrence of behavior.

training or conditioning, the meat powder is referred to as an **unconditioned stimulus.** Similarly, because salivation occurred automatically in the presence of meat, also without the need for any training or experience, this response of salivating is referred to as an **unconditioned response.**

Whereas the meat will produce salivation without any previous experience or training, other stimuli, such as a bell, will not produce salivation. Because these stimuli have no effect on the response in question, they are referred to as **neutral stimuli.** Pavlov's experiments showed that if a previously neutral stimulus is paired with an unconditioned stimulus, the neutral stimulus becomes a **conditioned stimulus** and gains the power to prompt a response similar to that produced by the unconditioned stimulus. In other words, after the bell and the meat are presented together, the ringing of the bell alone causes the dog to salivate. This process is referred to as **classical conditioning.** A diagram of Pavlov's theory is shown in Figure 5.1. In experiments such as these, Pavlov and his colleagues showed how learning could affect what were once thought to be involuntary, reflexive behaviors, such as salivating.

Pavlov's emphasis on observation and careful measurement and his systematic exploration of several aspects of learning helped to advance the scientific study of learning. Pavlov also left other behavioral theorists with significant mysteries, such as the process by which neutral stimuli take on meaning.

Thorndike: The Law of Effect

Pavlov's work inspired researchers in the United States such as E. L. Thorndike (Hilgard & Bower, 1966). Thorndike, like many of the early behavioral learning theorists, linked behavior to physical reflexes. In his early work he also viewed most behavior as a response to stimuli in the environment. This view that stimuli can prompt responses was the forerunner of what became known as stimulus-response (S-R) theory. Early learning theorists noted that certain reflexes, such as the knee jerking upward when it is tapped, occur without processing by the brain. They hypothesized that other behavior was also determined in a reflexive way by stimuli that are present in the environment rather than by conscious or unconscious thoughts.

Thorndike went beyond Pavlov by showing that stimuli that occurred after a behavior had an influence on future behaviors. In many of his experiments, Thorndike placed cats in boxes from which they had to escape to get food. He observed that over time, the cats learned how to get out of the box more and more quickly by repeating the behaviors that led to escape and not repeating the behaviors that were ineffective. From these experiments, Thorndike developed his **Law of Effect,** which states that if an act is followed by a satisfying change in the environment, the likelihood that the act will be repeated in similar situations increases. However, if a behavior is followed by an unsatisfying change in the environment, the chances that the behavior will be repeated decrease. Thus, Thorndike showed that the consequences of one's present behavior play a crucial role in determining one's future behavior.

Skinner: Operant Conditioning

Some human behaviors are clearly prompted by specific stimuli. Just like Pavlov's dogs, we salivate when we are hungry and see appetizing food. We also lend credibility to Thorndike's early emphasis on reflexive behavior when we learn things—such as how to ride a bicycle—so well that the brain seems to respond reflexively. However, B. F. Skinner proposed that reflexive behavior accounts for only a small proportion of all actions. Skinner proposed another class of behavior, which he labeled operant behaviors because they operate on the environment in the apparent absence of any unconditioned stimuli, such as food. Like Thorndike's, Skinner's work focused

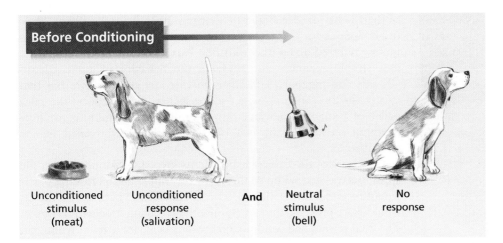

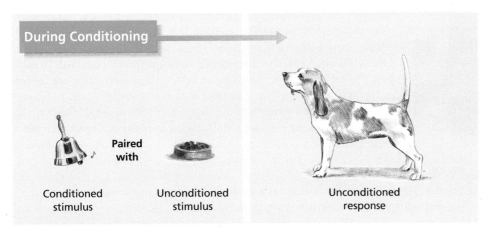

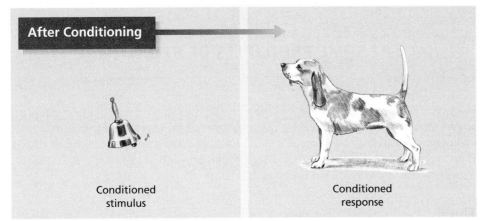

FIGURE 5.1
Classical Conditioning
In classical conditioning, a neutral stimulus (such as a bell) that at first prompts no response becomes paired with an unconditioned stimulus (such as meat) and gains the power of that stimulus to cause a response (such as salivation).

on the relation between behavior and its consequences. For example, if an individual's behavior is immediately followed by pleasurable consequences, the individual will engage in that behavior more frequently. The use of pleasant and unpleasant consequences to change behavior is often referred to as **operant conditioning.**

Skinner's work focused on placing subjects in controlled situations and observing the changes in their behavior produced by systematic changes in the consequences

CERTIFICATION POINTER

Most teacher certification tests will require you to know that when a teacher reinforces a student who raises her hand to speak, she is using operant conditioning.

How does this Skinner box work? What type of conditioning is the rat undergoing? How does that type of conditioning take place, and how is it different from the type of conditioning Pavlov studied?

of their behavior (see Bigge & Shermis, 2004; Iversen, 1992). Skinner is famous for his development and use of a device that is commonly referred to as the **Skinner box.** Skinner boxes contain a very simple apparatus for studying the behavior of animals, usually rats and pigeons. A Skinner box for rats consists of a bar that is easy for the rat to press, a food dispenser that can give the rat a pellet of food, and a water dispenser. The rat cannot see or hear anything outside of the box, so all stimuli are controlled by the experimenter.

In some of the earliest experiments involving Skinner boxes, the apparatus was first set up so that if the rat happened to press the bar, it would receive a food pellet. After a few accidental bar presses, the rat would start pressing the bar frequently, receiving a pellet each time. The food reward had conditioned the rat's behavior, strengthening bar pressing and weakening all other behaviors (such as wandering around the box). At this point, the experimenter might do any of several things. The food dispenser might be set up so that several bar presses were now required to obtain food, or so that some bar presses produced food but others did not, or so that bar presses no longer produced food. In each case the rat's behavior would be recorded. One important advantage of the Skinner box is that it allows for careful scientific study of behavior in a controlled environment (Bigge & Shermis, 2004; Delprato & Midgley, 1992). Anyone with the same equipment can repeat Skinner's experiments.

> **ON THE WEB**
>
> The B. F. Skinner Foundation website at **www.bfskinner.org** aims to improve the understanding of human behavior through the work of B. F. Skinner.

CONNECTIONS

See Chapter 11, Effective Learning Environments, for classroom applications, including applied behavioral analysis.

Skinner box

An apparatus developed by B. F. Skinner for observing animal behavior in experiments in operant conditioning.

consequences

Pleasant or unpleasant conditions that follow behaviors and affect the frequency of future behaviors.

ᙯHAT ARE SOME PRINCIPLES OF BEHAVIORAL LEARNING?

Principles of behavioral learning include the role of consequences, reinforcers, punishers, immediacy of consequences, shaping, extinction, schedules of reinforcement, maintenance, and the role of antecedents. Each of these principles will be discussed in the sections that follow (also see Bigge & Shermis, 2004; Kazdin, 2001; Malott, Malott, & Trojan, 2000; Miltenberger, 2001).

The Role of Consequences

Skinner's pioneering work with rats and pigeons established a set of principles of behavior that have been supported in hundreds of studies involving humans as well as animals. Perhaps the most important principle of behavioral learning theories is that behavior changes according to its immediate **consequences.** Pleasurable consequences strengthen behavior; unpleasant consequences weaken it. In other words, pleasurable consequences increase the frequency with which an individual engages in a behavior, whereas unpleasant consequences reduce the frequency of a behavior. If students enjoy reading books, they will probably read more often. If they find stories boring or

Teachers are a primary source of reinforcement in children's lives. What type of secondary reinforcement is this teacher demonstrating? What are the possible outcomes of this reinforcement?

are unable to concentrate, they may read less often, choosing other activities instead. Pleasurable consequences are called reinforcers; unpleasant consequences are called punishers.

Reinforcers

A **reinforcer** is defined as any consequence that strengthens (that is, increases the frequency of) a behavior. Note that the effectiveness of the reinforcer must be demonstrated. We cannot assume that a particular consequence is a reinforcer until we have evidence that it strengthens behavior for a particular individual. For example, candy might generally be considered a reinforcer for young children, but after a big meal a child might not find candy pleasurable, and some children do not like candy at all. A teacher who says, "I reinforced him with praise for staying in his seat during math time, but it didn't work," may be misusing the term reinforced if there is no evidence that praise is in fact a reinforcer for this particular student. No reward can be assumed to be a reinforcer for everyone under all conditions.

Primary and Secondary Reinforcers Reinforcers fall into two broad categories: primary and secondary. **Primary reinforcers** satisfy basic human needs. Some examples are food, water, security, warmth, and sex. **Secondary reinforcers** are reinforcers that acquire their value by being associated with primary reinforcers or other well-established secondary reinforcers. For example, money has no value to a young child until the child learns that money can be used to buy things that are themselves primary or secondary reinforcers. Grades have little value to students unless their parents notice and value good grades, and parents' praise is of value because it is associated with love, warmth, security, and other reinforcers. Money and grades are examples of secondary reinforcers because they have no value in themselves but have been associated with primary reinforcers or with other well-established secondary

reinforcer
A pleasurable consequence that maintains or increases a behavior.

primary reinforcer
Food, water, or other consequence that satisfies a basic need.

secondary reinforcer
A consequence that people learn to value through its association with a primary reinforcer.

Table 5.1

Consequences in Behavioral Learning	
Strengthens Behavior	*Discourages Behavior*
Positive Reinforcement *Example:* Rewarding or praising	**No Reinforcement** *Example:* Ignoring
Negative Reinforcement *Example:* Excusing from an undesirable task or situation	**Removal Punishment** *Example:* Forbidding a desirable task or situation
	Presentation Punishment *Example:* Imposing an undesirable task or situation

reinforcers. There are three basic categories of secondary reinforcers. One is social reinforcers, such as praise, smiles, hugs, or attention. When Ms. Esteban recognized Rebecca, she was inadvertently giving Rebecca a social reinforcer: her own attention. Other types of secondary reinforcers are activity reinforcers (such as access to toys, games, or fun activities) and token (or symbolic) reinforcers (such as money, grades, stars, or points that individuals can exchange for other reinforcers).

CERTIFICATION POINTER

Teacher certification tests are likely to require you to know that when a teacher says, "If you get an A on tomorrow's test you won't have to do homework the rest of the week," she's using negative reinforcement (escape from an unpleasant consequence, assuming homework is unpleasant!).

positive reinforcer
Pleasurable consequence given to strengthen behavior.

negative reinforcer
Release from an unpleasant situation, given to strengthen behavior.

Premack Principle
Rule stating that enjoyable activities can be used to reinforce participation in less enjoyable activities.

Positive and Negative Reinforcers   Most often, reinforcers that are used in schools are things given to students. These are called **positive reinforcers** and include praise, grades, and stars. However, another way to strengthen a behavior is to have the behavior's consequence be an escape from an unpleasant situation or a way of preventing something unpleasant from occurring. For example, a parent might release a student from doing the dishes if the student completes his or her homework. If doing the dishes is seen as an unpleasant task, release from it will be reinforcing. Reinforcers that are escapes from unpleasant situations are called **negative reinforcers.**

This term is often misinterpreted to mean punishment, as in "I negatively reinforced him for being late by having him stay in during recess" (Martella, Nelson, & Marchand-Martella, 2003). One way to avoid this error in terminology is to remember that reinforcers (whether positive or negative) strengthen behavior, whereas punishment is designed to weaken behavior. (See Table 5.1.)

The Premack Principle   One important principle of behavior is that we can promote less-desired (low-strength) activities by linking them to more-desired activities. In other words, access to something desirable is made contingent on doing something less desirable. For example, a teacher might say, "As soon as you finish your work, you may go outside" or "Clean up your art project, and then I will read you a story." These are examples of the Premack Principle (Premack, 1965). The **Premack Principle** is sometimes called "Grandma's Rule" from the age-old statement "Eat your vegetables, and then you may play." Teachers can use the Premack Principle by alternating more enjoyable activities with less enjoyable ones and making participation in the enjoyable activities depend on successful completion of the less enjoyable ones. For example, in elementary school it may be a good idea to schedule music, which most students consider an enjoyable activity, after completion of a difficult subject so that students will know that if they fool around in the difficult subject, they will be using up part of their desired music time (Martella et al., 2003).

Theory into **PRACTICE**

Classroom Uses of Reinforcement

INTASC

4 Multiple Instructional Strategies

The behavioral learning principle most useful for classroom practice is also the simplest: Reinforce behaviors you wish to see repeated. This principle may seem obvious, but in practice it is not as easy as it appears. For example, some teachers take the attitude that reinforcement is unnecessary, reasoning, "Why should I reinforce them? They're just doing what they're supposed to do!"

The main guidelines for the use of reinforcement to increase desired behavior in the classroom are as follows (see Jones & Jones, 2004; Kauffman et al., 2002; Marzano, 2003; Miltenberger, 2001).

1. **Decide what behaviors you want from students, and reinforce these behaviors when they occur.** For example, praise or reward good work. Do not praise or reward work that is not up to students' capabilities. As students begin a new task, they will need to be reinforced at every step along the way. Close approximations of what you hope to accomplish as a final product must receive positive feedback. Break down new behaviors (classroom assignments) into smaller parts and provide adequate rewards along the way.

2. **Tell students what behaviors you want; when they exhibit the desired behaviors and you reinforce them, tell them why.** Present students with a rubric that itemizes the criteria you will use when evaluating their work and include the point value for each criterion. Students then will be able to discriminate their own strengths and weaknesses from the feedback they receive from you.

3. **Reinforce appropriate behavior as soon as possible after it occurs.** Delayed reinforcement is less effective than immediate reinforcement. When you are grading an assignment, present feedback to the students as soon as possible. It is important that students know how they are doing in class, so don't delay with their grades. When constructing an assignment, you should always consider the grading scheme that you will use and how long it will take you to provide the intended feedback.

Intrinsic and Extrinsic Reinforcers

Often, the most important reinforcer that maintains behavior is the pleasure inherent in engaging in the behavior. For example, most people have a hobby that they work on for extended periods without any reward. People like to draw, read, sing, play games, hike, or swim for no reason other than the fun of doing it. Reinforcers of this type are called **intrinsic reinforcers,** and people can be described as being intrinsically motivated to engage in a given activity. Intrinsic reinforcers are contrasted with **extrinsic reinforcers,** praise or rewards given to motivate people to engage in a behavior that they might not engage in without it. There is evidence that reinforcing children for certain behaviors they would have done anyway can undermine long-term intrinsic motivation (Deci, Koestner, & Ryan, 1999; Sethi, Drake, Dialdin, & Lepper, 1995). Research on this topic finds that the undermining effect of extrinsic reinforcers occurs only in a limited set of circumstances, in which rewards are provided to children for engaging in an activity without any standard of performance, and only if the activity is one that children would have done on their own without any reward (Cameron & Pierce, 1994, 1996; Eisenberger, Pierce, & Cameron, 1999). Verbal praise and other types of feedback are extrinsic reinforcers that have been found to increase, not

CONNECTIONS

For more on intrinsic and extrinsic motivation, see Chapter 10, page 334.

intrinsic reinforcers
Behaviors that a person enjoys engaging in for their own sake, without any other reward.

extrinsic reinforcers
Praise or rewards given to motivate people to engage in behavior that they might not engage in without them.

decrease, intrinsic interest. What this research suggests for practice is that teachers should be cautious about giving tangible reinforcers to children for activities they would have done on their own. However, for most school tasks, which most students would not have done on their own, there is no basis for concern that use of extrinsic reinforcers will undermine intrinsic motivation, especially if those reinforcers are social and communicate recognition of students' growing mastery and independence.

ON THE WEB

For a debate on the issue of intrinsic versus extrinsic motivation visit the website at **www.restud.com/PDF/intrinsicresfeb4.pdf.**

Theory into **PRACTICE**

Practical Reinforcers

Anything that children like can be an effective reinforcer, but there are obvious practical limitations on what should be used in classrooms. One general principle of positive reinforcement is that it is best to use the least elaborate or tangible reinforcer that will work. In other words, if praise or self-reinforcement will work, don't use certificates. If certificates will work, don't use small toys. If small toys will work, don't use food. However, do not hesitate to use whatever practical reinforcer is necessary to motivate children to do important things. In particular, try all possible reinforcement strategies before even thinking of punishment (described next). A few categories of reinforcers and examples of each appear here (also see Burden, 2000; Kauffman et al., 2002; Martella et al., 2003). These are arranged from least tangible to most tangible.

Self-reinforcement. Students may be taught to praise themselves, give themselves a mental pat on the back, check off progress on a form, give themselves a short break, or otherwise reinforce themselves for completing a task or staying out of trouble.

Praise. Phrases such as "Good job," "Way to go," "I knew you could do it," and other verbal praise can be effective, but the same message can often be delivered with a smile, a wink, a thumbs-up signal, or a pat on the back. In cooperative learning and peer tutoring, students can be encouraged to praise each other for appropriate behavior.

Attention. The attention of a valued adult or peer can be a very effective reinforcer for many children. Listening, nodding, or moving closer may provide a child with the positive attention she or he is seeking. For outstanding performance or for meeting goals over a longer time period, students might be allowed a special time to visit with the custodian, help in the office, or take a walk with the principal.

Grades and recognition. Grades and recognition (e.g., certificates of accomplishment) can be effective both in giving students positive feedback on their efforts and in communicating progress to parents, who are likely to reinforce good reports themselves. Public displays of good work, notes from the principal, and other honors can have the same effect. Quiz scores, behavior ratings, and other feedback given frequently can be more effective than report card grades given for months of work.

Call home. Calling or sending a note to a child's parents to recognize success can be a powerful reinforcer.

Home-based reinforcement. Parents can be effective partners in a reinforcement system. Teachers can work out with parents an arrangement in which parents give their children special privileges at home if the children meet well-specified standards of behavior or performance.

Privileges. Children can earn free time, access to special equipment (e.g., soccer balls), or special roles (such as running errands or distributing papers). Children or groups who behaved well can simply be allowed to line up first for recess or dismissal or to have other small privileges.

Activity reinforcers. On the basis of achieving preestablished standards, students can earn free time, videos, games, or access to other fun activities. Activity reinforcers lend themselves particularly well to group contingencies, in which a whole class can earn free time or special activities if the whole class achieves a standard.

Tangible reinforcers. Children may earn points for achievement or good behavior that they can exchange for small toys, erasers, pencils, marbles, comic books, stickers, and so on. Tangible reinforcers usually work better if children have a choice among several options (Fisher & Mazur, 1997).

Food. Raisins, fruit, peanuts, or other healthy snacks can be used as reinforcers.

CONNECTIONS

For more on working with parents to reinforce behavior, see Chapter 11, page 374.

CONNECTIONS

For more on the use of activity reinforcers, see Chapter 11, pages 372 and 377.

Punishers

Consequences that weaken behavior are called punishers. Note that there is the same catch in the definition of **punishment** as in the definition of reinforcement: If an apparently unpleasant consequence does not reduce the frequency of the behavior it follows, it is not necessarily a punisher. For example, some students like being sent to the principal's office or out to the hall, because it releases them from the classroom, which they see as an unpleasant situation (Driscoll, 2000; Kauffman et al., 2002; Martella et al., 2003). Some students like to be scolded, because it gains them the teacher's attention and perhaps enhances their status among their peers. As with reinforcers, the effectiveness of a punisher cannot be assumed but must be demonstrated. Punishment can take two primary forms.

Presentation Punishment   **Presentation punishment** is the use of unpleasant consequences, or **aversive stimuli,** as when a student is scolded.

Removal Punishment   **Removal punishment** is the withdrawal of a pleasant consequence. Examples include loss of a privilege, having to stay in during recess, or having to stay after school. One frequently used form of removal punishment in classrooms is **time out,** in which a student who misbehaves is required to sit in the corner or in the hall for several minutes (see Nelson & Carr, 2000). Teachers often use time out when they believe that the attention of other students is serving to reinforce misbehavior; time out deprives the miscreant of this reinforcer. The use of time out as a consequence for misbehavior has generally been found to reduce the misbehavior (Costenbader & Reading-Brown, 1995).

For example, White and Bailey (1990) evaluated use of a sit-and-watch consequence for physical education classes. Children who misbehaved were told what they

punishment
Unpleasant consequences used to weaken behavior.

presentation punishment
An aversive stimulus following a behavior, used to decrease the chances that the behavior will occur again.

aversive stimulus
An unpleasant consequence that a person tries to avoid or escape.

removal punishment
Withdrawal of a pleasant consequence that is reinforcing a behavior, designed to decrease the chances that the behavior will recur.

time out
Procedure of removing a student from a situation in which misbehavior was being reinforced.

CERTIFICATION POINTER

For teacher certification tests you will probably need to know that unless an unpleasant consequence reduces the frequency of the behavior it follows, it may not be a punisher.

had done wrong and were given a 3-minute sand timer and asked to sit and watch until the sand ran out. The program was first tried in an alternative class for fourth- and fifth-graders with serious behavior problems. Figure 5.2 summarizes the findings. After a baseline of up to 343 disruptive behaviors in 10 minutes was observed, a behavioral checklist program was tried, in which teachers rated each child's behavior and sent poorly behaved children to the office or deprived them of a free period. This reduced misbehavior but did not eliminate it. However, when the sit-and-watch procedure was introduced, misbehavior virtually disappeared. The same sit-and-watch method was used in a regular fourth-grade physical education class, and the results were similar.

FIGURE 5.2
Reducing Disruptive Behavior with Sit and Watch

Number of disruptive behaviors per 10-minute observation period.

From A. G. White and J. S. Bailey, "Reducing Disruptive Behaviors of Elementary Physical Education Students with Sit and Watch," *Journal of Applied Behavior Analysis, 3,* 1990, p. 357. Adapted by permission.

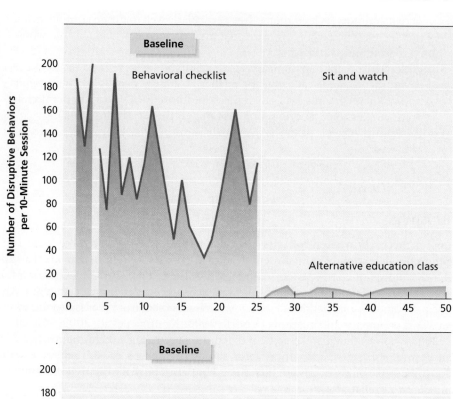

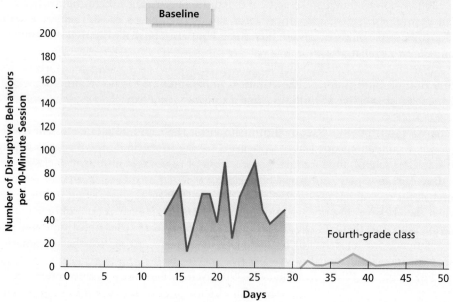

The issue of if, when, and how to punish has been a source of considerable controversy among behavioral learning theorists. Some have claimed that the effects of punishment, especially presentation (aversive) punishment, are only temporary, that punishment produces aggression, and it causes individuals to avoid settings in which it is used (Kazdin, 2001; Miltenberg, 2001; Weinstein, 1999). Even behavioral learning theorists who do support the use of punishment agree that it should be resorted to only when reinforcement for appropriate behavior has been tried and has failed; that when punishment is necessary, it should take the mildest possible form; and that punishment should always be used as part of a careful plan, never inconsistently or out of frustration. Physical punishment in schools (such as spanking) is illegal in most places (Evans & Richardson, 1995) and is universally opposed by behavioral learning theorists on ethical as well as scientific grounds (see Kazdin, 2001; Malott et al., 2000).

Immediacy of Consequences

One very important principle of behavioral learning theories is that consequences that follow behaviors closely in time affect behavior far more than delayed consequences do. If we waited a few minutes to give a rat in a Skinner box its food pellet after it pressed a bar, the rat would take a long time to learn the connection between bar pressing and food, because by the time the food arrived, the rat might be doing something other than bar pressing. A smaller reinforcer that is given immediately generally has a much larger effect than does a large reinforcer that is given later (Kulik & Kulik, 1988). This concept explains much about human behavior. It suggests, for example, why people find it so difficult to give up smoking or overeating. Even though the benefits of giving up smoking or of losing weight are substantial and well known, the small but immediate reinforcement of just one cigarette or one doughnut often overcomes the behavioral effect of the large but delayed reinforcers. In the classroom the principle of immediacy of consequences is also very important. Particularly for younger students, praise for a job well done that is given immediately can be a stronger reinforcer than a good grade given much later. Moving close to a student who is misbehaving, touching his or her shoulder, or making a gesture (e.g., finger to lips to ask for silence) may be much more effective than a scolding or warning given at the end of class (Jones & Jones, 2004; Kauffman et al., 2002).

Immediate feedback serves at least two purposes. First, it makes clear the connection between behavior and consequence. Second, it increases the informational value of the feedback. In practice, few classroom teachers can provide individual feedback immediately to all their students. However, the same results can be obtained by giving students answers right after they complete their work. In dealing with misbehavior, teachers can apply the principle of immediacy of consequences by responding immediately and positively when students are not misbehaving—in effect, by catching them in the act of being good!

Shaping

Immediacy of reinforcement is important to teaching, but so is the decision as to what to reinforce. Should a kindergarten teacher withhold reinforcement until a child can recite the entire alphabet? Certainly not. It would be better to praise children for recognizing one letter, then for recognizing several, and finally for learning all 26 letters. Should a music teacher withhold reinforcement until a young student has played a piano piece flawlessly? Or should the teacher praise the first halting run-through? Most students need reinforcement along the way. When teachers guide students toward goals by reinforcing the many steps that lead to success, they are using a technique called **shaping.**

shaping
The teaching of a new skill or behavior by means of reinforcement for small steps toward the desired goal.

INTASC

3 Adapting Instruction for Individual Needs

Personal Reflection

Modifying Behavior

Vanessa was the precocious 8-year-old daughter of a friend. Her mother was trying to teach her to keep her room tidy. Vanessa would leave her toys and clothes littered all over her floor. Her mother would nag her to pick up her things, threaten to give away her toys to less fortunate children, and occasionally deprive Vanessa of her favorite TV show until she cleaned up her room. None of these strategies worked very well or for very long. Then one day, Vanessa's mother learned about behavior modification in her educational psychology class and she decided to try using it to get her daughter to tidy up her room. She created a chart, showed it to Vanessa, and explained that every evening for one week they would record the number of objects on her bedroom floor to establish a baseline. After that, Vanessa would get a sticker on the chart for every day that there were no objects on her bedroom floor. In that first week, which was supposed to be the baseline, there were no objects left on Vanessa's floor! Just the simple fact of charting her behavior with a clear goal was enough feedback to get Vanessa to pick up her clothes and toys. After that, Vanessa's room was the cleanest room in the house.

Children are thinking, feeling beings who do more than just respond to rewards and punishments, and we need to be prepared as parents and teachers to learn from them what is meaningful to them, not just what is reinforcing.

Reflect on This. Why do you think the charting strategy was so effective for Vanessa? Describe a time when you used a behavior modification strategy to change something about yourself. Was it successful? How would behavior modification strategies for elementary children differ from strategies used with middle school or high school students?

The term *shaping* is used in behavioral learning theories to refer to the teaching of new skills or behaviors by reinforcing learners for approaching the desired final behavior (Bigge & Shermis, 2004; Driscoll, 2000). For example, in teaching children to tie their shoelaces, we would not simply show them how it is done and then wait to reinforce them until they do the whole job themselves. Rather, we would first reinforce them for tying the first knot, then for making the loops, and so on, until they can do the entire task. In this way we would be shaping the children's behavior by reinforcing all those steps that lead toward the final goal.

Shaping is an important tool in classroom instruction. Let's say we want students to be able to write paragraphs with a topic sentence, three supporting details, and a concluding sentence. This task has many parts: being able to recognize and then produce topic sentences, supporting details, and concluding sentences; being able to write complete sentences using capitalization, punctuation, and grammar correctly; and being able to spell. If a teacher taught a lesson on all these skills, asked students to write paragraphs, and then scored them on content, grammar, punctuation, and spelling, most students would fail and would probably learn little from the exercise.

Instead, the teacher might teach the skills step by step, gradually shaping the final skill. Students might be taught how to write first topic sentences, then supporting details, then concluding sentences. Early on, they might be held responsible only for paragraph content. Later, the requirement for reinforcement might be increased to include grammar and punctuation. Finally, spelling might be added as a criterion for success. At each stage, students would have a good chance to be reinforced, because the criterion for reinforcement would be within their grasp. The principle here is that

extinction
The weakening and eventual elimination of a learned behavior as reinforcement is withdrawn.

Whether teaching children new physical skills or academic skills, teachers and coaches begin with the basics and build from there. What techniques can they use to shape children's behaviors?

students should be reinforced for behaviors that are within their current capabilities but that also stretch them toward new skills.

Extinction

By definition, reinforcers strengthen behavior. But what happens when reinforcers are withdrawn? Eventually, the behavior will be weakened, and ultimately, it will disappear. This process is called **extinction** of a previously learned behavior.

Extinction is rarely a smooth process. When reinforcers are withdrawn, individuals often increase their rate of behavior for a while. For example, think of a door that you've used as a shortcut to somewhere on campus you go frequently. Imagine that one day the door will not open. You may push even harder for a while, shake the door, turn the handle both ways, perhaps even kick the door. You are likely to feel frustrated and angry. However, after a short time you will realize that the door is locked and go away. If the door is permanently locked (without your knowing it), you may try it a few times over the next few days, then perhaps once after a month; only eventually will you give up on it.

Your behavior when confronted by the locked door is a classic extinction pattern. Behavior intensifies when the reinforcer is first withdrawn, then rapidly weakens until the behavior disappears. Still, the behavior may return after much time has passed. For example, you could try the door again a year later to see whether it is still locked. If it is, you will probably leave it alone for a longer time, but probably not forever.

A dinosaur goes through extinction.

The characteristic **extinction burst,** the increase in levels of a behavior in the early stages of extinction, has important consequences for classroom management. For example, imagine that you have decided to extinguish a child's inappropriate calling out of answers (instead of raising his hand to be recognized) by ignoring him until he raises his hand quietly. At first, ignoring the child is likely to increase his calling-out behavior, a classic extinction burst. You might then mistakenly conclude that ignoring isn't working, when in fact continuing to ignore inappropriate call-outs is exactly the right strategy if you keep it up (Kauffman et al., 2002; Martella et al., 2003). Worse, you might finally decide to give in and recognize the child after his third or fourth call-out. This would teach the child the worst possible message: that calling out works eventually if you keep doing it. This would probably result in an increase in the very behavior you were trying to reduce, as children learn that "if at first you don't succeed, try, try again" (O'Leary, 1995). This was the case in the vignette presented at the beginning of this chapter. Ms. Esteban at first ignored Rebecca's calling out, so Rebecca called out even louder. Then she called on Rebecca, unintentionally communicating to her that only loud and persistent calling out would be reinforced.

Extinction of a previously learned behavior can be hastened when some stimulus or cue informs the individual that behaviors that were once reinforced will no longer be reinforced. In the case of the locked door, a sign saying, "Door permanently locked—use other entrance," would have greatly reduced the number of times you tried the door before giving up on it. Call-outs would be reduced much more quickly if the teacher told the class, "I will no longer respond to anyone unless they are silent and are raising their hand," and then ignored all other attempts to get her attention.

Schedules of Reinforcement

The effects of reinforcement on behavior depend on many factors, one of the most important of which is the **schedule of reinforcement** (see Kazdin, 2001; Miltenberger, 2001). This term refers to the frequency with which reinforcers are given, the amount of time that elapses between opportunities for reinforcement, and the predictability of reinforcement.

Fixed Ratio (FR)   One common schedule of reinforcement is the **fixed-ratio (FR) schedule,** in which a reinforcer is given after a fixed number of behaviors. For example, a teacher might say, "As soon as you finish ten problems, you may go outside." Regardless of the amount of time it takes, students are reinforced as soon as they finish 10 problems. This is an example of an FR10 schedule (10 behaviors for one reinforcer). One common form of a fixed-ratio schedule is one in which each behavior is reinforced. This is called continuous reinforcement (CRF), or FR1. Putting money in a soda machine is (usually) an example of continuous reinforcement, because one behavior (inserting coins) results in one reinforcer (a soda). Giving correct answers in class is also usually continuously reinforced. The student gives a good answer, and the teacher says, "Right! Good answer!"

One important process in instruction is gradually increasing reinforcement ratios. Early in a sequence of lessons, it may be necessary to reinforce students for every correct answer, such as a single math problem. However, this is inefficient in the long run. As soon as students are answering math problems correctly, it may be possible to reinforce every 5 problems (FR5), every 10 (FR10), and so on. Thinning out the reinforcement schedule in this way makes the student more able to work independently without reinforcement and makes the behavior more resistant to extinction. Ultimately, students might be asked to do entire projects on their own, receiving no reinforcement until the project is completed. As adults, we often take on tasks that

extinction burst
The increase in levels of a behavior in the early stages of extinction.

schedule of reinforcement
The frequency and predictability of reinforcement.

fixed-ratio (FR) schedule
Reinforcement schedule in which desired behavior is rewarded following a fixed number of behaviors.

take years to complete and years to produce a desired outcome. (Writing an educational psychology text is one such task!)

Fixed-ratio schedules are effective in motivating individuals to do a great deal of work—especially if the fixed ratio starts with continuous reinforcement (FR1) to get the individual going and then moves to high requirements for reinforcement. One reason that high requirements for reinforcement produce higher levels of behavior than low requirements is that reinforcing too frequently can make the value of the reinforcer wear off. Students who were praised for every math problem would soon grow tired of being praised, and the reinforcer might lose its value.

Variable Ratio (VR)   A **variable-ratio (VR) schedule** of reinforcement is one in which the number of behaviors required for reinforcement is unpredictable, although it is certain that the behaviors will eventually be reinforced. For example, a slot machine is a variable-ratio reinforcer. It may pay off after 1 pull one time and after 200 the next, and there is no way to predict which pull will win. In the classroom a variable-ratio schedule exists when students raise their hands to answer questions. They never know when they will be reinforced by being able to give the correct answer, but they may expect to be called on about 1 time in 30 in a class of 30. This would be called a VR30 schedule, because, on the average, 30 behaviors are required for one reinforcer. Variable-ratio schedules tend to produce high and stable rates of behavior. In fact, almost all gambling games involve VR schedules, and so they can be quite literally addicting. Similarly, use of frequent random checks of student work can help to addict students to steady, careful work.

Variable-ratio schedules are highly resistant to extinction. Even after behaviors are no longer being reinforced, people may not give up working for a long time. Because they have learned that it may take a lot of work to be rewarded, they keep on working in the mistaken belief that the next effort might just pay off.

Fixed Interval (FI)   In **fixed-interval schedules,** reinforcement is available only at certain periodic times. The final examination is a classic example of a fixed-interval schedule. Fixed-interval schedules create an interesting pattern of behavior. The individual may do very little until just before reinforcement is available, then put forth a burst of effort as the time for reinforcement approaches. This pattern can be demonstrated with rats and pigeons on fixed-interval schedules, but it is even more apparent in students who cram at the last minute before a test or who write their monthly book reports the night before they are due. These characteristics of fixed-interval schedules suggest that frequent short quizzes may be better than infrequent major exams for encouraging students to give their best effort all the time rather than putting in all-nighters before the exam (Crooks, 1988).

Variable Interval (VI)   In a **variable-interval schedule,** reinforcement is available at some times but not at others, and we have no idea when a behavior will be reinforced. An example of this is a teacher making spot checks of students who are doing assignments in class. Students are reinforced if they are working well at the particular moment the teacher comes by. Since they cannot predict when the teacher will check them, students must be doing good work all the time. People may obey traffic laws out of respect for the law and civic responsibility, but it also helps that the police randomly check drivers' compliance with the law. Troopers hide on overpasses or behind hills so that they can get a random sampling of drivers' behavior. If they were always in plain sight, they would be a signal to drive carefully, so the necessity for driving carefully at other times would be reduced.

variable-ratio (VR) schedule
Reinforcement schedule in which desired behavior is rewarded following an unpredictable number of behaviors.

fixed-interval schedule
Reinforcement schedule in which desired behavior is rewarded following a constant amount of time.

variable-interval schedule
Reinforcement schedule in which desired behavior is rewarded following an unpredictable amount of time.

Teaching Dilemmas: Cases to Consider

INTASC **2 Knowledge of Human Development and Learning**

Dealing with Behavior Problems

Sam, a boy with a talkative and bubbly personality, has just entered Angela Hairston's kindergarten class at Elliott Elementary School. Sam has had a complicated medical history since birth, culminating a year ago in back surgery to correct spinal scoliosis, followed by many months in a full-body cast. Last year, after the surgery, Sam was in Diana Braddock's preschool class at Elliott, where, after a rough start, he made good academic and social progress. Now, however, after two weeks of school, Angela is afraid that Sam doesn't have the maturity to be in kindergarten. She meets with Diana Braddock and Sam's mother, Janet, to discuss her concerns.

Angela: Thank you both for taking the time to meet with me this afternoon. I'm concerned because Sam is starting to exhibit some of the same behaviors he showed at the beginning of his preschool year with you, Diana.

Diana: Sam certainly demonstrated separation anxiety when he began preschool. I remember the tantrums he would throw when Janet dropped him off for school. Then he would complain that he felt sick, begin to cry, and even make himself throw up so he could go home.

Janet: Sam became overly dependent on me when he had his back surgery and was in the body cast. But Diana and I worked out a plan that seemed to help Sam get over his problems last year.

Angela: Well, it appears that Sam is having what psychologists call an extinction burst of that behavior now that he's started kindergarten. I was at my wits' end yesterday, Janet, when I had to call you for the second time this week to pick Sam up because he had had a thirty-minute tantrum and made himself sick. Diana, tell me again how you helped Sam last year.

Diana: Sure. Janet and I talked about Sam's overdependence on adults and how that could negatively affect his academic progress. We also talked about his need to develop better social skills with his classmates so that he didn't always need to be the center of attention.

Janet: I told Diana how I thought my dad was reinforcing Sam's dependence. Whenever I picked Sam up from preschool because he was "sick," I'd have to take him to work with me. I work for my dad, who has a small business in town. Sam would sit in the reception area while I worked, and the customers would give him their undivided attention, because Sam would just turn on the charm.

Diana: Janet and I decided that whenever Sam left school "sick," Janet would ask her father and the customers not to give Sam any attention. Instead, she would tell Sam to rest in a side room until she could take him home and put him to bed.

Janet: Sam got "sick" several more times, but once he realized that Dad, the customers—and I, too—weren't going to give him any attention at the store, he didn't play sick anymore.

Diana: Meanwhile, at school, I had made Sam and one of his classmates the "Attendance Helpers" who took the absence report to the school secretary every day. I rotated Sam's partner often so that he could form one-on-one relationships with several classmates. And Mrs. Thompson's third-grade class developed a buddy system to help Sam interact with teachers and children in more appropriate ways.

Janet: By winter, Sam had made friends with several children in his class.

Diana: And everyone enjoyed being with him since he didn't demand center stage anymore.

Angela: It's been a big help to hear about all you did for Sam last year. It seems like you did all the right things to help him get over his separation anxiety and to get along better with his peers. I guess I'll just have to try the same techniques again to help him adjust to kindergarten. Janet, I hope you'll support me in this.

Janet: Oh, yes, Mrs. Roberts. I really want Sam to have a good year in kindergarten.

⊘ Questions for Reflection

1. Do you think that Mrs. Roberts is correct in saying that Sam is showing an extinction burst in the way he is behaving in kindergarten? Why or why not?

2. How effective do you think it will be to repeat in kindergarten the plan Diana used to extinguish Sam's behavior in preschool?

3. If you were Mrs. Roberts, what, if anything, would you do to reinforce Sam's behavior as it improves? What type of schedule of reinforcement would you use?

Source: Adapted from "Kindergarten Is Big Business" by Linda K. Elksnin, Diane Birschbach, and Susan P. Gurganus, from Allyn & Bacon's Custom Cases in Education, edited by Greta Morine-Dershimer, Daniel Hallahan, and James Kauffman. Copyright © 2000 by Pearson Education. Adapted by permission of the publisher.

Like variable-ratio schedules, variable-interval schedules are very effective for maintaining a high rate of behavior and are highly resistant to extinction. For example, let's say a teacher has a policy of having students hand in their seatwork every day. Rather than checking every paper, the teacher pulls three papers at random and

Table 5.2			
Schedules of Reinforcement			
Specific response patterns during reinforcement and extinction characterize each of the four types of schedules.			
Schedule	*Definition*	*Response Patterns*	
		During Reinforcement	**During Extinction**
Fixed ratio	Constant number of behaviors required for reinforcement	Steady response rate; pause after reinforcement	Rapid drop in response rate after required number of responses passes without reinforcement
Variable ratio	Variable number of behaviors required for reinforcement	Steady, high response rate	Response rate stays high, then drops off
Fixed interval	Constant amount of time passes before reinforcement is available	Uneven rate, with rapid acceleration at the end of each interval	Rapid drop in response rate after interval passes with no reinforcement
Variable interval	Variable amount of time passes before reinforcement is available	Steady, high response rate	Slow decrease in response rate

gives these students extra credit if their seatwork was done well. This variable-interval schedule would probably motivate students to do their seatwork carefully. If the teacher secretly stopped spot-checking halfway through the year, the students might never know it, figuring that their own paper just hadn't been pulled to be checked rather than realizing that reinforcement was no longer available for anyone.

Table 5.2 defines and gives additional examples of schedules of reinforcement.

Maintenance

The principle of extinction holds that when reinforcement for a previously learned behavior is withdrawn, the behavior fades away. Does this mean that teachers must reinforce students' behaviors indefinitely or they will disappear?

Not necessarily. For rats in a Skinner box, the withdrawal of reinforcement for bar pressing will inevitably lead to extinction of bar pressing. However, humans live in a much more complex world that is full of natural reinforcers for most of the skills and behaviors that we learn in school. For example, students may initially require frequent reinforcement for behaviors that lead to reading. However, once they can read, they have a skill that unlocks the entire world of written language, a world that is highly reinforcing to most students. After a certain point, reinforcement for reading may no longer be necessary, because the content of reading material itself maintains the behavior. Similarly, poorly behaved students may need careful, systematic reinforcement for doing schoolwork. After a while, however, they will find out that doing schoolwork pays off in grades, in parental approval, in ability to understand what is going on in class, and in knowledge. These natural reinforcers for doing schoolwork were always available, but the students could not experience them until their schoolwork was improved by more systematic means.

This kind of **maintenance** of behavior also occurs with behaviors that do not need to be reinforced because they are intrinsically reinforcing, which is to say that engaging in these behaviors is pleasurable in itself. For example, many children love

maintenance
Continuation (of behavior).

to draw, to figure out problems, or to learn about things even if they are never rein-forced for doing so. Many of us even complete books of crossword puzzles or other problem-solving activities, even though after we have completed them, no one will ever check our work.

The concept of resistance to extinction, discussed earlier (in the section on sched-ules of reinforcement), is central to an understanding of maintenance of learned be-havior. As was noted, when new behaviors are being introduced, reinforcement for correct responses should be frequent and predictable. However, once the behaviors are established, reinforcement for correct responses should become less frequent and less predictable. The reason for this is that variable schedules of reinforcement and schedules of reinforcement that require many behaviors before reinforcement is given are much more resistant to extinction than are fixed schedules or easy ones. For ex-ample, if a teacher praises a student every time the student does a math problem but then stops praising, the student may stop doing math problems. In contrast, if the teacher gradually increases the number of math problems a student must do to be praised and praises the student at random intervals (a variable-ratio schedule), then the student is likely to continue to do math problems for a long time with little or no reinforcement from the teacher.

The Role of Antecedents

We have seen that the consequences of behavior strongly influence behavior. Yet it is not only what follows a behavior that has influence. The stimuli that precede a behav-ior also play an important role (Kazdin, 2001).

Cueing **Antecedent stimuli,** events that precede a behavior, are also known as **cues,** because they inform us what behavior will be reinforced and/or what behavior will be punished. Cues come in many forms and give us hints as to when we should change our behavior and when we should not. For example, during a math session, most teachers will reinforce students who are working on problems. However, after the teacher has announced that math is over and it is time for lunch, the consequences change. The ability to behave one way in the presence of one stimulus—"It's math time"—and a different way in the presence of another stimulus—"It's time for lunch"—is known as stimulus discrimination.

Discrimination When is the best time to ask your boss for a raise? When the company is doing well, the boss looks happy, and you have just done something especially good? Or when the company has just gotten a poor earnings report, the boss is glowering, and you have just made a costly error? Obviously, the first situation is more likely to lead to success. You know this because you have learned to discriminate between good and bad times to ask your boss to do something for you. **Discrimination** is the use of cues, sig-nals, or information to know when behavior is likely to be reinforced. The company's financial condition, the boss's mood, and your recent performance are discriminative stimuli with regard to the chances that your request for a raise will be successful. For students to learn discrimination, they must have feedback on the correctness or incor-rectness of their responses. Studies of discrimination learning have generally found that students need to know when their responses are incorrect as well as correct.

Learning is largely a matter of mastering more and more complex discriminations. For example, all letters, numbers, words, and mathematical symbols are discriminative stimuli. A young child learns to discriminate between the letters *b* and *d*. An older student learns the distinction between the words *effective* and *efficient*. An educational psychology student learns to discriminate negative reinforcement from punishment. A

CERTIFICATION POINTER

Teacher certification tests may require you to know that holding up your hand to get students' attention is cueing, an antecedent stimulus that informs students what be-haviors will be reinforced.

antecedent stimuli
Events that precede behaviors.

cues
Signals as to what behavior(s) will be rein-forced or punished.

discrimination
Perception of and response to differences in stimuli.

teacher learns to discriminate facial and verbal cues indicating that students are bored or interested by a lecture.

Applying the concept of discriminative stimuli to classroom instruction and management is easy: Teachers should tell students what behaviors will be reinforced. In theory, a teacher could wait until students did something worthwhile and then reinforce it, but this would be incredibly inefficient. Rather, teachers should give students messages that say, in effect, "To be reinforced (e.g., with praise, grades, or stars), these are the things you must do." In this way, teachers can avoid having students spend time and effort on the wrong activities. If students know that what they are doing will pay off, they will usually work hard.

Generalization   If students learn to stay in their seats and do careful work in math class, will their behavior also improve in science class? If students can subtract 3 apples from 7 apples, can they also subtract 3 oranges from 7 oranges? If students can interpret symbolism used by Shakespeare, can they also interpret symbolism used in African folk tales? These are all questions of **generalization,** or transfer of behaviors learned under one set of conditions to other situations. Generalization cannot be taken for granted. Usually, when a classroom management program is successfully introduced in one setting, students' behaviors do not automatically improve in other settings. Instead, students learn to discriminate among settings. Even young children readily learn what is encouraged and what is forbidden in kindergarten, at home, and at various friends' houses. Their behavior may be quite different in each setting, according to the different rules and expectations.

For generalization to occur, it usually must be planned for. A successful classroom management program used in social studies class may be transferred to English class to ensure generalization to that setting. Students may need to study the use of symbolism by many authors in many cultures before they acquire the skill to interpret symbolism in general.

Obviously, generalization is most likely to occur across similar settings or across similar concepts. A new behavior is more likely to generalize from reading class to social studies class than to recess or home settings. However, even in the most similar-appearing settings, generalizations may not occur. For example, many students will demonstrate complete mastery of spelling or language mechanics and then fail to apply this knowledge to their own compositions. Teachers should not assume that because students can do something under one set of circumstances, they can also do it under a different set of circumstances.

Techniques for Increasing Generalization   Schloss and Smith (1998) describe 11 techniques for increasing the chances that a behavior learned in one setting, such as a given class, will generalize to other settings, such as other classes or, more important, real-life applications (also see Martella et al., 2003). Some of these strategies involve teaching in a way that makes generalization easier. For example, arithmetic lessons involving money will probably transfer better to real life if they involve manipulating real or simulated coins and bills than if they involve only problems on paper. Another teaching strategy known to contribute to generalization is using many examples from different contexts. For example, students are more likely to be able to transfer the concept of supply and demand to new areas if they learn examples relating to prices for groceries, prices for natural resources, values of collectibles (such as baseball cards), and wages for common and rare skills than if they learn only about grocery pricing. An obvious strategy for increasing generalization is "on-the-job training": teaching a given skill in the actual environment in which it will be used, or in a simulation of such an environment.

generalization
Carryover of behaviors, skills, or concepts from one setting or task to another.

After initial instruction has taken place, there are many ways to increase generalization. One is to repeat instruction in a variety of settings. For example, after teaching students to use a given test-taking strategy in mathematics, such as "skip difficult problems and go back to them after answering the easy ones," a teacher might give students the opportunity to use this same strategy on a science test, a grammar test, and a health test. Another after-teaching technique is to help students make the link between a new skill and natural reinforcers in the environment so as to maintain that skill. For example, when children are learning to read, they can be given a regular homework assignment to read books or magazines that are of high interest to them, even if those materials are not "good literature." Initially, new reading skills may be better maintained by comic books than by literary classics, because for some children the comic books tie their new skill more immediately to the pleasure of reading, making generalization to nonschool settings more likely. Finally, a teacher can increase generalization by directly reinforcing generalization—for example, by praising a student who connects a new idea to a different context or uses a skill in a new application.

𝓗OW HAS SOCIAL LEARNING THEORY CONTRIBUTED TO OUR UNDERSTANDING OF HUMAN LEARNING?

CONNECTIONS

For the relation of social learning theory to social construction of meaning, see Chapter 8, page 243.

CONNECTIONS

For the relation of social learning theory to Vygotskian and neo-Piagetian views of development, see Chapter 2, pages 43 and 44.

Social learning theory is a major outgrowth of the behavioral learning theory tradition. Developed by Albert Bandura, **social learning theory** accepts most of the principles of behavioral theories but focuses to a much greater degree on the effects of cues on behavior and on internal mental processes, emphasizing the effects of thought on action and action on thought (Bandura, 1986).

Bandura: Modeling and Observational Learning

Bandura noted that the Skinnerian emphasis on the effects of the consequences of behavior largely ignored the phenomena of **modeling**—the imitation of others' behavior—and of vicarious experience—learning from others' successes or failures. He felt that much of human learning is not shaped by its consequences but is more efficiently learned directly from a model (Bandura, 1986; Schunk, 2000). The physical education teacher demonstrates jumping jacks, and students imitate. Bandura calls this no-trial learning, because students do not have to go through a shaping process but can reproduce the correct response immediately.

Bandura's (1986) analysis of **observational learning** involves four phases: the attentional, retention, reproduction, and motivational phases.

social learning theory
Learning theory that emphasizes not only reinforcement but also the effects of cues on thought and of thought on action.

modeling
Imitation of others' behavior.

observational learning
Learning by observation and imitation of others.

> **ON THE WEB**
>
> For more on social learning theory go to **http://tip.psychology.org/bandura.html**.

   1. Attentional phase: The first phase in observational learning is paying attention to a model. In general, students pay attention to role models who are attractive, successful, interesting, and popular. This is why so many students copy the dress, hairstyle, and mannerisms of pop culture stars. In the classroom the teacher gains the students' attention by presenting clear and interesting cues, by using novelty or surprise, and by motivating students.

   2. Retention phase: Once teachers have students' attention, it is time to model the behavior they want students to imitate and then give students a chance to practice or rehearse. For example, a teacher might show how to write the letter *A*. Then students would imitate the teacher's model by trying to write *A*'s themselves.

3. Reproduction: During the reproduction phase, students try to match their behavior to the model's. In the classroom the assessment of student learning takes place during this phase. For example, after seeing the letter *A* modeled and practicing it several times, can the student reproduce the letter so that it looks like the teacher's model?

4. Motivational phase: The final stage in the observational learning process is motivation. Students will imitate a model because they believe that doing so will increase their own chances to be reinforced. In the classroom the motivational phase of observational learning often entails praise or grades given for matching the teacher's model. Students pay attention to the model, practice it, and reproduce it because they have learned that this is what the teacher likes and they want to please the teacher. When the child makes a recognizable *A*, the teacher says, "Nice work!"

Vicarious Learning   Although most observational learning is motivated by an expectation that correctly imitating the model will lead to reinforcement, it is also important to note that people learn by seeing others reinforced or punished for engaging in certain behaviors (Bandura, 1986). This is why magazine distributors always include happy winners in their advertisements to induce people to enter promotional contests. We may consciously know that our chances of winning are one in several million, but seeing others so handsomely reinforced makes us want to imitate their contest-entering behavior.

Classroom teachers use the principle of **vicarious learning** all the time. When one student is fooling around, teachers often single out others who are working well and reinforce them for doing a good job. The misbehaving student sees that working is reinforced and (it is hoped) gets back to work. This technique was systematically studied by Broden, Hall, Dunlap, and Clark (1970). Two disruptive second-graders, Edwin and Greg, sat next to each other. After a baseline period, the teacher began to notice and praise Edwin whenever he was paying attention and doing his classwork. Edwin's behavior improved markedly under this condition. Of greater interest, however, is that Greg's behavior also improved, even though no specific reinforcement for appropriate behavior was directed toward him. Apparently, Greg learned from Edwin's experience. In the case of Ms. Esteban and Rebecca at the opening of this chapter, other students saw Rebecca get Ms. Esteban's attention by calling out answers, so they modeled their behavior on Rebecca's.

One of the classic experiments in social learning theory is a study done by Bandura (1965). Children were shown one of three films. In all three, an adult modeled aggressive behavior. In one film the model was severely punished. In another the model was praised and given treats. In a third the model was given no consequences. After viewing one of the films, the children were observed playing with toys. The children who had seen the model punished engaged in significantly fewer aggressive acts in their own play than did the children who had seen the model rewarded or had viewed the no-consequences film.

INTASC

2 Knowledge of Human Development and Learning

CERTIFICATION POINTER

Teacher certification tests may require you to know that learning vicariously means that you learn from observing or hearing about another's experiences.

vicarious learning
Learning based on observation of the consequences of others' behavior.

Theory into **PRACTICE**

Observational Learning

Have you ever tried to teach someone to tie his or her shoes? Imagine explaining this task to someone without the use of a model or imitation! Such a simple task, and one that many of us take for granted, can be quite a milestone for a kindergartner. Learning to tie our shoes is certainly a prime example of how observational learning works.

Acquiring new skills by observing the behaviors of others is a common part of everyday life. In many situations children watch others talking and acting, and they witness the consequences of those activities as well. Such observations provide models that teach children strategies to use at other times and places.

Although the major focus of research on observational learning has been on specific behaviors, studies have also shown that attitudes, too, may be acquired through observation (Miller, 1993). Teachers and parents alike are concerned with the models emulated by children. The value of these models goes beyond the specific abilities they possess and includes the attitudes they represent. In the classroom the teacher must be certain to exemplify a standard of behavior consistent with the expectations he or she has for the students. For instance, if promptness and politeness are characteristics the teacher wants to foster in the students, then the teacher must be certain to demonstrate those traits.

In cooperative learning groups, the success of the group may depend on the models present in that group. Peers have a strong influence on the behaviors of the individual. For example, when teachers place students in math groups, it may be just as important to include students who possess a high motivation for learning in a group as it is to include students with strong math skills. The attitudes and behaviors that accompany high motivation will be imitated by fellow students.

CONNECTIONS

For more on self-regulated learning, see Chapter 8, page 248.

Self-Regulated Learning   Another important concept in social learning theory is **self-regulation** (Boekaerts, Pintrich, & Zeidner, 2000; Schunk & Pajares, 2004; Zimmerman, 2000). Bandura (1997) hypothesized that people observe their own behavior, judge it against their own standards, and reinforce or punish themselves. We have all had the experience of knowing we've done a job well and mentally patting ourselves on the back, regardless of what others have said. Similarly, we all know when we've done less than our best. To make these judgments, we have to have expectations for our own performance. One student might be delighted to get 90 percent correct on a test, while another might be quite disappointed.

Students can be taught to use self-regulation strategies, and they can be reminded to do so in a variety of contexts so that self-regulation becomes a habit. For example, students might be asked to set goals for the amount of time they expect to study each evening and to record whether or not they meet their goals. Children who are studying multiplication facts might be asked to time themselves on how quickly and accurately they can complete a 50-item facts test and then to try to beat their own record. Students might be asked to grade their own essays in terms of content, mechanics, and organization, and to see whether they can match the teacher's ratings. Each of these strategies puts students in control of their own learning goals, and each is likely to build a general strategy of setting and meeting personal goals and personal standards (Schunk & Zimmerman, 2003).

As with any skill, self-regulated learning skills are likely to remain limited to one situation or context unless they are applied in many contexts. For example, children who learn to set study goals for themselves when working alone may not transfer these skills to situations in which they are working in groups or in the presence of a

self-regulation
Rewarding or punishing one's own behavior.

teacher (Schunk & Pajares, 2004; Zimmerman, 2000), although they can readily learn to make these generalizations if they are taught or reminded to do so. Similarly, children may not transfer self-regulated learning strategies from English to math, or even from computations to problem solving (Boekaerts, 1995). For this reason, students need many opportunities to use goal-setting and self-evaluation strategies in a variety of contexts, to monitor and celebrate their progress, and to understand how, when, and why they should self-regulate.

Meichenbaum's Model of Self-Regulated Learning

Students can be taught to monitor and regulate their own behavior. Self-regulated learning strategies of this kind are often called **cognitive behavior modification** (Harris, Graham, & Pressley, 2001; Manning & Payne, 1996). For example, Meichenbaum (1977) developed a strategy in which students are trained to say to themselves, "What is my problem? What is my plan? Am I using my plan? How did I do?" This strategy has also been used to reduce disruptive behavior of students at

How do community summer reading programs encourage young children to read? How is this a form of self-regulated learning?

many grade levels (Martella et al., 2003; Workman & Katz, 1995). Manning (1988) taught disruptive third-graders self-statements to help them remember appropriate behavior and to reinforce it for themselves. As one instance, for appropriate hand-raising, students were taught to say to themselves while raising their hands, "If I scream out the answer, others will be disturbed. I will raise my hand and wait my turn. Good for me. See, I can wait!" (Manning, 1988, p. 197). Similar strategies have been successfully applied to help students monitor their own achievement. For example, poor readers have been taught to ask themselves questions as they read and to summarize paragraphs to make sure they comprehend text (Bornstein, 1985).

The steps involved in self-instruction are described by Meichenbaum (1977) as follows:

1. An adult model performs a task while talking to self out loud (cognitive modeling).
2. The child performs the same task under the direction of the model's instructions (overt, external guidance).
3. The child performs the task while instructing self aloud (overt self-guidance).
4. The child whispers the instructions to self as he or she goes through the task (faded, overt self-guidance).
5. The child performs the task while guiding his or her performance via private speech (covert self-instruction). (p. 32)

Note the similarity of Meichenbaum's self-regulated learning strategy to the Vygotskian approach to scaffolded instruction described in Chapter 2. Both approaches emphasize modeling private speech and gradually moving from teacher-controlled to student-controlled behaviors, with the students using private speech to talk themselves through their tasks. Encouraging self-regulated learning is a means of teaching students to think about their own thinking. Self-regulated learning strategies not only have been found to improve performance on the task students were taught, but also

CONNECTIONS

For the related concept of teaching self-questioning strategies to develop metacognitive skills, see Chapter 6, page 192.

CONNECTIONS

For more on Vygotsky, see Chapter 2, page 43.

cognitive behavior modification
Procedures based on both behavioral and cognitive principles for changing one's own behavior by means of self-talk and self-instruction.

have generalized to other tasks (Harris, Graham, & Pressley, 2001; Schunk & Zimmerman, 2003).

One example of a way to help children engage in self-regulated learning is providing students, when assigning a long or complex task, with a form for monitoring their progress. For example, a teacher might assign students to write a report on the life of Martin Luther King Jr. Students might be given the following self-monitoring checklist:

TASK COMPLETION FORM

☐ Located material on Martin Luther King Jr. in the library

☐ Read and took notes on material

☐ Wrote first draft of report

☐ Checked draft for sense

☐ Checked draft for mechanics:

  ☐ Spelling

  ☐ Grammar

  ☐ Punctuation

☐ Composed typed or neatly handwritten final draft

The idea behind this form is that breaking down a complex task into smaller pieces encourages students to feel that they are making progress toward their larger goal. Checking off each step allows them to give themselves a mental pat on the back that reinforces their efforts (Manning & Payne, 1996). After seeing many checklists of this kind, students might be asked to make up their own, to learn how to chart their own progress toward a goal. Along similar lines, Trammel, Schloss, and Alper (1994) found that having children with learning disabilities keep records and make graphs of their homework completion significantly increased the amount of homework they did (see also Martella, Marchand-Martella, & Cleanthous, 2001). A review by Robinson, Robinson, and Katayama (1999) found that cognitive behavior modification strategies can have a substantial impact, especially on reducing hyperactive, impulsive, and aggressive behaviors (e.g., Binder, Dixon, & Ghezi, 2000). Several of the studies reviewed found these effects to be long-lasting.

Self-Reinforcement   Drabman, Spitalnik, and O'Leary (1973) designed and evaluated a classic procedure to teach students to regulate their own behavior. They asked teachers to rate student behaviors each day and reinforce students when they earned high ratings. Then they changed the program: They asked students to guess what rating the teacher had given them. The students were reinforced for guessing correctly. Finally, the reinforcers were gradually removed. The students' behavior improved under the reinforcement and guessing conditions, and it remained at its improved level long after the program was ended. The authors explained that students who were taught to match the teacher's ratings developed their own standards for appropriate behavior and reinforced themselves for meeting those standards.

Information about one's own behavior has often been found to change behavior (Rosenbaum & Drabman, 1982), even when that information is self-provided. For example, researchers have increased on-task behavior by having children mark down every few minutes whether or not they have been studying in the last few minutes (Maag, Rutherford, & DiGangi, 1992; Webber et al., 1993). When coupled with self-reinforcement, self-observation often has important effects on student behavior (Jenson et al., 1988). Many of us use this principle in studying, saying to ourselves that we will not take a break for lunch until we have finished reading a certain amount of material.

Students who feel confident in their ability to use metacognitive and self-motivational behaviors are likely to be high in self-efficacy—the belief that one's own efforts (rather than luck or other people or other external or uncontrollable factors) determine one's success or failure. Self-efficacy beliefs are perhaps the most important factor (after ability) in determining students' success in school (Bandura, 1997; Schunk & Zimmerman, 2003).

Strengths and Limitations of Behavioral Learning Theories

The basic principles of behavioral learning theories are as firmly established as any in psychology and have been demonstrated under many different conditions. These principles are useful for explaining much of human behavior; they are even more useful in changing behavior.

It is important to recognize, however, that behavioral learning theories are limited in scope. With the exception of social learning theorists, behavioral learning theorists focus almost exclusively on observable behavior. This is one reason why so many of the examples presented in this chapter involve the management of behavior (see Driscoll, 2000). Less visible learning processes, such as concept formation, learning from text, problem solving, and thinking, are difficult to observe directly and have therefore been studied less often by behavioral learning theorists. These processes fall more into the domain of cognitive learning. Social learning theory, which is a direct outgrowth of behavioral learning theories, helps to bridge the gap between the behavioral and cognitive perspectives.

Behavioral and cognitive theories of learning are often posed as competing, opposite models. There are indeed specific areas in which these theories take contradictory positions. However, it is more accurate to see them as complementary rather than competitive—that is, as tackling different problems (Kazdin, 2001; Miltenberger, 2001).

CONNECTIONS

For more on self-efficacy beliefs and student success, see Chapter 10, pages 321 and 322.

CERTIFICATION POINTER

The idea that behavioral learning theories apply best to observable behavior (rather than thinking, for example) may appear on teacher certification tests.

Chapter Summary

What Is Learning?

Learning involves the acquisition of abilities that are not innate. Learning depends on experience, including feedback from the environment.

What Behavioral Learning Theories Have Evolved?

Early research into learning studied the effects of stimuli on reflexive behaviors. Ivan Pavlov contributed the idea of classical conditioning, in which neutral stimuli can acquire the capacity to evoke behavioral responses through their association with unconditioned stimuli that trigger reflexes. E. L. Thorndike developed the Law of Effect, emphasizing the role of the consequences of present behavior in determining future

THE INTENTIONAL TEACHER

Using What You Know about Behavioral and Social Learning Theory to Improve Teaching and Learning

Intentional teachers are concerned with the outcome of their teaching—what happens when learning goals are met? Robert Mager (1997) asks, "How can you tell the difference between people who have met a goal and those who haven't?" By observing what they do—in short, their behaviors.

One role of the intentional teacher is functioning as an instructional designer, carefully planning what new abilities learners will acquire. Sometimes called "behavioral" or "performance" objectives, such outcome statements often imply two performance levels. Again, Mager reminds us to "always state the *main intent*" of an objective. Many important outcomes state performances that *cannot be observed*. You can't see your students adding or composing or comparing or relating, but these "cognitive" actions are often the real goal you intend to help your students achieve. For these "covert," unobservable behaviors, Mager suggests that you, in your role as a designer of instruction, think of "indicator behaviors," observable actions that will show not only you but others, and most important the students themselves, that they can indeed "add," "compose," "compare," "relate," or perform any other meaningful mental behavior aimed at in your lesson.

❶ What do I expect my students to know and be able to do at the end of this lesson? How does this contribute to course objectives and to students' needs to become capable individuals?

In considering any plan to improve classroom behavior, remember that we tend to use the term "classroom behavior" in too limited a way, equating "behavior" with "being good" (i.e., sitting still and being quiet). Watch for indications of interest and engagement as students work individually or in groups. For example, as your students work in spirited project groups, you might briefly interrupt their work to ask questions: "Are you on task? Have you said at least one nice thing about someone else's idea?" The questions help students check their own behavior.

Before the school year begins, you should develop a discipline plan that supports appropriate behavior and seeks to extinguish negative behaviors, and then update that plan in light of student behavior. For example, before your noisy sixth period begins, you might rehearse: "I will recognize only those who make an appropriate bid for the floor. *No matter what.* I will ignore attention-seeking behaviors. I will use praise to reinforce on-task behavior."

❷ What knowledge, skills, needs, and interests do my students have that must be taken into account in my lesson?

Particular reinforcers vary in their effectiveness for individuals and groups. Determine what kinds of reinforcers are effective for particular students. For example, you might hand out a survey early in the year that asks open-ended questions such as: "If you had time to do any practical fun activity in the classroom, what would you do?" and "When you do a good job in school, what response from teachers makes you the happiest?" and "What message from your teacher to your parents would make you feel most proud?" You would take note of the survey responses to determine useful consequences for various behaviors for this class and particular individuals.

Reinforcers are most effective when they immediately follow the behavior. Provide immediate feedback so that students have knowledge of the results of their actions and learn to link behavior to its consequences.

❸ What do I know about the content, child development, learning, motivation, and effective teaching strategies that I can use to accomplish my objectives?

An intentional teacher breaks down complex skills and performances into smaller bits so that students learn gradually by logical steps. For example, you might give students an opportunity to discriminate and to generalize among examples and settings by suggesting the relevant characteristics and information to look for. In teaching second-graders about mammals, you might provide 40 large pictures of animals, pointing out characteristics of mammals. The students could then sort the

behavior. B. F. Skinner continued the study of the relationship between behavior and consequences. He described operant conditioning, in which reinforcers and punishers shape behavior.

What Are Some Principles of Behavioral Learning?

Reinforcers increase the frequency of a behavior, and punishers decrease its frequency. Reinforcement can be primary or secondary, positive or negative. Intrinsic reinforcers are rewards inherent in a behavior itself. Extrinsic reinforcers are praise or rewards.

pictures into mammals and nonmammals, and you might praise them for their accuracy. In teaching high school students about justice, you might have them sort a set of examples of various forms of civil disobedience into "justifiable" and "not justifiable."

You can increase the likelihood of students' generalizing (transferring) their learning to new situations by using real-life applications and many examples from different contexts. For instance, after studying a variety of graphs with your students, you might prepare a bulletin board and invite students to fill it with examples of graphs from newspapers, advertisements, and other print sources.

❹ What instructional materials, technology, assistance, and other resources are available to help accomplish my objectives?

Bandura and Meichenbaum developed these ideas—modeling, observational learning, self-directedness. Some activities that build on the concepts of observational and self-regulated learning follow.

Consider teaching cognitive behavior modification and self-regulation directly. For example, you might plan an art activity for your students designed to create an "illuminated" initial for their name. You model the tasks, describing out loud how you outline the letter, select your favorite color for the letter, and select symbols and designs to decorate the letter, based on your personal interests. You might guide the students through these steps, directing them to "make a big outline of your initial and choose your favorite color to fill it in." "Now choose some designs that represent your own interests—sports, hobbies, et cetera—and decorate the letter." "Now make the initial of your last name and talk yourself through it in a whisper as we just did together." "Finally, put both your initials together, reminding yourself as you work of these steps but not saying anything out loud, just in your mind."

You might sum up the activity by pointing out that this is a process students can use to direct themselves through any task they wish to manage themselves: Think of the steps, say them to themselves in a whisper as they plan the tasks, and then do the steps, talking to themselves silently. You might say, "Talking to yourself can be a great way to get things done!" In other subject areas for this class, you might make use of similar modeling examples.

❺ How will I plan to assess students' progress toward my objectives?

In all subject areas and in all grades, you will have developed a number of specific assignments with measurable expected outcomes. You might make a policy of involving students in determining the criteria for grading such assignments, and inform students with each assignment of what the decided-upon criteria for performance are.

As an intentional teacher, you should recognize that behavioral learning theories are one set of tools that can help you support positive changes in student behavior and learning. You should develop your observational skills and modify your actions in light of what you perceive of students' reactions to instruction. You should rely on constant observation of your class, developing the "withitness" that is a characteristic of effective teachers.

❻ How will I respond if individual children or the class as a whole are not on track toward success? What is my back-up plan?

Gather information on the effects of your instruction by watching students' responses, and change strategies if changes are needed. For example, you might do quick visual sweeps of your class to make note of nonverbal hints from students that they are interested or bored, getting it or lost. Check in with students who are struggling and give them additional explanations, or assign them a peer tutor.

Punishment involves weakening behavior by either introducing aversive consequences or removing reinforcers. The Premack Principle states that a way to increase less-enjoyed activities is to link them to more-enjoyed activities.

Shaping through timely feedback on each step of a task is an effective teaching practice based on behavioral learning theory. Extinction is the weakening and gradual disappearance of behavior as reinforcement is withdrawn.

Schedules of reinforcement are used to increase the probability, frequency, or persistence of desired behavior. Reinforcement schedules may be based on ratios or intervals and may be fixed or variable.

Antecedent stimuli serve as cues indicating which behaviors will be reinforced or punished. Discrimination involves using cues to detect differences between stimulus situations, whereas generalization involves responding to similarities between stimuli. Generalization is transfer or carryover of behaviors learned under one set of conditions to other situations.

How Has Social Learning Theory Contributed to Our Understanding of Human Learning?

Social learning theory is based on a recognition of the importance of observational learning and self-regulated learning. Bandura noted that learning through modeling—directly or vicariously—involves four phases: paying attention, retaining the modeled behavior, reproducing the behavior, and being motivated to repeat the behavior. Bandura proposed that students should be taught to have expectations for their own performances and to reinforce themselves. Meichenbaum proposed steps for self-regulated learning that represent a form of cognitive behavior modification.

Behavioral learning theories are central to the application of educational psychology in classroom management, discipline, motivation, instructional models, and other areas. Behavioral learning theories are limited in scope, however, in that they describe only observable behavior that can be directly measured.

Research
Navigator.com

Key Terms

Review the following key terms from the chapter. Then, to explore research on these topics and how they relate to education today, connect to Research Navigator™ through this book's Companion Website or directly at www.researchnavigator.com.

antecedent stimuli   152
aversive stimulus   143
behavioral learning theories   134
classical conditioning   136
cognitive behavior modification   157
cognitive learning theories   134
conditioned stimulus   136
consequences   138
cues   152
discrimination   152
extinction   146
extinction burst   148
extrinsic reinforcers   141
fixed-interval schedule   149
fixed-ratio (FR) schedule   148
generalization   153
intrinsic reinforcers   141
Law of Effect   136
learning   134
maintenance   151
modeling   154
negative reinforcer   140
neutral stimuli   136

observational learning   154
operant conditioning   136
positive reinforcer   140
Premack Principle   140
presentation punishment   143
primary reinforcer   139
punishment   143
reinforcer   139
removal punishment   143
schedule of reinforcement   148
secondary reinforcer   139
self-regulation   156
shaping   145
Skinner box   138
social learning theory   154
stimuli (stimulus)   135
time out   143
unconditioned response   136
unconditioned stimulus   136
variable-interval schedule   149
variable-ratio (VR) schedule   149
vicarious learning   155

Self-Assessment: Practicing for Licensure

Directions: The chapter-opening vignette addresses indicators that are often assessed in state licensure exams. Re-read the chapter-opening vignette, and then respond to the following questions.

1. Julia Esteban, first-grade teacher at Tanner Elementary School, calls on her students when they do not raise their hands, a practice that goes against an established rule in the class. Which of the following types of conditioning can Ms. Esteban use to teach her students about appropriate hand-raising behaviors?

   a. classical conditioning
   b. operant conditioning
   c. modeled conditioning
   d. assisted conditioning

2. Which of the following explanations best summarizes Julia Esteban's problem with her students' failure to raise their hands prior to speaking?

   a. Ms. Esteban is using negative reinforcement rather than positive reinforcement.
   b. Ms. Esteban has failed to apply the Premack Principle when her students break the hand-raising rule.
   c. Ms. Esteban allows her students to make decisions about classroom rules, a practice that research studies have shown to be unsuccessful.
   d. Ms. Esteban should note that pleasurable consequences (rewarding appropriate behaviors) increase a behavior while unpleasant consequences weaken the frequency of a behavior.

3. According to research on behavioral learning theories, which strategy might Ms. Esteban use to get her students to raise their hand prior to speaking?

   a. Reward those students who follow the rule.
   b. Punish those students who do not follow the rule.
   c. Ignore those students who follow the rule.
   d. Wait before administering any type of consequence for rule-breakers.

4. Imagine that Ms. Esteban's students have a difficult time breaking their habit of speaking out of turn. Which of the following techniques might she use to reinforce close approximations of the behaviors she wants her students to exhibit?

   a. extinction
   b. maintenance
   c. shaping
   d. discrimination

5. Which type of reinforcement schedule is Ms. Esteban using if she reinforces her students' appropriate behavior after so many behaviors, but the students do not know when the reinforcement will be applied?

   a. continuous
   b. fixed ratio schedule
   c. fixed interval schedule
   d. variable ratio schedule

6. Explain how classical conditioning and operant conditioning are alike and different. Give at least one example of each.

7. Describe Albert Bandura's social learning theory. Bandura's analysis of observational learning involves four phases—describe each phase.

Information Processing and Cognitive Theories of Learning

Verona Bishop's biology class was doing a unit on human learning. At the start of one lesson, Ms. Bishop did an experiment with her students. For 3 seconds, using an overhead projector, she flashed a diagram of a model of information processing identical to the one in Figure 6.1. Then she asked students to recall what they noticed. Some mentioned that they saw boxes and arrows. Some saw the words *memory* and *forgotten* and inferred that the figure had something to do with learning. One student even saw the word *learning*, though it wasn't in the figure.

"Come now," said Ms. Bishop. "You noticed a lot more than that! You just may not have noticed what you noticed. For example, what did you smell?"

The whole class laughed. They all recalled smelling the broccoli cooking in the cafeteria. The students caught on to the idea and began to recall all the other details they had noticed that had nothing to do with the diagram: the sounds of a truck going by, details of the classroom and the people in it, and so on.

After this discussion, Ms. Bishop said, "Isn't the brain amazing? In only three seconds you received an enormous amount of information. You didn't even know you were noticing the smell of the broccoli until I reminded you about it, but it was in your mind just the same. Also, in only three seconds your mind was already starting to make sense of the information in the figure. Cheryl thought she saw the word *learning*, which wasn't there at all. But her mind leaped to that word because she saw words like *memory* that relate to learning.

"Now imagine that you could keep in your mind forever everything that occurred in the three seconds you looked at the diagram: the arrows, the boxes, the words, the truck, the broccoli—everything. In fact, imagine that you could keep everything that ever entered your mind. What would that be like?"

"You'd be a genius!" ventured Samphan.

"You'd go crazy!" countered Jamal.

"I think Jamal is closer to the truth," said Ms. Bishop. "If your mind filled up with all this useless junk, you'd be a blithering idiot! One of the most important things we're going to learn about learning is that it is an active process of focusing in on important information, screening out unimportant information, and using what is already in our minds to decide which is which."

Ms. Bishop turned on the overhead projector again.

"When we study this diagram in more detail, you'll use what you already know about learning, memory, forgetting, and diagrams to make sense of it. I hope you'll always remember the main ideas it's trying to show you. You'll soon forget the boxes and arrows, and even the smell of the broccoli will fade from your memory, but the parts of this diagram that make sense to you and answer questions you care about may stay in your memory your whole life!"

USING YOUR

Experience

Cooperative Learning   Jot down two or three ways in which you try to memorize lists and study new concepts. Share with other students a strategy that you use to learn information better.

Cooperative Learning   What is your picture of learning, memory, and forgetting? After drafting your own picture, meet with four or five classmates to compose a summary illustration or diagram of human memory and cognition based on your individual ideas. After 10 minutes, share with the class.

INTASC

2 Knowledge of Human Development and Learning

The human mind is a meaning maker. From the first microsecond you see, hear, taste, or feel something, you start a process of deciding what it is, how it relates to what you already know, and whether it is important to keep in your mind or should be discarded. This whole process may take place consciously, unconsciously, or both. This chapter describes how information is received and processed in the mind, how memory and loss of memory work, and how teachers can help students understand and remember critical information, skills, and ideas. This chapter also presents cognitive theories of learning, theories that relate to processes that go on within the minds of learners, and means of helping students use their minds more effectively to learn, remember, and use knowledge.

information-processing theory
Cognitive theory of learning that describes the processing, storage, and retrieval of knowledge in the mind.

sensory register
Component of the memory system in which information is received and held for very short periods of time.

WHAT IS AN INFORMATION-PROCESSING MODEL?

Information constantly enters our minds through our senses. Most of this information is almost immediately discarded, and we may never even be aware of much of it. Some is held in our memories for a short time and then forgotten. For example, we may remember the seat number on a baseball ticket until we find our seats, at which point we will forget the number. However, some information is retained much longer, perhaps for the rest of our lives. What is the process by which information is absorbed, and how can teachers take advantage of this process to help students retain critical information and skills? These are questions that have been addressed by cognitive learning theorists and that have led to **information-processing theory,** a dominant theory of learning and memory since the mid-1970s.

Research on human memory (see, e.g., Anderson, 1995; Bransford, Brown, & Cocking, 1999; Byrnes, 2001; Ericsson & Kintsch, 1995; Solso, 2001) has helped learning theorists to describe the process by which information is remembered (or forgotten). This process, usually referred to as the Atkinson–Shiffrin model of information processing (Atkinson & Shiffrin, 1968), is illustrated in Figure 6.1.

Sensory Register

The first component of the memory system that incoming information meets is the sensory register, shown at the left of Figure 6.1. **Sensory registers** receive large amounts of information from each of the senses (sight, hearing, touch, smell, taste) and hold it for a very short time, no more than a couple of seconds. If nothing happens to information held in a sensory register, it is rapidly lost.

Ingenious experiments have been used to detect sensory registers. A person might be shown a display like that in Figure 6.2 for a very short period of time, say 50 milliseconds. The person is usually able to report seeing 3, 4, or 5 of the letters but not all 12 of them. In a classic early experiment, Sperling (1960) presented a display like Figure 6.2 to people. After the display disappeared, he signaled viewers to try to recall the top, middle, or bottom row. He found that people could recall any one row almost perfectly. Therefore they must have seen all the letters in the 50 milliseconds and retained them for a short period of time. However, when people tried to recall all 12 letters, the time it took them to do so apparently exceeded the amount of time the letters lasted in their sensory registers, so they lost some of the letters.

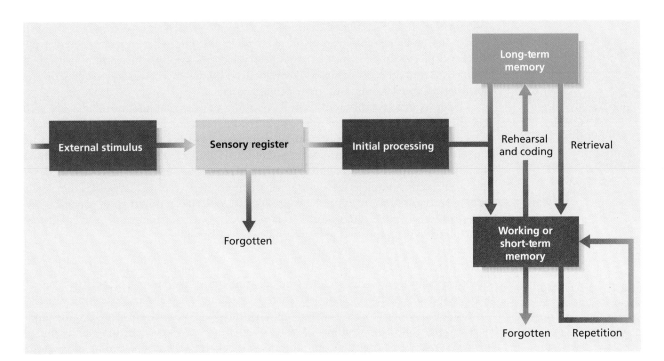

FIGURE 6.1
The Sequence of Information Processing
Information that is to be remembered must first reach a person's senses, then be attended to and transferred from the sensory register to the working memory, then be processed again for transfer to long-term memory.
From Charles G. Morris, *Psychology: An Introduction* (8th ed.), p. 233. Copyright © 1993. Adapted by permission of Prentice Hall, Upper Saddle River, New Jersey.

FIGURE 6.2
Display Used in Sensory Register Experiments
This is a typical display used by G. A. Sperling to detect the existence and limits of the sensory register. People who were shown the display for an instant and then asked to recall a specific row were usually able to do so. However, they were not able to recall all 12 letters.
From G. A. Sperling, "The Information Available in Brief Visual Presentations," *Psychological Monographs, 74,* 1960, American Psychological Association.

The existence of sensory registers has two important educational implications. First, people must pay attention to information if they are to retain it. Second, it takes time to bring all the information seen in a moment into consciousness. For example, if students are bombarded with too much information at once and are not told which aspects of the information they should pay attention to, they may have difficulty learning any of the information at all.

Perception   When the senses receive stimuli, the mind immediately begins working on some of them. Therefore the sensory images of which we are conscious are not exactly the same as what we saw, heard, or felt; they are what our senses perceived. **Perception** of stimuli is not as straightforward as reception of stimuli. Instead, it involves mental interpretation and is influenced by our mental state, past experience, knowledge, motivations, and many other factors.

First, we perceive different stimuli according to rules that have nothing to do with the inherent characteristics of the stimuli. If you are sitting in a building, for example, you may not pay much attention to, or even hear, a fire engine's siren. If you are driving a car, you pay a great deal more attention. If you are standing outside a burning building waiting for the firefighters to arrive, you pay even more attention. Second, we do not perceive stimuli as we see or sense them but as we know (or assume) they really are. From across a room, a book on a bookshelf looks like a thin strip of paper, but we infer that it is a three-dimensional rectangular form with many pages. You might see just the edge of a table and mentally infer the entire table.

perception
A person's interpretation of stimuli.

attention
Active focus on certain stimuli to the exclusion of others.

Attention   When teachers say to students, "Pay attention" or "Lend me your ears," they are using the words *pay* and *lend* appropriately. Like money, **attention** is a limited resource. When a teacher asks students to spend their limited attention capacity on whatever the teacher is saying, students must give up actively attending to other stimuli, shifting their priorities so that other stimuli are screened out. For example, when people listen intently to an interesting speaker, they are unaware of minor body sensations (such as itches or hunger) and other sounds or sights. An experienced speaker knows that when the audience looks restless, its attention is no longer focused on the lecture but might be turning toward considerations of lunch or other activities; it is time to recapture the listeners' attention.

Gaining Attention   How can teachers focus students' attention on the lesson at hand, and in particular on the most important aspects of what is being taught?

There are several ways to gain students' attention, all of which go under the general heading of arousing student interest. One way is to use cues that indicate "This is important." Some teachers raise or lower their voices to signal that they are about to impart critical information. Others use gestures, repetition, or body position to communicate the same message.

Another way to gain attention is to increase the emotional content of material. Some publications accomplish this by choosing very emotional words. This is probably why newspaper headlines say "Senate Kills Mass Transit Proposal" rather than "Senate Votes Against Mass Transit Proposal."

Unusual, inconsistent, or surprising stimuli also attract attention. For example, science teachers often introduce lessons with a demonstration or magic trick to engage student curiosity.

Finally, informing students that what follows is important to them will catch their attention. For example, teachers can ensure attention by telling students, "This will be on tomorrow's test." Of course, learners make their own decisions about what is important, and they learn more of what they think is important than of other material because they pay more attention to it. Students can be taught to identify what is important in texts and then to devote more attention to those aspects.

Short-Term or Working Memory

Information that a person perceives and pays attention to is transferred to the second component of the memory system: the **short-term memory** (Solso, 2001). Short-term memory is a storage system that can hold a limited amount of information for a few seconds. It is the part of memory in which information that is currently being thought about is stored. The thoughts we are conscious of having at any given moment are being held in our short-term memory. When we stop thinking about something, it disappears from our short-term memory. Another term for short-term memory is **working memory** (Anderson, 1995; Ericsson & Kintsch, 1995). This term emphasizes that the most important aspect of short-term memory is not its duration, but the fact that it is active. Working memory is where the mind operates on information, organizes it for storage or discarding, and connects it to other information.

As depicted in Figure 6.1, information may enter working memory from sensory registers or from the third basic component of the memory system: long-term memory. Often, both things happen at the same time. When you see a robin, your sensory register transfers the image of the robin to your working memory. Meanwhile, you may (unconsciously) search your long-term memory for information about birds so that you can identify this particular one as a robin. Along with that recognition may come a lot of other information about robins, memories of past experiences with robins, or feelings about robins—all of which were stored in long-term memory but are brought into consciousness (working memory) by your mental processing of the sight of the robin.

One way to hold information in working memory is to think about it or say it over and over. You have probably used this strategy to remember a phone number for a short time. This process of maintaining an item in working memory by repetition is called **rehearsal** (Baddeley, 1999). Rehearsal is important in learning because the longer an item remains in working memory, the greater the chance that it will be transferred to long-term memory. Without rehearsal, items will probably not stay in working memory for more than about 30 seconds. Because working memory has a limited capacity, information can also be lost from it by being forced out by other information. You have probably had the experience of looking up a telephone number, being interrupted briefly, and finding that you had forgotten the number.

CERTIFICATION POINTER

For teacher certification tests, you may be expected to detail various strategies for gaining students' attention, such as lowering your voice, using a gesture or surprise, and increasing the emotional content.

INTASC

2 Knowledge of Human Development and Learning

short-term or working memory
The component of memory in which limited amounts of information can be stored for a few seconds.

rehearsal
Mental repetition of information, which can improve its retention.

Teachers must allocate time for rehearsal during classroom lessons. Teaching too much information too rapidly is likely to be ineffective, because unless students are given time to mentally rehearse each new piece of information, later information is likely to drive it out of their working memories. When teachers stop a lesson to ask students whether they have any questions, they are also giving students a few moments to think over and mentally rehearse what they have just learned. This helps students to process information in working memory and thereby to establish it in long-term memory. This mental work is critical when students are learning new, difficult material.

Working Memory Capacity   Working memory is believed to have a capacity of five to nine bits of information (Miller, 1956). That is, we can think about only five to nine distinct things at a time. However, any particular bit may itself contain a great deal of information. For example, think how difficult it would be to memorize the following shopping list:

flour	orange juice	pepper	mustard
soda pop	parsley	cake	butter
relish	mayonnaise	oregano	canned tomatoes
potatoes	milk	lettuce	syrup
hamburger	hot dogs	eggs	onions
tomato paste	apples	spaghetti	buns

This list has too many bits of information to remember easily. All 24 food items would not fit into working memory in random order. However, you could easily memorize the list by organizing it according to familiar patterns. As shown in Table 6.1, you might mentally create three separate memory files: breakfast, lunch, and dinner. In each, you expect to find food and beverages; in the lunch and dinner files, you expect to find dessert as well. You can then think through the recipes for each item on the menus. In this way, you can recall what you have to buy and you need maintain only

Table 6.1

Example of Organization of Information to Facilitate Memory

A 24-item shopping list that would be very hard to remember in a random order can be organized into a smaller number of familiar categories, making the list easier to recall.

Breakfast	*Lunch*	*Dinner*
Pancakes: • Flour • Milk • Eggs • Butter • Syrup Beverage: Orange juice	Hot Dogs: • Hot dogs • Buns • Relish • Mustard Potato Salad: • Potatoes • Mayonnaise • Parsley Beverage: Soda pop Dessert: Apple	Spaghetti: • Spaghetti • Onions • Hamburger • Canned tomatoes • Tomato paste • Oregano • Pepper Salad: • Lettuce Beverage: Milk Dessert: Cake

a few bits of information in your working memory. When you enter the store, you are thinking, "I need food for breakfast, lunch, and dinner." First, you bring the breakfast file out of your long-term memory. It contains food (pancakes) and beverage (orange juice). You might think through how you make pancakes step by step and buy each ingredient, plus orange juice as a beverage. When you have done this, you can discard breakfast from your working memory and replace it with the lunch file and then the dinner file, going through the same processes. Note that all you did was to replace 24 little bits of information with 3 big bits that you could then separate into their components.

Working memory can be thought of as a bottleneck through which information from the environment reaches long-term memory. The limited capacity of working memory is one aspect of information processing that has important implications for the design and practice of instruction (Sweller, van Merrienboer, & Paas, 1998). For example, you cannot present students with many ideas at once unless the ideas are so well organized and well connected to information already in the students' long-term memories that their working memories (with assistance from their long-term memories) can accommodate them, as in the case of the shopping list just discussed.

As another illustration of the limited capacity of working memory, Mayer (2001) compared a lesson on lightning storms that included a number of extraneous words, pictures, and music to a lesson without these elements. The simpler lesson produced higher performance on a transfer test. Apparently the more coherent lesson used working memory capacity more effectively (see Mayer, 2003).

Individual Differences in Working Memory Individuals differ, of course, in the capacity of their working memories to accomplish a given learning task. One of the main factors in enhancing this capacity is background knowledge. The more a person knows about something, the better able the person is to organize and absorb new information (Engle, Nations, & Cantor, 1990; Kuhara-Kojima & Hatano, 1991). However, prior knowledge is not the only factor. Individuals also differ in their abilities to organize information and can be taught to consciously use strategies for making more efficient use of their working memory capacity (Levin & Levin, 1990; Peverly, 1991; Pressley & Harris, 1990). Strategies of this kind are discussed later in this chapter.

Long-Term Memory

Long-term memory is that part of our memory system where we keep information for long periods of time. Long-term memory is thought to be a very large-capacity, very long-term memory store. In fact, many theorists believe that we may never forget information in long-term memory; rather, we might just lose the ability to find the information within our memory. For this reason, some theorists use the term *permanent memory* (Byrnes, 1996). We do not live long enough to fill up our long-term memory. The differences among sensory registers, working (short-term) memory, and long-term memory are summarized in Table 6.2.

Ericsson and Kintsch (1995) hypothesize that people store not only information but also learning strategies in long-term memory for easy access. This capacity, which Ericsson and Kintsch call long-term working memory, accounts for the extraordinary skills of experts (such as medical diagnosticians) who must match current information with a vast array of patterns held in their long-term memories.

"Mrs. Lee, can I be excused? My working memory capacity is full."

long-term memory
The components of memory in which large amounts of information can be stored for long periods of time.

Table 6.2

Characteristics of Components of Cognitive Storage Systems

Storage Structure	Processes				Cause of Failure to Recall
	Code*	Capacity	Duration	Retrieval	
Sensory "store"	Sensory features	12–20 items† to huge	250 msec.–4 sec.	Complete, given proper cueing	Masking or decay
Short-term memory	Acoustic, visual, semantic, sensory features identified and named	7 ± 2 items	About 12 sec.; longer with rehearsal	Complete, with each item being retrieved every 35 msec.	Displacement, interference, decay
Long-term memory	Semantic, visual knowledge; abstractions; meaningful images	Enormous, virtually unlimited	Indefinite	Specific and general information available, given proper cueing	Interference, organic dysfunctioning, inappropriate cues

*How information is represented
†Estimated

Source: From Robert L. Solso, *Cognitive Psychology,* sixth edition, p. 240. Published by Allyn & Bacon, Boston, MA. Copyright © 2001 by Pearson Education. Reprinted by permission of the publisher.

episodic memory
A part of long-term memory that stores images of our personal experiences.

semantic memory
A part of long-term memory that stores facts and general knowledge.

procedural memory
A part of long-term memory that stores information about how to do things.

Theorists divide long-term memory into at least three parts: episodic memory, semantic memory, and procedural memory (Eichenbaum, 2003; Squire et al., 1993; Tulving, 1993). **Episodic memory** is our memory of personal experiences, a mental movie of things we saw or heard. When you remember what you had for dinner last night or what happened at your high school prom, you are recalling information stored in your long-term episodic memory. Long-term **semantic memory** contains the facts and generalized information that we know; concepts, principles, or rules and how to use them; and our problem-solving skills and learning strategies. Most things that are learned in class lessons are retained in semantic memory. **Procedural memory** refers to "knowing how" in contrast to "knowing that" (Solso, 2001). The abilities to drive, type, and ride a bicycle are examples of skills that are retained in procedural memory.

Episodic, semantic, and procedural memory store and organize information in different ways. Information in episodic memory is stored in the form of images that are organized on the basis of when and where events happened. Information in semantic memory is organized in the form of networks of ideas. Information in procedural memory is stored as a complex of stimulus–response pairings (Anderson, 1995). Recent brain studies (e.g., Bransford, Brown, & Cocking, 1999; Byrnes & Fox, 1998; Solso, 2001) have suggested that operations relating to each of these types of long-term memory take place in different parts of the brain. Let's examine in detail what we mean by these three kinds of memory.

Episodic Memory   Episodic memory contains images of experiences organized by when and where they happened (Tulving, 1993). For example, answer this question: In the house in which you lived as a child, when you entered your bedroom, was the head of your bed to the right, left, or away from or pointed toward you? If you are like most people, you answered this question by imagining the bedroom and seeing where the head of the bed was. Now consider this question: What did you do on the night of your senior prom or dance? Most people answer this question by imagining themselves back on that night and describing the events. Finally, suppose you are asked to recall the names of your high school classmates. One psychologist asked graduate students to come to a specific place for 1 hour a day and try to remember the names. Over the course of a month, the students continued to recall new names. Interestingly, they used space and time cues, which are associated with episodic memory, to imagine incidents that allowed them to recall the names. For example, they might recall the day their social studies teacher came to school dressed as an Arctic explorer and then mentally scan the faces of the students who were there.

These demonstrations indicate that images are important in episodic memory and that cues related to space and time help us to retrieve information from this part of memory. You have probably taken an exam and said to yourself, "I should know this answer. I remember reading this section. It was right on the bottom left corner of the page with the diagram in the upper right."

Episodic memories are often difficult to retrieve, because most episodes in our lives are repeated so often that later episodes get mixed up in memory with earlier ones, unless something happens during the episode to make it especially memorable. For example, few people remember what they had for lunch a week ago, much less years ago. However, there is a phenomenon called **flashbulb memory** in which the occurrence of an important event fixes mainly visual and auditory memories in a person's mind. For example, people who happened to be eating breakfast at the moment they first heard about the attack on the World Trade Center or about Princess Diana's death may well remember that particular meal (and other trivial aspects of the setting) forever. The reason for this is that the unforgettable event of that moment gives us access to the episodic (space and time) memories relating to what would usually be forgotten details.

Martin (1993) has speculated that educators could improve retention of concepts and information by explicitly creating memorable events involving visual or auditory images. For example, uses of projects, plays, simulations, and other forms of active learning could give students vivid images that they could remember and then use to retrieve other information presented at about the same time. In support of this idea, there is much evidence that pictures illustrating text help children to remember the text even when the pictures are no longer presented (Small, Lovett, & Scher, 1993). The pictures presumably tie the semantic information to the child's episodic memory, making the information easier to retrieve. There is also evidence that students often create their own mental pictures, which then help them remember material they have studied (Robinson, Robinson, & Katayama, 1999).

Semantic Memory   Semantic (or declarative) memory is organized in a very different way. It is mentally organized in networks of connected ideas or relationships called **schemata** (singular: *schema*) (Anderson, 1995; Flavell et al., 1993; Voss & Wiley, 1995). Recall that Piaget introduced the word *scheme* to describe a cognitive framework that individuals use to organize their perceptions and experiences. Cognitive processing theorists similarly use the terms *schema* and *schemata* to describe networks of concepts that individuals have in their memories that enable them to understand and incorporate new information. A schema is like an outline, with different concepts or ideas grouped under larger categories. Various aspects of schemata may be related by series of propositions, or relationships. For example, Figure 6.3 illustrates a simplified schema for the concept "bison," showing how this concept is related to other concepts in memory.

In the figure, the concept "bison" is linked to several other concepts. These may be linked to still more concepts (such as "How did Plains Indians hunt bison?") and to

CONNECTIONS

For more on the concept of schemes, see Chapter 2, page 31.

flashbulb memory
Important events that are fixed mainly in visual and auditory memory.

schemata
Mental networks of related concepts that influence understanding of new information; the singular is *schema*.

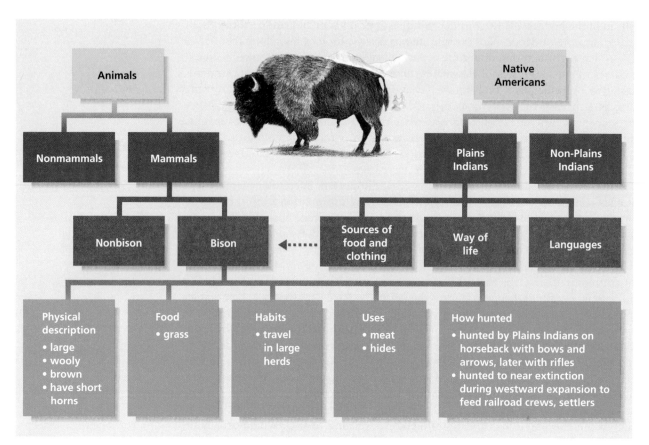

FIGURE 6.3
Schema for the Concept "Bison"

Information in long-term semantic memory is organized in networks of related ideas. The concept
"bison," for example, falls under the more general concepts "mammals" and "animals" and is
related to many other ideas that help to differentiate it from other concepts in memory.

broader categories or concepts (such as "How have conservationists saved many species from extinction?"). Schema theory (Anderson, 1995) holds that we gain access to
information held in our semantic long-term memory by mentally following paths like
those illustrated in Figure 6.3. For example, you might have deep in your memory the
idea that the Spanish introduction of the horse to North America revolutionized how
the Plains Indians hunted bison. To get to that bit of information, you might start
thinking about characteristics of bison, then think about how Plains Indians hunted
bison on horseback, then recall (or imagine) how they hunted bison before they had
horses. Many pathways can be used to get at the same bit of information. In fact, the
more pathways you have leading to a piece of information and the better established
those pathways are, the better access you will have to information in long-term semantic memory (Solso, 2001). Recall that the problem of long-term memory is not that
information is lost but that our access to information is lost.

One clear implication of schema theory is that new information that fits into a
well-developed schema is retained far more readily than is information that does not
fit into a schema. Schema theory will be covered in more detail later in this chapter.

Procedural Memory Procedural memory is the ability to recall how to do something, especially a physical task. This type of memory is apparently stored in a series

of stimulus–response pairings. For example, even if you have not ridden a bicycle for a long time, as soon as you get on one, the stimuli begin to evoke responses. When the bike leans to the left (a stimulus), you "instinctively" shift your weight to the right to maintain balance (a response). Other examples of procedural memory include handwriting, typing, and running skills. Neurological studies show that procedural memories are stored in a different part of the brain than are semantic and episodic memories; procedural memories are stored in the cerebellum, whereas semantic and episodic memories are stored in the cerebral cortex (Black, 2003; Byrnes & Fox, 1998; Eichenbaum, 2003).

Factors That Enhance Long-Term Memory

Contrary to popular belief, people retain a large portion of what they learn in school. Semb and Ellis (1994), in reviewing research on this topic, note that laboratory studies of retention of nonsense words and other artificial material greatly underestimate the degree to which information and skills learned in school can be retained (also see Ellis, Semb, & Cole, 1998). Long-term retention of information that is learned in school varies a great deal according to the type of information. For example, concepts are retained much longer than names (Conway, Cohen, & Stanhope, 1991). In general, retention drops rapidly in the first few weeks after instruction but then levels off (Bahrick & Hall, 1991). Whatever students have retained about 12 to 24 weeks after instruction, they may retain forever.

Several factors contribute to long-term retention. One, not surprisingly, is the degree to which students had learned the material in the first place (Bahrick & Hall, 1991). It is interesting to note that the effects of ability on retention are unclear (Semb & Ellis, 1994). Higher-ability students score better at the end of a course but often lose the same percentage of what they had learned as lower-ability students do.

Instructional strategies that actively involve students in lessons contribute to long-term retention. For example, MacKenzie and White (1982) contrasted students in eighth and ninth grades learning geography under three conditions: traditional classroom instruction, traditional instruction plus fieldwork, and traditional instruction plus fieldwork plus active processing of information involved in fieldwork. Twelve weeks later (after summer vacation), the active processing group had lost only 10 percent of the information, while the other two groups had lost more than 40 percent. Similarly, Specht and Sandling (1991) contrasted undergraduates who learned accounting from traditional lectures with others who learned it through role playing. After 6 weeks, the traditionally taught students lost 54 percent of their problem-solving performance, whereas the role-playing group lost only 13 percent.

Other Information-Processing Models

Atkinson and Shiffrin's (1968) model of information processing outlined in Figure 6.1 is not the only one accepted by cognitive psychologists. Several alternative models do not challenge the basic assumptions of the Atkinson–Shiffrin model but elaborate aspects of it, particularly aspects relating to the factors that increase the chances that information will be retained in long-term memory. These alternative theories are as follows.

Levels-of-Processing Theory   One widely accepted model of information processing is called **levels-of-processing theory** (Craik, 2000; Craik & Lockhart, 1972), which holds that people subject stimuli to different levels of mental processing and retain only the information that has been subjected to the most thorough processing. For example, you might perceive a tree but pay little attention to it. This is the lowest

levels-of-processing theory
Explanation of memory that links recall of a stimulus with the amount of mental processing it receives.

People use procedural memory to recall how to do physical tasks. This type of memory is stored in a different part of the brain from semantic and episodic memories. How can teachers encourage procedural memory in their students?

level of processing, and you are unlikely to remember the tree. Second, you might give the tree a name, such as *maple* or *oak*. Once named, the tree is somewhat more likely to be remembered. The highest level of processing, however, is giving meaning to the tree. For example, you might remember having climbed the tree or having commented on the tree's unusual shape, or you might have wondered whether the tree would fall on your house if it were struck by lightning. According to levels-of-processing theory, the more you attend to the details of a stimulus, the more mental processing you must do with a stimulus and the more likely you are to remember it. This was illustrated in a classic study by Bower and Karlin (1974), who had Stanford undergraduates look at yearbook pictures from Yale. Some of the students were told to classify the pictures as "male" or "female," and some were told to classify them as "very honest" or "less honest." The students who had to categorize the faces as very honest or less honest remembered them far better than did those who merely categorized them as male or female. Presumably, the honesty raters had to do a much higher level of mental processing with the pictures than did the gender raters, and for this reason they remembered the faces better. More recently, Kapur et al. (1994) had students read a series of nouns. One group was asked to identify which words contained the letter "a." Another group had to identify the nouns as "living" or "nonliving." As in the Bower and Karlin study and many others, the students who had to sort the words into "living" and "nonliving" recalled many more words. More interesting, however, was that brain imaging revealed that the "living/nonliving" students were activating a portion of their brains associated with enhanced memory performance, while the other students were not. This experiment adds important evidence to the idea that the brain treats "deep processing" and "shallow processing" differently (see Craik, 2000).

Dual Code Theory   A concept that is related to levels-of-processing theory is Paivio's **dual code theory of memory,** which hypothesizes that information is retained in long-term memory in two forms: visual and verbal (corresponding to episodic and semantic memory, respectively) (Clark & Paivio, 1991; Mayer & Moreno, 1998; Sadoski, Goetz, & Fritz, 1993). This theory predicts that information represented both visually and verbally is recalled better than information represented only one way. For example, you remember a face better if you also know a name, and you remember a name better if you can connect it to a face (Mayer, 2003).

Parallel Distributed Processing Model   The Atkinson–Shiffrin model of learning emphasized in this chapter is felt by many modern researchers to be a bit too simplistic in proposing a sequence of steps by which information is processed. Lewandowsky and Murdock (1989) have described a **parallel distributed processing model** based on the idea that information is processed simultaneously in the three parts of the memory system, each part operating on the same information at the same time. For example, when reading this paragraph, you are not looking at individual letters, forming them into words and meanings, and then working with them in short-term memory to file them in long-term memory. Instead, you are immediately using information in your long-term memory to interpret the words and meanings. Even at the first stages of

dual code theory of memory

Theory suggesting that information coded both visually and verbally is remembered better than information coded in only one of those two ways.

parallel distributed processing model

A model based on the idea that information is processed simultaneously in the sensory register, working memory, and long-term memory.

perception, what you see is heavily influenced by what you expect to see, which means that your long-term memory is operating at the same time as your sensory register and short-term memory.

Connectionist Models   A major alternative to the Atkinson–Shiffrin model has been taking shape in recent years. This model, called *connectionism* (Bates & Elman, 2002; Smolensky, 2000), is closely associated with parallel distributed processing theories. It emphasizes the idea that knowledge is stored in the brain in a network of connections, not in a system of rules or in storage of individual bits of information. In this view, experience leads to learning by strengthening certain connections, often at the expense of others. For example, a little boy may learn the concept "dog" by seeing many quite different-looking animals and hearing them referred to as dogs (Rumelhart & McClelland, 1986). Each time the child sees a new dog, connections are strengthened between the concept "dog" and attributes that are common to dogs, while false connections, caused by unique characteristics of particular dogs, are weakened. Let's say the boy's family has a poodle, and he therefore believes that dogs bark, wag their tails, and have curly hair. As he meets more dogs, the "bark" and "wag" connections are strengthened and the "curly hair" connection is weakened by experience. Other dog attributes are also strengthened, until the child can readily identify any dog, even if he has never seen that breed of dog before. Similarly, a young girl may confidently and correctly use the word *went*, because she hears it frequently and finds it very useful in her own speech. However, over time she experiences a different pattern: past tenses in English are usually formed by the addition of -*ed*. The connection "past tense = -*ed*" is strengthened by experience and may even become stronger than the existing "past tense of go = *went*" connection; as a result, the child may start using the word *goed*. But as the network of connections becomes more complex and the child sees that *goed* does not match other people's usage, she is able to maintain both connections, "past tense of go = *went*" and "past tense = -*ed*," and to apply them appropriately. Note that even though the child's behavior becomes rulelike, no explicit teaching or learning of rules is assumed. Instead, through direct experience the child strengthens connections that work and weakens ones that do not (Bereiter, 1991; Driscoll, 1994; Iran-Nejad, Marsh, & Clements, 1992; Schneider & Graham, 1992).

Connectionist models are consistent with current research on the brain, which has established that information is not held in any one location but is distributed in many locations and connected by intricate neural pathways (Solso, 2001). However, the implications of connectionism for teaching and learning are not clear. A straightforward application would be to place a greater emphasis on experience-based teaching and to deemphasize the teaching of rules (such as grammar or arithmetic rules); but researchers in this tradition (e.g., Bereiter, 1991; Schneider & Graham, 1992) are careful to note that the connectionist model does have a place for rule-based teaching.

Research on the Brain

In the past, research on learning, memory, and other cognitive functions took place using methods one step away from the brain itself. Scientists used ingenious experiments to learn about brain function from subjects' responses to particular stimuli or tests, examined individuals with unusual brain damage, or made inferences from experiments on animals. However, in recent years neuroscientists have developed a capacity to actually watch healthy brains in operation, using brain imaging methods such as functional magnetic resonance imaging (fMRI) (Eichenbaum, 2003; Goswami, 2004; Shaywitz, 2003). Scientists can now observe what parts of the brain are activated when an individual hears a symphony, reads a book, speaks a second language,

CONNECTIONS

For more on language acquisition during the preschool years, see Chapter 3, page 68.

connectionist models
Theories proposing that knowledge is stored in the brain in a network of connections, not in systems of rules or in individual bits of information.

INTASC

2 **Knowledge of Human Development and Learning**

or solves a math problem. This capability has led to an explosion of research on the brain (see, for example, Bransford, Brown, & Cocking, 1999; Bruer, 1999; Goswami, 2004; Solso, 2001; Sprenger, 1999).

It has long been known that specific mental functions are carried out in specific locations in the brain. For example, vision is localized in the visual cortex, hearing in the auditory cortex (see Figure 6.4). However, new research is finding that the brain is even more specialized than was thought previously. When you think about a face, you activate a different part of the brain than when you think about a chair, a song, or a feeling. If you are bilingual in, say, Spanish and English, slightly different areas of your brain are activated when you speak each language. The two hemispheres of the brain have somewhat different functions; the left hemisphere is more involved in language, while the right is more involved in spatial and nonverbal information. However, despite the specialization within the brain, almost all tasks we perform involve both hemispheres and many parts of the brain working together (Black, 2003; Saffran & Schwartz, 2003).

Many findings from brain research might have importance for education and child development. One has to do with early development, where studies find that the amount of stimulation early in a child's development relates to the number of neural connections, or synapses, which are the basis for higher learning and memory (Black, 2003; Bruer, 1999). The finding that the brain's capacity is not set at birth, but is influenced by early experience, has had an electrifying impact on the world of early childhood research and education policy (National Research Council, 2003). Further, some research is suggesting that extensive training can change brain structures, even into adulthood. For example, a study of London cabdrivers found that their training caused increased activity in a part of the brain that processes directions (Maguire et

FIGURE 6.4
Brain Physiology and Functions

Each part of the brain specializes in a particular category of functions.

Adapted from Wood, Wood, & Boyd, *The World of Psychology* (5th ed.), p. 53. Published by Allyn & Bacon, Boston, MA. Copyright © 2005 by Pearson Education. Reprinted by permission of the publisher.

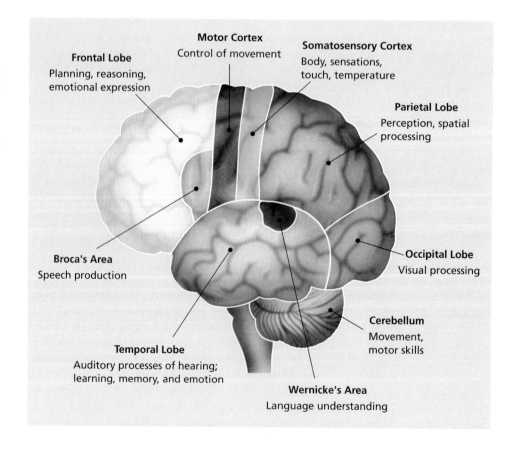

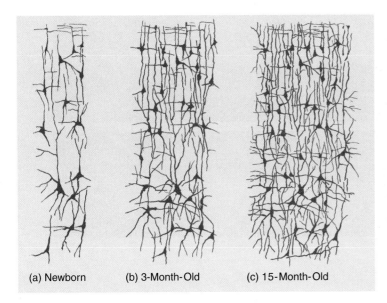

(a) Newborn   (b) 3-Month-Old   (c) 15-Month-Old

FIGURE 6.5
Development of Neural Connections, from Birth through 15 Months of Age
Neural connections in children's brains develop rapidly from birth through infancy.

From Richard Fabes and Carol Lynn Martin, *Exploring Child Development: Transactions and Transformations*, p. 119. Published by Allyn & Bacon, Boston, MA. Copyright © 2000 by Pearson Education. Reprinted by permission of the publisher.

al., 2000), and that children who receive intensive tutoring in reading develop brain structures like those of proficient readers (Shaywitz, 2003; Shaywitz & Shaywitz, 2004; Turkeltaub et al., 2003).

Another important finding is initially counterintuitive. Up to the age of 18 months, infants generate enormous numbers of neurons and connections between neurons (see Figure 6.5). After that point, they begin to lose them. What is happening is that the brain sloughs off connections that are not being used, so that the remaining connections are efficient and well organized. This process is strongly affected by the environment in which the child lives, and continues through early childhood. The plasticity of the brain, or its susceptibility to change by the environment, is highest at the earliest ages and diminishes over time (Kolb & Whishaw, 1998).

A third important finding of brain research is the discovery that as a person gains in knowledge and skill, his or her brain becomes more efficient. For example, Solso (2001) compared the brain activation of an expert artist to that of novices. On a task familiar to the artist—drawing faces—only a small portion of his brain was active, while novices had activity in many parts of their brains (see Figure 6.6). In another series of studies, Eden et al. (1996) compared the brain activation of children with dyslexia with that of normal readers while they were reading. The children with dyslexia activated auditory as well as visual areas of their brains, as though they had to laboriously translate the letters into sounds and then the sounds into meaning. The proficient readers skipped the auditory step entirely. The same difference has been documented between children just learning to read and the same children after they become good readers (Turkeltaub et al., 2003). Research long ago noted the importance of automaticity, or seemingly effortless performance made possible by extensive experience and practice, in the development of expertise. The brain studies show how automaticity can actually allow the brain to skip steps in solving problems.

Recent studies (Shawitz, 2003) have found that proficient readers primarily activate three regions of the left brain. In contrast, dyslexics overactivate a region in the front of the brain called Broca's area, which controls speaking. In other words, poor readers seem to use an inefficient pathway (print to speech to understanding) while good readers use a more efficient pathway (print to understanding.) More broadly, individuals with learning disabilities have been found to use less efficient brain processes than other learners (Blair, 2004).

CERTIFICATION POINTER
Teacher certification tests will require you to know that as individuals learn more, their brains become more efficient. This leads to automaticity, the effortless performance that comes with the development of expertise.

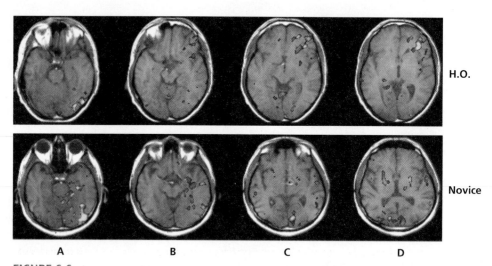

FIGURE 6.6
Brain Activity of an Artist and a Non-Artist While Drawing

fMRI scans made on an accomplished artist, H.O., and a non-artist control subject showing right parietal activity for both people (see column A). This area is involved in facial perception, but it appears that the non-artist is demanding more energy to process faces than H.O. In columns C and D, there is an increase in blood flow in the right frontal area of the artist, suggesting a higher-order abstraction of information.

From Robert L. Solso, *Cognitive Psychology* (6th ed.). Published by Allyn & Bacon, Boston, MA. Copyright © 2001 by Pearson Education. Reprinted by permission of the publisher.

These and many other findings of brain research reinforce the conclusion that the brain is not a filing cabinet for facts and skills but is engaged in a process of organizing information to make it efficiently accessible and usable. The process of discarding connections and selectively ignoring or excluding information, as well as the process of making orderly connections among information, is as important, or perhaps more important, than adding information. The progress of brain research has quite naturally led to a call for applications to the practice of education. For example, Caine & Caine (1997) and Howard (2000) suggest that brain research justifies a shift away from linear, hierarchical teaching toward complex, thematic, and integrated activities. Langer (1997) cites brain research to attack a teaching focus on memorization, suggesting more of an emphasis on flexible thinking. Gardner (2000) claims that brain research supports the importance of early stimulation, of activity in learning, and of music and emotions. All of these and other prescriptions may turn out to be valid, but at present the evidence for them, when it exists at all, comes from traditional educational psychology, not from brain research itself. Further, the prescriptions from brain research are remarkably similar to the principles of progressive education described a century ago by John Dewey, without the benefit of modern brain research (see Ellis, 2001d). It may be that brain research will someday vindicate Dewey or lead to clear prescriptions for practice, but the rush to make grand claims for educational methods based on brain research has already led to a substantial body of cautionary literature (e.g., Bruer, 1999; Coles, 2004; Ellis, 2001d; Jensen, 2000; Stanovich, 1998).

"And this is the part of the brain that's responsible for sleep."

WHAT CAUSES PEOPLE TO REMEMBER OR FORGET?

Why do we remember some things and forget others? Why can we sometimes remember trivial things that happened years ago but not important things that happened yesterday? Most forgetting occurs because information in working memory was never transferred to long-term memory. However, it can also occur because we have lost our access to information that is in long-term memory.

Forgetting and Remembering

Over the years, researchers have identified several factors that make it easier or harder to remember information (see Schacter, 2001).

Interference   One important reason people forget is **interference** (Anderson, 1995; Dempster & Corkill, 1999). Interference happens when information gets mixed up with, or pushed aside by, other information. One form of interference occurs when people are prevented from mentally rehearsing newly learned information. In one classic experiment, Peterson and Peterson (1959) gave subjects a simple task: the memorization of sets of three nonsense letters (such as FQB). The subjects were then immediately asked to count backward by 3s from a three-digit number (e.g., 287, 284, 281, etc.) for up to 18 seconds. At the end of that time the subjects were asked to recall the letters. They had forgotten far more of them than had subjects who had learned the letters and then simply waited for 18 seconds to repeat them. The reason for this is that the subjects who were told to count backward were deprived of the opportunity to rehearse the letters mentally to establish them in their working memories. As was noted earlier in this chapter, teachers must take into account the limited capacity of working memory by allowing students time to absorb or practice (that is, mentally rehearse) new information before giving them additional instruction.

interference
Inhibition of recall of certain information by the presence of other information in memory.

According to research on memory and forgetting, what factors determine how well this student remembers the information she learns in class?

Retroactive Inhibition   Another form of interference is called **retroactive inhibition.** This occurs when previously learned information is lost because it is mixed up with new and somewhat similar information. For example, young students may have no trouble recognizing the letter *b* until they are taught the letter *d*. Because these letters are similar, students often confuse them. Learning the letter *d* thus interferes with the previously learned recognition of *b*. In the same way, a traveler might know how to get around in a particular airport but then lose that skill to some extent after visiting many similar airports.

Of all the reasons for forgetting, retroactive inhibition is probably the most important. This phenomenon explains, for example, why we have trouble remembering frequently repeated episodes, such as what we had for dinner a week ago. Last night's dinner will be forgotten because memories of dinners that come after it will interfere, unless something remarkable happens to clearly distinguish last night's dinner from the dinners that will follow.

Theory into **PRACTICE**

Reducing Retroactive Inhibition

There are two ways to help reduce retroactive inhibition for students. The first is by not teaching similar and confusing concepts too closely in time. The second is to use different methods to teach similar concepts. The first way to reduce retroactive inhibition implies that one of several confusing or similar concepts should be taught thoroughly before the next is introduced. For example, students should be completely able to recognize the letter *b* before the letter *d* is introduced. If these letters are introduced at close to the same time, learning of one may inhibit learning of the other. When the new letter is introduced, the teacher must carefully point out the differences between *b* and *d,* and students must practice discriminating between the two until they can unerringly say which is which. As another example, consider the following lists of Spanish and English word pairs:

A	B
llevar—to carry	*perro*—dog
llorar—to cry	*gato*—cat
llamar—to call	*caballo*—horse

List B is much easier to learn. The similarities among the Spanish words in list A (they all are verbs, start with *ll,* end with *ar,* and have the same number of letters and syllables) make them very difficult to tell apart. The English words in list A are also somewhat difficult to discriminate among, because all are verbs that start with a *c*. In contrast, the words in list B are easy to discriminate from one another. Because of the problem of retroactive inhibition, presenting all the word pairs in list A in the same lesson would be a poor instructional strategy. Students would be likely to confuse the three Spanish words because of their similar spellings. Rather, students should be completely familiar with one word pair before the next is introduced.

Another way to reduce retroactive inhibition is to use different methods to teach similar concepts or to vary other aspects of instruction for each concept. For example, in social studies a teacher might teach about Spain by using lectures and discussion, about France by using group projects, and about Italy by using films. This would help students avoid confusing information about one country with information about the others.

retroactive inhibition
Decreased ability to recall previously learned information, caused by learning of new information.

Most things that are forgotten were never firmly learned in the first place. The best way to ensure long-term retention of material taught in school is to make certain that students have mastered the essential features of the material. This means assessing students' understanding frequently and reteaching if it turns out that students have not achieved adequate levels of understanding.

Proactive Inhibition   **Proactive inhibition** occurs when learning one set of information interferes with learning later information. A classic case is that of a North American learning to drive on the left side of the road in England. It may be easier for a North American nondriver to learn to drive in England than for an experienced North American driver, because the latter has so thoroughly learned to stay to the right—a potentially fatal error in England.

Individual Differences in Resistance to Interference   In a 1999 article, Dempster and Corkill raise the possibility that the ability to focus on key information and screen out interference is at the heart of cognitive performance. Reviewing research from many fields, including brain research, they note strong relationships between measures of resistance to interference and school performance. For example, among children with similar IQs, those with learning disabilities perform much worse on measures of resistance to interference (see Forness & Kavale, 2000). Children with attention deficit hyperactivity disorders (ADHD) are very poor at screening out irrelevant stimuli. If you think about the stereotype of the "absent minded professor," the ability to focus one's attention on a given problem, to the exclusion of all else, may be a hallmark of extraordinary intellect.

Facilitation   It should also be noted that learning one thing can often help a person learn similar information. For example, learning Spanish first may help an English-speaking student later learn Italian, a similar language. This would be a case of **proactive facilitation.** Learning a second language can also help with an already established language. It is often the case, for example, that English-speaking students find that the study of Latin helps them understand their native language better. This would be **retroactive facilitation.**

   For another example, consider teaching. We often have the experience that learning to teach a subject helps us understand the subject better. Because later learning (e.g., learning to teach addition of fractions) increases our understanding of previously learned information (addition of fractions), this is a prime example of retroactive facilitation. Table 6.3 summarizes the relationships among retroactive and proactive inhibition and facilitation.

Primacy and Recency Effects   One of the oldest findings in educational psychology is that when people are given a list of words to learn and then tested immediately afterward, they tend to learn the first few and last few items much better than those in the middle of the list. The tendency to learn the first things presented is called the **primacy effect;** the tendency to learn the last things is called the **recency effect.** The most common explanation for the primacy effect is that we pay more attention and devote more mental effort to items presented first. As was noted earlier in this chapter, mental rehearsal is important in establishing new information in long-term memory. Usually, much more mental rehearsal is devoted to the first items presented than to later items (Anderson, 1995). Recency effects, in contrast, are due in large part to the fact that little or no other information intervenes between the final items and the test.

proactive inhibition
Decreased ability to learn new information, caused by interference from existing knowledge.

proactive facilitation
Increased ability to learn new information due to the presence of previously acquired information.

retroactive facilitation
Increased comprehension of previously learned information due to the acquisition of new information.

primacy effect
The tendency for items at the beginning of a list to be recalled more easily than other items.

recency effect
The tendency for items at the end of a list to be recalled more easily than other items.

Table 6.3		
Retroactive and Proactive Inhibition and Facilitation		
Summary of the effects on memory of retroactive and proactive inhibition and facilitation.		
Effect on Learning	*Effect on Memory*	
	Inhibition (Negative)	Facilitation (Positive)
Later learning affects earlier learning	Retroactive inhibition (*Example:* Learning *d* interferes with learning *b*.)	Retroactive facilitation (*Example:* Learning to teach math helps with previously learned math skills.)
Earlier learning affects later learning	Proactive inhibition (*Example:* Learning to drive in the U.S. interferes with learning to drive in the U.K.)	Proactive facilitation (*Example:* Learning Spanish helps with later learning of Italian.)

Teachers should consider primacy and recency effects, which imply that information taught at the beginning or the end of the period is more likely to be retained than other information. To take advantage of this, teachers might organize their lessons to put the most essential new concepts early in the lesson and then to summarize at the end. Many teachers take roll, collect lunch money, check homework, and do other noninstructional activities at the beginning of the period. However, it is probably a better idea to postpone these activities, to start the period right away with important concepts and only toward the end of the period deal with necessary administrative tasks.

Automaticity   Information or skills may exist in long-term memory, but may take so much time or so much mental effort to retrieve that they are of limited value when speed of access is essential. The classic case of this is reading. A child may be able to sound out every word on a page, but if he or she does so very slowly and laboriously, the child will lose comprehension and will be unlikely to read for pleasure (National Reading Panel, 2000). For reading and for other skills in which speed and limited mental effort are necessary, existence in long-term memory is not enough. **Automaticity** is required; that is, a level of rapidity and ease such that a task or skill involves little or no mental effort. For a proficient reader reading simple material, decoding requires almost no mental effort. Neurological studies show that the brain becomes more efficient as a person becomes a skilled reader (Eden et al., 1996). A beginning reader with serious learning disabilities uses both auditory and visual parts of the brain during reading, trying laboriously to sound out new words. In contrast, a skilled reader uses only a small, well-defined portion of the brain relating to visual processing.

Automaticity is primarily gained through practice far beyond the amount needed to establish information or skills in long-term memory. A soccer player knows after 10 minutes of instruction how to kick a ball, but the player practices this skill thousands of times until it becomes automatic. A chess player quickly learns the rules of chess but spends a lifetime learning to quickly recognize patterns that suggest winning moves. Bloom (1986), who studied the role of automaticity in the performances of gifted pianists, mathematicians, athletes, and others, called automaticity "the hands and feet of genius."

automaticity
A level of rapidity and ease such that tasks can be performed or skills utilized with little mental effort.

massed practice
Technique in which facts or skills to be learned are repeated often over a concentrated period of time.

distributed practice
Technique in which items to be learned are repeated at intervals over a period of time.

enactment
A learning process in which individuals physically carry out tasks.

By practicing scales far beyond the amount needed to establish the skills in their long-term memories, these young musicians can gain automaticity. How will this benefit them?

Practice

The most common method for committing information to memory is also the most mundane: practice. Does practice make perfect?

Practice is important at several stages of learning. As was noted earlier in this chapter, information received in working memory must be mentally rehearsed if it is to be retained for more than a few seconds. The information in working memory must usually be practiced until it is established in long-term memory (Willingham, 2004).

Massed and Distributed Practice   Is it better to practice newly learned information intensively until it is thoroughly learned, a technique called **massed practice?** Or is it more effective to practice a little each day over a period of time—**distributed practice?** Massed practice allows for faster initial learning, but for most kinds of learn-

ing, distributed practice is better for retention, even over short time periods. This is especially true of factual learning (Dempster, 1989; Willingham, 2002); cramming factual information the night before a test could get you through that test, but the information probably won't be well integrated into your long-term memory. Long-term retention of all kinds of information and skills is greatly enhanced by distributed practice. This is the primary purpose of homework: to provide practice on newly learned skills over an extended period of time to increase the chances that the skills will be retained.

Enactment   Everyone knows that we learn by doing. It turns out that research on **enactment** supports this commonsense conclusion. That is, in learning how to perform tasks of many kinds, individuals learn much better if they are asked to enact the tasks (to physically carry them out) than if they simply read the instructions or watch a teacher enact the task (Cohen, 1989). For example, students learn much more from a lesson on drawing geometric solids (such as cubes and spheres) if they have an opportunity to draw some rather than just watching the teacher do so.

HOW CAN MEMORY STRATEGIES BE TAUGHT?

INTASC

4 Multiple Instructional Strategies

Many of the things that students learn in school are facts that must be remembered. These form the framework on which more complex concepts depend. Factual material must be learned as efficiently and effectively as possible to leave time and mental energy for meaningful learning, such as problem-solving, conceptual, and creative activities. If students can memorize the routine things more efficiently, they can free their minds for tasks that involve understanding and reasoning. Some learning involves memorization of facts or of arbitrary associations between terms. For example, *pomme,* the French word for *apple,* is an arbitrary term associated with an object. The capital of Iowa could just as well have been called *Iowapolis* as *Des Moines.* Students often learn things as facts before they understand them as concepts or skills. For instance, students may learn the formula for the volume of a cylinder as an arbitrary fact long before they understand why the formula is what it is.

> **ON THE WEB**
>
> For techniques and resources for improving memory go to **www.mindtools.com.**

Verbal Learning

In many studies psychologists have examined **verbal learning,** or how students learn verbal materials, in laboratory settings (Raaijmakers & Shiffrin, 1992). For example, students might be asked to learn lists of words or nonsense syllables. Three types of verbal learning tasks that are typically seen in the classroom have been identified and studied extensively: the paired-associate learning task, the serial learning task, and the free-recall learning task.

1. **Paired-associate learning** involves learning to respond with one member of a pair when given the other member of the pair. Usually there is a list of pairs to be memorized. In typical experiments, the pairs are arbitrary. Educational examples of paired-associate tasks include learning the states' capitals, the names and dates of Civil War battles, the addition and multiplication tables, the atomic weights of the elements, and the spelling of words.
2. **Serial learning** involves learning a list of terms in a particular order. Memorization of the notes on the musical staff, the Pledge of Allegiance, the elements in atomic weight order, and poetry and songs are serial learning tasks. Serial learning tasks occur less often in classroom instruction than paired-associate tasks do.
3. **Free-recall learning** tasks also involve memorizing a list, but not in a special order. Recalling the names of the 50 states, types of reinforcements, kinds of poetic feet, and the organ systems in the body are examples of free-recall tasks.

The following sections describe these three verbal learning tasks in more detail.

Paired-Associate Learning

In paired-associate learning, the student must associate a response with each stimulus. For example, the student is given a picture of a bone (the stimulus) and must respond

verbal learning
Learning of words (or facts expressed in words).

paired-associate learning
Learning of items in linked pairs so that when one member of a pair is presented, the other can be recalled.

serial learning
Memorization of a series of items in a particular order.

free-recall learning
Learning of a list of items in any order.

FIGURE 6.7
Example of the Use of Images to Aid Recall
An English-speaking student learning French can easily remember that the French word for fencing is *l'escrime* by linking it to the English word *scream* and picturing a fencer screaming.

tibia, or is given the symbol *Au* and must respond *gold.* One important aspect of the learning of paired associates is the degree of familiarity the student already has with the stimuli and the responses. For example, it would be far easier to learn to associate foreign words with English words, such as *dog—chien* (French) or *dog—perro* (Spanish) than to learn to associate two foreign words, such as *chien—perro.*

Imagery Many powerful memory techniques are based on forming mental images to help remember associations. For example, the French word for fencing is *l'escrime,* pronounced "le scream." It is easy to remember this association (*fencing—l'escrime*) by forming a mental picture of a fencer screaming while being skewered by an opponent, as illustrated in Figure 6.7.

One ancient method of enhancing memory by use of **imagery** is the creation of stories to weave together information (Egan, 1989). For example, images from Greek myths and other sources have long been used to help people recall the constellations.

Theory into **PRACTICE**

Keyword Mnemonics

One of the most extensively studied methods of using imagery and **mnemonics** (memory devices) to help paired-associate learning is the **keyword method,** which was originally developed for teaching foreign language vocabulary but was later applied to many other areas (Carney et al., 2004). The example used earlier of employing vivid imagery to recall the French word *l'escrime* is an illustration of the keyword method. In that case, the keyword was *scream.* It is called a keyword because it evokes the connection between the word *l'escrime* and the mental picture. The Russian word for building, *zdanie,* pronounced "zdan'-yeh," might be recalled by using the keyword *dawn* and imagining the sun coming up behind a building with an onion dome on top.

imagery
Mental visualization of images to improve memory.

mnemonics
Devices or strategies for aiding the memory.

keyword method
A strategy for improving memory by using images to link pairs of items.

Atkinson and Raugh (1975) used this method to teach students a list of 120 Russian words over a three-day period. Other students were given English translations of the Russian words and allowed to study as they wished. At the end of the experiment, the students who used the keyword method recalled 72 percent of the words, while the other students recalled only 46 percent. This result has been repeated dozens of times, using a wide variety of languages (Pressley, Levin, & Delaney, 1982), with students from preschoolers to adults. However, young children seem to require pictures of the mental images they are meant to form, while older children (starting in upper elementary school) learn equally well making their own mental images (Willoughby, Porter, Belsito, & Yearsley, 1999). Furthermore, having students work in pairs or cooperative groups has been found to enhance vocabulary learning using mnemonic strategies (Jones, Levin, Levin, & Beitzel, 2000).

The images that are used in the keyword method work best if they are vivid and active, preferably involving interaction. For example, the German word for *room, zimmer* (pronounced "tsimmer"), might be associated with the keyword *simmer.* The German word would probably be better recalled by using an image of a distressed person in a bed immersed in a huge, steaming cauldron of water in a large bedroom than by using an image of a small pot of water simmering in the corner of a bedroom. The drama, action, and bizarreness of the first image make it memorable; the second is too commonplace to be easily recalled.

Similarly, Rummel, Levin, and Woodward (2003) showed students pictures to help them recall a link between various theorists of intelligence and their contributions. For example, to link Binet and measurement of higher mental processes, Rummel and colleagues showed students a race car driver protecting his *brain* with a *bonnet.* A review of many studies involving various mnemonic strategies found substantial positive effects, on average (Hattie, Bibbs, & Purdie, 1996). However, it should be noted that most of the research done on the use of mnemonic strategies has taken place under rather artificial, laboratory-like conditions, using materials that are thought to be especially appropriate for these strategies. Evaluations of actual classroom applications of these strategies show more mixed results, and there are questions about the long-term retention of material learned by means of keywords (Carney & Levin, 1998; Wang & Thomas, 1995).

Serial and Free-Recall Learning

Serial learning is learning facts in a particular order. Learning the events on a timeline, learning the order of operations in long division, and learning the relative hardnesses of minerals are examples of serial learning. Free-recall learning is learning a list of items that need not be remembered in order, such as the names of the Canadian provinces.

Loci Method   A mnemonic device for serial learning that was used by the ancient Greeks employs imagery associated with a list of locations (see Anderson, 1990). In the **loci method** the student thinks of a very familiar set of locations, such as rooms in her or his own house, and then imagines each item on the list to be remembered in one specific location. Vivid or bizarre imagery is used to place the item in the location. Once the connections between the item and the room or other location are established, the learner can recall each place and its contents in order. The same locations can be mentally cleared and used to memorize a different list. However, they should always be used in the same order to ensure that all items on the list were remembered.

loci method
A strategy for remembering lists by picturing items in familiar locations.

Pegword Method   Another imagery method useful for serial learning is called the **pegword method** (Krinsky & Krinsky, 1996). To use this mnemonic, the student might memorize a list of pegwords that rhyme with the numbers 1 to 10. To use this method, the student creates mental images relating to items on the list to be learned with particular pegwords. For example, in learning the order of the first 10 U.S. presidents, you might picture George Washington eating a bun (1) with his wooden teeth, John Adams tying his shoe (2), Thomas Jefferson hanging by his knees from a branch of a tree (3), and so on.

Initial-Letter Strategies   One memory strategy that involves a reorganization of information is taking initial letters of a list to be memorized and making a more easily remembered word or phrase. For example, many trigonometry classes have learned about the imaginary SOH CAH TOA tribe, whose letters help us recall that sine = opposite/hypotenuse; cosine = adjacent/hypotenuse; tangent = opposite/adjacent. Many such **initial-letter strategies** exist for remembering the relative distances of the planets from the sun. The planets, in order, are Mercury, Venus, Earth, Mars, Jupiter, Saturn, Uranus, Neptune, and Pluto. Students are taught a sentence in which the first letters of the words are the first letters of the planets in order, such as "My very educated monkey just served us nine pizzas."

In a similar fashion, acronyms help people remember the names of organizations. Initial-letter strategies may also help students remember procedural knowledge, such as steps in a process.

ᗯHAT MAKES INFORMATION MEANINGFUL?

Consider the following sentences:

1. Enso flrs hmen matn snoi teha erso iakt siae otin tnes esna nrae.
2. Easier that nonsense information to makes than sense is learn.
3. Information that makes sense is easier to learn than nonsense.

Which sentence is easiest to learn and remember? Obviously, sentence 3. All three sentences have the same letters, and sentences 2 and 3 have the same words. Yet to learn sentence 1, you would have to memorize 52 separate letters, and to learn sentence 2, you would have to learn 10 separate words. Sentence 3 is easiest because to learn it you need only learn one concept, a concept that readily fits your common sense and prior knowledge about how learning takes place. You know the individual words, you know the grammar that connects them, and you already have in your mind a vast store of information, experiences, and thoughts about the same topic. For these reasons, sentence 3 slides smoothly into your understanding.

The message in sentence 3 is what this chapter is all about. Most human learning, particularly school learning, involves making sense out of information, sorting it in our minds until it fits in a neat and orderly way, and using old information to help assimilate new learning. We have limited ability to recall rote information—how many telephone numbers can you remember for a month? However, we can retain meaningful information far more easily. Recall that most of the mnemonic strategies discussed in the previous section involve adding artificial meaning to arbitrary associations in order to take advantage of the much greater ease of learning meaningful information.

The message in sentence 3 has profound implications for instruction. One of the teacher's most important tasks is to make information meaningful to students by presenting it in a clear, organized way; by relating it to information already in students'

pegword method
A strategy for memorization in which images are used to link lists of facts to a familiar set of words or numbers.

initial-letter strategies
Strategies for learning in which initial letters of items to be memorized are made into a more easily remembered word or phrase.

minds; and by making sure that students have truly understood the concepts being taught and can apply them to new situations.

Rote versus Meaningful Learning

Ausubel (1963) discussed the distinction between rote learning and meaningful learning. **Rote learning** refers to the memorization of facts or associations, such as the multiplication tables, the chemical symbols for the elements, words in foreign languages, or the names of bones and muscles in the human body. Much of rote learning involves associations that are essentially arbitrary. For example, the chemical symbol for gold (*Au*) could just as well have been *Go* or *Gd*. In contrast, **meaningful learning** is not arbitrary, and it relates to information or concepts learners already have. For example, if we learn that silver is an excellent conductor of electricity, this information relates to our existing information about silver and about electrical conductivity. Further, the association between "silver" and "electrical conductivity" is not arbitrary. Silver really is an excellent conductor, and while we could state the same principle in many ways or in any language, the meaning of the statement "Silver is an excellent conductor of electricity" could not be arbitrarily changed.

Uses of Rote Learning   We sometimes get the impression that rote learning is "bad" and meaningful learning is "good." This is not necessarily true. For example, when the doctor tells us we have a fractured *tibia*, we hope that the doctor has mastered the rote association between the word tibia and the leg bone it names. The mastery of foreign language vocabulary is an important case of rote learning. However, rote learning has gotten a bad name in education because it is overused. We can all remember being taught to parrot facts that were supposed to be meaningful but that we were forced to learn as rote, meaningless information. William James, in a book called *Talks to Teachers on Psychology* (1912), gave an excellent example of this kind of false learning:

> A friend of mine, visiting a school, was asked to examine a young class in geography. Glancing at the book, she said: "Suppose you should dig a hole in the ground, hundreds of feet deep, how should you find it at the bottom—warmer or colder than on top?" None of the class replying, the teacher said: "I'm sure they know, but I think you don't ask the question quite rightly. Let me try." So, taking the book, she asked: "In what condition is the interior of the globe?" and received the immediate answer from half the class at once. "The interior of the globe is in a condition of igneous fusion." (p. 150)

Clearly, the students had memorized the information without learning its meaning. The information was useless to them because it did not tie in with other information they had.

Inert Knowledge   The "igneous fusion" information that students had memorized in the class James' friend visited is an example of what Bransford, Burns, Delclos, and Vye (1986) call **inert knowledge.** This is knowledge that could and should be applicable to a wide range of situations but is applied only to a restricted set of circumstances. Usually, inert knowledge consists of information or skills learned in school that we cannot apply in life. For example, you may know people who could pass an advanced French test but would be unable to communicate in Paris, or who can solve volume problems in math class but have no idea how much sand to order to fill a sandbox. Many problems in life arise not from a lack of knowledge but from an inability to use the knowledge we already have.

An interesting experiment by Perfetto, Bransford, and Franks (1983) illustrates the concept of inert knowledge. In the experiment, college students were given problems such as the following: "Uriah Fuller, the famous Israeli superpsychic, can tell you the score of any baseball game before the game starts. What is his secret?"

INTASC

4 Multiple Instructional Strategies

rote learning
Memorization of facts or associations that might be essentially arbitrary.

meaningful learning
Mental processing of new information that relates to previously learned knowledge.

inert knowledge
Learned information that could be applied to a wide range of situations but whose use is limited to restricted, often artificial applications.

Before seeing the problems, some of the students were given a list of sentences to memorize that were clearly useful in solving the problems; among the sentences was "Before it starts, the score of any game is 0 to 0." Students who were told to use the sentences in their memories as clues performed much better on the problem-solving task than did other students, but students who memorized the clues but were not told to use them did no better than students who never saw the clues. What this experiment tells us is that having information in your memory does not guarantee that you can bring it out and use it when appropriate. Rather, you need to know how and when to use the information you have.

Teachers can help students learn information in a way that will make it useful as well as meaningful to them. Effective teaching requires an understanding of how to make information accessible to students so that they can connect it to other information, think about it, and apply it outside of the classroom (Willingham, 2003).

Schema Theory

As was noted earlier, meaningful information is stored in long-term memory in networks of connected facts or concepts called schemata. Recall the representation of the concept "bison" presented in Figure 6.3, showing how this one concept was linked to a wide range of other concepts. The most important principle of **schema theory** is that information that fits into an existing schema is more easily understood, learned, and retained than information that does not fit into an existing schema (Anderson & Bower, 1983). The sentence "Bison calves can run soon after they are born" is an example of information that will be easily incorporated into your "bison" schema, because you know that (1) bison rely on speed to escape from predators and (2) more familiar animals (such as horses) that also rely on speed have babies that can run very early. Without all this prior knowledge, "Bison calves can run soon after they are born" would be more difficult to assimilate mentally and more easily forgotten.

Hierarchies of Knowledge   It is thought that most well-developed schemata are organized in hierarchies similar to outlines, with specific information grouped under general categories, which are grouped under still more general categories. Recall Figure 6.3, on p. 174. Note that in moving from the top to the bottom of the figure, you are going from general (animals and Native Americans) to specific (how Native Americans hunted bison). The concepts in the figure are well anchored in the schema. Any new information relating to this schema will probably be learned and incorporated into the schema much more readily than would information relating to less established schemata or rote learning that does not attach to any schema.

One important insight of schema theory is that meaningful learning requires the active involvement of the learner, who has a host of prior experiences and knowledge to bring to understanding and incorporating new information (Alexander, 1992). What you learn from any experience depends in large part on the schema you apply to the experience.

The Importance of Background Knowledge   One of the most important determinants of how much you can learn about something is how much you already know about it (Alexander, Kulikowich, & Jetton, 1994, 1995; Schneider, 1993). A study in Japan by Kuhara-Kojima and Hatano (1991) illustrates this clearly. College students were taught information about baseball and music. Those who knew a great deal about baseball but not about music learned much more about baseball; the converse was true of those who knew a lot about music and little about baseball. In fact, background knowledge was much more important than general learning ability in predicting how much the students would learn. Learners who know a great deal about a subject have more well-developed schemata for incorporating new knowledge. Not

schema theory
Theory stating that information is stored in long-term memory in schemata (networks of connected facts and concepts), which provide a structure for making sense of new information.

Teaching Dilemmas: Cases to Consider

Differing Approaches

Helen Baker and George Kowalski, both eleventh-grade U.S. history teachers, are talking in George's classroom after school. Helen has taught for seven years and George for twenty-one years at Garfield High School, home of the current state high school basketball champions. Both teachers are members of the Social Studies Department's curriculum committee, which is in the process of revising the U.S. history course.

Helen: I wanted to talk to you about our disagreement about the curriculum revision. I thought that if you and I could work out our differences, maybe the committee would get out of the stalemate we're in.

George: Well, Helen, as I see it, you contend that students first need to master the facts of U.S. history before they can move on to higher-order thinking, like problem solving and working with abstract concepts. My view is just the reverse. For generations we've taught students facts, and they forget them right after the test is over. That's because we don't ask them to use the facts in higher-order thought. To me, that's the only way you can learn to think abstractly and solve problems.

Helen: But, George, trying to think abstractly and solve problems must be based on knowledge. Otherwise, problem solving is a pointless exercise—it amounts to a sharing of ignorance among the uninformed.

George: But I don't think that's as pointless as the other extreme—sticking to lecture and discussion and objective tests on key names, dates, terms, and events!

Helen: I know you use a lot of small-group and independent study work and give essay-type tests. I heard some students talking about how your questions really blew their minds. I think one was "What would the United States be like today if the South had won the Civil War?"

George (chuckling): Yes, that stirred them up a bit!

Helen: But, George, believe it or not, I've asked my students to write on that question from time to time when we're on the Civil War, and their answers were terrible—totally devoid of facts. The kids just wrote their opinions.

George: That's my point, Helen! Students have to learn how to use facts—and practice organizing and incorporating them into answers. Basketball players look terrible the first time they try a slam-dunk. But after they learn the technique, it's easy!

Helen: I think where we really disagree is on strategy. I maintain that learning the facts is the first step and higher-order thinking follows. You begin by posing problems and questions and hope that the kids will learn the facts to answer the questions. That seems like throwing kids into a lake and asking them to swim.

George: Sure, the facts and fundamentals are important, but in my experience, kids just forget them. But if you compel kids to determine and then use the facts, they'll remember them long after the test. I'll bet some of the things they learn in my course are still with them when they're adults.

Helen: Well, George, I just can't see how we are going to reconcile our two positions. Can you?

@ Questions for Reflection

1. How do Helen's and George's positions differ on the nature of information processing, memory, and forgetting? What are the merits and drawbacks of each approach?

2. What does the latest brain-based research tell us that might help settle the argument between Helen and George?

3. Extend the dialogue with a third character who brings a problem-solving approach to the impasse.

---

surprisingly, interest in a given subject contributes to background knowledge in it, as well as depth of understanding and willingness to use background knowledge to solve new problems (Tobias, 1994). However, learners often do not spontaneously use their prior knowledge to help them learn new material. Teachers must link new learning to students' existing background knowledge (Fennema, Franke, Carpenter, & Carey, 1993; Pressley, Harris, & Marks, 1992; Spires & Donley, 1998).

How do metacognitive skills help students learn?

metacognition
Knowledge about one's own learning or about how to learn ("thinking about thinking").

The term **metacognition** means knowledge about one's own learning (Flavell, 1985; McCormick, 2003) or about how to learn. Thinking skills and study skills are examples of **metacognitive skills.** Students can be taught strategies for assessing their own understanding, figuring out how much time they will need to study something, and choosing an effective plan of attack to study or solve problems (McCormick, 2003). For example, in reading this book, you are bound to come across a paragraph that you don't understand on first reading. What do you do? Perhaps you re-read the paragraph more slowly. Perhaps you look for other clues, such as pictures, graphs, or glossary terms to help you understand. Perhaps you read further back in the chapter to see whether your difficulty arose because you did not fully understand something that came earlier. These are all examples of metacognitive skills; you have learned how to know when you are not understanding and how to correct yourself (Schunk & Zimmerman, 1997). Another metacognitive strategy is the ability to predict what is likely to happen or to tell what is sensible and what is not. For example, when you first read the word *modeling* in Chapter 5, you knew right away that this did not refer to building models of ships or airplanes, because you knew that meaning would not fit in the context of this book.

> **CONNECTIONS**
>
> The term *modeling* is discussed in Chapter 5, page 154, in relation to Bandura's social learning theory.

> **ON THE WEB**
>
> For an overview of metacognition visit **www.ncrel.org/skrs/areas/issues/students/learning/lr1metn.htm.**

While most students do gradually develop adequate metacognitive skills, some do not. Teaching metacognitive strategies to students can lead to a marked improvement in their achievement (Alexander, Graham, & Harris, 1998; Hattie et al., 1996). Students can learn to think about their own thinking processes and apply specific learning strategies to think themselves through difficult tasks (Butler & Winn, 1995; Pressley, Harris, & Marks, 1992; Schunk, 2000). **Self-questioning strategies** are particularly effective (Zimmerman, 1998). In self-questioning, students look for common elements in a given type of task and ask themselves questions about these elements. For example, many researchers (e.g., Dimino, Gersten, Carnine, & Blake, 1990; Stevens, Madden, Slavin, & Farnish, 1987) have taught students to look for characters, settings, problems, and problem solutions in stories. Instructors start with specific questions and then let students find these critical elements on their own. Paris, Cross, and Lipson (1984) and King (1992) found that students comprehended better if they were taught to ask themselves *who, what, where,* and *how* questions as they read. Englert, Raphael, Anderson, Anthony, and Stevens (1991) gave students planning sheets to help them plan creative writing. Among the questions students were taught to ask themselves were: For whom am I writing? What is being explained? What are the steps? Essentially, students are taught to talk themselves through the activities they are engaged in, asking themselves or each other the questions a teacher would ask. Students have been successfully taught to talk themselves through mathematics problem solving (Cardelle-Elawar, 1990), spelling (Block & Peskowitz, 1990), creative writing (Zellermayer, Salomon, Globerson, & Givon, 1991), reading (Chin, 1998; Kucan & Beck, 1997), and many other subjects (see Chan, Burtis, Scardamalia, & Bereiter, 1992; Guthrie, Bennett, & Weber, 1991; McInerney & McInerney, 1998).

metacognitive skills Methods for learning, studying, or solving problems.

self-questioning strategies Learning strategies that call on students to ask themselves who, what, where, and how questions as they read material.

WHAT STUDY STRATEGIES HELP STUDENTS LEARN?

How are you reading this book? Are you underlining or highlighting key sentences? Are you taking notes or summarizing? Are you discussing the main ideas with a classmate? Are you putting the book under your pillow at night and hoping the information will somehow seep into your mind? Students have used these and many other strategies ever since the invention of reading, and such strategies have been studied almost as long. Even Aristotle wrote on the topic. Yet educational psychologists are still debating which study strategies are most effective (see Mayer, 1996; Pressley, Yokoi, Van Meter, van Etten, & Freebern, 1997).

Research on effective study strategies is confusing at best. Few forms of studying are found to be always effective, and fewer still are never effective. Clearly, the value of study strategies depends on their specifics and on the uses to which they are put (Weinstein & Hume, 1998; Zimmerman, 1998). Research on the most common study strategies is summarized in the following sections.

Note-Taking

A common study strategy that is used both in reading and in learning from lectures is **note-taking.** Note-taking can be effective for certain types of material, because it can require mental processing of main ideas, as one makes decisions about what to write. However, the effects of note-taking have been found to be inconsistent. Positive effects are most likely when note-taking is used for complex conceptual material in which the critical task is to identify the main ideas (Rickards, Fajen, Sullivan, & Gillespie, 1997). Also, note-taking that requires some mental processing is more effective than simply writing down what was read (Kiewra, 1991; Kiewra et al., 1991; Slotte & Lonka, 1999). For example, Bretzing and Kulhavy (1981) found that writing paraphrase notes (stating the main ideas in different words) and taking notes in preparation to teach others the material were effective note-taking strategies, because they required a high degree of mental processing of the information.

One apparently effective means of increasing the value of students' note-taking is for the teacher to provide partial notes before a lecture or reading, giving students categories to direct their own note-taking. Several studies have found that this practice, combined with student note-taking and review, increases student learning (Robinson et al., 2004).

Underlining

Perhaps the most common study strategy is underlining or highlighting. Yet despite the widespread use of this method, research on underlining generally finds few benefits (Anderson & Armbruster, 1984; Gaddy, 1998; Snowman, 1984). The problem is that most students fail to make decisions about what material is most critical and simply underline too much. When students are asked to underline the one sentence in each paragraph that is most important, they do retain more, probably because deciding which is the most important sentence requires a higher level of processing (Snowman, 1984).

Summarizing

Summarizing involves writing brief statements that represent the main ideas of the information being read. The effectiveness of this strategy depends on how it is used (King, 1991; Slotte & Lonka, 1999). One effective way is to have students write one-sentence summaries after reading each paragraph (Wittrock, 1991). Another is to have students prepare summaries that are intended to help others learn the material—partly because this activity forces the summarizer to be brief and to consider seriously what is important and what is not (Brown, Bransford, Ferrara, &

note-taking
A study strategy that requires decisions about what to write.

summarizing
Writing brief statements that represent the main idea of the information being read.

Campione, 1983). However, it is important to note that several studies have found no effects of summarization, and the conditions under which this strategy increases comprehension or retention of written material are not well understood (Wittrock, 1991; Wittrock & Alesandrini, 1990).

Writing to Learn

A growing body of evidence supports the idea that having students explain in writing the content they are learning helps them understand and remember it (Klein, 1999). For example, Fellows (1994) had sixth-graders in a 12-week science unit on states of matter write about their understandings of the concepts at several points in the unit. A control group studied the same content without writing. The writing group retained substantially more of the content at post-test. This and other studies find that focused writing assignments help children learn the content they are writing about. However, evidence is much more mixed regarding the effects of less focused "journal writing," in which students keep logs of their ideas and observations.

Outlining and Mapping

A related family of study strategies requires the student to represent the material studied in skeletal form. These strategies include outlining, networking, and mapping. **Outlining** presents the main points of the material in a hierarchical format, with each detail organized under a higher-level category. In networking and **mapping,** students identify main ideas and then diagram connections between them (Hyerle, 1995; Robinson & Skinner, 1996). For example, the schematic representation of the concept "bison" shown in Figure 6.3 might have been produced by students themselves as a network to summarize factual material about bison and their importance to Plains Indians (see Clark, 1990; Rafoth, Leal, & De Fabo, 1993).

Research on outlining, networking, and mapping is limited and inconsistent but generally finds that these methods are helpful as study aids (Katayama & Robinson, 1998; Robinson & Kiewra, 1995).

> **CERTIFICATION POINTER**
>
> When responding to the case studies in certification tests you may be asked to design a lesson that includes strategies for helping students learn relationships between ideas using concept mapping.

The PQ4R Method

One of the best-known study techniques for helping students understand and remember what they read is a procedure called the **PQ4R method** (Thomas & Robinson, 1972), which is based on an earlier version known as SQ3R, developed by F. P. Robinson (1961). The acronym stands for *preview, question, read, reflect, recite,* and *review.*

Research has shown the effectiveness of the PQ4R method for older children (Adams, Carnine, & Gersten, 1982), and the reasons seem clear. Following the PQ4R procedure focuses students on the meaningful organization of information and involves them in other effective strategies, such as question generation, elaboration, and distributed practice (opportunities to review information over a period of time) (Anderson, 1990).

outlining
Representing the main points of material in hierarchical format.

mapping
Diagramming main ideas and the connections between them.

PQ4R method
A study strategy that has students preview, question, read, reflect, recite, and review material.

> **ON THE WEB**
>
> For a description of PQR4 visit the West Virginia University Learning Center website at **www.rfl.wvu.edu/learningcenter/id49.htm.**

Theory into **PRACTICE**

Teaching the PQ4R Method

Explain and model the steps of the PQ4R method for your students, using the following guidelines:

1. **Preview.** Survey or scan the material quickly to get an idea of the general organization and major topics and subtopics. Pay attention to headings and subheadings, and identify what you will be reading about and studying.
2. **Question.** Ask yourself questions about the material before you read it. Use headings to invent questions using the *wh* words: *who, what, why, where.*
3. **Read.** Read the material. Do not take extensive written notes. Try to answer the questions that you posed prior to reading.
4. **Reflect on the material.** Try to understand and make meaningful the presented information by (1) relating it to things you already know, (2) relating the subtopics in the text to primary concepts or principles, (3) trying to resolve contradictions within the presented information, and (4) trying to use the material to solve problems suggested by the material.
5. **Recite.** Practice remembering the information by stating points out loud and asking and answering questions. You may use headings, highlighted words, and notes on major ideas to generate those questions.
6. **Review.** In the final step, actively review the material, focusing on asking yourself questions; re-read the material only when you are not sure of the answers.

Personal
Reflection

Defining *Effective*

On a recent trip to China, I visited four schools of education in different parts of the country. In each of these universities, I saw a remarkable phenomenon. Early each morning, students would distribute themselves outside, on benches or on the grass or, often, standing up, and would read their assignments out loud, all by themselves. I heard students at one university reading an English assignment that was a dialogue that happened to explain what they were doing—it stated that to get ahead in life, one must study hard by reading assignments out loud, repeating each section three times.

Is this widespread Chinese study strategy in fact effective? I don't know. It seemed to me that it would have made a lot more sense for the students to read to each other and give each other feedback, rather than just read to the air. Yet the usual alternative, in North American and European universities I've visited, is silent study, not paired study.

Studying is at the core of the educational experience, so much so that we often take it for granted. We know something about how to help students maximize the effectiveness of their studying, but I think we should know a great deal more. Perhaps three times out loud has real advantages. Wouldn't it be interesting to evaluate?

@ Reflect on This. Make a case for why the Chinese method for processing information might be effective. In studying for your classes, do you memorize or do you learn? What have you found to be the best way for you to learn new information and retain it?

Analogies   Like advance organizers, use of explanatory analogies (comparisons or parallels) can contribute to understanding by linking new information to well-established background knowledge. For example, a teacher could introduce a lesson on the human body's disease-fighting mechanisms by telling students to imagine a battle and to consider it as an analogy for the body's fight against infection. Similarly, a teacher could preface a lesson on termite societies by asking students to think of the hierarchy of citizens within a kingdom, using that as an analogy for such insect societies. **Analogies** can help students learn new information by relating it to concepts they already know (Bulgren, Deshler, Schumaker, & Lenz, 2000; McDaniel & Dannelly, 1996).

One interesting study (Halpern, Hansen, & Riefer, 1990) found that analogies work best when they are most different from the process being explained. For example, college students' learning about the lymph system was aided more by an analogy of the movement of water through a sponge than by one involving the movement of blood through veins. What this probably illustrates is that it is more important that analogies be thoroughly familiar to the learner than that they relate in any direct way to the concepts being taught.

Elaboration   Cognitive psychologists use the term **elaboration** to refer to the process of thinking about material to be learned in a way that connects the material to information or ideas that are already in the learner's mind (Ayaduray & Jacobs, 1997). As an example of the importance of elaboration, Stein, Littlefield, Bransford, and Persampieri (1984) conducted a series of experiments in which students were given lists of phrases to learn, such as "The gray-haired man carried the bottle." Some students were given the same phrases embedded in a more elaborate sentence, such as "The gray-haired man carried the bottle of hair dye." These latter students recalled the phrases much better than did those who did not receive the elaboration, because the additional words tied the phrase to a well-developed schema that was already in the students' minds. The connection between *gray-haired man* and *bottle* is arbitrary until we give it meaning by linking these words with the *hair dye* idea.

Teachers can apply this principle—that elaborated information is easier to understand and remember—to helping students comprehend lessons. Students may be asked to think of connections between ideas or to relate new concepts to their own lives. For example, it might help students to understand the U.S. annexation of Texas and California if they consider these events from the perspective of Mexicans or if they compare the events to a situation in which a friend borrows a bicycle and then decides not to give it back. In discussing a story or novel, a teacher might ask students from time to time to stop and visualize what is happening or what's about to happen as a means of helping them to elaborate their understanding of the material. Elaboration can be taught as a skill to help students comprehend what they read (Willoughby, Porter, Belsito, & Yearsley, 1999).

Organizing Information

Recall the shopping list discussed earlier in this chapter. When the list was presented in random order, it was very difficult to memorize, partly because it contained too many items to be held in working memory all at once. However, when the list was organized in a logical way, it was meaningful and therefore easy to learn and remember. The specific foods were grouped according to familiar recipes (e.g., flour, eggs, and milk were grouped under "pancakes"); and the recipes and other foods were grouped under "breakfast," "lunch," and "dinner."

Material that is well organized is much easier to learn and remember than material that is poorly organized (Durso & Coggins, 1991). Hierarchical organization, in

analogies
Images, concepts, or narratives that compare new information to information students already understand.

elaboration
The process of connecting new material to information or ideas already in the learner's mind.

which specific issues are grouped under more general topics, seems particularly helpful for student understanding. For example, in a classic study by Bower, Clark, Lesgold, and Winzenz (1969), one group of students was taught 112 words relating to minerals in random order. Another group was taught the same words, but in a definite order. Figure 6.8 shows the hierarchy within which the words were organized. The students were taught the words at levels 1 and 2 in the first of four sessions; those at levels 1, 2, and 3 in the second session; and those at levels 1 through 4 in the third and fourth sessions. The students in this second group recalled an average of 100 words, in comparison to only 65 for the group that received the random presentation—demonstrating the effectiveness of a coherent, organized presentation. In teaching complex concepts, not only is it necessary that material be well organized, it is also important that the organizing framework itself be made clear to students (Kallison, 1986). For example, in teaching about the minerals shown in Figure 6.8, the teacher might refer frequently to the framework and mark transitions from one part of it to another, as follows:

> "Recall that alloys are combinations of two or more metals."
> "Now that we've covered rare and common metals and alloys, let's move on to the second category of minerals: stones."

Using Questioning Techniques   One strategy that helps students learn from written texts, lectures, and other sources of information is the insertion of questions requiring students to stop from time to time to assess their own understanding of what the text or teacher is saying (Pressley et al., 1990). Presenting questions before the introduction of the instructional material can also help students learn material related to the questions (Hamaker, 1986; Hamilton, 1985), as can having students generate their own questions (Rosenshine, Meister, & Chapman, 1996).

FIGURE 6.8
The Hierarchical Structure for Minerals

From "Hierarchical Retrieval Schemes in Recall of Categorized Word Lists" by G. H. Bower et al., from *Journal of Verbal Learning and Verbal Behavior*, Volume 8, 323–343, copyright © 1969 by Academic Press. Reprinted by permission of Elsevier.

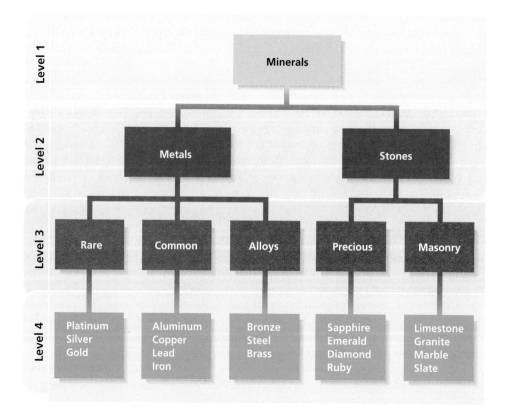

Using Conceptual Models   Another means that teachers can use to help students comprehend complex topics is the introduction of conceptual models, or diagrams showing how elements of a process relate to one another. Figure 6.1, which illustrates information processing, is a classic example of a conceptual model. Use of such models organizes and integrates information. Examples of topics that lend themselves to use of conceptual models are electricity, mechanics, computer programming, and the processes by which laws are passed. When models are part of a lesson, not only do students learn more, but they are also better able to apply their learning to creatively solve problems (see Hiebert, Wearne, & Taber, 1991; Mayer & Gallini, 1990; Winn, 1991). Knowledge maps, a variation on conceptual models, can be used to teach a wider variety of content. A knowledge map graphically shows the main concepts of a topic of study and the links between them. Giving students knowledge maps after a lesson has been shown to increase their retention of the lesson's content (O'Donnell, Dansereau, & Hall, 2002).

Graphs, charts, tables, matrices, and other means of organizing information into a comprehensible, visual form, have all been found to aid comprehension, memory, and transfer (Carney & Levin, 2002; Shah, Mayer, & Hegarty, 1999). However, these devices lose their effectiveness if they contain too much information that is not quickly communicated by the visuals (Robinson, Robinson, & Katayama, 1999; Schnotz, 2002; Vekiri, 2002). Atkinson et al. (1999) described a method to confront this problem by combining mnemonics with tables. To teach about the characteristics of various sharks, teachers made tables in which humorous pictures linked the names of the sharks with their characteristics. For example, dogfish sharks live near shore in moderate depth and have sawlike teeth, so the mnemonic showed dogs emerging from a submarine in shallow water holding saws to cut down a "No Dogs Allowed" sign on shore. Fifth-graders retained much more about the characteristics of nine sharks using this method than did students who saw other kinds of displays.

Chapter Summary

What Is an Information-Processing Model?

The three major components of memory are the sensory register, short-term or working memory, and long-term memory. The sensory registers are very short-term memories linked to the senses. Information that is received by the senses but not attended to will be quickly forgotten. Once information is received, it is processed by the mind in accord with our experiences and mental states. This activity is called perception.

Short-term or working memory is a storage system that holds five to nine bits of information at any one time. Information enters working memory from both the sensory register and the long-term memory. Rehearsal is the process of repeating information in order to hold it in working memory.

Long-term memory is the part of the memory system in which a large amount of information is stored for an indefinite time period. Cognitive theories of learning stress the importance of helping students relate information being learned to existing information in long-term memory.

The three parts of long-term memory are episodic memory, which stores our memories of personal experiences; semantic memory, which stores facts and generalized knowledge in the form of schemata; and procedural memory, which stores knowledge of how to do things. Schemata are networks of related ideas that guide our understanding and action. Information that fits into a well-developed schema is easier to learn than information that cannot be so accommodated. Levels-of-processing theory suggests that learners will remember only the things that they process. Students are processing

THE INTENTIONAL TEACHER

Using What You Know about Cognitive Theories of Learning to Improve Teaching and Learning

Intentional teachers know how information is received, processed, and stored in memory. They demonstrate that teaching is more than telling; they help students connect new information with what they already know, and encourage students to apply information in other contexts. Incorporating research findings about cognition into the classroom allows intentional teachers to help students build lasting and meaningful understandings.

1 What do I expect my students to know and be able to do at the end of this lesson? How does this contribute to course objectives and to students' needs to become capable individuals?

Meaningful information tends to be remembered best. Review your goals and objectives to ensure that you plan for meaningful learning.

For example, if you are teaching about the human body, you might make sure to focus on functions and connections among organs, not just identification. If you are teaching about parts of speech, you might ask students to generate their own examples of sentences using adjectives or adverbs, not just locate adjectives and adverbs in sentences you create.

2 What knowledge, skills, needs, and interests do my students have that must be taken into account in my lesson?

The more students know about a subject, the better they can organize and relate new information. Find out what your students already know about the topics you study.

In your history class, you might begin a unit on the Vietnam War by spending a period charting what students already know about the war. Recognizing that emotion and personal meaning and relevance can help students process information deeply so that they can remember better, you might invite them to share personal stories of family members who might have participated in that combat.

For your science unit on sea life, you might determine in the initial class session that your students are fascinated by whales. You might discuss with them how scientists differentiate among species of whales and help them generate a list of characteristics common to all whales that vary according to the species. You could guide their selection of categories to assure that they list relevant characteristics, and give them a reading passage from the text as homework, asking them to write down the questions that come to their minds as they read for discussion in the next session.

3 What do I know about the content, child development, learning, motivation, and effective teaching strategies that I can use to accomplish my objectives?

To make information meaningful and memorable, you should engage students in using new knowledge and skills to create their own new products. In teaching a foreign language, for instance, you might have students make up their own sentences and dialogues using new vocabulary or verb forms. For example, you might ask students in teams to make up gossip about a boy, a girl, a couple, a group of girls, and a school principal,

information when they manipulate it, look at it from different perspectives, and analyze it. Dual code theory further suggests the importance of using both visual and verbal coding to learn bits of information. Other elaborations of the information-processing model are parallel distributed processing, and connectionist models.

Technology that enables scientists to observe the brain in action has led to rapid advances in brain science. Findings have shown how specific parts of the brain process specific types of information in concert with other specific brain sites. As individuals gain expertise, their brain function becomes more efficient. Early brain development is a process of adding neural connections and then sloughing off those that are not used.

What Causes People to Remember or Forget?

Interference theory helps explain why people forget. It suggests that students can forget information when it gets mixed up with, or pushed aside by, other information. Interference theory states that two situations cause forgetting: retroactive inhibition, when learning a second task makes a person forget something that was learned previously, and proactive inhibition, when learning one thing interferes with the retention of things learned later. The primacy and recency effects state that people best remem-

enabling them to use different pronouns, verbs, and adjectives in realistic contexts.

④ What instructional materials, technology, assistance, and other resources are available to help accomplish my objectives?

Schema theory suggests that new information is added to existing networks of connected ideas. With the computer lab teacher, you might explore software for diagramming information, and for building data bases. You could plan to demonstrate the use of these programs and then provide follow-up lab time or classroom opportunities for the students to make use of these tools to develop materials for their portfolios in appropriate content areas. Many current software programs allow inclusion of visual as well as verbal material, addressing more than one form of information processing and encouraging students to think about and monitor their learning of the material being manipulated.

⑤ How will I plan to assess students' progress toward my objectives?

Students need to demonstrate different kinds of understanding: rote learning, meaningful learning, and the ability to use information in new contexts. Give them tasks that allow you to check for different uses of knowledge: Are they forgetting? Are they transferring? Are they applying? Adjust your instruction based on your results. For example, as the teacher of an advanced foreign language class, you could assess students' recall of vocabulary terms, their ability to describe rules and structures of the language, and their ability to communicate in the language you are teaching. You might find that students have good recall of vocabulary but struggle with expressing their own thoughts, so you could plan for opportunities for them to speak in simulated realistic contexts, such as a party, a restaurant, an airport, or a picnic.

⑥ How will I respond if individual children or the class as a whole are not on track toward success? What is my back-up plan?

Students demonstrate success when they show they can control their own learning. Check to see that students use self-questioning strategies and metacognition to assess their own learning. For example, before you hand your fourth-graders a reading passage on reptiles, you might prompt them to ask themselves questions as they read, and suggest they record their findings. After they complete the passage, you could ask them which sections of text were difficult and what they do when they encounter difficult text. Their answers tell you how far they have progressed toward actively monitoring their own learning.

ber information that is presented first and last in a series. Automaticity is gained by practicing information or skills far beyond the amount needed to establish them in long-term memory so that using such skills requires little or no mental effort. Practice strengthens associations of newly learned information in memory. Distributed practice, which involves practicing parts of a task over a period of time, is usually more effective than massed practice. Enactment also helps students to remember information.

How Can Memory Strategies Be Taught?

Teachers can help students remember facts by presenting lessons in an organized way and by teaching students to use memory strategies called mnemonics. Three types of verbal learning are paired-associate learning, serial learning, and free-recall learning. Paired-associate learning is learning to respond with one member of a pair when given the other member. Students can improve their learning of paired associates by using imagery techniques such as the keyword method. Serial learning involves recalling a list of items in a specified order. Free-recall learning involves recalling the list in any order. Helpful strategies are the loci method, the pegword method, rhyming, and initial-letter strategies.

What Makes Information Meaningful?

Information that makes sense and has significance to students is more meaningful than inert knowledge and information learned by rote. According to schema theory, individuals' meaningful knowledge is constructed of networks and hierarchies of schemata.

How Do Metacognitive Skills Help Students Learn?

Metacognition helps students learn by thinking about, controlling, and effectively using their own thinking processes.

What Study Strategies Help Students Learn?

Note-taking, selective directed underlining, summarizing, writing to learn, outlining, and mapping can effectively promote learning. The PQ4R method is an example of a strategy that focuses on the meaningful organization of information.

How Do Cognitive Teaching Strategies Help Students Learn?

Advance organizers help students process new information by activating background knowledge. Analogies, information elaboration, organizational schemes, questioning techniques, and conceptual models are other examples of teaching strategies that are based on cognitive learning theories.

Key Terms

Research Navigator.com

Review the following key terms from the chapter. Then, to explore research on these topics and how they relate to education today, connect to Research Navigator™ through this book's Companion Website or directly at www.researchnavigator.com.

Self-Assessment: Practicing for Licensure

Directions: The chapter-opening vignette addresses indicators that are often assessed in state licensure exams. Re-read the chapter-opening vignette, and then respond to the following questions.

1. According to information-processing theory, which component of the memory system did Verona Bishop's students first use during the 3-second experiment?

   a. sensory register
   b. short-term memory
   c. working memory
   d. long-term memory

2. Verona Bishop asks her students, "[I]magine that you could keep everything that ever entered your mind. What would that be like?" One student responds, "You'd be a genius!" Another responds, "You'd go crazy!" Why does Ms. Bishop side with the second student?

   a. Genius is an inherited trait not associated with memory.
   b. There is no correlation between genius and paying attention to environmental clues.
   c. Being bombarded with too much information at once decreases learning.
   d. People with mental illness absorb more environmental information than do people without mental illness.

3. During the 3-second memory experiment, Verona Bishop asks her students to recall things not associated with the overhead information she presented. What type of memory are students using when they recall smells, sounds, and details of the classroom and the people in it?

   a. semantic memory
   b. procedural memory
   c. dual-code memory
   d. episodic memory

4. Cheryl, one of Verona Bishop's students, recalled seeing the word *learning* on the overhead screen, even though it was not there. How does Ms. Bishop explain this phenomenon?

   a. Ms. Bishop actually said the word during the 3-second experiment, so Cheryl picked it up there.
   b. Humans have a tendency to learn the first and last bits of information presented, so Cheryl thought of the word *learning* after the 3-second experiment.
   c. *Learning* and *memory,* a word that was actually presented, are closely related and most likely stored closely together in memory. When one is recalled, so is the other.

   d. Because the students had only 3 seconds to review the information, Cheryl's report of what she remembered contained guesses.

5. Consider that some of Verona Bishop's students attempted to memorize the information on the overhead screen in a random fashion. Which of the following learning strategies are they using?

   a. free-recall learning
   b. serial learning
   c. paired-associate learning
   d. process learning

6. Verona Bishop summarizes her experiment by telling her students that they will forget some details of the experiment but remember others. Why is this so?

   a. According to levels-of-processing theory, we tend to retain information that has been subject to thorough processing. If the students gave meaning to the information, it is likely to be remembered.
   b. According to dual-code theory, visual information is more likely to be retained than verbal information. If the students saw the information, it is more likely to be remembered than if they heard it.
   c. According to the parallel distributed processing model, information that is processed simultaneously in two parts of the memory system—the sensory register and working memory—is most likely to be recalled. If the students processed the information simultaneously in both systems, the information is likely to be remembered.
   d. According to connectionist models of memory, only those students who built a network of connections in their memory systems will retain the information. Students using a system of rules or storing individual bits of information separately will forget.

7. Review the current research on the brain. What do we know about how it works? What is the connection between brain function and memory?

8. Describe several memory strategies that you can teach your students to help them remember the facts, concepts, and ideas presented to them in a lesson.

The Effective Lesson

Jennifer Logan's eighth-grade physical science class is a happy mess. Students are working in small groups at lab stations, filling all sorts of bottles with water and then tapping them to see how various factors affect the sound. One group has set up a line of identical bottles and put different amounts of water in each one so that tapping the bottles in sequence makes a crude musical scale. "The amount of water in the bottle is all that matters," one group member tells Ms. Logan, and her groupmates nod in agreement. Another group has an odd assortment of bottles and has carefully measured the same amount of water into each. "It's the shape and thickness of the bottles that make the difference," says one group member. Other groups are working more chaotically, filling and tapping large and small, narrow and wide, and thick and thin bottles with different amounts of water. Their theories are wild and varied.

After a half hour of experimentation, Ms. Logan calls the class together and asks group members to describe what they did and what they concluded. Students loudly uphold their group's point of view. "It's the amount of water!" "It's the height of the bottles!" "It's the thickness of the bottles!" "No, it's their shape!" "It's how hard you tap the bottles!" Ms. Logan moderates the conversation but lets students confront each other's ideas and give their own arguments.

The next day, Ms. Logan teaches a lesson on sound. She explains how sound causes waves in the air and how the waves cause the eardrum to vibrate, transmitting sound information to the brain. She has two students come to the front of the class with a Slinky and uses the Slinky to illustrate how sound waves travel. She asks many questions of students, both to see whether they are understanding and to get them to take the next mental step. She then explains how sound waves in a tube become lower in pitch the longer the tube is. To illustrate this, she plays a flute and a piccolo. Light bulbs are starting to click on in the students' minds, and Ms. Logan can tell from the responses to her questions that the students are starting to get the idea. At the end of the period, Ms. Logan lets the students get back into their groups to discuss what they have learned and to try to apply their new knowledge to the bottle problem.

When the students come into class on the third day of the sound lesson, they are buzzing with excitement. They rush to their lab stations and start filling and tapping bottles to test out the theories they came up with the day before. Ms. Logan walks among the groups, listening in on their conversations. "It's not the amount of water, it's the amount of air," she hears one student say. "It's not the bottle; it's the air," says a student in another group. She helps one group that is still floundering to get on track. Finally, Ms. Logan calls the class together to discuss their findings and conclusions. Representatives of some of the groups demonstrate the experiments they used to show how it was the amount of air in each bottle that determined the sound.

"How could we make one elegant demonstration to show that it's only the amount of air that controls the sound?" asks Ms. Logan.

The students buzz among themselves and then assemble all their bottles into one experiment. They make one line of identical bottles with different amounts of water. Then to demonstrate that it is the air, not the water, that matters, they put the same amount of water in bottles of different sizes. Sure enough, in each case, the more air space left in the bottle, the lower the sound.

Ms. Logan ends the period with a homework assignment: to read a chapter on sound in a textbook. She tells the students that they will have an opportunity to work in their groups to make certain that every group member understands everything in the sound lesson, and then there will be a quiz in which students will have to show individually that they can apply their new knowledge. She reminds them that their groups can be "superteams" only if everyone knows the material.

The bell rings, and the students pour into the hallway, still talking excitedly about what they have learned. Some groupmates promise to call each other that evening to prepare for the group study the next day. Ms. Logan watches them file out. She's exhausted, but she knows that this group of students will never forget the lessons they've learned about sound, about experiments, and, most important, about their ability to use their minds to figure out difficult concepts. *⊘*

USING YOUR

Experience

Creative Thinking Write the phrase *Effective Lesson* in the middle of a sheet of paper and circle it. Brainstorm all the types of instructional approaches you can think of that make an effective lesson. Now list the types of instructional approaches that Ms. Logan uses.

Critical Thinking How does Ms. Logan motivate the students? What strategies does she use to encourage retention of the material?

The lesson is where education takes place. All other aspects of schooling, from buildings to buses to administration, are designed to support teachers in delivering effective lessons; they do not educate in themselves. Most teachers spend most of their class time teaching lessons. The typical elementary or secondary school teacher may teach 800 to 1,000 class lessons each year!

Conducting effective lessons is at the heart of the teacher's craft. Some aspects of lesson presentation have to be learned on the job; good teachers get better at it every

Personal Reflection

Balancing Instruction

I once went along with some colleagues from another university to visit a school that was using an exciting discovery science program they'd developed. We watched a teacher present an outstanding lesson, and then the students broke into small groups to work on experiments designed to lead them to discover a key scientific principle. The students got right to work and carried out the experiments with great enthusiasm. Gradually, through-out the class, groups were coming to the same conclusion—which was wrong! I asked the teacher what she did if students "discovered" the wrong answer.

She looked around in a conspiratorial way, and drew me back into a corner out of sight of my friends. "I *teach* them," she whispered.

Discovery learning can be a wonderful part of instruction for topics that lend them-selves to it, but discovery needs to be balanced with direct instruction, to make sure that students both learn the joy and excitement of discovery and the basic knowledge and skills needed to be proficient in any subject.

@ *Reflect on This.* *What subjects might lend themselves more to discovery learning? As the teacher of this class, how would you turn this lesson around to* teach *them to arrive at the correct answer?*

INTASC

5 Classroom Motivation and Management

7 Instructional Planning Skills

year. Yet educational psychologists have studied the elements that go into effective lessons, and we know a great deal that is useful in day-to-day teaching at every grade level and in every subject (Good & Brophy, 2003; Sternberg & Horvath, 1995). This chapter and the four that follow it present the principal findings of this research and translate them into ways of thinking about the practical demands of everyday teaching.

As Ms. Logan's lesson illustrates, effective lessons use many teaching methods. In four periods on one topic, she used direct instruction as well as discussion, coopera-tive learning, and other constructivist techniques. These methods are often posed as different philosophies, and the ideological wars over which is best go on incessantly (see Berg & Clough, 1990/91; Hunter, 1990/91; Joyce, Weil, & Calhoun, 2004; Pressley et al., 2003). Yet few experienced teachers would deny that teachers must be able to use all of them and must know when to use each.

This chapter focuses on the strategies that teachers use to transmit information to students in ways that are most likely to help students understand, incorporate, and use new concepts and skills. Chapter 8 focuses on student-centered methods, in which students play an active role in structuring learning for themselves and for each other. However, the teaching strategies presented in these two chapters should be seen not as representing two sharply conflicting philosophies of education, but as complementary approaches to be used at different times for different purposes.

CERTIFICATION POINTER

You may be asked on your teacher certification test to describe techniques for planning instruction that incorporate learning theory, subject matter, and particular student develop-mental levels.

WHAT IS DIRECT INSTRUCTION?

At times, the most effective and efficient way to teach students is for the teacher to present information, skills, or concepts in a direct fashion (Bligh, 2000; Good & Brophy, 2003; Gunter, Estes, & Schwab, 2003). The term **direct instruction** is used to describe lessons in which the teacher transmits information directly to students,

direct instruction
Approach to teaching in which the teacher trans-mits information directly to the students; lessons are goal-oriented and structured by the teacher.

structuring class time to reach a clearly defined set of objectives as efficiently as possible. Direct instruction is particularly appropriate for teaching a well-defined body of information or skills that all students must master (Gersten, Taylor, & Graves, 1999; Gunter, Estes, & Schwab, 2003). It is held to be less appropriate when deep conceptual change is an objective or when exploration, discovery, and open-ended objectives are the object of instruction. However, recent research has supported the idea that direct instruction can be more efficient than discovery in conceptual development as well. Klahr and Nigam (in press) compared third-graders directly taught to do experiments that isolate the effects of one variable to those who carried out their own experiments without direct instruction. Those who received direct instruction performed much better in setting up new experiments.

A great deal of research was done in the 1970s and 1980s to discover the elements of effective direct instruction lessons. Different authors describe these elements differently (see Evertson, Emmer, Clements, Sanford, & Worsham, 1994; Gagné & Briggs, 1979; Good et al., 1983; Hunter, 1995; Rosenshine & Stevens, 1986). Researchers and teachers generally agree as to the sequence of events that characterize effective direct instruction lessons. First, the teacher brings students up to date on any skills they might need for today's lesson (e.g., the teacher might briefly review yesterday's lesson if today's is a continuation) and tells students what they are going to learn. Then the teacher devotes most of the lesson time to teaching the skills or information, giving students opportunities to practice the skills or express the information, and questioning or quizzing students to determine whether or not they are learning the objectives.

A brief description of the parts of a direct instruction lesson follows. The next section of this chapter will cover each part in detail.

1. **State learning objectives and orient students to the lesson:** Tell students what they will be learning and what performance will be expected of them. Whet students' appetites for the lesson by informing them how interesting, important, or personally relevant it will be to them.
2. **Review prerequisites:** Go over any skills or concepts students need in order to understand today's lesson.
3. **Present new material:** Teach the lesson, presenting information, giving examples, demonstrating concepts, and so on.
4. **Conduct learning probes:** Pose questions to students to assess their level of understanding and correct their misconceptions.
5. **Provide independent practice:** Give students an opportunity to practice new skills or use new information on their own.
6. **Assess performance and provide feedback:** Review independent practice work or give a quiz. Give feedback on correct answers, and reteach skills if necessary.
7. **Provide distributed practice and review:** Assign homework to provide distributed practice on the new material. In later lessons, review material and provide practice opportunities to increase the chances that students will remember what they learned and will be able to apply it in different circumstances.

HOW IS A DIRECT INSTRUCTION LESSON TAUGHT?

INTASC

6 Communication Skills

The general lesson structure takes vastly different forms in different subject areas and at different grade levels. Teachers of older students may take several days for each step of the process, ending with a formal test or quiz. Teachers of younger students may go through the entire cycle in a class period, using informal assessments at the end. Tables 7.1 and 7.2 present two quite different lessons to illustrate how direct instruction would be applied to different subjects and grade levels. The first lesson, "Subtraction

Table 7.1

Sample Lesson for Basic Math: Subtraction with Renaming

Lesson Part	Teacher Presentation
1. State learning objective and orient students to lesson.	"There are 32 students in this class. Let's say we were going to have a party, and I was going to get one cupcake for each student in the class. But 5 of you said you didn't like cupcakes. How many cupcakes would I need to get for the students who do like cupcakes? Let's set up the problem on the chalkboard the way we have before, and mark the tens and ones . . ." tens ones 3 2 Students – 5 Don't like cupcakes "All right, let's subtract: 2 take away 5 is . . . *hey!* We can't do that! Five is more than 2, so how can we take 5 away from 2? We can't! "In this lesson we are going to learn how to subtract when we don't have enough ones. By the end of this lesson, you will be able to show how to rename tens as ones so that you can subtract."
2. Review prerequisites.	"Let's review subtraction when we have enough ones." Put on the chalkboard and have students solve: 47 56 89 – 3 – 23 – 8 How many tens are in 23?____ How many ones are in 30?____ Give answers, discuss all items missed by many students.
3A. Present new material (first subskill).	Have table monitors help hand out 5 bundles of 10 popsicle sticks each and 10 individual sticks to each student. Using an overhead projector, explain how to use sticks to show 13, 27, 30. Have students show each number at their own desks. Walk around to check.
4A. Conduct learning probes (first subskill).	Have students show 23 using their sticks. Check desks. Then have students show 40. Check desks. Continue until all students have the idea.
3B. Present new material (second subskill).	Using an overhead projector, explain how to use sticks to show 6 minus 2 and 8 minus 5. Then show 13 and try to take away 5. Ask for suggestions on how this could be done. Show that by removing the rubber band from the tens bundle, we have a total of 13 ones and can remove 5. Have students show this at their desks. Walk around to check.
4B. Conduct learning probes (second subskill).	Have students show 12 (check) and then take away 4 by breaking apart the ten bundle. Then have students show 17 and take away 9. Continue until all students have the idea.
3C. Present new material (third subskill).	Give students worksheets showing tens bundles and single units. Explain how to show renaming by crossing out a bundle of ten and rewriting it as 10 units and then subtracting by crossing out units.
4C. Conduct learning probes (third subskill).	Have students do the first items on the worksheet one at a time until all students have the idea.
5. Provide independent practice.	Have students continue, completing the worksheet on their own.
6. Assess performance and provide feedback.	Show correct answers to worksheet items on overhead projector. Have students mark their own papers. Ask how many got item 1, item 2, and so on, and discuss all items missed by more than a few students. Have students hand in papers.
7. Provide distributed practice and review.	Hand out homework, and explain how it is to be done. Review lesson content at start of following lesson and in later lessons.

Table 7.2	
Sample Lesson for History: The Origins of World War II	
Lesson Part	*Teacher Presentation*
1. State learning objective and orient students to lesson.	"Today we will begin to discuss the origins and causes of World War II—perhaps the most important event in the twentieth century. The political situation of the world today—the map of Europe, the political predominance of the United States, the problems of the Eastern European countries formerly under Soviet domination, even the problems of the Middle East—all can be traced to the rise of Hitler and the bloody struggle that followed. I'm sure many of you have relatives who fought in the war or whose lives were deeply affected by it. Raise your hand if a relative or someone you know well fought in World War II."
	• "Germany today is peaceful and prosperous. How could a man like Hitler have come to power? To understand this, we must first understand what Germany was like in the years following its defeat in World War I and why an unemployed Austrian painter could come to lead one of the largest countries in Europe."
	• "By the end of this lesson you will understand the conditions in Germany that led up to the rise of Hitler, the reasons he was successful, and the major events of his rise to power."
2. Review prerequisites.	Have students recall from the previous lesson:
	• The humiliating provisions of the Treaty of Versailles —Reparations —Demilitarization of the Ruhr —Loss of territory and colonies
	• The lack of experience with democracy in Germany
3. Present new material.	Discuss with students:
	• Conditions in Germany before the rise of Hitler —Failure of the Weimar Republic —Economic problems, inflation, and severe impact of the U.S. Depression —Belief that Germany lost World War I because of betrayal by politicians —Fear of Communism
	• Events in Hitler's rise to power —Organization of National Socialist (Nazi) Party —Beer-Hall Putsch and Hitler's imprisonment —*Mein Kampf* —Organization of Brown Shirts (S.A.) —Election and appointment as chancellor
4. Conduct learning probes.	Questions to students throughout lesson should assess student comprehension of the main points.
5. Provide independent practice.	Have students independently write three reasons why the situation in Germany in the 1920s and early 1930s might have been favorable to Hitler's rise, and have students be prepared to defend their answers.
6. Assess performance and provide feedback.	Call on randomly selected students to read and justify their reasons for Hitler's success. Discuss well-justified and poorly justified reasons. Have students hand in papers.
7. Provide distributed practice and review.	Review lesson content at start of next lesson and in later lessons.

with Renaming," is an example of the first of a series of lessons directed at a basic math skill. In contrast, the second lesson, "The Origins of World War II," is an example of a lesson directed at higher-order understanding of critical events in history and their causes and interrelationships. Note that the first lesson (Table 7.1) proceeds step by step and emphasizes frequent learning probes and independent practice to help students thoroughly learn the concepts being taught, whereas the second lesson (Table 7.2) is characterized by an alternation between new information, discussion, and questions to assess comprehension of major concepts.

The sequence of activities outlined in these two lessons flows along a logical path, from arousing student interest to presenting new information to allowing students to practice their new knowledge or skills to assessment. This orderly progression is essential to direct instruction lessons at any grade level and in any subject, although the various components and how they are implemented would, of course, look different for different subjects and grades.

State Learning Objectives

The first step in presenting a lesson is planning it in such a way that the reasons for teaching and learning the lesson are clear. What do you want students to know or be able to do at the end of the lesson? Setting out objectives at the beginning of the lesson is an essential step in providing a framework into which information, instructional materials, and learning activities will fit.

> **ON THE WEB**
>
> For tips on writing quality learning objectives visit **http://captain.park.edu/facultydevelopment/writing_learning_objectives.htm.**

CONNECTIONS
For in-depth coverage of instructional objectives, writing lesson plans, and using taxonomies, see Chapter 13, pages 440–450.

CERTIFICATION POINTER
For teacher certification tests, you may be asked to suggest techniques for building bridges between curriculum objectives and students' experiences.

Theory into **PRACTICE**

Planning a Lesson

The first step of a lesson, stating learning objectives or outcomes, represents a condensation of much advance **lesson planning** (see Burden & Byrd, 2003; Dick, Carey, & Carey, 2001; Karges-Bone, 2000). As a teacher planning a lesson, you will need, at the least, to answer the following questions:

1. What will students know or be able to do after the lesson? What will be the outcomes of their learning? How will you know when and how well students have achieved these learning outcomes or objectives?
2. What prerequisite skills are needed to learn this content? How will you make sure students have these skills?
3. What information, activities, and experiences will you provide to help students acquire the knowledge and skills they need in order to attain the learning outcomes? How much time will be needed? How will you use in-class and out-of-class time? How will seatwork and homework assignments help students to achieve the learning objectives?
4. How will you arouse students' interest in the content? How will you motivate them to learn? How will you give them feedback on their learning?
5. What books and materials will you use to present the lesson? When will you preview or test all the materials and create guidelines for students' responses to them? Are all materials accurate, pedagogically sound, fair to different cultures, and appropriate in content and grade level?

lesson planning
Procedure that includes stating learning objectives such as what the students should know or be able to do after the lesson; what information, activities, and experiences the teacher will provide; how much time will be needed to reach the objective; what books, materials, and media support the teacher will provide; and what instructional method(s) and participation structures will be used.

6. What methods of teaching will you incorporate? For example, will you use reading, lecture, role playing, videotape viewing, demonstration, or writing assignments?
7. What participation structures will you use: whole-group or small-group discussions, cooperative learning groups, ability groups, individual assignments? What learning tasks will groups and individuals perform? How will you organize, monitor, and evaluate groups?

EDUCATION TOUCHES THE FUTURE

J. BRAVO

"Dang. I'm not even ready for fifth period!"

Orient Students to the Lesson

At the beginning of a lesson, the teacher needs to establish a positive **mental set,** or attitude of readiness, in students: "I'm ready to get down to work. I'm eager to learn the important information or skills the teacher is about to present, and I have a rough idea of what we will be learning." This mental set can be established in many ways. First, teachers should require students to be on time to class and should start the lesson immediately when the period begins (Evertson et al., 1994). This establishes a sense of seriousness of purpose that is lost in a ragged start. Second, teachers need to arouse students' curiosity or interest in the lesson they are about to learn. The teacher in the first sample lesson (Table 7.1) did this by introducing subtraction with renaming as a skill that would be necessary in connection with counting cupcakes for a class party, a situation of some reality and interest to young students. In the second sample lesson (Table 7.2), the teacher advertised the importance of the lesson on the basis that understanding the origins and events of World War II would help students understand events today, and made the lesson personally relevant to students by having them think of a relative who either fought in World War II or was deeply affected by it. In the chapter-opening vignette, Ms. Logan whetted students' curiosity about sound by giving them an opportunity to experiment with it before the formal lesson.

A lesson on genetics might be introduced as follows:

Did you ever wonder why tall parents have taller-than-average children and red-haired children usually have at least one red-haired parent? Think of your own family. If your father and mother are both taller than average, then you will probably be taller than average. Well, today we are going to have a lesson on the science called genetics, in which we will learn how characteristics of parents are passed on to their children.

This introduction might be expected to grab students' interest because it makes the subject personally relevant.

Humor or drama can also establish a positive mental set. One teacher occasionally used a top hat and a wand to capture student interest by "magically" transforming adjectives into adverbs (e.g., *sad* into *sadly*). Popular and instructionally effective children's television programs, such as *Sesame Street* and *Between the Lions,* use this kind of device constantly to get young children's attention and hold their interest in basic skills. Finally, in starting a lesson teachers must give students a road map of where the lesson is going and what they will know at the end. Stating lesson objectives clearly has generally been found to enhance student achievement of those objectives (Gronlund, 2000). Giving students an outline of the lesson in advance may also help them to incorporate new information (Bligh, 2000).

mental set
Students' attitude of readiness to begin a lesson.

Theory into **PRACTICE**

Communicating Objectives to Students

Teacher education programs include training in creating lesson plans, beginning with a consideration of instructional objectives and learning outcomes. Sharing lesson plans with students is a good idea, because research suggests that knowledge of objectives can lead to improvements in student achievement. Practical suggestions follow for sharing lesson objectives with students.

1. The objectives you communicate to students should be broad enough to encompass everything the lesson will teach. Research suggests that giving students too narrow a set of objectives may lead them to devalue or ignore other meaningful aspects of a lesson. In addition, broad objectives provide greater flexibility for adapting instruction as needed once the lesson is under way.

2. The objectives you communicate should be specific enough in content to make clear to students what the outcomes of their learning will be—what they will know and be able to do and how they will use their new knowledge and skills.

3. Consider stating objectives both orally and in writing and repeating them during the lesson to remind students why they are learning. Teachers often use verbal and written outlines or summaries of objectives. Providing demonstrations or models of learning products or outcomes is also effective. For example, an art teacher might show a student's drawing that demonstrates use of perspective to illustrate what students will be able to produce themselves, or a math teacher might show a math problem that students could not do at the beginning of a series of lessons but will be able to do at the end.

4. Consider using questioning techniques to elicit from students their own statements of objectives or outcomes. Their input will likely both reflect and inform your lesson plan. Some teachers ask students to express their ideas for meeting objectives or demonstrating outcomes, because research suggests that students who have a stake in the lesson plan and a sense of control over their learning will be more motivated to learn.

Review Prerequisites

For the next major task in a lesson, teachers need to ensure that students have mastered prerequisite skills and to link information that is already in their minds to the information you are about to present. If today's lesson is a continuation of yesterday's and you are reasonably sure that students understood yesterday's lesson, then the review might just remind them about the earlier lesson and ask a few quick questions before beginning the new one. For instance, you might say, "Yesterday we learned how to add the suffix *-ed* to a word ending in *y*. Who will tell us how this is done?"

As today's lesson—adding other suffixes to words ending in *y*—is a direct continuation of yesterday's, this brief reminder is adequate. However, if you are introducing a new skill or concept that depends on skills learned much earlier, then more elaborate discussion and assessment of prerequisite skills may be needed.

Sometimes teachers need to assess students on prerequisite skills before starting a lesson. In the first sample lesson (Table 7.1), the teacher briefly quizzed students on subtraction without renaming and numeration skills in preparation for a lesson

CONNECTIONS

For more about the importance of activating students' prior knowledge, see Chapter 6, page 197.

on subtraction with renaming. If students had shown poor understanding of either prerequisite skill, the teacher would have reviewed those skills before going on to the new lesson.

Another reason teachers should review prerequisites is to provide advance organizers. As defined in Chapter 6, advance organizers are introductory statements by the teacher that remind students of what they already know and give them a framework for understanding the new material to be presented. In the second sample lesson (Table 7.2), the teacher set the stage for the new content (Hitler's rise to power) by reviewing the economic, political, and social conditions in Germany that made Hitler's success possible.

CONNECTIONS

See page 198 in Chapter 6 for a definition of advance organizers.

Present New Material

Here begins the main body of the lesson, the point at which the teacher presents new information or skills.

CONNECTIONS

See page 199 in Chapter 6 for a discussion of retention of well-organized information.

Lesson Structure   Lessons should be logically organized. Recall from Chapter 6 that information that has a clear, well-organized structure is retained better than less clearly presented information (Fuchs et al., 1997). A lesson on the legislative branch of the U.S. government might be presented as follows:

The Legislative Branch of the Federal Government (First Lesson)

I. Functions and nature of the legislative branch (Congress)
   A. Passes laws
   B. Approves money for executive branch
   C. Has 2 houses—House of Representatives and Senate
II. House of Representatives
   A. Designed to be closest to the people—representatives elected to 2-year terms—proportional representation
   B. Responsible for originating money bills
III. Senate
   A. Designed to give greater continuity to legislative branch—senators elected to 6-year terms—each state has 2 senators
   B. Approves appointments and treaties made by executive branch

This would be a beginning lesson; subsequent lessons would present how laws are introduced and passed, checks and balances on legislative power, and so on. The lesson has a clear organization that the teacher should point out to students. For example, you might pause at the beginning of the second topic and say, "Now we are going to learn about the lower house of Congress, the House of Representatives." This helps students form a mental outline that will help them remember the material. Research finds that a clearly laid out structure and transitional statements about the structure of the lesson increase student understanding (Lorch, Lorch, & Inman, 1993).

Lesson Emphasis   In addition to making clear the organization of a lesson by noting when the next subtopic is being introduced, instructionally effective teachers give clear indications about the most important elements of the lesson by saying, for example, "It is particularly important to note that . . ." (Alexander & Jetton, 1996). Repeat important points and bring them back into the lesson whenever appropriate. For example, in teaching about the presidential veto in the lesson on the legislative branch of government, a teacher might say:

Here again, we see the operation of the system of checks and balances we discussed earlier. The executive can veto legislation passed by the Congress, which in turn can withhold funds for actions of the executive. Remember, understanding how this system of checks and balances works is critical to an understanding of how the U.S. government works.

In this way, the teacher emphasizes one of the central concepts of the U.S. government—the system of checks and balances among the executive, legislative, and judicial branches—by bringing it up whenever possible and by labeling it as important.

One classic experiment found that teachers who used the lesson presentation strategies outlined in this section were more successful than other teachers in increasing student achievement (Clark et al., 1979). The researchers studied the effectiveness of teachers who reviewed main ideas, stated objectives at the beginning of the lesson, outlined lesson content, signaled transitions between parts of the lesson, indicated important points in the lesson, and summarized the parts of the lesson as the lesson proceeded. These teachers' students learned more than did students whose teachers did not do those things.

Lesson Clarity One consistent feature of effective lessons is clarity—the use of direct, simple, and well-organized language to present concepts (Land, 1987; McCaleb & White, 1980; Smith & Land, 1981). Wandering off into digressions or irrelevant topics or otherwise interrupting the flow of the lesson detracts from clarity. Clear presentations avoid the use of vague terms that do not add to the meaning of the lesson, such as the italicized words in the following sentence (from Smith & Land, 1981): "*Maybe* before we get to *probably* the main idea of the lesson, you should review a few prerequisite concepts."

Explanations Research finds that effective teachers also use many explanations and explanatory words (such as *because, in order to,* and *consequently*) and frequently use a pattern of **rule–example–rule** when presenting new concepts (Van Patten et al., 1986). For example:

> Matter may change forms, but it is never destroyed. If I were to burn a piece of paper, it would appear that the paper was gone, but in fact it would have been combined with oxygen atoms from the air and changed to a gas (mostly carbon dioxide) and ash. If I could count the atoms in the paper plus the atoms from the air before and after I burned the paper, we could see that the matter involved did not disappear, but merely changed forms.

Note that the teacher stated the rule ("Matter . . . is never destroyed"), gave an example, and restated the rule in the explanation of how the example illustrates the rule. Also note that a rule–example–rule sequence was used in this textbook to illustrate the rule–example–rule pattern!

Worked Examples Worked examples are an age-old strategy for teaching certain kinds of problem solving, especially in mathematics (Atkinson, Derry, Renkl, & Wortham, 2000). For example, a teacher might pose a problem and then work it out on a chalkboard or overhead, explaining his or her thinking at each step. In this way, the teacher models the strategies an expert would use to solve the problem, so that students can use similar strategies on their own. Research on worked examples generally finds that they are effective if they alternate with problems students do on their own (e.g., one worked example followed by several problems of the same type) (Atkinson et al., 2000; Sweller, van Merrienboer, & Paas, 1998). Teaching students to stop during worked examples to explain to themselves (Renkl, Stark, Gruber, & Mandl, 1998) or to explain to a partner (Renkl, 1998) what is going on in each step enhances the effects of worked examples. Worked examples are particularly effective

rule–example–rule
Pattern of teaching concepts by presenting a rule or definition, giving examples, and then showing how examples illustrate the rule.

By working through examples with students, a teacher can demonstrate problem solving and decision making. Why is this an important instructional strategy? Why is hands-on experience important for students?

for students who are new to a given topic or skill (Kalyuga, Chandler, Tuovinen, & Sweller, 2001).

Demonstrations, Models, and Illustrations   Cognitive theorists emphasize the importance of students' seeing and, when appropriate, having hands-on experience with concepts and skills. Visual representations are maintained in long-term memory far more readily than is information that is only heard (Hiebert et al., 1991; Sousa, 2001). Showing, rather than just telling, is particularly essential for children who are acquiring English (August & Hakuta, 1997). Recall how Ms. Logan gave her students both hands-on experience (filling and tapping bottles) and a visual analogy (the Slinky representing sound waves) to give the students clear and lasting images of the main principles of sound. However, manipulatives (such as counting blocks) can be counterproductive to learning if they do not clearly relate to the concept being taught (Campbell & Mayer, 2004).

Embedded Video   Video, television, and DVD have long been used in education. However, a new use is showing particular promise. This is video or DVD material that is embedded in on-screen text or class lessons, used to illustrate key concepts. Research on embedded video finds that it helps children learn and retain information to the degree that it is easy to understand and it clearly links to the main content (Mayer & Moreno, 2002). For example, a year-long study by Chambers and colleagues (2004) found that adding brief animations and puppet videos to illustrate letter sounds and sound blending significantly increased first-graders' progress in reading.

CONNECTIONS

For more on the importance of attention in learning, see Chapter 6, page 169.

Maintaining Attention   Straight, dry lectures can be boring, and bored students soon stop paying attention to even the most carefully crafted lesson. For this reason teachers should introduce variety, activity, or humor to enliven the lecture and maintain student attention. For example, the use of humor has been found to increase student achievement (Droz & Ellis, 1996; Ziv, 1988), and illustrating a lecture with easily understood graphics can help to hold students' attention. On the other hand, too much variation in mode of presentation can hurt achievement if it distracts students from the lesson content (Wyckoff, 1973). Several studies have established that students learn more from lessons that are presented with enthusiasm and expressiveness than from dry lectures (Patrick, Hisley, & Kempler, 2000). In one sense, teaching is performing, and it appears that some of the qualities we would look for in a performer are also those that increase teachers' effectiveness (see Timpson & Tobin, 1982).

Content Coverage and Pacing One of the most important factors in effective teaching is the amount of content covered. In general, students of teachers who cover more material learn more than other students do (e.g., Barr, 1987; Barr & Dreeben, 1983). This does not necessarily mean that teachers should teach faster; obviously, there is such a thing as going too fast and leaving students behind. Yet research on instructional pace does imply that most teachers could increase their pace of instruction (Good et al., 1983), as long as degree of understanding is not sacrificed. In addition to increasing content coverage, a relatively rapid pace of instruction can help with classroom management.

Conduct Learning Probes

Imagine an archer who shoots arrows at a target but never finds out how close to the bull's-eye the arrows fall. The archer wouldn't be very accurate to begin with and would certainly never improve in accuracy. Similarly, effective teaching requires that teachers be constantly aware of the effects of their instruction. All too often, teachers mistakenly believe that if they have covered a topic well and students appear to be paying attention, then their instruction has been successful. Students often believe that if they have listened intently to an interesting lecture, they know the material presented. Yet this might not be true. If teachers do not regularly probe students' understanding of the material being presented, students might be left with serious misunderstandings or gaps in knowledge.

The term **learning probe** refers to a variety of ways of asking for brief student responses to lesson content. Learning probes give the teacher feedback on students' levels of understanding and allow students to try out their understanding of a new idea to find out whether they have it right. Learning probes can take the form of questions to the class, as in the sample lesson on World War II presented in Table 7.2, or brief written or physical demonstrations of understanding, as in the sample subtraction lesson in Table 7.1.

Checks for Understanding Whether the response to the learning probe is written, physical, or oral, the purpose of the probe is checking for understanding (Rosenshine & Stevens, 1986). That is, teachers use learning probes not so much to teach or to provide practice as to find out whether students have understood what they just heard. Teachers use the probes to set their pace of instruction. If students are having trouble, teachers must slow down and repeat explanations. If all students show understanding, the teacher can move on to new topics. The following interchange shows how a teacher might use learning probes to uncover student strengths and misunderstandings and then adjust instruction accordingly. The teacher, Mr. Swift, has written several sentences containing conversation on an overhead projector transparency, and students are learning the correct use of commas and quotation marks.

Mr. Swift: Now we are ready to punctuate some conversation. Everyone get out a sheet of paper and copy this sentence, adding punctuation where needed: Take the criminal downstairs Tom said condescendingly. Is everyone ready? . . . Carl, how did you punctuate the sentence?

CONNECTIONS

For more on the impact of time on learning, see Chapter 11, page 352.

learning probe
A method, such as questioning, that helps teachers find out whether students understand a lesson.

Carl: Quote take the criminal downstairs quote comma Tom said condescendingly period.

Mr. Swift: Close, but you made the most common error people make with quotation marks. Maria, what did you write?

Maria: I think I made the same mistake Carl did, but I understand now. It should be: Quote take the criminal downstairs comma quote Tom said condescendingly period.

Mr. Swift: Good. How many got this right the first time? [Half of class raises hands.] Okay, I see we still have some problems with this one. Remember, commas and periods go inside the quotation mark. I know that sometimes this doesn't make much sense, but if English always made sense, a lot of English teachers would be out of work! Think of quotation marks as wrappers for conversation, and the conversation, punctuation and all, goes inside the wrapper. Let's all try another. Drive carefully Tom said recklessly. Samphan?

Samphan: Quote drive carefully comma quote Tom said recklessly period.

Mr. Swift: Great! How many got it? [All but one or two raise hands.] Wonderful, I think you're all with me. The quotation marks "wrap up" the conversation, including its punctuation. Now let's all try one that's a little harder: I wonder Tom said quizzically whether quotation marks will be on the test.

This interchange contains several features worth noting. First, Mr. Swift had all students work out the punctuation, called on individuals for answers, and then asked all students whether they got the right answers. This is preferable to asking only one or two students to work (say, on the chalkboard) while the others watch, thus wasting the time of most of the class. When all students have to figure out the punctuation and no one knows on whom Mr. Swift will call, all students actively participate and test their own knowledge, and Mr. Swift gets a quick reading on the level of understanding of the class as a whole.

Note also that when Mr. Swift found that half the class missed the first item, he took time to reteach the skill students were having trouble with, using a different explanation from the one he had used in his first presentation. By giving students the mental image of quotation marks as wrappers, he helped them to remember the order of punctuation in conversation. When almost all students got the second item, he moved to the next step, because the class had apparently mastered the first one.

Finally, note that Mr. Swift had plenty of sentences prepared on the overhead projector, so he did not have to use class time to write out sentences. Learning probes should always be brief and should not be allowed to destroy the tempo of the lesson. By being prepared with sentences for learning probes, Mr. Swift was able to maintain student involvement and interest. In fact, he might have done even better if he had given students photocopies with unpunctuated sentences on them to reduce the time used in copying the sentences.

Questions   Questions to students in the course of the lesson serve many purposes (Dantonio & Beisenherz, 2001). Teachers use questions as Socrates used them, to prompt students to take the next mental step; for example, "Now that we've learned that heating a gas makes it expand, what do you suppose would happen if we cool a gas?" (Tredway, 1995). Teachers also use questions to encourage students to think further about information they learned previously or to get a discussion started; for example, "We've learned that if we boil water, it becomes water vapor. Now, water vapor is a colorless, odorless, invisible gas. In that case, why do you suppose we can see steam coming out of a tea kettle?" With guidance, a class discussion would eventually arrive at the answer, which is that the water vapor recondenses when it hits the relatively cool air and that what is visible in steam is water droplets, not vapor. Teachers often find

Why are questions valuable learning probes? What value can students gain by learning to ask good questions of each other?

it helpful to have students generate their own questions, either for themselves or for each other (King, 1992). A great deal of evidence indicates that students gain from generating their own questions (Foos, Mora, & Tkacz, 1994; Rosenshine, Meister, & Chapman, 1996; Wittrock, 1991), especially questions that relate to students' existing background knowledge about a topic they are studying (King, 1994).

Finally, teachers can use questions as learning probes (Airsian, 1994). In fact, any question is to some degree a learning probe, in that the quality of response will indicate to the teacher how well students are learning the lesson. Research on the frequency of questions indicates that teachers who ask more questions related to the lesson at hand are more instructionally effective than are those who ask relatively few questions (Dunkin & Biddle, 1974; Gall et al., 1978; Stallings & Kaskowitz, 1974). At all levels of schooling, factual questions generally help with factual skills (Clark et al., 1979) and questions that encourage students to think about concepts help with conceptual skills (Fagan, Hassler, & Szabo, 1981; Gall, 1984; Redfield & Rousseau, 1981).

ON THE WEB

For questioning techniques see the Questioning Toolkit at **www.fno.org.**

Wait Time   One issue related to questioning that has received much research attention is **wait time,** the length of time the teacher waits for a student to answer a question before giving the answer or going on to another student. Research has found that teachers tend to give up too rapidly on students whom they perceive to be low achievers, a practice that tells those students that the teacher expects little from them (Rowe, 1974; Tobin & Capie, 1982).

Teachers who wait approximately 3 seconds after asking a student a question obtain better learning results than do those who give up more rapidly (Tobin, 1986). Furthermore, following up with students who do not respond has been associated with higher achievement (Anderson, Evertson, & Brophy, 1979; Larrivee, 1985). Waiting for students to respond or staying with them when they do not communicates

wait time
Length of time that a teacher waits for a student to answer a question.

positive expectations for them. On the other hand, there is such a thing as waiting too long. A study by Duell (1994) found that a wait time as long as 6 seconds had a small negative effect on the achievement of university students.

Calling Order In classroom questioning, **calling order** is a concern. Calling on volunteers is perhaps the most common method, but this allows some students to avoid participating in the lesson by keeping their hands down (Brophy & Evertson, 1974).

Common sense would suggest that when the question is a problem to be worked (as in math), all students should work the problem before any individual is called on. When questions are not problems to be worked, it is probably best to pose the question to the class as a whole and then ask a randomly chosen student (not necessarily a volunteer) to answer. Some teachers even carry around a class list on a clipboard and check off the students called on to make sure that all get frequent chances to respond, or put students' names on popsicle sticks and draw them at random from a can (Freiberg, 1999; Weinstein & Mignano, 1997). One teacher put her students' names on cards, shuffled them before class, and randomly selected cards to decide which student to call on. This system worked well until one student found the cards after class and removed his name from the deck!

In conducting learning probes, teachers might find it especially important to ask questions of students who usually perform above, at, and below the class average to be sure that all students understand the lesson.

Choral Response Researchers generally favor the frequent use of **choral responses** when there is only one possible correct answer (Becker & Carnine, 1980; Hunter, 1982; Rosenshine & Stevens, 1986). For example, the teacher might say, "Class, in the words listed on the board [*write, wring, wrong*], what sound does the *wr* make?" To which the class responds together, "Rrrr!" Similarly, when appropriate, teachers can ask all students to use hand signals to indicate true or false, to hold up a certain number of fingers to indicate an answer in math, or to write a short answer on a small chalkboard and hold it up on cue (Hunter, 1982). Research finds this type of all-pupil response has a positive effect on student learning (McKenzie, 1979; McKenzie & Henry, 1979). In the subtraction with renaming example used earlier in this chapter, recall that all students worked with popsicle sticks at their desks, and the teacher walked around to check their work. All-student responses give students many opportunities to respond and give the teacher information on the entire class's level of knowledge and confidence.

Provide Independent Practice

The term **independent practice** refers to work students do in class on their own to practice or express newly learned skills or knowledge. For example, after hearing a lesson on solving equations in algebra, students need an opportunity to work several equations on their own without interruptions, both to crystallize their new knowledge and to help the teacher assess their knowledge. Practice is an essential step in the process of transferring new information in working memory to long-term memory.

Independent practice is most critical when students are learning skills, such as mathematics, reading, grammar, composition, map interpretation, or a foreign language. Students can no more learn arithmetic, writing, or Spanish without practicing than they could learn to ride a bicycle from lectures alone. By contrast, independent practice is less necessary for certain concept lessons, such as the lesson on the origins of World War II outlined in Table 7.2 or a science lesson on the concept of magnetic attraction. In lessons of this kind, teachers can use independent practice to let students rehearse knowledge or concepts on their own, as the teacher did in the World War II

calling order The order in which students are called on by the teacher to answer questions during the course of a lesson.

choral responses Responses to questions made by an entire class in unison.

independent practice Component of instruction in which students work by themselves to demonstrate and rehearse new knowledge.

lesson, but rehearsal is not as central to this type of lesson as practice of skills is to a subtraction lesson.

Seatwork   Classic research on **seatwork,** or in-class independent practice, suggests that it is typically both overused and misused (Anderson, 1985; Brophy & Good, 1986). Several researchers have found that student time spent receiving instruction directly from the teacher is more productive than time spent in seatwork (Brophy & Evertson, 1974; Evertson, Emmer, & Brophy, 1980; Good & Grouws, 1977). For example, Evertson and colleagues (1980) found that the most effective seventh- and eighth-grade math teachers in their study spent about 16 minutes on lecture–demonstration and 19 minutes on seatwork, while the least effective teachers spent less than 7 minutes on lecture–demonstration and about 25 minutes on seatwork. Yet studies of elementary mathematics and reading classes found students spending 50 to 70 percent of their class time doing seatwork (Fisher et al., 1978; Rosenshine, 1980). Anderson, Brubaker, Alleman-Brooks, and Duffy (1985) have noted that time spent on seatwork is often wasted for students who lack the motivation, reading skills, or self-organization skills to work well on their own. Many students simply give up when they run into difficulties. Others fill out worksheets with little care for correctness, apparently interpreting the task as finishing the paper rather than learning the material.

Effective Use of Independent Practice Time   A set of recommendations for effective use of independent practice time, derived from the work of Anderson (1985), Evertson and colleagues (2000), and Good and colleagues (1983), follows.

1. Do not assign independent practice until you are sure students can do it. This is probably the most important principle. Independent practice is practice, not instruction, and the students should be able to do most of the items they are assigned to do on their own (Brophy & Good, 1986). In cognitive terms, practice serves as rehearsal for transferring information from working memory to long-term memory. For this to work, the information must first be established in students' working memories.

A high success rate on independent practice work can be accomplished in two ways. First, assignments should be clear and self-explanatory and should cover content on which all students can succeed. Second, students should rarely be given independent practice worksheets until they have indicated in learning probes that they can handle the material. For example, a teacher might use the first items of a worksheet as learning probes, assigning them one at a time and discussing each one after students have attempted it until it is clear that all or almost all students have the right idea.

2. Keep independent practice assignments short. There is rarely a justification for long independent practice assignments. About 10 minutes of work is adequate for most objectives, but this is far less than what most teachers assign (Rosenshine, 1980). Massed practice (e.g., many items at one sitting) has a limited effect on retention. Students are more likely to profit from relatively brief independent practice in class supplemented by distributed practice such as homework (Dempster, 1989; Krug, Davis, & Glover, 1990).

3. Give clear instructions. In the lower grades, ask students to read aloud or paraphrase the instructions to be sure that they have understood them.

4. Get students started, and then avoid interruptions. When students start on their independent practice work, circulate among them to be sure that everyone is under way before attending to the problems of individual students or other tasks. Once students have begun, avoid interrupting them.

5. Monitor independent work. It is important to monitor independent work (see Medley, 1979), for example, by walking around the class while students are doing

CONNECTIONS
For more on working memory and long-term memory, see Chapter 6, pages 169 and 171.

CERTIFICATION POINTER
Your teacher certification test may require you to choose the *least* effective teaching strategy to achieve a particular curriculum objective. You should know that one of the least effective strategies for having students practice a skill they have just learned is to have them doing long, independent seatwork, on which they do not get feedback.

seatwork
Work that students are assigned to do independently during class.

their assignment. This helps to keep students working and makes the teacher easily available for questions. Teachers can also look in on students who may be struggling, to give them additional assistance.

6. Collect independent work and include it in student grades. A major problem with seatwork as it is often used is that students see no reason to do their best on it because it has little or no bearing on their grades. Students should usually know that their seatwork will be collected and will count toward their grade. To this end, it is a good idea to save a few minutes at the end of each class period to briefly read answers to assigned questions and allow students to check their own papers or exchange papers with partners. Then students may pass in their papers for spot checking and recording. This procedure gives students immediate feedback on their seatwork and relieves the teacher of having to check all papers every day. Make this checking time brief to avoid taking time from instruction.

CONNECTIONS
For in-depth coverage of assessment, see Chapter 13.

INTASC

8 Assessment of Student Learning

Assess Performance and Provide Feedback

Every lesson should contain an assessment of the degree to which students have mastered the objectives set for the lesson. The teacher might do this assessment informally by questioning students, might use independent work as an assessment, or might give a separate quiz. One way or another, however, teachers should assess the effectiveness of the lesson and should give the results of the assessment to students as soon as possible (Gusky, 2003). For example, research has found frequent use of classroom assessment of the content of instruction improves children's reading skills (Taylor, Pearson, Clark, & Walpole, 2000). Students need to know when they are right and when they are wrong if they are to use feedback to improve their performance. In addition to assessing the results of each lesson, teachers need to test students from time to time on their learning of larger units of information. In general, more frequent testing results in greater achievement than does less frequent testing, but any testing is much more effective than none at all (Bangert-Drowns, Kulik, & Kulik, 1986). Feedback to students is important, but feedback to teachers on student performance is probably even more important. If students are learning everything they are taught, it might be possible to pick up the pace of instruction. On the other hand, if assessment reveals serious misunderstandings, instructors can re-teach the lesson or take other steps to get students back on track. If some students mastered the lesson and some did not, it might be appropriate to give more instruction just to the students who need it.

Provide Distributed Practice and Review

Practice or review spaced out over time increases retention of many kinds of knowledge (Dempster, 1989). This has several implications for teaching. First, it implies that reviewing and recapitulating important information from earlier lessons enhances learning. Students particularly need to review important material at long intervals (e.g., monthly) to maintain previous skills. In addition, teachers should assign homework in most subjects, especially at the secondary level. Homework gives students a chance to practice skills learned in one setting at one time (school) and in another setting at a different time (home). Research on homework finds that it generally does increase achievement, particularly if teachers check it and give comments to students (Cooper et al., 1998; Keith, Reimers, Fehrmann, Pottebaum, & Aubey, 1986).

"My problem is just the opposite. My students want more homework and their parents want less. I'm a sex education teacher!"

Teaching Dilemmas: Cases to Consider

Designing Lessons

Mr. Benson has been teaching secondary social studies for several years. When he was a student, he had one remarkable history teacher who made the subject come alive for him and inspired him to become a teacher. When he was hired to teach world history in a high school, he thought that nothing could be better. But over the years he has come to realize that there is just too much to cover in the course, and he is growing frustrated. Today, he is attending a conference sponsored by the state social studies curriculum adoption committee. In a roundtable discussion with other high school teachers and a professor from a local state university, Mr. Benson learns that he is not alone.

Mr. Benson: My textbook has forty-three chapters, and there are only thirty-six weeks in the school year, so I'm behind before I even start. I teach every lesson in an organized way: On Mondays, we review what we studied last week, and I orient the class to this week's subject matter and learning objectives. On Tuesdays and Wednesdays, I present the new material and question students along the way to be sure they understand the main points. On Thursdays, I have the students work on independent projects, such as papers, debates, or media projects related to the week's material. On Fridays, I give the class a quiz, and we discuss the answers to the quiz, as well as remaining issues from the chapter.

Ms. Rodriguez: And you're trying to pack all of world history into this routine? How do your students handle it?

Mr. Benson: I'm starting to get a lot of remarks like, "I have other classes that I have to read for, too" and "I can't remember all this stuff." And I'm just not able to make history exciting for them, like it was for me as a student.

Mr. Johnson: We just can't teach everything. There is too much to learn. Entire college courses are devoted to single units or topics that we are expected to cover within a week or two.

Mr. Benson: But what can we leave out? I know that with state curriculum exams coming up this semester, we'll get the usual criticism afterward that the students just don't know the facts of history.

Mr. Smith: Is it more important that they know the current and up-to-date historical events than the ancient ones? I know I never get as far as the middle twentieth century, so how many kids really have a good understanding of World War II, the Korean War, or the Vietnam conflict?

Professor Forsyth: At our university, in our social studies methods courses, we're emphasizing "real history"—telling students specific stories that make history come alive. For instance, a lesson can focus on the civil rights movement in one southern community, and students can read some of the legal papers written by Thurgood Marshall about the movement. It's not just coverage of the subject that is important. Real history occurs when one gets a microscope and just looks at one single, small event until it is understood. Then the individual owns it.

Mr. Benson: That's what makes me love history, but if I were to have my students study something in depth and look at historical instances that enrich, I'd have even less time to teach. I have lesson plans to cover, a resource file that's too thick and never gets used, and ideas for cooperative learning activities and critical thinking questions that I never have time to include. How can I cover it all?

@ Questions for Reflection

1. Evaluate Mr. Benson's use of direct instruction as he describes it. What are the strengths of his approach? What might be its limitations?
2. How can Mr. Benson incorporate Professor Forsyth's "real history" approach into his teaching? What difference do you think this would make in his students' comprehension and appreciation of the subject matter? What difference could it make in their curriculum exam scores?
3. How can Mr. Benson and his colleagues cover it all? Or should they attempt to do so? Discuss your thoughts with your classmates.

Source: Adapted from "Breadth versus Depth: Curricular Conflicts in a Secondary Classroom" by J. Merrell Hansen, from Allyn & Bacon's Custom Cases in Education, edited by Greta Morine-Dershimer, Paul Eggen, and Donald Kauchak. Copyright © 2000 by Pearson Education. Adapted by permission of the publisher.

However, the effects of homework are not as clear in elementary schools as they are at the secondary level (Cooper & Valentine, 2001; Corno, 1996), and assigning excessively lengthy or boring homework can actually be detrimental to learning and motivation (Corno, 2000). Good and Brophy (2003) recommend 5 to 10 minutes of homework per subject for fourth-graders, increasing to 30 minutes or more per subject for college-bound high school students. Homework can provide a means for parents to become constructively engaged in their children's schooling (Epstein & Van Voorhis, 2001; Xu & Corno, 2003), but it can also become a significant source of conflict in the home, especially for children having difficulty with the content (Walker & Hoover-Dempsey, 2001).

WHAT DOES RESEARCH ON DIRECT INSTRUCTION METHODS SUGGEST?

Most of the principles of direct instruction discussed in this chapter have been derived from **process–product studies,** in which observers recorded the teaching practices of teachers whose students consistently achieved at a high level and compared them to those of teachers whose students made less progress. These principles have been assembled into specific direct instruction programs and evaluated in field experiments; that is, other teachers have been trained in the methods used by successful teachers, and their students' achievement has been compared to that of students whose teachers did not receive the training.

Many studies have found a correlation between student achievement and teachers' use of strategies associated with direct instruction (e.g., Gage & Needels, 1989; Weinert & Helmke, 1995). However, experimental studies that compare the achievement of students whose teachers have been trained in specific direct instruction strategies to that of students whose teachers have not received this training have shown more mixed results. In classic studies of a direct instruction math approach called the Missouri Mathematics Program (MMP), Good and Grouws (1979) and Good et al. (1983) found that fourth-graders whose teachers used the MMP methods learned more than did students whose teachers were not trained in MMP. Evaluations of another direct instruction model, Madeline Hunter's (1982, 1995) Mastery Teaching program, did not generally find that the students of teachers trained in the model learned more than other students (Mandeville, 1992; Mandeville & Rivers, 1991; Slavin, 1986). A more recent study of explicit teaching, a form of direct instruction, found that this method made no difference in reading achievement of low achievers unless the method was supplemented by peer tutoring (Simmons, Fuchs, Fuchs, Mathes, & Hodge, 1995). More successful have been direct instruction models that place a greater emphasis on building teachers' classroom management skills (e.g., Evertson, Weade, Green, & Crawford, 1985) and models that improve teachers' use of reading groups (Anderson et al., 1979).

Studies of Direct Instruction (DI, formerly called DISTAR), a direct instruction program built around specific teaching materials and structured methods, have found strong positive effects of this approach in elementary schools, particularly with low achievers and at-risk students (Adams & Engelmann, 1996; Carnine, Grosen, & Silbert, 1995; Ellis, 2001; Herman, 1999). One study (Meyer, 1984) followed the progress of students from an inner-city Brooklyn, New York, neighborhood who had been in DI classes in first through third grades and found that these students were considerably more likely to graduate from high school than were students in a similar Brooklyn school who had not been taught with DI. Other studies have also found positive long-term effects of this approach (Gersten & Carnine, 1984; Gersten & Keating, 1987; Meyer, Gersten, & Gutkin, 1983).

Although the research on direct instruction models has had mixed conclusions, most researchers agree that the main elements of these models are essential minimum skills that all teachers should have (see Gage & Needels, 1989). In fact, most of the recommendations from direct instruction research are so commonsensical that they seem obvious. A study by Wong (1995), however, found that the opposites of some direct instruction principles also seemed obvious to teachers and university students.

process–product studies
Research approach in which the teaching practices of effective teachers are recorded through classroom observation.

When studies find no differences between teachers trained in the models and other teachers, it is often because both groups of teachers already had most of the direct instruction skills before the training took place (see Slavin, 1986).

Advantages and Limitations of Direct Instruction

It is clear that direct instruction methods can improve the teaching of certain basic skills, but it is equally clear that much is yet to be learned about how and for what purposes they should be used. The prescriptions derived from studies of effective teachers cannot be applied uncritically in the classroom and expected to make a substantial difference in student achievement. Structured, systematic instructional programs based on these prescriptions can markedly improve student achievement in basic skills, but it is important to remember that the research on direct instruction has focused mostly on basic reading and mathematics, mostly in the elementary grades. For other subjects and at other grade levels we have less of a basis for believing that direct instruction methods will improve student learning.

How DO STUDENTS LEARN AND TRANSFER CONCEPTS?

INTASC

2 Knowledge of Human Development and Learning

4 Multiple Instructional Strategies

A very large proportion of all lessons focus on teaching concepts (see Klausmeier, 1992). A **concept** is an abstract idea that is generalized from specific examples. For example, a red ball, a red pencil, and a red chair all illustrate the simple concept "red." A green book is not an instance of the concept "red." If you were shown the red ball, pencil, and chair and asked to say what they have in common, you would produce the concept "red objects." If the green book were also included, you would have to fall back on the much broader concept "objects."

Of course, many concepts are far more complex and less well defined than the concept "red." For example, the concept "justice" is one that people might spend a lifetime trying to understand. This book is engaged primarily in teaching concepts; in fact, at this very moment you are reading about the concept "concept"!

Concept Learning and Teaching

Concepts are generally learned in one of two ways. Most concepts that we learn outside of school we learn by observation. For example, a child learns the concept "car" by hearing certain vehicles referred to as "cars." Initially, the child might include SUVs or motorcycles under the concept "car"; but as time goes on, the concept is refined until the child can clearly differentiate "car" from "noncar." Similarly, the child learns the more difficult concepts "naughty," "clean," and "fun" by observation and experience.

Other concepts are typically learned by definition. For example, it is very difficult to learn the concepts "aunt" or "uncle" by observation alone. One could observe hundreds of "aunts" and "nonaunts" without deriving a clear concept of "aunt." In this case the concept is best learned by definition: To be an aunt, one must be a female whose brother or sister (or brother- or sister-in-law) has children. With this definition, instances and noninstances of "aunt" can be readily differentiated.

Definitions Just as children can learn concepts in two ways, instructors can teach them in two ways. Teachers might give students instances and noninstances of a

concept
An abstract idea that is generalized from specific examples.

concept and later ask them to derive or infer a definition. Or teachers might give students a definition and then ask them to identify instances and noninstances. Some concepts lend themselves to the example–definition approach. For most concepts that are taught in school, it makes most sense to state a definition, present several instances (and noninstances, if appropriate), and then restate the definition, showing how the instances typify the definition. For example, we might define the concept "learning" as "a change in an individual caused by experience." Instances might include learning of skills, of information, of behaviors, and of emotions. Noninstances might include maturational changes, such as changes in behaviors or emotions caused by the onset of puberty. Finally, we might restate the definition and discuss it in light of the instances and noninstances.

Examples   Teaching concepts involves extensive and skillful use of examples. Tennyson and Park (1980, p. 59) suggest that teachers follow three rules when presenting examples of concepts:

1. Order the examples from easy to difficult.
2. Select examples that differ from one another.
3. Compare and contrast examples and nonexamples.

Consider the concept "mammal." Easy examples are dogs, cats, and humans, and nonexamples are insects, reptiles, and fish. No problem so far. But what about dolphins? Bats? Snakes that bear live young? Kangaroos? Each of these is a more difficult example or nonexample of the concept "mammal"; it challenges the simplistic belief, based on experience, that terrestrial animals that bear live young are mammals and that aquatic animals, birds, and other egg-layers are not. The easy examples (dogs versus fish) establish the concept in general, but the more difficult examples (snakes versus whales) test the true boundaries of the concept. Students should thoroughly understand simple examples before tackling the odd cases.

Teaching for Transfer of Learning

Students often get so wrapped up in preparing for tests, and teachers in preparing students to take tests, that both forget the primary purpose of school: to give students the skills and knowledge necessary for them to function effectively as adults. If a student can fill in blanks on a language arts test but cannot write a clear letter to a friend or a prospective employer, or can multiply with decimals and percents on a math test but cannot figure sales tax, then that student's education has been sadly misdirected. Yet all too frequently, students who do very well in school or on tests are unable to transfer their knowledge or skills to real-life situations.

Real-Life Learning   **Transfer of learning** from one situation to another depends on the degree to which the information or skills were learned in the original situation and on the degree of similarity between the situation in which the skill or concept was learned and the situation to which it is to be applied (Bransford, Brown, & Cocking, 1999; Pressley & Yokoi, 1994; Price & Driscoll, 1997; Smagorinsky & Smith, 1992). These principles, known since the beginning of the twentieth century, have important implications for teaching. We cannot simply assume that students will be able to transfer their school learning to practical situations, so we must teach them to use skills in situations like those they are likely to encounter in real life or in other situations to which we expect learning to transfer. Students must receive specific instruction in how to use their skills and information to solve problems and encounter a variety of problem-solving experiences if they are to be able to apply much of what they learned in school.

transfer of learning
The application of knowledge acquired in one situation to new situations.

This woman has been able to transfer knowledge about math concepts to help with her personal finances. As a teacher, how will you ensure that your students are able to transfer what they have learned in the classroom to real-life situations?

The most important thing to know about transfer of learning is that it cannot be assumed (Cox, 1997). Just because a student has mastered a skill or concept in one setting or circumstance, there is no guarantee whatsoever that the student will be able to apply this skill or concept to a new setting, even if the setting seems (at least to the teacher) to be very similar (Mayer & Wittrock, 1996). Classic examples are people who score well on tests of grammar and punctuation but cannot apply these skills in their own compositions (Smagorinsky & Smith, 1992) and people who can solve all sorts of math problems in school but do not apply their math knowledge in real life. As an example of this, Lave (1988) describes a man in a weight-loss program who was faced with the problem of measuring out a serving of cottage cheese that was three-quarters of the usual two-thirds cup allowance. The man, who had passed college calculus, measured out two-thirds of a cup of cottage cheese, dumped it out in a circle on a cutting board, marked a cross on it, and scooped away one quadrant. It never occurred to him to multiply $2/3 \times 3/4 = 1/2$, an operation that almost any sixth-grader could do on paper (but few could apply in a practical situation).

Initial Learning and Understanding   Not surprisingly, one of the most important factors in transfer of a skill or concept from one situation to another is how well the skill or concept was learned in the first place (Pressley & Yokoi, 1994). However, it matters a great deal how well students understood the material, and to what degree it was taught in a meaningful way (Bereiter, 1995; Mayer & Wittrock, 1996). In other words, material that is memorized by rote is unlikely to transfer to new situations no matter how thoroughly it was mastered.

Learning in Context   If transfer of learning depends in large part on similarity between the situation in which information is learned and that in which it is applied, then how can we teach in the school setting so that students will be able to apply their knowledge in the very different setting of real life?

One important principle of transfer is that the ability to apply knowledge in new circumstances depends in part on the variety of circumstances in which we have learned or practiced the information or skill (Bereiter, 1995). For example, a few

---

Table 7.3

Teaching of Concepts

Research demonstrates that to teach a new concept, teachers should first present examples of the concept used in similar contexts and then offer examples in widely different contexts. This approach promotes the students' abilities to transfer the concept to new situations. The example here comes from a classic study in which students learned new concepts from the traditional culture of cowboys.

Concept to be taught: *Minge*

Definition: To gang up on a person or thing.

Same-Context Examples	*Varied-Context Examples*
The three riders decided to converge on the cow.	The band of sailors angrily denounced the captain and threatened a mutiny.
Four people took part in branding the horse.	A group in the audience booed the inept magician's act.
They circled the wolf so it would not escape.	The junk dealer was helpless to defend himself from the three thieves.
All six cowboys fought against the rustler.	All six cowboys fought against the rustler.

Source: From John D. Bransford, *Human Cognition*, Wadsworth Publishing, 1979. (Adapted from an unpublished doctoral thesis titled *Structuring Decontextualized Forms of Knowledge* by Nitsch, 1977.) Reprinted by permission of John D. Bransford.

---

weeks' experience as a parking attendant, driving all sorts of cars, would probably be better than years of experience driving one kind of car for enabling a person to drive a completely new and different car (at least in a parking lot!).

In teaching concepts, one way to increase the chance that students will appropriately apply the concepts to new situations is to give examples from a range of situations. A set of classic experiments by Nitsch (1977) illustrated this principle. Students were given definitions of words and were then presented with examples to illustrate the concepts. Some received several examples in the same context; others received examples from mixed contexts. For example, *minge* is a cowboy word meaning "to gang up on." The examples are shown in Table 7.3.

Students who received only the same-context examples could identify additional examples in the same context but were less successful in applying the concepts to new contexts. By contrast, the students who learned with the varied-context examples had some difficulties in learning the concept at first but, once they did, were able to apply it to new situations. The best strategy was a hybrid in which students received the same-context examples first and then the varied-context examples.

Teachers can use many other ways to increase the probability that information or skills learned in one context will transfer to other contexts, particularly to real-life applications. For example, simulations can approximate real-life conditions, as when secondary students prepare for job interviews by acting out interviews with teachers or peers pretending to be interviewers. Teachers can also facilitate transfer by introducing skills learned in one setting into a new setting. For example, a history teacher might do well to find out what writing or grammar skills are being taught in English classes and then remind students to use these same skills in history essays (Anderson, Reder, & Simon, 1996; White & Frederiksen, 1998).

"I wasn't copying. I was transferring knowledge from one context to another!"

Transfer versus Initial Learning   What makes transfer tricky is that some of the most effective procedures for enhancing transfer are exactly the opposite of those for initial learning. As the Nitsch (1977) study illustrated, teaching a concept in many different contexts confused students if it was done at the beginning of a sequence of instruction, but it enhanced transfer if it was done after students understood the concept in one setting. This principle holds important implications for teaching. In introducing a new concept, teachers should use similar examples until students understand the concept and use diverse examples that still demonstrate the essential aspects of the concept (Reimann & Schult, 1996).

As one example of this, consider a series of lessons on evolution. In introducing the concept, a teacher should first use clear examples of how animals evolved in ways that increased their chances of survival in their environments, using such examples as the evolution of flippers in seals or the evolution of humps in camels. Then the teacher might present evolution in plants (e.g., evolution of a waxy skin on desert plants), somewhat broadening the concept. Next, the teacher might discuss the evolution of social behaviors (such as cooperation in lions, baboons, and humans); finally, the teacher might explore phenomena that resemble the evolutionary process (such as the modification of businesses in response to selective pressures of free-market economies). In this way, the teacher first establishes the idea of evolution in one clear context (animals) and then gradually broadens the concept until students can see how processes in quite different contexts demonstrate the principles of selective adaptation. If the teacher had begun the lessons with a mixed discussion of animals, plants, societies, and businesses, it would have been too confusing. If the teacher had never moved beyond the evolution of animals, the concept would not have had much chance of transferring to different contexts. After learning about the concept of evolution in many different contexts, students are much more likely to be able to distinguish scientific and metaphorical uses and apply the concept to a completely new context, such as the evolution of art in response to changes in society (Bransford, Brown, & Cocking, 1999).

It is important in teaching for transfer not only to provide many examples, but also to point out in each example how the essential features of the concept are reflected (Kosonen & Winne, 1995). In the evolution lessons the teacher might explain the central process as it applied to each particular case. The development of cooperation among lions, for instance, shows how a social trait evolved because groups of lions that cooperated were better able than others to catch game, to survive, and to ensure that their offspring would survive. Pointing out the essential elements in each example helps students apply a concept to new instances they have never encountered (Anderson, Reder, & Simon, 1996). Similarly, comparing cases or situations illustrates a given concept, and pointing out similarities and differences between them can enhance transfer (Bulgren et al., 2002; Gentner, Loewenstein, & Thompson, 2003).

Explicit Teaching for Transfer   Students can be explicitly taught to transfer skills to new circumstances. For example, Fuchs and colleagues (2003) evaluated an "explicit transfer" technique in third-grade math classes. Children in the explicit transfer condition were taught what transfer means and were given examples of how the same kind of story problems could be changed using different language, different contexts, and different numbers. They were also taught to look at story problems to see if they resembled problems they had done before. For example, one problem asked how many packages of lemon drops (10 to a package) you'd have to buy to get 32 lemon drops. They then presented the same problem worded differently, with additional questions added, with different contexts, and so on. Teaching students how to look for commonalities among story problems significantly enhanced their success on transfer tasks.

*H*OW ARE DISCUSSIONS USED IN INSTRUCTION?

INTASC

4 Multiple Instructional
Strategies

Teachers use discussions as part of instruction for many reasons (see Gall, 1987), as detailed in the sections below.

Subjective and Controversial Topics

Questions in many subjects do not have simple answers. There may be one right answer to an algebra problem or one right way to conjugate a German verb, but is there one right set of factors that explains what caused the Civil War? How were Shakespeare's writings influenced by the politics of his day? Should genetic engineering be banned as a danger to world health? These and many other questions have no clear-cut answers, so it is important for students to discuss and understand these issues instead of simply receiving and rehearsing information or skills. Such subjects as history, government, economics, literature, art, and music include many issues that lend themselves to discussion and multiple and diverse explanations. Research finds that discussing controversial issues increases knowledge about the issues as well as encouraging deeper understanding of the various sides of an issue (Johnson & Johnson, 1999).

Difficult and Novel Concepts

In addition to subjective and controversial subjects, discussions can clarify topics that do contain single right answers but which involve difficult concepts that force students to see something in a different way. For example, a science teacher could simply give a lesson on buoyancy and specific gravity. However, since this lesson would challenge a simplistic view of why things float ("Things float because they are light"), students might understand buoyancy and specific gravity better if they had an opportunity to make and defend their own theories about why things float and if they faced such questions as "If things float because they are light, then why does a battleship float?" and "If you threw certain objects in a lake, they would sink part way but not to the bottom. Why would they stop sinking?" In searching together for theories to explain these phenomena, students might gain an appreciation for the meaning of buoyancy and specific gravity that a lecture alone could not provide.

Affective Objectives

Teachers might also use discussions when affective objectives (objectives that are concerned with student attitudes and values) are of particular importance. For example, a course on civics or government contains much information to be taught about how our government works but also involves important values to be transmitted, such as civic duty and patriotism. A teacher could teach "six reasons why it is important to vote," but the real objective here is not to teach reasons for voting, but rather to instill respect for the democratic process and a commitment to register and vote when the time comes. Similarly, a discussion of peer pressure might be directed at giving students the skills and the willingness to say no when classmates pressure them to engage in illegal, unhealthy, or undesirable behaviors. A long tradition of research in social psychology has established that group discussion, particularly when group members must publicly commit themselves, is far more effective at changing individuals' attitudes and behaviors than is even the most persuasive lecture.

Whole-Class Discussions

Discussions take two principal forms. In one, the entire class discusses an issue, with the teacher as moderator (Gunter, Estes, & Schwab, 2003; Tredway, 1995). In the other, students form small groups (usually with four to six students in each group) to discuss a topic, and the teacher moves from group to group, aiding the discussion.

A **whole-class discussion** differs from a usual lesson because the teacher plays a less dominant role. Teachers may guide the discussion and help the class avoid dead ends, but should encourage the students to come up with their own ideas. The following vignette illustrates an inquiry-oriented discussion led (but not dominated) by a teacher, who wants students to explore and develop their own ideas about a topic using information they have recently learned:

Ms. Wilson: In the past few weeks we've been learning about the events leading up to the American Revolution. Of course, since we are all Americans, we tend to take the side of the revolutionaries. We use the term *Patriots* to describe them; King George probably used a less favorable term. Yet many of the colonists were Loyalists, and at times, the Loyalists outnumbered the Patriots. Let's think about how Loyalists would have argued against the idea of independence from Britain.

Beth: I think they'd say King George was a good king.

Vinnie: But what about all the things he did to the colonists?

Ms. Wilson: Give some examples.

Vinnie: Like the Intolerable Acts. The colonists had to put up British soldiers in their own houses, and they closed Boston Harbor.

Tanya: But those were to punish the colonists for the Boston Tea Party. The Loyalists would say that the Patriots caused all the trouble in the first place.

Ms. Wilson: Good point.

Frank: I think the Loyalists would say, "You may not like everything he does, but King George is still our king."

Richard: The Loyalists probably thought the Sons of Liberty were a bunch of thugs.

Ms. Wilson: Well, I wouldn't put it quite that way, but I think you're right. What did they do that makes you think that?

Ramon: They destroyed things and harassed the Loyalists and the British troops. Like they called them names and threw things at them.

Ms. Wilson: How do you think Loyalists would feel about the Boston Massacre?

Beth: They'd say those thugs got what they deserved. They'd think that it was Sam Adams's fault for getting everyone all stirred up.

Ms. Wilson: Let's think about it another way. We live in California. Our nation's capital, Washington, is three thousand miles away. We have to pay all kinds of taxes, and a lot of those taxes go to help people in Boston or Baltimore rather than people here. Many of the things our government does make people in California mad. We've got plenty of food, and we can make just about anything we want to right here. Why don't we have a California Revolution and have our own country?

Sara: But we're part of America!

Tanya: We can't do that! The army would come and put down the revolution!

Ms. Wilson: Don't you think that the Loyalists thought some of the same things?

Vinnie: But we can vote and they couldn't.

Ramon: Right. Taxation without representation!

Beth: I'll bet a lot of Loyalists thought the British would win the war and it would be better to stay on the side of the winners.

In this discussion the teacher was not looking for any particular facts about the American Revolution, but rather was trying to get students to use the information they had learned previously to discuss issues from a different perspective. Ms. Wilson

whole-class discussion
A discussion among all the students in the class with the teacher as moderator.

let the students determine the direction of the discussion to a substantial degree. Her main tasks were to keep the discussion rolling, to get students to use specifics to defend their positions, to ensure that many students participated, and to help the students avoid dead ends or unproductive avenues.

> **ON THE WEB**
>
> For an example of how to conduct an effective class discussion go to **www.ncrel.org/ sdrs/areas/issues/students/learning/lr1jungl.htm.**

CERTIFICATION POINTER

For your teacher certification test you will need to demonstrate your understanding of the principles and techniques associated with a variety of instructional strategies. For example, you might be asked to identify the curricular goals that whole-class discussion would be appropriate for and how you would structure the discussion so it would be effective.

Information before Discussion   Before beginning a discussion, teachers must ensure that students have an adequate knowledge base. There is nothing so dreary as a discussion in which the participants don't know much about the topic. The American Revolution discussion depended on students' knowledge of the main events preceding the Revolution. Teachers can sometimes use a discussion before instruction as a means of generating interest in a topic, but at some point they must give students information. In the chapter-opening vignette, for example, Ms. Logan let students discuss and experiment not only before presenting a formal lesson but also after the lesson, when they had more information.

Small-Group Discussions

In a **small-group discussion,** students work in four- to six-member groups to discuss a particular topic. Because small-group discussions require that students work independently of the teacher most of the time, young or poorly organized students need a great deal of preparation and, in fact, might not be able to benefit from them at all. However, most students at or above the fourth-grade level can profit from small-group discussions.

Like any discussion, most small-group discussions should follow the presentation of information through teacher-directed lessons, books, or videos, or following an opportunity for students to find information for themselves in the library or on the Internet. When students know something about a subject, they might start to work in their groups, pulling desks together if necessary to talk and hear one another more easily.

Each group should have a leader appointed by the teacher. Leaders should be responsible, well-organized students but should not always be the highest-achieving students. Groups may all discuss the same topic, or each may discuss a different subtopic of a larger topic that the whole class is studying. For example, in a unit on the Great Depression, one group might focus on causes of the Depression, another on the collapse of the banking system, a third on the social consequences of the Depression, and a fourth on the New Deal. The teacher should give each group a series of questions to answer on the topic to be discussed. For example, if the topic were the collapse of the banking system, the questions might be the following:

1. What was the connection between the stock market crash of 1929 and the failures of so many banks?
2. What caused savers to lose confidence in the banks?
3. Why did the banks not have enough funds to pay savers who wished to withdraw their money?
4. Why is a widespread run on banks unlikely today?

small-group discussion
A discussion among four to six students in a group working independently of a teacher.

The leader's role in each discussion group is to make sure that the group stays on the topic and questions assigned to it and to ensure that all group members participate.

These students are involved in a small-group discussion. What does research tell us about the effectiveness of small-group discussions?

A group recorder could be appointed to write down the group's ideas. At the end of the discussion the group members prepare a report on their activities or conclusions to present to the rest of the class.

Research on small-group discussions indicates that these activities can increase student achievement more than traditional lessons if the students are well prepared to work in small groups and if the group task is well organized (Sharan et al., 1984; Sharan & Shachar, 1988). Also, some research suggests that small-group discussions have greater effects on student achievement if students are encouraged to engage in controversy rather than to seek a consensus (Johnson & Johnson, 1999).

CERTIFICATION POINTER
A certification test question may ask you to respond to a case study by identifying the strengths and weaknesses of the instructional strategies employed in the case.

Chapter Summary

What Is Direct Instruction?

Direct instruction is a teaching approach that emphasizes teacher control of most classroom events and the presentation of structured lessons. Direct instruction programs call for active teaching; clear lesson organization; step-by-step progression between subtopics; and the use of many examples, demonstrations, and visual prompts.

How Is a Direct Instruction Lesson Taught?

The first part of a lesson is stating learning objectives and orienting students to the lesson. The principal task is to establish both a mental set, so that students are ready to work and learn, and a "road map," so that students know where the lesson is going.

Part two of a lesson is to review prerequisites or pretest to ensure that students have mastered required knowledge and skills. The review might function as an advance organizer for the lesson.

THE INTENTIONAL TEACHER

Using What You Know about Direct Instruction to Improve Teaching and Learning

Intentional teachers select their instructional strategies with purpose. They understand the benefits and shortcomings of the strategies they select, and they choose strategies based on their students, the content, and the context.

Intentional teachers capitalize on their power as directors of learning by using the components of effective instruction. They take responsibility for presenting clear lessons that carefully lead students toward mastery of objectives. They use their time well by providing a quick instructional pace, by checking for student understanding frequently, and by providing meaningful practice in which students learn to transfer information and skills to new settings. Intentional teachers relish their role as designers of learning experiences.

❶ What do I expect my students to know and be able to do at the end of this lesson? How does this contribute to course objectives and to my students' need to become capable individuals?

Effective instruction requires careful preparation, which begins with teachers' thoughtful selection and phrasing of learning objectives. Think in specific terms about content students are to master and plan your lesson to focus directly on those objectives. For example, you might begin planning a series of lessons on spiders for your second-graders with the goal: "Students will learn about spiders' bodies and behaviors." From that goal you would develop specific objectives to frame your lessons. You might list as your first objective "Students will be able to point to, label, and describe at least three features of a spider's anatomy."

Stating the objective and purpose for a lesson helps students prepare mentally for the information that follows. Begin your lessons with a clear declaration of *what* and *why* students are to learn. For example, you could begin a lesson as follows: "Take a look at the two rocks here on my table. By the time you leave today, you'll be able to state how each of these rocks was formed. That's important information, because it can give us clues about the conditions of the earth far back in time. It helps us solve earth's puzzles!"

❷ What knowledge, skills, needs, and interests do my students have that must be taken into account in my lesson?

Intentional teachers use preassessments to ensure that their objectives and instruction are appropriate for students' needs. For example, before teaching a unit on the metric system, you might give a ten-item pretest to determine their current knowledge of metrics, such as "Which unit would you use to measure how long something is: liter, meter, gram?"

Effective lessons include a review of prerequisite skills. Briefly review previous learnings that students will need in the current lesson. For example, in a unit on persuasive speech, you might ask students what they have learned makes an effective speech. After noting their ideas on the board, you could add to the list any of the points that you think they might have missed as being especially important for persuasive speeches—organization, clarity, poise, effective use of gestures.

❸ What do I know about the content, child development, learning, motivation, and effective teaching strategies that I can use to accomplish my objectives?

Effective presentation of information will require you to call on all your skills in incorporating appropriate humor, novelty, and variety. It is important to consider means other than text for presenting information. Use pictures, music, video, and real objects or models when the content permits. Clarity of speech and pronunciation and a pleasant tone are important when you are speaking or reading aloud to present information. (In doing so, you are also modeling your expectations for student speaking.) For example, in a lesson on trees for young children, you might bring in a variety of leaf forms. To introduce the concept of "conifers" you might bring not only pictures of the cone and foliage of a variety of conifers, but also actual cones and sample foliage. Learners can then use their tactile sense as well as their eyes to discriminate between the types of cones. They can use their beginning number awareness to differentiate between conifers by the number of needles in the "bundles" of their foliage. You could make a point of clarifying the new words in these lessons to help build vocabulary and develop linguistic skills.

Part three involves presenting the new material in an organized way, providing explanations and demonstrations, and maintaining attention.

Part four, conducting learning probes, elicits students' responses to lesson content. This practice gives teachers feedback and lets students test their ideas. Questioning techniques are important, including the uses of wait time and calling order.

Practice by the students should include variety. You help your students develop the ability to apply ideas in new contexts when you provide a range of activities. For example, you might offer your students a choice of activities to practice applying their new knowledge of explorers of the New World. You could direct them to select three of the explorers they have studied. They might map their general routes, write an imaginary journal entry for a member of the party after seeing an important landmark, or write an imaginary dialogue between two different explorers, comparing their experiences.

4 What instructional materials, technology, assistance, and other resources are available to help accomplish my objectives?

Effective instruction maintains a high degree of student attention. Visual input is especially important for students who are acquiring English. Pace lessons rapidly (without sacrificing student understanding), and use humor, novelty, and variety to support the lesson focus. For example, imagine a lesson on descriptive writing. Rather than rely upon mental images, you might bring in an assortment of odd kitchen utensils and toolbox treasures. Students could pass the items around, conjecturing about their uses. The objects' novelty might enhance students' written descriptions.

Students need time to process information. Use wait time after you ask a question, and follow through with students who do not express understanding. For example, you might pose a question to your literature students: "What emotion do you suppose our main character was experiencing at this point?" Instead of calling on the first student to raise a hand, you could say: "I see three hands up. I think I'll wait for more." After a few seconds, many hands are in the air, and you could select three or four students to share their responses.

5 How will I plan to assess students' progress toward my objectives?

During direct instruction, teachers conduct many learning probes. Check for understanding frequently, and modify your instruction based on results. For example, in a geometry lesson for young children, you might arrange students in small groups and give each group a set of large shapes. You could ask: "Please hold up a shape that has four corners. Please hold up a shape that reminds you of a stop sign. Please hold up the shape that has the fewest number of sides." You might note that students struggle with your last prompt but easily responded to the first two, and make a note to provide additional work on problem solving and vocabulary terms such as *least, most, more,* and *fewer.*

Active participation devices allow teachers to assess all of their students' understandings. Use strategies that provide feedback on every student's progress. For example, after working on different spellings of the long /a/ sound (as in "made"), you might distribute individual chalkboards, chalk, and erasers. You could recite a few words. Students silently write the words on their boards and then raise the boards for you to check. You would quickly—and silently—assess each student's mastery of spelling patterns, and make a list of students who require further instruction.

6 How will I respond if individual children or the class as a whole are not on track toward success? What is my back-up plan?

As follow-up to any unit of instruction, you might plan for a review and question session. Homework assignments for the unit would be reviewed and corrected by peers in these class sessions. You can actively encourage and answer questions about the content of the unit's lessons. You should have watched for the level of student understanding throughout the unit in the "learning probe" activities you have conducted, and your notes from these "probes" serve as a guide for your review of content.

Part five of a lesson is independent practice, or seatwork, in which students apply their new skill. Research shows that independent practice should be given as short assignments with clear instructions and no interruptions, and that it should be given only when students can do the assignments. Teachers should monitor work, collect it, and include it in assessments.

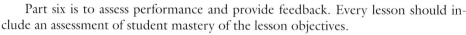

Part six is to assess performance and provide feedback. Every lesson should include an assessment of student mastery of the lesson objectives.

Part seven is to provide distributed practice, or homework, and review. Information is retained better when practice is spaced out over a period of time.

What Does Research on Direct Instruction Methods Suggest?

Research on particular direct instruction models shows mostly positive but inconsistent effects on student achievement. One program, DI (direct instruction), proved to be particularly successful for teaching reading and mathematics to low achievers and at-risk students.

How Do Students Learn and Transfer Concepts?

Students learn concepts through observation and definition. Concepts are taught through examples and nonexamples and through the rule–example–rule approach, in which teachers first state a definition, then give examples, and finally restate the definition. Unambiguous examples should be given before less obvious ones, and teachers should compare and contrast examples and nonexamples. Students transfer their learning to similar situations and must be taught to transfer concepts to different contexts and real-life situations. Material memorized by rote is unlikely to transfer.

How Are Discussions Used in Instruction?

In whole-group discussion the teacher plays a less dominant role than in a regular lesson. Students need an adequate knowledge base before beginning a discussion. In small-group discussion, each group should have a leader and a specific focus.

Key Terms

Research
Navigator.com

Review the following key terms from the chapter. Then, to explore research on these topics and how they relate to education today, connect to Research Navigator™ through this book's Companion Website or directly at www.researchnavigator.com.

calling order   222
choral responses   222
concept   227
direct instruction   209
independent practice   222
learning probe   219
lesson planning   213
mental set   214

process–product studies   226
rule–example–rule   217
seatwork   223
small-group discussion   234
transfer of learning   228
wait time   221
whole-class discussion   233

Self-Assessment: Practicing for Licensure

Directions: The chapter-opening vignette addresses indicators that are often assessed in state licensure exams. Re-read the chapter-opening vignette, and then respond to the following questions.

1. In the chapter-opening vignette, Ms. Logan uses a variety of instructional strategies in the lesson on sound. Which of the following statements from the vignette is an example of Ms. Logan using direct instruction?

   a. Students are working in small groups at lab stations.
   b. After a half hour of experimentation, Ms. Logan calls the class together.
   c. Representatives from some of the groups demonstrate the experiment.
   d. Ms. Logan teaches a lesson on sound.

2. If Ms. Logan were to use a direct instruction approach to a science lesson on gravity, which of the following steps would come first?

   a. conduct learning probes
   b. state the learning objective
   c. present new material
   d. provide independent practice

3. According to research on direct instruction, why should Ms. Logan conduct learning probes during her lesson on sound?

   a. to facilitate in teaching the lesson
   b. to provide students practice with the concepts presented
   c. to give the teacher feedback on the students' level of understanding
   d. to catch students who are not paying attention

4. Ms. Logan plays a flute and a piccolo to demonstrate how sound waves travel through air. She hopes this demonstration will help her students understand the experiment with the bottles of water. What principle of instruction is she using?

   a. reciprocal teaching
   b. distributed practice
   c. transfer of learning
   d. alternative assessment

5. After Ms. Logan's students work in groups to finish the lesson on sound, she tells them they will be tested individually to demonstrate their knowledge; however, their group can only be called "superteam" if everyone knows the material. What instructional strategy is the teacher using?

   a. cooperative learning
   b. small-group discussion
   c. direct instruction
   d. inquiry learning

6. Create a lesson using all of the steps of a direct instruction lesson.

7. What are some advantages and disadvantages of small-group discussions and whole-group discussions?

Student-Centered and Constructivist Approaches to Instruction

"You'll all recall," began Mr. Dunbar, "how last week we figured out how to compute the area of a circle and the volume of a cube. Today you're going to have a chance to discover how to compute the volume of a cylinder. This time, you're really going to be on your own. At each of your lab stations you have five unmarked cylinders of different sizes. You also have a metric ruler and a calculator, and you may use water from your sink. The most important resources you'll have to use, however, are your minds and your partners. Remember, at the end of this activity, everyone in every group must be able to explain not only the formula for volume of a cylinder, but also precisely how you derived it. Any questions? You may begin!"

The students in Mr. Dunbar's middle school math and science class got right to work. They were seated around lab tables in groups of four. One of the groups, the Master Minds, started off by filling all its cylinders with water.

"OK," said Miguel, "we've filled all of our cylinders. What do we do next?"

"Let's measure them," suggested Margarite. She took the ruler and asked Dave to write down her measurements.

"The water in this little one is 36 millimeters high and . . . just a sec . . . 42 millimeters across the bottom."

"So what?" asked Yolanda. "We can't figure out the volume this way. Let's do a little thinking before we start measuring everything."

"Yolanda's right," said Dave. "We'd better work out a plan."

"I know," said Miguel, "let's make a hypo . . . , hypotha . . . , what's it called?"

"Hypothesis," said Yolanda. "Yeah! Let's guess what we think the solution is."

"Remember how Mr. Dunbar reminded us about the area of a circle and the volume of a cube? I'll bet that's an important clue."

"You're right, Miguel," said Mr. Dunbar, who happened to be passing by. "But what are you guys going to do with that information?"

The Master Minds were quiet for a few moments. "Let's try figuring out the area of the bottom of one of these cylinders," ventured Dave. "Remember that Margarite said the bottom of the little one was 42 millimeters? Give me the calculator . . . now how do we get the area?"

Yolanda said, "I think it was pi times the radius squared."

"That sounds right. So 42 squared—"

"Not 42; 21 squared," interrupted Margarite. "If the diameter is 42, the radius is 21."

"OK, OK, I would have remembered. Now, 21 squared is . . . 441, and pi is about 3.14, so my handy-dandy calculator says . . . 13,847."

"Can't be," said Miguel. "Four hundred times three is twelve hundred, so 441 times 3.14 can't be thirteen thousand. I think you did something wrong."

"Let me do it again . . . 441 times 3.14 . . . you're right. Now it's about 1,385."

"So what?" said Yolanda.

"That doesn't tell us how to figure the volume!"

Margarite jumped in excitedly. "Just hang on for a minute, Yolanda. Now, I think we should multiply the area of the bottom by the height of the water."

"But why?" asked Miguel.

"Well," said Margarite, "when we did the volume of a cube, we multiplied length times width times height. Length times width is the area of the bottom. I'll bet we could do the same with a cylinder!"

"The girl's brilliant!" said Miguel. "Sounds good to me. But how could we prove it?"

"I've got an idea," said Yolanda. She emptied the water out of all the cylinders and filled the smallest one to the top. "This is my idea. We don't know what the volume of this cylinder is, but we do know that it's always the same. If we pour the same amounts of water into all four cylinders and use our formula, it should always come out to the same amount!"

"Let's try it!" said Miguel. He poured the water from the small cylinder into a larger one, refilled it, and poured it into another of a different shape.

The Master Minds measured the bases and the heights of the water in their cylinders, wrote down the measurements, and tried out their formula. Sure enough, their formula always gave the same answer for the same volume of water. In great excitement they called Mr. Dunbar to come see what they were doing. Mr. Dunbar asked each of the students to explain what they had done.

"Terrific!" he said. "Not only did you figure out a solution, but everyone in the group participated and understood what you did. Now I'd like you to help me out. I've got a couple of groups that are really stumped. Do you suppose you could help them? Don't give them the answer, but help them get on track. How about Yolanda and Miguel helping with the Brainiacs, and Dave and Margarite help with the Dream Team. OK? Thanks!"

USING YOUR

Experience

Cooperative Learning and Critical Thinking After reading this case, randomly select or appoint a four- to eight-member panel of "experts" on constructivism who sit in front of the class to explain why this method of teaching worked so well for Mr. Dunbar in his middle school math and science classroom. (Students might want to volunteer for the panel.) Members of the audience can ask questions once each panelist has spoken.

Critical Thinking Reflect on Mr. Dunbar's teaching style. How would you characterize it (e.g., Piagetian, Vygotskian, discovery, other)? How does he frame the task and interact with students? His addressing of students' prior learning and questioning are critical from a constructivist point of view. Why?

Learning is much more than memory. For students to really understand and be able to apply knowledge, they must work to solve problems, to discover things for themselves, to wrestle with ideas. Mr. Dunbar could have told his students that the formula for the volume of a cylinder is $\pi r^2 h$. With practice the students would have been able to feed numbers into this formula and grind out correct answers. But how much would it have meant to them, and how well could they have applied the ideas behind the formula to other problems? The task of education is not to pour information into students' heads, but to engage students' minds with powerful and useful concepts. The focus of this chapter is to examine ways of doing this.

WHAT IS THE CONSTRUCTIVIST VIEW OF LEARNING?

INTASC

4 Multiple Instructional Strategies

One of the most important principles of educational psychology is that teachers cannot simply give students knowledge. Students must construct knowledge in their own minds. The teacher can facilitate this process by teaching in ways that make information meaningful and relevant to students, by giving students opportunities to discover or apply ideas themselves, and by teaching students to be aware of and consciously use their own strategies for learning. Teachers can give students ladders that lead to higher understanding, yet the students themselves must climb these ladders.

Theories of learning based on these ideas are called **constructivist theories of learning.** The essence of constructivist theory is the idea that learners must individually discover and transform complex information if they are to make it their own (Anderson, Greeno, Reder, & Simon, 2000; Brown, Collins, & Duguid, 1989; Steffe & Gale, 1995; Tishman, Perkins, & Jay, 1995; Waxman, Padron, & Arnold, 2001). Constructivist theory sees learners as constantly checking new information against old rules and then revising rules when they no longer work. This view has profound implications for teaching, as it suggests a far more active role for students in their own learning than is typical in many classrooms. Because of the emphasis on students as active learners, constructivist strategies are often called *student-centered instruction.* In a student-centered classroom the teacher becomes the "guide on the side" instead of the "sage on the stage," helping students to discover their own meaning instead of lecturing and controlling all classroom activities (Weinberger & McCombs, 2001; Windschitl, 1999).

"2 + 2 = 4? What kind of constructivist answer is that?"

constructivist theories of learning
Theories that state that learners must individually discover and transform complex information, checking new information against old rules and revising rules when they no longer work.

Historical Roots of Constructivism

The constructivist revolution has deep roots in the history of education. It draws heavily on the work of Piaget and Vygotsky (recall Chapter 2), both of whom emphasized that cognitive change takes place only when previous conceptions go through a process of disequilibration in light of new information. Piaget and Vygotsky also emphasized the social nature of learning, and both suggested the use of mixed-ability learning groups to promote conceptual change.

CONNECTIONS

The work of Piaget and of Vygotsky is discussed on pages 31–47 of Chapter 2.

Social Learning   Modern constructivist thought draws most heavily on Vygotsky's theories (see John-Steiner & Mahn, 1996; Karpov & Bransford, 1995), which have been used to support classroom instructional methods that emphasize cooperative learning, project-based learning, and discovery. Four key principles derived from Vygotsky's ideas have played an important role. First is his emphasis on the social nature of learning (Hickey, 1997; O'Connor, 1998; Salomon & Perkins, 1998). Children learn, he proposed, through joint interactions with adults and more capable peers. On cooperative projects, like the one in Mr. Dunbar's class, children are exposed to their peers' thinking processes; this method not only makes the learning outcome available to all students, but also makes other students' thinking processes available to all. Vygotsky noted that successful problem solvers talk themselves through difficult problems. In cooperative groups, children can hear this inner speech out loud and can learn how successful problem solvers are thinking through their approaches.

CONNECTIONS

For more on the zone of proximal development, see Chapter 2, page 61.

Zone of Proximal Development   A second key concept is the idea that children learn best the concepts that are in their zone of proximal development. As discussed in Chapter 2, children are working within their zone of proximal development when they are engaged in tasks that they could not do alone but can do with the assistance of peers or adults. For example, if a child could not find the median of a set of numbers by himself but could do so with some assistance from his teacher, then finding medians is probably in his zone of proximal development. When children are working together, each child is likely to have a peer performing on a given task at a slightly higher cognitive level, exactly within the child's zone of proximal development.

Cognitive Apprenticeship   Another concept derived from Vygotsky's emphases both on the social nature of learning and on the zone of proximal development is **cognitive apprenticeship** (Greeno, Collins, & Resnick, 1996; Harpaz & Lefstein, 2000). This term refers to the process by which a learner gradually acquires expertise through interaction with an expert, either an adult or an older or more advanced peer. In many occupations, new workers learn their jobs through a process of apprenticeship, in which a new worker works closely with an expert, who provides a model, gives feedback to the less experienced worker, and gradually socializes the new worker into the norms and behaviors of the profession. Student teaching is a form of apprenticeship. Constructivist theorists suggest that teachers transfer this long-standing and highly effective model of teaching and learning to day-to-day activities in classrooms, both by engaging students in complex tasks and helping them through these tasks (as a master electrician would help an apprentice rewire a house) (Hamman, Berthelot, Saia, & Crowley, 2000; Newmann & Wehlage, 1993) and by engaging students in heterogeneous, cooperative learning groups in which more advanced students help less advanced ones through complex tasks.

ON THE WEB

For more on cognitive apprenticeship go to **http://mathforum.org/~sarah/Discussion. Sessions/Collins.html.**

cognitive apprenticeship The process by which a learner gradually acquires expertise through interaction with an expert, either an adult or an older or more advanced peer.

Mediated Learning   Finally, Vygotsky's emphasis on scaffolding, or mediated learning (Kozulin & Presseisen, 1995), is important in modern constructivist thought. Current interpretations of Vygotsky's ideas emphasize the idea that students should be given complex, difficult, realistic tasks and then be given enough help to achieve these tasks (rather than being taught little bits of knowledge that are expected someday to build up to complex tasks). This principle is used to support the classroom use of projects, simulations, explorations in the community, writing for real audiences, and other authentic tasks (Byerly, 2001; Holt & Willard-Holt, 2000). The term *situated* *learning* (Anderson, Greeno, Reder, & Simon, 2000; Prawat, 1992) is used to describe learning that takes place in real-life, authentic tasks.

Top-Down Processing

Constructivist approaches to teaching emphasize top-down rather than bottom-up instruction. The term *top-down* means that students begin with complex problems to solve and then work out or discover (with the teacher's guidance) the basic skills required. For example, students might be asked to write compositions and only later learn about spelling, grammar, and punctuation. This top-down processing approach is contrasted with the traditional bottom-up strategy, in which basic skills are gradually built into more complex skills. In top-down teaching, the tasks students begin with are complex, complete, and authentic, meaning that they are not parts or simplifications of the tasks that students are ultimately expected to perform but are the actual tasks. As one instance of a constructivist approach to mathematics teaching, consider an example from Lampert (1986). The traditional, bottom-up approach to teaching the multiplication of two-digit numbers by one-digit numbers (e.g., $4 \times 12 = 48$) is to teach students a step-by-step procedure to get the right answer. Only after students have mastered this basic skill are they given simple application problems, such as "Sondra saw some pencils that cost 12 cents each. How much money would she need to buy four of them?"

The constructivist approach works in exactly the opposite order, beginning with problems (often proposed by the students themselves) and then helping students figure out how to do the operations. Lampert's example of this appears in Figure 8.1.

For example, in the chapter-opening vignette, Mr. Dunbar used cooperative groups to help students derive a formula for the volume of a cylinder. Recall how the Master Minds bounced ideas off of each other, tried out and discarded false leads, and ultimately came up with a solution and a way to prove that their solution was correct. None of the students could have solved the problem alone, so the group work was helpful in arriving at a solution. More important, the experience of hearing others' ideas, trying out and receiving immediate feedback on proposed solutions, and arguing about different ways to proceed gave the Master Minds the cognitive scaffolding that Vygotsky, Bruner, and other constructivists hold to be essential to higher-order learning (Brooks & Brooks, 1993).

Cooperative Learning

Constructivist approaches to teaching typically make extensive use of cooperative learning, on the theory that students will more easily discover and comprehend difficult concepts if they can talk with each other about the problems. Again, the emphasis on the social nature of learning and the use of groups of peers to model appropriate ways of thinking and expose and challenge each other's misconceptions are key elements of Piaget's and Vygotsky's conceptions of cognitive change (Pontecorvo, 1993). Cooperative learning methods are described in more detail later in this chapter.

Discovery Learning

Discovery learning is an important component of modern constructivist approaches that has a long history in education innovation. In **discovery learning** (Bergstrom & O'Brien, 2001; Wilcox, 1993), students are encouraged to learn largely on their own through active involvement with concepts and principles, and teachers encourage students to have experiences and conduct experiments that permit them to discover principles for themselves. Bruner (1966), an advocate of discovery learning, put it this way: "We teach a subject not to produce little living libraries on that subject, but

INTASC

5 Classroom Motivation and Management

discovery learning
A constructivist approach to teaching in which students are encouraged to discover principles for themselves.

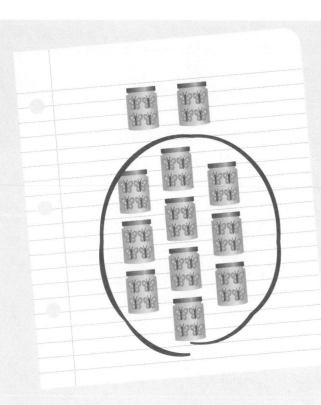

Teacher: Can anyone give me a story that could go with this multiplication . . . 12 × 4?

Student 1: There were 12 jars, and each had 4 butterflies in it.

Teacher: And if I did this multiplication and found the answer, what would I know about those jars and butterflies?

Student 1: You'd know you had that many butterflies altogether.

Teacher: Okay, here are the jars. *[Draws a picture to represent the jars of butterflies—see diagram.]* Now, it will be easier for us to count how many butterflies there are altogether if we think of the jars in groups. And, as usual, the mathematician's favorite number for thinking about groups is?

Student 2: 10

Teacher: Each of these 10 jars has 4 butterflies in it. *[Draws a loop around 10 jars.]*

Teacher: Suppose I erase my circle and go back to looking at the 12 jars again all together: Is there any other way I could group them to make it easier for us to count all the butterflies?

Student 3: You could do 6 and 6.

Teacher: Now, how many do I have in this group?

Student 4: 24

Teacher: How did you figure that out?

Student 4: 8 and 8 and 8. *[He puts the 6 jars together into 3 pairs, intuitively finding a grouping that made the figuring easier for him.]*

Teacher: That's 3 × 8. It's also 6 × 4. Now how many are in this group?

Student 3: 24. It's the same. They both have 6 jars.

Teacher: And how many are there altogether?

Student 5: 24 and 24 is 48.

Teacher: Do we get the same number of butterflies as before? Why?

Student 5: Yeah, because we have the same number of jars and they still have 4 butterflies in each.

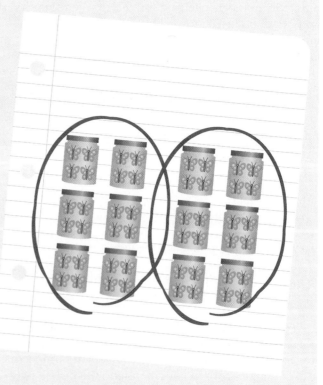

FIGURE 8.1

Mathematical Stories for Teaching Multiplication

From Magdalene Lampert, "Knowing, Doing and Teaching Multiplication," *Cognition and Instruction, 3,* 1986, pp. 305–342. Reprinted by permission of Lawrence Erlbaum Associates, Inc.

Teaching Dilemmas: Cases to Consider

Developing Self-Regulating Techniques

Ms. Sanchez has just finished reading *Clifford's Birthday Party* with her first-grade class. This week the students are working on activities related to the story. Ms. Sanchez describes the activities and explains that students should select three activities from the sheet to complete that morning. Activities include writing a story about Clifford, arranging word cards into sentences from the story, and writing a letter to Clifford about his birthday. Students move from center to center working on the activities. Thirty minutes before lunch, Ms. Sanchez asks the students to join her on the rug.

Ms. Sanchez: We had a lot of different activities this morning, and I wanted to know how you did. Were you successful?

Jessica: I didn't get all three of my activities done.

Ms. Sanchez: Could someone help Jessica by telling her how you planned your activities so that you finished them?

José: I kept working and if my friends talked to me too much, I took my work to another place in the room.

Crystal: I asked my friend to help me spell some of the words so I could write the story about Clifford. I got to use big words!

Ms. Sanchez: I see. José knew that he had to watch out and not get distracted so he could focus on his reading. Crystal knew that she should try to spell the words, but that friends can really help us learn new things. Those are good ideas to help us concentrate. Here is another question. Some of you were working with words from the book; you were putting them together so that they were just like the sentences in the story. How did you do that?

Susanna: First, I took out the word that started with a capital letter because I knew it would be the first word.

Ms. Sanchez: You thought about the beginning of the sentence. Did you think about the end, too?

Susanna: Yes, it had a period.

Juwan: I read all the words and kept changing them till they made sense.

Ms. Sanchez: Did you know all the words in the sentence, Tamika?

Tamika: No, I sounded one out. It started with *cl.* I knew *clap,* and I used that to figure out *close.*

Ms. Sanchez: So I hear that some people used the capital letters and punctuation as clues; some kept asking if the words made sense, and some used the letters they already knew to help them sound out new words. Those are all good strategies. You all knew that the sentence was supposed to make sense, just like the story, and you used different ways to do that. Before we go to lunch, I would like to check to see how many students marked off the activities they completed today. [Only half of the students raise their hands.] Do that now. One way you could remember is to make a small mark by each activity you are choosing. Then, before you move on to the next center, mark it off in the box. Any other ideas?

Pasqual: I remember the work I did, and that helps me remember at the end.

Ms. Sanchez: Yes, when you remember the Clifford story you wrote, you can find that on your activity sheet and check it off. Tomorrow, I hope everyone will try some of these good ideas to help them think about how they do their work.

@ Questions for Reflection

1. Some instructional techniques that teachers can use to help students develop self-regulation include modeling, pointing out successful performance, giving feedback for improvement, providing instructions, asking questions, and providing cognitive structures (e.g., identifying the theme of a story as "heroes" or reminding students to use strategies). Find some examples of these strategies in the dialogue, critique their effectiveness, and change two to be more effective.

2. Could you characterize this instruction as metacognitive? Why or why not?

3. Imagine that Jessica has just announced that she didn't complete her three activities or that she didn't know how to write the letter to Clifford. Rewrite or role-play the dialogue from that point on using different approaches to help her understand and solve her problem.

rather to get a student to think . . . for himself, to consider matters as an historian does, to take part in the process of knowledge-getting. Knowing is a process, not a product" (1966, p. 72).

Discovery learning has applications in many subjects. For example, some science museums have a series of cylinders of different sizes and weights, some hollow and some solid. Students are encouraged to race the cylinders down a ramp. By careful experimentation the students can discover the underlying principles that determine the cylinders' speed. Computer simulations can create environments in which students can discover scientific principles (DeJong & van Joolingen, 1998). After-school enrichment programs (Bergstrom & O'Brien, 2001) and innovative science programs (Singer et al., 2000) are particularly likely to be based on principles of discovery learning.

Discovery learning has several advantages. It arouses students' curiosity, motivating them to continue to work until they find answers. Students also learn independent problem-solving and critical-thinking skills, because they must analyze and manipulate information. However, discovery learning can also lead to errors and wasted time. For this reason, *guided* discovery learning is more common than pure discovery learning (Pressley et al., 2003). In guided discovery the teacher plays a more active role, giving clues, structuring portions of an activity, or providing outlines.

CONNECTIONS

For more on the motivational aspects of self-regulated learning, see Chapter 10, page 343.

Self-Regulated Learning

A key concept of constructivist theories of learning is a vision of the ideal student as a self-regulated learner (Paris & Paris, 2001). **Self-regulated learners** are ones who have knowledge of effective learning strategies and how and when to use them (Bandura, 1991; Dembo & Eaton, 2000; Schunk & Zimmerman, 1997; Winne, 1997). For example, they know how to break complex problems into simpler steps or to test out alternative solutions (Greeno & Goldman, 1998); they know how and when to skim and how and when to read for deep understanding; and they know how to write to persuade and how to write to inform (Zimmerman & Kitsantas, 1999). Further, self-regulated learners are motivated by learning itself, not only by grades or others' approval (Boekaerts, 1995; Corno, 1992; Schunk, 1995), and they are able to stick to a long-term task until it is done. When students have both effective learning strategies and the motivation and persistence to apply these strategies until a job is done to their satisfaction, then they are likely to be effective learners (Williams, 1995; Zimmerman, 1995) and to have a lifelong motivation to learn (Corno & Kanfer, 1993). Programs that teach children self-regulated learning strategies have been found to increase students' achievement (Fuchs et al., 2003; Mason, 2004).

CONNECTIONS

For more on scaffolding, see Chapter 2, page 46.

Scaffolding

As was noted in Chapter 2, scaffolding is a practice based on Vygotsky's concept of assisted learning. According to Vygotsky, higher mental functions, including the ability

Early in the scaffolding process, the teacher may provide more structure and then gradually turn responsibility over to the student. What are the possible benefits of this strategy?

to direct memory and attention in a purposeful way and to think in symbols, are mediated behaviors. Mediated externally by culture, these and other behaviors become internalized in the learner's mind as psychological tools. In assisted learning, or **mediated learning,** the teacher is the cultural agent who guides instruction so that students will master and internalize the skills that permit higher cognitive functioning. The ability to internalize cultural tools relates to the learner's age or stage of cognitive development. Once acquired, however, internal mediators allow greater self-mediated learning.

In practical terms, scaffolding might include giving students more structure at the beginning of a set of lessons and gradually turning responsibility over to them to operate on their own (Palincsar, 1986; Rosenshine & Meister, 1992, 1994). For example, students can be taught to generate their own questions about material they are reading. Early on, the teacher might suggest the questions, modeling the kinds of questions students might ask, but students later take over the question-generating task. For another example of scaffolding, see Figure 8.2.

Research has measured parents' use of scaffolding while helping fifth-graders with math homework. Researchers measured the degree to which adults shifted their level of intervention to fit the child's zone of proximal development. When the child is having difficulty, the adult who stays within this region increases his or her directiveness just enough to provide support but not so much as to take over the task, then reduces directiveness when the child begins to succeed. Findings revealed that making use of this principle predicted gains in children's learning of mathematics. A later section in this chapter describes reciprocal teaching, a method that uses scaffolding in just this way. Scaffolding is closely related to cognitive apprenticeship; experts working with apprentices typically engage them in complex tasks and then give them decreasing amounts of advice and guidance over time.

Here is a brief example of an adult scaffolding a young child's efforts to put a difficult puzzle together.

Jason: I can't get this one in. *(Tries to insert a piece in the wrong place)*

Adult: Which piece might go down here? *(Points to the bottom of the puzzle)*

Jason: His shoes. *(Looks for a piece resembling the clown's shoes but tries the wrong one)*

Adult: Well, what piece looks like this shape? *(Points again to the bottom of the puzzle)*

Jason: The brown one. *(Tries it and it fits; then attempts another piece and looks at the adult)*

Adult: There you have it! Now try turning that piece just a little. *(Gestures to show him)*

Jason: There! *(Puts in several more, commenting to himself, "Now a green piece to match," "Turn it [meaning the puzzle piece]," as the adult watches)*

FIGURE 8.2
Scaffolding

From Laura E. Berk, *Infants, Children, and Adolescents* (2nd ed.), p. 328. Published by Allyn & Bacon, Boston, MA. Copyright © 1996 by Pearson Education. Reprinted by permission of the publisher.

APA's Learner-Centered Psychological Principles

In 1992 the American Psychological Association's Task Force on Psychology in Education published a document called *Learner-Centered Psychological Principles: Guidelines for School Redesign and Reform* (American Psychological Association, 1992, 1997; see also Alexander & Murphy, 1994). Revised in 1997, this publication presents a consensus view of principles of learning and motivation among prominent educational psychologists primarily working within the constructivist tradition. Table 8.1 shows the APA's 14 principles.

The Learner-Centered Psychological Principles paint a picture of the learner as actively seeking knowledge by (1) reinterpreting information and experience for himself or herself, (2) being self-motivated by the quest for knowledge (rather than being motivated by grades or other rewards), (3) working with others to socially construct

self-regulated learners
Students who have knowledge of effective learning strategies and how and when to use them.

mediated learning
Assisted learning; an approach in which the teacher guides instruction by means of scaffolding to help students master and internalize the skills that permit higher cognitive functioning.

Table 8.1	
Learner-Centered Psychological Principles: Cognitive and Metacognitive Factors	
Principle	*Explanation*
Principle 1 Nature of the learning process	The learning of complex subject matter is most effective when it is an intentional process of constructing meaning from information and experience.
Principle 2 Goals of the learning process	The successful learner, over time and with support and instructional guidance, can create meaningful, coherent representations of knowledge.
Principle 3 Construction of knowledge	The successful learner can link new information with existing knowledge in meaningful ways.
Principle 4 Strategic thinking	The successful learner can create and use a repertoire of thinking and reasoning strategies to achieve complex learning goals.
Principle 5 Thinking about thinking	Higher-order strategies for selecting and monitoring mental operations facilitate creative and critical thinking.
Principle 6 Context of learning	Learning is influenced by environmental factors, including culture, technology, and instructional practices.
Principle 7 Motivational and emotional influences on learning	What and how much is learned is influenced by the learner's motivation. Motivation to learn, in turn, is influenced by the individual's emotional states, beliefs, interests and goals, and habits of thinking.
Principle 8 Intrinsic motivation to learn	The learner's creativity, higher-order thinking, and natural curiosity all contribute to motivation to learn. Intrinsic motivation is stimulated by tasks that are of optimal novelty and difficulty, are relevant to personal interests, and provide for personal choice and control.
Principle 9 Effects of motivation on effort	Acquisition of complex knowledge and skills requires extended learner effort and guided practice. Without learners' motivation to learn, the willingness to exert this effort is unlikely without coercion.
Principle 10 Developmental influences on learning	As individuals develop, they encounter different opportunities and experience different constraints for learning. Learning is most effective when differential development within and across physical, intellectual, emotional, and social domains is taken into account.
Principle 11 Social influences on learning	Learning is influenced by social interactions, interpersonal relations, and communication with others.
Principle 12 Individual differences in learning	Learners have different strategies, approaches, and capabilities for learning that are a function of prior experience and heredity.
Principle 13 Learning and diversity	Learning is most effective when differences in learners' linguistic, cultural, and social backgrounds are taken into account.
Principle 14 Standards and assessment	Setting appropriately high and challenging standards and assessing the learner and learning progress—including diagnostic, process, and outcome assessment—are integral parts of the learning process.

Source: From American Psychological Association, *Learner-centered psychological principles: A framework for school redesign and reform,* pp. 4–7. Copyright © 1997 by the American Psychological Association. Adapted by permission.

meaning, and (4) being aware of his or her own learning strategies and capable of applying them to new problems or circumstances.

Constructivist Methods in the Content Areas

Constructivist and student-centered methods have come to dominate current thinking in all areas of curriculum (see Gabler & Schroeder, 2003; Gagnon & Collay,

2001; Henson, 2004; Mayer, 2001). The following sections describe constructivist approaches in reading, mathematics, and science.

Reciprocal Teaching in Reading One well-researched example of a constructivist approach based on principles of question generation is **reciprocal teaching** (Palincsar & Brown, 1984). This approach, designed primarily to help low achievers in elementary and middle schools learn reading comprehension, involves the teacher working with small groups of students. Initially, the teacher models questions students might ask as they read, but students are soon appointed to act as "teacher" to generate questions for each other. Figure 8.3 below presents an example of reciprocal teaching in use. Note in the example how the teacher directs the conversation about crows at first but then turns the responsibility over to Jim (who is about to turn it over to another

reciprocal teaching
A small-group teaching method based on principles of question generation; through instruction and modeling, teachers foster metacognitive skills primarily to improve the reading performance of students who have poor comprehension.

Teacher: The title of this story is "Genius with Feathers." Let's have some predictions. I will begin by guessing that this story will be about birds that are very smart. Why do I say that?

First student: Because a genius is someone very smart.

Second student: Because they have feathers.

Teacher: That's right. Birds are the only animals that have feathers. Let's predict now the kind of information you might read about very smart birds.

Third student: What kinds of birds?

Teacher: Good question. What kinds would you guess are very smart?

Third student: Parrots or blue jays.

First student: A cockatoo.

Teacher: What other information would you want to know? *[No response from students]*

Teacher: I would like to know what these birds do that is so smart. Any ideas?

Second student: Some birds talk.

Fourth student: They can fly.

Teacher: That's an interesting one. As smart as people are, they can't fly. Well, let's read this first section now and see how many of our predictions were right. I will be the teacher for this section. *[All read the section silently.]*

Teacher: Who is the genius with feathers?

First student: Crows.

Teacher: That's right. We were correct in our prediction that this story would be about birds, but

we didn't correctly guess which kind of bird, did we? My summary of the first section would be that it describes the clever things that crows do, which make them seem quite intelligent.

Let's read on. Who will be the teacher for this section? Jim?

Jim: How do crows communicate with one another?

Teacher: Good question! You picked right up on our prediction that this is about the way crows communicate. Whom do you choose to answer your question?

Jim: Barbara.

Barbara: Crows have built-in radar and a relay system.

Jim: That's a good part of it. The answer I wanted was how they relay the messages from one crow to the other crow.

Teacher: Summarize now.

Jim: This is about how crows have developed a system of communication.

Teacher: That's right. The paragraph goes on to give examples of how they use pitch and changes in interval, but these are supporting details. The main idea is that crows communicate through a relay system, Jim?

Jim: It says in this section that crows can use their communication system to play tricks, so I predict the next section will say something about the tricks crows play. I would like Sue to be the next teacher.

Teacher: Excellent prediction. The last sentence of a paragraph often suggests what the next paragraph will be about. Good, Jim.

FIGURE 8.3
Example of a Reciprocal Teaching Lesson
From Anne Marie Palinscar, "The Role of Dialogue in Providing Scaffolded Instruction," *Educational Psychologist, 21,* 1986, pp. 73–98. Adapted by permission of Lawrence Erlbaum Associates, Inc.

student as the example ends). The teacher is modeling the behaviors she wants the students to be able to do on their own and then changes her role to that of facilitator and organizer as the students begin to generate the actual questions. Research on reciprocal teaching has generally found this strategy to increase the achievement of low achievers (Alfassi, 1998; Carter, 1997; Lysynchuk, Pressley, & Vye, 1990; Palincsar & Brown, 1984; Rosenshine & Meister, 1994).

Theory into PRACTICE

Introducing Reciprocal Teaching

In introducing reciprocal teaching to students, you might begin as follows: "For the coming weeks we will be working together to improve your ability to understand what you read. Sometimes we are so busy figuring out what the words are that we fail to pay much attention to what the words and sentences mean. We will be learning a way to pay more attention to what we are reading. I will teach you to do the following activities as you read:

1. To think of important questions that might be asked about what is being read and to be sure that you can answer those questions.
2. To summarize the most important information that you have read.
3. To predict what the author might discuss next in the passage.
4. To point out when something is unclear in the passage or doesn't make sense and then to see if we can make sense of it.

"These activities will help you keep your attention on what you are reading and make sure that you are understanding it.

"The way in which you will learn these four activities is by taking turns in the role of teacher during our reading group sessions. When I am the teacher, I will show you how I read carefully by telling you the questions I made up while reading, by summarizing the most important information I read, and by predicting what I think the author might discuss next. I will also tell you if I found anything I read to be unclear or confusing and how I made sense out of it.

"When you are the teacher, you will first ask the rest of us the questions you made up while reading. You will tell us if our answers are correct. You will summarize the most important information you learned while reading. You will also tell us if you found anything in the passage to be confusing. Several times throughout the story you will also be asked to predict what you think might be discussed next in the passage. When you are the teacher, the rest of us will answer your questions and comment on your summary.

"These are activities that we hope you will learn and use, not only when you are here in reading class, but whenever you want to understand and remember what you are reading—for example, in social studies, science, or history."

Daily Procedures

1. Pass out the passage for the day.
2. Explain that you will be the teacher for the first segment.
3. Instruct the students to read silently whatever portion of the passage you determine is appropriate. At the beginning, it will probably be easiest to work paragraph by paragraph.
4. When everyone has completed the first segment, model the following:

   • "The question that I thought a teacher might ask is . . ."

- Have the students answer your question. They may refer to the text if necessary. "I would summarize the important information in this paragraph in the following way . . ."
- "From the title of the passage, I would predict that the author will discuss . . ."
- If appropriate, "When I read this part, I found the following to be unclear . . ."

5. Invite the students to make comments regarding your teaching and the passage. For example:

- "Was there more important information?"
- "Does anyone have more to add to my prediction?"
- "Did anyone find something else confusing?"

6. Assign the next segment to be read silently. Choose a student to act as teacher for this segment. Begin with students who are more verbal and who you think will have less difficulty with the activities.

7. Coach the student teacher through the activities as necessary. Encourage the other students to participate in the dialogue, but always give the student teacher for that segment the opportunity to go first and lead the dialogue. Be sure to give the student teacher plenty of feedback and praise for his or her participation.

8. As the training days go by, try to remove yourself more and more from the dialogue so that the student teacher initiates the activities herself or himself with students providing feedback. Your role will continue to be monitoring, keeping students on track, and helping them over obstacles. Throughout the training, however, continue to take your turn as teacher, modeling at least once a session.

Questioning the Author   Another constructivist approach for reading is Questioning the Author (Beck & McKeown, 2001). In this method, children in grades 3–9 are taught to see the authors of factual material as real, fallible people and to then engage in simulated "dialogues" with the authors. As the students are reading a text, the teacher stops them from time to time to ask questions such as "What is the author trying to say, or what does she want us to know?" and then follows up with questions such as "How does that fit in with what she said before?" Ultimately, the students themselves take responsibility for formulating questions of the author's intent and meaning. A study of fifth- and sixth-graders found that students who experienced this technique recalled more from texts than did a comparison group, and were far more likely to describe the purpose of reading as *understanding* rather than just memorizing the text (McKeown & Beck, 1998).

Writing Process Models   A widely used set of approaches to the teaching of creative writing, writing process models (Calkins, 1983; Graves, 1983) engage students in small peer response teams in which they work together to help one another plan, draft, revise, edit, and "publish" compositions. That is, children may review each other's drafts and give helpful ideas for improvements in content as well as mechanics (e.g., spelling, punctuation), and ultimately present compositions for some authentic purpose (such as a poetry reading or a literary review). In the process of responding to others' compositions, children gain insight into the process of writing and revision.

Research on writing process methods has found positive effects of these strategies (Harris & Graham, 1996). Strategies that provide specific scaffolding, such as instruction in graphic organizers to help children use metacognitive strategies for planning and evaluating their own work, have been particularly effective (De La Paz & Graham, 2002; Englert et al., 1991).

Constructivist Approaches to Mathematics Teaching in the Primary Grades Carpenter and colleagues (1994) described four approaches to early mathematics instruction for the early elementary grades. In all four, students work together in small groups; teachers pose problems and then circulate among groups to facilitate the discussion of strategies, join students in asking questions about strategies they have proposed, and occasionally offer alternative strategies when students appear to be stuck. In Supporting Ten-Structured Thinking (STST) (Fuson, 1992), children use base-10 blocks to invent procedures for adding and subtracting large numbers. Conceptually Based Instruction (CBI) (Hiebert & Wearne, 1993) makes extensive use of physical, pictorial, verbal, and symbolic presentations of mathematical ideas and gives students opportunities to solve complex problems using these representations and to contrast different representations of the same concepts. Similarly, the Problem Centered Mathematics Project (PCMP) (Murray, Olivier, & Human, 1992) leads children through stages, from modeling with counters to solving more abstract problems without counters. Cognitively Guided Instruction (CGI) (Carpenter & Fennema, 1992; Fennema, Franke, Carpenter, & Carey, 1993), unlike STST and CBI, does not have a specific curriculum or recommended set of activities but provides extensive professional development for teachers of primary mathematics, focusing on principles similar to those used in the other programs. There is good evidence that this program increases student achievement not only on measures related to higher-level thinking in mathematics, which is the program's focus, but also on computational skills (Carpenter & Fennema, 1992; Carpenter, Fennema, Peterson, Chiang, & Loef, 1989).

In these and other constructivist approaches to mathematics, the emphasis is on beginning with real problems for students to solve intuitively and letting students use their existing knowledge of the world to solve problems any way they can (Greeno & Goldman, 1998; Hiebert et al., 1996; Schifter, 1996). The problem and solutions in Figure 8.1 illustrate this approach. Only at the end of the process, when students have achieved a firm conceptual understanding, are they taught formal, abstract representations of the mathematical processes they have been working with (see Clements & Battista, 1990).

Constructivist Approaches in Science Discovery, group work, and conceptual change have long been emphasized in science education, so it is not surprising that many elementary and secondary science educators have embraced constructivist ideas (see Greeno & Goldman, 1998). In this subject, constructivism translates into an emphasis on hands-on, investigative laboratory activities (Bainer & Wright, 1998; Singer, Marx, Krajcik, & Chambers, 2000; White & Frederiksen, 1998); identifying misconceptions and using experimental approaches to correct these misconceptions (Hand & Treagust, 1991; Sandoval, 1995); and cooperative learning (Pea, 1993; Wheatley, 1991).

CERTIFICATION POINTER

For teacher certification tests, you may be expected to choose alternative teaching strategies to achieve particular instructional goals.

Research on Constructivist Methods

Research comparing constructivist and traditional approaches to instruction is often difficult to interpret, because constructivist methods are themselves very diverse and are usually intended to produce outcomes that are qualitatively different from those of traditional methods. For example, many researchers argue that acquisition of skills and basic information must be balanced against constructivist approaches (Airsian & Walsh, 1997; Harris & Graham, 1996). But what is the appropriate balance, and for which objectives (Harris & Alexander, 1998; von Glaserfeld, 1996; Waxman, Padrón, & Arnold, 2001)? Also, much of the research on constructivist methods is descriptive rather than comparative. However, there are studies showing positive effects of constructivist approaches on traditional achievement measures in mathematics (e.g., Carpenter & Fennema, 1992), science (e.g., Neale, Smith, & Johnson, 1990), reading (e.g., Duffy & Roehler, 1986), and writing (e.g., De La Paz & Graham, 2002). Furthermore, a study by Knapp (1995) found a correlation between use of more constructivist approaches and achievement gains in high-poverty schools. Weinberger and McCombs (2001) found that students who reported more learner-centered methods used in their

Technology can help a teacher provide students with multiple representations of concepts. How does technology reinforce constructivist learning?

classrooms performed at a higher level than other students. Langer (2001) also found that secondary schools that performed better than expected used more constructivist approaches than lower-achieving schools. On the other hand, other studies found better results for explicit teaching than for constructivist approaches (Baker, Gerstein, & Lee, 2002; Klahr & Nigam, 2004; Kroesbergen, Van Luit & Maas, 2004). Much more research is needed to establish the conditions under which constructivist approaches are effective for enhancing student achievement.

How IS COOPERATIVE LEARNING USED IN INSTRUCTION?

In **cooperative learning** instructional methods, or peer-assisted learning (Rohrbeck, Ginsburg-Block, Fantuzzo, & Miller, 2003), students work together in small groups to help each other learn. Many quite different approaches to cooperative learning exist. Most involve students in four-member, mixed-ability groups (e.g., Slavin, 1994a), but some methods use dyads (e.g., Fantuzzo, Polite, & Grayson, 1990; Maheady, Harper, & Mallette, 1991; O'Donnell & Dansereau, 1992), and some use varying group sizes (e.g., Cohen, 1994b; Johnson & Johnson, 1999; Kagan, 1992; Sharan & Sharan, 1992). Typically, students are assigned to cooperative groups and stay together as a group for many weeks or months. They are usually taught specific skills that will help them work well together, such as active listening, giving good explanations, avoiding putdowns, and including other people.

Cooperative learning activities can play many roles in lessons (Webb & Palincsar, 1996). Recall the chapter-opening vignette in Chapter 7: Ms. Logan used cooperative learning for three distinct purposes. At first, students worked as discovery groups, helping each other figure out how water in bottles could tell them about principles of sound. After the formal lesson, students worked as discussion groups. Finally, students had an opportunity to work together to make sure that all group members had learned everything in the lesson in preparation for a quiz, working in a group study format. In the vignette at the beginning of this chapter, Mr. Dunbar used cooperative groups to solve a complex problem.

INTASC

4 Multiple Instructional Strategies

5 Classroom Motivation and Management

CERTIFICATION POINTER

On your teacher certification test, you may be required to suggest an appropriate way of assigning students in a case study to cooperative learning groups.

cooperative learning
Instructional approaches in which students work in small mixed-ability groups.

> **ON THE WEB**
>
> For newsletters and resources for cooperative learning visit the website of the International Association for the Study of Cooperation in Education at **www.iasce.net.**

Cooperative Learning Methods

CONNECTIONS

To learn about the benefits of cooperative learning methods in promoting harmony in culturally diverse classrooms, see Chapter 4, page 111.

Many quite different cooperative learning methods have been developed and researched. The most extensively evaluated cooperative learning methods are described in the following sections.

Student Teams–Achievement Divisions (STAD)   In **Student Teams–Achievement Divisions (STAD)** (Slavin, 1994a), students are assigned to four-member learning teams that are mixed in performance level, gender, and ethnicity. The teacher presents a lesson, and then students work within their teams to make sure that all team members have mastered the lesson. Finally, all students take individual quizzes on the material, at which time they may not help one another.

Students' quiz scores are compared to their own past averages, and points are awarded on the basis of the degree to which students meet or exceed their own earlier performance. These points are then summed to form team scores, and teams that meet certain criteria may earn certificates or other rewards. In a related method called Teams–Games–Tournaments (TGT), students play games with members of other teams to add points to their team scores.

**Student Teams–
Achievement
Divisions (STAD)**

A cooperative learning method for mixed-ability groupings involving team recognition and group responsibility for individual learning.

STAD and TGT have been used in a wide variety of subjects, from mathematics to language arts to social studies, and have been used from second grade through college. The STAD method is most appropriate for teaching well-defined objectives with single right answers, such as mathematical computations and applications, language usage and mechanics, geography and map skills, and science facts and concepts. However, it can easily be adapted for use with less well-defined objectives by incorporating more open-ended assessments, such as essays or performances. STAD is described in more detail in the next Theory into Practice.

By working together these students learn from each other. What are some advantages of cooperative learning?

Student Teams–Achievement Divisions (STAD)

An effective cooperative learning method is called Student Teams–Achievement Divisions, or STAD (Slavin, 1994a, 1995a). STAD consists of a regular cycle of teaching, cooperative study in mixed-ability teams, and quizzes, with recognition or other rewards provided to teams whose members excel.

STAD consists of a regular cycle of instructional activities, as follows:

- **Teach:** Present the lesson.
- **Team study:** Students work on worksheets in their teams to master the material.
- **Test:** Students take individual quizzes or other assessments (such as essays or performances).
- **Team recognition:** Team scores are computed on the basis of team members' scores, and certificates, a class newsletter, or a bulletin board recognizes high-scoring teams.

The following steps describe how to introduce students to STAD:

1. Assign students to teams of four or five members each. Four are preferable; make five-member teams only if the class is not divisible by four. To assign the students, rank them from top to bottom on some measure of academic performance (e.g., past grades, test scores) and divide the ranked list into quarters, placing any extra students in the middle quarters. Then put one student from each quarter on each team, making sure that the teams are well balanced in gender and ethnicity. Extra (middle) students may become fifth members of teams.

2. Make a worksheet and a short quiz for the lesson you plan to teach. During team study (one or two class periods) the team members' tasks are to master the material you presented in your lesson and to help their teammates master the material. Students have worksheets or other study materials that they can use to practice the skill being taught and to assess themselves and their teammates.

3. When you introduce STAD to your class, read off team assignments.

   - Have teammates move their desks together or move to team tables, and allow students about 10 minutes to decide on a team name.
   - Hand out worksheets or other study materials (two of each per team).
   - Suggest that students on each team work in pairs or threes. If they are working problems (as in math), each student in a pair or threesome should work the problem and then check with his or her partner(s). If anyone missed a question, that student's teammates have a responsibility to explain it. If students are working on short-answer questions, they might quiz each other, with partners taking turns holding the answer sheet or attempting to answer the questions.
   - Emphasize to students that they are not finished studying until they are sure that all their teammates will make 100 percent on the quiz.
   - Make sure that students understand that the worksheets are for studying—not for filling out and handing in. That is why it is important for students to have the answer sheets to check themselves and their teammates as they study.

- Have students explain answers to one another instead of just checking each other against the answer sheet.
- When students have questions, have them ask a teammate before asking you.
- While students are working in teams, circulate through the class, praising teams that are working well and sitting in with each team to hear how the members are doing.

4. Distribute the quiz or other assessment, and give students adequate time to complete it. Do not let students work together on the quiz; at this point they must show what they have learned as individuals. Have students move their desks apart if this is possible. Either allow students to exchange papers with members of other teams or collect the quizzes to score after class.

5. Figure individual and team scores. Team scores in STAD are based on team members' improvements over their own past records. As soon as possible after each quiz, you should compute individual team scores, and write a class newsletter (or prepare a class bulletin board) to announce the team scores. If at all possible, the announcement of team scores should be made in the first period after the quiz. This makes the connection between doing well and receiving recognition clear to students, increasing their motivation to do their best. Compute team scores by adding up the improvement points earned by the team members and dividing the sum by the number of team members who are present on the day of the quiz.

6. Recognize team accomplishments. As soon as you have calculated points for each student and figured team scores, you should provide some sort of recognition to any teams that averaged 20 improvement points or more. You might give certificates to team members or prepare a bulletin board display. It is important to help students value team success. Your own enthusiasm about team scores will help. If you give more than one quiz in a week, combine the quiz results into a single weekly score. After 5 or 6 weeks of STAD, reassign students to new teams. This allows students to work with other classmates and keeps the program fresh.

Cooperative Integrated Reading and Composition (CIRC)

A comprehensive program for teaching reading and writing in the upper elementary grades; students work in four-member cooperative learning teams.

Jigsaw

A cooperative learning model in which students are assigned to six-member teams to work on academic material that has been broken down into sections for each member.

Cooperative Integrated Reading and Composition (CIRC) Cooperative Integrated Reading and Composition (CIRC) (Stevens & Slavin, 1995a) is a comprehensive program for teaching reading and writing in the upper elementary grades. Students work in four-member cooperative learning teams. They engage in a series of activities with one another, including reading to one another, making predictions about how narrative stories will come out, summarizing stories to one another, writing responses to stories, and practicing spelling, decoding, and vocabulary. They also work together to master main ideas and other comprehension skills. During language arts periods, students engage in writing drafts, revising and editing one another's work, and preparing for publication of team books. Three studies of the CIRC program have found positive effects on students' reading skills, including improved scores on standardized reading and language tests (Stevens et al., 1987; Stevens & Slavin, 1991, 1995a).

Jigsaw In **Jigsaw** (Aronson, Blaney, Stephen, Sikes, & Snapp, 1978), students are assigned to six-member teams to work on academic material that has been broken down into sections. For example, a biography might be divided into early life, first accomplishments, major setbacks, later life, and impact on history. Each team member reads his or her section. Next, members of different teams who have studied the same sections meet in expert groups to discuss their sections. Then the students return to their teams and take turns teaching their teammates about their sections. Since the only way students can learn sections other than their own is to listen carefully to their teammates, they are motivated to support and show interest in one another's work. In a modification of this approach called Jigsaw II (Slavin, 1994a), students work in four- or five-member teams, as in STAD. Instead of each student being assigned a unique section, all students read a common text, such as a book chapter, a short story, or a biography. However, each student receives a topic on which to become an expert. Students with the same topics meet in expert groups to discuss them, after which they return to their teams to teach what they have learned to their teammates. The students take individual quizzes, which result in team scores, as in STAD.

Learning Together   **Learning Together,** a model of cooperative learning developed by David Johnson and Roger Johnson (1999), involves students working in four- or five-member heterogeneous groups on assignments. The groups hand in a single completed assignment and receive praise and rewards based on the group product. This method emphasizes team-building activities before students begin working together and regular discussions within groups about how well they are working together.

Group Investigation   **Group Investigation** (Sharan & Sharan, 1992) is a general classroom organization plan in which students work in small groups using cooperative inquiry, group discussion, and cooperative planning and projects. In this method, students form their own two- to six-member groups. After choosing subtopics from a unit that the entire class is studying, the groups break their subtopics into individual tasks and carry out the activities that are necessary to prepare group reports. Each group then makes a presentation or display to communicate its findings to the entire class.

Cooperative Scripting   Many students find it helpful to get together with classmates to discuss material they have read or heard in class. A formalization of this age-old practice has been researched by Dansereau (1985) and his colleagues. In it, students work in pairs and take turns summarizing sections of the material for one another. While one student summarizes, the other listens and corrects any errors or omissions. Then the two students switch roles, continuing in this manner until they have covered all the material to be learned. A series of studies of this **cooperative scripting** method has consistently found that students who study this way learn and retain far more than students who summarize on their own or who simply read the material (Newbern, Dansereau, Patterson, & Wallace, 1994). It is interesting that while both participants in the cooperative pairs gain from the activity, the larger gains are seen in the sections that students teach to their partners rather than in those for which they serve as listeners (Spurlin, Dansereau, Larson, & Brooks, 1984). More recent studies of various forms of peer tutoring find similar results (Fuchs & Fuchs, 1997; King, 1997, 1998).

Research on Cooperative Learning

Cooperative learning methods fall into two broad categories (Slavin, Hurley, & Chamberlain, 2003). One category might be called group study methods (Slavin,

Learning Together
A cooperative learning model in which students in four- or five-member heterogeneous groups work together on assignments.

Group Investigation
A cooperative learning model in which students work in small groups using cooperative inquiry, group discussion, and cooperative planning and projects, and then make presentations to the whole class on their findings.

cooperative scripting
A study method in which students work in pairs and take turns orally summarizing sections of material to be learned.

"At least I'm glad to see that you're finally working well as a group."

1996b), in which students primarily work together to help one another master a relatively well-defined body of information or skills—what Cohen (1994b) calls "well-structured problems." The other category is often called project-based learning or active learning (Stern, 1996). Project-based learning methods involve students working in groups to create a report, experiment, mural, or other product (Webb & Palinscar, 1996). Project-based learning methods such as those described by Blumenfeld, Marx, Soloway, and Krajcik (1996); Cohen (1994a), Palincsar, Anderson, and David (1993); and Sharan and Sharan (1992) focus on ill-structured problems, which typically have less of a clear expected outcome or instructional objective. Methods of this kind are often referred to as collaborative learning methods (Webb & Palinscar, 1996).

Most research comparing cooperative learning to traditional teaching methods has evaluated group study methods such as STAD, Jigsaw II, CIRC, and Johnson's methods. More than 100 studies have compared achievement of students in such methods to that of students in traditional classrooms over periods of at least 4 weeks (Slavin, 1995a). The results have consistently favored cooperative learning as long as two essential conditions are met. First, some kind of recognition or small reward must be provided to groups that do well so that group members can see that it is in their interest to help their groupmates learn (O'Donnell, 1996). Second, there must be individual accountability. That is, the success of the group must depend on the individual learning of all group members, not on a single group product. For example, groups might be evaluated on the basis of the average of their members' scores on individual quizzes or essays (as in STAD), or students might be individually responsible for a unique portion of a group task (as in Group Investigation). Without this individual accountability there is a danger that one student might do the work of the others, or that some students might be shut out of group interaction because they are thought to have little to contribute (O'Donnell & O'Kelly, 1994; Slavin, 1995a).

Studies of cooperative learning methods that incorporate group goals and individual accountability show substantial positive effects on the achievement of students in grades 2 through 12 in all subjects and in all types of schools (Ellis, 2001b; Rohrbeck et al., 2003; Slavin, 1995a; Slavin, Hurley, & Chamberlain, 2003). A review of group learning with technology also found positive effects for well-structured methods (Lou, Abrami, & d'Apollonia, 2001). Effects are similar for all grade levels and for all types of content, from basic skills to problem solving (Qin, Johnson, & Johnson, 1995). Cooperative learning methods are usually used for only a portion of a student's school day and school year (Antil, Jenkins, Wayne, & Vadasy, 1998), but one study found that students in schools that used a variety of cooperative learning methods in almost all subjects for a 2-year period achieved significantly better than did students in traditionally organized schools (Stevens & Slavin, 1995b). These effects were particularly positive for the highest achievers (compared to equally high achievers in the control group) and for the special-education students. Other studies have found equal effects of cooperative learning for high, average, and low achievers and for boys and girls (Slavin, 1995a). There is some evidence that these methods are particularly effective for African American and Latino students (Boykin, 1994; Calderón et al.,

CONNECTIONS

For more on how cooperative learning methods benefit the social integration of students with special education needs in the general education classroom, see Chapter 12, page 431.

1998; Hurley, 2000; Slavin, Hurley, & Chamberlain, 2003). A review of peer assisted learning by Rohrbeck and colleagues (2003) found that effects were strongest on younger, urban, low-income, and minority students. More informal cooperative learning methods, lacking group goals and individual accountability, have not generally had positive effects on student achievement (Chapman, 2001; Klein & Schnackenberg, 2000; Slavin, 1995; Slavin et al., 2003).

In addition to group goals and individual accountability, a few classroom practices can contribute to the effectiveness of cooperative learning. For example, students in cooperative groups who are taught communication and helping skills (Fuchs, Fuchs, Kazdan, & Allen, 1999; Webb & Farrivar, 1994) or are given specific structured ways of working with each other learn more than do students in cooperative groups without these enhancements (Baker, Gersten, & Lee, 2002; Emmer & Gerwels, 2002; Mathes et al., 2003). In addition, students who are taught metacognitive learning strategies (Fantuzzo, King, & Heller, 1992; Friend, 2001; Hoek, Terwel, & van den Eeden, 1997; Jones et al., 2000; Kramarski & Mevarech, 2003) learn more than do students in usual cooperative groups. For example, King (1999) taught students generic question forms to ask each other as they studied, such as "compare and contrast _____ and _____ ," or "how does _____ affect _____?" Students in classes that used these discourse patterns learned more than students using other forms of cooperative learning. A great deal of research has shown that students who give extensive

Personal Reflection

Working Together

I once visited a seventh-grade math class that was using a form of cooperative learning. The students had been taught advanced problem-solving strategies, and the teacher was extraordinarily capable. She posed to the students an exciting question involving a king who decided to release some prisoners according to a mathematical pattern that the students had to discover. The students were asked to work together in groups of four to solve the problem.

The students, in their groups, got right to work, excitedly using their problem-solving strategies to try to find the answer. Everything looked wonderful until I began to listen in on some of the teams. What was happening was that in most teams, one or two students had taken over the task. Other students were just watching them work. Once a watching student, who happened to be of an ethnic minority, offered a suggestion. "Quiet!" said one of the working students. "We've almost got the answer!"

This experience reinforced for me the importance of group goals and individual accountability in cooperative learning. The teacher's instructions were perfect from a math perspective but disastrous from a cooperative learning perspective. By having the group arrive at a simple solution as quickly as possible, students felt to be less able (or less aggressive) by their peers were sure to be sidelined. Imagine that the goals of the activity were not only to solve the problem but also to ensure that every member of the group could later explain the solution or solve a similar problem working alone. In this case, it would be essential to all students to make sure that everyone was involved and that everyone was learning to solve the problems.

@ Reflect on This. How might the math teacher have structured the cooperative learning to ensure that all students would be involved and all would learn to solve similar problems?

INTASC

5 Classroom Motivation and Management

explanations to others learn more in cooperative groups than do those who give or receive short answers or no answers (Nattiv, 1994; Webb, 1992; Webb, Trooper, & Fall, 1995).

There is less research on the effects of project-based forms of cooperative learning focused on ill-structured problems; but the studies that do exist show equally favorable results of cooperative methods designed for such problems (Blumenfeld et al., 1996; Lazarowitz, 1995; Thousand & Villa, 1994). In particular, a study by Sharan and Shachar (1988) found substantial positive effects of the Group Investigation method on higher-order objectives in language and literature, and studies by Cohen (1994a) have shown that the more consistently teachers implement her Complex Instruction program, the better children achieve.

In addition to boosting achievement, cooperative learning methods have had positive effects on such outcomes as improved intergroup relations (Slavin, 1995b), self-esteem, attitudes toward school, and acceptance of children with special educational needs (Schmuck & Schmuck, 1997; Shulman, Lotan, & Whitcomb, 1998; Slavin, 1995a; Slavin et al., 2003). Studies find that cooperative learning is very widely used (e.g., Antil et al., 1998; Puma et al., 1997), but the forms of cooperative learning most often used are informal methods lacking group goals and individual accountability. If this method is to achieve its full potential, educators will need to focus on more research-based strategies.

CERTIFICATION POINTER

On your teacher certification test, you may be asked to determine when you would *not* employ a particular cooperative learning strategy.

*H*OW ARE PROBLEM-SOLVING AND THINKING SKILLS TAUGHT?

INTASC

4 Multiple Instructional Strategies

Students cannot be said to have learned anything useful unless they have the ability to use information and skills to solve problems. For example, a student might be quite good at adding, subtracting, and multiplying but have little idea of how to solve this problem: "Sylvia bought four hamburgers at $1.25 each, two orders of french fries at 65 cents, and three large sodas at 75 cents. How much change did she get from a 10-dollar bill?"

Sylvia's situation is not an unusual one in real life, and the computations involved are not difficult. However, many students (and even some otherwise competent adults) would have difficulty solving this problem. The difficulty of most applications problems in mathematics lies not in the computations but in knowing how to set the problem up so that it can be solved. **Problem solving** is a skill that can be taught and learned (Bransford & Stein, 1993; Martinez, 1998; Mayer & Wittrock, 1996).

The Problem-Solving Process

General Problem-Solving Strategies   Students can be taught several well-researched strategies to use in solving problems (see, for example, Beyer, 1998; Derry, 1991; Tishman, Perkins, & Jay, 1995). Bransford and Stein (1993) developed and evaluated a five-step strategy called IDEAL:

problem solving

The application of knowledge and skills to achieve certain goals.

I   Identify problems and opportunities
D   Define goals and represent the problem
E   Explore possible strategies
A   Anticipate outcomes and act
L   Look back and learn

IDEAL and similar strategies begin with careful consideration of what problem needs to be solved, what resources and information are available, and how the problem can be represented (e.g., in a drawing, outline, or flowchart) and then broken into steps that lead to a solution. For example, the first step is to identify the goal and figure out how to proceed. Newell and Simon (1972) suggest that the problem solver repeatedly ask, "What is the difference between where I am now and where I want to be? What can I do to reduce that difference?" In solving Sylvia's problem, the goal is to find out how much change she will receive from a 10-dollar bill after buying food and drinks. We might then break the problem into substeps, each with its own subgoal:

1. Figure how much Sylvia spent on hamburgers.
2. Figure how much Sylvia spent on french fries.
3. Figure how much Sylvia spent on sodas.
4. Figure how much Sylvia spent in total.
5. Figure how much change Sylvia gets from $10.00.

Means–Ends Analysis   Deciding what the problem is and what needs to be done involves a **means–ends analysis.** Learning to solve problems requires a great deal of practice with different kinds of problems that demand thought. All too often, textbooks in mathematics and other subjects that include many problems fail to present problems that will make students think. For example, they might give students a set of word problems whose solutions require the multiplication of two numbers. Students soon learn that they can solve such problems by looking for any two numbers and multiplying them. In real life, however, problems do not line themselves up neatly in categories. We might hear, "Joe Smith got a 5 percent raise last week, which amounted to $1,200." If we want to figure out how much Joe was making before his raise, the hard part is not doing the calculation, but knowing what calculation is called for. In real life this problem would not be on a page titled "Dividing by Percents." The more different kinds of problems students learn to solve, and the more

means–ends analysis
A problem-solving technique that encourages identifying the goal (ends) to be attained, the current situation, and what needs to be done (means) to reduce the difference between the two conditions.

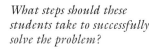

What steps should these students take to successfully solve the problem?

they have to think to solve the problems, the greater the chance that, when faced with real-life problems, students will be able to transfer their skills or knowledge to the new situation.

Extracting Relevant Information   Realistic problems are rarely neat and tidy. Imagine that Sylvia's problem was as follows:

> Sylvia walked into the fast-food restaurant at 6:18 with three friends. Between them, they bought four hamburgers at $1.25 each, two orders of french fries at 65 cents, and three large sodas at 75 cents. Onion rings were on sale for 55 cents. Sylvia's mother told her to be in by 9:00, but she was already 25 minutes late by the time she and her friends left the restaurant. Sylvia drove the 3 miles home at an average of 30 miles per hour. How long was Sylvia in the restaurant?

The first part of this task is to clear away all the extraneous information to get to the important facts. The means–ends analysis suggests that only time information is relevant, so all the money transactions and the speed of Sylvia's car can be ignored. Careful reading of the problem reveals that Sylvia left the restaurant at 9:25. This and her arrival time of 6:18 are all that matters for solving the problem. Once we know what is relevant and what is not, the solution is easy.

Representing the Problem   For many kinds of problems, graphic representation might be an effective means of finding a solution. Adams (1974) provides a story that illustrates this:

> A Buddhist monk has to make a pilgrimage and stay overnight in a temple that is at the top of a high mountain. The road spirals around and around the mountain. The monk begins walking up the mountain at sunrise. He walks all day long and finally reaches the top at about sunset. He stays all night in the temple and performs his devotions. At sunrise the next day the monk begins walking down the mountain. It takes him much less time than walking up, and he is at the bottom shortly after noon. The question is: Is there a point on the road when he was coming down that he passed at the same time of day when he was coming up the mountain?

This can seem to be a difficult problem because people begin to reason in a variety of ways as they think about the man going up and down. Adams points out one representation that makes the problem easy: Suppose there were two monks, one leaving the top at sunrise and one starting up at sunrise. Would they meet? Of course they would.

In addition to drawings, there are many other ways of representing problems. Students may be taught to make diagrams, flowcharts, outlines, and other means of summarizing and depicting the critical components of a problem (Katayama & Robinson, 1998; Robinson & Kiewra, 1995; van Meter, 2001).

Teaching Creative Problem Solving

Most of the problems students encounter in school might require careful reading and some thought, but little creativity. However, many of the problems we face in life are not so cut-and-dried. Life is full of situations that call for creative problem solving, as in figuring out how to change or end a relationship without hurt feelings or how to repair a machine with a bent paper clip (Sternberg, 1995).

The following sections describe a strategy for teaching creative problem solving (Beyer, 1997; Frederiksen, 1984a).

Incubation Creative problem solving is quite different from the analytical, step-by-step process that was used to solve Sylvia's problems. In creative problem solving, one important principle is to avoid rushing to a solution; instead, it is useful to pause and reflect on the problem and think through, or incubate, several alternative solutions before choosing a course of action. Consider the following simple problem:

> Roger baked an apple pie in his oven in three quarters of an hour. How long would it take him to bake three apple pies?

Many students would rush to multiply 45 minutes by 3. However, if they took some time to reflect, most would realize that baking three pies in the same oven would actually take about the same amount of time as baking one pie! In teaching this process, teachers must avoid putting time pressures on students. Instead of speed, they should value ingenuity and careful thought.

Suspension of Judgment In creative problem solving, students should be encouraged to suspend judgment, to consider all possibilities before trying out a solution. One specific method based on this principle is called *brainstorming* (Osborn, 1963), in which two or more individuals suggest as many solutions to a problem as they can think of, no matter how seemingly ridiculous. Only after they have thought of as many ideas as possible is any idea evaluated as a possible solution. The point of brainstorming is to avoid focusing on one solution too early and perhaps ignoring better ways to proceed.

Appropriate Climates Creative problem solving is enhanced by a relaxed, even playful environment (Tishman et al., 1995). Perhaps even more important, students who are engaging in creative problem solving must feel that their ideas will be accepted.

People who do well on tests of creative problem solving seem to be less afraid of making mistakes and appearing foolish than do those who do poorly. Successful problem solvers also seem to treat problem-solving situations more playfully (Benjafield, 1992). This implies that a relaxed, fun atmosphere is important in teaching problem solving. Students should certainly be encouraged to try different solutions and not be criticized for taking a wrong turn.

Analysis One method of creative problem solving that is often suggested is to analyze and juxtapose major characteristics or specific elements of a problem (Chen & Daehler, 2000; Lesgold, 1988). For example, careful analysis of the situation might help solve the following problem:

> A tennis tournament was set up with a series of rounds. The winner of each match advanced to the next round. If there were an odd number of players in a round, one player (chosen at random) would advance automatically to the next round. In a tournament with 147 players, how many matches would take place before a single winner would be declared?

We might solve this problem the hard way, making diagrams of the various matches. However, careful analysis of the situation would reveal that each match would produce exactly one loser. Therefore it would take 146 matches to produce 146 losers (and one winner).

Engaging Problems One key to the teaching of problem solving is providing problems that intrigue and engage children. The same problem-solving skills could be involved in a context that is either compelling or boring to students, and this matters in the outcomes. For example, Bottge (2001) found that low-achieving secondary

CERTIFICATION POINTER

Teacher certification tests will require you to know appropriate strategies for engaging students in active learning to promote the development of creative problem-solving skills.

students, many with serious learning disabilities, could learn complex problem-solving skills relating to building a cage for a pet or setting up a car racing track. Since John Dewey proposed it a hundred years ago, the motivational value of connecting problem solving to real life or simulations of real life has been demonstrated many times (Holt & Willard-Holt, 2000; Torp & Sage, 1998; Westwater & Wolfe, 2000).

Feedback   Provide practice with feedback. Perhaps the most effective way to teach problem solving is to provide students with a great deal of practice on a wide variety of problem types, giving feedback not only on the correctness of their solutions but also on the process by which they arrived at the solutions (Swanson, 1990). The role of practice with feedback in solving complex problems cannot be overemphasized. Mr. Dunbar's students, in the chapter-opening vignette, could not have arrived at the solution to their problem if they had not had months of practice and feedback on simpler problems.

Teaching Thinking Skills

One of the oldest dreams in education is that there might be some way to make students smarter—not just more knowledgeable or skillful but actually better able to learn new information of all kinds (Beyer, 1998). Perhaps someday someone will come up with a "smart pill" that will have this effect; but in the meantime, several groups of researchers have been developing and evaluating instructional programs that are designed to increase students' general thinking skills.

The most widely known and extensively researched of several thinking-skills programs was developed by an Israeli educator, Reuven Feuerstein (1980). In this program, called **Instrumental Enrichment,** students work through a series of paper-and-pencil exercises that are intended to build such intellectual skills as categorization, comparison, orientation in space, and numerical progressions. Figure 8.4 shows one example of an activity designed to increase analytic perception. The Instrumental Enrichment treatment is meant to be administered for 3 to 5 hours per week over a period of at least 2 years, usually to underachieving or learning-disabled adolescents. Studies of this duration have found that the program has positive effects on tests of aptitude, such as IQ tests, but generally not on achievement (Savell, Twohig, & Rachford, 1986; Sternberg & Bhana, 1986).

Another approach to the teaching of thinking skills is to incorporate them in daily lessons and classroom experiences—to create a "culture of thinking" (Sternberg, 2002; Tishman et al., 1995). As an example of integrating thinking skills into daily lessons, Tishman, Perkins, and Jay (1995) describe an impromptu discussion in a class that has been taught a generic strategy for problem solving. This strategy is built around a four-step process (state, search, evaluate, and elaborate) that is summarized in Table 8.2. In their example, Ms. Mandly's sixth-graders discuss why plants in terrariums the class planted a month earlier are starting to die and what they might do about it. The class learned the steps summarized in Table 8.2 and had a poster identical to the table posted in the classroom. The discussion went as follows:

Ms. Mandly: Let's take a look at the poster. How can we build a strategy to deal with this situation? Which building blocks can we use?

Rory: We should use the search step, to search for a solution to the problem.

Marc: Yeah, but we're not even exactly sure what the problem is. We don't know if the plants in the terrarium are wilted because they have too much water or too little.

Instrumental Enrichment

A thinking skills program in which students work through a series of paper-and-pencil exercises that are designed to develop various intellectual abilities.

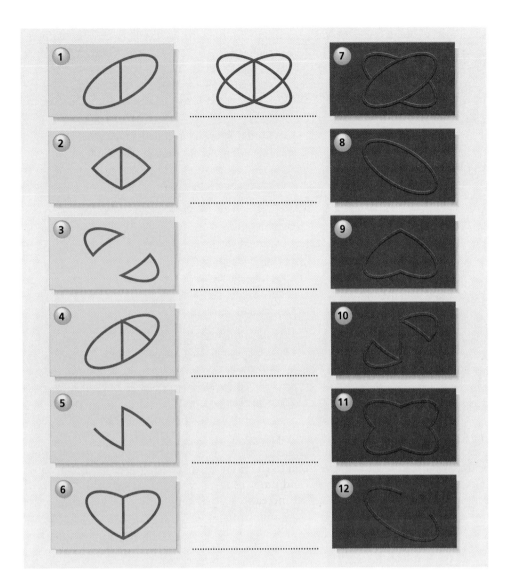

FIGURE 8.4
Examples from Analytic Perception

Look at the three columns at the right. For each drawing in the left column, there is a drawing in the right column that completes it to make the form shown in the middle column. Write the number of the form in the right column needed to complete the form in the first column. The student must select the appropriate drawing from the right to complete the one on the left to obtain a figure identical to the model in the middle column on this page. The task requires representation, internalization and labeling of the model, definition of the missing parts, systematic work, and comparison to the model for self-criticism.

From Reuven Feuerstein, "Instrumental Enrichment: A Selected Sample of Material for Review Purposes." Jerusalem: The Hadassah-Wizo-Canada Research Institute, May 1973, p. 5. Reprinted by permission of the author.

Ms. Mandly: Are you suggesting we also need a state step, Marc?

Marc (after a moment of looking at the poster): Yes. In two ways: I think we need to state the problem and we need to state our goal.

Ms. Mandly: That sounds reasonable. Any other building blocks we can use?

Marc: Yeah, that might not be enough. What if you take care of a terrarium, and it still wilts? Other people in your group will want to know what went wrong.

Ms. Mandly: It sounds like we have two goals here. One, decide how to care for the terrarium. And two, make a plan for keeping track of the terrarium's care.

After more discussion, students agreed on exactly what outcomes they wanted and moved to the "search" step. Looking at the search tactics, they decided to brainstorm lots of different possible solutions. Ms. Mandly kept track of their ideas on the blackboard and occasionally reminded them to keep in mind some key tactics: to look for hidden ideas and to look for different kinds of ideas. Some of the ideas students came up with are the following:

1. Have a sign-up list.

Table 8.2

Thinking Skills: Build a Strategy

	Strategy Building Blocks	
When . . .	*Strategy Step*	*Tactics*
When you need to be clear about what you're doing or where you're going . . .	State . . . either the problem, the situation, or your goal(s).	Identify the different dimensions of the situation. Identify the parts of the situation you will focus on. State precisely what you want to change or what you want your outcome to be. Be specific!
When you need to think broadly about something . . .	Search . . . for ideas, options, possibilities, purposes, features, assumptions, causes, effects, questions, dimensions, hypotheses, facts, or interpretations.	Brainstorm. Look for different kinds of ideas. Look at things from different points of view. Look for hidden ideas. Build on other people's ideas. Use categories to help you search.
When you need to assess, rate, or decide something . . .	Evaluate . . . options, plans, ideas, theories, or objects.	Look for lots of reasons. Consider the immediate and long-term consequences. List all the pros and cons, paying attention to both. Try to be objective; avoid bias. Use your imagination: How will it affect others?
When you need to think about the details of something . . .	Elaborate . . . possibilities, plans, options, hypotheses, or ideas.	Make a detailed plan: Say what will happen at each step. Visualize what it will look/feel/seem like *in detail*. Ask yourself: What resources will be used? How will it happen? Who will be affected? How long will it take? Think about the different parts. Draw a picture or write a description; imagine *telling* someone about it.

Source: From Shari Tishman, David N. Perkins, and Eileen Jay, *The Thinking Classroom.* Copyright © 1995 by Allyn & Bacon. Reprinted by permission.

2. Let the teacher decide who should water.
3. Have one person volunteer to do it all.
4. Make a rotating schedule for each group.
5. Make a rotating schedule, plus have weekly group meetings to discuss progress.

After students reviewed and evaluated their brainstormed list, they unanimously agreed that option 5—rotating schedule plus weekly meetings—was best.

They then went on to step 4: elaborate, and make a plan. They designed a rotation schedule for each terrarium group, and with Ms. Mandly's help they picked a time for weekly group meetings. Working through the "elaborate step," they invented a detailed checklist for the designated weekly waterer, to help track factors that might contribute to the terrarium's health, such as how much water has been given, the date of watering, the temperature of the classroom, and so on (Tishman et al., 1995).

In the course of discussing the terrarium problem, the students were learning a broadly applicable strategy for approaching and solving complex problems. By calling on this and other strategies frequently as they are appropriate in a classroom context, Ms. Mandly not only gave students useful strategies but also communicated the idea that strategy use is a normal and expected part of daily life.

Critical Thinking

One key objective of schooling is enhancing students' abilities to think critically, to make rational decisions about what to do or what to believe (Marzano, 1995). Examples of **critical thinking** include identifying misleading advertisements, weighing competing evidence, and identifying assumptions or fallacies in arguments. As with any other objective, learning to think critically requires practice; students can be given many dilemmas, logical and illogical arguments, valid and misleading advertisements, and so on (Halpern, 1995). Effective teaching of critical thinking depends on setting a classroom tone that encourages the acceptance of divergent perspectives and free discussion. There should be an emphasis on giving reasons for opinions rather than only giving correct answers. Skills in critical thinking are best acquired in relation to topics with which students are familiar. For example, students will learn more from a unit evaluating Nazi propaganda if they know a great deal about the history of Nazi Germany and the culture of the 1930s and 1940s. Perhaps most important, the goal of teaching critical thinking is to create a critical spirit, which encourages students to question what they hear and to examine their own thinking for logical inconsistencies or fallacies.

Why is critical thinking particularly important when using the Internet for research or help with homework?

Beyer (1988) identified 10 critical-thinking skills that students might use in judging the validity of claims or arguments, understanding advertisements, and so on:

1. Distinguishing between verifiable facts and value claims
2. Distinguishing relevant from irrelevant information, claims, or reasons
3. Determining the factual accuracy of a statement
4. Determining the credibility of a source
5. Identifying ambiguous claims or arguments
6. Identifying unstated assumptions
7. Detecting bias
8. Identifying logical fallacies
9. Recognizing logical inconsistencies in a line of reasoning
10. Determining the strength of an argument or claim. (p. 57)

Beyer notes that this is not a sequence of steps but rather a list of possible ways in which a student might approach information to evaluate whether or not it is true or sensible. The key task in teaching critical thinking to students is to help them

CERTIFICATION POINTER

When responding to the case studies in certification tests, you may be asked to design a lesson that includes strategies for teaching critical thinking skills.

critical thinking
The ability to make rational decisions about what to do or what to believe.

THE INTENTIONAL TEACHER

Using What You Know about Student-Centered and Constructivist Approaches to Improve Teaching and Learning

Intentional teachers keep sight of one of the overarching goals of education: to foster students' ability to solve real, complex problems. Intentional teachers work toward this lofty goal by ensuring that schooling provides more than a series of lectures and discrete workbook exercises. Intentional teachers furnish opportunities for students to build their own knowledge, to work with others in discovering important ideas, and to attack challenging real-life issues.

❶ What do I expect my students to know and to be able to do at the end of this lesson? How does this contribute to course objectives and to my students' need to become capable individuals?

Intentional teachers build in regular opportunities for students to approach complex, difficult, realistic tasks. Check your goals and curriculum: Where and how often do you encourage students to construct knowledge through student-centered approaches? For example, you might provide regular opportunities for students to study and use mathematics in realistic settings. The class might, for instance, develop, administer, analyze, and act on a schoolwide survey about a current issue, such as the purchase of playground equipment.

Intentional teachers think about the balance between direct, teacher-centered instructional approaches and constructivist, student-centered approaches. Select your teaching strategies based on your goals for students, and realize that a balance of both kinds of approaches might be best for promoting a variety of learning outcomes. For example, imagine that you feel pressed to cover a great deal of information in your government class; as a result, you find yourself lecturing almost daily. Then you recall that your major goal is to help your students become citizens who make informed decisions about complicated issues. Therefore, you review your plan book to ensure that you are using discovery approaches regularly. You begin with a discovery lesson the very next day by distributing nickels and asking students to draw inferences about the culture that created them.

❷ What knowledge, skills, needs, and interests do my students have that must be taken into account in my lesson?

Background knowledge affects students' ability to build meaning and solve problems. Gather information about your students' earlier school experiences by conversing with last year's teacher or teachers: Do your learners come with previous experiences in group work? What do their records suggest about their preferences and attitudes toward novelty?

Intentional teachers make use of top-down processing by beginning instruction with holistic problems or issues and moving to analysis of their parts. You might begin your lessons with real problems within the context of a supportive atmosphere. For example, you might begin a math class with a question: "If there are five flavors of fruity candies in this bag, how many flavor combinations can I create?" You could note the students' widely varying initial guesses, and then pass out bags of candy and allow them to get to work on the problem. When it becomes evident that they are stymied, you could suggest that they try a charting strategy to work on a single part of the problem: How many combinations of *just two* flavors are there? You and your class could devise the chart below, quickly finding patterns and discovering that there are 10 flavor combinations of two candies. Students should discern that they simply need to make similar charts for 3-, 4-, and 5-flavor combinations to arrive at their answer.

Flavor 1	1-1 1-2 1-3 1-4 1-5 (symbols represent flavor 1 with flavors 2, 3, 4, and 5)				
Flavor 2	2-1	2-2	2-3	2-4	2-5
Flavor 3	3-1	3-2	3-3	3-4	3-5
Flavor 4	4-1	4-2	4-3	4-4	4-5
Flavor 5	5-1	5-2	5-3	5-4	5-5

learn not only how to use each of these strategies but also how to tell when each is appropriate.

ON THE WEB

For articles and resources on critical thinking go to **www.criticalthinking.org**, the website of the Foundation for Critical Thinking.

Teach strategies for problem solving: include drawing pictures, acting out situations, and making diagrams. Model a variety of problem-solving strategies, using them as scaffolds to keep students working within their zone of proximal development.

❸ What do I know about the content, child development, learning, motivation, and effective teaching strategies that I can use to accomplish my objectives?

As students work on a cooperative project, watch them. What does their nonverbal behavior tell you about how well they are working with peers? How willing are they to take risks? When you see that students are unwilling to accept peers' ideas, you might stop the lesson and provide instruction on working well with others: "When someone gives a new idea, wait before you say no. Think for twenty seconds about how that idea might work. Watch, I'll pretend I'm in your group and you tell me a new idea . . ."

❹ What instructional materials, technology, assistance, and other resources are available to help accomplish my objectives?

Emotion, personal meaning, and relevance can help students process information deeply so that they remember better. Begin your lesson in ways that capture student interest, and provide instruction that focuses on developing understanding beyond surface-level features.

You begin a lesson on density by displaying two bottles of soda (one full, one with some air in it) in an aquarium: One sinks, but the other floats! The students' curiosity is piqued and they actively engage themselves in discovering the rule that allows for the cans' behavior. At the lesson's close, you create a powerful visual image of an immense iceberg floating in the chilling sea. You ask students to explain, using their new understanding of density, why the iceberg floats despite its vast size.

Your discussions with colleagues, both in the current setting in which you work, and with former classmates, can serve to help you identify new materials and other resources that will benefit your efforts to become a more intentional, student-centered teacher.

❺ How will I plan to assess students' progress toward my objectives?

Students' outputs provide information about success. Examine students' work for evidence of sense-making, of critical thinking, and of creativity. Imagine that you've just collected a stack of essays on students' analysis of a current environmental issue: destruction of the rain forests. You might begin your assessment by listing two questions to help you focus on students' knowledge construction: (a) How well do students marshal factual details to support their position? (b) What evidence is there of creative, inventive thinking?

One of the most challenging aspects of a student-centered orientation to teaching is how to determine whether students have met learning goals and attained intended objectives. Assess your instruction using multiple measures.

Review your plan book and check to see how many realistic opportunities you provided in the last week. Audio or videotape yourself teaching and analyze the kinds of questions and prompts you use. Ask your students for feedback on your teaching, using survey questions like this one: "The teacher _____ [never/sometimes/often/always] gives us opportunities to figure things out on our own."

❻ How will I respond if individual children or the class as a whole are not on track toward success? What is my back-up plan?

How can you, as an intentional teacher seeking to incorporate constructivist approaches, help prepare your students for this change from "tell me what I'm supposed to do" to the practices of group learning, inquiry, and open-ended thinking?

To help your students become more self-directed, not only utilize cooperative approaches wherever possible, but also provide direct instruction in helping and communication skills at the start of cooperative learning lessons. You can provide instruction on how to give feedback in group work, recalling that research has shown that students who give and/or receive extensive explanations learn more in cooperative settings. These techniques will help students to reach group goals.

Chapter Summary

What Is the Constructivist View of Learning?

Constructivists believe that knowing is a process and that learners must individually and actively discover and transform complex information to make it their own. Constructivist approaches emphasize top-down processing, in which students begin with complex problems or tasks and discover the basic knowledge and skills needed to solve the problems or perform the tasks. Constructivist approaches also emphasize cooperative learning, questioning or inquiry strategies, and other metacognitive skills.

Discovery learning and scaffolding are constructivist learning methods based on cognitive learning theories. Bruner's discovery learning highlights students' active self-learning, curiosity, and creative problem solving. Scaffolding, based on Vygotsky's views, calls for teacher assistance to students at critical points in their learning.

How Is Cooperative Learning Used in Instruction?

In cooperative learning, small groups of students work together to help one another learn. Cooperative learning groups are used in discovery learning, discussion, and study for assessment. Cooperative learning programs such as Student Teams–Achievement Divisions (STAD) are successful because they reward both group and individual effort and improvement and because groups are responsible for the individual learning of each group member.

How Are Problem-Solving and Thinking Skills Taught?

Problem-solving skills are taught through a series of steps, including, for example, means–ends analysis and problem representation. Creative problem solving requires incubation time, suspension of judgment, conducive climates, problem analysis, the application of thinking skills, and feedback. Thinking skills include, for example, planning, classifying, divergent thinking, identifying assumptions, identifying misleading information, and generating questions. Thinking skills can be taught through programs such as Instrumental Enrichment; creating a culture of thinking in the classroom is another useful technique.

Key Terms

Research
Navigator.com

Review the following key terms from the chapter. Then, to explore research on these topics and how they relate to education today, connect to Research Navigator™ through this book's Companion Website or directly at www.researchnavigator.com.

cognitive apprenticeship   244
constructivist theories of learning   243
Cooperative Integrated Reading and
   Composition (CIRC)   258
cooperative learning   272
cooperative scripting   259
critical thinking   269
discovery learning   245
Group Investigation   259
Instrumental Enrichment   266

Jigsaw   258
Learning Together   259
means–ends analysis   263
mediated learning   249
problem solving   262
reciprocal teaching   251
self-regulated learners   249
Student Teams–Achievement Divisions
   (STAD)   256

Self-Assessment: Practicing for Licensure

Directions: The chapter-opening vignette addresses indicators that are often assessed in state licensure exams. Re-read the chapter-opening vignette, and then respond to the following questions.

1. Mr. Dunbar, in his lesson on the volume of a cylinder, asks his students to figure out how to measure volume through experimentation. What type of learning strategy is he using?
   a. direct instruction
   b. classical conditioning
   c. discovery learning
   d. teacher-mediated discussion

2. Why didn't Mr. Dunbar just tell his students that the formula for finding the volume of a cylinder is $\pi r^2 h$?
   a. He believes that students will gain deeper understanding if they work it out for themselves.
   b. He thought the lesson would take less time if the students could figure it out.
   c. He knows that discovery learning is superior to direct instruction.
   d. He is applying teaching strategies suggested by B. F. Skinner and other behaviorists.

3. In which of the following examples is Mr. Dunbar demonstrating Vygotsky's "zone of proximal development" concept?
   a. Mr. Dunbar says, "Today we are going to have a chance to discover how to compute the volume of a cylinder."
   b. Mr. Dunbar assigns his students to sit around the lab tables in groups of four.
   c. Mr. Dunbar, as he is passing by the Master Minds group, says, "You're right, Miguel, but what are you going to do with that information?"
   d. Mr. Dunbar praises the Master Minds group for figuring out the answer on its own.

4. Mr. Dunbar effectively uses cooperative learning strategies in his lesson on the volume of cylinders. He does all of the following except
   a. give recognition to the groups when they solve the problem.
   b. assure that each group contains members who have similar abilities.
   c. make certain that each group member learns.
   d. mixes students in terms of race, ethnicity, gender, and special needs.

5. Which of the following cooperative learning strategies is Mr. Dunbar using?
   a. Group Investigation
   b. Learning Together
   c. Jigsaw
   d. STAD

6. Describe an example of discovery learning. What is the teacher's role in a discovery lesson? What strengths and limitations exist with discovery learning?

7. How can teachers improve students' problem-solving abilities?

Accommodating Instruction to Meet Individual Needs

$\mathcal{M}$r. Arbuthnot is in fine form. He is presenting a lesson on long division to his fourth-grade class and feels that he's never been so clear, so interesting, and so well organized. When he asks questions, several students raise their hands; when he calls on them, they always know the answers. "Arbuthnot, old boy," he says to himself, "I think you're really getting to these kids!"

At the end of the period he passes out a short quiz to see how well his students have learned the long-division lesson. When the papers are scored, he finds to his shock and disappointment that only about a third of the class got every problem right. Another third missed every problem; the remaining students fell somewhere in between. "What went wrong?" he thinks. "Well, no matter, I'll set the situation right in tomorrow's lesson."

The next day, Mr. Arbuthnot is even better prepared, uses vivid examples and diagrams to show how to do long division, and gives an active, exciting lesson. Even more hands than before go up when he asks questions, and the answers are usually correct. However, some of the students are beginning to look bored, particularly those who got perfect papers on the quiz and those who got none right.

Toward the end of the period he gives another brief quiz. The scores are better this time, but there is still a group of students who got none of the problems correct. He is crestfallen. "I had them in the palm of my hand," he thinks. "How could they fail to learn?"

To try to find out what went wrong, Mr. Arbuthnot goes over the quiz papers of the students who missed all the problems. He immediately sees a pattern. By the second lesson, almost all students were proceeding correctly in setting up the long-division problems. However, some were making consistent errors in subtraction. Others had apparently forgotten their multiplication facts. Their problems were not with division at all; the students simply lacked the prerequisite skills.

"Well," thinks Mr. Arbuthnot, "at least I was doing great with some of the kids." It occurs to him that one of the students who got a perfect paper after the first lesson might be able to give him an idea about how to teach the others better. He asks Teresa how she grasped long division so quickly.

"It was easy," she says. "We learned long division last year!" ◎

USING YOUR

Experience

Critical Thinking   List all of the ways in which Mr. Arbuthnot could be more effective in addressing student individual differences. Then list all of the ways in which he is effective in addressing student needs.

Cooperative Learning   Work with a group of four or five classmates. Pass a sheet of paper around the group, and ask each member to write down an idea to help Mr. Arbuthnot become more effective in addressing students' needs. After one idea is added, the sheet is passed to the next person in the group, who adds an idea and passes the sheet and so on. Share some of these ideas with the class.

INTASC

3 Adapting Instruction for Individual Needs

6 Communication Skills

7 Instructional Planning Skills

WHAT ARE ELEMENTS OF EFFECTIVE INSTRUCTION BEYOND A GOOD LESSON?

As Mr. Arbuthnot learned to his chagrin, effective instruction takes a lot more than effective lectures. He gave a great lesson on long division, yet it was appropriate for only some of his students, those who had the needed prerequisites but had not already learned long division. To make his lesson effective for all of his students, he needed to adapt it to meet their diverse needs. Furthermore, the best lesson in the world won't work if students are not motivated to learn it or if inadequate time is allotted to allow all students to learn.

If the quality of lectures were all that mattered in effective instruction, we could probably find the best lecturers in the world, videotape their lessons, and show the tapes to students. If you think about why videotaped lessons would not work very well by themselves, you will realize how much more is involved in effective instruction than simply giving good lectures. First, the video teacher would have no idea what students already know. A particular lesson might be too advanced or too easy for a particular group of students. Second, some students might be learning the lesson quite well while others would be missing key concepts and falling behind. The video teacher would have no way of knowing which students needed additional help and, in any case, would have no way of providing it. There would be no way to question students to find out whether they were getting the main points and then to reteach any concept they had missed. Third, the video teacher would have no way of motivating students to pay attention to the lesson or to really try to learn it. If students failed to pay attention or misbehaved, the video teacher could not do anything about it. Finally, the video teacher would never know at the end of a lesson whether students had actually learned the main concepts or skills.

This analysis of video teaching illustrates why teachers must be concerned with many elements of instruction in addition to the presentation of information. Teachers must know how to adapt their instruction to the students' levels of knowledge. They must motivate students to learn, manage student behavior, group students for instruction, and assess the students' learning.

To help make sense of all these elements of effective instruction, educational psychologists have proposed models of effective instruction. These models explain the critical features of high-quality lessons and how they relate to one another to enhance learning.

Carroll's Model of School Learning and QAIT

One of the most influential articles ever published in the field of educational psychology was a paper by John Carroll titled "A Model of School Learning" (1963, 1989). In it he describes teaching in terms of the management of time, resources, and activities to ensure student learning. Carroll proposed that learning is a function of (1) time actually spent on learning and (2) time needed to learn. That is, learning is greater the more time students spend on learning in relation to the amount of time they need to learn. Time needed is a product of aptitude and ability to learn; time actually spent depends on clock time available for learning, quality of instruction, and student perseverance.

Slavin (1987d) described a model focusing on the alterable elements of Carroll's model, those that the teacher or school can directly change. It is called the **QAIT model** (quality, appropriateness, incentive, time) of effective instruction.

1. **Quality of instruction:** The degree to which presentation of information or skills helps students easily learn the material. Quality of instruction is largely a product of the quality of the curriculum and of the lesson presentation itself.

2. **Appropriate levels of instruction:** The degree to which the teacher makes sure that students are ready to learn a new lesson (that is, have the necessary skills and knowledge to learn it) but have not already learned the lesson. In other words, the level of instruction is appropriate when a lesson is neither too difficult nor too easy for students.

3. **Incentive:** The degree to which the teacher makes sure that students are motivated to work on instructional tasks and to learn the material being presented.

4. **Time:** The degree to which students are given enough time to learn the material being taught.

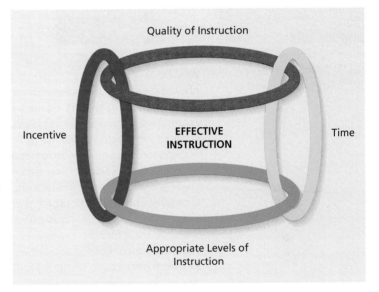

FIGURE 9.1
The QAIT Model
Each of the elements of the QAIT model is like a link in a chain, and the chain is only as strong as the weakest link.

For instruction to be effective, each of these four elements must be adequate. No matter how high the quality of instruction, students will not learn a lesson if they lack the necessary prior skills or information, if they lack the motivation, or if they lack the time they need to learn the lesson. On the other hand, if the quality of instruction is low, then it makes no difference how much students already know, how motivated they are, or how much time they have. Figure 9.1 illustrates the relationship among the elements in the QAIT model.

Quality of Instruction   Quality of instruction refers to the set of activities most people first think of when they think of teaching: lecturing, calling on students, discussing, helping students with seatwork, and so on. When instruction is high in quality, the information presented makes sense to students, is interesting to them, and is easy to remember and apply.

The most important aspect of quality of instruction is the degree to which the lesson makes sense to students. To ensure that lessons make sense, teachers must present material in an orderly, organized way. They need to relate new information

QAIT model
A model of effective instruction that focuses on elements teachers can directly control: quality, appropriateness, incentive, and time.

What are some of the challenges to the effectiveness of the QAIT model in a crowded classroom?

to what students already know. They need to use examples, demonstrations, pictures, and diagrams to make ideas vivid for students. They might use such cognitive strategies as advance organizers and memory strategies. Sometimes a concept will not make sense to students until they discover it or experience it themselves or until they discuss it with others.

Another important aspect of quality of instruction is the degree to which the teacher monitors how well students are learning and adapts the pace of instruction so that it is neither too fast nor too slow. For example, teachers should ask questions frequently to determine how much students have grasped. If the answers show that students are keeping up with the lesson, the teacher might move along a little more rapidly. But if students' answers show that they are having trouble keeping up, the teacher might review parts of the lesson and slow down the pace.

Appropriate Levels of Instruction   Perhaps the most difficult problem of classroom organization is dealing with the fact that students come into class with different levels of prior knowledge, skills, and motivation, and with different learning rates (Tomlinson, 2000, 2004). This was Mr. Arbuthnot's main dilemma. Student diversity requires teachers to provide appropriate levels of instruction. Teaching a class of 30 students (or even a class of 10) is fundamentally different from one-to-one tutoring because of the inevitability of student-to-student differences that affect the success of instruction. Teachers can always be sure that if they teach one lesson to the whole class, some students will learn the material much more quickly than others. In fact, some students might not learn the lesson at all; they might lack important prerequisite skills or adequate time (because to give them enough time would waste too much of the time of students who learn rapidly). Recognition of these instructionally important differences leads many teachers to search for ways of individualizing instruction, adapting instruction to meet students' different needs, or grouping students according to their abilities.

However, some of these solutions create problems of their own that could be more serious than the ones they are meant to solve. For example, a teacher might give all students materials that are appropriate to their individual needs and allow students to work at their own rates. This solves the problem of providing appropriate levels of instruction but creates serious new problems of managing the activities of 20 or 30 students doing 20 or 30 different things. A teacher may group students by ability (e.g., Redbirds, Bluebirds, and Yellowbirds) so that each group will have a relatively narrow range of abilities. However, this creates problems, too, because when the teacher is working with the Redbirds, the Bluebirds and Yellowbirds must work without supervision or help. Effective ways of adapting instruction to meet student needs are discussed later in this chapter.

INTASC

5 **Classroom Motivation and Management**

Incentive   Thomas Edison once wrote that "genius is one per cent inspiration and ninety-nine per cent perspiration." The same could probably be said of learning. Learning is work. This is not to say that learning isn't or can't be fun or stimulating—far from it. But it is true that students must exert themselves to pay attention, to conscientiously perform the tasks required of them, and to study; and students must somehow be motivated to do these things. This incentive, or motivation, might come from characteristics of the tasks themselves (e.g., the interest value of the material being learned), from characteristics of students (such as their curiosity or positive orientation toward learning), or from rewards provided by the teacher or the school (such as grades and certificates).

If students want to know something, they will be motivated to exert the necessary effort to learn it. This is why there are students who can rattle off the names, batting averages, number of home runs, and all sorts of other information about every player of the Chicago Cubs but can't name the 50 states or perform basic multiplication. To such students, baseball facts are of great interest, so they are willing to invest a great deal of effort to master them. Some information is naturally interesting to some or all students, but teachers can do much to create interest in a topic by arousing students' curiosity or by showing how knowledge gained in school can be useful outside of school. For example, baseball fans might be much more interested in learning about computing proportions if they are convinced that this information is necessary for computing batting averages.

However, not every subject can be made fascinating to all students at all times. Most students need some kind of recognition or reward if they are to exert maximum effort to learn skills or concepts that might seem unimportant at the moment but will be critical for later learning. For this reason, schools use praise, feedback, grades, certificates, stars, prizes, and other rewards to increase student motivation.

Time   The final element of the QAIT model is time. Instruction takes time. More time spent teaching something does not necessarily mean more learning, but if instructional quality, appropriateness of instruction, and incentive are all high, then more time on instruction will pay off in greater learning. The amount of time that is available for learning depends largely on two factors. The first is the amount of time that the teacher (1) schedules for instruction and (2) actually uses to teach. The other is the amount of time students pay attention to the lesson. Both kinds of time are affected by classroom management and discipline strategies. If students are well behaved, are well motivated, and have a sense of purpose and direction and if teachers are well prepared and well organized, then there is plenty of time for students to learn whatever teachers want to teach. However, many factors, such as interruptions, behavior problems, and poor transitions between activities, eat away at the time available for learning (see Hong, 2001).

HOW ARE STUDENTS GROUPED TO ACCOMMODATE ACHIEVEMENT DIFFERENCES?

From the day they walk into school, students differ in their knowledge, skills, motivations, and predispositions toward what is about to be taught. Some students are already reading when they enter kindergarten; others need much time and support to learn to read well. A teacher starting a new lesson can usually assume that some students already know a great deal about the lesson's content, some know less but will master the content early on, and some might not be able to master the content at all within the time provided (see Biemiller, 1993). Some have the prerequisite skills and knowledge they need in order to learn the lesson, while others do not. This was Mr. Arbuthnot's problem: Some of his students were not ready to learn long division, while others had already learned it before he began. Some of his students lacked basic multiplication and subtraction skills that are crucial for long division. Others already knew long division before he began his lesson, and many probably learned it during

CONNECTIONS

The rewards and general principles of motivation are discussed throughout Chapter 10.

CONNECTIONS

Principles of classroom management and discipline are discussed throughout Chapter 11.

CONNECTIONS

To learn more about student differences in general intelligence, specific aptitudes, and abilities and learning styles, see Chapter 4, page 121.

INTASC

3 Adapting Instruction for Individual Needs

the first lesson and did not need the second. If Mr. Arbuthnot stops to review multiplication and division, he will be wasting the time of the better-prepared students. If he sets his pace of instruction according to the needs of his more able students, those with learning problems will never catch up. How can Mr. Arbuthnot teach a lesson that will work for all of his students, who are performing within the normal range but differ in prior knowledge, skills, and learning rates?

Accommodating instruction to student differences is one of the most fundamental problems of education and often leads to politically and emotionally charged policies (Atkins & Ellsessor, 2003; Loveless, 1998). For example, most countries outside of North America attempt to deal with the problem of student differences, or student heterogeneity, by testing children at around 10 to 12 years of age and assigning them to different types of schools, only one of which is meant to prepare students for higher education. These systems have long been under attack and are changing in some countries (such as the United Kingdom) but remain in others (such as Germany). In the United States a similar function is carried out by assignment of students to college preparatory, general, and vocational **tracks.** Tracking, in which students are assigned to a specified curriculum sequence within which they take all their academic courses, has rapidly diminished in the 1980s and 1990s. Today, most secondary schools place students in ability-grouped classes separately by subject area; a student may be in a high-level math class but in a middle- or low-level English class (Loveless, 1998). Many secondary schools allow students, in consultation with counselors, to choose the level of each class, perhaps changing levels if a course turns out to be too difficult or too easy. All of these strategies, which result in students' attending classes that are more or less homogeneous in performance level, are called **between-class ability grouping** (Slavin, 1991). This is the predominant form of ability grouping in middle, junior high, and high schools and is sometimes used in elementary schools. Another common means of accommodating instruction to student differences in elementary schools is **within-class ability grouping,** as in the use of reading groups (Bluebirds, Redbirds, Yellowbirds) that divide students according to their reading performance (Lou et al., 1996). The problem of accommodating student differences is so important that many educators have suggested that instruction be completely individualized so that students can work independently at their own rates. This point of view has led to the creation of individualized instructional programs and computer-based instruction. Others have suggested retaining more children in a grade until they meet grade-level requirements, which reduces the range of skills in each class but also creates its own problems (see Grave & DePerna, 2000; Reynolds, Temple, & McCoy, 1997; Rothstein, 1998).

Each of the many ways of accommodating students' differences has its own benefits, but each introduces its own problems, which sometimes outweigh the benefits. This chapter discusses the research on various means of accommodating classroom instruction to student differences. Some student differences can be easily accommodated (see Gregory & Chapman, 2001; Tomlinson, 2003). For example, teachers can often accommodate different learning styles by, for example, augmenting oral presentations with visual cues—perhaps writing on the chalkboard or showing pictures and diagrams to emphasize important concepts. A teacher can accommodate other differences in learning styles by varying classroom activities, as in alternating active and quiet tasks or individual and group work. Teachers can sometimes work with students on an individual basis and adapt instruction to their learning styles—for example, by reminding impulsive students to take their time or by teaching overly reflective students strategies for skipping over items with which they are having problems so that they can complete tests on time.

Differences in prior knowledge and learning rates are more difficult to deal with. Sometimes the best way to deal with these differences is to ignore them: to teach the

tracks
Curriculum sequences to which students of specified achievement or ability level are assigned.

between-class ability grouping
The practice of grouping students in separate classes according to ability level.

within-class ability grouping
A system of accommodating student differences by dividing a class of students into two or more ability groups for instruction in certain subjects.

whole class at a single pace, perhaps offering additional help to low-achieving students and giving extra extension or enrichment activities to students who tend to finish assignments rapidly (see Meyer & Rose, 2000; Pettig, 2000; Tomlinson, 2000; Tomlinson, Kaplan, & Renzulli, 2001). Appropriate use of cooperative learning methods, in which students of different performance levels can help each other, can be an effective means of helping all children learn (Schniedewind & Davidson, 2000; Slavin, 1995a). Some subjects lend themselves more than others to a single pace of instruction for all (Slavin, 1993a). For example, it is probably less important to accommodate student achievement differences in social studies, science, and English than in mathematics, reading, and foreign languages. This is because in the latter subjects, skills build directly on one another, so teaching at one pace to a heterogeneous class might do a disservice to both low and high achievers; low achievers might fail because they lack prerequisite skills, and high achievers might become bored at what is for them a slow pace of instruction. This was the case in Mr. Arbuthnot's mathematics class.

The following sections discuss strategies for accommodating student achievement differences.

Between-Class Ability Grouping

Probably the most common means of dealing with instructionally important differences is to assign students to classes according to their abilities. This between-class ability grouping can take many forms. In high schools there might be college preparatory and general tracks that divide students on the basis of measured ability. In some junior high and middle schools, students are assigned to one class by general ability, and they then stay with that class, moving from teacher to teacher. For example, the highest-performing seventh-graders might be assigned to class 7–1, middle-performing students to 7–5, and low-performing students to 7–12. In other junior high and middle schools (and in many high schools), students are grouped separately by ability for each subject, so a student might be in a high-performing math class and an average-performing science class (Slavin, 1993b). In high schools this is accomplished by course placements. For example, some ninth-graders take Algebra I, while others who do not qualify for Algebra I take general mathematics. Elementary schools use a wide range of strategies for grouping students, including many of the patterns that are used in secondary schools. Often, students in elementary schools will be assigned to a mixed-ability class for homeroom, social studies, and science but regrouped by ability for reading and math. Elementary schools are less likely than secondary schools to use ability grouping between classes but more likely to use ability grouping within classes, especially in reading (McPartland, Coldiron, & Braddock, 1987). At any level, however, provision of separate special-education programs for students with serious learning problems is one form of between-class ability grouping, as is provision of separate programs for academically gifted and talented students.

Research on Between-Class Ability Grouping   Despite the widespread use of between-class ability grouping, research on this strategy does not support its use. Researchers have found that although ability grouping might have slight benefits for students who are assigned to high-track classes, these benefits are balanced by losses for students who are assigned to low-track classes (Ireson, in press; Oakes & Wells, 1998; Pallas, Entwisle, Alexander, & Stluka, 1994; Slavin, 1987b, 1990).

ON THE WEB

To read the position of the National Association of School Psychologists on ability grouping see **www.nasponine.org/information/pospaper_ag.html**.

CONNECTIONS

Programs for students who are gifted and who have special needs are discussed in Chapter 12, pages 408 and 411.

CERTIFICATION POINTER

For teacher certification tests, you may be asked to describe the strengths and weaknesses of between-class ability grouping. You should know that research does not support most forms of between-class ability grouping.

Why is between-class ability grouping so ineffective? Several researchers have explored this question. The primary purpose of ability grouping is to reduce the range of student performance levels that teachers must deal with so that they can adapt instruction to the needs of a well-defined group. However, grouping is often done on the basis of standardized test scores or other measures of general ability rather than according to performance in a particular subject. As a result, the reduction in the range of differences that are actually important for a specific class may be too small to make much difference (Oakes, 1995). Furthermore, concentrating low-achieving students in low-track classes seems to be harmful because it exposes them to too few positive role models (Page, 1991). Then, too, many teachers do not like to teach such classes and might subtly (or not so subtly) communicate low expectations for students in them (Weinstein, 1996). Studies find that teachers actually do not make many adaptations to the needs of students in low-ability groups (Ross, Smith, Lohr, & McNelis, 1994). Several studies have found that the quality of instruction is lower in low-track classes than in middle- or high-track classes. For example, teachers of low-track classes are less enthusiastic, are less organized, and teach more facts and fewer concepts than do teachers of high-track classes (Gamoran, Nystrand, Berends, & LePore, 1995; Muskin, 1990; Oakes, 1995; Raudenbush, Rowan, & Cheong, 1993). Instruction in mixed-ability, untracked classes more closely resembles that in high- and middle-track classes than that in low-track classes (Goodlad, 1983; Oakes, 1985). Perhaps the most damaging effect of tracking is its stigmatizing effect on students who are assigned to the low tracks; the message these students get is that academic success is not within their capabilities (Oakes & Guiton, 1995; Page, 1991). Schafer and Olexa (1971) interviewed one noncollege–prep girl who said that she carried her general-track books upside down to avoid being humiliated while walking down the hall. One student described in an interview how he felt when he went to junior high school and found out that he was in the basic track:

> I felt good when I was with my [elementary] class, but when they went and separated us—that changed us. That changed our ideas, our thinking, the way we thought about each other, and turned us to enemies toward each other—because they said I was dumb and they were smart.
>
> When you first go to junior high school you do feel something inside—it's like an ego. You have been from elementary to junior high, you feel great inside . . . you get this shirt that says Brown Junior High . . . and you are proud of that shirt. But then you go up there and the teacher says—"Well, so and so, you're in the basic section, you can't go with the other kids." The devil with the whole thing—you lose—something in you—like it goes out of you. (Schafer and Olexa, 1971, pp. 62–63)

Students in lower-track classes are far more likely than other students to become delinquent and truant and drop out of school (Goodlad, 1983; Oakes, 1985; Rosenbaum, 1980). These problems are certainly due in part to the fact that students in low-track classes are low in academic performance to begin with. However, this is probably not the whole story. For example, students who are assigned to the low track in junior high school experience a rapid loss of self-esteem (Goodlad, 1983), as the preceding interview illustrates. Slavin and Karweit (1982) found that fifth- and sixth-graders in urban elementary schools were absent about 8 percent of the time. When these same students entered the tracked junior high school, absenteeism rose almost immediately to 26 percent, and the truancy was concentrated among students assigned to the bottom-track classes. The change happened too rapidly to be attributed entirely to characteristics of students. Something about the organization of the junior

Some of these students are reading well above grade level, whereas others are still only learning to read. As a teacher, how might you accommodate instruction to their different abilities? What are the advantages and disadvantages of such strategies as between-class and within-class ability groupings?

high school apparently convinced a substantial number of students that school was no longer a rewarding place to be.

One of the most insidious aspects of tracking is that it often creates low-track classes that are composed predominantly of students from lower socioeconomic backgrounds and from minority groups, while upper-track classes are more often composed of children from higher socioeconomic levels (Braddock & Dawkins, 1993; Cooper, 1998; Dornbusch, 1994). There is evidence that this difference is due in part to discrimination (intended or not) against African American and Latino students (Hoffer & Nelson, 1993). A study by Yonezawa, Wells, and Serena (2002) found that even in high schools in which students are theoretically given a "free choice" of academic levels, African American and Latino students disproportionately ended up in low-level classes. The creation of groupings that are so often associated with social class and race is impossible to justify in light of the lack of evidence that such groupings are educationally necessary.

Although individual teachers can rarely set policies on between-class ability grouping, it is useful for all educators to know that research does not support this practice at any grade level, and tracking should be avoided whenever possible. This does not mean that all forms of between-class grouping should be abandoned, however. For example, there is probably some justification for acceleration programs, such as offering Algebra I to mathematically talented seventh-graders or offering advanced placement classes in high school (e.g., Swiatek & Benbow, 1991). Also, some between-class grouping is bound to occur in secondary schools, because some students choose to take advanced courses and others do not. However, the idea that having high, middle, and low sections of the same course can help student achievement has not been supported by research. Mixed-ability classes can be successful at all grade levels, particularly if other, more effective means of accommodating student differences are used. These include within-class ability grouping, tutoring for low achievers, and certain individualized instruction programs that are described in this chapter, as well as cooperative learning strategies.

CONNECTIONS

Cooperative learning strategies are described in Chapter 8, page 255.

Untracking

For many years, educators and researchers have challenged the use of between-class ability grouping at all levels. Influential groups such as the National Governors' Association (1993) and the Carnegie Corporation of New York (1989) recommended moving away from traditional ability grouping practices, and a number of guides to untracking and examples of successful untracking have been published (e.g., Burris, Heubert, & Levin, 2004; Cooper, 1998; Fahey, 2000; Hubbard & Mehan, 1998; Oakes, Quartz, Ryan, & Lipton, 2000). **Untracking** recommendations focus on having students in mixed-ability groups and holding them to high standards but providing many ways for them to reach those standards, including extra assistance for students who are having difficulties keeping up (Corno, 1995; Hubbard & Mehan, 1998). Use of appropriate forms of cooperative learning and project-based learning has often been recommended as a means of opening up more avenues to high performance for all children (Cohen, 1992; Hubbard & Mehan, 1998; Pool & Page, 1995). Yet the road to untracking is far from easy, especially in middle schools and high schools (Cooper, 1998; Oakes et al., 2000; Rubin, 2003). In particular, untracking often runs into serious opposition from the parents of high achievers. Oakes and colleagues (2000) and Wells, Hirshberg, Lipton, & Oakes (1995) have pointed out that untracking requires changes in thinking about children's potentials, not only changes in school or classroom practices. Teachers, parents, and students themselves, these researchers claim, must come to see the goal of schooling as success for every child, not as sorting students into categories, if untracking is to take hold (Hubbard & Mehan, 1997; Oakes, Quartz, Ryan, & Lipton, 2000). This change in perception is difficult to bring about; perhaps, as a result, the move toward untracking is going slowly at the secondary level (Hallinan, 2004).

Regrouping for Reading and Mathematics

Another form of ability grouping that is often used in the elementary grades is **regrouping.** In regrouping plans, students are in mixed-ability classes most of the day but are assigned to reading and/or math classes on the basis of their performance in these subjects. For example, at 9:30 A.M. the fourth-graders in a school may move to different teachers so that they can receive reading instruction that is appropriate to their reading levels. One form of regrouping for reading, the **Joplin Plan,** regroups students across grade lines. For example, a reading class at the fourth-grade, first-semester reading level may contain third-, fourth-, and fifth-graders.

One major advantage of regrouping over all-day ability grouping is that in regrouping plans the students spend most of the day in a mixed-ability class. Thus low achievers are not separated out as a class and stigmatized. Perhaps for these reasons, regrouping plans, especially the Joplin Plan, have generally been found to increase student achievement (Gutiérrez & Slavin, 1992; Slavin, 1987b).

Nongraded (Cross-Age Grouping) Elementary Schools

A form of grouping that was popular in the 1960s and early 1970s that is returning in various forms today is nongraded organization, or cross-age grouping (Fogarty, 1993; Pavan, 1992). **Nongraded programs** (or cross-age grouping programs) combine children of different ages in the same classes. Most often, students aged 5 to 7 or 6 to 8 may be mixed in a nongraded primary program. Students work across age lines but are often flexibly grouped for some instruction according to their needs and performance levels (Kasten & Lolli, 1998). A review of research on the nongraded programs of the 1960s and 1970s found that these programs had a positive effect

---

CONNECTIONS

Various forms of cooperative and project-based learning are described in Chapter 8, page 255.

untracking
A focus on having students in mixed-ability groups and holding them to high standards but providing many ways for students to reach those standards.

regrouping
A method of ability grouping in which students in mixed-ability classes are assigned to reading or math classes on the basis of their performance levels.

Joplin Plan
A regrouping method in which students are grouped across grade lines for reading instruction.

nongraded programs
Programs, generally at the primary level, that combine children of different ages in the same class. Also called *cross-age grouping programs.*

on achievement when they focused on flexible grouping for instruction but were less effective when they had a strong focus on individualized instruction (Gutiérrez & Slavin, 1992). The nongraded elementary school ultimately became the open classroom, which emphasized individualized learning activities and deemphasized teacher instruction. Research on the open classroom similarly failed to find achievement benefits (Giaconia & Hedges, 1982). There has been little research on today's application of the nongraded primary program (see Pavan, 1992), but one study did find achievement benefits for a nongraded school (Tanner & Decotis, 1994).

Sometimes cross-grade grouping is used out of necessity, because there are too few children at a given grade level to make up a whole class. Such combination classes (e.g., grades 3–4 or 5–6) have not been found to enhance student achievement and might even be harmful (Burns & Mason, 2002; Veenman, 1995, 1997).

Within-Class Ability Grouping

Another way to adapt instruction to differences in student performance levels is to group students within classes, as is typical in elementary school reading classes. For example, a third-grade teacher might have the Rockets group using a 3–1 (third-grade, first-semester) text, the Stars group using a 3–2 (third-grade, second-semester) text, and the Planets group using a 4–1 (fourth-grade, first-semester) text.

Within-class ability grouping is far more common in elementary schools than in secondary schools (McPartland et al., 1987), and it is very common in elementary reading classes. Surveys of principals have found that more than 90 percent of elementary reading teachers use multiple reading groups (Puma et al., 1997), whereas only 15 to 18 percent of elementary math teachers do so (Good, Mulryan, & McCaslin, 1992; Mason, 1995). Within-class ability grouping is rare in subjects other than reading or mathematics. In reading, teachers typically have each group working at a different point in a series of reading texts and allow each group to proceed at its own pace. Teachers who group in math might use different texts with the different groups or, more often, allow groups to proceed at their own rates in the same book, so the higher-performing group will cover more material than the lower-performing group. In many math classes the teacher teaches one lesson to the whole class and then meets with two or more ability groups during times when students are doing seatwork to reinforce skills or provide enrichment as needed.

> **CERTIFICATION POINTER**
> You may be asked on your teacher certification test to describe a technique for grouping students within a reading class to meet a wide range of student reading abilities.

Research on Within-Class Ability Grouping   Research on the achievement effects of within-class ability grouping has taken place almost exclusively in elementary mathematics classes. The reason is that researchers want to look at teaching situations in which some teachers use within-class ability grouping and others do not, and this is typically true only in elementary math. Until recently, almost all elementary reading teachers used reading groups, whereas in elementary subjects other than math, and in secondary classes, very few teachers did. Most studies that have evaluated within-class ability grouping methods in math (in which the different groups proceed at different paces on different materials) have found that students in the ability-grouped classes learned more than did students in classes that did not use grouping (Slavin, 1987b). Students of high, average, and low achievement levels seem to benefit equally from within-class ability grouping (Lou et al., 1996). One study by Mason and Good (1993) found that teachers who flexibly grouped and regrouped students according to their needs had better math achievement outcomes than did those who used permanent within-class groups.

The research suggests that small numbers of ability groups are better than large numbers (Slavin & Karweit, 1984). Smaller numbers of groups have the advantage of allowing more direct instruction from the teacher and using less seatwork time and transition time. With three groups this rises to two-thirds of class time. Teachers who try to teach more than three reading or math groups might also have problems with classroom management. Dividing the class into more than three groups does not decrease the magnitude or range of differences within each group enough to offset these problems (see Hiebert, 1983).

It is important to note that the research finding benefits of within-class grouping in elementary mathematics was mostly done many years ago with traditional teaching methods that were intended primarily to teach computation rather than problem solving. As mathematics moves toward the use of constructivist approaches that are more directed at problem solving, discovery, and cooperative learning, within-class grouping might become unnecessary (Good et al., 1992). The main point to be drawn from research on within-class ability grouping is not that it is desirable but that if some form of grouping is thought to be necessary, grouping within the class is preferable to grouping between classes. Beyond its more favorable achievement outcomes, within-class grouping can be more flexible and less stigmatizing and occupies a much smaller portion of the school day than between-class grouping does (Rowan & Miracle, 1983).

ᗯHAT IS MASTERY LEARNING?

One means of adapting instruction to the needs of diverse students is called **mastery learning** (Guskey, 1995). The basic idea behind mastery learning is to make sure that all or almost all students have learned a particular skill to a preestablished level of mastery before moving on to the next skill.

Mastery learning was first proposed as a solution to the problem of individual differences by Benjamin Bloom (1976), who based his recommendations in part on the earlier work of John Carroll (1963). As was discussed earlier in this chapter, Carroll had suggested that school learning was related to the amount of time needed to learn what was being taught and the amount of time spent on instruction.

One implication of Carroll's model is that if time spent is the same for all students and all students receive the same kind of instruction, then differences in student achievement will primarily reflect differences in student aptitude. However, in 1968, Bloom proposed that rather than providing all students with the same amount of instructional time and allowing learning to differ, perhaps we should require that all or almost all students reach a certain level of achievement by allowing time to differ. That is, Bloom suggested that we give students as much time and instruction as they need to bring them all to a reasonable level of learning. If some students appear to be in danger of not learning, then they should be given additional instruction until they do learn.

The assumption underlying mastery learning is that almost every student can learn the essential skills in a curriculum. This assumption is both communicated to the students and acted on by the teacher, whose job it is to provide the instruction necessary to make the expectation come true.

Forms of Mastery Learning

The problem inherent in any mastery learning strategy is how to provide the additional instructional time to students who need it. In some of the research on mastery learning, this additional instruction was given outside of regular class time, such as after school or during recess. Students who failed to meet a preestablished **mastery criterion** (such as 90 percent correct on a quiz) following a lesson were given this

mastery learning

A system of instruction that seeks to enable all students to achieve instructional objectives by allowing learning time to vary as needed.

mastery criterion

A standard that students must meet to be considered proficient in a skill.

extra **corrective instruction** until they could earn a 90 percent score on a similar quiz. Research on mastery learning programs that provide corrective instruction in addition to regular class time has generally found achievement gains, particularly for low achievers (Bloom, 1984; Kulik, Kulik, & Bangert-Drowns, 1990; Slavin, 1987c).

Forms of mastery learning that require additional instructional time are not easily applicable to elementary or secondary education, in which amounts of time available are relatively fixed. For example, it is possible to have students stay after school to receive corrective instruction for a few weeks, but this would be difficult to arrange over the long haul. Also, there is some question whether the additional time required for corrective instruction in mastery learning might not be better spent in covering more material.

Theory into **PRACTICE**

Applying the Principles of Mastery Learning

There's a classic Rolling Stones song called "Time Is on My Side." There probably couldn't be a less appropriate theme song for teachers. Yet because a significant element of mastery learning is the varying of time to meet individual needs, we cannot discuss the application of this approach without addressing realistic strategies for working within the time constraints of today's classrooms.

The basic assumption of mastery learning is that almost all students can learn the essential knowledge and skills within a curriculum when the learning is broken into its component parts and presented sequentially. To implement this approach effectively, teachers must meet several challenges.

The first challenge is to divide the content and/or skills into small units that you can present sequentially using sound teaching strategies. Then you will need to assess your students. The data you obtain will help you determine where in the sequence of the curriculum your instruction should begin. Quality assessment will allow you to link your instructional activities to individual student needs.

While you are involved in actual instructional activities, another challenge you will face is how to address the variations in student learning. For students who quickly grasp concepts, you will need to promote learning by developing relevant enrichment opportunities. This extension of basic concepts will allow these students to remain engaged in appropriate higher-level learning activities while simultaneously allowing you to extend the learning opportunities of the students who need more time to master the basics.

To increase the effectiveness of the instructional process and subsequent student learning, you should engage in ongoing **formative evaluations:** frequent assessments of student learning that will enable you to adjust your instruction to meet the individual needs of your students. You will then need to prepare **summative evaluations,** or final evaluations on each objective. These are likely to reveal that some learners still have not reached a mastery level of the basic knowledge/skills within the time frame you have provided. You will need to develop creative ways for reteaching, presenting alternative learning opportunities, and/or extending practice. Strategies such as after-school corrective instruction, peer or cross-age tutoring, or use of paraprofessionals can help students achieve mastery of the essentials.

Because a mastery learning approach can be labor and time intensive, you will want to be selective in its application. Identifying the key aspects of the curriculum to which mastery learning is most relevant and limiting the use of

corrective instruction
Educational activities given to students who initially fail to master an objective; designed to increase the number of students who master educational objectives.

formative evaluations
Evaluations designed to determine whether additional instruction is needed.

summative evaluations
Final evaluations of students' achievement of an objective.

this approach to situations where prerequisite knowledge/skills are *essential* for future learning will enhance your ability to apply mastery learning principles effectively. You and your students will feel you've made a wise investment of time and energy when the payoff is increased achievement for all.

One form of mastery learning varies the instructional time given to students with different needs by providing corrective instruction to students who need it while allowing those who do not need it to do enrichment work. For example, a high school earth science teacher might teach a lesson on volcanoes and earthquakes. At the end of the lesson, students would be quizzed. Those who scored less than 80 percent would receive corrective instruction on concepts they had problems with, while the remaining students would do **enrichment activities,** such as finding out about the recent San Francisco earthquake or the historical Mount Vesuvius eruption that buried the ancient city of Pompeii.

Research on Mastery Learning

Research on the earliest conceptualization of mastery learning is much less clear than research on later-developed forms of this approach (see Ellis, 2001f; Slavin, 1987c). Studies of at least 4 weeks' duration in which instructional time was the same for mastery and nonmastery classes generally found either no differences in effectiveness or small and short-lived differences favoring the mastery groups. Some of the most promising forms of mastery learning are ones that combine this approach with cooperative learning, in which students work together to help each other learn in the first place and then help groupmates who need corrective instruction (Guskey, 1990; Mevarech & Kramarski, 1997).

The central problem of mastery learning is that it involves a trade-off between the amount of content that can be covered and the degree to which students master each concept (Slavin, 1987c). The time needed to bring all or almost all students to a preestablished level of mastery must come from somewhere. If corrective instruction is provided during regular class time, it must reduce content coverage. And, as was noted in Chapter 7, content coverage is one of the most important predictors of achievement gain (Cooley & Leinhardt, 1980). This is not at all to say that mastery learning should be used only when additional time for corrective instruction is available; it is merely to emphasize that teachers should be aware of the trade-off involved and make decisions accordingly.

CONNECTIONS
For more on the relation between content coverage and achievement gain, see Chapter 7, page 217.

INTASC
3 Adapting Instruction for Individual Needs

enrichment activities
Assignments or activities designed to broaden or deepen the knowledge of students who master classroom lessons quickly.

WHAT ARE SOME WAYS OF INDIVIDUALIZING INSTRUCTION?

The problem of providing all students with appropriate levels of instruction could be completely solved if schools could simply assign each student his or her own teacher. Not surprisingly, studies of one adult–one student tutoring find substantial positive effects of tutoring on student achievement (Wasik & Slavin, 1993). One major reason for the effectiveness of tutoring is that the tutor can provide **individualized instruction,** tailoring instruction precisely to a student's needs. If the student learns quickly, the tutor can move to other tasks; if not, the tutor can figure out what the problem is, try another explanation, or just spend more time on the task.

What type of tutoring is taking place in this picture? What other means of individualizing instruction are available to you as a teacher?

There are situations in which tutoring by adults is feasible and necessary. Peer tutors (usually older students working with younger ones) can also be very effective. In addition, educational innovators have long tried to simulate the one-to-one teaching situation by individualizing instruction. Teachers have long found ways to informally accommodate the needs of different learners in heterogeneous classrooms (Tomlinson, 1999). Individualized instruction, or programmed instruction methods, in which students worked at their own level and pace were popular in the 1960s and 1970s (Fletcher, 1992), but this type of instruction has been replaced by forms of computer-based instruction. These strategies are discussed in the following sections.

Peer Tutoring

Students can help one another learn. In **peer tutoring,** one student teaches another. There are two principal types of peer tutoring: **cross-age tutoring,** in which the tutor is several years older than the student being taught, and same-age peer tutoring, in which a student tutors a classmate. Cross-age tutoring is recommended by researchers more often than same-age tutoring—partly because of the obvious fact that older students are more likely to know the material, and partly because students might accept an older student as a tutor but resent having a classmate appointed to tutor them (Topping & Ehly, 1998). Sometimes peer tutoring is used with students who need special assistance, in which case a few older students might work with a few younger students. Other tutoring schemes have involved, for example, entire fifth-grade classes tutoring entire second-grade classes. In these cases, half of the younger students might be sent to the older students' classroom while half of the older students go to the younger students' classroom. Otherwise, peer tutoring may take place in the cafeteria, the library, or another school facility.

Peer tutoring among students of the same age can be easier to arrange and has also been found to be very effective (e.g., King, 1997; Simmons, Fuchs, Fuchs, Mathes, & Hodge, 1995). Among classmates of the same age and performance level, reciprocal peer tutoring, in which students take turns as tutors and tutees, can be both practical

INTASC

6 Communication Skills

individualized instruction
Instruction tailored to particular students' needs, in which each student works at her or his own level and rate.

peer tutoring
Tutoring of one student by another.

cross-age tutoring
Tutoring of a younger student by an older one.

CONNECTIONS

For more on reciprocal teaching, see Chapter 8, page 251.

and effective (Fantuzzo, King, & Heller, 1992; Greenwood et al., 1993; Mathes, Torgeson, & Allor, 2001).

Adequate training and monitoring of tutors are essential (Jenkins & Jenkins, 1987). Tutors who have been taught specific tutoring strategies produce much better results than do those who have not had such training (Fuchs, Fuchs, Bentz, Phillips, & Hamlett, 1994; Merrill, Reiser, Merrill, & Landes, 1995). Also, involving parents in support of a tutoring program enhances its effectiveness (Fantuzzo, Davis, & Ginsburg, 1995).

Research on Peer Tutoring   Research evaluating the effects of peer tutoring on student achievement has generally found that this strategy increases the achievement of both tutees and tutors (Fantuzzo et al., 1992; King, Staffieni, & Adelgais, 1998; Simmons et al., 1995; Van Keer, 2004). In fact, some studies have found greater achievement gains for tutors than for tutees (Rekrut, 1992), and peer tutoring is sometimes used as much to improve the achievement of low-achieving older students as to improve that of the students being tutored (Top & Osguthorpe, 1987). As many teachers have noted, the best way to learn something thoroughly is to teach it to someone else. High achievers who tutor other students usually enjoy and value this activity (Thorkildsen, 1993).

> **ON THE WEB**
>
> For more on peer tutoring see the Northwest Regional Educational Laboratory at **www.nwrel.org.**

Adult Tutoring

One-to-one adult-to-child tutoring is one of the most effective instructional strategies known, and it essentially solves the problem of appropriate levels of instruction. The principal drawback to this method is its cost. However, it is often possible, on a small scale, to provide adult tutors for students who are having problems learning in the regular class setting. For example, adult volunteers such as parents, college students, or senior citizens are often willing to tutor students (Hopkins, 1998; Juel, 1996; Neuman, 1995). Volunteer tutors who are well supervised and who use well-structured materials can have a positive effect on children's reading performance (Baker, Gersten, & Keating, in press; Tingley, 2001; Wasik, 1997). Tutoring is an excellent use of school aides (Hock, Schumaker, & Deshler, 2001); some school districts hire large numbers of paraprofessional aides precisely for this purpose. In fact, research has found few achievement benefits of classroom aides unless they are doing one-to-one tutoring (see Slavin, 1994b).

There are some circumstances in which the high costs of one-to-one tutoring can be justified. One of these is that of first-graders who are having difficulties learning to read. Failing to learn to read in the lower grades of elementary school is so detrimental to later school achievement that an investment in tutors who can prevent reading failure is worthwhile. A one-to-one tutoring program, Reading Recovery, uses highly trained, certified teachers to work with first-graders who are at risk for failing to learn to read. Research on this strategy has found that students who received tutoring in first grade read significantly better than comparable students (D'Agostino & Murphy, 2004; Pinnell, Lyons, DeFord, Bryk, & Seltzer, 1994). Another effective program, Success for All, makes extensive use of one-to-one tutoring for at-risk first-graders (Slavin and Madden, 2001). Reading Recovery and Success for All are discussed later in this chapter. Other one-to-one tutoring programs for at-risk first-graders have also found substantial positive effects (see Meyer et al., 2002; O'Connor et al., 2002; Rabiner, 2003; Wasik & Slavin, 1993). In addition, an evaluation of a structured phonetic tutoring program for low-achieving second- and third-graders also found strong and lasting effects on students' reading performance (Blachman et al., 2004; Denton et al., 2004).

Theory into **PRACTICE**

Effectively Using Tutoring Methods to Meet Individual Needs

Peer tutoring is an effective way to improve learning for both the tutee and the tutor, and no one doubts the value of this strategy for meeting individual needs within a classroom. However, it takes more than simply pairing off students to make peer tutoring result in improved learning.

Although you are likely to use informal tutoring practices in your classroom every day (e.g., asking one student to help another student with a problem), establishing a formalized tutoring program requires more involved planning. The following strategies can help you create and sustain an effective program within your classroom. As with most initiatives, if you can work with your building administrator and other teachers to establish a schoolwide tutoring program, you will be able to serve the needs of all students more successfully.

To establish a tutoring program, recognize that specific skills need to be developed in both the tutors and tutees. Whether the tutors are same-age peers, older students, or even adults, use care in selecting tutors. It is always wise to begin with volunteers. Consider not only the knowledge base of the tutors (i.e., their proven proficiency with the subject matter) but also their ability to convey their knowledge clearly.

Typically, training will be minimal and will include basic instruction in modeling, prompting responses from tutees, using corrective feedback and praise/reinforcement, alternating teaching methods and materials (i.e., using multisensory methods), and recording and reporting progress. If this is a schoolwide initiative, classroom teachers or even parents or paraprofessionals can train students who will tutor as part of an extracurricular service activity.

Students receiving tutoring need to be clear about their role in this process. It would be counterproductive to force any student into a tutorial relationship. Therefore, initially select only students who express a willingness to work with a tutor. Steadily make tutoring a part of the natural learning activities within a classroom or an entire school. In this collaborative model, every student at some point in time will have the opportunity to be both tutor and tutee. Even students with less knowledge and skills might be able to find peers or younger students with whom they can work. Many students with special-education needs have gained confidence and improved their own abilities by working with younger students.

During the training process help all students to understand that the tutor represents the teacher and therefore should be respected accordingly. In addition, tutees and tutors must understand that the goal of the activity is to have each tutee reach a clear understanding of the concepts, not merely complete an assignment. To make this clear, you might want to use various role-playing activities during the training process. Demonstrate appropriate and inappropriate forms of instruction, feedback, reinforcement, and so on; then allow the participants to practice under supervised conditions. Corrective feedback within this controlled environment will allow you to feel more confident as the tutor–tutee pairs work together without your direct supervision.

CERTIFICATION POINTER

For your teacher certification test, you will probably need to demonstrate your understanding of appropriate applications of cross-age tutoring. For example, you might be asked to identify the curricular goals that cross-age tutoring would be appropriate for and how you would structure the tutoring so that it would be effective.

> Whether you decide to begin this process solely within your own classroom or to develop a schoolwide tutorial program, keep these issues in mind:
>
> 1. Tutors need to be trained in specific instructional practices.
> 2. Tutors and tutees need to have a clear understanding of their roles and expectations.
> 3. Tutors and tutees need to receive supervision and feedback about their work, particularly during the early stages of the tutoring process.
> 4. Teachers need to work with the tutors to create effective and efficient ways of recording and reporting the progress of the sessions.

INTASC

6 Communication Skills

How is Technology Used in Education?

The decreasing costs and increasing availability of microcomputers and other technologies in schools have led educators at all levels to become more interested in technology, particularly as a means of meeting students' diverse needs.

ON THE WEB

The International Society for Technology in Education (ISTE) has developed standards for technology use in education. It provides guidance for teachers in:

- Planning and designing learning environments supported by technology
- Integrating technology-enhanced experiences that address content standards
- Applying technology to assess and track student learning
- Using technology to enhance productivity and professional practice
- Understanding the social, ethical, and legal issues in the use of technology

You can find the complete ISTE National Educational Technology Standards for Teachers (NETS-T) at **iste@iste.org.**

There are three general types of technology applications in education. First, teachers use technology in their classroom teaching, to plan instruction and present content to their classes. Second, students use technology to explore, practice, and prepare papers and presentations. Finally, teachers and administrators use technology to accomplish administrative tasks associated with their profession, such as assessment, record keeping, reporting, and management tasks. Examples of these three types of technology applications are described next.

Technology for Instruction

Word processors, electronic spreadsheets, and presentation software are the most common electronic technologies that teachers use for instruction. Teachers use word processors for numerous teaching tasks, such as preparing student worksheets, tests, transparencies, classroom signs, and posters. Simple desktop publishing features allow teachers to use simple graphics and art to make texts appealing to students. Word processing makes it easy for teachers to adapt documents to meet specific students' needs. Teachers can make customized presentations of data and create clear summaries for students to use as study guides.

Electronic spreadsheets organize and compute numerical data, producing charts and graphs to illustrate the information. Spreadsheets are particularly helpful for teaching mathematics because they allow teachers to display numeric data visually, such as the impact of changes on variable values.

Presentation software helps teachers make professional presentations with a pre-arranged group of electronic slides. These presentations can include multimedia elements such as graphics, sound, special effects, animation, and video clips that make the presentations more appealing. These presentations can be printed to provide students with an outline of the presentation. More advanced multimedia and Web authoring systems help teachers create their own multimedia tutorials and Web pages to support their lessons.

Increasingly, technology is being used to combine text and visual content, such as animations or video. This multimedia approach has been found to enhance students' learning as long as the text and visuals directly support each other. For example, adding diagrams or animations to show how lightning works has been found to enhance the text, but adding motivational but nonexplanatory text (such as a picture of an airplane being hit by lightning) adds little to learning (Mayer, 2001). Similarly, a recent study of first-grade reading found that adding video content on letter sounds, sound blending, and vocabulary to teacher-led reading lessons significantly increased students' learning (Chambers et al., 2004).

The many technological tools available make teachers' lessons more dynamic. Initial fears that computers might replace teachers are unfounded. Teachers do make effective use of computer simulations, presentation software, spreadsheets, and other software, but these clearly enhance rather than replace teacher instruction.

Technology for Learning

In 1998, there were approximately 8.6 million computers in U.S. elementary and secondary schools, or one for every six students, and the number was growing by about 15 percent each year (Becker, 2001). There was an average of 69 computers in each elementary school, 98 in each middle school, and 122 in each high school. The computers were almost evenly divided between classrooms and computer labs (Anderson & Ronnkvist, 1999).

Computer use varies considerably across settings. In secondary schools, computers are concentrated in classes on computer use, and in business and vocational courses. When computers are used in traditional academic courses, they are most often used in English classes as word processors. Self-contained elementary classes are much

---

Teaching Dilemmas: Cases to Consider

Should Computers Be in Labs or Classrooms?

Imagine that your school is writing a grant to the state department of education to obtain funds to purchase computers for your 560 students. You are on the committee that is writing the grant and you need to explain where the computers will be located and how they will be used. The funds available allow only for one computer per class or for one computer lab.

Some benefits of having all the computers in a lab include (1) a whole class is able to work on the same software at the same time, (2) networking the computers is easier and less expensive, and (3) security is easier. However, the lab location requires careful scheduling, reducing flexibility and making integrating computers into the curriculum more difficult.

Having computers distributed among the classrooms means constant availability and easier integration into teachers' lessons. The teachers need to have a greater knowledge of hardware and software and cannot have everyone working on a project together. The cost of supporting the computers in classrooms is higher, and the security is more difficult.

Questions for Reflection

1. How would your answer be different if your school were an elementary, middle, or high school?
2. How would you spend the school's technology money? Would you put all of the computers in a computer lab, or would you distribute them among the classrooms?
3. Which uses of computers lend themselves to labs and which to distribution among many classes?

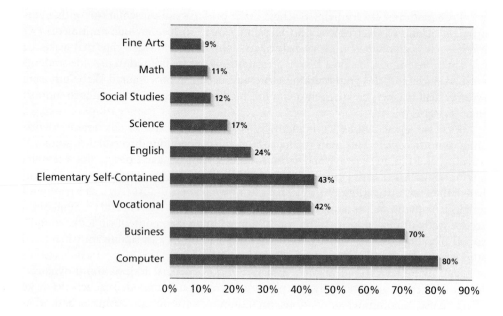

FIGURE 9.2
Frequent Computer Use by Subject Taught (Percent of Teachers Reporting 20+ Uses by Typical Student in Class during Year)

Source: Adapted from Becker, H. J. (2001). *How are teachers using computers in instruction?* Paper presented at the annual meeting of the American Educational Research Association, Seattle.

more likely to report extensive computer use than secondary academic subject classes (see Figure 9.2).

The most common use of computers in elementary and secondary schools is for word processing, followed by CD-ROM reference software (see Figure 9.3). Computers have replaced typewriters and encyclopedias, but instructional uses of computers are largely limited to word processing, games, and remediation (Becker, 2001).

Technology is used for a wide variety of purposes by students in classrooms. The applications of technology use by students fall into the following categories: word processing and publishing, spreadsheets and databases, computer-assisted instruction, the Internet, multimedia, integrated learning systems, and computer programming (see Geisert & Futrell, 2000; Goldman-Segall & Maxwell, 2003; Schwartz & Beichner,

CONNECTIONS

To learn about the use of computers for students with disabilities, see Chapter 12, page 429.

FIGURE 9.3
Software Used by Frequent Computer-Using Teachers (Elementary and Secondary Academic Subjects)

Source: Adapted from Becker, H. J. (2001). *How are teachers using computers in instruction?* Paper presented at the annual meeting of the American Educational Research Association, Seattle.

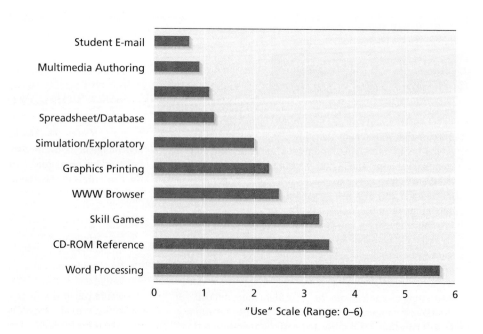

1999; Zhao & Frank, 2003). See Chapter 12 for a discussion of the use of technology in special education and mainstreaming (Blamires, 1999; Woodward & Cuban, 2001).

Word Processing and Publishing   By far the most common application of computers, especially in grades 4 through 12, is **word processing** or **desktop publishing.** As a result, English teachers are more likely than teachers of other subjects to make frequent use of computers in the secondary grades (Becker, 2001). Increasingly, students are asked to write compositions on classroom computers. A key advantage of word processing over paper-and-pencil composition is that word processing facilitates revision. Spell checkers and other utilities help students to worry less about mechanics and focus on the meaning and organization of their compositions. As writing instruction has moved toward an emphasis on a process of revision and editing, this capability has become very important. Word processing is probably the best-researched application of computers to instruction. Studies of word processing show that students who use computers write more, revise more, and take greater pride in their writing than do paper-and-pencil writers (Cochran-Smith, 1991). Writing quality tends to be somewhat better when students have access to word processors (Goldberg, Russell, & Cook, 2003; Kamil, Intrator, & Kim, 2000; Kwik, 2003). This writing effect may be enhanced when each student has a laptop, instead of having to share a small number of computers (Lowther, Ross, & Morrison, 2003). Of course, word processing itself has become an essential skill in a vast range of occupations, so teaching students to use word processing programs (e.g., in high school business courses) has obvious value.

Spreadsheets   As with word processing, use of **spreadsheets** in education is an extension of software that is widely used by adults. Typically, spreadsheets can convert raw data into graphs, charts, and other data summaries so that students can easily organize information and see the effects of various variables on outcomes. For example, a student could enter data for the number of tadpoles caught in each of five ponds at three times. By assigning a formula to a given column, the student could customize the spreadsheet program to total the numbers for each pond and each time. Changing any number would automatically change row and column totals. The spreadsheet program could then show the data in raw, numeric form or convert the data into a graph. Students are increasingly using spreadsheets to record data from science experiments and to reinforce mathematics skills.

Databases   A **database** is a computer program that keeps a lot of information that will be referred to later on and sometimes manipulated. Students can learn to search CD-ROM (ROM stands for read-only memory) databases such as encyclopedias, atlases, road maps, catalogs, and so on to find information for a variety of instructional purposes. Databases of this type can be particularly important in project-based learning, because they may put a great deal of information into easy reach for open-ended reports and other projects. Access to CD-ROM technology is growing rapidly; in 1995–1996, 54 percent of schools had this capability (ETS, 1996). After word processing, CD-ROM encyclopedias and related programs are among the most popular applications of computer technology in schools (Becker, 2001).

In many databases, students can use **hypertext** and **hypermedia** to search a database (such as an encyclopedia) by clicking on a word or picture. This leads the student to related or more detailed information on a specific portion of the text. Hypermedia can similarly provide pictures, music, video footage, or other information to illuminate and extend the information on a CD-ROM database (Bortnick, 1995; Dillon & Gabbard, 1998). Hypermedia has exciting possibilities for allowing learners to follow their interests or resolve gaps in understanding more efficiently than with traditional

word processing or desktop publishing
A computer application for writing compositions that lends itself to revising and editing.

spreadsheets
Computer programs that convert data into tables, charts, and graphs.

databases
Computer programs that contain large volumes of information, such as encyclopedias and atlases.

hypertext and hypermedia
Related information that appears when a computer user clicks on a word or picture.

These students use instructional software to learn. What does research say about the advantages and disadvantages of computer-based instruction? Are certain types of computer-assisted instruction more effective?

text, but so far, research on use of hypermedia finds limited and inconsistent effects on student learning that depend on both the type of material being studied and the nature of the learners (Dillon & Gabbard, 1998; Kamil, Intrator, & Kim, 2000).

Computer-Assisted Instruction   Applications of **computer-assisted instruction** (CAI) range in complexity from simple drill and practice software to complex problem-solving programs.

Drill and Practice.   One common application of microcomputers in education is to provide students with **drill and practice** on skills or knowledge. For example, many software programs provide students with practice on math facts or computations, geography, history facts, or science. Computer experts often frown on drill and practice programs, calling them "electronic page turning," and the programs are generally less than exciting. They typically replace independent seatwork and do have several major advantages over seatwork, including immediate feedback, record keeping, and, in many cases, appealing graphics and variations in pace or level of items depending on the student's responses. This can increase students' motivation to do work that might otherwise be boring (Kamil, Intrator, & Kim, 2000; Leu, 2000). Drill and practice programs should not be expected to teach by themselves, but they can reinforce skills or knowledge that students have learned elsewhere.

Tutorial Programs.   More sophisticated than drill and practice programs, **tutorial programs** are intended to teach new material and present appropriate correction and review based on the student's responses. The best tutorial programs come close to mimicking a patient human tutor. Increasingly, tutorial programs use speech and graphics to engage students' attention and present new information. Students are typically asked many questions, and the program branches in different directions depending on the answers, reexplaining if the student makes mistakes or moving on if a student responds correctly. Very sophisticated computer-managed programs that simulate the behaviors of expert human tutors are being developed and applied in a variety of settings (Lever-Duffy, McDonald, & Mizell, 2003). Computer tutorials

computer-assisted instruction

Individualized instruction administered by computer.

drill and practice

Application of computer technology to provide students with practice of skills and knowledge.

tutorial programs

Computer programs that teach new material, varying their content and pace according to the student's responses.

have been found to be particularly effective in the natural and social sciences (Kulik, 2003).

Instructional Games.   Most children are first introduced to computers through video games, and many educators (and parents) have wondered whether the same intensity, motivation, and perseverance that they see in children playing video games could be brought to the classroom. Many **instructional games** have been designed; most are simple extrapolations of drill and practice designs into a game format, but some are more creative. For example, the popular program "Where in the World Is Carmen Sandiego?" is designed to teach geography by engaging children in tracking a gang of criminals through various countries. Computer games are among the most common applications of computer software in schools (Becker, 2001).

Simulations.   **Simulation software** involves students in an interactive model of some sort of reality. Students operate within a simulated environment and, by doing so, learn about that environment from the inside. For example, one of the earliest simulations, "Oregon Trail," gives students limited allocations of food, water, money, horses, and other resources, and students must use these resources wisely to successfully move their wagon trains to the West. Other popular simulations let children build their own civilizations, build new forms of life, and so on. Simulations are engaging, fun, and creative, and recent evidence indicates that they can improve achievement compared to traditional teaching methods, particularly in science (Kulik, 2003).

Problem-Solving Programs.   The goal of developing students' critical thinking skills has led to the creation of numerous CAI programs that are designed as problem-solving activities. One innovative **problem-solving program** is the Jasper series, developed and researched at Vanderbilt University (Cognition and Technology Group at Vanderbilt, 1996). In this program, students are shown videos in which a character, Jasper Woodbury, faces a series of challenges that require applications of mathematics and thinking skills. Students must solve the problems Jasper faces before they see his solution. In addition to working with computers, students work in cooperative groups on offline activities that are related to the stories. Evaluations found that in comparison to matched controls, students in classes that used the Jasper program performed similarly in math computations and concepts but better in word problems and planning.

Internet   Perhaps the fastest-growing technology applications in U.S. schools involve the **Internet** (Lev, 2000; Lewin, 2001; Provenzo, 1999). Internet access for schools is becoming almost universal. In 1998, more than 90 percent of schools had Internet access, and the proportion was rapidly rising (Anderson & Ronnkvist, 1999; Shields & Behrman, 2000). The Internet gives schools access to vast stores of information, including databases on every imaginable subject, libraries throughout the world, and other specialized information (Levin, Jukes, Dosaj, & Macdonald, 2000; Linn & Slotta, 2000; Provenzo, 1999). Students can use the Internet to do WebQuests, in which they search the Internet on a given topic or theme. In a project called GLOBE (www.globe.gov), students collect local data on soil and water quality and contribute it to a real national scientific investigation (Means & Coleman, 2000). The Internet can also enable students to communicate with students in other schools, including those far away. Through this capability students can create international projects and carry out cooperative projects with other schools (Lewin, 2001; Means, 2000/2001), and so on. Classes and schools have set up their own Web pages (Havens, 2003), and have created their own virtual museums or encyclopedias by collecting and synthesizing information from many sources.

instructional games
Drill and practice exercises presented in a game format.

simulation software
Computer programs that model real-life phenomena to promote problem-solving abilities and motivate interest in the areas concerned.

problem-solving program
Program designed specifically to develop students' critical thinking skills.

Internet
A large and growing telecommunications network of computers around the world that communicate electronically.

Teachers use Internet-based communications such as e-mail, conferencing, list-servs (electronic mailing lists), chat rooms, and video conferencing to connect students to others in other areas of the world. Through these interactions students are exposed to perspectives different from their own (Lever-Duffy, McDonald, & Mizell, 2003).

CERTIFICATION POINTER

A teacher certification question may ask you to suggest a strategy for using technology to help students learn various instructional objectives.

> **ON THE WEB**
>
> For an example of a website that provides information for WebQuests see **www.edhelper.com.**

There is little research on the achievement outcomes of Internet involvement (Leu, 2000; Wallace, 2004; Yang & Wang, 2004). There are also serious concerns about how to limit children's access to pornography or other inappropriate materials that can be found on the Web (see National Research Council, 2001; Wartella & Jennings, 2000). Yet it seems that the Internet is here to stay, at least as a tool to supplement school libraries with a broad range of information.

multimedia

Electronic material such as graphics, video, animation, and sound, which can be integrated into classroom projects.

CD-ROM

A computer database designed for "read-only memory" that provides massive amounts of information, including pictures and audio; it can be of particular importance to students doing projects and research activities.

videodiscs

Interactive computer technology (might include videos, still pictures, and music).

digital photographs

Photographs that can be loaded into a computer and shared electronically.

integrated learning systems

Commercially developed comprehensive, multipurpose packages of interlinked management instructional software, running on a computer network.

computer programming

Creating instructions for a computer to perform specific functions.

Multimedia   Students can be encouraged to make their own **multimedia** projects—an update of the old-fashioned group report (Simpkins, Cole, Tavalin, & Means, 2002). In project-based multimedia learning, students design, plan, and produce a product or performance, integrating media objects such as graphics, video, animation, and sound. An example is a seventh-grade class that created a social studies and science multimedia presentation about the Black Plague, integrating animations of how the plague virus attacks and the perspectives of fourteenth-century farmers (Simkins, Cole, Tavalin, & Means, 2002).

Students can use a wide array of graphics tools to create their multimedia presentations, including CD-ROMs and videodiscs, digital photos, concept mapping, and graphic organizers. **CD-ROM** databases include clip art, photographs, illustrations, music, and sometimes video. **Videodiscs** make available enormous resources, including videos, films, still pictures, and music. Both CD-ROMs and videodiscs can be valuable in student projects, explorations, and reports. Students can use them to create multimedia reports that combine audio, video, music, and pictures. **Digital photographs** can be used as a stimulus for writing or to illustrate projects. For example, students might take digital photographs of animals on a field trip to the zoo. Back in the classroom, these serve as a reminder to students of what they saw and also are used to illustrate their reports on the trip.

Integrated Learning Systems   Early in the microcomputer revolution, schools typically assembled hardware and software from many sources, often with little coordination. Today, schools are increasingly purchasing **integrated learning systems**—entire packages of hardware and software, including most of the types of software described above. Integrated learning systems provide many terminals that are linked to each other and to computers that teachers use to monitor individual student work (Lever-Duffy, McDonald, & Mizell, 2003). Research on the effectiveness of commercial integrated learning systems has found positive and educationally meaningful effects on student achievement, but only in mathematics instruction (Kulik, 2003).

Computer Programming   Some researchers have proposed that learning **computer programming** (learning to teach the computer, rather than being taught by it) will increase children's achievement and ability to solve problems. Much of the research on teaching computer programming to elementary students focused on the computer language Logo, which was designed to be accessible to young children. Children draw on the computer's display screen by directing the movements of a graphic turtle, a figure that can move around the screen in response to messages that the programmer sends to it. Seymour Papert (1980), one of the creators of Logo and a leading supporter of the use of computer programming to expand children's intellectual power, argued that students who learn Logo will gain in general thinking skills. Others have made similar arguments for the teaching of other computer languages. Research is unclear on the degree to which this is true. When learning computer programming has effects on thinking skills or other cognitive skills, such as mathematics, the effects are generally restricted to the problem-solving skills that are most similar to those involved in the programming itself (Blume, 1984; Palumbo, 1990).

Technology for Administration

Teachers use a variety of technologies to accomplish the many administrative tasks associated with their work, such as grading, creating reports, writing class newsletters, making invitations, and sending individual notes to parents. E-mail makes it easier for teachers to communicate with teaching assistants, administrators, parents, and others. Part of every teacher's job involves organizing, maintaining, and retrieving different types of data. This ranges from creating student rosters and logging students' contact information, to tracking coverage of the district's language arts objectives. Teachers are beginning to use portfolio assessment software to document student achievement. These programs allow teachers to collect and display the information when it comes time to report to parents (Bitter & Pierson, 2005).

"It's one of those computer viruses. Keep her off the Internet for a week and she'll be fine."

Since the No Child Left Behind Act, schools are being held more accountable for their students' achievement than in the past. School districts are using technology to monitor the progress of individual students, teachers, and schools using database management systems. In addition to tracking students' achievements, these school management systems allow districts to monitor enrollment, attendance, and school expenditures. Data management software makes it easier for teachers to enter, retrieve, and update records and to create accurate, customized, professional reports for administrators or parents. They can track which students are mastering what content areas so that they can better target specific instruction to the students who need it the most.

Research on Computer-Assisted Instruction

Can computers teach? Most reviews of research on the effects of computer-assisted instruction (CAI) conclude that computer-based instruction has small- to moderate-sized positive effects on achievement (Aviram, 2000; Healy, 1998; Kulik & Kulik, 1991; Kulik, 2003). As was noted earlier, there is also evidence favoring specific applications of CAI, especially word processing (Bangert-Drowns, 1993; Goldberg et al., 2003).

CAI is often effective when it is used in addition to regular classroom instruction; it has smaller and less consistent achievement effects when it entirely replaces classroom instruction. Kulik's (2003) review of instructional technology found promising results for some integrated learning systems for mathematics, a few science tutorial programs, and a couple of reading programs. However, the potential of computers to improve U.S. education remains unclear. Some reviewers have argued that when the content of instruction is carefully controlled, computers are

INTASC

3 Adapting Instruction for Individual Needs

no more effective than other instructional methods (Bebell, O'Dwyer, Russell, & Seeley, 2004; Clark, 2001) or have small and variable effects (Blok, Oosterdam, Otter, & Overmaat, 2002). Researchers today generally agree that the computer itself is not magic. What matters is the curriculum, instruction, and social context surrounding the use of the computer (Cognition and Technology Group at Vanderbilt, 1996; Kozma, 1994). Asking whether computers enhance learning is like asking whether chalkboards enhance learning. In either case, it depends on how they are used.

A review of research by Lou, Abrami, and d'Apollonia (2001) found that having students work on computers in small groups was, on average, more effective than having them work individually, as long as students used well-specified cooperative learning approaches like those described in Chapter 8. Simply asking students to work together, however, produced no benefit. Outcomes were also enhanced when students worked in pairs rather than larger groups.

Leaving aside issues of effectiveness, it is clear that students do not all have the same access to computers. Middle-class children are considerably more likely than children of a lower socioeconomic status to have access to computers at home (Becker, 2000; Education Commission of the States, 2000; Holloway, 2000), although the digital divide is rapidly diminishing in schools (Becker, 2001). Within schools, boys tend to spend much more time on computers than do girls (Sutton, 1991; Volman & van Eck, 2001). To the extent that computers become increasingly effective and important in providing state-of-the-art instruction, these inequities must be addressed.

Use of computers and research on CAI are developing so rapidly that it is difficult to anticipate what the future will bring (see McCain & Jukes, 2000; Means et al., 2003). At this time, however, computers are rarely being used to provide basic instruction. In fact, many studies find that even in technology-rich schools, computers are turned off most of the day, and computer use occupies a tiny portion of each student's academic time (e.g., Cuban, Kirkpatrick, & Peck, 2001; Ganesh & Berliner, 2004). In secondary schools, computers are used primarily to teach programming and word processing, and in elementary schools they are used chiefly for enrichment. Many schools that originally bought computers for CAI have ended up using them to teach computer programming or computer literacy, giving students hands-on experience with the computer but not depending on it to achieve major instructional objectives (Dugger, 2001; Zhao & Frank, 2003). Of course as computers become ubiquitous in the world of work, exposure to them becomes important in its own right (Thornburg, 2002); but in helping students learn traditional subjects, computers continue to play a minor role. The majority of teachers still feel uncomfortable with computers and are poorly prepared to use them (Becker, 2001). Several decades into the computer revolution, with billions spent on computer hardware and software (Anderson & Becker, 2001), there is still a long way to go before computers fundamentally change the practice of education (see Becker & Ravitz, 2001; Cuban, 2001; McCain & Jukes, 2000; Salomon, 2002).

Cutting Edge Educational Technologies

In addition to computers, there are other digital technologies that are making their way into the schools. In the coming years, you will be probably be using some of these in your classroom.

personal digital assistants (PDAs)
Hand-held computing devices.

Personal Digital Assistants   **Personal digital assistants (PDAs)** or palmtop computers are hand-held computing devices that offer calendars, appointment books,

Personal Reflection

Computers in Education

I once visited an elementary school in suburban Atlanta that was a special demonstration site for computer use in education. A computer company representative proudly showed me all the cutting-edge technology the school was using, and I spoke with the principal and several teachers, who were excited about what the computers could help them do.

I spent about an hour in a math class. Like all the classes in the school, it had a lot of technology in it, but not enough computers for every child. Therefore, students were rotated from teacher directed to computer activities.

The computer activity involved using a mouse to manipulate blocks to represent arithmetic. The computer program was clever, appealing, and intuitive, and the students seemed to like it. However, the overall instructional plan was a disaster. The teacher's lessons were constantly being interrupted. When children rotated off of the computers, she had to reteach the portion of the lesson she'd just taught to students who'd been on the computer.

In another math class, I saw similar problems. In that class, children were working on graphs in small groups. In each case, one child had his or her hands on the key-

board, while three children watched. The working children seemed to be having fun. The watching children offered suggestions from time to time but weren't getting the concepts. I took a few watching children aside and asked them to explain the graph the group was creating. They had no idea.

Computers can be powerful tools in the classroom, but they are not magic. Computer activities need to coordinate with noncomputer activities and teacher instruction and should not dominate instructional planning. Even today, after many years of waiting for the "computer revolution," even the most technology-rich schools often have difficulty figuring out the right place for computers and other technology in students' instructional days and fail to reap the great potential technology can offer.

@ Reflect on This. How were computers used in your classes when you were in grade school? High school? How do you see technology changing in schools? Do you think access to technology is equal across all social groups? What might be the impact of differences on student learning across social groups?

phone books, and word processing. Teachers can use PDAs as classroom management tools to make notes on classroom activities and track student behavior and achievement. This information is then transferred into computerized lesson plans, grade books, and student files. Students can use PDAs to take notes and access the Internet during class.

Electronic Whiteboards   An **electronic whiteboard** is a display surface that can be saved to a computer file. The file can also be edited, and notes or illustrations that have been written on it can be printed. It allows teachers to project computer files and make more dynamic demonstrations of concepts. For example, in a math lesson, a teacher can divide a geometric figure in various ways on the whiteboard to demonstrate what portions of the figure are represented by various fractions. Students who were absent or who did not get the information quickly enough can access the whiteboard information later on a computer. The teacher can refer back to previously erased material in a way not possible with blackboards or regular whiteboards.

Liquid Crystal Display (LCD) Projectors   As they come down in price, **LCD projectors** will replace traditional overhead projectors and television monitors as tools for displaying images and video from either a computer or a video source such as a DVD player or VCR.

Memory Sticks   Compact, portable **memory sticks**, the size of a key ring, make it possible to transfer computer programs and files easily from one computer to another

electronic whiteboard
A display surface that makes it possible to save to a computer file, edit, and print notes or illustrations that have been written on it.

LCD projectors
Display images and video from computer or video sources.

memory sticks
Small, portable devices that transfer computer programs and files easily from one computer to another.

just by inserting them into a port on the computer. This will make it easier for teachers to store student work and record student progress in digital portfolios that they can access from home or school.

As we prepare students to enter the workforce of the twenty-first century, it is clear that the ability to work with evolving technologies is critical. The School Technology and Readiness Report of the CEO Forum (www.ceoforum.org) calls for schools to develop in their students the following skills:

- Digital-age literacy (including basic scientific, mathematical, and technological literacy)
- Inventive thinking (including curiosity, creativity, adaptability, and higher-order thinking)
- Effective communication (including interpersonal skills and personal and social responsibility)
- High productivity (effective use of real-world tools, ability to prioritize, plan and manage for results) (Thornburg, 2002)

INTASC

3 Adapting Instruction for Individual Needs

10 Partnerships

WHAT EDUCATIONAL PROGRAMS EXIST FOR STUDENTS PLACED AT RISK?

Any child can succeed in school. Any child can fail. The difference between success and failure depends primarily on what the school, the parents, community agencies, and the child himself or herself do to create conditions that are favorable for learning (Thomas & Bainbridge, 2001). Before school entry we cannot predict very well which individual children will succeed or fail, but there are factors in a child's background that make success or failure more likely (on the average). For example, students who come from impoverished or single-parent homes, those who have marked developmental delays, or those who exhibit aggressive or withdrawn behavior are more likely to experience problems in school than are other students. These children are often referred to as **students at risk** (Barr & Parrett, 1995; Manning & Baruth, 1995). The term *at risk* is borrowed from medicine, in which it has long been used to describe individuals who do not have a given disease but are more likely than average to develop it. For example, a heavy smoker or a person with a family history of cancer might be at risk for lung cancer, even though not all heavy smokers or people with family histories of cancer actually get the disease. High blood pressure is a known risk factor for heart attacks, even though most people with high blood pressure do not have heart attacks. Similarly, a given child from an impoverished home might do well in school, but 100 such children are likely to perform significantly worse, on the average, than 100 children from middle-class homes (Rossi & Stringfield, 1995).

Recently, the term *at risk* has often been replaced by the term *placed at risk* (Boykin, 2000). This term emphasizes the fact that it is often an inadequate response to a child's needs by school, family, or community that places the child at risk. For example, a child who could have succeeded in reading if he had been given appropriate instruction, a reading tutor, or eyeglasses could be said to be placed at risk by lack of these services.

Before children enter school, the most predictive risk factors relate to their socioeconomic status and family structure. After they begin school, however, such risk factors as poor reading performance, grade repetition, and poor behavior become more important predictors of later school problems (such as dropping out) than family background factors (Ensminger & Slusarcick, 1992).

CONNECTIONS

For more on factors such as poverty and limited English proficiency that might place students at risk of school failure, see Chapter 4, pages 99 and 112.

students at risk
Students who are subject to school failure because of their own characteristics and/or because of inadequate responses to their needs by school, family, or community.

Educational programs for students who are at risk fall into three major categories: compensatory education, early intervention programs, and special education. **Compensatory education** is the term used for programs designed to prevent or remediate learning problems among students who are from low-income families or who attend schools in low-income communities. Some intervention programs target at-risk infants and toddlers to prevent possible later need for remediation. Other intervention programs are aimed at keeping children in school. Compensatory and early intervention programs are discussed in the following sections. Special education, discussed in Chapter 12, is designed to serve children who have more serious learning problems as well as children with physical or psychological problems.

Compensatory Education Programs

Compensatory education programs are designed to overcome the problems associated with being brought up in low-income communities. Compensatory education supplements the education of students from disadvantaged backgrounds who are experiencing trouble in school or who are thought to be in danger of having school problems. Two such programs, Head Start and Follow Through, are designed to give disadvantaged preschool and primary school children the skills they need for a good start in school. These programs were discussed in Chapter 3. However, the largest compensatory education program, and the one that is most likely to affect regular classroom teachers, is called **Title I** (formerly "Chapter 1"), a federally funded program that gives schools money to provide extra services for students from low-income families who are having trouble in school (see Borman, Stringfield, & Slavin, 2001).

Title I is not merely a transfer of money from the federal government to local school districts. According to the federal guidelines, these funds must be used to "supplement, not supplant" local educational efforts. This means that most school districts cannot use the money to reduce class size for all students or increase teachers' salaries; the funds must go directly toward increasing the academic achievement of low achievers in schools that serve many disadvantaged students. The exception is that schools that serve very disadvantaged neighborhoods—neighborhoods in which at least 40 percent of the students qualify for a free lunch—can use Title I money to improve the school as a whole.

Title I Programs   Title I programs can take many forms. Most often, a special Title I teacher provides remedial help to students who are experiencing difficulties in reading and, in many cases, in other subjects as well (Puma, Jones, Rock, & Fernandez, 1993). Programs of this type are called **pull-out programs,** because the students are pulled out of their general education classes to take part in the programs.

Pull-out programs have been criticized for many years. One major problem with pull-out programs is that often the regular teacher and the Title I teacher do not coordinate their efforts, so the very students who need the most consistent and structured instruction may have to deal with two completely different approaches (Allington & McGill-Franzen, 1989; Meyers, Gelzheiser, Yelich, & Gallagher, 1990). One study found that half of a group of Title I teachers could not even name the reading text series that their students were using in the general education class; two-thirds could not name the specific book (Johnston et al., 1985). Johnston and colleagues (1985) argue that Title I programs must be directed at ensuring the success of students in the general education classroom and should therefore be closely coordinated with the general education teacher's instructional activities. For example, if a student is having trouble in the general education class with finding the main ideas of paragraphs, the

CONNECTIONS
To learn about factors such as problems of childhood and adolescence that might place students at risk of school failure, see Chapter 3, pages 82 and 89.

CONNECTIONS
Special education is discussed in detail in Chapter 12.

compensatory education
Programs designed to prevent or remediate learning problems among students from lower socioeconomic status communities.

Title I
Compensatory programs reauthorized under Title I of the Improving America's Schools Act (IASA) in 1994; formerly known as Chapter 1.

pull-out programs
Compensatory education programs in which students are placed in separate classes for remediation.

Title I teacher should be working on main ideas, perhaps using the same instructional materials that the classroom teacher is using.

Some school districts are avoiding the problems of pull-out programs by having the Title I teacher or aide work as a team teacher in the general education reading classroom (see Harpring, 1985). This way, two teachers can give reading lessons to two groups of students at the same time, a strategy that avoids some of the problems of within-class ability grouping. Team teaching can also increase the levels of communication and collaboration between the general education classroom teacher and the Title I teacher. However, such in-class models of Title I services have not been found to be any more effective than pull-out programs (Anderson & Pellicer, 1990; Borman et al., 1998).

Many other innovative programs have been found to accelerate the achievement gains of disadvantaged students. Among these are tutoring programs; continuous-progress programs, in which students are frequently assessed and regrouped as they proceed through a sequence of skills; and other structured instructional programs that have clear objectives and frequent assessments of students' attainment of these objectives (see Slavin & Madden, 1987; Slavin, Madden, & Karweit, 1989). The most effective approaches, however, are ones that prevent students from ever having academic difficulties in the first place (Hamburg, 1992; Slavin, Karweit, & Wasik, 1994). These include high-quality preschool and kindergarten programs (Berrueta-Clement et al., 1984; Reynolds, 1991), one-to-one tutoring for first-graders who are just beginning to have reading problems (Pinnell, 1990; Wasik & Slavin, 1993), and comprehensive school reform programs that help all children succeed the first time they are taught (Borman, 2002/2003; Borman et al., 2004).

Research on the Effects of Title I   Two major nationwide studies of the achievement effects of the programs offered under Title I have been carried out. The first, called the Sustaining Effects Study (Carter, 1984), found that Title I students did achieve better in reading and math than did similar low-achieving students who did not receive Title I services, but that these effects were not large enough to enable Title I students to close the gap with students performing at the national average. The greatest gains were for first-graders, while the benefits of Title I participation for students in fourth grade and above were slight.

A major study of the effects of the compensatory services funded under Title I, called *Prospects,* also compared elementary and middle school children receiving compensatory education services both to similar at-risk children not receiving services and to children who were never at risk. Prospects did not find any achievement benefits for children who received Title I services (Puma, Jones, Rock, & Fernandez, 1993). A more detailed analysis by Borman, D'Agostino, Wong, and Hedges (1998) found similarly disappointing outcomes, although there were some positive effects for children who were less disadvantaged and for those who received services during some years but not others. The most disadvantaged, lowest-achieving students were not narrowing their achievement gap with advanced peers.

While the Prospects data did not find overall positive effects of receiving compensatory services, results were positive in some situations. One particularly influential factor was the degree to which Title I services were closely coordinated with other school services (Borman, 1997; D'Agostino, Borman, Hedges, & Wong, 1998). In other words, schools that closely integrated remedial or instructional Title I services with the school's main instructional program, and especially schools that used Title I dollars to enhance instruction for all students in schoolwide projects, obtained the best outcomes. This kind of integration contrasts with the traditional practice of sending low-achieving students to remedial classes where instruction is poorly coordinated with that in the classes they are leaving.

Although a review of many studies did find positive effects on average (Borman & D'Agostino, 2001; Borman, 2002), no one familiar with the data would argue that Title I impacts are large. This is not a surprising conclusion, given that for most students Title I means no more than a 30-minute daily remedial session (Stringfield et al., 1997).

Research on effective practices in compensatory pull-out classes finds that, in general, practices that are effective in regular classes are also effective in pull-out classes. For example, more instructional time, more time on task, and other indicators of effective classroom management are important predictors of achievement gain in compensatory program classes (Crawford, 1989; Stein, Leinhardt, & Bickel, 1989). A large study of programs for students from high-poverty areas (Knapp, 1995; Knapp, Shields, & Turnbull, 1995) found that students in schools that emphasized instruction for deep understanding and meaning achieved significantly better than did students whose teachers emphasized drill and practice (also see Waxman, Padrón, & Arnold, 2001). Another large study, by Stringfield and colleagues (1997), evaluated a range of programs that are used in high-poverty schools. Two comprehensive school reform programs were particularly effective: Success for All and Comer's School Development Program, both of which are discussed later in this chapter. These and other findings have led Title I policy-makers increasingly to favor schoolwide programs in which Title I funds are used to improve instruction for all children in the school (Wong, Sunderman, & Lee, 1995). In particular, Title I schools are being encouraged to adopt proven, comprehensive reform models for the entire school (see Borman et al., 2001; Slavin & Fashola, 1998).

No Child Left Behind   In December 2001, the U.S. Congress passed the No Child Left Behind Act (NCLB) to supplement state and local efforts to improve education for all children and eliminate the achievement gap between students from different backgrounds. NCLB has provisions for increasing teacher quality, improving reading instruction, providing scientifically based practices, and holding schools accountable for their students' achievement.

ON THE WEB

For more details about No Child Left Behind see the U.S. Department of Education website **www.ed.gov/nclb.**

Under NCLB, each state must have established subject content standards for reading, math, and, beginning in 2005–2006, science. Most states already have standards for these subjects; some states have standards for other subjects as well. Schools, and increasingly school districts, decide what curricula, textbooks, materials, instruction, and support services they will implement to meet these state standards.

Although NCLB does not dictate what curricula or instructional methods schools must implement, Reading First and Early Reading First programs within NCLB were designed to support schools to implement scientifically based reading instruction. However, the Reading First definition of scientifically based is not rigorously applied, leading most states to permit reading programs that are not different from what was implemented before NCLB (Center on Education Policy, 2003). There is additional funding directed to remedial programs, after-school programs, and summer school programs as supplemental services to help bring students in low-achieving schools up to par.

Under NCLB, each year the state must administer tests in reading, language arts, and math to students in grades 3 to 8 and one year in high school. Performance on these tests determines students' level of proficiency—basic, proficient, or advanced (U.S. Department of Education, 2002). In each school, at least 95 percent of all students must take these high-stakes tests, including subgroups of children with limited English proficiency, children from economically disadvantaged families, children with disabilities, and children from each major racial or ethnic group. Schools and districts must make *adequate yearly progress* (AYP) toward the target of having all students reach the proficient level by 2014. Each year, schools must reduce the number of students in each subgroup not reaching proficiency by 10 percent. Incentives and sanctions are used to motivate schools to meet AYP. Sanctions begin for Title I schools not meeting AYP after two years. After five years of not meeting the target achievement level, the schools can be closed and restructured.

In 2003, states varied widely in the percentage of schools not reaching AYP, from Iowa with only 0.8 percent to Florida with 87 percent. The reasons for this vary. Some state tests are easier than others. Some states require a higher number of students in each subgroup in a school before that group's scores count toward AYP (Education Daily, August 19, 2003). Schools and districts in need of improvement receive technical assistance based on scientifically based practices.

According to the Education Trust (2003), high-poverty schools have a much higher proportion of unqualified teachers than do more advantaged schools. NCLB has also introduced minimum standards for qualifications of teachers and instructional aides. For Title I teachers this means holding at least a bachelor's degree and demonstrating subject area competency (Berry, Hoke, & Hirsch, 2004; Rebell & Hunter, 2004; U.S. Department of Education, 2002). Unavailability of highly qualified teachers, especially in inner-city and rural areas, may hinder administrators' attempts to meet this requirement.

Under NCLB, states must report the performance level of each school and each subgroup within the school. Parents of Title I students in low-performing schools can request supplemental educational services or ask that their child be transferred to a successful school (U.S. Department of Education, 2002).

CONNECTIONS

Chapter 14 presents the assessment aspects of No Child Left Behind.

Some critics of NCLB believe that it presents real obstacles to helping students and strengthening public schools because it focuses on sanctions rather than assistance, mandates rather than support for effective programs (National Education Association, 2004). The Center on Education Policy (2003) determined that because the federal government provides only 7 percent of the total funding for public schools, it may be impossible for poor school districts to make all the changes necessary to meet the NCLB requirements. Other criticisms of NCLB focus on the likelihood that severe accountability measures can lead schools to focus on a limited set of skills, at the expense of, for example, social studies, art, and music (Center on Education Policy, 2003; Goldberg, 2004; Marshak, 2003; Neill, 2003). Other concerns focus on the possibility that accountability pressures will lead to cheating, or the use of practices that increase scores without increasing learning (Peterson & West, 2003; RAND, 2003).

It is too early to know what the effects of No Child Left Behind will be on the futures of students in the United States. Factors outside of the control of schools, such as lack of community support, high student mobility, and children not prepared for kindergarten, make the challenge of having all students proficient by 2014 daunting (RAND, 2003). However, NCLB should at least focus attention on the achievement of all student subgroups, and it has started a useful conversation about scientifically based practice. For these reasons it may ultimately make a lasting difference.

Reading Recovery is particularly helpful for working with ESL/ELL children. How do such programs differ from traditional compensatory programs?

Early Intervention Programs

Traditionally, Title I and other compensatory education programs have overwhelmingly emphasized remediation. They typically provide services to children only after the children have already fallen behind. Such children might also end up in special education or might be retained. All of the remedial strategies have shown little evidence of effectiveness. In fact, there is evidence that providing such services only after children have failed can be very detrimental to student achievement, motivation, and other outcomes (e.g., Roderick, 1994; Shepard & Smith, 1989). Recently, increasing emphasis has been placed on prevention and **early intervention** rather than remediation in serving children placed at risk of school failure (see Powell, 1995; Slavin et al., 1994). For example, the findings of long-term benefits of preschool for low-income children (Schweinhart, Barnes, & Weikart, 1993) have led to a dramatic expansion of prekindergarten programs for 4-year-olds.

Programs that emphasize infant stimulation, parent training, and other services for children from birth to age 5 also have been found to have long-term effects on at-risk students' school success. An example is the Carolina Abecedarian program (Campbell & Ramey, 1994), which found long-term achievement effects of an intensive program for children from low-income homes who received services from infancy through school entry. Other programs have had similar effects (Garber, 1988; Wasik & Karweit, 1994). In addition to such preventive programs, there is evidence that early intervention can keep children from falling behind in the early grades. For example, Whitehurst et al. (1999) found lasting effects of an early intervention program emphasizing phonemic awareness (knowledge of how sounds blend into words) and other preliteracy strategies. A program called **Reading Recovery** (Lyons, Pinnell, & DeFord, 1993; Pinnell, DeFord, & Lyons, 1988) provides one-to-one tutoring from specially trained teachers to first-graders who are not reading adequately. This program is able to bring nearly all at-risk children to adequate levels of performance and can have long-lasting positive effects. Reading Recovery is used in more than 9,000 U.S. elementary schools. The cost-effectiveness of Reading Recovery and its long-term

CONNECTIONS

For more on prevention and early intervention, see Chapter 12, page 428.

early intervention
Programs that target at-risk infants and toddlers to prevent possible later need for remediation.

Reading Recovery
A program in which specially trained teachers provide one-to-one tutoring to first-graders who are not reading adequately.

effects have been somewhat controversial (Hiebert, 1996; Pinnell, Lyons, & Jones, 1996; Shanahan, 1998). Although there is little disagreement that Reading Recovery has a positive effect on the reading success of at-risk first-graders (see Lyons et al., 1993; Pinnell et al., 1994), there are conflicting findings concerning maintenance of these gains beyond first grade and concerning the question of whether positive effects for small numbers of first-graders represent the best use of limited funds for an entire age group of children (see Schachter, 2000).

In addition to Reading Recovery, several other programs have successfully used certified teachers, paraprofessionals, and even well-trained and well-supervised volunteers to improve the reading achievement of first-graders (Morris, Tyner, & Perney, 2000; Wasik, 1997; Wasik & Slavin, 1993). An Australian program that used a combination of curricular reform, one-to-one tutoring (Reading Recovery), family support, and other elements showed significant effects on first-graders' reading performance (Crévola & Hill, 1998).

Research on Reading Recovery, the Carolina Abecedarian program, and other preventive strategies shows that at-risk children can succeed if we are willing to give them high-quality instruction and intensive services early in their school careers (Slavin, 1997/98). Early intervention also ensures that children who do turn out to need long-term services are identified early—and that those whose problems can be solved early on are not needlessly assigned to special education (see Vellutino et al., 1996).

Comprehensive School Reform Programs

In recent years, a new form of school reform has become widespread, particularly in Title I schools. These *comprehensive school reform programs* are schoolwide approaches that introduce research-based strategies into every aspect of school functions: curriculum, instruction, assessment, grouping, accommodations for children having difficulties, parent involvement, and other elements (Herman, 1999; Slavin, 2000/2001; Stringfield, Ross, & Smith, 1996; Traub, 1999). Comprehensive reform models vary widely. Some, such as Success for All (Slavin & Madden, 2001) and Direct Instruction (Adams & Engelmann, 1996) provide specific student materials in each subject and detailed guides to using them, while others, such as Accelerated Schools (Hopfenberg & Levin, 1993) and the School Development Program (Comer, Haynes, Joyner, & Ben-Avie, 1996), provide more general guidelines for practice and then help school staffs develop their own approaches. America's Choice (Supovitz, Poglinco, & Snyder, 2001) and Modern Red Schoolhouse (Kilgore, Doyle, & Linkowsky, 1996) focus on infusing standards into school practices, and Co-nect (Goldberg & Richards, 1996) focuses on schoolwide infusion of technology. Collectively, these comprehensive school reform models were used in more than 6,000 U.S. schools in 2001–2002 and are growing rapidly. A federal funding program connected to Title I, called the Comprehensive School Reform Demonstration (CSRD), provides grants to schools to help them adopt "proven, comprehensive reform models," and this funding has contributed significantly to the growth of CSR.

The most widely used and extensively researched of the CSR programs is **Success for All** (Slavin & Madden, 2001), a program that focuses on prevention and early intervention for elementary schools serving disadvantaged programs. Success for All provides research-based reading programs for preschool, kindergarten, and grades 1 through 8; one-to-one tutoring for first-graders who need it; family support services; and other changes in instruction, curriculum, and school organization designed to ensure that students do not fall behind in the early grades. Longitudinal

Success for All

A comprehensive approach to prevention and early intervention for preschool, kindergarten, and grades 1 through 5, with one-to-one tutoring, family support services, and changes in instruction designed to prevent students from falling behind.

studies of Success for All have shown that students in this program read substantially better than do students in matched control schools throughout the elementary grades, and that they are far less likely to be assigned to special education or to fail a grade (see Borman & Hewes, 2001; Borman et al., 2003; Madden, Slavin, Karweit, Dolan, & Wasik, 1993; Muñoz, Dossett, & Judy-Gallans, 2004; Slavin & Madden, 2000, 2001). In 2004–2005, Success for All was used in more than 1,400 Title I schools.

Another widely researched comprehensive school reform model is James Comer's School Development Program (Comer et al., 1996). Comer's model emphasizes building connections with parents and communities and organizing school staff into collaborative teams to create engaging, effective instruction (Ramirez-Smith, 1995). Two recent randomized experiments evaluating the Comer model had mixed results, but found that schools making the most extensive use of the principles underlying the approach had the greatest achievement gains (Cook et al., 1999; Cook, Murphy, & Hunt, 2000). (For descriptions and reviews of research on these and other comprehensive school reform models, see Herman, 1999; Northwest Regional Educational Laboratory, 1998; Slavin & Fashola, 1998; Traub, 1999.)

After-School and Summer School Programs

Increasingly, Title I and other federal, state, and local education agencies are funding programs that extend learning time for students beyond the school day. Both after-school and summer school programs are expanding rapidly.

After-school programs typically combine some sort of academic activity, such as homework help, with sports, drama, and cultural activities (Friedman 2002/2003). However, studies of after-school programs generally find that for such programs to enhance student achievement, they need to incorporate well-organized coursework, such as individual or small-group tutoring, to extend the academic day (Fashola, 2002; McComb, Scott, & Little, 2003).

Summer school sessions are also increasingly seen in schools, particularly as a last chance for students to avoid being retained in their grade. Summer school has long been advocated as a solution to the "summer loss" phenomenon, in which children from families that are low in socioeconomic status tend to lose ground over the summer, whereas middle-class students tend to gain (Entwisle, Alexander, & Olson, 2001). Research on summer school generally finds benefits for children's achievement (Borman & Boulay, 2004).

Chapter Summary

What Are Elements of Effective Instruction beyond a Good Lesson?

Teachers must know how to adapt instruction to students' levels of knowledge. According to Carroll's model of school learning, effectiveness of instruction depends on time needed (a function of student aptitude and ability to understand instruction) and time actually spent learning (which depends on time available, quality of instruction, and student perseverance).

Slavin's QAIT model of effective instruction identifies four elements that are subject to the teacher's direct control: quality of instruction, appropriate level of instruction, incentive, and amount of time. The model proposes that instruction that is deficient in any of these elements will be ineffective.

THE INTENTIONAL TEACHER

Using What You Know about Accommodating Instruction to Meet Individual Needs

Intentional teachers see students' needs, not textbooks, as the starting point for planning and providing instruction. They expect students to have varied areas of strength and struggle, and they plan instruction that meets the needs of individual students. They monitor student progress carefully, and use resources beyond the classroom to meet the needs of students with varying capabilities. Intentional teachers expect to continue learning and mastering strategies that encourage all students to succeed.

❶ What do I expect my students to know and be able to do at the end of this lesson? How does this contribute to course objectives and to students' needs to become capable individuals?

Intentional teachers think about instructional quality in terms of many components. As you plan and assess your lessons, analyze the extent to which they focus on providing high-quality, appropriate instruction, student motivation, and appropriate use of classroom time (this chapter's QAIT). For example, imagine that you view a videotape of yourself teaching and are pleased to see that student levels of enthusiasm and engagement are high during most parts of the lesson. However, you note with dismay that you spent nearly 20 minutes of the 50-minute period handling routines and interruptions. You might resolve to try a few management strategies that will allow you and your students to use instructional time to fuller advantage.

❷ What knowledge, skills, needs, and interests do my students have that must be taken into account in my lesson?

All students bring a range of experiences and achievements to the classroom. Check students' prerequisite knowledge through strategies such as informal discussion, student drawings, and pre-tests. Then decide whether and how your instruction in specific instances should be modified to reflect differences in students' experiences. For example, you might discover that your math and science students display a wide range of reading achievement. These reading differences have little bearing on your mathematics instruction, but you might modify your science instruction carefully to accommodate students' diverse reading abilities. You might arrange for a variety of print materials and for peer tutoring, and devise skeleton outlines to guide students' reading.

❸ What do I know about the content, child development, learning, motivation, and effective teaching strategies that I can use to accomplish my objectives?

Skilled teachers use a variety of approaches and resources to accommodate student differences. When you find relevant student differences, consider a wide variety of strategies that can help you meet needs. Examples include mastery learning, grouping strategies, tutoring, and computer-based instruction. For example, imagine that one-third of your students are work-

How Are Students Grouped to Accommodate Achievement Differences?

Many schools manage student differences in ability and academic achievement through between-class ability grouping, tracking, or regrouping into separate classes for particular subjects during part of a school day. However, research shows that within-class groupings are more effective, especially in reading and math, and are clearly preferable to groupings that segregate or stigmatize low achievers. Untracking recommends students be in mixed-ability groups. The students are held to high standards and are provided with assistance to reach those goals. Nongraded elementary schools combine children of different ages in the same classroom. Students are flexibly grouped according to their needs and performance levels.

What Is Mastery Learning?

Mastery learning is based on the idea that all or almost all students should have mastered a particular skill before proceeding to the next skill. Amounts of instructional time should vary so that all students have as much time as they need to attain the targeted knowledge and skills. Mastery learning takes a variety of forms, all of which involve formative and summative evaluations, corrective instruction, and enrichment

ing substantially above your grade-level mathematics curriculum, but more than half are wrestling with most concepts and skills. Over coffee, you and an experienced colleague discuss your options. You consider four strategies that might work: (1) combining your students with your colleague's class for peer tutoring; (2) spending a portion of each period in mastery learning, in which you and your colleague would divide students into those who have or have not mastered particular skills; (3) calling in volunteer tutors from a local senior center; (4) arranging for tutorial and drill and practice work in mathematics at your school's computer lab.

❹ What instructional materials, technology, assistance, and other resources are available to help accomplish my objectives?

Effective teachers use grouping practices that are supported by research. Think about alternatives to between-class ability grouping. Consider options such as regrouping, within-class grouping, and cross-age grouping. For example, you might ask the principal of your high school to put you on a faculty meeting agenda to discuss alternatives to your school's traditional tracks for college preparatory, basic, and remedial courses. You could share an overview of the research on ability grouping, share some descriptions of schools that have engaged in untracking, and suggest that a committee of teachers, parents, and administrators explore the issue further.

❺ How will I plan to assess students' progress toward my objectives?

Effective teachers use a variety of ongoing assessments to monitor how well students are learning, and they use this information to adapt their instruction to accommodate individual needs. Assess student progress frequently and be prepared to modify future lessons based on your findings. For example, you might use semiweekly journal entries and weekly objective quizzes to check student progress in your biology class. To students who demonstrate that they have quickly mastered objectives, you might provide enrichment opportunities to study the content through websites, software packages, readings, and investigations. For students who need additional scaffolding, you provide more intensive instruction.

❻ How will I respond if individual children or the class as a whole are not on track toward success? What is my back-up plan?

Assumptions that accommodations are uniformly effective could prove faulty. Gather data to determine the extent to which your accommodations are having the desired effect. Check effects on attitude and self-esteem as well as achievement. For example, you might continually assess children's progress within their reading groups and accelerate students doing well, so that over time students not progressing as fast as others can receive more individual attention.

activities. Mastery learning is generally effective in teaching basic skills but may reduce coverage of content.

What Are Some Ways of Individualizing Instruction?

Peer and adult tutoring are all methods for individualizing instruction. Research shows clear benefits of cross-age peer tutoring.

How Is Technology Used in Education?

Technology in education is used for three general purposes. First, teachers use technology, such as word processors, multimedia, and presentation software, for planning and presenting lessons. Second, students use technology, such as word processing and CD-ROM reference software, for learning and preparing presentations. Computer-assisted instruction in the form of drill and practice, tutorials, instructional games, simulations, and the Internet are widespread. Third, teachers and administrators use technology for administrative tasks. Research on computer-based instruction demonstrates small to moderate positive effects on achievement.

What Educational Programs Exist for Students Placed at Risk?

Students who are at risk are any students who are likely to fail academically for any reason stemming from the student or from the student's environment. Reasons are diverse and might include poverty.

Educational programs for students who are at risk include compensatory education, early intervention programs, and special education. Federally funded compensatory education programs include, for example, Head Start, which aims to help preschool-age children from low-income backgrounds achieve school readiness, and Title I, which mandates extra services to low-achieving students in schools that have many low-income students. Extra services include pull-out programs, tutoring programs, and continuous-progress programs.

The No Child Left Behind Act holds schools accountable for their students' achievement. It calls for annual testing of students in reading, language arts, and math. After-school and summer school programs are increasingly funded by federal, state, and local education agencies to extend students' learning time. Research is mixed regarding the effectiveness of compensatory education programs.

Research also supports the effectiveness of many prevention and intervention programs such as Reading Recovery, and comprehensive school reform programs such as Success for All, the School Development Program, America's Choice, and Direct Instruction.

Key Terms

Research
Navigator.com

Review the following key terms from the chapter. Then, to explore research on these topics and how they relate to education today, connect to Research Navigator™ through this book's Companion Website or directly at www.researchnavigator.com.

between-class ability grouping   280
CD-ROM   298
compensatory education   303
computer-assisted instruction
   (CBI)   296
computer programming   298
corrective instruction   287
cross-age tutoring   289
database   295
desktop publishing   295
digital photographs   298
drill and practice   296
early intervention   307
electronic whiteboard   301
enrichment activities   288
formative evaluations   287
hypermedia   295
hypertext   295
individualized instruction   289
instructional games   297
integrated learning systems   298
Internet   297
Joplin Plan   284
liquid crystal display (LCD)
   projectors   301

mastery criterion   286
mastery learning   286
memory sticks   301
multimedia   298
nongraded programs   284
peer tutoring   289
personal digital assistants (PDAs)   300
problem-solving program   297
pull-out programs   301
QAIT model   277
Reading Recovery   307
regrouping   284
simulation software   297
spreadsheets   295
students at risk   302
Success for All   308
summative evaluations   287
Title I   303
tracks   280
tutorial programs   296
untracking   284
videodiscs   298
within-class ability grouping   280
word processing   295

Self-Assessment: Practicing for Licensure

Directions: The chapter-opening vignette addresses indicators that are often assessed in state licensure exams. Re-read the chapter-opening vignette, and then respond to the following questions.

1. How does Mr. Arbuthnot, the fourth-grade teacher in the chapter-opening vignette, incorporate John Carroll's Model of School Learning into his lesson?
   a. Mr. Arbuthnot tries to match the time spent on learning with the time students need to learn.
   b. Mr. Arbuthnot groups students according to their ability level.
   c. Mr. Arbuthnot expects students to learn the concepts of long division through group discussion and inquiry.
   d. Mr. Arbuthnot equates quality of instruction with quantity of instruction.

2. Imagine that Mr. Arbuthnot decides to divide his class into three groups: those who know long division, those who know some long division, and those who do not know long division. What type of ability group would he be using?
   a. tri-grade ability grouping
   b. high–low ability grouping
   c. within-class ability grouping
   d. between-class ability grouping

3. If Mr. Arbuthnot were to use a "mastery learning" approach to continue his lesson on long division, what would he most likely do next?
   a. assume that not all students can learn, and then move on
   b. continue teaching long division until all or almost all students have learned long division
   c. manipulate the amount of learning rather than the time it takes to learn
   d. arrange students according to their ability level

4. In the opening of the vignette, Mr. Arbuthnot teaches an engaging lesson on long division, and then gives students a quiz over the content learned. What type of evaluation is this?
   a. norm-referenced
   b. standardized
   c. minimum competency
   d. formative

5. Mr. Arbuthnot decides that he cannot work individually with all the students who have not yet mastered long division. He decides that some sort of tutoring might solve his problem. If he selects the type of tutoring that is most effective, according to research, which of the following will he use?
   a. cross-age peer tutoring
   b. same-age peer tutoring
   c. tutoring by certified teachers
   d. computer tutoring

6. Explain how Mr. Arbuthnot could integrate technology into his teaching. What does the research on computer-based instruction say?

7. Describe programs that exist for students placed at risk.

8. How does No Child Left Behind change what teachers do with their students?

Motivating Students to Learn

The students in Cal Lewis's tenth-grade U.S. history

class were all in their seats before the bell rang, eagerly awaiting the start of the period. But Mr. Lewis himself was nowhere to be seen. Two minutes after the bell, in he walked dressed as George Washington, complete with an eighteenth-century costume and powdered wig and carrying a gavel. He gravely took his seat, rapped the gavel, and said, "I now call to order this meeting of the Constitutional Convention."

The students had been preparing for this day for weeks. Each of them represented one of the 13 original states. In groups of two and three, they had been studying all about their states, the colonial era, the American Revolution, and the United States under the Articles of Confederation. Two days earlier, Mr. Lewis had given each group secret instructions from their "governor" on the key interests of their state. For example, the New Jersey and Delaware delegations were to insist that small states be adequately represented in the government, whereas New York and Virginia were to demand strict representation by population.

In preparing for the debate, each delegation had to make certain that any member of the delegation could represent the delegation's views. To ensure this, Mr. Lewis had assigned each student a number from one to three at random. When a delegation asked to be recognized, he would call out a number, and the student with that number would respond for the group.

Mr. Lewis, staying in character as George Washington, gave a speech on the importance of the task they were undertaking and then opened the floor for debate. First, he recognized the delegation from Georgia, represented by Beth Andrews. Beth was a shy girl, but she had been well prepared by her fellow delegates and knew that they were rooting for her.

"The great state of Georgia wishes to raise the question of a Bill of Rights. We have experienced the tyranny of government, and we demand that the people have a guarantee of their liberties!"

Beth went on to propose elements of the Bill of Rights that her delegation had drawn up. While she was talking, Mr. Lewis was rating her presentation on historical accuracy, appropriateness to the real interests of her state, organization, and delivery. He would use these ratings in evaluating each delegation at the end of each class period. The debate went on. The North Carolina delegates argued in favor of the right of states to expand to the West; the New Jersey delegation wanted western territories made into new states. Wealthy Massachusetts wanted taxes to remain in the states where they were collected; poor Delaware wanted national taxes. Between debates, the delegates had an opportunity to do some "horse trading," promising to vote for proposals important to other states in exchange for votes on issues important to them. At the end of the week, the class voted on 10 key issues. After the votes were taken and the bell rang, the students poured into the hall still arguing about issues of taxation, representation, powers of the executive, and so on.

After school, Rikki Ingram, another social studies teacher, dropped into Mr. Lewis's classroom. "I see you're doing your Constitutional Convention again this year. It looks great, but how can you cover all of U.S. history if you spend a month on just the Constitution?"

Cal smiled. "Don't you remember how boring high school social studies was?" he said. "It sure was for me. I know I'm sacrificing some coverage to do this unit, but look how motivated these kids are!" He picked up a huge sheaf of notes and position papers written by the South Carolina delegation. "These kids are working their tails off, and they're learning that history is fun and useful. They'll remember this material for the rest of their lives!"

USING YOUR *Experience*

Critical Thinking Rikki Ingram seems concerned that Mr. Lewis's class is not covering the material well enough. What do you think are the advantages, disadvantages, and interesting or unclear aspects of Mr. Lewis's teaching strategy?

Cooperative Learning With another student, relate stories of a social studies or other high school teacher who tried methods similar to Mr. Lewis's method of teaching. As a pair, retell your stories to a student from another pair.

INTASC

5 Classroom Motivation and Management

Motivation is one of the most important ingredients of effective instruction. Students who want to learn can learn just about anything. But how can teachers ensure that every student wants to learn and will put in the effort needed to learn complex material?

Mr. Lewis knows the value of motivation, so he has structured a unit that taps many aspects of motivation. By having students work in groups and be evaluated on the basis of presentations made by randomly selected group members, he has created a situation in which students are encouraging each other to excel. Social motivation of this kind is very powerful, especially for adolescents. Mr. Lewis is rating students' presentations according to clear, comprehensive standards and giving them feedback each day. He is tying an important period in history to students' daily lives by having them take an active role in debating and trading votes. All of these strategies are designed not just to make history fun but to give students many sources of motivation to learn and remember the history they have studied. Mr. Lewis is right. The students will probably never forget their experience in his class and are likely to approach new information about revolutionary history and the Constitution with enthusiasm throughout their lives.

This chapter presents the many ways in which teachers can enhance students' desire to learn academic material and the theories and research behind each method.

WHAT IS MOTIVATION?

One of the most critical components of learning, motivation is also one of the most difficult to measure. What makes a student want to learn? The willingness to put effort into learning is a product of many factors, ranging from the student's personality and abilities to characteristics of particular learning tasks, incentives for learning, settings, and teacher behaviors.

All students are motivated. The question is: Motivated to do what? Some students are motivated more to socialize or watch television than to do schoolwork. The educator's job is not to increase motivation per se but to discover, prompt, and sustain students' motivations to learn, and to engage in activities that lead to learning. Imagine that Cal Lewis had come to class in eighteenth-century costume but had not structured tasks and evaluations to induce students to study U.S. history. The students might have been amused and interested, but we cannot assume that they would have been motivated to do the work necessary to learn the material.

Psychologists define **motivation** as an internal process that activates, guides, and maintains behavior over time (Murphy & Alexander, 2000; Pintrich, 2003; Schunk, 2000; Stipek, 2002). In plain language, motivation is what gets you going, keeps you going, and determines where you're trying to go.

Motivation can vary in both intensity and direction (Ryan & Deci, 2000). Two students might be motivated to play video games, but one of them might be more strongly motivated to do so than the other. Or one student might be strongly motivated to play video games, and the other equally strongly motivated to play football. Actually, though, the intensity and direction of motivations are often difficult to separate. The intensity of a motivation to engage in one activity might depend in large part on the intensity and direction of motivations to engage in alternative activities. If someone has only enough time and money to go to the movies or to play video games, motivation to engage in one of these activities is strongly influenced by the intensity of motivation to engage in the other. Motivation is not only important in getting students to engage in academic activities. It is also important in determining how much students will learn from the activities they perform or the information to which they are exposed. Students who are motivated to learn something use higher cognitive processes in learning about it and absorb and retain more from it (Driscoll, 2000; Jetton & Alexander, 2001; Pintrich, 2003). An important task for teachers is planning how they will support student motivation.

Motivation to do something can come about in many ways (Stipek, 2002). Motivation can be a personality characteristic; individuals might have lasting, stable interests in participating in such broad categories of activities as academics, sports, or social activities. Motivation can come from intrinsic characteristics of a task: By making U.S. history fun, social, active, and engaging, Cal Lewis made students eager to learn it. Motivation can also come from sources extrinsic to the task, as when Cal Lewis rated students' performances in the Constitutional Convention simulation.

motivation
The influence of needs and desires on the intensity and direction of behavior.

WHAT ARE SOME THEORIES OF MOTIVATION?

The first half of this chapter presents contemporary theories of motivation, which seek to explain why people are motivated to do what they do. The second half discusses the classroom use of incentives for learning and presents strategies for increasing students' motivations to learn and to do schoolwork.

Motivation and Behavioral Learning Theory

The concept of motivation is closely tied to the principle that behaviors that have been reinforced in the past are more likely to be repeated than are behaviors that have not been reinforced or that have been punished. In fact, rather than using the concept of motivation, a behavioral theorist might focus on the degree to which students learn to do schoolwork to obtain desired outcomes (see Bandura, 1986; Bigge & Shermis, 2004; Wielkiewicz, 1995).

CONNECTIONS

For more on reinforcement of behaviors, see Chapter 5, page 139.

Why do some students persist in the face of failure while others give up? Why do some students work to please the teacher, others to make good grades, and still others out of interest in the material they are learning? Why do some students achieve far more than would be predicted on the basis of their ability and some achieve far less? Examination of reinforcement histories and schedules of reinforcement might provide answers to such questions, but it is usually easier to speak in terms of motivations to satisfy various needs.

Rewards and Reinforcement   One reason that reinforcement history is an inadequate explanation for motivation is that human motivation is highly complex and context-bound. With very hungry animals we can predict that food will be an effective reinforcer. With humans, even hungry ones, we can't be sure what will be a reinforcer and what will not, because the reinforcing value of most potential reinforcers is largely determined by personal or situational factors. As an example of this, think about the value of $50 for an hour's light work. Most of us would view $50 as a powerful reinforcer, more than adequate to get us to do an hour of light work. But consider these four situations:

1. Mr. Scrooge offers Bill $60 to paint his fence. Bill thinks this is more than enough for the job, so he does his best work. However, when he is done, Mr. Scrooge says, "I don't think you did sixty dollars' worth of work. Here's fifty."
2. Now consider the same situation, except that Mr. Scrooge originally offers Bill $40 and, when Bill is finished, praises him for an excellent job and gives him $50.
3. Dave and Barbara meet at a party, like each other immediately, and after the party take a long walk in the moonlight. When they get to Barbara's house, Dave says, "Barbara, I enjoyed spending time with you. Here's fifty dollars I'd like you to have."
4. Marta's aunt offers her $50 to teach little Pepa how to play baseball next Saturday. However, if Marta agrees to do so, she will miss her chance to try out for the school baseball team.

In situations 1, 3, and 4, $50 is not a good reinforcer at all. In situation 1, Bill's expectations have been raised and then dashed by Mr. Scrooge. Even though the amount of monetary reward is the same in situation 2, this situation is much more likely to make Bill want to paint Mr. Scrooge's fence again, because in this case his reward exceeds his expectation. In situation 3, Dave's offer of $50 is insulting and would certainly not increase Barbara's interest in going out with him in the future.

In situation 4, although Marta's aunt's offer would seem generous to Marta under most circumstances, it is insufficient reinforcement this particular Saturday, because it interferes with a more highly valued activity.

Determining the Value of an Incentive   These situations illustrate an important point: The motivational value of an incentive cannot be assumed, because it might depend on many factors (Chance, 1992; Strong, Silver, & Robinson, 1995). When teachers say, "I want you all to be sure to hand in your book reports on time, because they will count toward your grade," the teachers might be assuming that grades are effective incentives for most students. However, some students might not care about grades, perhaps because their parents don't or because they have a history of failure in school and have decided that grades are unimportant. If a teacher says to a student, "Good work! I knew you could do it if you tried!" this might be motivating to a student who had just completed a task he thought was difficult, but punishing to one who thought the task was easy (because the teacher's praise implies that he had to work especially hard to complete the task). As in the case of Bill and Mr. Scrooge, students' expectations for rewards determine the motivational value of any particular reward. And it is often difficult to determine students' motivations from their behavior, because many different motivations can influence behavior. Sometimes one type of motivation clearly determines behavior; at other times, several motivations are influential.

Motivation and Human Needs

Whereas behavioral learning theorists (e.g., Bandura, 1986; Skinner, 1953) speak in terms of motivation to obtain reinforcers and avoid punishers, other theorists (e.g., Maslow, 1954) prefer the concept of motivation to satisfy needs. Some basic needs that we all must satisfy are those for food, shelter, love, and maintenance of positive self-esteem. People differ in the degree of importance they attach to each of these needs. Some need constant reaffirmation that they are loved or appreciated; others have a greater need for physical comfort and security. Also, the same person has different needs at different times; a drink of water would be much more appreciated after a four-mile run than after a four-course meal.

Maslow's Hierarchy of Needs   Given that people have many needs, which will they try to satisfy at any given moment? To predict this, Maslow (1954) proposed a hierarchy of needs, which is illustrated in Figure 10.1. In Maslow's theory, needs that are lower in this hierarchy must be at least partially satisfied before a person will try to satisfy higher-level needs. For example, a hungry person or someone who is in physical danger will be less concerned about maintaining a positive self-image than about obtaining food or safety; but once that person is no longer hungry or afraid, self-esteem needs might become paramount. One critical concept that Maslow introduced is the distinction between deficiency needs and growth needs. **Deficiency needs** (physiological, safety, love, and esteem) are those that are critical to physical and psychological well-being; these needs must be satisfied, but once they are, a person's motivation to satisfy them diminishes. In contrast, **growth needs,** such as the need to know and understand things, to appreciate beauty, or to grow and develop in appreciation of others, can never be satisfied completely. In fact, the more people are able to meet their need to know and understand the world around them, the greater their motivation might become to learn still more.

Self-Actualization   Maslow's theory includes the concept of desire for **self-actualization,** which he defines as "the desire to become everything that one is capable of becoming" (Maslow, 1954, p. 92). Self-actualization is characterized by acceptance

---

INTASC

2 Knowledge of Human Development and Learning

CERTIFICATION POINTER
Teacher certification tests will require you to identify which needs Maslow identified as deficiency needs and which he identified as growth needs.

deficiency needs
Basic requirements for physical and psychological well-being as identified by Maslow.

growth needs
Needs for knowing, appreciating, and understanding, which people try to satisfy after their basic needs are met.

self-actualization
A person's ability to develop his or her full potential.

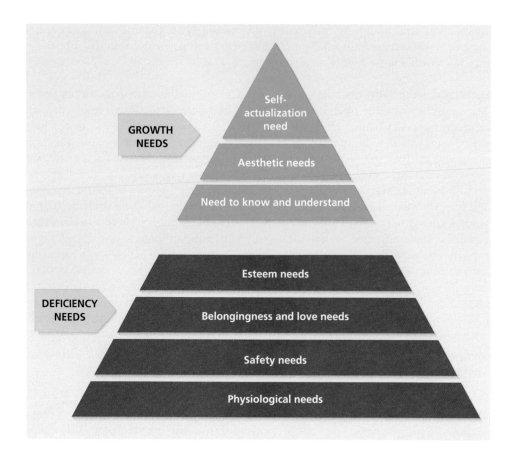

FIGURE 10.1
Maslow's Hierarchy of Needs

Maslow identifies two types of needs: deficiency needs and growth needs. People are motivated to satisfy needs at the bottom of the hierarchy before seeking to satisfy those at the top.

of self and others, spontaneity, openness, relatively deep but democratic relationships with others, creativity, humor, and independence—in essence, psychological health. Maslow places striving for self-actualization at the top of his hierarchy of needs, implying that achievement of this most important need depends on the satisfaction of all other needs. The difficulty of accomplishing this is recognized by Maslow (1968), who estimated that fewer than 1 percent of adults achieve self-actualization.

Implications of Maslow's Theory for Education   The importance of Maslow's theory for education is in the relationship between deficiency needs and growth needs. Obviously, students who are very hungry or in physical danger will have little psychological energy to put into learning. Schools and government agencies recognize that if students' basic needs are not met, learning will suffer. They have responded by providing free breakfast and lunch programs. The most important deficiency needs, however, are those for love and self-esteem. Students who do not feel that they are loved and that they are capable are unlikely to have a strong motivation to achieve the higher-level growth objectives, such as the search for knowledge and understanding for their own sake or the creativity and openness to new ideas that are characteristic of the self-actualizing person. A student who is unsure of his or her lovableness or capability will tend to make the safe choice: Go with the crowd, study for the test without interest in learning the ideas, write a predictable but uncreative essay, and so on. A teacher who can put students at ease and make them feel accepted and respected as individuals is more likely (in Maslow's view) to help them become eager to learn for the sake of learning and willing to risk being creative and open to new ideas. If students are to become self-directed learners, they must believe that the teacher will respond

CONNECTIONS

Motivational factors affecting the academic performance of students who are at risk of school failure are discussed in Chapter 9, page 307.

fairly and consistently to them and that they will not be ridiculed or punished for honest errors.

Motivation and Attribution Theory

Teresa usually gets good grades but receives a D on a certain quiz. The mark is inconsistent with her self-image and causes her discomfort. To resolve this discomfort, Teresa might decide to work harder to make certain that she never gets such a low grade again. On the other hand, she might try to rationalize her low grade: "The questions were tricky. I wasn't feeling well. The teacher didn't tell us the quiz was coming. I wasn't really trying. It was too hot." These excuses help Teresa account for one D—but suppose she gets several poor grades in a row. Now she might decide that she never did like this subject anyway or that the teacher shows favoritism to the boys in the class or is a hard grader. All of these changes in opinions and excuses are directed at avoiding an unpleasant pairing of inconsistent ideas: "I am a good student" and "I am doing poorly in this class, and it is my own fault."

Teresa is struggling to find a reason for her poor grades that does not require her to change her perception of herself as a good student. She attributes her poor performance to her teacher, to the subject matter, or to other students—external factors over which she has no control. Or, if she acknowledges that her poor performance is her own fault, she decides that it must be a short-term lapse due to a momentary (but reversible) lack of motivation or attention regarding this unit of instruction.

Attribution theory (see Graham & Weiner, 1996; Hareli & Weiner, 2002; Weiner, 1994, 2000) seeks to understand just such explanations and excuses, particularly when applied to success or failure (wherein lies the theory's greatest importance for education, in which success and failure are recurrent themes). Weiner (1994, 2000) suggests that most explanations for success or failure have three characteristics. The first is whether the cause is seen as internal (within the person) or external. The second is whether it is seen as stable or unstable. The third is whether it is perceived as controllable or not. A central assumption of attribution theory is that people will attempt to maintain a positive self-image (Thompson, Davidson, & Barber, 1995). Therefore, when they do well in an activity, they are likely to attribute their success to their own efforts or abilities; but when they do poorly, they will believe that their failure is due to factors over which they had no control (Vispoel & Austin, 1995). In particular, students who experience failure will try to find an explanation that enables them to save face with their peers (Juvonen, 2000). It has been demonstrated that if groups of people are given a task and then told that they either failed or succeeded (even though all, in fact, were equally successful), those who are told that they failed will say that their failure was due to bad luck, whereas those who are told that they succeeded will attribute their success to skill and intelligence (Weiner, 2000).

Attributions for others' behavior are also important. For example, students are more likely to respond to a classmate's request for help if they believe that the classmate needs help because of a temporary uncontrollable factor (such as getting hurt in a basketball game) than if they believe that help is needed because of a controllable factor (such as failure to study) (Juvonen & Weiner, 1993).

Attributions for Success and Failure   Attribution theory deals primarily with four explanations for success and failure in achievement situations: ability, effort, task difficulty, and luck. Ability and effort attributions are internal to the individual; task difficulty and luck attributions are external. Ability is taken to be a relatively stable, unalterable state; effort can be altered. Similarly, task difficulty is essentially a stable characteristic, whereas luck is unstable and uncontrollable. These four attributions and representative explanations for success and failure are presented in Table 10.1.

attribution theory
A theory of motivation that focuses on how people explain the causes of their own successes and failures.

Table 10.1		
Attributions for Success and Failure		
Attribution theory describes and suggests the implications of people's explanations of their successes and failures.		
Attribution		Stability
	Stable	**Unstable**
Internal	*Ability*	*Effort*
Success:	"I'm smart."	"I tried hard."
Failure:	"I'm stupid."	"I didn't really try."
External	*Task Difficulty*	*Luck*
Success:	"It was easy."	"I lucked out."
Failure:	"It was too hard."	"I had bad luck."

Source: From Bernard Weiner, "A Theory of Motivation for Some Classroom Experiences," *Journal of Educational Psychology, 71,* pp. 3–25. Copyright © 1979 by the American Psychological Association. Adapted by permission.

Table 10.1 shows how students often seek to explain success and failure differently. When students succeed, they would like to believe that it was because they are smart (an internal, stable attribution), not because they were lucky or because the task was easy or even because they tried hard (because "trying hard" says little about their likelihood of success in the future). In contrast, students who fail would like to believe that they had bad luck (an external, unstable attribution), which allows for the possibility of succeeding next time (Weiner, 1994, 2000). Of course, over time, these attributions might be difficult to maintain. As we illustrated in the case of Teresa, a student who gets one bad grade is likely to blame it on bad luck or some other external, unstable cause. After several bad grades, though, an unstable attribution becomes difficult to maintain; no one can be unlucky on tests week after week. Therefore, a student like Teresa might switch to a stable but still external attribution. For example, she could decide that the course is too difficult or make some other stable, external attribution that lets her avoid making a stable, internal attribution that would shatter her self-esteem: "I failed because I don't have the ability" (Juvonen, 2000). She might even reduce her level of effort so that she can maintain the idea that she could succeed if she really wanted to (Jagacinski & Nicholls, 1990).

Locus of Control and Self-Efficacy   One concept that is central to attribution theory is **locus of control** (Rotter, 1954). The word *locus* means *location*. A person with an internal locus of control is one who believes that success or failure is due to his or her own efforts or abilities. Someone with an *external locus of control* is more likely to believe that other factors, such as luck, task difficulty, or other people's actions, cause success or failure. Internal locus of control is often called self-efficacy, the belief that one's behavior makes a difference (Bandura, 1997; Pajares, 1996; Schunk & Pajares, 2004; Zimmerman, 1998). Locus of control or self-efficacy can be very important in explaining a student's school performance. For example, several researchers have found that students who are high in internal locus of control have better grades and test scores than do students of the same intelligence who are low in internal locus of control (Capella & Weinstein, 2001; Pajares & Graham, 1999; Zimmerman, 2000). Studies have found locus of control to be the second most important predictor (after ability) of a student's academic achievement (e.g., Bong, 2001; Pajares & Miller,

CONNECTIONS

Attributions for success or failure that are related to the socioemotional factors of self-esteem and peer relations are discussed in Chapter 3, pages 73, 80–82, and 88–89.

locus of control

A personality trait that determines whether people attribute responsibility for their own failure or success to internal or external factors.

1994; Pietsch, Walker, & Chapman, 2003; Zimmerman & Bandura, 1994). The reason is easy to comprehend. Students who believe that success in school is due to luck, the teacher's whims, or other external factors are unlikely to work hard. In contrast, students who believe that success and failure are due primarily to their own efforts can be expected to work hard (Pressley et al., 2003). In reality, success in a particular class is a product of both students' efforts and abilities (internal factors) and luck, task difficulty, and teacher behaviors (external factors). But the most successful students will tend to overestimate the degree to which their own behavior produces success and failure. Some experiments have shown that even in situations in which success and failure are completely due to luck, students who are high in internal locus of control will believe that it was their efforts that made them succeed or fail (see Weiner, 1992). (See Figure 10.2.)

It is important to note that locus of control can change and depends somewhat on the specific activity or situation. One difficulty in studying the effects of locus of control on achievement is that achievement has a strong effect on locus of control (Bong & Skaalvik, 2003; Weiner, 1992). For example, the same student

Despite being one of the most accomplished female athletes in the world, Mia Hamm often fought off self-doubt. Why is locus of control important to an athlete? How do locus of control and self-efficacy translate to the classroom? As a teacher, how can you influence self-efficacy?

---

1. If a teacher passes you to the next grade, would it probably be

   a. because she liked you, or

   b. because of the work you did? [*internal*]

2. When you do well on a test at school, is it more likely to be

   a. because you studied for it, or [*internal*]

   b. because the test was especially easy?

3. When you have trouble understanding something in school, is it usually

   a. because the teacher didn't explain it clearly, or

   b. because you didn't listen carefully? [*internal*]

4. Suppose your parents say you are doing well in school. Is it likely to happen

   a. because your school work is good, or [*internal*]

   b. because they are in a good mood?

5. Suppose you don't do as well as usual in a subject in school. Would this probably happen

   a. because you weren't as careful as usual, or [*internal*]

   b. because somebody bothered you and kept you from working?

FIGURE 10.2

Items from the Intellectual Achievement Responsibility Questionnaire

From V. C. Crandall, W. Katkovsky, and V. J. Crandall, "Children's Beliefs in Their Own Control of Reinforcement in Intellectual–Academic Achievement Situations," *Child Development, 36,* 1965, pp. 91–109. © The Society for Research in Child Development, Inc. Reprinted by permission.

might have an internal locus of control in academics (because of high academic ability) but an external locus of control in sports (because of low athletic ability). If this student discovered some unsuspected skill in a new sport, he or she might develop an internal locus of control in that sport (but probably still not in other sports).

Implications of Attributions and Self-Efficacy for Education In the classroom, students receive constant information concerning their level of performance on academic tasks, either relative to others or relative to some norm of acceptability. This feedback ultimately influences students' self-perceptions (Bandura, 1997; Schunk, 2004). Attribution theory is important in helping teachers understand how students might interpret and use feedback on their academic performance and in suggesting to teachers how they might give feedback that has the greatest motivational value (see Graham, 1997; Tollefson, 2000).

Motivation and Self-Regulated Learning

Self-regulated learning, discussed in Chapter 6, refers to "learning that results from students' self-generated thoughts and behaviors that are systematically oriented toward their learning goals" (Schunk & Zimmerman, 2003, p. 59). As this definition makes clear, self-regulated learning is closely related to students' goals. Students who are highly motivated to learn something are more likely than other students to consciously plan their learning, carry out a learning plan, and retain the information they obtain (Radosevich et al., 2004; Zimmerman, 2000). For example, students with high reading motivation are more likely to read on their own and to use effective comprehension strategies (Miller, Partelow, & Sen, 2004). This motivation can come from many sources. One is social modeling (Zimmerman & Kitsantas, 2002), such as seeing other students use self-regulated strategies. Another is goal-setting, in which students are encouraged to establish their own learning goals. A third is feedback that shows students that they are making good progress toward their learning goals, especially if the feedback emphasizes students' efforts and abilities. Schunk and Zimmerman (2003) argue that motivation to engage in self-regulated learning is not the same as achievement motivation in general, because self-regulated learning requires the learner to take independent responsibility for learning, not to simply comply with the teacher's demands. Fredericks, Blumenfeld, and Paris (2004) use the terms *engagement* and *investment* to describe motivation that leads students to engage in self-regulated learning, rather than just doing the work and following the rules. Algozzine et al. (2001) use the similar term *self-determination*, and describe a set of successful strategies for building self-determination among individuals with disabilities.

CONNECTIONS

For more on successful strategies for building self-determination, see Chapter 12, p. 428.

ON THE WEB

For articles on self-regulation strategies see **www.nyu.edu/education**.

Theory into PRACTICE

Giving Students Motivating Feedback

Students who believe that their past failures on tasks were due to lack of ability are unlikely to expect to succeed in similar tasks and are therefore unlikely to exert much effort (Ethington, 1991). Obviously, the belief that you will fail can be self-fulfilling. Students who believe that they will fail will be poorly motivated to do academic work, and this might in turn cause them to fail. Therefore, the most damaging idea a teacher can communicate to a student is that the student is "hopelessly stupid."

Few teachers would say such a thing directly to a student, but the idea can be communicated just as effectively in several other ways. One is to use a competitive grading system (e.g., grading on the curve) and to make grades public and relative student rankings important. This practice can make small differences in achievement level seem large, and students who receive the poorest grades might decide that they can never learn.

Alternatively, a teacher who deemphasizes grades and relative rankings but expresses the (almost always correct) expectation that all students in the class can learn is likely to help students see that their chances of success depend on their efforts—an internal but alterable attribution that lets students anticipate success in the future if they do their best.

A stable, internal attribution for success ("I succeed because I am smart") is also a poor motivator; able students, too, need to believe that it is their effort, not their ability, that leads to academic success. Teachers who emphasize the amount of effort as the cause of success as well as failure and who reward effort rather than ability are more likely to motivate all their students to do their best than are teachers who emphasize ability alone (Resnick, 1998).

Some formal means of rewarding students for effort rather than ability are the use of individualized instruction, in which the basis of success is progress at the student's own level; the inclusion of effort as a component of grading or as a separate grade; and the use of rewards for improvement.

CONNECTIONS

For more on individualized instruction, see Chapter 9, page 288.

CONNECTIONS

For more on grading student effort, see Chapter 13, page 480.

Motivation and Expectancy Theory

Expectancy theory is a theory of motivation based on the belief that people's efforts to achieve depend on their expectations of reward. Working within the framework of expectancy theory, Edwards (1954) and later Atkinson (1964) developed theories of motivation based on the following formula:

Motivation (M) = Perceived probability of success (Ps) × Incentive value of success (Is).

The formula is called an expectancy model, or **expectancy–valence model,** because it largely depends on the person's expectations of reward (see Pintrich, 2003; Stipek, 2002; Wigfield & Eccles, 2000). What this theory implies is that people's motivation to achieve something depends on the product of their estimation of their chance of success (perceived probability of success, Ps) and the value they place on success (incentive value of success, Is). For example, if Mark says, "I think I can make the honor roll if I try, and it is very important to me to make the honor roll," then he will probably work hard to make the honor roll. However, one very important aspect of the $M = Ps \times Is$ formula is that it is multiplicative, meaning that if people believe that their probability of success is zero or if they do not value success, then their motivation will be zero. If Mark would like very much to make the honor roll but believes that he hasn't a prayer of doing so, he will be unmotivated. If his chances are actually good but he doesn't care about making the honor roll, he will also be unmotivated. Wigfield (1995) found that students' beliefs that they were capable and their valuing of academic success were, taken together, more important than their actual ability in predicting their achievement.

Atkinson (1964) added an important aspect to expectancy theory in pointing out that under certain circumstances an overly high probability of success can be

expectancy theory
A theory of motivation based on the belief that people's efforts to achieve depend on their expectations of reward.

expectancy–valence model
A theory that relates the probability and the incentive value of success to motivation.

detrimental to motivation. If Mark is very able, it might be so easy for him to make the honor roll that he need not do his best. Atkinson (1958) explained this by arguing that there is a relationship between probability of success and incentive value of success such that success in an easy task is not as valued as is success in a difficult task. Therefore motivation should be at a maximum at moderate levels of probability of success. For example, two evenly matched tennis players will probably play their hardest. Unevenly matched players will not play as hard; the poor player might want very much to win but will have too low a probability of success to try very hard, and the better player will not value winning enough to exert his or her best effort. Confirming Atkinson's theory, more recent research has shown that a person's motivation increases as task difficulty increases up to a point at which the person decides that success is very unlikely or that the goal isn't worth the effort (DeBacker & Nelson, 1999). This and other research findings indicate that moderate to difficult (but not impossible) tasks are better than easy ones for learning and motivation (Brophy, 1999; Clifford, 1990; Wigfield & Eccles, 2000).

Implications of Expectancy Theory for Education   The most important implication of expectancy theory is the commonsense proposition that tasks for students should be neither too easy nor too difficult. If some students believe that they are likely to get an A no matter what they do, then their motivation will not be at a maximum. Similarly, if some students feel certain to fail no matter what they do, their motivation will be minimal. Therefore grading systems should be set up so that earning an A is difficult (but possible) for as many students as feasible and so that earning a low grade is possible for students who exert little effort. Success must be within the reach, but not the easy reach, of all students.

ℋOW CAN ACHIEVEMENT MOTIVATION BE ENHANCED?

INTASC

2 Knowledge of Human Development and Learning

One of the most important types of motivation for educational psychology is **achievement motivation** (McClelland & Atkinson, 1948), or the generalized tendency to strive for success and to choose goal-oriented, success/failure activities. For example, French (1956) found that given a choice of work partners for a complex task, achievement-motivated students tend to choose a partner who is good at the task, whereas affiliation-motivated students (who express the need for love and acceptance) are more likely to choose a friendly partner. Even after they experience failure, achievement-motivated students will persist longer at a task than will students who are less high in achievement motivation and will attribute their failures to lack of effort (an internal but alterable condition) rather than to external factors such as task difficulty or luck. In short, achievement-motivated students want and expect to succeed; when they fail, they redouble their efforts until they do succeed (see Weiner, 1992).

Not surprisingly, students who are high in achievement motivation tend to succeed at school tasks (Stipek, 2002). However, it is unclear which causes which: Does high-achievement motivation lead to success in school, or does success in school (due to ability or other factors) lead to high-achievement motivation? Initially, achievement motivation is strongly affected by family experiences (Turner & Johnson, 2003), but after children have been in school for a few years, success and motivation cause each other. Success breeds the desire for more success, which in turn breeds success (Wigfield, Eccles, & Rodriguez, 1998). In contrast, students who do not experience success in achievement settings will tend to lose the motivation to succeed in such settings and will turn their interest elsewhere (perhaps to social activities, sports, or even delinquent activities in which they might succeed). Achievement motivation tends to

achievement motivation
The desire to experience success and to participate in activities in which success depends on personal effort and abilities.

diminish over the school years, but it is unclear whether this trend is due to the nature of children or to the nature of middle and high schools (Eccles et al., 1993; Hidi & Harackiewicz, 2000; Stipek, 2002).

Motivation and Goal Orientations

Some students are motivationally oriented toward **learning goals** (also called task or **mastery goals**); others are oriented toward **performance goals** (Ames, 1992; Köller & Baumert, 1997; Pintrich, 2000). Students with learning goals see the purpose of schooling as gaining competence in the skills being taught, whereas students with performance goals primarily seek to gain positive judgments of their competence (and avoid negative judgments). Students who are striving toward learning goals are likely to take difficult courses and to seek challenges; students with performance goals focus on getting good grades, taking easy courses, and avoiding challenging situations.

Learning versus Performance Goals   Students with learning goals and those with performance goals do not differ in overall intelligence, but their classroom performance can differ markedly. When they run into obstacles, performance-oriented students tend to become discouraged, and their performance is seriously hampered. In contrast, when learning-oriented students encounter obstacles, they tend to keep trying, and their motivation and performance might actually increase (Pintrich, 2000; Schunk, 1996). Learning-oriented students are more likely to use metacognitive or self-regulated learning strategies (Greene et al., 2004; Pajares, Britner, & Valiante, 2000; Radosevich, et al., 2004; Vermetten, Lodewijks, & Vermunt, 2001). Performance-oriented students who perceive their abilities to be low are likely to fall

learning goals
The goals of students who are motivated primarily by desire for knowledge acquisition and self-improvement. Also called mastery goals.

performance goals
The goals of students who are motivated primarily by a desire to gain recognition from others and to earn good grades.

Personal Reflection

Using Different Styles

A professional acquaintance recently told me of a strong lesson she learned in her childhood that had a major impact on her work as a teacher. As a child growing up in a very athletic family, a lot was expected of Mary both athletically and academically. Her father, a baseball coach, pushed all the kids in the family hard to strive for success; and succeed they did, at the high school and collegiate level. Academically the pressure came from their mother, although in a much gentler and subtler way than from their father. Mary explained that her father never congratulated her for her achievements or showed any encouragement. Instead, he always focused on the mistakes and areas where she could improve. Eventually she came to realize that her academic and athletic drive were rooted in a fear of failure and a fear of disappointing her parents, and she often wondered what it would have been like to go into a competition or a test without fearing the possible outcome.

Once out of college and working as a teacher, coach, and youth sports league director, Mary discovered something else about herself. She couldn't criticize her kids. She never yelled in practice, never yelled in class, and didn't push her

students or athletes in the same way she had been pushed. She often wondered if she should be more vocal with the kids, but she just couldn't do it.

Mary explained that she knew how much she would have appreciated positive encouragement rather than constantly growing expectations when she was going through school, and she simply was unable to use criticism as a way of changing the behavior of her students and athletes. She certainly had her frustrations working with high school and middle school students, but she found it much more satisfying to use encouragement and reason.

@ Reflect on This. Why do you think Mary was unable to use the same strategies with her students and athletes that her parents had used with her? Identify a teacher or coach from your K–12 school days from whom you learned a lot or who brought out the best in you. What methods did this person use? Do you see yourself using some of those same methods as a teacher?

into a pattern of helplessness, for they believe that they have little chance of earning good grades (Midgley & Urdan, 2001; Pajares, Britner, & Valiante, 2000). Learning-oriented students who perceive their ability to be low do not feel this way; they are concerned with how much they themselves can learn, without regard for the performance of others (Fuchs et al., 1997; Kaplan & Midgley, 1997; Thorkildsen & Nicholls, 1998). Unfortunately, there is evidence that over their years in school, students tend to shift from learning or mastery goals to performance goals (Harackiewicz et al., 2000; Hicks-Anderman & Anderman, 1999; Stipek, 2002). Urdan and Maehr (1995) suggested a third goal orientation—social goals. That is, some students achieve to please the teacher, their parents, or their peers (Wentzel & Wigfield, 1998). In particular, there is a great deal of research indicating the powerful impact that a student's peer group can have on a student's own motivation (e.g., Lee & Smith, 1999; Ryan, 2000; Wentzel, 1999) and it is certainly the case that some students are motivated to learn in order to gain status in their peer group.

The most important implication of research on learning goals versus performance goals is that teachers should try to convince students that learning rather than grades is the purpose of academic work (Anderman et al., 2001; Ryan & Patrick, 2001; Wentzel, 2000). This can be done by emphasizing the interest value and practical importance of material students are studying and by deemphasizing grades and other rewards. For example, a teacher might say, "Today we're going to learn about events deep in the earth that cause the fiery eruptions of volcanoes!" rather than "Today we're going to learn about volcanoes. Pay attention so that you can do well on tomorrow's test." In particular, use of highly competitive grading or incentive systems should be avoided. When students perceive that there is only one standard of success in the classroom and that only a few people can achieve it, those who perceive their ability to be low will be likely to give up in advance (Ames, 1992). Table 10.2 (from Ames & Archer, 1988) summarizes the differences between the achievement goals of students with mastery (learning) goals and those of students with performance goals. Studies indicate that the types of tasks that are used in classrooms have a strong influence on students' adoption of learning goals. Use of tasks that are challenging, meaningful, and related to real life are more likely to lead to learning goals than are other tasks (Ames, 1992; Blumenfeld, 1992; Meece, 1991). Table 10.3 (from Maehr & Anderman, 1993) summarizes strategies that teachers can use to promote learning or task goals among students.

Table 10.2

Achievement Goal Analysis of Classroom Climate

Climate Dimensions	Mastery Goal	Performance Goal
Success defined as . . .	Improvement, progress	High grades, high normative performance
Value placed on . . .	Effort/learning	Normatively high ability
Reasons for satisfaction . . .	Working hard, challenge	Doing better than others
Teacher oriented toward . . .	How students are learning	How students are performing
View of errors/mistakes . . .	Part of learning	Anxiety eliciting
Focus of attention . . .	Process of learning	Own performance relative to others'
Reasons for effort . . .	Learning something new	High grades, performing better than others
Evaluation criteria . . .	Absolute progress	Normative

Source: From C. Ames and J. Archer, "Achievement Goals in the Classroom," *Journal of Educational Psychology, 80,* p. 261. Copyright © 1988 by the American Psychological Association. Reprinted by permission.

Table 10.3

School and Teacher Policies That Are Likely to Promote Learning or Task Goals

Area	Objectives	Examples of Possible Strategies
Task	Enhance intrinsic attractiveness of learning tasks. Make learning meaningful.	Encourage instruction that relates to students' backgrounds and experience. Avoid payment (monetary or other) for attendance, grades, or achievement. Foster goal-setting and self-regulation. Use extra classroom programs that make learning experiences relevant.
Autonomy/ Responsibility	Provide optimal freedom for students to make choices and take responsibility.	Give alternatives in making assignments. Ask for student comments on school life—and take them seriously. Encourage instructional programs that encourage students to take initiatives and evaluate their own learning. Establish leadership opportunities for *all* students.
Recognition	Provide opportunities for *all* students to be recognized for learning. Recognize *progress* in goal attainment. Recognize challenge seeking and innovation.	Foster personal-best awards. Reduce emphasis on honor rolls. Recognize and publicize a wide range of school-related activities of students.
Resources	Encourage the development and maintenance of strategies that enhance task–goal emphases.	Underwrite action taken by staff that is in accord with a task–goal emphasis.
Grouping	Build an environment of acceptance and appreciation of all students. Broaden the range of social interaction, particularly of at-risk students. Enhance social skills development.	Provide opportunities for cooperative learning, problem solving, and decision making. Allow time and opportunity for peer interaction. Foster the development of subgroups (teams, schools within schools, etc.) within which significant interaction can occur. Encourage multiple group membership to increase range of peer interaction. Eliminate ability-grouped classes.
Evaluation	Grading and reporting processes. Practices associated with use of standardized tests. Definition of goals and standards.	Reduce emphasis on social comparisons of achievement by minimizing public reference to normative evaluation standards (e.g., grades, test scores). Establish policies and procedures that give students opportunities to improve their performance (e.g., study skills, classes). Establish grading/reporting practices that portray student progress in learning. Encourage student participation in the evaluation process.
Time	Allow the learning task and student needs to dictate scheduling. Provide opportunities for extended and significant student involvement in learning tasks.	Allow students to *progress at their own rate* whenever possible. Encourage flexibility in the scheduling of learning experiences. Give teachers greater control over time usage through, for example, block scheduling.

Source: From M. L. Maehr and E. M. Anderman, "Reinventing Schools for Early Adolescents," *The Elementary School Journal, 93*(5), 1993, pp. 593–610. Copyright © 1993 by The University of Chicago Press. Adapted by permission.

Seeking Success versus Avoiding Failure   Atkinson (1964), extending McClelland's work on achievement motivation, noted that individuals might be motivated to achieve in either of two ways: to seek success or to avoid failure. He found that some people were more motivated to avoid failure than to seek success (failure avoiders), whereas others were more motivated to seek success than to avoid failure (success seekers). Success seekers' motivation is increased after a failure, as they intensify their efforts to succeed. Failure avoiders decrease their efforts after a failure (Weiner, 1986).

One very important characteristic of failure avoiders is that they tend to choose either very easy or very difficult tasks. For example, J. W. Atkinson and Litwin (1960) found that in a ring toss game, failure avoiders would choose to stand very near the target or very far away, and success seekers would choose an intermediate distance. They hypothesized that failure avoiders preferred either easy tasks (on which failure was unlikely) or such difficult tasks that no one would blame them if they failed.

Understanding that it is common for failure avoiders to choose impossibly difficult or ridiculously easy tasks for themselves is very important for the teacher. For example, a poor reader might choose to write a book report on the classic epic novel *War and Peace* but then, when told that was too difficult, might choose a simple children's book. Such students are not being devious but are simply doing their best to maintain a positive self-image.

Learned Helplessness and Attribution Training

CERTIFICATION POINTER

For a case study on your teacher certification test, you may be required to suggest an appropriate strategy for improving student motivation by training students to attribute their successes to controllable causes, especially effort.

An extreme form of the motive to avoid failure is called **learned helplessness,** which is a perception that no matter what one does, one is doomed to failure or ineffectuality: "Nothing I do matters." In academic settings, learned helplessness can be related to an internal, stable explanation for failure: "I fail because I'm stupid, and that means I will always fail" (Diener & Dweck, 1978). Students who experience repeated failures might develop a "defensive pessimism" to protect themselves from negative feedback (Martin, Marsh, & Debus, 2001).

Learned helplessness can arise from a child's upbringing (Hokoda & Fincham, 1995) but also from inconsistent, unpredictable use of rewards and punishments by teachers—a pattern that can lead students to believe that there is little they can do to be successful. Students with learning disabilities, for example, are more likely than other students to respond to failure with helpless behavior (Sideridis, in press). Teachers can prevent or alleviate learned helplessness by giving students (1) opportunities for success in small steps; (2) immediate feedback; and (3) most important, consistent expectations and follow-through (see Alderman, 1990). Focusing on learning goals rather than on performance goals (see the previous section) can reduce helplessness, because all students can attain learning goals to one degree or another (Dweck, 1986).

Changes in Achievement Motivation   Motivation-related personality characteristics can be altered. They are altered in the natural course of things when something happens to change a student's environment, as when students who have vocational but not academic skills move from a comprehensive high school in which they were doing poorly to a technical preparation program in which they find success. Such students might break out of a long-standing pattern of external locus of control and low-achievement motivation because of their newfound success experience. Late bloomers, students who have difficulty in their earlier school years but take off in their later years, might also experience lasting changes in motivation-related personality characteristics, as would students who are initially successful in school but who later experience difficulty keeping up. However, achievement motivation and attributions can also be changed directly by special programs designed for this purpose.

learned helplessness
The expectation, based on experience, that one's actions will ultimately lead to failure.

Several studies have found that learned helplessness in the face of repeated failure can be modified by an attribution training program that emphasizes lack of effort, rather than lack of ability, as the cause of poor performance (Forsterling, 1985; Robertson, 2000). For example, Schunk (1983) found that students who received statements attributing their past successes and failures to effort performed better than did students who received no feedback.

Theory into **PRACTICE**

Helping Students Overcome Learned Helplessness

The concept of learned helplessness derives from the theory that students might become academic failures through a conditioning process based on negative feedback from teachers, school experiences, peers, and students themselves. Numerous studies show that when students consistently fail, they eventually give up. They become conditioned to helplessness (Seligman, 1975).

Teachers at both the elementary and secondary levels can help to counter this syndrome in a variety of ways, including attribution training, goal restructuring, self-esteem programs, success-guaranteed approaches, and positive feedback systems. The following general principles are helpful for all students, especially students who have shown a tendency to accept failure.

Accentuate the positive. Get to know the student's strengths, then use these as building blocks. Every student has something she or he does well. But be careful that the strength is authentic; don't make up a strength. For example, a student might like to talk a lot but write poorly. Have the student complete assignments by talking rather than writing. As confidence is restored, slowly introduce writing.

Eliminate the negative. Do not play down a student's weaknesses. Deal with them directly but tactfully. In the above example, talk to the student about problems with writing. Then have the student develop a plan to improve on the writing. Discuss the plan, and together make up a contract about how the plan will be completed.

Go from the familiar to the new, using advance organizers or guided discovery. Some students have difficulties with concepts, skills, or ideas with which they are not familiar. Also, students relate better to lessons that are linked to their own experiences. For example, a high school math teacher might begin a lesson with a math problem that students might face in the real world, such as calculating the sales tax when purchasing a CD player. Further, the teacher can ask students to bring to class math problems they have encountered outside of school. The whole class can become involved in solving a student's math problem.

Create challenges in which students actively create problems and solve them using their own knowledge and skills.

INTASC

7 Instructional Planning Skills

Teacher Expectations and Achievement

On the first day of class, Mr. Erhard called roll. Soon he got to a name that looked familiar. "Wayne Clements?"

"Here!"

"Do you have a brother named Victor?"

"Yes."

"I remember Victor. He was a terror. I'm going to keep my eye on you!"

As he neared the end of the roll, Mr. Erhard saw that several boys were starting to whisper to one another in the back of the room. "Wayne! I asked the class to remain silent while I read the roll. Didn't you hear me? I knew I'd have to watch out for you!"

This dialogue illustrates how teachers can establish expectations for their students and how these expectations can be self-fulfilling. Mr. Erhard doesn't know it, but Wayne is generally a well-behaved, conscientious student, quite unlike his older brother, Victor. However, because of his experience with Victor, Mr. Erhard expects that he will have trouble with Wayne. When he sees several boys whispering, it is Wayne he singles out for blame, confirming for himself that Wayne is a troublemaker. After a few episodes of this treatment, we can expect Wayne to begin playing the role Mr. Erhard has assigned to him.

Research on teachers' expectations for their students has generally found that students live up (or down) to the expectations that their teachers have for them (Jussim & Eccles, 1995; Wigfield & Harold, 1992), particularly in the younger grades and when teachers know relatively little about their students' actual achievement levels (Raudenbush, 1984). Further, there is evidence that students in schools whose teachers have high expectations achieve more than those in other schools (Marks, Doane, & Secada, 1998). Of course, students' expectations for themselves are at least as important as those of their teachers. One study found that students whose self-perceptions exceeded their current performance later tended to increase in grades, while those whose self-perceptions were lower than their performance tended to drop in grades (Anderman, Anderman, & Griesinger, 1999).

Communicating Positive Expectations   It is important for teachers to communicate to their students the expectation that they can learn (see Babad, 1993). Obviously, it is a bad idea to state the contrary—that a particular student cannot learn—and few teachers would explicitly do so. There are several implicit ways in which teachers can communicate positive expectations of their students (or avoid negative ones).

1. Wait for students to respond. Rowe (1974) and others have noted that teachers wait longer for answers from students for whom they have high expectations than from other students. Longer wait times may communicate high expectations and increase student achievement (Tobin, 1987).

2. Avoid unnecessary achievement distinctions among students. Assessment results and grades should be a private matter between students and their teacher, not public information. Reading and math groups might be instructionally necessary in some classrooms, but teachers should avoid establishing a rigid hierarchy of groups, should treat the groups equally and respectfully, and should be prepared to move a student out of one group and into another when appropriate (see Gamoran, 1984; Rosenholtz & Simpson, 1984). Students usually know who is good in school and who is not, but teachers can still successfully communicate the expectation that all students, not just the most able ones, are capable of learning (Weinstein, Madison, & Kuklinski, 1995).

3. Treat all students equally. Call on students at all achievement levels equally often, and spend equal amounts of time with them. In particular, guard against bias. Research finds that teachers often unwittingly hold lower expectations for certain categories of students, such as minority-group students (Baron, Tom, & Cooper, 1985) or females (Kahle & Meece, 1993; Sadker, Sadker, & Long, 1997).

CONNECTIONS

For more on grouping students, see Chapter 9, page 279.

Expectations

Leonard Watkins and Elizabeth Olson are teachers at a diverse high school in a city school district. Elizabeth, a novice English teacher, has come to Leonard, who teaches math, for some advice on one of her students.

Elizabeth: Leonard, I'm having a problem with one of my students, and I'm hoping you'll help me out.

Leonard: I'm always glad to help. Let me guess. This is about Tyler, right?

Elizabeth: I'm afraid so. He's such a bright child, but he's not working up to his potential. Also, he just won't listen to me, and he frequently disrupts the class. You have him for math, and I know he does a lot better in your class.

Leonard: What have you tried so far?

Elizabeth: Well, I've asked him to come in after school to talk with me. He's told me about all the problems he has in his family, and how he feels the other kids would make fun of him if he did his best.

Leonard: Do these conversations help?

Elizabeth: A little. But he still comes in late and doesn't always hand in his assignments. He knows I care about him, but I don't think he respects me. I wondered if you had any ideas about ways I could make my teaching more appropriate to his needs.

Leonard: With all due respect, Elizabeth, I think you're already doing too much for that young man. He's getting away with murder!

Elizabeth: But I want to be fair.

Leonard: In my way of thinking, the fairest thing you can do, and the most beneficial for Tyler, is to hold him to the same standards as everyone else. You need to show him you have high expectations for him.

Elizabeth: But what should I do?

Leonard: You said it yourself, Tyler is a bright kid, and he is. But it's worthless to be bright if you don't act bright. If you tell Tyler that you expect excellence from him, he'll rise to your expectations. If you let him slide, he'll slide. In math class, for example, if he doesn't do his best work, I have him come in after school and do it over.

Elizabeth: That sounds right, but . . .

Leonard: Think of your own favorite teachers. I'll bet they were the ones who challenged you, who held you to high standards. Am I right?

Elizabeth: Yes, but . . .

Leonard: It's the same with Tyler. Your job is to help him be the great student you and I both know he can be!

@ Questions for Reflection

1. Reflect on the conversation between Leonard and Elizabeth. Below the surface, what are they really talking about? What are the major issues in their discussion?

2. Do you think Leonard is suggesting that Elizabeth be too tough on Tyler?

3. What specific actions could Elizabeth take to show positive and appropriate expectations for Tyler?

4. Is it possible for expectations to be too high? What if Elizabeth expresses high expectations for Tyler and then he doesn't meet them?

5. Imagine that Tyler is African American. Would that change any of your answers? How would Tyler's cultural background relate to the expectations his teachers have for him?

Anxiety and Achievement

Anxiety is a constant companion of education. Every student feels some anxiety at some time while in school; but for certain students, anxiety seriously inhibits learning or performance, particularly on tests (Everson, Smodlaka, & Tobias, 1994; Wigfield & Eccles, 1990).

The main source of anxiety in school is the fear of failure and, with it, loss of self-esteem (Hill & Wigfield, 1984). Low achievers are particularly likely to feel anxious in school, but they are by no means the only ones. We all know very able, high-achieving students who are also very anxious, maybe even terrified to be less than perfect at any school task.

Anxiety can block school performance in several ways (Naveh-Benjamin, 1991; Skaalvik, 1997). Anxious students might have difficulty learning in the first place, difficulty using or transferring knowledge they do have, and difficulty demonstrating their knowledge on tests (Bandalos, Yates, & Thorndike-Christ, 1995). Anxious students

The recent focus on high-stakes testing and achievement leaves students, administrators, and teachers anxious over the outcome of test scores. What can you do to alleviate some of that pressure with your students?

CONNECTIONS

Programs designed to train test-anxious children in test-taking skills are discussed in Chapter 14, page 501.

are likely to be overly self-conscious in performance settings, a feeling that distracts attention from the task at hand (Tobias, 1992). One particularly common form of debilitating anxiety is math anxiety. Many students (and adults) simply freeze up when given math problems, particularly word problems (Everson, Tobias, Hartman, & Gourgey, 1993).

Teachers can apply many strategies to reduce the negative impact of anxiety on learning and performance. Clearly, creating a classroom climate that is accepting, comfortable, and noncompetitive helps. Giving students opportunities to correct errors or improve their work before handing it in also helps anxious children, as does providing clear, unambiguous instructions (Wigfield & Eccles, 1989). In testing situations, teachers can do many things to help anxious students to do their best. They can avoid time pressure, giving students plenty of time to complete a test and check their work. Tests that begin with easy problems and only gradually introduce more difficult ones are better for anxious students, and tests with standard, simple answer formats help such students. Test-anxious children can be trained in test-taking skills and relaxation techniques, and these can have a positive impact on their test performance (Spielberger & Vagg, 1995).

How CAN TEACHERS INCREASE STUDENTS' MOTIVATION TO LEARN?

Learning takes work. Euclid, a Greek mathematician who lived around 300 B.C. and wrote the first geometry textbook, was asked by his king whether there were any shortcuts the king could use to learn geometry, as he was a very busy man. "I'm sorry," Euclid replied, "but there is no royal road to geometry." The same is true of every other subject: Students get out of any course of study only what they put into it.

The remainder of this chapter discusses the means by which students can be motivated to exert the effort learning requires. First, the issue of intrinsic motivation—the motivational value of the content itself—is presented. Extrinsic motivation—the use of praise, feedback, and incentives to motivate students to do their best—is then discussed.

Also in this section are specific strategies for enhancing student motivation and suggestions for solving motivational problems that are common in classrooms, including reward-for-improvement incentive systems.

Intrinsic and Extrinsic Motivation

Sometimes a course of study is so fascinating and useful to students that they are willing to do the work required to learn the material with no incentive other than the interest level of the material itself. For example, many students would gladly take auto mechanics or photography courses and work hard in them, even if the courses offered no credit or grades. For these students the favorite subject itself has enough **intrinsic incentive** value to motivate them to learn. Other students love to learn about par-

intrinsic incentive

An aspect of an activity that people enjoy and therefore find motivating.

ticular topics such as insects, dinosaurs, or famous people in history and need little encouragement or reward to do so (Covington, 1999; Gottfried & Fleming, 2001; Schraw, Flowerday, & Lehman, 2001). Students who have a strong "future time perspective" (i.e., are willing to do things today that may benefit them in the future) are often particularly motivated to learn, even without immediate incentives (Husman & Lens, 1999).

However, much of what must be learned in school is not inherently interesting or useful to most students in the short run. Students receive about 900 hours of instruction every year, and intrinsic interest alone will not keep them enthusiastically working day in and day out. In particular, students' intrinsic motivation generally declines from early elementary school through secondary school (Gottfried & Fleming, 2001; Sethi, Drake, Dialdin, & Lepper, 1995). For this reason, schools apply a variety of **extrinsic incentives,** rewards for learning that are not inherent in the material being learned (Brophy, 1998). Extrinsic rewards might range from praise to grades to recognition to prizes or other rewards.

In the vignette at the beginning of this chapter, Cal Lewis tried to enhance both intrinsic and extrinsic motivation. His simulation of the Constitutional Convention was intended to arouse students' intrinsic interest in the subject, and his ratings of students' presentations and his feedback at the end of each period were intended to provide extrinsic motivation.

"The school board decided not to raise teachers' salaries. We didn't want to undermine their intrinsic motivation."

Lepper's Experiment on the Impact of Rewards on Motivation   An important question in research on motivation concerns whether or not the providing of extrinsic rewards diminishes intrinsic interest in an activity. In a classic experiment exploring this topic, Lepper and colleagues (1973) gave preschoolers an opportunity to draw with felt-tip markers, which many of them did quite enthusiastically. Then the researchers randomly divided the children into three groups: One group was told that its members would receive a reward for drawing a picture for a visitor (a Good Player Award), one was given the same reward as a surprise (not dependent on the children's drawing), and one received no reward. Over the next 4 days, observers recorded the children's free-play activities. Children who had received a reward for drawing spent about half as much time drawing with felt-tip markers as did those who had received the surprise reward and those who had gotten no reward. The authors suggested that promising extrinsic rewards for an activity that is intrinsically interesting might undermine intrinsic interest by inducing children to expect a reward for doing what they had previously done for nothing. In a later study (Greene & Lepper, 1974), it was found that just telling children that they would be watched (through a one-way mirror) had an undermining effect similar to that of a promised reward.

Do Rewards Destroy Intrinsic Motivation?   In understanding the results of these studies, it is important to recall the conditions of the research. The students who were chosen for the studies were ones who showed an intrinsic interest in using marking pens; those who did not were excluded from the experiments. Also, drawing with felt-tip pens does not resemble most school tasks. Many children love to draw at home; but few, even those who are most interested in school subjects, would independently study grammar and punctuation, work math problems, or learn the valences of chemical elements. Further, many of our most creative and self-motivated scientists were heavily reinforced as students with grades, science fair prizes, and scholarships for doing science, and virtually all successful artists have been reinforced at some point

extrinsic incentive
A reward that is external to the activity, such as recognition or a good grade.

for engaging in artistic activities. This reinforcement certainly did not undermine the activities' intrinsic interest. Research on older students doing more school-like tasks has generally failed to replicate the results of the Lepper and colleagues (1973) experiment (Cameron & Pierce, 1994, 1996; Eisenberger & Cameron, 1998). In fact, the use of rewards more often increases intrinsic motivation, especially when rewards are contingent on the quality of performance rather than on mere participation in an activity (Lepper, 1983; Ryan & Deci, 2000), when the rewards are seen as recognition of competence (Rosenfield, Folger, & Adelman, 1980), when the task in question is not very interesting (Morgan, 1984), or when the rewards are social (e.g., praise) rather than material (Cameron, 2001; Cameron & Pierce, 1994; Chance, 1992; Miller & Hom, 1990; Ryan & Deci, 2000). Cameron (2001) summarizes the situation in which extrinsic rewards undermine intrinsic interest as follows: "A negative effect occurs when a task is of high interest, when the rewards are tangible and offered beforehand, and when the rewards are delivered without regard to success on the task or to any specified level of performance" (p. 40). This is a very narrow set of conditions, characterized by Bandura (1986, p. 246) as "of no great social import because rewards are rarely showered on people regardless of how they behave." However, Deci, Koestner, & Ryan (2001), while acknowledging that there are many forms of extrinsic rewards that have a positive or neutral impact on motivation, nevertheless argue that "the use of rewards as a motivational strategy is clearly a risky proposition, so we continue to argue for thinking about educational practices that will engage students' interest and support the development of their self-regulation" (Deci, Koestner, & Ryan, 2001, p. 50).

The research on the effects of extrinsic rewards on intrinsic motivation does counsel caution in the use of material rewards for intrinsically interesting tasks (see Lepper, 1998; Lepper, Keavney, & Drake, 1996; Ryan & Deci, 2000; Sansone & Harackiewicz, 2000). Teachers should attempt to make everything they teach as intrinsically interesting as possible and should avoid handing out material rewards when they are unnecessary, but teachers should not refrain from using extrinsic rewards when they are needed (Ryan & Deci, 2000). Often, extrinsic rewards may be necessary to get students started in a learning activity but may be phased out as students come to enjoy the activity and succeed at it (Stipek, 1993). Also, remember that in any given class, there are students who are intrinsically motivated to do a given activity and those who are not. To ensure that all students learn, strategic use of both intrinsic and extrinsic motivators is likely to be necessary.

How Can Teachers Enhance Intrinsic Motivation?

Classroom instruction should enhance intrinsic motivation as much as possible. Increasing intrinsic motivation is always helpful for learning, whether or not extrinsic incentives are also in use (Covington, 1999). This means that teachers must try to get their students interested in the material they are presenting and then present it in an appealing way that both satisfies and increases students' curiosity about the material itself. A discussion of some means of doing this follows (see also Brophy, 1999; Burden & Byrd, 2003; Covington, 1999; Stipek, 2002).

Arousing Interest   It is important to convince students of the importance and interest level of the material that is about to be presented, to show (if possible) how the knowledge to be gained will be useful to students (Bergin, 1999; Tomlinson, 2002). For example, intrinsic motivation to learn a lesson on percents might be increased by introducing the lesson as follows:

> Today we will begin a lesson on percents. Percents are important in our daily lives. For example, when you buy something at the store and a salesperson figures the sales tax, he or she is using percents. When we leave a tip for a waiter or waitress,

CERTIFICATION POINTER

On your teacher certification test, you should recognize the value of intrinsic motivation in promoting students' lifelong growth and learning.

CONNECTIONS

The importance of student interest in creative problem solving and other constructivist approaches is discussed in Chapter 8, page 264.

we use percents. We often hear in the news things like "Prices rose seven percent last year." In a few years, many of you will have summer jobs, and if they involve handling money, you'll probably be using percents all the time.

INTASC

4 Multiple Instructional Strategies

Introducing lessons with examples relating the material to students' cultures can be particularly effective. For example, in introducing astronomy to a class with many Latino children, a teacher could say, "Thousands of years ago, people in Mexico and Central America had calendars that accurately predicted the movement of the moon and stars for centuries into the future. How could they do this? Today we will learn about how planets, moons, and stars move in predictable paths." The purpose of these statements is to arouse student curiosity about the lesson to come, thereby enhancing intrinsic motivation to learn the material.

Another way to enhance students' intrinsic interest is to give them some choice about what they will study or how they will study it (Cordova & Lepper, 1996; Stipek, 2002). Choices need not be unlimited to be motivational. For example, students might be given a choice of writing about ancient Athens or Sparta, or a choice of working independently or in pairs.

Maintaining Curiosity   A skillful teacher uses a variety of means to further arouse or maintain curiosity in the course of the lesson. Science teachers, for instance, often use demonstrations that surprise or baffle students and induce them to want to understand why. A floating dime makes students curious about the surface tension of liquids. "Burning" a dollar bill covered with an alcohol–water solution (without harming the dollar bill) certainly increases curiosity about the heat of combustion. Guthrie and Cox (2001) found that giving students hands-on experience with science activities greatly increased their learning from books on related topics and provided more motivation.

Less dramatically, surprising or challenging students with a problem they can't solve with their current knowledge can arouse curiosity, and therefore intrinsic motivation (see Bottge, 2001). A seventh-grade teacher in England used this principle in a lesson on equivalent fractions. First, he had his students halve and then halve again $\frac{8}{13}$ and $\frac{12}{20}$. Working in pairs they instantly agreed on $\frac{4}{13}$ and $\frac{2}{13}$, $\frac{6}{20}$ and $\frac{3}{20}$. Then he gave them $\frac{13}{20}$. After a moment of hesitation, students came back with $\frac{6\frac{1}{2}}{20}$ and $\frac{3\frac{1}{4}}{20}$. "Crikey!" he said. "All these fractions inside fractions are making me nervous! Isn't there some other way we can do this?" "Round off?" suggested one student. "Use decimals?" suggested another. Finally, after much discussion and argument, the students realized that they could use their knowledge about equivalent fractions to find the solutions: $\frac{13}{40}$ and $\frac{13}{80}$. Getting the students into a familiar pattern and then breaking that pattern excited and engaged the whole class, making them question *their* question far more effectively than would have been possible by just teaching the algorithm in the first place. The element of surprise, challenging the students' current understanding, made them intensely curious about an issue they'd never before considered.

Using a Variety of Interesting Presentation Modes   The intrinsic motivation to learn something is enhanced by the use of interesting materials, as well as by variety in mode of presentation. For example, teachers can maintain student interest in a subject by alternating use of films, guest speakers, demonstrations, and so on, although the use of each resource must be carefully planned to be sure it focuses on the course objectives and complements the other activities. Use of computers can enhance most students' intrinsic motivation to learn (Lepper, 1985). What makes materials interesting are elements such as the use of emotional material (e.g., danger, sex, money, heartbreak, disaster), concrete rather than abstract examples, cause-and-effect relationships, and clear organization (Bergin, 1999; Jetton & Alexander, 2001; Schraw et al., 2001; Wade, 2001).

One excellent means of increasing interest in a subject is to use games or simulations. A simulation, or role play, is an exercise in which students take on roles and

CONNECTIONS

The importance of student interest in lesson content and presentation is discussed in Chapter 7, page 216.

This student has intrinsic incentive to learn about art projects. As a teacher, how could you maintain or extend his motivation? How could you present the same task to another student for whom the task does not have intrinsic value?

engage in activities appropriate to those roles. Cal Lewis used a simulation to teach students about the Constitutional Convention. Programs exist that simulate many aspects of government; for example, students may take roles as legislators who must negotiate and trade votes to satisfy their constituents' interests or as economic actors (farmers, producers, consumers) who run a minieconomy. Creative teachers have long used simulations that they designed themselves. For example, teachers can have students write their own newspaper; design, manufacture, and market a product; or set up and run a bank.

The advantage of simulations is that they allow students to learn about a subject from the inside. Although research on use of simulations (see VanSickle, 1986) finds that they are not usually or are no more effective than traditional instruction for teaching facts and concepts, studies do consistently find that simulations increase students' interest, motivation, and affective learning (Dukes & Seidner, 1978). They certainly impart a different affective knowledge of a subject.

Nonsimulation games can also increase motivation to learn a given subject. The spelling bee is a popular example of a nonsimulation game. Teams–Games–Tournament, or TGT (Slavin, 1995a), uses games that can be adapted to any subject. Team games are usually better than individual games; they provide an opportunity for teammates to help one another and avoid one problem of individual games, which is that more able students might consistently win. If all students are put on mixed-ability teams, all have a good chance of success (see Slavin, 1995a).

Helping Students Set Their Own Goals   One fundamental principle of motivation is that people work harder for goals that they themselves set than for goals set for them by others (Ryan & Deci, 2000). For example, a student might set a minimum number of books she expects to read at home or a score she expects to attain on an upcoming quiz. At the next goal-setting conference the teacher would discuss student attainment of (or failure to attain) goals and set new goals for the following week. During these meetings the teacher might help students learn to set ambitious but realistic goals and would praise them for setting and then achieving their goals. Goal-setting strategies of this kind have been found to increase students' academic performance and self-efficacy (Page-Voth & Graham, 1999; Shih & Alexander, 2000).

Principles for Providing Extrinsic Incentives to Learn

Teachers must always try to enhance students' intrinsic motivation to learn academic materials, but they must at the same time be concerned about extrinsic incentives for learning (Brophy, 1998; Hidi & Harackiewicz, 2000). Not every subject is intrinsically interesting to all students, and students must be motivated to do the hard work necessary to master difficult subjects. The following sections discuss a variety of incentives that can help motivate students to learn academic material.

Expressing Clear Expectations   Students need to know exactly what they are supposed to do, how they will be evaluated, and what the consequences of success will be. Often, students' failures on particular tasks stem from confusion about what they are being asked to do (see Anderson, Brubaker, Alleman-Brooks, & Duffy, 1985; Brophy, 1998). Communicating clear expectations is important. For example, a teacher might introduce a writing assignment as follows:

Teaching Dilemmas: Cases to Consider

Adapting Strategies

Carlos Suarez, a fourth-grade teacher with 10 years' experience, talks in his classroom after school to Ruth Duncan about Ruth's son Jeremy.

Carlos: I appreciate your taking time to come down today.

Ruth: Oh, I was glad to come. I must say, though, it's tricky. My husband and I run a store, and it's a 24-hour-a-day job. Anyway, how is Jeremy doing?

Carlos: I'm sure you've noticed from his report cards that Jeremy has not been reaching our minimum goals for him in several areas, especially math. He seems to have trouble applying himself in class. His attention wanders. Also, he doesn't always turn in his homework. What happens to the work I send home with him?

Ruth: Well, he certainly doesn't seem to sit down and dig into it on his own. I see some books come home, but when I ask him about what he's supposed to do, he says it's nothing.

Carlos: Hmm. I'd like to see that attitude change. Good work motivation develops early, and Jeremy needs to get a good start.

In math period the next day, the class is working on adding two-digit numbers with renaming. Carlos sets up a store activity with Pete and a reluctant Jeremy.

Carlos: Okay, my desk is the counter, and these empty pencil boxes are new video game cartridges, right? Each one has a price label. And you each have plenty of fake money. *So . . . May I help you, sir?*

Pete: Well, I'll take these two: $17 and $26.

Carlos: Fine. *Now, unfortunately, my cash register is broken, sir, so I need you to add up what you owe me.* Here, use the blackboard.

Pete (working): Seven and six makes thirteen, put down the three . . . *$33?* No, wait. I think I forgot something. We did this yesterday on that worksheet, right? Don't tell me, let me try again. *$43!*

Carlos: Correct. And a good job of sticking with the problem, Pete. *Here you are, sir, enjoy your purchases. Now, sir, what can I do for you?*

Jeremy: Nothing. I don't want to do this.

Carlos: Hey, Jeremy, this isn't hard. You made a good start on these kinds of problems when I worked with you yesterday, remember?

Jeremy: Maybe, but I still don't get it. It's not my fault, Mr. Suarez. I just can't do it. I hate math.

Carlos: Well, let me ask you, what do you like to do at home?

Jeremy: Like? I like riding my bike. I like helping my dad in his store.

Carlos: You help in the store? That's excellent. What do you do to help?

Jeremy: I don't know. Sometimes I just hang around. Or I arrange the displays. Sometimes I tell Dad if we're out of something, or I show people where things are.

Carlos: How about helping out with money? Do you put on price tags or work the cash register?

Jeremy: No, Mr. Suarez! I couldn't do any of that! I can't do math.

Carlos: Well, you just put your finger on the whole point. You need to learn to add and subtract here in school. Then you'll be able to have a lot more responsibility and do a lot of interesting things that you like to do.

Jeremy: I don't care. I'll learn math soon enough, I guess. Anyway, my mom and dad wouldn't ever let me use the cash register. They don't care about me doing math. Anyway, I could do most of those problems if I tried, I bet.

Carlos: You might be right about that. So how about trying?

Jeremy: Yeah, maybe, Mr. Suarez.

@ Questions for Reflection

1. How can Carlos help motivate Jeremy to learn? Is it possible for one person to motivate another, or is motivation something inside a person? How can Carlos encourage intrinsic motivation while using extrinsic motivation?

2. Drawing on what you know about the situation, develop a problem-solving approach for getting Jeremy motivated. How might you involve Jeremy's parents?

3. Is Carlos's approach focused on learning goals or performance goals? How might Carlos change his approach, if at all, depending on Jeremy's orientation toward learning or performance goals?

4. Model your problem-solving approach by extending the dialogue in writing or role play to the next day.

Today, I'd like you all to write a composition about what Thomas Jefferson would think of government in the United States today. I expect your compositions to be about two pages long, and I want them to compare and contrast the plan of government laid out by the nation's founders with the way government actually operates today. Your compositions will be graded on the basis of your ability to describe similarities and differences between the structure and function of the U.S. government in Thomas Jefferson's time and today, as well as on the originality and clarity of your writing. This will be an important part of your six weeks' grade, so I expect you to do your best!

Note that the teacher is clear about what students are to write, how much material is expected, how the work will be evaluated, and how important the work will be for the students' grades. This clarity assures students that efforts directed at writing a good composition will pay off—in this case, in terms of grades. If the teacher had just said, "I'd like you all to write a composition about what Thomas Jefferson would think about government in the United States today," students might write the wrong thing, write too much or too little, or perhaps emphasize the if-Jefferson-were-alive-today aspect of the assignment rather than the comparative-government aspect. They would be unsure how much importance the teacher intended to place on the mechanics of the composition as compared to its content. Finally, they would have no way of knowing how their efforts would pay off, lacking any indication of how much emphasis the teacher would give to the compositions in computing grades.

A study by Graham, MacArthur, and Schwartz (1995) shows the importance of specificity. Low-achieving fifth- and sixth-graders were asked to revise compositions either to "make [your paper] better" or to "add at least three things that will add information to your paper." The students with the more specific instructions wrote higher-quality, longer revisions because they had a clearer idea of exactly what was being asked of them.

CONNECTIONS

Feedback is also discussed in Chapter 7, page 224.

Providing Clear Feedback   The word **feedback** means information on the results of one's efforts. The term has been used throughout this book to refer both to information students receive on their performance and to information teachers obtain on the effects of their instruction. Feedback can serve as an incentive. Research on feedback has found that provision of information on the results of one's actions can be an adequate reward in some circumstances (Gibbons, Duffin, Robertson, & Thompson, 1998). However, to be an effective motivator, feedback must be clear and specific and must be given close in time to performance (Kulik & Kulik, 1988). This is important for all students, but especially for young ones. For example, praise for a job well done should specify what the student did well:

- "Good work! I like the way you used the guide words in the dictionary to find the words on your worksheet."
- "I like that answer. It shows you've been thinking about what I've been saying about freedom and responsibility."
- "This is an excellent essay. It started with a statement of the argument you were going to make and then supported the argument with relevant information. I also like the care you took with punctuation and word usage."

Specific feedback is both informative and motivational (Kulhavy & Stock, 1989). It tells students what they did right, so that they will know what to do in the future, and helps give them an effort-based attribution for success ("You succeeded because you worked hard"). In contrast, if students are praised or receive a good grade without any explanation, they are unlikely to learn from the feedback what to do next time to be successful and might form an ability attribution ("I succeeded because I'm smart") or an external attribution ("I must have succeeded because the teacher likes me, the task was easy, or I lucked out"). As was noted earlier in this chapter, effort attributions are most conducive to continuing motivation. Similarly, feedback about mistakes or failures can add to motivation if it focuses only on the performance itself (not on students' general abilities) and if it is alternated with success feedback (see Clifford, 1984, 1990).

feedback

Information on the results of one's efforts.

Providing Immediate Feedback   Immediacy of feedback is also very important (Kulik & Kulik, 1988). If students complete a project on Monday and don't receive any feedback on it until Friday, the informational and motivational value of the feedback will be diminished. First, if they made errors, they might continue all week making similar errors on related material that might have been averted by feedback on the performance. Second, a long delay between behavior and consequence confuses the relationship between the two. Young students, especially, might have little idea why they received a particular grade if the performance on which the grade is based occurred several days earlier.

Providing Frequent Feedback   Feedback should be delivered frequently to students to maintain their best efforts. For example, it is unrealistic to expect most students to work hard for 6 or 9 weeks in hope of improving their grade unless they receive frequent feedback. Research in the behavioral learning theory tradition has established that no matter how powerful a reward is, it might have little impact on behavior if it is given infrequently; small, frequent rewards are more effective incentives than are large, infrequent ones. Research on frequency of testing has generally found that it is a good idea to give frequent brief quizzes to assess student progress rather than infrequent long tests (Dempster, 1991). Research also indicates the importance of asking many questions in class so that students can gain information about their own level of understanding and can receive reinforcement (praise, recognition) for paying attention to lessons.

Increasing the Value and Availability of Extrinsic Motivators   Expectancy theories of motivation, discussed earlier in this chapter, hold that motivation is a product of the value an individual attaches to success and the individual's estimate of the likelihood of success (see Wigfield & Eccles, 2000). One implication of this is that students must value incentives that are used to motivate them. Some students are not particularly interested in teacher praise or grades but might value notes sent home to their parents, a little extra recess time, or a special privilege in the classroom.

Another implication of expectancy theory is that although all students must have a chance to be rewarded if they do their best, no student should have an easy time achieving the maximum reward. This principle is violated by traditional grading practices, because some students find it easy to earn A's and B's, whereas others believe that they have little chance of academic success no matter what they do. In this circumstance, neither high achievers nor low achievers are likely to exert their best efforts. This is one reason that it is important to reward students for effort, for doing better than they have done in the past, or for making progress, rather than only for getting a high score. For example, students can build a portfolio of compositions, projects, reports, or other work and can then see how their work is improving over time. Not all students are equally capable of achieving high scores; but all are equally capable of exerting effort, exceeding their own past record, or making progress, so these are often better, more equally available criteria for reward.

CONNECTIONS

For more on student portfolios, see Chapter 13, page 473.

$\mathcal{H}$OW CAN TEACHERS REWARD PERFORMANCE, EFFORT, AND IMPROVEMENT?

INTASC

4 Multiple Instructional Strategies

As has been noted many times in this chapter, incentive systems that are used in the classroom should focus on student effort, not ability. A principal means of rewarding students for putting forth their best efforts is to reward effort directly by praising students for their efforts or, as is done in many schools, by giving a separate effort grade or rating along with the usual performance grade or including effort as an important part of students' grades.

Using Praise Effectively

CONNECTIONS

For more on the use of praise as a reinforcer, see Chapter 11, page 366.

Praise serves many purposes in classroom instruction but is primarily used to reinforce appropriate behaviors and to give feedback to students on what they are doing right. Overall, it is a good idea to use praise frequently, especially with young children and in classrooms with many low-achieving students (Brophy, 1998; Evans, 1996). However, what is more important than the amount of praise given is the way it is given. Praise is effective as a classroom motivator to the extent that it is contingent, specific, and credible (Sutherland, Wehby, & Copeland, 2000). **Contingent praise** depends on student performance of well-defined behaviors. For example, if a teacher says, "I'd like you all to open your books to page ninety-two and work problems one to ten," then praise will be given only to the students who follow directions. Praise should be given only for right answers and appropriate behaviors.

Specificity means that the teacher praises students for specific behaviors, not for general "goodness." For example, a teacher might say, "Susan, I'm glad you followed my directions to start work on your composition," rather than, "Susan, you're doing great!"

CERTIFICATION POINTER

When responding to a case study on your certification test, you should know that providing praise that is contingent, specific, and credible can increase student motivation.

When praise is *credible*, it is given sincerely for good work. Brophy (1981) notes that when praising low-achieving or disruptive students for good work, teachers often contradict their words with tone, posture, or other nonverbal cues. Brophy's (1981) list of guidelines for effective praise appears in Table 10.4.

In addition to contingency, specificity, and credibility, Brophy's list includes several particularly important principles that reinforce topics discussed earlier in this chapter. For example, guidelines 7 and 8 emphasize that praise should be given for good

---

Table 10.4

Guidelines for Effective Praise

If used properly, praise can be an effective motivator in classroom situations.

Effective Praise

1. Is delivered contingently.

2. Specifies the particulars of the accomplishment.

3. Shows spontaneity, variety, and other signs of credibility; suggests clear attention to the student's accomplishment.

4. Rewards attainment of specified performance criteria (which can include effort criteria, however).

5. Provides information to students about their competence or the value of their accomplishments.

6. Orients students toward better appreciation of their own task-related behavior and thinking about problem solving.

7. Uses students' own prior accomplishments as the context for describing present accomplishments.

8. Is given in recognition of noteworthy effort or success at difficult tasks (for *this* student).

9. Attributes success to effort and ability, implying that similar successes can be expected in the future.

10. Focuses students' attention on their own task-relevant behavior.

11. Fosters appreciation of, and desirable attributions about, task-relevant behavior after the process is completed.

Source: From Jere Brophy, "Teacher Praise: A Functional Analysis," *Review of Educational Research, 51,* p. 26. Copyright © 1981 by the American Educational Research Association. Adapted by permission of the publisher.

contingent praise
Praise that is effective because it refers directly to specific task performances.

performance relative to a student's usual level of performance. That is, students who usually do well should not be praised for a merely average performance, but students who usually do less well should be praised when they do better. This relates to the principle of accessibility of reward discussed earlier in this chapter; rewards should be neither too easy nor too difficult for students to obtain.

Teaching Students to Praise Themselves

CONNECTIONS
For more on self-regulated learning, see Chapter 5, page 156.

There is increasing evidence that students can learn to praise themselves and that this increases their academic success. For example, children can learn to mentally give themselves a pat on the back when they finish a task or to stop at regular intervals to notice how much they have done (Corno & Kanfer, 1993; Ross, Rolheiser, & Hogaboam-Gray, 1998). This strategy is a key component of self-regulated learning (see Schunk & Zimmerman, 1997).

> **ON THE WEB**
>
> For more on how teachers can influence student motivation see **www.selu.edu/academics/faculty.**

Using Grades as Incentives

CONNECTIONS
Principles and procedures of grading are discussed in Chapter 13, page 480.

The grading systems that most schools use serve three quite different functions at the same time: evaluation, feedback, and incentive. This mix of functions makes grades less than ideal for each function. For example, because grades are based largely on ability rather than on effort, they are less than ideal for motivating students to exert maximum effort, as was noted earlier in this chapter. Also, grades are given too infrequently to be very useful as either feedback or incentives for young children who cannot see the connection between today's work and a grade to be received in 6 weeks. Grades are effective as incentives for older students, however. Experiments comparing graded and ungraded college classes (e.g., Gold, Reilly, Silberman, & Lehr, 1971) find substantially higher performance in the graded classes. Grades work as incentives in part because they increase the value of other rewards given closer in time to the behaviors they reinforce. For example, when students get stars on their papers, they value them in part because the stars are an indication that their grades in that subject might also be good. The accessibility problem of grades—the fact that good grades are too easy for some students but too difficult for others—can be partially diminished by the use of grading systems that have many levels. For example, low-performing students might feel rewarded if they simply pass or if they get a C, while their high-performing classmates might not be satisfied unless they get an A. Also, one major reason that students value grades is that their parents value them, and parents are particularly likely to praise their children for improvements in their grades. Even though good grades are not equally attainable by all students, improved grades certainly are, except by straight A students. One implication of this is that teachers should make it clear how performance on individual assignments and tests contribute to students' grades. Students often perceive that teachers *give* students their grades, not that students *earn* the grades.

Incentive Systems Based on Goal Structure

goal structure
The degree to which students are placed in competitive or cooperative relationships in the earning of classroom rewards.

One aspect of classroom incentive systems that has received considerable research attention in recent years is the **goal structure** of the classroom. This term refers to the degree to which students are in cooperation or competition with one another. If students are in competition, any student's success means another's failure. For example, if the teacher establishes a policy that only one-quarter of the class can get an A, then students are in

Praise is effective as a classroom motivator when it is contingent, specific, and credible. As a teacher, how will you use praise to motivate your students?

competition, because if any student gets an A, this means that another cannot get an A. Just the opposite is true of cooperation. If a group of four students is doing a laboratory exercise together, they will all succeed or fail together. If one student works hard, this increases the others' chances of success. A third goal structure is individualization, in which one individual's success or failure has no consequences for others. For example, if the teacher said, "I will give an A to all students who average at least 90 percent on all quizzes given this marking period," then the students would be under an individualized goal structure, because the success of any one student would have no consequences for the success of his or her classmates (see Johnson & Johnson, 1999).

Competitive Goal Structures   Competitive goal structures have been criticized for discouraging students from helping one another learn (Johnson & Johnson, 1999), for tending to set up a pecking order in the classroom (Ames, 1986), and for establishing a situation in which low achievers have little chance of success (Slavin, 1995a). Coleman (1961) noted long ago that an individual student's success in sports is strongly supported by other students because the sports hero brings glory to the team and the school, but that students do not encourage one another's academic achievements because in the competitive academic system, achievement brings success only to the individual.

CERTIFICATION POINTER

For teacher certification tests you may be expected to suggest ways of structuring your class so that students promote each other's learning (rather than competing with each other) in order to foster a positive climate for learning.

ON THE WEB

The Northwest Regional Laboratory has resources for teachers on sparking students' motivation at **www.nwrel.org**.

Chapter Summary

What Is Motivation?

Motivation is an internal process that activates, guides, and maintains behavior over time. There are different kinds, intensities, aims, and directions of motivation. Motivation to learn is critically important to students and teachers.

What Are Some Theories of Motivation?

In behavioral learning theory (Skinner and others), motivation is a consequence of reinforcement. However, the value of a reinforcer depends on many factors, and the strength of motivation may be different in different students.

In Maslow's human needs theory, which is based on a hierarchy of needs, people must satisfy their lower-level (deficiency) needs before they will be motivated to try to satisfy their higher-level (growth) needs. Maslow's concept of the need for self-actualization, the highest need, is defined as the desire to become everything one is capable of becoming.

Attribution theory seeks to understand people's explanations for their success or failure. A central assumption is that people will attempt to maintain a positive self-image; so when good things happen, people attribute them to their own abilities, whereas they tend to attribute negative events to factors beyond their control. Locus of control might be internal (success or failure is due to personal effort or ability) or external (success or failure is due to luck or task difficulty). Students who are self-regulated learners perform better than those who are externally motivated. Self-regulated learners consciously plan and monitor their learning and thus retain more.

Expectancy theory holds that a person's motivation to achieve something depends on the product of that person's estimation of his or her chance of success and the value he or she places on success. Motivation should be at a maximum at moderate levels of probability of success. An important educational implication is that learning tasks should be neither too easy nor too difficult.

How Can Achievement Motivation Be Enhanced?

Teachers can emphasize learning goals and positive or empowering attributions. Students with learning goals see the purpose of school as gaining knowledge and competence; these students tend to have higher motivation to learn than do students with the performance goals of positive judgments and good grades. Teachers can use special programs such as attribution training to help students out of learned helplessness, in which students feel that they are doomed to fail despite their actions. Teachers' expectations significantly affect students' motivation and achievement. Teachers can communicate positive expectations that students can learn and can take steps to reduce anxiety.

How Can Teachers Increase Students' Motivation to Learn?

An incentive is a reinforcer that people can expect to receive if they perform a specific behavior. Intrinsic incentives are aspects of certain tasks that in themselves have enough value to motivate students to do the tasks on their own. Extrinsic incentives include grades, gold stars, and other rewards. Teachers can enhance intrinsic motivation by arousing students' interest, maintaining curiosity, using a variety of presentation modes, and letting students set their own goals. Ways to offer extrinsic incentives include stating clear expectations; giving clear, immediate, and frequent feedback; and increasing the value and availability of rewards.

How Can Teachers Reward Performance, Effort, and Improvement?

Classroom rewards include praise, which is most effective when it is contingent, specific, and credible. Feedback and grades can serve as incentives. A general method of rewarding effort is to recognize students' improvement over their own past records. Teachers can use cooperative learning methods that emphasize cooperative goal structures over competitive goal structures and reward effort and improvement.

THE INTENTIONAL TEACHER

Using What You Know about Motivation to Improve Teaching and Learning

Intentional teachers know that, although students might be motivated by different things and to varying degrees, every student is motivated. They understand that many elements of motivation can be influenced by the teacher, and they capitalize on their ability to unearth and direct student motivation. They provide instruction that helps students find meaning in learning and in taking pride in their own accomplishments.

❶ What do I expect my students to know and be able to do at the end of this lesson? How does this contribute to course objectives and to students' needs to become capable individuals?

Intentional teachers plan how they will support student motivation. Think about how you will discover and sustain your students' drive to participate in learning. Consider principles of motivation in your long- and short-term planning. You might review major findings on motivation and jot down some guiding ideas on an index card that you clip to your plan book.

❷ What knowledge, skills, needs, and interests do my students have that must be taken into account in my lesson?

Motivation varies by student, situation, and domain. Determine your students' current motivation. You can gather information about your students' motivation from a variety of sources. For instance, you could observe the students during informal conversations and during instruction, or ask them to write journal entries on such prompts as "What accounts for your score on this test?" You could analyze their answers and your observations to gather information about three areas of motivation: (1) Where do students seem to be functioning in terms of Maslow's hierarchy of needs? (2) Do students seem to be seeking success or avoiding failure? (3) Do students use internal or external causal attributions? Stable or unstable? Controllable or uncontrollable? (4) Are students primarily oriented toward mastery, or learning, or just toward performance, or grades?

❸ What do I know about the content, child development, learning, motivation, and effective teaching strategies that I can use to accomplish my objectives?

For motivation to be high, students need to perceive that with effort, success is possible. Provide tasks that require effort but allow students to see that success is within reach. For example, imagine that you check your grade book at the end of the first marking period and find that some of your students have earned D's and F's across the board but that others have a string of apparently easy A's. You could begin your quest to improve instruction by meeting with students individually. You might ask how they earned their grades and what they expect to earn in the future. Based on your conversations, you could develop research projects at the student's correct level of difficulty and devise careful contracts so that students who have yet to achieve see that success is possible.

Some students display a performance orientation instead of the more useful learning orientation. Help students shift their focus from completion to mastery by emphasizing the practical importance of content. Deemphasize grades and rewards. For example, imagine that your secondary students seem overly concerned with their scores on essays and the grading curve. You might employ portfolio assessments and require students to analyze their growth over time. Students could grade themselves on improvement rather than on how their work compares to that of their peers.

Praise needs to be used effectively. Be certain that your praise is sincere, specific, and contingent on students' behavior. Try to reserve your praise for good performance, to focus on the behavior and not the student, and to be specific about what constitutes good performance: "Jamal, I like the way you blended those two colors. That really adds depth to the painting. It looks real!"

❹ What instructional materials, technology, assistance, and other resources are available to help accomplish my objectives?

Always be on the lookout for additional sources of motivation, intrinsic as well as extrinsic. For example, bring in parents or other speakers with life experience relevant to your lesson to excite students about the content. Students will be more interested in trigonometry if they hear a former artilleryman explain how he used trig every day in the army, or they might be more interested in persuasive essays if they hear from a volunteer for Amnesty International describe how she writes letters to attempt to gain freedom for prisoners of conscience.

❺ How will I plan to assess students' progress toward my objectives?

Students need to develop accurate attributions for their success. Observe your students to note whether they perceive that their efforts contribute to their learning. Intervene when students' attributions are inaccurate. Step up your efforts to help students set goals, take responsibility for their progress, and evaluate their work. Together, you and your students might devise a grading system that rewards performance, effort, and improvement.

❻ How will I respond if individual children or the class as a whole are not on track toward success? What is my back-up plan?

Maslow asserted that the goal of psychological health is self-actualization. Review your instruction and your students' learning to determine the extent to which you and the students are meeting the broad span of their needs and reaching their full potential. Consider the following. What evidence is there that (1) the environment is safe and comfortable and encourages students to take risks, (2) instruction is meaningful and lively, and (3) students are active participants in analyzing their growth and setting plans?

Key Terms

Review the following key terms from the chapter. Then, to explore research on these topics and how they relate to education today, connect to Research Navigator™ through this book's Companion Website or directly at www.researchnavigator.com.

achievement motivation   326
attribution theory   321
contingent praise   342
deficiency needs   319
expectancy theory   325
expectancy–valence model   325
extrinsic incentive   335
feedback   340
goal structure   343

growth needs   319
intrinsic incentive   334
learned helplessness   330
learning goals   327
locus of control   322
mastery goals   327
motivation   317
performance goals   327
self-actualization   319

Self-Assessment: Practicing for Licensure

Directions: The chapter-opening vignette addresses indicators that are often assessed in state licensure exams. Re-read the chapter-opening vignette, and then respond to the following questions.

1. According to behavioral learning theorists, why are Cal Lewis's students motivated to learn about the Constitutional Convention?

   a. to obtain reinforcers
   b. to satisfy growth needs
   c. to eliminate deficiency needs
   d. to maximize expectancy effects

2. Mr. Lewis's students see the purpose of lessons about the Constitutional Convention as a way to gain information about the history of the United States. What type of goal orientation is this?

   a. performance goal
   b. learning goal
   c. expectancy goal
   d. self-regulated goal

3. Beth Andrews, a shy girl in Mr. Lewis's class, proposes elements of the Bill of Rights to the convention members. If Beth has an internal locus of control, she is most likely to attribute her successful presentation to which of the following factors?

   a. the presentation requirements being easy
   b. favoritism by the teacher
   c. careful preparation
   d. good luck

4. Mr. Lewis wants his students to work hard regardless of their ability level or task difficulty. What type of attributions will he attempt to instill in his students?

   a. internal-stable
   b. internal-unstable
   c. external-stable
   d. external-unstable

5. Under what circumstances is it most important for Mr. Lewis to avoid the use of external incentives?

   a. when students are doing challenging work
   b. when the task communicates feedback about students' competence
   c. when students are motivated to do the work without extrinsic incentives
   d. when students have experienced a great deal of failure

6. Analyze Mr. Lewis's lesson and his students' willingness to participate from the four theories of motivation presented in the chapter: behavioral, human needs, attribution, and expectancy.

7. Describe ways in which a teacher can increase students' motivation to learn.

CHAPTER

11

Effective Learning Environments

The bell rang outside of Julia Cavalho's tenth-grade

English class. The sound was still echoing in the hall when Ms. Cavalho started her lesson. "Today," she began, "you will become thieves. Worse than thieves. Thieves steal only your money or your property. You—" (she looked around the class and paused for emphasis) "—will steal something far more valuable. You will steal an author's style. An author builds his or her style, word by word, sentence by sentence, over many years. Stealing an author's style is like stealing a boat that someone built by hand. It's despicable, but you're going to do it."

During her speech the students sat in rapt attention. Two students, Mark and Gloria, slunk in late. Mark made a funny "Oops, I'm late" face and did an exaggerated tiptoe to his desk. Ms. Cavalho ignored both of them, as did the class. She continued her lesson.

"To whom are you going to do this dirty deed? Papa Hemingway, of course. Hemingway of the short, punchy sentence. Hemingway of the almost excessive attention to physical detail. You've read *The Old Man and the Sea*. You've read parts of *The Sun Also Rises* and *For Whom the Bell Tolls*."

While Ms. Cavalho talked, Mark made an exaggerated show of getting out his books. He whispered to a neighboring student. Without stopping her lesson, Ms. Cavalho moved near Mark. He stopped whispering and paid attention.

"Today you will become Hemingway. You will steal his words, his pace, his meter, his similes, his metaphors, and put them to work in your own story."

Ms. Cavalho had students review elements of Hemingway's style, which the class had studied before.

"Everyone think for a moment. How would Hemingway describe an old woman going up the stairs at the end of a long day's work? Mai, what do you think?"

Mai gave her short description of the old woman.

"Sounds great to me. I like your use of very short sentences and physical description. Any other ideas? Kevin?"

Ms. Cavalho let several students give Hemingway-style descriptions, using them as opportunities to reinforce her main points.

"In a moment," she said, "you're going to get your chance to become Ernest Hemingway. As usual, you'll be working in your writing response groups. Before we start, however, let's go over our rules about effective group work. Who can tell me what they are?"

The students volunteered several rules: respect others, explain your ideas, be sure everyone participates, stand up for your opinion, keep voices low.

"All right," said Ms. Cavalho. "When I say begin, I'd like you to move your desks together and start planning your compositions. Ready? Begin."

The students moved their desks together smoothly and quickly and got right to work. During the transition, Ms. Cavalho called Mark and Gloria to her desk to discuss their lateness. Gloria had a good excuse, but Mark was developing a pattern of lateness and disruptiveness.

"Mark," said Ms. Cavalho, "I'm concerned about your lateness and your behavior in class. I've spoken to some of your other teachers, and they say you're behaving even worse in their classes than you do in mine. Please come here after school, and we'll see if we can come up with a solution to this problem."

Mark returned to his group and got to work. Ms. Cavalho circulated among the groups, giving encouragement to students who were working well. When she saw two girls who were goofing off, she moved close to them and put her hand on one girl's shoulder while looking at the plan for her composition. "Good start," she said. "Let's see how far you can get with this by the end of the period."

The students worked in a controlled but excited way through the end of the period, thoroughly enjoying "stealing" from Hemingway. The classroom sounded like a beehive with busy, involved students sharing ideas, reading drafts to each other, and editing each other's compositions. At the end of the day, Mark returned to Ms. Cavalho's classroom.

"Mark," she said, "we need to do something about your lateness and your clowning in class. How would you suggest that we solve this problem?"

"Gloria was late, too," Mark protested.

"We're not talking about Gloria. We're talking about you. You are responsible for your own behavior."

"OK, OK, I promise I'll be on time."

"That's not good enough. We've had this conversation before. We need a different plan this time. I know you can succeed in this class, but you're making it hard on yourself as well as disrupting your classmates."

"Let's try an experiment," Ms. Cavalho went on. "Each day, I'd like you to rate your own behavior. I'll do the same. If we both agree at the end of each week that you've been on time and appropriately behaved, fine. If not, I'll need to call your parents and see whether we can make another plan. Are you willing to give it a try?"

"OK, I guess so."

"Great. I'm expecting to see a new Mark starting tomorrow. I know you won't let me down!" ⓐ

Critical Thinking   What methods of classroom management does Ms. Cavalho use? What potential problems is she preventing?

Creative Thinking   Suppose Mark continues to be late for class. Plan a conference with his parents. What are the goals? How will they be implemented?

Critical and Creative Thinking   Analyze two variables, grade level and classroom management strategies, in a matrix. Using Ms. Cavalho's classroom as a starter, create this matrix with grade level on the horizontal (e.g., elementary, middle, and high school), and then brainstorm classroom management strategies down the vertical column. Finally, check off which management strategies are influential at different grade levels.

WHAT IS AN EFFECTIVE LEARNING ENVIRONMENT?

INTASC

5 Classroom Motivation and Management

6 Communication Skills

Providing an effective learning environment includes strategies that teachers use to create a positive, productive classroom experience. Often called **classroom management,** strategies for providing effective learning environments include not only preventing and responding to misbehavior but also, more important, using class time well, creating an atmosphere that is conducive to interest and inquiry, and permitting activities that engage students' minds and imaginations. A class with no behavior problems can by no means be assumed to be a well-managed class.

The most effective approaches to classroom management are those discussed in Chapters 6 through 10. Students who are participating in well-structured activities that engage their interests, who are highly motivated to learn, and who are working on tasks that are challenging yet within their capabilities rarely pose any serious management problems. The vignette involving Ms. Cavalho illustrates this. She has a well-managed class not because she behaves like a drill sergeant, but because she teaches interesting lessons, engages students' imaginations and energies, makes efficient use of time, and communicates a sense of purpose, high expectations, and contagious enthusiasm. However, even a well-managed class is sure to contain individual students who will misbehave. While Ms. Cavalho's focus is on preventing behavior problems, she is also ready to intervene when necessary to see that students' behaviors are within acceptable limits. For some students a glance, physical proximity, or a hand on the shoulder are enough. For others, consequences might be necessary. Even in these cases, Ms. Cavalho does not let behavior issues disrupt her lesson or her students' learning activities.

This chapter focuses on the creation of effective learning environments (also known as classroom management) and on discipline. Creating an effective learning environment involves organizing classroom activities, instruction, and the physical classroom to provide for effective use of time, to create a happy, productive learning environment, and to minimize disruptions. **Discipline** refers to methods used to prevent behavior problems or to respond to existing behavior problems so as to reduce

classroom management
Methods used to organize classroom activities, instruction, physical structure, and other features to make effective use of time, to create a happy and productive learning environment, and to minimize behavior problems and other disruptions.

discipline
Methods used to prevent behavior problems from occurring or to respond to behavior problems so as to reduce their occurrence in the future.

their occurrence in the future (see Charles, 2005; Levin & Nolan, 2004; Marzano, 2003).

There is no magic or charisma that makes a teacher an effective classroom manager. Setting up an effective learning environment is a matter of knowing a set of techniques that any teacher can learn and apply. This chapter takes an approach to classroom management and discipline that emphasizes prevention of misbehavior, on the theory that effective instruction itself is the best means of avoiding discipline problems. In the past, creating an effective learning environment has often been seen as a matter of dealing with individual student misbehaviors. Current thinking emphasizes management of the class as a whole in such a way as to make individual misbehaviors rare (Evertson & Harris, 1993). Teachers who present interesting, well-organized lessons, who use incentives for learning effectively, who accommodate their instruction to students' levels of preparation, and who plan and manage their own time effectively will have few discipline problems to deal with. Still, every teacher, no matter how effective, will encounter discipline problems sometimes, and this chapter also presents means of handling these problems when they arise.

𝒲HAT IS THE IMPACT OF TIME ON LEARNING?

Obviously, if no time is spent teaching a subject, students will not learn it. However, within the usual range of time allocated to instruction, how much difference does time make? This has been a focus of considerable research (see Adelman, Haslam, & Pringle, 1996; National Education Commission on Time and Learning, 1994). Although it is clear that more time spent in instruction has a positive impact on student achievement, the effects of additional time are often modest or inconsistent (Gijselaers & Schmidt, 1995; Karweit, 1989c). In particular, the typical differences in lengths of school days and school years among different districts have only a minor impact on student achievement (see Karweit, 1981; Walberg, 1988). What seems to be more important is how time is used in class. **Engaged time,** or **time on-task,** the number of minutes actually spent learning, is the time measure that is most frequently found to contribute to learning (e.g., Marks, 2000; Rowan, Correnti, & Miller, 2002). In other words, the most important aspect of time is the one that is under the direct control of the teacher: the organization and use of time in the classroom (Jones & Jones, 1998; Marzano, 2003).

Using Allocated Time for Instruction

Time is a limited resource in schools. A typical school is in session about 6 hours a day for 180 days each year. Time for educational activities can be expanded by means of homework assignments or (for some students) summer school, but the total time available for instruction is essentially set. Out of these 6 hours (or so) must come time for teaching a variety of subjects plus time for lunch, recess, and physical education; transitions between classes; announcements; and so on. In a 40- to 60-minute period in a particular subject, many quite different factors reduce the time available for instruction. Figure 11.1 illustrates how time scheduled for mathematics instruction in 12 second- to fifth-grade classes observed by Karweit and Slavin (1981) was whittled away.

The classes that Karweit and Slavin (1981) observed were in schools in and around a rural Maryland town. Overall, the classes were well organized and businesslike, with dedicated and hardworking teachers. Students were generally well behaved and respectful of authority. However, even in these very good schools, the average

engaged time

Time students spend actually learning; same as *time on-task.*

time on-task

Time students spend actively engaged in learning the task at hand.

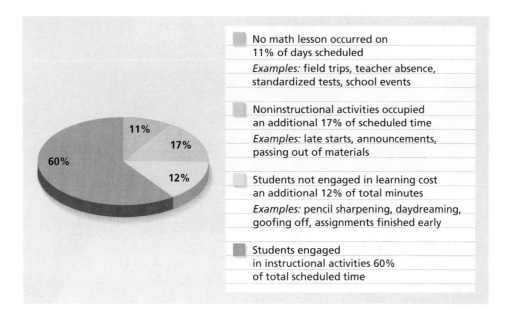

No math lesson occurred on 11% of days scheduled
Examples: field trips, teacher absence, standardized tests, school events

Noninstructional activities occupied an additional 17% of scheduled time
Examples: late starts, announcements, passing out of materials

Students not engaged in learning cost an additional 12% of total minutes
Examples: pencil sharpening, daydreaming, goofing off, assignments finished early

Students engaged in instructional activities 60% of total scheduled time

FIGURE 11.1
Where Does the Time Go?
Observations of elementary school mathematics classes showed that the time students actually spend learning in class is only about 60 percent of the time allocated for instruction.

Based on data from N. L. Karweit and R. E. Slavin, "Measurement and Modeling Choices in Studies of Time and Learning," *American Educational Research Journal, 18*(2). Copyright © 1981 by the American Educational Research Association. Adapted by permission of the publisher.

student spent only 60 percent of the time scheduled for mathematics instruction actually learning mathematics. First of all, about 20 class days were lost to such activities as standardized testing, school events, field trips, and teacher absences. On days when instruction was given, class time was lost because of late starts and noninstructional activities such as discussions of upcoming events, announcements, passing out of materials, and disciplining of students. Finally, even when math was being taught, many students were not actually engaged in the instructional activity. Some were daydreaming during lecture or seatwork times, goofing off, or sharpening pencils; others had nothing to do, either because they were finished with their assigned work or because they had not yet been assigned a task. The 60 percent figure estimated by Karweit and Slavin is, if anything, an overestimate. In a much larger study, Weinstein and Mignano (1993) found that elementary school students spent only about one-third of their time engaged in learning tasks (see also Hong, 2001; Meek, 2003).

A term for available instructional time is **allocated time:** the time during which students have an opportunity to learn. When the teacher is lecturing, students can learn by paying attention. When students have written assignments or other tasks, they can learn by doing them. A discussion follows of some common ways in which allocated time can be maximized (see Jones & Jones, 1995).

Preventing Lost Time   One way in which much instructional time disappears is through losses of entire days or periods. Many of these losses are inevitable because of such things as standardized testing days and snow days, and we certainly would not want to abolish important field trips or school assemblies just to get in a few more periods of instruction. However, frequent losses of instructional periods interrupt the flow of instruction and can ultimately deprive students of sufficient time to master the curriculum.

Making good use of all classroom time is less a matter of squeezing out a few more minutes or hours of instruction each year than of communicating to students that learning is an important business that is worth their time and effort. If a teacher finds excuses not to teach, students might learn that learning is not a serious enterprise. In studying an outstandingly effective inner-city Baltimore elementary school, Salganik (1980) described a third-grade teacher who took her class to the school library, which she found locked. She sent a student for the key, and while the class waited, the teacher

allocated time
Time during which students have the opportunity to learn.

Teachers' time for instruction is limited by the amount of time used for routine management concerns such as taking attendance. As a teacher, how will you prevent loss of instruction time?

whispered to her students, "Let's work on our doubles. Nine plus nine? Six plus six?" The class whispered the answers back in unison. Did a couple of minutes working on addition facts increase the students' achievement? Of course not. But it probably did help to develop a perception that school is for learning, not for marking time.

Preventing Late Starts and Early Finishes   A surprising amount of allocated instructional time is lost because the teacher does not start teaching at the beginning of the period. This can be a particular problem in self-contained elementary classes, in which there are no bells or fixed schedules to structure the period. It is also a problem in departmentalized secondary schools, where teachers might spend a long time dealing with late students or other problems before starting the lesson. A crisp, on-time start to a lesson is important for setting a purposive tone to instruction. If students know that a teacher does not start on time, they might be lackadaisical about getting to class on time; this attitude makes future on-time starts increasingly difficult. In Ms. Cavalho's class, students know that if they are late, they will miss something interesting, fun, and important. As a result, almost all of them are in class and ready to learn when the bell rings.

Teachers can also shortchange students if they stop teaching before the end of the period. This is less damaging than a ragged or late start but is still worth avoiding by planning more instruction than you think you'll need, in case you finish the lesson early (Evertson, 1982).

Preventing Interruptions   One important cause of lost allocated time for instruction is interruptions. Interruptions may be externally imposed, such as announcements or the need to sign forms sent from the principal's office; or they may be caused by teachers or students themselves. Interruptions not only directly cut into the time for instruction; they also break the momentum of the lesson, which reduces students' attention to the task at hand.

Avoiding interruptions takes planning. For example, some teachers put a "Do not disturb—learning in progress!" sign on the door to inform would-be interrupters to come back later. One teacher wore a special hat during small-group lessons to remind her other second-graders not to interrupt her during that time. Rather than signing forms or dealing with other "administrivia" at once, some teachers keep a box where students and others can put any forms and then deal with them after the lesson is over.

Anything the teacher can postpone doing until after a lesson should be postponed. For example, if the teacher has started a lesson and a student walks in late, the teacher should go on with the lesson and deal with the tardiness issue later.

Handling Routine Procedures Some teachers spend too much time on simple classroom routines. For example, some elementary teachers spend many minutes getting students ready for lunch or dismissal because they call students by name, one at a time. This is unnecessary. Early in the school year, many teachers establish a routine that only when the entire table (or row) is quiet and ready to go are students called to line up. Lining up for lunch then takes seconds, not minutes.

Other procedures must also become routine for students. They must know, for example, when they may go to the washroom or sharpen a pencil and not ask to do these things at other times. A teacher may collect papers by having students pass them to the front or to the left or by having table monitors collect the table's papers. Distribution of materials must also be planned for. Exactly how these tasks are done is less important than that students know clearly what they are to do. Many teachers assign regular classroom helpers to take care of distribution and collection of papers, taking messages to the office, erasing the blackboard, and other routine tasks that are annoying interruptions for teachers but that students love to do. Teachers should use student power as much as possible.

Minimizing Time Spent on Discipline Methods of disciplining students are discussed at length later in this chapter. However, one aspect of disciplining should be mentioned at this point. Whenever possible—which is almost always—disciplinary statements or actions should not interrupt the flow of the lesson. A sharp glance, silently moving close to an offending student, or a hand signal, such as putting finger to lips to remind a student to be silent, is usually effective for the kind of minor behavior problems that teachers must constantly deal with, and they allow the lesson to proceed without interruption. For example, Ms. Cavalho could have interrupted her lesson to scold Mark and Gloria, but that would have wasted time and disrupted the concentration and focus of the whole class. If students need talking to about discipline problems, the time to do it is after the lesson or after school, not in the middle of a lesson. If Diana and Martin are talking during a quiet reading time instead of working, it would be better to say, "Diana and Martin, see me at three o'clock," than to launch into an on-the-spot speech about the importance of being on-task during seatwork times.

Using Engaged Time Effectively

Engaged time (or time on-task) is the time individual students actually spend doing assigned work. Allocated time and engaged time differ in that allocated time refers to the opportunity for the entire class to engage in learning activities, whereas engaged time may be different for each student, depending on a student's attentiveness and willingness to work. Strategies for maximizing student time on-task are discussed in the following sections. Several studies have found teacher training programs based on principles presented in the following sections to increase student engagement and, in some cases, learning (Evertson & Harris, 1993; Jones & Jones, 1998).

Teaching Engaging Lessons The best way to increase students' time on-task is to teach lessons that are so interesting, engaging, and relevant to students'

CONNECTIONS

For more information about the importance of time use and time management in effective teaching, see Chapter 9, page 279.

"When I said you two needed to get engaged, this isn't what I had in mind!"

CONNECTIONS

For more information about arousing student interest and focusing student attention, see Chapter 7, page 218, and Chapter 6, page 168.

CONNECTIONS

For more information about active learning, see Chapter 8, page 259.

INTASC

4 Multiple Instructional
Strategies

interests that students will pay attention and eagerly do what is asked of them. Part of this strategy calls for the teacher to emphasize active, rapidly paced instruction with varied modes of presentation and frequent opportunities for student participation and to deemphasize independent seatwork, especially unsupervised seatwork (as in follow-up time in elementary reading classes). Research has consistently shown that student engagement is much higher when the teacher is teaching than during individual seatwork (Evertson & Harris, 1992). Giving students many opportunities to participate actively in lessons is also associated with greater learning (Finn & Cox, 1992), and engaged time is much higher in well-structured cooperative learning programs than in independent seatwork (Slavin, 1990).

Maintaining Momentum   Maintaining momentum during a lesson is a key to keeping task engagement high. *Momentum* refers to the avoidance of interruptions or slowdowns (Kounin, 1970). In a class that maintains good momentum, students always have something to do and, once started working, are not interrupted. Anyone who has tried to write a term paper only to be interrupted by telephone calls, knocks on the door, and other disturbances knows that these interruptions cause much more damage to concentration and progress than the amount of time they take.

Kounin (1970) gives the following example of teacher-caused slowdowns and interruptions:

> The teacher is just starting a reading group at the reading circle while the rest of the children are engaged in seatwork with workbooks. She sat in front of the reading group and asked, "All right, who can tell me the name of our next chapter?" Before a child was called on to answer, she looked toward the children at seatwork, saying: "Let's wait until the people in Group Two are settled and working." (Actually most were writing in their workbooks.) She then looked at John, who was in the seatwork group, naggingly asking, "Did you find your pencil?" John answered something which was inaudible. The teacher got up from her seat, saying, "I'd like to know what you did with it." Pause for about two seconds. "Did you eat it?" Another pause. "What happened to it? What color was it? You can't do your work without it." The teacher then went to her desk to get a pencil to give to John, saying, "I'll get you a pencil. Make sure the pencil is here tomorrow morning. And don't tell me you lost that one too. And make it a new one, and see that it's sharpened." (p. 104)

This teacher destroyed the momentum of a reading lesson by spending more than a minute dealing with a child in the seatwork group who did not have a pencil. Of course, during this interchange, the entire class—both the reading group and the seatwork group—were off-task; but what is worse, they required much more time to get resettled and back to work after the incident. Just as a lesson was getting under way and students were ready to listen, the teacher broke this chain of activities with a completely unnecessary reprimand for a behavior that could easily have been ignored.

Kounin found momentum to be strongly related to total time on-task, and Brophy and Evertson (1976) and Anderson, Evertson, and Brophy (1979) found momentum to be related to student achievement. It is significant that some of the features of effective lessons described in Chapter 7 are largely directed at maintaining momentum. For example, in one model of direct instruction (Good et al., 1983), the teacher has students try a few problems under his or her watchful eye ("controlled practice") before letting them start their seatwork, to make sure that the flow from lesson to seatwork is not interrupted by student questions and problems.

Maintaining Smoothness of Instruction   *Smoothness* is another term Kounin (1970) uses to refer to continued focus on a meaningful sequence of instruction. Smooth instruction avoids jumping without transitions from topic to topic or from the lesson to other activities, which produces "jarring breaks in the activity flow" (Kounin, 1970, p. 97). For example:

> The teacher was conducting a recitation with a subgroup. She was walking toward a child who was reciting when she passed by the fish bowl. She suddenly stopped walking toward the boy, and stopped at the fish bowl, saying: "Oh my, I forgot to feed the fish!" She then got some fish food from a nearby shelf and started to feed the fish, saying: "My, see how hungry it is." She then turned to a girl, saying: "See, Margaret, you forgot to feed the fish. You can see how hungry it is. See how quickly it comes up to eat." (Kounin, 1970, pp. 98–99)

This example illustrates how smoothness and momentum are related. The teacher jumped from her lesson to housekeeping to (unnecessary) disciplining, interrupting one student's recitation and making it virtually impossible for the other students to focus on the lesson. As with momentum, smoothness was found to be strongly associated with student time on-task (Kounin, 1970) and achievement (Anderson et al., 1979; Brophy & Evertson, 1976).

Managing Transitions   Transitions are changes from one activity to another; for example, from lecture to seatwork, from subject to subject, or from lesson to lunch. Elementary school classes have been found to have an average of 31 major transitions a day, occupying 15 percent of class time (Burns, 1984). Transitions are the seams of class management at which classroom order is most likely to come apart; Anderson and colleagues (1979) and Evertson, Emmer, and Brophy (1980) found that teachers' efficiency at managing transitions between activities was positively related to their students' achievement.

Following are three rules for the management of transitions:

1. When making a transition, the teacher should give a clear signal to which the students have been taught to respond. For example, in the elementary grades, some teachers use a bell to indicate to students that they should immediately be quiet and listen to instructions.

2. Before the transition is made, students must be certain about what they are to do when the signal is given. For example, a teacher might say, "When I say 'Go,' I want you all to put your books away and get out the compositions you started yesterday. Is everyone ready? All right, go!" When giving instructions to students to begin independent seatwork, the teacher can help them get started with the activity before letting them work independently, as in the following example:

> *Teacher:* Today we are going to find guide words for different pages in the dictionary. Everyone should have a ditto sheet with the words on it and a dictionary. Class, hold up your ditto sheet. [They do.] Now hold up your dictionary. [They do.] Good. Now turn to page eighty-two. [The teacher walks around to see that everyone does so.] Look at the top of the page, and put your finger on the first guide word. [The teacher walks around to check on this.] Class, what is the first guide word?
> *Class:* Carrot!
> *Teacher:* Good. The first guide word is carrot. Now look to the right on the same page. Class, what word do you see there?
> *Class:* Carve!
> *Teacher:* Right. The guide words are carrot and carve. Now turn to page five hundred fifty-five and find the guide words. [Students do this.] Class, what is the first guide word on page five hundred fifty-five?
> *Class:* Scheme!
> *Teacher:* Class, what is the second guide word?

CERTIFICATION POINTER   You may be asked on your teacher certification test to discuss why it is important for a teacher to plan carefully for transitions and describe what can happen if transitions are not implemented with care.

Class: Scissors!

Teacher: Great! Now do the first problem on your assignment sheet by yourselves, and then check with a partner to see if you agree.

The teacher will then check whether all or almost all students have the first item correct before telling them to complete the worksheet. The idea, of course, is to make sure that students know exactly what they are to do before they start doing it.

3. Make transitions all at once. Students should be trained to make transitions as a group, rather than one student at a time (Charles, 1989). The teacher should usually give directions to the class as a whole or to well-defined groups: "Class, I want you all to put away your laboratory materials and prepare for dismissal as quickly and quietly as you can. . . . I see that Table Three is quiet and ready. Table Three, please line up quietly. Table Six, line up. Table One . . . Table Four. Everyone else may line up quietly. Let's go!"

Maintaining Group Focus during Lessons Maintaining group focus means using classroom organization strategies and questioning techniques that ensure that all students in the class stay involved in the lesson, even when only one student is called on by the teacher. Two principal components of Kounin's concept of maintaining group focus were found to be significantly related to students' on-task behavior: accountability and group alerting.

Kounin (1970) uses the term **accountability** to mean "the degree to which the teacher holds the children accountable and responsible for their task performances during recitation sessions" (p. 119). Examples of tactics for increasing accountability are using choral responses, having all students hold up their work so the teacher can see it, circulating among the students to see what they are doing, and drawing other children into the performance of one child (e.g., "I want you all to watch what Suzanne is doing so you can tell me whether you agree or disagree with her answer"). Ms. Cavalho increased involvement and accountability by having all students prepare a Hemingway-like description and only then asking for a few of them to be read.

The idea behind these tactics is to maintain the involvement of all students in all parts of the lesson. A study of third- and fourth-graders found that students raised their hands an average of once every 6 minutes and gave an answer only once every 15 minutes, with some students hardly ever participating (Potter, 1977). This is not enough participation to ensure student attention. Teachers should be concerned not only about drawing all students into class activities but also about avoiding activities that relegate most students to the role of spectator for long periods. For example, a very common teaching error is to have one or two students work out a lengthy problem on the chalkboard or read an extended passage while the rest of the class has nothing to do. Such methods waste the time of much of the class, break the momentum of the lesson, and leave the door open for misbehavior (Gump, 1982).

Group alerting refers to questioning strategies that are designed to keep all students on their toes during a lecture or discussion. One example of group alerting is creating suspense before calling on a student by saying, "Given triangle ABC, if we know the measures of sides A and B and of angle AB, what else can we find out about the triangle? . . . [Pause] . . . Maria?" Note that this keeps the whole class thinking until Maria's name is called. The opposite effect would have been created by saying, "Maria, given triangle ABC . . . ," because only Maria would have been alerted. Calling on students in a random order is another example of group alerting, as is letting students know that they may be asked questions about the preceding reciter's answers. For example, the teacher might follow up Maria's answer with "What is the name of the postulate that Maria used? . . . Ralph?"

accountability
The degree to which people are held responsible for their task performances or decision outcomes.

group alerting
Questioning strategies that encourage all students to pay attention during lectures and discussions.

Maintaining Group Focus during Seatwork   During times when students are doing seatwork and the teacher is available to work with them, it is important to monitor the seatwork activities and to informally check individual students' work. That is, the teacher should circulate among the students' desks to see how they are doing. This allows the teacher to identify any problems students are having before they waste seatwork time practicing errors or giving up in frustration. If students are engaged in cooperative group work, students can check each other's work, but the teacher still needs to check frequently with each group to see that the students are on the right track.

Seatwork times provide excellent opportunities for providing individual help to students who are struggling to keep up with the class, but teachers should resist the temptation to work too long with an individual student. Interactions with students during seatwork should be as brief as possible, because if the teacher gets tied down with any one student, the rest of the class may drift off-task or run into problems of their own (Doyle, 1984).

Withitness   **Withitness** is another term coined by Kounin (1970). It describes teachers' actions that indicate awareness of students' behavior at all times. Kounin calls this awareness "having eyes in the back of one's head." Teachers who are with-it can respond immediately to student misbehavior and know who started what. Teachers who lack withitness can make the error of scolding the wrong student, as in the following instance:

> Lucy and John, who were sitting at the same table as Jane, started to whisper. Robert watched this, and he too got into the act. Then Jane giggled and said something to John. Then Mary leaned over and whispered to Jane. At this point, the teacher said, "Mary and Jane, stop that!" (adapted from Kounin, 1970, p. 80)

By responding only to Mary and Jane, who were the last to get involved in the whispering and giggling incident, the teacher indicated that she did not know what was going on. A single incident of this kind might make little difference, but after many such incidents, students recognize the teacher's tendency to respond inappropriately to their behavior.

Another example of a lack of withitness is responding too late to a sequence of misbehavior. Lucy and John's whispering could have been easily nipped in the bud, perhaps with just a glance or a finger to the lips. By the time the whispering had escalated to giggling and spread to several students, a full stop in the lesson was needed to rectify the situation.

A major component of withitness is scanning the class frequently and establishing eye contact with individual students. Several studies have found that more effective classroom managers frequently scan the classroom visually, to monitor the pace of activity as well as individual students' behaviors (Brooks, 1985; Emmer, Evertson, & Anderson, 1980; Evertson & Emmer, 1982). Effective classroom managers have the ability to interpret and act on the mood of the class as a whole. They notice when students are beginning to fidget or are otherwise showing signs of flagging attention, and they act on this information to change activities to recapture student engagement (Carter, Cushing, Sabers, Stein, & Berliner, 1988).

Overlapping   **Overlapping** refers to the teacher's ability to attend to interruptions or behavior problems while continuing a lesson or other instructional activity. For example, one teacher was teaching a lesson on reading comprehension when he saw a student looking at a book that was unrelated to the lesson. Without interrupting his lesson, the teacher walked over to the student, took her book, closed it, and put it

withitness
The degree to which the teacher is aware of and responsive to student behavior at all times.

overlapping
A teacher's ability to respond to behavior problems without interrupting a classroom lesson.

on her desk, all while continuing to speak to the class. This took care of the student's misbehavior without slowing the momentum of the lesson; the rest of the class hardly noticed that the event occurred. Similarly, Ms. Cavalho squelched a whispering incident just by moving closer to the whispering students while continuing her lesson.

Another example of a teacher doing a good job of overlapping is as follows:

> The teacher is at the reading circle and Lucy is reading aloud while standing. Johnny, who was doing seatwork at his desk, walks up toward the teacher, holding his workbook. The teacher glances at Johnny, then looks back at Lucy, nodding at Lucy, as Lucy continues to read aloud. The teacher remains seated and takes Johnny's workbook. She turns to Lucy, saying, "That was a hard word, Lucy, and you pronounced it right." She checks about three more answers to Johnny's book saying, "That's fine, you can go ahead and do the next page now," and resumes looking at the reading book as Lucy continues reading. (Kounin, 1970, p. 84)

CERTIFICATION POINTER

For your teacher certification test you may be asked to make suggestions for helping students stay on task in a particular case.

Johnny's interruption of the reading group might have been avoided altogether by a good classroom manager, who would have assigned enough work to keep all students productively busy during reading circle time and given clear instructions on what they were to do when they finished their seatwork. For example, Johnny's work could have been checked by a partner or teammate. However, interruptions are sometimes unavoidable, and the ability to keep the main activity going while handling them is strongly related to overall classroom order (Copeland, 1983; Kounin, 1970) and to achievement (Anderson et al., 1979; Brophy & Evertson, 1976).

Can Time On-Task Be Too High?

A class that is rarely on-task is certainly not a well-managed class. However, it is possible to go too far in the other direction, emphasizing time on-task to the exclusion of all other considerations (Weade & Evertson, 1988). For example, in a study of

INTASC

6 Communication Skills

Personal Reflection

Maintaining Control

I was once visiting a fifth-grade class in suburban Baltimore involved in a study we were doing at Johns Hopkins University. The teacher was presenting an interesting, well-organized lesson, and most of the students were paying attention. However, one girl had a comic book she was secretly reading, paying no attention to the lesson.

The veteran teacher was aware of everything going on in the class, and he soon noticed that the girl wasn't paying attention. Without interrupting his lesson in the slightest, he strolled sideways toward her desk, took the comic book, closed it, and put it on her desk. This was done so smoothly that few if any of the other students even seemed to notice it. This was a wonderful demonstration, I thought, of Kounin's principles of classroom management. The teacher dealt with the behavior without interrupting the flow of the lesson. Had he stopped and yelled at the girl, he would have broken the lesson, given the whole class an occasion for enjoying either the girl's defiance or her comeuppance, and taken much time to get back on track. The girl may have enjoyed such attention, and other students may have wanted to get in on the act. Instead, the girl received ample feedback (that her behavior was known and not appreciated), but the show went on.

Reflect on This. What is your temperament like normally? Do you think this will carry over to your teaching? How does a teacher's temperament affect the mood of a classroom?

time on-task in elementary mathematics, one teacher's class was found to be engaged essentially 100 percent of the time. The teacher accomplished this by walking up and down the rows of desks looking for the slightest flicker of inattention. This class learned very little math over the course of the year. An overemphasis on engaged time rather than on engaging instruction can produce what Bloome, Puro, and Theodorou (1989) call **mock participation,** in which students appear to be on-task but are not really engaged in learning.

Several studies have found that increasing time on-task in classes in which students were already reasonably well behaved did not increase student achievement (Blackadar & Nachtigal, 1986; Slavin, 1986; Stallings & Krasavage, 1986). An overemphasis on time on-task can be detrimental to learning in several ways. For example, complex tasks involving creativity and uncertainty tend to produce lower levels of time on-task than do simple cut-and-dried tasks (Doyle & Carter, 1984; Evertson & Randolph, 1995). Yet it would clearly be a poor instructional strategy to avoid complex or uncertain tasks just to keep time on-task high. Maintaining classroom order is an important goal of teaching, but it is only one of many (see Evertson & Randolph, 1995; Slavin, 1987a).

Classroom Management in the Student-Centered Classroom

It is important to note that most research on classroom management has taken place in traditionally organized classrooms, in which students have few choices as to what they do and few interactions with each other. In more student-centered classrooms, children are likely to be spending much of their time working with each other, doing open-ended projects, writing, and experimenting. Evertson and Randolph (1995) have discussed the shift that must take place in thinking about classroom management for such classrooms. Clearly, classroom management is more participatory in a student-centered classroom, with students centrally involved in setting standards of behavior. Equally clearly, the type of behavior to be expected will be different. It is impossible to imagine a student-centered classroom that is silent, for example. Yet in other respects the requirements for managing student-centered classrooms are not so different from those for managing traditional ones. Rules are still needed and must be consistently communicated to students and consistently enforced (Freiberg, Connell, & Lorentz, 2001). If students in student-centered classrooms are deeply involved and motivated by the variety, activity, and social nature of classroom activities, then disciplinary actions will be less necessary (Rogers & Freiberg, 1994). Inevitably, however, certain students' misbehavior will disrupt others' learning, and the teacher must have strategies to help students live up to norms that all members of the class have agreed to.

The following sections describe strategies for preventing misbehavior in any classroom context and responding effectively to misbehavior when it does occur.

WHAT PRACTICES CONTRIBUTE TO EFFECTIVE CLASSROOM MANAGEMENT?

Research has consistently shown that basic commonsense planning and groundwork go a long way toward preventing discipline problems from ever developing. Simple measures include starting the year properly, arranging the classroom for effective instruction, setting class rules and procedures, and making expectations of conduct clear to students (Marzano, 2003).

mock participation
Situation in which students appear to be on-task but are not engaged in learning.

The relationship you establish with your students will set the tone for learning in your classroom. What do you anticipate being the biggest challenge to establishing a productive classroom?

INTASC

7 Instructional Planning
Skills

Different grade levels and student groups present different management concerns. For instance, with younger students, teachers need to be concerned about socializing students to the norms and behaviors that are expected in school (Evertson, Emmer, & Worsham, 2000). Programs focusing on establishing consistent, schoolwide behavior expectations and on building positive relationships and school success through the use of cooperative learning have been effective in improving the behavior of elementary school children (Freiberg, Connell, & Lorentz, 2001; O'Donnell, Hawkins, Catalano, Abbott, & Day, 1995).

In middle school and high school, students can grasp the principles that underlie rules and procedures and can rationally agree to observe them (Emmer, Evertson, Clements, & Worsham, 2000). At the same time, some adolescents resist authority and place greater importance on peer norms. Aggressive behavior, truancy, and delinquency also increase as students enter adolescence (Tierno, 1993). In the upper grades, departmentalization, tracking, and class promotion might become management issues, especially with students who have established patterns of learned helplessness or academic failure. Teachers of older students need to be more concerned with motivating them toward more self-regulation in observing rules and procedures and in learning the course material. Programs that increase the clarity of rules, consistency of rule enforcement, and frequency of communication with the home have been very effective in improving adolescents' behavior (Gottfredson, Gottfredson, & Hybl, 1993).

Starting Out the Year Right

Emmer and colleagues (1980) and Evertson and Emmer (1982) studied teachers' actions at the beginning of the school year and correlated them with students' behaviors later in the year. They found that the first days of school were critical in establishing classroom order. They compared teachers whose classes were mostly on-task over the course of the school year with teachers whose classes were less consistently on-task and found that the better classroom managers engaged in certain activities during the first days of school significantly more often than did the less effective managers (Evertson et al., 2000). A list of six characteristics of effective classroom managers follows:

1. More effective managers had a clear, specific plan for introducing students to classroom rules and procedures and spent as many days as necessary carrying out their plan until students knew how to line up, ask for help, and so on.
2. More effective managers worked with the whole class initially (even if they planned to group students later). They were involved with the whole class at all times, rarely leaving any students without something to do or without supervision. For example, more effective managers seldom worked with an individual student unless the rest of the class was productively occupied (Doyle, 1984; Sanford & Evertson, 1981).
3. More effective managers spent extra time during the first days of school introducing procedures and discussing class rules (often encouraging students to suggest rules themselves). These teachers usually reminded students of class rules every day for at least the first week of school (Weinstein & Mignano, 1993).
4. More effective managers taught students specific procedures. For example, some had students practice lining up quickly and quietly; others taught students to respond to a signal, such as a bell, a flick of the light switch, or a call for attention.
5. As first activities, more effective managers used simple, enjoyable tasks. Materials for the first lessons were well prepared, clearly presented, and varied. These teachers asked students to get right to work on the first day of school and then gave them instructions on procedures gradually, to avoid overloading them with too much information at a time.
6. More effective managers responded immediately to stop any misbehavior.

Setting Class Rules

One of the first management-related tasks at the start of the year is setting class rules. Three principles govern this process. First, class rules should be few in number. Second, they should make sense and be seen as fair by students. Third, they should be clearly explained and deliberately taught to students (Doyle, 1990b; Metzger, 2002). A major purpose of clearly explaining general class rules is to give a moral authority for specific procedures (Freiberg, 1996). For example, all students will understand and support a rule such as "Respect others' property." This simple rule can be invoked to cover such obvious misbehaviors as stealing or destroying materials but also gives a reason for putting materials away, cleaning up litter, and refraining from marking up textbooks. Students may be asked to help set the rules, or they may be given a set of rules and asked to give examples of these rules. Class discussions give students a feeling of participation in setting rational rules that everyone can live by (Kauffman & Burbach, 1997; Nelson, Lott, & Glenn, 1997). When the class as a whole has agreed on a set of rules, offenders know that they are transgressing community norms, not the teacher's arbitrary regulations. One all-purpose set of class rules follows:

1. **Be courteous to others.** This rule forbids interrupting others or speaking out of turn, teasing or laughing at others, fighting, and so on.
2. **Respect others' property.**
3. **Be on-task.** This includes listening when the teacher or other students are talking, working on seatwork, continuing to work during any interruptions, staying in one's seat, being at one's seat and ready to work when the bell rings, and following directions.
4. **Raise hands to be recognized.** This is a rule against calling out or getting out of one's seat for assistance without permission.

Teaching Dilemmas: Cases to Consider

Rules of the Room

Althea Johnson, a third-grade teacher, is standing in front of her new class on the second day of school.

Althea: Okay, class. I want to spend a few minutes talking with you about class rules. Let's start by listing some on the board. Please raise your hands if you have a rule you'd like to suggest and wait until I call on you.

In a few minutes Althea has written the following on the board under the heading Rules:

- Do not talk in class.
- Do not run in the hallways.
- Do not put gum under your desk.
- Do not throw spitballs (or paper airplanes).
- Do not draw on your desk.
- Do not fight.
- Do not come late without a note from home.
- Do not yell in class.
- Do raise your hand to be called on.
- Do not bring radios to school.
- Do not pass notes to your friends.
- Do not write in your books.

Althea: Does everyone think these rules are fair? Hands? [Hands go up.] Okay, that's a good start. But I see two problems. First, this is a long list to remember. And second, most of them start with *"Do not."* I'd like to try to group these to create a few rules that tell us what we *should* do.

Her students offer ideas, and eventually the board shows the following rules, each with several examples underneath:

1. Respect the rights of others.
2. Respect other people's property.
3. Be courteous to others.
4. Be on-task.
5. Raise your hand to be called on.

Althea: Okay, we've all agreed that these rules are fair. But if somebody does forget and breaks a rule, what should happen? What should the consequences be? Clare?

Clare: You go to the principal's office.
Althea: Yes, that could be one consequence. Let's list more.

As before, Althea lists the students' suggestions under the heading Consequences:

- Go to the principal's office.
- Sit in the corner for half an hour.
- Miss recess.
- Stay after school.
- Get a letter sent home to your parents.

Althea: Who has a suggestion for encouraging people to want to keep the rules in the first place, not break them? A kind of reward? Mimi? Clare?
Mimi: Getting gold stars?
Clare: We could all get an extra recess if the whole class was good all day.
Billy (interrupting): We could all just stay home!
Althea: Billy, we've all agreed to raise hands and to be courteous. So are you trying to give the class an example of how not to behave?
Billy: Sorry, Mrs. Johnson.
Althea: Okay, now I want everyone to copy our basic rules and think about them. We'll talk a little more about rewards and consequences tomorrow.

@ Questions for Reflection

1. Do you agree with Althea that third-graders should be involved in setting class rules? How might a teacher of kindergarten or high school children approach the same task?
2. For the grade level you plan to teach, develop a problem-prevention plan of action for the first week of school. Model your plan by extending the dialogue in this case with another character; for example, have Althea talk with a novice teacher.

WHAT ARE SOME STRATEGIES FOR MANAGING ROUTINE MISBEHAVIOR?

The preceding sections of this chapter discussed means of organizing classroom activities to maximize time for instruction and minimize time for such minor disturbances as students talking out of turn, getting out of their seats without permission, and not paying attention. Provision of interesting lessons, efficient use of class time, and careful structuring of instructional activities will prevent most such minor behavior problems—and many more serious ones as well (Barr & Parrett, 2001). For example,

Kounin (1970) found that teacher behaviors that were associated with high time on-task were also associated with fewer serious behavior problems. Time off-task can lead to more serious problems; many behavior problems arise because students are frustrated or bored in school. Instructional programs that actively involve students and provide all of them with opportunities for success might prevent such problems.

However, effective lessons and good use of class time are not the only means of preventing or dealing with inappropriate behavior. Besides structuring classes to reduce the frequency of behavior problems, teachers must have strategies for dealing with behavior problems when they do occur (Emmer & Stough, 2001).

The great majority of behavior problems with which a teacher must deal are relatively minor disruptions, such as talking out of turn, getting up without permission, failing to follow class rules or procedures, and inattention—nothing really serious, but behaviors that must be minimized for learning to occur. Before considering disciplinary strategies, it is important to reflect on their purpose. Students should learn much more in school than the "Three Rs." They should learn that they are competent learners and that learning is enjoyable and satisfying. A classroom environment that is warm, supportive, and accepting fosters these attitudes (Fay, 2001). Furthermore, there is a strong link between attentive, nondisruptive behavior and student achievement (Finn, Pannozzo, & Voelkl, 1995; Wentzel, 1993).

A healthy classroom environment cannot be created if students do not respect teachers or teachers do not respect students. Though teachers should involve students in setting class rules and take student needs or input into account in organizing the classroom, teachers are ultimately the leaders who establish and enforce rules that students must live by. These class rules and procedures should become second nature to students. Teachers who have not established their authority in the classroom are likely to spend too much time dealing with behavior problems or yelling at students to be instructionally effective. Furthermore, the clearer the structure and routine procedures in the classroom, the more freedom the teacher can allow students (Mackenzie, 1997; Weinstein, 1999). The following sections discuss strategies for dealing with typical discipline problems (Evertson et al., 2003; Emmer et al., 2003; Jones & Jones, 1998; Kyle & Rogien, 2004; Walker & Shea, 1999; Weinstein & Migano, 1997).

The Principle of Least Intervention

In dealing with routine classroom behavior problems, the most important principle is that a teacher should correct misbehaviors by using the simplest intervention that will work (Kyle & Rogien, 2004; Nelson, Lott, & Glenn, 1997). Many studies have found that the amount of time spent disciplining students is negatively related to student achievement (Crocker & Brooker, 1986; Evertson et al., 1980). The teacher's main goal in dealing with routine misbehavior is to do so in a way that is both effective and avoids unnecessarily disrupting the lesson (Evertson & Harris, 1992; Jones & Jones, 1998). If at all possible, the lesson must go on while any behavior problems are dealt with. A continuum of strategies for dealing with minor misbehaviors, from least disruptive to most, is listed in Table 11.1 and discussed in the following sections.

Prevention

The easiest behavior problems to deal with are those that never occur in the first place. As was illustrated earlier in this chapter, teachers can prevent behavior problems by presenting interesting and lively lessons, making class rules and procedures clear, keeping students busy on meaningful tasks, and using other effective techniques of basic classroom management (Doyle, 1990b; Jones & Jones, 1995; Fay, 2001; Stipek, de la

Table 11.1		
Principle of Least Intervention		
Step	*Procedure*	*Example*
1	Prevention	Teacher displays enthusiasm, varies activities, keeps students interested.
2	Nonverbal cues	Tanya turns in paper late: teacher frowns.
3	Praise of correct behavior that is incompatible with misbehavior	"Tanya, I hear you completed your science fair project on time for the judging. That's great!"
4	Praise for other students	"I see most of you turned your papers in on time today. I really appreciate that."
5	Verbal reminders	"Tanya, please turn in your next paper on time."
6	Repeated reminders	"Tanya, it's important to turn your paper in on time."
7	Consequences	Tanya spends 10 minutes after class starting on the next paper assignment.

Sota, & Weishaupt, 1999). Ms. Cavalho's class is an excellent example of this. Her students rarely misbehave because they are interested and engaged.

Varying the content of lessons, using a variety of materials and approaches, displaying humor and enthusiasm, and using cooperative learning or project-based learning can all reduce boredom-caused behavior problems. A teacher can avert frustration caused by material that is too difficult or assignments that are unrealistically long by breaking assignments into smaller steps and doing a better job of preparing students to work on their own. Fatigue can be reduced if short breaks are allowed, activities are varied, and difficult subjects are scheduled in the morning, when students are fresh.

ON THE WEB

To learn more about classroom management go to the Teacher Talk Forum on the Center for Adolescent and Family Studies website, **www.indiana.edu/~cafs/**, and Temple University's Teacher's Connection at **www.temple.edu/CETP/temple_ teach/index.html.**

INTASC

6 Communication Skills

nonverbal cues
Eye contact, gestures, physical proximity, or touching that a teacher uses to communicate without interrupting verbal discourse.

Nonverbal Cues

Teachers can eliminate much routine classroom misbehavior without breaking the momentum of the lesson by the use of simple **nonverbal cues** (Woolfolk & Brooks, 1985). Making eye contact with a misbehaving student might be enough to stop misbehavior. For example, if two students are whispering, the teacher might simply catch the eye of one or both of them. Moving close to a student who is misbehaving also usually alerts the student to shape up. If these techniques fail, a light hand on the student's shoulder is likely to be effective (although touch should be used cautiously with adolescents, who may be sensitive about being touched). These nonverbal strategies all clearly convey the same message: "I see what you are doing and don't like it. Please get back to work." The advantage of communicating this message nonverbally is that the lesson need not be interrupted. In contrast, verbal reprimands can cause a ripple effect; many students stop working while one is being reprimanded (Kounin, 1970). Instead of interrupting the flow of concentration for many to deal with the behavior of one, nonverbal cues usually have an effect only on the student who is misbehaving, as was illustrated earlier in this chapter by the example of the teacher who continued his lesson while silently closing and putting away a book one student was reading. That student was the only one in the class who paid much attention to the whole episode.

Praising Behavior That Is Incompatible with Misbehavior

Praise can be a powerful motivator for many students. One strategy for reducing misbehavior in class is to make sure to praise students for behaviors that are incompatible with the misbehavior you want to reduce. That is, catch students in the act of doing right. For example, if students often get out of their seats without permission, praise them on the occasions when they do get to work right away.

Praising Other Students

It is often possible to get one student to behave by praising others for behaving. For example, if Polly is goofing off, the teacher might say, "I'm glad to see so many students working so well—Jake is doing a good job, Carol is doing well, José and Michelle are working nicely. . . ." When Polly finally does get to work, the teacher should praise her, too, without dwelling on her past inattention: "I see James and Walter and Polly doing a good job."

Verbal Reminders

If a nonverbal cue is impossible or ineffective, a simple verbal reminder might help to bring a student into line. The reminder should be given immediately after the student misbehaves; delayed reminders are usually ineffective. If possible, the reminder should state what students are supposed to be doing rather than dwelling on what they are doing wrong. For example, it is better to say, "John, please attend to your own work," than, "John, stop copying off of Alfredo's paper." Stating the reminder positively communicates more positive expectations for future behavior than does a negative statement (Evertson et al., 2003). Also, the reminder should focus on the behavior, not on the student. Although a particular student behavior may be intolerable, the student himself or herself is always accepted and welcome in the classroom.

Repeated Reminders

Most often a nonverbal cue, reinforcement of other students, or a simple reminder will be enough to end minor misbehavior. However, sometimes students test the teacher's resolve by failing to do what has been asked of them or by arguing or giving excuses. This testing will diminish over time if students learn that teachers mean what they say and will use appropriate measures to enforce an orderly, productive classroom environment.

When a student refuses to comply with a simple reminder, one strategy to attempt first is a repetition of the reminder, ignoring any irrelevant excuse or argument. Canter and Canter (2002), in a program called **Assertive Discipline,** call this strategy the *broken record.* Teachers should decide what they want the student to do, state this clearly to the student (statement of want), and then repeat it until the student complies. An example of the broken record from Canter and Canter (2002) follows:

Assertive Discipline
Method of giving a clear, firm, unhostile response to student misbehavior.

Teacher: "Craig, I want you to start your project now." (Statement of want)

Craig: "I will as soon as I finish my game. Just a few more minutes."

Teacher (firmly): "Craig, I understand, but I want you to start your project now." (Broken record)

Craig: "You never give me enough time with the games."

Teacher (calmly, firmly): "That's not the point. I want you to start your project now."

Craig: "I don't like doing my project."

Teacher (firmly): "I understand, but I want you to start your project."

Craig: "Wow, you really mean it. I'll get to work."

This teacher avoided a lengthy argument with a student by simply repeating the request. When Craig said, "You never give me enough time with the games," and, "I don't like doing my project," he was not inviting a serious discussion but was simply procrastinating and testing the teacher's resolve. Rather than going off on a tangent with him, the teacher calmly restated the request, turning aside his excuses with "That's not the point . . ." and "I understand, but. . . ." Of course, if Craig had had a legitimate issue to discuss or a valid complaint, the teacher would have dealt with it; but all too often students' arguments or excuses are nothing more than a means of drawing out an interaction with the teacher to avoid getting down to work (see Walker, Ramsey, & Gresham, 2003/2004a). Recall how Ms. Cavalho refused to be drawn into a discussion of Gloria's lateness when it was Mark's behavior that was at issue.

Applying Consequences

When all previous steps have been ineffective in getting the student to comply with a clearly stated and reasonable request, the final step is to pose a choice to the student: Either comply or suffer the consequences (Fisher & Mazur, 1997; Tierno, 1993). Examples of consequences are sending the student out of class, making the student miss a few minutes of recess or some other privilege, having the student stay after school, and calling the student's parents. A consequence for not complying with the teacher's request should be mildly unpleasant, short in duration, and applied as soon as possible after the behavior occurs. Certainty is far more important than severity; students must know that consequences follow misbehavior as night follows day. One disadvantage of using severe or long-lasting punishment (e.g., no recess for a week) is that it can create resentment in the student and a defiant attitude. Also, it might be difficult to follow through on severe or long-lasting consequences. Mild but certain consequences communicate, "I cannot tolerate that sort of behavior, but I care about you and want you to rejoin the class as soon as you are ready."

Before presenting a student with a consequence for noncompliance, teachers must be absolutely certain that they can and will follow through if necessary. When a teacher says, "You may choose to get to work right away, or you may choose to spend 5 minutes of your recess doing your work here," the teacher must be certain that someone will be available to monitor the student in the classroom during recess. Vague or empty threats ("You stop that or I'll make you wish you had!" or "You get to work or I'll have you suspended for a month!") are worse than useless. If teachers are not prepared to follow through with consequences, students will learn to shrug them off.

After a consequence has been applied, the teacher should avoid referring to the incident. For example, when the student returns from a 10-minute exclusion from class, the teacher should accept her or him back without any sarcasm or recriminations. The student now deserves a fresh start.

*H*OW IS APPLIED BEHAVIOR ANALYSIS USED TO MANAGE MORE SERIOUS BEHAVIOR PROBLEMS?

The previous section discussed how to deal with behaviors that might be appropriate on the playing field but are out of line in the classroom. There are other behaviors that are not appropriate anywhere. These include fighting, stealing, destruction of property, and gross disrespect for teachers or other school staff. These are far less common than routine classroom misbehavior but far more serious. Behavioral learning theories, described in Chapter 5, have direct application to classroom management. Simply put, behavioral learning theories hold that behaviors that are not reinforced or are punished will diminish in frequency. The following sections present **applied behavior analysis,** an analysis of classroom behavior in terms of behavioral concepts, and give specific strategies for preventing and dealing with misbehavior (Alberto & Troutman, 1999; Walker & Shea, 1999).

> **ON THE WEB**
>
> For articles on applied behavior analysis visit the website for the Cambridge Center for Behavioral Studies **www.behavior.org** and click on About Behavior Analysis.

How Student Misbehavior Is Maintained

A basic principle of behavioral learning theories is that if any behavior persists over time, it is being maintained by some reinforcer. To reduce misbehavior in the classroom, we must understand which reinforcers maintain misbehavior in the first place.

The most common reinforcer for classroom misbehavior is attention—from the teacher, the peer group, or both. Students receiving one-to-one tutoring rarely misbehave, both because they already have the undivided attention of an adult and because no classmates are present to attend to any negative behavior. In the typical classroom, however, students have to go out of their way to get the teacher's personal attention, and they have an audience of peers who might encourage or applaud their misdeeds.

Teacher's Attention Sometimes students misbehave because they want the teacher's attention, even if it is negative. This is a more common reason for misbehavior than many teachers think. A puzzled teacher might say, "I don't know what is wrong with Nathan. I have to stay with him all day to keep him working! Sometimes I get exasperated and yell at him. My words fall off him like water off a duck's back. He even smiles when I'm scolding him!"

When students appear to misbehave to gain the teacher's attention, the solution is relatively easy: Pay attention to these students when they are doing well, and ignore them (as much as possible) when they misbehave. When ignoring their actions is impossible, imposing time out (e.g., sending these students to a quiet corner or to the principal's office) might be effective.

Peers' Attention Another very common reason that students misbehave is to get the attention and approval of their peers. The classic instance of this is the class clown, who is obviously performing for the amusement of his or her classmates. However, many other forms of misbehavior are motivated primarily by peer attention and approval—in

applied behavior analysis
The application of behavioral learning principles to understanding and changing behavior.

This student misbehaves to get her peer's attention. Which responses to peer-supported misbehavior will you use in the classroom?

INTASC

4 Multiple Instructional Strategies

group contingencies
Class rewards that depend on the behavior of all students.

fact, few students completely disregard the potential impact of their behavior on their classmates. For example, students who refuse to do what the teacher has asked are consciously or unconsciously weighing the effect of their defiance on their standing among their classmates.

Even preschoolers and early elementary school students misbehave to gain peer attention, but beginning around the third grade (and especially during the middle school/junior high school years), it is particularly likely that student misbehavior is linked to peer attention and support. As students enter adolescence, the peer group takes on extreme importance, and peer norms begin to favor independence from authority. When older children and teenagers engage in serious delinquent acts (such as vandalism, theft, and assault), they are usually supported by a delinquent peer group.

Strategies for reducing peer-supported misbehavior are quite different from those for dealing with misbehavior that is meant to capture the teacher's attention. Ignoring misbehavior will be ineffective if the misbehavior is reinforced by peers. For example, if a student is balancing a book on his or her head and the class is laughing, the behavior can hardly be ignored, because it will continue as long as the class is interested (and will encourage others to behave likewise). Further, scolding might only attract more attention from classmates or, worse, enhance the student's standing among peers. Similarly, if two students are whispering or talking to each other, they are reinforcing each other for misbehaving, and ignoring their behavior will only encourage more of it.

There are two primary responses to peer-supported misbehavior. One is to remove the offender from the classroom to deprive her or him of peer attention. Another is to use **group contingencies,** strategies in which the entire class (or groups of students within the class) is rewarded on the basis of everyone's behavior. Under group contingencies, all students benefit from their classmates' good behavior, so peer support for misbehavior is removed. Group contingencies and other behavior management strategies for peer-supported misbehavior are described in more detail in the following sections.

Release from Unpleasant States or Activities   A third important reinforcer for misbehavior is release from boredom, frustration, fatigue, or unpleasant activities. As was explained in Chapter 5, escaping or avoiding an unpleasant stimulus is a reinforcer. Some students see much of what happens in school as unpleasant, boring, frustrating, or tiring. This is particularly true of students who experience repeated failure in school. But even the most able and motivated students feel bored or frustrated at times. Students often misbehave just to escape from unpleasant activities. This can be clearly seen with students who frequently ask permission to get a drink of water, go to the washroom, or sharpen their pencils. Such students are more likely to make these requests during independent seatwork than during cooperative learning activities or even a lecture, because seatwork can be frustrating or anxiety-provoking for students who have little confidence in their academic abilities. More serious misbehaviors can also be partially or completely motivated by a desire for release from boredom, frustration, or fatigue. A student might misbehave just to stir things up. Sometimes students misbehave precisely so that they will be sent out of the classroom. Obviously, sending such a student to the hall or the principal's office can be counterproductive.

The best solution for misbehaviors arising from boredom, frustration, or fatigue is prevention. Students rarely misbehave during interesting, varied, engaging lessons. Actively involving students in lessons can head off misbehaviors due to boredom or fatigue. Use of cooperative learning methods or other means of involving students in an active way can be helpful. A teacher can prevent frustration by using materials that ensure a high success rate for all, by making sure that all students are challenged but none is overwhelmed. Changing instruction and assessments to help students succeed can be an effective means of resolving frustration-related behavior problems.

CONNECTIONS

For more information about behavioral theory, see Chapter 5, page 138.

Principles of Applied Behavior Analysis

The behavior management strategies outlined earlier (e.g., nonverbal cues, reminders, mild but certain punishment) might be described as informal applications of behavioral learning theories. These practices, plus the prevention of misbehavior by the use of efficient class management and engaging lessons, will be sufficient to create a good learning environment in most classrooms.

However, more systematic methods are sometimes needed. In classrooms in which most students are well behaved but a few have persistent behavior problems, individual behavior management strategies can be effective. In classrooms in which many students have behavior problems, particularly when there is peer support for misbehavior, whole-class strategies or group contingencies might be needed. Such strategies are most often required when many low-achieving or poorly motivated students are put in one class, as often happens in special-education classes and in schools that use tracking or other between-class ability grouping methods.

Setting up and using any applied behavior analysis program requires following a series of steps that proceeds from the observation of the behavior through program implementation to program evaluation (see Schloss & Smith, 1994). The steps listed here are, to a greater or lesser extent, part of all applied behavior analysis programs:

CONNECTIONS

For more information about the problems of tracking, see Chapter 9, pages 279–283.

1. Identify target behavior(s) and reinforcer(s).
2. Establish a baseline for the target behavior.
3. Choose a reinforcer and criteria for reinforcement.
4. If necessary, choose a punisher and criteria for punishment.

5. Observe behavior during program implementation, and compare it to baseline.
6. When the behavior management program is working, reduce the frequency of reinforcement.

Individual behavior management strategies are useful for coping with individual students who have persistent behavior problems in school. **Behavior modification** is a systematic application of antecedents and consequences to change behavior (Alberto & Troutman, 1999; Walker & Shea, 1999).

Identify Target Behaviors and Reinforcers

The first step in implementing a behavior management program is to observe the misbehaving student to identify one or a small number of behaviors to target first and to see what reinforcers maintain the behavior(s). Another purpose of this observation is to establish a baseline against which to compare improvements. A structured individual behavior management program should aim to change only one behavior or a small set of closely related behaviors. Tackling too many behaviors at a time risks failure with all of them, because the student might not clearly see what he or she must do to be reinforced.

The first behavior targeted should be one that is serious; is easy to observe; and, most important, occurs frequently. For example, if a child gets into fights in the playground every few days but gets out of his or her seat without permission several times per hour, you might start with the out-of-seat behavior and deal with the fighting later. Ironically, the more frequent and persistent a behavior, the easier it is to extinguish. This is because positive or negative consequences can be applied frequently, making the connection between behavior and consequence clear to the student.

In observing a student, try to determine what reinforcer(s) are maintaining the target behavior. If a student misbehaves with others (e.g., talks without permission, swears, or teases) or if a student's misbehavior usually attracts the attention of others (e.g., clowning), then you might conclude that the behavior is peer-supported. If the behavior does not attract much peer attention but always requires teacher attention (e.g., getting out of seat without permission), then you might conclude that the behavior is supported by your own attention.

Establish Baseline Behavior

Observe the student to see how often the target behavior occurs. Before you do this, you will need to clearly define exactly what constitutes the behavior. For example, if the target behavior is "bothering classmates," you will have to decide what specific behaviors constitute "bothering" (perhaps teasing, interrupting, and taking materials).

Select Reinforcers and Criteria for Reinforcement

Typical classroom reinforcers include praise, privileges, and tangible rewards. Praise is especially effective for students who misbehave to get the teacher's attention. It is often a good idea to start a behavior management program by using praise for appropriate behavior to see whether this is sufficient. However, be prepared to use stronger reinforcers if praise is not enough (see McDaniel, 1993; Schloss & Smith, 1994). In addition to praise, many teachers find it useful to give students stars, "smilies," or other small rewards when students behave appropriately. Some teachers use a rubber stamp to mark students' papers with a symbol indicating good work. These small rewards make the teacher's praise more concrete and visible and let students take their work home and receive praise from their parents. Figure 11.2 provides suggestions for social reinforcers and preferred activities to encourage positive behavior.

Select Punishers and Criteria for Punishment, If Necessary

Behavioral learning theories strongly favor the use of reinforcers for appropriate behavior rather than

behavior modification
Systematic application of antecedents and consequences to change behavior.

Social Reinforcers

Praising Words and Phrases

"That's clever."

"Good thinking."

"That shows a great deal of work."

"You really pay attention."

"You should show this to your father."

"That was very kind of you."

"I'm pleased with that."

"Keep up the good work."

"I appreciate your help."

"Now you've got the hang of it."

"That's an interesting point."

"You make it look easy."

"I like the way you got started on your homework."

Nearness

Walking together

Sitting together

Eating lunch together

Playing games with the student

Working after school together

Physical Contact

Touching

Hugging

Shaking hands

Holding hands

Expressions

Smiling

Winking

Nodding up and down

Looking interested

Laughing

Preferred Activities

Going first

Running errands

Getting to sit where he or she wants to

Telling a joke to the class

Having a party

Doing artwork related to studies

Choosing the game for recess

Earning an extra or longer recess

Helping the teacher

Visiting another class

Playing a short game: connect the dots, tic-tac-toe

Taking a class pet home for the weekend

Being team captain

Seeing a movie

Playing with a magnet or other science equipment

Reading with a friend

Getting free time in the library

Being asked what he or she would like to do

Planning a class trip or project

FIGURE 11.2
Social Reinforcers and Preferred Activities

From Vernon F. Jones and Louise S. Jones, *Comprehensive Classroom Management* (4th ed.), p. 363. Copyright © 1995 by Allyn & Bacon. Adapted by permission.

punishers for inappropriate behavior. The reasons for this are practical as well as ethical. Punishment often creates resentment; so even if it solves one problem, it could create others (see Skinner, 1968). Even if punishment would work as well as reinforcement, it should be avoided because it is not conducive to the creation of a happy, healthy classroom environment (Webber & Scheuermann, 1993). Punishment of one kind or another is necessary in some circumstances, and it should be used without qualms when reinforcement strategies are impossible or ineffective. However, a program of punishment for misbehavior (e.g., depriving a student of privileges, never physical punishment) should always be the last option considered, never the first. A punisher is any unpleasant stimulus that an individual will try to avoid. Common punishers used in schools are reprimands, being sent out of class or to the principal's office, and detention or missed recess. Corporal punishment (e.g., spanking) is illegal in some states and districts and highly restricted in others, but regardless of laws or policies, it should never be used in schools. It is neither a necessary nor an effective response to misbehavior in school (Evans & Richardson, 1995; Gregory, 1995).

O'Leary and O'Leary (1972) list seven principles for the effective and humane use of punishment:

1. Use punishment sparingly.
2. Make it clear to the child why he or she is being punished.
3. Provide the child with an alternative means of obtaining some positive reinforcement.
4. Reinforce the child for behaviors that are incompatible with those you wish to weaken (e.g., if you punish for being off-task, also reinforce for being on-task).
5. Never use physical punishment.
6. Never punish when you are in a very angry or emotional state.
7. Punish when a behavior starts rather than when it ends.

One effective punisher is called **time out.** The teacher tells a misbehaving student to go to a separate part of the classroom, the hall, the principal's or vice principal's office, or another teacher's class. If possible, the place where the student is sent should be uninteresting and out of view of classmates. One advantage of time-out procedures is that they remove the student from the attention of her or his classmates. Therefore, time out may be especially effective for students whose misbehavior is motivated primarily by peer attention. The sit-and-watch procedure described in Chapter 5 is a good example of the use of time out. Students who misbehaved in a physical education class were given a sand timer and asked to sit and watch for 3 minutes. This consequence, applied immediately and consistently, soon virtually eliminated misbehavior (White & Bailey, 1990).

Teachers should assign time outs infrequently. When they do assign them, they should do so calmly and surely. The student is to go straight to the time-out area and stay there until the prescribed time is up. Time-out assignments should be brief; about 5 minutes is usually adequate. However, timing should begin only after the student settles down; if the student yells or argues, that time should not count. During time out, no one should speak to the student. Teachers should not scold the student during time out. Students should be told why they are being given time out but should not otherwise be lectured. If the principal's office is used, the principal should be asked not to speak to the student.

Reduce the Frequency of Reinforcement Once a reinforcement program has been in operation for a while and the student's behavior has improved and stabilized at a new level, the frequency of reinforcement can be reduced. Initially, reinforcers might be applied to every instance of appropriate behavior; as time goes on, every other instance, then every several instances, might be reinforced. Reducing the frequency of reinforcement helps to maintain the new behaviors over the long run and aids in extending the behaviors to other settings.

Applied Behavior Analysis Programs

Home-based reinforcement strategies and daily report card programs are examples of applied behavioral analysis involving individual students. A group contingency program is an example of an applied behavioral analysis in which the whole class is involved.

Home-Based Reinforcement Some of the most practical and effective classroom management methods are **home-based reinforcement strategies** (see Barth, 1979).

CONNECTIONS

For more information about sit-and-watch as a punishment for misbehavior, see Chapter 5, page 144 and Figure 5.2.

CERTIFICATION POINTER

For your teacher certification test you will need to demonstrate your understanding of appropriate applications of applied behavioral analysis.

time out

Removal of a student from a situation in which misbehavior was reinforced.

home-based reinforcement strategies

Behavior modification strategies in which a student's school behavior is reported to parents, who supply rewards.

Teachers give students a daily or weekly report card to take home, and parents are instructed to provide special privileges or rewards to students on the basis of these teacher reports. Home-based reinforcement is not a new idea; a museum in Vermont displays weekly report cards from the 1860s.

Home-based reinforcement has several advantages over other, equally effective behavior management strategies. First, parents can give much more potent rewards and privileges than schools can. For example, parents control access to such activities as television, trips to the store, and going out with friends. Parents also know what their own children like and can therefore provide more individualized privileges than the school can. Second, home-based reinforcement gives parents frequent good news about their children. Parents of disruptive children usually hear from the school only when their child has done something wrong. This is bad for parent–school relations and leads to much blame and finger-pointing. Third, home-based reinforcement is easy to administer. The teacher can involve any adults who deal with the child (other teachers, bus drivers, playground or lunch monitors) in the program by having the student carry a daily report card all day. Finally, over time, daily report cards can be replaced by weekly report cards and then biweekly report cards without loss in effectiveness, until the school's usual 6- or 9-week report cards can be used.

"Mrs. Jones, I'm just calling to say that Tommy had a great day in school today . . . Mrs. Jones? . . . Mrs. Jones?"

Daily Report Cards Figure 11.3 presents a daily report card for Homer Heath, an elementary school student. His teacher, Ms. Casa, rated his behavior and schoolwork at the end of each academic period, and she arranged to have the lunch monitor and the recess monitor rate his behavior when Homer was with them. Homer was responsible for carrying his report card with him at all times and for making sure that it was

STUDENT _Homer H._	DAILY REPORT CARD		DATE _March 21_
PERIOD	**BEHAVIOR**	**SCHOOLWORK**	**TEACHER**
Reading	1 2 ③ 4	1 ② 3 4	_Ms. Casa_
Math	1 2 3 ④	1 2 3 ④	_Ms. Casa_
Lunch	1 2 ③ 4		_Mr. Mason_
Recess	1 2 ③ 4		_Ms. Hauser_
Language	1 2 3 ④	1 2 3 ④	_Ms. Casa_
Science/Soc. Stud.	1 2 ③ 4	1 2 ③ 4	_Ms. Casa_

	1 = Poor 2 = Fair 3 = Good 4 = Excellent	1 = Assignments not completed 2 = Assignments completed poorly 3 = Assignments completed adequately 4 = Assignments completed—excellent!

Total rating ___33___   ☺   Score needed ___30___

FIGURE 11.3
Example of a Daily Report Card

Teachers who use a home-based reinforcement program must set up a daily report card so that a student's work and behavior can be assessed and reported to the student's parents.

From E. Dougherty and A. Dougherty, "The Daily Report Card," *Psy-chology in the Schools, 14,* pp. 191–195. Copyright © 1977 by the Clinical Psychology Publishing Co., Inc., Brandon, Vermont. Reprinted by permission.

marked and initialed at the end of each period. Whenever he made at least 30 points, his parents agreed to give him a special privilege: His father was to read him an extra story before bedtime and let him stay up 15 minutes longer than usual. Whenever he forgot to bring home his report card, his parents were to assume that he did not meet the criterion. If Homer had been a junior or senior high school student or if he had been in a departmentalized elementary school (where he changed classes for each subject), he would have carried his report card to every class, and each teacher would have marked it. Obviously, this approach requires some coordination among teachers, but the effort is certainly worthwhile if the daily report card dramatically reduces a student's misbehaviors and increases his or her academic output, as it has in dozens of studies evaluating this method (Barth, 1979).

Theory into PRACTICE

Using a Daily Report Card System

Steps for setting up and implementing a daily report card system are as follows:

1. Decide which behaviors to include in the daily report card. Choose a behavior or set of behaviors on which the daily report card is to be based. Devise a rating scheme for each behavior, and construct a standard report card form. Your daily report card might be more or less elaborate than the one in Figure 11.3. For example, you might break behavior down into more precise categories, such as getting along with others, staying on-task, and following class rules.

2. Explain the program to parents. Home-based reinforcement programs depend on parent participation, so it is critical to inform parents about the program and to obtain their cooperation. Parents should be told what the daily report card means and should be asked to reward their children whenever they bring home a good report card. In presenting the program to parents, teachers should explain what parents might do to reward their children. Communications with parents should be brief, positive, and informal and should generate a feeling that "we're going to solve this together." The program should focus on rewarding good behavior rather than punishing bad behavior. Examples of rewards parents might use at home (adapted from Walker & Shea, 1999) follow:

- Special activities with a parent (e.g., reading, flying a kite, building a model, shopping, playing a game, going to the zoo)
- Special foods
- Baking cookies or cooking
- Operating equipment that is usually reserved for adults (e.g., the dishwasher or vacuum cleaner)
- Access to special games, toys, or equipment
- Small rewards (such as coloring books, paper, comic books, erasers, or stickers)
- Additional play time, television time, and the like
- Having a friend spend the night
- Later bedtime or curfew

Parents should be encouraged to choose rewards that they can give every day (that is, nothing too expensive or difficult).

The best rewards are ones that build closeness between parent and child, such as doing special activities together. Many children who have behavior problems in school also have them at home and might have less than ideal relationships with their parents. Home-based reinforcement programs provide an opportunity for parents to show their love for their child at a time when the child has something to be proud of. A special time with Dad can be especially valuable as a reward for good behavior in school and for building the father–son or father–daughter relationship.

3. When behavior improves, reduce the frequency of the report. When home-based reinforcement works, it often works dramatically. Once the student's behavior has improved and has stabilized, it is time to decrease the frequency of the reports to parents (of course, keep the parents informed about this change). Report cards might then be issued only weekly (for larger but less frequent rewards). As was noted in Chapter 5, the best way to ensure maintenance is to thin out the reinforcement schedule—that is, to increase the interval between reinforcers.

Group Contingency Programs A **group contingency program** is a reinforcement system in which an entire group is rewarded on the basis of the behavior of the group members. Teachers have always used group contingencies, as in "We'll go to lunch as soon as all students have put their work away and are quiet." When the teacher says this, any one student can cause the entire class to be late to lunch. Or the teacher might say, "If the class averages at least ninety on tomorrow's quiz, then you'll all be excused from homework for the rest of the week." This group contingency will depend on the average performance of all group members rather than on any single student's performance.

One important advantage of group contingencies is that they are relatively easy to administer. Most often, the whole class is either rewarded or not rewarded, so the teacher need not do one thing with some students and something else with others. For example, suppose a teacher says, "If the whole class follows the class rules this morning, we will have five extra minutes of recess." If the class does earn the extra recess, they all get it together; the teacher does not have to arrange to have some students stay out longer while others are called inside.

The theory behind group contingencies is that when a group is rewarded on the basis of its members' behavior, the group members will encourage one another to do whatever helps the group gain the reward (Slavin, 1990). Group contingencies can turn the same peer pressure that often supports misbehaviors to pressure opposing misbehavior. When the class can earn extra recess only if all students are well behaved all morning, no one is liable to find it funny when Joan balances a book on her head or Quinn speaks disrespectfully to the teacher.

Group contingencies have been used successfully in many forms and for many purposes (Marzano, 2003). Barrish and colleagues (1969) divided a fourth-grade class into two teams during math period. When the teacher saw any member of a team disobeying class rules, the whole team received a check mark on the chalkboard. If a team had five or fewer check marks at the end of the period, all team members would take part in a free-time activity at the end of the day. If both teams got more than five check marks, the one that got fewer would receive the free time. A more recent study also found positive effects of the good-behavior game on the behavior of first-graders (Dolan et al., 1993).

CERTIFICATION POINTER

You teacher certification test may require you to describe types of classroom management procedures that would tend to make class discussions more productive.

group contingency program
A program in which rewards or punishments are given to a class as a whole for adhering to or violating rules of conduct.

Theory into **PRACTICE**

Establishing a Group Contingency Program

As was noted earlier, a group contingency behavior management program can be as simple as the statement "Class, if you are all in your seats, on-task, and quiet this morning, you may have 5 extra minutes of recess." However, a little more structure than this can increase the effectiveness of the group contingency.

1. Decide which behaviors will be reinforced. As in any whole-class behavior modification program, the first step in setting up a group contingency is to establish a set of class rules.

2. Set up a developmentally appropriate point system. There are essentially three ways to implement a group contingency behavior management program. One is simply to rate class behavior each period or during each activity. That is, an elementary school class might receive 0 to 5 points during each individual instructional period such as reading, language arts, and math. A secondary school class might receive one overall rating each period or separate ratings for behavior and completed assignments. The class would then be rewarded each day or week if they exceeded a preestablished number of points.

Another way to set up a group contingency program is to rate the class at various times during the day. For example, you might set a timer to ring on the average of once every 10 minutes (but varying randomly from 1 to 20 minutes). If the whole class is conforming to class rules when the timer rings, then the class earns a point. The same program can be used without the timer if the teacher gives the class a point every 10 minutes or so if all students are conforming to class rules. Canter and Canter (1992) suggest that teachers use a bag of marbles and a jar, putting a marble into the jar from time to time whenever the class is following rules. Each marble would be worth 30 seconds of extra recess. In secondary schools, where extra recess is not possible, each marble might represent 30 seconds of break time held at the end of the period on Friday.

3. Consider deducting points for serious misbehavior. The group contingency reward system by itself should help to improve student behavior. However, it might still be necessary to react to occasional serious misbehavior. For example, you might deduct 10 points for any instance of fighting or of serious disrespect for the teacher. When points must be deducted, do not negotiate with students about it. Just deduct them, explaining why they must be deducted and reminding students that they may earn them back if they follow class rules.

4. When behavior improves, reduce the frequency of the points and reinforcers. Initially, the group contingency should be applied every day. When the class's behavior improves and stabilizes at a new level for about a week, you may change to giving rewards once a week. Ultimately, the class may graduate from the point-and-reward system entirely, though feedback and praise based on class behavior should continue.

5. Combine group and individual contingencies if necessary. The use of group contingencies need not rule out individual contingencies for students who need them. For example, students who continue to have problems in a class using a group contingency might still receive daily or weekly report cards to take home to their parents.

Ethics of Behavioral Methods

The behavior analysis strategies described in this chapter can be powerful. Properly applied, they will usually bring the behavior of even the most disruptive students to manageable levels. However, there is a danger that teachers might use such techniques to overcontrol students. They could be so concerned about getting students to sit down, stay quiet, and look productive that they lose sight of the fact that school is for learning, not for social control. Many years ago, Winett and Winkler (1972) wrote an article titled "Current Behavior Modification in the Classroom: Be Still, Be Quiet, Be Docile," in which they warned that behavior modification–based classroom management systems are being misused if teachers mistakenly believe that a quiet class is a learning class. This point parallels the basic premise of the QAIT model of effective instruction presented in Chapter 9. Behavior management systems can increase time for learning; but unless the quality of instruction, appropriate levels of instruction, and incentives for learning are also adequate, the additional time might be wasted (Emmer & Aussiker, 1990).

CONNECTIONS

For more information about the QAIT model, see Chapter 9, page 277.

Some people object to applied behavior analysis on the basis that it constitutes bribing students to do what they ought to do anyway. However, all classrooms use rewards and punishers (such as grades, praise, scolding, suspension). Applied behavior analysis strategies simply use these rewards in a more systematic way and avoid punishers as much as possible.

Applied behavior analysis methods should be used only when it is clear that preventive or informal methods of improving classroom management are not enough to create a positive environment for learning. It is unethical to overapply these methods, but it might be equally unethical to fail to apply them when they could avert serious problems. For example, it might be unethical to refer a child to special education or to suspend, expel, or retain a child on the basis of a pattern of behavior problems before using positive behavior management methods long enough to see whether they can resolve the problem without more draconian measures.

How CAN SERIOUS BEHAVIOR PROBLEMS BE PREVENTED?

Everyone misbehaves. There is hardly a person on earth who has not at some time done something he or she knew to be wrong or even illegal. However, some people's misbehavior is far more frequent and/or serious than others', and students in this category cause their teachers and school administrators (not to mention their parents and themselves) a disproportionate amount of trouble and concern.

Serious behavior problems are not evenly distributed among students or schools. Most students who are identified as having severe behavior problems are male; from 3 to 8 times as many boys as girls are estimated to have serious conduct problems (Perkins & Borden, 2003). Serious delinquency is far more common among students from impoverished backgrounds, particularly in urban locations. Students with poor family relationships are also much more likely than other students to become involved in serious misbehavior and delinquency, as are students who are low in achievement and those who have attendance problems (see Hawkins et al., 2000; Herrenkohl et al., 2001; Perkins & Borden, 2003).

The school has an important role to play in preventing or managing serious misbehavior and delinquency, but the student and the school are only one part of the story. Delinquent behavior often involves the police, courts, and social service agencies, as well as students' parents and peers. However, there are some guidelines for prevention of delinquency and serious misbehaviors.

Preventive Programs

As noted earlier in this chapter, the easiest behavior problems to deal with are those that never occur. There are many approaches that have promise for preventing serious behavior problems. One is simply creating safe and prosocial classroom environments and openly discussing risky behaviors and ways to avoid them (Learning First Alliance, 2001; Stipek, de la Sota, & Weishaupt, 1999). Another is giving students opportunities to play prosocial roles as volunteers, tutors, or leaders in activities that benefit their school and community (Allen, 2003; Rosenberg, McKeon, & Dinero, 1999). Creating democratic, participatory classrooms can give students ways of achieving recognition and control in a positive environment, reducing the need to act out (Hyman & Snook, 2000). Smaller, less impersonal schools have been found to reduce bullying and violence (Pellegrini, 2002). Programs that improve academic achievement also often affect behavior as well (Barr & Parrett, 2001). These kinds of strategies embed preventive activities in the day-to-day lives of students, rather than singling them out for special treatment.

Identifying Causes of Misbehavior

Even though some types of students are more prone to misbehavior than others, these characteristics do not cause misbehavior. Some students misbehave because they perceive that the rewards for misbehavior outweigh the rewards for good behavior. For example, students who do not experience success in school might perceive that the potential rewards for hard work and good behavior are small, so they turn to other sources of rewards. Some, particularly those who are failing in many different domains, find their niche in groups that hold norms that devalue achievement and other prosocial behavior (Wentzel, 2003). The role of the delinquent peer group in maintaining delinquent behavior cannot be overstated. Delinquent acts among adolescents and preadolescents are usually done in groups and are supported by antisocial peer norms (Perkins & Borden, 2003; Walker, Colvin, & Ramsey, 1995).

Enforcing Rules and Practices

Expectations that students will conform to school rules must be consistently expressed. For example, graffiti or other vandalism must be repaired at once so that other students do not get the idea that misbehavior is common or accepted. On the other hand, rules should be enforced firmly but fairly; rigid applications of "zero tolerance" policies have often been found to be counterproductive (Skiba, 2000).

Enforcing School Attendance

Truancy and delinquency are strongly related; when students are out of school, they are often in the community making trouble. There are many effective means of reducing truancy (Haslinger, Kelly, & O'Lara, 1996; Lehr et al., 2003; Minke & Bear, 2000). Brooks (1975) had high school students with serious attendance problems carry cards to be signed by their teachers at the end of each period they attended. Students received a ticket for each period attended, plus bonus tickets for good behavior in class and for going 5 days without missing a class. The tickets were used in a drawing for a variety of prizes. Before the program began, the target students were absent 60 percent of all school days. During the program, absences dropped to 19 percent of school days. Over the same period, truancy among other students with attendance problems who were not in the program increased from 59 percent to 79 percent.

    Barber and Kagey (1977) markedly increased attendance in an entire elementary school by making full participation in once-a-month parties depend on student attendance. Several activities were provided during the parties, and students could earn access to some or all of them according to the number of days they attended class.

Fiordaliso, Lordeman, Filipczak, and Friedman (1977) increased attendance among chronically truant junior high school students by having the school call their parents whenever the students were present several days in a row. The number of days before calling depended on how severe the student's truancy had been. Parents of the most truant students, who had been absent 6 or more days per month, were called after the student attended for only 3 consecutive days.

Check and Connect

Check and Connect is a model that has school-based "monitors" work with students, families, and school personnel to improve the attendance and engagement of students in schools. The program has documented significant gains on attendance in elementary schools (Lehr, Sinclair, & Christenson, 2004) and on dropout and overall school success in middle schools (Sinclair, Christenson, Evelo, & Hurley, 1998). Check and Connect includes the following elements (Lehr et al., 2004, p. 284):

INTASC
10 Partnerships

- *Relationship building:* Fostering mutual trust and open communication, nurtured through a long-term commitment that is focused on students' educational success
- *Routine monitoring of alterable indicators:* Systemically checking warning signs of withdrawal (attendance, academic performance, behavior) that are readily available to school personnel and that can be altered through intervention
- *Individualized and timely intervention:* Providing support that is tailored to individual student needs, based on level of engagement with school, associated influences of home and school, and the leveraging of local resources
- *Long-term commitment:* Committing to stay with students and families for at least two years, including the ability to follow students during transitions across school levels and follow highly mobile youth from school to school and program to program
- *Persistence plus:* Maintaining a persistent source of academic motivation, a continuity of familiarity with the youth and family, and a consistency in the message that "education is important for your future"
- *Problem solving:* Promoting the acquisition of skills to resolve conflict constructively and to look for solutions rather than a source of blame
- *Affiliation with school and learning:* Facilitating students' access to and active participation in school-related activities and events.

Avoiding Tracking

Tracking (between-class ability grouping) should be avoided if possible (see Chapter 9). Low-track classes are ideal breeding grounds for antisocial delinquent peer groups (Howard, 1978). Similarly, behavioral and academic problems should be dealt with in the context of the regular class as much as possible, rather than in separate special-education classes (Madden & Slavin, 1983b; Safer, 1982).

Practicing Intervention

Classroom management strategies should be used to reduce inappropriate behavior before it escalates into delinquency. Improving students' behavior and success in school can prevent delinquency (Walker, Ramsey, & Gresham, 2003/2004a,b). For example, Hawkins et al. (2001) used preventive classroom management methods such as those emphasized in this chapter along with interactive teaching and cooperative learning to help low-achieving seventh-graders. In comparison with control-group students, the students who were involved in the program were suspended and expelled less often, had better attitudes toward school, and were more likely to expect to complete high school. Use of applied behavior analysis programs for misbehavior in class can also contribute to the prevention of delinquency (Walker & Gresham, 2003). Group contingencies can be especially effective with predelinquent students, because this strategy can deprive students of peer support for misbehavior.

Requesting Family Involvement

Involve the student's home in any response to serious misbehavior. When misbehavior occurs, parents should be notified. If misbehavior persists, parents should be involved in establishing a program, such as a home-based reinforcement program, to coordinate home and school responses to misbehavior.

> **ON THE WEB**
>
> For more on how schools can establish a climate that reduces behaviors such as ridicule, bullying, and violence, go to **www.dontlaugh.org** or **www.nomorebullies.com**.

Using Peer Mediation

CERTIFICATION POINTER

A teacher certification question may ask you to respond to a case study by suggesting ways of helping students develop the social skills that would help resolve conflicts presented in the case.

Students can be trained to serve as peer mediators, particularly to resolve conflicts between fellow students. Students who are having problems with other students might be asked to take these problems to peer mediators rather than to adults for resolution, and the peer mediators themselves might actively look for interpersonal problems among their classmates and offer help when they occur. Peer mediators have been found to be effective in resolving a variety of interpersonal problems, from insults and perceptions of unfairness among students to stealing to physical aggression (Johnson & Johnson, 2001; Troop & Asher, 1999). However, peer mediators need to be carefully trained and monitored if they are to be effective (Latham, 1997a). Figure 11.4 shows a guide for peer mediators used in one conflict management program.

These students are demonstrating peer mediation as a way to resolve a conflict. As a teacher, how would you advise student mediators to handle conflicts with a group of students?

1. Introduce yourselves: "Hi, my name is _____. I'm conflict manager and this is my partner _____."
2. Ask the parties: "Do you want to solve the problem with us or with a teacher?" If necessary, move to a quiet place to solve the problem.
3. Explain to the parties: "First you have to agree to four rules":
   a. Agree to solve the problem.
   b. No name-calling.
   c. Do not interrupt.
   d. Tell the truth.
4. Conflict Manager #1 asks Person #1: "What happened? How do you feel?" Conflict Manager #1 repeats what Person #1 said, using active listening: "So, what you're saying is . . ."
5. Conflict Manager #2 asks Person #2: "What happened? How do you feel?" Conflict Manager #2 repeats what Person #2 said, using active listening: "So, what you're saying is . . ."
6. Ask Person #1: "Do you have a solution?" Ask Person #2: "Do you agree with the solution?" If no: "Do you have another solution?" and so on until disputants have reached a solution agreeable to both of them.
7. Have disputants tell each other what they have just agreed to: "So will you tell each other what you've just agreed to?"
8. Congratulate them both: "Thank you for working so hard to solve your problem. Congratulations."
9. Fill out Conflict Manager Report Form.

FIGURE 11.4
Peer Conflict Management
From Classroom Law Project, 6318 S. W. Corbett, Portland, OR 97201. Adapted by permission.

Judiciously Applying Consequences

Avoid the use of suspension (or expulsion) as punishment for all but the most serious misbehavior (see Chobot & Garibaldi, 1982; Curwin & Mendler, 1999). Suspension often exacerbates truancy problems, both because it makes students fall behind in their work and because it gives them experience in the use of time out of school. In-school suspension, detention, and other penalties are more effective.

When students misbehave, they should be punished; but when punishment is applied, it should be brief. Being sent to a time-out area or detention room is a common punishment and is effective for most students. Loss of privileges may be used. However, whatever punishment is used should not last too long. It is better to make a misbehaving student miss two days of football practice than to throw him off the team, in part because once the student is off the team, the school could have little else of value to offer or withhold. Every child has within himself or herself the capacity for good behavior as well as for misbehavior. The school must be the ally of the good in each child at the same time that it is the enemy of misbehavior. Overly harsh penalties or penalties that do not allow the student to reenter the classroom on an equal footing with others risk pushing students into the antisocial, delinquent subculture. When a student has paid her or his debt by losing privileges, experiencing detention, or whatever the punishment might be, he or she must be fully reaccepted as a member of the class.

Chapter Summary

What Is an Effective Learning Environment?

Creating effective learning environments involves strategies that teachers use to maintain appropriate behavior and respond to misbehavior in the classroom. Keeping

THE INTENTIONAL TEACHER

Using What You Know about Effective Learning Environments to Improve Teaching and Learning

Intentional teachers are leaders in their classrooms who take responsibility for managing time, activities, and behaviors. At the core of their success as classroom managers is high-interest, meaningful instruction. Intentional teachers use instructional time to its fullest by structuring a positive, consistent environment with reasonable rules and time-conscious procedures. They proactively prevent misbehavior and have planned out a range of responses to misbehavior should it occur despite prevention. Intentional teachers' actions reflect their understanding that effective learning environments result from careful planning and vigilant monitoring.

❶ What do I expect my students to know and be able to do at the end of this lesson? How does this contribute to course objectives and to students' needs to become capable individuals?

Students learn best when they are productively engaged in instruction. Develop a management plan that aims to prevent misbehavior. Before the school year begins, list some of the strategies that you can employ to help your students make good choices about their behavior. At the top of your list type in bold: **Provide instruction that taps students' curiosity and creativity!** Next, list key terms and brief reminders about actions that can help to prevent misbehavior, such as:

> *Fairness*—Show genuine concern for the students and consider their perspectives. Apply consequences consistently and without emotion.
> *Withitness*—remember to monitor all corners of the room.

Research indicates that some teachers lose half—or more—of their instructional time. Make a plan to use your students' time well, and guard your instructional minutes carefully. Commit to teach bell-to-bell, beginning your lessons with an opener—usually a practice exercise or a brain teaser—that is on the overhead projector as students arrive, and closing the lessons with a brief period of independent work during which you can work with students who had difficulties with the lesson.

❷ What knowledge, skills, needs, and interests do my students have that must be taken into account in my lesson?

Bored or frustrated students might find greater rewards in avoiding schoolwork than in completing it. Provide instruction that engages students' curiosity and attends to the various preparation levels students bring to the classroom. For example, imagine that a small cluster of students has been unruly during the beginning of your unit on computation with decimals. You could do a task analysis of the concepts and skills required in the unit and find that this small group of students is missing some prerequisite skills: They have not yet committed basic math facts to memory. So that students can succeed with decimal computations, you might allow them to use their fact tables. At the same time, you could plan to introduce math facts games to help your students master basic operations.

❸ What do I know about the content, child development, learning, motivation, and effective teaching strategies that I can use to accomplish my objectives?

Different kinds of misbehavior require different levels of intervention. Develop a range of responses to misbehavior, begin-

students interested and engaged and showing enthusiasm are important in preventing misbehavior. Creating an effective learning environment is a matter of knowing a set of techniques that teachers can learn and apply.

What Is the Impact of Time on Learning?

Methods of maximizing allocated time include preventing late starts and early finishes, preventing interruptions, handling routine procedures smoothly and quickly, minimizing time spent on discipline, and using engaged time effectively. Engaged time, or time on-task, is the time individual students spend actually doing assigned work. Teachers can maximize engaged time by teaching engaging lessons, maintaining momentum, maintaining smoothness of instruction, managing transitions, maintaining group focus, practicing withitness, and overlapping. In a student-centered classroom, classroom management is more participatory, with students involved in setting standards of behavior; yet rules are still needed and must be consistently communicated and enforced.

ning with the lowest level of intensity. When students exhibit serious misbehaviors, consider the motivation for their behavior, and respond in ways that take into account the individual and the problem. You can address most misbehavior through low-level interventions such as nonverbal cues, physical proximity, and hints. A few students, though, demonstrate persistent misbehavior. You might develop home-based reinforcement programs in which students can earn added time at their favorite activities if their school behavior improves.

❹ What instructional materials, technology, assistance, and other resources are available to help accomplish my objectives?

Effective managers start the year by teaching and reinforcing classroom rules and procedures. Spend time during the first days of school teaching students your expectations for behavior. Perhaps you could interview a few experienced colleagues about their first-day-of-school plans. From their suggestions, you might develop a plan to (1) devise a set of classroom rules through class discussion, (2) develop consequences for instances when students choose to violate or ignore those rules, and (3) teach the students procedures for submitting homework, collecting work for an absent paper, and working effectively in small groups.

❺ How will I plan to assess students' progress toward my objectives?

Collect ongoing information about your use of allocated and engaged time. Ask yourself whether you are devoting enough time to each subject and whether students are engaged during that time in experiences that result in meaningful learning. Review your use of time by, first, examining your schedule to determine whether allocated time is appropriate. Then, for a week, you might track start and end times for each of your lessons to determine where minutes may be lost. Finally, examine students' work to assess the degree to which students demonstrate that their on-task behavior has resulted in significant learning.

Teachers need to review students' responses to their efforts to redirect behavior. Consider changing strategies when misbehavior persists or when you are spending too much time correcting it. For example, when you overhear some of your students bragging about being members of your Three O'Clock Club (after-school detention), you are forced to reconsider its effectiveness as a punishment.

❻ How will I respond if individual children or the class as a whole is not on track toward success? What is my back-up plan?

Take frequent "temperature readings" of the motivational climate of your classroom environment. Gather information from several sources to determine that your strategies are productive and that students are happy and learning. For example, ask students to write an anonymous journal entry on their perceptions of how the class is going. You might ask, in particular, whether they feel they have enough say in what happens in the classroom. After searching for patterns in the entries, you might spend a class period on a classroom meeting to set new goals.

What Practices Contribute to Effective Classroom Management?

Practices that contribute to effective classroom management include starting the year properly and developing rules and procedures. Class rules and procedures should be explicitly presented to students and applied promptly and fairly.

What Are Some Strategies for Managing Routine Misbehavior?

One principle of classroom discipline is good management of routine misbehavior. The principle of least intervention means using the simplest methods that will work. There is a continuum of strategies from least to most disruptive: prevention of misbehavior; nonverbal cues such as eye contact, which can stop a minor misbehavior; praise of incompatible, correct behavior; praise of other students who are behaving; simple verbal reminders given immediately after students misbehave; repetition of verbal reminders; and application of consequences when students refuse to comply. For serious behavior problems, swift and certain consequences must be applied. A call to the student's parents can be effective.

How Is Applied Behavior Analysis Used to Manage More Serious Behavior Problems?

The most common reinforcer for both routine and serious misbehavior is attention from teacher or peers. When the student misbehaves to get the teacher's attention, one effective strategy is to pay attention to correct behavior while ignoring misbehavior as much as possible; scolding often acts as a reinforcer of misbehavior.

Individual behavior management strategies are useful for students with persistent behavior problems in school. After establishing baseline behavior, the teacher selects reinforcers such as verbal praise or small, tangible rewards, and punishers such as time outs (removing a child from a situation that reinforces misbehavior). The teacher also establishes criteria for applying reinforcement and punishment.

Home-based reinforcement strategies might involve giving students daily or weekly report cards to take home and instructing parents to provide rewards on the basis of these reports. The steps to setting up such a program include deciding on behaviors to use for the daily report card and explaining the program to parents.

Group contingency programs are those in which an entire group is rewarded on the basis of the behavior of the group members.

One objection to behavior management techniques is that they can be used to overcontrol students. Behavior management strategies should always emphasize praise and reinforcement, reserving punishment as a last resort.

How Can Serious Behavior Problems Be Prevented?

There are few sure methods of preventing delinquency, but some general principles include clearly expressing and consistently enforcing classroom rules, reducing truancy however possible, avoiding the use of between-class ability grouping, using preventive classroom management strategies, involving parents in any response to serious misbehavior, using peer mediation, avoiding the use of suspension, applying only brief punishment, and reintegrating students after punishment. Check and Connect is one program that incorporates many of these principles.

Research Navigator.com

Key Terms

Review the following key terms from the chapter. Then, to explore research on these topics and how they relate to education today, connect to Research Navigator™ through this book's Companion Website or directly at www.researchnavigator.com.

accountability   358
allocated time   353
applied behavior analysis   369
Assertive Discipline   367
behavior modification   372
classroom management   351
discipline   351
engaged time   352
group alerting   358
group contingencies   370

group contingency program   377
home-based reinforcement strategies   374
mock participation   361
nonverbal cues   366
overlapping   359
time on-task   352
time out   374
withitness   359

Self-Assessment: Practicing for Licensure

Directions: The chapter-opening vignette addresses indicators that are often assessed in state licensure exams. Re-read the chapter-opening vignette, and then respond to the following questions.

1. Ms. Cavalho works hard to prevent behavior problems and disruption in her classroom. Which of the following terms refers to her interaction with Mark?

   a. management
   b. discipline
   c. learning environment
   d. instruction

2. According to research, how could Ms. Cavalho increase student achievement in her classroom?

   a. increase allocated time for instruction by 10 percent above what is normal
   b. increase engaged time to 100 percent of the allocated classroom time
   c. increase engaged time by 10 percent above what is normal
   d. decrease allocated time by starting late and finishing early

3. Ms. Cavalho continues her lesson on writing style even as Mark attempts to interrupt. This is called

   a. engaged time.
   b. allocated time.
   c. momentum.
   d. overlapping.

4. Ms. Cavalho uses the "Principle of Least Intervention" in her classroom. She works to prevent inappropriate behavior first, then if that does not work, she gives nonverbal cues and verbal reminders about how to act. She has used these strategies with Mark. Assume that Mark's behavior does not change after their discussion. What should she do next?

   a. apply consequences
   b. give praise for appropriate behavior
   c. ask students to solve the problem
   d. ignore the behavior

5. Daily report cards, group contingency programs, home-based reinforcement programs, and individual behavior management programs are all based on

   a. assertive discipline practices.
   b. delinquency prevention.
   c. behavioral learning theory.
   d. the principle of least intervention.

6. Discuss ethical considerations in the use of individual and group behavior management programs.

7. Explain how you would prevent the following misbehaviors: speaking out of turn, teasing, physical fighting.

Learners with Exceptionalities

Elaine Wagner, assistant principal at Pleasantville Elementary School, came in to work one day and was stopped by the school secretary. "Good morning," the secretary said. "There's a Helen Ross here to see you. She is interested in enrolling her children. She's waiting in your office. Looks nervous—I gave her some coffee and settled her down."

"Thanks, Beth," said Ms. Wagner. She went into her office and introduced herself to Ms. Ross.

"I appreciate your seeing me," said Ms. Ross. "We're planning to move to Pleasantville next fall, and I wanted to look at the schools before we move. We have one child, Tommy, going into second grade, and Annie is going into kindergarten. I'm really concerned about Tommy. In the school he's in now, he's not doing very well. It's spring, and he's hardly reading at all. His teacher says he might have a learning disability, and the school wants to put him in special education. I don't like that idea. He's a normal, happy kid at home, and it would crush him to find out he's 'different,' but I want to do what's best for him. I guess the main thing I want to see is what you do for kids like Tommy."

"Well," said Ms. Wagner, "the most important thing I can tell you about our school is that our philosophy is that every child can learn, and it is our job to find out how to reach each one. I can't tell you exactly what we'd do with Tommy, of course, since I don't know him, but I can assure you of a few things. First, we'll attend to his reading problem right away. We believe in prevention and early intervention. If Tommy is having serious reading problems, we'll probably arrange to give him one-to-one tutoring so that he can catch up quickly with the other second-graders. Second, we'll try to keep him in his regular classroom if we possibly can. If he needs special-education services, he'll get them, but in this school we try everything to solve a child's learning problems before we refer him or her for testing that might lead to special-education placement. Even if Tommy does qualify for special education, we'll structure his program so that he is with his regular class as much as possible. We will develop an individualized education plan for him. Finally, I want to assure you that you will be very much involved in all decisions that have to do with Tommy and that we'll talk with you frequently about his progress and ask for your help at home to make sure that Tommy is doing well."

"Ms. Wagner, that all sounds great. But how can you give Tommy the help he needs and still let him stay in his regular class?"

"Why don't I take you to see some of our classes in operation right now?" said Ms. Wagner. "I think you'll see what I mean."

Ms. Wagner led the way through the brightly lit corridors lined with student projects, artwork, and compositions. She turned in at Mr. Esposito's second-grade class. There, she and Ms. Ross were met by a happy, excited buzz of activity. The children were working in small groups, measuring each other's heights and the lengths of fingers and feet. Some children were trying to figure out how to measure the distance around each other's heads. Another teacher, Ms. Park, was working with some of the groups.

Ms. Wagner and Ms. Ross stepped back into the hall. "What I wanted to show you," said Ms. Wagner, "is how we integrate our students with special needs into the general education classroom. Could you tell which students were special-needs students?"

"No," admitted Ms. Ross.

"That's what we hope to create—a classroom in which children with special needs are so well integrated that you can't pick them out. Ms. Park is the special-education teacher for the younger grades, and she teams with Mr. Esposito during math and reading periods to serve all of the second-graders who need special services. Ms. Park will help any child who is having difficulty, not just students with special needs, since a large part of her job is to prevent students from ever needing special education. Sometimes she'll work with individual kids or small groups that need help. She often teaches skills children will be learning in advance, so they will be better prepared in class. For example, she might have gone over measurement with some of the kids before this lesson so that they'd have a leg up on the concept."

Ms. Wagner led the way to a small room near the library room. She pointed through a window at a teacher working with one child. "What you see there is a tutor working with a first-grader who is having difficulty in reading. If your Tommy were here, this is what we might be doing with him. We try to do anything we can to keep kids from falling behind in the first place so that they can stay out of special education and progress along with their classmates."

Ms. Wagner showed Ms. Ross all over the school. In one class a child with a visual disability was reading text from a computer that had inch-high letters. In another they saw a child with Down syndrome working in a cooperative learning group on a science project. In a third classroom a child using a wheelchair was leading a class discussion.

Ms. Ross was fascinated.

"I had no idea a school could be like this. I'm so excited that we're moving to Pleasantville. This looks like the perfect school for both of my children. I only wish we could have moved here two years ago!" *(@)*

Cooperative Learning   In groups of five, discuss Tommy Ross and students like him. One person assumes the role of Ms. Wagner; one is his future homeroom teacher, Mr. Esposito; one is Ms. Ross; one is the special-education teacher, Ms. Park; and one is the special-education director for the district. Discuss how Tommy will be screened for a potential learning disability in reading, and list some strategies that his teachers might use if, in fact, he does have a learning disability.

Cooperative Learning   Divide groups of four classmates into pairs. The pairs interview a partner about what a learning disability in reading might look like (i.e., how a reading disability might be identified) and what a teacher might do to address this situation. The two interviewers share what they have learned within their group. Roles are then reversed. The two new interviewers tell their group what they have learned about reading disabilities.

Pleasantville Elementary School is organized around two key ideas: that all children can learn, and that it is the school's responsibility to find ways to meet each child's needs in the general education classroom to the maximum extent possible. Pleasantville Elementary is organized to identify children's strengths as well as their problems and to provide the best program it can for each child. Every school has children with exceptionalities who can do well in school when they are given the specific supports they need to learn. This chapter describes children with exceptionalities and programs that are designed to help them achieve their full potential.

INTASC

2 Knowledge of Human Development and Learning

3 Adapting Instruction for Individual Needs

$\mathcal{W}$HO ARE LEARNERS WITH EXCEPTIONALITIES?

In one sense, every child is exceptional. No two children are exactly alike in their ways of learning and behaving, in their activities and preferences, in their skills and motivations. All students would benefit from programs uniquely tailored to their individual needs.

However, schools cannot practically meet the precise needs of every student. For the sake of efficiency, students are grouped into classes and given common instructional experiences designed to provide the greatest benefit to the largest number at a moderate cost. This system works reasonably well for the great majority of students. However, some students do not fit easily into this mold. Some students have physical or sensory disabilities, such as hearing or vision loss or orthopedic disabilities, that restrict their ability to participate in the general education classroom program without special assistance. Other students have mental retardation, emotional or behavioral disorders, or learning disabilities that make it difficult for them to learn in the general education classroom without assistance. Finally, some students have such outstanding talents that the general education classroom teacher is unable to meet their unique needs without help.

To receive special-education services, a student must have one of a small number of categories of disabilities or disorders. These general labels, such as "specific learning disabilities," "mental retardation," and "orthopedic impairments," cover a wide diversity of problems.

Labels tend to stick, making change difficult, and the labels themselves can become handicaps for the student. Education professionals must avoid using labels in a way that unintentionally stigmatizes students, dehumanizes them, segregates them socially from their peers, or encourages discrimination against them in any form (Trent, Artiles, & Englert, 1998). Teachers of learners with exceptionalities need to be sensitive to the political and social dimensions of these students' differences (Hartwell, 2001; Heward & Cavanaugh, 1997). The term **learners with exceptionalities** may be used to describe any individuals whose physical, mental, or behavioral performance is so different from the norm—either higher or lower—that additional services are needed to meet the individuals' needs.

The terms disability and handicap are not interchangeable. A **disability** is a functional limitation a person has that interferes with the person's physical or cognitive abilities. A **handicap** is a condition imposed on a person with disabilities by society, the physical environment, or the person's attitude. For example, a student who uses a wheelchair is handicapped by a lack of access ramps. Handicap is therefore not a synonym for disability (Hallahan & Kauffman, 1997).

"People-First" Language

Individuals with disabilities and their families have fought for, and earned, many rights that were once reserved only for their nondisabled peers. As we recognize those rights, we must also ensure that our language and choice of vocabulary and terminology convey the appropriate message of respect. In referring to people with disabilities, there are two basic principles to keep in mind (Smith, 2001). The first is to *put people first*. An example of this would be to refer to Frankie as a student with a learning disability, not a "learning disabled child." He is a student first; the fact that he has a learning disability is secondary. The second principle is to *avoid making the person equal the disability* (Smith, 2001). There are many characteristics to each student and the disability is only one. To define the child in terms of the disability does him or her an injustice.

As with any rule, there are exceptions. Individuals with visual disabilities may also be referred to as blind, and the term *blind* may come first (i.e., the blind student, blind individuals). Individuals who are deaf are the other exception. Table 12.1 summarizes a generally accepted language of disabilities.

Even though labels are neither exact nor unchanging and might be harmful in some situations, they are a useful shorthand for educators to use to indicate the type and extent of a student's exceptionalities—as long as the limitations of the labels are taken into consideration. The following sections discuss characteristics of students with the types of exceptionalities that are most commonly seen in schools.

Types of Exceptionalities and the Numbers of Students Served

Some exceptionalities, such as loss of vision and hearing, are relatively easy to define and measure. Others, such as mental retardation, learning disabilities, and emotional disorders, are much harder to define, and their definitions have evolved over time. In fact, recent decades have seen dramatic changes in these categories (Keogh & MacMillan, 1996). Since the mid-1970s, the numbers of children in categories of disabilities that are most easily defined, such as physical impairments, have re-

---

learners with exceptionalities

Any individuals whose physical, mental, or behavioral performance is so different from the norm—either higher or lower—that additional services are needed to meet the individuals' needs.

disability

The limitation of a function, such as cognitive processing or physical or sensory abilities.

handicap

A condition imposed on a person with disabilities by society, the physical environment, or the person's attitude.

Table 12.1		
"People-First" Language*		
DO say:	Students with . . . Students who have . . . Individuals with . . . Individuals who have . . . Children with . . . Youth with . . . Toddlers with . . . Adults with . . .	disabilities mental retardation learning disabilities speech impairments language impairments severe emotional disturbance behavioral disorders cerebral palsy physical disabilities hearing impairments visual disabilities
EXCEPTIONS:	People . . . Toddlers . . . Students . . . Youth . . . Individuals . . . The deaf The blind Blind students Deaf individuals	who face physical challenges who use a wheelchair who are blind who have low vision who are deaf who are hearing impaired who are hard of hearing
DON'T say:	The . . .	disabled/learning disabled handicapped disturbed crippled wheelchair bound retarded

*Adapted from Smith, 2001.

mained fairly stable. However, the number of students categorized as learning disabled has steadily increased, and the use of the category "mentally retarded" has diminished.

Figure 12.1 shows the percentages of all students, ages 3 to 21, receiving special-education services in 2000–2001. There are several important pieces of information in this figure. First, notice that the overall percentage of students receiving special education was about 12 percent; that is, 1 out of 8 students, ages 3 to 21, was categorized as exceptional. Of these, the largest proportion were categorized as having specific learning disabilities (6 percent of all students) or speech disabilities (2.3 percent). Table 12.2 shows the percentages of students ages 3 to 21 receiving special-education services who had various disabilities in 2000–2001 (U.S. Department of Education, 2002). Specific learning disabilities (45.2 percent of all students with disabilities), speech and language impairments (17.2 percent), and mental retardation (9.5 percent) are far more common than physical or sensory disabilities. In a class of 25 a teacher might, on the average, have one or two students with learning disabilities and one with a speech impairment. In contrast, only about 1 class in 40 is likely to have a student who has hearing or vision loss or a physical disability.

FIGURE 12.1
Percentage of Children Ages 3 to 21 Served under IDEA, Part B, by Disability during the 2000–2001 School Year

From U.S. Department of Education, Office of Special Education and Rehabilitative Services, *Annual Report to Congress on the Implementation of the Individuals with Disabilities Education Act,* Washington, DC, 2002.

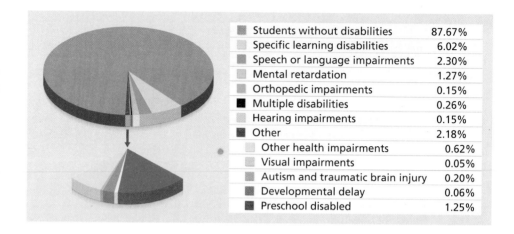

Students without disabilities	87.67%
Specific learning disabilities	6.02%
Speech or language impairments	2.30%
Mental retardation	1.27%
Orthopedic impairments	0.15%
Multiple disabilities	0.26%
Hearing impairments	0.15%
Other	2.18%
Other health impairments	0.62%
Visual impairments	0.05%
Autism and traumatic brain injury	0.20%
Developmental delay	0.06%
Preschool disabled	1.25%

Not all disabilities qualify students for special education services. Table 12.3 on pages 396–397 lists the categories of disabilities in the current U.S. special-education law, IDEA '97, and briefly describes each.

Students with Mental Retardation

Just over one percent of all students ages 6 to 21 have mental retardation (U.S. Department of Education, 2000). There are several definitions of **mental retardation.** In 1992 the American Association on Mental Retardation (AAMR) defined mental retardation as follows:

Mental retardation refers to substantial limitations in present functioning. It is characterized by significantly subaverage intellectual function, existing

Table 12.2

Number of Children Ages 3 to 21 Served under IDEA, Part B, by Disability, during the 2000–2001 School Year

Type of Disability	Number Served	Percentage of All Students with Disabilities
Specific learning disabilities	2,842,000	45.2
Speech or language impairments	1,084,000	17.2
Mental retardation	599,000	9.5
Hearing impairments	70,000	1.1
Orthopedic impairments	72,000	1.1
Other health impairments	292,000	4.6
Visual impairments	25,000	0.4
Multiple disabilities	121,000	1.9
Autism and traumatic brain injury	94,000	1.5
Developmental delay	28,000	0.4
Preschool disabled	592,000	9.4
All disabilities	**6,293,000**	**100.0**

mental retardation
A condition, usually present at birth, that results in below-average intellectual skills and poor adaptive behavior.

concurrently with related limitations in two or more of the following applicable adaptive skill areas: communication, self-care, home living, social skills, community use, self-direction, health and safety, functional academics, leisure and work. Mental retardation manifests before age 18. (Luckasson et al., 1992, p. 1)

This definition means that people with mental retardation have low scores on tests of intelligence and also show difficulty in maintaining the standards of personal independence and social responsibility that would be expected for their age and cultural group (Luckasson et al., 1992; MacLean, 1996). In addition, these impairments in intelligence and adaptive behavior become apparent sometime between conception and age 18.

Causes of Mental Retardation   Among the many causes of mental retardation are genetic inheritance; chromosomal abnormalities, such as Down syndrome (Turner & Alborz, 2003); diseases passed between mother and fetus in utero, such as rubella (German measles) and syphilis; fetal chemical dependency syndromes caused by a mother's abuse of alcohol or cocaine during pregnancy; birth accidents that result in oxygen deprivation; childhood diseases and accidents, such as encephalitis traumatic brain injury; and toxic contamination from the environment, such as lead poisoning (McDonnell, Hardman, & McDonnell, 2003).

Intelligence Quotient (IQ)   To understand how severity of impairment in children with mental retardation is classified, it is first important to recall the concept of **IQ,** or **intelligence quotient,** derived from scores on standardized tests (see Dennis & Tapsfield, 1996; McArdle & Woodcock, 1998). Students with IQs above 70 are generally regarded as being in the normal range. Slightly more than 2 percent of students have IQs below this range. However, consistent with AAMR recommendations, education professionals do not use IQs alone to determine the severity of cognitive impairment. They take into account a student's school and home performance, scores on other tests, and cultural background. Recall from Chapter 4 that IQ tests have been criticized for cultural bias (Hilliard, 1992).

CONNECTIONS

For more on IQ, see Chapter 4, page 121.

CONNECTIONS

For more about IQ testing, see Chapter 14, page 504.

Classifications of Mental Retardation   In the past, individuals with mental retardation were largely categorized according to their IQ scores. For example, the 1983 AAMR manual listed four degrees of severity of mental retardation in terms of ranges of IQ, including mild retardation (IQs 50–55 to 70–75), moderate retardation (IQs 35–40 to 50–55), severe retardation (IQs 20–25 to 35–40), and profound retardation (IQs below 20–25) (Luckasson et al., 1992). This categorization is still widely used. In an older classification system, students with mild retardation, typically with IQs between 55 and 70, were regarded as "educable" (EMR); that is, able to learn basic academic skills up to a fifth-grade level. Students with moderate retardation (IQs 40–55) were classified as "trainable" (TMR); that is, able to learn independent self-care and job skills for sheltered workshops (MacMillan & Forness, 1992). Children with IQs below 50 were often termed "custodial" and usually received out-of-school services. These IQ-based classification systems have been challenged by some professionals who believe that the emphasis in present-day special education is that all people can learn and that education and training cannot be clearly differentiated (Smith & Luckasson, 1995). However, some school districts use this or a similar simplified system of classification (MacLean, 1996).

Current AAMR definitions emphasize the capabilities of individuals with mental retardation in two main areas—intellectual functioning and adaptive skills—and categorize individuals on the basis of the supports they need (Smith, 2001).

intelligence quotient (IQ)
An intelligence test score that should be near 100 for people of average intelligence.

Table 12.3

IDEA '97 Disability Categories

Category	Definitions/Characteristics
Learning disability	"The term 'specific *learning disability*' means a disorder in one or more of the basic psychological processes involved in understanding or in using language, spoken or written, which disorder may manifest itself in imperfect ability to listen, think, speak, read, write, spell, or do mathematical calculations. Such term includes such conditions as perceptual disabilities, brain injury, minimal brain dysfunction, dyslexia, and developmental aphasia. Such term does not include a learning problem that is primarily the result of visual, hearing, or motor disabilities, of mental retardation, of emotional disturbance, or of environmental, cultural, or economic disadvantage" (PL 105-17).
Speech or language disorder	Language is a code made up of rules governing word construction, meaning, grouping (sentences), and pragmatics (appropriate use that varies by situation). A person with a *receptive language* problem cannot understand the language code; a person with an *expressive language* problem has not mastered the rules of codes well enough to share thoughts, ideas, and feelings completely. Someone who has a *speech problem* may use the correct language code, but the message will not sound right. Stuttering and rough, hoarse, or nasal sounding voices are all examples of speech problems. Speech and language problems can exist together, or individually (ASHA, 2001).
Mental retardation	"*Mental retardation* refers to substantial limitations in present functioning. It is characterized by significantly subaverage intellectual functioning, existing concurrently with related limitations in two or more of the following applicable adaptive skills areas: communication, self-care, home living, social skills, community use, self-direction, health and safety, functional academics, leisure, and work. Mental retardation manifests before age 18" (Luckasson, R., Coulter, D. L., Polloway, E. A., Reis, S., Schalock, R. L., Snell, M. E., Spitalnik, D. M., & Stark, J. A., 1992). A classification system, based on the intensity of support needed by the individual, has four levels: intermittent, limited, extensive, and pervasive.
Emotional or behavioral disorders (EBD)	The term *emotional disturbance* ". . . means a condition exhibiting one or more of the following characteristics over a long period of time and to a marked degree that adversely affects a child's educational performance: • An inability to learn that cannot be explained by intellectual, sensory, or health factors; • An inability to build or maintain satisfactory interpersonal relationships with peers and teachers; • Inappropriate types of behavior or feelings under normal circumstances; • A general pervasive mood of unhappiness or depression; • A tendency to develop physical symptoms of fears associated with personal or school problems. The term includes children who are schizophrenic. The term does not include children who are socially maladjusted, unless it is determined that they have an emotional disturbance" (U.S. Department of Education, 1999, p. 12422).
Orthopedic impairments	An *orthopedic impairment* is a condition that ". . . adversely affects a child's educational performance. The term includes impairments caused by congenital anomaly (e.g., clubfoot, absence of some member, etc.), impairments caused by disease (e.g., poliomyelitis, bone tuberculosis, etc.), and impairments from other causes (e.g., cerebral palsy, amputations, and fractures or burns that cause contractures)" (U.S. Department of Education, 1999, p. 12422).
Other health impairments	Individuals with *other health impairments* have ". . . limited strength, vitality or alertness, including a heightened alertness to environmental stimuli that results in limited alertness with respect to the educational environment, that is due to chronic or acute health problems such as asthma, attention deficit hyperactivity disorder, diabetes, epilepsy, a heart condition, hemophilia, lead poisoning, leukemia, nephritis, rheumatic fever, and sickle cell anemia; and adversely affects a child's educational performance" (U.S. Department of Education, 1999, p. 12422).

Table 12.3		(continued)
Category	**Definitions/Characteristics**
Deafness and hard of hearing	Individuals who are *deaf* or profoundly hard of hearing " . . . have hearing abilities that provide them with little useful hearing even if they use hearing aids" and cannot use hearing as the primary avenue for accessing information. Those who are *hard of hearing* can process information from sound, usually with the help of a hearing aid (Smith, 2001). Hearing loss is measured in decibels and categorized by levels: • Mild—15–40 dB—cannot hear a whispered conversation in a quiet atmosphere at close range; • Moderate—40–60 dB—cannot hear normal conversation in a quiet atmosphere at close range; • Severe—60–90 dB—cannot hear speech; can only hear loud noises such as a vacuum cleaner or lawn mower at close range; • Profound—over 90 dB—cannot hear speech; may only hear extremely loud noises such as a chain saw at close range or the vibrating component of loud sound (Alexander Graham Bell Association for the Deaf and Hard of Hearing, 2001).
Visual disabilities	Visual disabilities are often divided into two groups, low vision and blindness. *Low vision* is "a level of vision which, with standard correction, hinders an individual in the planning and/or execution of a task, but which permits enhancement of the functional vision through the use of optical or nonoptical devices, environmental modifications and/or techniques" (Corn, 1989, p. 28). *Blindness* refers to individuals without functional use of vision who must be educated through tactile and other sensory channels (Smith, 2001).
Autism	*Autism* is a " . . . developmental disability significantly affecting verbal and nonverbal communication and social interaction, generally evident before age 3, that adversely affects a child's performance. Other characteristics often associated with autism are engagement in repetitive activities and stereotyped movements, resistance to environmental change or change in daily routines, and unusual responses to sensory experiences. The term does not apply if a child's educational performance is adversely affected primarily because the child has a serious emotional disturbance" (U.S. Department of Education, 1999, p. 12422).
Deaf-blindness	"*Deaf-blindness* means concomitant hearing and visual impairments, the combination of which causes such severe communication and other developmental and learning needs that the persons cannot be appropriately educated in special education programs solely for children and youth with hearing impairments or severe disabilities, without supplementary assistance to address their education needs due to these dual, concurrent disabilities" (U.S. Department of Education, 1999, p. 12422).
Traumatic brain injury	*Traumatic brain injury (TBI)* is " . . . an acquired injury to the brain caused by an external physical force, resulting in total or partial functional disability or psychosocial impairment, or both, that adversely affects a child's educational performance. The term applies to open or closed head injuries resulting in impairments in one or more areas, such as cognition; language; memory; attention; reasoning, abstract thinking; judgment; problem solving; sensory, perceptual, and motor abilities; psychosocial behavior; physical functions; information processing; and speech. The term does not apply to brain injuries that are congenital or degenerative, or to brain injuries induced by birth trauma" (U.S. Department of Education, 1999, p. 12422).

Table 12.4 defines four categories of services people with mental retardation might need and gives examples of these services.

However the categories are defined, children with mild retardation, who need intermittent or limited support, are rarely identified before school entry (Luckasson,

Table 12.4	
Definitions and Examples of Intensities of Supports, 1992	
Type of Support	*Definition and Examples*
Intermittent	Supports on an as-needed basis. Characterized by episodic nature, person not always needing the support(s), or short-term supports needed during the life-span transitions (e.g., job loss or an acute medical crisis). Intermittent supports may be high or low intensity when provided.
Limited	An intensity of supports characterized by consistency over time, time-limited but not of an intermittent nature, might require fewer staff members and less cost than more intense levels of support (e.g., time-limited employment training or transitional supports during the school to adult period).
Extensive	Supports characterized by regular involvement (e.g., daily) in at least some environments (such as work at home) and not time-limited (e.g., long-term support and long-term home living support).
Pervasive	Supports characterized by their constancy, high intensity; provided across environments; potential life-sustaining nature. Pervasive supports typically involve more staff members and intrusiveness than do extensive or time-limited supports.

Source: From R. Luckasson, D. Coulter, E. Polloway, S. Reiss, R. Schalock, M. Snell, D. Spitalnik, and J. Stark, *Mental Retardation: Definitions, Classification, and Systems of Supports,* p. 26. Copyright 1992 by American Association on Mental Retardation. Reprinted by permission.

Schalock, Snell, & Spitalnik, 1996). Approximately 89 percent of children with mental retardation have mild mental retardation (U.S. Department of Education, 1994).

There is increasing evidence that as many as 50 percent of all cases of mental retardation could have been prevented by improving prenatal care; ensuring proper nutrition; preventing accidents, diseases, and ingestions of poisons (such as lead paint) among children; and providing children with safe, supportive, and stimulating environments in early childhood (Smith & Luckasson, 1995). Studies of intensive early intervention programs emphasizing infant stimulation, effective preschool programs, parent support programs, and other services have shown lasting impacts on the performance of children who are at risk for mental retardation (Bradley et al., 1994; Campbell & Ramey, 1994; Garber, 1988; Noonan & McCormick, 1993; Ramey et al., 1992). Even children with more pervasive mental retardation benefit substantially from intensive prevention programs in their early childhood years (Casto & Mastropieri, 1986).

The following Theory into Practice section suggests ways in which general education classroom teachers can help students who have mental retardation to acquire adaptive behavior skills. Specific ways of modifying instruction for students with special needs are discussed later in this chapter.

Theory into PRACTICE

Teaching Adaptive Behavior Skills

Instructional objectives for helping students who have mental retardation to acquire adaptive behavior skills are not very different from those that are valuable for all students. Every student needs to cope with the demands of school, develop interpersonal relationships, develop language skills, grow emotionally, and take care of personal needs. Teachers can help students by directly instructing or supporting students in the following areas (see Hardman, Drew, Egan, & Wolf, 1996; Wehmeyer, 2001):

1. **Coping with the demands of school:** Attending to learning tasks, organizing work, following directions, managing time, and asking questions.
2. **Developing interpersonal relationships:** Learning to work cooperatively with others, responding to social cues in the environment, using socially acceptable language, responding appropriately to teacher directions and cues, and enhancing social awareness.
3. **Developing language skills:** Understanding directions, communicating needs and wants, expressing ideas, listening attentively, and using appropriate voice modulation and inflection.
4. **Socioemotional development:** Seeking out social participation and interaction (decreasing social withdrawal) and being motivated to work (decreasing work avoidance, tardiness, and idleness).
5. **Personal care:** Practicing appropriate personal hygiene, dressing independently, taking care of personal property, and moving successfully from one location to another.

INTASC

3 Adapting Instruction for Individual Needs

Students with Learning Disabilities

Learning disabilities (LD) are not a single condition but a wide variety of specific disabilities that are presumed to stem from some dysfunction of the brain or central nervous system. The following definition is adapted from the National Joint Committee on Learning Disabilities (1988, p. 1):

> Learning disabilities is a general term for a diverse group of disorders characterized by significant difficulties in the acquisition and use of listening, speaking, reading, writing, reasoning, or computing. These disorders stem from the individual and may occur across the life span. Problems in self-regulatory behaviors, social perception, and social interaction may exist with learning disabilities but do not by themselves constitute a learning disability. Learning disabilities may occur with other handicapping conditions but are not the result of those conditions.

Older definitions of learning disability include specific reference to *dyslexia,* a severely impaired ability to read; *dysgraphia,* an impaired ability to write; and *dyscalculia,* an impaired ability to learn mathematics. The source of these conditions in brain dysfunction can seldom be proved, however, and these terms must be used with caution (Smith & Luckasson, 1995).

Identifying Students with Learning Disabilities   Different interpretations of the many definitions of *learning disability* have led state and local school districts to vary widely in their eligibility requirements and provisions for students with learning disabilities (Bender, 2004; Spear-Swerling & Sternberg, 1998). The increasing numbers of students identified as having learning disabilities have contributed to the confusion. In 2000–2001, for example, 45.2 percent of all students ages 3–21 with disabilities were identified as having specific learning disabilities (U.S. Department of Education, 2002). However, the growing numbers of students in this category are due to a shift in its definition, not to a change in the total number of children at risk.

learning disabilities (LD) Disorders that impede academic progress of people who are not mentally retarded or emotionally disturbed.

Education professionals have the task of distinguishing students with learning disabilities from students who are nondisabled low achievers and students with mild mental retardation (Smith, 2001). In some school districts a student who falls more than two grade levels behind expectations and has an IQ in the normal range is likely to be called *learning disabled*. Some characteristics of students with learning disabilities follow:

- Normal intelligence or even giftedness
- Discrepancy between intelligence and performance
- Delays in achievement
- Attention deficit or high distractibility
- Hyperactivity or impulsiveness
- Poor motor coordination and spatial relation ability
- Difficulty solving problems
- Perceptual anomalies, such as reversing letters, words, or numbers
- Difficulty with self-motivated, self-regulated activities
- Overreliance on teacher and peers for assignments
- Specific disorders of memory, thinking, or language
- Immature social skills
- Disorganized approach to learning

Definitions of learning disabilities have historically required that there be a serious discrepancy between actual performance and the performance that might have been predicted on the basis of one or more tests of cognitive functioning, such as an IQ test (Meyer, 2000; Siegel, 2003). In practice, many children are identified as having a learning disability as a result of having substantial differences between some subscales of an IQ test and others or between one ability test and another. This emphasis on discrepancies has increasingly come under attack in recent years, however. For example, Fletcher and colleagues (1994) studied children ages 7.5 to 9.5 who were failing in reading. Some of these children had major discrepancies between their IQs and their performance; others had (low) IQ scores consistent with their poor performance. On an extensive battery of assessments, the discrepant and "nondiscrepant" children were nearly identical. In either case, what they lacked were skills that were closely related to reading. Many other studies (e.g., Francis, Shaywitz, Shaywitz, Stuebing, & Fletcher, 1996; Metsala, Stanovich, & Brown, 1998; Stanovich, Siegel, & Gottard, 1997) have found the same result. These studies have undermined the idea that there is a sharp-edged definition of learning disabilities as distinct from low achievement (see Hessler, 2001; Stuebing et al., 2002).

Based on this research, the 2004 reauthorization of the main U.S. special-education law, IDEA, eliminated the use of discrepancy as part of the definition of learning disabilities, and asked that states develop new definitions defining learning disabilities as a failure to respond to high-quality instruction based on well-validated principles.

The studies also point to a very different emphasis for prevention and treatment. There has been a long tradition of searching for exotic treatments for learning disabilities, from engaging children in activities to increase their hand–eye coordination to placing colored filters over reading material to experimenting with children's diets. Such treatments are based on the assumption that there is something qualitatively different about the brains of children with learning disabilities. Yet very few such children show any evidence of neurological dysfunction. Exotic treatments may work with some children, but for the great majority of children with learning disabilities, effective prevention and treatment focuses far more directly on the problems that brought the child to the attention of the special-education system—most often reading problems, which are involved in more than 90 percent of referrals for students with possible learning disabilities (Kavale & Reese, 1992; Slavin, 1996a). For example, use of research-based interventions for at-risk students in kindergarten have had substantial impacts on children who otherwise might have been categorized as learning disabled (Cavanaugh et al., 2004).

Characteristics of Students with Learning Disabilities   On the average, students with learning disabilities tend to have lower academic self-esteem than do nondisabled students, although in nonacademic arenas their self-esteems are like those of other children (Bear, Minke, & Manning, 2001; Elbaum & Vaughn, 2001; Gresham & MacMillan, 1997; Kelly & Norwich, 2004; Manning, Bear, & Minke, 2001). On most social dimensions, children with learning disabilities resemble other low achievers (Larrivee & Horne, 1991). Boys are more likely than girls to be labeled as learning disabled. African Americans, Latinos, and children from families in which the head of household has not attended college tend to be overrepresented in special-education classes, while female students are underrepresented (Heward & Cavanaugh, 1997). There is a great deal of concern about the overidentification of boys and minority students in special education (Meyer, Harry, & Sapon-Shevin, 1997). The 2004 reauthorization of the U.S. special-education law, IDEA, requires states and the federal government to monitor racial differences in special-education placements and to change policies that perpetuate them.

Theory into **PRACTICE**

Teaching Students with Learning Disabilities

There are many types of learning disabilities, and issues in teaching students with learning disabilities differ by age level. However, a few broad principles apply across many circumstances. In general, effective teaching for students with learning disabilities uses the same strategies that are effective with other students, except that there might be less margin for error. In other words, a student with learning disabilities is less likely than other students to learn from poor instruction. General concepts of effective teaching for students with learning disabilities include these (see Bender, 2004; Lerner, 1997; Smith, 1998):

Emphasize prevention. Many of the learning deficits that cause a child to be categorized as having learning disabilities can be prevented. For example, high-quality early childhood programs and primary-grades teaching significantly reduce the number of children identified with learning disabilities (Conyers, Reynolds, & Ou, 2003; Slavin, 1996a; Snow, Burns, & Griffin, 1998). One-to-one tutoring for first-graders struggling with reading can be particularly effective in preventing reading disabilities (Elbaum, Vaughn, Hughes, & Moody, 2000; Lyons et al., 1993; Morris, Tyner, & Perney, 2000; Wasik & Slavin, 1993). Use of early reading strategies emphasizing phonics, beneficial to most children, is essential to a large proportion of children at risk for reading disabilities (Cavanaugh et al., 2004; Schneider, Roth, & Ennemoser, 2000; Snow, Burns, & Griffin, 1998; Torgeson et al., 1999). Clearly, the easiest learning disabilities to deal with are those that never appear in the first place.

Recognizing that the great majority of children labeled as having learning disabilities have problems in reading, the 2004 reauthorization of IDEA encourages schools to provide scientifically validated reading programs to students who are at risk, and it allows schools to spend up to 15 percent of

INTASC

5 Classroom Motivation and Management

7 Instructional Planning Skills

their IDEA funding for prevention and early intervention to help struggling students before they fall far enough behind to require a disability diagnosis.

Teach learning-to-learn skills. Many students with learning disabilities lack good strategies for studying, test-taking, and so on. These skills can be taught. Many studies have shown that students with learning disabilities who are directly taught study strategies and other cognitive strategies perform significantly better in school (Bryant, Ugel, Thompson, & Hampff, 1999; Deshler, Ellis, & Lenz, 1996; Gersten et al., 2001; Harris, Graham, & Pressley, 2001; Jitendra et al., 2004; Swanson, 2001; Swanson & Hoskyn, 1998).

Give frequent feedback. Students with learning disabilities are less likely than other students to be able to work productively for long periods of time with little or no feedback. They do better in situations in which they get frequent feedback on their efforts, particularly feedback about how they have improved or how they have worked hard to achieve something. For example, children with learning disabilities are likely to do better with brief, concrete assignments that are immediately scored than with long-term assignments. If long-term projects or reports are assigned, the students should have many intermediate goals and should get feedback on each (see Deshler et al., 1996).

Use teaching strategies that engage students actively in lessons. Students with learning disabilities are particularly unlikely to learn from long lectures. They tend to do best when they are actively involved. This implies that teachers who have such students in their classes should make extensive use of hands-on projects, cooperative learning, and other active learning methods, although it is important that these activities be well structured and have clear goals and roles (see Putnam, 1998a; Slavin, 1995a; Swanson & Hoskyn, 1998).

Use effective classroom management methods. Because of their difficulties with information processing and language, many students with learning disabilities experience a great deal of frustration in school and respond by engaging in minor (or major) misbehavior. Effective classroom management methods can greatly reduce this misbehavior, especially strategies that emphasize prevention. For example, students with learning disabilities are likely to respond well to a rapid pace of instruction with much variety and many opportunities to participate and respond successfully (Bauer & Shea, 1999; Rivera & Smith, 1997; Mather & Goldstein, 2001).

Coordinate supplementary services with classroom instruction. Many students with learning disabilities will need some sort of supplementary services, such as small-group tutorials, resource teachers, one-to-one tutoring, or computer-assisted instruction. Whatever these services are, they should be closely aligned with the instruction being given in academic classes. For example, if a student is working on *Treasure Island* in class, a tutor should also work on *Treasure Island*. If a student's math class is working on fractions, so should the resource teacher. Of course, there are times when supplementary services cannot be coordinated fully with classroom instruction, as when a student needs work on study strategies or prerequisite skills. However, every effort should be made to create as much linkage as possible so that the student can see an immediate learning payoff for his or her efforts in the supplementary program. The students having the greatest difficulties in learning should not have to balance two completely different kinds of teaching on different topics.

Students with Attention Deficit Hyperactivity Disorder

Students with **attention deficit hyperactivity disorder (ADHD)** have difficulties maintaining attention because of a limited ability to concentrate (Mash & Wolfe, 2003). ADHD includes impulsive actions, attention deficits, and sometimes hyperactive behavior. These characteristics differentiate students with ADHD from students with learning disabilities, who have attention deficits for other unknown reasons (American Psychiatric Association, 1994). Children with ADHD do not qualify for special education unless they also have some other disability condition that is defined in the law (Aleman, 1990). There is much debate about whether ADHD exists as a distinct diagnostic category (Pellegrini & Horvat, 1995; Swanson, Mink, & Bocian, 1999). Prevalence estimates for ADHD suggest that 3 to 5 percent of all children might have the disorder. Research indicates that males with ADHD outnumber females in ratios varying from 4:1 to 9:1 (American Psychiatric Association, 1994; Parker, 1990). Children with ADHD may be impulsive, acting before they think or without regard for the situation they are in, and often can be inattentive and may find it hard to sit still. Medications for ADHD are widely prescribed, and a variety of drugs have been found to make hyperactive children more manageable and improve their academic performance (DuPaul, Barkley, & McMurray, 1991; Evans et al., 2000). They can also have side effects, such as insomnia, weight loss, and blood pressure changes (Wilens, 1998).

Theory into **PRACTICE**

Students with ADHD: The Role of the Teacher

Attention deficit hyperactivity disorder (ADHD) is usually associated with inattention, impulsivity, and hyperactivity. Educational implications of ADHD are that students might have significant academic, behavior, and social problems stemming from the inability to pay attention. Specific suggestions for the general education classroom teacher who has students with ADHD include the following (see Schlozman & Schlozman, 2000; Smith, 2001; Teeter, 2000):

- Make sure students understand all classroom rules and procedures.
- Consider carefully the seating arrangements of students with ADHD to prevent distractions and to keep these students in proximity to the teacher.
- Adhere to the principles of effective classroom management.
- Understand that certain behaviors, although not desirable, are not meant to be noncompliant—students might not be able to control their behaviors.
- Allow students who are hyperactive to have many opportunities to be active.
- Refrain from implementing a behavior management system that is predicated mostly on the use of punishment or threats.
- Group students with ADHD wisely, taking into consideration the purpose of the group and the other students who will be members of the group.
- Teach students to manage their own behaviors—this includes self-monitoring, self-evaluation, self-reinforcement, and self-instruction (Binder, Dixon, & Ghezi, 2000; Robinson, Smith, Miller, & Brownell, 1999).
- Maintain ongoing communication with the students' homes by using daily report cards or other instruments to convey information (see Chapter 11).
- Collaborate with special-education personnel to develop behavioral and instructional plans for dealing with attention problems.

INTASC

3 Adapting Instruction for Individual Needs

5 Classroom Motivation and Management

7 Instructional Planning Skills

CERTIFICATION POINTER

☞ For a case study on your teacher certification test, you may be asked to suggest how to help a student with a very limited attention span to focus on a lecture and organize the concepts.

attention deficit hyperactivity disorder (ADHD)

A disorder characterized by difficulties maintaining attention because of a limited ability to concentrate; includes impulsive actions and hyperactive behavior.

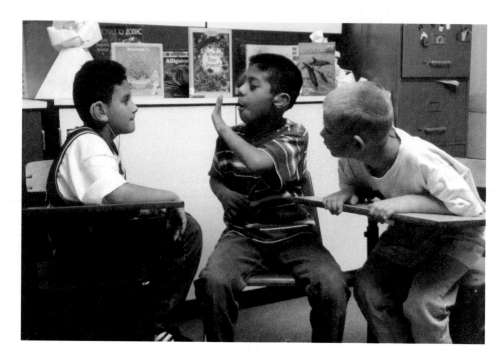

Students with a hearing impairment, no matter how slight or severe, can easily fall through the cracks in a busy classroom. As a teacher, what considerations might you need to make in order to fully support the needs of a hearing impaired student?

Students with Speech or Language Impairments

Some of the most common disabilities are problems with speech and language. About 1 in every 40 students has a communication disorder serious enough to warrant speech therapy or other special-education services.

Although the terms speech and language are often used interchangeably, they are not the same. Language is the communication of ideas using symbols and includes written language, sign language, gesture, and other modes of communication in addition to oral speech. Speech refers to the formation and sequencing of sounds. It is quite possible to have a speech disorder without a language disorder or to have a language disorder without a speech disorder (Bernstein & Tiegerman-Farber, 2002).

Students with Speech Disorders   There are many kinds of **speech disorders.** The most common are articulation (or phonological) disorders, such as omissions, distortions, or substitutions of sounds. For example, some students have difficulty pronouncing *r*'s, saying "sowee" for "sorry." Others have lisps, substituting *th* for *s*, saying "thnake" for "snake."

Misarticulated words are common and developmentally normal for many children in kindergarten and first grade but drop off rapidly through the school years. Moderate and extreme deviations in articulation diminish over the school years, with or without speech therapy. For this reason, speech therapists often decide not to work with a child who has a mild articulation problem. However, speech therapy is called for if a student cannot be understood or if the problem is causing the student psychological or social difficulties (such as being teased).

Speech disorders of all kinds are diagnosed by and treated by speech pathologists or speech therapists. The classroom teacher's role is less important here than with other disability areas. However, the classroom teacher does have one crucial role to play: displaying acceptance of students with speech disorders. Most speech disorders will eventually resolve themselves. The lasting damage is more often psychological than phonological; students with speech disorders often are subjected to a great deal of teasing and social rejection. Teachers can model acceptance of the child with speech

speech disorders

Oral articulation problems, occurring most frequently among children in the early elementary school grades.

disorders in several ways. First, teachers should be patient with students who are stuttering or having trouble producing words and never finish a student's sentence or allow others to do so. Second, teachers should avoid putting students who have speech problems into high-pressure situations that require quick verbal responses. Third, teachers should refrain from correcting students' articulation in class.

Students with Language Disorders   **Language disorders** are impairments of the ability to understand language or to express ideas in one's native language (Bernstein & Tiegerman-Farber, 2002). Problems due to limited English-speaking proficiency (LEP) for students whose first language is not English are not considered language disorders.

Difficulties in understanding language (receptive language disorders) or in communicating (expressive language disorders) might result from such physical problems as hearing or speech impairment. If not, they are likely to indicate mental retardation or learning disabilities. Many students come to school with what appear to be receptive or expressive language disorders but that in fact result from a lack of experience with standard English either because they speak a language other than English or a dialect of English (Battle, 1996; Bonner-Tompkins, 2001). Preschool programs that are rich in verbal experience and direct instruction in the fundamentals of standard English have been found to be effective in overcoming language problems that are characteristic of children from disadvantaged homes.

Students with Emotional and Behavioral Disorders

All students are likely to have emotional problems at some point in their school career; but about 1 percent have such serious, long-lasting, and pervasive emotional or psychiatric disorders that they require special education. As in the case of learning disabilities, students with serious emotional and behavioral disorders are far more likely to be boys than girls, by a ratio of more than 3 to 1 (U.S. Department of Education, 1994).

Students with **emotional and behavioral disorders** have been defined as ones whose educational performance is adversely affected over a long period of time to a marked degree by any of the following conditions:

1. An inability to learn that cannot be explained by intellectual, sensory, or health factors
2. An inability to build or maintain satisfactory interpersonal relationships with peers and teachers
3. Inappropriate types of behavior or feelings under normal circumstances
4. A general, pervasive mood of unhappiness or depression
5. A tendency to develop physical symptoms, pains, or fears associated with personal or school problems.

Causes of Emotional and Behavioral Disorders   Serious and long-term emotional and behavioral disorders may be the result of numerous potential causal factors in the makeup and development of an individual (Jones, Dohrn, & Dunn, 2004). Neurological functioning, psychological processes, a history of maladaptations, self-concept, and lack of social acceptance all play a role (Hardman, Drew, & Winston-Egan, 1996; Roeser, Eccles, & Strobel, 1998). Some of the same factors, including family dysfunction and maltreatment (Thompson & Wyatt, 1999), also play a role in disturbances that might temporarily affect a child's school performance.

Many factors that affect families can disrupt a student's sense of security and self-worth for a period of time. Changes in the family structure, for example, might leave a

CONNECTIONS

Problems due to limited English proficiency are discussed in Chapter 4, page 112.

CONNECTIONS

For more on preschool programs that help overcome problems of children from disadvantaged homes, see Chapter 3, page 76.

language disorders
Impairments in one's ability to understand language or to express ideas in one's native language.

emotional and behavioral disorders
Exceptionalities characterized by problems with learning, interpersonal relationships, and control of feelings and behavior.

child depressed, angry, insecure, defensive, and lonely, especially in the case of divorce, relocation to a new community, the addition of a younger sibling, the addition of a new stepparent, or the death or serious illness of a family member.

One problem in identifying serious emotional and behavioral disorders is that the term covers a wide range of behaviors, from aggression or hyperactivity to withdrawal or inability to make friends (Epstein & Cullinan, 1992) to anxiety and phobias (King & Ollendick, 1989). Also, children with emotional disorders quite frequently have other disabilities, such as learning disabilities or mental retardation, and it is often hard to tell whether an emotional problem is causing the diminished academic performance or school failure is causing the emotional problem.

Characteristics of Students with Emotional and Behavioral Disorders Scores of characteristics are associated with emotional and behavioral disorders (Rosenberg et al., 2004). The important issue is the degree of the behavior problem. Virtually any behavior that is exhibited excessively over a long period of time might be considered an indication of emotional disturbance. However, most students who have been identified as having emotional and behavioral disorders share some general characteristics. These include poor academic achievement, poor interpersonal relationships, and poor self-esteem (Lewis & Sullivan, 1996). Quay and Werry (1986) noted four general categories: conduct disorder, anxiety–withdrawal, immaturity, and socialized–aggressive disorder. For example, children with **conduct disorders** are frequently characterized as disobedient, distractible, selfish, jealous, destructive, impertinent, resistive, and disruptive. Quay and Werry noted that the first three of these categories represent behaviors that are maladaptive or sources of personal distress. However, socialized–aggressive behavior, which relates to frequent aggression against others, seems to be tied more to poor home conditions that model or reward aggressive behavior and might therefore be adaptive (though certainly not healthy or appropriate). The inclusion of conduct disorders in classifications of emotional and behavioral disorders is controversial. By law, students with conduct disorders must also have some other recognized disability or disorder to receive special-education services. IDEA has long protected children who have emotional and behavioral disorders from ordinary punishments (such as suspension) for disruptive behavior. The 2004 reauthorization maintains this protection for behaviors related to the child's disability, but not for unrelated behaviors.

Students Exhibiting Aggressive Behavior Students with conduct disorders and socialized–aggressive behaviors might frequently fight, steal, destroy property, and refuse to obey teachers (Jones, Dohrn, & Dunn, 2004). These students tend to be disliked by their peers, their teachers, and sometimes their parents. They typically do not respond to punishment or threats, though they might be skilled at avoiding punishment. Aggressive children not only pose a threat to the school and to their peers, but also put themselves in grave danger. Aggressive children, particularly boys, often develop serious emotional problems later in life, have difficulty holding jobs, and become involved in criminal behavior (Loeber & Stouthamer-Loeber, 1998). Effective approaches for these children include behavior management strategies like those described in Chapter 11 (see Jones et al., 2004).

Students with Withdrawn and Immature Behavior Children who are withdrawn, immature, low in self-esteem, or depressed typically have few friends or play with children much younger than themselves. They often have elaborate fantasies or daydreams and either very poor or grandiose self-images. Some might be overly anxious about their health and feel genuinely ill when under stress. Some students exhibit school phobia by refusing to attend, or by running away from, school.

CONNECTIONS

Behavior management programs for students exhibiting aggressive behavior are described in Chapter 11, page 371.

conduct disorders

Socioemotional and behavioral disorders that are indicated in individuals who, for example, are chronically disobedient or disruptive.

Unlike children who are aggressive, who can appear quite normal when they are not being aggressive, children who are withdrawn and immature often appear odd or awkward at all times. They almost always suffer from a lack of social skills (see Troop & Asher, 1999).

Students with Autism

In 1990, autism became a formal category of disability. The U.S. Department of Education (1991) defined **autism** as a developmental disability that significantly affects social interaction and verbal and nonverbal communication. It is usually evident before the age of three and has an adverse affect on educational performance. Children with autism are typically extremely withdrawn and have such severe difficulties with language that they might be entirely mute. They often engage in self-stimulation activities such as rocking, twirling objects, or flapping their hands. However, they might have normal or even outstanding abilities in certain areas. The term *autism spectrum disorder* is now being used to describe a broad range of severity, including a mild form of autism called *Asperger's syndrome* (National Research Council, 2001; Sweeney & Hoffman, 2004). For unknown reasons, autism is far more prevalent among boys than among girls (Friend & Bursuck, 1999). It is thought to be caused by some sort of brain damage or other brain dysfunction, although this is not clear (Matson, 1994). There are promising treatments for autism, including methods of teaching people with autism to build relationships with others (Koegel & Koegel, 1995) and teaching them alternative means of communicating (Quill, 2000).

Students with Sensory, Physical, and Health Impairments

Sensory impairments are problems with the ability to see or hear or otherwise receive information through the body's senses. Physical disorders include conditions such as cerebral palsy, spina bifida, spinal cord injury, and muscular dystrophy. Health disorders include, for example, acquired immune deficiency syndrome (AIDS); seizure disorders; diabetes; cystic fibrosis; sickle-cell anemia (in African American students); and bodily damage from chemical addictions, child abuse, or attempted suicide (Hardman et al., 1996).

Students with Visual Disabilities   Most students' visual problems are correctable by glasses or other types of corrective lenses. A **vision loss** is considered a disability only if it is not correctable. It is estimated that approximately 1 out of every 1,000 children has a visual disability. Individuals with such disabilities are usually referred to as *blind* or *visually impaired*. A legally blind child is one whose vision is judged to be 20/200 or worse in the better eye even with correction or whose field of vision is significantly narrower than that of a person with normal vision. Partially sighted persons, according to this classification system, are those whose vision is between 20/70 and 20/200 in the better eye with correction (Rogow, 1988).

It is a misconception to assume that individuals who are legally blind have no sight. More than 80 percent of students who are legally blind can read large- or regular-print books (Levin, 1996). This implies that many students with vision loss can be taught by means of a modification of usual teaching materials. Classroom teachers should be aware of the signs that indicate that a child is having a vision problem. Undoubtedly, children who have difficulty seeing also have difficulty in many areas of learning, because classroom lessons typically use a tremendous amount of visual material. Several possible signs of vision loss include the following: (1) child often tilts head; (2) child rubs eyes often; (3) child's eyes are red, inflamed, crusty, or water excessively; (4) child has difficulty reading small print or can't discriminate letters; (5) child complains of

autism
A category of disability that significantly affects social interaction, verbal and nonverbal communication, and educational performance.

sensory impairments
Problems with the ability to receive information through the body's senses.

vision loss
Degree of uncorrectable inability to see well.

Peers-helping-peers can provide multiple benefits for all parties involved, including the teacher. Describe these benefits.

dizziness or headaches after a reading assignment (Smith & Luckasson, 1995; Sornson, 2001). If you notice any of these problems, you should refer the student for appropriate vision screening.

Students Who Are Deaf or Hard of Hearing   **Hearing disabilities** can range from complete deafness to problems that can be alleviated with a hearing aid. The appropriate classification of an individual with hearing loss depends on the measures required to compensate for the problem. Simply having a student sit at the front of the classroom might be enough to compensate for a mild hearing loss. Many children can communicate adequately by listening to your voice and watching your lips. Others might need a hearing aid, and those with more severe problems will need to use a nonverbal form of communication such as sign language (see Radziewicz & Antonellis, 2002). Flexner (2001) argues that a broad range of children can benefit from amplification of the teacher's voice. Following are several suggestions to keep in mind:

1. Seat children with hearing problems in the front of the room, slightly off center toward the windows. This will allow them to see your face in the best light.
2. If the hearing problem is predominantly in one ear, students should sit in a front corner seat so that their better ear is toward you.
3. Speak at the student's eye level whenever possible.
4. Give important information and instructions while facing the class. Avoid talking while facing the chalkboard.
5. Do not use exaggerated lip movements when speaking.
6. Learn how to assist a child who has a hearing aid.

hearing disabilities
Degree of deafness; uncorrectable inability to hear well.

giftedness
Exceptional intellectual ability, creativity, or talent.

Students Who Are Gifted and Talented

Who are the gifted and talented? Almost all children, according to their parents; and in fact many students do have outstanding talents or skills in some area. **Giftedness** was once defined almost entirely in terms of superior IQ or demonstrated ability, such as outstanding performance in mathematics or chess, but the definition now encompasses students with superior abilities in a wide range of activities, including the arts

ON THE WEB

WEB-BASED RESOURCES FOR SPECIAL NEEDS EDUCATORS

Family Friendly Fun with Special Needs: www.family-friendly-fun.com

This site offers a great collection of resources for use with children with special needs on a variety of topics.

Special Needs Resource: www.edbydesign.com/specneedsres/links.html

This site showcases international students, assistive technologies, and other resources for special learners.

Internet Resources for Special Children: www.irsc.org

This organization is dedicated to providing information, activities, and support for learners with special needs.

Special Needs Opportunity Windows: http://snow.utoronto.ca

Professional development, student activities, and parent resource materials are just a few of the many areas contained on this site.

DREAMMS for Kids, Inc.: www.dreamms.org

Developmental Research for the Effective Advancement of Memory and Motor Skills is a nonprofit parent and professional service agency that specializes in Assistive Technology (AT)-related research, development, and information dissemination.

CAST (Center for Applied Special Technology): www.cast.org

CAST is an educational, not-for-profit organization that uses technology to expand opportunities for all people, including those with disabilities.

NCIP (National Center to Improve Practice in Special Education): www2.edc.org/NCIP

The National Center to Improve Practice in Special Education was federally funded from 1992 to 1998 to improve educational outcomes for students with disabilities by promoting the effective use of assistive and instructional technologies among educators and related personnel serving these students.

Alliance for Technology Access: www.ataccess.org

The Alliance for Technology Access (ATA) is a network of community-based resource centers, developers and vendors, affiliates, and associates dedicated to providing information and support services to children and adults with disabilities and increasing their use of standard, assistive, and information technologies.

Closing the Gap: www.closingthegap.com

Closing the Gap is a rich source for information on innovative applications of computer technology for persons with disabilities. This site provides a comprehensive examination of the most current uses of technology by persons with disabilities and the professionals who work with them.

Internet Special Education Resources (ISER): www.iser.com

ISER is a nationwide directory of professionals who serve the learning disabilities and special-education communities. This site helps parents and caregivers find local special-education professionals to help with learning disabilities and attention deficit hyperactivity disorder assessment, therapy, advocacy, and other special needs.

Adaptive Technologies: www.washington.edu/doit

The University of Washington has an extensive collection of publications and videos concerning technologies to help people with disabilities.

(Olszewski-Kubilius, 2003). High IQ is still considered part of the definition of gifted and talented (Steiner & Carr, 2003), and most students who are so categorized have IQs above 130. However, some groups are underidentified as gifted and talented, including females, students with disabilities, underachievers, and students who are members of racial or ethnic minority groups (Ford, 1996; Smith & Luckasson, 1995; Subotnik, 1997).

The 1978 Gifted and Talented Act stated that

the gifted and talented are children . . . who are identified . . . as possessing demonstrated or potential abilities that give evidence of high performance capabilities in areas such as intellectual, creative, specific academic or leadership ability or in the performing or visual arts and to by reason thereof require services or activities not ordinarily provided by the school (Public Law 95-561, Section 902).

This definition is meant to include students who possess extraordinary capabilities in any number of activities, not just in those areas that are part of the school curriculum. According to these rather vague criteria (see Gallagher, 1992), somewhere between 3 and 5 percent of all students are "gifted and talented." However, the percentage of students identified as gifted and talented varies from less than 1 percent in North Dakota to almost 10 percent in New Jersey (National Center for Education Statistics, 1988). This does not mean that New Jersey's students are especially talented; rather, it indicates the vast diversity in defining and identifying the gifted and talented in different states.

Characteristics of Gifted and Talented Students   Intellectually gifted children typically have strong motivation (Dai, Moon, & Feldhusen, 1998; Gottfried & Gottfried, 2004). They also are academically superior; usually learn to read early; and, in general, do excellent work in most school areas (Gallagher, 1992). One of the most important studies of the gifted, begun by Lewis Terman in 1926, followed 1,528 individuals who had IQs over 140 as children. Terman's research exploded the myth that high-IQ individuals were brainy but physically and socially inept. In fact, Terman found that children with outstanding IQs were larger, stronger, and better coordinated than other children and became better adjusted and more emotionally stable adults (Terman & Oden, 1959). Gifted students also have high self-concepts (Hoge & Renzulli, 1993), although they can suffer from perfectionism (Parker, 1997).

Education of Gifted Students   How to educate gifted students is a matter of debate (see Gallagher, 1995; Smutny, 2003; Willard-Holt, 2003; Winebrenner, 2000). Some programs for gifted and talented children involve special secondary schools for students who are gifted in science or in the arts. Some programs are special classes for high achievers in regular schools (see Olszewski-Kubilius, 2003). One debate in this area concerns acceleration versus enrichment. Advocates of acceleration (e.g., Pendarvis & Howley, 1996; Van Tassel-Baska, 1989) argue that gifted students should be encouraged to move through the school curriculum rapidly, perhaps skipping grades and going to college at an early age. Others (e.g., Feldhusen, 1996; Gallagher, 1992; Renzulli & Reis, 1997) maintain that rather than merely moving students through school more rapidly, programs for the gifted should engage them in more creative and problem-solving activities.

Research on the gifted provides more support (in terms of student achievement gains) for acceleration than for enrichment (Kulik & Kulik, 1997; Swiatek & Benbow, 1991). However, this could be because the outcomes of enrichment, such as creativity or problem-solving skills, are difficult to measure. **Acceleration programs** for the gifted often involve the teaching of advanced mathematics to students at early ages. A variation on the acceleration theme is a technique called curriculum compacting, in which teachers may skip over portions of the curriculum that the very able students do not need (Willard-Holt, 2003).

Enrichment programs take many forms. Many successful enrichment programs have involved self-directed or independent study (Parke, 1983; Reiss & Cellerino, 1983). Others have provided gifted students with adult mentors (Nash, Borman, & Colson, 1980). Renzulli (1994) suggests an emphasis on three types of activities: general exploratory activities, such as projects that allow students to find out

acceleration programs
Rapid promotion through advanced studies for students who are gifted or talented.

enrichment programs
Programs in which assignments or activities are designed to broaden or deepen the knowledge of students who master classroom lessons quickly.

about topics on their own; group training activities, such as games and simulations to promote creativity and problem-solving skills; and individual and small-group investigations of real problems, such as writing books or newspapers, interviewing elderly people to write oral histories, and conducting geological or archaeological investigations.

One problem with enrichment programs for the gifted and talented is simply stated: Most of the activities that are suggested for gifted and talented students would benefit all students. In recognition of this, many schools are now infusing activities that are characteristic of enrichment programs into the curriculum for all students, thereby meeting the needs of gifted and talented students without physically separating them from their peers (see Feldhusen, 1998; Holloway, 2003; Page, 2000; Renzulli, 1994; Treffinger, 1998; Van Tassel-Baska, 1998). Examples of such activities include increased use of projects, experiments, independent study, and cooperative learning.

WHAT IS SPECIAL EDUCATION?

Special education is any program provided for children with disabilities instead of, or in addition to, the general education classroom program. The practice of special education has changed dramatically in recent years and is still evolving (see Hallahan & Kauffman, 2003; Sorrells, Rieth, & Sindelar, 2004). Federal legislation has been critical in setting standards for special-education services administered by states and local districts.

Public Law 94-142 and IDEA

As recently as the mid-1960s, education of children with exceptionalities was quite different from what it is today. Many "handicapped" students received no special services at all. Those who did get special services usually attended separate schools or institutions for people with mental retardation, emotional disturbances, or vision or hearing loss. In the late 1960s the special-education system came under attack (see, e.g., Christoplos & Renz, 1969; Dunn, 1968; Semmel, Gerber, & MacMillan, 1994). Critics argued that people who had serious disabilities were too often shut away in state institutions with inadequate educational services or were left at home with no services at all and that mildly disabled children (particularly those with mild mental retardation) were being isolated in special programs that failed to teach them the skills they needed to function in society. Four million of the eight million disabled students of school age were not in school.

As a result, in 1975, Congress passed **Public Law 94-142,** the Education for the Handicapped Act. P.L. 94-142, as it is commonly called, profoundly affected both special and general education throughout the United States. It prescribed the services that all disabled children must receive and gave the children and their parents legal rights that they had not previously possessed. A basic tenet of P.L. 94-142 was that every disabled child is entitled to special education appropriate to the child's needs at public expense. This means, for example, that school districts or states must provide special education to children who are severely retarded or disabled.

P.L. 94-142 was extended beyond its original focus in two major pieces of legislation. In 1986, Public Law 99-457 extended the entitlement to free, appropriate education to children ages 3 to 5. It also added programs for seriously disabled infants

CERTIFICATION POINTER

Teacher certification tests will require you to identify areas of exceptionality in learning, including learning disabilities, visual and perceptual difficulties, and specific physical challenges.

special education
Programs that address the needs of students with mental, emotional, or physical disabilities.

Public Law 94-142
Federal law enacted in 1975 requiring provision of special-education services to eligible students.

Individuals with Disabilities Education Act (IDEA)

P.L. 101-476, a federal law enacted in 1990 that changed the name of P.L. 94-142 and broadened services to adolescents with disabilities.

IDEA '97

Public Law 105-17, enacted in 1997 to reauthorize IDEA (P.L. 101-476) and add provisions for greater parental and classroom teacher involvement in the education of students with special needs.

least restrictive environment

Provision in IDEA that requires students with disabilities to be educated with nondisabled peers to the maximum extent appropriate.

CERTIFICATION POINTER

On your teacher certification test, you should know that the placement of students in the "least restrictive" educational environment developed as a result of efforts to normalize the lives of children with disabilities.

mainstreaming

The temporal, instructional, and social integration of eligible children with exceptionalities with peers without exceptionalities based on an ongoing, individually determined educational planning and programming process.

Individualized Education Program (IEP)

A program tailored to the needs of a learner with exceptionalities.

and toddlers. Public Law 101-476, which passed in 1990, changed the name of the special-education law to the **Individuals with Disabilities Education Act (IDEA),** required that schools plan for the transition of adolescents with disabilities into further education or employment starting at age 16, and replaced the term *handicapped children* with the term *children with disabilities.*

In 1997, Public Law 105-17, the Individuals with Disabilities Education Act Amendments of 1997, or **IDEA '97,** was passed to reauthorize and strengthen the original act (National Information Center for Children and Youth with Disabilities, 1998). Among the goals of this law are raising educational expectations for children with disabilities, increasing the role of parents in the education of their children with disabilities, assuring that regular classroom teachers are involved in planning for and assessment of these children, including students with disabilities in local and state assessments, and supporting professional development for all who educate children with disabilities (U.S. Department of Education, 1998). The six major provisions of IDEA '97 are summarized in Table 12.5.

IDEA was further updated in 2004 under Public Law 108-446, known as the Individuals with Disabilities Education Improvement Act. This revision emphasized prevention and early intervention, allowing schools to spend special-education funds to prevent children from needing special-education services. It changed the definition of learning disabilities to eliminate the concept of discrepancy between IQ and achievement, asked states to monitor and correct racial disparities in assignment to special education, and coordinated IDEA with other reforms, especially No Child Left Behind (see Chapter 9).

Least Restrictive Environment The provision of IDEA that is of greatest importance to general education classroom teachers is that students with disabilities must be assigned to the **least restrictive environment** that is appropriate to their needs. This provision gives a legal basis for the practice of **mainstreaming,** a term that has now been replaced with the word *inclusion.* This means that general education classroom teachers are likely to have in their classes students with mild disabilities (such as learning disabilities, mild mental retardation, physical disabilities, or speech problems) who might leave class for special instruction part of the day. It also means that classes for students with more serious disabilities are likely to be located in general education school facilities and that these students will probably attend some activities with their nondisabled peers.

Individualized Education Program (IEP) Another important requirement of IDEA is that every student with a disability must have an **Individualized Education Program (IEP)** that guides the services the student receives. The IEP describes a student's problems and delineates a specific course of action to address these problems. Generally, it is prepared by a special services committee composed of school professionals such as special-education teachers, special-education supervisors, school psychologists, the principal, counselors, and/or classroom teachers. Special services teams go by different names in different states; for example, they may be called child study teams or appraisal and review teams. The student's parent must consent to the IEP. The idea behind the use of IEPs is to give everyone concerned with the education of a child with a disability an opportunity to help formulate the child's instructional program. The requirement that a parent sign the IEP is designed to ensure parental awareness of and approval of what the school proposes to do for the child. A parent might hold the school accountable if the child does not receive the promised services.

The law requires that evaluations of students for possible placement in special-education programs be done by qualified professionals. Although general education classroom and special-education teachers will typically be involved in the evaluation

Table 12.5

The Six Principles of IDEA '97

The Six Principles	Key Points
Free appropriate public education	"The term *free appropriate public education* means special education and related services that: (A) have been provided at public expense, under public supervision and direction, and without charge; (B) meet the standards of the State educational agency; (C) include an appropriate preschool, elementary, or secondary school education in the State involved; and (D) are provided in conformity with the individualized education program required under section 614(d)." [Section 602(8)]
Appropriate evaluation	Evaluation procedures should assure that all children with disabilities are appropriately assessed for purposes of: • eligibility determination, • educational programming, • individual performance monitoring, • and should be selected and administered so as to avoid racial or cultural discrimination. In addition, IDEA '97 adds that: • no child should be subjected to unnecessary tests and assessments, and that • LEAs (local education agencies) should not be unnecessarily burdened with the associated expenses.
Individualized Education Program	Must be developed by a multidisciplinary team and contain statements of: • present levels of educational performance, including how the disability affects involvement and progress in the general curriculum; • measurable annual goals, including benchmarks or short-term objectives; • the special education and related services to be provided; • program modifications or supports provided for the child; • an explanation of the extent, if any, to which the child will not participate with nondisabled students in the regular class and in extracurricular and nonacademic activities; • any modifications for administration of State and district-wide assessment or alternative assessment methods; • initiation date and the anticipated frequency, location, and duration of services; • transition service needs of the child, beginning at age 14 and updated annually; • needed transition services of the child, beginning at age 16; • information to the child, at least one year before reaching the age of majority under State law, of rights that will transfer upon reaching the age of majority; • procedures for measuring progress and informing parents of that progress. [Section 614(d)(1)(A)]
Least restrictive environment	LRE is based on the presumptions that children with disabilities are: • most appropriately educated with their nondisabled peers; removal from the general educational setting occurs only when that education—even with the use of supplementary aids and services—cannot be achieved satisfactorily. [Section 612(a)(5)(A)]
Parent and student participation in decision making	When developing the IEP, parents must: • be notified; • give consent; • have their input solicited and considered. Students can: • be active members of their own IEP team.
Procedural safeguards	Procedural safeguards were developed to: • protect rights; • ensure that information is provided; • give a way for disputes to be resolved.

process, teachers are not generally allowed to give the psychological tests (such as IQ tests) that are used for placement decisions.

IDEA gives children with disabilities and their parents legal safeguards with regard to special-education placement and programs. For example, if parents believe that a child has been diagnosed incorrectly or assigned to the wrong program or if they are unsatisfied with the services a child is receiving, they may bring a grievance against the school district. Also, the law specifies that parents be notified about all placement decisions, conferences, and changes in program.

For children with special needs who are under the age of 3, a specialized plan focusing on the child and his or her family is typically prepared. This is called an Individualized Family Service Plan (IFSP). At the other end of the education system, an Individualized Transition Plan (ITP) is often written for adolescents with special needs before their 17th birthday (Sax & Thoma, 2002). The ITP anticipates the student's needs as he or she makes the transition from school to work and to adult life.

An Array of Special-Education Services

An important aspect of an IEP is a special-education program that is appropriate to the student's needs. Every school district offers children with special needs an array of services intended to be flexible enough to meet the unique needs of all. In practice, these services are often organized as a continuum going from least to most restrictive, as follows:

1. Direct or indirect consultation and support for general education teacher
2. Special education up to 1 hour per day
3. Special education 1 to 3 hours per day; resource program
4. Special education more than 3 hours per day; self-contained special education
5. Special day school
6. Special residential school
7. Home/hospital.

In general, students with more severe disabilities receive more restrictive services than do those with less severe disabilities. For example, a student with severe mental retardation is unlikely to be placed in a general education classroom during academic periods, whereas a student with a speech problem or a mild learning disability is likely to be in a general education classroom for most or all of the school day. However, severity of disability is not the sole criterion for placement; also considered is the appropriateness of the various settings for an individual student's needs. For example, a student in a wheelchair with a severe orthopedic disability but no learning problems could easily attend and profit from general education classes, whereas a student with a hearing deficit might not.

With the exception of students who have physical or sensory disabilities, few students received special education outside of the school building. The great majority of students who have learning disabilities or speech impairments attend general education classes part or most of the day, usually supplemented by 1 or more hours per day in a special-education resource room. This is also true for the majority of students with physical disabilities and almost half of all students with emotional disorders. Most other students with special needs attend special classes located in their school buildings. The continuum of services available to students with disabilities, from least to most restrictive, is described in the following sections.

General Education Classroom Placement   The needs of many students with disabilities can be met in the general education classroom with little or no outside assistance.

For example, students who have mild vision or hearing loss may simply be seated near the front of the room. Students with mild to moderate learning disabilities may have their needs met in the general education classroom if the teacher uses strategies for accommodating instruction to student differences. For example, the use of instructional aides, tutors, or parent volunteers can allow exceptional students to remain in the general education classroom. Classroom teachers can often adapt their instruction to make it easier for students to succeed. For example, one teacher noticed that a student with perceptual problems was having difficulties with arithmetic because he could not line up his numbers. She solved the problem by giving him graph paper to work on.

Research generally shows that the most effective strategies for dealing with students who have learning and behavior problems are those used in the general education classroom (Lloyd, Singh, & Repp, 1991). Special-education options should usually be explored only after serious efforts have been made to meet students' needs in the general education classroom (see Putnam, 1998b; Smith, Polloway, Patton, & Dowdy, 1998).

CONNECTIONS

Strategies for accommodating instruction to student differences are discussed in Chapter 9, page 279.

Collaboration with Consulting Teachers and Other Professionals

In **collaboration,** several professionals work cooperatively to provide educational services. Students with disabilities who are included in the general education classroom benefit from professionals such as the consulting resource room teacher, school psychologist, speech and language specialists, and other professionals who collaborate with the general education teacher to develop and implement appropriate educational experiences for the students. Many school districts provide classroom teachers with consultants to help them adapt their instruction to the needs of students with disabilities. Consulting teachers typically are trained in special education as well as general education. They might come into the classroom to observe the behavior of a student, but most often they suggest solutions to the general education teacher rather than work directly with students (Warger & Pugach, 1996). Research finds that well-designed consulting models can be effective in assisting teachers to maintain students with mild disabilities, particularly those with learning disabilities, in the general education classroom (Rosenfield & Gravois, 1996; Snell & Janney, 2000).

INTASC

10 Partnerships

For some types of disabilities, itinerant (traveling) teachers provide special services to students a few times a week. This pattern of service is typical of programs for students with speech and language disorders.

Resource Room Placement

Many students with disabilities are assigned to general education classes for most of their school day but participate in resource programs at other times. Most often, resource programs focus on teaching reading, language arts, mathematics, and occasionally other subjects. A resource room program usually involves a small number of students working with a special-education teacher. Ideally, the resource teacher meets regularly with the classroom teacher to coordinate programs for students and to suggest ways in which the general education classroom teacher can adapt instruction when the students are in the general education class (Larrivee, Semmel, & Gerber, 1997).

Sometimes resource teachers work in the general education classroom. For example, a resource teacher might work with one reading group while the general education classroom teacher works with another. This arrangement avoids pulling students out of class—which is both inefficient (because of the transition time required) and potentially demeaning, because the students are excluded from class for some period of time. Team teaching involving general education and special-education teachers also enhances communication between the teachers (Hardin & McNelis, 1996).

collaboration
Process in which professionals work cooperatively to provide educational services.

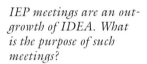

Special-Education Class Placement with Part-Time Inclusion   Many students with disabilities are assigned to special classes taught by a special-education teacher but are integrated with nondisabled students part of the school day. These students join other students most often for music, art, and physical education; somewhat less often for social studies, science, and mathematics; and least often for reading. One important difference between this category of special services and the resource room model is that in the resource room, the student's primary placement is in the general education class; the classroom teacher is the homeroom teacher and generally takes responsibility for the student's program, with the resource teacher providing extra support. In the case of a student who is assigned to special education and is integrated part of the day, the situation is reversed. The special-education teacher generally serves as the homeroom teacher and takes primary responsibility.

Self-Contained Special Education   A self-contained special-education program is a class located in a school separately from the general education instructional program. Until the mainstreaming movement began in the early 1970s, this (along with separate schools for children with mental retardation) was the typical placement for students with disabilities. Students in self-contained programs are taught by special-education teachers and have relatively few contacts with the general education instructional program.

Some students attend separate, special, day schools. These are typically students with severe disabilities, such as severe retardation or physical disabilities, or students whose presence might be disruptive to the general education school, such as those with serious emotional disturbances. In addition, small numbers of students with disabilities attend special residential schools for students with profound disabilities who require special treatment.

Related Services   IDEA '97 guarantees "related services" for children with disabilites. These are services required by a child with a disability to benefit from gen-

IEP meetings are an outgrowth of IDEA. What is the purpose of such meetings?

eral or special education. For example, school psychologists are often involved in the process of diagnosing students with disabilities and sometimes participate in the preparation of IEPs (Reschly, 2003). In addition, they may counsel the student or consult with the teacher about behavioral and learning problems. Speech and language therapists generally work with students on a one-to-one basis, though they may provide some small-group instruction for students with similar problems. These therapists also consult with teachers about ways to address student difficulties. Physical and occupational therapists treat motor difficulties under the direction of a physician.

School social workers and pupil personnel workers serve as a major link between the school and the family and are likely to become involved when problems at home are affecting students' school performance or behavior.

Classroom teachers have important roles in the education of children with disabilities. They are important in referring students to receive special services, in participating in the assessment of students, and in preparing and implementing IEPs. The

Teaching Dilemmas: Cases to Consider

INTASC   **2** Knowledge of Human Development and Learning
            8 Assessment of Student Learning

Referring a Student

Roger Bond is a second-grade teacher at a rural elementary school in the Southwest. He's scheduled an appointment with his principal, Ana Garza, to discuss a child.

Roger: Thanks for meeting with me. I wanted to talk with you about one of my children, Callie Williams. She's really struggling with her reading, and I think she should be in special ed. I know you were a special-ed teacher before you were principal, so I thought you could help.

Ana: I'll do my best. I know Callie, and I know she had some trouble in first grade, too. What do you think the problem is?

Roger: Well, she seems to be able to decode, but she reads very slowly and loses comprehension.

Ana: That's a common problem with second-graders. What makes Callie stand out?

Roger: Well, besides her reading she has a lot of problems with distractibility, and she's always misbehaving in class.

Ana: I see. Have you given her any reading tests to see where her problem is?

Roger: I thought they'd do that when she got referred for special ed. She did get a low score on the state reading test.

Ana: Right, but that doesn't tell you where her problem is.

Roger: Well, if you'll tell me how to start the process, we can get her the testing she needs.

Ana: Not so fast! My philosophy is that you don't start a child toward special education until you've tried everything else.

Roger: But then won't she just get worse? Also, she's disrupting my class and making it hard for other kids to learn. A special-education teacher would have more expertise in helping students with difficulties, and a smaller class size.

Ana: Assigning a child to special ed is a major step. Let's try some other things first, and we'll watch her carefully. If we've really tried everything, then we'll start the IEP process to see if she qualifies for special ed, but not before!

Roger: Well . . . OK. What should I do?

Ana: First, let's find out what her reading problem is. I'll ask Ms. Jackson, our reading specialist, to give her an individual assessment. If she needs special help with reading fluency, which I suspect, we can assign her to a tutor.

Roger: But what about her behavior?

Ana: Let's look into that, too. The county is doing a series of workshops on behavior management. I'm going to see if I can get you in.

Roger: OK, I'll give it a try. But frankly, I'm surprised. Because you are a former special-ed teacher, I thought you'd back me up.

Ana: If Callie needs special education, I'll see that she gets it. But my experience tells me that special ed isn't magic. Wherever she is, Callie will need good instruction and good classroom management.

Roger: All right. Thanks.

@ *Questions for Reflection*

1. Is Ana Garza right to deny Roger's request for a special-education evaluation? Is she depriving Callie of services she's entitled to, or is she doing the right thing?

2. What if Callie had been an English language learner? How might the conversation between Roger and Ana have been different?

3. What should Roger do to help Callie? How can Ms. Garza and others in the school help him succeed?

Theory into Practice section that follows describes the process by which classroom teachers seek special-education services for students (see Hallahan & Kauffman, 1997; Smith, 2001).

In Figure 12.2 a flowchart shows how the IEP process operates. Figure 12.3 on pages 420–421 is an example of an IEP.

FIGURE 12.2
Flowchart for the Individualized Education Program Process

From Diane Pedrotty Rivera and Deborah Deutsch Smith, *Teaching Students with Learning and Behavior Problems* (3rd ed.), p. 52. Copyright © 1997 by Allyn & Bacon. Reprinted by permission.

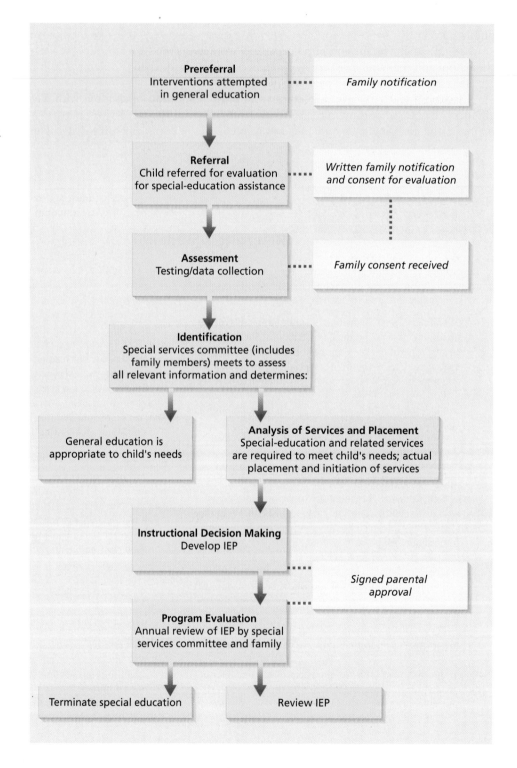

Preparing IEPs

Initial referral. The process of preparing an Individualized Education Program begins when a student is referred for assessment. Referrals for special-education assessment can be made by parents, physicians, principals, or teachers. Classroom teachers most often initiate referrals for children with suspected learning disabilities, mental retardation, speech impairment, or emotional disturbance. Most other disabilities are diagnosed before students enter school. In most schools, initial referrals are made to the building principal, who contacts the relevant school district staff.

Screening and assessment. As soon as the student is referred for assessment, an initial determination is made to accept or reject the referral. In practice, almost all referrals are accepted. The evaluation and placement team may look at the student's school records and interview classroom teachers and others who know the student. If the team members decide to accept the referral, they must obtain parental permission to do a comprehensive assessment.

Members of the special services team include professionals designated by the school district plus the parents of the referred student and, if appropriate, the referred student. If the referral has to do with learning or emotional problems, a school psychologist or guidance counselor will usually be involved. If the referral has to do with speech or language problems, a speech pathologist or speech teacher will typically serve on the team. The building principal usually chairs the team but may designate a special-education teacher or other professional to do so.

The referred student is then given tests to assess strengths and weaknesses. For learning and emotional problems, these tests are usually given by a school psychologist. Specific achievement tests (such as reading or mathematics assessments) are often given by special-education or reading teachers. Parents must give permission for any specialized assessments. Increasingly, portfolios of student work, teacher evaluations, and other information collected over extended time periods are becoming important parts of the assessment process (Gomez, Grave, & Block, 1991).

If appropriate, the school may try a prereferral intervention before deciding on placement in special education (see Mamlin & Harris, 1998; Rosenfield & Gravois, 1996). For example, a child having serious reading problems might be given a tutor for a period of time before being determined to have a reading disability. For a child with a behavior problem, a home-based reinforcement program or other behavior management program might be set up. If these interventions worked, then the child might not be assigned to special education but could be served within the general education program. Even if a child does need special-education services, the prereferral intervention is likely to provide important information about the kind of services most likely to work.

Writing the IEP. When the comprehensive assessment is complete, the special services team members meet to consider the best placement for the student. If they determine that special education is necessary, they will prepare an IEP. An example of an IEP appears in Figure 12.3. Usually, the special-education teacher and/or the classroom teacher prepares the

INTASC

8 Assessment of Student Learning

CONNECTIONS

For more on home-based reinforcement strategies, see Chapter 11, page 374.

Quentinburg Public Schools—Special-Education Department

Individualized Education Program

Student Name: Jillian Carol

School: Jefferson Elementary

Primary lang.: Home-English Student-English

Program start date: 8/28/04

Date of Birth: 4/2/93

Grade: 5

Date of meeting: 8/28/04

Review date: 8/28/05

Services required

General Education   Full-time participation with support from paraprofessional or special-education teacher at least three hours weekly

Resources   Incidental as needed

Self-Contained   Speech/language therapy for language development

Related Services   40 minutes/week

Other

Justification for Placement (include justification for any time spent not in general education): Student's needs indicate that learning can appropriately take place in the general education classroom with appropriate supports provided. Supports will include adapted materials as well as adult assistance up to three hours per week. Incidental time noted in the resource room is intended to preserve the option of one-to-one assistance on specific goals and objectives as needed, as determined by the teachers.

Tests Used

Intellectual   WISC-III (Full Scale IQ = 64)

Educational   Woodcock Reading, Keymath

Behavioral   NA

Speech/language

Other

Vision   Within normal limits

Hearing   Within normal limits

Strengths (present level of functioning)

Jillian enjoys talking with peers and adults.

Jillian is polite and well mannered.

Jillian generally responds appropriately to directions.

Jillian likes to tell stories she creates.

Weaknesses (present level of functioning)

1. Below grade level in word identification (3.1) and reading comprehension (3.2)

2. Below grade level in vocabulary usage (2.1)

3. Below grade level in math computation and problem solving (1.6)

FIGURE 12.3

Sample Individualized Education Program

From Marilyn Friend and William D. Bursuck, *Including Students with Special Needs: A Practical Guide for Classroom Teachers* (2nd ed.), pp. 55–56. Copyright © 1999 by Allyn & Bacon. Reprinted by permission.

Annual Goal: Jillian will improve her reading skills to approximately a 3.9 level.
STO 1: Jillian will read from a 3rd-grade reader at 80 words per minute with fewer than 3 errors per minute.
STO 2: Jillian will answer with 80% accuracy comprehension questions about reading passages at a third-grade level.
Evaluation: Oral performance   **Person(s):** Special-education teacher

Annual Goal: Jillian will use vocabulary at approximately a 3.0 level
STO 1: Jillian will tell a story using vocabulary from third-grade reading materials.
STO 2: Jillian will use 3rd-grade vocabulary when talking about her out-of-school activities.
STO 3: Jillian will learn at least 40 vocabulary words by using a word bank.
Evaluation: Oral performance, checklist   **Person(s):** Special-education teacher
                                            Classroom teacher

Annual Goal: Jillian will compute and problem solve at approximately a 2.5 level
STO 1: Jillian will write answers to basic addition and subtraction facts with 100% accuracy.
STO 2: Jillian will accurately compute two-digit addition and subtraction problems without regrouping with 90% accuracy.
STO 3: Jillian will correctly solve word problems written at her reading level and at approximately a 2.5 difficulty level with 90% accuracy.
Evaluation: Written performance   **Person(s):** Special-education teacher
                                            Classroom teacher

Team Signatures

LEA Representative   Eva Kim
Parent   Julia Carol
Special-Education Teacher   Vera Delaney
General Education Teacher
Psychologist   Nadine Showalter
Counselor
Speech/Language Therapist   Ed Briggs
Other
Other

IEP. The student's parent(s) must sign a consent form regarding the place-ment decision, and in many school districts a parent must also sign the IEP. This means that parents can (and in some cases do) refuse to have their children placed in special-education programs. At a minimum, the IEP must contain the following information (see Bateman & Linden, 1998).

1. **Statements indicating the child's present level of performance.** These typically include the results of specific tests as well as descriptions of class-room functioning. Behavior rating checklists, work samples, or other obser-vation forms may be used to clarify a student's strengths and weaknesses.

2. **Goals indicating anticipated progress during the year.** For example, a student might have goals of reading at a fourth-grade level as measured by a standardized test, of improving classroom behavior so that disciplinary referrals are reduced to zero, or of completing a bricklaying course in a vocational education program.

3. **Intermediate (shorter-term) instructional objectives.** A student who is having difficulties in reading might be given a short-term objective (STO) of completing a certain number of individualized reading comprehension units per month, or a student with emotional and behavior problems might be expected to get along with peers better and avoid fights.

4. **A statement of the specific special-education and related services to be provided as well as the extent to which the student will participate in general education programs.** The IEP might specify, for example, that a student would receive two 30-minute sessions with a speech therapist each week. An IEP for a student with a learning disability might specify 45 min-utes per day of instruction from a resource teacher in reading plus consul-tation between the resource teacher and the classroom teacher on ways to adapt instruction in the general education classroom. A student with mental retardation might be assigned to a self-contained special-education class, but the IEP might specify that the student participate in the general physi-cal education program. The IEP would specify any adaptations necessary to accommodate students in the general education class, such as wheelchair ramps, large-type books, or cassette tapes.

5. **The projected date for the initiation of services and the anticipated duration of services.** Once the IEP has been written, the student must receive services within a reasonable time period. Students may not be put on a waiting list; the school district must provide or contract for the indicated services.

6. **Evaluation criteria and procedures for measuring progress toward goals on at least an annual basis.** The IEP should specify a strategy for remediat-ing the student's deficits. In particular, the IEP should state what objectives the student is to achieve and how those objectives are to be attained and measured. It is critical to direct special-education services toward a well-specified set of learning or behavior objectives rather than simply deciding that a student falls into some category and therefore should receive some service. Ideally, special education for students with mild disabilities should be a short-term, intensive treatment to give students the skills needed in a general education classroom. All too often, a student who is assigned to spe-cial education remains there indefinitely, even after the problem for which the student was initially referred has been remediated.

IEPs must be updated at least once a year. The updating provides an opportunity for the team to change programs that are not working or to reduce or terminate special-education services when the student no longer needs them.

$\mathcal{W}$HAT IS INCLUSION?

The least restrictive environment clause of P.L. 94-142 revolutionized the practice of special education as well as general education. As has already been noted, it requires that exceptional students be assigned to the least restrictive environment that is appropriate to their needs. Refer to Figure 12.4 for definitions of least restrictive environment and inclusion. This provision has resulted in greatly increased contact between students with disabilities and students without disabilities. In general, students with all types of disabilities have moved one or two notches up the continuum of special-education services. Students who were once placed in special schools are now generally put in separate classrooms in general education schools. Students who were once placed in separate classrooms in general education schools, particularly students with mild retardation and learning disabilities, are now most often assigned to general education classes for most of their instruction. A growing movement for **full inclusion** calls for including all children in general education classes, with appropriate assistance (see Gartner & Lipsky, 1987; Porter & Stone, 1998; Sapon-Shevin, 2001, 2003).

Proponents of full inclusion argue that pull-out programs discourage effective partnerships between general and special educators in implementing IEPs and that students in pull-out programs are stigmatized when they are segregated from other

INTASC

4 Multiple Instructional Strategies

full inclusion
Arrangement whereby students who have disabilities or are at risk receive all their instruction in a general education setting; support services are brought to the student.

**FIGURE 12.4
Terminology: Inclusive Education**

Mainstreaming means:

"the temporal, instructional, and social integration of eligible exceptional children with normal peers based on an ongoing, individually determined educational planning and programming process" (Kaufman et al., 1975, pp. 40–41).

Least restrictive environment means:

the provision in Public Law 94-142 (renamed the Individuals with Disabilities Education Act, or IDEA) that requires students with disabilities to be educated to the maximum extent appropriate with their nondisabled peers.

Inclusive education means:

"that students attend their home school with their age and grade peers. It requires that the proportion of students labeled for special services is relatively uniform for all of the schools within a particular district. . . . Included students are not isolated into special classes or wings within the school" (National Association of State Boards of Education, 1992, p. 12).

Full inclusion means that

students who are disabled or at risk receive all their instruction in a general education setting; support services come to the student.

Partial inclusion means that

students receive most of their instruction in general education settings, but the student may be pulled out to another instructional setting when such a setting is deemed appropriate to the student's individual needs.

INTASC

9 Professional Commitment
   and Responsibility

Personal Reflection

The Struggle over Inclusion

I was once doing a study intended to improve outcomes for children with learning disabilities. The project focused both on integrating children in regular classes and making sure that pull-out special-education teachers were using content and methods closely aligned with those used in the general education classroom.

I remember visiting a special-education teacher who was very resistant to the concept of teaching children the same content they were seeing in their regular classes. "I think of this (pull-out) class as a club," she said, "a safe place where kids can escape from the pressures they experience the rest of the day."

I was astonished. As part of the research, I'd seen her kids in their general education classes. They were eager to learn what the other kids were learning and were frustrated that they had trouble doing it. The teacher had an opportunity to help them succeed on the content that the kids themselves thought they should learn, much less the school and the state.

Children with learning disabilities want to succeed, and they can do so with additional help. Because they experience a lot of frustration, they need emotional support too, but to my way of thinking, children are happiest when they're succeeding, and they need to have every chance to make it where it matters most to them, in the regular class.

@ Reflect on This. What are the possible positive benefits this teacher's children might realize as a result of her belief? What are the potential negative ramifications of her approach? What do you consider to be the best approach to inclusion, and what do you see as your biggest challenge as the classroom teacher?

students. These proponents suggest that special-education teachers or paraprofessionals team with classroom teachers and provide services in the general education classroom (Fisher, Sax, & Grove, 2000; Hanline & Daley, 2002; McLesky & Waldron, 2002; Ruder, 2000; Sapon-Shevin, 2001; Vaughn, Bos, & Schumm, 2000). Opponents of full inclusion argue that general education classroom teachers lack appropriate training and materials and are already overburdened with large class sizes and inadequate support services, and they worry that children with special needs might not receive necessary services (CASE, 1993; Kauffman, Lloyd, Baker, & Riedel, 1995; National Education Association, 1992; Shanker, 1994/1995).

Many (perhaps most) classroom teachers have students with disabilities, who are usually receiving some type of special-education services part of the day. Most of these integrated students are categorized as having learning disabilities, speech impairments, mild retardation, or emotional disorders. High-quality inclusion models can improve the achievement and self-confidence of these students. Inclusion also allows students with disabilities to interact with peers and to learn conventional behavior. However, inclusion also creates challenges. When integrated students are performing below the level of the rest of the class, some teachers struggle to adapt instruction to these students' needs—and to cope with the often negative attitudes of the nondisabled students toward their classmates with disabilities (McLeskey & Waldron, 2002; Pearl et al., 1998), which might defeat attempts at social integration. Unfortunately, some classroom teachers are uncomfortable about having students with disabilities in their classes, and many feel poorly prepared to accommodate these students' needs (Schumm & Vaughn, 1992; Semmel, Abernathy, Butera, & Lesar, 1991). Inclusion

This student with physical impairments is in a full inclusion program. According to research, how effective are full inclusion and mainstreaming compared to other approaches? As a teacher, how might you foster this boy's social acceptance by peers?

provides an opportunity for more effective services but is by no means a guarantee that better services will actually be provided (see Fuchs & Fuchs, 1995; Kauffman, McGee, & Brigham, 2004; Riehl, 2000).

Research on Inclusion

Research on inclusion, often referred to as mainstreaming, has focused on students with learning disabilities, mild retardation, and mild emotional disorders, whose deficits can be termed "mild academic disabilities" (Holloway, 2001; Manset & Semmel, 1997). Several studies have compared students with mild academic disabilities in special-education classes to those in general education classes. When the general education teacher uses an instructional method that is designed to accommodate a wide range of student abilities, students with mild disabilities generally learn much better in the general education classroom than in special-education classes. One classic study on this topic was done by Calhoun and Elliott (1977), who compared students with mild mental retardation and emotional disorders in general education classes with students with the same disabilities in special-education classes. General education classes as well as special-education classes used the same individualized materials, and teachers (trained in special education) were rotated across classes to ensure that the only difference between the general and special programs was the presence of nondisabled classmates. The results of the Calhoun and Elliott (1977) study, depicted in Figure 12.5, suggest the superiority of general education class placement. Other studies (e.g., Gottlieb & Weinberg, 1999; Manset & Semmel, 1997; Reynolds & Wolfe, 1999; Saleno & Garrick-Duhaney, 1999; Waldron & McLesky, 1998) have found more mixed results.

Research on programs for general education classrooms that contain students with learning disabilities indicates that one successful strategy is to use individualized instructional programs. For example, the Cooperative Integrated Reading and Composition (CIRC) program described in Chapter 8 has been found to improve

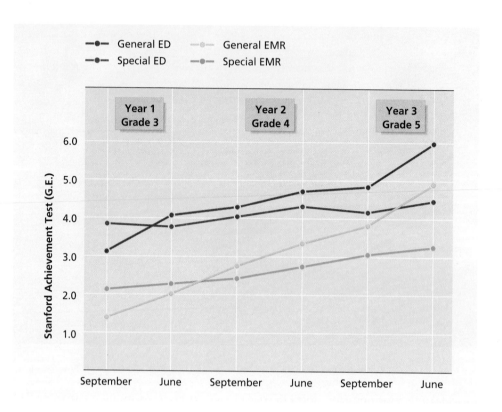

FIGURE 12.5

Achievement of Students in General Education and Special-Education Classes

In a classic study, placement in general education classes rather than special-education classes resulted in higher achievement levels over 3 years for students who are emotionally disturbed (ED) and educable mentally retarded (EMR).

From N. A. Madden and R. E. Slavin, "Mainstreaming Students with Mild Handicaps," *Review of Educational Research, 53*(4), 1983, p. 525. Copyright © 1983 by the American Educational Research Association. Reprinted by permission of the publisher. Based on data from G. Calhoun and R. Elliott, "Self-Concept and Academic Achievement of Educable Retarded and Emotionally Disturbed," *Exceptional Children, 44*, pp. 379–380. Copyright © 1977 by The Council for Exceptional Children. Reprinted with permission.

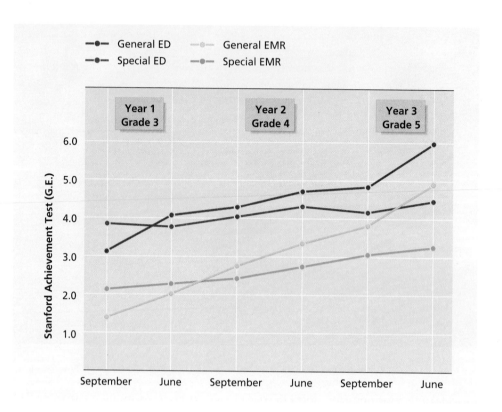

CONNECTIONS

Cooperative Integrated Reading and Composition (CIRC) is discussed in Chapter 8, page 258.

CONNECTIONS

For more on STAD, see Chapter 8, page 256.

INTASC

10 Partnerships

the achievement of mainstreamed students with learning disabilities, in comparison to mainstreamed students in traditionally organized classes (Slavin, Madden, & Leavey, 1984a, 1984b; Stevens & Slavin, 1995a).

Improving the social acceptance of students with academic disabilities is a critical task of inclusion. One consistently effective means of doing this is to involve the students in cooperative learning teams with their nondisabled classmates (Nevin, 1998; Putnam, 1998a). For example, a study of Student Teams–Achievement Divisions (STAD) in classes containing students with learning disabilities found that STAD reduced the social rejection of the students with learning disabilities while significantly increasing their achievement (Madden & Slavin, 1983a). Other cooperative learning programs have found similar effects on the social acceptance of students with mild academic disabilities (Slavin et al., 1984b; Slavin & Stevens, 1991; Stevens & Slavin, 1995a).

A key element in effective inclusion is maintaining close coordination between classroom and special teachers (Choate, 2002; Friend & Bursuck, 2002; Smith, Polloway, Patton, & Dowdy, 2004). Studies of pull-out programs for students with learning disabilities often find that special-education teachers have little knowledge of the school's general education curriculum and do little to integrate their instruction with it (Allington & McGill-Franzen, 1989). An experiment by Fuchs, Fuchs, and Fernstrom (1993) showed how coordination could improve student performance and accomplish full integration of all students with learning disabilities into general education classes over a period of time. In this study, children in pull-out math programs were given frequent curriculum-based measures assessing their progress relative to the school's math program. Special-education teachers examined the requirements for success in the general education class and prepared children specifically to succeed in that setting. As the children reached a criterion level of skills in math, they were transitioned into the general education class and then followed up to ensure that they were succeeding there. Over the course of a school year, all 21 students involved in the study were successfully transitioned to full-time general education class placement and learned significantly more than matched control students did.

There is very little research on the outcomes of full inclusion programs that integrate children who generally would not have been integrated in traditional mainstreaming models. There are descriptions of outstanding full inclusion programs (e.g., Mahony, 1997; Raison, Hanson, Hall, & Reynolds, 1995; Villa & Thousand, 2003) but there have also been reports of full inclusion disasters (e.g., Baines, Baines, & Masterson, 1994). Research comparing inclusive and special-education programs finds few differences (e.g., Fuchs & Fuchs, 1995; Hunt & Goetz, 1997; Manset & Semmel, 1997; Zigmond, Jenkins, Fuchs, Deno, & Fuchs, 1995). However, the goals of including students with even the most profound disabilities in general education classrooms are difficult to measure (see McLeskey & Waldron, 2002; Zigmond et al., 1995). Full inclusion is a goal worth striving toward with care, caution, and flexibility (Capper, Kampschroer, & Keyes, 2000; Downing, 2001). Research in this area is under way and should produce better information about the conditions under which full inclusion works best.

Adapting Instruction

Teacher behaviors that are associated with effective teaching for students with disabilities in the general education classroom are essentially the same as those that improve achievement for all students (Swanson & Hoskyn, 1998). Nevertheless, some adaptations in instructional strategies will help teachers to better meet the needs of students with disabilities. Whether they use individualized instruction, cooperative learning, or other means of accommodating student differences, teachers need to know how to adapt lessons to address students' needs. When students have difficulty with instruction or materials in learning situations, the recommendation is frequently to adapt or modify the instruction or the materials (see Bauer & Shea, 1999; Janney & Snell, 2000). The particular adaptation that is required depends on the student's needs and could be anything from format adaptation to the rewriting of textbook materials. The following Theory into Practice describes three common types of adaptations for accommodating integrated students (also see Browder, 2001; Choate, 2004; Smith et al., 2004).

INTASC

3 Adapting Instruction for Individual Needs

Theory into **PRACTICE**

Adapting Instruction for Students with Special Needs

Format adaptations for written assignments. Teachers can change the format in which a task is presented without changing the actual task. Such a change might be needed for a variety of reasons: (1) an assignment is too long; (2) the spacing on the page is too close to allow the student to focus on individual items; (3) the directions for the task are insufficient or confusing; or (4) the models or examples for the task are either absent, misleading, or insufficient. The critical concept here is that while task and response remain the same, the teacher makes adaptations in the way the material is presented (Kleinert & Kearns, 2001).

Occasionally, the directions for a task or assignment must be simplified. For example, you might substitute in a set of directions the word *circle* for *draw a ring around*. You could also teach students the words that are commonly found in directions (Bender, 2004; Smith et al., 2004). By teaching students how to understand such words, you will help them to be more independent learners. Models or examples presented with a task may also be changed to more closely resemble the task.

Content adaptations. In some instances, students might require an adaptation in the content being presented, such as when so much new information is presented that the student cannot process it quickly or when the student lacks a prerequisite skill or concept necessary to complete a task.

One way to adapt the amount of content being presented is to isolate each concept (Bos & Vaughn, 1999) and require mastery of each concept as a separate unit before teaching the next concept. Although this type of adaptation involves smaller units of material, the same content will be covered in the end.

Adaptations that are required because students lack essential prerequisites might be as simple as explaining vocabulary or concepts before teaching a lesson. More complex adaptations are required when students lack prerequisite skills or concepts that cannot be explained easily or when students do not have a skill they need to learn the lesson. For example, if the math lesson involves solving word problems that require the division of three-digit numerals and a student has not yet learned how to divide three-digit numerals, this skill will have to be taught before the student can address the word problems.

Adaptations in modes of communication. Some students require adaptations in either the way in which they receive information or the way in which they demonstrate their knowledge of specific information (Bender, 2004). Many students cannot learn information when their only means of getting it is through reading but can learn if the information is made available in other forms. Be creative in considering the possibilities. You might have students watch a demonstration, filmstrip, film, videotape, television program, computer program, or play. Or you might have them listen to an audiotape, lecture/discussion, or debate.

A different type of adaptation might be required if a student cannot respond as the task directs. If a student has a writing problem, for example, you might ask the student to tell you about the concept in a private conversation and record the student's response on a tape recorder, or ask the student to present an oral report to the class. Or you might let the student represent the knowledge by drawing a picture or diagram or by constructing a model or diorama.

Teaching Learning Strategies and Metacognitive Awareness

Many students do poorly in school because they have failed to learn how to learn. Programs that are directed at helping students learn such strategies as note-taking, summarization, and memorization methods have been very successful with children and adolescents who have learning disabilities (Mastropieri & Scruggs, 1998; Schumaker & Deshler, 1992). Increasingly, research is identifying a variety of strategies for teaching students with learning disabilities to use metacognitive strategies to comprehend what they read (Gersten et al., 2001) and to build "self-determination" skills, such as the ability to work independently (Algozzine et al., 2001).

Prevention and Early Intervention

INTASC

4 Multiple Instructional Strategies

6 Communication Skills

The debate over inclusion versus special education for children with learning problems revolves around concerns about children whose academic performance is far below that of their agemates. However, many of these children could have succeeded in school in the first place if they had had effective prevention and early intervention programs (Snow, Burns, & Griffin, 1998). Slavin (1996a) proposed a policy of "neverstreaming," which avoids the mainstreaming/special-education dilemma by focusing attention on intensive early intervention that is capable of bringing at-risk learners to performance levels high enough to remove any need for special-education services.

There is strong evidence that a substantial portion of students who are now in the special-education system could have been kept out of it if they had had effective early intervention. Studies of high-quality early childhood programs such as the Perry Preschool (Berrueta-Clement et al., 1984), the Abecedarian Project (Ramey & Ramey, 1992), and the Milwaukee Project (Garber, 1988) all showed substantial reductions in special-education placements for students with learning disabilities and mild mental retardation (Siegel, 2003). Programs that provide one-to-one tutoring to first-graders who are struggling in reading have also shown reductions in the need for special-education services for students with learning disabilities (Dev, Doyle, & Valente, 2002; Lyons, 1989; Silver & Hagin, 1990; Slavin, 1996a). Success for All, which combines effective early childhood programs, curriculum reform, and one-to-one tutoring, has reduced special-education placement by more than half (Borman & Hewes, 2003; Slavin, 1996a; Slavin & Madden, 2001) and has substantially increased the reading achievement of children who have already been identified as needing special-education services (Ross, Smith, Casey, & Slavin, 1995; Smith et al., 1994). These and other findings suggest that the number of children who need special-education services could be greatly reduced if prevention and early intervention programs were more widely applied.

CONNECTIONS

For more on the Success for All approach, see Chapter 9, page 308.

Computers and Students with Disabilities

Computers provide opportunities for individualized instruction for students with disabilities. The use of computers to help children with exceptionalities has four major advantages (Curry, 2003; Hasselbring & Williams-Glaser, 2000; Kamil et al., 2000; Latham, 1997c). First, computers can help to individualize instruction in terms of method of delivery, type and frequency of reinforcement, rate of presentation, and level of instruction. Second, computers can give immediate corrective feedback and emphasize the active role of the child in learning (Ryba, Selby, & Nolan, 1995). Third, computers can hold the attention of children who are easily distractible. Fourth, computer instruction is motivating and patient. For students with physical disabilities, computers can permit greater ease in learning and communicating information. For example, computers can enlarge text or read text aloud for children with visual disabilities (Kamil et al., 2000).

CONNECTIONS

For more on computer-based instruction, see Chapter 9, page 292.

Children in special-education programs seem to like learning from computers. Poorly motivated students have become more enthusiastic about their studies. They feel more in control because they are being taught in a context that is positive, reinforcing, and nonthreatening. However, findings as to the actual learning benefits of computer-assisted instruction for students with disabilities have been inconsistent (Carnine, 1989; MacArthur, Ferretti, Okolo, & Cavalier, 2001; Malouf, Wizer, Pilato, & Grogan, 1990).

One valuable approach using computers is to provide children who are academically disabled with activities in which they can explore, construct, and communicate.

CERTIFICATION POINTER

When responding to a case study on your certification test, you should be familiar with adaptive technologies for assisting students with disabilities.

INTASC

6 Communication Skills

Word processors serve this purpose (Bender, 2004), and other programs have been specifically designed for children with disabilities (Meyer & Rose, 2000; Wagmeister & Shifrin, 2000). Refer to Figure 12.6 for examples of computers and other technology for students with disabilities.

Buddy Systems and Peer Tutoring

One way to help meet the needs of students with disabilities in the general education classroom is to provide these students with assistance from nondisabled classmates, using either a buddy system for noninstructional needs or peer tutoring to help with learning problems.

A student who volunteers to be a special-education student's buddy can help that student cope with the routine tasks of classroom life. For example, a buddy can guide

FIGURE 12.6
Adaptive Technologies for Students with Disabilities

For Students with Limited Motor Control

- Cursor and mouse enhancements allow students who do not have sufficient fine motor control to use a keyboard. Mouse enhancement utilities can be trained to recognize gestures made with mouse commands. Other features include high visibility, color, and animated cursors.
- Key definition programs allow students to define function keys on their keyboard to complete common tasks with fewer keystrokes.
- Virtual keyboard software displays a picture of a computer keyboard on the screen. Students can "type" on this virtual keyboard using a mouse, trackball, or similar pointing device, instead of pushing keys on a real keyboard.

For Students with Visual Impairments

- Magnification software programs ease reading on a computer monitor by displaying text in large fonts (from 2 to 16 times the normal view) and with foreground and background colors of the user's choice.
- Scanners allow students to scan documents that are then converted into editable word processing and spreadsheet documents. These can be magnified and edited on the screen or read aloud by a speech synthesizer.
- Speech synthesizers read aloud what is displayed on the screen—the contents of the active window, menu options, or text that has been typed. They can save documents in audio format as well. There are speaking calendars and talking calculators that read out every operation, as well as mathematical results.
- Braille readers and writers permit students to access the Internet, send and receive e-mail, and create documents by converting text into Braille.

For Students with Hearing Impairments

- Voice recognition software converts spoken words into written text. It can be programmed to execute particular commands, e.g., taking a user to favorite websites with a single voice command.

For Students with Learning Disabilities

- Some word processing programs have a word prediction and abbreviation–expansion program that makes writing faster and easier for those with physical or learning disabilities who use a keyboard to write. Both features help reduce the number of keystrokes needed for typing and can make writing more productive.
- Concept mapping software helps students understand the relationship among concepts by constructing, navigating, sharing, and criticizing knowledge models represented as concept maps.

a student with vision loss, help a student who is academically disabled to understand directions, or deliver cues or prompts as needed in some classes. In middle school and high school settings, a buddy can take notes for a student with hearing loss or learning disabilities by making photocopies of his or her own notes. The buddy can also ensure that the student with a disability has located the correct textbook page during a lesson and has the materials necessary for a class. The buddy's primary responsibility is to help the student with special needs adjust to the general education classroom, to answer questions, and to provide direction for activities. Use of this resource allows the general education classroom teacher to address more important questions related to instructional activities.

Another way of helping students within the general education classroom is to use peer tutoring (Fantuzzo, King, & Heller, 1992; Scruggs & Richter, 1986). Teachers who use peers to tutor in their classroom should ensure that these tutors are carefully trained. This means that the peer tutor must be taught how to provide assistance by modeling and explaining, how to give specific positive and corrective feedback, and when to allow the student to work alone. Peer tutors and tutees may both benefit: the special-education student by acquiring academic concepts and the tutor by gaining a better acceptance and understanding of students with disabilities. Sometimes, older students with disabilities tutor younger ones; this generally benefits both students (Osguthorpe & Scruggs, 1986; Top & Osguthorpe, 1987).

Special-Education Teams

When a student with disabilities is integrated into the general education classroom, the classroom teacher often works with one or more special educators to ensure the student's successful integration (Friend & Bursuck, 2002; Smith et al., 2004; Snell & Janney, 2000). The classroom teacher might participate in conferences with special-education personnel, the special-education personnel might at times be present in the classroom, or the classroom teacher might consult with a special educator at regular intervals. Whatever the arrangement, the classroom teacher and the special educator(s) must recognize that each has expertise that is crucial to the student's success. The classroom teacher is the expert on classroom organization and operation on a day-to-day basis, the curriculum of the classroom, and the expectations placed on students for performance. The special educator is the expert on the characteristics of a particular group of students with disabilities, the learning and behavioral strengths and deficits of the mainstreamed student, and instructional techniques for a particular kind of disability. All this information is important to the successful integration of students, which is why communication between the general education and special-education teachers is so necessary (Pawlowski, 2001; Tucker, 2001).

Communication should begin before students are placed in the general education classroom and should continue throughout the placement. Both teachers must have up-to-date information about the student's performance in each setting to plan and coordinate an effective program. Only then can instruction targeted at improving the student's performance in the general education classroom be designed and presented. In addition, generalization of skills and behaviors from one setting to the other will be enhanced (see Fuchs, Fuchs, Bahr, Fernstrom, & Stecker, 1990).

Social Integration of Students with Disabilities

Placement of students in the general education classroom is only one part of their integration into that environment. These students must be integrated socially as well as instructionally (see Wilkins, 2000). The classroom teacher plays a critical role in this process. Much has been written about the effects of teacher expectations on student

CONNECTIONS
For more on peer tutoring, see Chapter 9, page 289.

CERTIFICATION POINTER
For teacher certification tests you may be expected to suggest ways of structuring peer tutoring to help meet the needs of students with disabilities.

INTASC
10 Partnerships

CONNECTIONS
For more on teaching adaptive skills to help students in their socioemotional development, see Chapter 3, page 83.

INTASC
6 Communication Skills

Teaching Dilemmas: Cases to Consider

INTASC **8** Assessment of Student Learning
10 Partnerships

Finding What Works

Arlisa is two weeks into her teaching practicum in Ruth Runson's kindergarten class at Central Elementary School. Kwan, a student with special needs who receives help from Amanda, the special-education resource teacher, has surprised Arlisa with an uncharacteristic outburst, screaming at her when she asked him a question and then moving into a corner with his back toward her. Later in the day, Arlisa, Ruth Runson, and Amanda discuss Kwan's situation.

Ruth: Arlisa, don't be disheartened about the way Kwan acted today. This is a common episode for him.

Arlisa: I'm not disheartened, but I don't think I understand the nature of Kwan's special needs, so I don't know what to do in situations like this one.

Amanda: Kwan is very intelligent for his age—he reads very well already—but he has socializing problems.

Ruth: Often, Kwan won't talk to me, either. When he acts like that, just leave him alone until he comes around.

Arlisa: I don't think it's that Kwan won't talk. Earlier this week on the playground, several other kindergarten boys were chasing him and Mary. Kwan was yelling at the boys to leave Mary alone. I stopped the boys and then asked Kwan what had happened. Kwan tried to yell at me, so I took the moment to try to help him with his communication. I encouraged him to calm down and speak to me, rather than yelling, to tell me what was wrong. Eventually, he calmed down enough to shout at me about what had happened, but his shouting seemed more out of frustration with the boys than intentional. I called the boys back, we talked, and the issue was resolved. Kwan and Mary left to play together.

Ruth: I'm surprised, Arlisa, that Kwan listened to you and actually tried to talk! And Kwan hasn't chosen a classmate to play with since the first day of school. Maybe you should capitalize on Kwan's willingness to listen to you.

Amanda: I agree, Arlisa. When we work one-on-one, Kwan has told me that his classmates are too loud on the bus and at circle time. I've scheduled him for a hearing test, but meanwhile I've gotten him a pair of ear plugs to wear on the bus. The driver says this seems to calm him down.

Arlisa: Amanda, what strategies can I use to get Kwan to talk to me, instead of shouting or sulking?

Amanda: Well, he seems to sulk when we ask him to make a decision before he's ready, like when you ask him what he wants to do during choosing time. You should tell him it's okay, and that he should speak to you when he has decided what he wants to do. Then move on to the other children. When he shouts at you, or when he simply points at what he wants, remind him to tell you what he needs or wants. Remind him that it is hard to listen to him when he shouts.

Ruth: He often starts sulking or has an outburst when another child comes to take his or her turn at the computer he has been using. I think that giving him a time limit on the computers will encourage him to play with the other children.

Amanda: That's a good idea, Ruth. And I can work with Kwan and a few other children on additional computer activities during my scheduled time with him to reinforce those ideas.

Arlisa: Isn't there something we can do to build on his strengths, like his reading abilities?

Amanda: That's another good idea. I could start writing responses to him on sticky notes and putting them on his shirt. Then, when he rejoins the entire class, both of you could ask him to read the sticky notes to you. This will reinforce his good reading abilities while also encouraging him to talk.

Arlisa: Do you really think these strategies will help Kwan?

Ruth: We'll try them and see. Amanda and I are still talking with Kwan's parents, diagnosing his needs, and putting together an IEP for him. Then we'll have a better idea of how to help him.

ⓐ Questions for Reflection

1. List the special needs that Kwan seems to demonstrate. What additional instructional adaptations might you suggest to help Kwan succeed in kindergarten?

2. Evaluate the level of collaboration demonstrated among the three teachers. If you were Ruth Runson, the classroom teacher, how would you capitalize on the support offered by Amanda, the special-education teacher? If you were Amanda, how would you propose additional accommodations that Ruth and Arlisa could make for Kwan?

3. Kwan's exceptionalities have not been clearly diagnosed yet, but how has his label as a child with special needs already served as a barrier during the first two weeks of kindergarten? How can the three teachers work to remove this barrier?

Source: Adapted from "Student Diversity: Barriers to Getting to Know Our Students" by A. Johnson, from *Allyn & Bacon's Custom Cases in Education,* edited by Greta Morine-Dershimer, Paul Eggen, and Donald Kauchak. Copyright © 2000 by Pearson Education. Adapted by permission of the publisher.

Consider these tips for including secondary students in the general education classroom:

Secondary Students with Learning Disabilities

1. Specifically teach self-recording strategies such as asking, "Was I paying attention?"
2. Relate new material to knowledge that the student with learning disabilities already has, drawing specific implications from familiar information.
3. Teach the use of external memory enhancers (e.g., lists and note-taking).
4. Encourage the use of other devices to improve class performance (e.g., tape recorders).

Secondary Students with Emotional or Behavioral Disorders

1. Create positive relationships within your classroom through the use of cooperative learning teams and group-oriented assignments.
2. Use all students in creating standards for conduct as well as consequences for positive and negative behaviors.
3. Focus your efforts on developing a positive relationship with the student with behavior disorders by greeting him or her regularly, informally talking with him or her at appropriate times, attending to improvement in his or her performance, and becoming aware of his or her interests.
4. Work closely with the members of the teacher assistance team to be aware of teacher behaviors that might adversely or positively affect students' performance.
5. Realize that changes in behavior often occur very gradually, with periods of regression and sometimes tumult.

FIGURE 12.7
Including Secondary Students with Disabilities in the General Education Classroom
From Michael L. Hardman, Clifford J. Drew, and M. Winston Egan, *Human Exceptionality* (5th ed.). Copyright © 1996 by Allyn & Bacon. Adapted by permission.

achievement and behavior. In the case of students with disabilities, the teacher's attitude toward these students is important not only for teacher–student interactions but also as a model for the nondisabled students in the classroom. The research on attitudes toward individuals with disabilities provides several strategies that might be useful to the general education classroom teacher who wants to promote successful social integration by influencing the attitudes of nondisabled students. One strategy is to use cooperative learning methods (Nevin, 1998; Slavin & Stevens, 1991; Stevens & Slavin, 1995a). Social skills training has been found to improve the social acceptance of children with disabilities (Troop & Asher, 1999). For practical ways to include secondary students with disabilities in the general education classroom, see Figure 12.7.

CONNECTIONS

For more on the effects of teacher expectations on student achievement and behavior, see Chapter 10, page 331.

Chapter Summary

Who Are Learners with Exceptionalities?

Learners with exceptionalities are students who have special-educational needs in relation to societal or school norms. An inability to perform appropriate academic tasks for any reason inherent in the learner makes that learner exceptional. A handicap is a condition or barrier imposed by the environment or the self; a disability is a functional limitation that interferes with a person's mental, physical, or sensory abilities. Classification systems for learners with exceptionalities are often arbitrary and debated, and the use of labels may lead to inappropriate treatment or damage students' self-concepts.

THE INTENTIONAL TEACHER

Using What You Know about Learners with Exceptionalities to Improve Teaching and Learning

Intentional teachers relish their responsibility to reach each of their students. They create inclusive environments and commit to fostering learning for all. Intentional teachers serve as members of professional teams in order to collaborate to meet the needs of students with special needs.

❶ What do I expect my students to know and be able to do at the end of this lesson? How does this contribute to course objectives and to students' needs to become capable individuals?

Think about the goals you have established for student learning. Consider the extent to which each of these goals is appropriate for learners with special needs. Work with other professionals to develop formal goal statements, including Individualized Education Programs that shape appropriate goals and instruction for your students with special needs. For example, imagine that Michael and Renee, two students with learning disabilities in reading, struggle with the text for your class, so you consult with the special-education teacher. He reviews the students' IEPs with you, noting that reading comprehension is a goal for both students this year. Together you converse about possible adjustments to your course goals for Michael and Renee, and you discuss appropriate instructional modifications. You chat with the students' parents, who give you additional insights about strategies they have found to be successful.

❷ What knowledge, skills, needs, and interests do my students have that must be taken into account in my lesson?

Identification of students' special-educational needs may begin before students enter formal schooling. When students with documented special needs are assigned to your class, talk with students (as appropriate), their parents, and professionals about students' preferences and past successes. Review past records as appropriate. For example, imagine that Angela, a junior who is visually impaired, joins your class. You might set up an informal conference with Angela, her parents, and the resource teacher. They provide you with information about strategies that help Angela, and she talks openly about her likes and her pet peeves. They also refer you to one of your colleagues who was particularly successful last year at providing a supportive environment without dwelling too much on Angela's vision. You might seek assistive technology, such as a computer that greatly enlarges text, to help Angela participate successfully in class.

❸ What do I know about the content, child development, learning, motivation, and effective teaching strategies that I can use to accomplish my objectives?

Students might have special needs that have not been identified. Observe carefully for signs that students need extra support. For example, imagine that Sheila, who sits in a back row, often looks out the window or looks puzzled during your lessons. Noticing some differences in her enunciation, you suspect

About 9 percent of students in the United States receive special education. Examples of learners with exceptionalities are students with mental retardation, specific learning disabilities, speech or language disorders, emotional disorders, behavioral disorders, and vision or hearing loss. Students who are gifted and talented are also regarded as exceptional and may be eligible for special accelerated or enrichment programs. Clearly identifying learners with exceptionalities and accommodating instruction to meet their needs are continual challenges.

What Is Special Education?

Special-education programs serve children with disabilities instead of, or in addition to, the general education classroom program.

Public Law 94-142 (1975), which was amended by P.L. 99-457 (1986) to include preschool children and seriously disabled infants and is now called the Individuals with Disabilities Education Act (IDEA) according to P.L. 101-476 (1990), mandates that every child with a disability is entitled to appropriate special education at public expense. Strengthened by P.L. 105-17 (1997), IDEA '97 calls for greater involvement of parents and classroom teachers in the education of children with disabilities. The

a hearing impairment and refer her for testing. In the meantime, you move her to the front row and provide visual input to support your direct instruction.

❹ What instructional materials, technology, assistance, and other resources are available to help accomplish my objectives?

Teachers need to create a social environment that fosters acceptance for every student. Think about how you will encourage students to accept and help each other as individuals. For example, imagine that Jarred, a student with cerebral palsy, is placed in your classroom. You and your students might hold a classroom meeting to discuss ways to welcome a new student. You could also talk about areas in which classmates have helped each other this year and the idea that you all have benefited by working with each other because of your varied strengths. You might hand out a "job application" for the position of "buddy" to new students, as several students clamor to be Jarred's buddy.

❺ How will I plan to assess students' progress toward my objectives?

Teachers need to use information from a variety of sources to determine success for students with special needs. What evidence do you have that students maintain positive self-concepts? That their classmates' self-concepts are similarly enriched? That stu-

dents are learning? Collect information that enables you to determine whether students are progressing on an individual basis. For example, imagine that you meet for a midyear review of Patrick's Individualized Education Program. To the review you bring anecdotal notes that you collected as students demonstrated their capacity to care about and help each other. You share vignettes of Patrick's sense of humor and impressive knowledge of dinosaurs. You show his portfolio, which demonstrates marked growth in his letter recognition and drawing. You commit to providing more intensive work in mathematics, though, because he shows less growth in shape and number recognition.

❻ How will I respond if individual children or the class as a whole are not on track toward success? What is my back-up plan?

Instruction should meet individual needs. Select from a variety of strategies to modify your instruction when you find that it does not challenge each student. For example, imagine that some of your students are struggling despite your attempts to provide relevant and engaging instruction. You reread your notes on instructional modifications such as individualized instruction, cooperative learning, computers, and peer tutoring. You might choose peer tutoring to capitalize on your students' social tendencies. You could train peer tutors in learning strategies and work out a schedule so that peer tutors and tutees can meet during class for 20 minutes three times per week.

least restrictive environment clause means that students with special needs must be mainstreamed into general education classes as much as possible. A requirement of IDEA is that every student with a disability must have an Individualized Education Program (IEP). The idea behind the use of IEPs is to give everyone concerned with the education of a child with a disability an opportunity to help formulate the child's instruction program. An array of services is available for exceptional students, including support for the general education teacher, special education for part of the day in a resource room, special education for more than 3 hours per day in a special-education classroom, special day schools, special residential schools, and home/hospitals.

What Is Inclusion?

Inclusion means placing students with special needs in general education classrooms for at least part of the time. Full inclusion of all children in general education classes with appropriate assistance is a widely held goal. Research has shown that inclusion is effective in raising many students' performance levels, especially when cooperative learning, buddy systems, peer tutoring, computer instruction, modifications in lesson presentation, and training in social skills are a regular part of classroom learning.

Research has also shown that some disabilities, especially reading disabilities, can be prevented through programs of prevention and early intervention.

Key Terms

Review the following key terms from the chapter. Then, to explore research on these topics and how they relate to education today, connect to Research Navigator™ through this book's Companion Website or directly at www.researchnavigator.com.

acceleration programs   410
attention deficit hyperactivity disorder (ADHD)   403
autism   407
collaboration   415
conduct disorders   406
disability   392
emotional and behavioral disorders   405
enrichment programs   410
full inclusion   423
giftedness   408
handicap   392
hearing disabilities   408
Individualized Education Program (IEP)   412

Individuals with Disabilities Education Act (IDEA)   412
IDEA '97   412
intelligence quotient (IQ)   395
language disorders   405
learners with exceptionalities   392
learning disabilities (LD)   399
least restrictive environment   412
mainstreaming   412
mental retardation   394
Public Law 94-142   411
sensory impairments   407
special education   411
speech disorders   404
vision loss   407

Self-Assessment: Practicing for Licensure

Directions: The chapter-opening vignette addresses indicators that are often assessed in state licensure exams. Re-read the chapter-opening vignette, and then respond to the following questions.

1. Elaine Wagner, assistant principal at Pleasantville Elementary School, meets with Helen Ross about her son, Tommy, who is having a difficult time in another school. She explains to Ms. Ross that Tommy would need to meet certain criteria to receive special-education services. Which of the following examples is an indication that someone needs special-education services?

   a. The student must have an IQ at or below 120.
   b. The student must have at least one of a small number of categories of disabilities.
   c. The student must be below the 50th percentile in his or her academic work.
   d. All parents who request special-education services for their children must receive them.

2. Suppose you are going to be Tommy's new teacher. If his mother were to ask you about the difference between handicap and disability, what would you say?

   a. A disability is a condition in which a person has difficulty with cognitive functioning, while a handicap is a condition in which a person has difficulty with physical functioning.
   b. A disability is a condition in which a person has barriers placed on him or her by society, while a handicap is the disabling condition.
   c. A disability is a functional limitation a person has that interferes with her or his physical or cognitive abilities. A handicap is a condition imposed on a person with disabilities by society, the physical environment, or the person's attitude.
   d. The terms disability and handicap are synonymous.

3. Which of the following public laws gave parents like Helen Ross an increased role in making decisions about the education of their children?

   a. Public Law 94-142, The Education for the Handicapped Act
   b. Public Law 99-457, the amendment to P.L. 94-142
   c. Public Law 101-476, the Individuals with Disabilities Education Act
   d. Public Law 105-17, the Individuals with Disabilities Education Act amendments

4. Assistant Principal Elaine Wagner tells Helen Ross that even if Tommy needs special-education services, he will be placed in the "least restrictive environment." What does this mean for Tommy?

   a. Tommy will be placed in the general education classes as much as possible, and only removed for special-education services if necessary.
   b. Tommy will be placed in a special-education room that does not restrict his movements or academic choices.
   c. Tommy will be eligible for any and all special-education services.
   d. Tommy will receive public funds to pay for his private special-education services.

5. Helen Ross, Tommy's mother, asks Elaine Wagner, "Your school's philosophy on inclusion sounds just right for Tommy. Why don't all schools adopt it? What disadvantages are there?" Ms. Wagner, who is current on her knowledge about inclusion, would most likely make which of the following responses?

   a. Data show that students enrolled in inclusion programs do not do as well academically as those who are enrolled in special-education classrooms.
   b. General education classroom teachers sometimes lack appropriate training and materials and are already overburdened with large class sizes and inadequate support services.
   c. Special-education experts are not convinced that there is such a thing as a learning disability. They believe that all students should be in a general education classroom.
   d. Many parents of general education students do not feel it is fair to adapt instruction to meet the needs of students with disabilities.

6. How would you go about developing an individualized learning plan for Tommy if it is determined that he has a reading disability?

7. Describe the advantages and disadvantages that might occur when students with special needs are enrolled in the general education classroom.

Assessing Student Learning

M*r. Sullivan was having a great time teaching about*

the Civil War, and his eleventh-grade U.S. history class was having fun, too. Mr. Sullivan was relating all kinds of anecdotes about the war. He described a battle fought in the nude (a group of Confederates was caught fording a river), the time Stonewall Jackson lost a battle because he took a nap in the middle of it, and several stories about women who disguised their gender to fight as soldiers. He told the story of a Confederate raid (from Canada) on a Vermont bank. He passed around real minié balls and grapeshot. In fact, Mr. Sullivan had gone on for weeks about the battles, the songs, and the personalities and foibles of the generals. Finally, after an interesting math activity in which students had to figure out how much Confederate money they would need to buy a loaf of bread, Mr. Sullivan had students put away all their materials to take a test.

The students were shocked. The only question was: What were the main causes, events, and consequences of the Civil War?

Mr. Sullivan's lessons are fun. They are engaging. They use varied presentation modes. They integrate skills from other disciplines. They are clearly accomplishing one important objective of social studies: building enjoyment of the topic. However, as engaging as Mr. Sullivan's lessons are, there is little correspondence between what he is teaching and what he is testing. He and his students are on a happy trip, but where are they going? ◎

USING YOUR

Experience

Cooperative Learning   In a group of four or five students, draw a value line from 1 to 100, with 1 representing poor teaching and 100 representing great teaching. Take turns marking where you would place Mr. Sullivan on this scale. Let each person explain his or her rating. Now review the ratings and change them as appropriate. Discuss better ways in which Mr. Sullivan might teach and then assess his students.

This chapter discusses an important topic: evaluation. The most important idea in the chapter is that a teacher's lesson objectives are the means by which instruction and evaluation are linked together. The objectives are the teacher's plan for what students should know and be able to do at the end of a course of study; their lessons must be designed to accomplish these objectives; and their evaluation of students must tell them the extent to which each student has actually mastered those objectives by the end of the course (Carr & Harris, 2001; Marzano, Pickering, & Pollock, 2001). Put another way, every teacher should have a clear idea of where the class is going, how it will get there, and how to know whether it has arrived.

WHAT ARE INSTRUCTIONAL OBJECTIVES AND HOW ARE THEY USED?

INTASC

7 Instructional Planning Skills

What do you want your students to know or be able to do at the end of today's lesson? What should they know at the end of a series of lessons on a particular subject? What should they know at the end of the course? Knowing the answers to these questions is one of the most important prerequisites for intentional, high-quality instruction. A teacher is like a wilderness guide with a troop of tenderfeet. If the teacher does not have a map or a plan for getting the group where it needs to go, the whole group will surely be lost. Mr. Sullivan's students are having a lot of fun, but because their teacher has no plan for how his lessons will give them essential concepts relating to the Civil War, they will be unlikely to learn these concepts.

Setting out objectives at the beginning of a course is an essential step in providing a framework into which individual lessons will fit. Without such a framework it is easy to wander off the track, to spend too much time on topics that are not central to the course. One high school biology teacher spent most of the year teaching biochemistry; her students knew all about the chemical makeup of DNA, red blood cells, chlorophyll, and starch but little about zoology, botany, anatomy, or other topics that are usually central to high school biology. Then in late May the teacher panicked, because she realized that the class had to do a series of laboratory exercises before the end of the year. On successive days they dissected a frog, an eye, a brain, and a pig fetus! Needless to say, the students learned little from those hurried labs and little about biology in general. This teacher did not have a master plan but was deciding week by week (or perhaps day by day) what to teach, thereby losing sight of the big picture—the scope of knowledge that is generally agreed to be important for a high school student to learn in biology class. Few teachers follow a plan rigidly once they make it, but the process of making it is still very helpful (Clark & Peterson, 1986).

An **instructional objective,** sometimes called a behavioral objective, is a statement of skills or concepts that students are expected to know at the end of some

instructional objective

A statement of skills or concepts that students should master after a given period of instruction.

period of instruction. Typically, an instructional objective is stated in such a way as to make clear how the objective will be measured (see Mager, 1975). Some examples of instructional objectives are as follows:

- Given 100 division facts (such as 27 divided by 3), students will give correct answers to all 100 in 3 minutes.
- When asked, students will name at least five functions that characterize all living organisms (respiration, reproduction, etc.).
- In an essay, students will be able to compare and contrast the artistic styles of van Gogh and Gauguin.
- Given the statement "Resolved: The United States should not have entered World War I," students will be able to argue persuasively either for or against the proposition.

Note that even though these objectives vary enormously in the type of learning involved and in the performance levels they address, they have several things in common. Mager (1975), whose work began the behavioral objectives movement, described objectives as having three parts: performance, conditions, and criteria. Explanations and examples are given in Table 13.1.

CONNECTIONS

For more on lesson planning and lesson objectives as components of effective instruction, see Chapter 7, page 213.

Planning Lesson Objectives

In practice, the skeleton of a behavioral objective is condition–performance–criterion. First, state the conditions under which learning will be assessed, as in the following:

- Given a 10-item test, students will be able to . . .
- In an essay the student will be able to . . .
- Using a compass and protractor, the student will be able to . . .

The second part of an objective is usually an action verb that indicates what students will be able to do, for example (from Gronlund, 2000):

- Write
- Distinguish between
- Identify
- Match
- Compare and contrast

Table 13.1			
Parts of a Behavioral Objectives Statement			
	Performance	*Conditions*	*Criterion*
Definition	An objective always says what a learner is expected to do.	An objective always describes the conditions under which the performance is to occur.	Whenever possible, an objective describes the criterion of acceptable performance.
Question Answered	What should the learner be able to do?	Under what conditions do you want the learner to be able to do it?	How well must it be done?
Example	Correctly use adjectives and adverbs.	Given 10 sentences with missing modifiers, . . .	. . . the student will correctly choose an adjective or adverb in at least 9 of the 10 sentences.

Finally, a behavioral objective generally states a criterion for success, such as the following:

- . . . all 100 multiplication facts in 3 minutes.
- . . . at least five of the nations that sent explorers to the New World.
- . . . at least three similarities and three differences between U.S. government under the Constitution and the Articles of Confederation.

Sometimes a criterion for success cannot be specified as the number correct. Even so, success should be specified as clearly as possible, as in the following:

- The student will write a two-page essay describing the social situation of women as portrayed in *A Doll's House*.
- The student will think of at least six possible uses for an eggbeater other than beating eggs.

Writing Specific Objectives   Instructional objectives must be adapted to the subject matter being taught (Hamilton, 1985). When students must learn well-defined skills or information with a single right answer, specific instructional objectives should be written as follows:

- Given 10 problems involving addition of two fractions with like denominators, students will solve at least 9 correctly.
- Given 10 sentences lacking verbs, students will correctly choose verbs that agree in number in at least 8 sentences. Examples: My cat and I [has, have] birthdays in May. Each of us [want, wants] to go to college.
- Given a 4-meter rope attached to the ceiling, students will be able to climb to the top in less than 20 seconds.

Some material, of course, does not lend itself to such specific instructional objectives, and it would be a mistake in such cases to adhere to objectives that have numerical criteria (TenBrink, 1986). For example, the following objective could be written:

- The student will list at least five similarities and five differences between the situation of immigrants to the United States in the early 1900s and that of immigrants today.

However, this objective asks for lists, which might not demonstrate any real understanding of the topic. A less specific but more meaningful objective might be the following:

- In an essay the student will compare and contrast the situation of immigrants to the United States in the early 1900s and that of immigrants today.

This general instructional objective would allow students more flexibility in expressing their understanding of the topic and would promote comprehension rather than memorization of lists of similarities and differences.

Writing Clear Objectives   Instructional objectives should be specific enough to be meaningful. For example, an objective concerning immigrants might be written as follows:

- Students will develop a full appreciation for the diversity of peoples who have contributed to the development of U.S. society.

This sounds nice, but what does "full appreciation" mean? Such an objective neither helps the teacher prepare lessons nor helps students understand what is to be taught and how they will be assessed. Mager (1975, p. 20) lists more slippery and less slippery words used to describe instructional objectives:

Words Open to Many Interpretations	Words Open to Fewer Interpretations
to know	to write
to understand	to recite
to appreciate	to identify
to fully appreciate	to sort
to grasp the significance	to solve
to enjoy	to construct

Performing a Task Analysis   In planning lessons, it is important to consider the skills required in the tasks to be taught or assigned. For example, a teacher might ask students to use the school library to write a brief report on a topic of interest. The task seems straightforward enough, but consider the separate skills involved:

Why is careful planning a critical step in learning and assessing learning? What kinds of ongoing assessment can you build into your lessons that will help you determine if your students are meeting the objectives you establish?

- Knowing alphabetical order
- Using the card catalog to find books on a subject
- Using a book index to find information on a topic
- Getting the main idea from expository material
- Planning or outlining a brief report
- Writing expository paragraphs
- Knowing language mechanics skills (such as capitalization, punctuation, and usage)

These skills could themselves be broken down into subskills. The teacher must be aware of the subskills involved in any learning task to be certain that students know what they need to know to succeed. Before assigning the library report task, the teacher would need to be sure that students knew how to use the card catalog and book indexes, among other things, and could comprehend and write expository material. The teacher might teach or review these skills before sending students to the library.

Similarly, in teaching a new skill, it is important to consider all the subskills that go into it. Think of all the separate steps involved in long division, in writing chemical formulas, or in identifying topic sentences and supporting details. For that matter, consider the skills that go into making a pizza, as illustrated in Figure 13.1.

This process of breaking tasks or objectives down into their simpler components is called **task analysis** (see Gagné 1977; Gardner, 1985). In planning a lesson, a three-step process for task analysis may be used:

1. Identify prerequisite skills. What should students already know before you teach the lesson? For example, for a lesson on long division, students must know their subtraction, multiplication, and division facts and must be able to subtract and multiply with renaming.

2. Identify component skills. In the actual lesson, what subskills must students be taught before they can learn to achieve the larger objective? To return to the long-division example, students will need to learn estimating, dividing, multiplying, subtracting, checking, bringing down the next digit, and then repeating the process. Each of these steps must be planned for, taught, and assessed during the lesson.

3. Plan how component skills will be assembled into the final skill. The final step in task analysis is to assemble the subskills back into the complete process being taught. For example, students might be able to estimate, to divide, and to multiply, but this does not necessarily mean that they can do long division. The subskills must be integrated into a complete process that students can understand and practice.

task analysis
Breaking tasks down into fundamental subskills.

FIGURE 13.1

Example of a Task Analysis

Before students can practice the main skill (making pizza), they must be able to use an oven, make dough, and make sauce. These skills must all be learned before the main skill can be mastered. They are independent of one another and can be learned in any order. Before making dough or making sauce, students must be able to read a recipe and measure ingredients. Finally, to read a recipe the learner first has to learn how to decode abbreviations.

From Robert F. Mager, *Preparing Instructional Objectives*, p. 100. Copyright © 1984 by Lake Publishing Company, Belmont, CA 94002. Adapted by permission.

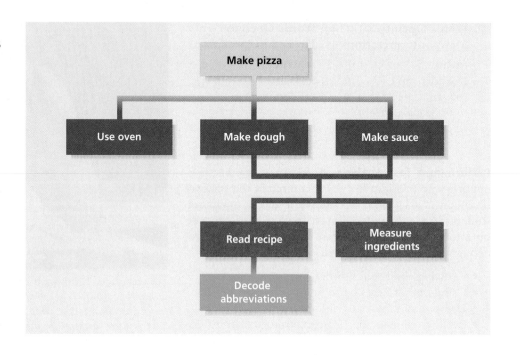

Backward Planning   Just as lesson objectives are more than the sum of specific task objectives, the objectives of a course of study are more than the sum of specific lesson objectives. For this reason it makes sense to start by writing broad objectives for the course as a whole, then objectives for large units, and only then specific behavioral objectives (see Gronlund, 2000). This is known as **backward planning.** For example, Mr. Sullivan would have done well to have identified the objective of his Civil War unit as follows: "Students will understand the major causes, events, and consequences of the Civil War." Then he might have written more detailed objectives relating to causes, events, and consequences, and could have planned units and individual lessons around these objectives. A detailed example of the backward planning process is illustrated in Table 13.2 and described in the next Theory into Practice.

Up to now, this chapter has focused on planning of instruction according to specific instructional objectives. But how does this fit into the larger task of planning an entire course?

Theory into **PRACTICE**

Planning Courses, Units, and Lessons

In planning a course, it is important for a teacher to set long-term, middle-term, and short-term objectives before starting to teach (Brown, 1988; Shavelson, 1987). Before the students arrive for the first day of class, the teacher needs to have a general plan of what will be covered all year, a more specific plan for what will be in the first unit (a connected set of lessons), and a very specific plan for the content of the first lessons (as shown in Table 13.2). Increasingly, states are establishing standards for each subject, and these standards should guide teachers' planning, especially if there are also state assessments based on the standards (see Chapter 14).

backward planning

Planning instruction by first setting long-range goals, then setting unit objectives, and finally planning daily lessons.

Table 13.2

Example of Objectives for a Course in Life Science

Teachers can allocate instructional time for a course by (a) deciding what topics to cover during the year or semester, (b) deciding how many weeks to spend on each topic, (c) choosing units within each topic, (d) deciding how many days to spend on each, and (e) deciding what each day's lesson should be.

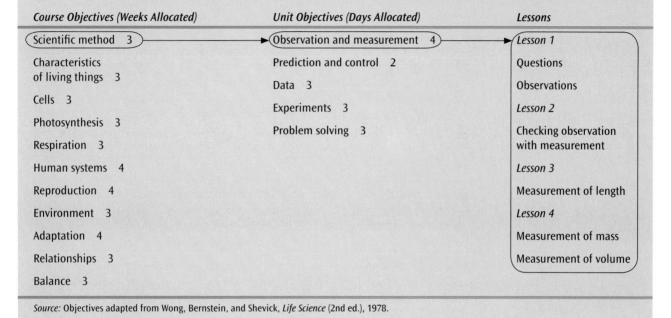

Course Objectives (Weeks Allocated)	Unit Objectives (Days Allocated)	Lessons
Scientific method 3	Observation and measurement 4	Lesson 1
Characteristics of living things 3	Prediction and control 2	Questions
Cells 3	Data 3	Observations
Photosynthesis 3	Experiments 3	Lesson 2
Respiration 3	Problem solving 3	Checking observation with measurement
Human systems 4		Lesson 3
Reproduction 4		Measurement of length
Environment 3		Lesson 4
Adaptation 4		Measurement of mass
Relationships 3		Measurement of volume
Balance 3		

Source: Objectives adapted from Wong, Bernstein, and Shevick, *Life Science* (2nd ed.), 1978.

Table 13.2 implies a backward planning process. First the course objectives are established. Then unit objectives are designated. Finally, specific lessons are planned. The course objectives list all the topics to be covered during the year. The teacher might divide the number of weeks in the school year by the number of major topics to figure what each will require. More or less time could be reserved for any particular topic, as long as adequate time is allowed for the others. A whole semester could be spent on any one of the topics in Table 13.2, but this would be inappropriate in a survey course on life science. The teacher must make hard choices before the first day of class about how much time to spend on each topic to avoid spending too much time on early topics and not having enough time left to do a good job with later ones. Some history teachers always seem to find themselves still on World War I in mid-May and have to compress most of the twentieth century into a couple of weeks!

Table 13.2 shows approximate allocations of weeks to each of the topics to be covered. These are just rough estimates to be modified as time goes on.

Unit objectives and unit tests. After course objectives have been laid out, the next task is to establish objectives for the first unit and to estimate the number of class periods to spend on each objective. It is a good idea to write a unit test as part of the planning process. Writing a test in advance helps you to focus on the important issues to be covered. For example, in a

CERTIFICATION POINTER

For your teacher certification test you may be asked to take a goal from a state curriculum standard and write a behavioral objective to meet that standard.

4-week unit on the Civil War you might decide that the most important things students should learn are the causes of the war, a few major points about the military campaigns, the importance of the Emancipation Proclamation, Lincoln's assassination, and the history of the Reconstruction period. These topics would be central to the unit test on the Civil War. Writing this test would put into proper perspective the importance of the various issues that should be covered.

The test that you prepare as part of your course planning might not be exactly the test that you give at the end of the unit. You may decide to change, add, or delete items to reflect the content you actually covered. But this does not diminish the importance of having decided in advance exactly what objectives you wanted to achieve and how you were going to assess them.

Many textbooks provide unit tests and objectives, making your task easier. However, even if you have ready-made objectives and tests, it is still important to review their content and change them as necessary to match what you expect to teach.

If you prepare unit tests from scratch, use the guide to test construction presented later in this chapter. Be sure that the test items cover the various objectives in proportion to their importance to the course as a whole (that is, that the more important objectives are covered by more items), and include items that assess higher-level thinking as well as factual knowledge.

Lesson plans and lesson assessments. The final step in backward planning is to plan daily lessons. Table 13.2 shows how a given unit objective might be broken down into daily lessons. The next step is to plan the content of each lesson. A lesson plan consists of an objective; a plan for presenting information; a plan for giving students practice (if appropriate); a plan for assessing student understanding; and, if necessary, a plan for reteaching students (or whole classes) if their understanding is inadequate.

Linking Objectives and Assessment

INTASC

8 Assessment of Student Learning

Because instructional objectives are stated in terms of how they will be measured, it is clear that objectives are closely linked to **assessment.** An assessment is any measure of the degree to which students have learned the objectives set out for them. Most assessments in schools are tests or quizzes, or informal verbal assessments such as questions in class. However, students can also show their learning by writing an essay, painting a picture, doing a car tune-up, or baking a pineapple upside-down cake.

One critical principle of assessment is that assessments and objectives must be clearly linked. Students learn some proportion of what they are taught; the greater the overlap between what was taught and what is tested, the better students will score on the test and the more accurately any need for additional instruction can be determined (Carr & Harris, 2001; Marzano, Pickering, & Pollock, 2001). Teaching should be closely linked to instructional objectives, and both should clearly relate to assessment. If any objective is worth teaching, it is worth testing, and vice versa. This idea was illustrated by Mager as follows:

assessment

A measure of the degree to which instructional objectives have been attained.

> During class periods of a seventh grade algebra course, a teacher provided a good deal of skillful guidance in the solution of simple equations. . . . When it came time for an examination, however, the test items consisted mainly of word problems, and the students did rather poorly. The teacher's justification for this "sleight of test" was that the students didn't "really understand" algebra if they

could not solve word problems. Perhaps the teacher was right. But the skill of solving equations is considerably different from the skill of solving word problems; if he wanted his students to learn how to solve word problems, he should have taught them how to do so. (Mager, 1975, p. 82)

Mager's algebra teacher really had one objective in mind (solving word problems) but taught according to another (solving equations). If he had coordinated his objectives, his teaching, and his assessment, he and his students would have been a lot happier, and the students would have had a much better opportunity to learn to solve algebra word problems.

One way to specify objectives for a course is to actually prepare test questions before the course begins (see Gronlund, 2000). This allows the teacher to write general **teaching objectives** (clear statements of what students are expected to learn through instruction) and then to clarify them with very specific **learning objectives** (specific behaviors students are expected to exhibit at the end of a series of lessons), as in the following examples:

Teaching Objective	Specific Learning Objective (Test Questions)
a. Ability to subtract three-digit numbers renaming once or twice	a1. $237 - 184$ a2. $412 - 298$ a3. $596 - 448$
b. Understanding of use of language to set mood in Edgar Allan Poe's "The Raven"	b1. How does Poe reinforce the mood of "The Raven" after setting it in the first stanza?
c. Ability to identify the chemical formulas for common substances	Write the chemical formulas for the following: c1. Water _____ c2. Carbon dioxide _____ c3. Coal _____ c4. Table salt _____

Using Taxonomies of Instructional Objectives

In writing objectives and assessments, it is important to consider different skills and different levels of understanding. For example, in a science lesson on insects for second-graders, you might want to impart both information (the names of various insects) and an attitude (the importance of insects to the ecosystem). In other subjects you might try to convey facts and concepts that differ by type. For example, in teaching a lesson on topic sentences in reading, you might have students first repeat a definition of topic sentence, then identify topic sentences in paragraphs, and finally write their own topic sentences for original paragraphs. Each of these activities demonstrates a different kind of understanding of the concept "topic sentence," and this concept has not been adequately taught if students can do only one of these activities. These various lesson goals can be classified by type and degree of complexity. A taxonomy, or system of classification, helps a teacher to categorize instructional activities.

Bloom's Taxonomy In 1956, Benjamin Bloom and some fellow researchers published a **taxonomy of educational objectives** that has been extremely influential in the research and practice of education ever since. Bloom and his colleagues categorized objectives from simple to complex or from factual to conceptual. The key elements of what is commonly called Bloom's taxonomy (Anderson & Sosniak, 1994; Bloom, Englehart, Furst, Hill, & Krathwohl, 1956; Kreitzer & Madaus, 1994; Marzano, 2001) for the cognitive domain are (from simple to complex):

CONNECTIONS

For information on thinking skills and critical thinking, see Chapter 8, page 269.

teaching objectives
Clear statements of what students are intended to learn through instruction.

learning objectives
Specific behaviors that students are expected to exhibit at the end of a series of lessons.

taxonomy of educational objectives
Bloom's ordering of objectives from simple learning tasks to more complex ones.

1. Knowledge (recalling information): The lowest level of objectives in Bloom's hierarchy, knowledge refers to objectives such as memorizing math facts or formulas, scientific principles, or verb conjugations.

2. Comprehension (translating, interpreting, or extrapolating information): Comprehension objectives require that students show an understanding of information as well as the ability to use it. Examples include interpreting the meaning of a diagram, graph, or parable; inferring the principle underlying a science experiment; and predicting what might happen next in a story.

3. Application (using principles or abstractions to solve novel or real-life problems): Application objectives require students to use knowledge or principles to solve practical problems. Examples include using geometric principles to figure out how many gallons of water to put into a swimming pool of given dimensions and using knowledge of the relationship between temperature and pressure to explain why a balloon is larger on a hot day than on a cold day.

4. Analysis (breaking down complex information or ideas into simpler parts to understand how the parts relate or are organized): Analysis objectives involve having students see the underlying structure of complex information or ideas. Examples of analysis objectives include contrasting schooling in the United States with education in Japan, understanding how the functions of the carburetor and distributor are related in an automobile engine, and identifying the main idea of a short story.

5. Synthesis (creation of something that did not exist before): Synthesis objectives involve using skills to create completely new products. Examples include writing a composition, deriving a mathematical rule, designing a science experiment to solve a problem, and making up a new sentence in a foreign language.

6. Evaluation (judging something against a given standard): Evaluation objectives require making value judgments against some criterion or standard. For example, students might be asked to compare the strengths and weaknesses of two home computers in terms of flexibility, power, and available software.

What stage in Bloom's taxonomy are the students taking part in here? How could a teacher incorporate all of Bloom's stages into this lesson?

Because Bloom's taxonomy is organized from simple to complex, some people interpret it as a ranking of objectives from trivial (knowledge) to important (synthesis, evaluation). However, this is not the intent of the taxonomy. Different levels of objectives are appropriate for different purposes and for students at different stages of development.

The primary importance of Bloom's taxonomy is in its reminder that we want students to have many levels of skills. All too often, teachers focus on measurable knowledge and comprehension objectives and forget that students cannot be considered proficient in many skills until they can apply or synthesize those skills. On the other side of the coin, some teachers fail to make certain that students are well rooted in the basics before heading off into higher-order objectives.

Using a Behavior Content Matrix   One way to be sure that your objectives cover many levels is to write a **behavior content matrix.** This is simply a chart that shows how a particular concept or skill will be taught and assessed at different cognitive levels. Examples of objectives in a behavior content matrix appear in Table 13.3. Note that for each topic, objectives are listed for some but not all levels of Bloom's taxonomy. Some topics do not lend themselves to some levels of the taxonomy, and there is no reason that every level should be covered for every topic. However, using a behavior content matrix in setting objectives forces you to consider objectives above the knowledge and comprehension levels.

behavior content matrix
A chart that classifies lesson objectives according to cognitive level.

Table 13.3

Examples of Objectives in a Behavior Content Matrix

A behavior content matrix can remind teachers to develop instructional objectives that address skills at various cognitive levels.

Type of Objective	Example 1: The Area of a Circle	Example 2: Main Idea of a Story	Example 3: The Colonization of Africa
Knowledge	Give the formula for area of a circle.	Define *main idea.*	Make a time line showing how Europeans divided Africa into colonies.
Comprehension		Give examples of ways to find the main idea of a story.	Interpret a map of Africa showing its colonization by European nations.
Application	Apply the formula for area of a circle to real-life problems.		
Analysis		Identify the main idea of a story.	Contrast the goals and methods used in colonizing Africa by the different European nations.
Synthesis	Use knowledge about the areas of circles and volumes of cubes to derive a formula for the volume of a cylinder.	Write a new story based on the main idea of the story read.	Write an essay on the European colonization of Africa from the perspective of a Bantu chief.
Evaluation		Evaluate the story.	

Affective Objectives   Learning facts and skills is not the only important goal of instruction. Sometimes the feelings that students have about a subject or about their own skills are at least as important as how much information they learn. Instructional goals related to attitudes and values are called **affective objectives.** Many people would argue that a principal purpose of a U.S. history or civics course is to promote values of patriotism and civic responsibility, and one purpose of any mathematics course is to give students confidence in their ability to use mathematics. In planning instruction, it is important to consider affective as well as cognitive objectives. Love of learning, confidence in learning, and development of prosocial, cooperative attitudes are among the most important objectives teachers should have for their students.

Research on Instructional Objectives

Three principal reasons are given for writing instructional objectives. One is that this exercise helps to organize the teacher's planning. As Mager (1975) puts it, if you're not sure where you're going, you're liable to end up someplace else and not even know it. Another is that establishing instructional objectives helps to guide evaluation. Finally, it is hypothesized that development of instructional objectives improves student achievement.

Although it would be a mistake to overplan or to adhere rigidly to an inflexible plan (see Shavelson, 1987), most experienced teachers create, use, and value objectives and assessments that are planned in advance (Brown, 1988).

It is important to make sure that instructional objectives that are communicated to students are broad enough to encompass everything the lesson or course is supposed to teach. There is some danger that giving students too narrow a set of objectives might focus them on some information to the exclusion of other facts and concepts (Klauer, 1984).

Perhaps the most convincing support for the establishment of clear instructional objectives is indirect. Cooley and Leinhardt (1980) found that the strongest single factor predicting student reading and math scores was the degree to which students were actually taught the skills that were tested. This implies that instruction is effective to the degree to which objectives, teaching, and assessment are coordinated with one another. Specification of clear instructional objectives is the first step in ensuring that classroom instruction is directed toward giving students critical skills, those that are important enough to test.

Why Is Evaluation Important?

Evaluation, or assessment, refers to all the means used in schools to formally measure student performance (McMillan, 2004; Popham, 2005). These include quizzes and tests, written evaluations, and grades. Student evaluation usually focuses on academic achievement, but many schools also assess behaviors and attitudes. Many elementary schools provide descriptions of students' behavior (such as "follows directions," "listens attentively," "works with others," "uses time wisely"). In upper elementary, middle, and high school the prevalence of behavior reports diminishes successively, but even many high schools rate students on such criteria as "works up to ability," "is prepared," and "is responsible."

Why do teachers use tests and grades? They use them because, one way or another, they must periodically check and communicate about students' learning. Tests and grades tell teachers, students, and parents how students are doing in school. Teachers can use tests to determine whether their instruction was effective and to find out which students need additional help. Students can use tests to find out whether their studying strategies are paying off. Parents need grades to learn how their children

affective objectives
Objectives that have to do with student attitudes and values.

evaluation
Measurement of student performance in academic and, sometimes, other areas; used to determine appropriate teaching strategies.

are doing in school; grades usually serve as the one consistent form of communication between school and home. Schools sometimes need grades and tests to make student placements. States and school districts need tests to evaluate schools and, in some cases, teachers. Ultimately, colleges use grades and standardized test scores to decide whom to admit and employers use grade-based evidence of attainment such as diplomas and other credentials in hiring decisions. Teachers must therefore evaluate student learning; few would argue otherwise. Fortunately, research on the use of tests finds that students learn more in courses that use tests than in those that do not (Dempster, 1991).

Student evaluations serve six primary purposes (see Gronlund, 2003):

1. Feedback to students
2. Feedback to teachers
3. Information to parents
4. Information for selection and certification
5. Information for accountability
6. Incentives to increase student effort

Evaluation as Feedback

Imagine that a store owner tried several strategies to increase business—first advertising in the newspaper, then sending fliers to homes near the store, and finally holding a sale. However, suppose that after trying each strategy, the store owner failed to record and compare the store's revenue. Without taking stock this way, the owner would learn little about the effectiveness of any of the strategies and might well be wasting time and money. The same is true of teachers and students. They need to know as soon as possible whether their investments of time and energy in a given activity are paying off by the increasing of their learning.

Feedback for Students   Like the store owner, students need to know the results of their efforts (Bangert-Drowns, Kulik, Kulik, & Morgan, 1991; Munk & Bursuck, 1998). Regular evaluation gives them feedback on their strengths and weaknesses. For example, suppose a teacher had students write compositions and then gave back written evaluations. Some students might find out that they needed to work more on content, others on the use of modifiers, still others on language mechanics. This information would help students to improve their writing much more than would a grade with no explanation.

To be useful as feedback, evaluations should be as specific as possible. For example, Cross and Cross (1980/1981) found that students who received written feedback in addition to letter grades were more likely than other students to believe that their efforts, rather than luck or other external factors, determined their success in school.

Feedback to Teachers   One of the most important (and often overlooked) functions of evaluating student learning is to provide feedback to teachers on the effectiveness of their instruction. Teachers cannot expect to be optimally effective if they do not know whether students have grasped the main points of their lessons. Asking questions in class and observing students as they work gives the teacher some idea of how well students have learned; but in many subjects brief, frequent quizzes, writing assignments, and other student products are necessary to provide more detailed indications of students' progress. Evaluations also give information to the principal and the school as a whole, which can be used to guide overall reform efforts by identifying where schools or subgroups within schools are in need of improvement (Hanna & Dettmer, 2004; Lane & Beebe-Frankenberger, 2004; Trumbull & Farr, 2000).

CONNECTIONS

For more on feedback as a component of effective teaching, see Chapter 7, page 224.

INTASC

8 Assessment of Student Learning
9 Professional Commitment and Responsibility

Evaluation as Information

A report card is called a report card because it reports information on student progress. This reporting function of evaluation is important for several reasons.

Information to Parents   First, routine school evaluations of many kinds (test scores, stars, and certificates as well as report card grades) keep parents informed about their children's schoolwork. For example, if a student's grades are dropping, the parents might know why and might be able to help the student get back on track. Second, grades and other evaluations set up informal home-based reinforcement systems. Recall from Chapter 11 that many studies have found that reporting regularly to parents when students do good work and asking parents to reinforce good reports improves student behavior and achievement (Barth, 1979). Without much prompting, most parents naturally reinforce their children for bringing home good grades, thereby making grades important and effective as incentives (Natriello & Dornbusch, 1984).

CONNECTIONS

For more on information to parents, see Chapter 11, page 374.

Information for Selection   Some sociologists see the sorting of students into societal roles as a primary purpose of schools: If schools do not actually determine who will be a butcher, a baker, or a candlestick maker, they do substantially influence who will be a laborer, a skilled worker, a white-collar worker, or a professional. This sorting function takes place gradually over years of schooling. In the early grades, students are sorted into reading groups and, in many cases, into tracks that might remain stable over many years (Slavin, 1987c, 1990). Tracking becomes more widespread and systematic by junior high or middle school, when students begin to be selected into different courses (McPartland, Coldiron, & Braddock, 1987). For example, some ninth-graders are allowed to take Algebra I while others take prealgebra or general mathematics. In high school, students are often steered toward college preparatory, general, or vocational tracks or toward advanced, basic, or remedial levels of particular courses; and of course a major sorting takes place when students are accepted into various colleges and training programs. Throughout the school years, some students are selected into special-education or gifted programs or into other special programs with limited enrollments.

Closely related to selection is certification, a use of tests to qualify students for promotion or for access to various occupations. For example, many states and local districts have minimum competency tests that students must pass to advance from grade to grade or to graduate from high school. Bar exams for lawyers, board examinations for medical students, and tests for teachers such as the National Teachers' Examination are examples of certification tests that control access to professions.

This child discusses her report card with her mother. As a teacher, how can you ensure that report cards provide feedback, information, and incentive?

Information for Accountability   Often, evaluations of students serve as data for the evaluation of teachers, schools, districts, or even states. Every state has some form of statewide testing program that allows the states to rank every school in terms of student performance (Gandal & Vranek, 2001; Linn, 2000). In addition to state tests, school districts often use tests for similar purposes (for example, in grades not tested by the state). These test scores are also often used in evaluations of principals, teachers, and superintendents. Consequently, these tests are taken very seriously.

Evaluation as Incentive

One important use of evaluations is to motivate students to give their best efforts. In essence, high grades, stars, and prizes are given as rewards for good work. Students value grades and prizes primarily because their parents value them. Some high school students also value grades because they are important for getting into selective colleges.

CONNECTIONS

For information on using grades as incentives, see Chapter 10, page 343.

$\mathcal{H}$ow Is Student Learning Evaluated?

Evaluation strategies must be appropriate for the uses that are made of them (McMillan, 2004; Trice, 2000). To understand how assessments can be used most effectively in classroom instruction, it is important to know the differences between formative and summative evaluation and between norm-referenced and criterion-referenced interpretation.

INTASC

8 Assessment of Student Learning

Formative and Summative Evaluations

The distinction between formative and summative evaluations was explained in the discussion of mastery learning in Chapter 9, but this distinction also applies to a broader range of evaluation issues. Essentially, a *formative evaluation* asks, "How well are you doing and how can you be doing better?" A *summative evaluation* asks, "How well did you do?" Formative, or diagnostic, tests are given to discover strengths and weaknesses in learning and to make midcourse corrections in pace or content of instruction. Formative evaluations might even be made "on the fly" during instruction through oral or brief written learning probes (see Chapter 7). Formative evaluation is useful to the degree that it is informative, closely tied to the curriculum being taught, timely, and frequent (McMillan, 2004). For example, frequent quizzes that are given and scored immediately after specific lessons might serve as formative evaluations, providing feedback to help both teachers and students improve students' learning.

In contrast, summative evaluation refers to tests of student knowledge at the end of instructional units (such as final exams). Summative evaluations may or may not be frequent, but they must be reliable and (in general) should allow for comparisons among students. Summative evaluations should also be closely tied to formative evaluations and to course objectives.

CONNECTIONS

For the discussion of mastery learning, see Chapter 9, page 286.

CERTIFICATION POINTER

For your teacher certification test you may be given a case illustrating an evaluation of student performance and you will need to categorize that evaluation as formative or summative.

Norm-Referenced and Criterion-Referenced Evaluations

Interpretation in order to attach a degree of value to a student's performance is an important step in an evaluation. The distinction between norm-referencing and criterion-referencing refers to how students' scores are interpreted.

Norm-referenced interpretations focus on comparisons of a student's scores with those of other students. Within a classroom, for example, grades commonly are used to give teachers an idea of how well a student has performed in comparison with classmates. A student might also have a grade-level or school rank; and in standardized testing, student scores might be compared with those of a nationally representative norm group.

Criterion-referenced interpretations focus on assessing students' mastery of specific skills, regardless of how other students did on the same skills. Criterion-referenced evaluations are best if they are closely tied to specific objectives or well-specified domains of the curriculum being taught. Table 13.4 compares the principal

CONNECTIONS

For more on standardized testing, see Chapter 14.

norm-referenced interpretations
Assessments that compare the performance of one student against the performance of others.

criterion-referenced interpretations
Assessments that rate how thoroughly students have mastered specific skills or areas of knowledge.

Table 13.4

Comparison of Two Approaches to Achievement Testing

Norm-referenced tests and criterion-referenced tests serve different purposes and have different features.

Feature	Norm-Referenced Testing	Criterion-Referenced Testing
Principal use	Survey testing	Mastery testing
Major emphasis	Measures individual differences in achievement	Describes tasks students can perform
Interpretation of results	Compares performance to that of other individuals	Compares performance to a clearly specified achievement domain
Content coverage	Typically covers a broad area of achievement	Typically focuses on a limited set of learning tasks
Nature of test plan	Table of specifications is commonly used	Detailed domain specifications are favored
Item selection procedures	Items selected to provide maximum discrimination among individuals (to obtain high score variability); easy items typically eliminated from the test	Includes all items needed to adequately describe performance; no attempt is made to alter item difficulty or to eliminate easy items to increase score variability
Performance standards	Level of performance determined by *relative* position in some known group (e.g., student ranks fifth in a group of 20)	Level of performance commonly determined by *absolute* standards (e.g., student demonstrates mastery by defining 90 percent of the technical terms)

Source: Adapted from Norman E. Gronlund, *How to Make Achievement Tests and Assessments* (5th ed.). Copyright © 1993 by Allyn & Bacon. Reprinted by permission.

features and purposes of criterion-referenced and norm-referenced testing (see also Popham, 2005; Shepard, 1989a).

Formative evaluation is almost always criterion-referenced. In formative testing, teachers want to know, for example, who is having trouble with Newton's laws of thermodynamics, not which student is first, fifteenth, or thirtieth in the class in physics knowledge. Summative testing, in contrast, can be either criterion-referenced or norm-referenced. Even if it is criterion-referenced, however, teachers usually want to know on a summative test how each student did in comparison with other students.

Matching Evaluation Strategies with Goals

Considering all the factors discussed up to this point, what is the best strategy for evaluating students? The first answer is that there is no one best strategy (Popham, 2005). The best means of accomplishing any one objective of evaluation might be inappropriate for other objectives. Therefore, teachers must choose different types of evaluation for different purposes. At a minimum, two types of evaluation should be used: one directed at providing incentive and feedback and the other directed at ranking individual students relative to the larger group.

Evaluation for Incentive and Feedback   Traditional grades are often inadequate as incentives to encourage students to give their best efforts and as feedback to teachers and students. The principal problem is that grades are given too infrequently, are too

CERTIFICATION POINTER

Your teacher certification test may require you to evaluate when it would be more appropriate to use a criterion-referenced versus a norm-referenced test.

INTASC

5 Classroom Motivation and Management

6 Communication Skills

far removed in time from student performance, and are poorly tied to specific student behaviors. Recall from Chapter 5 that the effectiveness of reinforcers and of feedback diminishes rapidly if there is much delay between behavior and consequences. By the same token, research has found that achievement is higher in classrooms where students receive immediate feedback on their quizzes than in classrooms where feedback is delayed (Bangert-Drowns, Kulik, Kulik, & Morgan, 1991; Crooks, 1988).

CONNECTIONS
Rewards and motivation are discussed in Chapter 5, page 139.

Another reason that grades are less than ideal as incentives is that they are usually based on comparative standards. In effect, it is relatively easy for high-ability students to achieve A's and B's but very difficult for low achievers to do so. As a result, some high achievers do less work than they are capable of doing, and some low achievers give up. As was noted in Chapter 10, a reward that is too easy or too difficult to attain, or that is felt to be a result of ability rather than of effort, is a poor motivator (DeBacker & Nelson, 1999; Wigfield & Eccles, 2000).

CONNECTIONS
For more on what rewards make poor motivators, see Chapter 10, page 334.

CONNECTIONS
For more on rewards that are too easy to attain, see Chapter 10, p. 341.

For these reasons, traditional grades should be supplemented by evaluations that are better designed for incentive and feedback. For example, teachers might give daily quizzes of 5 or 10 items that are scored in class immediately after completion, or they might have students write daily "mini-essays" on a topic the class is studying. These give both students and teachers the information they need to adjust their teaching and learning strategies and to rectify any deficiencies revealed by the evaluations. If teachers make quiz results important by having them count toward course grades or by giving students with perfect papers special recognition or certificates, then quiz scores also serve as effective incentives, rewarding effective studying behavior soon after it occurs. It is important to have a clear and objective set of criteria that student work is compared with so students can see exactly why they scored as they did. If the criteria are illustrated using a rubric that has descriptions of different levels of achievement (scores) as well as examples of student work at the highest levels of achievement (or better yet, that is typical of each possible score students might receive according to the rubric), then students can see exactly how their achievement compares with the criteria.

Evaluation for Comparison with Others   There are times when teachers need to know and to communicate how well students are doing in comparison to others. This information is important to give parents (and students themselves) a realistic picture of student performance. For example, students who have outstanding skills in science ought to know that they are exceptional, not only in the context of their class or school, but also in a broader state or national context. In general, students need to form accurate perceptions of their strengths and weaknesses to guide their decisions about their futures.

Comparative evaluations are traditionally provided by grades and by standardized tests. Unlike incentive/feedback evaluations, comparative evaluations need not be conducted frequently. Rather, the emphasis in comparative evaluations must be on fair, unbiased, reliable assessment of student performance. Comparative evaluations should assess what students can do and nothing else. Student grades should be based primarily on demonstrated knowledge of the course content, not on politeness, good behavior, neatness, or punctuality, because the purpose of a grade is to give an accurate assessment of student attainment, not to reward or punish students for their behavior. However, grades are often imperfect as comparative evaluators, because many teachers consider subjective factors when assigning grades. One solution in secondary schools is for teachers in a given department to get together to write departmental exams for each course. For example, a high school science department might decide on common objectives for all chemistry classes and then make up common unit tests and/or final exams. This would ensure that students in all classes were evaluated according to the same criteria.

CONNECTIONS
For more on grades and standardized tests, see Chapter 14.

To be fair, comparative evaluations and other summative assessments of student performance must be firmly based on the objectives established at the beginning of the course and must be consistent with the formative incentive/feedback evaluations in format, as well. No teacher wants a situation in which students do well on week-to-week assessments but then fail the summative evaluations because there is a lack of correspondence between the two forms of evaluation. For example, if the summative test uses essay questions, then the formative tests leading up to it should also include essay questions.

There are two keys to reliable summative assessment. First, teachers should use multiple assessment opportunities. No student should receive a grade based on just one test since too much can go wrong with only one assessment. Second, teachers should test learning when it is completed, not as it is developing. Some teachers may base grades on formative assessments, but assessments used as incentives and for feedback are inadequate for grading because they do not evaluate students' eventual learning. It is better to collect summative evaluation information as students complete instructional units as well as to use major unit and final tests.

*H*ow are tests constructed?

Once you know the concept domains to be assessed in a test of student learning, it is time to write test items. From 5 to 15 percent of all class time is used in written testing (Dorr-Bremme & Herman, 1986; Haertel, 1986). Writing good achievement tests is therefore a critical skill for effective teaching. This section presents some basic principles of achievement testing and practical tools for test construction (see Carey, 2001; Gredler, 1999; Gronlund, 2003; Trice, 2000). Achievement testing is taken up again in Chapter 14 in relation to standardized tests.

CONNECTIONS

For more on achievement testing in relation to standardized tests, see Chapter 14, page 506.

Principles of Achievement Testing

Gronlund (2000) listed six principles to keep in mind in preparing achievement tests. These are paraphrased as follows:

1. Achievement tests should measure clearly defined learning objectives that are in harmony with instructional objectives. Perhaps the most important principle of achievement testing is that the tests should correspond with the course objectives and with the instruction that is actually provided (Carr & Harris, 2001; Gorin & Blanchard, 2004; Hanna & Dettmer, 2004; Linn, 2000). An achievement test should never be a surprise for students; rather, it should assess the students' grasp of the most important concepts or skills the lesson or course is supposed to teach. Further, assessments should tap the true breadth of objectives of the course, not just the easy-to-measure elements. For example, a test in a course on twentieth-century art should probably ask students to discuss or to compare artworks. Although it would be much easier to ask students just to match artists with their paintings, such a test would not cover the likely range of course objectives (see Frederiksen, 1984b).

CONNECTIONS

For more on the characteristics and uses of standardized achievement tests, see Chapter 14, page 512.

2. Achievement tests should measure a representative sample of the learning tasks included in the instruction. With rare exceptions (such as multiplication facts), achievement tests do not assess every skill or fact students are supposed to have learned. Rather, they sample from among all the learning objectives. If students do not know in advance what questions will be on a test, then they must study the entire course content to do well. However, the test items must be representative of all the objectives (contents and skills) that were covered. For example, if an English literature course spent 8 weeks on Shakespeare and 2 weeks on other Elizabethan authors, the test should have about 4 times as many items relating to Shakespeare as to the others. Items that are chosen to represent a particular objective must be central to that objective. There is no place in achievement testing for tricky or obscure questions. For example, a unit test on the American Revolution should ask questions relating to the causes, principal events, and outcomes of that struggle, not who rowed George Washington across the Delaware. (*Answer:* John Glover and his Marblehead Marines.)

3. Achievement tests should include the types of test items that are most appropriate for measuring the desired learning outcomes. Items on achievement tests should correspond as closely as possible to the ultimate instructional objectives (Carr & Harris, 2001; Strong, Silver, & Perini, 2001). For example, in mathematics problem solving, one of the teacher's goals might be to enable students to solve problems like the ones they will encounter outside of school. Matching items or multiple choice might be inappropriate for this kind of exam, because in real life we do not select from a menu of possible solutions to a problem.

4. Achievement tests should fit the particular uses that will be made of the results. Each type of achievement test has its own requirements. For example, a test that is used for diagnosis would focus on particular skills with which students might need help. A diagnostic test of elementary arithmetic might contain items on subtraction involving zeros in the minuend (e.g., 307 minus 127), a skill with which many students have trouble. In contrast, a test that is used to predict future performance might assess a

These students are taking achievement tests. What are the principles for preparing achievement tests?

student's general abilities and breadth of knowledge. Formative tests should be very closely tied to material that has recently been presented, whereas summative tests should survey broader areas of knowledge or skills.

5. Achievement tests should be as reliable as possible and should be interpreted with caution. A test is reliable to the degree that students who were tested a second time would fall in the same rank order. In general, writers of achievement tests increase reliability by using relatively large numbers of items and by using few items that almost all students get right or that almost all students miss (Hopkins, 1998). The use of clearly written items that focus directly on the objectives that are actually taught also enhances test reliability. Still, no matter how rigorously reliability is built into a test, there will always be some error of measurement. Students have good and bad days or can be lucky or unlucky guessers. Some students are test-wise and usually test well; others are text-anxious and test far below their actual knowledge or potential. Therefore no single test score should be viewed with excessive confidence. Any test score is only an approximation of a student's true knowledge or skills and should be interpreted as such.

6. Achievement tests should improve learning. Achievement tests of all kinds, particularly formative tests, provide important information on students' learning progress. Stiggins (2004), for example, urges that assessments *for* learning are more important than assessments *of* learning. Achievement testing should be seen as part of the instructional process and should be used to improve instruction and guide student learning (Darling-Hammond & Falk, 1997; Trumbull & Farr, 2000). This means that achievement test results should be clearly communicated to students soon after the test is taken; in the case of formative testing, students should be given the results immediately. Teachers should use the results of formative and summative tests to guide

CONNECTIONS

For more on the reliability of achievement tests, see Chapter 14, page 518.

instruction, to locate strong and weak points in students' understandings, and to set an appropriate pace of instruction.

Theory into **PRACTICE**

Making Assessments Fair

Although fairness in assessment is something everyone believes in, defining fairness in assessment is not straightforward. Indeed, the latest edition of the *Standards for Educational and Psychological Testing* gives four definitions and acknowledges that many more are in the literature (AERA/APA/NCME, 1999). For our purposes, we might define fairness as being honest, impartial, and free from discrimination.

Besides being ethical, fairness makes good instructional sense. Fair testing encourages students to spend more effort on learning because they will come to see that success depends only on what they know and can do.

Fairness in assessment arises from good practice in four phases of testing: writing, administering, scoring, and interpreting assessments. Practices that lead to fairness in these areas are considered separately below.

Writing assessments. Base assessments on course objectives. Students expect a test to cover what they have been learning. They also have a right to a test that neither "tricks" them into wrong answers nor rewards them if they can get a high score through guessing or bluffing.

Cover the full range of thinking skills and processes. Assuming instruction has included higher-order thinking, so should an assessment based on that instruction prompt students to use the material intellectually, not merely repeat memorized knowledge. Further, if a teacher's tests cover only memorization, the students will emphasize only memorization of facts in their preparation.

Cover course content proportionally to coverage in instruction. The content areas on the test should be representative of what students have studied. The best guide to appropriate proportions is the relative amounts of instructional time spent on those topics.

Test what is important for students to know and be able to do rather than isolated trivia. The best guide to the content most appropriate for the test is to cover what is important for students to come away with from the course. When writing a test, ask yourself whether each task is what other teachers would agree is important when teaching that course. Better, ask a colleague to review your draft test.

Avoid contexts and expressions that are more familiar and/or intriguing to some students than to others. One challenge in writing tests is to make sure none of your students are advantaged or disadvantaged because of their different backgrounds. For example, music, sports, or celebrity-related examples might be appealing to some students but not others. Language or topics should not be used if they are more well known or interesting to some students than to others. If that proves impossible, then at least make sure the items that favor some students are balanced with others that favor the rest.

Giving assessments. Make sure students have had equal opportunities to learn the material on the assessment. Whether or not students have learned as much as they can, at least they should have had equal chances to do so. If some students are given extra time or materials that are withheld from others, the others likely will not feel they have been treated fairly.

Announce assessments in plenty of time for students to prepare for them. Since students' learning styles differ, some will keep up to date with their studying and others will prefer to put in extra effort when it is most needed. Surprise assessments reward the former and punish the latter. But these styles are not part of the material to be learned. Not only is it more fair to announce assessments in advance, it also serves as a motivator for students to study.

Make sure students are familiar with the formats they will be using to respond. If some students are not comfortable with the types of questions on an assessment, they will not have an equal chance to show what they can do. If that might be the case, some practice with the format beforehand is recommended to help them succeed.

Give plenty of time. Most tests in education do not cover content that will eventually be used under time pressure. Thus, most assessments should reward quality instead of speed. Only by allowing enough time so virtually all students have an opportunity to answer every question will the effects of speed be eliminated as a barrier to performance.

Scoring assessments. Make sure the rubric used to score responses awards full credit to an answer that is responsive to the question asked as opposed to requiring more information than requested for full credit. If the question does not prompt the knowledgeable student to write an answer that receives full credit, then it should be changed. It is unfair to reward some students for doing more than has been requested in the item; not all students will understand the real (and hidden) directions since they have not been told.

Interpreting assessments. Base grades on summative, end-of-unit assessments rather than formative assessments that are used to make decisions about learning as it is progressing. The latter are intended as diagnostic and to be used to help accomplish learning. Since grades certify attainment, they should be determined based on assessments made after learning has taken place.

Base grades on several assessment formats. Since students differ in their preferred assessment formats, some are advantaged by selected-response tests, others by essay tests, others by performance assessments, and still others by papers and projects.

Base grades on several assessments over time. As with assessment formats, grades should also depend on multiple assessments taken at different times.

Make sure factors that could have resulted in atypical performance for a student are used to minimize the importance of the student's score on that assessment. If it is known that a student has not done her or his best, then basing a grade or other important decision on that assessment is not only unfair; it is inaccurate.

ON THE WEB

DiscoverySchool.com has rubrics for every kind of assessment imaginable, as well as lesson plans and other useful information for educators. Visit their website at **www.school.discovery.com/schrockguide/assess.html.**

Using a Table of Specifications

Achievement tests should measure well-specified objectives. The first step in the test development process is to decide which concept domains the test will measure and

Table 13.5

Table of Specifications for a Chemistry Unit

This table of specifications classifies test items (circled numbers) and objectives according to six categories ranging from knowledge of terms to ability to apply knowledge.

A. Knowledge of Terms	B. Knowledge of Facts	C. Knowledge of Rules and Principles	D. Skill in Using Processes and Procedures	E. Ability to Make Translations	F. Ability to Make Applications
Atom (1)		Boyle's law (12)			
Molecule (2)		Properties of a gas (13)		Substance into diagram (22)	
Element (3)		Atomic theory (16)			Writing and solving equations to fit experimental situations
Compound (4)	Diatomic gases (11)	Chemical formula (19)		Compound into formula (21)	(28)
Diatomic (5)					(23)
Chemical formula (6)		Avogadro's hypothesis (14)			(24)
Avogadro's number (7)		Gay-Lussac's law (15)			(25)
Mole (8)		Grams to moles (18)			(26)
Atomic weight (9)		Molecular weight (17)	Molecular weight (20)		(27)
Molecular weight (10)					(29)

Source: From B. S. Bloom, J. T. Hastings, and G. F. Madaus, *Handbook on Formative and Summative Evaluation of Student Learning,* p. 121. Copyright © 1971 by McGraw-Hill, Inc. Reproduced with permission of The McGraw-Hill Companies.

how many test items will be allocated to each concept. Gronlund (2000) and Bloom, Hastings, and Madaus (1971) suggest that teachers make up a **table of specifications** for each instructional unit listing the various objectives taught and different levels of understanding to be assessed. The levels of understanding might correspond to Bloom's taxonomy of educational objectives (Bloom et al., 1956; Marzano, 2001). Bloom and colleagues (1971) suggest classifying test items for each objective according to six categories, as shown in Table 13.5, a table of specifications for a chemistry unit.

The table of specifications varies for each type of course and is nearly identical to behavior content matrixes, discussed earlier in this chapter. This is as it should be; a behavior content matrix is used to lay out objectives for a course, and the table of specifications tests those objectives.

Once you have written items corresponding to your table of specifications, look over the test in its entirety and evaluate it against the following standards:

table of specifications
A list of instructional objectives and expected levels of understanding that guides test development.

1. Do the items emphasize the same things you emphasized in day-to-day instruction? (Recall how Mr. Sullivan, in the chapter-opening vignette, ignored this common-sense rule.)
2. Has an important area of content or any objective been overlooked or under-emphasized?
3. Does the test cover all levels of instructional objectives included in the lessons?
4. Does the language of the items correspond to the language and reading level you used in the lessons?
5. Is there a reasonable balance between what the items measure and the amount of time that will be required for students to develop a response?
6. Did you write model answers or essential component outlines for the short essay items? Does the weighting of each item reflect its relative value among all the other items?

Evaluation that is restricted to information acquired from paper-and-pencil tests provides only certain kinds of information about students' progress in school. Other sources and strategies for appraisal of student work must be used, including checklists, interviews, classroom simulations, role-playing activities, and anecdotal records. To do this systematically, you may keep a journal or log to record concise and cogent evaluative information on each student throughout the school year.

Writing Selected-Response Test Items

Test items that can be scored correct or incorrect without the need for interpretation are referred to as **selected-response items.** Multiple-choice, true–false, and matching items are the most common forms. Note that the correct answer appears on the test and the student's task is to select it. There is no ambiguity about whether the student has or has not selected the correct answer. This section discusses these types of test items and their advantages and disadvantages.

Multiple-Choice Items   Considered by some educators to be the most useful and flexible of all test forms (Gronlund, 2000; Haladyna, 1997, 1999), **multiple-choice items** can be used in tests for most school subjects. The basic form of the multiple-choice item is a **stem** followed by choices, or alternatives. The stem may be a question or a partial statement that is completed by one of several choices. No truly optimum number of choices exists, but four or five are most common—one correct response and others that are referred to as **distractors.**

Here are two types of multiple-choice items, one with a question stem and the other with a completion stem:

1. What color results from the mixture of equal parts of yellow and blue paint?
   a. black
   b. gray
   c. green [*correct choice*]
   d. red
2. The actual election of the U.S. president to office is done by
   a. all registered voters.
   b. our congressional representatives.
   c. the Electoral College. [*correct choice*]
   d. the Supreme Court.

When writing a multiple-choice item, keep two goals in mind. First, a capable student should be able to choose the correct answer and not be distracted by the wrong

selected-response items
Test items in which respondents can select from one or more possible answers, without requiring the scorer to interpret their response.

multiple-choice items
Test items that usually consist of a stem followed by choices or alternatives.

stem
A question or partial statement in a test item that is completed by one of several choices.

distractors
Incorrect responses that are offered as alternative answers to a multiple-choice question.

alternatives. Second, you should minimize the chance that a student who is ignorant of the subject matter can guess the correct answer. To achieve this, the distractors (the wrong choices; also sometimes called foils) must look plausible to the uninformed; their wording and form must not identify them readily as bad answers. Hence, one of the tasks in writing a good multiple-choice item is to identify two, three, or four plausible, but not tricky, distractors.

Theory into **PRACTICE**

Writing Multiple-Choice Tests (Format Suggestions)

Here are some guidelines for constructing multiple-choice items (see Haladyna, 1997):

1. Make the stem sufficiently specific to stand on its own without qualification. In other words, the stem should contain enough information to set the context for the concepts in it. Here is an example of a stem for which insufficient context has been established:

   Applied behavior analysis can be

   a. classical conditioning.
   b. punishment.
   c. reinforcement contingencies.
   d. self-actualization.

An improved version of this stem is as follows:

   What is the main emphasis of modern classroom use of applied behavior analysis?

   a. classical conditioning
   b. punishment
   c. reinforcement contingencies [*correct choice*]
   d. self-actualization

2. Avoid long and complicated stems unless the purpose of the item is to measure a student's ability to deal with new information or to interpret a paragraph. The stem should not be too wordy; a test is not the place to incorporate instruction that should have been given in the lessons. Writing the item stems as simple sentences in question form often helps to focus them appropriately.

3. The stem and every choice in the list of potential answers ought to fit grammatically. In addition, phrases or words that would commonly begin each of the alternatives should be part of the stem. It is also a sound idea to have the same grammatical form (say, a verb) at the beginning of each choice. For example:

   The task of statistics is to

   a. *make* the investigation of human beings more precise and rigorous.
   b. *make* the social sciences as respectable as the physical sciences.
   c. *predict* human behavior.
   d. *reduce* large masses of data to an interpretable form. [*correct choice*]

4. Take special care in using no-exception words such as "never," "all," "none," and "always." These words, called specific determiners, are most commonly

found in incorrect statements because the admission of no exceptions usually makes statements wrong. In multiple-choice items these words often give clues to the test-wise but concept-ignorant student. Hill (1977) notes also that words allowing qualification, such as *often, sometimes, seldom, usually, typically, generally,* and *ordinarily,* are most often found in correct statements (or responses that are true) and, along with the no-exception words, this type of specific determiner should be avoided whenever possible, or at least distributed among correct answers and distractors.

5. Avoid making the correct choice the only one that is qualified (e.g., by an "if" clause). Also, it should be neither the longest nor shortest of the alternatives (usually the longest, because absolutely correct answers often require qualification and precision). These features make a choice stand out, called **clang.** If the choices vary considerably in length, then having at least two short ones and at least two long ones will reduce clang.

6. Do not allow an item to be answered on the basis of information contained in another item on the same test. This is another form of clang because it allows a student to identify the answer without knowing it beforehand.

7. Avoid overinclusive options that contain other options. For example, the choices "dogs" and "setters" should not be in the same item since a setter is a type of dog. Similarly, be cautious in using "all of the above" as an alternative, because it also often reduces the possible correct choices to one or two alternatives. Here is an example illustrating how a student might know very little and get the correct answer. By knowing that only one of the choices is incorrect, a student will reduce the number of plausible choices from four to two:

What type of research is best for investigating the effects of a new instructional program on mathematics achievement?

a. correlational
b. experimental [*correct choice*]
c. historical
d. all of the above

The student who knows that "historical" is not a good choice also knows that *d* must be incorrect, and the answer must be *a* or *b*.

8. After a test, discuss the items with students, and note their interpretations of the wording of the items. Students often interpret certain phrases quite differently from the way the teacher intended. Such feedback will help you revise items for the next test, as well as informing you about students' understandings.

9. Do not include a choice that is transparently absurd. All choices should seem plausible to a student who has not studied or otherwise become familiar with the subject.

Besides these guidelines for writing multiple-choice items, here are some suggestions about format:

- List the choices vertically rather than side by side.
- Use letters rather than numerals to label the choices, especially on scientific and mathematical tests.
- Use word structures that make the stem agree with the choices according to acceptable grammatical practice. For example, a completion-type stem

clang
Features that make a choice stand out in multiple-choice questions.

would require that each of the choices begin with a lowercase letter (unless it begins with a proper noun).

- Avoid repeating the same word or phrase in the stem and in only one alternative.
- Avoid overusing one letter position as the correct choice, as well as a pattern in the correct answers. Instead, correct choices should appear in random letter positions.

As an illustration of how test "wiseness" rather than knowledge can help students pass a test, take the brief test in Figure 13.2.

true–false items

A form of multiple-choice test items, most useful when a comparison of two alternatives is called for.

matching items

Test items that are presented in two lists, each item in one list matching one or more items in the other list.

True–False Items   **True–false items** can be seen as one form of multiple choice. The main drawback of true–false items is that students have a 50 percent chance of guessing correctly. For this reason, they should rarely be used.

Matching Items   **Matching items** are commonly presented in the form of two lists, say *A* and *B*. For each item in list *A*, the student has to select one item in list *B*. The basis for choosing must be clearly explained in the directions. Matching items can be used to cover a large amount of content; that is, a large (but not unmanageably so) number of concepts should appear in the two lists. Each list should cover related

FIGURE 13.2
A Test of Test "Wiseness"

The following test is about a made-up country, Quizzerland. Use your test wiseness to guess the answers to these very bad items.

1. What is the main currency used in Quizzerland?
   a. dollar
   b. peso
   c. quark
   d. pound

2. Describe the pattern of annual rainfall in Quizzerland.
   a. mostly rainy in the highlands, dry in the lowlands
   b. rainy
   c. dry
   d. snowy

3. How many children are there in Quizzerlandian families?
   a. never more than 2
   b. usually 2–3
   c. always at least 3
   d. none

4. What would be the correct response to any question asked here?
   a.
   b.
   c.
   d.

Answers:
   1. c (process of elimination)
   2. a (longer item with qualifications is usually correct)
   3. b ("always" and "never" items are usually wrong)
   4. d (this response hasn't been used yet)

content (use more than one set of matching items for different types of material). The primary cognitive skill that matching exercises test is *recall*.

Matching items can often be answered by elimination because many teachers maintain a one-to-one correspondence between the two lists. To engage students in the content, not the format, teachers should either include more items in list *B* than in list *A* or allow re-use of the items in list *B*.

Writing Constructed-Response Items

Constructed-response items require the student to supply rather than to select the answer. They also usually require some degree of judgment in scoring.

The simplest form is fill-in-the-blank items, which can often be written to reduce or eliminate ambiguity in scoring. Still, unanticipated responses might lead to ambiguous answers, causing questions in the mind of the instructor on how to score. Constructed response items also come in short and long essay forms.

Fill-in-the-Blank Items   When there is clearly only one possible correct answer, an attractive format is completion, or "fill in the blank," as in the following examples:

1. The largest city in Germany is _____.
2. What is 15 percent of $198.00? _____
3. The measure of electric resistance is the _____.

The advantage of these **completion items** is that they can reduce the element of test-wiseness to near zero. For example, compare the following items:

1. The capital of Maine is _____.
2. The capital of Maine is

   a. Sacramento.
   b. Augusta.
   c. Juneau.
   d. Boston.

A student who has no idea what the capital of Maine is could pick Augusta from the list in item 2 because it is easy to rule out the other three cities. In item 1, however, the student has to know the answer. Completion items are especially useful in arithmetic, in which use of multiple choice may help to give the answer away or reward guessing. For example:

    4037
   − 159

   a. 4196
   b. 4122
   c. 3878 [*correct answer*]
   d. 3978

If students subtract and get an answer other than any of those listed, they know that they have to keep trying. In some cases they can narrow the alternatives by estimating rather than knowing how to compute the answer.

It is critical to avoid ambiguity in completion items. In some subject areas this can be difficult, because two or more answers will reasonably fit a fragment that does not specify the context. Here are two examples:

1. The Battle of Hastings was in _____. [Date or place?]
2. "H2O" represents _____. [Water or two parts hydrogen and one part oxygen?]

completion items
Fill-in-the-blank test items.

If there is any ambiguity possible, it is probably best to move to a selection type of item such as multiple choice.

Writing and Evaluating Essay Tests

Short essay questions allow students to respond in their own words. The most common form for a **short essay item** includes a question for the student to answer. The answer may range from a sentence or two to a page of, say, 100 to 150 words. A **long essay item** requires more length and more time, allowing greater opportunity for students to demonstrate organization and development of ideas. Although they differ in length, the methods available to write and score them are similar.

The essay form can elicit a wide variety of responses, from giving definitions of terms to comparing and contrasting important concepts or events. These items are especially suited for assessing students' ability to analyze, synthesize, and evaluate. Hence teachers might use them to appraise students' progress in organizing data and applying concepts at the highest levels of instructional objectives. Of course, these items depend heavily on writing skills and the ability to phrase ideas, so exclusive use of essays might cause the teacher to underestimate the knowledge and effort of a student who has learned the material but is a poor writer.

One of the crucial mistakes teachers make in writing essay items is failing to specify clearly the approximate detail required in the response and its expected length. Stating how much weight an item has relative to the entire test is generally not sufficient to tell students how much detail must be incorporated in a response. Here's an illustration of this point:

Poor Essay Item

Discuss the role of the prime minister in Canadian politics.

Improvement

In five paragraphs or less, identify three ways in which the Canadian prime minister and the U.S. president differ in their obligations to their respective constituencies. For each of the three, explain how the obligations are different.

Note that the improved version expresses a length (five paragraphs or less), the aspect to be treated (differences between the prime minister and the president), the number of points to be covered (three; while some teachers might write "at least three," that would introduce ambiguity into the task), how the points should be selected (differ in their obligations to their respective constituencies), and the direction and degree of elaboration needed (explain how the obligations are different). This item points the student toward the desired response and allows the teacher greater opportunity to explain the criteria by which student responses will be judged.

An essay item should contain specific information that students are to address. Some teachers are reluctant to name the particulars that they wish the student to discuss, because they believe that supplying a word or phrase in the instructions is giving away too much information. But if an item is ambiguous, different students will interpret it differently. Consequently, they will be responding to different questions and the test will almost surely not be fair to all of them.

Essay items have a number of advantages in addition to letting students state ideas in their own words. Essay items are not susceptible to correct guesses. They can be used to measure creative abilities, such as writing talent or imagination in constructing hypothetical events. Essay items might require students to combine several concepts in their response. They can assess organization and fluency.

On the negative side is the problem of reliability in scoring essay responses. Some studies demonstrate that independent marking of the same essay response by several

short essay item
A test question the answer to which may range from a sentence or two to a page of 100 to 150 words.

long essay item
A test question requiring an answer of more than a page.

teachers results in appraisals ranging from excellent to a failing grade. This gross difference in evaluations indicates a wide range of marking criteria and standards among teachers of similar backgrounds.

A second drawback of essay items is that essay responses take considerable time to evaluate. The time you might have saved by writing one essay item instead of several other kinds of items must be paid back in grading the essays.

Third, essay items in general take considerable response time from students. Consequently, they typically cannot be used to cover broad ranges of content. Nevertheless, essay items allow teachers the opportunity to see how well students can use the material they have been taught. Breadth is sacrificed for depth.

Here are some additional suggestions for writing essay items:

1. As with any item format, match the items with the instructional objectives.
2. Do not use such general directives in an item as "discuss," "give your opinion about . . . ," "tell all you know about. . . ." Rather, carefully choose specific response verbs such as "compare," "contrast," "identify," "list and define," and "explain the difference."
3. Write a response to the item before you give the test to estimate the time students will need to respond. About four times the teacher's time is a fair estimate.
4. Rewrite the item to point students clearly toward that response.
5. Require all students to answer all items. Although it seems attractive to allow student choice in which items to answer, that is fundamentally an unfair practice. First, students differ in their ability to make the best selections. Second, the items will not be of equivalent difficulty. And third, some students who know they will have a choice can increase their score by studying very carefully only part of the material.

After writing an essay item—and clearly specifying the content that is to be included in the response—you must have a clear idea of how you will score various elements of a student's response. Of course, you want to use the same standards and criteria for all students' responses to that item. The first step is to write a model response or a detailed outline of the essential elements students are being directed to include in their responses. You will compare students' responses to this model. If you intend to use evaluative comments but no letter grades, your outline or model will serve as a guide for pointing out to students the omissions and errors in their responses, as well as the good points of their answers. If you are using letter grades to score the essays, you will compare elements of students' responses with the contents of your model and give suitable credit to responses that match the relative weights of elements in the model.

If possible, you should ask a colleague to assess the validity of the elements and their weights in your model response. Going a bit further and having the colleague apply the model criteria to one or more student responses could increase the reliability of your scoring. Be sure to offer to do the same for them!

One issue relating to essay tests is whether and how much to count grammar, spelling, and other technical features. If you do count these, give students separate grades in content and in mechanics so that they will know the basis on which their work was evaluated.

A powerful use of assessment in instruction is to generate one or more scoring rubrics that can be shared with students well in advance of the test. The rubrics, like the example, should be generic, in that they can be applied to a broad range of essays. Students can see what aspects of their achievement will contribute to a positive evaluation and can practice to make sure their work illustrates those critical elements. One rubric for high school math problem solving appears in Figure 13.3.

Level 3

The response indicates application of a reasonable strategy that leads to a correct solution in the context of the problem. The representations are essentially correct. The explanation and/or justification is logically sound, clearly presented, fully developed, supports the solution, and does not contain significant mathematical errors. The response demonstrates a complete understanding and analysis of the problem.

Level 2

The response indicates application of a reasonable strategy that may be incomplete or undeveloped. It may or may not lead to a correct solution. The representations are fundamentally correct. The explanation and/or justification supports the solution and is plausible, although it may not be well developed or complete. The response demonstrates a conceptual understanding and analysis of the problem.

Level 1

The response indicates little or no attempt to apply a reasonable stategy or applies an inappropriate strategy. It may or may not have the correct answer. The representations

are incomplete or missing. The explanation and/or justification reveals serious flaws in reasoning. The explanation and/or justification may be incomplete or missing. The response demonstrates a minimal understanding and analysis of the problem.

Level 0

The response is completely incorrect or irrelevant. There may be no response, or the response may state, "I don't know."

Explanation refers to the student using the language of mathematics to communicate how the student arrived at the solution.

Justification refers to the student using mathematical principles to support the reasoning used to solve the problem or to demonstrate that the solution is correct. This could include the appropriate definitions, postulates, and theorems.

Essentially correct representations may contain several minor errors such as missing labels, reversed axes, or scales that are not uniform.

Fundamentally correct representations may contain several minor errors such as missing labels, reversed axes, or scales that are not uniform.

FIGURE 13.3
Generic Rubric for Brief Constructed Response Items in High School Mathematics in Maryland
From W. D. Schafer, G. Swanson, N. Bené, & G. Newberry, "Effects of Teacher Knowledge of Rubrics on Student Achievement in Four Content Areas," *Applied Measurement in Education, 14,* 2001, pp. 151–170.

Theory into **PRACTICE**

Detecting Bluffing in Students' Essays

Students who are not well prepared for essay tests are likely to try to bluff their way through. Gronlund (2003, p. 113) offers the following advice: Students can obtain higher scores on essay questions by clever bluffing. Although this requires skill in writing and some knowledge of the topic, credit should not be given unless the question is specifically answered. Some common types of bluffing are listed below.

1. Student repeats the question in statement form (slightly paraphrased) and tells how important the topic is (e.g., "The role of assessment in teaching is extremely important. It is hard to imagine effective instruction without it.").
2. Student writes on a well-known topic and fits it to the question (e.g., a student who knows testing well but knows little about performance assessment and is asked to compare testing and performance assessment might describe testing in considerable detail and frequently state that performance

assessment is much superior for evaluating the type of learning measures by the test).

3. Student liberally sprinkles the answer with basic concepts whether they are understood or not (e.g., asked to write about any assessment technique, the importance of "validity" and "reliability" is mentioned frequently).

4. Student includes the teacher's basic beliefs wherever possible (e.g., "The intended learning outcomes must be stated in performance terms before this type of test is constructed or selected.").

Bluffing is most effective where plans have not been made for careful scoring of the answers.

Writing and Evaluating Problem-Solving Items

In many subjects, such as mathematics and the physical and social sciences, instructional objectives include the development of skills in problem solving, so it is important to assess students' performance in solving problems (Haladyna, 1997). A **problem-solving assessment** requires students to organize, select, and apply complex procedures that have at least several important steps or components. It is important to appraise the students' work in each of these steps or components.

CONNECTIONS

For more on problem solving, see Chapter 8, page 262.

Here are a seventh-grade-level mathematical problem and a seventh-grader's response to it. In the discussion of evaluating problem solving to follow, the essential components are described in specific terms, but they can be applied to all disciplines.

Problem

Suppose two gamblers are playing a game in which the loser must pay an amount equal to what the other gambler has at the time. If Player A won the first and third games, and Player B won the second game, and they finished the three games with $12 each, with how much money did each begin the first game? How did you get your answer?

A student's response:

After game	A had	B had
3	$12.00	$12.00
2	6.00	18.00
1	15.00	9.00
In the beginning	$ 7.50	$16.50

When I started with Game 1, I guessed and guessed, but I couldn't make it come out to 12 and 12.

Then I decided to start at Game 3 and work backward. It worked!

How will you objectively evaluate such a response? As in evaluating short essay items, you should begin your preparation for appraising problem-solving responses by writing either a model response or, perhaps more practically, an outline of the essential components or procedures that are involved in problem solving. As with essays, problem-solving responses may take several different yet valid approaches. The outline must be flexible enough to accommodate all valid possibilities.

problem-solving assessment
Test that calls for organizing, selecting, and applying complex procedures that have at least several important steps or components.

Theory into **PRACTICE**

INTASC

6 Communication Skills

Peer Evaluations

An evaluation technique often used in cooperative learning, especially in creative writing and (less often) mathematics problem solving, is to have students rate each others' work on a specific set of criteria, before the teacher rates them on the same criteria. The peer evaluation does not contribute to a student's score or grade, but gives the student feedback that he or she can use to revise the composition or product. Figure 13.4 shows a peer response guide that might be used for a comparison–contrast writing assignment. The partner, and then the teacher, would put a check mark in each space to indicate that the student has done an adequate job in that category. The partner and the teacher would also mark the student's paper to make suggestions for improvement. Peer evaluation provides a formative evaluation for the writer, but it also gives the evaluator an invaluable opportunity to take the teacher's perspective and gain insight into what constitutes good writing.

Evaluating problem-solving items. Problem solving involves several important components that fit most disciplines. Those include understanding the problem to be solved, attacking the problem systematically, and arriving at a reasonable answer. Following is a detailed checklist of elements common to most problem solving that can guide your weighting of elements in your evaluation of a student's problem-solving abilities.

Problem-solving evaluation elements

☐ 1. Problem organization
  ☐ a. representation by table, graph, chart, etc.
  ☐ b. representation fits the problem
  ☐ c. global understanding of the problem

FIGURE 13.4
Example of a Partner Response Form for a Comparison–Contrast–Comparison

Criterion	Partner	Teacher
Content		
1. Shows how concepts are similar		
2. Shows how concepts are different		
3. Well organized		
4. Good opening sentence		
5. Good concluding sentence		
Mechanics		
1. Spelling correct		
2. Grammar correct		
3. Punctuation correct		
4. At least 2 pages		

☐ 2. Procedures (mathematical: trial-and-error, working backward, experimental process, empirical induction)
    ☐ a. A viable procedure was attempted.
    ☐ b. The procedure was carried to a final solution.
    ☐ c. Computation (if any) was correct.
☐ 3. Solution (mathematical: a table, number, figure, graph, etc.)
    ☐ a. answer was reasonable
    ☐ b. answer was checked
    ☐ c. answer was correct
☐ 4. Logic specific to the detail or application of the given information was sound.

If you wish to give partial credit for an answer that contains correct elements or want to inform students about the value of their responses, you must devise ways to do this consistently. The following points offer some guidance:

1. Write model responses before giving partial credit for such work as essay writing, mathematical problem solving, laboratory assignments, or any work that you evaluate according to the quality of its various stages.
2. Tell students in sufficient detail the meaning of the grades you give to communicate the value of the work.

The following examples illustrate outlines of exemplary student work from mathematics and social studies or literature.

From mathematics. Students are given the following problem:

In a single-elimination tennis tournament, 40 players are to play for the singles championship. Determine how many matches must be played.

Evaluation

☐ a. Evidence that the student understood the problem, demonstrated by depiction of the problem with a graph, table, chart, equation, etc. (*3 points*)

☐ b. Use of a method for solving the problem that had potential for yielding a correct solution—for example, systematic trial and error, empirical induction, elimination, working backward. (*5 points*)

☐ c. Arrival at a correct solution. (*3 points*)

The three components in the evaluation were assigned points according to the weight the teacher judged each to be worth in the context of the course of study and the purpose of the test. Teachers can give full credit for a correct answer even if all the work is not shown in the response, provided that they know that students can do the work in their heads. But it is important to guard against the **halo effect.** This occurs when a teacher knows which student wrote which response and alters the grading of the paper depending on her or his opinion of the student. The same response should receive the same score no matter who wrote it. Use of a detailed rubric, or scoring guide, in evaluation is a way to make scoring more objective and thus to avoid any halo effects.

From social studies or literature. Students are asked to respond with a 100-word essay to the following item:

halo effect
Bias due to carryover of a general attitude about a respondent, as when a teacher knows which student wrote which response and alters the grading depending on his or her opinion of the student.

Compare and contrast the development of Inuit and Navajo tools on the basis of the climates in which these two peoples live.

Evaluation

☐ a. The response gives evidence of specific and accurate recall of the climates in which the Inuit and Navajos live (*1 point*) and of Inuit and Navajo tools. (*1 point*)

☐ b. The essay develops with continuity of thought and logic. (*3 points*)

☐ c. An accurate rationale is provided for the use of the various tools in the respective climates. (*3 points*)

☐ d. An analysis comparing and contrasting the similarities and differences between the two groups and their tool development is given. (*8 points*)

☐ e. The response concludes with a summary and closure. (*1 point*)

These two examples should suggest ways to evaluate items in other subject areas as well. Giving partial credit for much of the work students do certainly results in a more complete evaluation of student progress than does scoring the work as merely right or wrong. The examples show how to organize objective assessments for evaluating work that does not lend itself to the simple forms of multiple-choice, true–false, completion, and matching items. Points do not have to be used to evaluate components of the responses. In many situations, some kind of evaluative descriptors might be more meaningful. **Evaluative descriptors** are statements describing strong and weak features of a response to an item, a question, or a project. In the mathematics example a teacher's evaluative descriptor for item *a* might read, "You have drawn an excellent chart showing that you understand the meaning of the problem, and that is very good, but it seems you were careless when you entered several important numbers in your chart."

Note that each of these examples are much like rubrics and can be generalized to broad ranges of topics. If teachers and students discuss these during instruction, students will have a device that helps them understand what they are working toward and both teachers and students have a common language that they can use during instruction and in their formative assessments.

INTASC

8 Assessment of Student Learning

WHAT ARE AUTHENTIC, PORTFOLIO, AND PERFORMANCE ASSESSMENTS?

After much criticism of standardized testing (e.g., Rothberg, 2001; Shepard, 2000; Thompson, 2001), critics have developed and implemented alternative assessment systems that are designed to avoid the problems of typical multiple-choice tests. The key idea behind the testing alternatives is that students should be asked to document their learning or demonstrate that they can actually do something real with the information and skills they have learned in school (Campbell, 2000; Carey, 2001; Marzano, Pickering, & Pollock, 2001). For example, students might be asked to keep a portfolio, design a method of measuring wind speed, draw a scale model of a racing car, or write something for a real audience. Such tests are referred to as *authentic assessments* or *performance assessments* (Ellis, 2001a; Stiggins, 2000; Weber, 1999; Wiggins, 1999). One goal of these "alternative assessments" is to demonstrate achievement in realistic contexts. In reading, for example, the authentic assessment movement has led to the development of tests in which students are asked to read and inter-

evaluative descriptors
Statements describing strong and weak features of a response to an item, a question, or a project.

pret longer sections and show their metacognitive awareness of reading strategies (Roeber & Dutcher, 1989; Valencia, Pearson, Peters, & Wixson, 1989). In science, authentic assessments might involve having students set up and carry out an experiment. In writing, students might be asked to write real letters or newspaper articles. In math, students might solve complex physical problems that require insight and creativity. Authentic tests sometimes require students to integrate knowledge from different domains; for example, to use algebra in the context of reading about and performing a science experiment and to write up the results.

See Figure 13.5 for assessment criteria for a science concept map.

Portfolio Assessment

One popular form of alternative assessment is called **portfolio assessment:** the collection and evaluation of samples of student work over an extended period (Carey, 2001; McMillan, 2004; Rolheiser, Bower, & Stevahn, 2000). Teachers may collect student compositions, projects, and other evidence of higher-order functioning and use this evidence to evaluate student progress over time. For example, many teachers have students maintain portfolios of their writings that show the development

portfolio assessment
Assessment of a collection of the student's work in an area showing growth, self-reflection, and achievement.

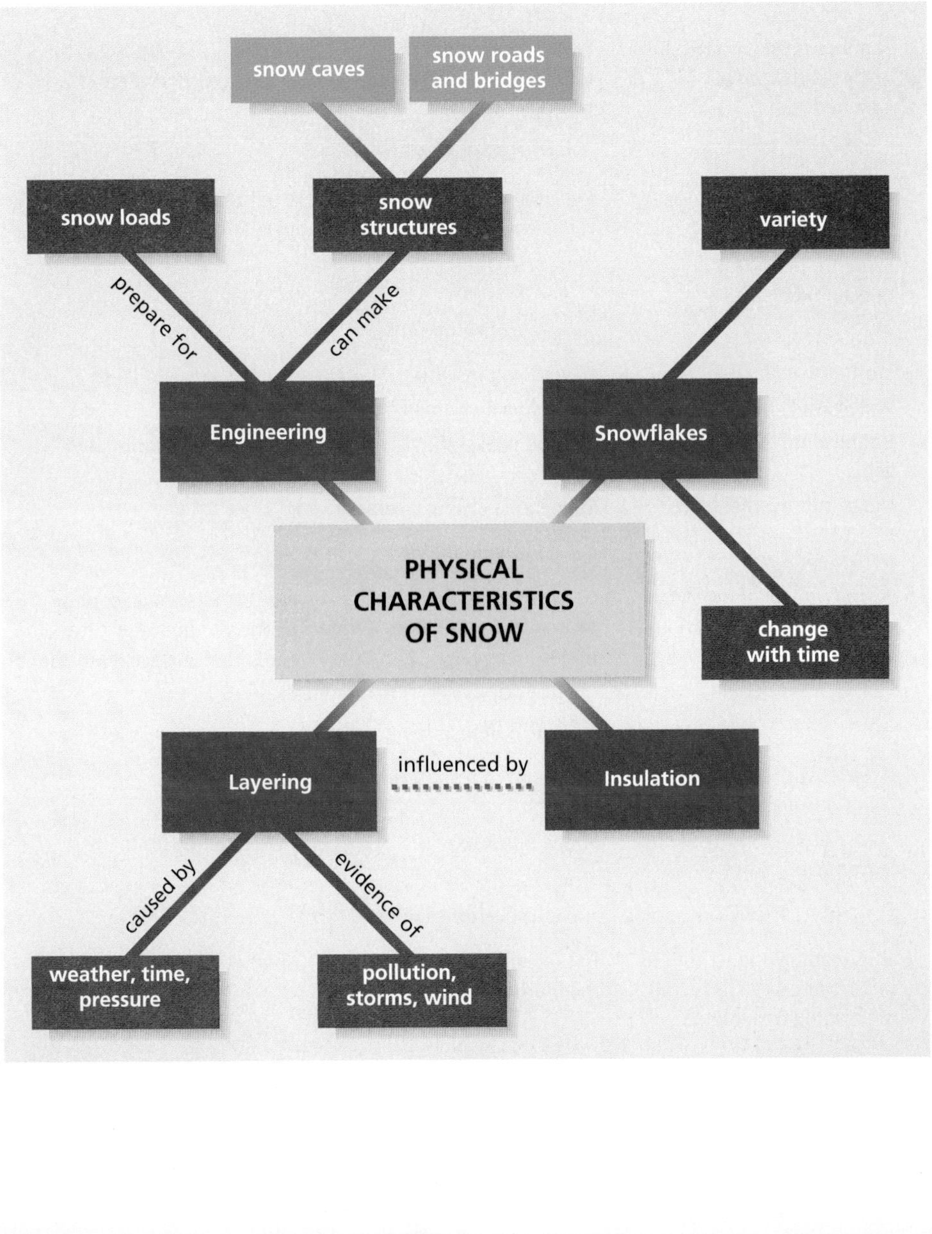

FIGURE 13.5
Assessment Criteria for a Science Concept Map

Sample assessment criteria for visual concept maps or mindmaps might consist of the following: a clear, central focus; an adequate number of key concepts, ideas; appropriate detail; pertinent examples; accurate relationships among data; and neatness, clarity, and legibility.

From Linda Campbell, Bruce Campbell, and Dee Dickinson, *Teaching and Learning Through Multiple Intelligences.* Copyright © 1996 by Allyn & Bacon. Reprinted by permission.

of a composition from first draft to final product; journal entries, book reports, art-work, computer printouts, or papers showing development in problem solving (Arter, 1991; Shaklee, Barbour, Ambrose, & Hansford, 1997; Wolf et al., 1991). Portfolios are increasingly being maintained in computers to supplement paper files (Diehm, 2004; Wiedmer, 1998). Refer to Figure 13.6 for sample criteria for evaluating student writing portfolios.

Portfolio assessment has important uses when teachers want to evaluate students for reports to parents or other within-school purposes. When combined with a consistent and public rubric, portfolios showing improvement over time can provide power-

FIGURE 13.6

Sample of Criteria for Evaluating Students' Writing Ability through Portfolio Assessment

From Cathy Collins Block, *Teaching the Language Arts: Expanding Thinking through Student Centered Instruction.* Copyright © 1993 by Allyn & Bacon. Reprinted by permission.

Continua of Descriptors		
Strong Performance ◄──────────────────► Needs Improvement		
Versatility		
Wide variety of reading and writing across genre	Some variety	Little or no variety Collection shows little breadth or depth
Process		
Samples reveal discoveries or pivotal learning experiences	Process illustrated in inflexible or mechanistic ways	Minimal use of process to reflect on achievements
Response		
Engaged with story Discusses key issues Evidence of critical questioning	Personal reflection but focus is narrow	Brief retelling of isolated events
Self-Evaluations		
Multidimensional Wide variety of observations Establishing meaningful goals Notes improvement	Developing insights Some specifics noted Limited goal setting Vague idea of improvement	Single focus, global in nature Goal setting too broad or nonexistent
Individual Pieces		
Strong control of a variety of elements: organization, cohesion, surface features, etc.	Growing command evidenced; some flaws, but major ideas clear	Needs to improve: sophistication of ideas, text features, and surface features
Problem Solving		
Wrestles with problems using various resources Enjoys problem solving and learning new ways	Uses limited resources Wants quick fix	Seems helpless Frustrated by problems
Purposefulness/Uses		
Uses reading and writing to satisfy various goals including sharing with others	Uses reading and writing to meet others' goals	Apathetic, resistant

ful evidence of change to parents and to students themselves. However, innovators have also proposed that portfolio assessment be used as part of assessments for school accountability. This use is more controversial (Herbert, 1998; Taylor, 1994), as a student's product can often be greatly influenced by his or her teacher's or classmates' input (Gearhart & Herman, 1995). Also, evidence about the reliability of portfolio assessment scoring is largely disappointing. Different raters can give very different ratings of the same portfolios (Cheung, 1995; Herman & Winters, 1994; Koretz, Stecher, & Deibert, 1993). Nevertheless, portfolio assessments may be used in combination with other assessments that students take in a structured testing setting, and through the use of multiple measures, adequate reliability and validity may be possible.

CERTIFICATION POINTER

A teacher certification question may ask you to respond to a case study by suggesting a way to implement portfolio assessment that would be appropriate for the case.

> **ON THE WEB**
>
> For reports, newsletters, and other publications about assessment, particularly performance and portfolio assessment visit **www.cresst.org,** the National Center for Research on Evaluation, Standards, and Student Testing (CRESST), located at UCLA.

Theory into **PRACTICE**

Using Portfolios in the Classroom

Planning and organization

- Develop an overall flexible plan for student portfolios (see Shaklee et al., 1997). What purposes will the portfolios serve? What items will be required? When and how will they be obtained? What criteria will be applied for reflection and evaluation?
- Plan sufficient time for students to prepare and discuss portfolio items. Portfolio assessments take more time and thought than correcting paper-and-pencil tests does.
- Begin with one aspect of student learning and achievement, and gradually include others as you and the students learn about portfolio procedures. The writing process, for instance, is particularly well suited to documentation through portfolios.
- Choose items to be included in portfolios that will show developing proficiency on important goals and objectives. Items that address multiple objectives help to make portfolio assessments more efficient.
- Collect at least two types of items: required indicators (Arter & McTighe, 2001; Murphy & Underwood, 2000) or core items and optional work samples. Required or core indicators are items collected for every child that will show how each child is progressing. Optional work samples show individual student's unique approaches, interests, and strengths.
- Place a list of goals and objectives in the front of each portfolio, along with a list of required indicators and a place for recording optional items, so that you and the students can keep track of contents.

Implementation

- In order to save time, to ensure that portfolio items are representative of students' work, and to increase authenticity, embed the development of portfolio items into ongoing classroom activities.

- Give students responsibility for preparing, selecting, evaluating, and filing portfolio items and keeping portfolios up to date. Young children will need guidance with this.

- For selected portfolio items, model reflection and self-assessment for students to help them become aware of the processes they used, what they learned and have yet to learn, and what they might need to do differently next time.

- Be selective. A portfolio is not a haphazard collection of work samples, audio or videotapes, pictures, websites, and other products. It is a thoughtful selection of items that exemplify children's learning. Random inclusion of items quickly becomes overwhelming.

- Use information in portfolios to place learners on a sequence of developing skills. For example, Wiggins (1994) presented a developmental spelling sequence that was used in a performance assessment program in a New Jersey district. This appears in Figure 13.7.

- Analyze portfolio items for insight into students' knowledge and skills. As you do this, you will understand more of the students' strengths and needs, thinking processes, preconceptions, misconceptions, error patterns, and developmental benchmarks (Athanases, 1994).

- Use portfolio information to document and celebrate students' learning, to share with parents and other school personnel, and to improve and target classroom instruction. If portfolios are not linked to improving instruction, they are not working. (For guides to portfolio evaluation, see Murphy & Underwood, 2000; Rolheiser, Bower, & Stevahn, 2000; Stiggins, 2000.)

FIGURE 13.7
Scoring Guidelines for Spelling

This figure is from the South Brunswick, New Jersey, schools. Adapted from Grant Wiggins, "Toward Better Report Cards," *Educational Leadership, 52*(2), 1994, pp. 28–37. Copyright © 1994 by the Center on Learning, Assessment, and School Structure. Reprinted by permission of the author.

Look at the child's spelling list. Were most of the spellings *Precommunicative, Semiphonetic, Phonetic, Transitional,* or *Correct*? This is the child's probable developmental level. You might feel that a child truly falls between two of the categories, but try to select just one category per child.

1. **Precommunicative** spellers are in the "babbling" stage of spelling. Children use letters for writing words but the letters are strung together randomly. The letters in precommunicative spelling do correspond to sounds.

2. **Semiphonetic** spellers know that letters represent sounds. They often abbreviate spellings to represent initial and/or final sounds. Example: E = eagle; A = eighty.

3. **Phonetic** spellers spell words the way they sound. The speller perceives and represents all of the phonemes in a word, though spellings may be unconventional. Example: EGL = eagle; ATE = eighty.

4. **Transitional** spellers think about how words appear visually; a visual memory of spelling patterns is apparent. Spellings exhibit conventions of English orthography, such as vowels in every syllable, correctly spelled inflection endings, and frequent English letter sequences. Example: EGUL = eagle; EIGHTEE = eighty.

5. **Correct** spellers develop over years of word study and writing. Correct spelling can be categorized by instruction levels; for example, correct spelling for a body of words that can be spelled by the average fourth-grader would be fourth-grade-level correct spelling.

Performance Assessment

Tests that involve actual demonstrations of knowledge or skills in real life are called **performance assessments** (Foster & Noyce, 2004; McMillan, 2004; Popham, 2005; Trice, 2000). For example, ninth-graders might be asked to conduct an oral history project, reading about a significant recent event and then interviewing the individuals involved. The quality of the oral histories, done over a period of weeks, would indicate the degree of the students' mastery of the social studies concepts involved. Wiggins (1993b) also describes assessments used in the last 2 weeks of school in which students must apply everything they have learned all year to analyze a sludge that mixes a variety of solids and liquids. Some schools are requiring elaborate "exhibitions," such as projects developed over many months, as demonstrations of competence (Sills-Briegel, Fisk, & Dunlop, 1996). More time-limited performance assessments might ask students to set up experiments, respond to extended text, write in various genres, or solve realistic math problems (Egeland, 1996).

A model for performance assessment is the doctoral thesis, an extended project required for Ph.D. candidates that is intended to show not only what students know, but also what they can do (Archibald & Newmann, 1988). Driver's tests, tests for pilots' licenses, and performance tests in medicine are also common examples of performance assessments (Swanson, Norman, & Linn, 1995).

ON THE WEB

To view articles and multimedia related to assessment and other education topics, go to the website of the George Lucas Foundation at **www.glef.org**.

How Well Do Performance Assessments Work?

One of the most important criticisms of traditional standardized tests is that they can focus teachers on teaching a narrow range of skills that happen to be on the test (see Popham, 2004; Shepard, 1989b). How might performance assessments be better? At

performance assessments
Assessments of students' ability to perform tasks in real-life contexts, not just to show knowledge. Also called *authentic assessments.*

This student's performance is being evaluated by his classmates. What are the advantages and disadvantages of using a performance or group activity as a method for evaluating students?

least in theory, it should be possible to create tests that would require such a broad understanding of subject matter that the test would be worth teaching to. Wiggins (1989, p. 41) puts it this way: "We should 'teach to the test.' The catch is to design and then teach to . . . tests so that practicing for and taking the tests actually enhances rather than impedes education."

For example, consider the performance test in science shown in Figure 13.8. Imagine that you know that your students will have to conduct an experiment to solve a problem like the one posed in the figure (but not that exact problem). The only way to teach such a test will be to expose students to a broad range of information about electricity, experimentation, and problem-solving strategies (see Shepard, 1995).

Beyond all the practical problems and expense of administering and scoring performance tests, it is not yet clear whether the new tests will solve all the problems of standardized testing (Cizek, 1993; Messick, 1994; Moss, 1992; Shepard, 1993b; Worthen & Spandel, 1993). For example, Shavelson, Baxter, and Pine (1992) studied performance assessments in science (Figure 13.8 is taken from their study). They found that student performance on such assessments could be reliably rated, but different performance assessments produced very different patterns of scores, and student scores were still related more closely to student aptitude than to what students were actually taught (see also Educational Testing Service, 1995; Linn, 1994; Supovitz & Brennan, 1997). Further, the hope that performance assessments would show

CERTIFICATION POINTER

You may be asked on your teacher certification test to give an example of a performance goal and then to write a behavioral objective, an activity, and an assessment of student learning that would accomplish the goal.

FIGURE 13.8

Example of a Performance Assessment Activity

From R. J. Shavelson, G. P. Baxter, and J. Pine, "Performance Assessments: Political Rhetoric and Measurement Reality," *Educational Researcher, 21*(2), p. 23. Copyright © 1992 by the American Educational Research Association. Reprinted by permission of the publisher.

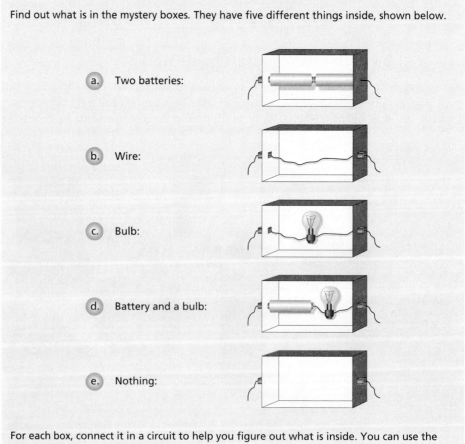

Find out what is in the mystery boxes. They have five different things inside, shown below.

a. Two batteries:

b. Wire:

c. Bulb:

d. Battery and a bulb:

e. Nothing:

For each box, connect it in a circuit to help you figure out what is inside. You can use the bulbs, batteries, and wires any way you like.

smaller differences between students of different ethnic backgrounds has not generally been realized (Klein et al., 1997).

Scoring Rubrics for Performance Assessments

Performance assessments are typically scored according to rubrics that specify in advance the type of performance that is expected for each activity (Arter & McTighe, 2001; Lewin & Shoemaker, 1998). Figure 13.7 illustrated a very general rubric for spelling. However, rubrics can be written for individual tasks. Figure 13.9 shows one rubric (from Taylor, 1994) that was developed for an essay on character development in stories students have read.

Performance assessment tasks are similar to essay items in that students might approach them in multiple ways. It is therefore also important for performance assessments that the criteria for scoring be understood by students. One way to do this is to write a few generic rubrics that are flexible enough to apply to the full range of student performance. Figure 13.3 gave an example of a generic rubric that has been applied to outcomes in high school mathematics. It has been suggested that using rubrics such as this in classroom instruction can enhance student achievement (Schafer, Swanson, Bené, & Newberry, 2001).

Performance
Essay on Character Development in Literature

Performance Criteria
- Character is identified.
- At least three aspects of the character's development during the course of the story are described.
- Appropriate support for each character aspect is given using excerpts from the story.
- Character's contribution to the story's plot is described.
- At least three excerpts from the story are given as support for writer's ideas about the character's contribution to the story.
- Text references used for support are appropriate.

Scoring Rubric

4 points	Essay is complete, thorough, and insightful in describing the character's development and contribution to the story. Adequate support is given to encourage us to consider the writer's point of view. All excerpts from the text enhance our understanding of the writer's view of the character.
3 points	Essay is complete in describing the character's development and contribution to the story. Adequate support is given to encourage us to consider the writer's point of view. Most excerpts from the text enhance our understanding of the writer's view of the character.
2 points	Essay is complete in its description of either the character's development *or* the character's contribution to the story. Some support is given to help us consider the writer's point of view. Most excerpts from the text enhance our understanding of the writer's view of the character for the element described.
1 point	Essay is mostly complete in its description of either the character's development or the character's contribution to the story. Support is given for the writer's point of view, but it is not always convincing. Few excerpts from the text enhance our understanding of the writer's view of the character for the element described.
0 points	The written essay was not completed, is significantly lacking in performance of all criteria, or is off-task.

FIGURE 13.9
Sample Scoring Rubric: Targeted Performance, Performance Criteria, and a Description of Performances at Different Score Points

From Catherine Taylor, "Assessment for Measurement or Standards," *American Educational Research Journal, 31*(2), pp. 231–262. Copyright © 1994 by the American Educational Research Association. Reprinted by permission of the publisher.

Psychology Fair Rubric

✔ **Our Psychology Project . . .**

☐ (25 pts) Provides background information—it cites other studies, explains our interest in the topic, and presents a rationale for the topic. [The better the background information, the more detailed, and the more it "fits," the more points you earn.]

   Brief example: "We are interested in how dress affects behavior. We always felt better when we were dressed up and also thought that less violence occurs between people who 'dress up.' Cohen and Cohen (1987) found that students who wore uniforms performed 10 percent better on exams and were cited for fewer office referrals. Thus we wanted to look into this topic further."

☐ (25 pts) Gives a description of the study (an abstract—a *general* statement in 100 words or fewer about your project).

   Brief example: "This study investigates the relationship between academic performance and the use of uniforms in schools. Three schools in Derry County, Pennsylvania, were surveyed on issues of academic performance and office referrals. The use of uniforms showed an increase in achievement and decreased behavioral problems."

☐ (40 pts) Has a measurable hypothesis with specific variables defined and identified.

☐ (25 pts) Includes at least one graph, chart, or other visual aid which *summarizes the data*. Someone should be able to look at your graph/chart and clearly see what the variables and results were.

☐ (10 pts) Includes a clean copy of any survey or other scale that was used to gather data.

☐ (40 pts) Includes a written procedure that tells the observer *exactly* what we did.
   Brief example: "We took 3 days to survey 100 students and 30 teachers."

☐ (30 pts) Includes a section that explains the data and tells whether the hypothesis was accurate.

   Brief example: "Our data reflect that our hypothesis was correct: The 30 percent increase in scores reflects the improved achievement of students while . . ." [Again, develop your explanation. If you only say "We were right" or "Our hypothesis is correct/wrong" you will not receive more than half the points.]

☐ (30 pts) Includes a section explaining the significance of the study—why it is important.

   Brief example: "This is an important study because it reflects a bias that many people may not be aware of, as well as a way in which students can improve scores and reduce their own behavioral problems. It further . . ."

☐ (50 pts) Is interactive. That is, observers can take the test, view the screen, do the quiz, and so on. [This can be done in a variety of ways. For instance, if the test is long have observers do part of it, or show a video of your procedure.]

Total Points Possible: 275

FIGURE 13.10
Semester-Long Assessment

From Chuck Greiner, High School Psychology teacher, James M. Bennett High School, Salisbury, MD.

Planning for performance assessments takes time, and avoiding the pitfalls of subjectivity in rating performances takes practice (Popham, 2005). However, a few well-thought-out, well-written items for a performance assessment could serve, for example, as a summative evaluation for all or most of your educational objectives for an entire unit. (See Figure 13.10.)

*H*OW ARE GRADES DETERMINED?

INTASC

5 Classroom Motivation and Management

One of the most perplexing and often controversial tasks a teacher faces is grading student work (Guskey & Bailey, 2001; Marzano, 2000; Munk & Bursuck, 1998;

Trumbull & Farr, 2000). Is grading necessary? It is clear that some form of summative student evaluation is necessary, and grading of one kind or another is the predominant form used in most schools.

Establishing Grading Criteria

Many sets of grading criteria exist, but regardless of the level of school that teachers teach in, they generally agree on the need to explain the meaning of grades they give (Gusky & Bailey, 2001; Marzano, 2000). Grades should communicate at least the relative value of a student's work in a class. They should also help students to understand better what is expected of them and how they might improve.

Teachers and schools that use letter grades attach the following general meanings to the letters:

A = superior; exceptional; outstanding attainment
B = very good, but not superior; above average
C = competent, but not remarkable work or performance; average
D = minimum passing, but serious weaknesses are indicated; below average
F = failure to pass; serious weaknesses demonstrated

Assigning Letter Grades

All school districts have a policy or common practice for assigning report card grades. Most use A-B-C-D-F or A-B-C-D-E letter grades, but many (particularly at the elementary school level) use various versions of outstanding-satisfactory-unsatisfactory (Marzano, 2000). Some simply report percentage grades. The criteria on which grades are based vary enormously from district to district. Secondary schools usually give one grade for each subject taken, but most elementary schools and some secondary schools include ratings on effort or behavior as well as on performance.

The criteria for giving letter grades might be specified by a school administration, but grading criteria are most often set by individual teachers using very broad guidelines (Canady & Hotchkiss, 1993). In practice, few teachers could get away with giving half their students A's or with failing too many students; but between these two extremes, teachers may have considerable leeway. (See Frisbie & Waltman, 1993; Guskey & Bailey, 2001; Marzano, 2000.)

Absolute Grading Standards   Grades may be given according to absolute or relative standards. Absolute grading standards might consist of preestablished percentage scores required for a given grade, as in the following example:

Grade	Percentage Correct
A	90–100 percent
B	80–89 percent
C	70–79 percent
D	60–69 percent
F	Less than 60 percent

In another form of absolute standards, called criterion-referenced grading, the teacher decides in advance what performances constitute outstanding (A), above-average (B), average (C), below-average (D), and inadequate (F) mastery of the instructional objective.

Absolute percentage standards have one important disadvantage: Student scores might depend on the difficulty of the tests they are given. For example, a student can pass a true–false test (if a passing grade is 60 percent) by knowing only 20 percent of the answers and guessing on the rest (getting 50 percent of the remaining 80 percent

Teaching Dilemmas: Cases to Consider

Establishing a Grading System

Rachel Greenberg is a beginning social studies teacher in a large urban high school. In preparation for a social studies department meeting, she talks with Antonio Watts in the teachers' lounge.

Rachel: Antonio, do you have a minute to tell me about the school's grading policy?

Antonio: Sure. Where do you want to begin?

Rachel: Well, we do have a policy, I assume?

Antonio: I guess you could say so. If you look on the report cards, you'll notice that 94 to 100 is an A, 88 to 94 is a B, and so forth. Anything below 70 is failing.

Rachel: What if no one gets in the 94 to 100 range?

Antonio: Then either you don't give any A's, if you think the test was fair, or you adjust the scale by adding on points to every student's score. There's no rigid policy, but if you give too many A's and B's, that could become a problem.

Rachel: How many are too many?

Antonio: Well, certainly there should be more B's than A's and more C's than either A's or B's. You try to approximate the normal bell-shaped curve in a general, flexible way. It all depends on the students' ability level. In an advanced placement history course, I seldom give D's or F's. In the sophomore-level world history course, however, the number of D's and F's fairly closely approximates the number of A's and B's.

Rachel: What if a teacher puts a mastery learning plan into effect, and it works so well that everyone achieves at practically 100 percent? What happens to the bell-shaped curve then?

Antonio: Well, that happened a few years back. One young teacher did give almost all A's and B's. It came to light when the students began comparing grades at report card time. Some other teachers and parents were quite upset. The administration smoothed things over with the parents and other teachers. As for the young teacher, he's at another school now. I hear he's doing a fine job.

Rachel: Oh. Another question: In my history classes I plan to emphasize individual and small-group projects. I

am interested in cooperative learning approaches with mixed-ability groups.

Antonio: Group projects are nice, but grading them can be very subjective and hard to defend. I'd go easy on that.

Rachel: So you'd recommend objective tests, not essay tests?

Antonio: Right. Good objective tests are hard to write, but they're worth it because students and parents have a hard time arguing grading bias, favoritism, or subjectivity when you give objective tests. Also, I figure that objective tests help prepare the kids to succeed on standardized achievement tests.

Rachel: I see what you mean, but I try to keep outcomes in mind—overall objectives like verbal information, intellectual skills, cognitive strategies, and so on. But teaching for those outcomes may not always leave time for teaching to objective tests. What if some of my students get D's and F's? I'm a little afraid of some of the parents.

Antonio: I think communication is the key. If the students—and their parents—think you're fair, you'll have few problems. Spell out very clearly what you expect and what the grading procedures are. After all, our society was founded on competition. Our kids have to learn how to deal with failure as well as success. And parents should understand that too.

Rachel: Thanks, Antonio! I don't know if I altogether agree with you about the value of failure, but I really appreciate your support.

@ Questions for Reflection

1. Do you agree with the advice Rachel received? Why or why not? For the grade level you plan to teach, what departmentwide evaluation strategy would you propose for your subject area?

2. If you were on a committee to evaluate and revise this school's evaluation and grading policies and procedures, what would you recommend and why?

3. Extend the dialogue to express an evaluation approach that would work best for the way Rachel wants to teach.

of the items by chance). On a difficult test on which guessing is impossible, however, 60 percent could be a very high score. For this reason, use of absolute percentage criteria should be tempered with criterion-referenced standards. That is, a teacher might use a 60-70-80-90 percent standard in most circumstances but establish (and announce to students) tougher standards for tests that students are likely to find easy and easier standards for more difficult tests.

Another disadvantage is that the ranges of the grades are typically different, especially for F. A student who receives an F may be very close to a D or may be hopelessly far from "passing." This is true for the other grades, too, but the large range of

F (0 percent to 60 percent) emphasizes the uncertainty. Moreover, the consequences of an F are often quite severe.

Relative Grading Standards   A **relative grading standard** exists whenever a teacher gives grades according to the students' rank in their class or grade. The classic form of relative grading is specifying what percentage of students will be given A's, B's, and so on. A form of this practice is called *grading on the curve*, because students are given grades on the basis of their position on a predetermined distribution of scores.

Relative grading standards have the advantage of placing students' scores in relation to one another, without regard to the difficulty of a particular test. However, relative grading standards also have serious drawbacks (see Guskey, 1994). One is that because they hold the number of A's and B's constant, students in a class of high achievers must get much higher scores to earn an A or B than students in low-achieving classes—a situation that is likely to be widely seen as unfair. Teachers often deal with this problem by giving relatively more A's and B's in high-achieving classes than in others. Another disadvantage of relative grading is that it creates competition among students; when one student earns an A, this diminishes the chances that others may do so. Competition can inhibit students from helping one another and can hurt social relations among classmates (Krumboltz & Yeh, 1996).

Strict grading on the curve and guidelines for numbers of A's and B's have been disappearing in recent years. For one thing, there has been a general grade inflation; more A's and B's are given now than in the past, and C is no longer the expected average grade but often indicates below-average performance. As one indication of current practices with respect to grading, Anderson (1994) summarized a national survey of eighth-graders who were asked to report their English grades since sixth grade. The results were as follows:

Mostly A's: 31 percent
Mostly B's: 38 percent
Mostly C's: 23 percent
Mostly D's: 6 percent
Mostly less than D's: 2 percent

Results were similar in mathematics, and grades were only slightly lower in high-poverty schools than in middle-class schools. It is likely that these self-reported grades are somewhat higher than what students actually received, but it is nevertheless likely that the average grade today is B, not C.

The most common approach to grading involves teachers looking at student scores on a test, taking into account test difficulty and the overall performance of the class, and assigning grades in such a way that about the "right number" of students earn A's and B's and the "right number" fail. Teachers vary considerably in their estimates of what these right numbers should be, but schools often have unspoken norms about how many students should be given A's and how many should fail (see Fitzpatrick, 1989; Hoge & Coladarci, 1989).

Performance Grading

One of the most important limitations of traditional grades is that while they might give some indication of how students are doing in comparison to others, they provide no information about what students know and can do. A student who gets a B in English might be disappointed or breathe a sigh of relief, depending on what she expected. However, this grade does not tell her or her parents or teachers what she can do, what she needs to do to progress, or where her strengths or weaknesses are. Furthermore, giving a single grade in each subject can reinforce the idea that students

relative grading standard
Grades given according to a student's rank in his or her class or grade.

are more able or less able, or perhaps more motivated or less motivated, rather than the idea that all students are growing.

One response to these limitations that is used in some schools is an alternative approach to grading called *performance grading*. In performance grading, teachers determine what children know and can do and then report this in a way that is easy for parents and students to understand.

Figure 13.11 (from Wiggins, 1994) shows one page of a language arts assessment keyed to fifth-grade exit standards, or expectations of what a fifth-grader should know. A parent of a student who receives a form like this could see how the student is progressing toward the kind of performance the school district has defined as essential. Note that the form does provide information on how the student is doing in comparison to other students, but that the emphasis is on growth over time.

Scoring Rubrics for Performance Grading A key requirement for the use of performance grading is collection of work samples from students that indicate their level of performance on a developmental sequence. Collecting and evaluating work that students are already doing in class (such as compositions, lab reports, or projects) is called portfolio assessment (Herbert, 1998; Shaklee et al., 1997), discussed earlier in this chapter. An alternative is to give students tests in which they can show their abilities to apply and integrate knowledge, skills, and judgment. Most performance grading schemes use some combination of portfolios and on-demand performance tests. In either case the student performance may be evaluated against rubrics, which describe, for example, partially proficient, proficient, and advanced performance, or which indicate a student's position on a developmental sequence (recall Figures 13.6, 13.7, 13.9, 13.10, and 13.11).

Other Alternative Grading Systems

Several other approaches to grading are used in conjunction with innovative instructional approaches. In *contract grading,* students negotiate a particular amount of work or level of performance that they will achieve to receive a certain grade. For example, a student might agree to complete five book reports of a given length in a marking period to receive an A. **Mastery grading,** an important part of mastery learning, involves establishing a standard of mastery, such as 80 or 90 percent correct on a test. All students who achieve that standard receive an A; students who do not achieve it the first time receive corrective instruction and then retake the test to try to achieve the mastery criterion. Finally, many teachers give grades based on improvement or effort usually in combination with traditional grades. In this way a student who is performing at a low level relative to others can nevertheless receive feedback indicating that he or she is on a path leading to higher performance (see Tomlinson, 2001).

Letting Students Retake Tests Many teachers allow students to retake tests, especially if they failed the first time. This can be a good idea if it gives students an opportunity to do additional studying and master the material the class is studying. For example, a student might be given 2 days to study the content that was tested and then take an alternative form of the test. (Giving the same test to the student is not recommended since that would allow the student to study only the questions that were asked.) The student might then be given a grade that is one letter grade lower than he or she scored on the second test, since the student had an advantage in having an extra opportunity to study. There is some danger that if students know that they can retake tests, they might not study until after attempting the first test; but in general, allowing students a second chance is a good way to allow those who are willing to put in extra effort to improve a poor grade. On the other hand, this practice requires that

mastery grading
Grading requiring an established standard of mastery, such as 80 or 90 percent correct on a test. Students who do not achieve it the first time may receive corrective instruction and then retake the test to try to achieve mastery.

Cherry Creek School District
Polton Community Elementary
School Fairplay Progress Report
(Language Arts Section)

Student Name _____   Grade 3 _____ 4 _____
Teacher _____   School Year _____

Performance-based graduation requirements focus on student mastery of the proficiencies. The curriculum and written progress report are geared toward preparing students for this task. A date (for example, 11/02) indicates where a student is performing on a continuum of progress based on the fifth-grade exit standards.

	Basic	Proficient	Advanced
Language Arts Proficiency 1 Listens, interpreting verbal and nonverbal cues to construct meaning.	Actively listens, demonstrates understanding, and clarifies with questions and paraphrasing.	Actively listens for purpose, demonstrates understanding, and clarifies with questions and paraphrasing.	Actively listens for purpose, demonstrates understanding, clarifies with questions and paraphrasing, classifies, analyzes, and applies information.
Language Arts Proficiency 2 Conveys meaning clearly and coherently through speech in both formal and informal situations.	Appropriately speaks to inform, explain, demonstrate, or persuade. Organizes a speech and uses vocabulary to convey a message.	Appropriately speaks to inform, explain, demonstrate, or persuade. Organizes a formal speech and uses vocabulary to convey a message.	Appropriately speaks to inform, explain, demonstrate, or persuade. Organizes a formal speech with details and transitions adapting subject and vocabulary. Uses eye contact, gestures, and suitable expression for an audience and topic.
Language Arts Proficiency 3 Reads to construct meaning by interacting with the text, by recognizing the different requirements of a variety of printed materials, and by using appropriate strategies to increase comprehension.	Reads varied material, comprehends at a literal level. Recalls and builds knowledge through related information. Begins to use strategies to develop fluency, adjusting rate when reading different material.	Reads varied material, comprehends literally and interpretively. Synthesizes and explores information, drawing inferences. Critiques author's intent, analyzes material for meaning and value. Applies strategies to increase fluency, adjusting rate when reading different material.	Reads varied material, comprehends and draws inferences, recalls and builds knowledge through related information. Applies strategies to increase fluency, adjusting rate when reading different material.
Language Arts Proficiency 4 Produces writing that conveys purpose and meaning, uses effective writing strategies, and incorporates the conventions of written language to communicate clearly.	Appropriately writes on assigned or self-selected topics. Clear main ideas, few details. Weak elements in the beginning, middle, end. Sentence structure lacks variety and contains errors.	Appropriately writes on assigned or self-selected topics. Clear main ideas, interesting details, clear organization, sequencing, varied sentence structure, edits to reduce errors. Appropriate voice and word choice.	Appropriately writes on assigned or self-selected topics. Connects opinions, details, and examples. Effective organization and sequencing, meaningful sentence structure, edits to eliminate most errors. Appropriate voice and word choice.

As compared to the class in the area of Language Arts, your child

Note: The teacher places a check in one box per marking period to indicate child's status in language arts.

	1	2	3	Marking Periods
				Displays strong performance
				Demonstrates appropriate development
				Needs practice and support

FIGURE 13.11 Sample Performance Grading

From Grant Wiggins, "Toward Better Report Cards," *Educational Leadership, 52*(2), 1994, pp. 28–37. Copyright © 1994 by the Center on Learning, Assessment, and School Structure. Reprinted by permission of the author.

the teacher write more test items, and the second form of the test might not have the same difficulty as the first.

Assigning Report Card Grades

Most schools give report cards four or six times per year, that is, every 6 or 9 weeks. Report card grades are most often derived from some combination of the following factors (Guskey & Bailey, 2001; Marzano, 2000):

- Scores on quizzes and tests
- Scores on papers and projects
- Scores on homework
- Scores on seatwork
- Class participation (academic behaviors in class, answers to class questions, and so on)
- Deportment (classroom behavior, tardiness, attitude)
- Effort.

These are listed in order from most formal and reliable measures of achievement to least valid as a learning indicator. The first two are summative assessments and virtually everyone would consider them appropriate for grading. The next two are typically formative and thus indicate how learning is progressing when it is still incomplete. They are less appropriate since they do not convey information about status at the end of instructional units. The final three might contribute to achievement, but they are not achievement. Basing grades on them could miscommunicate information to others about students. Teachers often give different weights to various factors, stating (for example) that grades will be based 30 percent on quizzes, 30 percent on a final test, 20 percent on homework, and 20 percent on class participation. This helps communicate to students what is most important to the teacher.

Personal Reflection

Assigning Grades

I think grading is one of the most difficult tasks for any teacher, but especially for a beginning teacher. I remember my first grading experience, as a student teacher of high school social studies.

My greatest dilemma involved a girl I'll call Jane. She seemed very nice and very bright. Yet she frequently failed to do assignments, skipped class from time to time, and generally did very little. I agonized over Jane. Was there something I was doing wrong? Was there anything I could do? I called her in a few times to tell her that she was headed for trouble, and she always promised to do better, but her resolution never lasted very long.

I spoke with my mentor teacher, who told me I had to give Jane a failing grade. I did so, but not before several sleepless nights. It's terrible to admit, but among all the wonderful students I had that year, Jane's is the only name I still remember.

Of course, with the passage of time and experience, I realize that I didn't fail Jane, she failed herself. I'll never know why, but I'll never forget this hard introduction to one painful reality of teaching.

Reflect on This. Why do you think a teacher might feel he or she "failed" when a student fails a class? What can you do to make sure you can always justify the grades you give students?

One important issue arises when scores are to be combined for grading—how to treat missing work, such as homework assignments. Some teachers assign a "zero" to missing work. But a zero can be devastating (it is so far from even a passing grade that it is virtually impossible for the student to recover). This practice can only be viewed as punitive. A better strategy would be to use a system whereby grades are converted to a reasonable set of numerical grades (e.g., A = 4, B = 3, etc.) and give an F for the missing work. To illustrate the difference in these two strategies, consider a female student who misses one assignment out of five. If she is given a zero for the missing work, and her scores for the assignments are 92, 86, 0, 73, and 91; her average score would be 68.4, or a D in a 60-70-80-90 grading scheme. Converting the scores using the letter grades, on the other hand, would give her a mean of 2.6, which would be a solid C.

Sometimes a student's performance on a test or a quiz seems unusually poor for him or her. Such atypical assessments might be due to nonacademic reasons such as a disruption at home or in school. A private conversation with the student about the test or quiz might uncover a problem that should be looked into and the student might be given an opportunity to retake the test. Some teachers drop the lowest score a student receives on quizzes to avoid penalizing them for one unusual slippage.

One important principle in report card grading is that grades should never be a surprise. Students should always know how their grades will be computed, whether classwork and homework are included, and whether class participation and effort are taken into account. Being clear about standards for grading helps a teacher avert many complaints about unexpectedly low grades and, more important, lets students know exactly what they must do to improve their grades (Guskey, 2001).

Many schools give an "interim" grade at the middle of a marking period. These give students an early idea of how they are doing, and a warning if they seem headed for trouble. A variation on this practice is to provide an interim grade only if students are headed for a D or F. Further, adding comments to the grade to explain what the student needs to do to earn a higher grade can be very helpful in maintaining motivation and improving performance (Black et al., 2004).

Another important principle is that grades should be private. There is no need for students to know one another's grades; making grades public only invites invidious comparisons among students. Finally, it is important to restate that grades are only one method of student evaluation. Written evaluations that add information can provide useful information to parents and students (Marzano, 2000). Computerized gradebooks are now widely available and widely used. Guskey (2002), however, warns that teachers should be careful when using this time-saving software and avoid letting the program make decisions that the teacher should make.

Chapter Summary

What are Instructional Objectives and How Are They Used?

Research supports the use of instructional, or behavioral, objectives, which are clear statements about what students should know and be able to do at the end of a lesson, unit, or course. These statements also specify the conditions of performance and the criteria for assessment. In lesson planning, task analysis contributes to the formulation of objectives, and backward planning facilitates the development of specific objectives from general objectives in a course of study. Objectives are closely linked with assessment. Bloom's taxonomy of educational objectives classifies educational objectives from simple to complex, including knowledge, comprehension, application, analysis,

THE INTENTIONAL TEACHER

Using What You Know about Assessing Student Learning to Improve Teaching and Learning

Intentional teachers assess student learning in ways that align with both their goals and their instruction. They use assessment results to adjust their instruction and to provide important feedback to students, families, and communities. Intentional teachers know that no one measure is ideal for every circumstance, and they implement a range of assessments that fits their purposes and circumstances.

❶ What do I expect my students to know and be able to do at the end of this lesson? How does this contribute to course objectives and to students' needs to become capable individuals?

One cardinal rule of assessing learning is that tests should be tied directly to learning goals and to instruction. Specify in advance what students are to learn. Design instruction to help students learn those things, and then assess their learning in relation to the specified goals.

The variety and range of objectives to which teachers should teach is large. Write objectives in different domains (for example, cognitive and affective) and at different levels of specificity (for example, long-term goals and lesson objectives, and goals for different levels of understanding according to Bloom's taxonomy). For example, you might begin your year-long planning by examining your state's and district's expected outcomes for the grade and subject you teach. Then you might spread out the teacher's editions of your five texts, flipping each open to the scope and sequence chart that specifies content and learning objectives. This process allows you to examine and evaluate

the variety and levels of understanding set by your curricular materials.

❷ What knowledge, skills, needs, and interests do my students have that must be taken into account in my lesson?

Formative assessments allow teachers to discover their students' experiences, preferences, and needs. Use frequent formative assessments to gather information about students' attitudes and prior knowledge. For example, to begin a unit on geology, you might conduct interviews with small groups. You could display a variety of rocks and minerals and listen as students converse about the rocks. Your notes document students' enthusiasm about the topic and their extensive out-of-class experiences studying rocks. You could use this information to create a more sophisticated unit than you might have if students had no prior knowledge of rocks and minerals.

❸ What do I know about the content, child development, learning, motivation, and effective teaching strategies that I can use to accomplish my objectives?

Students' levels of preparation might affect their performance on tests and other measures. Check to see that your measures truly assess the objective you intended to assess. For example, imagine that a cluster of students who typically are highly successful in solving the challenging word problems you present in mathematics each week score surprisingly low on the problem-solving items of a school-based achievement test. When you

synthesis, and evaluation. A behavior content matrix helps to ensure that objectives cover many levels.

Why Is Evaluation Important?

Formal measures of student performance or learning are important as feedback for students and teachers, as information for parents, as information for selection and certification, as information for assessing school accountability, and as incentives for increasing student effort.

How Is Student Learning Evaluated?

Strategies for evaluation include formative evaluation; summative evaluation; norm-referenced evaluation, in which a student's scores are compared with other students' scores; and criterion-referenced evaluation, in which students' scores are compared to a standard of mastery. Students are evaluated through tests or performances. The appropriate method of evaluation is based on the goal of evaluation. For example,

review the items, you wonder whether students' reading ability—and not their problem-solving abilities—accounted for their low scores. To test your hunch, you read similar problems aloud to the students. They solve the problems accurately. This leads you to seek tutorial or other assistance for these students.

4 **What instructional materials, technology, assistance, and other resources are available to help accomplish my objectives?**

Assessments should be challenging for all but impossible for none. Use assessments that are fair measures of the objectives and not of general aptitude. Check that your assessments are applied consistently to all students. For example, you might write weekly quizzes with a general format in mind: Put recall-level items first, reasoning that they provide immediate success for all or most students in demonstrating knowledge. Subsequent items test higher levels of understanding and stretch even the best-prepared students to apply content to new situations.

5 **How will I plan to assess students' progress toward my objectives?**

Assessment equals feedback. Use information from assessments to adjust your instruction and future assessments. Imagine that in reviewing your students' writing portfolios, you discern some trends that offer strong guidance for your instruction. For instance, students' reflections indicate that they seem to find particular meaning in writing autobiographical pieces, and less relevance in other forms of writing. You might build on

their interests in autobiography by including prewriting experiences that tap into students' life experiences, no matter what the genre.

Evaluations need to be important to students if they are to serve as incentives for effort. Assure that your students perceive the objectives as important and the assessments as fair, consistent, and driven by clear criteria. For example, if you were assigning a shelf-building project in a woodworking class, you might display a set of samples of varying quality. You could ask the students to brainstorm the qualities of a well-made shelf, and discuss the real-life consequences of poorly constructed shelves, with students laughing at the imagined disasters that accompany shoddy work. You might develop a scoring rubric based on the criteria they have generated, and distribute it as students begin their work.

6 **How will I respond if individual children or the class as a whole are not on track toward success? What is my back-up plan?**

Successful assessments are valid and reliable for the setting. Check the validity and reliability of your measures with the help of students and peers. For example, after writing a summative exam for a given unit, hand the exam to a peer and ask him or her to assess whether the questions appropriately emphasize particular sections of content. When students complete the exam, ask them to turn over their test papers and evaluate the exam for fairness. You might invite them to write the things they know from the unit that were *not* assessed in your test.

if the goal of testing is to find out whether students have mastered a key concept in a lesson, a criterion-referenced formative quiz or a performance would be the most appropriate.

How Are Tests Constructed?

Tests are constructed to elicit evidence of student learning in relation to the instructional objectives. Achievement tests should be constructed in keeping with six principles: They should (1) measure clearly defined learning objectives, (2) measure a representative sample of the learning tasks included in instruction, (3) include the types of test items most appropriate for measuring the desired learning outcomes, (4) fit the uses that will be made of the results, (5) be as reliable as possible and be interpreted with caution, and (6) improve learning. A table of specifications helps in the planning of tests that correspond to instructional objectives. Types of test items include multiple-choice, true–false, completion, matching, short essay, and problem-solving items. Each type of test item has optimal uses, advantages, and disadvantages. For example, if you want to learn how students think about, analyze, synthesize, or evaluate some aspect of course content, a short essay test might be most appropriate, provided that you have time to administer it and evaluate students' responses.

What Are Portfolio and Performance Assessments?

Portfolio assessment and performance assessment avoid the negative aspects of pencil-and-paper multiple-choice tests by requiring students to demonstrate their learning through work samples or direct real-world applications. Performance assessments are usually scored according to rubrics that specify in advance the type of performance expected.

How Are Grades Determined?

Grading systems differ in elementary and secondary education. For example, informal assessments might be more appropriate at the elementary level, whereas letter grades become increasingly important at the secondary level. Grading standards might be absolute or relative (grading on the curve). Performance grading is a way for teachers to determine what children know and can do. A key requirement for performance grading is judicious collection of work samples from students that indicate level of performance. Another approach is to give students tests in which they can show their abilities. Other systems include contract grading and mastery grading. Report card grades typically average scores on tests, homework, seatwork, class participation, deportment, and effort.

Key Terms

Research Navigator.com

Review the following key terms from the chapter. Then, to explore research on these topics and how they relate to education today, connect to Research Navigator™ through this book's Companion Website or directly at www.researchnavigator.com.

affective objectives   450
assessment   446
backward planning   444
behavior content matrix   449
clang   463
completion items   465
criterion-referenced
   interpretations   453
distractors   461
evaluation   450
evaluative descriptors   472
halo effect   471
instructional objective   440
learning objectives   447
long essay item   466
mastery grading   484

matching items   464
multiple-choice items   461
norm-referenced interpretations   453
performance assessments   477
portfolio assessment   473
problem-solving assessment   469
relative grading standard   483
selected-response items   461
short essay item   466
stem   461
table of specifications   460
task analysis   443
taxonomy of educational
   objectives   447
teaching objectives   447
true–false items   464

Self-Assessment: Practicing for Licensure

Directions: The chapter-opening vignette addresses indicators that are often assessed in state licensure exams. Re-read the chapter-opening vignette, and then respond to the following questions.

1. Mr. Sullivan is having a difficult time connecting what he is teaching and what he is testing. Which of the following evaluation tools will most likely help Mr. Sullivan make the connection?

   a. a multiple-choice test
   b. instructional objectives
   c. traditional teaching strategies
   d. open-book testing

2. Mr. Sullivan might use a chart showing how a concept or skill will be taught at different cognitive levels in relation to an instructional objective. What is this chart called?

   a. task analysis
   b. backward planning
   c. behavior content matrix
   d. table of specifications

3. Mr. Sullivan might improve the connection between what he teaches and what he tests by following which of the following pieces of advice?

   a. Include all instructional content in the test.
   b. Make a test that includes all item types: true–false, multiple choice, matching, short answer, essay, and problem solving.
   c. Be free from the confines of instructional objectives.
   d. Design a test that fits the particular uses that will be made of the results.

4. Which of the following types of evaluation is Mr. Sullivan using?

   a. summative
   b. aptitude
   c. affective
   d. task analysis

5. Why would Mr. Sullivan construct a table of specifications?

   a. Indicate the type of learning to be assessed for different instructional objectives.
   b. Measure a student's performance against a specified standard.
   c. Make comparisons among students.
   d. Identify conditions of mastery.

6. Write a brief essay explaining why evaluation is important.

7. Write instructional objectives, create a table of specifications using Bloom's taxonomy, develop a lesson plan, and write a short test for a topic of study.

Standardized Tests

Jennifer Tranh is a fifth-grade teacher at Lincoln Elementary School. Recently she met with the parents of one of her students, Anita McKay.

"Hello, Mr. and Mrs. McKay," said Ms. Tranh when Anita's parents arrived. "I'm so glad you could come. Please take a seat, and we'll start right in. First, I wanted to tell you what a delight it is to have Anita in my class. She is always so cheerful, so willing to help others. Her work is coming along very well in most subjects, although there are a few areas I'm a bit concerned about. Before I start, though, do you have any questions for me?"

Mr. and Mrs. McKay explained to Ms. Tranh that they thought Anita was having a good year and that they were eager to hear how she was doing.

"All right. First of all, I know you've seen the results of Anita's California Achievement Tests. We call those 'CATs' for short. Most parents don't understand these test scores, so I'll try to explain them to you. First, let's look at math. As you know, Anita has always been a good math student, and her scores and grades reflect this. She got an A on her last report card and a percentile score of 90 on math computations. That means that she scored better than 90 percent of all fifth-graders in the country. She did almost as well on math concepts and applications—her score is in the 85th percentile."

"What does this 'grade equivalent' mean?" asked Mrs. McKay.

"That's a score that's supposed to tell how a child is achieving in relation to his or her grade level. For example, Anita's grade equivalent of 6.9 means that she is scoring more than a year ahead of the fifth-grade level."

"Does this mean she could skip sixth-grade math?" asked Mr. McKay.

Ms. Tranh smiled. "I'm afraid not. It's hard to explain, but a grade equivalent score of 6.9 is supposed to be what a student at the end of sixth grade would score on a fifth-grade test. It doesn't mean that Anita already knows sixth-grade material. Besides, we take any student's testing information with a grain of salt. We rely much more on day-to-day performance and classroom tests to tell how they are doing. In this case the standardized CAT scores are pretty consistent with what we see Anita doing in class. But let me show you another example that shows less consistency. I'm sure you noticed that even though

Anita's reading grades have been pretty good, her scores in reading comprehension were much lower than her scores in most other areas. She got a percentile score of only 30. This is almost a year below grade level. I think Anita is a pretty good reader, so I was surprised. I gave her another test, the Gray Oral Reading Test. This test is given one-on-one, so it gives you a much better indication of how well students are reading. On the Gray, Anita scored at grade level. This score is more indicative of where I see her reading in class, so I'm not concerned about her in this area.

"On the other hand, there is a concern I have about Anita that is not reflected in her standardized tests. She scored near the 70th percentile in both language mechanics and language expression. This might make you think Anita's doing great in language arts, and she is doing well in many ways. However, I'm concerned about Anita's writing. I keep a portfolio of student writing over the course of the year. This is Anita's here. She's showing some development in writing, but I think she could do a lot better. As you can see, her spelling, punctuation, and grammar are excellent, but her stories are very short and factual. As you know, we don't give grades in writing. We use a rating form that shows the student's development toward proficient writing. Based on her portfolio I rated her at proficient, but to go to advanced, I'd like to see her write more and really let her imagination loose. She tells great stories orally, but I think she's so concerned about making a mistake in mechanics that she writes very conservatively. On vacation you might encourage her to write a journal or to do other writing wherever it makes sense."

"But if her standardized test scores are good in language," said Mrs. McKay, "doesn't that mean that she's doing well?"

"Test scores tell us some things, but not everything," said Ms. Tranh. "The CAT is good on simple things such as math computations and language mechanics, but it is not so good at telling us what children can actually do. That's why I keep portfolios of student work in writing, in math problem solving, and in science. I want to see how children are really developing in their ability to apply their skills to doing real things and solving real problems. In fact, now that we've gone over Anita's grades and standardized tests, let's look at her portfolios, and I think you'll get a much better idea of what she's doing here in school."

USING YOUR
Experience

Cooperative Learning and Creative Thinking   Act out this parent–teacher conference about test scores. Have volunteers for the roles of Mrs. McKay, Mr. McKay, and Ms. Tranh. One volunteer can act as moderator to clarify any miscommunications and to keep the conference moving.

Critical Thinking   What do you know from reading this case? What do you still want to know? And what did you learn here? Has Ms. Tranh told us everything we need to know about Anita's standardized test scores and portfolio assessments in writing, math, and science?

Jennifer Tranh's conversation with the McKays illustrates some of the uses and limitations of grades and standardized tests. The CATs and the Gray Oral Reading Test give Ms. Tranh information that does relate Anita's performance in some areas to national norms, and Anita's grades give Ms. Tranh some idea of how Anita is doing relative to her classmates; but neither standardized tests nor grades provide the detail or comprehensiveness reflected in portfolios of Anita's work and other observations of Anita's performance. Taken together, the cautiously interpreted standardized tests, the grades, the portfolios of Anita's work, and other classroom assessments provide a good picture of Anita's performance. Each has value and all the information should be evaluated in making educational decisions.

WHAT ARE STANDARDIZED TESTS AND HOW ARE THEY USED?

INTASC

8 Assessment of Student Learning

Do you remember taking SATs, ACTs, or other college entrance examinations? Did you ever wonder how those tests were constructed, what the scores meant, and the degree to which your scores represented what you really knew or could really do? The SATs and other college entrance examinations are examples of **standardized tests.** Unlike the teacher-made tests discussed in Chapter 13, a standardized test is typically given under the same "standardized" conditions to thousands of students who are similar to those for whom the test is designed. This allows the test publisher to establish norms to which any individual score can be compared. For example, if a representative national sample of fourth-graders had an average score of 37 items correct on a 50-item standardized test, then we might say that fourth-graders who score above 37 are "above the national norm" on this test and those who score below 37 are "below the national norm."

Traditional standardized tests have been subjected to a great deal of criticism and controversy, and today a wide variety of assessments are used. However, standardized tests of many kinds continue to be used for a wide range of purposes at all levels of education. This chapter discusses how and why standardized tests are used and how scores on these tests can be interpreted and applied to important educational decisions. It discusses the use of standardized tests in holding districts, schools, and teachers accountable for student performance, and No Child Left Behind, a major federal initiative focused primarily on accountability. It also includes information on criticisms of standardized testing and on alternatives that are being developed, debated, and applied.

Standardized tests are usually used to offer a yardstick against which to compare individuals or groups of students that teacher-made tests cannot provide. For example, suppose a child's parents ask a teacher how their daughter is doing in math. The teacher says, "Fine, she got a score of 81 percent on our latest math test." For some purposes this information would be adequate. But for others the parents might want to know much more. How does 81 percent compare to the scores of other students in this class? How about other students in the school, the district, the state, or the whole country? In some contexts the score of 81 percent might help to qualify the girl for a special program for the mathematically gifted; in others it might suggest the need for remedial instruction. Also, suppose the teacher found that the class averaged 85 percent correct on the math test. How is this class doing compared to other math classes or to students nationwide? A teacher-made test cannot yield this information.

Standardized tests are typically carefully constructed to provide accurate information about students' levels of performance. Most often, curriculum experts establish

standardized tests
Tests that are usually commercially prepared for nationwide use and designed to provide accurate and meaningful information on students' performance relative to that of others at their age or grade levels.

what students at a particular age should know and be able to do in a particular subject. Then questions are written to assess the various skills or information students are expected to possess. The questions are tried out on various groups of students. Items that almost all students get right or almost all miss are usually dropped, as are items that students find unclear or confusing. Patterns of scores are carefully examined. If students who score well on most items do no better than lower-scoring students on a particular item, then that item will probably be dropped.

Eventually, a final test will be developed and given to a large selected group of students from all over the country. Attempts are usually made to ensure that this group resembles the larger population of students who will ultimately use the test. For example, a test of geometry for eleventh-graders might be given to a sampling of eleventh-graders in urban, rural, and suburban locations; in different regions of the country; in private as well as public schools; and to students with different levels of preparation in mathematics. Care will be taken to include students of all ethnic backgrounds. This step establishes the **norms** for the test, which provide an indication of how an average student will score (Hopkins, 1998). Finally, a testing manual is prepared, explaining how the test is to be given, scored, and interpreted. The test is now ready for general use. The test development process creates tests whose scores have meaning outside of the confines of a particular classroom or school. These scores are used in a variety of ways. Explanations of some of the most important functions of standardized testing follow (see Bracey, 1998).

Selection and Placement

CONNECTIONS

For discussions of between- and within-class ability grouping, see Chapter 9, pages 281 and 284.

Standardized tests are often used to select students for entry or placement in specific programs. For example, the SAT (Scholastic Assessment Test) or ACT (American College Testing Program) that you probably took in high school might have been used to help your college admissions board decide whether to accept you as a student. Similarly, admission to special programs for gifted and talented students might depend on standardized test scores. Standardized tests might also be used, along with other information, to help educators decide whether to place students in special-education programs or to assign students to ability groups. For example, high schools may use standardized tests in deciding which students to place or counsel into college preparatory, general, or vocational programs. Elementary schools may use them to place students in reading groups. Some colleges use them to decide whether entering students have met prerequisites for certain courses. Standardized tests are sometimes used to determine eligibility for grade-to-grade promotion, graduation from high school, or entry into an occupation. For example, most states use standardized tests as part of the teacher certification process.

Diagnosis

norms
Standards that are derived from the test scores of a sample of people who are similar to those who will take the test and that can be used to interpret scores of future test takers.

Standardized tests are often used to diagnose individual students' learning problems or strengths. For example, a student who is performing poorly in school might be given a battery of tests to determine whether he or she has a learning disability or mental retardation. At the same time the testing might identify specific deficits that need remediation. Teachers frequently employ diagnostic tests of reading skills, such as the Gray Oral Reading Test that Ms. Tranh used, to identify a student's particular reading problem. For example, a diagnostic test might indicate that a student's decoding skills are fine but that his or her reading comprehension is poor; or that a student has good computation skills but lacks problem-solving skills. More fine-grained diagnostic tests might tell a teacher that a physics student is doing well in states of matter but not scientific measurement, or that a foreign language student is doing well in grammar but not so well in expression. Sophisticated assessments can help teachers determine students' cognitive styles and the depth of their understanding of complex concepts (Carver, Lehrer, Connell, & Erickson, 1992; Nichols, 1994).

Evaluation

Perhaps the most common use of standardized testing is to evaluate students' progress and teachers' and schools' effectiveness. For example, districts and states use tests to evaluate the gains that schools make in overall student performance (see "Accountability"). Parents often want to know how their children are doing in comparison with what is typical of children at their grade level. For individual students, standardized test scores are meaningful as evaluation only if teachers use them along with other information, such as students' actual performance in school and in other contexts, as Ms. Tranh did. Many students who score poorly on standardized tests excel in school, college, or occupations; either they have trouble taking tests or they have important skills that are not measured by such tests. On the other hand, some students demonstrate their achievement best on standardized tests.

The primary goal of President Bush's No Child Left Behind program has been to level the playing field for students throughout the country, no matter where they attend school. How can high-stakes testing help "level the playing field?"

School Improvement

Standardized tests can contribute to improving the schooling process. The results of some standardized tests provide information about appropriate student placement and diagnostic information that is important in remediation. In addition, achievement tests can guide curriculum development and revision when areas of weakness appear (see Hopkins, 1998; Schmoker, 1999). Standardized tests can play a role in guidance and counseling as well. This is true not only for achievement and aptitude testing but also for more specialized types of measures, such as vocational interest inventories and other psychological scales that are used in the counseling of students.

Schools often turn to academic achievement tests to evaluate the relative success of competing educational programs or strategies. For example, if a teacher or school tries out an innovative teaching strategy, tests can help reveal whether it was more successful than previous methods. Statewide and districtwide test results often serve as a yardstick by which citizens can judge the success of their local schools. Tests are sometimes used to indicate the relative teaching strengths and weaknesses of the school's faculty. However, educating students is a complex process, and standardized tests provide only a small portion of the information that is necessary for evaluating teachers, programs, or schools.

Accountability

A growing trend since the mid-1970s has been the effort to hold teachers, schools, and districts accountable for what students learn. All U.S. states, most Canadian provinces, and Britain (among other countries) have implemented regular standardized testing programs and publish the results on a school-by-school basis. Many districts supplement these state tests with their own tests, including "benchmark assessments" that are given several times each year to help guide instruction toward meeting state standards. Not surprisingly, principals and other administrators watch these scores the way business owners watch their profit sheets. More and more, standardized tests are becoming "high-stakes" tests, which means that their results have serious consequences for educators and (increasingly) for students themselves. For example, many states and districts now require that students score at a given level on state tests in order to be promoted from grade to grade or to graduate from high school. Many states and districts issue school report cards listing such data as test scores, attendance, retentions, and suspensions; these might be reported in newspapers or otherwise publicized. Test scores are frequently used in decisions about hiring, firing, promotion, and transfer of principals and superintendents, and often teachers.

ON THE WEB

To learn more about accountability and state-level assessment issues, visit the website for the Council of Chief State School Officers (CCSSO) at **www.ccsso.org**. CCSSO is an organization of public officials who lead K–12 education in the 50 states.

Chicago studies of grade-to-grade promotion standards found higher student motivation (Roderick & Engel, 2001) and higher achievement (Roderick, Jacob, & Bryk, 2002) than before the standards were implemented. Also, school districts often establish special remedial programs, such as summer school or after-school programs (Fashola, 2001), and these can help students pass the tests and qualify for promotion or graduation.

The accountability movement stems in part from the public's loss of confidence in education. Legislators (among others), upset by examples of students graduating from high school unable to read or compute, have demanded that schools establish higher standards and that students achieve them.

The accountability movement has many critics, however (Rotberg, 2001; Shepard, 2000; Sirotnik, 2002; Thompson, 2001). Many argue that schools will teach only what is tested, emphasizing reading and mathematics at the expense of, for instance, science and social studies (Shepard, 1995), and emphasizing easily measured objectives (such as punctuation) over more important hard-to-measure objectives (such as composition). Many educators point out that accountability assessments fail to take into account differences in the challenges faced by schools. A school or classroom might test low because the students are from disadvantaged backgrounds rather than because they were given poor instruction. Students in high-poverty schools may have fewer opportunities to learn because their funding is often lower than that of other schools (Orfield & Kornhaber, 2001; Starratt, 2003). High student mobility, especially prevalent in low-SES urban areas, might mean that schools are held accountable for students they have only had for a few weeks or months. School performance year-to-year is unstable, and schools may be rewarded or punished based on minor variations of no statistical importance (Linn & Haug, 2002). High-stakes testing can lead schools and districts to try to adopt policies that artificially inflate scores by removing potentially low-scoring students from the testing pool, such as assigning more children to special education, categorizing more students as limited English proficient, or retaining more students (Allington & McGill-Franzen, 1992; Linn, 2000). Many observers have noted that teachers, under extraordinary pressure, sometimes use unethical strategies to increase students' scores (Cizek, 1999; Popham, 2005).

Several researchers (e.g., Amrein & Berliner, 2003; Bracey, 2003; Ellmore & Fuhrman, 2001; Neill, 2003) have questioned whether increased accountability actually leads to higher achievement. Carnoy and Loeb (2002) found only slight differences in NAEP score gains favoring states with strong accountability systems in comparisons with other states, whereas Neill and Gaylor (2001) and Amrein and Berliner (2003) found that states with strong accountability systems had *lower* gains on NAEP than other states.

Regardless of these criticisms, the demand for accountability is here to stay (Gandel & Vranek, 2001; Scherer, 2001). One advantage of accountability is that it does increase the pressure on schools and teachers to pay attention to students who might otherwise fall through the cracks and to help those who need help the most. States are increasingly reporting "disaggregated" scores, meaning that they are separately held accountable for gains of students of each ethnicity, limited English proficient students, and so on. This can focus school leaders on means of ensuring that all groups are making progress (Scheurich, Skrla, & Johnson, 2000). Another advantage is that accountability encourages schools to search out improved instructional methods and guarantees routine evaluation of any innovations schools try (Kennedy, 2003; Streifer, 2002; Gandel & McGiffert, 2003; Lane & Beebe-Frankenberger, 2004).

State accountability tests are based on state standards (Strong, Silver, & Perini, 2001). For a teacher, a principal, or a subject matter specialist, knowing what these standards are is a key to helping students achieve higher test performance (Carr & Harris, 2001). Goals that are understood are more likely to be reached than goals that are unclear.

The standards on which accountability tests are based are usually developed by diverse groups of stakeholders, including teachers, parents, employers, and researchers who express their judgments about what should be taught and learned. Through a consensus-building process, a state or district pools the thinking of educators and noneducators in defining the content domains it demands through its assessments. This process forces education leaders and policymakers to make clear what it is they want children to learn, which can then help them set policies in line with these objectives (Gandel & Vranek, 2001).

Accountability under No Child Left Behind   The No Child Left Behind (NCLB) legislation is intended to move all children to success on their state standards by 2014. The assessment provisions of NCLB are as follows (see Center on Education Policy, 2003; The Education Trust, 2003; Stecher, Hamilton, & Gonzales, 2003; U.S. Department of Education, 2002).

> **CONNECTIONS**
> Chapter 9 provides an overview of No Child Left Behind.

1. *Annual testing.* All states must put in place annual tests of student performance, initially in reading and math, with science to be added in 2006–2007. Before NCLB, most states tested children for accountability purposes only in selected grades. Now, states must test in grades 3 through 8, plus one high school grade. Some states develop their own tests, some contract with companies to create customized tests, and some purchase commercial tests such as those described in this chapter.

2. *Disaggregated reporting of scores.* Under NCLB, states now must report test scores for each school according to each subgroup in the school: each ethnic group, students in special education, students in poverty, and limited English proficient students. There must be a minimum number of students in a given category for it to be considered a subgroup for NCLB, and this number varies widely from state to state. Schools and districts are held accountable for each subgroup, so it is no longer possible to look successful by succeeding on average if one or more subgroups are failing to make good progress.

3. *Adequate yearly progress.* All subgroups in all schools are now expected to make adequate yearly progress (AYP) on all state

"Well now, let's see who made adequate yearly progress this year . . ."

assessments. This is defined differently in each state, but in essence each subgroup must either be scoring at a high level or have an increasing percentage of students in all subgroups who score at the proficient level each year. Further, subgroups are not considered to be making adequate progress if there are too many missing students (to avoid situations in which schools fail to obtain tests from some low-achieving students). The AYP requirement is, for most schools, the most important aspect of NCLB, as it makes school and district leaders very anxious to ensure that every group is making progress.

4. *Consequences for not meeting AYP.* Schools with one or more subgroups not meeting their state's AYP standards may be subject to various consequences, depending on how many years they fail to meet AYP. Schools not meeting AYP for two years or more must offer their children supplemental educational services, usually small-group tutorials held after school or over the summer. Also, such schools are supposed to offer parents the opportunity to transfer to a more successful school, although in practice very few parents have taken advantage of this. As schools fail to meet AYP for more years, they may be subject to more severe consequences, eventually leading to the possibility of reconstitution (replacing the staff with a new staff), closure, or takeover by the state.

Criticisms of NCLB   Although the NCLB Act was supported by Republicans and Democrats (and by both candidates in the 2004 election), its accountability provisions have unleashed a firestorm of criticism from educators. Among the main criticisms:

1. *Excessive and narrow testing.* Many educators are concerned that NCLB continues a trend toward excessive testing of children on standardized, mostly multiple-

Personal Reflection

Mixed Messages

A friend recently told me about a decision by a local school board in her state that had outraged parents in the community, as well as state health education officials. The school district had decided to reduce recess time at all of the elementary schools in the district from 20 minutes each day to 10 minutes. School officials argued that the change was necessary in order to allow more time to help students focus on core academic courses and thereby help raise the district's testing scores.

My friend, a health advocate and former health education specialist, is outraged by the conflicting messages about child health she feels exist today. Daily we hear news reports about the growing concern over the general health of our nation's children, particularly with regard to obesity, asthma, and diabetes. Yet at the same time, each year more and more school districts reduce programs not considered part of the core curriculum, such as physical education and health education, all in the name of improving test scores and meeting the requirements of No Child Left Behind.

My friend worries that the focus on high-stakes testing will affect more than just children's physical health. She wonders, also, about students' social development. Are we sacrificing important areas of children's development for the sake of test scores?

@ Reflect on This. What are some potential negative ramifications of cutbacks to noncore-curricular programs in schools? Who has to pick up the slack in these areas when schools no longer offer such programs? Do you think all communities are affected equally by such cutbacks, regardless of socioeconomic conditions?

choice tests (Popham, 2003; Sadker & Zittleman, 2004; Wasserman, 2001). In particular, because NCLB focuses on reading, math, and (soon) science, educators are concerned that social studies, art, music, and anything involving creativity or deep understanding will be pushed out (Wasserman, 2001). Elmore (2003) has expressed concern about NCLB's excessive focus on testing and insufficient focus on building the capacity of teachers.

2. *State-to-state variations in standards.* Because NCLB leaves up to the states the testing, passing standards, and other elements that go into determining whether schools have met AYP, there is enormous variation from state to state. For example, a study by the Northwest Evaluation Association (2003) found that an eighth-grader who performed at the proficient level in Montana would be at the 36th percentile on an NWEA exam, whereas a similar student in Wyoming would score at the 89th percentile on the same test. In addition, states vary in how many students are needed to constitute a subgroup, so states with high requirements (some require fifty students, some as few as five) may not be held accountable for their students in special education or other subgroups, whereas other states with identical test scores may have many schools not meeting AYP because they are accountable for a larger number of subgroups. As a result, some states have the majority of their schools not meeting AYP, whereas others have hardly any schools not meeting AYP. For example, as noted in Chapter 9, in 2003, 87 percent of Florida schools failed to meet AYP, compared to 0.8 percent of Iowa schools.

3. *NCLB is underfunded.* NCLB brought with it a substantial increase in federal education funding, but far less than the amount many of its advocates had hoped (Council on Education Policy, 2004). The problem is that much of the new funding is taken up by the requirements for additional testing, supplemental educational services, and helping parents transfer their children to new schools. Clearly, meeting the ambitious goals of NCLB will require a significant investment (see Orfield & Kornhaber, 2001).

"Of course we still make time for art. Right now, for example, we're practicing shading in boxes."

Time will tell whether NCLB will lead to significant and lasting improvements in the performance of U.S. schools. The best thing that can be said about NCLB is that something had to be done; the performance of U.S. students, and the gaps between scores of majority and minority students, are unacceptable (see Chapter 4).

CONNECTIONS

See Chapter 4 for a description of the achievement gap between majority and minority students.

ON THE WEB

For a description of the basics and updated news on No Child Left Behind from the office of the U.S. Secretary of Education visit **www.nclb.gov.**

Theory into **PRACTICE**

Teaching Test-Taking Skills

As standardized testing has taken on increasing importance in the evaluation of students, teachers, and schools, so too has the preparation of students to take these tests. Of course, the best way to prepare students for tests is to do a good job of teaching them the material. However, schools also need to help many students to become test-wise, to show what they really know on standardized tests, and to get as good a score as possible.

CONNECTIONS

For more on teaching test-taking skills in the context of teaching metacognitive awareness and study skills, see Chapter 6, page 192.

Many ethical issues are involved in helping students do well on standardized tests (Smith, 1991; Popham, 2005). For example, one way to help students score well would be to know the test items in advance and teach students the answers. Clearly, this would be cheating. A much more ethically ambiguous case arises when teachers know what subjects will be on the test and teach only material that they know will be tested. For example, if a standardized test did not assess Roman numerals, a math teacher might skip this topic to spend more time on an objective that would be tested. This practice is criticized as "teaching to the test." It could be argued that it is unfair to test students on material that they have not been taught and that instruction should therefore be closely aligned with tests (Popham, 2004, 2005). On the other hand, a standardized test can assess only a small sample of all objectives that are taught in school. Gearing instruction toward the objectives that will be on the test, to the exclusion of all others, would produce a very narrow curriculum.

Because of the temptation to limit instruction to the content of upcoming tests, it is important to maintain test security. Specific items on a test should never be shared with teachers in advance of the administration date. Beyond matching instructional content with test objectives, there are many ways to help students learn to do well on tests in general. Research has found that students can be taught to be test-wise and that this increases their standardized test scores (Bangert-Drowns et al., 1991; Scruggs, White, & Bennion, 1986). Students can also be taught coping strategies to deal with their anxiety about testing. These strategies can sometimes help children approach tests with more confidence and less stress (Schutz & Davis, 2000; Zeidner, 1995).

Questions have been raised about the effectiveness of programs that prepare students for the SAT. Since the SAT measures cognitive skills, it is perhaps to be expected that instructional programs can improve scores. The consensus among researchers is that coaching (especially long-term coaching) is effective for the SAT, particularly for minority and low-achieving students (Becker, 1990a; Messick, 1982) when it focuses on the skills the SAT measures.

Some ways of helping students to prepare for standardized tests follow (see Hill & Wigfield, 1984):

1. Give students practice with similar item formats. For example, if a test will use multiple-choice formats, give students practice with similar formats in routine classroom quizzes and tests. If a test will use an unusual format such as verbal analogies (e.g., Big:Small::Honest: _____), give students practice with this type of item.

2. Suggest that students skip over difficult or time-consuming items and return to them later.

3. If there is no penalty for guessing on a test, suggest to students that they always fill in some answer. If there is a penalty for guessing, students should still be encouraged to guess, especially if they can narrow down the options by eliminating one or more choices.

4. Suggest that students read all options on a multiple-choice test before choosing one. Sometimes more than one answer is correct but only one of them will be the better answer.

5. Suggest to students that they use all available time. If they finish early, they should go back over their answers.

What is the main difference between standardized and nonstandardized tests? How are standardized test results used in student selection, placement, diagnosis, and evaluation? How are state assessments constructed, and how do they hold teachers and schools accountable for what students learn?

WHAT TYPES OF STANDARDIZED TESTS ARE GIVEN?

Three kinds of standardized tests are commonly used in school settings: aptitude tests, norm-referenced achievement tests, and criterion-referenced achievement tests (Aiken, 2003; Popham, 2005). An **aptitude test** is designed to assess students' abilities. It is meant to predict the ability of students to learn or to perform particular types of tasks rather than to measure how much the students have already learned. The most widely used aptitude tests measure general intellectual aptitude; but many other, more specific tests measure particular aptitudes, such as mechanical or perceptual abilities or reading readiness. The SAT, for example, is meant to predict a student's aptitude for college studies. An aptitude test is successful to the degree that it predicts performance. For example, a reading readiness test given to kindergartners that did not accurately predict how well the students would read when they reached first or second grade would be of little use.

Achievement tests are used to (1) predict students' future performance in a course of study, (2) diagnose students' difficulties, (3) serve as formative tests of students' progress, and (4) serve as summative tests of learning.

Norm-referenced achievement tests are assessments of a student's knowledge of a particular content area, such as mathematics, reading, or Spanish. What makes these tests norm-referenced is that their results can be compared with those of a representative group of students. They are purposely constructed to reveal differences among students. Those differences are expected to be due to quality of instruction and student learning rather than differences from school to school in curricula. Norm-referenced achievement tests thus assess some but not all of the skills that are taught in any one school. A norm-referenced achievement test cannot range too broadly because it is designed for nationwide use and the curricula for any given subject vary from district to district. For example, if some seventh-graders learn about base-2 arithmetic or Venn diagrams but others do not, then these topics will be unlikely to appear on a national mathematics test.

A criterion-referenced achievement test also assesses a student's knowledge of subject matter, but rather than comparing the achievement of an individual student against national norms, it is designed to measure the degree to which the student has mastered certain well-specified skills. The information that a criterion-referenced test produces is quite specific: "Thirty-seven percent of Ontario fifth-graders can fill in the names of the major Western European nations on an outline map" or "Ninety-three percent of twelfth-graders at Alexander Hamilton High School know that increasing the temperature of a gas in a closed container increases the gas's pressure." Sometimes criterion-referenced test scores are used in comparisons between schools or between districts, but typically no representative norming group is used. If a group of curriculum experts decides that every fifth-grader in Illinois should be able to fill in an outline map of South America, then the expectation for that item is 100 percent; it is of less interest whether Illinois fifth-graders score better or worse on this item than students in other states. What is more important is that, overall, students improve each year on this item.

Aptitude Tests

Although aptitude tests, norm-referenced achievement tests, and criterion-referenced tests are distinct from one another in theory, there is in fact considerable overlap

aptitude test
A test designed to measure general abilities and to predict future performance.

achievement tests
Standardized tests measuring how much students have learned in a given context.

"According to your vocational aptitude test, you're best suited to a job filling in bubbles with a #2 pencil."

CONNECTIONS

To learn more about student differences in general intelligence, specific aptitudes, and abilities and learning styles, see Chapter 4, page 121.

CONNECTIONS

For a discussion of the use of IQ scores in the classification of learners with exceptionalities or for special-education services, see Chapter 12, page 395.

among them. For example, aptitudes are usually measured by evaluating achievement over a very broadly defined domain. School learning can thus affect students' aptitude test scores, and a student who scores well on one type of test will usually score well on another (Popham, 2005).

The following subsections discuss the types of aptitude tests most often given in schools.

General Intelligence Tests   The most common kind of aptitude tests given in school are tests of **intelligence,** or general aptitude for school learning. The intelligence quotient, or IQ, is the score that is most often associated with intelligence testing, but other types of scores are also used.

Intelligence tests are designed to provide a general indication of individuals' aptitudes in many areas of intellectual functioning. Intelligence itself is seen as the ability to deal with abstractions, to learn, and to solve problems (Sternberg, 2000), and tests of intelligence focus on these skills. Intelligence tests give students a wide variety of questions to answer and problems to solve.

The Measurement of IQ   The measurement of the intelligence quotient (IQ) was introduced in the early 1900s by Alfred Binet, a French psychologist, to identify children with such serious learning difficulties that they were unlikely to profit from regular classroom instruction. The scale that Binet developed to measure intelligence assessed a wide range of mental characteristics and skills, such as memory, knowledge, vocabulary, and problem solving. Binet tested a large number of students of various ages to establish norms (expectations) for overall performance on his tests. He then expressed IQ as a ratio of **mental age** (the average test scores received by students of a particular age) to **chronological age,** multiplied by 100. For example, 6-year-olds (chronological age [CA] = 6) who scored at the average for all 6-year-olds (mental age [MA] = 6) would have an IQ of 100 (6/6 × 100 = 100). Six-year-olds who scored at a level typical of 7-year-olds (MA = 7) would have IQs of about 117 (7/6 × 100 = 117).

Over the years the mental age/chronological age comparison has been dropped, and IQ is now defined as having a mean of 100 and a standard deviation of 15 (a *standard deviation* is a measure of how spread out scores are, defined later in this chapter) at any age. Most scores fall near the mean, with small numbers of scores extending well above and below the mean. In theory, about 68 percent of all individuals will have IQs within one standard deviation of the mean; that is, from 85 (one standard deviation below the mean) to 115 (one standard deviation above), and 95 percent will be found in the range up to two standard deviations from the mean (between 70 and 130).

Intelligence tests are designed to provide a general indication of an individual's aptitudes in many areas of intellectual functioning. The most widely used tests contain many different scales. Figure 14.1 shows items like those used on the Wechsler Adult Intelligence Scale (Wechsler, 1955). Each scale measures a different component of intelligence. Most often, a person who scores well on one scale will also do well on others, but this is not always so. The same person might do very well on general comprehension and similarities, less well on arithmetic reasoning, and poorly on block design, for example.

Intelligence tests are administered either to individuals or to groups. Tests that are administered to groups, such as the Otis-Lennon Mental Ability Tests, the Lorge-Thorndike Intelligence Tests, and the California Test of Mental Maturity, are often

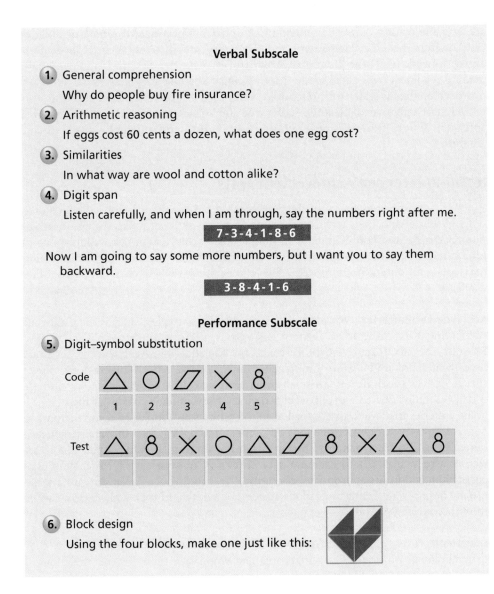

Verbal Subscale

1. General comprehension

   Why do people buy fire insurance?

2. Arithmetic reasoning

   If eggs cost 60 cents a dozen, what does one egg cost?

3. Similarities

   In what way are wool and cotton alike?

4. Digit span

   Listen carefully, and when I am through, say the numbers right after me.

   7 - 3 - 4 - 1 - 8 - 6

   Now I am going to say some more numbers, but I want you to say them backward.

   3 - 8 - 4 - 1 - 6

Performance Subscale

5. Digit–symbol substitution

   Code

   Test

6. Block design

   Using the four blocks, make one just like this:

FIGURE 14.1
Illustrations of Items Used in Intelligence Testing

Intelligence tests focus on skills such as dealing with abstractions and solving problems. This sample of items resembles those used on the Wechsler Adult Intelligence Scale.

From Robert L. Thorndike and Elizabeth P. Hagen, *Measurement and Evaluation in Psychology and Education* (4th ed.), pp. 302–303. Copyright © 1986. Reprinted by permission of Prentice Hall, Upper Saddle River, New Jersey.

given to large groups of students as general assessments of intellectual aptitude. These tests are not as accurate or detailed as are intelligence tests administered individually to people by trained psychologists, such as the Wechsler Intelligence Test for Children-Fourth Edition (WISC-IV) or the Stanford-Binet test. For example, students who are being assessed for possible placement in special education usually take an individually administered test (most often the WISC-IV), along with other tests.

IQ scores are important because they are correlated with school performance (Ceci, 1992). That is, students who have higher IQs tend, on the average, to get better grades, score higher on achievement tests, and so on. By the time a child is about age six, IQ estimates tend to become relatively stable, and most people's IQs remain about the same into adulthood. However, some people will experience substantial changes in their estimated IQ, often because of schooling or other environmental influences (Ceci, 1991).

Multifactor Aptitude Tests   One other form of aptitude test that provides a breakdown of more specific skills is the **multifactor aptitude battery.** Many such tests

intelligence
General aptitude for learning, often measured by ability to deal with abstractions and to solve problems.

mental age
The average test score received by individuals of a given chronological age.

chronological age
The age of an individual in years.

multifactor aptitude battery
A test that predicts ability to learn a variety of specific skills and types of knowledge.

are available, with a range of content and emphases. They include scholastic abilities tests such as the SAT; elementary and secondary school tests, such as the Differential Aptitude Test, the Cognitive Abilities Test, and the Test of Cognitive Skills; reading readiness tests, such as the Metropolitan Reading Readiness Test; and various developmental scales for preschool children. At a minimum, most of these tests provide not only overall aptitude scores but also subscores for verbal and nonverbal aptitudes. Often, subscores are even more finely divided to describe more specific abilities.

Norm-Referenced Achievement Tests

Whereas aptitude tests focus on general learning potential and knowledge acquired both in school and out, achievement tests focus on skills or abilities that are traditionally taught in schools. In general, standardized achievement tests fall into one of four categories: achievement batteries, diagnostic tests, single-subject achievement measures, and criterion-referenced achievement measures (Aiken, 2003; Gronlund, 2003).

Achievement Batteries   Standardized **achievement batteries,** such as the California Achievement Test, the Iowa Tests of Basic Skills, the Comprehensive Test of Basic Skills, the Stanford Achievement Test, and the Metropolitan Achievement Tests, are used to measure individual or group achievement in a variety of subject areas. These survey batteries include several small tests, each in a different subject area, and are usually administered to a group over a period of several days. Many of the achievement batteries that are available for use in the schools are similar in construction and content. However, because of slight differences among the tests in the instructional objectives and subject matter sampled within the subtests, it is important before selecting a particular test to examine it carefully for its match with a specific school curriculum and for its appropriateness relative to school goals. Achievement batteries usually have several forms for various age or grade levels so that achievement can be monitored over a period of several years.

Diagnostic Tests   **Diagnostic tests** differ from achievement batteries in that they generally focus on a specific content area and emphasize the skills that are thought to be important for mastery of that subject matter. Diagnostic tests produce much more detailed information than do other achievement tests. For example, a standardized mathematics test often produces scores for math computations, concepts, and applications, whereas a diagnostic test would give scores on more specific skills, such as adding decimals or solving two-step word problems. Diagnostic tests are available mostly for reading and mathematics and are intended to show specific areas of strength and weakness in these skills. The results can be used to guide remedial instruction or to structure learning experiences for students who are expected to learn the skill.

achievement batteries
Standardized tests that include several subtests designed to measure knowledge of particular subjects.

diagnostic tests
Tests of specific skills used to identify students' needs and to guide instruction.

Subject Area Achievement Tests   Teachers make up most classroom tests for assessing skills in specific subjects. However, school districts can purchase specific subject achievement tests for almost any subject. A problem with many of these tests is that unless they are tied to the particular curriculum and instructional strategies that are used in the classroom, they might not adequately represent the content that has been taught. If standardized achievement tests are considered for evaluating learning in specific areas, the content of the test should be closely examined for its match with the district curriculum, the instruction the students have received, and the district's or state's standards and assessments.

Criterion-Referenced Achievement Tests

Criterion-referenced tests differ from norm-referenced standardized tests in several ways (Aiken, 2003). Such tests can take the form of a survey battery, a diagnostic test, or a single-subject test. In contrast to norm-referenced tests, which are designed for use by schools with varying curricula, criterion-referenced tests are most meaningful when constructed around a well-defined set of objectives. For many tests, these objectives can be chosen by the school district, building administrator, or teacher to be applied in a specific situation. The items on the test are selected to match specific instructional objectives, often with three to five items measuring each objective. Therefore, the tests can indicate which objectives individual students or the class as a whole have mastered. Test results can be used to guide future instruction or remedial activities. For this reason these tests are sometimes referred to as objective-referenced tests.

Criterion-referenced tests differ from other achievement tests in the way in which they are scored and in how the results are interpreted. On criterion-referenced tests, it is generally the score for each objective that is important. Results could show, for example, how many students can multiply two digits by two digits or how many can write a business letter correctly. Moreover, students' scores on the total test or on specific objectives are interpreted with respect to some criterion of adequate performance independent of group performance. Examples of criterion-referenced tests include tests for drivers and pilots, which were designed to determine who can drive or fly, not who is in the top 20 percent of drivers or pilots. Tests for teachers are also criterion referenced.

Score reports for criterion-referenced tests are frequently in the form of the number of items that the student got correct on each objective. From these data the teacher can gauge whether the student has mastered the objective.

Standard Setting

When tests are used for making decisions about degree(s) of mastery of a subject or topic, some procedure must be employed to determine the test score cutoff point(s) indicating various proficiency levels (Kane, 1994). Most procedures for the establishment of a **cutoff score** rely on the professional judgment of representative groups of teachers and other educators. Qualified professionals might examine each item in a test and judge the probability that a student with a given level of proficiency would get the item correct. They then base the cutoff score for mastery or proficiency on these probabilities. Standards set using procedures like this are common in licensing exams as well as in many state and district accountability programs.

ℋOW ARE STANDARDIZED TESTS INTERPRETED?

After students take a standardized test, the tests are usually sent for computer scoring to the central office or the test publisher. The students' raw scores (the number correct on each subtest) are translated into one or more **derived scores,** such as percentiles, grade equivalents, or normal curve equivalents, which relate the students' scores to those of the group on which the test was normed. These statistics are described in the following sections (see Aiken, 2000; McMillan, 2001).

Percentile Scores

A **percentile score,** or percentile rank (sometimes abbreviated in test reports as % ILE), indicates the percentage of students in the norming group who scored lower than

---

CONNECTIONS

For more on the definitions of norm-referenced and criterion-referenced testing, see Chapter 13, page 453.

CERTIFICATION POINTER

On your teacher certification test you may need to know that a criterion-referenced test would give you better information about how much each student has learned about a particular aspect of the curriculum than a norm-referenced test.

cutoff score
The score designated as the minimum necessary to demonstrate mastery of a subject.

derived scores
Values computed from raw scores that relate students' performances to those of a norming group, e.g., percentiles and grade equivalents.

percentile score
A derived score that designates what percentage of the norming group earned raw scores lower than a particular score.

The sight of a child taking a standardized test is a common one these days. What might the results tell us about this child?

a particular score. For example, if a student achieved at the median for the norming group (that is, if equal numbers of students scored better and worse than that student), the student would have a percentile rank of 50, because his or her scores exceeded those of 50 percent of the others in the norming group. If you ranked a group of 30 students from bottom to top on test scores, the 25th student from the bottom would score in the 83rd percentile (25/30 × 100 = 83.3).

Grade-Equivalent Scores

Grade-equivalent scores relate students' scores to the average scores obtained by students at a particular grade level. Let's say a norming group achieved an average raw score of 70 on a reading test at the beginning of fifth grade. This score would be established as a grade equivalent of 5.0. If a sixth-grade norming group achieved a test score of 80 in September, this would be established as a grade equivalent of 6.0. Now let's say that a fifth-grader achieved a raw score of 75. This is halfway between the score for 5.0 and that for 6.0, so this student would be assigned a grade equivalent of 5.5. The number after the decimal point is referred to as "months," so a grade equivalent of 5.5 would be read "five years, five months." In theory, a student in the third month of fifth grade should have a score of 5.3 (five years, three months), and so on. Only the ten months of the regular academic year, September to June, are counted.

The advantage of grade equivalents is that they are easy to interpret and make some intuitive sense. For example, if an average student gains one grade equivalent each year, we call this achieving at expected levels. If we know that a student is performing 2 years below grade level (say, a ninth-grader is scoring at a level typical of seventh-graders), this gives us some understanding of how poorly the student is doing.

However, grade-equivalent scores should be interpreted as only a rough approximation (Gronlund, 2003). For one thing, students do not gain steadily in achievement from month to month. For another, scores that are far from the expected grade level do not mean what they appear to mean. A fourth-grader who scores at, say, the 7.4 grade equivalent is by no means ready for seventh-grade work; this score just means that the fourth-grader has thoroughly mastered fourth-grade work and has scored as well as a seventh-grader would on the fourth-grade test. Obviously, the average seventh-grader knows a great deal more than what would be on a fourth-grade test, so there is no real comparison between a fourth-grader who scores at a 7.4 grade equivalent and a seventh-grader who does so. The two tests they took would have been very different.

Shifting definitions of grade-level expectations can also confuse the interpretation of scores. For example, New York City school administrators were pleased during the late 1980s to report that 67 percent of students were reading at or above grade level. However, there was a national discussion about what is called the "Lake Wobegon Effect." (In Garrison Keillor's mythical town of Lake Wobegon, "All the children are above average.") Far more than 50 percent of students were scoring "above average" (Cannell, 1987). Test makers renormed their tests, and as a result, administrators in New York City could then claim that only 49 percent of their students were reading at or above grade level (Fiske, 1989). Today, the Lake Wobegon Effect is again in full force, and most standardized tests again produce scores that put many more than 50 percent of students "at grade level" or "above national norms." Because the norms vary from test to test, statements about how many students are at a given level should

CERTIFICATION POINTER

For your teacher certification test you may need to know that a student's grade-equivalent score of 7.3 on a standardized math test would indicate that the student performed as well as an average seventh-grader in the third month of school on that same test, but if students are in a grade level below 7, a grade equivalent of 7.3 does not imply the ability to do seventh-grade work.

grade-equivalent scores
Standard scores that relate students' raw scores to the average scores obtained by norming groups at different grade levels.

always be taken with a grain of salt. What is more meaningful is how students are changing over time, or how one group compares to another on the same test.

Standard Scores

Several kinds of scores describe test results according to their position on the normal curve. A normal curve describes a distribution of scores in which most fall near the mean, or average, with a symmetrically smaller number of scores appearing the farther we go above or below the mean. A frequency plot of a **normal distribution** produces a bell-shaped curve. For example, Figure 14.2 shows a frequency distribution from a test with a mean score of 50. Each × indicates one student who got a particular score; there are 10 ×'s at 50, so we know that 10 students got this score. Nine students got 49s and nine got 51s, and so on, and very few students made scores above 60 or below 40. Normal distributions like the one shown in Figure 14.2 are common in nature; for example, height and weight are normally distributed throughout the general adult population. Standardized tests are designed so that extremely few students will get every item or no item correct, so scores on them are typically normally distributed.

Standard Deviation   One important concept related to normal distributions is the **standard deviation,** a measure of the dispersion of scores. The standard deviation is, roughly speaking, the average amount that scores differ from the mean. For example, consider these two sets of scores:

Set *A*		Set *B*
85		70
70		68
65	< Mean >	65
60		62
45		60
Standard deviation: 14.6		Standard deviation: 4.1

Note that both sets have the same mean (65) but that otherwise they are quite different, Set *A* being more spread out than Set *B*. This is reflected in the fact that

normal distribution
A bell-shaped symmetrical distribution of scores in which most scores fall near the mean, with progressively fewer occurring as the distance from the mean increases.

standard deviation
A statistical measure of the degree of dispersion in a distribution of scores.

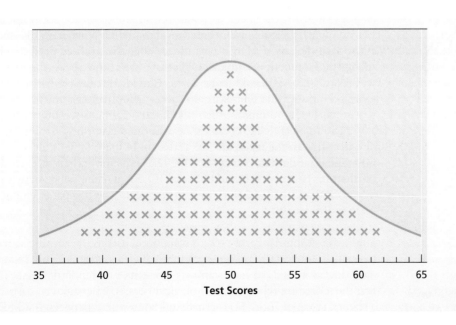

FIGURE 14.2
Frequency of Scores Forming a Normal Curve
If 100 people take a test and the score for each is marked by an x on a graph, the result could suggest a normal curve. In a normal distribution, most scores are at or near the mean (in this case, 50), and the number of scores progressively decreases farther from the mean.

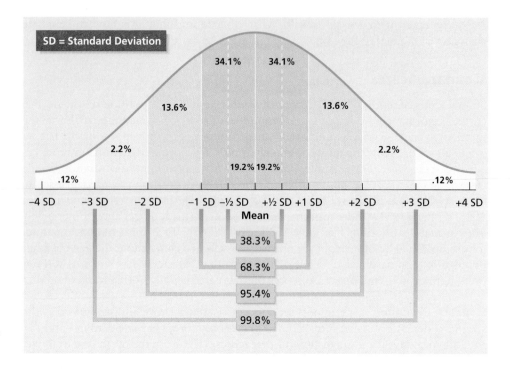

FIGURE 14.3
Standard Deviation

When test scores are normally distributed, knowledge of how far a given score lies from the mean in terms of standard deviations indicates what percentage of scores are higher and lower.

"Mr. Rodriguez, I can't make it in today to give the state tests. I'm feeling two standard deviations below the mean!"

Set *A* has a much larger standard deviation (14.6) than does Set *B* (4.1). The standard deviation of a set of scores indicates how spread out the distribution will be. Furthermore, when scores or other data are normally distributed, we can predict how many scores will fall a given number of standard deviations from the mean. This is illustrated in Figure 14.3, which shows that in any normal distribution, about 34 percent of all scores fall between the mean and one standard deviation above the mean (+1 SD), and a similar number fall between the mean and one standard deviation below the mean (–1 SD). If you go out two standard deviations from the mean, about 95 percent of the scores are included.

Scores on standardized tests are often reported in terms of how far they lie from the mean as measured in standard deviation units. For example, IQ scores are normed so that there is a mean of 100 and a standard deviation of 15. This means that the average person will score 100, someone scoring one standard deviation above the mean will score 115, someone scoring one standard deviation below will score 85, and so on. Therefore, in theory about 68 percent of all IQ scores (that is, a little more than two-thirds) fall between 85 (–1 SD) and 115 (+1 SD). SAT scores are also normed according to standard deviations, with the mean for the Verbal and Quantitative scales set at 500 and a standard deviation of 100. That puts more than two-thirds of all scores between 400 and 600. For IQ, 95 percent will be between 70 (–2 SD) and 130 (+2 SD); for the SAT scale, the comparable range is from 300 to 700.

Stanines   A standard score that is sometimes used is the **stanine score** (from the words <u>standard</u> <u>nine</u>). Stanines have a mean of 5 and a standard deviation of 2, so each stanine represents 0.5 standard deviation. Stanine scores are reported as whole numbers, so a person who earned a stanine score of 7 (+1 SD) actually fell somewhere between 0.75 SD and 1.25 SD above the mean.

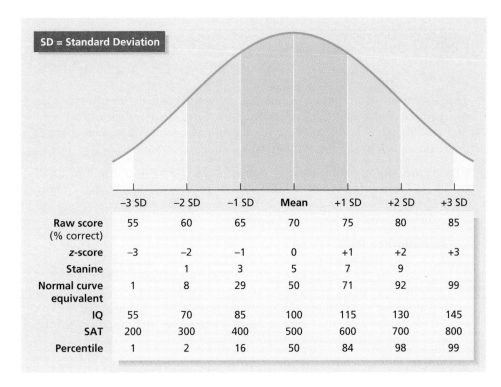

	−3 SD	−2 SD	−1 SD	Mean	+1 SD	+2 SD	+3 SD
SD = Standard Deviation							
Raw score (% correct)	55	60	65	70	75	80	85
z-score	−3	−2	−1	0	+1	+2	+3
Stanine		1	3	5	7	9	
Normal curve equivalent	1	8	29	50	71	92	99
IQ	55	70	85	100	115	130	145
SAT	200	300	400	500	600	700	800
Percentile	1	2	16	50	84	98	99

FIGURE 14.4
Relationships among Various Types of Scores
Raw scores that are normally distributed can be reported in a variety of ways. Each reporting method is characterized by its mean, by the range between high and low scores, and by the standard deviation interval.

Normal Curve Equivalents   Another form of a standard score that is sometimes used is the **normal curve equivalent** (NCE). A normal curve equivalent can range from 1 to 99, with a mean of 50 and a standard deviation of approximately 21. NCE scores are similar to percentiles, except that intervals between NCE scores are equal (which is not the case with percentile scores). Another standard score, used more often in statistics than in reporting standardized test results, is the **z-score,** which sets the mean of a distribution at 0 and the standard deviation at 1. Figure 14.4 shows how a set of normally distributed raw scores with a mean percent correct of 70 percent and a standard deviation of 5 would be represented in z-scores, stanines, normal curve equivalents, percentile scores, and equivalent IQ and SAT scores.

Note the difference in the figure between percentile scores and all standard scores (z-score, stanine, NCE, IQ, and SAT). Percentile scores are bunched up around the middle of the distribution, because most students score near the mean. This means that small changes in raw scores near the mean can produce large changes in percentiles (percentages of students below the score). In contrast, changes in raw scores that are far above or below the mean make a smaller difference in percentiles. For example, an increase of 5 points on the test from 70 to 75 moves a student from the 50th to the 84th percentile, an increase of 34 percentile points; but 5 more points (from 75 to 80) increases the student's percentile rank by only 14 points. At the extreme, the same 5-point increase, from 80 to 85, results in an increase of only 1 percentile point, from 98 to 99.

This characteristic of percentile ranks means that changes in percentiles should be interpreted cautiously. For example, one teacher might brag, "My average kids increased 23 percentile points [from 50 to 73], while your supposedly smart kids gained only 15 percentile points [from 84 to 99]. I really did a great job with them!" In fact, the bragging teacher's students gained only 3 points in raw score, or 0.6 standard deviations, while the other teacher's students gained 10 points in raw score, or 2 standard deviations!

stanine score

A type of standardized score ranging from 1 to 9, having a mean of 5 and a standard deviation of 2.

normal curve equivalent

A set of standard scores ranging from 1 to 99, having a mean of 50 and a standard deviation of about 21.

z-score

A standard score having a mean of 0 and a standard deviation of 1.

Theory into **PRACTICE**

Interpreting Standardized Test Scores

This section presents a guide to interpreting test reports for one widely used standardized test of academic performance, the Terra Nova, published by CTB/McGraw-Hill (1997). Other widely used nationally standardized tests (such as the CAT, the Iowa, and the Stanford) use similar report formats.

Class record sheet. Figure 14.5 on pages 514–515 shows portions of an actual Terra Nova (CTBS/5) pre/post class record sheet for children (whose names have been changed) in a Title I second-grade reading class. The main information on the form is as follows.

Identification Data
Look first at the top of the form. It identifies the tests taken at the end of the previous year (pre) and at the end of the current year (post). The grade (2.7) indicates that at the time of post-testing, students were in month seven of second grade (April; September is month zero). Information at the bottom left shows testing dates, school, district, test norm, and "quarter month" (i.e., weeks since school began).

Scores
Under each column, test scores are shown in two metrics. NP refers to national percentiles; NCE, to normal curve equivalent. For example, look at the fifth child, Marvin Miller. At the end of first grade, his national percentile score in reading was 49, indicating that he scored better than 49 percent of all first-graders. By second grade, his percentile score had increased to 76. In NCEs, however, he increased from 49 to 65. The test form shows a gain of 16 NCEs; NCE scores can be added and subtracted, because they are on an equal interval scale, whereas percentile scores cannot. Now look at the second student, Brittany Duphily. In reading, her percentile scores (and NCEs) dropped from first to second grade. Does this mean that she knows less in second grade than she did in first? Not at all. However, she did perform less well in second grade compared to other second-graders. To understand this, consider a girl who is the third fastest runner in the fourth grade, but a year later is the twelfth fastest in the fifth grade. The girl has not slowed down, and probably can run faster than before, but other runners are making better progress.

Summary
At the bottom of the form is a summary of the test scores for second-graders in the entire district (a class or school summary would look the same). The scores are presented as median percentiles (the score of the middle child in the district) and the national percentile of the median, which indicates how well the district is doing among all districts. In this district, for example, the middle second-grader is scoring better than 35.3 percent of all second-graders in reading. The last set of numbers shows the mean NCEs for all second-graders and the difference between first-grade NCEs (42.5) and second-grade NCEs (41.6). The difference, a loss of 0.9 NCEs, is very small, essentially indicating that children in this district score at about the

same reading level in first and second grades, in comparison to children in other districts.

Individual profile report. Like most standardized tests, the Terra Nova provides a detailed analysis of the test performance of each child. Figure 14.6 (page 516) shows an example for a third-grader, Maria Olthof (a real report, but not her real name). The form gives the following information:

Norm-Referenced Scores

At the top of the report is a list of Maria's scores on 14 scales listed six ways. The first is grade equivalent. In reading, Maria's grade equivalent is 2.0, indicating that her score is like that which would be obtained by an average child just starting second grade. Her NCE of 35 also indicates that she is performing significantly below grade level. (In general, an NCE of 50 is considered "at grade level.") Skip over scale score, which is not interpretable. Maria's local percentile indicates that she is reading extremely poorly in comparison to other children in her class, school, or district (however "local" was defined). A percentile of 1 is the lowest possible score.

Number correct is self-explanatory. In reading, Maria's national percentile indicates that she is scoring better than only 24 percent of all third-graders in the United States. "NP range" indicates the likely range of national percentile scores that Maria might receive if she took the same test many times. That is, there is always a range of scores a student might get, depending on luck, inadvertent errors, testing conditions, motivation, and so on—all factors that could vary each time a student took a test even if his or her level of knowledge or skill stayed the same. The chart on the upper right shows this national percentile range with a diamond indicating the actual percentile score. The shading between the 25th and 75th percentiles indicates the "normal range"; Maria's reading score is below that range, although her own "NP range" suggests that on a very good day she might score within the normal range.

Note that at the bottom of the national percentile chart is a scale indicating stanines. Recall that stanine scores range from 1 to 9, with a score of 5 indicating the national average.

Performance on Objectives

The remainder of the individual profile report breaks Maria's test down into subskills in each area. This breakdown can provide some useful information to explain overall scores. For example, look at Maria's mathematics scores. She scores very well on an "objectives performance index" in every subscale of math but one: problem solving. For Maria, this one low score could be due to her reading problems; or she might need additional work with this skill. However, subscale analyses of this kind should be interpreted very cautiously. The small number of items involved and the lack of a clear connection to the material Maria is studying mean that classroom assessments, perhaps supplemented by more fine-tuned diagnostic tests in mathematics, would give a much better indicator of Maria's strengths, weaknesses, and instructional needs.

CERTIFICATION POINTER

For your teacher certification test you may need to be able to select, construct, and use assessment strategies and instruments appropriate to the learning outcomes being evaluated.

PRE-POST CLASS RECORD SHEET
CLASS: GRD.2 TCH 3

PRE-TEST: CTBS/5 MA
POST-TEST: CTBS/5 MA

GRADE 2.7

TITLE 1 READING

STUDENTS / FORM-LEVEL	SCORES	READ	VOCAB	READING CMPST	LANG	MECH	LANGUAGE CMPST	MATH	COMPU	MATHEMATICS CMPST	TOTAL SCORE ++	SCI	SOCIAL STDY	SPELL	WORD ANLYS
BEACHY JULIA M BIRTH DATE: 5/ 4/90	PRE NP	98			94			76			94				
PRE GRADE: 1.7 A-11	POST NP	55			81			62			70				
POST GRADE: 2.7 A-12	PRE NCE	94			83			65			82				
CODES/PRE: 3916720000......:....	POST NCE	53			69			57			61				
CODES/POST: 391672......1:.....	DIFF	-41			-14			-8			-21				
DUPHILY BRITTN D BIRTH DATE: 9/25/90	PRE NP	79			70			88			82				
PRE GRADE: 1.7 A-11	POST NP	53			58			70			62				
POST GRADE: 2.7 A-12	PRE NCE	67			61			74			70				
CODES/PRE: 6613080000......:....	POST NCE	52			54			61			57				
CODES/POST: 661308......1:.....	DIFF	-15			-7			-13			-13				
HARRISON ROBERT L BIRTH DATE: 5/23/90	PRE NP	44			30			19			28				
PRE GRADE: 1.7 A-11	POST NP	63			34			42			46				
POST GRADE: 2.7 A-12	PRE NCE	47			39			32			37				
CODES/PRE: 4039710000......:....	POST NCE	57			41			46			48				
CODES/POST: 403971......1:.....	DIFF	10			2			14			11				
KNOX CARLY M BIRTH DATE: 7/ 9/90	PRE NP	99			*99			99			99				
PRE GRADE: 1.7 A-11	POST NP	84			64			56			71				
POST GRADE: 2.7 A-12	PRE NCE	99			99			99			99				
CODES/PRE: 8441620000......:....	POST NCE	71			57			53			62				
CODES/POST: 844162......1:.....	DIFF	-28			-42			-46			-37				
MILLER MARVIN R BIRTH DATE: 5/11/90	PRE NP	49			85			70			73				
PRE GRADE: 1.7 A-11	POST NP	76			86			39			71				
POST GRADE: 2.7 A-12	PRE NCE	49			72			61			63				
CODES/PRE: 2905390000......:....	POST NCE	65			73			44			62				
CODES/POST: 290539......1:.....	DIFF	16			1			-17			-1				
MOORE RICHAR J BIRTH DATE: 8/26/90	PRE NP	58			66			86			75				
PRE GRADE: 1.7 A-11	POST NP	54			76			80			72				
POST GRADE: 2.7 A-12	PRE NCE	54			59			73			64				
CODES/PRE: 352384......:....	POST NCE	52			65			68			63				
CODES/POST: 352384......1:.....	DIFF	-2			6			-5			-1				

SCHOOL: SCHOOL 1
DISTRICT: ANY DISTRICT
CITY: ANY CITY
STATE: CA

PRE-TEST DATE: 4/14/97
  QUARTER MONTH: 31
  NORMS: CTBS/5 1996
  PATTERN (IRT)

POST-TEST DATE: 4/22/98
  QUARTER MONTH: 31
  NORMS: CTBS/5 1996
  PATTERN (IRT)

++ TOTAL SCORE CONSISTS OF READING, LANGUAGE, MATHEMATICS

NP: NATIONAL PERCENTILE
NCE: NORMAL CURVE EQUIVALENT
DIFF: DIFFERENCE (POST-SCORE MINUS PRE-SCORE)
    DIFFERENCES ARE NOT REPORTED FOR NATIONAL PERCENTILES

*: MAXIMUM OR MINIMUM SCORE

CTBID: 982680273549001-03-00094-000051

FIGURE 14.5
Sample Class Record Sheet for a Standardized Test

When a class of students takes a standardized test as a pre-test and a post-test, the results may be compared by means of a form similar to the one shown here.

Published by CTB/McGraw-Hill, 20 Ryan Ranch Road, Monterey, CA 93940-5703. Copyright © 1986 by McGraw-Hill, Inc. All rights reserved. Reproduced with permission of CTB/McGraw-Hill LLC.

PRE-POST CLASS RECORD SHEET

DISTRICT: ANY DISTRICT

PRE-TEST: CTBS/5 MA
POST-TEST: CTBS/5 MA

TITLE 1 READING

GRADE 2

DISTRICT SUMMARY

SCORES	READING			LANGUAGE			MATHEMATICS			TOTAL SCORE ++	SCI	SOCIAL STDY	SPELL	WORD ANLYS
	READ	VOCAB	CMPST	LANG	MECH	CMPST	MATH	COMPU	CMPST					
PRE MDNP	40.4			39.2			34.3			33.0				
POST MDNP	35.3			32.5			36.3			34.0				
PRE NPMN	36			39			36			36				
POST NPMN	35			35			38			36				
PRE MNCE	42.5			44.0			42.5			42.5				
POST MNCE	41.6			42.1			43.4			42.3				
DIFF	-0.9			-1.9			0.9			-0.2				
** NUMBER OF STUDENTS = 95	91			91			93			90				

PRE-TEST FORM/LEVEL
A-11

POST-TEST FORM/LEVEL
A-12

++ TOTAL SCORE CONSISTS OF READING, LANGUAGE, MATHEMATICS

MDNP: MEDIAN NATIONAL PERCENTILE
NPMN: NATIONAL PERCENTILE OF MEAN NORMAL CURVE EQUIVALENT
MNCE: MEAN NORMAL CURVE EQUIVALENT
DIFF: DIFFERENCE (POST-SCORE MINUS PRE-SCORE)
      DIFFERENCES ARE NOT REPORTED FOR NATIONAL PERCENTILES

**: SUMMARIES DO NOT INCLUDE
    STUDENTS WHO WERE RETAINED
    OR WHO SKIPPED A GRADE

PRE-TEST DATE: 4/14/97
  QUARTER MONTH: 31
  NORMS: CTBS/5 1996
  PATTERN (IRT)
POST-TEST DATE: 4/22/98
  QUARTER MONTH: 31
  NORMS: CTBS/5 1996
  PATTERN (IRT)

CITY: ANY CITY
STATE: CA

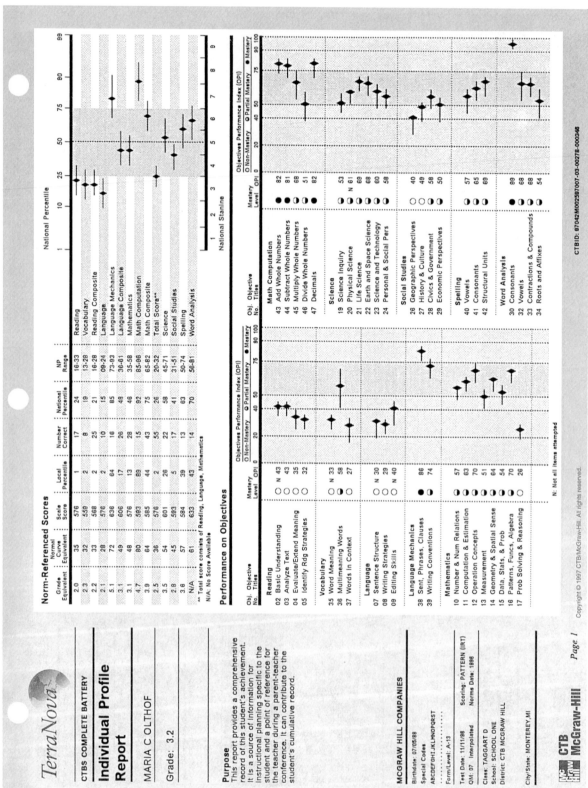

FIGURE 14.6

Sample Individual Test Record for a Standardized Test

Reports for individuals who take standardized tests may include overall scores and scores on specific content objectives.

WHAT ARE SOME ISSUES CONCERNING STANDARDIZED AND CLASSROOM TESTING?

The use of standardized tests to assess teachers, schools, and districts has increased dramatically in recent years. As noted earlier, all states now have statewide testing programs in which students at selected grade levels take criterion-referenced performance tests and/or standardized achievement tests. Education departments use scores on these tests to evaluate the state's educational program as a whole and to compare the performance of individual school districts, schools, and teachers. These comparisons go under the general heading of accountability programs. Accountability is one of several issues related to uses and abuses of standardized tests. Issues concerning testing, standards, and related topics are among the most hotly debated questions in U.S. education (Chatterji, 2002; Gallagher, 2003). In recent years there have been many developments and proposals for change in testing. These are discussed in the following sections.

validity
A measure of the degree to which a test is appropriate for its intended use.

content evidence
A measure of the match between the content of a test and the content of the instruction that preceded it.

Test Validity

We use test scores to make inferences about the students we are measuring. The **validity** of a test is the extent to which those inferences are justified (Aiken, 2003; McMillan, 2001). The types of evidence that are used to evaluate the validity of a test vary according to the test's purpose. For example, if a test is being selected to help teachers and administrators determine which students are likely to have some difficulty with one or more aspects of instruction, primary interest will be in how well the test predicts future academic performance. However, if the aim is to describe the current achievement levels of a group of students, primary interest will focus on the accuracy of that description. In short, validity deals with the relevance of a test for its intended purpose (Aiken, 2003).

Because of the various roles that tests are expected to play in schools and in the education process, three classes of evidence of validity are of concern to test users: content, criterion-related, and consequential.

Content Evidence of Validity The most important criterion for the usefulness of a test—especially an achievement test—is whether it assesses what the user wants it to assess (Popham, 2005; Shepard, 1993a). This criterion is called **content evidence.** Content evidence in achievement testing is an assessment of the degree of overlap between what is taught (or what should be taught) and what is tested. It is determined through careful comparison of the content of a test with state or district standards or with the objectives of a course or program. For example, if a test emphasized dates and facts in history but curricula and state or local standards emphasized key ideas of

These students will take nationwide standardized aptitude and achievement tests this year. Will the results be equally fair to them all? Why or why not?

CONNECTIONS

For more on using a table of specifications, see Chapter 13, page 459.

criterion-related evidence

A type of evidence about validity that exists when scores on a test are related to scores from another measure of an associated trait.

predictive evidence

A type of criterion-related evidence that exists when scores on a test are related to scores from a measure of a trait that the test could be used to predict.

readiness tests

Tests to assess a student's levels of the skills and knowledge necessary for a given activity.

concurrent evidence

A type of criterion-related evidence that exists when scores on a test are related to scores from another measure of the same or a very similar trait.

convergent evidence

A type of evidence about validity that exists when scores on a test are related to scores from one or more measures of other traits when educational or psychological theory about these traits predicts they should be related.

discriminant evidence

A type of evidence about validity that exists when scores on a test are unrelated to scores from one or more measures of other traits when educational or psychological theory about these traits predicts these traits should be unrelated.

reliability

A measure of the consistency of test scores obtained from the same students at different times.

history, the test could not be considered valid (Baker, 1994). A table of specifications provides excellent content evidence, as do the opinions of acknowledged experts that the domain of content covered on the test is consistent with its domain of objectives.

Criterion-Related Evidence of Validity   **Criterion-related evidence** is gathered by looking at relationships between scores on the test and other sets of scores. These are compared with expectations based on understandings about these various assessments. For example, **predictive evidence** of a test's validity might be a measure of its ability to help predict future behavior. If we are using a test to predict students' future school performance, one way to examine the test's validity is to relate the test scores to some measure of students' subsequent performance. If an appropriate level of correspondence exists between the test and later performance, the test can then be used to provide predictive information for students.

For example, test scores on SATs and ACTs have been shown to relate to a reasonable degree to performance in college; many college admissions officers therefore use these scores (along with high school grades and other information) in deciding which applicants to accept. Reading readiness tests and other school **readiness tests** are often used to route children into transitional first grades, extra-year kindergarten programs, and so on; this practice has come under fire in recent years, however, in large part because of the poor predictive evidence of validity of these measures (see Ellwein et al., 1991; Shepard, 1991).

Another criterion-related form is called **concurrent evidence** of validity. At issue is whether the test measures the same domain as another test. For example, if a group IQ test were to be substituted for an individual IQ test, one would first want to know whether they yielded comparable scores. By giving the two tests to the same students in a study, the relationship between their scores could be evaluated.

Both predictive and concurrent forms of evidence are called **convergent evidence** since the scores are expected to show clear relationships. Another form of concurrent evidence is called **discriminant evidence.** Achievement tests, for example, might be expected to show a *lack* of relationship with some variables. For example, a test of mechanical aptitude should relate to a test taker's ability to assemble a machine, but should *not* correlate too well with verbal aptitude, which is a different skill, or with gender, which has nothing to do with the skill being measured.

Test Reliability

Whereas validity relates to the skills and knowledge measured by a test, the **reliability** of a test relates to the accuracy with which these skills and knowledge are measured (Aiken, 2003). Test scores are supposed to result from the knowledge and skill of the students being measured. But when a test is administered, aspects related to both the test itself and the circumstances surrounding its administration could cause the results to be inaccurate. In theory, if a student were to take equivalent tests twice, he or she should obtain the same score both times. The extent to which this would not occur is the subject of reliability. Random features of the assessment such as ambiguous test items, differences in specific item content, lucky or unlucky guessing, inconsistent motivation, and anxiety all affect test scores and could cause results for different administrations of equivalent tests to differ. If it could be shown that individuals received similar scores on two administrations of the same test, then some confidence could be placed in the test's reliability. If the scores were greatly inconsistent, it would be difficult to place much faith in a particular test score. Generally, the longer the test and the more similar the items are to each other, the greater is the reliability.

Reliability is commonly measured using a coefficient that has a theoretical range from 0 to 1. The higher the number, the more reliable the test. In general, good standardized achievement tests should have coefficients in the .90 range or higher. The question of reliability might be thought of as how consistently the test measures something about students. Validity relates to the question of how meaningful a test score is for something we care about. Thus, a test cannot have validity without reliability, but a test can be reliable without being valid. As an example of reliability without validity, consider your reaction if your instructor assigned course grades on the basis of student height. He or she would have a highly reliable assessment (height can be determined quite accurately), but the scores would not be valid indicators of your knowledge or skill. On the other hand, imagine a test of creativity in which students were asked to describe innovative uses for a can opener. If raters could not agree on how to score students' responses, or if this test did not correlate with other plausible indicators of creativity, then the scale would lack reliability and therefore could not be considered valid.

Test Bias

Some major criticisms of traditional standardized tests relate to issues of validity and reliability (see Linn, 2000). Critics argue that such tests

- Give false information about the status of learning in the nation's schools (Bracey, 2003).
- Are unfair to (or biased against) some kinds of students (e.g., students from diverse backgrounds, those with limited proficiency in English, females, and students from low-income families) (see Lissitz & Schafer, 2002; Orfield & Kornhaber, 2001; Scheurich et al., 2000; Suzuki et al., 2000).
- Tend to corrupt the processes of teaching and learning, often reducing teaching to mere preparation for testing (Cizek, 1999; Darling-Hammond & Falk, 1997; Rotberg, 2001).
- Focus time, energy, and attention on the simpler skills that are easily tested and away from higher-order thinking skills and creative endeavors (Campbell, 2000; Popham, 2003).

One major issue in the interpretation of standardized test scores is the possibility of **bias** against students from low-income or diverse backgrounds (Lissitz & Schafer, 2002; Suzuki, Ponterotto, & Meller, 2000). In one sense, this is a question of test validity: A test that gave an unfair advantage to one or another category of student could not be considered valid. Of greatest concern is the possibility that tests could be biased because their items assess knowledge or skills that are common to one group or culture but not another. For example, a test that includes a reading comprehension passage about a trip to the beach could be biased against students who live far from a beach or cannot afford to travel to a beach. A passage about Halloween could be unfair to Jehovah's Witnesses, who do not celebrate Halloween.

Test publishers routinely assess bias in test items (called *item bias*). Items that exhibit lower (or higher) scores for student demographic groups (e.g., gender or race groups) than expected on the basis of the test as a whole are flagged for evaluation. These items are usually referred to a committee with representatives from a broad range of demographic groups, which is likely to exclude the item. A related issue is sensitivity. It should go without saying that test items with any kind of overt cultural or gender stereotyping should be rejected. For example, a test whose items always refer to doctors as "he" or give Hispanic names only to menial workers should not be used. Publishers of widely used tests almost always edit them in an effort to rule out cultural or gender bias, but tests should nevertheless be read carefully for possible stereotyping or other unfair elements.

CERTIFICATION POINTER

Your teacher certification test is likely to require you to understand assessment-related issues such as test validity, test reliability, bias, and scoring concerns.

bias

An undesirable characteristic of tests in which item content discriminates against certain students on the basis of socioeconomic status, race, ethnicity, or gender.

Teaching Dilemmas: Cases to Consider

INTASC   **8   Assessment of Student Learning**

Dealing with High-Stakes Testing

Jerry Natkin is beginning his seventh year of teaching English. Roscoe Carnes is beginning his fourth year as an art teacher. It is early September, and the two friends sit talking in the teachers' lounge of a high school in a medium-sized city.

Roscoe: What's on your agenda in the English department this year, Jerry? Any new plans or projects?

Jerry: Well, it may seem early to be worrying about this, but we're determined to do something about the standardized test results in this school.

Roscoe: What's the matter with them?

Jerry: The scores are still declining. We looked back over 10 years of results. On average, last year's students scored a couple of percentage points below the kids of 5 years ago and even farther below the scores from 10 years ago. I wonder if these kids just aren't learning.

Roscoe: Did you consider that they might be learning a lot but simply can't show what they know on standardized achievement tests?

Jerry: Maybe. But regardless, the issue is how to get the scores up. I think that in the English department, we should at least make sure that our courses are covering the content of the state standardized test. As I see it, with some changes in course content and classroom testing procedures, we can easily increase the school's overall average score and also our number of state finalists each year.

Roscoe: But, Jerry, that sounds like teaching to the test.

Jerry: It is. What's wrong with that?

Roscoe: Is it ethical? Should tests determine curriculum? Is doing well on standardized tests the reason kids go to school? Is testing fair to all students? Those tests contain cultural and class biases, you know. Anyway, the state exam is practically all multiple choice. If you teach to the exam, you run the risk of lowering your standards—minimums do have a way of becoming maximums. What about higher-order learning like problem solving and creative thinking?

Jerry: Higher-order thinking is always part of English, Roscoe. Don't worry! But I'm convinced we can include higher-order objectives and cover the test better. Also, we need to push the kids more.

Roscoe: How?

Jerry: I'd like to involve the parents. Get them to work with their kids at home, using sample test items and such. You know, kids who score higher on tests make better grades and do better in life. We've got to coach them.

Roscoe: I'd argue with you on that. How would you coach all the kids? Would it be fair to pick only some for special treatment? And what does "doing better in life" mean? Better income? Isn't there more to life than that?

Jerry: Sure, sure. Of course achievement tests aren't everything. And they aren't perfect either. But they're there, and we need them—for feedback! How else can we as teachers know what we've accomplished? We get to see kids make measurable progress.

Roscoe: But I don't think standardized tests are a good measure of students' actual abilities or meaningful knowledge. Maybe your scores tell you something about English proficiency, but I can't measure my kids' progress that way.

Jerry: I bet you could. You could measure creativity.

Roscoe: And then teach to the creativity test? Jerry, do you really think standardized test scores should be guiding your instructional goals as an English teacher?

Questions for Reflection

1. Using a problem-solving approach, address Jerry's concerns about declining test scores. How would you evaluate Jerry's plan to improve scores? Is it a good idea? Will it work? What could his department do to increase parents' involvement? How could students be coached?

2. Using a problem-solving approach, address Roscoe's concerns about overrelying on test scores. Do standardized tests lead to lower minimum standards? How could that be avoided? Where should the line be drawn; should achievement tests be used for diagnosis? For prediction? For placement? Why or why not? Can cultural and class biases be removed? How else could student achievement be measured? How else could teachers get feedback?

3. Model your solutions by adding one or more new characters and extending the dialogue in writing or role play.

Computer Test Administration

The use of computers to administer tests is becoming more common. In its simplest form, the same multiple-choice items (in the same order) are administered to students as they would take them if they sat for the typical, paper-and-pencil test. However, the use of a computer makes it possible to tailor the selection of items to the performance of the student. When this is done, the administration is called **computer-adaptive** (Wainer, 2000). Typically, a single item is administered first, and depending on whether the student was successful or unsuccessful, a harder or an easier item, respectively, is presented next. As the test progresses, a running estimate of the student's performance over the entire test is continually updated. This can result in real time savings; students can commonly take tests in under one-third the time for a paper-and-pencil administration with the same degree of accuracy. Also, computer-adaptive testing can zero in on a particular set of skills at the forward edge of what a student knows, giving more accurate information on those skills while avoiding wasting time on items that are very easy or impossible for the student.

> **ON THE WEB**
>
> For more on issues related to the principles of educational assessment go to the website of the National Council on Measurement in Education (NCME) at **www.ncme.org.**

Chapter Summary

What Are Standardized Tests and How Are They Used?

The term *standardized* describes tests that are uniform in content, administration, and scoring and therefore allow for the comparison of results across classrooms, schools, and school districts. Standardized tests such as the SAT and CTBS measure individual performance or ability against standards, or norms, that have been established for many other students in the school district, state, or nation for which each test was designed. Standardized test scores are used for selection and placement, such as grade promotion or college admission; for diagnosis and remediation; for evaluation of student proficiency or progress in content areas; and for evaluation of teaching strategies, teachers, and schools. No Child Left Behind is causing all states to make more extensive use of standardized tests. NCLB, and standardized testing in general, have raised much controversy.

What Types of Standardized Tests Are Given?

Aptitude tests, such as tests of general intelligence and multifactor batteries, predict students' general abilities and preparation to learn. IQ tests administered to individuals or groups attempt to measure individual aptitude in the cognitive domain. Achievement tests assess student proficiency in various subject areas. Diagnostic tests focus on specific subject matter to discover strengths or weaknesses in mastery. Norm-referenced testing interprets scores in comparison with the scores of other people who took the test, and criterion-referenced testing interprets scores based on fixed performance criteria.

How Are Standardized Tests Interpreted?

Scores that are derived from raw scores include percentiles, the percentage of scores in the norming group that fall below a particular score; grade equivalents, the grade and month at which a particular score is thought to represent typical performance; and standard scores, the students' performance in relation to the normal distribution of scores. Standard scores include stanines (based on the standard deviation of scores),

computer-adaptive
An approach to assessment in which a computer is used to present items and each item presented is chosen to yield the best new information about the examinee based on her or his prior responses to earlier items.

THE INTENTIONAL TEACHER

Using What You Know about Standardized Tests to Improve Teaching and Learning

Intentional teachers know that standardized tests can provide some—albeit limited—information about how teachers, schools, and students are performing. They can interpret standardized scores and use results from standardized tests for decision making. Intentional teachers rely on other assessment measures to complete the complicated picture of student learning.

❶ What do I expect my students to know and be able to do at the end of this lesson? How does this contribute to course objectives and to students' needs to become capable individuals?

Teachers do well to explore the role of standardized testing in their locale. Talk with experienced colleagues and your administrators to determine the extent to which standardized tests play a role in your professional practice. Ask about district and local expectations for your use of standardized tests. Imagine that after a lunchtime conversation with some experienced peers, you (a first-year teacher in this district) perceive a sense of urgency surrounding standardized testing in this district. Knowing that parents and community members are highly interested in year-end results, you might take some time to reflect on your own position on standardized testing. You might ask yourself, "To what extent do standardized tests measure what we value here? What information do standardized tests provide that can be useful to my school? How do we continue to

teach complex thinking and still help our students prepare for tests?" You might call your experienced colleagues and arrange a second lunch date to discuss your answers to tough questions such as these.

❷ What knowledge, skills, needs, and interests do my students have that must be taken into account in my lesson?

Teachers can use formal, standardized tests to provide information about their students' needs. Consider the use of diagnostic tests to identify learning problems and cognitive strengths. For example, imagine that Mindy reads at a level that appears to be far above that of her peers. She gives sophisticated analyses of the stories she reads, and although she is a willing learner, she sometimes appears bored with the curriculum. You might call the school psychologist to learn the procedure for obtaining formal testing to determine whether special services for students who are gifted and talented would be appropriate for Mindy.

❸ What do I know about the content, child development, learning, motivation, and effective teaching strategies that I can use to accomplish my objectives?

The assessments that teachers use should provide information about each of their students in several domains. Ask yourself

normal curve equivalents (based on a comparison of scores with the normal distribution), and z-scores (the location of scores above or below the mean).

What Are Some Issues Concerning Standardized and Classroom Testing?

Tests and test items must have validity, the quality of testing what is intended to be tested. Predictive validity means that the test accurately predicts future performance. Reliability means that test results are consistent when the test is administered at different places or times. Test bias in any form compromises validity. Other issues related to standardized testing include ethics in the content of tests, student preparation for testing, the uses of test scores, the relationship of tests to the curriculum, and computer administration of tests.

Key Terms

Research
Navigator.com

Review the following key terms from the chapter. Then, to explore research on these topics and how they relate to education today, connect to Research Navigator™ through this book's Companion Website or directly at www.researchnavigator.com.

INTASC **7 Instructional Planning Skills**   **9 Professional Commitment and Responsibility**
        8 Assessment of Student Learning

about one of your students—pick one at random—and consider how much you understand about this student's progress. Adjust your use of standardized tests, grades, and other assessment measures to provide more complete information about student learning. Although you might have taken a quick glance at each of your students' standardized scores from the previous year and you have your gradebook filled with letter grades at hand, you might still find yourself unable to give an accurate, trustworthy picture of many students' efforts to date. To round out your understanding of student learning, you could resolve to collect performance-based data through observations and attitudinal data through journal entries and interest inventories.

4 What instructional materials, technology, assistance, and other resources are available to help accomplish my objectives?

The public is increasingly interested in maintaining teachers' and schools' accountability. Check current sources such as your school's annual statement and newspaper reports to determine public perceptions of your success. To what extent do you consider public information a valid measure of schools' (and your!) success? Imagine that a recent newspaper article puts your mean students' district-wide performance at the 48th percentile. The headline of the article is "PLEASANT CITY'S SEVENTH-GRADERS SCORE WELL ON STANDARDIZED TESTS!" How should you interpret this?

5 How will I plan to assess students' progress toward my objectives?

Teachers should be careful consumers when using standardized measures. Check information related to the content, predictive, and construct validity of the tests employed in your district. Ask for information related to test bias. If the information booklet that accompanies the teacher's packet on the statewide test does not provide information about test bias, call the question hot line and ask how the authors have screened for bias against students from minority groups and students acquiring English.

6 How will I respond if individual children or the class as a whole are not on track toward success? What is my back-up plan?

If your students take a standardized test that has consequences for them (such as grade-to-grade promotion), make sure to examine test scores to make sure that they make sense. If a test score seems too low for a student who you see doing well in class, ask if the student can be retested, perhaps using a different test format.

Self-Assessment: Practicing for Licensure

Directions: The chapter-opening vignette addresses indicators that are often assessed in state licensure exams. Re-read the chapter-opening vignette, and then respond to the following questions.

1. Ms. Tranh speaks to Anita's parents about the many measures of achievement she has to assess Anita's academic ability. Which of the following types of assessment would Ms. Tranh use to predict Anita's future performance?

   a. placement test
   b. achievement test
   c. aptitude test
   d. diagnostic test

2. Which of the following interpretations would Ms. Tranh make if Anita were to score at the mean of a standardized test?

   a. percentile = 90, stanine = 0, z = 20
   b. NCE = 50, z = 0, percentile = 50
   c. GE = 7.2, stanine = 5, NCE = 45
   d. z = 1, NCE = 60, percentile = 50

3. Ms. Tranh tells Mr. and Mrs. McKay that Anita's grade equivalent score on the CAT is 6.9. What does this mean?

   a. Anita is almost ready for seventh-grade work.
   b. Anita found the test very easy.
   c. Anita has done as well as an end-of-year sixth-grader.
   d. Anita scored at the 6.9 percentile.

4. Ms. Tranh compares her students' scores on a math test with those of another class. She finds that the students' average score in both classes is 75, but the students in her class have scores that are much more spread out. This means that Ms. Tranh's results will have a larger

   a. mean.
   b. median.
   c. standard deviation.
   d. normal curve.

5. If Anita scored consistently on the CAT over multiple applications, it can be said that the test has

   a. predictive validity.
   b. content validity.
   c. construct validity.
   d. reliability.

6. Write a short essay describing the advantages and major criticisms of standardized tests.

7. What are the advantages and disadvantages of absolute grading and relative grading standards?

Appendix: Developing Your Portfolio

What Is a Portfolio?

A portfolio is not merely a file of course projects and assignments, nor is it a scrapbook of teaching memorabilia. A portfolio is an organized, goal-driven documentation of your professional growth and achieved competence in the complex act called teaching. Although it is a collection of documents, a portfolio is tangible evidence of the wide range of knowledge, dispositions, and skills that you possess as a growing professional. What's more, documents in the portfolio are self-selected, reflecting your individuality and autonomy.

There are actually two kinds of portfolios that you will be developing: a working portfolio and a presentation portfolio. A working portfolio is characterized by your ongoing systematic collection of selected work in courses and evidence of community activities. This collection would form a framework for self-assessment and goal setting. Later, you would develop a presentation portfolio by winnowing your collection to samples of your work that best reflect your achieved competence, individuality, and creativity as a professional educator.

What Is a Working Portfolio?   A working portfolio is always much larger and more complete than a presentation portfolio. It contains unabridged versions of the documents you have carefully selected to portray your professional growth. For example, it might contain entire reflective journals, complete units, unique teacher-made materials, and a collection of videos of your teaching. Working portfolios are often stored in a combination of computer disks, notebooks, and even boxes.

What Is a Presentation Portfolio?   A presentation portfolio is compiled for the expressed purpose of giving others an effective and easy-to-read portrait of your professional competence. A presentation portfolio is selective and streamlined because other people usually do not

Excerpted from Dorothy M. Campbell et al. (2001). *How to Develop a Professional Portfolio: A Manual for Teachers* (2nd ed.). Boston: Allyn & Bacon.

have the time to review all the material in your working portfolio. In making a presentation portfolio, you will find that less is more. For example, since you would be unlikely to take to an interview all your teacher-made learning materials, you might rely on photographs. Most reviewers would not want to assess several videos of your teaching but would be interested in one well-edited and annotated video. Sample pages from a large project would replace an entire project. The two types of portfolios differ in that all documents in a presentation portfolio should be preceded by an explanation of the importance or relevance of the document so that the reviewer understands the context of your work. Because it is important that a presentation portfolio not be cumbersome or unwieldy, we recommend the use of a notebook.

How Do I Organize My Portfolio?

There is one essential way in which working portfolios and presentation portfolios are alike. From their inception, both need to have a well-established organizational system. There is no one standard way to organize a portfolio, but to be effective it must have a system of organization that is understandable and meaningful to you and other educators. We suggest organizing your portfolio around a set of goals you are trying to achieve. This makes sense when one of your purposes for a portfolio is to demonstrate to others that you are achieving success in meeting standards set for excellence in the teaching profession.

Many professional organizations are setting goals for the teachers of the twenty-first century. These organizations include state departments of education, professional societies such as the National Association for the Education of Young Children or the National Council of Teachers of Mathematics, interagency groups, and university schools of education. The professional goals established by these organizations are called by a variety of names, including standards, principles, performance domains, outcomes, and competencies. They are all attempts to reflect the knowledge, skills, and dispositions that define excellent teachers and therefore are goals for you as a preservice teacher to achieve.

You should become familiar with a number of documents that outline sets of standards for your discipline, your state, and your own university department. As you study these standards, choose or adapt a set of goals that makes sense to you in your particular situation. Regardless of the goals or standards chosen, everything collected for your portfolio should be organized around the chosen goal statements.

What Evidence Should I Include in My Portfolio?

For every standard, you will include artifacts that demonstrate you have met this principle. An artifact is tangible evidence of knowledge that is gained, skills that are mastered, values that are clarified, or dispositions and attitudes that are characteristic of you. Artifacts cannot conclusively prove the attainment of knowledge, skills, or dispositions, but they provide indicators of achieved competence. For example, lesson and unit plans are pieces of evidence that might provide strong indication of your ability to plan curriculum or use a variety of teaching strategies. A video of your teaching might be a convincing indicator of your ability to manage and motivate a group of students. The same artifact may document more than one standard. At first, many artifacts will be collected. Later, artifacts will be selectively placed within each of the standards. Those artifacts that represent your growth and very best professional work should be included as evidence in your professional portfolio. Ask yourself: Would I be proud to have my future employer and peer group see this? Is this an example of what my future professional work might look like? Does this represent what I stand for as a professional educator? If not, what can I do to revise or rearrange so that it represents my best efforts?

Who Is the Audience for My Portfolio?

Information contained in the portfolio will be of interest to individuals who will be assessing your performance and measuring your accountability. While a student, your portfolio will be reviewed by your university faculty and advisors. Moreover, your portfolio will be an excellent way for you to introduce yourself to cooperating teachers and administrators during field experiences and student teaching. During job interviews, your portfolio is likely to be reviewed by superintendents, principals, teachers, and in some cases even school board members. As you begin your teaching career, your portfolio will be a helpful vehicle for mentors, in-service education

coordinators, and other colleagues. In some school districts, a portfolio will be relied on by supervisory staff charting ongoing career development or making tenure and promotion decisions. There is also a good possibility that your portfolio will one day be used to facilitate licensing by professional organizations, state agencies, or national consortiums. Most importantly, the portfolio provides you, the author, with an informative and accurate picture of your professional development and growth.

What Are Some Artifact Possibilities?

Article Summaries or Critiques   You may have written a summary or evaluation of an article from a professional journal as a class assignment. When including these in your portfolio, choose critiques that address the desired topic very specifically. The title of the article should be reflective of a chosen standard, making an obvious connection. This document is especially helpful if your professor has made positive remarks about your work and these remarks are about the outcome you wish to document.

The article summary or critique may show your ability to analyze any number of teaching skills. For example, suppose you critiqued an article titled "Getting Parents Involved in Their Children's Education." If you discussed your own ideas about parent involvement in your critique, this document may be able to reflect your knowledge of school-home-community cooperation.

Assessments   Any forms of assessment you have used or developed to measure child performance would be included in this type of document. Examples of assessments are performance tasks, portfolios, teacher-written tests, informal observations or notes, evaluations from lesson plans, formative assessment notes or charts, and summative charts of student developmental levels. You may want to include the actual assessment instrument you have written, with the children's work on it, if applicable (only one copy is necessary). In addition, you may include notes in a personal journal from observations made during the administration of a standardized test. Your ability to assess children's performance, diagnose progress, and use tests wisely is reflected in this document. In addition, your understanding of child development may be evident.

Awards and Certificates   Copies of letters, awards, or certificates that verify your outstanding contribution to the field of education fit in this category. These could include honors conferred, memberships in honorary professional organizations, community recognition, and volunteer recognition. Your professional commitment is reflected in these types of documents.

Bulletin Board Ideas After creating a bulletin board, make a copy of your design or take a photograph of the board. Make sure all spelling, punctuation, and grammar are standard English. This document can be used to show your ability to think creatively, use materials in interesting ways, or motivate students.

Case Studies A case study is a thorough examination of a student's growth over a period of time. When using this as a document, make sure the student is anonymous. Generally, case studies are quite long; therefore, you may want to include a specific part of the paper for documentation of a standard. Your knowledge of child development as well as your observation skills may be evident in this document.

Classroom Management Philosophy This is a written summary of your philosophy of classroom management. Make sure to cite the research and theories that have guided you in the way you influence student behavior and encourage development of self-control. Classroom management skills and knowledge of human development are evident in this document.

Computer Programs This includes examples of various programs you have utilized, developed, or incorporated in your teaching that provide evidence of your ability to use materials in a challenging and appropriate way to encourage active learning.

Also appropriate are programs that demonstrate your ability to conduct online searches and research. Examples include ERIC, Education Index, and Internet programs that link teachers worldwide. You can document your abilities by providing the hard copies of these searches along with an explanation of the reason for your computer searches. These documents reflect your willingness to seek further professional growth.

Cooperative Learning Strategies Have you planned or taught a lesson using a cooperative learning technique? Cooperative learning is a method of teaching in which students work collaboratively in small groups to solve a problem. This type of group work must be obvious in your lesson. You may want to include a copy of the lesson plan and, if the lesson was actually taught, a statement assessing the effectiveness of the cooperative learning technique. This will document your ability to use cooperative learning as a strategy as well as your ability to manage and motivate a class of students.

Curriculum Plans These documents are written plans, or programs, or both designed to organize curriculum. Your curriculum plans can reflect all experiences you have developed for the child while engaged in the process of schooling. Examples may include lesson plans, units, thematic units, learning centers, extracurricular programs, or school–community ventures. These documents portray your instructional planning skills or your ability to use many and varied instructional strategies.

Essays You can use papers from education courses, English composition, or any other class in which you were required to write an essay. Examine the topic you addressed in your paper to be sure its main idea reflects one of the standards you are using.

Goal Statements Professional goals are based on your needs, interests, philosophy of education, and perception of your role as a teacher. Goal statements assist you in determining where you want to be and provide you with information about how to get there.

Think about the important results you should accomplish in your role as a teacher and record these as goal statements. Remember that any short-term goals you establish should be tied to the longer-term goals you have identified in conjunction with your philosophy of education. Periodically review and evaluate your accomplishments in relation to your goal statements. You may wish to list your accomplishments associated with each goal. You will establish new goals as you refine your philosophy of education, your role as a teacher, and your expectations. It is important to keep your list of goal statements current. These statements might appear at the beginning of your portfolio or as documentation of your professional commitment.

Individualized Plans Children with special needs sometimes need tasks to be structured in ways that will allow them to use their strengths and compensate for their specific learning difficulties. Ways in which lesson and unit plans have been adapted for specific students should be documented. Make sure the learning need is defined and clearly addressed. This artifact could document your skills in meeting individual needs, your instructional strategies skills, and your knowledge of child development.

Journals You may have kept journals during field classes or observation assignments. Include them if they address your observations of students as they relate to the desired standard. If necessary, highlight the appropriate sections of the journals. Make sure dates and times are included but not the names of schools or teachers visited.

Lesson Plans   Copies of your lesson plans should include all components of a workable plan: objectives, materials, introduction, procedures, closing, and evaluation.

Sometimes plans may be used for more than one standard. In this case, highlight the specific part of the plan that documents the standard. Your ability to execute instructional planning and to use a variety of instructional strategies will be most obviously documented with lesson plans; however, it is possible that knowledge of content, use of environments and materials, communication skills, and knowledge of human development could be documented here.

Media Competencies   This type of document includes evidence and descriptions of the various forms of media you are able to incorporate in your instruction. This could include teaching resources such as the slide projector, camcorder and VCR, overhead projector, 16mm projector, computers and printers, interactive video, laser discs, and cable and electronic (educational) television.

You will also want to include evidence of your ability to incorporate technology into the classroom. Examples of how you have used e-mail, remote databases, and distance learning equipment to research and to communicate with students and colleagues regionally, nationally, and internationally should be highlighted. A printout or floppy disk of your Internet address(es), listing of professional online news group and listserv memberships you hold, and examples of printed texts will provide documentation of your ability to share and retrieve information via the Internet.

Projects   Projects can include any type of assignment that involved problem solving, group presentations, creating materials, investigating phenomena in classrooms, or researching current information. In a presentation portfolio, include paper copies only and make photographs of anything too large to fit in a notebook. If this is a group project, make that clear but indicate the extent of your input. (Be careful about this one; it is not helpful to brag about doing all the work.)

The documentation possibilities of this artifact depend on the project. Examine the standards to determine whether the project reflects instructional planning skills, professional commitment, the ability to meet individual needs, or knowledge of content.

References   References might include statements, evaluations, or both, from your supervisors of your academic work, experiences in the classroom, other work experience with children, or outside employment.

Try to connect the reference with one of your selected standards. For instance, the reference might de-

scribe a lesson you taught in a field course or in student teaching. You could use this document to illustrate your competence in the area of instructional strategies. In addition, you may want to place reference letters from your cooperating teachers in a special tabbed section of the portfolio.

Research Papers   When selecting a research paper to include in your portfolio, you will need to consider several factors. The content of the research paper might make it appropriate for inclusion under a particular standard. It might, for instance, highlight your knowledge of an academic subject.

Subscriptions   If you subscribe to a journal that specifically addresses the standard in its title, include a copy of the cover of the journal, along with the address label showing your name. You might also briefly mention any ideas, instructional techniques, or other helpful information you gathered from reading the journal. Generally, professional commitment is well documented with subscriptions; however, you may find other standards to document with this artifact, depending on the type of journal to which you subscribe.

Teacher-Made Materials   These materials may include games, manipulatives, puppets, big books, charts, videotapes, films, photographs, transparencies, teaching aids, costumes, posters, or artwork. Because many of these items are cumbersome, include only paper copies or photographs of the materials. If you do not have copies of the actual materials you have made, you may want to highlight sections of a well-designed lesson plan that show how you would use creative teaching materials. Materials that support learning theory and were designed to suit this purpose are most helpful. Your materials should reflect your ability to encourage active learning and a variety of instructional strategies.

Transcripts   A copy of your official transcript can be used in a variety of ways. You may wish to use it to document your knowledge in subject areas such as chemistry, geography, or education courses. Highlight the courses and the grade you wish to document. Include a brief, typewritten explanation of why this transcript is included. You may even include other information, such as a syllabus from the course that you have highlighted, to show that you have taken essay or other types of tests on the subject.

Unit Plans   A unit plan is an integrated plan for instruction on a topic developed over several days or even weeks. Often, units are developed within a discipline, and lessons are organized to build on knowledge acquired in previous lessons. Unit plans generally include purposes, objectives, content outlines, activities, instructional resources, and evaluation methods. (Interdisciplinary units have been described under the entry called Theme Studies.) Unit plans are particularly good for documenting your ability to use a variety of instructional strategies and instructional planning skills.

Volunteer Experience Descriptions This document might include a list and brief description of volunteer experiences and services provided to the school and community. You should focus on how these activities have enhanced your abilities while providing a contribution to society. You should also emphasize the importance of maintaining positive school–community collabora-

tion through teacher, parent, and student interaction. Depending on what you learned from these experiences, make sure they address the standard under which you have placed this document.

Work Experience Descriptions These are statements you have written to describe work experiences. These might include work with students in both traditional and nontraditional settings and work for which you were compensated or that you performed on a voluntary basis. To be of most interest, these statements should include not only a summary of the setting and your responsibilities but also a reflective statement addressing the intangible aspects of the work experience. In writing these statements, be sure to address how these work experiences relate to the specific standard.

References

Abbott-Shim, M., Lambert, R., & McCarty, F. (2003). A comparison of school readiness outcomes for children randomly assigned to a Head Start program and the program's wait list. *Journal of Education for Students Placed at Risk, 8*(2), 191–214.

Aboud, F., & Fenwick, V. (1999). Exploring and evaluating school-based interventions to reduce prejudice. *Journal of Social Issues, 55*(4), 767–786.

Achilles, C. M., Finn, J. D., & Bain, H. P. (1997/98). Using class size to reduce the equity gap. *Educational Leadership, 55*(4), 40–43.

Adams, A., Carnine, D., & Gersten, R. (1982). Instructional strategies for studying content area texts in the intermediate grades. *Reading Research Quarterly, 18,* 27–53.

Adams, G. L., & Engelmann, S. (1996). *Research on Direct Instruction: 25 years beyond DISTAR.* Seattle, WA: Educational Achievement Systems.

Adams, J. L. (1974). *Conceptual blockbusting.* San Francisco: Freeman.

Adelman, N. E., Haslam, M. B., & Pringle, B. A. (1996). *The uses of time for teaching and learning.* Washington, DC: U.S. Department of Education.

AERA/APA/NCME. (1999). *The standards for educational and psychological testing.* Washington, DC: American Educational Research Association.

Aiken, L. R. (2000). *Psychological testing and assessment* (10th ed.). Boston: Allyn & Bacon.

Aiken, L. R. (2003). *Psychological testing and assessment* (11th ed.). Boston: Allyn & Bacon.

Airsian, P. W. (1994). *Classroom assessment* (2nd ed.). New York: McGraw Hill.

Airsian, P. W., & Walsh, M. E. (1997). Constructivist cautions. *Phi Delta Kappan, 78*(6), 444–449.

Alba, R. D. (1990). *Ethnic identity.* New Haven, CT: Yale University Press.

Alberto, P., & Troutman, A. (1999). *Applied behavior analysis for teachers* (5th ed.). Columbus, OH: Charles E. Merrill.

Alderman, M. K. (1990). Motivation for at-risk students. *Educational Leadership, 48*(1), 27–30.

Aleman, S. R. (1990). *Attention deficit disorder.* Washington, DC: Education and Public Welfare Division of the Congressional Research Service.

Alexander, G. A., Graham, S., & Harris, K. R. (1998). A perspective on strategy research: Progress and prospects. *Educational Psychology Review, 10*(2), 129–154.

Alexander, P. A. (1992). Domain knowledge: Evolving themes and emerging concerns. *Educational Psychologist, 27,* 33–51.

Alexander, P. A., & Jetton, T. L. (1996). The role of importance and interest in the processing of text. *Educational Psychology Review, 8*(1), 89–121.

Alexander, P. A., & Murphy, P. K. (1994, April). *The research base for APA's learning-centered psychological principles.* Paper presented at the annual meeting of the American Educational Research Association, San Francisco, CA.

Alexander, P. A., Kulikowich, J. M., & Jetton, T. L. (1994). The role of subject-matter knowledge and interest in the processing of linear and nonlinear texts. *Review of Educational Research, 64,* 201–252.

Alexander, P. A., Kulikowich, J. M., & Jetton, T. L. (1995). Interrelationship of knowledge, interest, and recall: Assessing a model of domain learning. *Journal of Educational Psychology, 87*(4), 559–575.

Alfassi, M. (1998). Reading for meaning: The efficacy of reciprocal teaching in fostering reading comprehension in high school students in remedial reading classes. *American Educational Research Journal, 35*(2), 309–332.

Algozzine, B., Browder, D., Karvonen, M., Test, D. W., & Wood, W. M. (2001). Effects of interventions to promote self-determination for individuals with disabilities. *Review of Educational Research, 71*(2), 219–277.

Allen, R. (2003). The democratic aims of service learning. *Educational Leadership, 60*(6), 51–54.

Allington, R. L., & McGill-Franzen, A. (1989). School response to reading failure: Instruction for Chapter 1 and special education students in grades two, four, and eight. *Elementary School Journal, 89*(5), 529–542.

Allington, R. L., & McGill-Franzen, A. (1992). Does high-stakes testing improve school effectiveness? *ERS Spectrum, 10*(2), 3–12.

Alvermann, D. E., et al. (1985). Prior knowledge activation and the comprehension of compatible and incompatible text. *Reading Research Quarterly, 20,* 420–436.

Ambert, A. M. (1997). *Parents, children, and adolescents: Interactive relationships and development in context.* New York: Haworth.

American Association of University Women. (1992). *How schools shortchange girls.* Washington, DC: Author.

American Psychiatric Association. (1994). *Diagnostic and statistical manual of mental disorders* (4th ed.). Washington, DC: Author.

American Psychological Association. (1992). Working draft report of the APA Presidential Task Force on Psychology in Education.

American Psychological Association. (1997). *Learner-centered psychological principles: A framework for school redesign and reform.* Washington, DC: Author.

Ames, C. (1986). Effective motivation: The contribution of the learning environment. In R. S. Feldman (Ed.), *The social psychology of education.* Cambridge, England: Cambridge University Press.

Ames, C. (1992). Classrooms: Goals, structures, and student motivation. *Journal of Educational Psychology, 84,* 261–271.

Ames, C., & Archer, J. (1988). Achievement goals in the classroom: Students' learning strategies and motivation processes. *Journal of Educational Psychology, 80,* 260–267.

Amrein, A., & Berliner, D. (2003). The effects of high-stakes testing on student motivation and learning. *Educational Leadership, 60*(5), 32–38.

Anderman, E. M., Anderman, L. H., & Griesinger, T. (1999). The relation of present and possible academic selves during early adolescence to grade point average and achievement goals. *The Elementary School Journal, 100*(1), 3–18.

Anderman, E. M., Eccles, J. S., Yoon, K. S., Roeser, R., Wigfield, A., & Blumenfeld, P. (2001). Learning to value mathematics and reading: Relations to mastery and performance-oriented instructional practices. *Contemporary Educational Psychology, 26*(1), 76–95.

Anderson, J. (1994). *What do student grades mean? Differences across schools.* Washington, DC: U.S. Department of Education, Office of Educational Research and Improvement.

Anderson, J. R. (1985). *Cognitive psychology and its implications* (2nd ed.). San Francisco: Freeman.

Anderson, J. R. (1990). *Cognitive psychology and its implications* (3rd ed.). New York: Freeman.

Anderson, J. R. (1995). *Learning and memory: An integrated approach.* New York: Wiley.

Anderson, J. R., & Bower, G. (1983). *Human associative memory.* Washington, DC: Winston.

Anderson, J. R., Greeno, J. G., Reder, L. M., & Simon, H. (2000). Perspectives on learning, thinking, and activity. *Educational Researcher, 29*(4), 11–13.

Anderson, J. R., Reder, L. M., & Simon, H. A. (1996). Situated learning and education. *Educational Researcher, 25*(4), 5–11.

Anderson, L. M., Blumenfeld, P., Pintrich, P. R., Clark, C. M., Marx, R. W., & Peterson, P. (1995). Educational psychology for teachers: Reforming our courses, rethinking our roles. *Educational Psychologist, 30*(3), 143–157.

Anderson, L. M., Brubaker, N. L., Alleman-Brooks, J., & Duffy, G. G. (1985). A qualitative study of seatwork in first-grade classrooms. *Elementary School Journal, 86,* 123–140.

Anderson, L. M., Evertson, C. M., & Brophy, J. E. (1979). An experimental study of effective teaching in first-grade reading groups. *Elementary School Journal, 79,* 193–223.

Anderson, L. W., & Pellicer, L. O. (1990). Synthesis of research on compensatory and remedial education. *Educational Leadership, 48*(1), 10–16.

Anderson, L. W., & Sosniak, L. A. (Eds.). (1994). *Bloom's taxonomy: A forty-year perspective.* Chicago: University of Chicago Press.

Anderson, R. E., & Becker, H. J. (2001). School investments in instructional technology: Teaching, learning, and computing: 1998 survey (Rep. No. 8). Center for Research on Information Technology and Organizations, University of California, Irvine, and University of Minnesota.

Anderson, R. E., & Ronnkvist, A. (1999). *The presence of computers in American schools.* Irvine, CA: University of California, Center for Research on Information Technology and Organizations.

Anderson, T. H., & Armbruster B. B. (1984). Studying. In P. D. Pearson (Ed.), *Handbook of reading research.* New York: Longman.

Andrich, D., & Styles, I. (1994). Psychometric evidence of intellectual growth spurts in early adolescence. *Journal of Early Adolescence, 14*(3), 328–344.

Anthony, J. L., & Lonigan, C. J. (2004). The nature of phonological awareness: Converging evidence from four studies of preschool and early grade school children. *Journal of Educational Psychology, 96*(1), 43–55.

Antil, L., Jenkins, J., Wayne, S., & Vadasy, P. (1998). Cooperative learning: Prevalence, conceptualizations, and the relation between research and practice. *American Educational Research Journal, 35*(3), 419–454.

Archibald, D., & Newmann, F. (1988). *Beyond standardized testing: Authentic academic achievement in the secondary school.* Reston, VA: NASSP Publications.

Armstrong, T. (1994). *Multiple intelligences in the classroom.* Alexandria, VA: Association for Supervision and Curriculum Development.

Arnold, M. L. (2000). Stage, sequence, and sequels: Changing conceptions of morality, post-Kohlberg. *Educational Psychology Review, 12*(4), 365–383.

Aronson, E. A. (1995). *The social animal.* New York: Freeman.

Aronson, E., Blaney, N., Stephan, C., Sikes, J., & Snapp, M. (1978). *The jigsaw classroom.* Beverly Hills, CA: Sage.

Arter, J. A. (1991). *Using portfolios in instruction and assessment: State of the art summary.* Portland, OR: Northwest Regional Educational Laboratory.

Arter, J., & McTighe, J. (2001). *Scoring rubrics in the classroom.* Thousand Oaks, CA: Corwin.

Athanases, S. Z. (1994). Teachers' reports of the effects of preparing portfolios of literacy instruction. *The Elementary School Journal, 94*(4), 421–439.

Atkins, J., & Ellsesser, J. (2003). Tracking: The good, the bad, and the questions. *Educational Leadership, 61*(2), 44–47.

Atkinson, J. W. (1958). Towards experimental analysis of human motivation in terms of motive expectancies and incentives. In J. W. Atkinson (Ed.), *Motives in fantasy, action, and society*. Princeton, NJ: Van Nostrand.

Atkinson, J. W. (1964). *An introduction to motivation*. Princeton, NJ: Van Nostrand.

Atkinson, J. W., & Litwin, G. H. (1960). Achievement motive and test anxiety as motives to approach success and avoid failure. *Journal of Abnormal and Social Psychology, 60*, 52–63.

Atkinson, R. C., & Raugh, M. R. (1975). An application of the mnemonic keyword method to the acquisition of Russian vocabulary. *Journal of Experimental Psychology: Human Learning and Memory, 104*, 126–133.

Atkinson, R. C., & Shiffrin, R. M. (1968). Human memory: A proposed system and its component processes. In K. Spence & J. Spence (Eds.), *The psychology of learning and motivation*, Vol. 2. New York: Academic Press.

Atkinson, R. K., Derry, S. J., Renkl, A., & Wortham, D. (2000). Learning from examples: Instructional principles from the worked examples research. *Review of Educational Research, 70*(2), 181–214.

Atkinson, R. K., Levin, J. R., & Atkinson, L. A. (1998, April). *Mnemonic matrices for acquiring science facts and concepts: An illustration of applying through remembering*. Paper presented at the annual meeting of the American Educational Research Association, San Diego, CA.

Atkinson, R., Levin, J., Atkinson, L., Kiewra, K., Meyers, T., Kim, S., Renandya, W., & Hwang, Y. (1999). Matrix and mnemonic text-processing adjuncts: Comparing and combining their components. *Journal of Educational Psychology, 91*(2), 342–357.

Atwater, E. (1996). *Adolescence*. Upper Saddle River, NJ: Prentice-Hall.

August, D., & Hakuta, K. (1997). *Improving schooling for language-minority children: A research agenda*. Washington, DC: National Research Council.

Ausubel, D. P. (1963). *The psychology of meaningful verbal learning*. New York: Grune and Stratton.

Ausubel, D. P. (1978). In defense of advance organizers: A reply to the critics. *Review of Educational Research, 48*, 251–258.

Ausubel, D. P., & Youssef, M. (1963). Role of discriminability in meaningful parallel learning. *Journal of Educational Psychology, 54*, 331–336.

Aviram, A. (2000). From "computers in the classroom" to mindful radical adaptation by education systems to the emerging cyber culture. *Journal of Educational Change, 1*(4), 331–352.

Ayduray, J., & Jacobs, G. M. (1997). Can learner strategy instruction succeed? The case of higher order questions and elaborate responses. *System, 25*(4), 561–570.

Babad, E. (1993). Pygmalion—25 years after: Interpersonal expectancies in the classroom. In P. D. Blanck (Ed.), *Interpersonal expectations: Theory, research, and application* (pp. 125–152). Cambridge, England: Cambridge University Press.

Baddeley, A. (1999). *Essentials of human memory*. Philadelphia: Psychology Press.

Bahrick, H. P., & Hall, L. K. (1991). Lifetime maintenance of high school mathematics. *Journal of Experimental Psychology, 120*, 20–33.

Baillargeon, R., Graber, M., DeVos, J., & Black, J. (1990). Why do young infants fail to search for hidden objects? *Cognition, 36*, 255–284.

Bainer, D. L., & Wright, D. (1998, April). *Evaluating a constructivist professional development program to improve science teaching*. Paper presented at the annual meeting of the American Educational Research Association, San Diego, CA.

Baines, L., Baines, C., & Masterson, C. (1994). Mainstreaming: One school's reality. *Phi Delta Kappan, 76*(1), 39–40, 57–64.

Baker, E. L. (1994). Learning-based assessments of history understanding. *Educational Psychologist, 29*(2), 97–106.

Baker, S., Gersten, R., & Keating, T. (in press). When less may be more: A two-year longitudinal evaluation of a volunteer tutoring program requiring minimal training. *Reading Research Quarterly*.

Baker, S., Gersten, R., & Lee, D. S. (2002). A synthesis of empirical research on teaching mathematics to low-achieving students. *The Elementary School Journal, 103*(1), 51–73.

Balfanz, R., & Legters, N. (2004). *Locating the dropout crisis*. Baltimore, MD: Johns Hopkins University, Center for Social Organization of Schools.

Balfanz, R., & MacIver, D. (2000). Transforming high-poverty urban middle schools into strong learning institutions: Lessons from the first five years of the Talent Development Middle School. *Journal of Education for Students Placed at Risk, 5*(1 & 2), 137–158.

Bandalos, D. L., Yates, K., & Thorndike-Christ, T. (1995). Effects of math self-concept, perceived self-efficacy, and attributions for failure and success on test anxiety. *Journal of Educational Psychology, 87*(4), 611–623.

Bandura, A. (1965). Influence of models' reinforcement contingencies on the acquisition of imitative responses. *Journal of Personality and Social Psychology, 28*(2), 117–148.

Bandura, A. (1986). *Social foundations of thought and action: A social-cognitive theory*. Englewood Cliffs, NJ: Prentice-Hall.

Bandura, A. (1991). Social cognitive theory of self-regulation. *Organizational Behavior and High Performance, 50*, 248–287.

Bandura, A. (1997). *Self-efficacy: The exercise of control*. New York: Freeman.

Bangert-Drowns, R. L. (1993). The word processor as an instructional tool: A meta-analysis of word processing in writing instruction. *Review of Educational Research, 63*(1), 69–93.

Bangert-Drowns, R. L., Kulik, C. C., Kulik, J. A., & Morgan, M. (1991). The instructional effect of feedback in test-like events. *Review of Educational Research, 61*(2), 213–238.

Bangert-Drowns, R. L., Kulik, J. A., & Kulik, C. L. (1986, April). *Effects of frequent classroom testing*. Paper presented at the annual meeting of the American Education Research Association, San Francisco, CA.

Banks, J. A. (1993). *Multiethnic education: Theory and practice* (3rd ed.). Boston: Allyn & Bacon.

Banks, J. A. (1995). Historical development, dimensions, and practice. In J. A. Banks & C. A. M. Banks (Eds.), *Handbook of multicultural education.* New York: Macmillan.

Banks, J. A. (1995c). Multicultural education: Its effects on students' racial and gender role attitudes. In J. A. Banks & C. A. M. Banks (Eds.), *Handbook of multicultural education.* New York: Macmillan.

Banks, J. A. (1997). Multicultural education: Characteristics and goals. In J. A. Banks & C. A. M. Banks (Eds.), *Multicultural education: Issues and perspectives* (pp. 3–31). Boston: Allyn & Bacon.

Banks, J. A. (1999). *An introduction to multicultural education* (2nd ed.). Boston: Allyn & Bacon.

Banks, J. A. (2001). Multicultural education: Goals, possibilities, and challenges. In C. F. Diaz (Ed.), *Multicultural education in the 21st century.* New York: Longman.

Barber, R. M., & Kagey, J. R. (1977). Modification of school attendance for an elementary population. *Journal of Applied Behavior Analysis, 10,* 41–48.

Baron, R., Tom, D., & Cooper, H. (1985). Social class, race, and teacher expectations. In J. Duser (Ed.), *Teacher expectations.* Hillsdale, NJ: Erlbaum.

Barr, R. (1987). Content coverage. In M. J. Dunkin (Ed.), *International encyclopedia of teaching and teacher education.* New York: Pergamon.

Barr, R. D., & Parrett, W. H. (1995). *Hope at last for at-risk youth.* Boston: Allyn & Bacon.

Barr, R. D., & Parrett, W. H. (2001). *Hope fulfilled for at-risk and violent youth* (2nd ed.). Boston: Allyn & Bacon

Barr, R., & Dreeben, R. (1983). *How schools work.* Chicago: University of Chicago Press.

Barrish, H. H., Saunders, M., & Wolf, M. M. (1969). Good behavior game: Effects of individual contingencies for group consequences on disruptive behavior in a classroom. *Journal of Applied Behavior Analysis, 2,* 119–124.

Barth, R. (1979). Home-based reinforcement of school behavior: A review and analysis. *Review of Educational Research, 49,* 436–458.

Barton, P. (2003). *Parsing the achievement gap: Baselines for tracking progress.* Princeton, NJ: Educational Testing Service.

Bateman, B., & Linden, M. (1998). *Better IEPs* (3rd ed.). Longmont, CO: Sapris West.

Bates, E. A., & Elman, J. L. (2002). Connectionism and the study of change. In M. H. Johnson, Y. Munakata, & R. O. Gilmore (Eds.), *Brain development and cognition: A reader.* Malden, MA: Blackwell.

Battin-Pearson, S., Newcomb, M., Abbott, R., Hill, K., Catalano, R., & Hawkins, D. (2000). Predictors of early high school dropout: A test of five theories. *Journal of Educational Psychology, 92*(3), 568–582.

Battistich, V., Watson, M., Solomon, D., Lewis, C., & Schaps, E. (1999). Beyond the three R's: A broader agenda for school reform. *The Elementary School Journal, 99*(5), 415–432.

Battle, D. (1996). Language learning and use by African American children. *Topics in Language Disorders, 16,* 22–37.

Bauer, A. M., & Shea, T. M. (1999). *Inclusion 101: How to teach all learners.* Baltimore: Brookes.

Baumeister, R. F., & Leary, M. R. (1995). The need to belong: Desire for interpersonal attachments as a fundamental human motivation. *Psychological Bulletin, 117*(3), 497–529.

Baxter, S. (1994). The last word on gender differences. *Psychology Today, 27*(2), 51–53.

Bear, G. G., & Rys, G. S. (1995). Moral reasoning, classroom behavior, and sociometric status among elementary school children. *Developmental Psychology, 30,* 633–638.

Bear, G. G., Minke, K. M., & Manning, M. A. (2001). *Self-concept among students with learning disabilities: A meta-analysis.* Submitted for publication.

Bebell, D., O'Dwyer, L., Russell, M., & Seeley, K. (2004). *Estimating the effect of computer use at home and in school on student achievement.* Paper presented at the annual meeting of the American Educational Research Association, San Diego, CA.

Beck, I., & McKeown, M. (2001). Inviting students into the pursuit of meaning. *Educational Psychology Review, 13*(3), 225–242.

Becker, B. E., & Luthar, S. S. (2002). Social-emotional factors affecting achievement outcomes among disadvantaged students: Closing the achievement gap. *Educational Psychologist, 37*(4), 197–214.

Becker, H. J. (1990). Coaching for the scholastic aptitude test: Further synthesis and appraisal. *Review of Educational Research, 60*(3), 373–417.

Becker, H. J. (2000). Who's wired and who's not: Children's access to and use of computer technology. *Children and Computer Technology, 10*(2), 44–75.

Becker, H. J. (2001, April). *How are teachers using computers in instruction?* Paper presented at the annual meeting of the American Educational Research Association, Seattle, WA.

Becker, H. J., & Ravitz, J. L. (2001, April). *Computer use by teachers: Are Cuban's predictions correct?* Paper presented at the annual meeting of the American Educational Research Association, Seattle, WA.

Becker, W., & Carnine, D. (1980). Direct instruction: An effective approach for educational intervention with the disadvantaged and low performers. In B. Lahey & A. Kazdin (Eds.), *Advances in child clinical psychology.* New York: Plenum.

Bee, H., & Boyd, D. (2003). *Lifespan development.* Boston: Pearson.

Behrman, R. E. (1997). Children and poverty. *The Future of Children, 7*(2), 4–160.

Bender, W. N. (2004). *Learning disabilities: Characteristics, identification, and teaching strategies* (5th ed.). Boston: Pearson.

Benjafield, J. G. (1992). *Cognition.* Englewood Cliffs, NJ: Prentice-Hall.

Benson, P. (1997). *All kids are our kids.* San Francisco: Jossey-Bass.

Bereiter, C. (1991). Implications of connectionism for thinking about rules. *Educational Researcher, 20*(3), 10–16.

Bereiter, C. (1995). A dispositional view of transfer. In A. McKeough, J. Lupart, & A. Marini (Eds.), *Teaching for transfer: Fostering generalization in learning*. Mahwah, NJ: Erlbaum.

Berg, C. A., & Clough, M. (1990/91). Hunter lesson design: The wrong one for science teaching. *Educational Leadership, 48*(4), 73–78.

Bergin, D. (1999). Influences on classroom interest. *Educational Psychologist, 34*(2), 87–98.

Bergstrom, J. M., & O'Brien, L. A. (2001). Themes of discovery. *Educational Leadership, 58*(7), 29–33.

Berk, L. E. (2001). *Development through the lifespan* (2nd ed.). Boston: Allyn & Bacon.

Berk, L. E. (2003). *Development through the lifespan* (3rd ed.). Boston: Pearson.

Berko, J. (1985). The child's learning of English morphology. *Word, 14,* 150–177.

Bernard-Powers, J. (2001). Gender effects in schooling. In C. F. Diaz (Ed.), *Multicultural education for the 21st century*. New York: Longman.

Bernstein, D. K., & Tiegerman-Farber, E. (2002). *Language and communication disorders in children* (5th ed.). Boston: Allyn & Bacon.

Berrueta-Clement, J. R., Schweinhart, L. J., Barnett, W. S., Epstein, A. S., & Weikart, D. P. (1984). *Changed lives*. Ypsilanti, MI: High/Scope.

Berry, B., Hoke, M., & Hirsch, E. (2004). The search for highly qualified teachers. *Phi Delta Kappan, 85*(9), 684–689.

Bettmann, E. H., & Friedman, L. J. (2004). The Anti-Defamation League's A Word of Difference Institute. In W. G. Stephan & W. P. Vogt (Eds.), *Education Programs for Improving Intergroup Relations*. New York: Teachers College Press.

Beyer, B. K. (1988). *Developing a thinking skills program*. Boston: Allyn & Bacon.

Beyer, B. K. (1998). *Improving student thinking: A comprehensive approach*. Boston: Allyn & Bacon.

Biddle, B., & Berliner, D. (2002). Unequal school funding in the United States. *Educational Leadership, 59*(8), 48–59.

Bielinski, J., & Davison, M. (1998). Gender differences by item difficulty interactions in multiple-choice mathematics items. *American Educational Research Journal, 35*(3), 455–476.

Biemiller, A. (1993). Lake Wobegon revisited: On diversity in education. *Educational Researcher, 22*(9), 7–12.

Bigge, M. L., & Shermis, S. S. (2004). *Learning theories for teachers* (6th ed.). Boston: Pearson.

Bigler, R. (1999). The use of multicultural curricula and materials to counter racism in children. *Journal of Social Issues, 55*(4), 687–705.

Binder, L. M., Dixon, M. R., & Ghezi, P. M. (2000). A procedure to teach self-control to children with attention deficit hyperactivity disorder. *Journal of Applied Behavior Analysis, 33,* 233–237.

Bitter, G. G., & Pierson, M. E. (1999). *Using technology in the classroom* (4th ed.). Boston: Allyn & Bacon.

Black, J. (2003). Environment and development of the nervous system. In M. Gallagher & R. J. Nelson (Eds.), *Handbook of psychology: Vol. 3. Biological psychology* (pp. 655–665). Hoboken, NJ: Wiley.

Black, M. M., & Krishnakumar, A. (1998). Children in low-income, urban settings. Interventions to promote mental health and well-being. *American Psychologist, 53*(6), 635–646.

Black, P., Harrison, C., Lee, C., Marshall, B., & Dylan, W. (2004). Working inside the black box: Assessment for learning in the classroom. *Phi Delta Kappan, 86*(1), 8–21.

Blackadar, A. R., & Nachtigal, P. (1986). *Cotapaxi/Westcliffe follow-through project: Final evaluation report*. Denver, CO: Mid-Continental Regional Educational Laboratory.

Blair, C. (2004). Learning disability, intelligence, and fluid cognitive functions of the prefrontal cortex: A developmental neuroscience approach. *Learning Disabilities: A Contemporary Journal, 2*(1), 22–29.

Blamires, M. (Ed.). (1999). *Enabling technology for inclusion*. Thousand Oaks, CA: Corwin.

Bligh, D. (2000). *What's the use of lectures?* San Francisco: Jossey-Bass.

Block, K. K., & Peskowitz, N. B. (1990). Metacognition in spelling: Using writing and reading to self-check spelling. *Elementary School Journal, 91,* 151–164.

Blok, H., Oostdam, R., Otter, M. E., & Overmaat, M. (2002). Computer-assisted instruction in support of beginning reading instruction: A review. *Review of Educational Research, 721*(1), 101–130.

Bloom, B. S. (1976). *Human characteristics and school learning*. New York: McGraw-Hill.

Bloom, B. S. (1984). The 2 sigma problem: The search for methods of instruction as effective as one-to-one tutoring. *Educational Researcher, 13,* 4–16.

Bloom, B. S. (1986). Automaticity: The hands and feet of genius. *Educational Leadership, 43,* 70–77.

Bloom, B. S., Englehart, M. B., Furst, E. J., Hill, W. H., & Krathwohl, O. R. (1956). *Taxonomy of educational objectives: The classification of educational goals. Handbook 1: The cognitive domain*. New York: Longman.

Bloom, B. S., Hastings, J. T., & Madaus, G. F. (1971). *Handbook on formative and summative evaluation of student learning*. New York: McGraw-Hill.

Bloome, D., Puro, P., & Theodorou, E. (1989). Procedural displays and classroom lessons. *Curriculum Inquiry, 19*(3), 265–291.

Blume, G. W. (1984, April). *A review of research on the effects of computer programming on mathematical problem solving*. Paper presented at the annual meeting of the American Educational Research Association, New Orleans, LA.

Blumenfeld, P. C. (1992). Classroom learning and motivation: Clarity and expanding goal theory. *Journal of Educational Psychology, 84,* 272–281.

Blumenfeld, P. C., Marx, R. W., Soloway, E., & Krajcik, J. (1996). Learning with peers: From small group cooperation to collaborative communities. *Educational Researcher, 25*(8), 37–40.

Boden, M. A. (1980). *Jean Piaget.* New York: Viking Press.

Bodine, R. J., Crawford, D. K., & Schrumpf, F. (1994). *Creating the peaceable school: A comprehensive program for teaching conflict resolution.* Champaign, IL: Research Press.

Boekaerts, M. (1995). Self-regulated learning: Bridging the gap between metacognitive and metamotivational theories. *Educational Psychologist, 30*(4), 195–200.

Boekaerts, M., Pintrich, P. R., & Zeidner, M. (Eds.). (2000). *Handbook of self-regulation.* San Diego, CA: Academic Press.

Bong, M. (2001). Between- and within-domain relations of academic motivation among middle and high school students: Self-efficacy, task-value, and achievement goals. *Journal of Educational Psychology, 93*(1), 23–34.

Bong, M., & Skaalvik, E. (2003). Academic self-concept and self-efficacy: How different are they really? *Educational Psychology Review, 15*(1), 1–40.

Bonner-Tompkins, E. (2001, May/June). Effective practices for serving limited English proficient students with disabilities. *Gaining Ground.* Council of Chief State School Officers.

Borg, M. (1998). Tests of the internal/external frames of reference model with subject-specific academic self-efficacy and frame-specific academic concepts. *Journal of Educational Psychology, 90*(1), 102–110.

Borman, G. (2002/2003). How can Title I improve achievement? *Educational Leadership, 60*(4), 49–53.

Borman, G. D. (1997). *A holistic model of the organization of categorical program students' total educational opportunities.* Unpublished doctoral dissertation, University of Chicago.

Borman, G. D., & Boulay, M. (2004). *Summer learning: Research, policies, and programs.* Mahwah, NJ: Erlbaum.

Borman, G. D., & Overman, L. T. (2004). Academic resilience in mathematics among poor and minority students. *The Elementary School Journal, 104*(3), 177–195.

Borman, G. D., D'Agostino, J. V., Wong, K. K., & Hedges, L. V. (1998). The longitudinal achievement of Chapter I students: Preliminary evidence from the Prospects study. *Journal of Education for Students Placed at Risk, 3*(4), 363–399.

Borman, G., & Hewes, G. (2001). *Long-term effects and cost effectiveness of Success for All.* Baltimore: Johns Hopkins University, Center for Research on the Education of Students Placed at Risk.

Borman, G., & Hewes, G. (2003). Long-term effects and cost effectiveness of Success for All. *Educational Evaluation and Policy Analysis, 24*(2), 243–266.

Borman, G., Stringfield, S., & Slavin, R. (Eds.). (2001). *Title I: Compensatory education at the crossroads.* Mahwah, NJ: Erlbaum.

Borman, G. D., Hewes, G. M., Overman, L. T., & Brown, S. (2003). Comprehensive school reform and achievement: A meta-analysis. *Review of Educational Research, 73*(2), 125–230.

Bornstein, P. H. (1985). Self-instructional training: A commentary and state-of-the-art. *Journal of Applied Behavior Analysis, 18,* 69–72.

Bortnick, R. (1995). Interactive learning and hypermedia technology. In J. H. Block, S. T. Everson, & T. R. Guskey (Eds.), *School improvement programs* (pp. 77–90). New York: Scholastic.

Bos, C. S., & Vaughn, S. (2002). *Strategies for teaching students with learning and behavior problems.* Boston: Allyn & Bacon.

Bottge, B. A. (2001). Using intriguing problems to improve math skills. *Educational Leadership, 58*(6), 68–72.

Bower, G. H., & Karlin, M. B. (1974). Depth of processing pictures of faces and recognition memory. *Journal of Experimental Psychology, 103,* 751–757.

Bower, G. H., Clark, M. C., Lesgold, A. M., & Winzenz, D. (1969). Hierarchical retrieval schemes in recall of categorized word lists. *Journal of Verbal Learning and Verbal Behavior, 8,* 323–343.

Bowman, B. (1993). Early childhood education. *Review of Research in Education, 19,* 101–134.

Boykin, A. W. (1994a). Afrocultural expression and its implications for schooling. In E. Hollins et al. (Eds.), *Teaching diverse populations.* Albany: State University of New York Press.

Boykin, A. W. (1994b). Harvesting culture and talent: African American children and educational reform. In R. Rossi (Ed.), *Schools and students at risk* (pp. 116–130). New York: Teachers College Press.

Boykin, A. W. (2000). The talent development model of schooling: Placing students at promise for academic success. *Journal of Education for Students Placed at Risk, 5*(1 & 2), 3–25.

Bracey, G. W. (1998). *Put to the test: An educator's and consumer's guide to standardized testing.* Bloomington, IN: Phi Delta Kappan.

Bracey, G., & Stellar, A. (2003). Long-term studies of preschool: Lasting benefits far outweigh costs. *Phi Delta Kappan, 84*(10), 780–783.

Braddock, J. H., & Dawkins, M. P. (1993). Ability grouping, aspirations, and attainments: Evidence from the National Educational Longitudinal Study of 1988. *Journal of Negro Education, 62*(3), 1–13.

Braddock, J. H., Dawkins, M. P., & Wilson, G. (1995). Intercultural contact and race relations among American youth. In W. D. Hawley & A. W. Jackson (Eds.), *Toward a common destiny: Improving race and ethnic relations in America.* San Francisco: Jossey-Bass.

Bradley, R. H., Whiteside, L., Mundfrom, D. J., Casey, P. H., Caldwell, B. M., & Barrett, K. (1994). Impact of the Infant Health and Development Program (IHDP) on the home environments of infants born prematurely and with low birthweight. *Journal of Educational Psychology, 80,* 531–541.

Branch, C. (1998). *Adolescent gangs: Old issues, new approaches.* Philadelphia: Brunner/Mazel.

Bransford, J. D., & Stein, B. S. (1993). *The ideal problem solver* (2nd ed.). New York: W. H. Freeman.

Bransford, J. D., Burns, M. S., Delclos, V. R., & Vye, N. J. (1986). Teaching thinking: Evaluating evaluations and broadening the data base. *Educational Leadership, 44*(2), 68–70.

Bransford, J., Brown, A., & Cocking, R. (Eds.). (1999). *How people learn: Brain, mind, experience, and school.* Washington, DC: National Academy Press.

Bretzing, B. B., & Kulhavy, R. W. (1981). Note taking and passage style. *Journal of Educational Psychology, 73,* 242–250.

Broden, M., Hall, R. V., Dunlap, A., & Clark, R. (1970). Effects of teacher attention and a token reinforcement system in a junior high school special education class. *Exceptional Children, 36,* 341–349.

Bronfenbrenner, U., & Morris, P. A. (1998). The ecology of developmental processes. In W. Damon (Ed.), *Handbook of child psychology* (Vol. 1, pp. 993–1029). New York: Wiley.

Brooks, B. D. (1975). Contingency management as a means of reducing school truancy. *Education, 95,* 206–211.

Brooks, D. M. (1985). Beginning of the year in junior high: The first day of school. *Educational Leadership, 42,* 76–78.

Brooks, J. G., & Brooks, M. G. (1993). *The case for constructivist classrooms.* Alexandria, VA: Association for Supervision and Curriculum Development.

Brophy, J. (1981). Teacher praise: A functional analysis. *Review of Educational Research, 51,* 5–32.

Brophy, J. (1999). Toward a model of the value aspects of motivation in education: Developing appreciation for particular learning domains and activities. *Educational Psychologist, 34*(2), 75–85.

Brophy, J. E. (1998). *Motivating students to learn.* Boston: McGraw-Hill.

Brophy, J. E., & Evertson, C. M. (1974). Process-product correlations in the Texas teacher effectiveness study: Final report (Research Reports No. 74-4). Austin: Research and Development Center for Teacher Education. University of Texas.

Brophy, J. E., & Evertson, C. M. (1976). *Learning from teaching: A developmental perspective.* Boston: Allyn & Bacon.

Brophy, J. E., & Good, T. L. (1986). Teacher behavior and student achievement. In M. C. Wittrock (Ed.), *Handbook of research on teaching* (3rd ed.). New York: Macmillan.

Browder, D. M. (2001). *Curriculum and assessment for students with moderate and severe disabilities.* New York: Guilford.

Brown, A. L., Bransford, J. D., Ferrara, R. A., & Campione, J. C. (1983). Learning, remembering, and understanding. In J. Flavell & E. M. Markman (Eds.), *Handbook of child psychology* (4th ed.) (Vol. 3, pp. 515–629). New York: Wiley.

Brown, B. B. (1990). Peer groups and peer cultures. In S. S. Feldman & G. R. Elliot (Eds.), *At the threshold: The developing adolescent* (pp. 171–196). Cambridge, MA: Harvard University Press.

Brown, D. S. (1988). Twelve middle-school teachers' planning. *Elementary School Journal, 89,* 69–88.

Brown, J. S., Collins, A., & Duguid, P. (1989). Situated cognition and the culture of learning. *Educational Research, 18,* 32–42.

Bruer, J. T. (1999). Neural connections: Some you use, some you lose. *Phi Delta Kappan, 81*(4), 264–277.

Bruner, J. S. (1966). *Toward a theory of instruction.* New York: Norton.

Bryant, A. L., & Zimmerman, M. A. (2002). Examining the effects of academic beliefs and behaviors on changes in substance use among urban adolescents. *Journal of Educational Psychology, 94*(3), 621–637.

Bryant, D. M., Clifford, R. M., & Peisner, E. S. (1991). Best practices for beginners: Developmental appropriateness in kindergarten. *American Educational Research Journal, 28*(4), 783–803.

Bryant, D. P., Ugel, N., Thompson, S., & Hampff, A. (1999). Instructional strategies for content-area reading instruction. *Intervention in School and Clinic, 34*(5), 293–302.

Bulgren, J. A., Lenz, B. K., Schumaker, J. B., Deshler, D. D., & Marquis, J. G. (2002). The use and effectiveness of a comparison routine in diverse secondary content classrooms. *Journal of Educational Psychology, 94*(2), 356–371.

Bulgren, J., Deshler, D., Schumaker, J., & Lenz, B. (2000). The use and effectiveness of analogical instruction in diverse secondary content classrooms. *Journal of Educational Psychology, 92*(3), 426–441.

Burden, P. R. (2000). *Powerful classroom management strategies: Motivating students to learn.* Thousand Oaks, CA: Corwin.

Burden, P., & Byrd, D. (2003). *Methods for effective teaching.* Boston: Allyn & Bacon.

Burns, R. B. (1984). How time is used in elementary schools: The activity structure of classrooms. In L. W. Anderson (Ed.), *Time and school learning: Theory, research, and practice.* London: Croom Helm.

Burns, R. B., & Mason, D. A. (2002). Class composition and student achievement in elementary schools. *American Educational Research Journal, 39*(1), 207–233.

Burris, C., Heubert, J., & Levin, H. (2004). Math acceleration for all. *Educational Leadership, 61*(5), 68–71.

Burt, M. R., Resnick, G., & Novick, E. R. (1998). *Building supportive communities for at-risk adolescents.* Washington, DC: American Psychological Association.

Bus, A. G., & van Ijzendoorn, M. H. (1999). Phonological awareness and early reading: A meta-analysis of experimental training studies. *Journal of Educational Psychology, 91*(3), 403–414.

Bussey, K. (1992). Lying and truthfulness: Children's definitions, standards, and evaluative reactions. *Child Development, 63,* 129–137.

Butler, D. L., & Winne, P. H. (1995). Feedback and self-regulated learning. *Review of Educational Research, 65*(3), 245–281.

Byerly, S. (2001). Linking classroom teaching to the real world through experiential instruction. *Phi Delta Kappan, 82*(9), 697–699.

Byrne, B., Fielding-Barnsley, R., & Ashley, L. (2000). Effects of preschool phoneme identity training after six years: Outcome level distinguished from rate of response. *Journal of Educational Psychology, 92*(4), 659–667.

Byrnes, J. (2001). *Cognitive development and learning* (2nd ed.). Boston: Allyn & Bacon.

Byrnes, J. P. (1996). *Cognitive development and learning in instructional contexts.* Boston: Allyn & Bacon.

Byrnes, J. P., & Fox, N. A. (1998). The educational relevance of research in cognitive neuroscience. *Educational Psychology Review, 10*(3), 297–342.

Caine, R. M., & Caine, G. (1997). *Education on the edge of possibility.* Alexandria, VA: Association for Supervision and Curriculum Development.

Calderón, M. (1994, April). *Cooperative learning as a powerful staff development tool for school renewal.* Paper presented at the annual meeting of the American Educational Research Association, New Orleans.

Calderón, M., Hertz-Lazarowitz, R., & Slavin, R. E. (1998). Effects of bilingual cooperative integrated reading and Composition on students making the transition from Spanish to English reading. *Elementary School Journal, 99*(2), 153–165.

Calderón, M. (2001). Curricula and methodologies used to teach Spanish-speaking limited English proficient students to read English. In R. Slavin and M. Calderón (Eds.), *Effective programs for Latino students.* Mahwah, NJ: Erlbaum.

Calderón, M. E., & Minaya-Rowe, L. (2003). *Designing and implementing two-way bilingual programs.* Thousand Oaks, CA: Corwin.

Calderón, M., August, D., Slavin, R. E., Durán, D., Madden, N. A., & Cheung, A. (2004). *The evaluation of a bilingual transition program for Success for All.* Baltimore, MD: Johns Hopkins University, Center for Research on the Education of Students Placed at Risk.

Calhoun, G., & Elliott, R. (1977). Self-concept and academic achievement of educable retarded and emotionally disturbed children. *Exceptional Children, 44,* 379–380.

Calkins, L. M. (1983). *Lessons from a child: On the teaching and learning of writing.* Exeter, NH: Heinemann.

Cameron, J. (2001). Negative effects of reward on intrinsic motivation—a limited phenomenon: Comment on Deci, Koestner, and Ryan (2001). *Review of Educational Research, 71*(1), 29–42.

Cameron, J., & Pierce, W. D. (1994). Reinforcement, reward, and intrinsic motivation: A meta-analysis. *Review of Educational Research, 64,* 363–423.

Cameron, J., & Pierce, W. D. (1996). The debate about rewards and intrinsic motivation: Protests and accusations do not alter the results. *Review of Educational Research, 66*(1), 39–51.

Campbell, D. (2000). Authentic assessment and authentic standards. *Phi Delta Kappan, 81*(5), 405–407.

Campbell, F. A., & Ramey, C. T. (1994). Effects of early intervention on intellectual and academic achievement: A follow-up study of children from low-income families. *Child Development, 65,* 684–698.

Campbell, F. A., & Ramey, C. T. (1995). Cognitive and school outcomes for high-risk African American students at middle adolescence: Positive effects of early intervention. *American Educational Research Journal, 32,* 743–772.

Campbell, J., & Mayer, R. E. (2004, April). *Concrete manipulatives: For whom are they beneficial?* Paper presented at the annual meeting of the American Educational Research Association, San Diego, CA.

Campbell, L., Campbell, B., & Dickinson, D. (1996). *Teaching and learning through multiple intelligences.* Boston: Allyn & Bacon.

Canada, G. (2000). Raising better boys. *Educational Leadership, 57*(4), 14–17.

Canady, R. L., & Hotchkiss, P. R. (1993). It's a good score! Just a bad grade. In K. M. Cauley, F. Linder, & J. H. McMillan (Eds.), *Annual Editions: Educational Psychology 93/94.* Guilford, CT: Dushkin.

Canfield, J., & Siccone, F. (1995). *101 ways to develop students' self-esteem and responsibility.* Boston: Allyn & Bacon.

Cannell, J. J. (1987). *Nationally normed elementary achievement testing in America's public schools: How all fifty states are above the national average.* Daniels, WV: Friends for Education.

Canter, L., & Canter, M. (1992). *Assertive discipline: Positive behavior management for today's classroom.* Santa Monica, CA: Lee Canter & Associates.

Canter, L., & Canter, M. (2002). *Assertive discipline: Positive behavior management for today's schools.* Seal Beach, CA: Lee Canter & Associates.

Cappella, E., & Weinstein, R. (2001). Turning around reading achievement: Predictors of high school students' academic resilience. *Journal of Educational Psychology, 93*(4), 758–771.

Capper, C. A., Kampschroer, E. F., & Keyes, M. W. (2000). *Meeting the needs of students of all abilities: How leaders go beyond inclusion.* Bloomington, IN: Phi Delta Kappan.

Capron, C., & Duyme, M. (1991). Children's IQ's and SES of biological and adoptive parents in a balanced cross-fostering study. *Cahiers de Psychologie Cognitive, 11,* 323–348.

Cardelle-Elawar, M. (1990). Effects of feedback tailored to bilingual students' mathematics needs on verbal problem solving. *Elementary School Journal, 91,* 165–175.

Cardellichio, T., & Field, W. (1997). Seven strategies that encourage neural branching. *Educational Leadership, 54*(6), 33–36.

Carey, L. M. (2001). *Measuring and evaluating school learning* (3rd ed.). Boston, MA: Allyn & Bacon.

Carlo, M. S., August, D., McLaughlin, B., Snow, C. E., Dressler, C., Lippman, D., Lively, T., & White, C. (2004). Closing the gap: Addressing the vocabulary needs of English language learners in bilingual and mainstream classrooms. *Reading Research Quarterly, 39*(2), 188–215.

Carnegie Corporation of New York. (1989). *Turning points: Preparing American youth for the 21st century.* New York: Author.

Carnegie Corporation of New York. (1994). *Starting points: Meeting the needs of our youngest children.* New York: Author.

Carnegie Corporation of New York. (1996). *Years of promise: A comprehensive learning strategy for America's children.* New York: Author.

Carney, R. N., & Levin, J. R. (1998). Do mnemonic memories fade as time goes by? Here's looking anew! *Contemporary Educational Psychology, 23*(3), 276–297.

Carney, R. N., & Levin, J. R. (2002). Pictorial illustrations still improve students' learning from text. *Educational Psychology Review, 14*(1), 5–26.

Carnine, D. (1989). Teaching complex content to learning disabled children: The role of technology. *Exceptional Children, 55,* 524–533.

Carnine, D., Grosen, B., & Silbert, J. (1995). Direct instructions to accelerate cognitive growth. In J. H. Block, S. T. Everson, & T. R. Guskey (Eds.), *School improvement programs* (pp. 129–152). New York: Scholastic.

Carnoy, M., & Loeb, S. (2002). Does external accountability affect student outcomes? A cross-state analysis. *Educational Evaluation and Policy Analysis, 24*(4), 305–331.

Carpenter, T. P., & Fennema, E. (1992). Cognitively guided instruction: Building on the knowledge of students and teachers. *International Journal of Educational Research, 17,* 457–470.

Carpenter, T. P., Fennema, E., Fuson, K., Hiebert, J., Human, P., Murray, H., Olivier, A., & Wearne, D. (1994, April). *Teaching mathematics for learning with understanding in the primary grades.* Paper presented at the annual meeting of the American Educational Research Association, New Orleans, LA.

Carpenter, T. P., Fennema, E., Peterson, P. L., Chiang, C. P., & Loef, M. (1989). Using knowledge of children's mathematics thinking in classroom teaching: An experimental study. *American Educational Research Journal, 26,* 499–531.

Carr, J. F., & Harris, D. E. (2001). *Succeeding with standards: Linking curriculum, assessment, and action planning.* Alexandria, VA: ASCD.

Carroll, J. B. (1963). A model of school learning. *Teachers College Record, 64,* 723–733.

Carroll, J. B. (1989). The Carroll model: A 25-year retrospective and prospective view. *Educational Researcher, 18,* 26–31.

Carter, C. J. (1997). Why reciprocal teaching? *Educational Leadership, 54*(6), 64–68.

Carter, K., Cushing, K., Sabers, D., Stein, P., & Berliner, D. (1988). Expert-novice differences in perceiving and processing visual classroom information. *Journal of Teacher Education, 39*(3), 25–31.

Carter, R. T., & Goodwin, A. L. (1994). *Racial Identity and Education, 20,* 291–336.

Carver, S. M., & Klahr, D. (2001). *Cognition and instruction: Twenty five years of progress.* Mahwah, NJ: Erlbaum.

Carver, S. M., Lehrer, R., Connell, T., & Erickson, J. (1992). Learning by hypermedia design: Issues of assessment and implementation. *Educational Psychologist, 27*(3), 385–404.

Case, R. (1998). The development of conceptual structures. In W. Damon (Ed.), *Handbook of child psychology* (Vol. 2, pp. 851–898). Hoboken, NJ: Wiley.

CASE. (1993). *CASE position paper on delivery of services to students with disabilities.* Washington, DC: Council for Administrators of Special Education.

Casto, G., & Mastropieri, M. A. (1986). The efficacy of early intervention programs: A meta-analysis. *Exceptional Children, 52,* 417–424.

Cavanaugh, C., Kim, A.-H., Wanzek, J., & Vaughn, S. (2004). Kindergarten reading interventions for at-risk students: Twenty years of research. *Learning Disabilities: A Contemporary Journal, 2*(1), 1–8.

Ceci, S. J. (1991). How much does schooling influence general intelligence and its cognitive components? A reassessment of the evidence. *Developmental Psychology, 27,* 703–722.

Ceci, S. J. (1992). The new intelligence theorists: Old liberals in new guises? *Educational Researcher, 21*(6), 25–27.

Center on Education Policy (2003). *State and federal efforts to implement the No Child Left Behind Act.* Washington, DC: Author.

Center on Education Policy (2004). *Title I funds: Who's gaining, who's losing, and why.* Washington, DC: Author.

Centers for Disease Control. (1998). *Youth risk behavior surveillance—United States, 1997.* Atlanta, GA: Author.

Chambers, B., Cheung, A., Gifford, R., Madden, N., & Slavin, R. E. (2004). *Achievement effects of embedded multimedia in a Success for All reading program.* Manuscript submitted for publication.

Chan, C. K. K., Burtis, P. J., Scardamalia, M., & Bereiter, C. (1992). Constructive activity in learning from text. *American Educational Research Journal, 29,* 97–118.

Chance, P. (1992). The rewards of learning. *Phi Delta Kappan, 74*(3), 200–207.

Chapman, E. (2001, April). *More on moderations in cooperative learning outcomes.* Paper presented at the annual meeting of the American Educational Research Association, Montreal.

Chapman, J., Tunmer, W., & Prochnow, J. (2000). Early reading-related skills and performance, reading self-concept, and the development of academic self-concept: A longitudinal study. *Journal of Educational Psychology, 92*(4), 703–708.

Charles, C. M. (1989). *Building classroom discipline: From models to practice* (3rd ed.). New York: Longman.

Charles, C. M. (2005). *Building classroom discipline* (8th ed.). Boston: Pearson.

Chatterji, M. (2002). Models and methods for examining standards-based reforms and accountability initiatives: Have the tools of inquiry answered pressing questions on improving schools? *Review of Educational Research, 72*(3), 345–386.

Chen, Z., & Daehler, M. (2000). External and internal instantiation of abstract information facilitates transfer in insight problem solving. *Contemporary Educational Psychology, 25*(4), 423–449.

Cheung, K. C. (1995). On meaningful measurement: Issues of reliability and validity from a humanistic constructivist information-processing perspective. *Educational Research and Evaluation, 1*(1), 90–107.

Chin, C. W. T. (1998, April). *Synthesizing metacognitive interventions: What training characteristics can improve reading performance?* Paper presented at the annual meeting of the American Educational Research Association, San Diego, CA.

Chinn, C. A., & Brewer, W. F. (1993). The role of anomalous data in knowledge acquisition. *Review of Educational Research, 63*(1), 1–49.

Choate, J. (2004). *Successful inclusive teaching* (4th ed.). Boston: Pearson.

Chobot, R., & Garibaldi, A. (1982). In-school alternatives to suspension: A description of ten school district programs. *The Urban Review, 14,* 71–75.

Chomsky, C. (1969). *The acquisition of syntax in children from 5 to 10.* M.I.T. Press Research Monogram No. 57. Cambridge, MA: M.I.T. Press.

Christian, D., & Genesee, F. (Eds.). (2001). *Bilingual education.* Alexandria, VA: TESOL.

Christoplos, F., & Renz, P. (1969). A critical examination of special education programs. *Journal of Special Education, 3,* 371–379.

Cizek, G. J. (1993). Innovation or enervation? Performance assessment in perspective. In K. M. Cauley, F. Linder, & J. H. McMillan (Eds.), *Annual Editions: Educational Psychology 93/94.* Guilford, CT: Dushkin.

Cizek, G. J. (1999). *Cheating on tests: How to do it, detect it, and prevent it.* Mahwah, NJ: Erlbaum.

Clark, C. M., & Peterson, P. L. (1986). Teachers' thought processes. In M. C. Wittrock (Ed.), *Handbook of research on teaching* (3rd ed.). New York: Macmillan.

Clark, C. M., Gage, N. L., Marx, R. W., Peterson, P. L., Stayrook, N. G., & Winne, P. H. (1979). A factorial experiment on teacher structuring, soliciting, and reacting. *Journal of Educational Psychology, 71,* 534–552.

Clark, J. (1990). *Patterns of thinking: Integrating learning skills with content teaching.* Boston: Allyn & Bacon.

Clark, J. M., & Paivio, A. (1991). Dual coding theory and education. *Educational Psychology Review, 3*(3), 149–210.

Clark, R. E. (Ed.). (2001). *Learning from media: Arguments, analysis, and evidence.* Greenwich, CT: Information Age.

Clements, D. H., & Battista, M. T. (1990). Constructivist learning and teaching. *Arithmetic Teacher, 38,* 34–37.

Clifford, M. M. (1984). Thoughts on a theory of constructive failure. *Educational Psychologist, 19,* 108–120.

Clifford, M. M. (1990). Students need challenge, not easy success. *Educational Leadership, 48*(1), 22–26.

Clifford, R. M., Early, D. M., & Hills, T. W. (1999). Almost a million children in school before kindergarten: Who is responsible for early childhood services? *Young Children, 12,* 48–51.

Cline, Z. (1998). *Buscando su voz en dos culturas:* Finding your voice in two cultures. *Phi Delta Kappan, 79*(9), 699–705.

Cobb, N. (1995). *Adolescence.* Mountain View, CA: Mayfield.

Cochran-Smith, M. (1991). Word processing and writing in elementary classrooms: A critical review of related literature. *Review of Educational Research, 61*(1), 107–155.

Cognition and Technology Group at Vanderbilt. (1996). Looking at technology in context: A framework for understanding technology and education research. In D. C. Berliner & R. C. Calfee (Eds.), *Handbook of educational psychology* (pp. 807–840). New York: Macmillan.

Cohen, E. G. (1984). Talking and working together: Status, interaction, and learning. In P. Peterson, L. C. Wilkinson, & M. Hallinan (Eds.), *The social context of instruction: Group organization and group processes.* New York: Academic Press.

Cohen, E. G. (1986). *Designing groupwork: Strategies for the heterogeneous classroom.* New York: Teachers College Press.

Cohen, E. G. (1992, April). *Complex instruction in the middle school.* Paper presented at the annual meeting of the American Educational Research Association, San Francisco, CA.

Cohen, E. G. (1994a). *Designing groupwork: Strategies for the heterogeneous classroom* (2nd ed.). New York: Teachers College Press.

Cohen, E. G. (1994b). Restructuring the classroom: Conditions for productive small groups. *Review of Educational Research, 64*(1), 1–35.

Cohen, E. G. (2004). Producing equal-status interaction amidst classroom diversity. In W. G. Stephan & W. P. Vogt (Eds.), *Education Programs for Improving Intergroup Relations.* New York: Teachers College Press.

Cohen, L. B., & Cashon, C. H. (2003). Infant perception and cognition. In R. M. Lerner, M. A. Easterbrooks, & J. Mistry (Eds.), *Handbook of psychology: Vol. 6. Developmental psychology* (pp. 65–89). Hoboken, NJ: Wiley.

Cohen, R. L. (1989). Memory for action events: The power of enactment. *Educational Psychology Review, 1*(1), 57–80.

Coie, J. D., Dodge, K. A., & Kupersmidt, J. (1990). Peer group behavior and social status. In S. R. Asher & J. D. Coie (Eds.), *Peer rejection in children* (pp. 17–59). New York: Cambridge University Press.

Colby, C., & Kohlberg, L. (1984). Invariant sequence and internal consistency in moral judgment stages. In W. Kurtines & J. Gewirts (Eds.), *Morality, moral behavior, and moral development.* New York: Wiley-Interscience.

Cole, D. A. (1991). Change in self-perceived competence as a function of peer and teacher evaluation. *Developmental Psychology, 27,* 682–688.

Coleman, J. (1961). *The adolescent society.* New York: Free Press.

Coles, G. (2004). Danger in the classroom: "Brain Glitch" research and learning to read. *Phi Delta Kappan, 85*(5), 344–357.

Coley, R. (2001). *Differences in the gender gap: Comparisons across racial/ethnic groups in education and work.* Princeton: Educational Testing Service, Policy Information Center. Retrieved from www.ets.org/research/pic.

Coley, R. L., & Chase-Lansdale, P. L. (1998). Adolescent pregnancy and parenthood. *American Psychologist, 53*(2), 152–166.

Comer, J. P. (1990). *Maggie's American dream.* New York: Plume.

Comer, J. P., Haynes, N. M., Joyner, E. T., & Ben-Avie, M. (1996). *Rallying the whole village: The Comer process for reforming education.* New York: Teachers College Press.

Connor, C. M., Son, S. H., Hindman, A. H., & Morrison, F. J. (2004). *Teacher qualifications, classroom practices, and family characteristics: Complex effects on first-graders' vocabulary and early reading outcomes.* Ann Arbor: University of Michigan, Department of Psychology.

Conway, M. A., Cohen, G., & Stanhope, N. (1991). Very long-term memory of knowledge acquired through formal education: Twelve years of cognitive psychology. *Journal of Experimental Psychology: General, 120,* 395–409.

Conyers, L., Reynolds, A., & Ou, S. (2003). The effect of early childhood intervention and subsequent special education services: Findings from the Chicago child–parent centers. *Educational Evaluation and Policy Analysis, 25*(1), 75–95.

Cook, J. L., & Cook, G. (2005). *Child development: Principles and perspectives.* Boston: Pearson.

Cook, T. D., Habib, F., Phillips, M., Settersten, R. A., Shagle, S., & Degirmencioglu, M. (1999). Comer's school development program in Prince George's County, Maryland: A theory-based evaluation. *American Educational Research Journal, 36*(3), 543–597.

Cook, T., Murphy, R. F., & Hunt, H. D. (2000). Comer's school development program in Chicago: A theory-based evaluation. *American Educational Research Journal, 37*(2), 535–597.

Cooley, W. W., & Leinhardt, G. (1980). The instructional dimensions study. *Educational Evaluation and Policy Analysis, 2,* 7–26.

Cooper, H., & Valentine, J. C. (2001). Using research to answer practical questions about homework. *Educational Psychologist.*

Cooper, H., Lindsay, J. J., Nye, B., & Greathouse, S. (1998). Relationships among attitudes about homework, amount of homework assigned and completed, and student achievement. *Journal of Educational Psychology, 90*(1), 70–83.

Cooper, R. (1998). Urban school reform: Student responses to detracking in a racially mixed high school. *Journal of Education for Students Placed at Risk, 4*(3), 259–275.

Cooper, R., & Slavin, R. E. (2004). Cooperative learning: An instructional strategy to improve intergroup relations. In W. G. Stephan & W. P. Vogt (Eds.), *Education programs for improving intergroup relations.* New York: Teachers College Press.

Copeland, W. D. (1983, April). *Classroom management and student teachers' cognitive abilities: A relationship.* Paper presented at the annual convention of the American Educational Research Association, Montreal.

Cordova, D. I., & Lepper, M. R. (1996). Intrinsic motivation and the process of learning: Beneficial effects of contextualization, personalization, and choice. *Journal of Educational Psychology, 88*(4), 715–730.

Corkill, A. J. (1992). Advance organizers: Facilitators of recall. *Educational Psychology Review, 4,* 33–67.

Corno, L. (1992). Encouraging students to take responsibility for learning and performance. *Elementary School Journal, 95,* 69–84.

Corno, L. (1995). The principles of adaptive teaching. In A. C. Ornstein (Ed.), *Teaching: Theory into practice.* Boston: Allyn & Bacon.

Corno, L. (1996). Homework is a complicated thing. *Educational Researcher, 25*(8), 27–30.

Corno, L. (2000). Looking at homework differently. *The Elementary School Journal, 100*(5), 529–548.

Corno, L., & Kanfer, R. (1993). The role of volition in learning and performance. *Review of Research in Education, 19,* 301–341.

Cortés, C. E. (1995). Knowledge construction and popular culture: The media as multicultural educator. In J. A. Banks & C. A. M. Banks (Eds.), *Handbook of research on multicultural education.* New York: Macmillan.

Cose, E. (2004). *Beyond Brown v. Board: The final battle for excellence in American education.* A report by Ellis Close to the Rockefeller Foundation.

Costenbader, V., & Reading-Brown, M. (1995). Isolation timeout used with students with emotional disturbance. *Exceptional Children, 61,* 353–363.

Council of Chief State School Officers. (1990). *School success for limited English proficient students: The challenge and state response.* Washington, DC: Author.

Covington, M. (1999). Caring about learning: The nature and nurturing of subject-matter appreciation. *Educational Psychologist, 34*(2), 127–136.

Cox, B. D. (1997). The rediscovery of the active learner in adaptive contexts: A developmental-historical analysis of transfer of training. *Educational Psychologist, 32,* 41–55.

Craik, F. I. M. (2000). Memory: Coding processes. In A. Kazdin (Ed.), *Encyclopedia of psychology.* Washington, DC: American Psychological Association.

Craik, F. I. M., & Lockhart, R. S. (1972). Levels of processing: A framework for memory research. *Journal of Verbal Thinking and Verbal Behavior, 11,* 671–684.

Crawford, J. (1989). Instructional activities related to achievement gain in Chapter I classes. In R. E. Slavin, N. L. Karweit, & N. A. Madden (Eds.), *Effective programs for students at risk.* Boston: Allyn & Bacon.

Crévola, C. A., & Hill, P. W. (1998). Evaluation of a whole-school approach to prevention and intervention in early literacy. *Journal of Education for Students Placed at Risk, 3*(2), 133–157.

Creswell, J. W. (2002). Research design: *Qualitative, quantitative, and mixed methods approaches* (2nd ed.). Thousand Oaks, CA: Sage.

Crocker, R. K., & Brooker, G. M. (1986). Classroom control and student outcomes in grades 2 and 5. *American Educational Research, 23,* 1–11.

Crooks, T. J. (1988). The impact of classroom evaluation practices on students. *Review of Educational Research, 58,* 438–481.

Cross, L. H., & Cross, G. M. (1980/1981). Teachers' evaluative comments and pupil perception of control. *Journal of Experimental Education, 49,* 68–71.

Cross, W. E. (1995). Oppositional identity and African American youth: Issues and prospects. In W. D. Hawley & A. W. Jackson (Eds.), *Toward a common destiny: Improving race and ethnic relations in America.* San Francisco: Jossey-Bass.

Cuban, L., Kirkpatrick, H., & Peck, C. (2001). High access and low use of technology in high school classrooms: Explaining an apparent paradox. *American Educational Research Journal, 38*(4), 813–834.

Cummings, E. M., Braungart-Rieker, J. M., & Du Rocher-Schudlich, T. (2003). Emotion and personality development in childhood. In R. M. Lerner, M. A. Easterbrooks, & J. Mistry (Eds.), *Handbook of psychology: Vol. 6. Developmental psychology* (pp. 211–239). Hoboken, NJ: Wiley.

Cummins, J. (1998). Language issues and educational change. In A. Hargreaves et al. (Eds.), *International handbook of educational change* (pp. 440–459). Dordrecht, The Netherlands: Kluwer.

Curry, C. (2003). Universal design accessibility for all learners. *Educational Leadership, 61*(2), 55–60.

Curwin, R. E., & Mendler, A. N. (1999). Zero tolerance for zero tolerance. *Phi Delta Kappan, 81*(2), 119–120.

D'Agostino, J. V., & Murphy, J. A. (2004). Meta-analysis of Reading Recovery in United States schools. *Educational Evaluation and Policy Analysis, 26*(1), 23–28.

Dai, D., Moon, S., & Feldhusen, J. (1998). Achievement motivation and gifted students: A social cognitive perspective. *Educational Psychologist, 33*(1), 45–63.

Dansereau, D. F. (1985). Learning strategy research. In J. Segal, S. Chipman, & R. Glaser (Eds.), *Thinking and learning skills: Relating instruction to basic research, Vol. 1.* Hillsdale, NJ: Erlbaum.

Dantonio, M., & Beisenherz, P. (2001). *Learning to question, questioning to learn.* Boston: Allyn & Bacon.

Danziger, S. H., Sandefur, G., & Weinberg, D. H. (Eds.). (1994). *Confronting poverty.* Cambridge, MA: Harvard University Press.

Darling-Hammond, L. (1995). Inequality and access to knowledge. In J. A. Banks & C. A. M. Banks (Eds.), *Handbook of research on multicultural education* (pp. 465–483). New York: Macmillan.

Darling-Hammond, L., & Falk, B. (1997). Using standards and assessments to support student learning. *Phi Delta Kappan, 79*(3), 190–201.

Darling-Hammond, L., Ancess, J., & Ort, S. W. (2002). Reinventing high school: Outcomes of the coalition campus schools project. *American Educational Research Journal, 39*(3), 639–673.

Darling-Hammond, L., Gendler, T., & Wise, A. D. (1990). *The teaching internship: Practical preparation for a licensed profession.* Santa Monica, CA: RAND.

Das, J. P. (1995). Some thoughts on two aspects of Vygotsky's work. *Educational Psychologist, 30*(2), 993–997.

Davidman, L., & Davidman, P. (Eds.). (2001). *Teaching with a multicultural perspective: A practical guide.* New York, NY: Addison-Wesley.

De Jong, T., & van Joolingen, W. R. (1998). Scientific discovery learning with computer simulations of conceptual domains. *Review of Educational Research, 68*(2), 179–201.

de La Paz, S., & Graham, S. (2002). Explicitly teaching strategies, skills, and knowledge: Writing instruction in middle school classrooms. *Journal of Educational Psychology, 94*(2), 687–698.

De Lisi, R., & Staudt, J. (1980). Individual differences in college students' performance on formal operations tasks. *Journal of Applied Developmental Psychology, 1,* 201–208.

de Ribaupierre, A., & Rieben, L. (1995). Individual and situational variability in cognitive development. *Educational Psychologist, 30*(1), 5–14.

DeBacker, T., & Nelson, R. M. (1999). Variations on an expectancy-value model of motivation in science. *Contemporary Educational Psychology, 24*(2), 71–94.

Deci, E. L., Koestner, R., & Ryan, R. M. (1999). A meta-analytic review of experiments examining the effects of extrinsic rewards on intrinsic motivation. *Psychological Bulletin, 125,* 627–668.

Deci, E., Koestner, R., & Ryan, R. (2001). Extrinsic rewards and intrinsic motivation in education: Reconsidered once again. *Review of Educational Research, 71*(1), 1–27.

Deci, E., Koestner, R., & Ryan, R. (2001). The pervasive negative effects of rewards on intrinsic motivation: Response to Cameron (2001). *Review of Educational Research, 71*(1), 43–51.

Delamont, S. (2002). Gender and education. In D. L. Levinson, P. W. Cookson, Jr., & A. R. Sadovnik (Eds.), *Education and sociology: An encyclopedia* (pp. 273–279). New York: Routledge Falmer.

Delpit, L. (1995). *Other people's children: Cultural conflict in the classroom.* New York: New Press.

Delprato, D. J., & Midgley, B. D. (1992). Some fundamentals of B. F. Skinner's behaviorism. *American Psychologist, 47,* 1507–1520.

Dembo, M., & Eaton, M. (2000). Self-regulation of academic learning in middle-level schools. *The Elementary School Journal, 100*(5), 472–490.

Dempster, F. N. (1989). Spacing effects and their implications for theory and practice. *Educational Psychology Review, 1,* 309–330.

Dempster, F. N. (1991). Synthesis of research on reviews and tests. *Educational Leadership, 72*(8), 71–76.

Dempster, F., & Corkill, A. (1999). Interference and inhibition in cognition and behavior: Unifying themes for educational psychology. *Educational Psychology Review, 11*(1), 1–74.

Dennis, I., & Tapsfield, P. (Eds.). (1996). *Human abilities: Their nature and measurement.* Mahwah, NJ: Erlbaum.

Denton, C. A., Anthony, J. L., Parker, R., & Hasbrouck, J. E. (2004). Effects of two tutoring programs on the English reading development of Spanish-English bilingual students. *The Elementary School Journal, 104*(4), 289–305.

Derry, S. J. (1991). Strategy and expertise in solving word problems. In C. McCormick, G. Miller, & M. Pressley (Eds.), *Cognitive strategies research: From basic research to educational applications.* New York: Springer-Verlag.

Deshler, D. D., Ellis, E. S., & Lenz, B. K. (1996). *Teaching students with learning disabilities: Strategies and methods.* (2nd ed.). Denver: Love.

Dev, P., Doyle, B. A., & Valente, B. (2002). Labels needn't stick: "At risk" first graders rescued with appropriate intervention. *Journal of Education for Students Placed at Risk, 7*(3), 327–332.

DeVries, R. (1997). Piaget's social theory. *Educational Researcher, 26*(2), 4–17.

Deyhle, D., & Swisher, K. (1995). Research in American Indian and Alaskan native education: From assimilation to self-determination. In M. W. Apple (Ed.), *Review of research in education, 22* (pp. 113–194). Washington, DC: American Educational Research Association.

Dianda, M., & Flaherty, J. (1995, April). *Effects of Success for All on the reading achievement of first graders in California bilingual programs.* Paper presented at the annual meeting of the American Educational Research Association, San Francisco, CA.

Diaz, C. (2001). *Multicultural education for the 21st century.* Boca Raton, FL: Addison-Wesley.

Diaz-Rico, L. T. (2004). *Teaching English learners: Strategies and methods.* Boston: Pearson.

Dick, W., Carey, L., & Carey, J. (2001). *The systematic design of instruction* (5th ed.). New York: Longman.

Diehm, C. (2004). From worn-out to web-based: Better student portfolios. *Phi Delta Kappan, 85*(10), 792–795.

Diener, C. I., & Dweck, C. S. (1978). An analysis of learned helplessness: Continuous changes in performance, strategy, and achievement cognitions following failure. *Journal of Personality and Social Psychology, 36,* 451–462.

Dillon, A., & Gabbard, R. (1998). Hypermedia as an educational technology: A review of the quantitative research literature on learner comprehension, control, and style. *Review of Educational Research, 68*(3), 322–349.

Dimino, J., Gersten, R., Carnine, D., & Blake, G. (1990). Story grammar: An approach for promoting at-risk secondary students' comprehension of literature. *Elementary School Journal, 91,* 19–32.

Dolan, L. J., Kellam, S. G., Brown, C. H., Werthamer-Larsson, L., Rebok, G. W., Mayer, L. S., Laudolff, J., Turkkan, J. S.,

Ford, C., & Wheeler, L. (1993). The short-term impact of two classroom-based preventive interventions on aggressive and shy behaviors and poor achievement. *Journal of Applied Developmental Psychology, 4,* 317–345.

Dooling, D. J., & Lachman, R. (1971). Effects of comprehension on retention of prose. *Journal of Experimental Psychology, 8,* 216–222.

Dornbusch, S. (1994). *Off the track.* Paper presented at the annual meeting of the Society for Research on Adolescence, San Diego, CA.

Dorr-Bremme, D. W., & Herman, J. (1986). *Assessing school achievement: A profile of classroom practices.* Los Angeles: Center for the Study of Evaluation, UCLA.

Downing, J. E. (2001). *Including students with severe and multiple disabilities in typical classrooms.* Baltimore: Brookes.

Doyle, W. (1984). How order is achieved in classrooms: An interim report. *Journal of Curriculum Studies, 16,* 259–277.

Doyle, W. (1990b). Classroom management techniques. In O. Moles (Ed.), *Student discipline strategies.* Albany: State University of New York Press.

Doyle, W., & Carter, K. (1984). Academic tasks in classrooms. *Curriculum Inquiry, 14,* 129–149.

Drabman, R., Spitalnik, R., & O'Leary, K. (1973). Teaching self-control to disruptive children. *Journal of Abnormal Psychology, 82,* 10–16.

Driscoll, M. P. (1994). *Psychology of learning for instruction.* Boston: Allyn & Bacon.

Driscoll, M. P. (2000). *Psychology of learning for instruction* (2nd ed.). Boston: Allyn & Bacon.

Droz, M., & Ellis, L. (1996). *Laughing while learning: Using humor in the classroom.* Longmont, CO: Sopris West.

Dryfoos, J. G. (1998). *Safe passage: Making it through adolescence in a risky society.* New York: Oxford University Press.

Dryfoos, J. G. (2003). *Adolescents at risk: Prevalence and prevention.* New York: Oxford University Press.

Duck, L. (2000). The ongoing professional journey. *Educational Leadership, 57*(8), 43–45.

Duell, O. K. (1994). Extended wait time and university student achievement. *American Educational Research Journal, 31*(2), 397–414.

Duffy, G. G., & Roehler, L. R. (1986). The subtleties of instructional mediation. *Educational Leadership, 43*(7), 23–27.

Dugger, W. (2001). Standards for technological literacy. *Phi Delta Kappan, 82*(7), 513–517.

Duke, N. K. (2000). For the rich it's richer: Print experiences and environments offered to children in very low- and very high-socioeconomic status first-grade classrooms. *American Educational Research Journal, 37*(2), 441–478.

Dukes, R., & Seidner, C. (1978). *Learning with simulations and games.* Beverly Hills, CA: Sage.

Dunkin, M. J., & Biddle, B. J. (1974). *A study of teaching.* New York: Holt, Rinehart and Winston.

Dunn, L. M. (1968). Special education for the mentally retarded—is it justified? *Exceptional Children, 35,* 5–22.

Dunn, R., & Dunn, K. (1993). *Teaching secondary students through their individual learning styles.* Boston: Allyn & Bacon.

Dunn, R., Beaudrey, J. S., & Klavas, A. (1989). Survey of research on learning styles. *Educational Leadership, 46*(6), 50–58.

DuPaul, G. J., Barkley, R. A., & McMurray, M. B. (1991). Therapeutic effects of medication on ADHD: Implications for school psychologists. *School Psychology Review, 20,* 203–219.

Durán, R. P. (1994). Cooperative learning for language-minority students. In R. DeVillar, C. Faltis, & J. Cummins (Eds.), *Cultural diversity in schools.* Albany: State University of New York Press.

Durso, F. T., & Coggins, K. A. (1991). Organized instruction for the improvement of word knowledge skills. *Journal of Educational Psychology, 83,* 108–112.

Dweck, C. S. (1986). Motivational processes affecting learning. *American Psychologist, 41,* 1040–1048.

Ebeling, D. G. (2000). Adapting your teaching to any learning style. *Phi Delta Kappan, 82*(3), 247–248.

Eccles, J. S., Wigfield, A., & Byrnes, J. (2003). Cognitive development in adolescence. In R. M. Lerner, M. A. Easterbrooks, & J. Mistry (Eds.), *Handbook of psychology: Vol. 6. Developmental psychology* (pp. 325–350). Hoboken, NJ: Wiley.

Eccles, J. S., Wigfield, A., Midgley, C., Reuman, D., MacIver, D., & Feldlaufer, H. (1993). Negative efforts of traditional middle schools on students' motivation. *The Elementary School Journal, 93*(5), 553–574.

Echevarria, J., Vogt, M. E., & Short, D. (2004). *Making content comprehensible for English learners: The SIOP model.* Boston: Allyn & Bacon.

Eckensberger, L. H. (1994). Moral development and its measurement across cultures. In W. J. Lonner & R. S. Malpass (Eds.), *Psychology and culture* (pp. 75–79). Boston: Allyn & Bacon.

Eden, G. F., Van Meter, J. W., Rumsey, J. M., Maisog, J. M., Woods, R. P., & Zeffird, T. A. (1996). Abnormal processing of visual motion in dyslexia revealed by functional brain imaging. *Nature, 382,* 66–69.

Education Commission of the States. (2000). *Technology: Equitable access in schools.* Denver, CO: Author.

Educational Testing Service. (1995). *Performance assessment: Different needs, difficult answers.* Princeton, NJ: Author.

Educational Testing Service. (1996). *Computers in classrooms: The status of technology in U.S. schools.* Princeton, NJ: Author.

Edwards, W. (1954). The theory of decision making. *Psychology Bulletin, 51,* 380–417.

Egan, K. (1989). Memory, imagination, and learning: Connected by the story. *Phi Delta Kappan, 70,* 455–459.

Egeland, P. (1996). Pulleys, planes, and student performance. *Educational Leadership, 54*(4), 41–45.

Ehri, L. C., Nunes, S. R., Stahl, S. A., & Willows, D. M. (2001). Systematic phonics instruction helps students learn to read: Evidence from the National Reading Panel's meta-analysis. *Review of Educational Research, 71*(3), 393–447.

Eichenbaum, H. (2003). Memory systems. In M. Gallagher & R. J. Nelson (Eds.), *Handbook of psychology: Vol. 3. Biological psychology* (pp. 543–558). Hoboken, NJ: Wiley.

Einerson, M. (1998). Fame, fortune, and failure: Young girls' moral language surrounding popular culture. *Youth and Society, 30,* 241–257.

Eisenberg, N., & Mussen, P. H. (1989). *The roots of prosocial behavior in children.* New York: Cambridge University Press.

Eisenberger, R., & Cameron, J. (1998). Reward, intrinsic interest, and creativity: New findings. *American Psychologist, 53*(6), 676–679.

Eisenberger, R., Pierce, W. D., & Cameron, J. (1999). Effects of rewards on intrinsic motivation—negative, neutral, and positive: Comment on Deci, Koestner, and Ryan (1999). *Psychological Bulletin, 125,* 677–691.

Eisner, E. W. (1982). The contribution of painting to children's cognitive development. *Journal of Education, 164,* 227–237.

Elbaum, B., & Vaughn, S. (2001). School-based interventions to enhance the self-concept of students with learning disabilities: A meta-analysis. *The Elementary School Journal, 101*(3), 303–330.

Elbaum, B., Vaughn, S., Hughes, M., & Moody, S. (2000). How effective are one-to-one tutoring programs in reading for elementary students at risk for reading failure? A meta-analysis of the intervention research. *Journal of Educational Psychology 92*(4), 605–619.

Elkind, D. (1989). Developmentally appropriate practice: Philosophical and practical implications. *Phi Delta Kappan, 71*(2), 113–117.

Ellis, A. K. (2001a). Authentic and performance assessment. In A. K. Ellis (Ed.), *Research on educational innovations.* Larchmont, NY: Eye on Education.

Ellis, A. K. (2001b). Cooperative learning. In A. K. Ellis (Ed.), *Research on educational innovations.* Larchmont, NY: Eye on Education.

Ellis, A. K. (2001c). Direct instruction. In A. K. Ellis (Ed.), *Research on educational innovations.* Larchmont, NY: Eye on Education.

Ellis, A. K. (2001d). Innovations from brain research. In A. K. Ellis (Ed.), *Research on educational innovations.* Larchmont, NY: Eye on Education.

Ellis, A. K. (2001f). Teaching for intelligence. In A. K. Ellis (Ed.), *Research on educational innovations.* Larchmont, NY: Eye on Education.

Ellis, J., Semb, G. B., & Cole, B. (1998). Very long-term memory for information taught in school. *Contemporary Educational Psychology, 23,* 419–433.

Ellwein, M. C., Walsh, D. J., Eads, G. M., II, & Miller, A. (1991). Using readiness tests to route kindergarten students: The snarled intersection of psychometrics, policy, and practice. *Educational Evaluation and Policy Analysis, 13*(2), 159–175.

Elmore, R. F., & Fuhrman, S. H. (2001). Holding schools accountable: Is it working? *Phi Delta Kappan, 83*(1), 67–72.

Emerson, M. J., & Miyake, A. (2003). The role of inner speech in task switching: A dual-task investigation. *Journal of Memory and Language, 48,* 148–168.

Emmer, E. T., & Aussiker, A. (1990). School and classroom discipline programs: How well do they work? In O. C. Moles (Ed.), *Student discipline strategies.* Albany: State University of New York Press.

Emmer, E. T., & Gerwels, M. C. (2002). Cooperative learning in elementary classrooms: Teaching practices and lesson characteristics. *The Elementary School Journal, 103*(1), 75–91.

Emmer, E. T., & Stough, L. M. (2001). Classroom management: A critical part of educational psychology, with implications for teacher education. *Educational Psychologist, 36*(2), 103–112.

Emmer, E. T., Evertson, C. M., Clements, B., & Worsham, M. E. (2000). *Classroom management for elementary teachers* (5th ed.). Boston: Allyn & Bacon.

Emmer, E., Evertson, C., & Anderson, L. (1980). Effective classroom management at the beginning of the school year. *Elementary School Journal, 80,* 219–231.

Emmer, E., Evertson, C., & Worsham, M. (2003). *Classroom management for secondary teachers* (6th ed.). Boston: Allyn & Bacon.

Engle, R. W., Nations, J. K., & Cantor, J. (1990). Is "working memory capacity" just another name for word knowledge? *Journal of Educational Psychology, 82*(4), 799–804.

Englert, C. S., Raphael, T. E., Anderson, L. M., Anthony, H. M., & Stevens, D. D. (1991). Making strategies and self-talk visible: Writing instruction in regular and special education classrooms. *American Educational Research Journal, 28,* 337–372.

Ensminger, M. E., & Slusarcick, A. L. (1992). Paths to high school graduation or dropout: A longitudinal study of a first grade cohort. *Sociology of Education, 65,* 95–113.

Entwisle, D. R., Alexander, K. L., & Olson, L. (1997). *Children, schools, and inequality.* Boulder, CO: Westview.

Entwisle, D., Alexander, L., & Olson, L. S. (2001). Keep the faucet flowing: Summer learning and home environment. *American Educator, 25*(3), 10–15.

Epstein, J. L., & Van Voorhis, F. L. (2001). More than minutes: Teachers' roles in designing homework. *Educational Psychologist, 36*(3), 181–193.

Epstein, J. L., Sanders, M. G., Salinas, K., Simon, B., Van Voorhis, F., & Jansorn, N. (2002). *School, family and community partnerships: Your handbook for action* (2nd ed.). Thousand Oaks, CA: Corwin.

Epstein, M. H., & Cullinan, D. (1992). Emotional/behavioral problems. In M. C. Alkin (Ed.), *Encyclopedia of educational research* (6th ed.) (pp. 430–432). New York: Macmillan.

Ericcson, K. A., & Kintsch, W. (1995). Long-term working memory. *Psychological Review, 102,* 211–245.

Erickson, F. (1997). Culture in society and in educational practices. In J. A. Banks & C. A. M. Banks (Eds.), *Multicultural education: Issues and perspectives* (pp. 32–60). Boston: Allyn & Bacon.

Erikson, E. H. (1963). *Childhood and society* (2nd ed.). New York: Norton.

Erikson, E. H. (1968). *Identity, youth and crisis.* New York: Norton.

Erikson, E. H. (1980). *Identity and the life cycle* (2nd ed.). New York: Norton.

Ethington, C. A. (1991). Testing a model of achievement behaviors. *American Educational Research Journal, 28,* 155–172.

Evans, E. D., & Richardson, R. C. (1995). Corporal punishment: What teachers should know. *Teaching Exceptional Children, 27*(2), 33–36.

Evans, S. W., Pelham, W. E., Smith, B. H., Bukstein, O., Gnagy, E. M., Greiner, A. R., Altenderfer, L., & Baron-Myak, C. (2000). Dose-response effect of methylphenidate on ecologically valid measures of academic performance and classroom behavior in adolescents with ADHD. *Experimental and Clinical Psychopharmacology, 9*(2), 163–175.

Evans, T. D. (1996). Encouragement: The key to reforming the classrooms. *Educational Leadership, 54*(1), 81–85.

Everson, H., Smodlaka, I., & Tobias, S. (1994). Exploring the relationship of test anxiety and metacognition on reading test performance: A cognitive analysis. *Anxiety, Stress, and Coping, 7,* 85–96.

Everson, H., Tobias, S., Hartman, H., & Gourgey, A. (1993). Test anxiety and the curriculum: The subject matters. *Anxiety, Stress, and Coping, 6,* 1–8.

Evertson, C. M. (1982). Differences in instructional activities in higher- and lower-achieving junior high English and math classes. *Elementary School Journal, 82,* 329–350.

Evertson, C. M., & Emmer, E. T. (1982). Effective management at the beginning of the year in junior high classes. *Journal of Educational Psychology, 74,* 485–498.

Evertson, C. M., & Harris, A. H. (1992). What we know about managing classrooms. *Educational Leadership, 49*(7), 74–78.

Evertson, C. M., & Harris, A. H. (1993). What we know about managing classrooms. In K. M. Cauley, F. Linder, & J. H. McMillan (Eds.), *Annual editions: Educational psychology 93/94.* Guilford, CT: Dushkin.

Evertson, C. M., & Randolph, C. H. (1995). Classroom management in the learning-centered classroom. In A. C. Ornstein (Ed.), *Teaching: Theory into practice.* Boston: Allyn & Bacon.

Evertson, C. M., Emmer, E. T., & Brophy, J. E. (1980). Predictors of effective teaching in junior high mathematics classrooms. *Journal for Research in Mathematics Education, 11,* 167–178.

Evertson, C. M., Emmer, E. T., & Worsham, M. E. (2000). *Classroom management for elementary teachers* (5th ed.). Boston: Allyn & Bacon.

Evertson, C. M., Emmer, E. T., & Worsham, M. E. (2003). *Classroom management for elementary teachers* (6th ed.). Boston: Allyn & Bacon.

Evertson, C. M., Emmer, E. T., Clements, B. S., Sanford, J. P., & Worsham, M. E. (1994). *Classroom management for elementary teachers* (3rd ed.). Boston: Allyn & Bacon.

Evertson, C. M., Weade, R., Green, J., & Crawford, J. (1985). *Effective classroom management and instruction: An exploration of models.* Nashville, TN: Vanderbilt University.

Fabes, R. A., & Martin, C. L. (2000). *Exploring child development.* Boston: Allyn & Bacon.

Fagan, E. R., Hassler, D. M., & Szabo, M. (1981). Evaluation of questioning strategies in language arts instruction. *Research in the Teaching of English, 15,* 267–273.

Fahey, J. A. (2000). Who wants to differentiate instruction? We did . . . *Educational Leadership, 58*(1), 70–72.

Fantuzzo, J. W., Davis, G. V., & Ginsburg, M. D. (1995). Effects of parent involvement in isolation or in combination with peer tutoring on student self-concept and mathematics achievement. *Journal of Educational Psychology, 87*(2), 272–281.

Fantuzzo, J. W., King, J. A., & Heller, L. R. (1992). Effects of reciprocal peer tutoring on mathematics and school adjustment: A component analysis. *Journal of Educational Psychology, 84,* 33–39.

Fantuzzo, J. W., Polite, K., & Grayson, N. (1990). An evaluation of reciprocal peer tutoring across elementary school settings. *Journal of School Psychology, 28,* 309–323.

Farmer, T., Leung, M.-C., Pearl, R., Rodkin, P., Cadwallader, T., & Van Acker, R. (2002). Deviant or diverse peer groups? The peer affiliations of aggressive elementary students. *Journal of Educational Psychology, 94* (3), 611–620.

Fashola, O. S. (2001) *Building effective after-school programs: Research and practice.* Thousand Oaks, CA: Corwin.

Fashola, O. S., & Slavin, R. E. (1998). Effective dropout prevention and college attendance programs for students placed at risk. *Journal of Education for Students Placed at Risk, 3*(2), 159–183.

Fashola, O. S. (2002). *Building effective after school programs.* Thousand Oaks, CA: Corwin.

Fay, J. (2001). The classroom of your dreams. In B. Sornson (Ed.), *Preventing early learning failure.* Alexandria, VA: ASCD.

Feingold, A. (1992). Sex differences in variability in intellectual abilities: A new look at an old controversy. *Review of Educational Research, 62*(1), 61–84.

Feldhusen, J. F. (1996). How to identify and develop special talents. *Educational Leadership, 53*(5), 66–69.

Feldhusen, J. F. (1998). Programs for the gifted few or talent development for the many? *Phi Delta Kappan, 79*(10), 734–738.

Feldman, D. H. (2003). Cognitive development in childhood. In R. M. Lerner, M. A. Easterbrooks, & J. Mistry (Eds.), *Handbook of psychology: Vol. 6. Developmental psychology* (pp. 195–210). Hoboken, NJ: Wiley.

Fellows, N. J. (1994). A window into thinking: Using student writing to understand conceptual changes in science learning. *Journal of Science Teaching, 31,* 985–1001.

Fennema, E., Carpenter, T. P., Jacobs, V. R., Franke, M. L., & Levi, L. W. (1998). A longitudinal study of gender differences in young children's mathematical thinking. *Educational Researcher, 27*(5), 6–11.

Fennema, E., Franke, M. L., Carpenter, T. P., & Carey, D. A. (1993). Using children's mathematical knowledge in instruction. *American Educational Research Journal, 30*(3), 555–583.

Fenson, L., Dale, P. S., Reznick, J. S., Bates, E., Thal, D. J., & Pethick, S. J. (1994). Variability in early communicative development. *Monographs of the Society for Research in Child Development, 59*(5), No. 242.

Ferguson, R., & Mehta, J. (2004). An unfinished journey: The legacy of Brown and the narrowing of the achievement gap. *Phi Delta Kappan, 85*(9), 656–669.

Feuerstein, R. (1980). *Instrumental enrichment: An intervention program for cognitive modifiability.* Baltimore: University Park Press.

Feuerstein, R., & Kozulin, A. (1995). The Bell Curve: Getting the facts right. *Educational Leadership, 52*(7), 71–74.

Fielding, L. G., Anderson, R. C., & Pearson, P. D. (1990). *How discussion questions influence children's story understanding* (Tech. Rep. No. 490). Champaign: University of Illinois, Center for the Study of Reading.

Finn, C. (2003). Small classes in American schools: Research, practice, and politics. *Phi Delta Kappan, 83*(7), 551–559.

Finn, J. D., & Achilles, C. M. (1999). Tennessee's Class Size Study: Findings, implications, misconceptions. *Educational Evaluation and Policy Analysis, 21*(2), 97–109.

Finn, J. D., & Cox, D. (1992). Participation and withdrawal among fourth-grade pupils. *American Educational Research Journal, 29*(1), 141–162.

Finn, J. D., Pannozzo, G. M., & Achilles, C. M. (2003). The "why's" of class size: Student behavior in small classes. *Review of Educational Research, 73*(3), 321–368.

Finn, J. D., Pannozzo, G. M., & Voelkl, K. E. (1995). Disruptive and inattentive-withdrawn behavior and achievement among fourth graders. *The Elementary School Journal, 95*(5), 421–434.

Fiordaliso, R., Lordeman, A., Filipczak, J., & Friedman, R. M. (1977). Effects of feedback on absenteeism in the junior high school. *Journal of Educational Research, 70,* 188–192.

Fisher, C. W., Berliner, D. C., Filby, N. N., Marliave, R., Cahen, L. S., Dishaw, M. M., & Moore, J. E. (1978). *Teaching behaviors, academic learning time, and student achievement: Final report of Phase III-B, beginning teacher evaluation study.* (Tech. Report V-1). San Francisco: Far West Laboratory for Educational Research and Development.

Fisher, D., Sax, C., & Grove, K. (2000). The resilience of changes promoting inclusiveness in an urban elementary school. *The Elementary School Journal, 100*(3), 213–228.

Fisher, W. W., & Mazur, J. E. (1997). Basic and applied research on choice responding. *Journal of Applied Behavior Analysis, 30,* 387–410.

Fiske, E. B. (1989, July 12). The misleading concept of "average" on reading tests changes, and more students fall below it. *The New York Times.*

Fitzgerald, H. E., Mann, T., Cabrera, N., & Wong, M. M. (2003). Diversity in caregiving contexts. In R. M. Lerner, M. A. Easterbrooks, & J. Mistry (Eds.), *Handbook of psychology: Vol. 6. Developmental psychology* (pp. 135–167). Hoboken, NJ: Wiley.

Fitzgerald, J. (1995). English as a second language instruction in the United States: A research review. *Journal of Reading Behavior, 27,* 115–152.

Fitzpatrick, A. R. (1989). Social influences in standard setting: The effects of social interaction on group judgments. *Review of Educational Research, 59*(3), 315–328.

Flanagan, C. (1993). Gender and social class: Intersecting issues in women's achievement. *Educational Psychologist, 28*(4), 357–378.

Flavell, J. H. (1985). *Cognitive development* (2nd ed.). Englewood Cliffs, NJ: Prentice-Hall.

Flavell, J. H. (1986, January). Really and truly. *Psychology Today,* 38–44.

Flavell, J. H. (1996). Piaget's legacy. *Psychological Science, 7*(4), 200–203.

Flavell, J. H., Green, F. L., Flavell, E. R., & Grossman, J. B. (1997). The development of children's knowledge about inner speech. *Child Development, 68,* 39–47.

Flavell, J. H., Miller, P. H., & Miller, S. A. (1993). *Cognitive development.* Englewood Cliffs, NJ: Prentice Hall.

Fletcher, J. D. (1992). Individualized systems of instruction. In M. C. Alkin (Ed.), *Encyclopedia of educational research* (6th ed.) (pp. 612–620). New York: Macmillan.

Fletcher, J. M., Shaywitz, S. E., Shankweiler, D. P., Katz, L., Liberman, I. Y., Stvebing, K. K., Francis, D. J., Fowler, A. E., & Shaywitz, B. A. (1994). Cognitive profiles of reading disability: Comparisons of discrepancy and low achievement definitions. *Journal of Educational Psychology, 86,* 6–23.

Flexner, C. (2001). Enhancing the listening environment for early learning success. In B. Sornson (Ed.), *Preventing early learning failure.* Alexandria, VA: ASCD.

Flouri, E., & Buchanan, A. (2004). Early father's and mother's involvement and child's later educational outcomes. *British Journal of Educational Psychology, 74*(2), 141–153.

Fogarty, R. (Ed.). (1993). *The multiage classroom.* Palatine, IL: IRI/Skylight.

Foos, P. W., Mora, J. J., & Tkacz, S. (1994). Student study techniques and the generation effect. *Journal of Educational Psychology, 86*(4), 567–576.

Ford, D. Y. (1996). *Reversing underachievement among gifted black students: Promising practices and programs.* New York: Teachers College Press.

Forness, S. R., & Kavale, K. A. (2000). What definitions of disabilities say and don't say: A critical analysis. *Journal of Learning Disabilities, 33*(3), 239–256.

Forsterling, F. (1985). Attribution retraining: A review. *Psychological Bulletin, 98,* 495–512.

Foster, D., & Noyce, P. (2004). The mathematics assessment collaborative: Performance testing to improve instruction. *Phi Delta Kappan, 85*(5), 367–374.

Francis, D. J., Shaywitz, S. E., Shaywitz, B. A., Stuebing, K. K., & Fletcher, J. M. (1996). Developmental lag versus deficit models of reading disability: A longitudinal, individual growth curves analysis. *Journal of Educational Psychology, 88*(1), 3–17.

Franklin, R. D., Allison, D. B., & Gorman, B. S. (Eds.). (1997). *Design and analysis of single-case research.* Mahwah, NJ: Erlbaum.

Frederiksen, N. (1984a). Implications of cognitive theory for instruction in problem solving. *Review of Educational Research, 54,* 363–407.

Frederiksen, N. (1984b). The real test bias: Influences of testing on teaching and learning. *American Psychologist, 39,* 193–202.

Fredricks, J. A., Blemenfeld, P. C., & Paria, A. H. (2004). School engagement: Potential of the concept, state of the evidence. *Review of Educational Research, 74*(1), 59–109.

Freiberg, H. J. (1996). From tourists to citizens in the classroom. *Educational Leadership, 54*(1), 32–36.

Freiberg, H. J., Connell, M. L., & Lorentz, J. (2001). Effects of consistency management on student mathematics achievement on seven Chapter I elementary schools. *Journal of Education for Students Placed at Risk, 6*(3), 249–270.

French, E. G. (1956). Motivation as a variable in work partner selection. *Journal of Abnormal and Social Psychology, 55,* 96–99.

Friedman, L. (1995). The space factor in mathematics: Gender differences. *Review of Educational Research, 65*(1), 22–50.

Friedman, L. (2003). Promoting opportunity after school. *Educational Leadership, 60*(4), 79–82.

Friend, M., & Bursuck, W. (2002). *Including students with special needs* (3rd ed.). Boston: Allyn & Bacon.

Friend, M., & Bursuck, W. D. (1999). *Including students with special needs: A practical guide for classroom teachers* (2nd ed.). Boston: Allyn & Bacon.

Friend, R. (2001). Effects of strategy instruction on summary writing of college students. *Contemporary Educational Psychology, 26*(1), 3–24.

Frisbie, D. A., & Waltman, K. K. (1993). Developing a personal grading plan. In K. M. Cauley, F. Linder, & J. H. McMillan (Eds.), *Annual editions: Educational psychology 93/94.* Guilford, CT: Dushkin.

Fuchs, D., & Fuchs, L. S. (1995). What's special about special education? *Phi Delta Kappan, 76*(7), 522–530.

Fuchs, D., & Fuchs, L. S. (1997). Peer-assisted learning strategies: Making classrooms more responsive to diversity. *American Educational Research Journal, 34*(1), 174–206.

Fuchs, D., Fuchs, L. S., & Fernstrom, P. (1993). A conservative approach to special education reform: Mainstreaming through transenvironmental programming and curriculum-based measurement. *American Educational Research Journal, 30,* 149–177.

Fuchs, D., Fuchs, L. S., Bahr, M. W., Fernstrom, P., & Stecker, P. M. (1990). Mainstream assistance teams: A scientific basis for the art of consultation. *Exceptional Children, 56,* 493–513.

Fuchs, L. S., Fuchs, D., Bentz, J., Phillips, N. B., & Hamlett, C. L. (1994). The nature of student interactions during peer tutoring with and without prior training and experience. *American Educational Research Journal, 31*(1), 75–103.

Fuchs, L. S., Fuchs, D., Hamlett, C. L., & Stecker, P. M. (1991). Effects of curriculum-based measurement and consultation on teacher planning and student achievement in mathematics operations. *American Educational Research Journal, 28*(3), 617–641.

Fuchs, L. S., Fuchs, D., Karns, K., Hamlett, C. L., Katzaroff, M., & Dutka, S. (1997). Effects of task-focused goals on low-achieving students without learning disabilities. *American Educational Research Journal, 34*(3), 513–543.

Fuchs, L. S., Fuchs, D., Kazden, S., & Allen, S. (1999). Effects of peer-assisted learning strategies in reading with and without training in elaborated help giving. *The Elementary School Journal, 99*(3), 201–221.

Fuchs, L., Fuchs, D., Finelli, R., Courey, S., & Hamlett, C. (2003). Expanding schema-based transfer instruction to help third graders solve real-life mathematical problems. *American Educational Research Journal, 41*(2), 419–445.

Fuchs, L., Fuchs, D., Prentice, K., Burch, M., Hamlett, C., Owen, R., et al. (2003). Enhancing third-grade students' mathematical problem solving with self-regulated learning strategies. *Journal of Educational Psychology, 94*(2), 306–315.

Furman, W., & Buhrmester, D. (1992). Age and sex differences in perceptions of networks of personal relationships. *Child Development, 63*, 103–115.

Fuson, K. C. (1992). Research on whole number addition and subtraction. In D. Grouws (Ed.), *Handbook of research on mathematics teaching and learning* (pp. 243–275). New York: Macmillan.

Gabler, I. C., & Schroeder, M. (2003). Constructivist methods for the secondary classroom. Boston, MA: Allyn & Bacon.

Gaddy, M. L. (1998, April). *Reading and studying from highlighted text: Memory for information highlighted by others.* Paper presented at the annual meeting of the American Educational Research Association, San Diego, CA.

Gage, N. L. (1991). The obviousness of social and educational research results. *Educational Researcher, 20*(1), 10–16.

Gage, N. L. (1994). The scientific status of the behavioral sciences: The case of research on teaching. *Teaching and Teacher Education, 10*(5), 565–577.

Gage, N. L., & Needels, M. C. (1989). Process-product research on teaching: A review of criticism. *Elementary School Journal, 89*, 253–300.

Gagné, R. (1977). *The conditions of learning* (3rd ed.). New York: Holt, Rinehart and Winston.

Gagné, R., & Briggs, L. (1979). *Principles of instructional design* (2nd ed.). New York: Holt, Rinehart and Winston.

Gagnon, G. W., & Collay, M. (2001). *Designing for learning: Six elements in constructivist classrooms.* Thousand Oaks, CA: Corwin.

Galambos, N. L., & Costigan, C. L. (2003). Emotional and personality development in adolescence. In R. M. Lerner, M. A. Easterbrooks, & J. Mistry (Eds.), *Handbook of psychology: Vol. 6. Developmental psychology* (pp. 351–372). Hoboken, NJ: Wiley.

Gall, M. (1984). Synthesis of research on teachers' questioning. *Educational Leadership, 42,* 40–47.

Gall, M. D. (1987). Discussion methods. In M. J. Dunkin (Ed.), *International encyclopedia of teaching and teacher education.* New York: Pergamon.

Gall, M., Ward, B., Berliner, D., Cahen, L., Winne, P., Glashoff, J., & Stanton, G. (1978). Effects of questioning techniques and recitation on student learning. *American Educational Research Journal, 15,* 175–199.

Gallagher, A. M., & DeLisi, R. (1994). Gender differences in scholastic aptitude test: Mathematics problem solving among high ability students. *Journal of Educational Psychology, 86*(2), 204–211.

Gallagher, C. J. (2003). Reconciling a tradition of testing with a new learning paradigm. *Educational Psychology Review, 15*(1), 83–99.

Gallagher, J. J. (1992). Gifted persons. In M. C. Alkin (Ed.), *Encyclopedia of educational research* (6th ed.) (pp. 544–549). New York: Macmillan.

Gallagher, J. J. (1995). Education of gifted students: A civil rights issue? *Phi Delta Kappan, 76*(5), 408–410.

Gallimore, R., & Goldenberg, C. (2001). Analyzing cultural models and settings to connect minority achievement and school improvement research. *Educational Psychologist, 36*(1), 45–56.

Gamoran, A. (1984, April). *Egalitarian versus elitist use of ability grouping.* Paper presented at the annual convention of the American Educational Research Association, New Orleans, LA.

Gamoran, A., Nystrand, M., Berends, M., & LePore, P. C. (1995). An organizational analysis of the effects of ability grouping. *American Educational Research Journal, 32,* 687–715.

Gandal, M., & McGiffert, L. (2003). The power of testing. *Educational Leadership, 60*(5), 39–42.

Gandal, M., & Vranek, J. (2001). Standards: Here today, here tomorrow. *Educational Leadership, 59*(1), 6–13.

Ganesh, T., & Berliner, D. (2004, April). *Practices of computer use in elementary education: Perceived and missed opportunities.* Paper presented at the annual meeting of the American Educational Research Association, San Diego, CA.

Garbarino, J. (1997). Educating children in a socially toxic environment. *Educational Leadership, 54*(7), 12–16.

Garber, H. L. (1988). *The Milwaukee Project: Preventing mental retardation in children at risk.* Washington, DC: American Association on Mental Retardation.

Garcia, J. (1993). The changing image of ethnic groups in textbooks. *Phi Delta Kappan, 75*(1), 29–35.

Gardner, H. (1995). Reflections on multiple intelligences: Myths and messages. *Phi Delta Kappan, 77,* 200–209.

Gardner, H. (2000). *Intelligence reframed: Multiple intelligences for the 21st century.* New York: Basic Books.

Gardner, H. (2003, April). *Multiple intelligences after twenty years.* Paper presented at the annual meetings of the American Educational Research Association, Chicago, IL.

Gardner, H., & Hatch, T. (1989). Multiple intelligences go to school. *Educational Researcher, 18*(8), 6.

Gardner, M. K. (1985). Cognitive psychological approaches to instructional task analysis. In E. W. Gordon (Ed.), *Review of research in education, Vol. 12* (pp. 157–195). Washington, DC: American Educational Research Association.

Gartner, A., & Lipsky, D. K. (1987). Beyond special education: Toward a quality system for all students. *Harvard Educational Review, 57,* 367–395.

Garvey, C. (1990). *Play* (enlarged ed.). Cambridge, MA: Harvard University Press.

Gay, G. (2004). The importance of multicultural education. *Educational Leadership, 61*(4), 30–34.

Ge, X., Conger, R. D., & Elder, G. H. (2001). The relation between puberty and psychological distress in adolescent boys. *Journal of Research on Adolescence, 11,* 49–70.

Gearhart, M., & Herman, J. L. (1995). *Portfolio assessment: Whose work is it?* Los Angeles: UCLA, Center for the Study of Evaluation.

Geisert, P. G., & Futrell, M. K. (2000). *Teachers, computers, and curriculum: Microcomputers in the classroom* (3rd ed.). Boston: Allyn & Bacon.

Gelman, R. (1979). Preschool thought. *American Psychologist, 34,* 900–905.

Gelman, R. (2000). Domain specificity and variability in cognitive development. *Child Development, 71,* 854–856.

Gelman, R., & Brenneman, K. (1994). Domain specificity and cultural variation are not inconsistent. In L. A. Hirschfeld & S. Gelman (Eds.), *Mapping the mind: Domain specificity in cognition and culture.* New York: Cambridge University Press.

General Accounting Office. (1995). *Early childhood centers: Services to prepare children for school often limited.* Washington, DC: Author.

Gentner, D., Loewenstein, J., & Thompson, L. (2002). Learning and transfer: A general role for analogical encoding. *Journal of Educational Psychology, 94*(2), 393–408.

Gersten, R., Fuchs, L. S., Williams, J. P., & Baker, S. (2001). Teaching reading comprehension strategies to students with learning disabilities: A review of research. *Review of Educational Research, 71*(2), 279–320.

Gersten, R., Taylor, R., & Graves, A. (1999). Direct instruction and diversity. In R. Stevens (Ed.), *Teaching in American schools* (pp. 81–106). Upper Saddle River, NJ: Merrill/Prentice-Hall.

Giaconia, R. M., & Hedges, L. V. (1982). Identifying features of effective open education. *Review of Educational Research, 52,* 579–602.

Gibbons, A. S., Duffin, J. R., Robertson, D. J., & Thompson, B. (1998, April). *Effects of administering feedback following extended problem solving.* Paper presented at the annual meeting of the American Educational Research Association, San Diego, CA.

Gijselaers, W. H., & Schmidt, H. G. (1995). Effects of quantity of instruction on time spent on learning and achievement. *Educational Research and Evaluation, 1*(2), 183–201.

Gilligan, C. (1982). *In a different voice: Sex differences in the expression of moral judgment.* Cambridge, MA: Harvard University Press.

Gilligan, C. (1985). *Remapping development.* Paper presented at the biennial meeting of the Society for Research in Child Development, Toronto.

Gilligan, C., & Attanucci, J. (1998). Two moral orientations: Gender differences and similarities. *Merrill-Palmer Quarterly, 34,* 223–237.

Glantz, M. D., Johnson, J., & Huffman, L. (Eds.). (2002). *Resilience and development: Positive life adaptations.* New York: Kluwer.

Glassman, Michael. (2001). Dewey and Vygotsky: Society, experience, and inquiry in educational practice. *Educational Researcher, 30*(4), 3–14.

Glazer, S. M., & Burke, E. M. (1994). *An integrated approach to early literacy.* Boston: Allyn & Bacon.

Goddard, R. D., Hoy, W. K., & Hoy, A. W. (2000). Collective teacher efficacy: Its meaning, measure, and impact on student achievement. *American Educational Research Journal, 37*(2), 479–507.

Goelman, H., Andersen, C. J., Anderson, J., Gouzouasis, P., Kendrick, M., Kindler, A. M., et al. (2003). In W. M. Reynolds & G. E. Miller (Eds.), *Handbook of psychology: Vol. 7. Educational psychology* (pp. 285–331). Hoboken, NJ: Wiley.

Gold, R. M., Reilly, A., Silberman, R., & Lehr, R. (1971). Academic achievement declines under pass-fail grading. *Journal of Experimental Education, 39,* 17–21.

Goldberg, A., Russell, M., & Cook, A. (2003). The effect of computers on student writing: A meta-analysis of studies from 1992 to 2002. *Journal of Technology, Learning, and Assessment, 2*(1), 1–51. Available from www.jtla.org.

Goldberg, B., & Richards, J. (1996). The Co-NECT design for school change. In S. Stringfield, S. Ross, & L. Smith (Eds.), *Bold plans for school restructuring: The new American schools development corporation designs.* Mahwah, NJ: Erlbaum.

Goldberg, M. F. (2004). The test mess. *Phi Delta Kappan, 85*(5), 361–366.

Goldman-Segall, R., & Maxwell, J. W. (2003). Computers, the Internet, and new media for learning. In W. M. Reynolds & G. E. Miller (Eds.), *Handbook of psychology: Vol. 7. Educational psychology* (pp. 393–427). Hoboken, NJ: Wiley.

Goldschmidt, P., & Wang, J. (1999). When can schools affect dropout behavior? A longitudinal multilevel analysis. *American Educational Research Journal, 36*(4), 715–738.

Goleman, D. (1995). *Emotional intelligence: Why it can matter more than IQ.* New York: Bantam.

Gomez, M. L., Grave, M. E., & Block, M. N. (1991). Reassessing portfolio assessment rhetoric and reality. *Language Arts, 68,* 620–628.

Good, T. L., & Brophy, J. E. (1997). *Looking in classrooms* (7th ed.). New York: Longman.

Good, T. L., Mulryan, C., & McCaslin, M. (1992). Grouping for instruction in mathematics: A call for programmatic research on small group processes. In D. Grouws (Ed.), *Handbook of research on mathematics teaching and learning* (pp. 165–196). New York: Macmillan.

Good, T., & Brophy, J. (2003). *Looking in classrooms*. Boston: Allyn & Bacon.

Good, T., & Grouws, D. (1977). Teaching effects: A process-product study in fourth grade mathematics classes. *Journal of Teacher Education, 28,* 49–54.

Good, T., & Grouws, D. (1979). The Missouri Mathematics Effectiveness Project: An experimental study in fourth-grade classrooms. *Journal of Educational Psychology, 71,* 355–362.

Good, T., Grouws, D., & Ebmeier, H. (1983). *Active mathematics teaching*. New York: Longman.

Goodlad, J. I. (1983). *A place called school*. New York: McGraw-Hill.

Goodman, K. S., & Goodman, Y. M. (1989). Introduction: Redefining education. In L. B. Bird (Ed.), *Becoming a whole language school: The Fair Oaks story* (pp. 3–10). Katonah, NY: Richard C. Owen.

Gordon, E. W., & Bhattacharyya, M. (1994). Race and intelligence. In R. J. Sternberg (Ed.), *Encyclopedia of human intelligence*. New York: Macmillan.

Gorin, J. S., & Blanchard, J. S. (2004, April). *The effect of curriculum alignment on elementary mathematics and reading achievement*. Paper presented at the annual meeting of the American Educational Research Association, San Diego, CA.

Goswami, U. (2004). Neuroscience and education. *British Journal of Educational Psychology, 74*(1), 1–14.

Gottfredson, D. C., Gottfredson, G. D., & Hybl, L. G. (1993). Managing adolescent behavior: A multiyear, multi-school study. *American Educational Research Journal, 30*(1), 179–215.

Gottfried, A. E., & Fleming, J. S. (2001). Continuity of academic intrinsic motivation from childhood through late adolescence: A longitudinal study. *Journal of Educational Psychology, 93*(1), 3–13.

Gottfried, A. E., & Gottfried, A. W. (2004). Toward the development of a conceptualization of gifted motivation. *Gifted Child Quarterly, 48*(2), 121–132.

Gottlieb, J., & Weinberg, S. (1999). Comparison of students referred and not referred for special education. *The Elementary School Journal, 99*(3), 187–200.

Graham, S. (1991). A review of attribution theory in achievement contexts. *Educational Psychology Review, 3*(1), 5–39.

Graham, S., & Weiner, B. (1996). Theory and principles of motivation. In D. C. Berliner & R. C. Calfee (Eds.), *Handbook of educational psychology* (pp. 63–84). New York: Macmillan.

Graham, S., MacArthur, C., & Schwartz, S. (1995). Effects of goal setting and procedural facilitation on the revising behavior and writing performance of students with writing and learning problems. *Journal of Educational Psychology, 87*(2), 230–240.

Grave, M. E., & DePerna, J. (2000). Redshirting and early retention: Who gets the "gift of time" and what are its outcomes? *American Educational Research Journal, 37*(2), 509–534.

Graves, D. (1983). *Writing: Teachers and children at work*. Exeter, NH: Heinemann.

Gredler, M. E. (1999). *Classroom assessment and learning*. New York, NY: Longman.

Green, M. (1989). *Theories of human development*. New York: Prentice Hall.

Greenbowe, T., Herron, J. D., Nurrenbern, S., Staver, J. R., & Ward, C. R. (1981). Teaching preadolescents to act as scientists: Replication and extension of an earlier study. *Journal of Educational Psychology, 73,* 705–711.

Greene, B. A., Miller, R. B., Crowson, M., Duke, B. L., & Akey, K. L. (2004). Predicting high school students' cognitive engagement and achievement: Contributions of classroom perceptions and motivation. *Contemporary Educational Psychology, 29*(4), 462–482.

Greene, D., & Lepper, M. R. (1974). How to turn play into work. *Psychology Today, 8,* 49–54.

Greene, J. P. (1997). A meta-analysis of the Rossell & Baker review of bilingual education research. *Bilingual Research Journal, 21*(2/3).

Greenfield, P., & Cocking, R. (Eds.). (1994). *Cross-cultural roots of minority child development*. Hillsdale, NJ: Erlbaum.

Greeno, J. G., Collins, A. M., & Resnick, L. R. (1996). Cognition and learning. In D. C. Berliner & R. C. Calfe (Eds.), *Handbook of educational psychology* (pp. 15–46). New York: Macmillan.

Greeno, J., & Goldman, S. (Eds.). (1998). *Thinking practices in mathematics and science learning*. Mahwah, NJ: Erlbaum.

Greenwood, C. R., Terry, B., Utley, C. A., Montagna, D., & Walker, D. (1993). Achievement, placement, and services: Middle school benefits of Classwide Peer Tutoring used at the elementary level. *School Psychology Review, 22*(3), 497–516.

Gregory, G. H., & Chapman, C. (2001). *Differentiated instructional strategies: One size doesn't fit all*. Thousand Oaks, CA: Corwin.

Gregory, J. F. (1995). The crime of punishment: Racial and gender disparities in the use of corporal punishment in U.S. public schools. *Journal of Negro Education, 64*(4), 454–462.

Gresham, F. M., & MacMillan, D. L. (1997). Social competence and affective characteristics of students with mild disabilities. *Review of Educational Research, 67*(4), 377–415.

Gronlund, N. E. (2000). *How to write and use instructional objectives* (6th ed.). Upper Saddle River, NJ: Merrill/Prentice-Hall.

Gronlund, N. E. (2003). *Assessment of student achievement* (7th ed.). Boston: Allyn & Bacon.

Grossman, H. (1995). *Teaching in a diverse society*. Boston: Allyn & Bacon.

Grossman, H., & Grossman, S. H. (1994). *Gender issues in education*. Boston: Allyn & Bacon.

Grusec, J. E., & Goodnow, J. J. (1994). Impact of parental discipline methods on the child's internalization of values. *Developmental Psychology, 30*, 4–19.

Guay, F., Marsh, H. W., & Boivin, M. (2003). Academic self-concept and academic achievement: Developmental perspectives on their causal ordering. *Journal of Educational Psychology, 95*(1), 124–136.

Guilford, J. P. (1988). Some changes in the Structure-of-Intellect model. *Educational and Psychological Measurement, 48*, 1–4.

Gump, P. V. (1982). School settings and their keeping. In D. L. Duke (Ed.), *Helping teachers manage classrooms* (pp. 98–114). Alexandria, VA: Association for Supervision and Curriculum Development.

Gunter, M. A., Estes, T. H., & Schwab, J. (2003). *Instruction: A models approach* (4th ed.). Boston: Allyn & Bacon.

Guskey, T. (2003). How classroom assessments improve learning. *Educational Leadership, 60*(5), 7–11.

Guskey, T. R. (1990). Cooperative mastery learning strategies. *The Elementary School Journal, 91*(1), 33–42.

Guskey, T. R. (1994). Making the grade: What benefits students? *Educational Leadership, 52*(2), 14–19.

Guskey, T. R. (1995). Mastery learning. In J. H. Block, S. T. Everson, & T. R. Guskey (Eds.), *School improvement programs* (pp. 91–109). New York: Scholastic.

Guskey, T. R. (2001). Helping standards make the grade. *Educational Leadership, 59*(1), 20–27.

Guskey, T. R. (2002). Computerized gradebooks and the myth of objectivity. *Phi Delta Kappan, 83*(10), 775–780.

Guskey, T. R., & Bailey, J. M. (2001). *Developing grading and reporting systems for student learning*. Thousand Oaks, CA: Corwin.

Gustafsson, J. E. (1994). General intelligence. In R. J. Sternberg (Ed.), *Encyclopedia of human intelligence*. New York: Macmillan.

Guthrie, J. T., & Cox, K. (2001). Classroom conditions for motivation and engagement in reading. *Educational Psychology Review, 13*(3), 283–302.

Guthrie, J. T., Bennett, S., & Weber, S. (1991). Processing procedural documents: A cognitive model for following written directions. *Educational Psychology Review, 3*, 249–265.

Gutiérrez, R., & Slavin, R. E. (1992). Achievement effects of the nongraded elementary school: A best evidence synthesis. *Review of Educational Research, 62*(4), 333–376.

Freiberg, H. J. (Ed.). *Beyond behaviorism: Changing the classroom management paradigm*. Boston: Allyn & Bacon.

Haertel, E. (1986, April). *Choosing and using classroom tests: Teachers' perspectives on assessment*. Paper presented at the annual meeting of the American Educational Research Association, San Francisco, CA.

Hakuta, K., & McLaughlin, B. (1996). Bilingualism and second language learning: Seven tensions that define the research. In D. C. Berliner & R. C. Calfee (Eds.), *Hand-

book of educational psychology* (pp. 603–621). New York: Macmillan.

Hakuta, K., Butler, Y. G., & Witt, D. (2000). *How long does it take English learners to attain proficiency?* The University of California Linguistic Minority Research Institute, Policy Report 2000-1.

Haladyna, T. M. (1997). *Writing test items to evaluate higher order thinking*. Boston: Allyn & Bacon.

Haladyna, T. M. (1999). *Developing and validating multiple-choice tests*. Mahwah, NJ: Erlbaum.

Hallahan, D. P., & Kauffman, J. M. (1997). *Exceptional learners: Introduction to special education* (7th ed.). Boston: Allyn & Bacon.

Hallahan, D., & Kauffman, J. (2003). *Exceptional learners* (9th ed.). Boston: Allyn & Bacon.

Halle, T. G., Kurtz-Coster, B., & Mahoney, J. L. (1997). Family influence on school achievement in low-income, African-American children. *Journal of Educational Psychology, 89*(3), 527–537.

Halpern, D. F. (1995). *Thought and knowledge: An introduction to critical thinking* (3rd ed.). Hillsdale, NJ: Erlbaum.

Halpern, D. F., & LaMay, M. L. (2000). The smarter sex: A critical review of sex differences in intelligence. *Educational Psychology Review, 12*(2), 229–246.

Halpern, D. F., Hansen, C., & Riefer, D. (1990). Analogies as an aid to understanding and memory. *Journal of Educational Psychology, 82*, 298–305.

Hamaker, C. (1986). The effects of adjunct questions on prose learning. *Review of Educational Research, 56*, 212–242.

Hamburg, D. A. (1992). *Today's children: Creating a future for a generation in crisis*. New York: Times Books.

Hamilton, R. J. (1985). A framework for the evaluation of the effectiveness of adjunct questions and objectives. *Review of Educational Research, 55*, 47–85.

Hamman, D., Berthelot, J., Saia, J., & Crowley, E. (2000). Teacher's coaching of learning and its relation to students' strategic learning. *Journal of Educational Psychology, 92*(2), 342–348.

Hand, B., & Treagust, D. F. (1991). Student achievement and science curriculum development using a constructive framework. *Schools, Science, and Mathematics, 91*, 172–176.

Hanline, M. F., & Daley, S. (2002). "Mom, will Haelie always have possibilities?" *Phi Delta Kappan, 84*(1), 73–76.

Hanna, G. S., & Bettmer, P. A. (2004). *Assessment for effective teaching: Using context-adaptive planning*. Boston: Pearson.

Hanson, S. L., Morrison, D. R., & Ginsburg, A. L. (1989). The antecedents of teenage fatherhood. *Demography, 26*, 579–596.

Harackiewicz, J., Barron, K., Tauer, J., & Carter, S. (2000). Short-term and long-term consequences of achievement goals: Predicting interest and performance over time. *Journal of Educational Psychology, 92*(2), 316–330.

Hardin, D. E., & McNelis, S. J. (1996). The resource center: Hub of inclusive activities. *Educational Leadership, 53*(5), 41–43.

Hardman, J. L., Drew, C., & Winston-Egan, M. (1996). *Human exceptionality: Society, school, and family* (5th ed.). Boston: Allyn & Bacon.

Hareli, S., & Weiner, B. (2002). Social emotions and personality inferences: A scaffold for a new direction in the study of achievement motivation. *Educational Psychologist, 37*(3), 183–189.

Hargreaves, A. (1996). Transforming knowledge: Blurring the boundaries between research, policy, and practice. *Educational Evaluation and Policy Analysis, 18*(2), 105–122.

Harpaz, Y., & Lefstein, A. (2000). Communities of thinking. *Educational Leadership, 58*(3), 54–57.

Harpring, S. A. (1985, April). *In-class alternatives to traditional Chapter I pullout programs.* Paper presented at the annual meeting of the American Educational Research Association, Chicago, IL.

Harris, K. R., & Alexander, P. A. (1998). Integrated, constructivist education: Challenge and reality. *Education Psychology Review, 10*(2), 155–127.

Harris, K. R., & Graham, S. (1996). Memo to constructivists: Skills count, too. *Educational Leadership, 53*(5), 26–29.

Harris, K. R., Graham, S., & Pressley, M. (2001). Cognitive strategies in reading and written language. In N. N. Singh & I. Beale (Eds.), *Current perspectives in learning disabilities: Nature, theory and treatment.* New York: Springer-Verlag.

Hart, B., & Risley, T. R. (1995). *Meaningful differences in the everyday experience of young American children.* Baltimore: Brookes.

Harter, S. (1998). The development of self-representations. In W. Damon (Ed.), *Handbook of child psychology* (Vol. 3, pp. 553–618). New York: Wiley.

Harter, S., Whitesell, N. R., & Kowalski, P. (1992). Individual differences in the effects of educational transitions on young adolescents' perceptions of competence and motivational orientation. *American Educational Research Journal, 29,* 777–807.

Hartup, W. W. (1996). The company they keep: Friendships and their developmental significance. *Child Development, 67,* 1–13.

Hartwell, R. E. (2001). Understanding disabilities. *Educational Leadership, 58*(7), 72–75.

Haslinger, J., Kelly, P., & O'Lara, L. (1996). Countering absenteeism, anonymity, and apathy. *Educational Leadership, 54*(1), 47–49.

Haspe, H., & Baddeley, J. (1991). Moral theory and culture: The case of gender. In W. Kurtines & J. L. Gewirtz (Eds.), *Handbook of moral behavior and development* (Vol. 1, pp. 223–250). Mahwah, NJ: Erlbaum.

Hasselbring, T., & Williams-Glaser, C. H. (2000). Use of computer technology to help students with special needs. *Children and Computer Technology, 10*(2), 102–122.

Hattie, J., & Marsh, H. W. (1996). The relationship between research and teaching: A meta-analysis. *Review of Educational Research, 66*(4), 507–542.

Hattie, J., Bibbs, J., & Purdie, N. (1996). Effects of learning skills interventions on student learning: A meta-analysis. *Review of Educational Research, 66*(2), 99–136.

Hatzichriston, C., & Hopf, D. (1996). A multiperspective comparison of peer sociometric status groups in childhood and adolescence. *Child Development, 67,* 1085–1102.

Hauser-Cram, P., Sirin, S. R., & Stipek, D. (2003). When teachers' and parents' values differ: Teachers' ratings of academic competence in children from low-income families. *Journal of Educational Psychology, 95*(4), 813–820.

Havens, J. (2003). Student web pages—a performance assessment they'll love. *Phi Delta Kappan, 84*(9), 710–711.

Hawkins, J. D., Guo, J., Hill, K., Battin-Pearson, S., & Abbott, R. (2001). Long-term effects of the Seattle social development intervention on school bonding trajectories. *Applied Developmental Sciences, 5,* 225–236.

Hawkins, J. D., Herrenkohl, T. I., Farrington, D. P., Brewer, D., Catalano, R. F., Harachi, T. W., & Cothern, L. (2000). *Predictors of youth violence.* Washington, DC: Office of Juvenile Justice and Delinquency Prevention.

Haycock, K. (2001). Closing the achievement gap. *Educational Leadership, 58*(6), 6–11.

Healy, J. (1998). *Failure to connect.* New York: Simon & Schuster.

Hein, K. (1993). "Getting real" about HIV in adolescents. *American Journal of Public Health, 83,* 492–494.

Henry, S. L., & Pepper, F. C. (1990). Cognitive, social, and cultural effects on Indian learning style: Classroom implications. *Journal of Educational Issues of Language Minority Students, 7,* 85–97.

Henson, K. T. (2004). *Constructivist teaching strategies for diverse middle-level classrooms.* Boston: Pearson.

Henson, R. K. (2002). From adolescent angst to adulthood: Substantive implications and measurement dilemmas in the development of teacher efficacy research. *Educational Psychologist, 37*(3), 137–150.

Henze, R. (2001). Segregated classroom, integrated intent. *Journal of Education for Students Placed at Risk, 6*(1 & 2), 133–155.

Herbert, E. A. (1998). Lessons learned about student portfolios. *Phi Delta Kappan, 79*(8), 583–585.

Herman, J. L., & Winters, L. (1994). Portfolio research: A slim collection. *Educational Leadership, 52*(2), 48–55.

Herman, R. (1999). *An educator's guide to schoolwide reform.* Arlington, VA: Educational Research Service.

Herrenkohl, T. I., Maguin, E., Hill, K. G., Hawkins, J. D., & Abbott, R. D. (2001). Developmental risk factors for youth violence. *Journal of Adolescent Health, 26,* 176–186.

Herrnstein, R. J., & Murray, C. (1994). *The bell curve: Intelligence and class structure in American life.* New York: Free Press.

Hessler, G. L. (2001). Who is really learning disabled? In B. Sornson, (Ed.), *Preventing early learning failure.* Alexandria, VA: ASCD.

Heward, W. L., & Cavanaugh, R. A. (1997). Educational equality for students with disabilities. In J. A. Banks &

C. A. M. Banks (Eds.), *Multicultural education: Issues and perspectives* (pp. 301–333). Boston: Allyn & Bacon.

Heymann, S. J., & Earle, A. (2000). Low-income parents: How do working conditions affect their opportunity to help school-age children at risk? *American Educational Research Journal, 37*(3), 833–848.

Heyns, B. (2002). Summer learning. In D. L. Levinson, P. W. Cookson, Jr., & A. R. Sadovnik (Eds.), *Education and sociology: An encyclopedia* (pp. 645–650). New York: Routledge Falmer.

Hickey, D. T. (1997). Motivational contemporary socio-constructivist instructional perspectives. *Educational Psychologist, 32*(3), 175–193.

Hicks-Anderman, L., & Anderman, E. M. (1999). Social predictors of changes in students' achievement goal orientations. *Contemporary Educational Psychology, 24*(1), 21–37.

Hicks-Bartlett, S. (2004). Forging the chain: "Hands across the campus" in action. In W. G. Stephan & W. P. Vogt (Eds.), *Education Programs for Improving Intergroup Relations.* New York: Teachers College Press.

Hidi, S., & Harackiewicz, J. M. (2000). Motivating the academically unmotivated: A critical issue for the 21st century. *Review of Educational Research, 70*(2), 151–179.

Hiebert, E. (1983). An examination of ability groupings for reading instruction. *Reading Research Quarterly, 18,* 231–255.

Hiebert, E. H. (1996). Revisiting the question: What difference does Reading Recovery make to an age cohort? *Educational Researcher, 25*(7), 26–28.

Hiebert, J., & Wearne, D. (1993). Instructional tasks, classroom discourse, and student learning in second grade. *American Educational Research Journal, 30,* 393–425.

Hiebert, J., Carpenter, T. P., Fennema, E., Fuson, K., Human, P., Murray, H., Olivier, A., & Wearne, D. (1996). Problem solving as a basis for reform in curriculum and instruction: The case of mathematics. *Educational Researcher, 25*(4), 12–21.

Hiebert, J., Wearne, D., & Taber, S. (1991). Fourth graders' gradual construction of decimal fractions during instruction using different physical representations. *Elementary School Journal, 91,* 321–341.

Hilgard, E. R., & Bower, G. H. (1966). *Theories of learning.* New York: Appleton-Century-Crofts.

Hill, J. R. (1977). *Measurement and evaluation in the classroom.* Columbus, OH: C. E. Merrill.

Hill, K., & Wigfield, A. (1984). Test anxiety: A major educational problem and what can be done about it. *Elementary School Journal, 85,* 105–126.

Hill, N. E. (2001). Parenting and academic socialization as they relate to school readiness: The roles of ethnicity and family income. *Journal of Educational Psychology, 93*(4), 686–697.

Hilliard, A. G. (1992). The pitfalls and promises of special education practice. *Exceptional Children, 59,* 168–172.

Hilliard, A. G. (1994). Misunderstanding and testing intelligence. In J. I. Goodlad & P. Keating (Eds.), *Access to knowledge: The continuing agenda for our nation's schools.* New York: The College Board.

Hillocks, G. (1984). What works in teaching composition: A meta-analysis of experimental treatment studies. *American Journal of Education, 93,* 133–170.

Hock, M., Schumaker, J., & Deshler, D. D. (2001). The case for strategic tutoring. *Educational Leadership, 58*(7), 50–52.

Hodgkinson, H. (2001). Educational demographics: What teachers should know. *Educational Leadership, 58*(4), 6–11.

Hoek, D., Terwel, J., & van den Eeden, P. (1997). Effects of training in the use of social and cognitive strategies: An intervention study in secondary mathematics in cooperative groups. *Educational Research and Evaluation, 3*(4), 364–389.

Hoff, E. (2003). Language development in childhood. In R. M. Lerner, M. A. Easterbrooks, & J. Mistry (Eds.), *Handbook of psychology: Vol. 6. Developmental psychology* (pp. 171–193). Hoboken, NJ: Wiley.

Hoffer, T., & Nelson, C. (1993, April). *High school effects on coursework in science and mathematics.* Paper presented at the annual meeting of the American Educational Research Association, Chicago, IL.

Hoffman, M. L. (1993). Affective and cognitive processes in moral internalization. In E. T. Higgins, D. Ruble, & W. Hartup (Eds.), *Social cognition and social development* (pp. 236–274). Cambridge, England: Cambridge University Press.

Hoffman, S. D., Foster, E. M., & Furstenberg, F. F. (1993). Reevaluating the costs of teenage childbearing. *Demography, 30,* 1–13.

Hogan, T., Rabinowitz, M., & Craven, J. A., III. (2003). Representation in teaching: Inferences from research of expert and novice teachers. *Educational Psychologist, 38*(4), 235–247.

Hoge, R. D., & Coladarci, T. (1989). Teacher-based judgments of academic achievement: A review of literature. *Review of Educational Research, 59*(3), 297–313.

Hoge, R. D., & Renzulli, J. S. (1993). Exploring the link between giftedness and self-concept. *Review of Educational Research, 63,* 449–465.

Hokoda, A., & Fincham, F. D. (1995). Origins of children's helpless and mastery achievement patterns in the family. *Journal of Educational Psychology, 87,* 375–385.

Holloway, J. (2003). Grouping gifted students. *Educational Leadership, 61*(2), 89–91.

Holloway, J. H. (2000). The digital divide. *Educational Leadership, 58*(2), 90–91.

Holloway, J. H. (2001). Inclusion and students with learning disabilities. *Educational Leadership, 58*(6), 88–89.

Holt, D. G., & Willard-Holt, C. (2000). Let's get real: Students solving authentic corporate problems. *Phi Delta Kappan, 82*(3), 243–246.

Hong, L. K. (2001). Too many intrusions on instructional time. *Phi Delta Kappan, 82*(9), 712–714.

Hopfenberg, W. S., & Levin, H. M. (1993). *The accelerated schools resource guide.* San Francisco: Jossey-Bass.

Hopkins, C. J. (1998). "I'm here to help—what do you want me to do?" A primer for literacy tutors. *The Reading Teacher, 52*(3), 310–312.

Hopkins, K. D. (1998). *Educational and psychological measurement and evaluation* (8th ed.). Boston: Allyn & Bacon.

Horgan, D. D. (1995). *Achieving gender equality: Strategies for the classroom.* Boston: Allyn & Bacon.

Howard, E. R. (1978). *School discipline desk book.* West Nyack, NY: Parker.

Howard, P. (2000). *The owner's manual for the brain: Everyday applications from mind-brain research.* Austin, TX: Bard.

Howes, C., & Matheson, C. C. (1992). Sequences in the development of competent play with peers: Social and social pretend play. *Developmental Psychology, 28,* 961–974.

Howes, C., & Rodning, C. (1992). Attachment security and social pretend play negotiations: Illustrative study #5. In C. Howes, O. Unger, & C. C. Matheson (Eds.), *The collaborative construction of pretend: Social pretend play functions* (pp. 89–98). Albany: State University of New York Press.

Hubbard, L., & Mehan, H. (1997, March). *Scaling up an untracking program: A co-constructivist process.* Paper presented at the annual meeting of the American Educational Research Association, Chicago, IL.

Hubbard, L., & Mehan, H. (1998). Scaling up an untracking program: A co-constructed process. *Journal of Education for Students Placed at Risk, 4*(1), 83–100.

Hughes, F. P. (1995). *Children, play and development* (2nd ed.). Boston: Allyn & Bacon.

Hunt, P., & Goetz, L. (1997). Research on inclusive educational programs, practices, and outcomes for students with severe disabilities. *Journal of Special Education, 31*(1), 3–29.

Hunter, M. (1982). *Mastery teaching.* El Segundo, CA: TIP Publications.

Hunter, M. (1990/91). Hunter lesson design helps achieve the goals of science instruction. *Educational Leadership, 48*(4), 79–81.

Hunter, M. (1995). Mastery teaching. In J. H. Block, S. T. Everson, & T. R. Guskey (Eds.), *School improvement programs* (pp. 181–204). New York: Scholastic.

Hurley, E. A. (2000, April). *The interaction of culture with math achievement and group processes among African-American and European-American children.* Paper presented at the annual meeting of the American Educational Research Association, New Orleans, LA.

Hurn, C. J. (2002). IQ. In D. L. Levinson, P. W. Cookson, Jr., & A. R. Sadovnik (Eds.), *Education and sociology: An encyclopedia* (pp. 399–402). New York: Routledge Falmer.

Husman, J., & Lens, W. (1999). The role of the future in student motivation. *Educational Psychologist, 34*(2), 113–125.

Hyerle, D. (1995). Thinking maps: Seeing is understanding. *Educational Leadership, 53*(4), 85–89.

Hyman, I. A., & Snook, P. A. (2000). Dangerous schools and what you can do about them. *Phi Delta Kappan, 81*(7), 488–501.

Hymel, S., Bowker, A., & Woody, E. (1993). Aggressive versus withdrawn unpopular children: Variations in peer and self-perceptions in multiple domains. *Child Development, 64,* 879–896.

Inhelder, B., & Piaget, J. (1958). *The growth of logical thinking from childhood to adolescence.* New York: Basic Books.

Iran-Nejad, A., Marsh, G. E., & Clements, A. C. (1992). The figure and the ground of constructive brain functioning: Beyond explicit memory processes. *Educational Psychologist, 74,* 473–492.

Ireson, J., Hallam, S., & Hurley, C. (in press). What are the effects of ability grouping on GCSE attainment? *British Educational Research Journal.*

Iversen, I. H. (1992). Skinner's early research: From reflexology to operant conditioning. *American Psychologist, 47,* 1318–1328.

Jackson, J. F. (1999). What are the real risk factors for African American children? *Phi Delta Kappan, 81*(4), 308–312.

Jaffee, S., & Hyde, J. S. (2000). Gender differences in moral orientation: A meta-analysis. *Psychological Bulletin, 126,* 703–726.

Jagacinski, C. M., & Nicholls, J. G. (1990). Reducing effort to protect perceived ability: "They'd do it but I wouldn't." *Journal of Educational Psychology, 82,* 15–21.

Jagers, R. J., & Carroll, G. (2002). Issues in educating African American children and youth. In S. Stringfield & D. Land (Eds.), *Educating at-risk students* (pp. 48–65). Chicago: National Society for the Study of Education.

James, W. (1912). *Talks to teachers on psychology: And to students on some of life's ideals.* New York: Holt.

Janney, R., & Snell, M. E. (2000). *Modifying schoolwork.* Baltimore: Brookes.

Jenkins, J. R., & Jenkins, L. M. (1987). Making peer tutoring work. *Educational Leadership, 44*(6), 64–68.

Jensen, A. R. (1980). *Bias in mental testing.* New York: Free Press.

Jensen, E. (2000). Brain-based learning: A reality check. *Educational Leadership, 57*(7), 76–80.

Jenson, W., Sloane, H., & Young, K. (1988). *Applied behavior modification in education.* Englewood Cliffs, NJ: Prentice-Hall.

Jetton, T. L., & Alexander, P. A. (2001). Interest assessment and the content area literacy environment: Challenges for research and practice. *Educational Psychology Review, 13*(3), 303–318.

Jeynes, W. H., & Littell, S. W. (2000). A meta-analysis of studies examining the effect of whole language instruction on the literacy of low-SES students. *The Elementary School Journal, 101*(1), 21–34.

Jitendra, A., Edwards, L., Sacks, G., & Jacobson, L. (2004, April). *What research says about vocabulary instruction for students with learning disabilities.* Paper presented at the annual meeting of the American Educational Research Association, San Diego, CA.

Johnson, D. W., & Johnson, R. T. (1998). Cultural diversity and cooperative learning. In J. W. Putnam (Ed.), *Cooperative learning and strategies for inclusion* (pp. 67–85). Baltimore: Paul H. Brookes.

Johnson, D. W., & Johnson, R. T. (1999). *Learning together and alone: Cooperative, competitive, and individualistic learning.* Boston: Allyn & Bacon.

Johnson, D. W., & Johnson, R. T. (2001). *Teaching students to be peacemakers: A meta-analysis.* Paper presented at the annual convention of the American Educational Researchers Association, Seattle, WA.

Johnson, L. D., O'Malley, P. M., & Bachman, J. G. (2001). *Monitoring the future: National survey results on drug use, 1975–2000: Vol. 1, secondary school students.* Bethesda, MD: National Institute on Drug Abuse.

John-Steiner, V., & Mahn, H. (1996). Sociocultural approaches to learning and development: A Vygotskian framework. *Educational Psychologist, 31*(3 & 4), 191–206.

John-Steiner, V., & Mahn, H. (2003). Sociocultural contexts for teaching and learning. In W. M. Reynolds & G. E. Miller (Eds.), *Handbook of psychology: Vol. 7. Educational psychology* (pp. 125–151). Hoboken, NJ: Wiley.

Johnston, P., Allington, R., & Afflerbach, P. (1985). The congruence of classroom and remedial instruction. *Elementary School Journal, 85,* 465–477.

Jones, M., Levin, M., Levin, J., & Beitzel, B. (2000). Can vocabulary-learning strategies and pair-learning formats be profitably combined? *Journal of Educational Psychology, 92*(2), 256–262.

Jones, V. F., & Jones, L. S. (1995). *Comprehensive classroom management* (4th ed.). Boston: Allyn & Bacon.

Jones, V. F., & Jones, L. S. (1998). *Comprehensive classroom management* (5th ed.). Boston: Allyn & Bacon.

Jones, V., & Jones, L. (2004). *Comprehensive classroom management* (7th ed.). Boston: Pearson.

Jones, V., Dohrn, E., & Dunn, C. (2004). *Creating effective programs for students with emotional and behavior disorders.* Boston: Pearson.

Jordan, W. J., McPartland, J. M., Legters, N. E., & Balfanz, R. (2000). Creating a comprehensive school reform model: The talent development high school with career academies. *Journal of Education for Students Placed at Risk, 5*(1 & 2), 159–181.

Joyce, B. R., Calhoun, E., & Hopkins, D. (1999). *The new structure of school improvement.* Buckingham, England: Open University Press.

Joyce, B. R., Weil, M., & Calhoun, E. (2000). *Models of teaching* (6th ed.). Boston: Allyn & Bacon.

Joyce, B., Weil, M., & Calhoun, E. (2004). *Models of teaching* (7th ed.). Boston: Pearson.

Juel, C. (1996). What makes literacy tutoring effective? *Reading Research Quarterly, 31,* 268–289.

Jukes, I., Dosaj, A., & Macdonald, B. (2000). *Net.savvy: Building information literacy in the classroom* (2nd ed.). Thousand Oaks, CA: Corwin.

Jussim, L., & Eccles, J. (1995). Naturally occurring interpersonal expectancies. In N. Eisenberg (Ed.), *Social development: Review of personality and social psychology, 15* (pp. 74–108). Thousand Oaks, CA: Sage.

Juvonen, J. (2000). The social functions of attributional face-saving tactics among early adolescents. *Educational Psychology Review, 12*(1), 15–32.

Juvonen, J., & Weiner, B. (1993). An attributional analysis of students' interactions: The social consequences of perceived responsibility. *Educational Psychology Review, 5,* 325–345.

Juvonen, J., Nishina, A., & Graham, S. (2000). Peer harassment, psychological adjustment, and school functioning in early adolescence. *Journal of Educational Psychology, 92*(2), 349–359.

Kagan, S. (1992). *Cooperative learning resources for teachers.* San Juan Capistrano, CA: Resources for Teachers.

Kagan, S. (2001). Teaching for character and community. *Educational Leadership, 59*(2), 50–55.

Kagan, S. L., & Neuman, M. J. (1998). Lessons from three decades of transition research. *Elementary School Journal, 98*(4), 365–379.

Kagan, S., Zahn, G. L., Widaman, K. F., Schwartzwald, J., & Tyrrell, G. (1985). Classroom structural bias: Impact of cooperative and competitive classroom structures on cooperative and competitive individuals and groups. In R. E. Slavin et al. (Eds.), *Learning to cooperate, cooperating to learn.* New York: Plenum.

Kahle, J., & Meece, J. (1993). Research on gender issues in the classroom. In D. Gabel (Ed.), *Handbook of research on science teaching and learning.* New York: Macmillan.

Kahlenberg, R. E. (2000). The new economic school desegregation. *Educational Leadership, 57*(7), 16–19.

Kalichman, S. C. (1996). *Answering questions about AIDS.* Washington, DC: American Psychological Association.

Kallison, J. M. (1986). Effects of lesson organization on achievement. *American Educational Research Journal, 23,* 337–347.

Kalyuga, S., Chandler, P., Tuovinen, J., & Sweller, J. (2001). When problem solving is superior to studying worked examples. *Journal of Educational Psychology, 93*(3), 579–588.

Kamil, M. L., Intrator, S. M., & Kim, H. S. (2000). The effects of other technologies on literacy and literacy learning. In M. L. Kamil, P. B. Mosenthal, P. D. Pearson, & R. Barr (Eds.), *Handbook of Reading Research: Vol. 3.* (pp. 771–788). Mahwah, NJ: Erlbaum.

Kane, M. (1994). Validating the performance standards associated with passing scores. *Review of Educational Research, 64*(3), 425–461.

Kantor, H., & Lowe, R. (1995). Class, race, and the emergence of federal education policy: From the new deal to the great society. *Educational Researcher, 24*(3), 4–11.

Kaplan, A., & Midgley, C. (1997). The effect of achievement goals: Does level of perceived academic competence make a difference? *Contemporary Educational Psychology, 22*(4), 415–435.

Kapur, S., Craik, F. I. M., Tulving, E., Wilson, A. A., Hoyle, S., & Brown, G. M. (1994). Neuroanatomical correlates of encoding in episodic memory: Levels of processing effect. *Proceedings of the National Academy of Sciences, 91,* 2008–2011.

Karges-Bone, L. (2000). *Lesson planning: Long-range and short-range models for grades K–6.* Boston: Allyn & Bacon.

Karpov, Y. V., & Bransford, J. D. (1995). L. S. Vygotsky and the doctrine of empirical and theoretical learning. *Educational Psychologist, 30,* 61–66.

Karpov, Y. V., & Haywood, H. C. (1998). Two ways to elaborate Vygotsky's concept of mediation. *American Psychologist, 53*(1), 27–36.

Karweit, N. (1989). Time and learning: A review. In R. E. Slavin (Ed.), *School and classroom organization.* Hillsdale, NJ: Erlbaum.

Karweit, N. L. (1981). Time in school. *Research in Sociology of Education and Socialization, 2,* 77–110.

Karweit, N. L. (1994). Issues in kindergarten organization and curriculum. In R. E. Slavin, N. L. Karweit, & B. A. Wasik (Eds.), *Preventing early school failure.* Boston: Allyn & Bacon.

Karweit, N. L., & Slavin, R. E. (1981). Measurement and modeling choices in studies of time and learning. *American Educational Research Journal, 18,* 157–171.

Kasten, W. C., & Lolli, E. M. (1998). *Implementing multiage education.* Norwood, MA: Christopher–Gordon.

Katayama, A. D., & Robinson, D. H. (1998, April). *Study effectiveness of outlines and graphic organizers: How much information should be provided for students to be successful on transfer tests?* Paper presented at the annual meeting of the American Educational Research Association, San Diego, CA.

Kauffman, J. M., & Burbach, H. J. (1997). On creating a climate of classroom civility. *Phi Delta Kappan, 79*(4), 320–325.

Kauffman, J. M., Lloyd, J. W., Baker, J., & Riedel, T. M. (1995). Inclusion of all students with emotional or behavioral disorder? Let's think again. *Phi Delta Kappan, 76*(7), 542–546.

Kauffman, J. M., Mostert, M. P., Trent, S. C., & Hallahan, D. P. (2002). *Managing classroom behavior: A reflective case-based approach.* Boston: Allyn & Bacon.

Kauffman, J., McGee, K., & Brigham, M. (2004). Enabling or disabling? Observations on changes in special education. *Phi Delta Kappan, 85*(8), 613–620.

Kavale, K. A., & Reese, J. H. (1992). The character of learning disabilities: An Iowa profile. *Learning Disability Quarterly, 15,* 74–94.

Kazdin, A. E. (2001). *Behavior modification in applied settings* (6th ed.). Belmont, CA: Wadsworth.

Keith, T. Z., Reimers, T. M., Fehrmann, P. G., Pottebaum, S. M., & Aubey, L. W. (1986). Parental involvement, homework, and TV time: Direct and indirect effects on high school achievement. *Journal of Educational Psychology, 78,* 373–380.

Kelly, N., & Norwich, B. (2004). Pupils' perceptions of self and of labels: Moderate learning difficulties in mainstream and special schools. *British Journal of Educational Psychology, 74*(3), 411–435.

Kemple, J. J. (1997). *Career academies: Communities of support for students and teachers: Further findings from a 10-site evaluation.* New York: MDRC.

Kennedy, E. (2003). *Raising test scores for all students: An administrator's guide to improving standardized test performance.* Thousand Oaks, CA: Corwin.

Kennedy, J. H. (1990). Determinants of peer social status: Contributions of physical appearance, reputation, and behavior. *Journal of Youth and Adolescence, 19,* 233–244.

Kennedy, M. M. (1997). The connection between research and practice. *Educational Researcher, 26*(7), 4–12.

Keogh, B. K., & MacMillan, D. L. (1996). Exceptionality. In D. C. Berliner & R. C. Calfee (Eds.), *Handbook of educational psychology* (pp. 311–330). New York: Macmillan.

Kerr, M., Stattin, H., Biesecker, G., & Ferrer-Wreder, L. (2003). Relationships with parents and peers in adolescence. In R. M. Lerner, M. A. Easterbrooks, & J. Mistry (Eds.), *Handbook of psychology: Vol. 6. Developmental psychology* (pp. 395–419). Hoboken, NJ: Wiley.

Khmelkov, V., & Hallinan, M. (1999). Organizational effects on race relations in schools. *Journal of Social Issues, 55*(4), 627–645.

Kiewra, K. A. (1991). Aids to lecture learning. *Educational Psychologist, 26,* 37–53.

Kiewra, K. A., DuBois, N. F., Christian, D., McShane, A., Meyerhoffer, M., & Roskelley, D. (1991). Note-taking functions and techniques. *Journal of Educational Psychology, 83,* 240–245.

Kilgore, S., Doyle, D., & Linkowsky, L. (1996). The modern red schoolhouse. In S. Stringfield, S. Ross, & L. Smith (Eds.), *Bold plans for school restructuring: The new American schools development corporation designs.* Mahwah, NJ: Erlbaum.

Killen, M. (1996). *Children's autonomy, social competence, and interactions with adults and other children: Exploring connections and consequences.* San Francisco: Jossey-Bass.

Kim, S. E. (2001, April). *Meta-analysis of gender differences in test performance using HLM.* Paper presented at the annual meeting of the American Educational Research Association, Seattle, WA.

King, A. (1991). Effects of training in strategic questioning on children's problem-solving performance. *Journal of Educational Psychology, 83,* 307–317.

King, A. (1992). Facilitating elaborative learning through guided student-generated questioning. *Educational Psychologist, 27,* 111–126.

King, A. (1994). Guiding knowledge construction in the classroom: Effects of teaching children how to question and how to explain. *American Educational Research Journal, 31*(2), 338–368.

King, A. (1997). Ask to think—tell why: A model of transactive peer tutoring for scaffolding higher level complex learning. *Educational Psychologist, 32*(4), 221–235.

King, A. (1998). Transactive peer tutoring: Distributing cognition and metacognition. *Educational Psychology Review, 10*(1), 57–74.

King, A. (1999). Teaching effective discourse patterns for small-group learning. In R. J. Stevens (Ed.), *Teaching in American schools.* Upper Saddle River, NJ: Merrill/Prentice-Hall.

King, A., Staffieni, A., & Adelgais, A. (1998). Mutual peer tutoring: Effects of structuring tutorial interaction to scaffold peer learning. *Journal of Educational Psychology, 90*(1), 134–152.

King, E. W. (2002). Ethnicity. In D. L. Levinson, P. W. Cookson, Jr., & A. R. Sadovnik (Eds.), *Education and sociology: An encyclopedia* (pp. 247–253). New York: Routledge Falmer.

King, N. J., & Ollendick, T. H. (1989). Children's anxiety and phobic disorders in school settings: Classification, assessment, and intervention issues. *Review of Educational Research, 59*(4), 431–470.

Kirby, D. (2000). What does the research say about sexuality education? *Educational Leadership, 58*(2), 72–75.

Klahr, D., & Nigam, M. (2004). The equivalence of learning paths in early science instruction: Effects of direct instruction and discovery learning. *Psychological Science, 15*(10), 661–667.

Klauer, K. (1984). Intentional and incidental learning with instructional texts: A meta-analysis for 1970–1980. *American Educational Research Journal, 21,* 323–339.

Klein, J. D., & Schnackenberg, H. L. (2000). Effects of informal cooperative learning and the affiliation motive on achievement, attitude, and student interactions. *Contemporary Educational Psychology, 25*(1), 332–341.

Klein, P. D. (1999). Reopening inquiry into cognitive processes in writing-to-learn. *Educational Psychology Review, 11*(3), 203–270.

Klein, S. F. (1994). Continuing the journey toward gender equity. *Educational Researcher, 23*(8), 13–21.

Klein, S. P., Jovanovic, J., Stecher, B. M., McCaffrey, D., Shavelson, R. J., Haertel, E., Solano-Flores, G., & Comfort, K. (1997). Gender and racial/ethnic differences on performance assessments in science. *Educational Evaluation and Policy Analysis, 19*(2), 83–97.

Kleinert, H. L., & Kearns, J. F. (2001). *Alternate assessment: Measuring outcomes and supports for students with disabilities.* Baltimore: Paul H. Brookes.

Kline, P. (2001). Teaching to all of a child's intelligences. In B. Sornson (Ed.), *Preventing early learning failure.* Alexandria, VA: ASCD.

Klingner, J. K., & Vaughn, S. (2004). Strategies for struggling second-language readers. In T. L. Jetton & J. A. Dole (Eds.), *Adolescent literacy: Research and practice.* New York: Guilford Press.

Knapp, M. S. (1995). *Teaching for meaning in high-poverty classrooms.* New York: Teachers College Press.

Knapp, M. S., & Woolverton, S. (1995). Social class and schooling. In J. A. Banks & C. A. M. Banks (Eds.), *Handbook of research on multicultural education.* New York: Macmillan.

Knapp, M. S., Shields, P. M., & Turnbull, B. S. (1995). Academic challenge in high-poverty classrooms. *Phi Delta Kappan, 76*(10), 770–776.

Knight, C. B., Halpin, G., & Halpin, G. (1992, April). *The effects of learning environment accommodations on the achievement of second graders.* Paper presented at the annual meeting of the American Educational Research Association, San Francisco, CA.

Koch, J. (2003). Gender issues in the classroom. In W. M. Reynolds & G. E. Miller (Eds.), *Handbook of psychology: Vol. 7. Educational psychology* (pp. 259–281). Hoboken, NJ: Wiley.

Koegel, R. L., & Koegel, L. K. (Eds.). (1995). *Teaching children with autism: Strategies for initiating positive interactions and improving learning opportunities.* Baltimore: Paul H. Brookes.

Kogan, N. (1994). Cognitive styles. In R. J. Sternberg (Ed.), *Encyclopedia of human intelligence.* New York: Macmillan.

Kohlberg, L. (1963). The development of children's orientations toward moral order. I: Sequence in the development of human thought. *Vita Humana, 6,* 11–33.

Kohlberg, L. (1969). Stage and sequence: The cognitive-developmental approach to socialization. In D. A. Golsin (Ed.), *Handbook of socialization theory and research* (pp. 347–380). Chicago: Rand McNally.

Kohlberg, L. (1978). Revisions in the theory and practice of moral development. In W. Damon (Ed.), *New directions for child development* (No. 2, pp. 83–87). San Francisco: Jossey-Bass.

Kohlberg, L. (1980). High school democracy and educating for a just society. In M. L. Mosher (Ed.), *Moral education: A first generation of research and development* (pp. 20–57). New York: Praeger.

Kohlberg, L. (1984). *Essays on moral development.* San Francisco: Harper & Row.

Kolb, G., & Whishaw, I. Q. (1998). Brain plasticity and behavior. In J. T. Spence, J. M. Darley, & D. J. Foss (Eds.), *Annual review of psychology* (pp. 43–64). Palo Alto, CA: Annual Reviews.

Kóller, O., & Baumert, J. (1997, March). *The impact of different goal orientations on scholastic learning.* Paper presented at the annual meeting of the American Educational Research Association, Chicago, IL.

Konig, A. (1995, March/April). *Maternal discipline and child temperament as contributors to the development of internalization in your children.* Paper presented at the biennial meetings of the Society for Research in Child Development, Indianapolis, IN.

Koppelman, K., & Goodhart, L. (2005). *Understanding human differences: Multicultural education for a diverse America.* Boston: Pearson.

Koretz, D., Stecher, B., & Deibert, E. (1993). *The reliability of scores from the 1992 Vermont Portfolio Assessment Program* (Tech. Rep. No. 355). Los Angeles: UCLA, Center for the Study of Evaluation.

Kornhaber, M., Fierros, E., & Veenema, S. (2004). *Multiple Intelligences: Best Ideas from Research and Practice*. Boston: Allyn & Bacon.

Kosonen, P., & Winne, P. H. (1995). Effects of teaching statistical laws of reasoning about everyday problems. *Journal of Educational Psychology, 87*(1), 33–46.

Kostelnik, M. J. (1992). Myths associated with developmentally appropriate programs. *Young Children, 47*(4), 17–23.

Kounin, J. (1970). *Discipline and group management in classrooms*. New York: Holt, Rinehart and Winston.

Kozma, R. B. (1994). Will media influence learning? Reframing the debate. *Educational Technology Research and Development, 42*(2), 7–19.

Kozol, J. (1991). *Savage inequalities: Children in America's schools*. New York: Crown.

Kozulin, A., & Presseisen, B. Z. (1995). Mediated learning experience and psychological tools: Vygotsky's and Feuerstein's perspectives in a study of student learning. *Educational Psychologist, 30*, 67–75.

Kramarski, B., & Mevarech, Z. R. (2003). Enhancing mathematical reasoning in the classroom: The effects of cooperative learning and metacognitive training. *American Educational Research Journal, 40*(1), 281–310.

Krechevsky, M., Hoerr, T., & Gardner, H. (1995). Complementary energies: Implementing MI theory from the laboratory and from the field. In J. Oakes & R. H. Quartz (Eds.), *Creating new educational communities*. Chicago: University of Chicago Press.

Kreitzer, A. E., & Madaus, G. F. (1994). Empirical investigations of the hierarchical structure of the taxonomy. In L. W. Anderson & L. A. Sosniak (Eds.), *Bloom's taxonomy: A forty-year perspective*. Chicago: University of Chicago Press.

Krinsky, R., & Krinsky, S. G. (1996). Pegword mnemonic instruction: Retrieval times and long-term memory performance among fifth grade children. *Contemporary Educational Psychology, 21*(2), 193–207.

Kroesbergen, E. H., Van Luit, J. E. H., & Maas, C. J. M. (2004). Effectiveness of explicit and constructivist mathematics instruction for low-achieving students in the Netherlands. *The Elementary School Journal, 104*(3), 233–251.

Krug, D., Davis, T. B., & Glover, J. A. (1990). Massed versus distributed reading: A case of forgetting helping recall? *Journal of Educational Psychology, 82*, 366–371.

Krumboltz, J. D., & Yeh, C. J. (1996). Competitive grading sabotages good teaching. *Phi Delta Kappan, 78*(4), 324–326.

Kucan, L., & Beck, I. L. (1997). Thinking aloud and reading comprehension research: Inquiry, instruction, and social interaction. *Review of Educational Research, 67*(3), 271–299.

Kuhara-Kojima, K., & Hatano, G. (1991). Contribution of content knowledge and learning ability to the learning of facts. *Journal of Educational Psychology, 83*(2), 253–263.

Kulhavy, R. W., & Stock, W. A. (1989). Feedback in written instruction: The place of response certitude. *Educational Psychology Review, 1*(4), 279–308.

Kulik, C.-L., Kulik, J. A., & Bangert-Drowns, R. L. (1990). Effectiveness of mastery learning programs: A meta-analysis. *Review of Educational Research, 60*(2), 265–299.

Kulik, C.-L. C., & Kulik, J. A. (1991). Effectiveness of computer-based instruction: An updated analysis. *Computers in Human Behavior, 7*(1–2), 75–94.

Kulik, J. A. (2003). *Effects of using instructional technology in elementary and secondary schools: What controlled evaluation studies say. SRI Project Number P10446.001*. Arlington, VA: SRI International.

Kulik, J. A., & Kulik, C.-L. (1988). Timing of feedback and verbal learning. *Review of Educational Research Journal, 21*, 79–97.

Kulik, J. A., & Kulik, C.-L. (1997). Ability grouping. In N. Colangelo & G. A. Davis (Eds.), *Handbook of gifted education* (2nd ed.) (pp. 230–242). Boston: Allyn & Bacon.

Kupersmidt, J. B., & Coie, J. D. (1990). Preadolescent peer status, aggression, and school adjustment as predictors of externalizing problems in adolescence. *Child Development, 61*, 1350–1362.

Kyle, P., & Rogien, L. (2004). *Opportunities and options in classroom management*. Boston: Pearson.

Ladd, G. W., & Hart, C. H. (1992). Creating informal play opportunities: Are parents' and preschoolers' initiations related to children's competence with peers? *Developmental Psychology, 28*, 1179–1187.

Lahaderne, H. (1968). Attitudinal and intellectual correlates of attention: A study of four sixth-grade classrooms. *Journal of Educational Psychology, 59*, 320–324.

Lampert, M. (1986). Knowing, doing, and teaching multiplication. *Cognition and Instruction, 3*, 305–342.

Land, D., & Legters, N. (2002). The extent and consequences of risk in U.S. education. In S. Stringfield & D. Land (Eds.), *Educating at-risk students* (pp. 1–28). Chicago: National Society for the Study of Education.

Land, M. L. (1987). Vagueness and clarity. In M. J. Dunkin (Ed.), *International encyclopedia of teaching and teacher education*. New York: Pergamon.

Lane, K. L., & Beebe-Frankenberger, M. (2004). *School-based interventions: The tools you need to succeed*. Boston: Pearson.

Langer, E. (1997). *The power of mindful learning*. Reading, MA: Addison-Wesley.

Langer, J. A. (2001). Beating the odds: Teaching middle and high school students to read and write well. *American Educational Research Journal, 38*(4), 837–880.

Langer, J., & Killen, M. (1998). *Piaget, evolution, and development*. Mahwah, NJ: Erlbaum.

Larivée, S., Normandeau, S., & Parent, S. (2000). The French connection: Some contributions of French-language research in the post-Piagetian era. *Child Development, 71*, 823–839.

Larrivee, B. (1985). *Effective teaching behaviors for successful mainstreaming*. New York: Longman.

Larrivee, B., & Horne, M. D. (1991). Social status: A comparison of mainstreamed students with peers of different ability levels. *Journal of Special Education, 25*, 90–101.

Larrivee, B., Semmel, M. I., & Gerber, M. M (1997). Case studies of six schools varying in effectiveness for students with learning disabilities. *Elementary School Journal, 98*(1), 27–50.

Latham, A. S. (1997a). Peer counseling: Proceed with caution. *Educational Leadership, 55*(2), 77–78.

Latham, A. S. (1997b). Technology and LD students: What is best practice? *Educational Leadership, 55*(3), 88.

Laupa, M. (1991). Children's reasoning about three authority attributes: Adult status, knowledge, and social position. *Developmental Psychology, 27,* 321–329.

Lave, J. (1988). *Cognition in practice.* Boston: Cambridge Press.

Lazarowitz, R. (1995). Learning science in cooperative modes in junior and senior high schools: Cognitive and affective outcomes. In J. E. Pedersen & A. D. Digby (Eds.), *Secondary schools and cooperative learning* (pp. 185–227). New York: Garland.

Learning First Alliance. (1998). *Every child reading: An action plan.* Washington, DC: Author.

Learning First Alliance. (2001). *Every child learning: Safe and supportive schools.* Washington, DC: Author.

Lee, C. D. (2000, April). *The state of knowledge about the education of African Americans.* Paper presented at the annual meeting of the American Educational Research Association, New Orleans, LA.

Lee, J. (2004). Multiple facets of inequity in racial and ethnic achievement gaps. *Peabody Journal of Education, 79*(2), 51–73.

Lee, V. E., & Burkam, D. T. (2003). Dropping out of high school: The role of school organization and structure. *American Educational Research Journal, 40*(2), 353–393.

Lee, V. E., & Smith, J. B. (1999). Social support and achievement for young adolescents in Chicago: The role of school academic press. *American Educational Research Journal, 36*(4), 907–945.

Lehr, C. A., Hansen, A., Sinclair, M. F., & Christenson, S. L. (2003). Moving beyond dropout prevention to school completion: An integrative review of data based interventions. *School Psychology Review, 32,* 342–364.

Lehr, C. A., Sinclair, M. F., & Christenson, S. L. (2004). Addressing student engagement and truancy prevention during the elementary school years: A replication study of the Check & Connect model. *Journal of Education for Students Placed at Risk, 9*(3), 279–301.

Lepper, M. R. (1983). Extrinsic reward and intrinsic motivation: Implications for the classroom. In J. M. Levine & M. C. Wang (Eds.), *Teacher and student perceptions: Implications for learning* (pp. 281–317). Hillsdale, NJ: Erlbaum.

Lepper, M. R. (1985). Microcomputers in education. Motivational and social issues. *American Psychologist, 40,* 1–18.

Lepper, M. R. (1998). A whole much less than the sum of its parts. *American Psychologist, 53*(6), 675–676.

Lepper, M. R., Greene, D., & Nisbett, R. E. (1973). Undermining children's intrinsic interest with extrinsic rewards: A test of the overjustification hypothesis. *Journal of Personality and Social Psychology, 28,* 129–137.

Lepper, M. R., Keavney, M., & Drake, M. (1996). Intrinsic motivation and extrinsic rewards: A commentary on Cameron & Pierce's meta-analysis. *Review of Educational Research, 66*(1), 5–32.

Lerner, J. (1997). *Learning disabilities: Theories, diagnosis, and teaching strategies.* Boston: Houghton Mifflin.

Lesgold, A. (1988). Problem solving. In R. J. Sternberg & E. E. Smith (Eds.), *The psychology of human thought* (pp. 188–213). New York: Cambridge University Press.

Lessow-Hurley, J. (2005). *The foundations of dual language instruction.* Boston: Pearson.

Leu, D. J., Jr. (2000). Literacy and technology: Deictic consequences for literacy education in an information age. In M. L. Kamil, P. B. Mosenthal, P. D. Pearson, & R. Barr (Eds.), *Handbook of Reading Research: Vol. 3.* (pp. 743–770). Mahwah, NJ: Erlbaum.

Lever-Duffy, J., McDonald, J., & Mizell, A. (2003). *Teaching and learning with technology.* Boston: Pearson.

Levin, A. V. (1996). Common visual problems in the classroom. In R. H. A. Haslam & P. J. Valletutti (Eds.), *Medical problems in the classroom: The teacher's role in diagnosis and management* (pp. 161–180). Austin, TX: Pro-Ed.

Levin, J., & Nolan, J. F. (2004). *Principles of classroom management* (4th ed). Boston: Pearson.

Levin, J. R., O'Donnell, A. M., & Kratochwill, T. R. (2003). Educational/psychological intervention research. In W. M. Reynolds & G. E. Miller (Eds.), *Handbook of psychology: Vol. 7. Educational psychology* (pp. 557–581). Hoboken, NJ: Wiley.

Levin, M. E., & Levin, J. R. (1990). Scientific mnemonics: Methods for maximizing more than memory. *American Educational Research Journal, 27,* 301–321.

Levine, C., Kohlberg, L., & Hewer, A. (1985). The current formulation of Kohlberg's theory and a response to critics. *Human Development, 28,* 94–100.

Levine, D. U., & Levine, R. F. (1996). *Society and education* (9th ed.). Boston: Allyn & Bacon.

Levine, M. (2003). Celebrating diverse minds. *Educational Leadership, 61*(2), 12–18. Available online at www.ascd. org/index.cfm.

Levy, S. (1999). Reducing prejudice: Lessons from social-cognitive factors underlying perceiver differences in prejudice. *Journal of Social Issues, 55*(4), 745–765.

Lewandowsky, S., & Murdock, B. B. (1989). Memory for serial order. *Psychological Review, 96,* 25–57.

Lewin, L. (2001). *Using the Internet to strengthen curriculum.* Alexandria, VA: ASCD.

Lewin, L., & Shoemaker, B. J. (1998). *Great performances: Creating classroom-based assessment tasks.* Alexandria, VA: ASCD.

Lewis, M., & Sullivan, M. W. (Eds.). (1996). *Emotional development in atypical children.* Mahwah, NJ: Erlbaum.

Lickona, T. (1992). *Educating for character.* New York: Bantam.

Lieberman, A., & Miller, L. (1999). *Teachers—transforming their world and their work*. New York: Teachers College Press.

Lindeman, B. (2001). Reaching out to immigrant parents. *Educational Leadership, 58*(6), 62–66.

Linn, M. C., & Slotta, J. D. (2000). WISE science. *Educational Leadership, 58*(2), 29–32.

Linn, R. L. (1994). Performance assessment: Policy promises and technical measurement standards. *Educational Researcher, 23*(9), 4–14.

Linn, R. L. (2000). Assessments and accountability. *Educational Researcher, 29*(2), 4–15.

Linn, R., & Haug, C. (2002). Stability of school-building accountability scores and gains. *Educational Evaluation and Policy Analysis, 24*(1), 29–36.

Lissitz, R., & Schafer, W. (2002). *Assessment in educational reform: Both means and ends*. Boston: Allyn & Bacon.

Lloyd, J. W., Singh, N. N., & Repp, A. C. (Eds.). (1991). *The Regular Education Initiative: Alternative perspectives on concepts, issues, and models*. DeKalb, IL: Sycamore.

Loeber, R., & Stouthamer-Loeber, M. (1998). Development of juvenile aggression and violence. *American Psychologist, 53*(2), 242–259.

Lomawaima, K. T., & McCarty, T. L. (2002). When tribal sovereignty challenges democracy: American Indian education and the democratic ideal. *American Educational Research Journal, 39*(2), 279–305.

Lomotey, K., & Teddlie, C. (Eds.). (1997). *Forty years after the Brown decision: Social and cultural effects of school desegregation, vol. 14*. New York: AMS Press.

Lorch, R. F., Lorch, E. P., & Inman, W. E. (1993). Effects of signaling topic structure on text recall. *Journal of Educational Psychology, 85*, 281–290.

Losey, K. M. (1995). Mexican American students and classroom interaction: An overview and critique. *Review of Educational Research, 65*, 283–318.

Lou, Y., Abrami, P. C., & D'Apollonia, S. (2001). Small group and individual learning with technology: A meta-analysis. *Review of Educational Research, 71*(3), 449–521.

Lou, Y., Abrami, P. C., Spence, J. C., Poulsen, C., Chambers, B., & D'Apollonia, S. (1996). Within-class grouping: A meta-analysis. *Review of Educational Research, 66*(4), 423–458.

Loury, G. C. (2002). *The anatomy of racial inequality*. Cambridge, MA: Harvard University Press.

Loveless, T. (1998). The tracking and ability grouping debate. *Fordham Report, 2*(8), 1–27.

Lowther, D., Ross, S., & Morrison, G. (2003). *When each one has one: The influences on teaching strategies and student achievement of using laptops in the classroom*. Paper presented at the annual meeting of the American Educational Research Association, Seattle, WA.

Luckasson, R., Coulter, D., Polloway, E., Reiss, S., Schalock, R., Snell, M., Spitalnik, D., & Stark, J. (1992). *Mental retardation: Definitions, classification, and systems of supports* (9th ed.). Washington, DC: American Association on Mental Retardation.

Luckasson, R., Schalock, R. L., Snell, M. E., & Spitalnik, D. M. (1996). The 1992 AAMR definition and preschool children: Response from the committee on terminology and classification. *Mental Retardation, 247–253.*

Lyons, C. A., Pinnell, G. S., & DeFord, D. E. (1993). *Partners in learning: Teachers and children in reading recovery*. New York: Teachers College Press.

Lysynchuk, L. M., Pressley, M., & Vye, N. J. (1990). Reciprocal teaching improves standardized reading-comprehension performance in poor comprehenders. *Elementary School Journal, 90*, 469–484.

Ma, X., & Kishor, N. (1997). Attitude toward self, social factors, and achievement in mathematics: A meta-analytic review. *Educational Psychology Review, 9*(2), 89–120.

Maag, J. W., Rutherford, R. B., & DiGangi, S. A. (1992). Effects of self-monitoring and contingency reinforcement on on-task behavior and academic productivity of learning disabled students: A social validation study. *Psychology in the Schools, 29*, 157–172.

MacArthur, C., Ferretti, R., Okolo, C., & Cavalier, A. (2001). Technology applications for students with literacy problems: A critical review. *The Elementary School Journal, 101*(3), 273–302.

Macedo, D. (2000). The illiteracy of English-only literacy. *Educational Leadership, 57*(4), 63–67.

Macguire, E. A., Gadian, D. G., Johnsrude, I. S., Good, C. D., Ashburner, J., Frackowiak, R. S. J., & Frith, C. D. (2000). Navigation-related structural change in the hippocampi of taxi drivers. *Proceedings of the National Academy of Sciences, 97*(8) 4398–4403.

MacIver, D. J., Reuman, D. A., & Main, S. R. (1995). Social structuring of the school: Studying what is, illuminating what could be. *Annual Review of Psychology, 46*, 375–400.

MacKenzie, A. A., & White, R. T. (1982). Fieldwork in geography and long-term memory. *American Educational Research Journal, 19*, 623–632.

Mackenzie, R. J. (1997). Setting limits in the classroom. *American Educator, 21*(3), 32–43.

MacLean, W. E. (1996). *Ellis' handbook of mental deficiency, psychological theory, and research*. Mahwah, NJ: Erlbaum.

MacMillan, D. L., & Forness, S. R. (1992). Mental retardation. In M. C. Alkin (Ed.), *Encyclopedia of educational research* (6th ed.). New York: Macmillan.

Madden, N. A., & Slavin, R. E. (1983a). Effects of cooperative learning on the social acceptance of mainstreamed academically handicapped students. *Journal of Special Education, 17*, 171–182.

Madden, N. A., & Slavin, R. E. (1983b). Mainstreaming students with mild academic handicaps: Academic and social outcomes. *Review of Educational Research, 53*, 519–569.

Madden, N. A., Slavin, R. E., Karweit, N. L., Dolan, L. J., & Wasik, B. A. (1993). Success for All: Longitudinal effects of a restructuring program for inner-city elementary schools. *American Educational Research Journal, 30.*

Maehr, M. L., & Anderman, E. M. (1993). Reinventing schools for early adolescents: Emphasizing task goals. *The Elementary School Journal, 93*(5), 593–610.

Mager, R. F. (1975). *Preparing instructional objectives.* Belmont, CA: Fearon.

Maheady, L., Harper, G. F., & Mallette, B. (1991). Peer-mediated instruction: Review of potential applications for special education. *Reading, Writing, and Learning Disabilities, 7,* 75–102.

Maher, F. A., & Ward, J. V. (2002). *Gender and teaching.* Mahwah, NJ: Erlbaum.

Mahony, M. (1997). Small victories in an inclusive classroom. *Educational Leadership, 54*(7), 59–62.

Malott, R. W., Malott, M. E., & Trojan, E. A. (2000). *Elementary principles of behavior* (4th ed.). Upper Saddle River, NJ: Prentice-Hall.

Malouf, D. B., Wizer, D. R., Pilato, V. H., & Grogan, M. M. (1990). Computer-assisted instruction with small groups of mildly handicapped students. *Journal of Special Education, 24,* 51–68.

Mamlin, N., & Harris, K. R. (1998). Elementary teachers' referral to special education in light of inclusion and prereferral: "Every child is here to learn . . . but some of these children are in real trouble." *Journal of Educational Psychology, 90*(3), 385–396.

Mandeville, G. K. (1992). Does achievement increase over time? Another look at the South Carolina PET program. *The Elementary School Journal, 93*(2), 117–129.

Mandeville, G. K., & Rivers, J. L. (1991). The South Carolina PET study: Teachers' perceptions and student achievement. *Elementary School Journal, 91,* 377–407.

Manning, B. H. (1988). Application of cognitive behavior modification: First and third graders' self-management of classroom behaviors. *American Educational Research Journal, 25,* 193–212.

Manning, B. H., & Payne, B. D. (1996). Self-talk for teachers and students: Metacognitive strategies for personal and classroom use. Boston: Allyn & Bacon.

Manning, M. A., Bear, G. G., & Minke, K. M. (2001, April). *The self-concept of students with learning disabilities: Does educational placement matter?* Paper presented at the annual meeting of the American Educational Research Association, Seattle, WA.

Manning, M. L., & Baruth, L. G. (1995). *Students at risk.* Boston: Allyn & Bacon.

Manning, M. L., & Baruth, L. G. (2004). *Multicultural education of children and adolescents* (4th ed.). Boston: Pearson.

Manset, G., & Semmel, M. I. (1997). Are inclusive programs for students with mild disabilities effective? A comparative review of model programs. *Journal of Special Education, 31*(2), 155–180.

Mantzicopoulos, P. (2003). Flunking kindergarten after Head Start: An inquiry into the contribution of contextual and individual variables. *Journal of Educational Psychology, 95,* 268–278.

Marcia, J. E. (1991). Identity and self-development. In R. M. Lerner, A. C. Petersen, & E. J. Brooks-Gunn (Eds.), *Encyclopedia of adolescence* (Vol. 1, pp. 527–531). New York: Garland.

Marks, H. M. (2000). Student engagement in instructional activity: Patterns in the elementary, middle, and high school years. *American Educational Research Journal, 37*(1), 153–184.

Marks, H., Doane, K., & Secada, W. (1998). Support for student achievement. In F. Newmann et al. (Eds.), *Restructuring for student achievement: The impact of structure and culture in 24 schools.* San Francisco: Jossey-Bass.

Marsh, H. W. (1993). The multidimensional structure of academic self-concept: Invariance over gender and age. *American Educational Research Journal, 30,* 841–860.

Marsh, H. W., & Yeung, A. S. (1997). Casual effects of academic self-concept on academic achievement: Structural equation models of longitudinal data. *Journal of Educational Psychology, 89*(1), 41–54.

Marshak, D. (2003). No Child Left Behind: A foolish race into the past. *Phi Delta Kappan, 85*(3), 229–231.

Martella, R. C., Marchand-Martella, N. E., & Cleanthous, C. (2001). *ADHD: A comprehensive approach.* Dubuque, IA: Rendall/Hunt.

Martella, R. C., Nelson, J. R., & Marchand-Martella, N. E. (2003). *Managing disruptive behaviors in the schools.* Boston: Pearson.

Martin, A. J., Marsh, H. W., & Debus, R. L. (2001). Self-handicapping and defensive pessimism: Exploring a model of predictors and outcomes from a self-protection perspective. *Journal of Educational Psychology, 93*(1), 87–102.

Martin, J. (1993). Episodic memory: A neglected phenomenon in the psychology of education. *Educational Psychologist, 28*(2), 169–183.

Martinez, M. E. (1998). What is problem solving? *Phi Delta Kappan, 70*(8), 605–609.

Marzano, R. (2003). Using data: Two wrongs and a right. *Educational Leadership, 60*(5), 56–60.

Marzano, R. J. (1995). Critical thinking. In J. H. Block, S. T. Everson, & T. R. Guskey (Eds.), *School improvement programs* (pp. 57–76). New York: Scholastic.

Marzano, R. J. (2000). *Transforming classroom grading.* Alexandria: ASCD.

Marzano, R. J. (2001). *Designing a new taxonomy of educational objectives.* Thousand Oaks, CA: Corwin.

Marzano, R. J. (2003). *Classroom management that works: Research-based strategies for every teacher.* Alexandria: ASCD.

Marzano, R. J., Pickering, D. J., & Pollock, J. E. (2001). *Classroom instruction that works: Research-based strategies for increasing student achievement.* Alexandria: ASCD.

Mash, E. J., & Wolfe, D. A. (2003). Disorders of childhood and adolescence. In G. Stricker & T. A. Widigner (Eds.), *Handbook of psychology: Vol. 8. Clinical psychology,* (pp. 27–64). Hoboken, NJ: Wiley.

Maslow, A. (1968). *Toward a psychology of being.* New York: Wiley.

Maslow, A. H. (1954). *Motivation and personality*. New York: Harper & Row.

Mason, D. A. (1995). Grouping students for elementary school mathematics: A survey of principals in 12 states. *Educational Research and Evaluation, 1*(4), 318–346.

Mason, D. A., & Good, T. L. (1993). Effects of two-group and whole-class teaching on regrouped elementary students' mathematics achievement. *American Educational Research Journal, 30*(2), 328–360.

Mason, L. H. (2004). Explicit self-regulated strategy development versus reciprocal questioning: Effects on expository reading comprehension among struggling readers. *Journal of Educational Psychology, 96*(2), 283–296.

Mastropieri, M. A., & Scruggs, T. E. (1998). Enhancing school success with mnemonic strategies. *Intervention in School and Clinic, 33*(4), 201–208.

Matheny, K. B., Aycock, D. W., & McCarthy, C. J. (1993). Stress in school-aged children and youth. *Educational Psychology Review, 5*(2), 109–134.

Mather, N., & Goldstein, S. (2001). *Learning disabilities and challenging behaviors*. Baltimore: Brookes.

Mathes, P. G., Torgesen, J. K., Clancy-Menchetti, J., Santi, K., Nicholas, K., Robinson, C., & Grek, M. (2003). A comparison of teacher-directed versus peer-assisted instruction to struggling first-grade readers. *The Elementary School Journal, 103*(5), 461–479.

Mathes, P. G., Torgeson, J. K., & Allor, J. H. (2001). The effects of peer-assisted literacy strategies for first-grade readers with and without additional computer-assisted instruction in phonological awareness. *American Educational Research Journal, 38*(2), 371–410.

Matson, J. L. (Ed.). (1994). *Autism in children and adults: Etiology, assessment, and intervention*. Pacific Grove, CA: Brooks/Cole.

Mattingly, D. J., Prisllin, R., McKenzie, T. L., Rodriguez, J. L., & Kayzar, B. (2002). Evaluating evaluations: The case of parent involvement programs. *Review of Educational Research, 72*(4), 549–576.

May, D. C., & Kundert, D. K. (1997). School readiness practices and children at risk. *Psychology in the Schools, 34*, 73–84.

Mayer, R. (2001). *Multimedia learning*. New York: Cambridge University Press.

Mayer, R. E. (1992). Cognition and instruction: Their historic meeting within educational psychology. *Journal of Educational Psychology, 84*, 405–412.

Mayer, R. E. (1996). Learning strategies for making sense out of expository text: The SOI model for guiding three cognitive processes in knowledge construction. *Educational Psychology Review, 8*(4), 357–371.

Mayer, R. E. (2001). What good is educational psychology? The case of cognition and instruction. *Educational Psychologist, 36*(2), 83–88.

Mayer, R. E. (2003). Memory and information processes. In W. M. Reynolds & G. E. Miller (Eds.), *Handbook of psychology: Vol. 7. Educational psychology* (pp. 47–57). Hoboken, NJ: Wiley.

Mayer, R. E., & Gallini, J. K. (1990). When is an illustration worth ten thousand words? *Journal of Educational Psychology, 82*, 715–726.

Mayer, R. E., & Moreno, R. (1998). A split-attention effect in multi media learning: Evidence for dual processing systems in working memory. *Journal of Educational Psychology, 90*(2), 312–320.

Mayer, R. E., & Moreno, R. (2002). Animation as an aid to multimedia learning. *Educational Psychology Review, 14*(1), 87–100.

Mayer, R. E., & Wittrock, M. C. (1996). Problem-solving transfer. In D. C. Berliner & R. C. Calfee (Eds.), *Handbook of educational psychology* (pp. 47–62). New York: Macmillan.

McArdle, J. J., & Woodcock, R. W. (Eds.). (1998). *Human cognitive abilities in theory and practice*. Mahwah, NJ: Erlbaum.

McCain, T., & Jukes, I. (2000). *Windows on the future: Education in the age of technology*. Thousand Oaks, CA: Corwin.

McCaleb, J., & White, J. (1980). Critical dimensions in evaluating teacher clarity. *Journal of Classroom Interaction, 15*, 27–30.

McCallum, R. S., & Bracken, B. A. (1993). Interpersonal relations between school children and their peers, parents, and teachers. *Educational Psychology Review, 5*(2), 155–176.

McCarthy, B. (1997). A tale of four learners: 4 MAT's learning styles. *Educational Leadership, 54*(6), 46–51.

McClelland, D. C., & Atkinson, J. W. (1948). The projective expression of needs: II. The effect of different intensities of the hunger drive on thematic apperception. *Journal of Experimental Psychology, 38*, 643–658.

McComb, E. M., & Scott-Little, C. (2003). *After-school programs: Evaluations and outcomes*. Greensboro, NC: SERVE.

McCombs, B. L. (2003). Research to policy for guiding educational reform. In W. M. Reynolds & G. E. Miller (Eds.), *Handbook of psychology: Vol. 7. Educational psychology* (pp. 583–607). Hoboken, NJ: Wiley.

McCormick, C. B. (2003). Metacognition and learning. In W. M. Reynolds & G. E. Miller (Eds.), *Handbook of psychology: Vol. 7. Educational psychology* (pp. 79–102). Hoboken, NJ: Wiley.

McDaniel, M. A., & Dannelly, C. M. (1996). Learning with analogy and elaborative interrogation. *Journal of Educational Psychology, 88*(3), 508–519.

McDaniel, T. R. (1993). Practicing positive reinforcement: Ten behavior management techniques. In K. M. Cauley, F. Linder, & J. H. McMillan (Eds.), *Annual editions: Educational psychology 93/94*. Guilford, CT: Dushkin.

McDonnell, J., Hardman, M., & McDonnell, A. (2003). *An introduction to persons with moderate and severe disabilities*. Boston: Allyn & Bacon.

McHale, S. M., Dariotis, J. K., & Kauh, T. J. (2003). Social development and social relationships in middle childhood. In R. M. Lerner, M. A. Easterbrooks, & J. Mistry (Eds.), *Handbook of psychology: Vol. 6. Developmental psychology* (pp. 241–265). Hoboken, NJ: Wiley.

McInerney, V., & McInerney, D. M. (1998, April). *Metacognitive strategy training in self-questioning: The strengths of multimedia investigations of the comparative effects of two instructional approaches on self-efficacy and achievement.* Paper presented at the annual meeting of the American Educational Research Association, San Diego, CA.

McIntyre, T. (1992). The culturally sensitive disciplinarian. *Severe Behavior Disorders Monograph, 3,* 107–115.

McKenzie, G. (1979). Effects of questions and testlike events on achievement and on-task behavior in a classroom concept learning presentation. *Journal of Educational Research, 72,* 348–350.

McKenzie, G. R., & Henry, M. (1979). Effects of testlike events on on-task behavior, test anxiety, and achievement in a classroom rule-learning task. *Journal of Educational Psychology, 71,* 370–374.

McKeown, M. G., & Beck, I. L. (1998). Talking to an author: Readers taking charge of the reading process. In R. Calfoe & N. Nelson (Eds.), *The Reading—Writing Connection* (pp. 112–130). Chicago: National Society for the Study of Education.

McLeskey, J., & Waldron, N. L. (2002). School change and inclusive schools: Lessons learned from practice. *Phi Delta Kappan, 84*(1), 65–72.

McLoyd, V. C. (1998). Economic disadvantage and child development. *American Psychologist, 53*(2), 185–204.

McMillan, J. H. (2001). *Essential assessment concepts for teachers and administrators.* Thousand Oaks, CA: Corwin.

McMillan, J. H. (2004). *Classroom assessment: Principles and practice for effective instruction.* Boston: Pearson.

McPartland, J. M., Balfanz, R., Jordan, W. J., & Legers, N. (2002). Promising solutions for the least productive American high schools. In S. Stringfield & D. Land (Eds.), *Educating at-risk students* (pp. 148–170). Chicago: National Society for the Study of Education.

McPartland, J. M., Coldiron, J. R., & Braddock, J. H. (1987). *School structures and classroom practices in elementary, middle, and secondary schools* (Tech. Rep. No. 14). Baltimore: Johns Hopkins University, Center for Research on Elementary and Middle Schools.

Means, B. (2001). Technology use in tomorrow's schools. *Educational Leadership, 58*(4), 57–61.

Means, B., & Coleman, E. (2000). Technology supports for student participation in science investigations. In M. J. Jacobson & R. B. Kozma (Eds.), *Innovations in science and mathematics* (pp. 287–319). Mahwah, NJ: Erlbaum.

Means, B., Roschelle, J., & Penuel, W. (2003). Technology's contribution to teaching and policy: Efficiency, standardization, or transformation? *Review of Education in Research, 27,* 159–182.

Medley, D. M. (1979). The effectiveness of teachers. In P. L. Peterson & H. Walberg (Eds.), *Research on teaching: Concepts, findings, and implications* (pp. 11–27). Berkeley: McCutchan.

Meece, J. L. (1991). The classroom context and children's motivational goals. In M. Maehr & P. Pintrich (Eds.), *Advances in motivation and achievement* (vol. 7, pp. 261–286). Greenwich, CT: JAI Press.

Meek, C. (2003). Classroom crisis: It's about time. *Phi Delta Kappan, 84*(8), 592–595.

Meichenbaum, D. (1977). *Cognitive behavior modification: An integrative approach.* New York: Plenum.

Merickel, A., Linquanti, R., Parrish, T. B., Pérez, M., Eaton, M., & Esra, P. (2003). *Effects of the implementation of Proposition 227 on the education of English language learners, K–12: Year 3 report.* San Francisco: WestEd.

Merrill, D. C., Reiser, B. J., Merrill, S. K., & Landes, S. (1995). Tutoring: Guided learning by doing. *Cognition and Instruction, 13*(3), 315–372.

Mertler, C. A., & Charles, C. M. (2005). *Introduction to education research* (5th ed.). Boston: Pearson.

Messick, S. (1982). Issues of effectiveness and equity in the coaching controversy: Implications for educational and testing practice. *Educational Psychologist, 17,* 67–91.

Messick, S. (1994). The interplay of evidence and consequences in the validation of performance assessments. *Educational Researcher, 23*(2), 13–23.

Metsala, J. L., Stanovich, K. E., & Brown, G. D. A. (1998). Regularity effects and the phonological deficit model of reading disabilities: A meta-analytic review. *Journal of Educational Psychology, 90*(2), 279–293.

Metzger, M. (2002). Learning to discipline. *Phi Delta Kappan, 84*(1), 77–84.

Mevarech, Z. R., & Kramarski, B. (1997). Improve: A multidimensional method for teaching mathematics in heterogeneous classrooms. *American Educational Research Journal, 34*(2), 365–394.

Meyer, A., & Rose, D. H. (2000). Universal design for individual differences. *Educational Leadership, 58*(3), 39–43.

Meyer, B., Middlemiss, W., Theodorou, E., Brezinski, K., McDougall, J., & Bartlett, B. (2002). Effects of structure strategy instruction delivered to fifth-grade children using the internet with and without the aid of older adult tutors. *Journal of Educational Psychology, 94*(3), 486–519.

Meyer, L. H., Harry, B., & Sapon-Shevin, M. (1997). School inclusion: Multicultural issues in special education. In J. A. Banks & C. A. M. Banks (Eds.), *Multicultural education: Issues and perspectives* (pp. 334–360). Boston: Allyn & Bacon.

Meyer, M. (2000). The ability-achievement discrepancy: Does it contribute to an understanding of learning disabilites? *Educational Psychology Review, 12*(3), 315–338.

Meyers, J., Gelzheiser, L., Yelich, G., & Gallagher, M. (1990). Classroom, remedial and resource teachers' views of pullout programs. *Elementary School Journal, 90*(5), 531–545.

Mickelson, R. A. (2002). Race and education. In D. L. Levinson, P. W. Cookson, Jr., & A. R. Sadovnik (Eds.), *Education and sociology: An encyclopedia* (pp. 485–494). New York: Routledge Falmer.

Midgley, C. M. (1993). Motivation and middle level schools. In M. L. Maehr & P. R. Pintrick (Eds.), *Advances in motivation and achievement* (Vol. 8, pp. 217–274). Greenwich, CT: JAI Press.

Midgley, C., & Urdan, T. (2001). Academic self-handicapping and achievement goals: A further examination. *Contemporary Educational Psychology, 26*(1), 61–75.

Miller, A., & Hom, H. L., Jr. (1990). Influence of extrinsic and ego incentive value on persistence after failure and continuing motivation. *Journal of Educational Psychology, 82*(3), 539–545.

Miller, D., Partelow, L., Sen, A. (2004, April). *Self-regulatory reading processes in relation to fourth-graders' reading literacy.* Paper presented at the annual meeting of the American Educational Research Association, San Diego, CA.

Miller, G. A. (1956). The magical number seven, plus or minus two: Some limits on our capacity for processing information. *Psychological Review, 63,* 81–97.

Miller, P. H. (1993). *Theories of developmental psychology* (3rd ed.). New York: Freeman.

Miller, S., & Ferroggiaro, M. (1995). Class dismissed? *The American Prospect, 21,* 100–104.

Mills, C. J., Ablard, K. E., & Stumpf, H. (1993). Gender differences in academically talented young students' mathematical reasoning: Patterns across age and subskills. *Journal of Educational Psychology, 85*(2), 340–346.

Mills, G. E. (2000). *Action research: A guide for the teacher-researcher.* Columbus, OH: Merrill.

Miltenberger, R. G. (2001). *Behavior modification: Principles and procedures* (2nd ed.). Belmont, CA: Wadsworth.

Minke, K. M., & Bear, G. C. (Eds.). (2000). *Preventing school problems—promoting school success.* Bethesda, MD: National Association of School Psychologists.

Morgan, M. (1984). Reward-induced decrements and increments in intrinsic motivation. *Review of Educational Research, 54,* 5–30.

Morris, D., Tyner, B., & Perney, J. (2000). Early Steps: Replicating the effects of a first-grade reading intervention program. *Journal of Educational Psychology, 92,* 681–693.

Morris, J. E. (1999). What is the future of predominantly black urban schools? The politics of race in urban education policy. *Phi Delta Kappan, 81*(4), 316–319.

Morrison, P., & Masten, A. S. (1991). Peer reputation in middle childhood as a predictor of adaptation in adolescence: A seven-year follow-up. *Child Development, 62,* 991–1007.

Morrow, L. M. (1993). *Literacy development in the early years.* Boston: Allyn & Bacon.

Moss, P. A. (1992). Shifting conceptions of validity in educational measurement: Implications for performance assessment. *Review of Educational Research, 62*(3), 229–258.

Mosteller, F., & Boruch, R. (Eds.). (2002). *Evidence matters: Randomized trials in educational research.* Washington, DC: Brookings.

Munk, D. D., & Bursuck, W. D. (1998). Can grades be helpful and fair? *Educational Leadership, 55*(4), 44–47.

Muñoz, M. A., Dossett, D., & Judy-Gullans, K. (2004). Educating students placed at risk: Evaluating the impact of Success for All in urban settings. *Journal of Education for Students Placed at Risk, 9*(3), 261–277.

Murdock, T. B. (1999). The social context of risk: Status and motivational predictors of alienation in middle school. *Journal of Educational Psychology, 91*(1), 62–75.

Murdock, T. B., Hale, N. M., & Weber, M. J. (2001). Predictors of cheating among early adolescents: Academic and social motivations. *Contemporary Educational Psychology, 26*(1), 96–115.

Murphy, K. P., & Alexander, P. A. (2000). A motivated exploration of motivation technology. *Contemporary Educational Psychology, 25*(1), 3–53.

Murphy, S., & Underwood, T. (2000). *Portfolio practices: Lessons from schools, districts, and states.* Norwood, MA: Christopher–Gordon.

Murray, H., Olivier, A., & Human, P. (1992). The development of young students' division strategies. In W. Geeslin & K. Graham (Eds.), *Proceedings of the sixteenth international conference for the psychology of mathematics instruction* (Vol. 2, pp. 152–159). Durham, NH.

Muskin, C. (1990, April). *Equity and opportunity to learn in high school U.S. history classes: Comparisons between schools and ability groups.* Paper presented at the annual meeting of the American Educational Research Association, Boston, MA.

Nagy, P., & Griffiths, A. K. (1982). Limitations of recent research relating Piaget's theory to adolescent thought. *Review of Educational Research, 52,* 513–556.

Nash, W. R., Borman, C., & Colson, S. (1980). Career education for gifted and talented students: A senior high school model. *Exceptional Children, 46,* 404–405.

National Academy of Sciences. (1998). *The prevention of reading difficulties in young children.* Washington, DC: Author.

National Association for the Education of Young Children. (1997). *Developmentally appropriate practice in early childhood programs.* Washington, DC: Author.

National Center for Education Statistics. (2003). *The nation's report card: Reading 2003.* Washington, DC: Author.

National Center for Education Statistics. (2004). *Language minorities and their educational and labor market indicators—recent trends.* Washington, DC: U.S. Department of Education.

National Center for Education Statistics. (1988). *Digest of educational statistics.* Washington, DC: U.S. Department of Education, NCES.

National Center for Education Statistics. (1997). *The condition of education, 1997.* Washington, DC: U.S. Department of Education, NCES.

National Center for Education Statistics. (2001). *The condition of education, 2001.* Washington, DC: U.S. Department of Education, NCES.

National Education Association. (1992). *Education for all students with disabilities.* Washington, DC: Author.

National Education Commission on Time and Learning. (1994). *Prisoners of time: Schools and programs making time work for students and teachers.* Washington, DC: Author.

National Education Goals Panel. (1997). *Special early childhood report 1997.* Washington, DC: Author.

National Governors' Association. (1993). *Ability grouping and tracking: Current issues and concerns.* Washington, DC: Author.

National Information Center for Children and Youth with Disabilities. (1998). *Office of Special Education Programs' IDEA amendments of 1997 curriculum* [Internet]. Retrieved from: www.nichcy.org/Trainpkg/trainpkg.htm.

National Joint Committee on Learning Disabilities. (1988). (Letter to NJCLD member organization). Washington, DC: Author.

National Reading Panel. (2000). *Teaching children to read: An evidence-based assessment of the scientific research literature on reading and its implications for reading instruction.* Rockville, MD: National Institute of Child Health and Human Development.

National Reading Panel. (1999). *Teaching children to read.* Washington, DC: U.S. Department of Education.

National Research Council. (1995). *Losing generations: Adolescents in high-risk settings.* Hyattsville, MD: American Psychological Association.

National Research Council. (2000). *Improving intergroup relations among youth.* Washington, DC: NRC.

National Research Council. (2001). *Non-technical strategies to reduce children's exposure to inappropriate material on the Internet.* Washington, DC: National Academy Press.

Natriello, G. (2002). At-risk students. In D. L. Levinson, P. W. Cookson, Jr., & A. R. Sadovnik (Eds.), *Education and sociology: An encyclopedia* (pp. 49–54). New York: Routledge Falmer.

Natriello, G., & Dornbusch, S. M. (1984). *Teacher evaluative standards and student effort.* New York: Longman.

Nattiv, A. (1994). Helping behaviors and math achievement gain of students using cooperative learning. *The Elementary School Journal, 94*(3), 285–297.

Navaez, D., Getz, I., Rest, J. R., & Thoma, S. J. (1999). Individual moral judgment and cultural ideologies. *Developmental Psychology, 35,* 478–488.

Naveh-Benjamin, M. (1991). A comparison of training programs intended for different types of test-anxious students: Further support for an information-processing model. *Journal of Educational Psychology, 83,* 134–139.

Neale, D. C., Smith, D., & Johnson, V. G. (1990). Implementing conceptual change teaching in primary science. *Elementary School Journal, 91,* 109–131.

Neill, M. (2003). Leaving children behind: How No Child Left Behind will fail our children. *Phi Delta Kappan, 85*(3), 225–228.

Neill, M. (2003). The dangers of testing. *Educational Leadership, 60*(5), 43–46.

Neill, M., & Gaylor, K. (2001). Do high-stakes graduation tests improve learning outcomes? Using state-level NAEP data to evaluate the effects of mandatory graduation tests. In G. Orfield & M. L. Kornhaber (Eds.), *Raising standards or raising barriers? Inequality and high-stakes testing in public education* (pp. 107–126). New York: Century Foundation Press.

Nelson, J. R., & Carr, B. A. (2000). *The Think Time Strategy for schools.* Denver, CO: Sopris West.

Nelson, J., Lott, L., & Glenn, S. (1997). *Positive discipline in the classroom* (2nd ed.). New York: Ballantine.

Neufield, B., & Roper, D. (2003). *Coaching: A strategy for developing instructional capacity.* Providence, RI: Annenberg Institute.

Neuman, S. (2003). From rhetoric to reality: The case for high-quality compensatory prekindergarten programs. *Phi Delta Kappan, 85*(4), 286–291.

Neuman, S. B. (1995). Reading together: A community-based parent tutoring program. *The Reading Teacher, 49*(2), 120–129.

Neuman, S. B., & McCormick, S. (1995). *Single-subject experimental research.* Newark, DE: International Reading Association.

Neuman, S. B., & Roskos, K. (1993). Access to print for children of poverty: Differential effects of adult mediation and literacy enriched play settings on environmental and functional print tasks. *American Educational Research Journal, 30,* 95–122.

Nevin, A. (1998). Curriculum and instructional adaptations for including students with disabilities in cooperative groups. In J. W. Putnam (Ed.), *Cooperative learning and strategies for inclusion* (pp. 49–66). Baltimore: Paul H. Brookes.

Newbern, D., Dansereau, D. F., Patterson, M. E., & Wallace, D. S. (1994, April). *Toward a science of cooperation.* Paper presented at the annual meeting of the American Educational Research Association, New Orleans, LA.

Newcomb, A. F., & Bagwell, C. L. (1998). The developmental significance of children's friendship relations. In W. M. Bukowski, A. F. Newcomb, & W. W. Hartup (Eds.), *The company they keep: Friendships in childhood and adolescence* (pp. 289–312). New York: Cambridge University Press.

Newell, A., & Simon, H. (1972). *Human problem solving.* Englewood Cliffs, NJ: Prentice-Hall.

Newmann, F. M., & Wehlage, G. G. (1993). Five standards of authentic instruction. *Educational Leadership, 50*(7), 8–12.

Niaz, M. (1997). How early can children understand some form of "scientific reasoning"? *Perceptual and motor skills, 85,* 1272–1274.

NICHD Early Child Care Research Network. (2002). Early child care and children's development prior to school entry: Results from the NICHD study of early child care. *American Educational Research Journal, 39*(1), 133–164.

Nichols, P. D. (1994). A framework for developing cognitively diagnostic assessments. *Review of Educational Research, 64*(4), 575–603.

Nieto, S. (1997). School reform and student achievement: A multicultural perspective. In J. A. Banks & C. A. M. Banks (Eds.), *Multicultural education: Issues and perspectives* (pp. 387–407). Boston: Allyn & Bacon.

Nieto, S. M. (2003). Profoundly multicultural questions. *Educational Leadership, 60*(4), 6–10.

Nitsch, K. E. (1977). *Structuring decontextualized forms of knowledge.* Unpublished doctoral dissertation, Vanderbilt University.

Noddings, N. (1995). Teaching themes of care. *Phi Delta Kappan, 76,* 675–679.

Noonan, M. J., & McCormick, L. (1993). *Early intervention in natural environments.* Pacific Grove, CA: Brooks/Cole.

Northcutt, N., & McCoy, D. (2004). *Interactive qualitative analysis.* Thousand Oaks, CA: Sage.

Northwest Regional Educational Laboratory. (1998). *Catalog of school reform models.* Portland, OR: Author.

Nucci, L. (1987). Synthesis of research on moral development. *Educational Leadership, 44,* 86–92.

O'Connor, M. C. (1998). Can we trace the "efficacy of social constructivism"? In P. D. Pearson & A. Iran-Nejad (Eds.), *Review of research in education* (pp. 25–72). Washington, DC: American Educational Research Association.

O'Connor, R. E., Bell, K. M., Harty, K. R., Larkin, L. K., Sackor, S. M., & Zigmond, N. (2002). Teaching reading to poor readers in the intermediate grades: A comparison of text difficulty. *Journal of Educational Psychology, 94*(3), 474–485.

O'Donnell, A. M. (1996). Effects of explicit incentives on scripted and unscripted cooperation. *Journal of Educational Psychology, 88*(1), 74–86.

O'Donnell, A. M., & Dansereau, D. F. (1992). Scripted cooperation in student dyads: A method for analyzing and enhancing academic learning and performance. In R. Hertz-Lazarowitz & N. Miller (Eds.), *Interaction in cooperative groups: The theoretical anatomy of group learning* (pp. 120–144). New York: Cambridge University Press.

O'Donnell, A. M., & O'Kelly, J. (1994). Learning from peers: Beyond the rhetoric of positive results. *Educational Psychology Review, 6,* 321–349.

O'Donnell, A. M., Dansereau, D. F., & Hall, R. H. (2002). Knowledge maps as scaffolds for cognitive processing. *Educational Psychology Review, 14*(1), 71–86.

O'Donnell, J., Hawkins, J. D., Catalano, R. F., Abbott, R. D., & Day, L. E. (1995). Preventing school failure, drug use, and delinquency among low-income children: Long-term intervention in elementary schools. *American Journal of Orthopsychiatry, 65*(1), 87–100.

O'Leary, K. D., & O'Leary, S. G. (1972). *Classroom management: The successful use of behavior modification.* New York: Pergamon.

O'Leary, S. G. (1995). Parental discipline mistakes. *Current Directions in Psychological Science, 4*(1), 11–13.

O'Neil, J. (1991). A generation adrift? *Educational Leadership, 49*(1), 4–10.

Oakes, J. (1985). *Keeping track: How schools structure inequality.* New Haven, CT: Yale University Press.

Oakes, J. (1995). Two cities: Tracking and within-school segregation. In L. Miller (Ed.), *Brown plus forty: The promise.* New York: Teachers College Press.

Oakes, J., & Guiton, G. (1995). Matchmaking: The dynamics of high school tracking decisions. *American Educational Research Journal, 32*(1), 3–33.

Oakes, J., & Lipton, M. (1994). Tracking and ability grouping: A structural barrier to access and achievement. In J. I. Goodlad & P. Keating (Eds.), *Access to knowledge: The continuing agenda for our nation's schools.* New York: The College Board.

Oakes, J., & Wells, A. S. (1998). Detracking for high student achievement. *Educational Leadership, 55*(6), 38–41.

Oakes, J., Quartz, K., Ryan, S., & Lipton, M. (2000). *Becoming good American schools: The struggle for civic virtue in school reform.* San Francisco: Jossey-Bass.

Ogbu, J. (1999, April). *The significance of minority status.* Paper presented at the annual meeting of the American Educational Research Association, Montreal.

Okagaki, L. (2001). Triarchic model of minority children's school achievement. *Educational Psychologist, 36*(1), 9–20.

Okagaki, L., & Frensch, P. A. (1998). Parenting and children's school achievement: A multiethnic perspective. *American Educational Research Journal, 35*(1), 123–144.

Olszewski-Kubilius, P. (2003). Gifted education programs and procedures. In W. M. Reynolds & G. E. Miller (Eds.), *Handbook of psychology: Vol. 7. Educational psychology* (pp. 487–510). Hoboken, NJ: Wiley.

Olweus, D. (1994). Bullying at school: Basic facts and effects of a school-based intervention program. *Journal of Child Psychology and Psychiatry, 35,* 1171–1190.

Orfield, G., & Kornhaber, M. L. (Eds.). (2001). *Raising standards or raising barriers? Inequality and high-stakes testing in public education.* New York: Century Foundation Press.

Orfield, G., Frankenberg, E., & Lee, C. (2003). The resurgence of school segregation. *Educational Leadership, 60*(4), 16–21.

Osborn, A. F. (1963). *Applied imagination* (3rd ed.). New York: Scribner's.

Osguthorpe, R. T., & Scruggs, T. E. (1986). Special education students as tutors: A review and analysis. *Remedial and Special Education, 7*(4), 15–25.

Overton, W. F. (1998). Developmental psychology: Philosophy, concepts, and methodology. In W. Damon (Ed.), *Handbook of child psychology,* (Vol. 1, pp. 107–188). New York: Wiley.

Padrón, Y. N., Waxman, H. C., & Rivera, H. H. (2002). Issues in educating Hispanic students. In S. Stringfield & D. Land (Eds.), *Educating at-risk students* (pp. 66–88). Chicago: National Society for the Study of Education.

Page, R. N. (1991). *Lower track classrooms: A curricular and cultural perspective.* New York: Teachers College Press.

Page, S. W. (2000). When changes for the gifted spur differentiation for all. *Educational Leadership, 58*(1), 62–65.

Page-Voth, V., & Graham, S. (1999). Effects of goal setting and strategy use on the writing performance and self-efficacy of students with writing and learning problems. *Journal of Educational Psychology, 91*(2), 230–240.

Pajares, F. (1996). Self-efficacy beliefs in academic settings. *Review of Educational Research, 66*(4), 543–578.

Pajares, F., & Miller, M. D. (1994). Role of self-efficacy and self-concept beliefs in mathematical problem solving: A path analysis. *Journal of Educational Psychology, 86*(2), 193–203.

Pajares, F., Britner, S. L., & Valiante, G. (2000). Relation between achievement goals and self-beliefs of middle school students in writing and science. *Contemporary Educational Psychology, 25*(4), 406–422.

Pajares, R., & Graham, L. (1999). Self-efficacy, motivation constructs, and mathematics performance of entering middle school students. *Contemporary Educational Psychology, 24*(2), 124–139.

Palincsar, A. S. (1986). The role of dialogue in providing scaffolded instruction. *Educational Psychologist, 21,* 73–98.

Palincsar, A. S., & Brown, A. L. (1984). Reciprocal teaching of comprehension fostering and comprehension monitoring activities. *Cognition and Instruction, 2,* 117–175.

Palincsar, A. S., Brown, A. L., & Martin, S. M. (1987). Peer interaction in reading comprehension instruction. *Educational Psychologist, 22,* 231–253.

Pallas, A. M. (2002). High school dropouts. In D. L. Levinson, P. W. Cookson, Jr., & A. R. Sadovnik (Eds.), *Education and sociology: An encyclopedia* (pp. 315–320). New York: Routledge Falmer.

Pallas, A. M., Entwisle, D. R., Alexander, K. L., & Stluka, M. F. (1994). Ability-group effects: Instructional, social, or institutional? *Sociology of Education, 67,* 27–46.

Palumbo, D. B. (1990). Programming language/problem-solving research: A review of relevant issues. *Review of Educational Research, 60*(1), 65–89.

Papert, S. (1980). *Mindstorms: Children, computers, and powerful ideas.* New York: Basic Books.

Paris, S. G. (2001). Wisdom, snake oil, and the educational marketplace. *Educational Psychologist, 36*(4), 257–260.

Paris, S. G., & Paris, A. H. (2001). Classroom applications of research on self-regulated learning. *Educational Psychologist, 36*(2), 89–101.

Paris, S., Cross, D., & Lipson, M. (1984). Informal strategies for learning: A program to improve children's reading awareness and comprehension. *Journal of Educational Psychology, 76,* 1239–1252.

Parke, B. N. (1983). Use of self-instructional materials with gifted primary aged students. *Gifted Child Quarterly, 27,* 29–34.

Parker, H. C. (1990). *C.H.A.D.D.: Children with attention deficit disorders: Parents supporting parents.* Education position paper, Plantation, FL.

Parker, W. D. (1997). An empirical typology of perfectionism in academically talented children. *American Educational Research Journal, 34*(3), 545–562.

Parkhurst, J. T., & Asher, S. R. (1992). Peer rejection in middle school: Subgroup differences in behavior, loneliness, and interpersonal concerns. *Developmental Psychology, 28,* 231–241.

Parten, M. (1932). Social participation among preschool children. *Journal of Abnormal and Social Psychology, 27,* 243–269.

Patrick, B., Hisley, J., & Kempler, T. (2000). "What's everybody so excited about?": The effects of teacher enthusiasm on student intrinsic motivation and vitality. *Journal of Experimental Education, 68,* 217–236.

Pavan, B. N. (1992). The benefits of nongraded schools. *Educational Leadership, 50*(2), 22–25.

Pawlowski, K. F. (2001). The instructional support team concept in action. In B. Sornson (Ed.), *Preventing early learning failure.* Alexandria, VA: ASCD.

Pea, R. D. (1993). Learning scientific concepts through material and social activities: Conversational analysis meets conceptual change. *Educational Psychologist, 28*(3), 265–277.

Pearl, R., Farmer, T. W., Van Acker, R., Rodkin, P. C., Bost, K. K., Coe, M., & Henley, W. (1998). The social integration of students with mild disabilities in general education classrooms: Peer group membership and peer-assessed social behavior. *The Elementary School Journal, 99*(2), 167–185.

Peisner-Feinberg, E., Clifford, R., Yazejian, N., Culkin, M., Howes, C., & Kagan, S. L. (1998, April). *The longitudinal effects of childcare quality: Implications for kindergarten success.* Paper presented at the annual meeting of the American Educational Research Association, San Diego, CA.

Pellegrini, A. D. (2002). Bullying, victimization, and sexual harassment during the transition to middle school. *Educational Psychologist, 37*(3), 151–163.

Pellegrini, A. D., & Bartini, M. (2000). A longitudinal study of bullying, victimization, and peer affiliation during the transition from primary school to middle school. *American Educational Research Journal, 37*(3), 699–725.

Pellegrini, A. D., & Horvat, M. (1995). A developmental contextualist critique of attention deficit hyperactivity disorder. *Educational Researcher, 24*(1), 13–18.

Pendarvis, E., & Howley, A. (1996). Playing fair: The possibilities of gifted education. *Journal for the Education of the Gifted, 19,* 215–233.

Pepitone, E. A. (1985). Children in cooperation and competition: Antecedents and consequences of self-orientation. In R. E. Slavin, S. Sharan, S. Kagan, R. Hertz-Lazarowitz, C. Webb, & R. Schmuck (Eds.), *Learning to cooperate, cooperating to learn.* New York: Plenum.

Perfetto, G. A., Bransford, J. D., & Franks, J. J. (1983). Constraints on access in a problem solving context. *Memory and Cognition, 11,* 24–31.

Perkins, D. F., & Borden, L. M. (2003). Positive behaviors, problem behaviors, and resiliency in adolescence. In R. M. Lerner, M. A. Easterbrooks, & J. Mistry (Eds.), *Handbook of psychology: Vol. 6. Developmental psychology* (pp. 373–394). Hoboken, NJ: Wiley.

Perry, K., & Weinstein, R. (1998). The social context of early schooling and children's school adjustment. *Educational Psychologist, 33*(4), 177–194.

Persell, C. H. (1997). Social class and educational equality. In J. A. Banks & C. A. M. Banks (Eds.), *Multicultural edu-*

cation: Issues and perspectives (pp. 87–107). Boston: Allyn & Bacon.

Peterson, L. R., & Peterson, M. J. (1959). Short-term retention of individual verbal items. *Journal of Experimental Psychology, 58,* 193–198.

Peterson, P. E., & West, M. R. (Eds.). (2003). *No Child Left Behind? The politics and practice of school accountability.* Washington, DC: Brookings.

Petrill, S. A., & Wilkerson, B. (2000). Intelligence and achievement: A behavioral genetic perspective. *Educational Psychology Review, 12*(2), 185–199.

Pettig, K. L. (2000). On the road to differentiated practice. *Educational Leadership, 58*(1), 14–18.

Peverly, S. T. (1991). Problems with the knowledge-based explanation of memory and development. *Review of Educational Research, 61*(1), 71–93.

Phelan, P., Yu, H. C., & Davidson, A. L. (1994). Navigating the psychosocial pressures of adolescence: The voices and experiences of high school youth. *American Educational Research Journal, 31,* 415–447.

Phillips, J. L. (1975). *The origins of intellect: Piaget's theory* (2nd ed.). San Francisco: Freeman.

Piaget, J. (1952a). *The language and thought of the child.* London: Routledge and Kegan-Paul.

Piaget, J. (1952b). *The origins of intelligence in children.* New York: Basic Books.

Piaget, J. (1964). *The moral judgment of the child.* New York: Free Press.

Piaget, J., & Inhelder, B. (1956). *The child's conception of space.* Boston: Routledge and Kegan-Paul.

Pietsch, J., Walker, R., & Chapman, E. (2003). The relationship among self-concept, self-efficacy, and performance in mathematics during secondary school. *Journal of Educational Psychology, 95*(3), 589–603.

Pinnell, G. S. (1990). Success for low achievers through Reading Recovery. *Educational Leadership, 48*(1), 17–21.

Pinnell, G. S., DeFord, D. E., & Lyons, C. A. (1988). *Reading Recovery: Early intervention for at-risk first graders.* Arlington, VA: Educational Research Service.

Pinnell, G. S., Lyons, C. A., DeFord, D. E., Bryk, A. S., & Seltzer, M. (1994). Comparing instructional models for the literacy education of high risk first graders. *Reading Research Quarterly, 29,* 8–38.

Pinnell, G. S., Lyons, C., & Jones, N. (1996). Response to Hiebert: What difference does Reading Recovery make? *Educational Researcher, 25*(7), 23–25.

Pintrich, P. (2000). Multiple goals, multiple pathways: The role of goal orientation in learning and achievement. *Journal of Educational Psychology, 92*(3), 544–555.

Pintrich, P. R. (2003). A motivational science perspective on the role of student motivation in learning and teaching contexts. *Journal of Educational Psychology, 95*(4), 667–686.

Pintrich, P. R. (2003). Motivation and classroom learning. In W. M. Reynolds & G. E. Miller (Eds.), *Handbook of psychology: Vol. 7. Educational psychology* (pp. 103–122). Hoboken, NJ: Wiley.

Plomin, R. (1989). Environment and genes: Determinants of behavior. *American Psychologist, 44*(2), 105–111.

Polite, L., & Saenger, E. B. (2003). A pernicious silence: Confronting race in the elementary classroom. *Phi Delta Kappan, 85*(4), 274–278.

Pomerantz, E. M., Altermatt, E. R., & Saxon, J. L. (2002). Making the grade but feeling distressed: Gender differences in academic performance and internal distress. *Journal of Educational Psychology, 94*(2), 396–404.

Pontecorvo, C. (1993). Social interaction in the acquisition of knowledge. *Educational Psychology Review, 5*(3), 293–310.

Pool, H., & Page, J. A. (Eds.). (1995). *Beyond tracking: Finding success in inclusive schools.* Bloomington, IN: Phi Delta Kappan Educational Foundation.

Pope, A. W., & Bierman, K. L. (1999). Predicting adolescent peer problems and antisocial activities: The relative roles of aggression and dysregulation. *Developmental psychology, 35,* 335–346.

Popham, W. J. (2004). "Teaching to the test": An expression to eliminate. *Educational Leadership, 62*(3), 82–83.

Popham, W. J. (2005). *Classroom assessment: What teachers need to know* (4th ed.). Boston: Pearson.

Porter, G. L., & Stone, J. A. (1998). The inclusive school model: A framework and key strategies for success. In J. W. Putnam (Ed.), *Cooperative learning and strategies for inclusion* (pp. 229–248). Baltimore: Paul H. Brookes.

Portes, P. R. (1999). Social and psychological factors in the academic achievement of children of immigrants: A cultural history puzzle. *American Educational Research Journal, 36*(3), 489–507.

Potter, E. F. (1977, April). *Children's expectancy of criticism for classroom achievement efforts.* Paper presented at the annual convention of the American Educational Research Association, New York, NY.

Poulin, F., Cillessen-A. H. N., & Coie, J. D. (1997). Children's friends and behavioral similarity in the social contexts. *Social Development, 6,* 224–236.

Powell, D. R. (1995). *Enabling young children to succeed in school.* Washington, DC: American Educational Research Association.

Prawat, R. S. (1992). Teachers' beliefs about teaching and learning: A constructivist perspective. *American Journal of Education, 100*(3), 354–395.

Premack, D. (1965). Reinforcement theory. In D. Levine (Ed.), *Nebraska symposium on motivation.* Lincoln: University of Nebraska Press.

Pressley, M. (1998). *Reading instruction that works: The case for balanced teaching.* New York: Guilford.

Pressley, M. (2003). Psychology of literacy and literacy instruction. In W. M. Reynolds & G. E. Miller (Eds.), *Handbook of psychology: Vol. 7. Educational psychology* (pp. 333–355). Hoboken, NJ: Wiley.

Pressley, M., & Harris, K. R. (1990). What we really know about strategy instruction. *Educational Leadership, 48*(1), 31–34.

Pressley, M., & Harris, K. R. (1994). Increasing the quality of educational intervention research. *Educational Psychology Review, 6*(3), 191–208.

Pressley, M., & Yokoi, L. (1994). Motion for a new trial on transfer. *Educational Researcher, 23*(5), 36–38.

Pressley, M., Harris, K. R., & Marks, M. B. (1992). But good strategy instructors are constructivists! *Educational Psychology Review, 4*, 3–31.

Pressley, M., Levin, J. R., & Delaney, H. (1982). The mnemonic keyword method. *Review of Educational Research, 52*, 61–92.

Pressley, M., Roehrig, A. D., Raphael, L., Dolezal, S., Bohn, C., Mohan, L., Wharton-McDonald, R., Bogner, K., & Hogan, K. (2003). Teaching processes in elementary and secondary education. In W. M. Reynolds & G. E. Miller (Eds.), *Handbook of psychology: Vol. 7. Educational psychology* (pp. 153–175). Hoboken, NJ: Wiley.

Pressley, M., Tannenbaum, R., McDaniel, M. A., & Wood, E. (1990). What happens when university students try to answer prequestions that accompany textbook material? *Contemporary Educational Psychology, 15*, 27–35.

Pressley, M., Wood, E., Woloshyn, V. E., Martin, V., King, A., & Menke, D. (1992). Encouraging mindful use of prior knowledge: Attempting to construct explanatory answers facilitates learning. *Educational Psychologist, 27*, 91–109.

Pressley, M., Yokoi, L., van Meter, P., van Etten, S., & Freebern, G. (1997). Some of the reasons why preparing for exams is so hard: What can be done to make it easier? *Educational Psychology Review, 9*(1), 1–38.

Price, E. A., & Driscoll, M. P. (1997). An inquiry into the spontaneous transfer of problem-solving skill. *Contemporary Educational Psychology, 22*(4), 472–494.

Provenzo, E. F. (1999). *The Internet and the World Wide Web for preservice teachers.* Boston: Allyn & Bacon.

Puma, M. J., Jones, C. C., Rock, D., & Fernandez, R. (1993). *Prospects: The congressionally mandated study of educational growth and opportunity.* Interim Report. Bethesda, MD: Abt Associates.

Puma, M. J., Karweit, N., Price, C., Ricciuti, A., Thompson, W., & Vaden-Kiernan, M. (1997). *Prospects: Final report on student outcomes.* Cambridge, MA: Abt Associates.

Purcell-Gates, V., McIntyre, E., & Freppon, P. A. (1995). Learning written storybook language in school: A comparison of low-SES children in skills-based and whole language classrooms. *American Educational Research Journal, 32*, 659–685.

Putnam, J. W. (Ed.). (1998a). *Cooperative learning and strategies for inclusion* (2nd ed.). Baltimore: Paul H. Brookes.

Putnam, J. W. (1998b). The movement toward teaching and learning in inclusive classrooms. In J. W. Putnam (Ed.), *Cooperative learning and strategies for inclusion* (pp. 1–16). Baltimore: Paul H. Brookes.

Qin, Z., Johnson, D. W., & Johnson, R. T. (1995). Cooperative versus competitive efforts and problem solving. *Review of Educational Research, 65*, 129–143.

Quay, H. C., & Werry, J. S. (Eds.). (1986). *Psychopathological disorders of childhood* (3rd ed.). New York: Wiley.

Quill, K. A. (2000). *Do-watch-listen-say: Social and communication intervention for children with autism.* Baltimore: Brookes.

Raaijmakers, J. G. W., & Shiffrin, R. M. (1992). Models for recall and recognition. *Annual Review of Psychology, 43*, 205–234.

Rabiner, D. L., Malone, P., & the Conduct Problems Prevention Research Group (2003, February). *The impact of tutoring on early reading achievement for children with and without attention problems.* Paper presented at the annual meetings of the Society for Research on Child Development, Tampa, FL.

Radosevich, D., Vaidyanathan, V., Yeo, S., & Radosevich, D. (2004). Relating goal orientation to self-regulatory processes: A longitudinal field test. *Contemporary Educational Psychology, 29*(3), 207–229.

Radziewicz, C., & Antonellis, S. (2002). Considerations and implications for habilitation of hearing-impaired children. In D. K. Bernstein & E. Tiegerman-Farber, (Eds.), *Language and communication disorders in children* (5th ed.). Boston: Allyn & Bacon.

Rafoth, M. A., Leal, L., & De Fabo, L. (1993). *Strategies for learning and remembering: Study skills across the curriculum.* Washington, DC: National Education Association Professional Library.

Raison, J., Hanson, L. A., Hall, C., & Reynolds, M. C. (1995). Another school's reality. *Phi Delta Kappan, 76*(6), 480–484.

Ramey, C. T., & Ramey, S. L. (1992). *At risk does not mean doomed.* Birmingham: Civitan International Research Center, University of Alabama.

Ramey, C. T., & Ramey, S. L. (1998). Early intervention and early experience. *American Psychologist, 53*(2), 109–120.

Ramey, C. T., Bryant, D. M., Wasik, B. H., Sparling, J. J., Fendt, K. H., & LaVange, L. M. (1992). Infant health and development program for low birth weight, premature infants: Program elements, family participation, and child intelligence. *Pediatrics, 3*, 454–465.

Ramirez-Smith, C. (1995). Stopping the cycle of failure: The Comer model. *Educational Leadership, 52*(5), 14–19.

Range, L. M. (1993). Suicide prevention: Guidelines for schools. *Educational Psychology Review, 5*(2), 135–154.

Raudenbush, S. W. (1984). Magnitude of teacher expectancy effects on pupil IQ as a function of the credibility of expectancy induction: A synthesis of finds from 18 experiments. *Journal of Educational Psychology, 76*, 85–97.

Raudenbush, S. W., Rowan, B., & Cheong, Y. F. (1993). Higher order instructional goals in secondary schools: Class, teacher, and school influences. *American Educational Research Journal, 30*(3), 523–553.

Reason, P., & Bradbury, H. (Eds.). (2001). *Handbook of action research.* Thousand Oaks, CA: Sage.

Rebell, M., & Hunter, M. (2004). "Highly qualified" teachers: Pretense or legal requirement? *Phi Delta Kappan, 85*(9), 690–696.

Redfield, D. L., & Rousseau, E. W. (1981). A meta-analysis of experimental research on teacher questioning behavior. *Review of Educational Research, 51,* 237–245.

Reimann, P., & Schult, T. J. (1996). Turning examples into cases: Acquiring knowledge structures for analogical problem solving. *Educational Psychologist, 31,* 123–132.

Reimer, J., Paolitto, D. P., & Hersh, R. H. (1990). *Promoting moral growth: From Piaget to Kohlberg.* Prospect Heights, IL: Waveland Press.

Reiss, S., & Cellerino, M. (1983). Guiding gifted students through independent study. *Teaching Exceptional Children, 15,* 136–139.

Rekrut, M. D. (1992, April). *Teaching to learn: Cross-age tutoring to enhance strategy acquisition.* Paper presented at the annual meeting of the American Educational Research Association, San Francisco, CA.

Renkl, A. (1998, April). *Learning by explaining in cooperative arrangements: What if questions were asked?* Paper presented at the annual meeting of the American Educational Research Association, San Diego, CA.

Renkl, A., Stark, R., Gruber, H., & Mandl, H. (1998). Learning from worked-out examples: The effects of example variability and elicited self-explanations. *Contemporary Educational Psychology, 23,* 90–108.

Renzulli, J. S. (1994). *Schools for talent development: A practical plan for total school improvement.* Mansfield Center, CT: Creative Learning Press.

Renzulli, J. S., & Reis, S. M. (1997). The schoolwide enrichment model: New directions for developing high-end learning. In N. Colangelo & G. A. Davis (Eds.), *Handbook of gifted education* (2nd ed.) (pp. 136–154). Boston: Allyn & Bacon.

Reschly, D. J. (2003). School psychology. In W. M. Reynolds & G. E. Miller (Eds.), *Handbook of psychology: Vol. 7. Educational psychology* (pp. 431–453). Hoboken, NJ: Wiley.

Resnick, L. (1998, April). *From aptitude to effort: A new foundation for our schools.* Paper presented at the annual meeting of the American Educational Research Association, San Diego, CA.

Rest, J., Edwards, L., & Thoma, S. (1997). Designing and validating a measure of moral judgment: Stage preference and stage consistency approaches. *Journal of Educational Psychology, 89*(1), 5–28.

Rest, J., Narvaez, D., Bebeau, M., & Thoma, S. (1999). A Neo-Kohlbergian approach: The DIT and schema theory. *Educational Psychology Review, 11*(4), 291–324.

Reyes, P., Schriber, J. D., & Paredes, A. (Eds.). (1999). *Lessons from high-performing Hispanic schools: Creating learning communities.* New York: Teachers College Press.

Reynolds, A. (1995). The knowledge base for beginning teachers: Education professionals' expectations versus research findings on learning to teach. *Elementary School Journal, 95*(3), 199–221.

Reynolds, A. J. (1991). Early schooling of children at risk. *American Educational Research Journal, 28*(2), 392–422.

Reynolds, A., & Wolfe, B. (1999). Special education and school achievement: An exploratory analysis with a central-city sample. *Educational Evaluation and Policy Analysis, 21*(3), 249–269.

Reynolds, A., Temple, J., & McCoy, A. (1997). Grade retention doesn't work. *Education Week,* September 17, 1997, p. 36.

Reynolds, A., Temple, J., Robertson, D., & Mann, E. (2002). Age 21 cost-benefit analysis of the Title I Chicago child–parent centers. *Educational Evaluation and Policy Analysis, 24*(4), 267–303.

Reynolds, W. M., & Miller, G. E. (2003). Current perspectives in educational psychology. In W. M. Reynolds & G. E. Miller (Eds.), *Handbook of psychology: Vol. 7. Educational psychology* (pp. 3–20). Hoboken, NJ: Wiley.

Rhine, S. (1998). The role of research and teachers' knowledge base in professional development. *Educational Researcher, 27*(5), 27–31.

Rice, E. P. (1996). *The adolescent: Development, relationships, and culture.* Boston: Allyn & Bacon.

Rickards, J. P., Fajen, B. R., Sullivan, J. F., & Gillespie, G. (1997). Signaling, notetaking, and field independence—dependence in text comprehension and recall. *Journal of Educational Psychology, 89*(3), 508–517.

Riehl, C. J. (2000). The principal's role in creating inclusive schools for diverse students: A review of normative, empirical, and critical literature on the practice of educational administration. *Review of Educational Research, 70*(1), 55–81.

Rifkin, J. (1998). The sociology of the gene. *Phi Delta Kappan, 79*(9), 649–657.

Rivera, D. P., & Smith, D. D. (1997). *Teaching students with learning and behavior problems.* Boston: Allyn & Bacon.

Robertson, J. S. (2000). Is attribution training a worthwhile classroom intervention for K–12 students with learning difficulties? *Educational Psychology Review, 12*(1), 111–134.

Robinson, D. H., & Kiewra, K. A. (1995). Visual argument: Graphic organizers are superior to outlines in improving learning from text. *Journal of Educational Psychology, 87,* 455–467.

Robinson, D. H., & Skinner, C. H. (1996). Why graphic organizers facilitate search processes: Fewer words or computationally efficient indexing. *Contemporary Educational Psychology, 21*(2), 166–180.

Robinson, D. H., Robinson, S. L., & Katayama, A. D. (1999). When words are represented in memory like pictures: Evidence for spatial encoding of study materials. *Contemporary Educational Psychology, 24*(1), 38–54.

Robinson, D., Katayama, A., Beth, A., Odom, S., & Hsieh, Y. (2004). *Training students to take more graphic notes: A partial approach.* Austin, TX: University of Texas at Austin.

Robinson, F. P. (1961). *Effective study.* New York: Harper & Row.

Robinson, J. L., & Fitzgerald, H. E. (2002). Early Head Start: Contemporary perspective and promise. *Infant Mental Health Journal, 23,* 250–257.

Robinson, T., Smith, S., Miller, M., & Brownell, M. (1999). Cognitive behavior modification of hyperactivity-impulsivity and aggression: A meta-analysis of school-based studies. *Journal of Educational Psychology, 91*(2), 195–203.

Roderick, M. (1994). Grade retention and school dropout: Investigating the association. *American Educational Research Journal, 31*(4), 729–759.

Roderick, M., & Engel, M. (2001). The grasshopper and the ant: Motivational responses of low-achieving students to high-stakes testing. *Educational Evaluation and Policy Analysis, 23*(3), 197–227.

Roderick, M., Jacob, B., & Bryk, A. (2002). The impact of high-stakes testing in Chicago on student achievement in promotional gate grades. *Educational Evaluation and Policy Analysis, 24*(4), 333–357.

Roeber, E., & Dutcher, P. (1989). Michigan's innovative assessment of reading. *Educational Leadership 46*(7), 64–69.

Roeser, R., Eccles, J., & Sameroff, A. (2000). School as a context of early adolescents' academic and social-emotional development: A summary of research findings. *The Elementary School Journal, 100*(5), 443–472.

Roeser, R., Eccles, J., & Strobel, K. (1998). Linking the study of schooling and mental health: Selected issues and empirical illustrations at the level of the individual. *Educational Psychologist, 33*(4), 153–176.

Rogers, C., & Freiberg, H. J. (1994). *Freedom to learn* (3rd ed.). New York: Merrill.

Rogoff, B. (2003). *The cultural nature of human development.* London: Oxford University Press.

Rogoff, B., & Chavajay, P. (1995). What's become of research on the cultural basis of cognitive development? *American Psychologist, 50,* 859–877.

Rogow, S. M. (1988). *Helping the visually impaired child with developmental problems: Effective practice in home, school, and community.* New York: Teachers College Press.

Rohrbeck, C. A., Ginsburg-Block, M. D., Fantuzzo, J. W., & Miller, T. R. (2003). Peer-assisted learning interventions with elementary school students: A meta-analytic review. *Journal of Educational Psychology, 94*(2), 240–257.

Rolheiser, C., Bower, B., & Stevahn, L. (2000). *The portfolio organizer: Succeeding with portfolios in your classroom.* Alexandria, VA: ASCD.

Roopnarine, J. L., Ahmeduzzaman, M., Donnely, S., Gill, P., Mennis, A., Arry, L., Dingler, K., McLaughlin, M., & Talukder, E. (1992). Social-cognitive play behaviors and playmate references in same-age and mixed-aged classrooms over a 6-month period. *American Educational Research Journal, 29,* 757–776.

Rosenbaum, M. S., & Drabman, R. S. (1982). Self-control training in the classroom: A review and critique. *Journal of Applied Behavior Analysis, 12,* 264, 266, 467–485.

Rosenberg, M., Wilson, R., Maheady, L., & Sindelar, P. (2004). *Educating students with behavioral disorders.* Boston: Pearson.

Rosenberg, S. L., McKeon, L. M., & Dinero, T. E. (1999). Positive peer solutions: One answer for the rejected student. *Phi Delta Kappan, 81*(2), 114–118.

Rosenfield, D., Folger, R., & Adelman, H. F. (1980). When rewards reflect competence: A qualification of the overjus-

tification effect. *Journal of Personality and Social Psychology, 39,* 368–376.

Rosenfield, S. A., & Gravois, T. A. (1996). *Instructional consultation teams: Collaborating for change.* New York: Guilford.

Rosenholtz, S. J., & Simpson, C. (1984). The formation of ability conceptions: Developmental trend or social construction? *Review of Educational Research, 54,* 31–63.

Rosenshine, B. V. (1980). How time is spent in elementary classrooms. In C. Denham & A. Lieberman (Eds.), *Time to learn.* Washington, DC: National Institute of Education.

Rosenshine, B. V., & Stevens, R. J. (1986). Teaching functions. In M. C. Wittrock (Ed.), *Third handbook of research on teaching.* Chicago: Rand McNally.

Rosenshine, B., & Meister, C. (1992). The use of scaffolds for teaching higher-level cognitive strategies. *Educational Leadership, 49*(7), 26–33.

Rosenshine, B., & Meister, C. (1994). Reciprocal teaching: A review of research. *Review of Educational Research, 64,* 479–530.

Rosenshine, B., Meister, C., & Chapman, S. (1996). Teaching students to generate questions: A review of the intervention studies. *Review of Educational Research, 66*(2), 181–221.

Ross, J. A., Rolheiser, C., & Hogaboam-Gray, A. (1998, April). *Impact of self-evaluation training on mathematics achievement in a cooperative learning environment.* Paper presented at the annual meeting of the American Educational Research Association, San Diego, CA.

Ross, S. M., Smith, L. J., Casey, J., & Slavin, R. E. (1995). Increasing the academic success of disadvantaged children: An examination of alternative early intervention programs. *American Educational Research Journal, 32,* 773–800.

Ross, S. M., Smith, L. J., Lohr, L., & McNelis, M. (1994). Math and reading instruction in tracked first grade classes. *The Elementary School Journal, 95*(2), 105–119.

Rossi, R. J., & Stringfield, S. C. (1995). What we must do for students placed at risk. *Phi Delta Kappan, 71*(1), 73–76.

Rossman, G. B., & Rallis, S. F. (2003). *Learning in the field: An introduction to qualitative research* (2nd ed.). Thousand Oaks, CA: Sage.

Rotberg, I. C. (2001). A self-fulfilling prophecy. *Phi Delta Kappan, 83*(2), 170–171.

Rothstein, R. (1998). Bilingual education: The controversy. *Phi Delta Kappan, 79*(9), 672–678.

Rothstein, R. (2001). *Improving educational achievement: A volume exploring the role of investments in schools and other supports and services for families and communities.* Washington, DC: The Finance Project.

Rotter, J. (1954). *Social learning and clinical psychology.* Englewood Cliffs, NJ: Prentice-Hall.

Rowan, B., & Miracle, A. (1983). Systems of ability grouping and the stratification of achievement in elementary schools. *Sociology of Education, 56,* 133–144.

Rowan, B., Correnti, R., & Miller, R. (2002). *What large-scale, survey research tells us about teacher effects on student achievement: Insights from the Prospects study of elementary schools.* Philadelphia, PA: Consortium for Policy Research in Education, University of Pennsylvania.

Rowe, M. B. (1974). Wait time and rewards as instructional variables, their influence on language, logic, and fate control. I: Wait time. *Journal of Research in Science Teaching, 11,* 81–94.

Rubin, B. C. (2003). Unpacking detracking: When progressive pedagogy meets students' social worlds. *American Educational Research Journal, 40*(2), 539–573.

Ruble, D. N., Eisenberg, R., & Higgins, E. T. (1994). Developmental changes in achievement evaluation: Motivational implications of self-other differences. *Child Development, 65,* 1095–1110.

Ruder, S. (2000). We teach all. *Educational Leadership, 58*(1), 49–51.

Rumelhart, D. E., & McClelland, J. L. (Eds.). (1986). *Parallel distributed processing: Explorations in the microstructure of cognition.* Cambridge, MA: MIT Press.

Rummel, N., Levin, J. R., & Woodward, M. M. (2002). Do pictorial mnemonic text-learning aids give students something worth writing about? *Journal of Educational Psychology, 94*(2), 327–334.

Ryan, A. M. (2000). Peer groups as a context for the socialization of adolescents' motivation, engagement, and achievement in school. *Educational Psychologist, 35*(2), 10–11.

Ryan, A. M., & Patrick, H. (2001). The classroom social environment and changes in adolescents' motivation and engagement during middle school. *American Educational Research Journal, 38*(2), 437–460.

Ryan, R. M., & Deci, E. L. (2000). Intrinsic and extrinsic motivations: Classic definitions and new directions. *Contemporary Educational Psychology, 25*(1), 54–67.

Ryba, K., Selby, L., & Nolan, P. (1995). Computers empower students with special needs. *Educational Leadership, 53*(2), 82–84.

Sachs, J. (2000). The activist professional. *Journal of Educational Change, 1*(1), 77–95.

Sadker, M., & Sadker, D. (1994). *Failing at fairness: How America's schools cheat girls.* New York: Charles Scribner's Sons.

Sadker, M., Sadker, D., & Long, L. (1997). Gender and educational equality. In J. A. Banks & C. A. M. Banks (Eds.), *Multicultural education: Issues and perspectives* (pp. 131–149). Boston: Allyn & Bacon.

Sadker, M., Sadker, D., Fox, L., & Salata, M. (1994). Gender equality in the classroom. In J. I. Goodlad & P. Keating (Eds.), *Access to knowledge: The continuing agenda for our nation's schools.* New York: The College Board.

Sadoski, M., Goetz, E. T., & Fritz, J. B. (1993). Impact of concreteness on comprehensibility, interest, and memory of text: Implications for dual coding theory and text design. *Journal of Educational Psychology, 85*(2), 291–304.

Safer, D. J. (1982). *School programs for disruptive adolescents.* Baltimore: University Park Press.

Saffran, E. M., & Schwartz, M. F. (2003). Language. In M. Gallagher & R. J. Nelson (Eds.), *Handbook of psychology: Vol. 3. Biological psychology* (pp. 595–627). Hoboken, NJ: Wiley.

Saleno, S., & Garrick-Duhaney, L. (1999). The impact of inclusion on students with and without disabilities and their educators. *Remedial and Special Education, 20*(2), 114–126.

Salganik, M. W. (1980, January 27). Teachers busy teaching make city's 16 "best" schools stand out. *Baltimore Sun,* p. A4.

Salomon, G. (2002). Technology and pedagogy: Why don't we see the promised revolution? *Educational Technology, 42*(2), 71–75.

Salomon, G., & Perkins, D. N. (1998). Individual and social aspects of learning. In P. D. Pearson & A. Iran-Nejad (Eds.), *Review of research in education* (pp. 1–24). Washington, DC: American Educational Research Association.

Sand, B. (2004, April). *Divergent and convergent thinking and selected independent variables: A meta-analysis.* Paper presented at the annual meeting of the American Educational Research Association, San Diego, CA.

Sanders, M. G., Allen-Jones, G. L., & Abel, Y. (2002). Involving families and communities in the education of children and youth placed at-risk. In S. Stringfield & D. Land (Eds.), *Educating at-risk students* (pp. 171–188). Chicago: National Society for the Study of Education.

Sandoval, J. (1995). Teaching in subject matter areas: Science. *Annual Review of Psychology, 46,* 355–374.

Sanford, J. P., & Evertson, C. M. (1981). Classroom management in a low SES junior high: Three case studies. *Journal of Teacher Education, 32,* 34–38.

Sansone, C., & Harackiewicz, J. M. (Eds.). (2000). *Intrinsic and extrinsic motivation.* Orlando, FL: Academic Press.

Sapon-Shevin, M. (2001). Schools fit for all. *Educational Leadership, 58*(4), 34–39.

Savell, J. M., Twohig, P. T., & Rachford, D. L. (1986). Empirical status of Feuerstein's "Instrumental Enrichment" (FIE) technique as a method of teaching thinking skills. *Review of Educational Research, 56,* 381–409.

Savin-Williams, R. C., & Berndt, T. J. (1990). Friendship and peer relations. In S. S. Feldman & G. R. Elliot (Eds.), *At the threshold: The developing adolescent* (pp. 277–307). Cambridge, MA: Harvard University Press.

Sax, C. L., & Thoma, C. A. (2002). *Transition assessment: Wise practices for quality lives.* Baltimore: Brookes.

Scarr, S. (1998). American childcare today. *American Psychologist, 53*(2), 95–108.

Schacter, D. L. (2001). *The seven sins of memory: How the mind forgets and remembers.* Boston: Houghton Mifflin.

Schacter, J. (2000). Does individual tutoring produce optimal learning? *American Educational Research Journal, 37*(3), 801–829.

Schafer, W. D., Swanson, G., Bené, N., & Newberry, G. (2001). Effects of teacher knowledge of rubrics on student achievement in four content areas. *Applied Measurement in Education, 14,* 151–170.

Schafer, W. E., & Olexa, C. (1971). *Tracking and opportunity.* Scranton, PA: Chandler.

Schaps, E., Schaeffer, E., & McDonnell, S. (2001, September 12). What's right and wrong in character education today. *Education Week*, 40–41.

Scherer, M. (2001). How and why standards can improve student achievement: A conversation with Robert J. Marzano. *Educational Leadership, 59*(1), 14–19.

Scheurich, J., Skrla, L., & Johnson, J. (2000). Thinking carefully about equity and accountability. *Phi Delta Kappan, 82*(4), 293–299.

Schiff, M., & Lewontin, R. (1986). *Education and class: The irrelevance of IQ genetic studies.* Oxford: Clarendon Press.

Schifter, D. (1996). A constructivist perspective on teaching and learning mathematics. *Phi Delta Kappan, 77*(7), 492–499.

Schloss, P. J., & Smith, M. A. (1994). *Applied behavior analysis in the classroom.* Boston: Allyn & Bacon.

Schloss, P. J., & Smith, M. A. (1998). *Applied behavior analysis in the classroom* (2nd ed.). Boston: Allyn & Bacon.

Schlozman, S. C., & Schlozman, V. R. (2000). Chaos in the classroom: Looking at ADHD. *Educational Leadership, 58*(3), 28–33.

Schmoker, M. (1999). *Results: The key to continuous school improvement* (2nd ed.). Alexandria, VA: ASCD.

Schmuck, R. A., & Schmuck, P. A. (1997). *Group processes in the classroom.* Madison, WI: Brown & Benchmark.

Schneider, B. (2002). Social capital: A ubiquitous emerging conception. In D. L. Levinson, P. W. Cookson, Jr., & A. R. Sadovnik (Eds.), *Education and sociology: An encyclopedia* (pp. 545–550). New York: Routledge Falmer.

Schneider, W. (1993). Domain-specific knowledge and memory performance in children. *Educational Psychology Review, 5,* 257–273.

Schneider, W., & Graham, D. J. (1992). Introduction to connectionist modeling in education. *Educational Psychologist, 27*(4), 513–530.

Schneider, W., Roth, E., & Ennemoser, M. (2000). Training phonological skills and letter knowledge in children at risk for dyslexia: A comparison of three kindergarten intervention programs. *Journal of Educational Psychology, 92*(2), 284–295.

Schniedwind, N., & Davidson, E. (2000). Differentiating cooperative learning. *Educational Leadership, 58*(1), 24–27.

Schnotz, W. (2002). Towards an integrated view of learning from text and visual displays. *Educational Psychology Review, 14*(1), 101–120.

Schofield, J. W. (1995). Review of research on school desegregation's impact on elementary and secondary school students. In J. A. Banks & C. A. M. Banks (Eds.), *Handbook of research on multicultural education.* New York: Macmillan.

Schofield, J. W. (1997). Causes and consequences of the colorblind perspective. In J. A. Banks & C. A. M. Banks (Eds.), *Multicultural education: Issues and perspectives* (pp. 251–271). Boston: Allyn & Bacon.

Schraw, G., Flowerday, T., & Lehman, S. (2001). Increasing situational interest in the classroom. *Educational Psychology Review, 13*(3), 211–224.

Schumaker, J. B., & Deshler, D. D. (1992). Validation of learning strategy interventions for students with learning disabilities: Results of a programmatic research effort. In B. Y. L. Wong (Ed.), *Contemporary intervention research in learning disabilities.* New York: Springer-Verlag.

Schumm, J. S., & Vaughn, S. (1992). Reflections on planning for mainstreamed students: General classroom teachers; perspectives. *Remedial and Special Education, 12*(4), 18–27.

Schunk, D. (2000). *Learning theories* (3rd ed.). Upper Saddle River, NJ: Merrill/Prentice-Hall.

Schunk, D. H. (1983). Reward contingencies, and the development of children's skills and self-efficacy. *Journal of Educational Psychology, 75,* 511–518.

Schunk, D. H. (1995). Inherent details of self-regulated learning include student perceptions. *Educational Psychologist, 30,* 213–216.

Schunk, D. H. (1996). Goal and self-evaluative influences during children's cognitive skill learning. *American Educational Research Journal, 33*(2), 359–382.

Schunk, D. H., & Pajares, F. (2004, April). *Self-Efficacy in Education: Issues and future directions.* Paper presented at the annual meeting of the American Educational Research Association, San Diego, CA.

Schunk, D. H., & Zimmerman, B. J. (1997). Social origins of self-regulatory competence. *Educational Psychologist, 32*(4), 195–208.

Schunk, D. H., & Zimmerman, B. J. (2003). Self-regulation and learning. In W. M. Reynolds & G. E. Miller (Eds.), *Handbook of psychology: Vol. 7. Educational psychology* (pp. 59–78). Hoboken, NJ: Wiley.

Schutz, P. A., & Davis, H. A. (2000). Emotions and self-regulation during test taking. *Educational Psychologist, 35*(4), 243–246.

Schwartz, J. E., & Beichner, R. J. (1999). *Essentials of educational technology.* Boston: Allyn & Bacon.

Schwartz, N. H., Ellsworth, L. S., Graham, L., & Knight, B. (1998). Assessing prior knowledge to remember text: A comparison of advance organizers and maps. *Contemporary Educational Psychology, 23*(1), 65–89.

Schweinhart, L. J., & Weikart, D. P. (1998). High/Scope Perry Preschool Program effects at age twenty-seven. In J. Crane (Ed.), *Social programs that work* (pp. 148–162). New York: Russell Sage Foundation.

Schweinhart, L. J., Barnes, H. V., & Weikart, D. P. (1993). *Significant benefits: The High/Scope Perry Preschool study through age 27.* Ypsilanti, MI: High/Scope.

Scruggs, T. E., & Richter, L. (1986). Tutoring learning disabled students: A critical review. *Learning Disability Quarterly, 9,* 2–14.

Scruggs, T. E., White, K. R., & Bennion, K. (1986). Teaching test-taking skills to elementary-grade students: A meta-analysis. *Elementary School Journal, 87,* 69–82.

Secada, W. G., Chavez-Chavez, R., Garcia, E., Munoz, C., Oakes, J., Santiago-Santiago, I., & Slavin, R. (1998). *No more excuses: The final report of the Hispanic dropout project.* Washington, DC: U.S. Department of Education.

Seligman, M. E. P. (1975). *Helplessness: On depression, development, and death.* San Francisco: Freeman.

Selman, R. (1980). *The growth of interpersonal understanding.* New York: Academic Press.

Selman, R. L. (1981). The child as a friendship philosopher. In S. R. Asher & J. M. Gottman (Eds.), *The development of children's friendships* (pp. 242–272). Cambridge: Cambridge University Press.

Semb, G. B., & Ellis, J. A. (1994). Knowledge taught in school: What is remembered? *Review of Educational Research, 24,* 253–286.

Semmel, M. I., Abernathy, T. V., Butera, G., & Lesar, S. (1991). Teacher perceptions of the regular education initiative. *Exceptional Children, 58,* 26–33.

Semmel, M. I., Gerber, M. M., & MacMillan, D. L. (1994). Twenty-five years after Dunn's article: A legacy of policy analysis research in special education. *Journal of Special Education, 27,* 481–495.

Sethi, S., Drake, M., Dialdin, D. A., & Lepper, M. R. (1995, April). *Developmental patterns of intrinsic and extrinsic motivation: A new look.* Paper presented at the annual meeting of the American Educational Research Association, San Francisco, CA.

Shah, P., Mayer, R., & Hegarty, M. (1999). Graphs as aids to knowledge construction: Signaling techniques for guiding the process of graph comprehension. *Journal of Educational Psychology, 91*(4), 690–702.

Shaklee, B. D., Barbour, N. E., Ambrose, R., & Hansford, S. J. (1997). *Designing and using portfolios.* Boston: Allyn & Bacon.

Shanahan, T. (1998). On the effectiveness and limitations of tutoring reading. In P. D. Pearson & A. Iran-Nejad (Eds.), *Review of research in education* (pp. 217–234). Washington, DC: American Educational Research Association.

Shanker, A. (1994/95). Full inclusion is neither free nor appropriate. *Educational Leadership, 52*(4), 18–21.

Shapon-Shevin, M. (2003). Inclusion: A matter of social justice. *Educational Leadership 61*(2), 25–30.

Sharan, S., & Shachar, C. (1988). *Language and learning in the cooperative classroom.* New York: Springer.

Sharan, S., Kussell, P., Hertz-Lazarowitz, R., Bejarano, Y., Raviv, S., & Sharan, Y. (1984). *Cooperative learning in the classroom: Research in desegregated schools.* Hillsdale, NJ: Erlbaum.

Sharan, Y., & Sharan, S. (1992). *Expanding cooperative learning through group investigation.* New York: Teachers College Press.

Shavelson, R. J. (1987). Planning. In M. Dunkin (Ed.), *The international encyclopedia of teaching and teacher education* (pp. 483–486). New York: Pergamon.

Shavelson, R. J., Baxter, G. P., & Pine, J. (1992). Performance assessments: Political rhetoric and measurement reality. *Educational Researcher, 21*(4), 22–27.

Shaywitz, S. (2003). *Overcoming dyslexia: A new and complete science-based program for reading problems at any level.* New York: Knopf.

Shaywitz, S., & Shaywitz, B. (2004). Reading disability and the brain. *Educational Leadership, 61*(3), 7–11.

Shepard, L. A. (1989a). Norm-referenced vs. criterion-referenced tests. In *Annual editions: Educational psychology 89/90* (pp. 198–203). Guilford, CT: Duskin.

Shepard, L. A. (1989b). Why we need better assessments. *Educational Leadership, 46*(7), 4–9.

Shepard, L. A. (1991). The influence of standardized tests on early childhood curriculum, teachers, and children. In B. Spodek & O. N. Saracho (Eds.), *Yearbook in early childhood education.* New York: Teachers College Press.

Shepard, L. A. (1993a). Evaluating test validity. In L. Darling-Hammond (Ed.), *Review of Research in Education 19.* Washington, DC: American Educational Research Association.

Shepard, L. A. (1993b). The place of testing reform in educational reform: A reply to Cizek. *Educational Researcher, 22*(4), 10–13.

Shepard, L. A. (1995). Using assessment to improve learning. *Phi Delta Kappan, 52*(5), 38–43.

Shepard, L. A. (2000). The role of assessment in a learning culture. *Educational Researcher, 29*(7), 4–14.

Shepard, L. A., & Smith, M. L. (Eds.). (1989). *Flunking grades: Research and policies on retention.* New York: Falmer.

Shields, M., & Behrman, R. (2000). Children and computer technology: Analysis and recommendations. *Children and Computer Technology, 10*(2), 4–30.

Shih, S., & Alexander, J. (2000). Interacting effects of goal setting and self- or other-referenced feedback on children's development of self-efficacy and cognitive skill within the Taiwanese classroom. *Journal of Educational Psychology, 92*(3), 536–543.

Shore, R. (1998). *Ready schools.* Washington, DC: National Education Goals Panel.

Shulman, J., Lotan, R. A., & Whitcomb, J. A. (1998). *Groupwork in diverse classrooms: A cookbook for educators.* New York: Teachers College Press.

Shulman, L. S. (2000). Teacher development: Roles of domain expertise and pedagogical development. *Journal of Applied Developmental Psychology, 21,* 129–135.

Sideridis, G. (2004, March). *On the origins of helpless behavior of students with learning disabilities: Avoidance motivation?* Paper presented at the annual meeting of the American Education Research Association, San Diego, CA.

Siegel, L. S. (2003). Learning disabilities. In W. M. Reynolds & G. E. Miller (Eds.), *Handbook of psychology: Vol. 7. Educational psychology* (pp. 455–486). Hoboken, NJ: Wiley.

Siegler, R. S. (1991). *Children's thinking* (2nd ed.). Englewood Cliffs, NJ: Prentice-Hall.

Siegler, R. S. (1998). *Children's thinking* (3rd ed.). Upper Saddle River, NJ: Prentice Hall.

Sills-Briegel, T., Fisk, C., & Dunlop, V. (1996). Graduation by exhibition. *Educational Leadership, 54*(4), 66–71.

Simmons, D. C., Fuchs, L. S., Fuchs, P., Mathes, P., & Hodge, J. P. (1995). Effects of explicit teaching and peer tutoring on the reading achievement of learning-disabled and low-performing students in regular classrooms. *The Elementary School Journal, 95*(5), 387–408.

Simmons, R. G., & Blyth, D. A. (1987). *Moving into adolescence: The impact of pubertal change and school context.* New York: Aldine de Gruyter.

Sinclair, M. F., Christenson, S. L., Evelo, D. L., & Hurley, C. (1998). Dropout prevention for high-risk youth with disabilities: Efficacy of a sustained school engagement procedure. *Exceptional Children, 65*(1), 7–21.

Singer, J., Marx, R. W., Krajcik, J., & Chambers, J. C. (2000). Constructing extended inquiry projects: Curriculum materials for science education reform. *Educational Psychologist, 35*(4), 165–178.

Sirin, S. (2003, April). *Socioeconomic status and academic achievement: A meta-analytic review of research 1990–2000.* Paper presented at the annual meeting of the American Educational Research Association, Chicago, IL.

Sirotnik, K. A. (2002). Promoting responsible accountability in schools and education. *Phi Delta Kappan, 83*(9), 662–973.

Skaalvik, E. M. (1997). Self-enhancing and self-defeating ego orientation: Relations with task and avoidance orientation, achievement, self-perceptions, and anxiety. *Journal of Educational Psychology, 89*(1), 71–81.

Skiba, R. (2000). *Zero tolerance, zero evidence: An analysis of school disciplinary practice.* Bloomington, IN: Indiana Education Policy Center.

Skinner, B. F. (1953). *Science and human behavior.* New York: Macmillan.

Skinner, B. F. (1968). *The technology of teaching.* New York: Appleton-Century-Crofts.

Slaughter, D. T., & Epps, E. (1994). The home environment and academic achievement of black American children and youth. In J. Kretovics & E. Nussel (Eds.), *Transforming urban education.* Boston: Allyn & Bacon.

Slavin, R. E. (1986). The Napa evaluation of Madeline Hunter's ITIP: Lessons learned. *Elementary School Journal, 87,* 165–171.

Slavin, R. E. (1987a). A theory of school and classroom organization. *Educational Psychologists, 22,* 89–108.

Slavin, R. E. (1987b). Grouping for instruction in the elementary school. *Educational Psychologist, 22,* 109–127.

Slavin, R. E. (1987c). Ability grouping and student achievement in elementary schools: A best-evidence synthesis. *Review of Educational Research, 57,* 293–336.

Slavin, R. E. (1987d). Mastery learning reconsidered. *Review of Educational Research, 57,* 175–213.

Slavin, R. E. (1990). Ability grouping and student achievement in secondary schools: A best-evidence synthesis. *Review of Educational Research, 60,* 471–499.

Slavin, R. E. (1991). Cooperative learning and group contingencies. *Journal of Behavioral Education, 1,* 105–115.

Slavin, R. E. (1993a). Students differ: So what? *Educational Researcher, 22*(9), 13–14.

Slavin, R. E. (1993b). Ability grouping in the middle grades: Achievement effects and alternatives. *The Elementary School Journal, 93*(5), 535–552.

Slavin, R. E. (1994a). *Using student team learning* (4th ed.). Baltimore: Johns Hopkins University, Center for Research on Elementary and Middle Schools.

Slavin, R. E. (1994b). School and classroom organization in beginning reading: Class size, aides, and instructional grouping. In R. E. Slavin, N. L. Karweit, B. A. Wasik, & N. A. Madden (Eds.), *Preventing early school failure: Research on effective strategies.* Boston: Allyn & Bacon.

Slavin, R. E. (1995a). *Cooperative learning: Theory, research, and practice* (2nd ed.). Boston: Allyn & Bacon.

Slavin, R. E. (1995b). Cooperative learning and intergroup relations. In J. Banks (Ed.), *Handbook of research on multicultural education.* New York: Macmillan.

Slavin, R. E. (1996a). Neverstreaming: Preventing learning disabilities. *Educational Leadership, 53*(5), 4–7.

Slavin, R. E. (1996b). Research on cooperative learning achievement: What we know, what we need to know. *Contemporary Educational Psychology, 21,* 43–69.

Slavin, R. E. (1997/98). Can education reduce social inequality? *Educational Leadership, 55*(4), 6–10.

Slavin, R. E. (2000/01). Putting the school back in school reform. *Educational Leadership, 58*(4), 22–27.

Slavin, R. E. (2002). The intentional school: Effective elementary education for all children. In S. Stringfield & D. Land (Eds.), *Educating at-risk students* (pp. 111–127). Chicago: National Society for the Study of Education.

Slavin, R. E., & Cheung, A. (2004). *A synthesis of research on language of reading instruction for English language learners.* Baltimore, MD: Johns Hopkins University, Center for Research on the Education of Students Placed at Risk.

Slavin, R. E., & Fashola, O. S. (1998). *Show me the evidence: Proven and promising programs for America's schools.* Thousand Oaks, CA: Corwin.

Slavin, R. E., & Karweit, N. (1984, April). *Within-class ability groupings and student achievement: Two field experiments.* Paper presented at the annual convention of the American Educational Research Association, New Orleans, LA.

Slavin, R. E., & Karweit, N. L. (1982, August). *School organizational vs. developmental effects on attendance among young adolescents.* Paper presented at the annual convention of the American Psychological Association, Washington, DC.

Slavin, R. E., & Madden, N. A. (1987, April). *Effective classroom programs for students at risk.* Paper presented at the annual convention of the American Educational Research Association, Washington, DC.

Slavin, R. E., & Madden, N. A. (1999). Effects of bilingual and English as a second language adaptations of Success for All on the reading achievement of students acquiring English. *Journal of Education for Students Placed at Risk, 4*(4), 393–416.

Slavin, R. E., & Madden, N. A. (Eds.). (2001). *One million children: Success for All.* Thousand Oaks, CA: Corwin.

Slavin, R. E., & Stevens, R. J. (1991). Cooperative learning and mainstreaming. In J. W. Lloyd, N. N. Singh, & A. C. Repp (Eds.). *The regular education initiative: Alternative perspectives on concepts, issues, and models* (pp. 177–191). Sycamore, IL: Sycamore.

Slavin, R. E., Hurley, E. A., & Chamberlain, A. (2003). Cooperative learning and achievement: Theory and research. In W. M. Reynolds & G. E. Miller (Eds.), *Handbook of psychology: Vol. 7. Educational psychology* (pp. 177–198). Hoboken, NJ: Wiley.

Slavin, R. E., Hurley, E. A., & Chamberlain, A. (2003). Cooperative learning and achievement: Research and theory. In N. J. Smelser & P. B. Baltes (Eds.), *International Encyclopedia of the Social & Behavioral Sciences*. Oxford: Pergamon.

Slavin, R. E., Karweit, N. L., & Wasik, B. A. (1994). *Preventing early school failure: Research on effective strategies*. Boston: Allyn & Bacon.

Slavin, R. E., Madden, N. A., & Karweit, N. L. (Eds.). (1989). *Effective programs for students at risk*. Boston: Allyn & Bacon.

Slavin, R. E., Madden, N. A., & Leavey, M. (1984a). Effects of team assisted individualization on the mathematics achievement of academically handicapped and nonhandicapped students. *Journal of Educational Psychology, 76*, 813–819.

Slavin, R. E., Madden, N. A., & Leavey, M. B. (1984b). Effects of cooperative learning and individualized instruction on mainstreamed students. *Exceptional Children, 84*, 409–422.

Slavin, R. E. (2003). A reader's guide to scientifically based research. *Educational Leadership, 60*(5), 12–16.

Slavin, R. E., & Calderón, M. (Eds.). (2001), *Effective Programs for Latino Students*. Mahwah, NJ: Erlbaum.

Slavin, R. E., & Cheung, A. (2003). *Effective programs for English language learners: A best-evidence synthesis*. Baltimore, MD: Johns Hopkins University, Center for Research on the Education of Students Placed at Risk.

Slotte, V., & Lonka, K. (1999). Review and process effects of spontaneous note-taking on text comprehension. *Contemporary Educational Psychology, 24*(1), 1–20.

Smagorinsky, P., & Smith, M. W. (1992). The nature of knowledge in composition and literary understanding: The question of specificity. *Review of Educational Research, 62*(3), 279–305.

Small, M. Y., Lovett, S. B., & Scher, M. S. (1993). Pictures facilitate children's recall of unillustrated expository prose. *Journal of Educational Psychology, 85*, 520–528.

Smith, D. D. (1998). *Introduction to special education: Teaching in an age of challenge*. Boston: Allyn & Bacon.

Smith, D. D. (2001). *Introduction to special education: Teaching in an age of opportunity*. Boston: Allyn & Bacon.

Smith, D. D., & Luckasson, R. (1995). *Introduction to special education* (2nd ed.). Boston: Allyn & Bacon.

Smith, L. J., Ross, S. M., & Casey, J. P. (1994). *Special education analyses for Success for All in four cities*. Memphis, TN: University of Memphis, Center for Research in Educational Policy.

Smith, L., & Land, M. (1981). Low-interference verbal behaviors related to teacher clarity. *Journal of Classroom Interaction, 17*, 37–42.

Smith, M. L. (1991). Meanings of test preparation. *American Educational Research Journal, 28*(3), 521–542.

Smith, S. S. (2002). Desegregation. In D. L. Levinson, P. W. Cookson, Jr., & A. R. Sadovnik (Eds.), *Education and sociology: An encyclopedia* (pp. 141–149). New York, NY: Routledge Falmer.

Smith, T. E. C., Polloway, E. A., Patton, J. R., & Dowdy, C. A. (1998). *Teaching students with special needs in inclusive settings* (2nd ed.). Boston: Allyn & Bacon.

Smith, T., Polloway, E., Patton, J., & Dowdy, C. (2004). *Teaching students with special needs in inclusive settings* (4th ed.). Boston: Pearson.

Smolensky, P. (2000). Connectionist approaches in language. In R. A. Wilson & E. C. Keil (Eds.), *The MIT encyclopedia of the cognitive sciences* (pp. 188–190). Cambridge, MA: MIT Press.

Smutny, J. (2003). *Gifted education: Promising practices*. Bloomington, IN: Phi Delta Kappan.

Snell, M. E., & Janney, R. (2000). *Collaborative teaming*. Baltimore: Brookes.

Snow, C. E., Burns, S. M., & Griffin, P. (Eds.). (1998). *Preventing reading difficulties in young children*. Washington, DC: National Academy Press.

Snow, R. E. (1992). Aptitude theory: Yesterday, today, and tomorrow. *Educational Psychologist, 27*(1), 5–32.

Snowman, J. (1984). Learning tactics and strategies. In G. Phye & T. Andre (Eds.), *Cognitive instructional psychology*. New York: Academic Press.

Snyderman, M., & Rothman, S. (1987). Survey of expert opinion on intelligence and aptitude testing. *American Psychologist, 42*, 137–144.

Solso, R. L. (2001). *Cognitive psychology* (6th ed.). Boston: Allyn & Bacon.

Sornson, N. (2001). Vision and learning. In B. Sornson (Ed.), *Preventing early learning failure*. Alexandria, VA: ASCD.

Sorrells, A. M., Rieth, H., & Sindelar, P. (2004). *Critical issues in special education: Access, diversity, and accountability*. Boston: Pearson.

Sousa, D. (2001). *How the brain learns* (2nd ed.). Boston: Allyn & Bacon.

Spear-Swerling, L., & Sternberg, R. J. (1998). Curing our "epidemic" of learning disabilities. *Phi Delta Kappan, 79*(5), 397–401.

Specht, L. B., & Sandling, P. K. (1991). The differential effects of experiential learning activities and traditional lecture classes in accounting. *Simulation and Games, 2*, 196–210.

Spector, J. E. (1992). Predicting progress in beginning reading: Dynamic assessment of phonemic awareness. *Journal of Educational Psychology, 84*(3), 353–363.

Spencer, M. B., Noll, E., Stoltzfus, J., & Harpalani, V. (2001). Identify and school adjustment: Revisiting the "acting White" assumption. *Educational Psychologist, 36*(1), 21–30.

Sperling, G. A. (1960). The information available in brief visual presentations. *Psychological Monographs, 74*, No. 498.

Spielberger, C., & Vagg, P. (Eds.). (1995). *Test anxiety: Theory, assessment, and treatment*. Washington, DC: Taylor & Francis.

Spires, H. A., & Donley, J. (1998). Prior knowledge activation: Inducing engagement with informational texts. *Journal of Educational Psychology, 90*(2), 249–260.

Sprenger, M. (1999). *Learning and memory: The brain in action.* Alexandria, VA: Association for Supervision and Curriculum Development.

Spurlin, J. E., Dansereau, D. F., Larson, C. O., & Brooks, L. W. (1984). Cooperative learning strategies in processing descriptive text: Effects of role and activity level of the learner. *Cognition and Instruction, 1,* 451–463.

Squire, L. R., Knowlton, B., & Musen, G. (1993). The structure and organization of memory. *Annual Review of Psychology, 44,* 453–495.

Stahl, S. A., & Miller, P. D. (1989). Whole language and language experience approaches for beginning reading: A quantitative research synthesis. *Review of Educational Research, 59,* 87–116.

Stallings, J. A., & Kaskowitz, D. (1974). *Follow-through classroom observation evaluation 1972–73.* Menlo Park, CA: Standard Research Institute.

Stallings, J., & Krasavage, E. M. (1986). Program implementation and student achievement in a four-year Madeline Hunter follow-through project. *Elementary School Journal, 87,* 117–138.

Stanovich, K. (1998). Cognitive neuroscience and educational psychology: What season is it? *Educational Psychology Review, 10,* 419–426.

Stanovich, K. E., Siegel, L. S., & Gottard, A. (1997). Converging evidence for phonological and surface subtypes of reading disability. *Journal of Educational Psychology, 89*(10), 114–127.

Starratt, R. (2003). Opportunity to learn and the accountability agenda. *Phi Delta Kappan, 85*(4), 298–303.

Stecher, B., Hamilton, L., & Gonzalez, G. (2003). *Working smarter to leave no child behind.* Santa Monica, CA: RAND.

Steffe, L. P., & Gale, J. (Eds.). (1995). *Constructivism in education.* Hillsdale, NJ: Erlbaum.

Stein, B. S., Littlefield, J., Bransford, J. D., & Persampieri, M. (1984). Elaboration and knowledge acquisition. *Memory and Cognition, 12,* 522–529.

Stein, M. K., Leinhardt, G., & Bickel, W. (1989). Instructional issues for teaching students at risk. In R. E. Slavin, N. L. Karweit, & N. A. Madden (Eds.), *Effective programs for students at risk.* Boston: Allyn & Bacon.

Stein, N. (2000). Listening to—and learning from—girls. *Educational Leadership, 57*(4), 18–20.

Steiner, H. H., & Carr, M. (2003). Cognitive development in gifted children: Toward a more precise understanding of emerging differences in intelligence. *Educational Psychology Review, 15*(3), 215–246.

Stephan, W. G., & Vogt, W. P. (Eds.). (2004). *Education programs for improving intergroup relations.* New York: Teachers College.

Stephan, W., & Finlay, K. (1999). The role of empathy in improving intergroup relations. *Journal of Social Issues, 55*(4), 729–743.

Stern, D. (1996). *Active learning in students and teachers.* Paris: Organization for Economic Cooperation and Development.

Sternberg, R. (1990). *Metaphors of mind: Conceptions of the nature of intelligence.* New York: Cambridge University Press.

Sternberg, R. J. (1995). Investing in creativity: Many happy returns. *Educational Leadership, 53*(4), 80–84.

Sternberg, R. J. (2002). Raising the achievement of all students: Teaching for successful intelligence. *Educational Psychology Review, 14*(4), 383–393.

Sternberg, R. J. (2003). Contemporary theories of intelligence. In W. M. Reynolds & G. E. Miller (Eds.), *Handbook of psychology: Vol. 7. Educational psychology* (pp. 23–45). Hoboken, NJ: Wiley.

Sternberg, R. J. (Ed.). (2000). *Handbook of intelligence.* New York: Cambridge University Press.

Sternberg, R. J., & Bhana, K. (1986). Synthesis of research on the effectiveness of intellectual skills programs: Snake-oil remedies or miracle cures? *Educational Leadership, 44*(2), 60–67.

Sternberg, R. J., & Detterman, D. K. (Eds.). (1986). *What is intelligence?* Norwood, NJ: Ablex.

Sternberg, R. J., & Horvath, J. A. (1995). A prototype view of expert teaching. *Educational Researcher, 24*(6), 9–17.

Stevens, R. J., & Slavin, R. E. (1995a). The effects of Cooperative Integrated Reading and Composition (CIRC) on academically handicapped and non-handicapped students' achievement, attitudes, and metacognition in reading and writing. *Elementary School Journal, 95*(3), 241–262.

Stevens, R. J., & Slavin, R. E. (1995b). The cooperative elementary school: Effects on students' achievement, attitudes, and social relations. *American Educational Research Journal, 32,* 321–351.

Stevens, R. J., Madden, N. A., Slavin, R. E., & Farnish, A. M. (1987). Cooperative Integrated Reading and Composition: Two field experiments. *Reading Research Quarterly, 22,* 433–454.

Stice, E., Presnell, K., & Bearman, S. K. (2001). Relation of early menarche to depression, eating disorders, substance abuse, and comorbid psychopathology among adolescent girls. *Developmental Psychology, 37*(5), 608–619.

Stiggins, R. (2004). New assessment beliefs for a new school mission. *Phi Delta Kappan, 86*(1), 22–27.

Stiggins, R. J. (2000). *Student-involved classroom assessment* (3rd ed.). Bloomington, IN: Phi Delta Kappan.

Stipek, D. (2002). *Motivation to learn: Integrating theory and practice* (4th ed.). Boston: Allyn & Bacon.

Stipek, D. J. (1993). *Motivation to learn: From theory to practice* (2nd ed.). Boston: Allyn & Bacon.

Stipek, D. J., & Ryan, R. H. (1997). Economically disadvantaged preschoolers: Ready to learn but further to go. *Developmental Psychology, 33*(4), 711–723.

Stipek, D., de la Sota, A., & Weishaupt, L. (1999). Life lessons: An embedded classroom approach to preventing high-risk behaviors among preadolescents. *The Elementary School Journal, 99*(5), 433–452.

Stringfield, S., Millsap, M. A., Herman, R., Yoder, N., Brigham, N., Nesselrodt, P., Schaffer, E., Karweit, N., Levin, M., & Stevens, R. J. (1997). *Special strategies studies final report.* Washington, DC: U.S. Department of Education.

Stringfield, S., Ross, S., & Smith, L., (Eds.). (1996). *Bold plans for school restructuring: The New American Schools.* Hillsdale, NJ: Erlbaum.

Strong, R. W., Silver, H. F., & Perini, M. J. (2001). *Teaching what matters most.* Alexandria, VA: ASCD.

Strong, R., Silver, H. F., & Robinson, A. (1995). What do students want (and what really motivates them)? *Educational Leadership, 53*(1), 8–12.

Stuebing, K. K., Fletcher, J. M., LeDoux, J. M., Lyon, G. R., Shaywitz, S. E., & Shaywitz, B. A. (2002). *American Educational Research Journal, 39*(2), 469–518.

Stumpf, H., & Stanley, J. C. (1996). Gender-related differences on the College Board's advanced placement achievement tests 1982–1992. *Journal of Educational Psychology, 88*(2), 353–364.

Subotnik, R. (1997). Teaching gifted students in a multicultural society. In J. A. Banks & C. A. M. Banks (Eds.), *Multicultural education: Issues and perspectives* (pp. 361–385). Boston: Allyn & Bacon.

Supovitz, J. A., & Brennan, R. T. (1997). Mirror, mirror on the wall, which is the fairest test of all? An examination of the equitability of portfolio assessment relative to standardized tests. *Harvard Educational Review, 67*(3), 474–505.

Supovitz, J. A., Poglinco, S. M., & Snyder, B. A. (2001). *Moving mountains: Successes and challenges of the America's Choice comprehensive school reform design.* Philadelphia: University of Pennsylvania, Consortium for Policy Research in Education.

Susman, E. J., Dorn, L. D., & Schiefelbein, V. L. (2003). Puberty, sexuality, and health. In R. M. Lerner, M. A. Easterbrooks, & J. Mistry (Eds.), *Handbook of psychology: Vol. 6. Developmental psychology* (pp. 295–324). Hoboken, NJ: Wiley.

Sutherland, K., Wehby, J., & Copeland, S. (2000). Effect of rates of varying behavior-specific praise on the on-task behavior of students with EBD. *Journal of Emotional and Behavioral Disorders, 8,* 2–8, 26.

Sutton, R. E. (1991). Equity and computers in the schools: A decade of research. *Review of Educational Research, 61*(4), 475–503.

Suzuki, L. A., Ponterotto, J. G., & Meller, P. J. (Eds.). (2000). *Handbook of multicultural assessment* (2nd ed.). San Francisco: Jossey-Bass.

Swanson, D. B., Norman, G. R., & Linn, R. L. (1995). Performance-based assessment: Lessons from the health professions. *Educational Researcher, 24*(5), 5–11, 35.

Swanson, H. (2001). Research on interventions for adolescents with learning disabilities: A meta-analysis of outcomes related to higher-order processing. *The Elementary School Journal, 101*(3), 331–348.

Swanson, H. L. (1990). Influence of metacognitive knowledge and aptitude on problem solving. *Journal of Educational Psychology, 82,* 306–314.

Swanson, H. L., & Hoskyn, M. (1998). Experimental intervention research on students with learning disabilities: A meta-analysis of treatment outcomes. *Review of Educational Research, 68*(3), 277–321.

Swanson, L., Mink, J., & Bocian, K. (1999). Cognitive processing deficits in poor readers with symptoms of reading disabilities and ADHD: More alike than different? *Journal of Educational Psychology, 91*(2), 321–333.

Swanson, M. C., Mehan, H., & Hubbard, L. (1995). The AVID classroom: Academic and social support for low-achieving students. In J. Oakes & K. H. Quartz (Eds.), *Creating new educational communities.* Chicago: University of Chicago Press.

Sweller, J., van Merrienboer, J. J. G., & Paas, F. G. W. C. (1998). Cognitive architecture and instructional design. *Educational Psychology Review, 10*(3), 251–296.

Swiatek, M. A., & Benbow, C. P. (1991). Ten-year longitudinal follow-up of ability-matched accelerated and unaccelerated gifted students. *Journal of Educational Psychology, 83*(4), 528–538.

Swisher, K., & Schoorman, D. (2001). Learning styles: Implications for teachers. In C. F. Diaz (Ed.), *Multicultural education in the 21st century.* New York: Longman.

Tanner, C. K., & Decotis, J. D. (1994). The effects of a continuous-progress, non-graded program on primary school students. *ERS Spectrum, 12*(3), 41–47.

Taylor, B., Pearson, P., Clark, K., & Walpole, S. (2000). Effective schools and accomplished teachers: Lessons about primary-grade reading instruction in low-income schools. *The Elementary School Journal, 101*(2), 121–166.

Taylor, C. (1994). Assessment for measurement or standards: The peril and promise of large-scale assessment reform. *American Educational Research Journal, 31*(2), 231–262.

Taylor, D., & Lorimer, M. (2003). Helping boys succeed. *Educational Leadership, 60*(4), 68–70.

Teeter, P. A. (2000). *Interventions for ADHD.* New York: Guilford.

TenBrink, T. D. (1986). Writing instructional objectives. In J. Cooper (Ed.), *Classroom teaching skills* (3rd ed.). Lexington, MA: D. C. Heath.

Tennyson, R. D., & Park, O. (1980). The teaching of concepts: A review of instructional design literature. *Review of Educational Research, 50,* 55–70.

Terman, L. M., & Oden, M. H. (1959). The gifted group in mid-life. In *Genetic studies of genius,* Vol. 5. Stanford, CA: Stanford University Press.

Tharp, R. G., & Gallimore, R. (1988). *Rousing minds to life.* New York: Cambridge University Press.

The Education Trust (2003). *ESEA: Myths versus realities. Answers to questions about the No Child Left Behind Act.* Washington, DC: Author.

Thelen, E., & Smith, L. B. (1998). Dynamic systems theories. In W. Damon (Ed.), *Handbook of child psychology: Vol. 1. Theoretical models of human development* (pp. 563–633). Hoboken, NJ: Wiley.

Thoma, S. J., & Rest, J. R. (1999). The relationship between moral decision making and patterns of consolidation and transition in moral judgment development. *Developmental Psychology, 35*(2), 323–334.

Thomas, E. L., & Robinson, H. A. (1972). *Improving reading in every class: A sourcebook for teachers.* Boston: Allyn & Bacon.

Thomas, M. D., & Bainbridge, W. L. (2001). "All children can learn": Facts and fallacies. *Phi Delta Kappan, 82*(9), 660–662.

Thompson, M. S., Entwisle, D. R., Alexander, K. L., & Sundius, M. J. (1992). The influence of family composition on children's conformity to the student role. *American Educational Research Journal, 29*(2), 405–424.

Thompson, R. A., & Wyatt, J. M. (1999). Current research on child maltreatment: Implications for educators. *Educational Psychology Review, 11*(3), 173–202.

Thompson, R. A., Easterbrooks, M. A., & Padilla-Walker, L. M. (2003). Social and emotional development in infancy. In R. M. Lerner, M. A. Easterbrooks, & J. Mistry (Eds.), *Handbook of psychology: Vol. 6. Developmental psychology* (pp. 91–112). Hoboken, NJ: Wiley.

Thompson, S. (2001). The authentic standards movement and its evil twin. *Phi Delta Kappan, 82*(5), 358–362.

Thompson, T., Davidson, J. A., & Barber, J. G. (1995). Self-worth protection in achievement motivation: Performance effects and attributional behavior. *Journal of Educational Psychology, 87*(4), 598–610.

Thorkildsen, T. A. (1993). Those who can, tutor: High-ability students' conceptions of fair ways to organize learning. *Journal of Educational Psychology, 85*(1), 182–190.

Thorkildsen, T. A., & Nicholls, J. G. (1998). Fifth graders' achievement orientations and beliefs: Individual and classroom differences. *Journal of Educational Psychology, 90*(2), 179–201.

Thornburg, D. (2002). *The new basics: Education and the future of work in the telematic age.* Alexandria, VA: ASCD.

Thousand, J. S., & Villa, R. A. (1994). *Creativity and collaborative learning: A practical guide to empowering students and teachers.* Baltimore: Paul H. Brookes.

Tierno, M. J. (1993). Responding to the socially motivated behaviors of early adolescents: Recommendations for classroom management. In K. M. Cauley, F. Linder, & J. H. McMillan (Eds.), *Annual editions: Educational psychology 93/94.* Guilford, CT: Dushkin.

Timpson, W. M., & Tobin, D. N. (1982). *Teaching as performing: A guide to energizing your public presentation.* Englewood Cliffs, NJ: Prentice-Hall.

Tingley, J. (2001). Volunteer programs: When good intentions are not enough. *Educational Leadership, 68*(7), 53–55.

Tisak, M. S., & Tisak, J. (1990). Children's conceptions of parental authority, friendship, and sibling relationships. *Merrill-Palmer Quarterly, 36*, 347–368.

Tishman, S., Perkins, D. N., & Jay, E. (1995). *The thinking classroom.* Boston: Allyn & Bacon.

Tobias, S. (1992). The impact of test anxiety cognition in school learning. In K. A. Hagtvet & T. B. Johnsen (Eds.), *Advances in test anxiety research* (Vol. 7, pp. 18–31). Amsterdam: Swets & Zeitlinger.

Tobias, S. (1994). Interest, prior knowledge, and learning. *Review of Educational Research, 63*, 37–54.

Tobin, K. (1986). Effects of teacher wait time on discourse characteristics in mathematics and language arts classes. *American Educational Research Journal, 23*, 191–200.

Tobin, K. (1987). The role of wait time in higher cognitive level learning. *Review of Educational Research, 57*, 69–95.

Tobin, K. G., & Capie, W. (1982). Relationships between classroom process variables and middle-school science achievement. *Journal of Educational Psychology, 74*, 441–454.

Tollefson, N. (2000). Classroom applications of cognitive theories of motivation. *Educational Psychology Review, 12*(1), 63–84.

Tomlinson, C. (2002). Invitation to learn. *Educational Leadership, 60*(1), 6–11.

Tomlinson, C. (2003). Deciding to teach them all. *Educational Leadership, 61*(2), 6–11.

Tomlinson, C. A. (1999). *The differentiated classroom: Responding to the needs of all learners.* Alexandria, VA: Association for Supervision and Curriculum Development.

Tomlinson, C. A. (2000). Reconcilable differences? Standards-based teaching and differentiation. *Educational Leadership, 58*(1), 6–11.

Tomlinson, C. A. (2001). Grading for success. *Educational Leadership, 58*(6), 12–15.

Tomlinson, C. A. (2004). Differentiating instruction: A synthesis of key research and guidelines. In T. L. Jetton & J. A. Dole (Eds.), *Adolescent literacy, research and practice* (pp. 228–250). New York: The Guilford Press.

Tomlinson, C. A., Kaplan, S. N., & Renzulli, J. S. (2001). *The parallel curriculum: A model for planning curriculum for gifted students and whole classrooms.* Thousand Oaks, CA: Corwin.

Top, B. L., & Osguthorpe, R. T. (1987). Reverse-role tutoring: The effects of handicapped students tutoring regular class students. *Elementary School Journal, 87*, 413–423.

Topping, K., & Ehly, S. (Eds.). (1998). *Peer-assisted learning.* Mahwah, NJ: Erlbaum.

Torgesen, J. K., Wagner, R., Rashotte, C., Rose, E., Lindamood, P., Conway, T., & Garvan, C. (1999). Preventing reading failure in young children with phonological processing disabilities: Group and individual responses to instruction. *Journal of Educational Psychology, 91*(4), 579–593.

Torp, L., & Sage, S. (1998). *Problems as possibilities: Problem-based learning for K–12 education.* Alexandria, VA: Association for Supervision and Curriculum Development.

Torrance, E. P. (1986). Teaching creative and gifted learners. In M. C. Wittrock (Ed.), *Handbook of research on teaching* (3rd ed.). New York: Macmillan.

Trammel, D. L., Schloss, P. J., & Alper, S. (1994). Using self-recording evaluation and graphing to increase completion of homework assignments. *Journal of Learning Disabilities, 27*, 75–81.

Traub, J. (1999). *Better by design? A consumer's guide to schoolwide reform.* Washington, DC: Thomas Fordham Foundation.

Trawick-Smith, J. (1997). *Early childhood development: A multicultural perspective.* Upper Saddle River, NJ: Merrill/Prentice-Hall.

Tredway, L. (1995). Socratic seminars: Engaging students in intellectual discourse. *Educational Leadership, 53*(1), 26–29.

Treffinger, D. J. (1998). From gifted education to programming for talent development. *Phi Delta Kappan, 79*(10), 752–755.

Trent, S. C., Artiles, A. J., & Englert, C. S. (1998). From deficit thinking to social constructivism: A review of theory research and practice in special education. In P. D. Pearson & A. Iran-Nejad (Eds.), *Review of research in education* (pp. 277–307). Washington, DC: American Educational Research Association.

Trent, W. T. (1997). Outcomes of school desegregation: Findings from longitudinal research. *Journal of Negro Education, 66*(3), 255–257.

Triandis, H. (1995). *Individualism and collectivism.* Boulder, CO: Westview.

Trice, A. D. (2000). *A handbook of classroom assessment.* New York: Longman.

Troop, W. R., & Asher, S. R. (1999). Teaching peer relationship competence in schools. In R. J. Stevens (Ed.), *Teaching in American schools.* Upper Saddle River, NJ: Merrill/Prentice-Hall.

Trumbull, E., & Farr, B. (2000). *Grading and reporting student progress in an age of standards.* Norwood, MA: Christopher–Gordon.

Tschannen-Moran, M., & Woolfolk Hoy, A. (2001). Teacher efficacy: Capturing an elusive construct. *Teaching and teacher education, 17,* 783–805.

Tucker, J. A. (2001). Instructional support teams: It's a group thing. In B. Sornson (Ed.), *Preventing early learning failure.* Alexandria, VA: ASCD.

Tulving, E. (1993). What is episodic memory? *Current Directions in Psychological Science, 2,* 67–70.

Turiel, E. (1998). The development of morality. In W. Damon (Ed.), *Handbook of child psychology: Vol.3. Social, emotional, and personality development* (pp. 863–932). Hoboken, NJ: Wiley.

Turkeltaub, P. E., Gareau, L., Flowers, D. L., Zeffiro, T. A., & Eden, G. F. (2003). Development of neural mechanisms for reading. *Nature Neuroscience, 6,* 767–773.

Turkheimer, E. (1994). Socioeconomic status and intelligence. In R. J. Sternberg (Ed.), *Encyclopedia of human intelligence.* New York: Macmillan.

Turner, L. A., & Johnson, B. (2003). A model of mastery motivation for at-risk preschoolers. *Journal of Educational Psychology, 95*(3), 495–505.

Turner, S., & Alborz, A. (2003). Academic attainments of children with down's syndrome: A longitudinal study. *British Journal of Educational Psychology, 73*(4), 563–583.

U.S. Census Bureau. (2001). Web site (www.census.gov). *Population projections.*

U.S. Department of Education. (2002). *No Child Left Behind: A desktop reference.* Washington, DC: Author. (available at www.ed.gov/offices/OESE/reference)

U.S. Department of Education. (2003). *Identifying and implementing educational practices supported by rigorous evidence: A user-friendly guide.* Washington, DC: Author.

U.S. Department of Education, Office of Special Education and Rehabilitation Services. (1998, September). *IDEA '97 general information* [Internet]. Retrieved from: www.ed.gov/offices/OSERS/IDEA/overview.html.

U.S. Department of Education. (1994). *Sixteenth annual report to Congress on the implementation of the Individuals with Disabilities Education Act.* Washington, DC: Author.

U.S. Department of Education. (2000). *The 22nd annual report to Congress on the implementation of the Individuals with Disabilities Education Act.* Washington, DC: U.S. Government Printing Office.

U.S. Department of Justice. (1998). *Criminal behavior of gang members and at-risk youths.* Washington, DC: Author.

Urdan, T. C., & Maehr, M. L. (1995). Beyond a two-goal theory of motivation and achievement: A case for social goals. *Review of Educational Research, 65,* 213–243.

Valencia, S. W., Pearson, P. D., Peters, C. W., & Wixson, K. K. (1989). Theory and practice in statewide reading assessment: Closing the gap. *Educational Leadership, 46*(7), 57–63.

Van Horn, M. L., & Ramey, S. L. (2003). The effects of developmentally appropriate practices on academic outcomes among former Head Start students and classmates, grades 1–3. *American Educational Research Journal, 40*(4), 961–990.

Van Keer, H. (2004). Fostering reading comprehension in fifth grade by explicit instruction in reading strategies and peer tutoring. *British Journal of Educational Psychology, 74*(1), 37–70.

Van Laar, C. (2000). The paradox of low academic achievement but high self-esteem in African American students: An attributional account. *Educational Psychology Review, 12*(1), 33–62.

Van Laar, C. (2001). Understanding the impact of disadvantage on academic achievement. In F. Salili & R. Hoosain (Eds.), *Multicultural education: Issues, policies, and practices.* Greenwich, CT: Information Age Publishing.

Van Meter, P. (2001). Drawing construction as a strategy for learning from text. *Journal of Educational Psychology, 93*(1), 129–140.

Van Patten, J., Chao, C. I., & Reigeluth, C. M. (1986). A review of strategies for sequencing and synthesizing instruction. *Review of Educational Research, 56,* 437–471.

Van Sickle, R. L. (1986, April). *A quantitative review of research on instructional simulation gaming: A twenty-year perspective.* Paper presented at the annual convention of the American Educational Research Association, San Francisco, CA.

Van Tassel-Baska, F. S. (1989). Appropriate curriculum for gifted learners. *Educational Leadership 46*(6), 13–15.

Van Tassel-Baska, J. (1998). The development of academic talent: A mandate for educational best practice. *Phi Delta Kappan, 79*(10), 760–763.

Vasquez, J. A. (1993). Teaching to the distinctive traits of minority students. In K. M. Cauley, F. Linder, & J. H. McMillan (Eds.), *Annual editions: Educational psychology 93/94*. Guilford, CT: Dushkin.

Vasta, R., & Liben, L. S. (1996). The water-level task: An intriguing puzzle. *Current Directions in Psychological Science, 5*(6), 171–177.

Vaughn, S., Bos, C. L., & Schumm, J. S. (2000). *Teaching exceptional, diverse, and at-risk students in the general education classroom*. Boston: Allyn & Bacon.

Veenman, S. (1995). Cognitive and noncognitive effects of multi-grade and multi-age classes: A best evidence synthesis. *Review of Educational Research, 65*(4), 319–381.

Veenman, S. (1997). Combination classrooms revisited. *Educational Research and Evaluation, 3*(3), 262–276.

Vekiri, I. (2002). What is the value of graphical displays in learning? *Educational Psychology Review, 14*(3), 261–312.

Vellutino, F. R., Scanlon, D. M., Sipay, E. R., Small, S. G., Chen, R., Pratt, A., & Denckla, M. B. (1996). Cognitive profiles of difficult-to-remediate and readily remediated poor readers: Early intervention as a vehicle for distinguishing between cognitive and experimental deficits as basic causes of specific reading disability. *Journal of Educational Psychology, 88*(4), 601–638.

Verba, M. (1993). Cooperative formats in pretend play among young children. *Cognition and Instruction, 11*(3 & 4), 265–280.

Vermetten, Y. J., Lodewijks, H. G., & Vermunt, J. D. (2001). The role of personality traits and goal orientations in strategy use. *Contemporary Educational Psychology, 26*(2), 149–170.

Vernez, G. (1998). *Projected social context for education of children*. Washington, DC: RAND.

Viadero, D. (2000). Students in dire need of good teachers often get the least qualified or less experienced. *Education Week*, March 22, 2000, pp. 18–19.

Villa, R., & Thousand, J. (2003). Making inclusive education work. *Educational Leadership, 61*(2), 19–23.

Vispoel, W. P., & Austin, J. R. (1995). Success and failure in junior high school: A critical incident approach to understanding students' attributional beliefs. *American Educational Research Journal, 32*, 277–412.

Volman, M., & van Eck, E. (2001). Gender equity and information technology in education: The second decade. *Review of Educational Research, 71*(4), 613–634.

von Glaserfeld, E. (1996). Footnotes to the "many faces of constructivism." *Educational Researcher, 25*(6), 19.

Voss, J. F., & Wiley, J. (1995). Acquiring intellectual skills. *Annual Review of Psychology, 46*, 155–181.

Vygotsky, L. S. (1978). *Mind in society*. M. Cole, V. John-Steiner, S. Scribner, & E. Souberman (Eds.). Cambridge, MA: Harvard University Press.

Wade, S. E. (2001). Research on importance and interest: Implications for curriculum development and future research. *Educational Psychology Review, 13*(3), 243–261.

Wadsworth, B. (1996). *Piaget's theory of cognitive and affective development* (5th ed.). New York: Longman.

Wagmeister, J., & Shifrin, B. (2000). Thinking differently, learning differently. *Educational Leadership, 58*(3), 45–48.

Wainer, H. (2000). *Computerized adaptive testing: A primer* (2nd ed.). Mahwah, NJ: Erlbaum.

Walberg, H. (1988). Synthesis of research on time and learning. *Educational Leadership, 45*(6), 76–80.

Waldron, N., & McLesky, J. (1998). The effects of an inclusive school program on students with mild and severe learning disabilities. *Exceptional Children, 64*(3), 395–405.

Walker, H. M., & Gresham, F. M. (2003). School-related behavior disorders. In W. M. Reynolds & G. E. Miller (Eds.), *Handbook of psychology: Vol. 7. Educational psychology* (pp. 511–530). Hoboken, NJ: Wiley.

Walker, H., Colvin, G., & Ramsey, E. (1995). *Antisocial behavior in school: Strategies and best practices*. Pacific Grove, CA: Brooks/Cole.

Walker, H., Ramsey, E., & Gresham, F. (2003). Heading off disruptive behavior. *American Educator, 27*(4), 6–21.

Walker, H., Ramsey, E., & Gresham, F. (2003). How disruptive students escalate hostility and disorder—and how teachers can avoid it. *American Educator, 27*(4), 22–27.

Walker, J. E., & Shea, T. M. (1999). *Behavior management: A practical approach for educators* (7th ed.). Upper Saddle River, NJ: Merrill.

Walker, J. M. T., & Hoover-Dempsey, K. V. (2001, April). *Age-related patterns in student invitations to parental involvement in homework*. Paper presented at the annual meeting of the American Educational Research Association, Seattle, WA.

Walker, L. J. (1991). Sex differences in moral reasoning. In W. Kurtines & J. L. Gewirtz (Eds.), *Handbook of moral behavior and development* (Vol. 2, pp. 333–364). Mahwah, NJ: Erlbaum.

Walker, L. J., & Henning, K. H. (1997). Moral development in the broader context of personality. In S. Hala (Ed.), *The development of social cognition* (pp. 297–327). Hove, England: Psychology Press.

Wallace, R. (2004). A framework for understanding teaching with the internet. *American Educational Research Journal, 41*(2), 447–448.

Wallace-Broscious, A., Serafica, F. C., & Osipow, S. H. (1994). Adolescent career development: Relationships to self-concept and identity status. *Journal of Research on Adolescence, 4*(1), 122–149.

Wang, A. Y., & Thomas, M. H. (1995). Effect of keywords on long-term retention: Help or hindrance? *Journal of Educational Psychology, 87*, 468–475.

Wapner, S., & Demick, J. (Eds.). (1991). *Field dependence-independence: Cognitive style across the life span*. Hillsdale, NJ: Erlbaum.

Warger, C. L., & Pugach, M. C. (1996). Forming partnerships around curriculum. *Educational Leadership, 53*(5), 62–65.

Warrick, P. D., & Naglieri, J. A. (1993). Gender differences in planning, attention, simultaneous, and successive (PASS) cognitive processes. *Journal of Educational Psychology, 85*(4), 693–701.

Wartella, E., & Jennings, N. (2000). Children and computers: New technology—old concerns. *Children and Computer Technology, 10*(2), 31–43.

Wasik, B. A. (1997). Volunteer tutoring programs: Do we know what works? *Phi Delta Kappan, 79*(4), 283–287.

Wasik, B. A. (2001). Teaching the alphabet to young children. *Young Children, 56,* 34–45.

Wasik, B. A., & Karweit, N. L. (1994). Off to a good start: Effects of birth-to-three interventions on early school success. In R. E. Slavin, N. L. Karweit, & B. A. Wasik (Eds.), *Preventing early school failure.* Boston: Allyn & Bacon.

Wasik, B. A., & Slavin, R. E. (1993). Preventing early reading failure with one-to-one tutoring: A review of five programs. *Reading Research Quarterly, 28*(2), 178–200.

Wasik, B. A., Bond, M. A., & Hindman, A. (2002). Educating at-risk preschool and kindergarten children. In S. Stringfield & D. Land (Eds.), *Educating at-risk students* (pp. 89–110). Chicago: National Society for the Study of Education.

Wasley, P. A. (2002). Small classes, small schools: The time is now. *Educational Leadership, 59*(3), 6–10.

Watt, K. M., Powell, C. A., & Mendiola, I. D. (2004). Implications of one comprehensive school reform model for secondary school students underrepresented in higher education. *Journal of Education for Students Placed at Risk, 9*(3), 241–259.

Waxman, H. C., Gray, J. P., & Padron, N. (2002). Resiliency among students at risk of academic failure. In S. Stringfield & D. Land (Eds.), *Educating at-risk students* (pp. 29–48). Chicago: National Society for the Study of Education.

Waxman, H., Padrón, Y., & Arnold, K. (2001). Effective instructional practices for students placed at risk of academic failure. In G. Borman, S. Stringfield, & R. Slavin (Eds.), *Title I: Compensatory education at the crossroads.* Mahwah, NJ: Erlbaum.

Wayne, A. J., & Youngs, P. (2003). Teacher characteristics and student achievement gains: A review. *Review of Educational Research, 73*(1), 89–122.

Weade, R., & Evertson, C. M. (1988). The construction of lessons in effective and less effective classrooms. *Teaching and Teacher Education, 4,* 189–213.

Weaver-Hightower, M. (2003). The "boy turn" in research on gender education. *Review of Educational Research, 73*(4), 471–498.

Webb, N. M. (1992). Testing a theoretical model of student interaction and learning in small groups. In R. Hertz-Lazarowitz & N. Miller (Eds.), *Interaction in cooperative groups: The theoretical anatomy of group learning* (pp. 102–119). New York: Cambridge University Press.

Webb, N. M., & Farrivar, S. (1994). Promoting helping behavior in cooperative small groups in middle school mathematics. *American Educational Research Journal, 31*(2), 369–395.

Webb, N. M., & Palincsar, A. (1996). Group processes in the classroom. In D. C. Berliner & R. C. Calfee (Eds.), *Handbook of educational psychology* (pp. 841–876). New York: Macmillan.

Webb, N. M., Trooper, J. D., & Fall, R. (1995). Constructive activity and learning in collaborative small groups. *Journal of Educational Psychology, 87,* 406–423.

Webber, J., & Scheuermann, B. (1993). Managing behavior problems: Accentuate the positive . . . eliminate the negative! In K. M. Cauley, F. Linder, & J. H. McMillan (Eds.), *Annual editions: Educational psychology 93/94.* Guilford, CT: Dushkin.

Webber, J., Scheuermann, B., McCall, C., & Coleman, M. (1993). Research on self-monitoring as a behavior management technique in special education classrooms: A descriptive review. *Remedial and Special Education, 14*(2), 38–56.

Weber, E. (1999). *Student assessment that works: A practical approach.* Boston: Allyn & Bacon.

Wechsler, D. (1955). *Wechsler Adult Intelligence Scale.* New York: Psychological Corporation.

Wehmeyer, M. L. (2001). *Teaching students with mental retardation: Providing access to the general curriculum.* Baltimore: Brookes.

Weikart, D. P. (1995). Early childhood education. In J. H. Block, S. T. Everson, & T. R. Guskey (Eds.), *School improvement programs that work* (pp. 289–312). New York: Scholastic.

Weinberger, E., & McCombs, B. L. (2001, April). *The impact of learner-centered practices on the academic and non-academic outcomes of upper elementary and middle school students.* Paper presented at the annual convention of the American Educational Research Association, Seattle, WA.

Weiner, B. (1986). *An attributional theory of motivation and emotion.* New York: Springer.

Weiner, B. (1992). *Human motivation: Metaphors, theories, and research.* Newbury Park, CA: Sage.

Weiner, B. (1994). Integrating social and personal theories of achievement striving. *Review of Educational Research, 64,* 557–573.

Weiner, B. (2000). Intrapersonal and interpersonal theories of motivation from an attributional perspective. *Educational Psychology Review, 12*(1), 1–14.

Weinert, F. E., & Helmke, A. (1995). Interclassroom differences in instructional quality and interindividual differences in cognitive development. *Educational Psychologist, 30*(1), 15–20.

Weinstein, C. E., & Hume, L. M. (1998). *Study strategies for lifelong learning.* Washington, DC: American Psychological Association.

Weinstein, C. S. (1999). Reflections on best practices and promising programs: Beyond assertive discipline. In H. J. Freiberg (Ed.), *Beyond behaviorism: Changing the classroom management paradigm* (pp. 147–163). Boston: Allyn & Bacon.

Weinstein, C. S., & Mignano, A. J. (1997). *Elementary classroom management: Lessons from research and practice* (2nd ed.). New York: McGraw-Hill.

Weinstein, C., & Mignano, A. (1993). *Organizing the elementary school classroom: Lessons from research and practice.* New York: McGraw-Hill.

Weinstein, R. S. (1996). High standards in a tracked system of schooling: For which students and with what educational supports? *Educational Researcher, 25*(8), 16–19.

Weinstein, R. S., Madison, S. M., & Kuklinski, M. R. (1995). Raising expectations in schooling: Obstacles and opportunities for change. *American Educational Research Journal, 32,* 121–159.

Weissbourd, R. (2003). Moral teachers, moral students. *Educational Leadership, 60*(6), 6–11.

Wells, A. S. (1995). Reexamining social science research on school desegregation. *Teachers College Record, 96*(4), 681–690.

Wells, A. S., & Crain, R. L. (1997). *Stepping over the color line.* New Haven, CT: Yale University Press.

Wells, A. S., Hirshberg, D., Lipton, M., & Oakes, J. (1995). Bounding the case within its context: A constructivist approach to studying detracking reform. *Educational Researcher, 24*(5), 18–24.

Wentzel, K. R. (1993). Does being good make the grade? Social behavior and academic competence in middle school. *Journal of Educational Psychology, 85*(2), 357–364.

Wentzel, K. R. (1999). Social-motivational processes and interpersonal relationships: Implications for understanding motivation at school. *Journal of Educational Psychology, 91*(1), 76–97.

Wentzel, K. R. (2000). What is it that I'm trying to achieve? Classroom goals from a content perspective. *Contemporary Educational Psychology, 25*(1), 105–115.

Wentzel, K. R. (2003). School adjustment. In W. M. Reynolds & G. E. Miller (Eds.), *Handbook of psychology: Vol. 7. Educational psychology* (pp. 235–258). Hoboken, NJ: Wiley.

Wentzel, K. R., & Asher, S. R. (1995). The academic lives of neglected, rejected, popular, and controversial children. *Child Development, 66,* 754–763.

Wentzel, K. R., & Erdley, C. A. (1993). Strategies for making friends: Relations to social behavior and peer acceptance in early adolescence. *Developmental Psychology, 29,* 819–826.

Wentzel, K. R., Barry, C. M., & Caldwell, K. A. (2004). Friendships in middle school: Influences on motivation and school adjustment. *Journal of Educational Psychology, 96*(2), 195–203.

Wessler, S. L. (2001). Sticks and stones. *Educational Leadership, 58*(4), 28–33.

West, J., Hausken, E. G., & Collins, M. (1993). *Profile of preschool children's child care and early education program participation.* Washington, DC: U.S. Department of Education.

Westwater, A., & Wolfe, P. (2000). The brain-compatible curriculum. *Educational Leadership, 58*(3), 49–52.

Wheatley, G. H. (1991). Constructivist perspectives on science and mathematics learning. *Science Education, 75,* 9–21.

White, A. G., & Bailey, J. S. (1990). Reducing disruptive behaviors of elementary physical education students with sit and watch. *Journal of Applied Behavior Analysis, 3,* 353–359.

White, B. Y., & Frederiksen, J. R. (1998). Inquiry, modeling, and meta-cognition: Making science accessible to all students. *Cognition and Instruction, 16*(1), 3–118.

White, K. J., & Kistner, J. (1992). The influence of teacher feedback on young children's peer preferences and perceptions. *Developmental Psychology, 28,* 933–940.

Whitehurst, G. J., Epstein, J. N., Angell, A. L., Payne, A. C., Crone, D. A., & Fischel, J. E. (1994). Outcomes of an emergent literacy intervention in Head Start. *Journal of Educational Psychology, 86*(4), 542–555.

Whitehurst, G., Crone, D., Zevenbergen, A., Schultz, M., Velting, O., & Fischel, J. (1999). Outcomes of an emergent literacy intervention from Head Start through second grade. *Journal of Educational Psychology, 91*(2), 261–272.

Wiedmer, T. L. (1998). Digital portfolios: Capturing and demonstrating skills and levels of performance. *Phi Delta Kappan, 79*(8), 586–589.

Wielkiewicz, R. M. (1995). *Behavior management in the schools: Principles and procedures* (2nd ed.). Boston: Allyn & Bacon.

Wigfield, A. L. (1995, April). *Relationship of children's competence beliefs and achievement values to their performance and choice of different activities.* Paper presented at the annual meeting of the American Educational Research Association, San Francisco, CA.

Wigfield, A., & Eccles, J. (1989). Test anxiety in elementary and secondary students. *Educational Psychologist, 24,* 159–183.

Wigfield, A., & Eccles, J. (1990). Test anxiety in the school setting. In M. Lewis & S. M. Miller (Eds.), *Handbook of developmental psychopathology* (pp. 237–250). New York: Plenum.

Wigfield, A., & Eccles, J. (2000). Expectancy-value theory of achievement motivation. *Contemporary Educational Psychology, 25*(1), 68–81.

Wigfield, A., & Harold, R. (1992). Teacher beliefs and children's achievement self-perceptions: A developmental perspective. In D. Schunk & J. Meece (Eds.), *Student perceptions in the classroom* (pp. 95–121). Hillsdale, NJ: Erlbaum.

Wigfield, A., Eccles, J. S., & Rodriguez, D. (1998). The development of children's motivation in school contexts. In P. D. Pearson & A. Iran-Nejad (Eds.), *Review of research in education* (pp. 73–118). Washington, DC: American Educational Research Association.

Wiggins, G. (1989). Teaching to the (authentic) test. *Educational Leadership, 46*(7), 41–47.

Wiggins, G. (1993). Assessment: Authenticity, context, and validity. *Phi Delta Kappan, 75*(3), 200–214.

Wiggins, G. P. (1999). *Assessing student performance.* San Francisco: Jossey-Bass.

Wilcox, R. T. (1993). Rediscovering discovery learning. In K. M. Cauley, F. Linder, & J. H. McMillan (Eds.), *Annual Editions: Educational Psychology 93/94.* Guilford, CT: Dushkin.

Wilens, T. E. (1998). *Straight talk about psychiatric medications for kids.* New York: Guilford.

Wilkins, J. (2000). *Group activities to include students with special needs.* Thousand Oaks, CA: Corwin.

Willard-Holt, C. (2003). Raising expectations for the gifted. *Educational Leadership, 61*(2), 72–75.

Williams, J. E. (1995, April). *Use of learning and study skills among students differing in self-regulated learning efficacy.* Paper presented at the annual meeting of the American Educational Research Association, San Francisco, CA.

Willingham, D. (2002). Allocating student study time. *American Educator, 26*(2), 37–39.

Willingham, D. (2003). Students remember what they think about. *American Educator, 27*(2), 37–41.

Willingham, D. T. (2003). Why students think they understand—when they don't. *American Educator, 27*(4), 38–41.

Willingham, D. T. (2004). Practice makes perfect—but only if you practice beyond the point of perfection. *American Educator, 28*(1), 31–33.

Willoughby, T., Porter, L., Belsito, L., & Yearsley, T. (1999). Use of elaboration strategies by students in grades, two, four, and six. *The Elementary School Journal, 99*(3), 221–232.

Windschitl, M. (1999). The challenges of sustaining a constructivist classroom culture. *Phi Delta Kappan, 80*(10), 751–755.

Winebrenner, S. (2000). Gifted students need an education, too. *Educational Leadership, 58*(1), 52–56.

Winett, R. A., & Winkler, R. C. (1972). Current behavior modification in the classroom: Be still, be quiet, be docile. *Journal of Applied Behavior Analysis, 5,* 499–504.

Winn, W. (1991). Learning from maps and diagrams. *Educational Psychology Review, 3,* 211–247.

Winne, P. H. (1997). Experimenting to bootstrap self-regulated learning. *Journal of Educational Psychology, 89*(3), 397–410.

Wittrock, M. C. (1991). Generative teaching of comprehension. *Elementary School Journal, 92,* 169–184.

Wittrock, M. C., & Alesandrini, K. (1990). Generation of summaries and analogies and analytic and holistic abilities. *American Educational Research Journal, 27,* 489–502.

Wolf, D., Bixby, J., Glenn, J., & Gardner, H. (1991). To use their minds well: New forms of student assessment. *Review of Research in Education, 17,* 31–74.

Wong, K. K., Sunderman, G. L., & Lee, J. (1995). *When federal Title I works to improve student learning in inner-city schools: Final report on the implementation of schoolwide projects in Minneapolis and Houston.* Chicago: University of Chicago Press.

Wong, L. Y. S. (1995). Research on teaching: Process-product research findings and the feeling of obviousness. *Journal of Educational Psychology, 87,* 504–511.

Wood, D. J., Bruner, J. S., & Ross, G. (1976). The role of tutoring in problem solving. *Journal of Child Psychology and Psychiatry, 17,* 89–100.

Woodring, T. (1995). *Effects of peer education programs on sexual behavior, AIDS knowledge, and attitudes.* Paper presented at the annual meeting of the Eastern Psychological Association, Boston, MA.

Woodward, J., & Cuban, L. (Eds.). (2001). *Technology, curriculum, and professional development: Adapting schools to meet the needs of students with disabilities.* Thousand Oaks, CA: Corwin.

Woolfolk, A. E., & Brooks, D. M. (1985). Beyond words: The influence of teachers' nonverbal behaviors on students' perceptions and performances. *Elementary School Journal, 85,* 513–528.

Workman, E. A., & Katz, A. M. (1995). *Teaching behavioral self-control to students.* Austin, TX: Pro-Ed.

Worthen, B. R., & Spandel, V. (1993). Putting the standardized test debate in perspective. In K. M. Cauley, F. Linder, & J. H. McMillan (Eds.), *Annual Editions: Educational Psychology 93/94.* Guilford, CT: Dushkin.

Wyckoff, W. L. (1973). The effect of stimulus variation on learning from lecture. *Journal of Experimental Education, 41,* 85–90.

Xu, J., & Corno, L. (2003). Family help and homework management reported by middle school students. *The Elementary School Journal, 103*(5), 503–517.

Yeung, A. E., Marsh, H. W., & Suliman, R. (2000). Can two tongues live in harmony: Analysis of the national education longitudinal study of 1988 (NELS88) longitudinal data on the maintenance of home language. *American Educational Research Journal, 37*(4), 1001–1026.

Yeung, J., Linver, M., & Brooks-Gunn, J. (2002). How money matters for young children's development: Human capital and family process. *Child Development, 73,* 1861–1879.

Yonezawa, S., Wells, A. S., & Serna, I. (2002). Choosing tracks: "Freedom of choice" in detracking schools. *American Educational Research Journal, 39*(1), 37–67.

Zeidner, M. (1995). Adaptive coping with test situations: A review of the literature. *Educational Psychologist, 30*(3), 123–133.

Zellermayer, M., Salomon, G., Globerson, T., & Givon, H. (1991). Enhancing writing-related metacognitions through a computerized writing partner. *American Educational Research Journal, 28,* 373–391.

Zettergren, P. (2003). School adjustment in adolescence for previously rejected, average and popular children. *British Journal of Educational Psychology, 72*(3), 207–221.

Zhao, Y., & Frank, K. A. (2003). Factors affecting technology uses in schools: An ecological perspective. *American Educational Research Journal, 40*(4), 807–840.

Zigler, E., & Gilman, E. (1998). *The legacy of Jean Piaget.* Mahwah, NJ: Erlbaum.

Zigmond, N., Jenkins, J., Fuchs, D., Deno, S., & Fuchs, L. S. (1995). When students fail to achieve satisfactorily. *Phi Delta Kappan, 77*(4), 303–306.

Zimmerman, B. (2000). Self-efficacy: An essential motive to learn. *Contemporary Educational Psychology, 25*(1), 82–91.

Zimmerman, B. J. (1995). Self-regulation involves more than metacognition: A social cognitive perspective. *Educational Psychologist, 30,* 217–221.

Zimmerman, B. J. (1998, April). *Achieving academic excellence: The role of perceived efficacy and self-regulatory skill.* Paper presented at the annual meeting of the American Educational Research Association, San Diego, CA.

Zimmerman, B. J. (2000). Attaining self-regulation: A social cognitive perspective. In M. Boekaerts, P. R. Pintrich, & M. Zeidner (Eds.). *Handbook of self-regulation* (pp. 13–39). San Diego, CA: Academic Press.

Zimmerman, B. J., & Bandura, A. (1994). Impact of self-regulatory influences on writing course attainment. *American Educational Research Journal, 31,* 845–862.

Zimmerman, B. J., & Kitsantas, A. (2002). Acquiring writing revision and self-regulatory skill through observation and emulation. *Journal of Educational Psychology, 94*(2), 660–668.

Zimmerman, B., & Kitsantas, A. (1999). Acquiring writing revision skill: Shifting from process to outcome self-regulatory goals. *Journal of Educational Psychology, 91*(2), 241–250.

Zimmerman, B. J. (2000). Attaining self-regulation: A social-cognitive perspective. In M. Boekaerts, P. R. Pintrich, & M. Zeidner (Eds.). *Handbook of self-regulation* (pp. 13–39). San Diego, CA: Academic Press.

Zittleman, K., & Sadker, D. (2003). The unfinished gender revolution. *Educational Leadership, 60*(4), 59–62.

Ziv, A. (1988). Teaching and learning with humor: Experiment and replication. *Journal of Experimental Education, 57,* 5–18.

Name Index

Subject Index

Credits

Text Credit: p. 37, excerpt from *Winnie-the-Pooh* by A. A. Milne, illustrated by E. H. Shepard, copyright 1926 by E. P. Dutton, renewed 1954 by A. A. Milne. Used by permission of Dutton Children's Books, a Division of Penguin Young Readers Group, a Member of Penguin Group (USA) Inc., 345 Hudson Street, New York, NY 10014. All rights reserved.

Photo Credits: p. 1, © Geo Stock/Photodisc Green/Getty Images; p. 4, 8, © Will Hart; p. 12, © Richard Hutchings/PhotoEdit; p. 28, © John Terence Turner/Getty Images; p. 36, © Laura Dwight/CORBIS; p. 45, © BananaStock/Alamy Images; p. 50, © Will Hart; p. 55, © Bob Daemmrich/Stock Boston; p. 64, © Will Faller; p. 69, © David Young-Wolff/PhotoEdit; p. 74, © Will Faller; p. 76, © Nancy Sheehan Photography; p. 87, © Michael Newman/PhotoEdit; p. 91, © AP/Wide World Photos; p. 96, © Charles Thatcher/Getty Images; p. 102, © Alan Weiner/Getty Images; p. 115, © Michael Newman/PhotoEdit; p. 120 left, © Ezra Shaw/Getty Images; p. 120 right, © AP/Wide World Photos; p. 122, © Will Hart; p. 132, © Jim Cummins/Getty Images; p. 138, © Nina Leen/Time Life Pictures/Getty Images; p. 139, © Will Hart; p. 147 left, © LWA-Dann Tardiff/CORBIS; p. 147 right, © Jim Cummins/CORBIS; p. 157, © Bill Aron/PhotoEdit; p. 164, © Michael Newman/PhotoEdit; p. 176, © Kevin Fleming/CORBIS; p. 181, 185, © Will Hart; p. 197, © T. Lindfors/Lindfors Photography; p. 206, © Michael Newman/PhotoEdit; p. 218, © Syracuse Newspapers/Gloria Wright/The Image Works; p. 221, 229, © David Young-Wolff/PhotoEdit; p. 235, © Will Hart; p. 240, © Will Hart/PhotoEdit; p. 248, © David Young-Wolff/PhotoEdit; p. 255, © David McLain/Aurora & Quanta Productions Inc.; p. 256, © Mary Kate Denny/Getty Images; p. 263, © Will Hart; p. 269, © David Young-Wolff/PhotoEdit; p. 274, © Andy Sacks/Getty Images; p. 278, © Spencer Ainsley/The Image Works; p. 283, © Michael Newman/PhotoEdit; p. 289, © Mary Kate Denny/Getty Images; p. 296, © Jonathan Nourok/PhotoEdit; p. 307, © Michael Newman/PhotoEdit; p. 314, © Lawrence Migdale/PIX; p. 323, © STR/AFP/Getty Images; p. 334, 338, © Will Hart; p. 344, © Jose Luis Pelaez, Inc./CORBIS; p. 348, © Michael Newman/PhotoEdit; p. 354, © Mark Richards/PhotoEdit; p. 362, © Will Hart; p. 370, © Will Faller; p. 382, © Bill Aron/PhotoEdit; p. 388, © Richard Hutchings/Science Source/Photo Researchers, Inc.; p. 404, © Robin Sachs/PhotoEdit; p. 408, © Michael Newman/PhotoEdit; p. 416, © Robin Nelson/PhotoEdit; p. 425, © Bill Bachmann/PhotoEdit; p. 438, © Bob Daemmrich/The Image Works; p. 443, © Will Hart/PhotoEdit; p. 448, © Will Faller; p. 452, © Yellow Dog Productions/Getty Images; p. 457, © Tony Freeman/PhotoEdit; p. 477, © Michael Newman/PhotoEdit; p. 492, © Doug Corrance/Getty Images; p. 497, © AP/Wide World Photos; p. 508, © Charles Gupton/CORBIS; p. 517 top, © Philip Gould/CORBIS; p. 517 bottom, © Will Hart/PhotoEdit.